Fiḍālat al-Khiwān fī Ṭayyibāt al-Ṭaʿām wa-l-Al
Best of Delectable Foods and Dishes from al-

"One of only a handful of surviving medieval Spanish cookbooks, Ibn Razin's *Fiḍāla* has been long known to scholars, even if incompletely. By at least the 17th century, 55 of its 475 recipes had disappeared. Then in 2018 a complete 15th–16th century copy [missing only the first and the last folios] of the cookbook, originally composed in Tunis around 1260 CE, surfaced in the British Library. Alerted to the discovery, Nasrallah, a food historian, set out to produce the first complete English translation, preserving lbn Razin's culinary legacy while modernizing 24 of the recipes for the home cook. The book serves as Ibn Razin's ode to the cuisine of Muslim Spain, before having to flee the Iberian Peninsula's conquest by Christian armies. He nostalgically surveys a wide range of dishes, from everyday boiled fava beans to special-occasion *sinhaji*, an elaborate stew and forebear of Spain's classic olla podrida. This faithful translation is an important contribution to the history of Andalusi cuisine."
– Tom Verde in *AramcoWorld*, July 1, 2022.

„Dankzij dit boek krijgen we inzicht in gerechten, hoe ze met de jaren zijn veranderd of juist hetzelfde gebleven, en hoe gerechten de verschillende gemeenschappen met elkaar verbonden. Dat wekt bewondering en is een aansporing om te experimenteren met die oude methodes en receptuur ... Wat een bijzonder document heeft Al-Tujibi de wereld achtergelaten. Gelukkig maar. Wie beweert dat tijdreizen niet mogelijk is, heeft duidelijk nooit van dit magische boek gehoord."
– Hassnae Bouazza in NRC *Handelsblad*, zaterdag 11 maart/zondag 12 maart, 2023.

فضالة الخوان في طيبات الطعام والألوان

Fiḍālat al-Khiwān fī Ṭayyibāt al-Ṭaʿām wa-l-Alwān

Best of Delectable Foods and Dishes from al-Andalus and al-Maghrib

A Cookbook by Thirteenth-Century Andalusi Scholar Ibn Razīn al-Tujībī (1227–1293)

English Translation with Introduction and Glossary

By

Nawal Nasrallah

TUTA SUB AEGIDE PALLAS · 1683 ·

BRILL

LEIDEN | BOSTON

Originally published in hardback in 2021 as Volume 186 in the series *Islamic History and Civilization*.
This paperback edition contains a number of small corrections to the content.

Cover illustration: Sharing a meal of roasted meat, with bread and dipping sauce, al-Ḥarīrī, *al-Maqāmāt*, fol. 149r, detail (BnF, Department of manuscripts, Arab 3929), source: gallica.bnf.fr/BnF.

The Library of Congress Cataloging-in-Publication Data is available online at http://catalog.loc.gov
LC record available at http://lccn.loc.gov/2021035080

Typeface for the Latin, Greek, and Cyrillic scripts: "Brill". See and download: brill.com/brill-typeface.

ISSN 0929-2403
ISBN 978-90-04-68837-7 (paperback, 2024)
ISBN 978-90-04-46947-1 (hardback)
ISBN 978-90-04-46948-8 (e-book)

This book is printed on acid-free paper and produced in a sustainable manner.

Printed by Printforce, the Netherlands

تبدت لنا وسط الرصافة نخلة   تناءت بارض الغرب عن بلد النخيل
فقلت شبيهي في التغرب والنوى   وطول اكتئابي عن بني وعن اهلي
نشأتِ بأرض أنت فيها غريبة   فمثلك في الإقصاء والمنتأى مثلي

A date palm, al-ʿUmarī, *Masālik al-abṣār*, fol. 215r, detail

BNF, DEPARTMENT OF MANUSCRIPTS, ARAB 2771. SOURCE: GALLICA.BNF.FR/BNF

A date palm I saw standing in the middle of the Ruṣāfa garden,
Here in exile, far removed from the country of palms.
I said, you are like me,
Estranged and far removed from home and family,
You grew on a foreign land, banished and distant,
And we are alike in this.

Apostrophe to a date palm by Emir ʿAbd al-Raḥmān I (d. 788).

Contents

Preface xv
Acknowledgments xvii
List of Figures xviii
Notes on Translating the Text xxviii

Introduction 1
Part I: The Making of *Fiḍālat al-khiwān* 1
I.1 *The Text* 1
I.2 *Ibn Razīn al-Tujībī (1227–1293)* 15
I.3 Fiḍālat al-khiwān*: Sources* 21
Part II: Food and Foodways in al-Andalus 24
II.4 *Diet and Formation of a Cuisine* 24
II.4.1 A Shopping Tour around al-Andalus 34
II.5 *Elements of Andalusi Cuisine* 44
II.5.1 The Foods They Ate 53
II.5.2 *Al-Mujabbanāt* 55
II.5.3 Eating Out and Shopping: Regulating the Food Markets 57
II.6 *Food in Andalusi Social Contexts* 62
II.6.1 The Language of Food 68
Part III: The Andalusi Cuisine as Depicted in the Book of *Fiḍāla* 70
III.7 *In the Kitchen with* Fiḍālat al-khiwān 72
III.8 *In the Kitchen, Cooking al-Tujībī's Dishes* 80
Part IV: The Years They Ate Couscous Dangerously 94

***Edition and Translation of the* Best of Delectable Foods and Dishes**

[Ibn Razīn al-Tujībī's Introduction] 105

PART 1
On Bread, Tharāyid, *Soups* (Aḥsāʾ), *Pastries, and the Like; and It Has Five Chapters*

I.1 Part One, Chapter One: On Varieties of Bread (*Akhbāz*) 117

I.2 Part One, Chapter Two: On *Tharāyid* 121

I.3 Part One, Chapter Three: On Soups (*Aḥsāʾ*) and Porridges 148

I.4 Part One, Chapter Four: On Pastries, *Mujabbanāt*, and *Isfanj* 154

I.5 Part One, Chapter Five: On All Kinds of Dishes That Are Sopped in Broth like *Tharīd*; and Those Cooked in Ways Similar to Soup 188

PART 2
On Meats of Quadrupeds, and It Has Six Chapters

II.1 Part Two, Chapter One: On Beef (*Luḥūm Baqariyya*) 203

II.2 Part Two, Chapter Two: On Mutton (*Luḥūm Ḍaʾn*) 216

II.3 Part Two, Chapter Three: On Lamb (*Luḥūm Khirfān*) 260

II.4 Part Two, Chapter Four: On Young Goat Meat (*Luḥūm al-Jidāʾ*) 271

II.5 Part Two, Chapter Five: On Wild Meat (*Luḥūm al-Waḥsh*) 273

II.6 Part Two, Chapter Six: On Foods Incorporated into Dishes Cooked with Meat of Quadrupeds, and Which Are Akin to Making Meatballs (*Banādiq*) 282

PART 3
On Dishes with Various Types of Poultry, and It Has Seven Chapters

III.1 Part Three, Chapter One: On Meat of Geese (*Iwazz*) 293

III.2 Part Three, Chapter Two: On Chicken (*Dajāj*) 297

III.3 Part Three, Chapter Three: On Meat of Partridges (*Ḥajal*) 333

III.4 Part Three, Chapter Four: On Meat of Squabs (*Firākh Ḥamām*) 337

III.5 Part Three, Chapter Five: On Meat of Fat Turtledoves (*Yamām Musmina*) 341

III.6 Part Three, Chapter Six: On Meat of Starlings (*Zarāzīr*) 346

III.7 Part Three, Chapter Seven: On Meat of Sparrows (*ʿAṣāfīr*) 348

PART 4
It Has Three Chapters: On a Dish Called Ṣinhājī, *Stuffed Tripe, and* Ṣinhājī *Tongue*

IV.1 Part Four, Chapter One: On Cooking a Dish Called *Ṣinhājī* 353

IV.2 Part Four, Chapter Two: On Making Stuffed Tripe (*Karsh Maḥshuwwa*) 355

IV.3 Part Four, Chapter Three: On Making [*Ṣinhājī*] Tongue 357

PART 5
On Varieties of Dishes with Fish and Eggs, and It Has Two Chapters

V.1 Part Five, Chapter One: On [Dishes with] Various Types of Fish 361

V.2 Part Five, Chapter Two: On Varieties of Egg Dishes 383

PART 6
On Dairy Foods (Albān)*, and It Has Three Chapters*

VI.1 Part Six, Chapter One: A Recipe for Rennet-Curdled Milk (*ʿAqīd al-Laban al-Ḥalīb*) and What Is Made With It 393

VI.2 Part Six, Chapter Two: On Making *Rāyib* (Yogurt) and Extracting Butter 397

VI.3 Part Six, Chapter Three: On Ripening Hard Cheese in a Jar (*Khābiya*) and Ways for Cooking It; and Remedying Butter and Milk 400

PART 7
On Vegetables (Buqūl) *and the Like, and It Has Ten Chapters*

VII.1 Part Seven, Chapter One: On Dishes Made with Gourd (*Qarʿ*) 405

VII.2 Part Seven, Chapter Two: On Dishes with Eggplants (*Bādhinjān*) 412

VII.3 Part Seven, Chapter Three: On Dishes with Carrots (*Jazar*) 428

VII.4 Part Seven, Chapter Four: On Dishes Made with Desert Truffles (*Kamʾa*) 431

VII.5 Part Seven, Chapter Five: On Cooking Asparagus (*Isfarāj*), and It Has One Dish 434

VII.6 Part Seven, Chapter Six: On *Ḥarshaf*, Which Are *Qannāriyya* and *Afzan* 436

VII.7 Part Seven, Chapter Seven: On Cooking Mushrooms (*Fuṭr*), and It Has One Dish 438

VII.8 Part Seven, Chapter Eight: On Cooking with Spinach (*Isfānākh*), Blite (*Yarbūz*), Lettuce (*Khass*), and the Like 439

VII.9 Part Seven, Chapter Nine: On Cooking *Jināniyya* 441

VII.10 Part Seven, Chapter Ten: On Cooking Taros (*Qulqāṣ*), and It Has One Dish 443

PART 8
On Fava Beans (Fūl), *Chickpeas* (Ḥimmaṣ), *and the Like. It Has Three Chapters*

VIII.1 Part Eight, Chapter One: On Fresh and Dried Fava Beans (*Fūl*) 447

VIII.2 Part Eight, Chapter Two: On Dishes with Chickpeas (*Ḥimmaṣ*) 454

VIII.3 Part Eight, Chapter Three: On Cooking All Kinds of Lentils (*ʿAdas*), and It Has One Dish 457

PART 9
On Muʿassalāt *and All Sorts of Confectionary* (Ḥalwāʾ), *with All Kinds of Variations, Made with Honey and Sugar. It Has Seven Chapters*

IX.1 Part Nine, Chapter One: On Making *Muʿassal* and *Ghassānī* 461

IX.2 Part Nine, Chapter Two: On Making Varieties of Confectionary (*Ḥalwāʾ*) 463

IX.3 Part Nine, Chapter Three: On Making *Qāhiriyya* (Delicate Cairene Ring Cookies) and *Sanbūsak* (Marzipan) 471

IX.4 Part Nine, Chapter Four: On Making *Jawzīnaq* and *Lawzīnaj* (Walnut and Almond Confections) 475

IX.5 Part Nine, Chapter Five: On Making *Qaṣab Ḥulw* (Reeds of Candy) 477

IX.6 Part Nine, Chapter Six: On Making *Fānīdh* (Pulled Sugar Taffy) and *Ishqāqūl* (Rings of Solomon) 478

IX.7 Part Nine, Chapter Seven: On Varieties of Desserts from the Eastern Region (*Sharqiyya*) 480

PART 10
On Pickles and Condiments (Kawāmikh) *and Other Related Preparations for Varieties of Vinegar and* Murrī (*Fermented Liquid Sauce*)*; Remedying Olive Oil and Replacing It With Other Oils When Not Available; Remedying Overly Salty Foods and Raw Meat That Does Not Smell Fresh; and the Like. It Has Twelve Chapters*

x.1 Part Ten, Chapter One: On Making *Ṣināb* (Mustard Sauce) 485

x.2 Part Ten, Chapter Two: On Curing Olives (*Zaytūn*) 488

x.3 Part Ten, Chapter Three: On Pickling Lemons (*Taṣyīr al-Līm*) 492

x.4 Part Ten, Chapter Four: On Various Ways for Pickling Capers (*Taṣyīr al-Kabar*) 495

x.5 Part Ten, Chapter Five: On Pickling (*Taṣyīr*) Eggplants (*Bādhinjān*), Onions (*Baṣal*), and Turnips (*Lift*) 498

x.6 Part Ten, Chapter Six: On Pickling Fish (*Taṣyīr al-Ḥūt*) 503

x.7 Part Ten, Chapter Seven: On Making Varieties of Vinegar 506

x.8 Part Ten, Chapter Eight: On Making Sun-Fermented Liquid Sauce (*Murrī Naqīʿ*), Cooked Liquid Sauce (*Murrī Maṭbūkh*), and Other Kinds 518

x.9 Part Ten, Chapter Nine: On Making Oil (*Zayt*) with Ingredients other than Olives When They Are Not Available; and Remedying Olive Oil When It Spoils and Its Flavor or Aroma Deteriorates 534

x.10 Part Ten, Chapter Ten: On Extracting Oils (*Adhān*) When Needed for Some Dishes 537

x.11 Part Ten, Chapter Eleven: On Making Cured Meat (*Qadīd*) 539

x.12 Part Ten, Chapter Twelve: On Ways to Remedy Food 541

PART 11
On Cooking Jarād (*Locusts*), Qumrūn (*Freshwater Shrimps*), *and* Aghlāl (*Edible Land Snails*) 543

PART 12
On Handwashing Preparations (Ghāsūlāt), *and It Has One Chapter* 551

[Final Bonus Recipe:] Making *Muṣannab* (Juice of Sweet Grapes Preserved with Mustard Seeds) 559

Glossary

1 Beverages 563

2 Breads, Grains, Pasta, Noodles, and Sweet and Savory Pastries 569

3 Dairy 588

4 Desserts and Sweeteners 591

5 Dishes and Prepared Foods: Main and Side Dishes, Snacks, Condiments, Pickles, Dips, and Table Sauces 598

6 Fats and Oils 613

7 Fruits and Nuts 619

8 Ingredients Used in Dishes and Other Preparations: Herbs, Spices, Aromatics, Minerals, Food Colors, and Seasoning Sauces 652

9.1 In the Kitchen: Cooking and Serving Implements and Utensils 711

9.2 In the Kitchen: Culinary Techniques and Terms 731

10 Meats and Eggs 740

11 Medical Terms and Hygienic Preparations 767

12 Vegetables and Legumes 772

13 Weights and Measures 800

Appendix 1: *Bunk*, the Mystery Ingredient 803
Appendix 2: In the Kitchen with Ibn Razīn al-Tujībī: Modern Adaptations of Twenty-four Recipes from *Fiḍālat al-Khiwān* 814
Works Cited 855
Index of People and Places 866
General Index 868
Index of Ingredients 871
Index of Dishes and Other Preparations 878

Preface

The sophisticated cuisine that developed in the Iberian Peninsula when it was under Muslim rule is in full view in the thirteenth-century cookbook *Fiḍālat al-khiwān fī ṭayyibāt al-ṭaʿām wa-l-alwān* by the Andalusi scholar Ibn Razīn al-Tujībī. With its 475 delectable recipes that are masterfully structured and explained, it is indeed the middle jewel in the 'unique necklace' of medieval Arabic cookery books that survived from the eastern and western regions of the Arabo-Muslim world.

Published for the first time in English, this edition presents al-Tujībī's complete text, based not only on the partial Berlin and Madrid manuscripts but also on a newly discovered, complete manuscript at the British Library. I unexpectedly came across this new manuscript while working on the translation of this text. I was asked by the British Library to identify a very long culinary fragment in an anonymous pharmaceutical compendium of Maghribi origin (more on this in the introduction). To my delight it turned out to be none other than al-Tujībī's cookbook, and a complete copy at that, except for a missing folio at the beginning and another one at the end, material already provided by the two incomplete manuscripts of the book. This new discovery is now available for the first time in print format.

Born into an affluent and well-established Andalusi family in Murcia in al-Andalus, al-Tujībī had to flee the country due to the rapid decline of Muslim rule in al-Andalus and settle in North Africa, in Tunis, where he established himself as a revered scholar. His biographers mention works he authored, variously dealing with historical, cultural, and literary matters; but not a single word on his cookbook *Fiḍālat al-khiwān* or even a by-the-way mention of his gourmandise. Ironically, of all his works it was his cookbook that survived. It is indeed instructive, illustrating how material culture, even when it is not fully acknowledged, is present and influential in shaping cultural heritage.

Based on circumstantial and internal evidence, al-Tujībī's primary motive for writing his cookbook was most likely his desire to preserve the Andalusi cuisine he knew quite well from his years growing up in Murcia, where he led a life of luxury. A cuisine he cherished was in danger of being forgotten or lost due to multitudes of his countrymen fleeing al-Andalus just as he had. Given his literary interests, he was well aware of the value of a well-written cookbook, not only as a practical guide for cooking but also as a source for an enjoyable reading experience outside the kitchen, and in this he was indeed ahead of his time.

This is a key resource on medieval material culture in the western region of the Arabo-Muslim world and on the Arab culinary heritage in Iberia. It is only in this cookbook that we find recipes for cooking the salt-cured tuna called *mushammaʿ* that is now the Spanish delicacy *mojama*. The book's recipes function as prototypes for dishes that later metamorphosed but kept their Arabic origin; for instance, the grand *Ṣinhājī*, named after one of the largest Amazigh tribes in North Africa, became the festive Spanish hodge-podge stew called *olla podrida*, or *jūdhāba*, the savory-sweet chicken pie that was the precursor of the Moroccan *basṭīla*. It is also a testimony to the credibility of the diverse food-related anecdotes we encounter in Andalusi records, such as the reference to a lavish feast arranged by a dignitary that offered nothing but chicken dishes—al-Tujībī's chicken chapter has 49 recipes, aside from many others interspersed in other parts of the book—or Ibn Khaldūn's comment on the diet of the Andalusi and Maghrebi urbanites as mostly mutton and chicken—the mutton chapter contains no less than 46 recipes.

In my concern for producing an accurate translation of al-Tujībī's cookbook, I had to work with the three manuscripts available to us in addition to the edited Arabic text. When identifying ingredients, the medieval Arabic sources on botany, dietetics, agronomy, and horticulture, mostly hailing from al-Andalus and al-Maghrib, were indispensable.

The aim of the introduction and glossary, for which material was extensively explored, and they are illustrated throughout with miniatures and period artifacts, is to introduce readers to the wonders of cooking and foodways in al-Andalus and al-Maghrib. The 24 modernized recipes will give readers a taste of the cuisine and may lead to further experimentations with the recipes. Understandably, not everyone will want to try al-Tujībī's recipe for boiling and frying locusts or preparing the head of the sacrificial sheep for a *tharīd* dish by banging its nostrils "so that the maggots that bred inside the nose fall out," as al Tujībī meticulously details, but there are hundreds of other recipes waiting to be discovered and enjoyed.

Acknowledgments

I would like to express my gratitude to Brill for publishing this volume, my third with them, and to the editorial board for their appreciation of my work and their constant encouragement. I am thankful and grateful to my editor Teddi Dols for her unfailing support along the way. My thanks also extend to the anonymous reviewers of the manuscript for their comments and suggestions that helped improve the work in many ways, and to Rebekah Zwanzig for her thoroughness and efficiency in copyediting the text, and Pieter te Velde, Production Editor, and his team for their meticulous work and the care they took in the final shaping of the book. Professor Kaj Öhrnberg has always been graciously supportive of my projects and for this I am grateful. I would also like to extend my gratitude to my friends Nadia Hassani, for once again helping me with securing a copy of the Berlin manuscript, Dr. Melitta Weiss Adamson for her assistance with a German document, and Dr. Wasmaa Chorbachi, for her instrumental mediation on my behalf when trying to obtain a copy of the Moroccan manuscript of the Andalusi cookbook *Anwāʿ al-ṣaydala*, to which I refer frequently in my translation of al-Tujībī's cookbook and which itself is the subject of my forthcoming translation project, God willing. And once again, to my husband Shakir Mustafa I owe the greatest debt of gratitude for his inexhaustible patience and support.

Figures

1 The opening folio of al-Tujībī's cookbook with his full name, from the Madrid MS, fol. 1v 2
2 A folio from al-Tujībī's introduction detailing the divisions of the book's parts in the Berlin MS, fol. 1vd 4
3 An example of Maghribi script used in the Madrid MS with its characteristic run-on lines, fol. 82r 5
4 The first folio of *Fiḍālat al-khiwān* in the BL MS, fol. 101r 7
5 The last folio of *Fiḍālat al-khiwān* in the BL MS, fol. 204v 9
6 A map of Bijāya, W.658.274b, Piri Reis, *Book on Navigation*, detail 18
7 Figs, *tīn*, al-ʿUmarī, *Masālik al-abṣār*, fol. 215r, detail 25
8 Tuna fishes on the reverse of a Phoenician and Punic coin, ca. 200–150 BC 26
9 A map showing the closest point between al-Andalus and North Africa, with the cities of Gibraltar and Ceuta, W.658.264b, Piri Reis, *Book on Navigation*, detail 27
10 Farmers at work, *Kitāb al-Diryāq*, fol. NP, detail 30
11 Ancient Roman aqueducts in Spain 32
12 A medieval noria near Murcia 32
13 A water wheel driven by oxen, al-Ḥarīrī, *al-Maqāmāt*, fol. 69v, copied and illustrated by al-Wāsiṭī, detail 32
14 A pomegranate tree, Dioscorides, *Fī Hayūlā al-ṭibb*, translation by Ḥunayn b. Isḥāq, fol. 60v, detail 33
15 A joy ride along the river, al-Ḥarīrī, *al-Maqāmāt*, fol. 61r, copied and illustrated by al-Wāsiṭī, detail 36
16 Saffron, Dioscorides, *Kitāb al-Ḥashāʾish fī hāyūlā al-ʿilāj al-ṭibbī*, Arabic translation by Ḥunayn b. Isḥāq, Or. 289, fol. 14r, detail 37
17 *Almadraba*, tuna fishing, etching by Jean-Pierre Houël, *Voyage pittoresque des Isles de Sicile, de Malte et de Lipari*. Paris, 1782 39
18 Mulberry trees, al-ʿUmarī, *Masālik al-abṣār*, fol. 152r, detail 40
19 Having a good time drinking and listening to music, al-Ḥarīrī, *al-Maqāmāt*, fol. 165v 43
20 An olive tree, al-Qazwīnī, *ʿAjāʾib al-makhlūqāt wa ghārāʾib al-mawjūdāt*, fol. 164v, detail 45
21 Playing the *ʿūd* in an orchard, al-Ḥarīrī, *al-Maqāmāt*, fol. 69v, copied and illustrated by al-Wāsiṭī, detail 47
22 Asparagus, *isfarāj*, al-Ghāfiqī, *Kitāb al-Adwiya al-mufrada*, MS 7508, fol. 138v, detail 49
23 Market transactions, *Kitāb al-Diryāq*, fol. NP, detail 57

24 *Al-muḥtasib* 'market inspector' weighs bread, *Ralamb Costume Book*, 1657, p. 85 58
25 At the marketplace, al-Ḥarīrī, *al-Maqāmāt*, fol. 105r, copied and illustrated by al-Wāsiṭī, detail 59
26 Having drinks with *naql* (mezza dishes), al-Ḥarīrī, *al-Maqāmāt*, fol. 167v, detail 62
27 A tray with *ṭayfūr*s being carried to guests, al-Ḥarīrī, *al-Maqāmāt*, fol. 140r, copied and illustrated by al-Wāsiṭī, detail 75
28 A server feeding the stove's fire with fuel, *Kitāb al-Diryāq*, fol. NP, detail 77
29 *Anafe* 78
30 Garlic, Dioscorides, *Fī Hayūlā al-ṭibb*, translation by Ḥunayn b. Isḥāq, fol. 108r, detail 83
31 Catching river fish, Ibn al-Muqaffaʿ, *Kalīla wa Dimana*, fol. 60r, detail 88
32 Catching sea fish, Ibn al-Muqaffaʿ, *Kalīla wa Dimana*, fol. 33r, detail 89
33 A Morisco farmer, Christoph Weiditz, *Trachtenbuch* 'Costume book,' ca. 1530, pp. 55–6 95
34 A Morisco carrying bread, Christoph Weiditz, *Trachtenbuch* 'Costume book,' ca. 1530, p. 104 96
35 Two men sharing a dish, eating with their hands, al-Ḥarīrī, *al-Maqāmāt*, fol. 166r, copied and illustrated by al-Wāsiṭī, detail 97
36 Moriscos having a good time singing and dancing to music, Christoph Weiditz, *Trachtenbuch* 'Costume book,' ca. 1530, pp. 107–8 98
37 Al-Tujībī's full name as it appears in the Madrid MS, fol. 1v, detail 105
38 A host serving his guests, al-Ḥarīrī, *al-Maqāmāt*, fol. 47v, copied and illustrated by al-Wāsiṭī, detail 107
39 A table laden with bread, al-Ḥarīrī, *al-Maqāmāt*, fol. 149r, detail 118
40 Millet, *dukhn*, Dioscorides, *Ajzāʾ min risāla fī l-nabātāt*, fol. 24v, detail 120
41 Garlic, Dioscorides, *Kitāb al-Ḥashāʾish fī hāyūlā al-ʿilāj al-ṭibbī*, Arabic translation by Ḥunayn b. Isḥāq, Or. 289, fol. 93r, detail 143
42 Rice, Dioscorides, *Fī Hayūlā al-ṭibb*, translation by Ḥunayn b. Isḥāq, fol. 94r, detail 153
43 A wide and shallow flat-based serving bowl with inscriptions in pseudo-Arabic script, ca. fifteenth-century Valencia, Spain 185
44 Barley, Dioscorides, *Ajzāʾ min risāla fī l-nabātāt*, fol. 23r, detail 196
45 Boxwood, al-ʿUmarī, *Masālik al-abṣār*, fol. 262v, detail 199
46 A cow, Dioscorides, *Fī Hayūlā al-ṭibb*, translation by Ḥunayn b. Isḥāq, fol. 79r, detail 204
47 A plum tree, *ijjāṣ*, Dioscorides, *Ajzāʾ min risāla fī l-nabātāt*, fol. 18v, detail 208
48 Serving meat with *jalja*, al-Ḥarīrī, *al-Maqāmāt*, fol. 120r, detail 214
49 A ram, *kabsh*, Dioscorides, *Fī Hayūlā al-ṭibb*, translation by Ḥunayn b. Isḥāq, fol. 77r, detail 217

50 Turnips, *Kitāb al-Diryāq*, fol. NP, detail 222
51 Chard, *silq*, Dioscorides, *Kitāb al-Ḥashāʾish fī hāyūlā al-ʿilāj al-ṭibbī*, Arabic translation by Ḥunayn b. Isḥāq, Or. 289, fol. 84r, detail 224
52 Borage, *lisān al-thawr*, Dioscorides, *Kitāb Dīsqūrīdis fī mawādd al-ʿilāj*, fol. 151r, detail 226
53 Orach, *qaṭaf*, Dioscorides, *Kitāb al-Ḥashāʾish fī hāyūlā al-ʿilāj al-ṭibbī*, Arabic translation by Ḥunayn b. Isḥāq, Or. 289, fol. 83r, detail 227
54 Blite, *yarbūz*, Dioscorides, *Kitāb al-Ḥashāʾish fī hāyūlā al-ʿilāj al-ṭibbī*, Arabic translation by Ḥunayn b. Isḥāq, Or. 289, fol. 82v, detail 228
55 Asparagus, *isfarāj*, al-Ghāfiqī, *Kitāb al-Adwiya al-mufrada*, MS 7508, fol. 138v, detail 231
56 Cardoon, *qannāriyya*, called *kankar* in al-Mashriq, Dioscorides, *Kitāb al-Ḥashāʾish fī hāyūlā al-ʿilāj al-ṭibbī*, Arabic translation by Ḥunayn b. Isḥāq, Or. 289, fol. 111v, detail 237
57 Apples, Dioscorides, *Fī Hayūlā al-ṭibb*, translation by Ḥunayn b. Isḥāq, fol. 62r, detail 240
58 A quince tree, Dioscorides, *Fī Hayūlā al-ṭibb*, translation by Ḥunayn b. Isḥāq, fol. 62v, detail 241
59 A lamb, *kharūf*, Ibn al-Muqaffaʿ, *Kalīla wa Dimana*, fol. 101r, detail 261
60 A young goat with its mother, Ibn al-Muqaffaʿ, *Kalīla wa Dimana*, fol. 110r, detail 272
61 A stag, *ayyal*, al-Qazwīnī, *ʿAjāʾib al-makhlūqāt wa-gharāʾib al-mawjūdāt*, fol. 107r, detail 274
62 Rabbit, *arnab*, al-Qazwīnī, *ʿAjāʾib al-makhlūqāt wa-gharāʾib al-mawjūdāt*, fol. 96r, detail 277
63 A decorated plate, fifteenth-century Seville, Spain 280
64 A goose, al-Qazwīnī, *ʿAjāʾib al-makhlūqāt wa-gharāʾib al-mawjūdāt*, fol. 115r, detail 294
65 A chicken, al-Qazwīnī, *ʿAjāʾib al-makhlūqāt wa ghārāʾib al-mawjūdāt*, fol. 187r, detail 298
66 A young chicken, *farrūj*, al-Qazwīnī, *ʿAjāʾib al-makhlūqāt wa ghārāʾib al-mawjūdāt*, fol. 345r, detail 310
67 Mushrooms, *fuṭr*, Dioscorides, *Kitāb Dīsqūrīdis fī mawādd al-ʿilāj*, fol. 140v, detail 331
68 Partridges, *ḥajal*, Anonymous, *Kitāb Naʿt al-ḥayawān*, fol. 9r, detail 334
69 Turtledoves, folio from a Persian *Manāfiʿ al-ḥayawān* of Ibn Bakhtīshūʿ, (recto), detail 342
70 A starling, *zurzūr*, al-Qazwīnī, *ʿAjāʾib al-makhlūqāt wa-gharāʾib al-mawjūdāt*, fol. 120r, detail 346
71 Sparrows, Anonymous, *Kitāb Naʿt al-ḥayawān*, fol. 22v, detail 349

72 Fishing by net, al-Qazwīnī, *ʿAjāʾib al-makhlūqāt wa ghārāʾib al-mawjūdāt*, fol. 125v, detail 362
73 An eel, al-Ghāfiqī, *Kitāb al-Adwiya al-mufrada*, MS 7508, fol. 111r, detail 376
74 Fish, al-Ḥarīrī, *al-Maqāmāt*, fol. 61r, copied and illustrated by al-Wāsiṭī, detail 382
75 A hen sitting on eggs, Dioscorides, *Fī Hayūlā al-ṭibb*, translation by Ḥunayn b. Isḥāq, fol. 80r, detail 384
76 Gourds on the vine, Dioscorides, *Fī Hayūlā al-ṭibb*, translation by Ḥunayn b. Isḥāq, fol. 103v, detail 406
77 Eggplants, al-Ghāfiqī, *Kitāb al-Adwiya al-mufrada*, MS 7508, fol. 73r, detail 413
78 Last folio, 77v, in the Berlin MS 429
79 Carrots, al-Ghāfiqī, *Kitāb al-Adwiya al-mufrada*, MS, fol. 113r, detail 430
80 A desert truffle, *kamʾa*, al-Ghāfiqī, *Kitāb al-Adwiya al-mufrada*, MS 7508, fol. 250r, detail 432
81 Asparagus, *isfarāj*, al-Ghāfiqī, *Kitāb al-Adwiya al-mufrada*, MS 7508, fol. 138v, detail 435
82 Cultivated cardoon, *kankar*, Dioscorides, *Kitāb Dīsqūrīdis fī mawādd al-ʿilāj*, fol. 12v, detail 437
83 Mushrooms, Dioscorides, *Fī Hayūlā al-ṭibb*, translation by Ḥunayn b. Isḥāq, fol. 206v, detail 438
84 Blite, *yarbūz*, also known as *baqla Yamāniyya*, Dioscorides, *Fī Hayūlā al-ṭibb*, translation by Ḥunayn b. Isḥāq, fol. 100v, detail 440
85 Green fava beans, Dioscorides, *Fī Hayūlā al-ṭibb*, translation by Ḥunayn b. Isḥāq, fol. 96r, detail 448
86 Spring garlic, Dioscorides, *Kitāb al-Ḥashāʾish fī hāyūlā al-ʿilāj al-ṭibbī*, Arabic translation by Ḥunayn b. Isḥāq, Or. 289, fol. 93r, detail 450
87 Fresh chickpeas, al-Ghāfiqī, *Kitāb al-Adwiya al-mufrada*, MS 7508, fol. 185r, detail 455
88 Lentil plant, Dioscorides, *Kitāb al-Ḥashāʾish fī hāyūlā al-ʿilāj al-ṭibbī*, Arabic translation by Ḥunayn b. Isḥāq, Or. 289, fol. 78v, detail 457
89 Mustard plant, Dioscorides, *Ajzāʾ min risāla fī l-nabātāt*, fol. 42r, detail 486
90 Olives, al-ʿUmarī, *Masālik al-abṣār*, fol. 171v, detail 489
91 Fully ripe lemons, al-ʿUmarī, *Masālik al-abṣār*, fol. 202v, detail 493
92 Capers, al-Ghāfiqī, *Kitāb al-Adwiya al-mufrada*, MS 7508, fol. 274r, detail 496
93 Onions, Dioscorides, *Kitāb al-Ḥashāʾish fī hāyūlā al-ʿilāj al-ṭibbī*, Arabic translation by Ḥunayn b. Isḥāq, Or. 289, fol. 92v, detail 499
94 Turnips, Dioscorides, *Fī Hayūlā al-ṭibb*, translation by Ḥunayn b. Isḥāq, fol. 98v, detail 501
95 Salt-cured fish, Dioscorides, *Fī Hayūlā al-ṭibb*, translation by Ḥunayn b. Isḥāq, fol. 76v, detail 504

96 Grapes, al-ʿUmarī, *Masālik al-abṣār*, fol. 186r, detail 507
97 A fig tree, Dioscorides, *Fī Hayūlā al-ṭibb*, translation by Ḥunayn b. Isḥāq, fol. 69r, detail 508
98 Black pepper plant, *fulful aswad*, Dioscorides, *Ajzāʾ min risāla fī l-nabātāt*, fol. 41r, detail 509
99 A squill, *baṣal al-ʿunṣul*, Dioscorides, *Ajzāʾ min risāla fī l-nabātāt*, fol. 45r, detail 512
100 Mint, *naʿnaʿ*, Dioscorides, *Ajzāʾ min risāla fī l-nabātāt*, fol. 56v, detail 516
101 Two physicians filtering a medicinal preparation with a suspended straining vessel put on top of a large bowl, the same way *murrī* would have been strained, Arabic version of Dioscorides, *De Materia Medica*, fol. W. 675r, detail 521
102 *Buṭm*, al-Ghāfiqī, *Kitāb al-Adwiya al-mufrada*, MS 7508, fol. 68r, detail 535
103 A sweet almond tree, Dioscorides, *Fī Hayūlā al-ṭibb*, translation by Ḥunayn b. Isḥāq, fol. 66r, detail 538
104 A locust, al-Qazwīnī, *ʿAjāʾib al-makhlūqāt wa ghārāʾib al-mawjūdāt*, fol. 359v, detail 545
105 A fifteenth-century Morisca peddler carrying on her head what looks like a pot of simmering freshwater shrimps on a small portable stove. A stove would explain the thick piece of cloth put directly on her head to insulate her from the heat, Christoph Weiditz, *Trachtenbuch* 'Costume book,' ca. 1530, p. 44, detail 547
106 A citron tree branch showing the thorns, Dioscorides, *Fī Hayūlā al-ṭibb*, translation by Ḥunayn b. Isḥāq, fol. 63v, detail 548
107 A land snail, Dioscorides, *Kitāb al-Ḥashāʾish fī hāyūlā al-ʿilāj al-ṭibbī*, Arabic translation by Ḥunayn b. Isḥāq, Or. 289, fol. 59v, detail 549
108 A tenth-century ivory pyxis from the time of Umayyad Caliph ʿAbd al-Raḥmān III, used for keeping handwashing preparations, *ushnān* 554
109 Andalusi jar, by Diego Sánchez Sarabia, 1762 560
110 A pitcher, ca. fifteenth-century Spain 564
111 A physician ladling from a *sharāb* cauldron, folio from an Arabic translation of the *Materia Medica* of Dioscorides, detail 565
112 Stacked wine jars, al-Ḥarīrī, *al-Maqāmāt*, fol. 33r, copied and illustrated by al-Wāsiṭī, detail 567
113 A table with folded discs of bread arranged all around it, fol. 120r, detail 570
114 Rice, *aruzz*, Dioscorides, *Ajzāʾ min risāla fī l-nabātāt*, fol. 24r, detail 571
115 Wheat, the green head in the middle is used to make *farīk*, Dioscorides, *Ajzāʾ min risāla fī l-nabātāt*, fol. 22v, detail 579
116 Barley heads, in varying degrees of ripeness, Dioscorides, *Fī Hayūlā al-ṭibb*, translation by Ḥunayn b. Isḥāq, fol. 92v, detail 585

117 Ceylon cornel, *wars*, al-Ghāfiqī, *Kitāb al-Adwiya al-mufrada*, MS, fol. 149r, detail 594
118 Dishes spread on *khiwāns*, al-Ḥarīrī, *al-Maqāmāt*, fol. 47v, copied and illustrated by al-Wāsiṭī, detail 599
119 A fat-tailed sheep, al-Qazwīnī, *ʿAjāʾib al-makhlūqāt wa ghārāʾib al-mawjūdāt*, fol. 364r, detail 614
120 Olives, al-Qazwīnī, *ʿAjāʾib al-makhlūqāt wa ghārāʾib al-mawjūdāt*, fol. 164v, detail 617
121 A plum tree, *ijjāṣ*, Dioscorides, *Fī Hayūlā al-ṭibb*, translation by Ḥunayn b. Isḥāq, fol. 92v, detail 620
122 Acorns, al-ʿUmarī, *Masālik al-abṣār*, fol. 149v, detail 621
123 Hazelnuts, *bunduq*, al-ʿUmarī, *Masālik al-abṣār*, fol. 255r, detail 623
124 A pistachio tree, Dioscorides, *Fī Hayūlā al-ṭibb*, translation by Ḥunayn b. Isḥāq, fol. 66r, detail 625
125 Terebinth trees, Dioscorides, *Fī Hayūlā al-ṭibb*, translation by Ḥunayn b. Isḥāq, fol. 42r, detail 626
126 A walnut tree, Dioscorides, *Fī Hayūlā al-ṭibb*, translation by Ḥunayn b. Isḥāq, fol. 66v, detail 629
127 Capers, *kabar*, Dioscorides, *Kitāb al-Ḥashāʾish fī hāyūlā al-ʿilāj al-ṭibbī*, Arabic translation by Ḥunayn b. Isḥāq, Or. 289, fol. 99v, detail 631
128 A carob tree, Dioscorides, *Kitāb al-Ḥashāʾish fī hāyūlā al-ʿilāj al-ṭibbī*, Arabic translation by Ḥunayn b. Isḥāq, Or. 289, fol. 46v, detail 632
129 Green almonds, al-ʿUmarī, *Masālik al-abṣār*, fol. 201r, detail 634
130 Limes growing on a tree, al-Qazwīnī, *ʿAjāʾib al-makhlūqāt wa ghārāʾib al-mawjūdāt*, fol. 174v, detail 635
131 A chestnut tree, Dioscorides, *Fī Hayūlā al-ṭibb*, translation by Ḥunayn b. Isḥāq, fol. 58r, detail 640
132 A pinecone tree, Dioscorides, *Fī Hayūlā al-ṭibb*, translation by Ḥunayn b. Isḥāq, fol. 41r, detail 641
133 Male and female date palms, Dioscorides, *Fī Hayūlā al-ṭibb*, translation by Ḥunayn b. Isḥāq, fol. 59v, detail 644
134 Citrons at different stages of ripeness, Dioscorides, *Fī Hayūlā al-ṭibb*, translation by Ḥunayn b. Isḥāq, fol. 63v, detail 647
135 Borage, *abū khuraysh*, also called *lisān al-thawr*, Dioscorides, *Kitāb Dīsqūrīdis fī mawādd al-ʿilāj*, fol. 151r, detail 653
136 A cylindrical jar for keeping dried herbs and spices, decorated with a band of pseudo-Kufic letters, commonly used in spice stores and hospital pharmacies, fourteenth-century Valencia 654
137 Aniseed plant, *anīsūn*, *Kitāb al-Diryāq*, fol. NP, detail 655
138 Pellitory, Dioscorides, *Fī Hayūlā al-ṭibb*, translation by Ḥunayn b. Isḥāq, fol. 147r, detail 657

139 Onions, Dioscorides, *Fī Hayūlā al-ṭibb*, translation by Ḥunayn b. Isḥāq, fol. 107v, detail 658
140 A squill, Dioscorides, *Fī Hayūlā al-ṭibb*, translation by Ḥunayn b. Isḥāq, fol. 114v, detail 660
141 Herb fennel, *basbās*, Dioscorides, *Kitāb al-Ḥashāʾish fī hāyūlā al-ʿilāj al-ṭibbī*, Arabic translation by Ḥunayn b. Isḥāq, Or. 289, fol. 126r, detail 661
142 Cassia, *Kitāb al-Diryāq*, fol. NP, detail 664
143 Cultivated rue, *fayjan*, Dioscorides, *Fī Hayūlā al-ṭibb*, translation by Ḥunayn b. Isḥāq, fol. 137v, detail 666
144 Black pepper, Dioscorides, *Fī Hayūlā al-ṭibb*, translation by Ḥunayn b. Isḥāq, fol. 110v, detail 668
145 Fenugreek, *ḥulba*, al-Ghāfiqī, *Kitāb al-Adwiya al-mufrada*, MS, fol. 184r, detail 669
146 *Idhkhir*, *Kitāb al-Diryāq*, fol. NP, detail 670
147 A camphor tree being protected by a tiger, al-Qazwīnī, *ʿAjāʾib al-makhlūqāt wa gharāʾib al-mawjūdāt*, fol. 171v, detail 672
148 Cumin, al-Ghāfiqī, *Kitāb al-Adwiya al-mufrada*, MS, fol. 258r, detail 674
149 Common parsley, Dioscorides, *Fī Hayūlā al-ṭibb*, translation by Ḥunayn b. Isḥāq, fol. 143v, detail 675
150 Caraway, Dioscorides, *Ajzāʾ min risāla fī l-nabātāt*, fol. 63v, detail 676
151 Tragacanth, *kathīrāʾ*, al-Ghāfiqī, *Kitāb al-Adwiya al-mufrada*, MS, fol. 256r, detail 677
152 Coriander plant, *kuzbara*, Dioscorides, *Kitāb al-Ḥashāʾish fī hāyūlā al-ʿilāj al-ṭibbī*, Arabic translation by Ḥunayn b. Isḥāq, Or. 289, fol. 134r, detail 681
153 Marjoram, *marzanjūsh*, Dioscorides, *Kitāb Dīsqūrīdis fī mawādd al-ʿilāj*, fol. 33r, detail 684
154 A storax tree, Dioscorides, *Fī Hayūlā al-ṭibb*, translation by Ḥunayn b. Isḥāq, fol. 39r, detail 686
155 Mother of thyme, *nammām*, Dioscorides, *Ajzāʾ min risāla fī l-nabātāt*, fol. 58v, detail 690
156 Costus, *Kitāb al-Diryāq*, fol. NP, detail 692
157 Myrtle, Dioscorides, *Kitāb al-Ḥashāʾish fī hāyūlā al-ʿilāj al-ṭibbī*, Arabic translation by Ḥunayn b. Isḥāq, Or. 289, fol. 45v, detail 693
158 *Salīkha*, Dioscorides, *Kitāb al-Ḥashāʾish fī hāyūlā al-ʿilāj al-ṭibbī*, Arabic translation by Ḥunayn b. Isḥāq, Or. 289, fol. 8v, detail 694
159 Thyme, *ṣaʿtar*, Dioscorides, *Ajzāʾ min risāla fī l-nabātāt*, fol. 58r, detail 695
160 *Shaṭriyya*, Dioscorides, *Fī Hayūlā al-ṭibb*, translation by Ḥunayn b. Isḥāq, fol. 134r, detail 698
161 Nigella plant, Dioscorides, *Kitāb Dīsqūrīdis fī mawādd al-ʿilāj*, fol. 62r, detail 699

162 Varieties of Cyperus, *su'd*, Dioscorides, *Fī Hayūlā al-ṭibb*, translation by Ḥunayn b. Isḥāq, fol. 21v, detail 700
163 Varieties of spikenard, *Kitāb al-Diryāq*, fol. NP, detail 702
164 Garlic, Dioscorides, *Ajzāʾ min risāla fī l-nabātāt*, fol. 44v, detail 703
165 Licorice, *Kitāb al-Diryāq*, fol. NP, detail 705
166 Bay laurel, *ghār*, Dioscorides, *Kitāb al-Ḥashāʾish fī hāyūlā al-ʿilāj al-ṭibbī*, Arabic translation by Ḥunayn b. Isḥāq, Or. 289, fol. 23r, detail 707
167 Saffron, *Kitāb al-Diryāq*, fol. NP, detail 708
168 Ginger, Dioscorides, *Ajzāʾ min risāla fī l-nabātāt*, fol. 41v, detail 709
169 A shallow bowl, ca. fourteenth-century Spain 712
170 A serving vessel, *ghaḍāra*, late thirteenth-century Málaga, Spain 713
171 Esparto grass, *ḥalfā*, Dioscorides, *Ajzāʾ min risāla fī l-nabātāt*, fol. 88v, detail 714
172 *Jafna*, a large and wide serving bowl, fifteenth-century Valencia, Spain 715
173 A server tending to fire burning in the stove, al-Ḥarīrī, *al-Maqāmāt*, fol. 140r, copied and illustrated by al-Wāsiṭī, detail 716
174 Two physicians working on a medicinal preparation, using a large *miʿjana*, folio from an Arabic translation of the *Materia Medica* of Dioscorides, detail 719
175 Varieties of reeds, Dioscorides, *Fī Hayūlā al-ṭibb*, translation by Ḥunayn b. Isḥāq, fol. 48r, detail 723
176 Pitch, *zift*, extracting it and cooking it down, Dioscorides, *Fī Hayūlā al-ṭibb*, translation by Ḥunayn b. Isḥāq, fol. 43v, detail 729
177 Food preparations, folio from *Divan* of Jāmī, 52.20.4, detail 732
178 A server filtering wine, al-Ḥarīrī, *al-Maqāmāt*, fol. 33r, copied and illustrated by al-Wāsiṭī, detail 738
179 Cooked snails at a food stall in Morocco 741
180 A male goat, *tays*, al-Qazwīnī, *ʿAjāʾib al-makhlūqāt wa-gharāʾib al-mawjūdāt*, fol., detail 742
181 Rabbits, which look more like *arānib barriyya* 'hares,' Anonymous, *Kitāb Naʿt al-ḥayawān*, fol. 167v, detail 743
182 A sparrow, al-Qazwīnī, *ʿAjāʾib al-makhlūqāt wa-gharāʾib al-mawjūdāt*, fol. 121v, detail 745
183 A rooster, al-Qazwīnī, *ʿAjāʾib al-makhlūqāt wa-gharāʾib al-mawjūdāt*, fol. 127v, detail 745
184 A young chicken, al-Qazwīnī, *ʿAjāʾib al-makhlūqāt wa-gharāʾib al-mawjūdāt*, fol. 128v, detail 746
185 Partridges, *ḥajal*, al-Qazwīnī, *ʿAjāʾib al-makhlūqāt wa-gharāʾib al-mawjūdāt*, fol. 118v, detail 748
186 Pigeons, *ḥamām*, al-Qazwīnī, *ʿAjāʾib al-makhlūqāt wa-gharāʾib al-mawjūdāt*, fol. 117r, detail 749

187 An eel, Anonymous, *Kitāb Naʿt al-ḥayawān*, fol. 28v, detail 751
188 A duck and a goose, as described in the MS, Anonymous, *Kitāb Naʿt al-ḥayawān*, fol. 10v, detail 754
189 Locusts, Anonymous, *Kitāb Naʿt al-ḥayawān*, fol. 61v, detail 755
190 A ram and a male lamb, *kabsh* and *ḥamal*, Dioscorides, *Fī Hayūlā al-ṭibb*, translation by Ḥunayn b. Isḥāq, fol. 77r, detail 756
191 A wild ass, Anonymous, *Kitāb Naʿt al-ḥayawān*, fol. 152r, detail 759
192 A gazelle, Ibn al-Muqaffaʿ, *Kalīla wa Dimana*, fol. 53v, detail 760
193 Hedgehogs, Dioscorides, *Fī Hayūlā al-ṭibb*, translation by Ḥunayn b. Isḥāq, fol. 70r, detail 762
194 Tuna fish, Dioscorides, *Fī Hayūlā al-ṭibb*, translation by Ḥunayn b. Isḥāq, fol. 79r, detail 763
195 Turtledoves, *yamām*, also called *shifnīn*. Anonymous, *Kitāb Naʿt al-ḥayawān*, fol. 20v, detail 765
196 A pharmacy jar decorated with stylized inscriptions of the Arabic word *al-ʿāfiya* (العافية) 'good health,' from which the Spanish *alafia* is derived, fifteenth-century Spain 768
197 Lentils, Dioscorides, *Ajzāʾ min risāla fī l-nabātāt*, fol. 27v, detail 773
198 Eggplants, al-Ghāfiqī, *Kitāb al-Adwiya al-mufrada*, MS 7508, fol. 73r, detail 774
199 Radishes, Dioscorides, *Kitāb al-Ḥashāʾish fī hāyūlā al-ʿilāj al-ṭibbī*, Arabic translation by Ḥunayn b. Isḥāq, Or. 289, fol. 80v, detail 777
200 Green fava beans, Dioscorides, *Fī Hayūlā al-ṭibb*, translation by Ḥunayn b. Isḥāq, fol. 96r, detail 778
201 Mushrooms, Dioscorides, *Ajzāʾ min risāla fī l-nabātāt*, fol. 94v, detail 779
202 A vine of snake cucumbers, *qiththāʾ*, with young shoots, al-Qazwīnī, *ʿAjāʾib al-makhlūqāt wa ghārāʾib al-mawjūdāt*, fol. 200r, detail 780
203 *ʿAkkūb*, a variety of wild cardoon, Dioscorides, *Kitāb Dīsqūrīdis fī mawādd al-ʿilāj*, fol. 161r, detail 781
204 Cultivated cardoon, *kankar*, called *qannāriyya* in al-Andalus, al-Ghāfiqī, *Kitāb al-Adwiya al-mufrada*, MS, fol. 275v, detail 782
205 Fresh chickpeas, Dioscorides, *Ajzāʾ min risāla fī l-nabātāt*, fol. 26v, detail 783
206 Asparagus, Dioscorides, *Kitāb al-Ḥashāʾish fī hāyūlā al-ʿilāj al-ṭibbī*, Arabic translation by Ḥunayn b. Isḥāq, Or. 289, fol. 84v, detail 786
207 Carrots, cultivated (R) and wild (L), Dioscorides, *Ajzāʾ min risāla fī l-nabātāt*, fol. 61v, detail 787
208 Cultivated lettuce, Dioscorides, *Kitāb al-Ḥashāʾish fī hāyūlā al-ʿilāj al-ṭibbī*, Arabic translation by Ḥunayn b. Isḥāq, Or. 289, fol. 88v, detail 788
209 Unripe cucumbers, Dioscorides, *Fī Hayūlā al-ṭibb*, translation by Ḥunayn b. Isḥāq, fol. 103v, detail 789
210 Turnips, Dioscorides, *Ajzāʾ min risāla fī l-nabātāt*, fol. 29r, detail 792

211 Gourd, *qar*ʿ, al-Qazwīnī, *ʿAjāʾib al-makhlūqāt wa gharāʾib al-mawjūdāt*, fol. 190v, detail 793

212 Chard, Dioscorides, *Fī Hayūlā al-ṭibb*, translation by Ḥunayn b. Isḥāq, fol. 101v, detail 796

213 Blite, *yarbūz*, Dioscorides, *Ajzāʾ min risāla fī l-nabātāt*, fol. 31r, detail 798

214 A pair of scales, al-Qazwīnī, *ʿAjāʾib al-makhlūqāt wa gharāʾib al-mawjūdāt*, fol. 28r, detail 801

215 *Umm ghaylān*, al-ʿUmarī, *Masālik al-abṣār*, fol. 227v, detail 804

216 *Bunk*, al-Ghāfiqī, *Kitāb al-Adwiya al-mufrada*, MS, fol. 58r, detail 807

217 *Sanṭ* tree, al-ʿUmarī, *Masālik al-abṣār*, fol. 275v, detail 808

218 *Samura* tree, al-ʿUmarī, *Masālik al-abṣār*, fol. 241r, detail 809

Notes on Translating the Text

1. The following English translation of al-Tujībī's *Fiḍālat al-khiwān* is based on the newly discovered **British Library manuscript Or 5927**, which is a complete copy of al-Tujībī's text, containing 104 folios; missing a folio in the introduction of the author where the chapter list is provided, and a folio at the very end, which contains the continuation of recipe xii.6 and the last three recipes that follow. This manuscript is referred to as the BL MS in the translated text.

A number of folios in the manuscript have been misplaced. I rearranged them, putting them back where they belong, resulting in the following sequence of folios, as they occur in the translated text:

Fols. 101r–130v
Fols. 137–148v
Fols. 131r–136v
Fols. 149r–169v
Fols. 203r–204v
Fols. 170r–173v
Fols. 179r–179v
Fols. 174r–178v
Fols. 180r–202v

I also used the following two manuscripts of al-Tujībī's *Fiḍāla al-khiwān*, which are incomplete in varying degrees to amend the translated text wherever needed.

1.1. **Manuscript Wetzstein II 1207**, a faithful copy of the above BL MS, albeit incomplete. It contains 77 folios only, ending at the beginning of chapter vii.3 on carrots. It is referred to as the **Berlin MS** in the translated text.

1.2. **Manuscript 16** in the Gayangos Collection at the Library of the Spanish Academy of History in Madrid. It is complete in the sense that in its 134 folios, it has the opening folio that provides the author's full name, and it ends with the colophon. However, compared with the BL MS, it is missing many parts and recipes and slightly differs stylistically from it. It is referred to as the **Madrid MS** in the translated text.

2. The Arabic edited text was executed by Muḥammad Bin Shaqrūn and published in 1981,[1] with a new edition in 1984.[2] The editor based it on the incom-

1 Its title is
فن الطبخ في الاندلس والمغرب في بداية عصر بني مرين: فدالة الخوان في طيبات الطعام والالوان.
It is not clear why the original Arabic word فضالة occurs as فدالة in the title above.

plete Berlin manuscript, with its beautiful and lucid handwriting, and finished it with the Madrid manuscript. In his introduction, the editor complained of the often-challenging illegibility of the Madrid manuscript, which apparently led to a good deal of misreadings on his part. This rendered my dependence on the manuscripts necessary. My comments on the edited text in cases of misreadings or discrepancies are given in footnotes in the translated text.

3. Unless otherwise mentioned, all translations of proverbs, anecdotes, verses, and medieval Arabic excerpts are mine.

4. Al-Tujībī's cookbook has so far been published twice in translation: once in French in 1992[3] and once in Spanish in 2007.[4] I have conducted the following English translation independently of the above two; and notably, it contains al-Tujībī's complete text for the first time in any language.

5. On pronouncing the title word فضالة as *fiḍāla*:

The Arabic word in al-Tujībī's title, فضالة, has occurred as *fuḍāla* and *faḍāla* in sources related to the book. To my knowledge, these two versions are more often than not equated with 'remains' and 'leftovers.' *Fiḍāla*, on the other hand, is more likely to designate a state of being the best, from *fiḍāl*, which is suggestive of 'contending for excellence.'[5]

It is unlikely that al-Tujībī's intention was to display the abundance of the leftovers of the table. Rather, it would have more likely been to showcase the diversity of delicious dishes it offered, which was indeed his design, and explicitly established in his own introduction, where he says,

> My book deals with all varieties of foods. I included many of the dishes that I approved of and many more that I myself created. The majority are from al-Andalus, and only a small number from al-Mashriq—the finest among them—are included here.

2 Its title is
فضالة الخوان في طيبات الطعام والالوان: صور من فن الطبخ في الاندلس والمغرب في بداية عصر بني مرين لإبن رزين التجيبي.

3 Mezzine and Benkirane, *Délices de la table et les meilleurs genres de mets Fudalat al-khiwan fi tayibat at-tàam wa al alwān*, Fès 1997. Their translation is based on the edited Arabic text.

4 Marín, *Relieves de la mesas, acerca de la delicias de la comida y los diferentes platos*, Asturias 2007. Her translation is based on the edited Arabic text.

5 See, for instance, Ibn Manẓūr, *Lisān al-ʿArab*, s.v. فضل; Steingass, *Dictionary*, s.vv. *fiẓāl* and *fuẓāla*; and Lane, *Arabic-English Lexicon* vol. 6, s.v. فضل.

Introduction

Part 1: The Making of *Fiḍālat al-khiwān*

With 475 delectable dishes masterfully structured and explained, *Fiḍālat al-khiwān fī ṭayyibāt al-alwān* is beyond dispute the middle jewel in the 'unique necklace' of medieval Arabic cookery books that survived from the eastern and western regions of the Arabo-Muslim world. Its authorship is impressively established in the exordium of one of the manuscripts:

> The learned scholar, eloquent scribe, and most erudite Abū al-Ḥasan ʿAlī bin Muḥammad bin Abī al-Qāsim Ibn Muḥammad bin Abī Bakr Razīn al-Tujībī al-Andalusi.

It took a long while, however, to discover the author's identity after the first published mention of the manuscript in 1948 in Maxime Rodinson's seminal study of Arabic food works. It was only in 2009, with the publication of the groundbreaking Arabic study *Ibn Razīn al-Tujībī: Ḥayātuhu wa āthāruhu* (Ibn Razīn al-Tujībī: His life and works) by the Moroccan scholar Muḥammad Bin Sharīfa, that we knew who he was. Evidently, al-Tujībī, who grew up in al-Andalus, was living in Tunis when he wrote the book. Given his cultural and scholarly background and professional training as a scribe, it comes as no surprise that his cookbook is a chef-d'oeuvre in structure and content. The following discussion of al-Tujībī and his cookbook is meant to shed light on the circumstances surrounding the conception of the text and the gastronomic repertoire it displays.

1.1 *The Text*

> Even though most of the recipes might hardly ever get to be cooked and tried, including them will indeed rarely fail to please with their novelty and exquisiteness.
>
> IBN RAZĪN AL-TUJĪBĪ commenting on recipes in his book of *Fiḍāla*

The first scholar to draw attention to a cookery manuscript entitled *Kitāb Fuḍalat al-khiwān fī ṭayyibāt al-ṭaʿām wa-l-alwān* was Maxime Rodinson (1915–2004). In "Recherches sur les documents Arabes relatifs à la cuisine," first published in 1949,[1] Rodinson mentioned that this nameless manuscript was pre-

1 English trans., "Studies in Arabic Manuscripts," 104.

 | DOI:10.1163/9789004469488_002

FIGURE 1 The opening folio of al-Tujībī's cookbook with his full name, from the Madrid MS, fol. 1v

served in Berlin; only two-thirds of it. He speculated that it might have been of Maghribi origin, based on the inclusion of a dish called *Ṣinhājī* in the summary list of headings of parts and chapters copied in the manuscript.[2]

This manuscript has been kept at the library of the University of Tübingen in Berlin, MS no. 5473 (henceforward referred to as the **Berlin MS**). It is estimated to have been written in 1688. The opening page establishes ownership of the copy, stating that it came into the possession of al-Sayyid ʿAlī Mūsā al-Ḥasanī in 1244/1829, along with the book's title as it is given in the author's introduction. It is beautifully and lucidly written in Mashriqi script, but slightly damaged in a few places. Unfortunately, it is incomplete; almost a third of it is missing from the back, which leaves us with a last folio, 77v, with an incomplete recipe for cooking carrots.

A second manuscript of our book has been residing at the library of the Royal Academy of History in Madrid, in the Gayangos Collection, MS no. 16 (henceforward referred to as the **Madrid MS**). A few unrelated folios bound with the book suggest the existence of this manuscript in Morocco at the beginning of the reign of Sulṭān Mawlāi Ismāʿīl (ruled 1672–1727), which might also be the place where this copy was made.[3] Indeed, it was in the Moroccan city of Tetouan that Gayangos purchased it in 1850.[4]

Written in Maghribi script, this Madrid MS, though not complete, offers more of the original work than the Berlin MS. Its opening page offers the full name of the author in an attractive simply adorned exordium, and its last page is complete with the addition of an unrelated bonus recipe for *muṣannab* that deals with preserving the juice of sweet grapes with mustard seeds. On the

---

2 Rodinson found this information in a Berlin catalogue, W. Ahlwardt, *Verzeichniss der arabischen Handschriften* v, 1893, MS no. 5473. He also discloses that Lévi-Provençal told him of another Arabic manuscript from the western region that was owned by George Colin. Later, in the 1950s, Spanish historian and Arabist Huici Miranda (1880–1973) borrowed it from him and edited this anonymous and titleless text, giving it the title *Kitāb al-Ṭabīkh fī l-Maghrib wa-l-Andalus fī ʿAṣr al-Muwaḥḥidīn* (A cookery book from al-Maghrib and al-Andalus in the era of Almohads). It was published in 1961 in *Ṣaḥīfat Maʿhad al-Dirāsāt al-Islāmiyya fī Madrīd*, vols. 9 and 10, 22–256. A new edition of Huici Miranda's Spanish translation of this book was published in 2005, entitled *La cocina hispano-magrebí durante la época almohade según un manuscrito anónimo del siglo XIII*, containing Manuela Marín's introduction, "Ambrosio Huici Miranda y la historia de la alimentación en el Occidente islámico."

Another Arabic edition based on a better manuscript than the one Huici Miranda used, although still anonymous, has the title *Anwāʿ al-ṣaydala fī alwān al-aṭʿima* (A smorgasbord of Andalusi and Maghribi dishes and their salutary benefits). The Arabic edited edition was executed by ʿAbd al-Ghanī Abū al-ʿAzm in 2003.

3 As suggested by Bin Shaqrūn, editor of the Arabic text, in his introduction, p. 21.

4 Based on a handwritten note on a blank page at the end of the book.

FIGURE 2 A folio from al-Tujībī's introduction detailing the divisions of the book's parts in the Berlin MS, fol. 1vd

STAATSBIBLIOTHEK ZU BERLIN—PREUSSISCHER KULTURBESITZ, ORIENTABTEILUNG, MS WETZSTEIN II 1207

FIGURE 3 An example of Maghribi script used in the Madrid MS with its characteristic run-on lines, fol. 82r
© REAL ACADEMIA DE LA HISTORIA ESPAÑA, GAYANGOS COLLECTION, MS NO. 16

other hand, the manuscript suffers from a good number of lacunae; and several chapters are either entirely missing or do not include all the recipes. Altogether it offers 134 folios that are comfortably legible once one gets familiar with the idiosyncrasies of Maghribi script: the dot for ف is underneath, just one dot for the ق, and 'run-on words.' There are also some misplaced folios, and some repeated recipes, as well as those not copied in the same sequence as in the other manuscripts.

The first person to draw attention to the Madrid MS was the Spanish orientalist Fernando de la Granja Santamaría (1928–1999). It was in the late 1950s when he worked on it for his doctorate dissertation, editing and translating it into Spanish. It was submitted in 1960 but was never published.[5]

In 1981 the edited Arabic text of our book came out for the first time, executed by the Moroccan scholar Muḥammad Bin Shaqrūn.[6] A second edition was published in 1984 in Beirut.[7] In editing the book, Bin Shaqrūn used the Berlin and Madrid manuscripts, in addition to scattered folios of the book borrowed from a friend of his. Unfortunately, the editor's benefit from the Madrid MS seems to have been limited to some extent due to the fact that he could not secure a copy of it and had to pay several visits to the Madrid library to peruse it, which did not prove practical in his case.[8] And ever since, this edited Arabic text, frustratingly incomplete, has been our sole source for al-Tujībī's cookbook that is accessible in print form.

---

5 *La cocina arábigo-andaluza según un manuscrito inédito: tesis doctoral.* Facultad de Filosofía y Letras, Madrid, 1960. See Marín, "From al-Andalus to Spain," 37.

6 Published in Rabat under the title, *Fann al-ṭabkh fī al-Andalus wa-l-Maghrib fī bidāyat ʿaṣr banī Marīn: Fadālat* [*sic*] *al-khiwān fī ṭayyibāt al-ṭaʿām wa-l-alwān*. It is unclear why the word فضالة in the Arabic title occurred as فدالة.

7 This time entitled *Faḍālat al-khiwān fī ṭayyibāt al-ṭaʿām wa-l-alwān: ṣūra min fann al-ṭabkh fī al-Andalus wa-l-Maghrib fī bidāyat ʿaṣr banī Marīn.*

8 See the editor's introduction, p. 7.

That is, until a third manuscript, this time a complete one, unexpectedly came my way while I was working on the translation of the text and was about to tackle the dreaded incomplete sections. I got an email from the British Library curator of Arabic Scientific Manuscripts to the effect that while cataloguing manuscript Or. 5927, previously listed as an anonymous pharmaceutical compendium of Maghribi origin,[9] he discovered that it also contains a very long fragment of a cookbook (fols. 101r–204v).[10] My task was to identify this cookery fragment. I took one look at the first page and immediately recognized it as al-Tujībī's; I kept 'leafing' through it, and there I found all the text missing from the Berlin and the Madrid manuscripts. There, in front of me at last, was the complete document, minus a folio at the beginning containing list of the book's sections and the title of the book, which are already copied in the Berlin and the Madrid MSS; and a folio at the end, material for which is already provided in the Madrid MS.[11]

This newly discovered copy (henceforward referred to as **BL MS**) turned out to be identical with the Berlin MS, albeit complete and earlier in execution. The missing material from the Berlin and Madrid MSS that the BL MS provides includes the completion of the carrot chapter, vii.3, and the altogether missing chapters vii.4 on desert truffles, vii.5 on asparagus, vii.6 on cardoons, vii.7 on mushrooms, x.1 on mustard sauces, and x.6 on pickling fish. In addition, it contains more recipes in part viii on pulses and chapter x.2 on curing olives. Chapters x.3 and x.4 have more recipes with more details on pickling capers and lemons, and chapter x.5 on pickling vegetables is complete, with more

9 As catalogued in Hamarneh, *Catalogue of Arabic Manuscripts on Medicine and Pharmacy at the British Library* (Cairo, 1975), pp. 249–50. Catalogued earlier as an anonymous pharmacopeia, 219 folios, fifteenth to sixteenth century, in Ellis, and Edwards, *A Descriptive List of the Arabic Manuscripts Acquired by the Trustees of the British Museum Since 1894* (London, 1912), p. 47.

10 I am grateful to BL curator Dr. Bink Hallum, and to Dr. Leigh Chipman, independent scholar of medieval Islamic pharmacy and medicine, for suggesting my name to Hallum.

11 The manuscripts bound with al-Tujībī's cookbook are:

1. *Ṣināʿat al-yad*, which though catalogued as anonymous has its authorship by Ibn ʿAbd Rabbihi stated in its last folio, 67r. The author was well-known tenth-century Andalusi physician Saʿīd b. ʿAbd Rabbihi, nephew of renowned author of *al-ʿIqd al-farīd* (The unique necklace), Ibn ʿAbd Rabbihi. See Ibn Abī Uṣaybiʿa. *ʿUyūn al-anbāʾ* 326–7, for more on this physician.
2. A treatise on dietetics, which though entered as anonymous, upon examination, I discovered that it is no other than Ibn Zuhr's *Kitāb al-aghdhiya.*
3. An anonymous cookery document, which I discovered to be al-Tujībī's *Fiḍālat al-khiwān.*
4. An anonymous treatise on craft techniques.

FIGURE 4 The first folio of *Fiḍālat al-khiwān* in the BL MS, fol. 101r
ANONYMOUS TREATISE ON COOKERY, BRITISH LIBRARY: ORIENTAL MANUSCRIPTS, OR 5927, FF. 101R–204V, IN *QATAR DIGITAL LIBRARY* HTTPS://WWW.QDL.QA/ARCHIVE/81055/VDC_100069662454.0X000002

recipes. Chapter x.7 on making various types of vinegar is complete, with 16 recipes compared with the two incomplete recipes included in the Madrid MS. Added to these are a number of recipes scattered throughout and expressions and explanations not found in the other two MSS.

Like the Berlin MS, the BL MS is anonymous, and the title al-Tujībī provides in his introduction is also missing as it occurs in the missing folio at the beginning of the book. The manuscript is copied in Maghribi script, slightly different from that of the Madrid MS, and tends to get a bit harder to read with unaided eyes towards the end on account of some water damage in the upper parts of the folios.[12] There are also several places of misplaced folios, which I put back where they should be in the course of the translation. For a list of the folios' proper sequence, see p. XXVIII above.

Regarding the Madrid MS, stylistically it is not a faithful copy of the BL MS but more like an 'edited' version, which opts for a more elliptical use of the language. Instead of beginning almost all the recipes with the instruction to take the ingredient first and then do things with it, as is the case in the BL MS, the Madrid MS skips this formulaic beginning. For instance, *tu'khadh al-dajāj al-simān fatudhbaḥ* (take fat chickens and slaughter them) becomes *tudhbaḥ al-dajāj al-simān* (slaughter fat chickens). Additionally, the formulaic ending in the BL MS in almost all the recipes, *wa yu'kal hanīʾan in shāʾa-llāh taʿālā* (and eat it salubriously, God Almighty willing), and variations on it, are almost nonexistent in the Madrid MS.

Also, certain statements mentioned in the BL and Berlin MS are left out in the Madrid MS, and vice versa. Granted, although the three of them were made in al-Maghrib, they belong to different periods in the history of the region. In the BL MS, estimated to have been written around the fifteenth century, the closest to the time of the original book, a personal comment made by al-Tujībī, which reveals Murcia to be his hometown and in which he expresses wishes for the captured Valencia to be back in the hands of the Muslims (recipe i.3.11), is not found in the seventeenth-century Madrid MS, perhaps rendered pointless in its time. Similar is the case where parsley is used in one of the recipes. Whereas in the BL MS the Andalusi Romance ('Ajamiyya) *būshīn* is given, the Madrid MS does not include a name that was of little relevance in its time. The same with the *qunilyāt*, the European wild rabbits that were prevalent in al-Andalus but not in al-Maghrib. When these rabbits are used, as in recipes i.2.25 and ii.5.7, the Madrid MS adds 'if available.' Or as in the case when mention of

12 I was able to surmount this hurdle by manipulating the images with the help of Photoshop software.

FIGURE 5 The last folio of *Fiḍālat al-khiwān* in the BL MS, fol. 204v
ANONYMOUS TREATISE ON COOKERY, BRITISH LIBRARY: ORIENTAL MANUSCRIPTS, OR 5927, FF. 101R–204V, IN *QATAR DIGITAL LIBRARY* HTTPS://WWW.QDL.QA/ARCHIVE/81055/VDC_100069662454.0X000002

Byzantium is made, whereas the BL MS invokes God's destruction upon them, *ahlakahā Allāh*, the Madrid MS does not have it, simply because Byzantium had already been defeated and hence the curse would have been redundant. On the other hand, it was only the Madrid MS that preserved for us the most interesting and rarest medieval cookbook author's commentary on the significance of the written recipes, stressing their theoretical as well as practical purposes. Commenting on the recipes at the end of chapter i.2, al-Tujībī writes:

> Even though most of [the recipes in the chapter] might hardly ever get to be cooked and tried, including them will indeed rarely fail to please with their novelty and exquisiteness. This is also true of most of the other chapters in this book.[13]

The full text of the *Fiḍālat al-khiwān*, as the BL MS has recently revealed, is considerably long, comprising a total of 474 recipes grouped into 60 chapters, which in turn fall into 12 parts:

1. The first part is about foods and dishes incorporating grains, and it has five chapters and a total of 97 recipes. It starts with varieties of bread, followed by dishes of *tharīd*, in which bread is the principal ingredient. Grain-based soups and porridges follow and then pastries of all kinds, including those made with cheese, called *mujabbanāt*, and the doughnut-like *isfanj*. The part ends with grain-based dishes that are cooked or sopped in broth. This includes varieties of couscous, pasta, and noodles.
2. The second part has six chapters and 90 recipes that deal with dishes cooked with the meat of quadrupeds (*dhawāt al-arbaʿ*). It methodically starts with beef, followed by mutton and lamb, followed by young goats, and then the wild meat of animals like deer, oryxes, gazelles, rabbits, and the like. The part conveniently ends with a short chapter dealing with foods that are made with ground meat and are usually incorporated into the cooking dishes, such as meatballs, sausages, haggis-like stuffed tripe, and more.
3. With seven chapters and 79 recipes, the third part deals with various types of poultry, beginning with geese, followed by chickens, and then partridges, squabs, turtledoves, starlings, and sparrows.
4. The fourth part is a short one, with three chapters and three recipes only. This part is like a finale to the preceding two parts dealing with a variety of meats.

---

13 وفيما ذكرت من انواع الثرايد كفاية, وان كان اكثرها مما لا يكاد يعمل فقلما يخلو من زيادة مستطرفة, وكذلك اكثر فصول هذا الكتاب.

5. The fifth part deals with fish and eggs in two chapters and 44 recipes.
6. Dairy products, such as cheese, yogurt, and butter, are the subjects of the sixth part, with its three chapters and 13 recipes.
7. Part seven, with its ten chapters and 47 recipes, and part eight, with its three chapters and 13 recipes, tackle meatless dishes that use vegetables and pulses. Meatless dishes were usually offered as side dishes and snack foods. Gourds and eggplants are given a fair share of the recipes and, to a lesser extent, so are recipes with vegetables like carrots, desert truffles, asparagus, varieties of cardoon, and mushrooms, as well as leaf vegetables like spinach, lettuce, and taro. The pulses used are lentils, as well as fava beans and chickpeas, both fresh and dried.
8. Sweets are the subject of the ninth part with its seven chapters and 26 recipes. They range from starch-based thickened puddings with honey to confectionary, like nougat, and pulled taffy to chewy candy, delicate ring cookies, and almond and walnut brittle, among others.
9. The tenth part, with its 12 chapters and 51 recipes, deals with food preservation, such as preserving fish in vinegar, curing meat, pickling vegetables, curing olives, making the grain-based fermented *murrī* sauce, and making vinegar. It also deals with extracting oils and remedying foods.
10. The eleventh part is short, with three recipes that deal with small edible creatures: locusts, freshwater shrimps, and land snails.
11. Finally, eating is followed by handwashing, and the twelfth part duly contains eight recipes for handwashing preparations.

As the above structural outline clearly demonstrates, exemplary organization and control of material characterize the book of *Fiḍāla* as a culinary document from the medieval era. In this respect it is completely antithetical to the only other surviving Andalusi cookbook contemporaneous with al-Tujībī's, the anonymous *Anwāʿ al-ṣaydala fī alwān al-aṭʿima*,[14] which is marred with disorganization, although still impressively interesting for its frequent references to historical figures, most of whom are recognizable, as well as its anecdotes and various commentaries.

The organizing factor in this collection of recipes is the main ingredient in the dishes. In this controlled structure, it should not surprise us that the numerous cross-references in the book are accurate. In recipe iii.7.3 for cooking sparrows, for instance, al-Tujībī says, "cook them as was described in the second chapter of the third part of this book"; and in recipe iii.7.4, he directs the reader

14 "A smorgasbord of Andalusi and Maghribi dishes and their salutary benefits." See n. 2 above.

to a basting mix mentioned earlier in the "fifth chapter of the third part of this book," and so on. Of course, I always managed to find my way through al-Tujībī's maze of cross-references with the aid of Microsoft Office, but back then, this was a feat. This naturally reflects on al-Tujībī's writing skills and good memory, manifested throughout, which should not be surprising given that such faculties were indeed the tools of the trade for the attainment of scholarship at the time.

In the sources we have on him (see next section), al-Tujībī was highly praised as an amiable hospitable host, and yet none of them mentioned, not even casually, that cooking was a subject of interest to him. Based on his book, however, we can safely say that he indeed knew a thing or two about cooking and good eating. What distinguishes the book of *Fiḍāla* from the rest of the extant Arabic medieval cookbooks is the large number of lengthy recipes in which a given cooking process is detailed. For instance, in recipe iii.1.1 for cooking an elaborately stuffed goose in the cavity and underneath the skin, the instruction is to let it boil gently in a pot and check on it all the time by turning it with care; and the recipe continues, "To prevent the bird's skin from rupturing while boiling in the pot, let there be with you a large needle ready to prick the skin; thus, any steam [forming underneath it] will find a way to escape without breaking it." In a recipe for *mujabbana*, a cheese pastry (i.4.33), the description of forming the pieces and frying them is so detailed you can almost see what is being done to them,

> Take a piece of the cheese with your right hand, put it in the middle of the dough and gather its edges on it. Now, encase and press this *mujabbana* in your left hand; do this tightly so that it comes out through the thumb and index fingers; cut away the surplus dough, flatten the *mujabbana* [which is now] on top of the thumb [and index fingers] with the back of the right hand, press a single hole in the middle, and put it in the skillet.

In an omelet dish (recipe v.2.1), the pinwheels of folded thin omelets are to be fried in shallow oil, with the following details: "If the skillet gets too crowded with the pieces, take some out to make more room for the rest to fry easily. Turn the pieces over gently to avoid breaking them." This sort of empirical culinary knowledge can only be accumulated with experience and attention to details.

All the recipes follow formulaic beginnings and endings, starting with the cook taking an ingredient, such as, "take the best cuts of lamb," and then cooking instructions follow. Almost all the recipes end with the writer's wishes for the eaters to enjoy the dish in good health; a congenial gesture and a conventional device denoting the end of the recipe. Far from being tedious, these rhythmic repetitions set a regular pattern that draw prospective cooks to the recipes and get them going. Instructions in between are generally well explained, which comes as no surprise as we are dealing here with a trained scribe and a distinguished literary personage. Occasionally, the text uses ʿAjamiyya, which is Andalusi Romance. In recipe ii.1.9, dealing with a Christian meat dish, al-Tujībī gives the Andalusi name *būshīn* for *maqdūnis* 'Macedonian parsley.' In the same recipe, a table sauce that was called *ṣalṣ* in contemporary Egypt is called *jalja* here,[15] and *shalsha* in a fish dish, recipe v.1.5. The European wild rabbit indigenous to southern Spain, cooked in several recipes in chapter ii.5, is called *qunilya*, from the Spanish *conejo*. The sparrow is called *barṭāl* in recipe viii.1.7, from the Spanish *pardal*; the cutting board is *ṭalya*, as in recipe ii.6.4, and the delicate variety of thin bread is called *shabāt*.[16]

The Amazigh element is also present, principally in the names of dishes and ingredients but also in cooking practices characteristic of their cuisine. The fourth part is dedicated to dishes for which Ṣinhāj, one of the largest Amazigh tribes in North Africa, was famous. In recipe i.5.10, the Amazigh term *bāzīn* is used to designate a cone-shaped mass of bread. Some ingredients are given using their Amazigh names, such as *afzān* for wild cardoon, *tirfās* for desert truffles, and *zunbūʿ* for Damascus citron; otherwise called *kabbād* in al-Mashriq. And, of course, couscous, for which we have five recipes in chapter i.5.

Names of recipes are generally conventional; often calling a dish by the main ingredient, such as a meat cut or vegetable, or not giving it a name at all, of which we have many instances of referring to a recipe as *lawn ʾākhar* 'another dish variety.' Still, we do encounter dishes with some interesting names, such as *raʾs maymūn* 'the blessed head' (recipes i.4.24–5, i.2.44), *shāshiyyat ibn al-waḍīʿ* 'cap of the lowlife son' (recipe i.2.8) and *dajājat ʿumrūs* 'the chubby boy's chicken' (recipe iii.2.20). Of dishes pertaining to religious groups, al-Tujībī gives the Jewish *Yahūdiyya* chicken dish (recipe iii.2.21) and the Christian *rāhibī* prepared with beef (recipe ii.1.7). He also includes a *muthawwama* dish, cooked with garlic in celebration of the Christian New Year festival in January (recipe i.2.25). Of the dishes described as Mashriqi, which are claimed to have originated in the eastern region of the Arabo-Muslim world, al-Tujībī includes a good number, even though he professes in his introduction that he kept them to a minimum in favor of Andalusi ones.

Since we are told nothing about al-Tujībī's culinary aspirations or gastronomic involvements by the people who knew him (see the next section), we

15 As in the anonymous fourteenth-century Egyptian cookbook *Kanz al-fawāʾid*, English trans., *Treasure Trove*, chapter 16.

16 See glossary 2, s.v. *shabāt*, for more on this bread.

have only his cookbook to answer the question as to why he wrote it in the first place, and for whom. There is no indication in al-Tujībī's introduction that he was commissioned. Most likely he was motivated by the desire to preserve the Andalusi cuisine he knew quite well from his years growing up in Murcia, where he led a life of luxury. A cuisine he cherished was in danger of being forgotten or lost, with multitudes of his countrymen fleeing al-Andalus like himself. When he wrote the book in Tunis in the late 1260s, he had no qualms about declaring his bias towards Andalusi foods. In justifying his predilection, he says:

> I here state that in the field of cooking and whatever is related to it, Andalusis are indeed admirably earnest and advanced despite the fact that they started later [than people of al-Mashriq] in creating the most delectable dishes, and in spite of the constricting limitations of their borders, and their proximity to the abodes of the enemies of Islam.

It was not only Mashriqi dishes that he was prejudiced against. We also come across a recipe that reveals what he really thinks of foods consumed by people with whom he spent a good portion of his life in Ifrīqiya; first in Bijāya and then Tunis, where he stayed the rest of his life. At the end of recipe ix.3.4 for marzipan-like *sanbūsak* made the Andalusi way, al-Tujībī proudly protests, "This is the true *sanbūsak*. As for what people of Ifrīqiya make of *sanbūsak* stuffed with pounded meat, it is to be sure devoid of any flavor, and far from being delicious" (ليس فيه طعم ولا لذاذة). In the Madrid MS, this sentiment is given even a stronger tone, "Look at the *sanbūsaka* people of Ifrīqiya make! … It is neither commendable nor relished" (أنظر الذي يصنعه اهل افريقية ... فليس بمستحسن ولا مستطاب).

Given all the trouble it took al-Tujībī to put together this complex structure of a book and the great lengths he went to explain the complicated cooking processes for creating some of the elaborate stuffed dishes, not neglecting to include, wherever needed, useful tips to ensure successful results, it is feasible to assume that al-Tujībī would have wanted his book to be used as a practical culinary guide. He was also ahead of his time in advocating for the notion that cookbooks can indeed be read for entertainment as well, which comes as no surprise given his literary credentials. At the end of a long series of recipes for the favorite *tharāyid* dishes in chapter i.2, he declares:

> What I have mentioned of the varieties of *tharīd* dishes above should be sufficient, God Almighty willing. Still, even though most of them might hardly ever get to be cooked and tried, including them will indeed rarely fail to please with their novelty and exquisiteness. This is also true of most of the other chapters in this book.

1.2 *Ibn Razīn al-Tujībī* (1227–1293)

> She adorns trays and tables, a dazzling virgin in whose adoration people congregate. She comes out only when tightly squeezed in the palm of the hand and can only swim in the fountain after being pressed. She might cool down a lover's heart, but she is hot.
>
> A riddle in prose on fried *mujabbana* (cheese pastry) by IBN RAZĪN AL-TUJĪBĪ[17]

Up until recently, our knowledge of Ibn Razīn al-Tujībī has been indeed meager. From the exordium of the Madrid MS, we get his full name: Abū al-Ḥasan ʿAlī bin Muḥammad bin Abī al-Qāsim Ibn Muḥammad bin Abī Bakr Razīn al-Tujībī al-Andalusi; and from the profuse epithets that preceded his name, *al-faqīh, al-adīb, al-kātib al-muʿannā, al-ʿallāma* (the learned scholar, eloquent scribe, and most erudite), we get the idea that he was an esteemed man of letters, recognized in his own time and even beyond, perhaps for two or three more generations, as his passing away was duly acknowledged in the manuscript. Furthermore, internal evidence, in a recipe for cooking rice (i.3.11), reveals the region where he was born and the approximate time during which he might have written it.[18]

It was only in 2009, with the publication of *Ibn Razīn al-Tujībī: Ḥayātuhu wa āthāruhu* on his life and works by Moroccan scholar Muḥammad Bin Sharīfa, that we came to know more about him. Bin Sharīfa garnered his data from several medieval biographical catalogues,[19] from which we learn that Ibn Razīn al-Tujībī was born into an affluent and well-established Andalusi family in Murcia. It was distinguished for its high standing, social status, and nobility, which indeed justifies the epithet *al-ḥasīb* (highborn) attached to his name in sources

---

17 Quoted in Bin Sharīfa, *Ibn Razīn al-Tujībī* 105. For a useful brief survey of al-Tujībī's life and his cookbook, see Marín, "The cook-book of Ibn Razīn al-Tujībī," 516–7.

18 In this recipe he mentions that rice grew abundantly in *Mursiya baladī* "Murcia my hometown" and *Balansiya aʿādahā Allāh* "Valencia, may God return it to the Muslims." I will elaborate on this point shortly.

19 A catalogue of this sort was called *fihris* and *barnāmaj*, typically containing lists with brief lives of learned literary and religious scholars, with the names of their masters (*sheikhs*) and students. Of these, Bin Sharīfa mentions al-ʿAbdarī, *Riḥla*, al-Wādī Āshī, *Barnāmaj*, and others. The most important and the longest account was by Ibn Rushayd (d. 1321) in his *Riḥla*. The entire section related to al-Tujībī is included in Bin Sharīfa's biography of him, 44–125. Ibn Rushayd, a well-known traveler, judge, and author from the Maghreb, was al-Tujībī's devout follower and a close companion with whom he exchanged visitations. He is our only source for the little we know of al-Tujībī's personal life.

that mention him.[20] He was born around 1227.[21] His grandfather on his father's side was the well-to-do Abū al-Qāsim al-Shaqūrī. He married one of his freed mawlas, Nabīl al-Rūmī, to his daughter (al-Tujībī's aunt), and they had a son (al-Tujībī's cousin), whose name was Abū al-Qāsim Aḥmad b. Abī al-Ḥasan Nabīl. Al-Tujībī's father died when he was still young, and his cousin Abū al-Qāsim was the one to raise him. Al-Tujībī later expressed his gratitude for his cousin, whom he describes as an accomplished judge and who treated him like his own son and took care of his education.

Murcia, where al-Tujībī grew up, was a prosperous, well-populated, and fortified city in the southeast of al-Andalus.[22] It was often described as a beautiful place, whose air was pleasant and water sweet, and whose land was fertile, growing wheat and barley, mostly dependent on irrigation. It was renowned for its agricultural bounties, such as grapes and figs. It was said to be comparable to Seville, surrounded by numerous gardens and orchards, with a river that ran through it, with many watermills all along its banks. Its rolling countryside of Shanqanīra was where the wonderful wheat berries were grown; each head containing 80 to 100 kernels.[23] To get to the gate of Murcia, one would walk a stretch of a road under a canopy of trees, listening to the singing of birds and the burbling of flowing streams of water.[24]

Al-Tujībī's time, however, was a time of political turmoil, with the rapid decline of Muslim rule in al-Andalus. In 1242 Murcia surrendered to the Christian King Fernando III of Castile according to a treaty that turned it into a protectorate of the crown of Castile, allowing the population the right to continue with their normal lives and religious practices. Around 1247, however, the Christian monarchy breeched the treaty; Muslims left in large numbers, but others chose to stay as Mudejars.[25] Eventually, in 1266, and according to another

---

20 Such as Ibn Rushayd and al-ʿAbdarī, see Bin Sharīfa, *Ibn Razīn al-Tujībī* 13.

21 According to al-Wādī Āshī and al-ʿAbdarī, who were not sure of the exact year.

22 See, for instance, al-Idrīsī, *Nuzhat al-Mushtāq* ii. 558–9. Modern researchers believe that Murcia is Roman in origin, considering its Latin name and what remained of an ancient settlement. "However, if the roots are Roman, the tree is Arab. The city owes its existence to the Umayyads, to ʿAbd al-Raḥmān II, the great builder and organizer," in the words of González, "From the Roman to the Arab," 216. For a relatively recent publication on Murcia in Spanish, see Martínez, *La Murcia Andalusí* (711–1243).

23 See anonymous *Tārīkh al-Andalus* 136. The average number of kernels is 50.

24 See ibid., for instance.

25 Mudejars (in Arabic, *mudajjanūn*, sg. *mudajjan*) generally were Muslim subjects living within the Crowns of Castile and Aragon and were allowed to practice their usual religious activities. In reality, as Constable, *To Live Like a Moor* 9, explains, their lives "were increasingly restricted and impoverished, their religious practices curtailed." Mudejars

treaty, the city was annexed to the Castilian Crown. It was at the breeching of the treaty in 1247 that Ibn Razīn al-Tujībī and his cousin's family left Murcia. He was about 20 years of age.

The first station in al-Tujībī's life in exile was the Moroccan city of Sabta (Ceuta), where he stayed with his cousin until 1251. Ceuta at the time had become a refuge for a huge number of Andalusi immigrants, especially from the east, with many notables among them, including al-Tujībī's cousin and his father-in-law and their families. Ibn Razīn continued to pursue his studies at the hands of the literary masters (*sheikh*s) and religious scholars (*muḥaddith*s), while his cousin worked as a judge until he died in 1270 in Ceuta.

The second station was Bijāya, a Mediterranean port city in Ifrīqiya;[26] he moved there in 1251. He was 24 years old at the time and wished to go with the scholars he followed to that city. Bijāya at the time was ruled by the Hafsid dynasty (al-Ḥafṣiyyūn), and it was the second city in importance after Tunis, their capital. It was a prosperous and active Mediterranean port city, an important fort, and a cultural center attracting men of learning fleeing al-Andalus.

Ibn Razīn al-Tujībī spent eight years in this city actively engaged in reading, writing, and memorizing *ḥadīth*s until 1259. Of the most influential scholars he met there and followed was the renowned man of letters, the Andalusi Ibn ʾAbbār.[27] Al-Tujībī was one of his brightest students, from whom he earned a written license (*ijāza*) in 1256, allowing him to transmit all he had learnt from him in prose and verse.[28]

The last station was Tunis. He was 32 years old when he left Bijāya and settled there for the rest of his life; he died in 1293 at the age of 66. Tunis became his second home. It was the period in his life when he got married and settled down with a family of his own. It was also a period of intellectual maturity, during which he wrote many works variously dealing with historical, cultural, and literary matters, as we understand from the biographical catalogue *Barnāmaj* by al-Wādī Āshī, where he mentions five of them. Two chronicles, *al-Aḥbār al-Tūnisiyya fī al-akhbār al-Firansiyya*, on the French Crusades in Tunis, and *al-Durar al-thamīna fī khabar al-Qull wa fatḥ Qusnaṭīna*, on quelling an uprising in the Algerian city of Constantine. Three other works were anthologies of

---

were urged to leave the Iberian Peninsula, as the argument of North African jurists was that life as true Muslims in such conditions was not possible.

26 In medieval times, Ifrīqiya constituted the coastal regions of what today are western Libya, Tunisia, and eastern Algeria.

27 Abū ʿAbdallāh Muḥammad al-Quḍāʿī. He was native of Valencia, born in 1199, and died in Tunis in 1260. He was well known in al-Andalus and North Africa as a poet, historian, critic, linguist, and biographer, among other accomplishments.

28 See Bin Sharīfa, *Ibn Razīn al-Tujībī* 25–6.

FIGURE 6 A map of Bijāya, W.658.274b, Piri Reis, *Book on Navigation*, detail
THE WALTERS ART MUSEUM, W.658, ACQUIRED BY HENRY WALTERS

literary works in prose and verse: *Naẓm al-farīd fī muntakhab al-adab al-ṭārif wa-l-talīd*, *Janā al-zahr wa sanā al-zuhr*, and a collection of his own prose and poetry.[29]

With the exception of his cookbook *Fiḍālat al-khiwān*, as well as some extracts of his prose and poetry preserved in Ibn Rushayd's *Riḥla*,[30] and his own brief *barnāmaj* of the masters whom he listened to and who licensed him and his followers who listened to him and whom he licensed,[31] nothing else remains of his other works, even though there is evidence that they continued to be in circulation in Tunis and Granada up until end of the fifteenth century.[32]

29 Al-Wādī Āshī, *Barnāmaj* 70–1.

30 On Ibn Rushayd, see n. 19 above.

31 See Bin Sharīfa, *Ibn Razīn al-Tujībī*, 147–8. The Arabic term used for this practice of licensing was *ijāza*, mentioned above.

32 The latest allusions to al-Tujībī's works were made by the Muslim jurist Abū ʿAbdallāh b.

It is regrettable that we know very little about the domestic aspect of al-Tujībī's life in Tunis. We do not know how he earned his living; there is mention, however, of him taking temporary scribal tasks in the administration of the ruling Hafsids.[33] Otherwise, it seems he spent most of his time writing and exchanging visitations with peers and hosting aspiring scholars visiting Tunis seeking knowledge at his hands. They all raved about how amiable, kind, and gentle he was.

Although none of the existent sources ever associate his name with gourmandise, let alone mention a cookbook he wrote,[34] enough anecdotes do suggest that food indeed was one of the subjects dear to his heart. A case in point is a long prose riddle addressed to a friend on the subject of *mujabbana*, a popular cheese pastry in al-Andalus. He describes it in terms of a plump beautiful woman: blonde, delicious, a dazzling virgin in whose adoration people congregate. She comes out only when tightly squeezed in the palm of the hand and can only swim in the fountain after being pressed.[35]

He was also interested in reciting other poets' descriptions of foods, as in the case of a poem on muskmelon (*biṭṭīkh*),[36] or on how to live well:

> Five things in this world you need to seize, my friend, before the other five, and you will do well.
> A healthy body, prosperity, and leisure time, before you get overburdened, poor, and sick.
> Enjoy youth and live well, because before you know it, you will get old and die.[37]

In the opinion of his friends, visiting scholars, and seekers of knowledge who used to visit him in his home, he had a lovable and most obliging character. They were most impressed by his friendliness and praised his welcoming spirit and hospitality. It must have been in Tunis, where he settled in exile, that he wrote the book of *Fiḍāla*, as we may guess from his comment on an unusual

---

al-Azraq al-Andalusi (d. 1491), see Bin Sharīfa, *Ibn Razīn al-Tujībī* 130. See introduction ii.6.1 below for more on Ibn al-Azraq.

33 See Bin Sharīfa, *Ibn Razīn al-Tujībī* 134.

34 In any case, a book like this one dealing with the subject of food recipes would not have been considered serious enough to include in their accounts.

35 Al-Tujībī's text is cited in Bin Sharīfa, *Ibn Razīn al-Tujībī* 105–6. It is interesting to see the similarities between how al-Tujībī describes how *mujabbana* is formed here and his recipe i.4.33.

36 Bin Sharīfa, *Ibn Razīn al-Tujībī* 120.

37 Ibid., 122.

variety of bread made with *banīj* (proso millet), recipe i.1.5. He says, "Of all types of bread made with grains other than wheat, [*banīj*] is the Andalusis' favorite; they find it delicious and unusual and eat a good deal of it during the yield season of the grain in their country."[38] The reference to al-Andalus and Andalusis as 'they' and 'their country' may point to the possibility that by then al-Andalus was no longer his country of residence.

Similarly, we may infer as to when he wrote his cookbook from a recipe for cooking rice (i.3.11), in which he mentions that this grain grew abundantly in *Mursiya baladī* (Murcia my hometown) and *Balansiya aʿādahā Allāh* (Valencia, may God return it to the Muslims), which could be any time between its first capture by the Christians in 1238 and until around the 1270s, after which entertaining hopes of its returning to Muslim hands was unrealistic. Given what we know of his life, it would be reasonable then to have him write the cookbook in Tunis in the 1260s, and before his cousin's death in 1270. It is my suspicion that financially al-Tujībī was dependent on his loving and dedicated cousin, who brought him up as his own son and with whom he fled to Ceuta. While his cousin stayed and lived a comfortable life as a judge there, al-Tujībī left in pursuit of his passion for learning for many years and then settled in Tunis. After his cousin's death in 1270, evidently al-Tujībī's financial means dried out.

Ibn Rushayd, who was al-Tujībī's 'biographer' and a devout follower, has preserved in his *Riḥla* a poem in which al-Tujībī looks back to his prosperous past and contrasts it with the obscure present, comparing himself to an idle sword in its sheath. Around the year 1286, several years before al-Tujībī's death, Ibn Rushayd, who was also his close companion and with whom he exchanged visitations, gives us a rare glimpse into al-Tujībī's domestic life. He writes, "One day I visited him during my return to Tunis, and I did not see a single object of value; just the bare essentials, like tattered cobwebs that can hardly protect." He movingly commented that although he did not get from this world what was enough to support his family and children, he was not bitter or resentful but accepting of his lot of poverty with his familiar integrity, patience, and generosity of the soul.[39]

Al-Tujībī died in the afternoon on Friday, the twelfth of Shaʿbān, 692/ 1293, at the age of 66.[40] While his name went into obscurity within two centuries or so, his cookbook, *Fiḍālat al-khiwān*, alone got a life of its own, living in posterity, copied and copied again; of which, so far, we are fortunate to have three of them.

---

38 لاستطرافه عند الاندلسيين وكثرة استعمالهم له في فصل غلته ببلادهم.
39 Bin Sharīfa, *Ibn Razīn al-Tujībī* 32. See also n. 19 above.
40 Ibid., 39. Al-Tujībī's death was also reported by Ibn Rushayd.

I.3 Fiḍālat al-khiwān: *Sources*

> In *Kitāb Tafsīr al-adwiya* by Ibn Janāḥ, I have come across a variety of cured meat called *namaksūd*, which is meat cured with crushed salt.
>
> From *Fiḍālat al-khiwān*, recipe x.11

In his own introduction, al-Tujībī remarks that his book of *Fiḍāla* abounds with dishes that he approved of and many more that he himself created. The following is an attempt to reveal the sources he might have used in reproducing the dishes and foods that he favored and gave his signature of approval to.

i.3.1. In chapter x.11 for curing meat, al-Tujībī cites a source for a variety of salt-cured meat called *namaksūd*. According to this technique a whole ram (*kabsh*) or a side of it is salt-cured without cutting it into thin slices. He says he found it described in *Kitāb Tafsīr al-adwiya* (Book on explaining medicinal drugs) by **Ibn Janāḥ**. His source's full name is Abū al-Walīd Marwān b. Janāḥ al-Qurṭubī (d. 1050), a famous Andalusi Jewish rabbi, physician, and grammarian. The title of the book that al-Tujībī cites and copies almost verbatim is in fact *Kitāb al-Talkhīṣ*, and in the opinion of its editors, al-Tujībī's version of it is "a mere description of its content and not the actual title."[41] Al-Tujībī's explicit reference to his source here points to his unfamiliarity with this curing technique. Clearly, it was not something that he had tried himself; after describing it, he thus addresses the reader, "You may make it and test it for yourself."

This is by far the only source al-Tujībī openly declares to have used. While working on the translation of the book of *Fiḍāla*, I also discovered some other sources that he used, some copied verbatim and others with stylistic modifications, without acknowledgement.

i.3.2. **Ibn Zuhr** (d. 1161), Abū Marwān ʿAbd al-Malik, an Arab physician and surgeon born in Seville. For his introduction, al-Tujībī copies from his *Kitāb al-Aghdhiya*. The part dealing with observations on cooking utensils is derived from Ibn Zuhr's chapter on utensils, *Dhikr al-awānī* 136–8. Some of his passages

41 Bos et al, *Marwān ibn Janāḥ* 10. This is a fairly recent edition executed with an English translation, in two volumes. See also al-Tujībī's chapter x.11. By comparing the two texts, al-Tujībī seems to have used another copy, which displays a few stylistic and other differences. For instance, Ibn Janāḥ's "هذا اللحم قد سحق بالملح اي عرك به" reads as "وهو نوع اللحم المملح بالملح المسحوق" in al-Tujībī's; and "النمكسود يستعمل في الكبس صحيحا او مقسوما بنصفين" occurs in al-Tujībī's as "النمكسود يعمل من الكبش الصحيح او المقسوم بنصفين". Clearly, in the latter's version, *kabsh*, a ram, is being used in the process, whereas in the former, (item 627), *kabs*, pickling, is a reference to the curing process itself. Possibly, such a disparity could have been caused by a scribe's textual misreading.

are paraphrased and others are copied almost verbatim, with some stylistic changes and omissions. The section dealing with the order of having foods is also borrowed from Ibn Zuhr's chapter *Marātib al-aghdhiya*, 111–2.[42]

i.3.3. **Ibn al-Jazzār** (d. 980), Abū Jaʿfar Aḥmad al-Qayrawānī, was an Arab physician who spent his whole life in Qayrawān (Kairouan, in Tunisia today). Al-Tujībī's part xii, dealing with handwashing preparations, is entirely copied (with the exception of the last recipe) from his book, *Kitāb fī Funūn al-ṭīb wa-l-ʿiṭr*, 117–20.

i.3.4. The last recipe in the book, dealing with preserving sweet grape juice, is not related in subject matter to the last part on handwashing preparations. In the manuscript it is copied by the same hand, and there is no way to tell whether it was originally there or added in subsequent copies. Anyway, whoever did this must have copied it from either the eleventh-century agronomist **Ibn Baṣṣāl**'s *Kitāb al-Filāḥa* or the twelfth-century agronomist **Ibn al-ʿAwwām**'s *al-Filāḥa al-Andalusiyya*, where Ibn Baṣṣāl is cited as a source for this recipe.[43]

i.3.5. The book of *Fiḍāla* has a long chapter on making the liquid sauce *murrī*, both sun-fermented (*naqīʿ*) and cooked (*maṭbūkh*). Al-Tujībī must have copied it from some specialized pamphlets. Only in one case, recipe x.8.1, was I able to locate a surviving *murrī* recipe similar to his. It occurs in **al-Ṭighnarī**, *Zahrat al-bustān*, 139–43.[44] Al-Ṭighnarī mentions that the famous physician Abū al-Ḥasan Shihāb al-Muʿayṭī himself copied this recipe for him.[45]

i.3.6. I have also discovered some passages similar, in varying degrees, to al-Tujībī's text in *al-Filāḥa al-Rūmiyya* by **Qusṭā Ibn Lūqā** (d. 912), a Christian Syrian physician, translator, and agronomist:

---

42 I made the connection between Ibn Zuhr's *Kitāb al-Aghdhiya* and al-Tujībī's text independently. However, it has recently come to my attention that the Spanish scholar Expiración García Sánchez made a similar connection in 2005. I owe this information to the anonymous reviewer of this book, who provided the year of publication only. I am grateful to professor Kaj Öhrnberg for his assistance in locating the source: "Comida de enfermos, dieta de sanos: procesos culinarios y hábitos alimenticios en los textos médicos andalusiés," in *El banquete de las palabras* 72, n. 54.

Interestingly, I also found out that Ibn Zuhr's popular text was similarly copied, with some stylistic modifications, by al-Arbūlī (or al-Uryūlī), *al-Kalām ʿalā al-aghdhiya* 149–50. He was an Andalusi scholar and physician who lived in Granada in the fourteenth century.

43 See the last recipe for more details on these two sources.

44 Abū ʿAbd al-Malik al-Gharnāṭī, also called al-Ḥājj al-Gharnāṭī, was an agronomist, physician, and poet. He was alive in Seville in 1101.

45 It must have been a popular recipe. I also encountered it in the anonymous fourteenth-century *Kanz al-fawāʾid*, English trans., *Treasure Trove* 162–3.

1. Recipe x.9.1, which describes how to make *zayt* (olive oil) with ingredients other than olives, is similar to Qusṭā's text, 315, with some stylistic differences.
2. In al-Tujībī's recipe x.9.2, on remedying olive oil, there are similarities between the remedies offered there and those in Qusṭā's text, 318–9, 320; and, to some extent, the Andalusi agronomist al-Ṭighnarī, *Zahrat al-bustān* 208–9, who copied it from Qusṭā.

i.3.7. Al-Tujībī's *Fiḍāla*, furthermore, shares around 38 recipes with the anonymous cookbook *Anwāʿ al-ṣaydala fī alwān al-aṭʿima*, which, based on internal evidence, was authored/compiled by an Andalusi who lived in the western regions of al-Andalus, in the Seville/Cordova region,[46] most probably around the 1220s before the fall of Cordova and Seville, which took place in 1236 and 1248, respectively.[47] The overlap seems to occur in recipes mostly dealing with pastries and sweets but also with some savory ones. They are scattered throughout the book and almost always differ stylistically in varying degrees.[48] There is only one instance where the recipes are clearly identical, and that is the *narjisiyya* dish (*Fiḍāla* ii.2.17, *Anwāʿ al-ṣaydala* 136). There is another instance where it is obvious that a similar source is being used: in the short opening statement of al-Tujībī's fish chapter v.1, dealing with the proper way to prepare fish before using it in cooking the dishes (corresponding text in *Anwāʿ al-ṣaydala* 149), and the concluding paragraph (corresponding text in *Anwāʿ al-ṣaydala* 155), dealing with ways to avert the harms of eating fish. The similarities between the two cookbooks by no means indicate the possibility of one being the source for the other; rather, they point to drawing on similar popular sources.

The picture we get of how the book of *Fiḍāla* came to be written is that of an amalgam of elements, some of which drew on culinary sources in al-Tujībī's time from which he picked the recipes he 'approved of.' For issues pertaining to nutriments, maintaining one's health, and hygiene, there were physicians' books he could help himself to; and for chapters dealing with foods that required skills more complicated than those of daily cooking and needed

46 At several places in this cookbook, the author's references related to al-Andalus indicate that he was there when he did the book. For instance, he refers to the feasts "that are held in our abodes," p. 6; a *mujabbana* recipe "as our country people prepare them in west of al-Andalus, such as Cordova, Seville, and Sharīsh," p. 181.

47 Internal evidence is drawn from allusions to rulers, viziers, and the like. The latest mentioned is Abū Saʿīd, whose name is associated with *mujabbana* cheese pastries, p. 182. He was vizier to al-Nāṣir li-Dīn Allāh, who died in 1214.

48 Instances of overlapping in recipes are pointed out in the footnotes to the translated text wherever relevant.

a certain level of expertise, such as cheese making, curing olives, pickling, and making the labor-intensive fermented sauces, he drew on books of agronomy. A case in point is the first recipe in chapter x.2 on curing olives. After the necessary steps are taken to clean and pack them in a jar and submerge them in water, the instruction that follows is to "set them aside as was described above." Given this is the first recipe in al-Tujībī's chapter, obviously it is the case here that this chapter must have been taken from a source, most probably one specialized in pickling foods, where other olive recipes preceded this one.

The rest we may assume that he worked on himself; he could have developed some of the dishes and wrote the recipes himself; for others, he might have rewritten other cooks' recipes in his own words with details based on his own observations and personal experience. His role in transmitting and documenting an oral culinary tradition is certainly further revealed in recipe i.2.27, where he gives a variation on a *tharīd* dish of dried fava beans, which somebody told him about:

> I have also heard that when the crumbled bread is added to the cooked and mashed fava beans, milk is gradually poured into the pot until enough is added. After emptying it [into a *tharīd* bowl], it would be sprinkled with sugar, with bowls of honey (*'asal*) offered to eat with the *tharīd*. I personally have neither cooked it this way nor eaten it, but let those who wish to try it do so.

Part II: Food and Foodways in al-Andalus

II.4 *Diet and Formation of a Cuisine*

> بيت لا تين فيه جياع أهله
>
> A house empty of figs; its people are hungry indeed.
>
> An Arabic saying on the abundance of figs in al-Andalus.[49]

When they came to Iberia to establish colonies around 300 BC, the Carthaginians must have been so impressed by the number of rabbits they encountered that they called the region Ispania, which means 'Land of Rabbits.' The Romans

49 It is analogous to a similar saying on the abundance of dates in al-Mashriq. See al-Bakr, *Amthāl 'Arabiyya* 23.

FIGURE 7 Figs, *tīn*, al-ʿUmarī, *Masālik al-abṣār*, fol. 215r, detail
BNF, DEPARTMENT OF MANUSCRIPTS, ARAB 2771. SOURCE: GALLICA.BNF.FR/BNF

adopted the name when they took over the country a century later, and thus it hereafter became Hispania.[50] The Carthaginians, like their ancestors the Phoenicians, were seafarers trading in foods and goods like olive oil, wine, and pottery. In addition to precious metals like silver and gold, southern Ispania was also a rich source for sea salt and bluefin tuna, which was salt-preserved in 'factories' and traded all around the Mediterranean basin. In fact, so important was tuna to them that they featured it on their coins.[51]

50 See Crow, *Spain: The Root and the Flower* 7.
51 See Sevilla, *Delicioso* 18.

FIGURE 8
Tuna fishes on the reverse of a Phoenician and Punic coin, ca. 200–150 BC
COURTESY OF CLASSICAL NUMISMATIC GROUP, LLC: HTTPS://WWW.CNGCOINS.COM/COIN.ASPX?COINID=150289

To the subsequent invaders, the Romans, Hispania became Rome's breadbasket. Their most profitable trading goods were wine, olive oil, salted tuna, wax, wheat, honey, and the fermented fish sauce called garum,[52] which Arabs later called *murrī al-ḥūt* (fermented fish sauce). The lands exploited for agricultural purposes were mainly in the eastern and southern regions along the valley of the river of Ebro, which became Ibruh in Arabic. Crops at the time were naturally irrigated by rainfall during the wintertime, but more importantly, they were also artificially irrigated with the help of irrigation structures and devices, such as the complex networks of aqueducts with their pipes, tunnels, canals and bridges, and water-hauling structures. Waterwheel devices of noria (from Arabic *nāʿūra*), driven by water, and *sāqiya*, driven by animals, were "known but little used in ancient times."[53] Towards the end of the fifth century AD and with the decline and fall of the Western Roman Empire, Iberia fell under the rule of Germanic tribes, the Visigoths (Qūṭ in Arabic), who chose Toledo for their capital. They were herders who kept pigs and cooked with lard rather than olive oil. Accounts of foreign travelers visiting Iberia at the time reported cooked foods that were "rough and primitive."[54] The previously rich Iberian diet and cultivated lands fell into decline, but this ended when the Arabs arrived on the Iberian scene.

The year 711 marks the beginning of a long chapter in the history of Iberia when the Arabs ruled the region. This was when the Umayyad commander

---

52 Fish sauce was also produced much earlier in ancient Mesopotamia, where it was called *siqqu*.

53 See Watson, *Agricultural Innovation* 108, and 192, n. 15: "there does not … seem to be any hard evidence whatever of the use of any kind of noria in pre-Islamic Iberia." Similarly, Zozaya, in "Eastern Influences in al-Andalus" 459, notes that "references to waterwheels from Roman times describe a rather different kind of mechanism, developed as a draining system for mining operations."

54 Roden, *Food of Spain* 12. See also Chabrán, "Medieval Spain," for a brief overview of Spanish diet before the advent of the Muslim era, 128–31.

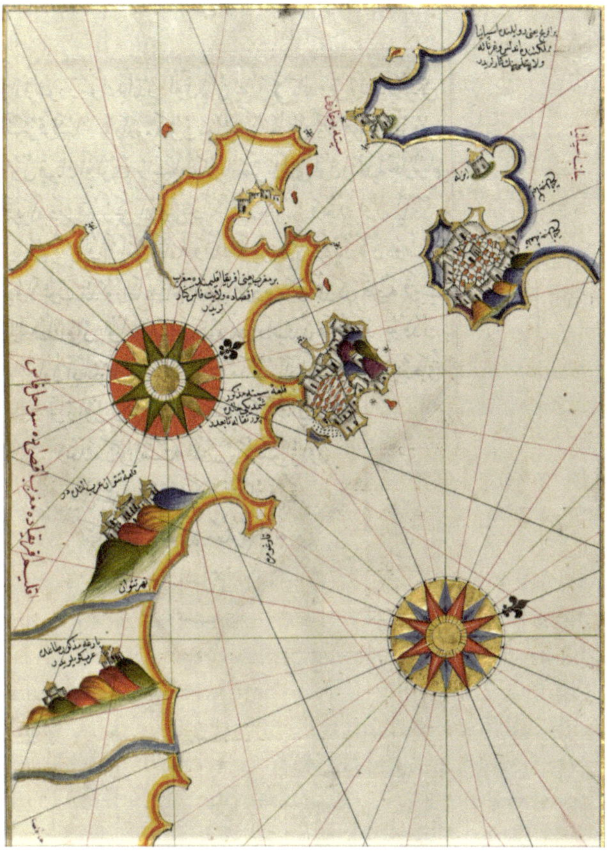

FIGURE 9 A map showing the closest point between al-Andalus and North Africa, with the cities of Gibraltar and Ceuta, W.658.264b, Piri Reis, *Book on Navigation*, detail
THE WALTERS ART MUSEUM, W.658, ACQUIRED BY HENRY WALTERS

Ṭāriq b. Ziyād led a large army, predominantly Amazigh, through the 12-mile-long strait from North Africa and landed in the rocky tip of southern Iberia. The place was later called Jabal Ṭāriq, 'mount of Tariq,' from which the name Gibraltar was derived. The series of expeditions to southern Iberia were in effect a continuation of the Arab Umayyad control of North Africa and the assimilation of Amazigh tribes into Islam. The brief outline that follows serves as a point of reference.

Al-Andalus was at first a province of the Umayyad caliphate (711–750), and when the Abbasids overthrew their dynasty, prince ʿAbd al-Raḥmān I fled the former capital of Damascus and established the Emirate of Cordova in 756.

The Caliphate of Cordova was declared in 929 by ʿAbd al-Raḥmān III, who appointed himself its first caliph. During this era, Cordova became the largest city in Europe and a leading cultural, intellectual, and economic center in the Arabo-Muslim world. The fall of the caliphate in 1031 gave rise to a period of fragmentation, and al-Andalus broke into sixty petty kingdoms, al-Taifa (*Duwal al-Ṭawāʾif*), of varying sizes and importance and were constantly competing and fighting with each other. The largest of these Taifa kingdoms was Seville. Meanwhile, al-Andalus was always in conflict with the Christian kingdoms in the north, and its fragmentation intensified their attacks to reclaim the lands taken by the Muslims. With the help of the Almoravids (*al-Murābiṭūn*), an imperial Amazigh, fundamentalist Muslim, Ṣinhājī dynasty based in Marrakesh, the Christian attacks were repelled, and al-Andalus became a province under the Almoravids' direct rule. Their dynasty lasted from 1091 to 1147, followed by a second Taifa fragmented period, and then another less conservative Amazigh dynasty, the Almohads (*al-Muwaḥḥidūn*), also based in Marrakesh, until the end of their rule over al-Andalus in 1228,[55] which was followed by a third Taifa fragmented period. Throughout the centuries of the Muslim presence in Iberia, al-Andalus's boundaries were in constant flux, ebbing and flowing depending on the progress of the Christian Reconquista, until eventually the big cities of Cordova and Seville fell to the Christians in 1236 and 1248, respectively. Thus, al-Andalus shrank to the single Emirate of Granada, ruled by the Nasrid dynasty in 1237, and the two centuries that followed were marked by cultural and economic prosperity, until Granada surrendered to the Christians in 1492.

As during Roman times, agricultural activities were heavily concentrated along the fertile eastern and southern coasts with little rain and hot summers. These were the areas where new crops brought by the Arabs via North Africa were cultivated successfully: rice, saffron, sugarcane, eggplants, spinach, watermelons, sour oranges (*nāranj*), Damascus citron (*zunbūʿ*), sorghum, and many more. The Arabs also played a big role in disseminating hard wheat to Iberia, where it became the principal variety of wheat used in making bread, pasta, and pastries. It was a pasta variety, the grain-shaped *fadāwīsh*, that gave its name to the Spanish *fideos*, noodles.[56] Couscous, the staple food of the North African Amazigh, which was principally made with hard wheat, must have traveled to Iberia with them in their early waves of migra-

55 They continued to rule in Africa until they lost to the Marinids, another Amazigh dynasty of Banū Marīn in 1269. They were based in Fez, and lasted from 1244–1465.

56 See Watson, *Agricultural Innovation* 21–3.

tion;[57] indeed, to them it was an indispensable travelers' victual. Couscous is now generally believed to be of Amazigh origin with ancient roots, and utensils like the ones we use were excavated in tombs that date back to the second century BC. During that period, an Amazigh king "unified the ancient Kingdom of Numidia by bringing together the northern part of modern Algeria, as well as Tunisia and Libya." Additionally, couscous utensils that date back to the ninth century were also excavated in a region southwest of the Algerian capital.[58]

Not all the immigrant crops, however, fared as well as the ones mentioned above. Fruit trees like date palms and coconut palms did not acclimatize well to the colder Iberian region; particularly the latter, judging from the Andalusi saying, (غارس النارجيل بالاندلس) "Like planting coconut palms in al-Andalus,"[59] to demonstrate futility.[60] The date palm, a tree closely associated with Arab/Muslim identity, was reintroduced to southern Iberia.[61] Growing them, however, was limited to the southern regions, and the dates produced were generally unpalatably astringent and not sweet enough due to the lack of heat.[62] With the exception of a pocket such as Elche, in the southeastern region of Alicante,[63] the cultivation of date palms, like the rest of the crops that proved difficult to acclimatize, fell into neglect in areas recaptured by the Christians, for reasons Watson attributed to "lacking skills, incentives, favorable attitudes, and receptive institutions."[64]

57 This would plausibly put the arrival of couscous in Iberia at a much earlier date than the thirteenth century, as was chosen by Charles Perry (see his article "Couscous," in *Oxford Companion to Food* 220). In fact, tenth-century Ibn Ḥawqal, *Ṣūrat al-arḍ* 99, affirms the cultivation and consumption of wheat, barley, and dates by the Amazigh.

58 "If Couscous be the Food of Love," https://www.france24.com/en/20180123-unesco-couscous-algeria-morocco-rivalry-unity, accessed May 4, 2020; cited in Gaul, "Light Enough to Travel: Couscous" 110. See also Wright, *Mediterranean Feast* 660–4.

59 Al-Bakr, *Amthāl ʿArabiyya* 43.

60 Interestingly, another Andalusi saying, (كغارس الزيتون في الهند) "Like planting olive trees in India," picks a thriving indigenous tree to express the same sentiment.

61 Based on Simon, *The Date Palm* 79–81, the tree was introduced by the Romans when this part of Iberia was a Roman colony, primarily to provide a dam-like barrier of trees to protect the coastal regions from recurrent floodings caused by high tides.

62 As described by two famous Andalusi agronomists, Ibn al-ʿAwwām, *al-Filāḥa al-Andalusiyya* ii 348, and al-Ṭighnarī, *Zahrat al-bustān* 363. See glossary 7, s.v. *tamr*.

63 The date palm forests for which the city was renowned continued to thrive even after the Christian reconquests, and still to this day. The Christians' main interest, however, was not the dates of the palm but its fronds, which were in demand for Easter festivities. Even more prized were the white fronds, obtained by tying the leaves in bunches so that the inner ones gradually lose their greenness and turn white. See Nasrallah, *Dates* 83–4, 100.

64 Watson, *Agricultural Innovation* 83.

FIGURE 10 Farmers at work, *Kitāb al-Diryāq*, fol. NP, detail
BNF, DEPARTMENT OF MANUSCRIPTS, ARAB 2964. SOURCE: GALLICA.BNF.FR/BNF

Another tree brought by the Arabs that fared better than the date palm is the sour orange *nāranj*. It was a well-loved sweet-smelling beautiful tree. However, the Arabs themselves who brought it started to see in it a bad omen and discouraged growing it. The eleven-century Andalusi agronomist al-Ṭighnarī explains that wherever the tree was grown and thrived, be it a city or a household, it brought with it calamities, as in the fall of Toledo into the hands of Christians in 1085.[65] As expected, if we go along with al-Ṭighnarī's observation, what was a bad omen for the Muslims was a good one for the Christians, and that was probably how the sour orange tree thrived in Spain.

During the early waves of the Muslim conquest of Iberia, the settlers consisted of many groups of Syrians, Yemenis, and other easterners, along with a majority of Amazigh from North Africa. They brought with them their ways and customs, the most important of which were their indigenous agricultural

65 Al-Ṭighnarī, *Zahrat al-bustān* 286–8.

knowledge and farming skills and techniques. For the new crops to succeed, irrigation systems had to be renewed and farming routines had to be adjusted. The growing season, usually winter in Iberia, had to be shifted to summer to accommodate the new plants that usually grew in the summer in their native lands, such as rice, eggplants, sugarcane, cotton, and watermelons. In addition, they followed the system of rotating planting sessions, thus lands were used more intensively. This also meant the need for efficient methods of irrigation. The ancient Roman irrigation systems of canals, aqueducts, and the like were in decline and had to be fixed and updated. Thus, lands started to be watered efficiently by devices like noria, the large waterwheel driven by water, as well as *sāqiya*, the waterwheel driven by animals, and *qanāt*, the underground canals.[66]

The Andalusi royal and private gardens also played an important role in adding variety to the Andalusi foods. As they started to be grown on a large scale, it was said of Emir ʿAbd al-Raḥmān I (d. 788) that he "collected in his garden rare plants from every part of the world. He sent agents to Syria and other parts of the east to procure new plants and seeds."[67] This was also how a favorite Andalusi variety of pomegranates, called *al-Safarī*, impressively large with fleshy and juicy arils, tiny seeds, and a smooth, sweet taste, came to be cultivated in al-Andalus. The story goes that one of ʿAbd al-Raḥmān's sisters sent him a large amount of choice pomegranates from the Levant (or from Baghdad according to al-Ṭighnarī), which he distributed among his courtiers. One of them, whose name was Safar b. ʿUbayd, planted the seeds in his estate in Rayya (Malaga) and took care of the plant and manipulated it until it produced a wonderful pomegranate variety. This was how it acquired the name *al-Safarī*, the origin of the Spanish *zafari*.[68] Such botanical gardens were often under the care of leading botanists and agronomists. For instance, the famous eleventh-century Ibn Baṣṣāl, who was employed by the king of Toledo, had to leave the city in 1085 after it was captured by the Christians, and he moved south to Seville, where he worked at the gardens of al-Muʿtamid, the last Taifa ruler of Seville.

Thus, the indigenous crops of grains, fruits, vegetables, and pulses, augmented with many newly adopted ones, and the impressive varieties of meat, both domesticated and wild, fish, and products like eggs and dairy, formed a rich dietary basis in the region.

66 See Watson, *Agricultural Innovation* 108.
67 See ibid., 118.
68 See al-Ṭighnarī, *Zahrat al-bustān* 212; and Ibn al-ʿAwwām, *al-Filāḥa al-Andalusiyya* ii 172.

FIGURE 11
Ancient Roman aqueducts in Spain
HTTPS://EN.WIKIPEDIA.ORG/WIKI/FILE:ROMAN_AQUEDUCT_TARRAGONA.JPG

FIGURE 12
A medieval noria near Murcia
PHOTO BY TOR EIGELAND (*ARAMCO WORLD* / SAWDIA)

FIGURE 13 A water wheel driven by oxen, al-Ḥarīrī, *al-Maqāmāt*, fol. 69v, copied and illustrated by al-Wāsiṭī, detail
BNF, DEPARTMENT OF MANUSCRIPTS, ARAB 5847. SOURCE: GALLICA.BNF.FR/BNF

FIGURE 14 A pomegranate tree, Dioscorides, *Fī Hayūlā al-ṭibb*, translation by Ḥunayn b. Isḥāq, fol. 60v, detail
FROM THE NEW YORK PUBLIC LIBRARY, SPENCER COLLECTION: HTTPS://DIGITALCOLLECTIONS.NYPL.ORG/ITEMS/5E66B3E8-A732-D471-E040-E00A180654D7

II.4.1 A Shopping Tour around al-Andalus

Praising al-Andalus, al-Ḥimyarī compares it to the Levant for its pleasant weather and wholesome air, to Yemen for its moderate temperatures, to India for its perfumes and aromas, to Ahwāz for its magnificent gardens and mountains, to China for its minerals and metals, and to Aden for its bounteous coasts.[69] Indeed, numerous descriptions of the cities, towns, and villages of al-Andalus in medieval Arabic geography books give the impression of a generous region brimming with produce, including fruits, honey, olive oil, fish, and livestock and their products.

Ishbīliya (Seville) was called the 'bride of Andalus.' It was described as a well-populated, large city, with a great river, al-Wādī al-Kabīr (Guadalquivir), running through it. It was lined on both sides with orchards of citron trees, blooming gardens, and parks. For 24 full miles, recreational boats went up and down the stream for joy rides and game hunting under the rich shades of trees while listening to the singing of birds. Of the river bounties were many excellent fish varieties, like *būrī* (flathead grey mullet, *Mugil cephalus*) and *shābil* (allis shad, *Alosa alosa*).[70] Its people were mostly affluent tradesmen dealing with olive oil, which they exported by land and sea to the eastern and western regions of the Arabo-Muslim world.

The sources for this oil were the 40-mile-long olive-tree groves on the evergreen Mount Sharaf, not far from Seville. The trees were so densely grown that one could walk in their unbroken shade for miles. The olives were distinguished for their high yield of excellent-quality oil, which would remain sweet and smooth for years. It was even said that their olives could be stored buried in the ground (*yuṭmar*) for 30 years, and when pressed, their yield of oil would be even more profuse than when pressed fresh.[71] Seville was also known for its first-rate honey, which could be stored for a long time without crystalizing, and for its dried figs, which would not deteriorate for years. Its safflower (*ʿuṣfur*) was deemed the best. Seville was indeed distinguished for its fertile soil; whatever was grown in it thrived. Its pastures, always green and luscious, were conducive to a profuse production of milk. It was also included as one of the southern regions where sugarcane cultivation succeeded.[72]

69 Al-Ḥimyarī, *Ṣifat Jazīrat al-Andalus* 3.

70 Anonymous, *Tārīkh al-Andalus* 114. For ways to cook these kinds of fish, see al-Tujībī's recipes in chapter v.1. See also Ibn Ḥazm, Ibn Saʿīd, and al-Shaqundī, *Faḍāʾil al-Andalus* 52.

71 Anonymous, *Tārīkh al-Andalus* 114.

72 As reported in ibid., 19–21; and al-ʿUdhrī, *Tarṣīʿ al-akhbār* 95–6.

Qurṭuba (Cordova) during the Umayyad times was said to be the Damascus of al-Andalus and its navel (*surra*) and the mother of all cities; praised for its sweet water and pleasant air. Its palaces, orchards, markets, mosques, and public baths were on both sides of the river of al-Wādī al-Kabīr. It had more than a thousand inns (*fanādiq*, sg. *funduq*) and *khān*s for travelers, bachelors, strangers, and the like, and no less than 80,452 shops. During the affluent days of Caliph ʿAbd al-Raḥmān III (d. 961), his household of concubines, slave girls, female servants, and female cooks amounted to 6,840. They daily consumed 13,000 pounds of meat, aside from poultry, game meat, and fish. For the thousands of Slavic guards and servants (*Ṣaqāliba*) at his palaces, 6,000 pounds of meat were allotted, not to mention game meat, poultry, and fish. It is also said that just for the fishpond at the palace of Madīnat al-Zahrā', 12,000 loaves of bread were soaked in a broth of cooked black chickpeas, 6 *qafīz* of them (a *qafīz* equals 60 pounds) daily.[73] Talking of chickpeas, another story tells how, during the days of ʿAbd al-Raḥmān III and his son al-Ḥakam after him, 5 *qafīz* of them used to be cooked outside the gates of the palace daily. While the broth was taken to the palace kitchens to cook with it, the remaining boiled chickpeas were distributed to the poor and the needy.[74] Cordova, however, started to decline in the eleventh century.[75]

Ṭulayṭula (Toledo) was another well-inhabited city with a large Jewish population. It was lusciously surrounded with orchards and gardens, and there were rivers running through it. The fruits that grew there were like no other, with watermills constantly working. The mountain to its north was a luscious pasture for the large herds of impressively fattened cows and sheep sold throughout al-Andalus. Wheat grown in Toledo was said to remain safe of worms for years to come; so much so that it stayed in the family's inherited possessions for generations.[76] Toledo was also known for its production of honey, as well as chestnuts, fine acorns, cherries, walnuts, and apples. Vegetables and fruits stored by burying them in the ground would stay unspoiled for a long time; a hundred years some would say. The soil of a small city adjoining Toledo, called Majrīṭ (Madrid), was used to make earthenware pots (*birām*) that were said to

73 See anonymous, *Tārīkh al-Andalus* 74–9.

74 See the anonymous thirteenth-century Andalusi cookbook *Anwāʿ al-ṣaydala* 55. The chickpea broth was believed to have all the goodness, as for the chickpeas themselves, they were said to be the food of peasants and gluttons. Chickpeas and their broth were believed to be an aphrodisiac. See, for instance, al-Tujībī's recipe i.2.14.

75 See anonymous, *Tārīkh al-Andalus* 80.

76 See al-Ḥimyarī, *Ṣifat Jazīrat al-Andalus* 132–3.

FIGURE 15 A joy ride along the river, al-Ḥarīrī, *al-Maqāmāt*, fol. 61r, copied and illustrated by al-Wāsiṭī, detail
BNF, DEPARTMENT OF MANUSCRIPTS, ARAB 5847. SOURCE: GALLICA.BNF.FR/BNF

remain good to use for 20 years without changing the flavor of the foods cooked in them, even in the summer.[77]

Balansiya (Valencia) was the city that gained for itself the name *Muṭayyib al-Andalus* on account of the abundance of sweet-smelling plants, fragrant air, and beautiful orchards. Al-Marrākushī explains that *al-muṭayyib* in al-Andalus designated a bouquet of fragrant flowers and herbs of narcissus, myrtle sprigs, and various kinds of aromatics (*mashmūmāt*).[78] Valencia was also renowned for the excellent quality of saffron grown there and for fine-quality rice. Both were valuable commodities traded all over al-Andalus. The city combined the bounties of land and sea with their luscious produce of vegetables and fruits and cattle. Its people from all walks of life were said to lead carefree lives, especially the affluent among them, who enjoyed listening to their female singers and bragged about the number of *ʿūd*s they owned.[79]

The southern city of **Shadhūna** (Medina-Sidonia) enjoyed land and sea bounties. Its land was said to be so fertile and plenteous with various crops, olive trees, cattle, and much more that during the famine of 754 in al-Andalus,

77 Anonymous, *Tārīkh al-Andalus* 95–6.
78 Al-Marrākushī, *Tārīkh al-Andalus* 246.
79 *ʿŪd* was their most popular string musical instrument.

FIGURE 16 Saffron, Dioscorides, *Kitāb al-Ḥashāʾish fī hāyūlā al-ʿilāj al-ṭibbī*, Arabic translation by Ḥunayn b. Isḥāq, Or. 289, fol. 14r, detail
UNIVERSITAIRE BIBLIOTHEKEN LEIDEN, HTTP://HDL.HANDLE.NET/1887.1/ITEM:1578266

multitudes of people moved there, and the city had enough means to accommodate them.[80] Its shores were the source for the most coveted ambergris (*ʿanbar*) obtained along the Arab coastlines. And it was also in Shadhūna that bluefin tuna was caught.

According to al-Ḥimyarī's account, tuna fish made their first appearance at the beginning of May; they would leave the Atlantic Ocean (*al-Baḥr al-Muḥīṭ*) and enter the Mediterranean Sea, called *al-Baḥr al-Rūmī* (the Byzantine sea).[81] The season for catching them would last for 40 days, after which they would go back to where they came from; only to return the following year.[82] Al-Ḥimyarī also describes how fish were caught with harpoons, which were long spears

80 Anonymous, *Tārīkh al-Andalus* 116. See also al-Ḥimyarī, *Ṣifat Jazīrat al-Andalus* 100.

81 As it was called when referring to the western side of the Mediterranean. On its eastern side, it was more commonly called *Baḥr al-Shām*, 'the Levantine sea.'

82 Al-Ḥimyarī, *Ṣifat Jazīrat al-Andalus* 101.

with wing-like heads and long ropes of hemp (*qinnab*) attached to their ends.[83] The thirteenth-century Andalusi botanist Ibn al-Bayṭār, in his entry on tuna (*tunn*), briefly mentions that when the grown tuna fish in *al-Baḥr al-Muẓlim*, 'the dark sea' (i.e., the Atlantic Ocean), entered the Mediterranean Sea, they were caught with nets. Apparently, to Ibn al-Bayṭār's contemporaries, tuna fish and their mysterious migratory ways made for a fascinating conversation subject during their social gatherings.[84]

The coastal areas of Shadhūna (Medina-Sidonia) and Sabta (Ceuta) were the places for catching tuna. The spot where tuna fish were captured was and still is called *almadraba*, a term originally adapted from the Arabic *al-maḍraba* (المضربة), literally 'the place to strike.'[85] The technique itself of catching tuna, however, is an ancient one, going back to Carthaginian times. As described in Fiona Dunlop's *Andaluz*:

> Located very close to shore in the exact passage of the migrating fish, a circle of fishing boats and forty or so men corral the tuna into a maze of vertical nets. As they thrash wildly in panic, the tuna are trapped and killed in an ever-tightening circle until, after two hours, comes the *levanta* (raising of the trap) when the extensive nets are lifted and the fish transferred to the boats.[86]

Tuna fish was consumed fresh and preserved in a salt-cured, air-dried form, called *tunn yābis* (dried tuna), and *mushammaʿ*, which is descriptive of its stiff, waxy texture.[87] It was in this dried form that tuna was traded in ancient times.

The western city of **Ashbūna** (Lisbon) was said to be so close to the Atlantic Ocean that its waves hit its walls. It was described as a bounteous region with numerous varieties of fish and rich, cultivated lands. Its apples were described as impressively huge, with a circumference of 3 spans (approx. 27 inches).

83 Al-Ḥimyarī, *al-Rawḍ al-miʿṭār* 303.

84 The expression Ibn al-Bayṭār uses is وينادم به ذكره, *al-Jāmiʿ* i 194. We now know that tuna fish go there to reproduce.

85 Pl. *maḍārib*. See Corriente, *Dictionary of Andalusi Arabic*, s.v. *d-r-b*, where it is explained as 'tunny fishery.' Medieval Arabic sources mentioned that nets were used in catching tuna fish, as in Ibn al-Bayṭār, *al-Jāmiʿ* i 194; and al-Ḥimyarī, *al-Rawḍ al-miʿṭār* 303, describes the tuna-catching harpoons as long spears with wing-like heads and long ropes of hemp (*qinnab*) attached to their ends.

86 Dunlop, *Andaluz* 290.

87 Etymologically, the Spanish *mojama* is derived from it.

FIGURE 17 *Almadraba*, tuna fishing, etching by Jean-Pierre Houël, *Voyage pittoresque des Isles de Sicile, de Malte et de Lipari*. Paris, 1782
HTTPS://EN.WIKIPEDIA.ORG/WIKI/ALMADRABA#/MEDIA/FILE:LA_PESCA_DEL_TONNO,_ACQUAFORTE_DI_JEAN-PIERRE_HOU%C3%ABL.JPG

Honey produced in Lisbon was highly praised. It was solid like sugar and could be kept in bags of cloth or paper.[88]

The big fish varieties in the coastal city of **Mālaqa** (Malaga) were legendary for their delicious flavor. The city itself is described in medieval Arabic sources as a well-loved destination (*maʿshūqa*). Its figs were renowned for their sweet, luscious taste. They were deemed the best in the world; sold in Baghdad as a novelty and exported to Egypt, the Levant, and even all the way to India and China. Ibn Ḥazm tells how an Amazigh was once asked about the figs of Malaga, and his answer was, "Do not ask me, just pour a whole basketful of them in my mouth."[89] Also aplenty were its olives, almonds, grapes, and pomegranates.[90] Its wine was said to be the best in all of al-Andalus.[91]

Ighranāṭa or **Gharnāṭa** (Granada),[92] as it was commonly called, was described as the most beautiful of cities and the most fortified. With a river running through it, many watermills were set up along its banks. It was built at the northern foot of the snow mountain (*Jabal al-Thalj*), abundant in trees of walnuts, chestnuts, apples, and mulberries (*farṣād*, also called *tūt al-ʿArab*) with their silkworms, and numerous flowers and herbs, such as excellent-quality

---

88 See anonymous, *Tārīkh al-Andalus* 97–9.
89 Ibn Ḥazm, Ibn Saʿīd, and al-Shaqundī, *Faḍāʾil al-Andalus* 52.
90 Anonymous, *Tārīkh al-Andalus* 123–4; and al-Ḥimyarī, *Ṣifat Jazīrat al-Andalus* 178.
91 Ibn Ḥazm, Ibn Saʿīd, and al-Shaqundī, *Faḍāʾil al-Andalus* 57.
92 Yāqūt al-Ḥamawī, *Muʿjam al-buldān* iv 195, proclaims that the name of the city means 'pomegranate' and that it was a ʿAjamiyya word (Andalusi Romance).

FIGURE 18 Mulberry trees, al-ʿUmarī, *Masālik al-abṣār*, fol. 152r, detail
BNF, DEPARTMENT OF MANUSCRIPTS, ARAB 2771. SOURCE: GALLICA.BNF.FR/BNF

spikenard. Its luscious countryside was compared to that of Damascus (*Ghūṭat Dimashq*). Granada was famous for its grapes and delicious raisins (*zabīb*). Sugarcane was said to have successfully grown along its coastal areas.[93]

Air in **Saraqusṭā** (Zaragoza) in the northeastern region seemed to have been dry enough to prevent any dried stored foods from molding or spoilage; wheat berries could stay good for a hundred years; dried grapes kept suspended would not mold for about six years; and four years for dried figs, peaches, cherries (*ḥabb*),[94] plums (*ijjāṣ*),[95] and cherry plums (*ihlīlaj*). Dried fava beans and chick-

93 Anonymous, *Tārīkh al-Andalus* 125–6; and al-Ḥimyarī, *Ṣifat Jazīrat al-Andalus* 23–4.
94 The full name for the cherries was *ḥabb al-mulūk*.
95 More commonly called *ʿayn al-baqar* in the Muslim West.

peas would not spoil for 20 years. Its fertile soil produced the most delicious of fruits in all of al-Andalus. It was also famous for its salt mines, from which the excellent white salt, called *milḥ andarānī*, was extracted.[96] In another northern port city, called **Ṭarkūna** (Tarragona), watermills worked with seawater channeled to them by means of mechanical devices. In this city, one could find plenty of walnuts, almonds, chestnuts, pistachios, and grapes, whose juice did not need fire or honey to thicken it.[97]

In the southern region, where bananas and sugarcane were introduced and flourished, was the coastal city of **Shalūbīnya** (Salobreña).[98] Sugarcane was its main production well into the sixteenth century. The southern inland city of **Jayyān** (Jaén) was built on the slope of a very high mountain. It was distinguished for its affordable prices, where meat and honey were plenty and cheap.[99] It was the best place to live in, as one of the Andalusi sayings goes, (يذكر البلدان ويسكن جيان) "While he chooses Jayyān for himself, he recommends other places to people."[100]

A remarkable diversity in human resources and agricultural bounty characterized the Andalusi foodways scene. The above sketches of main regions in al-Andalus show how such variety facilitated ease of access and convenience of mobility for the distribution of goods and produce to secure stable marketplaces, called *aswāq* (sg. *sūq*). The prosperous times of the Umayyad dynasty in Cordova marked the wide spread of markets and shops in towns, villages, and even the remotest of locations. We read in al-Maqqarī that for travelers on the road there were always available sources for water and all kinds of foods everywhere they went.[101]

Besides farming, the luscious Andalusi countryside was a place for raising poultry on a large scale, the most important of which were chicken, pigeons, and geese. Chickens were raised for their meat and eggs. The farmers followed simple methods for propagating large numbers of eggs by means of artificial incubation. They would grind dried chicken droppings, put them in glass ves-

---

96 Anonymous, *Tārīkh al-Andalus* 129.

97 Ibid., 132. Grape juice was usually reduced on the fire to make a kind of concentrated molasses, called *rubb*.

98 Al-Ḥimyarī, *Ṣifat Jazīrat al-Andalus* 111.

99 Ibid., 70.

100 Al-Bakr, *Amthāl 'Arabiyya* 54.

101 Al-Maqqarī, *Nafḥ al-ṭīb* i 226; and al-Ḥimyarī, *Ṣifat Jazīrat al-Andalus* 185. See also al-Khalīfāt, "Aswāq al-Andalus," a thoroughly researched study on markets during the Andalusi Umayyad Emirate, beginning in 756, and Caliphate, beginning in 929 and ending in 1030. Another comprehensive study of Andalusi markets is by Chalmeta, *El Zoco Medieval: Contribucion Al Estudio de La Historia del Mercado.*

sels, and arrange eggs in them with their pointed ends facing upwards. The eggs would then be covered with chicken feathers and again with ground chicken droppings. The eggs would be turned over twice a day for 20 days, after which chicks would hatch.[102]

There were also pigeon cotes in their farms, kept for their meat and droppings, used extensively to fertilize the soil.[103] Geese (*iwazz*) and ducks (*burak*) were widely raised for their meat. Ducks in particular were fattened with dough and dried figs. For fattening their livers, they were force-fed moistened pellets of ground toasted sesame seeds.[104] Of undomesticated animals, partridges were favored, apparently for the ease of catching them. Wheat berries were first boiled with seeds of henbane (*binj*) and then thrown in their way. They would be vulnerably dazed with them.[105] Another favorite was the *qunilyāt* (sg. *qunilya*), European wild rabbits,[106] which were smaller than hares. They were in great demand for their flavorful meat and excellent fur worn by all Andalusis, as al-Maqqarī reports.[107] Nets woven with hemp fibers were used to catch them.[108]

In Andalusi city plans, marketplaces were traditionally built at city centers next to mosques. In travelers' accounts of the region, they were described as spacious and clean, with crafts assigned separate spots. They also had easy access to *khāns*, inns, and public baths for the convenience of strangers and visitors. There were separate marketplaces for spices, such as *Sūq al-ʿAṭṭārīn* in Cordova, and for spices, herbs, aromatics, dyes, and scented distilled waters, such as those of roses, jasmine, musk, and ambergris; locally produced or imported. Prepared foods and drinks had their own *sūq*s as well.[109] The marketplaces of Seville had everything one needed; as the famous Andalusi saying goes, "Even if you are looking for milk of birds, you will find it there."[110] Apparently, the Sevillians were fun-loving people; they had a specialized marketplace for musical instruments. They used to say, if a singer died in Cordova, his musical instruments would be sold in Seville.[111] In the eyes of Andalusis, running a shop was

102 Ibn al-ʿAwwām, *al-Filāḥa al-Andalusiyya* vi 265–6.

103 Ibid., vi 239, 248.

104 Ibid., vi 255.

105 As suggested in al-Andalusī, *Kitāb fī l-Filāḥa* 78.

106 *Oryctolagus cuniculus*. The name of this rabbit species is derived from the Spanish *conejo*.

107 Al-Maqqarī, *Nafḥ al-ṭīb* i 198.

108 Al-Ishbīlī, *ʿUmdat al-ṭabīb* ii 512.

109 As described in Ibn Ḥayyān, *al-Muqtabis*, the fifth part, cited in al-Khalīfāt, "Aswāq al-Andalus" 146.

110 Ibn Ḥazm Ibn Saʿīd, and al-Shaqundī, *Faḍāʾil al-Andalus* 50.

111 Ibid., 52.

FIGURE 19
Having a good time drinking and listening to music, al-Ḥarīrī, *al-Maqāmāt*, fol. 165v
BNF, DEPARTMENT OF MANUSCRIPTS, ARAB 3929. SOURCE: GALLICA.BNF.FR/BNF

regarded as a respectable way to earn one's living; they had a saying, (صاحب دكان ما يحتاج بستان) "A shop owner does not need an orchard." Trade was as good as farming.

Stretched along the streets and alleys of cities like Cordova were places accommodating the daily needs of shoppers, such as fresh vegetable and fruit stalls, butcher shops, fishmonger stalls, dairy stores, bakeries, and the like. Apparently, prices were fixed, and shopkeepers were required to affix written prices next to the items sold. Customers who kneaded their daily bread at home and baked it at the neighborhood *furn* would usually pay by giving the bakery owner a portion of their bread.[112]

Trading with cattle was a profitable business. In Cordova alone it was estimated that between 70,000 and 100,00 heads of sheep were taken to the city markets daily; that is apart from cows. Salt-cured fish of all kinds was a popular item in the Cordovan food markets, and 20,000 dinars worth of them were sold daily.[113]

112 Fikrī, *Qurṭuba fī l-ʿAṣr al-Islāmī* 255.
113 Ibn Ghālib, *Farḥat al-anfus* 296.

Earthenware and ceramic utensils of various shapes and sizes for cooking, eating, and drinking purposes were made in cities like Cordova at specialized workshops. There were also workshops for making colorless glassware, which was quite fashionable at the time. The Cordovan polymath ʿAbbās Ibn Firnās (d. 887) was credited for devising the means for manufacturing it.[114]

Although al-Andalus was renowned for the generosity of its land and the affordability of its prices, it also went through periods when people suffered hardships because of natural and human-induced disasters, like wars. In times of famine, as when the locusts destroyed all the crops in al-Andalus during the times of the Cordovan Emir ʿAbd al-Raḥmān I, multitudes of people died of starvation and many more crossed the sea to the other side of the Mediterranean, al-ʿUdwa. Or when rivers raged with torrents, as in the year 798 when sections of the city of Cordova, including marketplaces, were destroyed.[115] However, the most memorable of all was preserved in the collective memory of the Andalusis as *Sanat Sittīn* (the year 60), which happened in 260 H (873 AD). So proverbial was it that subsequent catastrophes were compared to it.[116]

II.5 *Elements of Andalusi Cuisine*

كل الزيت ولا تمشي لطبيب

Do not go to the doctor, just eat olive oil.

An Andalusi saying in al-Zajjālī, *Amthāl al-ʿawām* ii 261

Two eventful flights during the early Arab presence in Iberia played pivotal roles in changing the course of history in the region. The Syrian Prince ʿAbd al-Raḥmān I fled to al-Andalus when the Abbasids overthrew the Umayyad dynasty in Damascus in 750. In 756 he established an emirate there that paved the way for a second Umayyad Caliphate in Cordova. A few decades later, a parallel flight happened when Abū al-Ḥasan ʿAlī b. Nāfiʿ, famously known as Ziryāb, fled Baghdad around 809 with his family and went to North Africa. He eventually became the chief singer in the court of Umayyad Emir ʿAbd al-Raḥmān II in 822 and remained in this position until his death in 857. In his new abode, he set the grounds for a rich, elegant cuisine to which the two thirteenth-century Andalusi cookbooks bear witness.

---

114 Fikrī, *Qurṭuba fī l-ʿAṣr al-Islāmī* 256.

115 See al-Khalīfāt, "Aswāq al-Andalus" 157.

116 Al-Bakr, *Amthāl ʿArabiyya* 38.

FIGURE 20 An olive tree, al-Qazwīnī, *ʿAjāʾib al-makhlūqāt wa gharāʾib al-mawjūdāt*, fol. 164v, detail
FROM THE NEW YORK PUBLIC LIBRARY, SPENCER COLLECTION: HTTPS://DIGITALCOLLECTIONS.NYPL.ORG/ITEMS/DAF7EAB0-28EB-0138-4299-0CDA5977DCD5

Before Ziryāb's arrival in al-Andalus, and even back to the older days of the Damascene Umayyad Caliphate of ʿAbd al-Raḥmān's ancestors, our information regarding their foodways is still meagre because we know of no culinary documents that survived from those periods, or whether they were written at all. What survived were for the most part anecdotes told by the Abbasids about Damascene Umayyad caliphs, mostly targeting Sulaymān b. ʿAbd al-Malik, the glutton (d. 717), whose favorite foods were grilled sheep and chicken. His demise was at the hands of a bowlful of bone marrow sprinkled with sugar, which he had after devouring two basketfuls of boiled eggs and figs.[117] Beyond doubt, the age-old *tharīda* dish of bread sopped in meat and vegetables was a staple, as it always has been. We can say the same about dishes cooked with grains such as *ḥarīra* and *jashīsha,* as well as *maḍīra* meat stew cooked with yogurt.[118] Also, with a majority population of Amazigh in al-Andalus, we may assume that couscous dishes were common.[119]

Ziryāb left Baghdad at a time when Abbasid gastronomy had reached a high level of sophistication. When he fled around 809, the half-brother of Hārūn al-Rashīd, Ibrāhīm b. al-Mahdī (779–839), famous for his innovative culinary skills, must already have written his cookbook. In fact, both Ibrāhīm and Ziryāb belonged to the same household. While the former was the son of Caliph al-Mahdī, Ziryāb was his *mawlā,* a freed slave. We can thereby say with confidence that Ziryāb could not have missed the chance of mastering the culinary arts with a gourmet like Ibrāhīm b. al-Mahdī around. However, Ziryāb's primary talent was not food but playing the musical instrument *al-ʿūd* masterfully and singing. Competition with his music master Isḥāq b. Ibrāhīm al-Mawṣilī (767–850) forced him to flee Baghdad. His music master was so jealous of him that he gave him only two options: be killed or leave the country altogether.

The most detailed account of how Ziryāb introduced Andalusis to Baghdadi gastronomy was recorded by the famous eleventh-century Cordovan historian Ibn Ḥayyān al-Qurṭubī.[120] We learn that Ziryāb was a name given to him in Baghdad by virtue of his sweet voice.[121] We also learn that he was an

117 See Ibn ʿAbd Rabbihi, *al-ʿIqd al-Farīd* viii 13–5.

118 See ibid, viii 4–5.

119 See above section ii.4, pp. 28–9 for more on couscous in the region.

120 Ibn Ḥayyān, *al-Sifr al-thānī* 307–35. The other account that includes Ziryāb's role in influencing Andalusi cuisine occurs in seventeenth-century al-Maqqarī, *Nafḥ al-ṭīb* iii 127–8, where Ibn Ḥayyān's detailed account was condensed to three sentences only.

121 *Ziryāb* is another name for a songbird called *shuḥrūr,* common blackbird (*Turdus merula*), suggesting Ziryāb's dark skin, eloquence, sweet nature, and beautiful voice. Another black bird associated with the word *ziryāb* is *ʿaqʿaq,* a magpie. Ibn Ḥayyān's account (p. 333) includes an episode when another court singer, jealous of Ziryāb, made fun of him by sug-

FIGURE 21 Playing the *ʿūd* in an orchard, al-Ḥarīrī, *al-Maqāmāt*, fol. 69v, copied and illustrated by al-Wāsiṭī, detail
BNF, DEPARTMENT OF MANUSCRIPTS, ARAB 5847. SOURCE: GALLICA.BNF.FR/BNF

accomplished charmer, a trend-setter in Andalusi high society. He introduced its elite to *martak*, or *mardāsanj* (white lead),[122] as a deodorizer instead of the perfumed powders and aromatics that stained their clothes. An important vegetable he drew their attention to was asparagus, which they called *isfarāj* (otherwise, *hilyawn* in al-Mashriq). Ibn Ḥayyān's text mentions precisely what

gesting to Emir ʿAbd al-Raḥmān, who was hunting for *ʿaqʿaq* birds in the mountains, that he need go no further, just let Ziryāb smear his butt and underarms with *shīrāz* (drained yogurt) and there you have it, your *ʿaqʿaq*.

Moreover, the word also designates anything that is golden, in this case it could have been descriptive of his 'golden' voice, or the golden hue of his complexion. See al-Zabīdī *Tāj al-ʿarūs*, s.v. زرب.

122 It is lead oxide, see al-Anṭākī, *Tadhkira* 325, for more on this ingredient.

Ziryāb did: He was the first to harvest asparagus that was growing in the wild in al-Andalus. Andalusis did not believe it to be an edible plant and neglected it; but Ziryāb was familiar with the cultivated variety from his days in Baghdad.

Ibn Ḥayyān's story goes that asparagus grew abundantly in the wild in al-Andalus; it was not cultivated in orchards as it was in al-Mashriq. Ziryāb saw the plant, recognized it, cooked it, and invited others to try it for themselves. He once invited one of the high-ranking people at the emir's palace and feasted him on the popular dishes he learnt from his days in Baghdad. The last dish he offered was a vegetable one of boiled asparagus, excellently cooked and masterfully sauced. The man balked at it and refused to eat it, but Ziryāb started eating it, urging his guest to try it. As soon as the guest had a taste of it, he bombarded Ziryāb with questions about it, saying it was the most delicious vegetable he had ever had. Ziryāb's response was, "Wait until you try it cooked with meat in a variety of ways. In addition to its delicious taste, it has the benefit of being a diuretic, it breaks down kidney stones, cleanses the bladder, balances the humors, and invigorates coitus."[123] "Tell me, where can I find it, may God bless you, so that I may bargain for its price?" the man earnestly asked. Ziryāb coolly responded, "God has saved you the trouble of doing this because He let it grow abundantly in the countryside (*fuḥūṣ*, sg. *faḥṣ*) for you and for everybody else, just send someone to get it for you." From that day on, asparagus became everybody's favorite, and people, high and low, started harvesting it when in season.

Ibn Ḥayyān furthermore credits Ziryāb with 'inventing' a green variety of a dish that Andalusis called *tafāyā*. Now, a plain-tasting dish like *tafāyā* was already well-known in al-Mashriq, albeit under a different name, *isfidhbāja*.[124] Quite possibly a simple meat dish like *tafāyā* was brought by the Amazigh to al-Andalus, and what Ziryāb was credited for was the more sophisticated variety, made green with cilantro juice, called *tafāyā khaḍrā'*. This variety requires extra care to preserve its greenness. Interestingly, the cook who was most well-known for this type of green stew in al-Mashriq was Hārūn al-Rashīd's half-brother Ibrāhīm b. al-Mahdī, who shared the same household with Ziryāb.[125]

---

123 In al-Tujībī's book of *Fiḍāla* we do indeed have a long asparagus recipe, ii.2.14, in which the dish is cooked with meat in many interesting ways. For a meatless asparagus dish, see chapter vii.5.

124 *Isfīdbāja* (*isfīd* 'white' + *bā*[*j*] 'broth'), as it was called in the eastern region (also occurs as *isfidhbāj* and *isbīdāj*). See, for instance, al-Warrāq, *Kitāb al-Ṭabīkh*, English trans., *Annals*, chapter 59.

125 See al-Warrāq, *Kitāb al-Ṭabīkh*, English trans., *Annals*, the last two recipes in chapter 59.

FIGURE 22 Asparagus, *isfarāj*, al-Ghāfiqī, *Kitāb al-Adwiya al-mufrada*, MS 7508, fol. 138v, detail
REPRODUCED BY PERMISSION OF THE OSLER LIBRARY OF THE HISTORY OF MEDICINE, MCGILL UNIVERSITY

For Ibrāhīm's green recipe a slow-burning portable stove was used to preserve the stew's vivid color.[126] Indeed, it must have been through Ziryāb that Andalusis were introduced to Ibrāhīm's recipes and possibly the cookbook he wrote. In the two Andalusi cookbooks that survived, we have recipes called *Ibrāhīmiyya* after his name,[127] a recipe said to be his,[128] and even a portion of a cookbook allegedly claimed to be his.[129]

---

126 It was called *nāfikh nafsihi* (see section iii.7 below, p. 78); alternatively, *kānūn ʿajlān* was called for, which was a portable stove made of clay, see al-Warrāq, *Kitāb al-Ṭabīkh*, English trans., *Annals*, glossary, 684–5.

127 Al-Tujībī's recipe iii.2.30, and a version of it in anonymous, *Anwāʿ al-ṣaydala* 24.

128 A meat dish cooked covered with bread, called *Maghmūm*, in anonymous, *Anwāʿ al-ṣaydala* 23.

129 A section in anonymous, *Anwāʿ al-ṣaydala* 128, is titled *Kitāb al-Ṭabkh li-Ibn Ibrāhīm bin al-Mahdī*. The recipes it includes, as David Waines suggests in *In a Caliph's Kitchen* 14, "may only be loosely related to Ibrahim's actual cookbook and be adaptations of a subsequent generation and locale."

Ibn Ḥayyān reports that *tafāyā* became the Andalusis' favorite dish, which they always served first before any other foods offered in their meals; it was particularly approved of by their physicians for its balanced properties that agreed with all eaters.[130] In al-Maqqarī's version, the green *tafāyā* dishes were served garnished with *sanbūsaq* (meat-filled pastries) and *kubāb* (meatballs).[131] Ibn Ḥayyān adds that of the Andalusis' other favorite dishes also attributed to Ziryāb were *baqliyyāt* (vegetable dishes),[132] but they were not as zealous about them as they were about *tafāyā*.[133] He further elaborates that Ziryāb introduced other dishes to the elite's kitchens, such as splendid varieties of luscious *tharāʾid*,[134] fine, well-seasoned cold dishes (*bawārid*),[135] dishes made with pounded meats drenched in sauces,[136] thin meat patties (*khafāʾif al-laḥm*),[137] and delectable bird dishes (*maṭāyib al-aṭyār*).

Ibn Ḥayyān's list continues with sweets of various kinds made with sugar and honey, such as *jawzīn* and *lawzīn* (walnut and almond pastries)[138] and *qaṭāʾif maḥshuwwa* (stuffed pancakes), which in al-Tujībī's cookbook, recipe i.4.16, they are indeed said to be of Abbasid origin. Other sweets mentioned are *fāwālīdh*, both dry and moist,[139] *muʿqadāt al-sukkar* (sugar candies), some

---

130 The dish is similarly praised in the thirteenth-century anonymous Andalusi cookbook *Anwāʿ al-ṣaydala* 58.

131 Addition found only in his *Nafḥ al-ṭīb* iii 127–8. For more on *tafāyā*, see introduction iii.8, pp. 85–6 below; and recipes ii.2.1–2.

132 Sg. *baqliyya*, erroneously copied as *taqliyya* (fried dish) in al-Maqqarī's account, *Nafḥ al-ṭīb* 128.

133 The Andalusi anonymous *Anwāʿ al-ṣaydala* 134 has preserved one such dish, *Ṣanʿat baqliyya li-Ziryāb* (making a *baqliyya* dish attributed to Ziryāb), of mutton cooked with chopped cabbages. Cf. a somewhat similar *kurunbiyya* dish in al-Tujībī's recipe ii.2.3. Al-Tujībī makes no mention of Ziryāb at all in his book.

134 They are dishes of bread sopped in rich broth, see al-Tujībī's chapter i.2.

135 Al-Warrāq's tenth-century Baghdadi cookbook, *Kitāb al-Ṭabīkh*, English trans., *Annals*, abounds with such recipes variously prepared with red meat, chicken, fish, and vegetables, see chapters 31, 33, 42, 45.

136 In Ibn Ḥayyān, *al-Sifr al-thānī* 322, this kind of food occurs as *al-mudaqqaqāt al-madsūsa fī l-ashriba* (المدقّقات المدسوسة في الأشربة). *Mudaqqaqāt* were any of the foods made with pounded meat, such as meatballs, sausages, and patties; see, for instance, al-Tujībī's chapter ii.6. Such dry foods were usually served drenched in liquid/liquidy sauces, such as vinegar, *murrī*, *ṣināb* 'mustard sauce,' and vinegar-based ones. They were variantly referred to as *jalja/shalsha*, *ṣibāgh*, and *maraq*; called *ashriba* in Ibn-Ḥayyān's text. In medieval lexicons, *ashriba* generally designated drinks. Syrups, which were often diluted with water to make drinks with them, were also called *ashriba*, see, for instance, glossary 1, s.v. *sharāb* 1.

137 See, for instance, *isfīriyya*, recipe ii.6.3.

138 See, for instance, recipes i.4.12–3 for pinwheel pastries.

139 An unusual plural of *fālūdhaj*, the starch-based *ḥalwā*. See, for instance, recipes ix.2.2–3 for the dry ones, and recipe ix.7.1 for the moist variety.

molded into figures,[140] and dry varieties (*mujassadāt*) made with pistachios and hazelnuts,[141] and many other similar well-relished sweet dainties (*raqāʾiq al-ḥulw al-multadhdha*); all served as *naql*.[142] Andalusis also learnt from Ziryāb how to make all kinds of digestives (*juwārishnāt*) and fruit conserves (*murabbayāt*) seasoned and scented with spices and aromatics, which have the power to remedy ailing stomachs and dissolve harmful vapors (*hāmiʿa lil-abkhira*).

It was Ziryāb, Ibn Ḥayyān asserts, who introduced these foods to al-Andalus and described how to make them. Cordovans followed his most refined ways and trivial ones alike; they, for instance, started toasting and salting their dried fava beans his way and called it al-Ziryābī after his name.[143] He would first soak the beans to soften them and then dry toast them slowly in an earthenware pan on very low heat. People preferred his method and abandoned theirs, according to which the beans were toasted on high heat, resulting in hardened texture. Ziryāb encouraged them to use refined glass vessels rather than their silver and gold ones. He recommended using table covers of soft leather, which could be cleaned quite easily, rather than serving food directly on wooden surfaces. Add to these varieties of perfumes and powders, some of which elite society was not aware of.

Interestingly, nowhere do we find in Ibn Ḥayyān's account given above (nor in al-Maqqarī's much shorter version of it) that Ziryāb was indeed the one to discourage Andalusis from serving the dishes haphazardly and showed them the proper order of dishes to have in a given meal; starting with soup (*shūrbā*), followed by appetizers (*muqaddamāt*) of meat dishes, and then refined and spiced bird dishes (*ṭuyūr mutabbala*), and ending with desserts. Aside from the details related to beginning the meals with *tafāyā*, which is not really a soup dish, and ending with desserts, this apparent fallacy has indeed been relentlessly circulating in books and journals for almost a century now.[144] In all probability, it was based on misreadings of, or reading too much into, the medieval texts mentioned above. It might well have all started in the 1930s with Lévi-Provençal's account of Arab civilization in Spain, in which he cited Angel

---

140 The expression Ibn Ḥayyān uses is *al-muṣaʿdāt lil-taṣwīr* (المصعّدات للتصوير), which involves shaping the pieces while they are still soft and malleable.

141 See, for instance, recipes in chapter ix.4 for nut brittles. For the term *mujassadāt*, see Ibn Manẓūr, *Lisān al-ʿArab*, s.v. جسد.

142 Generally, *naql* stands for nibbles and small dishes served as snacks and mezza-like foods during their drinking sessions, believed to slow down intoxication and keep hunger away.

143 Described as *al-fūl al-maqlū al-mamlūḥ* 'fried and salted fava beans,' as explained in al-Lakhmī, *Taqwīm al-lisān* 435. The latter source is cited by the editor of Ibn Ḥayyān, *al-Sifr al-thānī* 322 n. 4.

144 See, for instance, Lebling, "Ziryab" 390–2.

González Palencia, *El Islam y Occidente* (1931), who imprecisely gave al-Maqqarī as his source for this sort of information.[145]

In Ibn Ḥayyān's account of how Ziryāb taught Andalusis to wear white clothes for the hot season, there is an interesting early mention of the Christian religious festivals that occurred around the year, which apparently the Muslims adopted for regulating their annual activities, and they even celebrated with them from the days of their early presence in Iberia. Ibn Ḥayyān mentions that it was Ziryāb's idea that they change to wearing white clothes starting during what the Christian Andalusis called *Yawm al-Mahrajān*, also called *al-ʿAnṣara*.[146] Ibn Ḥayyān specified it as the sixth day before the end of the solar month Yūnya (June) of their Roman calendar. Ziryāb suggested that Andalusis resume wearing their colored clothes after three months, at the beginning of Uktūbar (October).[147]

Living in a land characterized by such diversity in temperatures and topographies as that of al-Andalus must have inevitably compelled its residents to be more attuned to matters of weather and changes of seasons than people living in Baghdad or Egypt for instance. The Andalusis' common proverbs and sayings interestingly reflected their awareness of these matters. They were like an almanac of sorts, as in the saying, (خروجك من يَنير اخير من خروجك من العنصر)[148] coming out of the New Year season (of January with spring and summer ahead) is better than coming out of ʿAnṣara (with autumn and winter ahead),[149] or (الميلاد لا يخذك برّ دارك ولا ورا واد), which is cautionary commentary on the sever-

145 Lévi-Provençal, *Ḥaḍārat al-ʿArab fī l-Andalus*, Arabic translation, 56. In the anonymous thirteenth-century Andalusi cookbook, *Anwāʿ al-ṣaydala* 58, there is mention how in high societies dishes were offered one after the other and not all at the same time. There is also mention of the order of serving the seven traditional Andalusi dishes for the wedding festivities in Cordova and Seville (p. 6), beginning with feminine ones such as vegetable dishes and simple stews of *tafāyā*, followed by masculine ones with stronger properties cooked with vinegar and the like, such as *mukhallal*, *jumlī*, *muthallath*, and *murrī*; ending with *muʿassal*, which is a starch-based thick pudding. No mention whatsoever is made of Ziryāb in this regard in *Anwāʿ al-ṣaydala*, and the details occur in a differently oriented context anyway.

Another Ziryāb story that needs to be debunked is that the name of the sweet *zalābiya* (syrupy fritters) was derived from *Ziryābiyya*, thus crediting him for inventing it. The truth is, *zalābiya* was known in the eastern region of al-Mashriq even before Ziryāb was born. Furthermore, etymologically, *zalābiya* is an ancient word; according to medieval lexicographers, the word occurred in Arabic verses from the pre-Islamic era. See, for instance, al-Zabīdī, *Tāj al-ʿarūs*, s.v. زلب.

146 It was June 24, on which the birth of Saint John was celebrated.

147 For celebrating these feasts, see section ii.6 below.

148 Al-Zajjālī, *Amthāl al-ʿawām* ii 205.

149 See p. 52 for more on this feast.

ity of winter weather. Once it is Christmas time, *Mīlād*, do not go out of your house or be on the road facing a river; it is the season of snow and flooding, which would prevent you from coming back home. Or this one, (مطر فبريل خير من فيض النيل) "April rains are better than the flooding of the Nile"; and (اذا جاز ابريل اعمل فوق البحر اسرير) "once April passes, you can spread a bed on the face of the sea."[150]

II.5.1 The Foods They Ate

With olive trees growing abundantly in al-Andalus, it should come as no surprise that olive oil was *the* preferred fat for all cooking purposes. Andalusis used it in savory and sweet dishes and even in frying, as they found ways for neutralizing its flavor and smell for such tasks. We learn from the Andalusi agronomist al-Ṭighnarī that olive oil was improved by treating it in a double boiler.[151] There were also ways to remedy olive oil and improve its flavor and smell, as suggested in al-Tujībī's recipe x.9.2. On top of all this, they strongly believed in its curative powers. Honey was the preferred sweetening agent despite the fact that sugarcane, one of the new crops brought to the region, was successfully grown in the southern coastal areas. It seems that was the general tendency in the western region. Writing about al-Maghrib, al-Qalqashandī observes that although sugarcane grew in the region and excellent qualities of sugar were produced, people did not care much for it and preferred to use honey, of which they had plenty.[152]

It is not certain how coriander, both the seeds and the herb, ended up being the most important of the seasoning ingredients in the cooking of the western region, even more important than parsley, whose use is almost negligible in al-Tujībī's recipes. By comparison, both coriander and parsley indiscriminately enjoyed popularity among cooks in al-Mashriq. It could simply have been that they loved its flavor. The protagonist in the *Portrait of Lozana*, for instance, giving an analogy on the obvious, once said, "Does coriander give food a better taste? Of course!"[153] The author/compiler of the thirteenth-century Andalusi cookbook stresses the use of coriander (seeds and cilantro) in all the dishes. His rational was that when eaten with food, coriander can slow down digestion and keep food in the stomach until it is fully digested.[154] On the other hand,

150 See al-Zajjālī, *Amthāl al-ʿawām* ii 18, 107, 349.

151 Al-Ṭighnarī, *Zahrat al-bustān* 210–1.

152 Qalqashandī, *Ṣubḥ al-aʿshā* v 176.

153 *Portrait of Lozana, the Lusty Andalusian Woman* 71. It was originally written by the sixteenth-century Francisco Delicado, English trans., Bruno Damiani.

154 Anonymous, *Anwāʿ al-ṣaydala* 53.

while tenth-century Baghdadi physician al-Rāzī describes coriander in similar terms, he specifically recommends it for people with diarrhea. Otherwise, he cautions strongly against overeating it, as this might cause mental confusion and even death.[155] Although it does not seem that anybody died because of coriander, still, it might have been the culprit in the collective condition of chronic constipation that Andalusis were known for being prone to. The Damascene physician Ibn Abī Uṣaybiʿa noted that while the people of al-Andalus needed 3 *dirhams* (9 grams) of scammonia to soften their bowels, people of al-Mashriq needed to only take ½ *dirham* (1½ grams).[156]

Judging from the surviving recipes, Andalusi cooks used garlic (*thūm*) more freely than their Mashriqi counterparts in dishes like braised chicken of *thūmiyya* (recipe iii.2.28) and chicken *tharīd*, called *muthawwama* (recipe i.2.25), cooked in celebration of the Christian Nayrūz day in January. Cooking with garlic in this way must have been a Christian preference that Andalusi Muslims adopted. Now that they were living in a colder region, garlic with its hot and dry properties was believed to be beneficial.[157]

Based on the two surviving cookbooks, Andalusi cuisine was the product of an inclusive kitchen. Dishes of partridge and chicken were described as Yahūdī;[158] and Christian ones, called *rāhibī* 'monks' dishes,' cooked with beef and sweetened with rose-petal jam and scented with rosewater (recipe ii.1.7), or beef pot roast served with *jalja*.[159] Amazigh couscous is prominent in this kitchen. A simplified version of it is given, among others, in which couscous is cooked in broth, like we do nowadays with rice; it was fast and delicious.[160] There are dishes called *al-ʿArabī*, *al-Qurashiyya*,[161] and *al-Ḥijāziyya* (from the Arabian Peninsula), cooked with cured meat; *Turkiyya* (Turkish), cooked with preserved lemons and cured olives; and *Ṣaqlabiyya* (of the Slavs), and so on. Additionally, Andalusi cuisine was not confined to the kitchens of courts and palaces; rather, it included other social strata, as in the peasant's dish of *badawiyya* or the suckling lamb dish cooked by shepherds in their sheepfolds, where a final sprinkle of black pepper or cinnamon is optional (recipe ii.3.2). In his

155 Al-Rāzī, *Manāfiʿ al-aghdhiya* 180.
156 Ibn Abī Uṣaybiʿa, *ʿUyūn al-anbāʾ* 190.
157 See also section iii.8, pp. 82–4, below.
158 See recipe iii.2.21 in al-Tujībī, *Fiḍāla*; and anonymous, *Anwāʿ al-ṣaydala* 42, 43, 45.
159 The Romance Andalusī for *ṣalṣa* 'dipping sauce.'
160 See al-Tujībī, *Fiḍāla* recipe i.5.3. In the anonymous Andalusi *Anwāʿ al-ṣaydala* 158, this dish is said to have been called *al-fityānī* in Marrakesh.
161 Most probably named after one of the Arab tribes in al-Andalus, who claimed to be descendants of Quraysh, the Prophet's tribe.

last part, al-Tujībī provides recipes for extravagantly prepared handwashing compounds, only to tell us that crushed chickpeas are what ordinary people like us would practically use (recipe xii.8).

II.5.2 *Al-Mujabbanāt*

Qayjaṭlī, nijabbin lak

If you make *qayjāṭa* for me, I will bring you fresh cheese.[162]

AL-ZAJJĀLĪ, *Amthāl al-ʿawām* ii 412

This was a famous Andalusi saying on collaboration and exchange of interests, and what better food to pick than their beloved cheese pastries of *mujabbanāt*? As a symbolic observation, the saying is also significant culturally and linguistically, playfully combining the Arabic *jubn* and the Andalusi Romance *qayjāṭ* for cheese.[163]

Al-mujabbana was one of the foodstuffs that evolved in al-Andalus and characterized Andalusi cuisine in the rest of the Arabo-Muslim world. It was made in a variety of ways: fried, when cheese was mixed with the dough, stuffed in it, or both; shaped, sometimes like doughnuts; or baked by layering thin sheets of dough with cheese (recipes i.4.33–9). The basic dough of the fried version was similar to that of *isfanj*, light and spongy fritters (recipes i.4.30–2). They were drenched in honey heated up with fresh butter, sprinkled with sugar and cinnamon, and served. We also learn from al-Tujībī's recipe i.4.33 that Andalusis preferred to have *al-mujabbana* not drenched with honey but sprinkled with Ceylon cinnamon, pounded aniseeds, and sugar, with a small vessel filled with honey served with them as a dip.

The eastern region was very familiar with *isfanj*, except that they called it *zalābiya sādhaja*, i.e., not shaped as latices (*mushabbaka*). From the tenth-century Baghdadi cookbook by al-Warrāq,[164] we learn that Levantines were the ones famous for making them this way; al-Warrāq called it *zalābiya Shāmiyya* and *ṣafanj*, which indeed is nothing other than *isfanj*. That *zalābiya* was another name for *isfanj* was later confirmed in the thirteenth-century Andalusi cookbook *Anwāʿ al-ṣaydala* 170.

---

162 Name of cheese pastry, which ultimately derives from the Spanish *queso* 'cheese,' and *quesito* for fresh cheese. For more on the etymology of the name *qayjāṭa*, see glossary 2, s.v. *mujabbanāt*.

163 See al-Tujībī's recipe i.4.35 for *qayjāṭa*.

164 Al-Warrāq, *Kitāb al-Ṭabīkh*, English trans., *Annals*, chapter 100.

Based on this, we may assume that the Andalusi *mujabbana* was an amalgam of the familiar *isfanj* and what was already known of the indigenous pastries incorporating fresh cheese, of which excellent varieties were brought from the luscious pastures of Iberia. Andalusis had a popular saying about the *mujabbana* of Sharīsh (Jerez), a city in the western region of al-Andalus close to Seville, which goes, "He who visits Sharīsh and does not eat its *mujabbana* is deprived indeed." The secret to Sharīsh *mujabbana* was the delicious flavor of cheese produced in the area, as al-Maqqarī notes.[165] This would also explain how *mujabbana* came to be closely associated with Christian feasts and festivals, such as the January Nayrūz feast and the Thursday in April before Easter Sunday. Aside from Christian festivals, *mujabbana* was consumed year-round, cooked in private kitchens and purchased from food markets. They were offered to guests at festive gatherings like weddings, circumcision parties, picnics, and the like.[166]

Apparently, the most popular time for eating *mujabbana* was in the morning and while still piping hot from the pan, as we learn from the Andalusi adage on things that are past their prime, (مجبنة الظهر خرج نارها وقلّ طلابها) "There is little demand for cold *mujabbana* offered at noon." *Mujabbana* was frequently described in verses, compared to the sun or to a pregnant virgin.[167] A *mujabbana* lover once said,

> Most beautiful when brought in with steam hovering all above the tray.
> Pick one up and it would burn your fingers with its heat,
> But cool and safe once inside you.[168]

Even our author al-Tujībī participated in this *mujabbana* culture, as we see him riddling about it in a prose composition, "She adorns trays and tables, a dazzling virgin in whose adoration people congregate. She comes out only when tightly squeezed in the palm of the hand and can only swim in the fountain after being pressed. She might cool down a lover's heart, but she is hot."[169]

Mujabbana with all its aura became to the Andalusis what the crescent-shaped stuffed cookies of *khushkanānaj* and the syrupy *qaṭāyif* pancakes, for instance, were to people of al-Mashriq in places like Baghdad and Egypt.

---

165 Al-Maqqarī, *Nafḥ al-ṭīb* i 184.
166 Bin Sharīfa, *al-Zajjālī: Amthāl al-ʿawām* i 235.
167 Ibid.
168 Cited in Bin Sharīfa, *Ibn Razīn al-Tujībī* 157.
169 Ibid., 105.

FIGURE 23 Market transactions, *Kitāb al-Diryāq*, fol. NP, detail
BNF, DEPARTMENT OF MANUSCRIPTS, ARAB 2964. SOURCE: GALLICA.BNF.FR /BNF

II.5.3 Eating Out and Shopping: Regulating the Food Markets

When Andalusis wanted to demonstrate excellence in quality, they would use *ḥimās al-ṭabbākh* 'meat grilled by a home cook,'[170] in contrast to *shiwāʾ al-sūq* 'meat grilled in the food market.' A common expression, of course, reflecting people's negative attitudes towards market food due to fears of a lack of skills and hygiene. Regardless, food markets flourished in al-Andalus, and people from all walks of life availed themselves of their services. They were particularly needed by people away from home and those staying in inns, who would usually be provided with a place to sleep but not food.

One reason behind the popularity of market food was the enforcement of rigorous standards. Generally, food offerings, called *akl al-sūq*, were up to acceptable standards, and it was the job of the market inspector, called *ṣāḥib al-sūq* (*al-muḥtasib* in the eastern region) to ensure that they were indeed so. There are surviving Andalusi manuals for market inspectors, who regulated the levels of quality and services at cookshops, where customers had the choice of eating on the premises or carrying their food out in *jirāb* (leather bags) or ves-

170 Al-Zajjālī, *Amthāl al-ʿawām* ii 188.

FIGURE 24
Al-muḥtasib 'market inspector' weighs bread, *Ralamb Costume Book*, 1657, p. 85
NATIONAL LIBRARY OF SWEDEN, SHELF MARK 8:O NR 10

sels with narrow tops.[171] To begin with, cooks were not allowed to work late at night or before dawn; their shops were required to be plastered with lime, easy to clean, and well-lit. While working on the dishes before putting them on the fire, the cook should have an apprentice to swat the flies away with a hand fan and cover the ones he finished working on with a piece of cloth.[172] Food ready to serve was to be emptied into wide bowls and pots so that the customers could have a better look at what they were purchasing. Additionally, cooks were not allowed to top their foods with *takhmīr*, made by whisking eggs with breadcrumbs and spices and spreading it on the face of food while it was cooking in a pot.[173] We see this frequently done in al-Tujībī's recipes, but in food markets there was always the possibility that venders would cheat by hiding substandard foods under *takhmīr*.

Evidently, food quality standards were meant to ensure consumers' well-being as well as honest commercial activity. Only fresh meat should be used in making *mirqās* (small sausage links) and *aḥrash* and *isfiriyya* (meat patties). Cooks who fried fish were cautioned against using too much flour to coat the pieces and were to avoid submerging them in brine, called *sharmūla*, when taken out of the pan. This was done to make the fish look good and weigh heavier on the scales.[174] Cooks who fried the popular *isfanj* fritters and *mujabbanāt*

171 Al-Saqaṭī, *Fī Ādāb al-ḥisba* 37.
172 Ibid., 35.
173 Ibn ʿAbd al-Raʾūf, *Fī Ādāb al-ḥisba* 96–7.
174 Ibn ʿAbd al-Raʾūf, *Fī Ādāb al-ḥisba* 97. The word *sharmūla*, which the author provides, was derived from the southern Hispanic Romance *salmúyra*, which is a hybrid of *sal* (salt) and *mūria* (*m-r-y*: sweet and sour condiment), as explained in Corriente, *Dictionary of Andalusi Arabic*, s.v. *sh-r-m-l*.

FIGURE 25 At the marketplace, al-Ḥarīrī, *al-Maqāmāt*, fol. 105r, copied and illustrated by al-Wāsiṭī, detail
BNF, DEPARTMENT OF MANUSCRIPTS, ARAB 5847. SOURCE: GALLICA.BNF.FR /BNF

cheese pastries, called *saffājīn* (sg. *saffāj*), used to sit on high chairs while frying, as illustrated in a line of verse describing them: "*Saffājīn*, you would take them for kings, / when they alight their pulpits (*manābir*), only to sit down on them."[175] These pastries used to sell like hot cakes, literally and figuratively, and the food inspectors were vigilant in preventing dishonest practices, such as using too much dough so the pastries might weigh heavier on the scales or adulterating the cheese filling by mixing it with flour.[176] *Mujabbana* makers had to follow specified proportions of ingredients. According to al-Saqaṭī, for *mujabbana* to pass the test, it must be brittle enough to break when you bite into it and leave greasy traces on your fingers.[177]

The test for good *harīsa* (wheat porridge with meat) was to put a two-pound weight on its face while still in the pot, if the weight did not sink, then the *harīsa* was thick enough and passed. But some *harīsa* makers who were aware of this test used to sink in a copper block at the place where the food inspector's weight

175 Quoted in al-Zajjālī, *Amthāl al-ʿawām* ii 385.
176 Al-Saqaṭī, *Fī Ādāb al-ḥisba* 37; and Ibn ʿAbdūn al-Ishbīlī, *Risāla* 45.
177 Al-Saqaṭī, *Fī Ādāb al-ḥisba* 38.

would be put, which of course meant it would not sink. Al-Saqaṭī highly praises *balāja* that looked and tasted good, made by a famous food market chef. *Balāja* was a kind of baked meatloaf made with ground organ meat or game meat mixed with eggs, breadcrumbs, and spices. Good *balāja* was not supposed to be thicker than the width of two fingers put together.[178] Whole sheep carcasses had to be weighed before and after roasting them; they had to be one-third of their weight lighter when done; otherwise, they would be returned to the *tannūr* oven. To test for done meat, the shoulder had to be easy to pull, and no bloody veins should be visible when the thigh was slightly slit. Incidentally, we learn that for Amazigh customers, only one-quarter of the sheep had to be reduced because they preferred the meat not too well done, as they would usually use knives to cut and eat grilled meat.[179]

Community ovens were required to be fueled with mountain wood.[180] Bakers were not allowed to sprinkle the face of bread with a solution of water and honey before baking it or brush it with oil after baking to make it look nice and glossy. The market inspector was required to examine the crumb of the bread as well, to make sure that the baker did not use inferior dough only to coat it when portioned with a thin layer of good-quality dough before baking it. Bread adulterated this way was called *mulabbas* (literally, clothed). Additionally, no large sizes were allowed for *buyyāt*, which was bread known to go stale fast, such as those made with whole wheat dough.[181]

As for candies and desserts sold in markets, our source this time is an interesting prose composition, titled *Risālat al-Ḥalwāʾ* (An epistle on desserts), by Ibn Shuhayd al-Andalusi (d. 1035), who lived at the beginning of the Taifa era. He tells how once he was with a group of friends and passed by a row of dessert sellers and how one of them happened to be a lover of sweets. He dribbled at the sight of the starch-based *fālūdhaj* made with honey, saying, look at them, sweeter than lovers' exchanges of saliva. He looked at the *khabīṣ*[182] and described it as valuable and yet so cheap. He then looked at the *qubayṭāʾ*, the pulled honey taffy,[183] and shouted, by God, this is melted white silver. Are they cooked with fire or light, because to me they look like full moons; and is it walnuts or almonds that they are kneaded with? He walked to the seller and

178 Ibid., 40.

179 Ibid.

180 Ibn ʿAbd al-Raʾūf, *Fī Ādāb al-ḥisba* 89, 91.

181 Ibn ʿAbdūn al-Ishbīlī, *Risāla* 43.

182 It is a variety of thick pudding, see al-Tujībī's recipe i.4.9.

183 Also called *qubbayṭ*, see al-Tujībī's recipe ix.2.5.

bought a whole pound for just two dirhams and immediately devoured them. He next saw the latticed fritters of *zalābiya*, which, apparently, he could not afford; then he passed by a seller of *ḥalwā* made with dates but could not buy any either. And so he sat at a corner crying. Ibn Shuhayd took pity on him and ordered a whole tray to be filled with all the desserts he craved, a pound of each.[184] Apparently, for people with reasonable means, the desserts available in the markets were not expensive.

Upholding known standards was indeed a big service for those who shopped for their daily cooking. Judging from the regulations set by inspectors, the markets were clean and organized. Fish sellers were not allowed to open shops in the marketplace centers, likewise with shops for slaughtering animals; trash was thrown outside the city walls, firewood sellers had special places to sell, coal was stored in dry places, vegetables were washed in running river water rather than ponds, and the like.[185] In their daily transactions, shoppers were protected by the market inspectors, who cautioned the sellers against mixing the bad with the good, the old with the new, or the cheap with the expensive. Shops of butchers selling mutton should be away from those that sold goat meat. Offal should not be sold with meat for the same price; egg sellers should have basins filled with water next to them to detect bad eggs, which usually float.[186] The list is long.

Mud was removed from market streets in winter, and streets were closed annually for a few days to repair them. Market inspector al-Jarsīfī, for instance, complains of reckless youths who used to sprinkle water at each other in marketplaces during Mahrajān Day, which would make the streets slippery.[187] Marketplaces were located close to mosques in the city centers. Nothing that caused dirt or bad smells was allowed to be sold in the vicinities of mosques. Other objects not allowed to be sold there included olive oil, *qunilya* rabbits, birds, and desert truffles (*tirfās*), which the inspectors disparagingly described as *fākihat al-khullāʿ*, that is, frivolous food of the shameless and the licentious.[188] Possibly it was one of the fun foods that people had as snacks (*naql*) during drinking sessions, in the manner of what we call mezza today.

184 Ibn Shuhayd al-Andalusi, *Risālat al-Tawābiʿ* 119–23.
185 Ibn ʿAbdūn al-Ishbīlī, *Risāla* 37, 38, 43.
186 Ibid.
187 Al-Jarsīfī, *Risāla* 124. For more on this festival, see section ii.6, pp. 67–8, below.
188 Ibn ʿAbdūn al-Ishbīlī, *Risāla* 43.

FIGURE 26 Having drinks with *naql* (mezza dishes), al-Ḥarīrī, *al-Maqāmāt*, fol. 167v, detail
BNF, DEPARTMENT OF MANUSCRIPTS, ARAB 3929. SOURCE: GALLICA.BNF.FR /BNF

11.6 *Food in Andalusi Social Contexts*

سمعت بنت السلطان الساعي يسعى، قالت كتعمل شبات بشحم؟

The sultan's daughter listened to the poor man's petition, and then asked,
"So you want to make *shabāt* with suet?"[189]

189 A saying from al-Zajjālī, *Amthāl al-ʿawām* ii 421. *Shabāt bi-shaḥm*, a delicate and rich pastry eaten drenched in honey, was associated with a life of leisure. A recipe for making it is in anonymous, *Anwāʿ al-ṣaydala* 180. The sultan's daughter sounds so much like Queen Marie Antoinette and her "let them eat brioche."

Andalusi ruling families, the elite around them, and those who enriched themselves from the economic prosperity that characterized periods of political stability enjoyed unprecedented lives of luxury, and they showed it. A memorable Andalusi feast that was often compared to the grand wedding of Abbasid Caliph al-Maʾmūn and Būrān was the huge celebration of the circumcision (*iʿdhār*) of the grandson of the Taifa ruler of Toledo, al-Maʾmūn Ibn Dhī al-Nūn, who reputedly accumulated an enormous wealth.[190] The feast lasted for several days. Soon after the circumcision, celebrations commenced with serving droves of the highest in rank endless varieties of foods, and they ate and ate to their hearts' desire, with servers swatting flies away from their foods with elaborately decorated swatters. When this group was done, they went to another hall where they cleansed their hands and anointed themselves after being sprinkled with rose water. Then followed droves after droves until the last group, the commoners, entered. They were treated to foods they had never seen or tasted before, and the text uncharitably describes how they hurriedly devoured, gulped, and swallowed the food.

The last king of the Taifa kingdom of Seville and Cordova, al-Muʿtamid Ibn ʿAbbād (d. 1095), was known for his extreme extravagance. It was said that he ordered the small town of Ṭiryāna (Triana), which faced Seville on the other bank of the river (the Guadalquivir), to completely whitewash the facades of all buildings and adorn them along the entire bank so that the promenading Sevillians on their side of the river would not be offended by any unsightly views; all expenses paid by Seville.

Another Ibn ʿAbbād story that went down in history as *yawm al-ṭīn* (the mud day) gives us a rare insight into his personal life and reveals how far he would go with his indulgences. One day his favorite wife, Iʿtimād al-Ramīkiyya, saw peasant girls heading to the markets to sell yogurt in containers they were carrying on their heads; they were trudging in mud. On a whim, she told al-Muʿtamid that she would like to do what those milkmaids did. Al-Muʿtamid, the story goes, ordered 'mud' to be made by kneading tremendous amounts of ambergris, musk, and camphor with rosewater, which was then spread in the palace court. He also ordered containers and ropes be made with pure silk threads (*ibrīsam*). So his wife plodded through the 'mud' with her slave girls, and it was great fun. Years later, after Ibn ʿAbbād's deposition and exile in Morocco, his wife once got frustrated with him and angrily told him that she had never seen a good day with him, at which he gently rebuked her, "Not even the mud day?" To which she apologized, so al-Maqqarī's story

190 A detailed account is found in al-Shantarīnī, *al-Dhakhīra* 127–37.

goes.[191] Al-Maqqarī also tells the story of the famous Almoravid Andalusi poet Ibn al-Zaqqāq (d. 1133). In his early years, studying hard until late at night, his father, who was very poor, once gently rebuked him, "Son, we are poor people, we cannot afford the oil you need to light your night hours of study."[192]

Teaching was said to be a profitable job for the popular ones among them, earning some of them what amounted to 4,000 dirhams a month. But they were also known for their generosity. Some of them were even reported to have offered daily meals to their students at the end of the day's teaching sessions. Hearty dishes would be served, like *tharīd* mounded with lamb and sweet olive oil or *tharīd* of milk moistened with ghee or butter; meals that would keep them full to the following day, one of the students reported.[193]

We learn from al-Maqqarī's excerpt from Ibn Saʿīd al-Maghribi that people of al-Andalus were fanatics about cleanliness,[194] with some who would rather spend the little they had on soap than on food. They were also known for leading frugal lives. Being careful with what they had now to spare themselves the indignity of asking later, undeservedly earned them a reputation for stinginess. They were generous, nevertheless, so Ibn Saʿīd seems to suggest, but in their own Andalusi way. To illustrate this, he tells how he and his father once passed by a village while traveling; it was cold and raining. They stopped at a house, and the owner immediately offered to host them if they gave him money to buy the needed coal, which they did. The man's son came closer to the fire to warm himself, for which his father rebuked him. Ibn Saʿīd's father asked the man why he did this, and the man said so that he learns not to take advantage of other people's money, and I want him to get used to the cold. When bedtime came, he said to his son, "Give the youth [i.e., Ibn Saʿīd] your overcoat to keep him warm," which the son did. Ibn Saʿīd said that when he woke up in the morning the child was fully awake, with a hand clutching the coat from a corner. When Ibn Saʿīd told his father about this, his explanation was that this was just Andalusis being Andalusis, generous but careful and cautious. "The boy gave you his coat, but since he did not know you, whether you would turn out to be honest or a thief, he stayed awake lest you should leave with it."[195] Al-Andalus was not the Arabia of the legendarily generous Ḥātim al-Ṭāʾī. Extreme winters, snowstorms,

191 Al-Maqqarī, *Nafḥ al-ṭīb* i 440.

192 Ibid., iii 289.

193 See Bin Sharīfa, *Al-Zajjālī: Amthāl al-ʿawām* i 233. This first volume is a valuable study of Andalusi society based on al-Zajjālī's collection of proverbs.

194 Al-Maqqarī took his excerpt from *al-Mughrib fī ḥulā al-Maghrib* by Ibn Saʿīd, the famous historian and poet.

195 Al-Maqqarī, *Nafḥ al-ṭīb* i 223–4.

famines, and the like taught Andalusis to be reservedly generous and economical with what they had. One of their sayings goes, (من اهترق زيت في دقيق يعمل الكعك) "If your oil falls into flour, make cookies with them"; or this one, (لا تهرق ما حتى تجد ما) "Do not throw out the water you have until you find water."[196]

Festive occasions, however, had no place for frugality. All households offered the best they could to celebrate their feasts; and there were many, Muslim, Jewish, and Christian. In addition to the major Muslim *ʿĪd*s of breaking the fast at the end of Ramaḍān, *ʿĪd al-Fiṭr*, and *ʿĪd al-Aḍḥā* after the Hajj, there was *ʿĀshūrāʾ* on the tenth day of Muḥarram, commemorating the martyrdom of al-Ḥusayn, grandson of the Prophet. Andalusis feasted mainly on fruits. The famous Cordovan poet Ibn Quzmān (d. 1160), who lived during the Almoravid rule, gives us a glimpse into his *ʿĀshūrāʾ* 'shopping list':

> We will buy acorns and chestnuts,
> And what do you say we also get some walnuts.
> And how about skinned almonds because we eat a lot of these.
> *Safarī* pomegranates, we've got to have them;[197] and maybe bananas.
> But definitely grilled meats and aged wine.[198]

For *ʿĪd al-Aḍḥā* all families were expected to sacrifice a ram, *kabsh*, and it was an occasion that caused financial hardships to many. In Ibn Quzmān's words, "A ram, which in the name of sacrifice the poor would buy./ They say it is to please God, but they really do it to please their kids."[199] Whether for God or kids, Ibn Quzmān could not wait to eat it. In one of his poems addressing it, he calls it *ḥabībī kabsh al-ʿīd*:

> My beloved ram of *ʿĪd*, I am your ally.
> Why are you shying away? Have mercy on your emaciated devotee.
> Why this distance between you and your lover, your friend?
> How far away is your grilled meat from me? And your cured meat?
> Here, put a clean pot on the fire, with salt, coriander, and the best of spices,

196 Al-Zajjālī, *Amthāl al-ʿawām* ii 322, 462.
197 This was an excellent variety of pomegranates, see glossary 7, s.v. *rummān*.
198 Ibn Quzmān, *Iṣābat al-aghrāḍ*, *zajal* 89, p. 283. Ibn Quzmān (d. 1160) lived in Cordova during the Almoravid period. He wrote his poetry in colloquial Andalusi Arabic, the language of ordinary people, rather than formal Arabic, as he did not expect any favors from the ruling classes, who disapproved of his licentious behavior.
199 Ibid., *zajal* 48, p. 162.

> Check the taste, and as soon as the pot's boiling sounds announce it's done,
> Beat your eggs, break your bread, and make us your *tharīd* dish.[200]

A festivity that Andalusi Muslims learnt from the Christians and applied to their cycle of feasts was *al-Shaʿbāniyya*. During the month of Shaʿbān, which occurs before the fasting month of Ramaḍān, it became their custom to arrange picnics, exchange visitations, and eat plenty of food to get ready for the fasting of Ramaḍān. The last day of Shaʿbān was particularly celebrated by congregating in parks, where Andalusis would recite poetry, play music, cross the river in joy rides, stroll along its banks, and eat to satiety, which gave rise to the saying, (شعبان شبعان) *"Shaʿbān is full."*[201] It was much like the Mardi Gras celebration before Lent.

One of the major feasts that Muslim Andalusis used to share with Christians was *ʿĪd Yanayyir*, which was the New Year in the Christian calendar, also called *Nayrūz/Nawrūz*.[202] The day before the New Year was believed to be a blessed time for getting married. For *Nawrūz*, people used to buy different foods, such as fruits, meat, and spices, as well as henna and incense to bring joy and merriment to their families; the rich among them exchanged gifts. What was most exciting about this feast was *madāʾin Yanayyir*. They were beautifully constructed miniature walled towns made with rich dough, colored green, red and the like, decorated, and then baked; thus described in verse:

> A walled city that magicians would puzzle,
> Built only with virgins' or sequestered women's hands.
> Like an adorned bride made with finest flour and saffron.
> With keys no other than your fingers ten.[203]

They were further decorated with fruits and nuts, such as almonds, chestnuts, dates, walnuts, acorns, figs, raisins, citrons, lemons, sugarcane, hazelnuts, and prunes, as well as candy figurines (*tamāthīl al-ḥalwā*). The grand trays thus decorated were called *naṣbāt*. They were either made at home or purchased from shops, each looking like an adorned bride. Of the estimated cost of such a *naṣba*, the arrangement of fruits and pastry cities was said to be as high as

---

200 Ibid., *zajal* 85, pp. 261–2.

201 See al-Zajjālī, *Amthāl al-ʿawām* ii 438.

202 *Nawrūz* was a feast of Persian origin, which Persians celebrated on the day of the spring equinox.

203 Ibn Saʿīd, *al-Mughrib* i 294.

70 dinars due to all the sugar and candies and fruits used. They made them the best they could, boasting how much money they spent on them, and offered them to their children to enjoy and celebrate.[204] Handsomely made dessert knives were especially used; apparently they were not sharp, which gave rise to an Andalusi saying on beautiful but useless objects, (سكين حلوى: يلمع ولا يقطع) "Dessert knife, it shines and glitters but can hardly cut."[205] It was also reported that in some places, huge casseroles of cured fish were made, costing at least 30 dinars each.[206] From al-Tujībī's cookbook (recipe i.2.25) we learn that they made a special *tharīd* dish for *Nawrūz* called *muthawwama*, which was roasted or grilled chicken served on bread sopped in garlic-flavored sauce and sprinkled with grated cheese.

Such extravagance, especially the expensive miniature cities that were meant to please the children, did not pass unnoticed. The Cordovan poet Ibn Quzmān sympathetically observes,

> These *naṣbāt*, they do look beautiful.
> By God, just looking at them would cheer you.
> Those with no children would surely be relieved,
> As for those who can afford them, they may indulge.[207]

To conservative Muslim Andalusis like the jurist Abū al-Qāsim al-ʿAzfī, these shows of excess were criticized on religious grounds, objecting to them as *bidʿa*, which is unacceptable newly introduced behavior. He in fact put the blame on men who would listen to wives eager to celebrate and show off.[208]

Another major seasonal Christian and Jewish feast that Muslims shared was *al-ʿAnṣara*, also called *ʿĪd al-Mahrajān*, Pentecost, on which the birthday of John the Baptist (Yaḥyā) was celebrated on the June 24. Women would decorate their houses and put cabbage leaves and green leaves in their pockets as a good omen. One of the ways to celebrate it was by lighting a pile of fire and jumping over it. It was also the custom to sprinkle water on each other. The market inspectors objected to such a practice as it caused the market streets to be too slippery for shoppers.[209] Like any other feasts, table spreads were served with

---

204 Bin Sharīfa, *al-Zajjālī: Amthāl al-ʿawām* i 239.
205 Al-Zajjālī, *Amthāl al-ʿawām* ii 422.
206 Bin Sharīfa, *al-Zajjālī: Amthāl al-ʿawām* i 239.
207 Ibn Quzmān, *Iṣābat al-aghrāḍ*, *zajal* 72, p. 222.
208 Abū al-Qāsim al-ʿAzafī (d. 1366) was a jurist and the emir of Ceuta; quoted in Bin Sharīfa, *al-Zajjālī*: *Amthāl al-ʿawām* i 239.
209 Al-Jarsīfī, *Risāla fī l-Ḥisba* 124.

varieties of dishes and desserts, especially *isfanj* fritters and cheese pastries of *mujabbanāt*.[210] Another Christian feast that Muslims joined in celebrating was *ʿĪd Khamīs Ibrīl* on the Thursday that preceded Easter Sunday in April. The principal foods made for this event were *mujabbanāt* and *isfanj*, consumed profusely outdoors during picnics in parks.[211] Around the same date, it was also the custom of Andalusi Jews to make bread and gift them to their Muslim neighbors on their *ʿĪd al-Fiṭr*.[212]

One of the paradoxes of Muslims sharing the land with Christians in al-Andalus was that the important religious feast of celebrating the birth of their own Prophet only became official in the thirteenth century when the conservative Muslim jurists wanted to replace Muslim celebrations of the Christian New Year, *ʿĪd Yanayyir*, with *ʿĪd al-Mawlid al-Nabawī*, the birth of the Prophet. It was a happy occasion, which people celebrated by lighting candles, having food treats, each according to their own means, wearing their best clothes, and going out on picnics in parks. The wealthy among the jurists used to hold feasts for friends and offer meals to the needy. Poems in praise of the Prophet were recited, and schoolboys used to ask their parents to buy candles to gift them to their teachers. It used to be that men and women celebrated the event together, as they were used to doing with the rest of their feasts, but this was frowned upon by the jurists, who considered this *bidʿa* (unwelcome new Muslim behavior) that had to stop.[213]

11.6.1 The Language of Food

Food poetry was a favorite pastime of Andalusis, as we have frequently witnessed in the above discussions; and poetry that was descriptive of food was particularly popular. Such subjects were often dealt with lightheartedly, as in the following verses describing *ḥarshaf* 'cardoon,' by Ibn Shuhayd al-Andalusi (d. 1035), who lived at the beginning of the Taifa era.

> Have your eyes ever set, my friend, on hedgehogs sold in baskets?
> Cardoons, large and sought after, with needles that an elephant's skin
> would pierce,

210 See al-Darrājī, *al-Taʾthīr al-ḥaḍārī* 117. The book's chapter dealing with Andalusi feasts, 103–25, is indispensable.

211 Ibid., 121.

212 Al-Wansharīsī, *al-Miʿyār al-Muʿrib* xi 111. This must have been done at the end of the seventh day of their *ʿīd*.

213 See Abū Muṣṭafā, *Jawānib min al-ḥayāt al-ijtimāʿiyya* 44–7; and Bin Sharīfa, *al-Zajjālī: Amthāl al-ʿawām* i 241.

Like the fangs of a ghoul's daughter. Stick one into the butt of a pain-in-the-neck bore,
And it would startle him into a jump, all the way to Egypt.
An appetizer for ignorant fools, and which numbskulls consider food.
I pledge never to offer it to my guests, nor with my wine consume.[214]

It was also a vehicle for light social criticism, as in the case of Ibn Quzmān cited above, but also a touching expression of nostalgia in exile, as in the case of Abū ʿAbdallāh b. al-Azraq al-Andalusī, who was the supreme judge of Granada during the Nasrid dynasty. He was sent to Egypt to seek help against the Christian armies in 1487 but failed in his mission and did not go back home. He died in Jerusalem in 1491. In a long poem bemoaning his life in exile, he brooded over the many foods he missed from home, even the simplest among them, such as eggs fried in plenty of delicious olive oil and the crispy fatty skin of grilled chicken. He missed the familiar *tharīd* dishes, especially the garlicky *muthawwama*, served with plenty of cheese and fattened young chickens, the fluffy fritters of *isfanj*, and cheese pastries of *mujabbana*. He also missed *shāshiyyat al-faqīr* (the poor man's cap), which would gladden even the hearts of the richest;[215] and of course couscous, which he described as noble and sublime. He especially missed the well-made couscous and remembered how he used to roll large morsels into balls and shove them into his mouth, so earnestly that they made his ears ring; and he goes on and on.[216] Interestingly, we have recipes in al-Tujībī's cookbook for almost all the dishes he mentions.

To some poets, food was the love of their lives:

Spare us the ways of lovers, their passions, and rendezvous.
Weep less on their relics, and do not despair when they leave.
It is not the cheeks and eyes of the beloveds that rational men would please.
More joyful to them is *thurda* of *tafāyā* with a plump young chicken.
When asked, whom do you love then, and for whom do you weep?
I say, "For *sikbājāt* and *jumliyyāt* dishes with tender roasts and delicate sheets of bread."

214 Ibn Shuhayd al-Andalusi, *Dīwān* 140.
215 See al-Tujībī's recipe i.2.8.
216 Cited by al-Maqqarī, *Nafḥ al-ṭīb* iii 298–303.

Wheat porridge to me is more luscious than the saliva of the beloved when embraced.[217]

On the other hand, there were also those with whom such an overindulgence did not sit well, and they condemned it, at least on health grounds:

You who eat whatever you crave,
Cursing doctors and their cures.
Know that you will reap what you planted.
Sickness, it is coming soon to you,
Disease, creeping on you by the day,
For ill-gotten foods are like sins.[218]

Part III: The Andalusi Cuisine as Depicted in the Book of *Fiḍāla*

Lozana: Does coriander give food a better taste? Of course!

Analogy on the obvious, from *Portrait of Lozana, the Lusty Andalusian Woman* 71[219]

In his *Fiḍālat al-khiwān*, Ibn Razīn al-Tujībī strikes not just the note of a serious cookbook writer but also that of an Andalusi gourmet with an attitude. In his introduction, he protests:

> I know of many people who wrote cookbooks in which they only included the most well-known of the dishes and neglected to point to so many issues. People of al-Mashriq have written a good deal of such stuff, which does not sound palatable to the ears and which people [here] find deplorable, even filthy; but to them it is the most elegant of foods.

It would indeed have helped had he given some examples to justify this strong aversion to things eastern, aside from attributing the differences "to the quality of their water and air and to the different natures of the needs and desires of people over there." He was similarly judgmental of the cooking of the people of

217 Cited by al-Shantarīnī, *al-Dhakhīra* i 557.

218 Cited by Ibn Saʿīd, *al-Mughrib* ii 100.

219 Originally written by the sixteenth-century Francisco Delicado, English trans. by Bruno Damiani.

Ifrīqiya,[220] which became his second home after he fled al-Andalus. Compared with the delectable marzipan-like *sanbūsak* Andalusis made (recipe ix.3.4), the meat-filled *sanbūsak* of the people of Ifrīqiya, al-Tujībī complains, is flavorless and simply unpalatable.

The author/compiler of the other contemporaneous Andalusi cookbook, anonymous, *Anwāʿ al-ṣaydala* 51, seems to have had a more tolerant attitude towards diversity in peoples' eating habits and gives several examples, such as of the people of Yemen who cook with tamarind and Persians who like to cook rice with sumac. He also tells how Egyptians favor the *marwazī* dish while Iraqis hate it because they think of it as medicine with the prunes, jujubes, and olive oil used to make it; and that many people like ghee whereas others do not tolerate even its smell. His conclusion is striking: If people dislike a certain food, they can expect others to be open to liking it.

Al-Tujībī's favoring of the Andalusi way of cooking is justified on the grounds that the population was "admirably earnest and advanced despite the fact that they started later [than people of al-Mashriq] in creating the most delectable dishes, and in spite of the constricting limitations of their borders and their proximity to the abodes of the enemies of Islam."[221] His fondness of what is local is indeed central to his overall design of the book. He chooses not to embellish it with anecdotes on famous caliphs and the like, or amusing ones on gluttons and gobblers, and other matters related to the benefits of foods offered at the table (*Fawāʾid al-mawāʾid*). Although he would have indeed been up to the task given his professional credentials as a scribe and man of letters, he aimed instead at being brief, limiting his choices only to the most favored of the cooked dishes, principally Andalusi ones.

As for the dishes, he says he chose many that he approved of, which we understand as meaning that they might have been picked from the circulating recipe books and pamphlets in his time; perhaps he needed to tweak them stylistically here and there, as we do not expect them to have been written by well-educated cooks. Al-Tujībī claims, as well, that he also included many more recipes that he himself created, a declaration that may suggest he was a practicing cook in his own right, and a creative one at that. Creativity, however, does not necessarily involve inventing dishes from scratch; rather, it could mean putting down on paper a recipe for a traditional dish that hitherto had been transmitted orally, or coming up with variations on already known dishes; his book abounds with these. The majority of the dishes, he says, are Andalusi, but

220 It included the coastal regions of what today are western Libya, Tunisia, and eastern Algeria.

221 Al-Tujībī's introduction, p. 108.

he picked from the eastern dishes only a small number, the finest among them. With a cookbook splendidly organized, with tasty recipes aptly detailed and lucidly written in grammatical Arabic, the erudite scholar Ibn Razīn al-Tujībī delivers, and we are in for a treat here.

III.7 *In the Kitchen with* Fiḍālat al-khiwān

To prepare the best of the Andalusi dishes that al-Tujībī offers in this collection of recipes, a well-equipped clean and spacious kitchen with a reliable source for clean water is expected; operated by several cooks and their small army of kitchen preppers and helpers to prepare the daily dishes and the occasional festive ones for weddings, circumcisions, religious feasts, and the like. Before hiring cooks, they were given the *tafāyā* test (see recipe ii.2.1); a good cook could manage to keep it white despite the many spices used, with well-balanced flavors and a pleasant aroma.[222]

The Andalusi kitchen was a busy place indeed. Servers carried trays of prepared bread discs and cookie pans to bake to perfection in the neighborhood brick oven, or earthenware *ṭājins* of prepared foods to brown there, and if it were a chicken, a goose, or a fish, somebody had to be there to turn the contents over several times to ensure they browned well. Coordination of activities and timing in the cooking processes was also important. In recipe i.2.18, for instance, a chicken grilled at home is to be served while still hot with a bread casserole, which has to be baked in the neighborhood brick oven. According to the recipe, these two activities should be timed accurately so that by the time the casserole arrives from the oven, the cook should have just finished grilling the chicken. Additionally, as displayed in the book of *Fiḍāla*, cooking was not solely restricted to the confines of the kitchen. A *muʿallak* festive dish, made with a fat suckling lamb in recipe ii.3.2, for instance, is said to be the kind of food that was mostly cooked by shepherds in the sheepfolds. There were also dishes, called *jināniyya*, which were prepared in orchards picnic style in the summer and fall (recipes i.2.26 and vii.9).

Pots of various shapes and sizes were needed, the most used of which were the earthenware ones, both glazed (*ḥantam/muzajjaj*) and unglazed (*fakhkhār*). Based on physicians' recommendations at the time, the unglazed ones should not be used more than once, whereas the glazed ones could be used up to five times. The rationale behind such practices was that the porous surfaces, especially those of the unglazed ones, are absorbent, and food trapped in them

---

222 See al-Saqaṭī, *Fī Ādāb al-ḥisba* 53. For a study of Andalusi cooking processes, see Marín, "Pots and Fire." For a survey of Andalusi cuisine, see Waines, "The Culinary Culture of al-Andalus."

would putrefy and mold. Regular washing could not efficiently guarantee the removal of all such particles. If these pots were used again, the putrefied particles in the pores would contaminate the cooking food and cause harm to the body.[223] Since the green-glazed ones were less porous, they could be reused several more times. This indeed explains the requirements for a new pot in a good number of recipes, such as those incorporating pulses and grains to preserve the purity of their tastes and various kinds of meat dishes, particularly those of stewed birds, and the simple *tafāyā*. Regarding big pots used in cooking foods like *tharīd*, which is an all-in-one dish (chapter i.2), the recipes ask for it to be well washed and cleaned before use.

In addition to the big stewing pot, a small pot (*qudayra*) was especially useful for small jobs, such as making dipping sauces and the like. It was also frequently used when attached to the rim of the large cooking stew pot after filling it with heated fresh water. The water would remain hot from the steam of the pot and would be used to replenish the liquid in the pot as needed. A couscoussier was an essential pot in the Andalusi kitchen, used for steaming *kuskusū* dishes. Its use is detailed in recipe i.5.1.

For precooking operations, large copper pots were needed, especially copper cauldrons (*ṭinjīr nuḥās*) with a rounded bottom for cooking honey-based desserts and syrups. Otherwise, tinned copper utensils were usually used for frying and cooking savory dishes. And there was the ubiquitous *ṭājin*, a versatile pan used on direct heat but more frequently for baking and roasting in the brick oven.[224] The *ṭājin*s used in al-Tujībī's recipes are variously made and shaped: large and small ones, wide, glazed and unglazed ones, and the unusual *ṭājin al-qaṭāyif*, specially made for cooking pancake-like pastries. As described in recipe i.4.15, it is made of glazed earthenware with a base textured with blind holes, which might have helped create interesting surface textures on the cooking pancakes. For frying tasks, a collection of skillets was needed, including the earthenware ones, skillets made of tinned iron or tinned copper, and a round metal pan set on flameless coal fire used for *kunāfa* crepes called *mir'āt Hindiyya* 'Indian mirror.' An iron griddle (*mafrash ḥadīd*) with a broad and flat surface was also needed to toast bread and grill thin slices of meat.

Although recommended by physicians of al-Tujībī's time for cooking, glass vessels were not offered as viable options.[225] We know, however, that they were made and used in affluent households when cooking Andalusi dishes. An inter-

---

223 As expounded by Ibn Zuhr, *Kitāb al-Aghdhiya* 137, whom al-Tujībī copies.

224 According to its description in the thirteenth-century Istanbul MS of al-Warrāq's cookbook, fol. 171r, it is a wide pan with relatively low sides.

225 See al-Tujībī's introduction, p. 109, below.

esting recipe in the anonymous fourteenth-century Egyptian cookbook *Kanz al-fawāʾid* describes how sparrows are left to simmer for hours in a glass pot on a quietly burning portable stove called *nāfikh nafsihi* (more on this below). The dish is said to be a North African and Andalusi specialty. It was, understandably, said to be one of the most exclusive foods, which kings and dignitaries used to eat to boost their libido (*quwwat al-bāh*).[226] In al-Tujībī's recipes, glass containers are used to store candies, pickles, vinegars, and the like. An interesting glass jar used for preserving lemons is described as a rectangular vessel, large enough for 50 lemons (recipe x.3.2).

For preparing dishes, a variety of bowls were used, the large and wide *jafna* for whipping eggs and the like, kneading bowls (*miʿjana*), wide and shallow ones called *ṣaḥfa* for mixing ingredients, and many more. For serving foods, large and wide bowls, called *mithrad*, were essential for the popular *tharīd* dishes; and for dishes that were not as soupy, glazed bowls, called *ghaḍāra*, were often used. They were usually large, but small ones were also used for serving snack foods like fried locusts and steamed snails. With the steamed snails, citron tree thorns were offered to pick their meat out. Related eating utensils were boxwood spoons (*malāʿiq baqs*), used with porridges,[227] and small ladles (*maghārif ṣighār*), which might have looked like today's round-bowled soup spoons, used for eating *tharīd* moistened with heated milk, offered with small bowlfuls of honey or melted fresh butter (recipes i.2.21–2); eating these dishes with spoons this way, al-Tujībī comments, "would be the utmost elegance."

Another interesting vessel, called a *ṭayfūr*,[228] is mentioned in recipe i.4.33 for serving *mujabbanāt* (cheese pastries) with a honey bowl in the middle, the way Andalusis preferred to have them, as al-Tujībī explains. Although the term *ṭayfūr* as referring to a vessel is not found in the medieval lexicons,[229] we encounter it in several medieval sources as *ṭayfūriyya*. It is used as a neat serving bowl filled with dried fruits; also mentioned as a small tray of gold and as a large platter filled with sweets, draped with a piece of silk fabric and offered as a gift.[230] And as we learn from reports on the medieval Spanish Inquisition

226 English trans., *Treasure Trove*, recipe 149.

227 It is yellow hardwood. Al-Ḥimyarī, *Ṣifat Jazīrat al-Andalus* 124, mentions that boxwood trees grew abundantly in Ṭurṭūsha (Tortosa) in the northeastern region of Catalonia. It was an important frontier city of the Umayyad Caliphate of Cordova.

228 With the definite article al-, it is pronounced *at-ṭayfūr*.

229 The word is only said to be a man's name, and the name of a small bird, with no further details. In Ghālib, *al-Mawsūʿa*, it is identified as *Aeglalites* (S), which is the little ringed plover.

230 As in Ibn Baṭṭūṭa *Tuḥfat al-nuẓẓār* i 255, and ii 104–5, and 258. For more on this vessel, see glossary 9.1.

FIGURE 27 A tray with *ṭayfūr*s being carried to guests, al-Ḥarīrī, *al-Maqāmāt*, fol. 140r, copied and illustrated by al-Wāsiṭī, detail
BNF, DEPARTMENT OF MANUSCRIPTS, ARAB 5847. SOURCE: GALLICA.BNF.FR/BNF

trials, it was called *ataifor*, used as a large communal dish for serving couscous (see part iv below). Another serving bowl, called a *mukhfiyya*, made of wood or glazed earthenware,[231] was used for keeping pulled sugar candies in recipe ix.6.1, and in recipes i.4.39–9 for serving *mujabbanāt*.

231 Perhaps called so because of its semigloss finish, see glossary 9.1.

Mortars (*mihrās*) made of copper, wood, and stone were used for different tasks, the most essential of which was crushing and pounding wet ingredients like meat and vegetable, usually with wooden ones. For pounding meat into paste to make sausages and meat patties, a wooden board, called a *ṭalya*, was used with an iron rod to beat the meat. A table (*māʾida*) was needed in the kitchen for rolling out sheets of bread and pastries. The knives specifically mentioned in al-Tujībī's cookbook were: a big one for shredding the meat of *harīsa* (wheat porridge) by stirring it with it in the pot; a knife with a very thin blade to cut a delicate cookie roll into bars before baking them; a sharp knife for carefully coring out the pulp of whole eggplants; and a small thin knife for making scores in olives before curing them; and the blunt back of the blade always came handy for mashing boiled leaf vegetables. A specially made wooden knife was used for daily scraping clean a leather jar (*qirba*) in which yogurt was left to ferment for three days (recipe vi.2.2). Only a cleaver (*sāṭūr*) could do the job required in recipe ii.2.28: breaking the ribs of a whole side of mutton from the inside, top to bottom, at three parallel places while keeping the outside uncut.

The small kitchen utensils available were: several types of sieves; a small quern (*ṭāḥūnat al-yad*), which is a small rotary hand-mill for coarsely crushing grains;[232] a grater, called an *iskarfāj*, for finely grating cheese; a decorating pair of copper tweezers (*minqāsh nuḥās*) for pastries; a funnel for stuffing sausage casings; and spoons of different sizes and materials. Add to these the familiar ladles, spatulas, and a *mikhṭāf* (iron hook) used in recipes i.4.33–4 to turn over frying cheese-filled pastries (*mujabbanāt*). Also needed were a rolling pin, a scraper, and threads for sewing up the cavities of stuffed sheep and birds and cutting boiled eggs into quarters for garnishes. A stack of cloths of different materials should be handy for making spice bundles, straining boiled honey, extracting the juice of pounded herbs, and the like. An interesting small mold, a *muʿakʿik*, was used for making perfectly rounded meatballs that were prepared for the luxurious dishes served at wedding festivities.[233]

Butter churning was one of the food preparations that might be more conveniently performed outside the kitchen. For this, a special churning vessel, called a *shakwa*, was needed. It was made with the skin of a kid or a lamb, used with a tripod, called a *ḥammāla*. It was vigorously pushed forwards and backwards to separate milk from fat, as described in recipe vi.2.3. Another operation that would be more fit for outdoors was pressing out grapes with a *miʿṣara* for the purpose of making vinegar with their juice (recipe x.7.1). Vinegars were

232 It is mentioned in the anonymous Andalusi cookbook *Anwāʿ al-ṣaydala* 173.

233 See recipe ii.6.1, n. 4.

FIGURE 28 A server feeding the stove's fire with fuel, *Kitāb al-Diryāq*, fol. NP, detail
BNF, DEPARTMENT OF MANUSCRIPTS, ARAB 2964. SOURCE: GALLICA.BNF.FR/BNF

often infused with flavors, such as mint, for which a simple distilling apparatus (*qādūs al-taqṭīr*) was needed (recipe x.7.16).

Although physical cleanliness of body and attire were required at all times for food handlers, cleanliness of a particular sort, called *ṭahāra*, was especially stressed in operations involving the handling of dairy, such as when taking care of vessels of fermenting yogurt (recipe vi.2.2), as well as those of the fermenting sauce of *murrī*, and all pickling and curing activities. In recipe x.2.4 for curing olives, there is a strict warning that nobody, man or woman, who is unclean (*najis*) should get near or handle them. Uncleanliness in this sense, *najāsa*, designates menstruating women and men and women who have not bathed after intercourse.

For cooking stews and other liquid dishes, a stove (*mustawqad*) must have been available in the kitchen even though the recipes' directions are, more often than not, to just cook or boil the pot, or to put it on the fire.[234] A portable

234 From other sources, we know that the nonmobile *mustawqad* was built as a rectangular

FIGURE 29
Anafe
© DISCOVER ISLAMIC ART | MUSEUM WITH NO FRONTIERS & ARCHAEOLOGICAL AREA AND MUSEUM OF MERTOLA, HTTP://WWW.CAMERTOLA.PT/

stove called a *kānūn al-nār*, mentioned in recipe i.4.15, is used only as a heat source to keep *qaṭāyif* batter warm and facilitate its fermentation. However, as we gather from the glass pot mentioned above, such portable stoves were certainly used for cooking purposes. The stove called *nāfikh nafsihi*, on top of which the glass pot was left to simmer, was a familiar cooking implement in the east and west Arabo-Muslim world. It was one of the stoves mentioned in tenth-century al-Warrāq's cookbook,[235] and it must have been used even much earlier. This stove got its name, 'the self-ventilating stove,' from the way it was made. Holes pierced in the base and sides of this stove were meant to keep air circulating and the fire going,[236] which rendered the service of a human blower unnecessary. The name apparently was reduced to *al-nāfikh* (pronounced *an-nāfikh*) for brevity; adopted in Spanish as *anafe*.[237] Heat in the stove was manipulated as required by the food being cooked and the stage of its cooking, using such expressions as *nār layyina*, 'gently-burning fire,' or *nār layyina muʿtadila*, 'moderately gentle fire.' When a pot was done cooking, the instruction is to remove the fire from underneath the pot and let it simmer on embers, called *ghaḍā*.

---

structure that was half a man's height, with outlets to drive out the smoke and let in fresh air. See al-Warrāq, *Kitāb al-Ṭabīkh*, English trans., *Annals* 87.

235 Al-Warrāq, *Kitāb al-Ṭabīkh*, English trans., *Annals*, chapter 59, p. 284.

236 As described by al-Khawārizmī, *Mafātīḥ al-ʿulūm* 278.

237 *Al-nāfikh* is still used in North Africa, sometimes referred to as *kānūn al-dār*.

Two types of ovens were used, usually built outside the kitchen and the living quarters of the house. The clay oven (*tannūr*), used for baking and roasting, was a cooking fixture in the Andalusi households of al-Tujībī's time. From the recipes, it is apparent that the Andalusi *tannūr* was no different from the one used in the eastern region. It was principally used for baking flat *tannūr* bread, as described in recipe i.1.2, as well as roasting. A whole lamb stuffed with couscous is roasted in recipe i.5.4; recipe ii.2.39 provides very interesting details on roasting a skewered yearling ram; and a ram is roasted by laying it flat on large bricks arranged in the bottom of a sealed *tannūr* in recipe ii.2.40.

From al-Tujībī's recipes we get the impression that domestic brick ovens built outside the living areas were mainly used for baking the daily bread and other simple tasks. Otherwise, delicate varieties of bread and pastries were sent to the neighborhood brick oven to brown at a distance from the fire. The browning of casserole dishes, poultry and fish put in clay vessels, called *ṭājin*, were similarly cooked. The recipe instructions in such cases is to 'send it to the *furn*,' and in cases when food in the casserole needs attention while in the oven, the instruction is to arrange for someone to be available for the task. Sometimes a recipe would give the option of cooking a meat casserole in the house (*fī l-dār*) instead, and here is the way to do it as described in recipe ii.1.7:

> Empty the contents of the pot into a glazed earthenware pan (*ṭājin muzajjaj*) and put it on moderate heat. Take another pan, made of iron or glazed earthenware, put strongly burning coals in it, and place it directly on the rim of first pan. Check on it periodically until the top browns and the liquid evaporates.

Grilling meat on an open coal fire (*shawī*) was popular. It was done with mutton, such as grilling a whole side slowly by suspending it skewered with burning fire placed all around it, as in recipe ii.2.38. Grilled meat was eaten with dipping sauces, such as *ṣināb* (mustard sauce), to which al-Tujībī dedicated a whole chapter (x.1), and vinegar-based ones, as they were believed to facilitate digestion. Geese were grilled rotisserie fashion by slowly turning them while basting.[238] To test for doneness, al-Tujībī suggests the following tips (recipe iii.1.2): "Hold a leg or a wing and pull it towards you, it should come off easily. Also, if you shake [either one], meat will fall off easily, or you can easily pull it off the bone. These are signs that the meat is fully cooked." Birds and grilled rabbits were eaten with dipping sauces made of cooked and mashed gar-

238 In the eastern region, meat grilled this way was called *kardanāj*, a word of Persian origin.

lic mixed with olive oil, and sometimes with grated hard cheese. Grilled squabs, young chicken, and sparrows were eaten with a sauce of drained yogurt mixed with olive oil and cooked and mashed garlic, as described in recipe vi.2.2. Sardines were grilled by placing them directly on flameless coals, as in recipe v.1.5, whereas a disjointed ram was grilled buried in a pit, as in recipe ii.2.41, which calls it *aknāf* (enclosed). In the eastern region it was more commonly called *mallīn*.[239]

In the opinion of medieval Arab physicians, grilling eggplant was believed to be the worst way to eat it, which explains the absence of such recipes in medieval cookbooks, except al-Tujībī's. He was certainly well aware of this, but grilled eggplant can be delicious. The way he got around this was by first giving the recipe: After burying eggplants in hot ashes, a fire is lighted all over and around them until they bake (p. 424). They are peeled and cut into large pieces, left to drain to get rid of their harmful liquids, and then chopped and mixed with mashed cooked garlic and olive oil and seasoned with salt and black pepper. He also gives alternative ways for grilling them in the *tannūr* by burying them in its embers or baking them in the *furn* 'brick oven' in an unglazed pan. He then responsibly ends the recipe with the caveat: "Do not eat too many eggplants prepared this way because they can agitate black bile."

III.8 *In the Kitchen, Cooking al-Tujībī's Dishes*

One of the most popular dishes in the western region was definitely *tharīd*, and in this respect the region was not any different from the rest of the Arabo-Muslim world. It is indeed an ancient Arab dish; said to be the Prophet's favorite. *Tharīd* is basically a large bowlful of bread broken into small pieces and drenched in rich broth with meat chunks and vegetables arranged all over it. Al-Tujībī's 27 recipes, moreover, manipulate its versatility to the utmost, incorporating varieties of red meat and birds, vegetables, and flat bread variously baked in the *tannūr*, *furn*, and *malla* (flat wide plate); ranging from the simple ones, such as *tharīda* with milk, recipe i.1.22, to the most complex, such as the one called *falyāṭil*, recipe i.2.17, made with bread composed of stacked thin sheets, and an interesting recipe that claims to invigorate coitus, recipe i.2.14.

All the medieval cookbooks are fastidious about the cleanliness of meats added to the pot to avoid a loathed greasy odor, called *zuhūma* and *zafar*, that

239 *Mallīn* is derived from *malla* 'baking by burying in sand.' In the anonymous Andalusi *Anwāʿ al-ṣaydala* 51, it is described as the preferred dish for weddings in the Levant. Today in Jordan it is a traditional Bedouin dish, called *zarb*, which is derived from *ḍarb*, literally 'beating,' originally used to reflect the custom of beating *malla* bread to get rid of sand grains that adhered to it while buried.

can spoil an otherwise good dish. But only in the book of *Fiḍāla* do we fine an instruction like this: After meticulously cleaning the heads of sheep, al-Tujībī directs the cook in *tharīd* recipe i.2.2 to "strike their nostrils on a stone so that the maggots (*dūd*) that bred inside their noses fall." I have seen this done by my mother, but usually no cookbooks will tell you this.

In cooking meat dishes, methods vary depending on whether you want the dish to be soupy or reduced. For the former, as in the *tharīd* dishes, meat is mixed with herbs and spices in a large pot, along with onion, and lots of olive oil and water to more than cover the meat before the cooking starts. For the dishes with reduced sauce, as those we find in the second part, meat with the ingredients mentioned above is first cooked without the water, and when it looks almost white, hot water is added only as needed.

Olive oil, abundant in the western region, is the principal variety of fat used throughout the book for everything, including sweets, with the occasional use of ghee, butter, and suet. It was the equivalent of the sesame oil abundantly used in the eastern region. Furthermore, plenty of olive oil is added in the meat dishes because it was believed to facilitate its digestion. It was also the preferred fat for making pastries and cookies, rather than ghee, which turns rancid fast. The general belief was that foods fried with it were easier to digest that those fried with ghee and suet.[240]

A common herb like *kuzbara* is used almost in every dish, both the seeds, *kuzbara yābisa* 'dry coriander' (which I translate as coriander), and the fresh green leaves, *kuzbara khaḍrā'* (which I translate as cilantro), whose juice was often combined with mint juice and used. This seems to have been a common feature in Andalusi cooking. The other Andalusi cookbook, the anonymous *Anwāʿ al-ṣaydala* 53, displays a similar tendency. In its entry on coriander seeds, the recommendation is to use it in all the dishes. Of its benefits, the entry states, coriander keeps food in the stomach and prevents it from leaving it quickly until it is completely digested. Apparently, using it profusely was not only because it made food taste better but also for its health benefits.

While both coriander and parsley, particularly the variety called *maqdūnis/baqdūnis* (Macedonian parsley, *Petroselinum macedonicum*), were abundantly used in the savory dishes of the eastern region, the use of Macedonian parsley was almost negligible in the western region.[241] In al-Tujībī's cookbook, it is used just a few times: incorporated into dipping sauces served with a pot

240 As explained in al-Arbūlī, *al-Kalām ʿalā l-aghdhiya* 144–5.

241 It is to be pointed out here that the argument offered in Marín, "Words for Cooking" 41–2, regarding the herb parsley is inexact. Marín's observation is that the "scarce use of parsley" in al-Tujībī's cookbook "matches its absence in the Eastern cookbooks." Parsley, the herb

roast (recipe ii.1.9), grilled rabbit (recipe ii.5.7), or fried fish (recipe v.1.8); and stuffed in pickled eggplants (recipe x.5.1). Lack of culinary interest in it cannot possibly be attributed to its scarcity in al-Andalus, as it grew abundantly there. It was as available and well-known in the western region as it was in the eastern region. Andalusis love for coriander, both the seeds and the herb alike, might be attributed to its much more pronounced flavor and fragrance than the timid parsley. In their daily cooking, they had very little use for parsley seeds. Economically speaking, perhaps propagating a plant like coriander, whose leaves and seeds were equally aromatic and bursting with flavor, cannot be underestimated, especially when, in the general medicinal opinion of their physicians and herbalists, whatever worked with parsley would work equally well with coriander.[242]

Besides the inevitable coriander and black pepper, other spices and herbs are used, albeit in a more controlled manner and limited in variety when compared with the lavish seasonings of the eastern dishes. Depending on what is being cooked in the book of *Fiḍāla*, additional spices might be added, such as cumin, cinnamon, ginger, cloves, spikenard, saffron, aniseeds, or fennel, in addition to small amounts of onion, citron leaves, or sprigs of herb fennel; and garlic (*thūm*).

A bolder use of garlic was made in preparing the dishes of al-Maghrib than what we witness in the surviving Mashriqi cookbooks. This liberal use of garlic must have been encouraged by the dominant medical belief that garlic was beneficial to people living in cold regions and during cold winters, which in fact applies to the conditions in al-Andalus more than say to a hot and humid region like Egypt, where garlic by comparison was sparingly used.[243] It was also believed to neutralize the bloating effects of beans and pulses. Anyway, whether for health reasons or otherwise, garlic was ubiquitous in the Andalusi dishes, mostly as a seasoning agent but also as the main ingredient, as in a braised chicken dish called *thūmiyya*, recipe iii.2.28, which uses 4 ounces of garlic; or a mutton dish with tender spring garlic, recipe ii.2.15; or a chicken *tharīd* called *muthawwama*, recipe i.2.25, where it is specified as the dish cooked for the day of Nayrūz. For the Iberian Christians, this was the New Year festival celebrated in January, in the depth of winter; it was a feast that ended up being celebrated by all Andalusis. It also clearly points to the possibility that cooking

---

and, to a much lesser extent, celery, were never absent in the eastern cookbooks. They are frequently used in the extant eastern recipes.

242 See Ibn al-Bayṭār, *al-Jāmiʿ* iv 310.

243 Judging from the surviving fourteenth-century anonymous Egyptian cookbook *Kanz al-fawāʾid*, English trans., *Treasure Trove*.

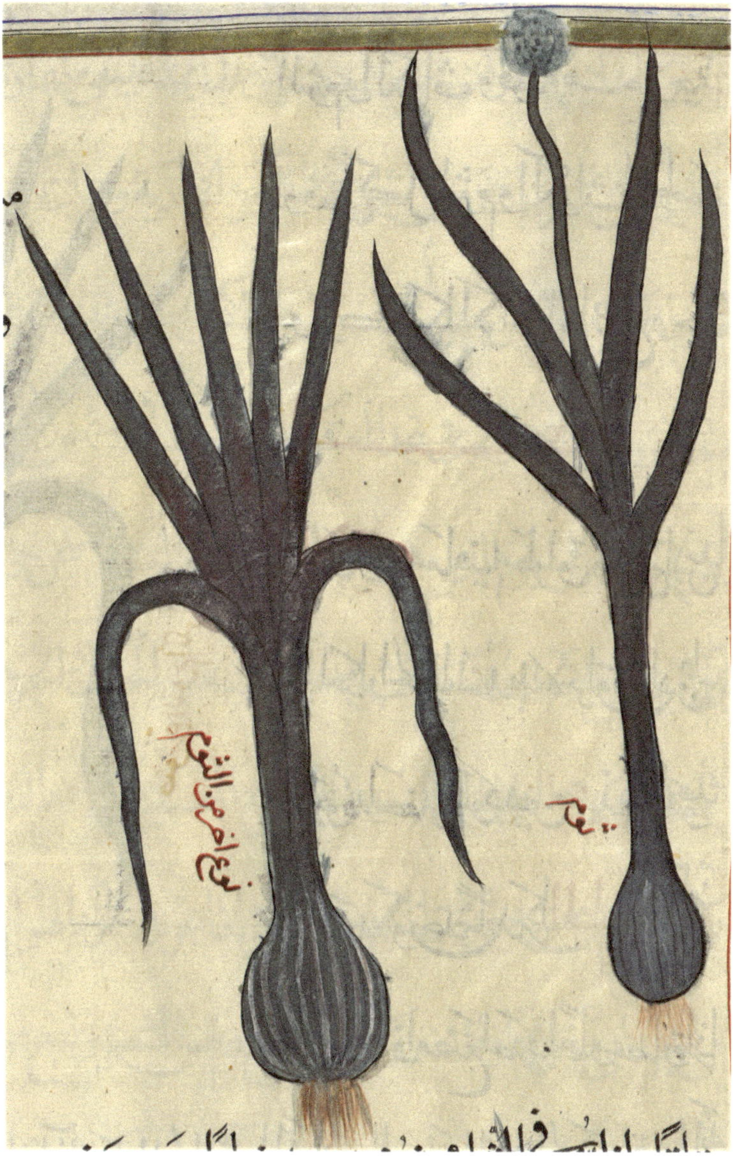

FIGURE 30 Garlic, Dioscorides, *Fī Hayūlā al-ṭibb*, translation by Ḥunayn b. Isḥāq, fol. 108r, detail
FROM THE NEW YORK PUBLIC LIBRARY, SPENCER COLLECTION: HTTPS://DIGITALCOLLECTIONS.NYPL.ORG/ITEMS/5E66B3E8-6E56-D471-E040-E00A180654D7

with garlic in this manner was indeed a Christian preference that the Andalusi Muslims liked and adopted. When cooking with garlic, the Andalusi cooks followed ways to ensure the neutralization of its powerful odor. In al-Tujībī's recipes garlic is always cooked, as when adding it to stews; if a whole head is added, the instruction is to discard it before serving the dish. In the *thūmiyya* dish, garlic is boiled first to get rid of the garlicky smell and then mashed and added. It is likewise treated before mixing it with sauces that accompany grilled meats.

Unlike the Mashriqi cuisine, known for incorporating fruits into stews and other dishes, only a few recipes in al-Tujībī's book use apples, quinces, raisins, and dried prunes, which Andalusis called *ʿayn al-baqar* (cows' eyes). This is also the case with juices of sour fruits. Mashriqi cooking, especially Egyptian, used plenty of acidic fruits to sour the dishes, the most important of which were juices of lemons, *nāranj* 'sour orange,' *utrujj* 'citron,' pomegranates, unripe grapes, and sumac. The Andalusi cooking by contrast had no interest in such juices; vinegar and *murrī* replaced them. These are differences that were not dictated by taste as much as by the necessity to adapt to the nature of the place where one lived. In the case of Egypt, for instance, due to the humidity and putridity of its air and heat, consuming foods and drinks with cold properties, which all these sour juices have, was the right thing to do.[244] On the other hand, Iberia, with its moderate weather verging on cold and moist, food was better served with seasonings that aided digestion with their hot and dry qualities, such as the fermented sauce called *murrī* and vinegar. The only part of the citron fruit used in al-Tujībī's recipes is the leaves, and the sour juices of unripe grapes, lemons, and Damascus citron (*zunbūʿ*) are mainly added in a preserved form, which the recipes call *khall* (vinegar).[245]

Although the space allotted to mutton in the part dealing with meat of quadrupeds establishes it as the most popular type of meat, beef, lamb, the meat of young goats, and wild meat are also cooked in equally interesting ways. In both the east and west of the medieval Arabo-Muslim world, beef was not thought of as the best of meats in terms of digestibility. Physicians described it as dense, cold in properties, and hard to digest; it was said to be fit for people physically active, such as menial workers. But once fully digested, it could be nutritious. Thanks to al-Tujībī's methodical organization based on ingredients, thus dedicating a whole chapter to dishes with beef, we can clearly see for the first time how beef was used and manipulated in the cooking processes to

---

244 See the anonymous Egyptian *Kanz al-fawāʾid*, English trans., *Treasure Trove* 48–9.

245 *Zunbūʿ* was more commonly known as *kabbād* in the eastern region, al-Mashriq, see glossary 7; also see glossary 8, s.v. *khall*.

facilitate its digestion.[246] Beef of unpastured cows, quickly fattened with barley grains (*baqar maʿlūf*), is mentioned in particular in two beef *tharīd* dishes in recipes i.2.4–5. Bones, with their plentiful marrow, as used in recipe i.2.5, are as essential as the meat itself. The directions to the food server are as follows:

> Once eating commences, take out the bones in the middle of the *tharīd* bowl and empty their marrow all over it. [To extract the remainder,] strike the bones hard at the base of a mortar and blow their fatty marrow [on the *tharīd* in the bowl]. Repeat with the vigorous striking and blowing of each bone until all the marrow inside comes out, all the while turning the *tharīd* bowl around so that each of its sides receives its share of it, and eat the dish salubriously.

It is to be assumed that meat from unpastured fattened cows and calves was also used in cooking the beef dishes in chapter ii.1. We find that all these dishes are seasoned with the fermented liquid sauce *murrī naqīʿ* and/or with vinegar. Both were believed to help the digestion of dense foods.

In the beef chapter we also see how a simple eastern dish of *Būrāniyya*, named after Būrān, wife of Abbasid Caliph al-Maʾmūn, gets a royal makeover in *Burāniyya* recipe ii.1.2; from a simple dish of fried eggplants, sometimes cooked with meat, to impressive oven-baked casseroles of cooked beef alternatively layered with eggplant patties or fried eggplant slices thinly enclosed with a spicy paste of pounded meat. In a fragrant beef dish called *rāhibī*, apparently inspired by Christian monks, beef is cooked with the familiar ingredients in addition to honey and saffron; its flavor is further enhanced with rose petal jam and then browned and reduced in the oven and given sprinkles of fragrant rosewater when taken out. In another Christian *rāhibī* beef dish, cooked as pot roast this time, it is served with vinegar-based dipping sauces, which al-Tujībī calls *shalsha* or *jalja* as they were called in al-ʿAjamiyya (Andalusi Romance).[247] Knife-cut small pieces of the meat are dipped in the sauce first and then eaten.

With its 46 recipes, chapter ii.2 on mutton is a feat, only comparable to the chicken chapter, iii.2, with its 49 recipes. It opens with the most common dish in the western region, *tafāyā*. *Tafāyā* is described as a plain-tasting dish, meaning it is neither sweet nor sour. Aside from the name, it is none other than the *isfidh-*

246 The rest of the cookbooks we have from the eastern region do not always specify the kinds of meat used in the dishes; more often than not mentioning it generically as *laḥm*, from which we assume, and rightly so, that it was mutton, unless otherwise specified.

247 In the Levant and Egypt, a more or less similar sauce was called *ṣalṣ*, pl. *ṣulūṣāt*. See fourteenth-century anonymous *Kanz al-fawāʾid*, English trans., *Treasure Trove*, chapter 16.

bāja of the eastern region.[248] By virtue of its simple, mild nature, *tafāyā* was categorized as feminine (*mu'annatha*), as opposed to the stronger masculine ones flavored with vinegar, *murrī*, and the like; it was praised for its balanced properties and recommended for weak stomachs.[249] It was also made green by adding fresh juice of cilantro or chard leaves and delightfully presented at the table with meatballs and egg yolks showing through, along with split boiled eggs and sprinklings of cinnamon and ginger.[250] When *tafāyā* was cooked, it was usually served first, before the other dishes. The formulaic ending of the *tafāyā* recipe meaningfully adds invoking the name of God, usually uttered at the start of the meal, before eating it salubriously (وسمّ الله تعالى وكل هنيئا). Mutton and lamb are cooked in a dizzying variety of dishes, some with vegetables, some fried, others sweetened with honey, and yet others are grilled or roasted after stuffing them with a variety of cooked birds. It also seems appropriate that al-Tujībī should include a variety of dishes incorporating rabbit meat, especially the European wild rabbit (*qunilya*), which was not readily available outside Spain, 'land of the rabbits.'[251]

Dishes incorporating geese, chicken, partridges, squabs, turtledoves, starlings, and sparrows, are all grouped in one spacious part, in which young fat chickens and capons get 'the lion's share,' 49 recipes no less, not counting the ones already included in *tharīd* chapter i.2, all dedicated to cooking them in the most interesting of ways. Some are ingeniously stuffed after being deboned; others stuffed underneath the skin. Turtledoves (*yamām*) in particular are cooked in an unfamiliar manner. Garlic cloves are first inserted in their nostrils and vents—one in each opening. They are then threaded on an iron skewer through their beaks and suspended in a large pot so that they dangle in the air with a large piece of bread spread in the bottom of the pot. The pot is then covered, sealed with a band of dough, and baked in the communal brick oven at a distance from the fire; to be served with the bread that has been moistened with the birds' fatty drippings (recipe iii.5.5). They are also baked encrusted in salt, recipe iii.5.6.

More than ten recipes are described as Mashriqi, although most of them do not differ substantially from the rest when it comes to spicing and cooking

---

248 The name is of Persian origin, meaning white broth (*isfīd* 'white' + *bāj* 'broth'). For comparison, see, for instance, al-Warrāq, *Kitāb al-Ṭabīkh*, English trans., *Annals*, chapter 59.

249 As described in the anonymous Andalusi *Anwāʿ al-ṣaydala* 58.

250 In medieval Arabic sources, such as Ibn Ḥayyān, *al-Sifr al-thānī* 322, the name of the famous singer Ziryāb was associated with it, see above section ii.5, pp. 44–52.

251 That was the meaning of Ispania, the name the Carthaginians, who established colonies in Iberia around 300 BC, chose to call it. See above section ii.4, pp. 24–5.

methods. However, a dish like *jūdhāba* (recipe iii.2.31) would indeed showcase the ingenuity of the Andalusi cooks in developing a borrowed Mashriqi dish; we can easily see in this the birth of the *bastilla* dish so well-known today in North African kitchens.

As a general rule, served dishes are almost always offered garnished in a variety of ways, including split boiled eggs, strips of thin meat patties, called *isfīriyya*, poached egg yolks, and the like, and sprinkled with cinnamon or ginger. Considerable thought went into the presentation of dishes destined for weddings and feasts to ensure lavish and grand displays to impress the guests. In addition to the abovementioned garnishes, a special recipe is exclusively given to the preparation of garnishes called *farsh*. They are meant to be scattered over the dishes before offering them to guests. They include lavish amounts of spicy meatballs perfectly shaped using a small mold called a *muʿakʿik*, poached egg yolks, small pieces of tripe, and split eggs, all colored intensely yellow with saffron. If in a daily dish chicken is cut into pieces, the recipe recommends offering the chickens whole if cooked for a wedding, as well as garnished with split eggs and tips of fresh mint stems (recipe iii.2.9).

As a finale to all the meat chapters, al-Tujībī offers a grand all-in-one dish called *Ṣinhājī* (recipe iv.1).[252] It incorporates all the meats, literally, along with a variety of vegetables, fruits like apples and quinces, sausages, chickpeas, preserved lemons, olives, and much more. To cook it, the recipe requires a glazed *ṭājin* (pan), the largest available. The dish does bring to mind the Spanish festive dish *olla podrida*—often called hodge-podge—famously described by Cervantes in *Don Quixote* ii at the wedding of Camacho, and it is very likely to have been its origin. A much simpler version is still cooked in Spain today.[253]

From the rivers and seas to which Andalusis had access, a great variety of fishes, called *ḥūt*, were caught and cooked in many interesting ways. In 33 recipes, fish is fried, braised in casseroles, baked in the brick oven encrusted in salt, baked stuffed and roasted in the *tannūr*, grilled in skewers, made into fried meatballs, and much more. For braising and baking fish casseroles, the preference is to send them to the community *furn*, where heat is more controlled; also to keep the house free of the cooking fish smells. The tuna dishes in al-Tujībī's chapter are the only ones that have survived from medieval times. Both fresh tuna and dried salted tuna, called *tunn yābis*, are used. Another name al-Tujībī gives to dried tuna is *mushammaʿ*, suggestive of its waxy texture (from *shamʿ* 'beeswax'). The term *mushammaʿ* was adopted in Spanish as *mojama*.

252 Named after Ṣinhāj, one of the largest Amazigh tribes in North Africa.

253 For an excellent discussion of *olla podrida*, see Nadeau, "Spanish Culinary History of Cervantes' 'Bodas de Camacho.'"

FIGURE 31 Catching river fish, Ibn al-Muqaffaʿ, *Kalīla wa Dimana*, fol. 60r, detail
BNF, DEPARTMENT OF MANUSCRIPTS, ARAB 3465. SOURCE: GALLICA.BNF.FR/BNF

Like chicken, eggs are aplenty in this cookbook. In the relatively small space allotted to them, an interesting mix of small dishes prepared with eggs is given, ranging from simply boiled ones and those cooked in hot ashes to the dainty omelet pinwheels made with *isfīriyya* (recipe v.2.1). After a thin omelet is fried in a small amount of oil, it is rolled like a reed and sliced. The resulting pieces

FIGURE 32 Catching sea fish, Ibn al-Muqaffaʿ, *Kalīla wa Dimana*, fol. 33r, detail
BNF, DEPARTMENT OF MANUSCRIPTS, ARAB 3465. SOURCE: GALLICA.BNF.FR /BNF

are fried once more until brown. Al-Tujībī fastidiously cautions, "Do not pour too much of the egg mix into the skillet as this would not result in well-folded egg rolls"; and when frying the sliced pieces and the "skillet gets too crowded, take some out to make more room for the rest to fry easily." When boiled eggs are done, he is careful to mention that they should be put in cold water first (recipe v.2.3). Even frying eggs is an art in itself; in recipe v.2.2, the eggs are individually broken one by one into a tinned skillet and then the white of each one is folded over its yolk so that the egg looks like a disc.

In addition to this chapter, eggs are used in almost all the meat dishes. The yolks are poached in stews and used as garnish, the whites are mixed with pounded meat as a binder, and boiled eggs are split into quarters to garnish many of the dishes. And of course there is *takhmīr*, a distinctive feature in the medieval Andalusi-Maghribi cuisine, most probably encouraged by the availability and affordability of chicken eggs in the region. By definition, *takhmīr* is 'covering,' which in the culinary context involved finishing off the cooking of meat dishes that had little sauce in them by first preparing a mix of eggs beaten with spices, often with the juices of fresh herbs like cilantro and mint, sometimes colored with saffron, and which was thickened with breadcrumbs. The mix would then be poured into the pot to cover the surface and left to set while the pot was on embers. It was a common method. Apparently, some cooks at the food markets took advantage of it and deceived customers by hiding their substandard dishes underneath. It was one of the duties of the Andalusi market inspector to check for this kind of punishable violation.[254]

Main dishes, called *alwān kibār*, always cooked with meat, abound in the book of *Fiḍāla*; some of them were even a meal by themselves, such as *al-Ṣinhājī*, mentioned above, and *al-kāmil* (recipe ii.2.40). They are all-in-one dishes that render offering other foods unnecessary. Andalusis would mock a person who exaggerates in pleasing others by saying (يعمل الكامل بزايد لون) "He makes *al-kāmil* and an extra dish with it."[255] Side dishes, called *alwān ṣighār*, are many and various. With few exceptions, they were invariably vegetarian; all quite tasty. They were either offered before the main dishes or eaten as snack foods. In the dairy section, we find delicious snack foods of fried cheese and drained yogurt of *shīrāz* and *akhlāṭ*. In recipe vi.1.2, al-Tujībī describes enticingly how to garnish drained yogurt and eat it:

> Whenever you want to eat *shīrāz*, take some out and put it in a wide shallow bowl. Level the surface with the ladle and let the *shīrāz* fill the bowl to its rim. Garnish it with olives and pickled young caper berries arranged all around the rim, with a pickled lemon put in the middle. Give the dish a light sprinkle of nigella seeds and a drizzle of sweet olive oil.

To be eaten with cleaned tender green onions, as the recipe suggests. "When it is time to eat the dish, hold an onion with your hand and pick up some *shīrāz* with it—just what amounts to a mouthful."

Meatless vegetable dishes, especially those made with eggplants and, to a lesser extent, gourds (chapters vii.1 and 2) are aplenty, with a variety of other vegetables given in shorter chapters (vii. 3–10), as well as pulses (viii.1–3). These small meatless dishes were not regarded as substantial foods. They were offered at the beginning of the meal before the ones containing meat. This was a reg-

---

254 Ibn 'Abd al-Ra'ūf, *Risāla fī Ādāb al-ḥisba* 97.

255 See al-Zajjālī, *Amthāl al-'awām* ii 482.

imen equally approved by their physicians, but for another reason. One of the dietetic rules al-Tujībī includes in his introduction on the order of foods eaten is that vegetable dishes (*baqliyyāt*) should be eaten first because they are believed to naturally soften the bowels (*yulayyin al-baṭn*).[256] Al-Tujībī also includes some curious snack foods that contain some sort of 'meat,' all served in small bowls. In part xi, locusts are eaten boiled or fried; freshwater shrimps (*qumrūn*), steamed or fried, are served with thyme; and boiled edible land snails (*aghlāl*) are offered with citron tree thorns to pick out the meat inside the shells. Apparently, al-Tujībī himself was not a fan of *qumrūn* and *aghlāl*; he thought they were disgusting, but he included them anyway because they were popular.

Durum wheat, the most important of the grains used in al-Andalus and North Africa, was used for making breads, pastries, and sweets with its *samīd* and *darmak* flours.[257] More importantly, it was the grain used for making *kuskusū* 'couscous,' which later became one of the sure identifiers of one's religious affiliation (see next section). Al-Tujībī describes in detail how to roll couscous grains until they look like small ants' heads, how to successfully cook it in the couscoussier (recipe i.5.1), and how to stuff a fat sheep with it (recipe i.5.4). He further attributes paucity in rice dishes in the Andalusi cuisine of his time to the fact that its cultivation was limited to the southeastern region, where his homeland Murcia and Valencia were (see recipe i.3.11).

In making pastries and sweets, honey rather than sugar is the principal sweetening agent used. This seems to have been the general preference of people of the western region. In his account of al-Maghrib, al-Qalqashandī makes a similar observation. Although sugarcane grew there and excellent qualities of sugar were produced, he says people did not care much for it and preferred to use honey, of which they had plenty.[258] Use of sugar in the book of *Fiḍāla* is much more limited in comparison to honey. Pastries and a few mutton dishes cooked with milk, for instance, are given light sprinkles of pounded sugar before serving. It is incorporated into stuffing for cookies, and it is the main ingredient in two candy recipes, ix.6.1–2, for *fānīdh* (pulled sugar taffy) and *ishqāqūl* (hard sugar candies).

Dainty cookies, called *kaʿk*, are luxuriously spiced with rosewater, ginger, spikenard, cinnamon, cloves, black pepper, and a small amount of camphor.

---

256 In the anonymous Andalusi cookbook *Anwāʿ al-ṣaydala* 58, *baqliyya* dishes, like *tafāyā*, are categorized as feminine (*muʾannatha*), i.e., seasoned plainly (*sādhaja*); they are neither sour nor sweet and are said to be served first in a given meal.

257 See glossary 2, for more on these types of flour.

258 Al-Qalqashandī, *Ṣubḥ al-aʿshā* v 176.

They are beautifully shaped into rings and decorated with a special pair of pincers. The gazelle's heels (*ka'b al-ghazāl*), recipe i.4.4, are no less impressive. Cylinders of dough stuffed with an aromatic almond filling are sliced into small pieces, like Newton cookies but much smaller, each the size of a fava bean. Excitedly, al-Tujībī adds,

> The kind of cookies mentioned here are indeed a novelty. Some of the ingenious cooks would add pounded skinned pine nuts to the filling, and when they slice the cylinders, they would insert a whole skinned pine nut inside each one of the cookies. But this would require patience and precision.

Besides the familiar pastries of *kunāfa*, *qaṭāyif*, *fālūdhaj*, and *khabīṣ* borrowed from the eastern region, there are others that are unique to the western region, such as *ra's maymūn* (the blessed head, recipe i.4.24), made to look like a human head; served on a platter with pine nuts, pistachios, and almonds stuck all over the head, probably to give it human features, drizzled with ghee warmed with honey, and sprinkled with fine sugar. Other popular pastries include: spongy yeasted fritters, called *isfanj*, made in different ways (recipes i.4.30–2), and the beloved *mujabbanāt* (cheese pastries), seven recipes in all (i.4.33–9), most commonly shaped like doughnuts and fried; served drenched in melted fresh butter and heated up honey. Apparently, this was how they were served in North Africa. As we learn from al-Tujībī, in al-Andalus they were served plain, arranged on a platter and sprinkled with crushed cinnamon, aniseeds, and sugar. A honey bowl was put in the middle of the platter, and the diners would eat the *mujabbanāt* in small bites, dipping them in honey before each bite. The most delicious of the *mujabbanāt* varieties in al-Tujībī's opinion is *qayjāṭa*, prepared like an oven-baked casserole and repeatedly moistened with milk while baking. In his words,

> Take the casserole out of the oven, … pour honey, which has been heated and mixed with black pepper and cassia, all over it after cutting it into crisscross lines. Keep it aside, covered, for about an hour until it cools a bit, and give it time to absorb the honey and serve it. It is the most delicious food.

I can almost imagine him salivating while writing this.

Al-Tujībī does not neglect to add a final part on handwashing preparations, called *ushnān*, which he obviously did not create himself. He copied (uncredited) a well-known authority in the field, the famous tenth-century Arab physician Ibn al-Jazzār.[259] These were all expensive, complex preparations originally made for caliphs and the elite. Apparently, he included them to impress his readers with the ways of the affluent. For practical purposes, he gives a recipe of his own—crushed and sifted chickpeas, adding that this is the *ushnān* that ordinary people like us would actually use.

Compared with other Arabic cookbooks from the medieval era, al-Tujībī only touches lightly on the then popular health-related recommendations and benefits based on the Galenic theory of the humors. This evidently was a deliberate choice on his part. After a short passage on the order of foods eaten to ensure good digestion in his introduction, he writes, "There is a good deal more to be said regarding the subject, but this would indeed take me beyond what I have intended for my book." Still, he found it necessary to attach a passage on averting the harms of eating fish at the end of the fish chapter. At another place, where he gives recipes for grilled eggplants, he is certainly aware of the physicians' low opinion of them. He included the recipes anyway and responsibly advised the eaters not to have too many of them.

Regarding the welfare of his brethren in the *bāh* 'coitus' department, al-Tujībī offers only one recipe, i.2.14, but a bombshell no less, with many ingredients well-known for their potency in this field, promoted as *ʿajība* (wonderful):

> Take fat young adult chickens ... put them in a new pot with olive oil, salt, cinnamon, and coriander seeds. After the pot comes to a boil, add white chickpeas, which have been soaked from early in the night before; also add the soaking liquid water. Add a suitable amount of onion juice, extracted by pounding it and squeezing out the juice. Also add ghee. When all this is done, add egg yolks. Pour the broth on crumbs of bread and sprinkle the dish with spikenard, cloves, ginger, black pepper, and cinnamon. Cover the bowl for a short while to allow it to absorb the liquid. It would even be better if sparrows are used instead of chicken; or both. It might also be cooked with carrots, as much as it can take, and it will be absolutely delicious and beneficial.

Amen.

259 See the above section i.3.3.

Part IV: The Years They Ate Couscous Dangerously

> She ate in a Muslim manner ... sitting with her relatives ... squatting around a tray on which they served couscous, and eating the couscous with their hands, pinching it into little balls.
>
> Guilt of a Toledan Morisca woman brought before the Inquisition, 1547.[260]

In 2016, a Spanish baker in Mallorca was asked about the history of the island's specialty pastry, *ensaïmada*, the coiled paper-thin sheets of pastry. He said,

> They say it comes from Arabic culture. For me it does not make sense because the Arabs do not eat pork and you use lard in *ensaïmada*. The story is that it comes from the Arabs or the Hebrews. But it is not confirmed. It is a supposition.[261]

Andalusi Muslims and Jews did indeed bake pastries similar to *ensaïmada*, and they called them *musammana* after the name of the fat used in layering the dough, which is *samn* 'ghee.' A variation of *musammana* was layered with rendered suet,[262] which is *shaḥm* in Arabic, a general name for solid fat and the origin of *saïm*. The suet used was, as expected, taken from sheep or goats. Muslims were able to make it either way, but Jews made them with ghee only because *shaḥm* is not Kosher. As to when Muslims and Jews started making the *musammana* with lard, and how indeed their eating a simple fare like couscous became a criminalizing act, here is what happened.

It began in 1492 when Granada surrendered to the besieging Castilian armies, and thus the almost eight centuries of Muslim control of the Iberian Peninsula came to an end. It was in effect the final act of what was called the *Reconquista*. A treaty of capitulation ensured the safety of the citizens of Granada and their possessions and freedom to practice their religious rites.[263] In that year, Granadan Jews faced two choices, convert to Christianity or leave; those who chose exile emigrated to places like North Africa, Italy, and regions under Ottoman control. The treaty that allowed Granadan Muslims to practice their religion freely was breeched in 1499, and they were forced to convert or leave.

260 Cited in Constable, *To Live Like a Moor* 104.
261 Madeleine Morrow, "An Island's History is Coiled in a Pastry," *Boston Globe*, Jan. 1, 2016: G9.
262 See al-Tujībī's recipes i.4.17–8.
263 See Makkī, "The Political History of al-Andalus" i 84.

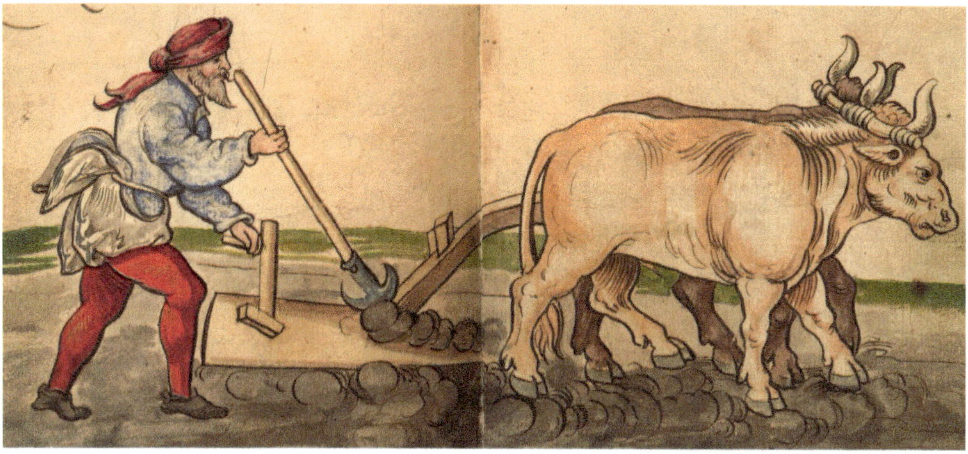

FIGURE 33 A Morisco farmer, Christoph Weiditz, *Trachtenbuch* 'Costume book,' ca. 1530, pp. 55–6
GERMANISCHES NATIONALMUSEUM, HS. 22474

It was thereafter the job of the Inquisition to identify heretics among those who converted from Judaism and Islam to Catholicism, known as conversos and Moriscos, and also referred to as New Christians. This all ended in 1609 with the final expulsion of all Moriscos, "the last act by Spain's Catholic monarchs to obliterate Spain's Muslim past."[264] During that period, the customs of the New Christians were under severe scrutiny; such as those related to the ways they dressed and behaved in public but also, more importantly, what they ate: "Many foods and foodways that had been seen as unremarkable and acceptable (and in some cases delicious and luxurious) in the thirteenth century were perceived as disgusting, un-Christian, and unacceptable."[265] Meat, expectedly, was one of the central issues that required close scrutiny given the various religious rituals involved in slaughtering and consuming the animal. To prove their true adherence to their newly acquired religion, Muslims and Jews had to cook with lard and only eat pork. There were even times when they were ordered to keep their doors open so that they did not cook foods their own way behind doors.

It was not only meat-related issues, such as slaughtering rituals, avoiding pork, and giving up Lent, but also avoiding wine as well as regional food habits

264 Dunlop, *Andaluz* 10.

265 Constable, *To Live Like a Moor* 104. Constable's book, particularly its chapter "Food and Foodways," 104–39, and Nadeau's *Food Matters*, are the most extensively researched resources on the subject in the English language. For the experience of the conversos during that period until their expulsion from Spain in 1492, see Gitlitz and Davidson, *A Drizzle of Honey*.

FIGURE 34 A Morisco carrying bread, Christoph Weiditz, *Trachtenbuch* 'Costume book,' ca. 1530, p. 104
GERMANISCHES NATIONALMUSEUM, HS. 22474

that attracted the inquisitors' scrutiny and condemnation. In 1572, Constable notes, a woman who had recently resettled from Granada, defends herself in court for not cooking with bacon by saying that where she came from people were used to cooking these dishes with olive oil.[266]

266 Constable, *To Live Like a Moor* 108.

FIGURE 35 Two men sharing a dish, eating with their hands, al-Ḥarīrī, *al-Maqāmāt*, fol. 166r, copied and illustrated by al-Wāsiṭī, detail
BNF, DEPARTMENT OF MANUSCRIPTS, ARAB 5847. SOURCE: GALLICA.BNF.FR /BNF

Couscous, on the other hand, was a grain dish in which none of the above rituals were involved, but how it nonetheless came to be equally blacklisted had everything to do with what one ate and how one ate it. These were seen as "critical markers of social and religious identity."[267] True Christians were expected to sit on chairs and eat from tables with utensils and not sit on the ground and eat their couscous with their hands *en ataifor*, that is, eat it from the traditional Andalusi communal tray, which in Arabic is called *ṭayfūr*.[268]

In fact, it was not only couscous that was seen as a recognizable identifier of the Morisco but also a host of other foods, like raisins, figs, butter, honey, rice, tripe, goat meat, fritters *buñuelos* that Arabs called *isfanj* (see recipes i.4.30–2), and eggplants; not that the Old Christians did not eat these foods—couscous and *buñuelos*, for instance, were widely eaten by everyone. There are even couscous recipes in a cookbook written by the sixteenth- to seventeenth-

267 Ibid., 105.
268 For more on this vessel, see the above section iii.7, pp. 74-5; also see glossary 9.1.

FIGURE 36 Moriscos having a good time singing and dancing to music, Christoph Weiditz, *Trachtenbuch* 'Costume book,' ca. 1530, pp. 107–8
GERMANISCHES NATIONALMUSEUM, HS. 22474

century head chef to Kings Philip III and IV.[269] And yet, these foods were considered distinguishably Morisco.

In the case of the staple couscous, singling it out as *the* incriminating dish was, in fact, for more critical reasons than just having it while squatting on the ground and pinching it into balls with one's hands. Couscous was a crowd-favorite dish traditionally served at weddings and feasts; enjoyed with friends while dancing and singing. The dish had become a central feature of collective activities deeply ingrained in Muslim cultural behavior. Couscous was customarily served in communal large trays and eaten by forming lumps of it with three fingers and pushing them into the mouth.[270] This was the way couscous was eaten in North Africa and al-Andalus alike. In his mid-sixteenth-century

269 His name is Francisco Martínez Montiño, cited in Nadeau, *Food Matters* 33–7, where a brief description of his cookbook *Arte de cocina* is given. In Montiño's recipes, a special couscous pan is required. For details on how he cooked it, see Nadeau, 125–6.

270 But washing hands meticulously before and after a meal has always been stressed in the Arabo-Muslim world.

account of Fez, Ḥasan b. Muḥammad al-Wazzān, known as Leo Africanus, describes to his European readers the unrefined eating habits even among the socially privileged, such as eating their food on the ground on low tables without using coverings of any sort, not even napkins, and no tools save their hands; and how couscous was offered in a communal plate with no spoons.[271]

Such fear of couscous lay in the danger that it might stand in the way of the true assimilation of the New Christians. Social gatherings and festivities they attended with Muslims, and which involved dancing to the tunes of ethnic music and sharing traditional foods, were particularly risky, as Constable goes on to explain, and aptly so,

> Eating familiar foods in a familiar fashion, for instance, enjoying a dish of couscous while sitting on the floor together with friends, could reinforce powerful Morisco bonds both with each other and with their common Muslim heritage. Equally problematic, in Old eyes, was for New Christians to mingle and share food with their previous coreligionists, lest eating with Muslims encourage converts to return to their old religion and its routines.[272]

While foods and ingredients like couscous and the pervasive coriander and cilantro that stamped the Andalusi cuisine with an unmistakable character gradually went into oblivion,[273] others fared better but were slowly divested of their Muslim identity. A striking example is eggplant, which was strongly associated with the Moriscos' foodways, and yet, as Nadeau aptly notes, "its Islamic identity was slowly erased, its 'otherness' consumed, and today eggplant is ubiquitous in Spanish cuisine."[274]

As to what other foods were cooking in the kitchens of the New Christians while they were still in Spain, we get valuable glimpses in a picaresque novel

---

271 Leo Africanus, Arabic trans., *Waṣf Ifrīqiyā* 253.

272 Constable, *To Live Like a Moor* 111. The common couscous, with the religious distinction it garnered at the time, is reminiscent of today's Middle Eastern staple falafel, satirically labeled as 'jihadi gateway food.' See https://momentmag.com/bachmann-takes-on-falafel/ , accessed April 29, 2020.

273 See Nadeau, "From *Kitāb al-ṭabīj* to the *Libre de Sent Soví*: Continuities and Shifts in the Earliest Iberian Cooking Manuals," 29–30, where the 'glaring' absence of the coriander plant in early modern Spanish cuisine is discussed, but no reasons are suggested for its rare appearance.

274 Nadeau, *Food Matters* 9; see also 12–44, for a detailed discussion of premodern Spanish cookbooks. Also recommended is a chapter on medieval Spanish food by Rafael Chabrán, "Medieval Spain," 125–52.

published in Venice in 1528 by Francisco Delicado, *La Lozana andaluza*.[275] Aldonza, the main character, is a penniless converso from Cordova who comes to the Spanish downtown in Rome to promote her skills. Boastingly, she enumerates the many dishes she learnt from her grandmother. She knows how to cook noodles (*fideos*), small meat pies (*ampanadillas*), couscous with chickpeas (*alcuzcuzu*), three ways of cooking rice (*arroz*), and small meatballs (*albondiguillas*) packed with cilantro (*culantro verde*). She knows how to make pastries, fried and then sprinkled with honey; she cooks turnips with cumin without lard, Murcia-style cabbages with caraway seeds, eggplant casserole (*cazuela de berengenas mojíes*), twice-baked eggplant casserole, marvelous Morisco-style casseroles, and many fish dishes, among others.[276]

It is intriguing to see how the dishes Aldonza learnt from her Cordovan grandmother, a converso, in many ways resemble those documented in the two extant thirteenth-century Andalusi cookbooks, especially the *fadāwīsh* (*fideos*), meat-stuffed *sanbūsak*, meatballs (*banādiq*) flavored with cilantro, couscous dishes with chickpeas, and the many eggplant casseroles. Although the two Andalusi cookbooks contain several rice dishes, they all end up being served mashed and porridge-like. What Aldonza describes in her account reveals that rice was cooked in many other ways. The *arroz entro* is a rice dish in which the grains are kept whole; and the *arroz seco* suggests that the grains are allowed to absorb all the moisture in the pot, resulting in what in thirteenth-century Baghdad was called *ruzz mufalfal* 'rice with separate grains.' *Arroz grasso*, which is rice cooked in fat, points to the emergence of a crowd-pleaser that would eventually replace the trays of couscous. It is the would-be paella, the signature dish of Valencia, which al-Tujībī singles out along with his hometown Murcia, as the rice-producing regions.

Aldonza's childhood memories of her grandmother's kitchen summarize a rich food culture. This kitchen, as Nadeau writes,

> stands as the nexus between the food habits of Jewish, Muslim, and Christian ethnicities, between elite and underprivileged communities, and across centuries. By going back in time to the thirteenth century and turning the pages of the Hispano-Muslim cooking manuals, one can ground the early modern court recipes in culinary heritage and see clear links between numerous grains, vegetables, and sweet dishes that

275 Delicado, English trans., *Portrait of Lozana the Lusty Andalusian Woman* 7–9.

276 See Nadeau, *Food Matters* 117–8; and García Sánchez, "La gastronomía Andalusí" 55.

Muslims and Jews prepared and consumed and how elite Christians ate centuries later.[277]

The Andalusi traces in modern Spanish cooking and foodways are indeed unmistakable, be they in names of foods, as in *albondigas* (meatballs), the existence of ingredients like eggplants, rice, and saffron, traditional utensils, such as *anafe*,[278] or varieties of dishes, as in *olla podrida* (hodge-podge); the list is long. Still, food studies exploring the extent and nature of influences and origins have only relatively recently turned to Muslim Spain. Writing in 2004, Manuela Marín, a prominent pioneer in the field, explains that the main reason behind the reluctance of scholars to look into the role the Arabs played in Spain was because "acknowledging Arab influences in Spain's life-style would have contributed to separate the country from the European context to which it had always aspired to belong,"[279] thus justifying glossing over an 800-year formative chapter in the history of Spain. To Marín, the research field is a 'minefield' that needs to be treaded carefully with "real examples of a cultural exchange."[280]

It is hoped that by making accessible a 'real example' of the culinary cultural exchanges that took place when the Arabs ruled Iberia, as is Ibn Razīn al-Tujībī's *Fiḍālat al-khiwān*, we get a more solid grasp of what happened in the Andalusi kitchens, its perseverance in face of adversity, and what was left behind and what survived in today's Spanish cooking.[281] By comparison, the story of the emigration of Andalusi cuisine to numerous cities in North Africa with the Muslims and Jews who escaped the persecution of the invading Christian armies and the Inquisition was a success story all along. Present-day cooking and dishes in North African countries testify to its survival. Suffice it to say that it was a dish like the sweet and savory *jūdhāba* chicken pie, made with multilayered paper-thin sheets of bread,[282] that gave the kitchens of al-Maghrib what is

277 Nadeau, *Food Matters* 136–7. See also Nadeau, "From *Kitāb al-ṭabīj* to the *Llibre de Sent Soví*," for a comparative discussion of the two surviving Arabic Andalusi cookbooks and the fourteenth-century anonymous *Book of Sent Soví*, the first existing culinary text of Catalan cooking.

278 See above, section iii.7, p. 78.

279 Marín, "From al-Andalus to Spain: Arab Traces in Spanish Cooking" 36–7.

280 Ibid., 38. Marín then presents an interesting analysis of evidence of Spanish food-related loan words from Arabic.

281 Of recipe cookbooks on Spanish cuisine with regional and historical backgrounds, see Roden, *The Food of Spain*; and Dunlop, *Andaluz*.

282 See al-Tujībī's recipe iii.2.31, which also suggests making it without meat, baklawa style. A comparable recipe is found in the thirteenth-century anonymous Andalusi *Anwāʿ al-*

now called *basṭīla* (bastilla) in Morocco, for which it is renowned; with regional variations in Algeria, where it is called *r'zīma* 'bundled,' and Tunisia, where the thin sheets of bread are called *malṣūqa* and the pie itself is *ṭājin malṣūqa*, with a simple meatless variety called *ūrṭa*.[283]

ṣaydala 175–7, which calls it *Umm al-Faraj* and specifies that it is a borrowed Mashriqī dish.

283 For Moroccan cookbooks, see Wolfert, *Couscous and Other Good Food from Morocco*; and Guinaudeau, *Traditional Moroccan Cooking: Recipes from Fez*. For the Tunisian *ūrṭa*, see Bellahsen, and Rouche, *Tunisia: Mediterranean Cuisine* 174–5.

Edition and Translation of the
Best of Delectable Foods and Dishes

فضالة الخوان في طيبات الطعام والألوان

∴

(101r)

بسم الله الرحمن الرحيم

صلى الله على سيدنا محمد وعلى آله وصحبه وسلم تسليما

In the name of God, the Compassionate, the Merciful. May He bless our Master Muḥammad and his family and companions and grant them salvation.

> The learned scholar, eloquent scribe, and most erudite Abū al-Ḥasan ʿAlī bin Muḥammad bin Abī al-Qāsim Ibn Muḥammad bin Abī Bakr Razīn al-Tujībī al-Andalusi, may God's mercy be on him, said:[1]

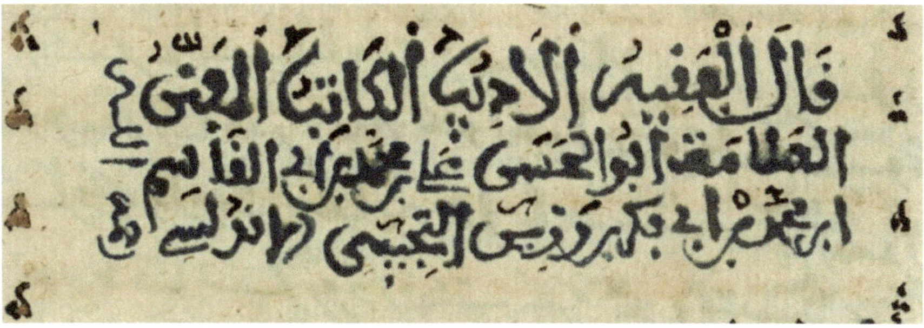
قال الفقيه الأديب الكاتب العلي
العلامة أبو الحسن علي بن محمد بن أبي القاسم
ابن محمد بن أبي بكر رزين التجيبي الأندلسي رحمه

FIGURE 37 Al-Tujībī's full name as it appears in the Madrid MS, fol. 1v, detail © REAL ACADEMIA DE LA HISTORIA ESPAÑA, GAYANGOS COLLECTION, MS NO. 16

[Ibn Razīn al-Tujībī's Introduction:]

Praise be to God, who chose humans as the best of His creations and distinguished them with an asset. "Say, who has prohibited the land's delights that

1 This paragraph is available only in the Madrid MS, fol. 1v. Neither the BL MS nor the incomplete Berlin MS include it.

God has brought forth for His worshippers and the delectables of His bounties?"[2] God has been benevolent to them, lavishly showering them with His countless blessings. He made them different from each other in the foods they crave and their varieties and innovations and allowed them to enjoy His bounty. "And eat of the delectables that We have blessed you with,"[3] and be thankful and grateful for them. Prayers be upon our Master Muḥammad, God's Messenger, our intercessor and protector, and most noble to God of all people on earth. May He bless him and his family and companions until the Day of Judgment.

Now to our subject.[4] Attention to food and the meticulous care taken in cooking the dishes as dictated by the best-tried and most-precise methods are what would delight the hospitable most and in which the affluent persistently display varying degrees of attention and concern. This is due to the fact that food is the mainstay for good health and is the principal means for keeping balanced the humoral temperaments of human beings.[5] The most praiseworthy among those people are the ones who are generously disposed; they shun stinginess because they themselves are endowed with the most generous of souls. Their bright fires are invitations in the darkness of nights; neither do they hesitate to protect neighbors in need. Their homes are as welcoming as their hearts are. They willingly accept as their lot toiling [in the service of their guests] and are not content with less than the highest esteem.[6] Their generosity should not be described as shimmering mirages on flats of salt,[7] nor should

---

2 Q 7:32, my translation.

3 Q 2:57, my translation.

4 In the Madrid MS, fols. 1v–2r, the following statement, up to 'the human being' is replaced with the following:

> When I wrote this book, being inspired by God Almighty to compile in it all ways of cooking for the benefit of people of understanding (*ʾulī al-albāb*), I named it *Kitāb Fiḍālat al-ikhwān fī ṭayyibāt al-alwān* (كتاب فضالة الاخوان في طيبات الالوان), and what is related to them, including exquisite foods, spices, condiments and pickles, remedying foods, and making handwashing preparations (*ushnān*). All carefully compiled and meticulously tried, the way they should be.

Notice the modified book title. According to Ibn Manẓūr, *Lisān al-ʿArab*, s.v. خون, *ikhwān* is synonymous with *khiwān*. See also n. 34 below.

5 The reference here is based on the Galenic theory of the humors. See glossary, s.v. *mizāj*.

6 The two words used here are نصب *naṣab* (toil) and رفع *rafʿ* (elevating), based on the Madrid MS, fol. 3r, which clearly copies the words as such. Al-Tujībī seems to be playing on these words, as *naṣb* and *rafʿ* are also grammatical terms that designate the accusative and nominative cases.

7 *Sibākh*, as it occurs in the Madrid MS, fol. 3.

FIGURE 38 A host serving his guests, al-Ḥarīrī, *al-Maqāmāt*, fol. 47v, copied and illustrated by al-Wāsiṭī, detail
BNF, DEPARTMENT OF MANUSCRIPTS, ARAB 5847. SOURCE: GALLICA.BNF.FR/BNF

it be said of them that the whitest garments in their households are those of their cooks.[8]

To start the subject, priority should certainly be given to [the Prophet's saying that] "vinegar is the best of appetizers"[9] and that the blessed *tharīd* renders offering more foods unnecessary.[10] Additionally, had I chosen to discuss foods at length, I would have mentioned al-Ma'mūn and the most famous stories told about him;[11] I would have also included Būrān,[12] whose name was asso-

8 The cook of a generous host was supposed to be seen wearing a garment, called *sirbāl*, all stained and smudged with smoke.

9 *"Niʿma al-idām al-khall,"* a famous saying by the Prophet Muḥammad. *Idām* (pl. *udum*) is usually a condiment, dip, or sauce eaten with bread before the main meal. According to this saying, a simple and affordable dip like vinegar will always be welcome.

10 *"Al-Baraka fī l-tharīd"* is another famous saying by the Prophet, who favored this dish of broken pieces of bread sopped in a rich broth with meat, see chapter i.2 below.

11 Based on the BL MS, fol. 101r, I amended the edited text here by replacing خبزا الشعيرا 'barley bread'—irrelevant in the given context—with خبرا شهيرا 'famous anecdotes.' Al-Ma'mūn is a famous Abbasid caliph (d. 833), son of Hārūn al-Rashīd.

12 She was wife of Abbasid Caliph al-Ma'mūn; her wedding ceremony was legendary for its lavishness (d. 884). She was credited for inventing eggplant dishes, called *Būrāniyyāt* after her name. See, for instance, *Burāniyya* recipe ii.1.2 below.

ciated with the creation of a beloved dish. I would also have added a variety of anecdotes related to the benefits of foods offered at the table[13] and amusing anecdotes on gluttons and gobblers. Instead, my inclination was to be brief, limiting my choices only to the most favored of the cooked dishes.

I know of many people who wrote cookbooks in which they only covered the most well-known of the dishes and neglected to point to so many issues. People of al-Mashriq have written a good deal of such stuff,[14] which does not sound palatable to the ears and which people [here] find deplorable, even filthy; but to them it is the most elegant of foods. This might well be attributed to the quality of their water and air and to the different natures of the needs and desires of people over there. In justification of my bias towards the Andalusi dishes, I would say that in the field of cooking and whatever is related to it, Andalusis are indeed admirably earnest and advanced despite the fact that they started later [than people of al-Mashriq] in creating the most delectable dishes, and in spite of the constricting limitations of their borders and their proximity to the abodes of the enemies of Islam; indeed, so much so, that they could see each other's fires.[15]

My book deals with all varieties of foods. (**101v**) I included many of the dishes that I approved of and many more that I myself created. The majority are from al-Andalus, and only a small number from al-Mashriq—the finest among them—are included here. In addition, many chapters deal with the most popular of the prepared foods that are worked into the cooking dishes or are associated with them specifically or generally, such as pickles and condiments (*kawāmikh*),[16] varieties of vinegar (*khulūl*), and the like.

I say, it is most essential that cooking at unwholesome places should be avoided and that the cook should refrain from objectionable conduct.[17] Also

13 *Fawā'id al-mawā'id*, as it occurs in the BL MS, fol. 101r; and the Madrid MS, fol. 2r. Otherwise, in the Berlin MS, fol. 1ra, it is copied as *farāyid al-fawāyid* 'unique benefits,' assumedly those related to food.

14 *Al-Mashāriqa* were people of the eastern region of the Arabo-Islamic world, which included Iraq, the Levant, and Egypt, where cookbooks were written.

15 تداني 'being so close that they could see each other,' as in the BL MS, fol. 101r; and ترائى 'seeing each other,' as in the Madrid MS fol. 2v.

16 Evidently, calling pickled foods and condiments like mustard sauce *kawāmikh* was an Andalusi usage of the term. We encounter the same terminology in the fourteenth-century *al-Kalām 'alā l-aghdhiya* 146, by Andalusi scholar al-Arbūlī. In the eastern region, al-Mashriq, however, *kawāmikh* specifically designated dairy-based fermented condiments. See, for instance, recipes in al-Warrāq's tenth-century Baghdadi cookbook *Kitāb al-Ṭabīkh*, English trans., *Annals*, chapter 40.

17 In the BL MS, fol. 101v, and the Madrid MS, fol. 3r, the word *siyar* 'conduct' precedes *al-dhamīma* 'objectionable.' The following observations on cooking utensils are derived from

to be shunned is cooking in an earthenware pot (*qidr al-fakhkhār*) more than once. This indeed has been urged by some physicians.[18] [One of them] says that cooking in silver and gold vessels would have indeed been the best were they affordable and permissible by Islamic law. Therefore, earthenware vessels and green-glazed ones (*ḥantam*) can be used, provided the earthenware ones are not used more than once in cooking food and the green-glazed ones not more than five times.[19] He also cautions against cooking in vessels of copper (*awānī al-nuḥās*) due to the copper's unfavorable properties. He favors iron vessels (*āniyat al-ḥadīd*), provided they are always washed and kept clean and free of rust (*ṣada'*). If regularly used in cooking the dishes, he further points out, iron vessels can be beneficial in many ways, the least of which would be fortifying all the bodily functions.[20] He also mentions that pots and serving vessels made of tin (*qaṣdīr*) are good enough.

Other [physicians] also say that eating and drinking with glass vessels, and even cooking in them if possible,[21] is quite agreeable and well-accepted. They further recommend that when the cooked foods are [ladled into the serving] bowls,[22] they should be covered only with objects that allow steam to escape, such as a sieve (*munkhul*). As they maintain, if the steam stays in and has no way of escaping, it will cause the food to acquire a toxic property (*quwwa summiyya*), especially fish and all grilled foods. Additionally, food cooking in a pot or a similar vessel should be covered with a lid with a tiny hole in it. The best vessels used for frying are those made of silver and gold; those made of tin (*qaṣdīr*) and lead (*raṣāṣ*) are next. Those made of copper (*nuḥās*) are not good because they spoil whatever is being fried in them, especially foods that contain a good

---

Ibn Zuhr, *Kitāb al-Aghdhiya* 136–8, in his chapter on utensils *Dhikr al-awānī*. Some of his passages are paraphrased and others are copied verbatim, with some stylistic changes and omissions.

18 Al-Tujībī's direct source for the following information on cooking and eating utensils is Ibn Zuhr, *Kitāb al-Aghdhiya*, mentioned in the above note.

19 The rationale behind such practices, as given by Ibn Zuhr, is that their porous surfaces, especially those of the unglazed ones, *fakhkhār*, are absorbent and food trapped in them would putrefy and mold; regular washing cannot efficiently get to them. If these pots are used again, the putrefied particles in the pores would contaminate the cooking food and cause harm to the body. The green-glazed ones, *ḥantam*, are less porous and hence they can be used more often, up to five times.

20 Ibn Zuhr, *Kitāb al-Aghdhiya* 137, see n. 17 above, mentions that it has what today we call 'a Viagra-like effect.'

21 There is an interesting recipe in the anonymous fourteenth-century Egyptian cookbook *Kanz al-fawā'id*, English trans., *Treasure Trove*, recipe 149, where sparrows are left to simmer for hours in a glass pot. The dish is said to be a Maghribi and Andalusi specialty.

22 *Ṣiḥāf*, sg. *ṣaḥfa*, are common serving bowls that are wide and shallow.

deal of fat, such as *mirqās*,[23] *qalāyā* (fried dishes), and the like. The properties of these dishes are already considerably off balance; imagine how much more so they will be when they get further affected by the properties of copper.[24]

Dense foods (*ghalīẓ*)[25] must be eaten first so that they settle in the lowest part of the stomach, which is stronger than its upper part. The same should be done with dairy foods (*albān*), *tharāyid*,[26] cheese (*jubn*), porridges (*harāyis*), noodle dishes (*iṭriya*), meat of fattened cows and sheep, cured meat (*qadīd*), fish (*ḥūt*), and parched beans and grains.[27] These are eaten first so that they digest well. Vegetable dishes (*baqliyyāt*) are also eaten first to soften the bowels. Whatever is overly salty should be served in the middle of the meal. Sweets should be served last.[28] Fruits and well-done grilled meats are better eaten first.[29] The same should be done with desserts containing eggs that have been hardened in cooking, as well as desserts having sesame seeds (*simsim*) or linseeds (*bazr kattān*). However, these foods must be avoided altogether if one's stomach is dominated by yellow bile.[30] Still, if they are eaten anyway, then let them be left till later;[31] unless the stomach is extremely weak, in which case they must be eaten first because priority should be given to having them be well digested.[32] (**Berlin MS 1v**) There is much more to be said regarding the subject,[33]

23 They are small sausages, see recipe ii.6.4 below.

24 Based on the Galenic theory of the humors, fried foods are overly hot and moist in properties, and hence unbalanced. In this respect, they share the same nature with copper, which is described as hot and female. See glossary 11, s.v. *mizāj*.

25 This passage is also borrowed from Ibn Zuhr, *Kitāb al-Aghdhiya* 111–2, in his section on the order of having foods *marātib al-aghdhiya*.

26 Sg. *tharīd*, which is a dish of broken pieces of bread sopped in rich broth with meat, see chapter i.2 below.

27 *Ḥubūb maqluwwa*. *Maqluwwa*, literally designates frying in fat. The word is also used when grains and beans are parched in a large flat pan.

28 Desserts, hot and moist in properties, were believed to aid digestion, which was described in terms of cooking.

29 The rationale behind this is that fruits go through the system fast and need to leave the stomach before having the meal; otherwise, they will be trapped and spoil. Grilled meat, when well done, requires longer and stronger digestion.

30 *Khalṭ ṣafrāwī*. It is one of the four humors of the body, generated by the digested food in the stomach and the liver. Yellow bile is hot and dry in properties, and the mentioned seeds, with their similarly hot and dry properties, will cause excessive heat in the stomach.

31 This is because yellow bile, with its intense heat, will manage to digest such foods.

32 Here ends fol. 101v of the BL MS, followed by two blank folios (fols. 101ar–101av). Luckily, the Berlin MS, which is an incomplete copy of it, has them.

33 See, for instance, al-Tujībī's contemporary Ibn Khalṣūn, *Kitāb al-Aghdhiya* 48–50, where much more detailed discussions on such dietary regulations are given; and the tenth-

but this would indeed take me beyond what I have intended for my book, which I called *Fiḍālat al-khiwān fī ṭayyibāt al-ṭaʿām wa-l-alwān*[34] and divided into twelve parts:[35]

Part One: On bread (*akhbāz*, sg. *khubz*), *tharāyid* (sg. *tharīd*, bread sopped in rich broth), soups (*aḥsāʾ*, sg. *ḥasāʾ*), pastries,[36] and others. It has five chapters:
Chapter one, on bread.
Chapter two, on *tharāyid*.
Chapter three, on soups and porridges (*jashāʾish*, sg. *jashīsh*).
Chapter four, on pastries, and varieties of *mujabbanāt* (cheese pastries), *isfanj* (fritters, *buñuelos*), and the like.
Chapter five, on all kinds of dishes that, like *tharīd*, are sopped in broth, and those cooked in ways similar to soup.

Part Two: On meats of quadrupeds, and it has six chapters:
Chapter one, on dishes made with beef (*luḥūm baqariyya*).
Chapter two, on dishes made with mutton (*luḥūm ghanamiyya*).[37]
Chapter three, on dishes made with lamb (*luḥūm khirfān*).[38]
Chapter four, on dishes made with meat of young goats (*luḥūm jidāʾ*).[39]
Chapter five, on dishes made with wild meat (*luḥūm waḥshiyya*).
Chapter six, on foods made with the meat of quadrupeds, such as *banādiq* (meatballs),[40] *mirqās* (small sausages), *aḥrash* (thin meat patties), *harīsa* (wheat porridge), and the like.

Part Three: On poultry, and it has seven chapters:
Chapter one, on dishes with geese (*luḥūm iwazz*).
Chapter two, on dishes with chicken (*luḥūm dajāj*).
Chapter three, on dishes with partridges (*luḥūm ḥajal*).

---

century Andalusi compendium by Ibn ʿAbd Rabbihi, *al-ʿIqd al-farīd* viii, on foods and drinks.

34 In the Madrid MS, fol. 3v, the title at this place is modified to فضالة الاخوان في طيبة الالوان *Fiḍālat al-ikhwān fī ṭībat al-alwān*. See also n. 4 above. According to Ibn Manẓūr, *Lisān al-ʿArab*, s.v. خون, *ikhwān* is synonymous with *khiwān*.

35 The wording of some of the headings of the book's chapters themselves slightly differ from the following list. In the case of part four, they also differ in order.

36 In this book, they are called *ṭaʿām al-khubz* 'bread-like foods.'

37 *Ghanam* is a generic name for adult sheep (*ḍaʾn*) and goats (*māʿiz*). The heading of the chapter in the text itself uses the term *ḍaʾn*.

38 Sg. *kharūf*. It is a male sheep, less than a year old.

39 Sg. *jadī* 'kid.' It is a male goat less than a year old.

40 The name is derived from *bunduq* 'hazelnuts.' See glossary 5.

Chapter four, on dishes with squabs (*firākh ḥamām*).
Chapter five, on dishes with turtledoves (*luḥūm yamām*).
Chapter six, on dishes with starlings (*luḥūm zarāzīr*).
Chapter seven, on dishes with sparrows (*luḥūm ʿaṣāfīr*).

(**Berlin MS 2r**) **Part Four:** On a dish called *Ṣinhājī*[41] and cooking tongue (*lisān*) and tripe (*karsh*). It has three chapters:
Chapter one, on *Ṣinhājī*.
Chapter two, on tongue.
Chapter three, on tripe.

Part Five: On fish (*ḥītān*, sg. *ḥūt*) and eggs (*bayḍ*), and it has two chapters:
Chapter one, on fish.
Chapter two, on varieties of egg dishes.

Part Six: On dairy foods (*albān*), and it has three chapters:
Chapter one, on curdling milk (*ʿaqd al-laban*) and what is made with it.
Chapter two, on making *rāyib* (yogurt) and extracting butter (*zubd*).
Chapter three, on making hard cheese (*jubn yābis*) and dishes made with it; and remedying butter and milk (*laban*).

Part Seven: On vegetables (*buqūl*) and other [foods] pertaining to them. It has ten chapters:
Chapter one, on gourds (*qarʿ*).
Chapter two, on dishes with eggplants (*bādhinjān*).
Chapter three, on dishes with carrots (*jazar*).
Chapter four, on desert truffles (*kamʾa*).
Chapter five, on asparagus (*isfarāj*).[42]
Chapter six, on dishes made with *ḥarshaf* (cardoons),[43] [which are] *qannāriyya* (cultivated cardoons)[44] and *afzān* (wild cardoons).[45]

---

41 It is specialty of Ṣinhāj, one of the largest Amazigh tribes in North Africa, which played an important role in the history of North Africa and the Sahara.

42 This was its common name in the Muslim West; *hilyawn* was its Mashriqi name. In the Madrid MS, fol. 4v, it is copied as *isfāranj*.

43 Copied as *khurshuf* in the Madrid MS, fol. 4v; *Cynara cardunculus*, a generic name for the cardoon plant. This will be made clear in the chapter heading itself. See glossary 12.

44 *Cynara cardunculus var. altilis DC*. This is the Andalusi Romance (ʿAjamiyyat al-Andalus) for what was in the eastern region more commonly known as *kankar*. It was also known as *ḥarshaf bustānī* 'cultivated cardoon.' See Ibn al-Bayṭār, *al-Jāmiʿ* iv 271–2.

45 Copied as *afzan* in the chapter heading itself. It is identified as the name Maghribi

Chapter seven, on cooking mushrooms (*fuṭr*).
Chapter eight, on dishes with spinach (*isfānākh*), blite leaves (*yarbūz*),[46] lettuce (*khass*),[47] and the like.
Chapter nine, on *jināniyya* (a dish cooked with orchard produce).
Chapter ten, on taros (*qulqās*).

Part Eight: On varieties of dishes with beans and pulses, such as fava beans, chickpeas, and the like. It has three chapters:
Chapter one, on fresh and dried fava beans (*fūl*).
Chapter two, on varieties of dishes with chickpeas (*ḥimmaṣ*).
Chapter three, on lentils (*ʿadas*).

Part Nine: On *muʿassalāt*[48] and varieties of confectionary. It has seven chapters:[49]
Chapter one, on making *muʿassal* and *ghassānī*.[50]
Chapter two, on confections (*ḥalwā*).
Chapter three, on *Qāhiriyya* (delicate ring cookies) and *sanbūsak* (marzipan).[51]
Chapter four, on *jawzīnaq* and *lawzīnaq* (walnut and almond confections).[52]

Amazigh gave to *ḥarshaf barrī* 'wild cardoon' (*Cynara cardunculus var. sylvestris*). See Ibn al-Bayṭār, *al-Jāmiʿ* ii 271, s.v. *ḥarshaf*.

In the Madrid MS, fol. 4v, the word occurs as *laṣīf*/*laṣif* 'gundelia,' which indeed is another variety of wild cardoon, more commonly called *ʿakkūb* in the eastern region. See glossary 12, s.v. *ḥarshaf*.

46 The word is inaccurately copied as *yarbūn* in the Berlin MS, fol. 2r. Blite is a variety of wild amaranth, also known as *baqla Yamāniyya* 'Yemeni vegetable.' See glossary 12 for more on this leaf vegetable.

47 It is copied as *khaṣṣ* in the Madrid MS, fol. 4v, which is a dialectal pronunciation. In the Andalusi Ibn Zuhr, *Kitāb al-Aghdhiya* 137, for instance, *nuḥās* 'copper' is copied as *nuḥāṣ*.

48 Sg. *muʿassal*, a starch-based thickened pudding, sweetened with honey. It was called *fālūdhaj* in the eastern region, see glossary 4.

49 The editor of the Arabic text inexplicably chose to scramble the sequence of this part's chapters. I here followed the order given in the Berlin MS, fol. 2r, and the Madrid MS, fol. 4v, which correspond with the sequence given in the text itself below.

50 It is like *muʿassal* but made with white honey and no saffron. Based on the medieval lexicons, it may be translated to 'gorgeous.' Judging from the *ghassānī* recipes, the name may also be attributed to its fair color. See, for instance, Ibn Manẓūr, *Lisān al-ʿArab*, s.v. غسن, where a fair-skinned handsome man is called *ghassānī*.

51 This confection is unlike the *sanbūsak* we encounter in the medieval cookbooks from the eastern region, which were usually prepared as fried, filled pastries.

52 In the BL MS, fol. 189r–v, *lawzīnaq* is copied as *lawzīnaj* in the chapter heading and the recipe.

Chapter five, on making reeds of candy (*qaṣab ḥulw*).
Chapter six, on making *fānīdh* (pulled sugar taffy) and *ishqāqūl* (rings of Solomon).[53]
Chapter seven, on varieties of desserts from the eastern region (*Sharqiyya*).

Part Ten: On *kawāmikh* (pickled foods and condiments)[54] and other related preparations for varieties of vinegar (*khulūl*, sg. *khall*) and *murrī* (liquid fermented sauce); extracting oils (*adhān*, sg. *duhn*); remedying olive oil (*zayt*) when it goes bad; and remedying foods. It has twelve chapters:
Chapter one, on making *ṣināb* (mustard sauce).
Chapter two, on curing olives.
Chapter three, on pickling lemons (*līm*).[55]
Chapter four, on pickling capers (*kabar*).
Chapter five, on pickling eggplants (*bādhinjān*).
Chapter six, on pickling fish (*ḥūt*).
Chapter seven, on making varieties of vinegar.
Chapter eight, on making varieties of *murrī* (liquid fermented sauce).
Chapter nine, on making oil (*zayt*) from varieties of seeds;[56] and remedying olives.
Chapter ten, on extracting oils (*adhān*).[57]
Chapter eleven, on making cured meat (*qadīd*).
Chapter twelve, on remedying foods and the like.

(**102r**)[58] **Part Eleven:** On cooking locusts (*jarād*) and freshwater shrimps (*qumrūn*).[59]

Part Twelve: On handwashing preparations (*ghāsūlāt*).

53 *Ishqāqūl* is mentioned only in the Madrid MS, fol. 4v.
54 See n. 16 above.
55 The word for pickling is *taṣyīr*, see glossary 9.2.
56 These are made to replace olive oil (*zayt*) when it is not available.
57 Sg. *duhn*, commonly used to designate oil extracted from nuts and seeds other than olives. Olive oil is called *zayt*.
58 Here resumes the text of BL MS, fol. 102r, and it continues uninterrupted to the folio before the last, which is missing.
59 This was the Andalusi variant of what was called *rūbyān* in Iraq and *farandas* in Egypt. See Ibn al-Bayṭār, *al-Jāmiʿ* ii 445.

PART 1

القسم الأول

في الأخباز والثرايد والاحساء وطعام الخبز وغير ذلك وهو خمسة فصول

On Bread, Tharāyid,[1] *Soups* (Aḥsāʾ), *Pastries,*[2] *and the Like; and It Has Five Chapters*

1 Sometimes copied as *tharāʾid*. Sg. *tharīda,* it is a dish of bread sopped in rich broth and meat.

2 In this book, they are called *ṭaʿām al-khubz* 'bread-like foods.'

CHAPTER I.1

Part One, Chapter One: On Varieties of Bread (*Akhbāz*)

I.1.1 Bread Baked in the *Furn* (Brick Oven)

Take semolina flour (*samīd*),[1] moisten it with water, add salt to it, and set it aside just long enough to dampen it. Press and rub it very well (*yuʿarrak*), and then add fresh yeast (*khamīr*) and knead it by adding water little by little until it has enough to bind it into dough.

Put a small amount of fine flour (*duqāq*)[2] on the dough to coat it with,[3] and shape it into discs as desired. Put the pieces in the folds of a linen or woolen cloth (*mindīl*), drape them with sheets of sheep skin or similar objects, and set them aside to ferment. The dough is fully fermented when it rises and sounds hollow when tapped. Bake the discs in the brick oven, but handle them with care. [Take them out when fully baked,] clean them [of any ashes or stones that might have stuck to them], and put them in a container and use them as needed.[4]

If the flour used is *darmak* (fine white flour) or other similar kinds, there is no need to moisten it and set it aside [as was done with semolina above]. Just add yeast and salt to it and immediately knead it into dough. The water used must always be warm enough regardless of the variety of flour, God Almighty willing.

1 It is flour of durum wheat (*Triticum durum*). For this type of flour and other varieties, see glossary 2.

2 دقاق; it is used here to designate 'very finely ground flour,' as explained in Corriente, *Dictionary of Andalusi Arabic*, s.v. *d-q-q*. The word is erroneously printed in the edited Arabic text as *ruqāq* (رقاق) 'thin bread', which is irrelevant in context. The purpose of sprinkling flour on the dough must have been to prevent it from sticking to the hands.

3 The verb used is *yulatt*. Based on Hans Wehr, *Dictionary*, s.v. لتّ, of the relevant meanings suggested are, 'coat' and 'roll in.' Otherwise, *yulatt* generally designates rubbing and mixing fat into dry ingredients.

4 The resulting bread would be crusty, with a spongy fluffy inside.

 | DOI:10.1163/9789004469488_004

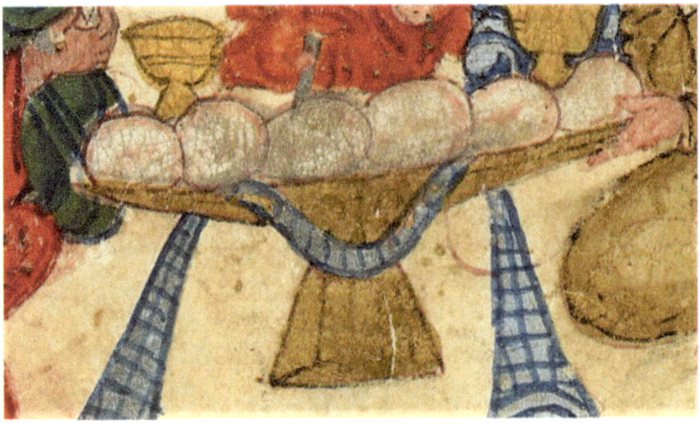

FIGURE 39 A table laden with bread, al-Ḥarīrī, *al-Maqāmāt*, fol. 149r, detail
BNF, DEPARTMENT OF MANUSCRIPTS, ARAB 3929.
SOURCE: GALLICA.BNF.FR/BNF

1.1.2 Bread Baked in the *tannūr* (Clay Oven)[5]

Take semolina flour (*samīd*) and make dough with it by moistening and kneading it as was previously mentioned; and set it aside to ferment. When it is almost fully fermented, light a strong fire in the *tannūr* until [its inner walls] heat up and look white, and then wipe out the smoke [with a wet piece of cloth]. Shape the dough into [flat] discs and quickly stick them to the inner wall of the *tannūr* one after the other,[6] wetting the hands with water before each one is done. Pass wetted grape leaves (*waraq karm*) on the faces of the discs to give them a glossier look.

Close the top opening of the oven (*fam al-tannūr*) and its lower hole to prevent heat from escaping and air from getting in. If the fire is too hot, gather the burning coals to the middle of the *tannūr* floor and put stones under the place where the bread discs are baking to prevent them from burning. Check on them for doneness, and when you take them out, wipe them [with a piece of cloth to remove any clinging ashes], and use them,[7] God Almighty willing.

5 The details this recipe provides clearly point to the fact that the Andalusi *tannūr* was similar to the one used in al-Mashriq. See glossary 9.1 for more on this oven.

6 The detail that the discs are stuck to the inner side of the *tannūr* (في جنب التنور من داخله) occurs only in the Madrid MS, fol. 5r.

7 The instruction here indicates that the bread is at its best when freshly baked; cf. the bread baked in a brick oven in the previous recipe, which is kept in containers and used as needed.

I.1.3 Bread Baked in the *malla*[8] or on an Iron Pan (*ṭājin ḥadīd*)

Take semolina flour (*samīd*), knead it as was mentioned earlier, and set it aside to ferment. Place the *malla* on a moderate fire (*muʿtadila*), and when it gets hot, shape the dough into discs, which you then put on the *malla* one after the other. Care should be taken while baking, turning them until they are fully done, and then use them,[9] God Almighty willing.

I.1.4 (102v) Unleavened Bread (*khubz faṭīr*)

Take semolina flour (*samīd*) and knead it as was mentioned earlier; do not use any leaven and add less water. Knead the dough thoroughly, and then shape it into very thin discs, the thinnest you can get them.[10] Make small holes all over them, wipe their faces with water, and bake them in the *furn* (brick oven). They are made the same way when baked in the *tannūr* (clay oven) or *malla* (earthenware plate).

I.1.5 Baking Bread with *banīj* (Proso Millet)[11]

Take flour of *banīj*, put it in a large kneading bowl (*miʿjana*), add salt, and then knead it very well with the addition of a small amount of water; adding too much water will spoil it. Shape it into thick discs (*khashin*) if baked in the *furn* (brick oven); otherwise, make the discs thin (*raqīq*)[12] for the *tannūr* (clay

---

8 Originally, *malla* was a pit in which flattened dough was baked in hot ashes and stones. The allusions to *malla* in this book suggest an earthenware or iron plate heated by placing it on the fire. This must have been the Andalusi usage of the term. The thirteenth-century Andalusi physician Ibn Khalṣūn, *Kitāb al-Aghdhiya* 92, explains that *khubz al-malla* is *khubz al-ṭabaq*, which is flat thin bread baked on a flat wide plate (called *ṭābaq* in the eastern region of al-Mashriq). As for the original *malla* bread baked in a pit, Ibn Khalṣūn calls it *khubz al-ramād* 'ash bread.'

9 See n. 7 above.

10 *Araqq māyumkin. Raqīq*, adj., usually designates thinness, the opposite of which is *thakhīn* 'thick,' as clearly explained in Ibn Manẓūr, *Lisān al-ʿArab*, s.v. رقق.

11 Written as *banīj* in Ibn Zuhr, *Kitāb al-Aghdhiya* 12. In Ibn Zuhr's opinion, bread made with it is deemed the most delicious after those made with wheat and barley, adding that it agrees with the digestive system (*taʾlafuhu al-ṭabīʿa*). It is a wild variety of millet, known as proso millet, *Panicum miliaceum*. See glossary 2.

12 The word for *raqīq* (رقيق) 'thin' is erroneously printed in the edited Arabic text as *daqīq* (دقيق) 'small.'

FIGURE 40 Millet, *dukhn*, Dioscorides, *Ajzāʾ min risāla fī l-nabātāt*, fol. 24v, detail
BNF, DEPARTMENT OF MANUSCRIPTS, ARAB 4947. SOURCE: GALLICA.BNF.FR/BNF

oven) and *malla* (earthenware plate). Sprinkle sesame seeds (*simsim*), aniseeds (*anīsūn*), and fennel seeds (*nāfiʿ*) on them, and bake them immediately; delaying the baking will spoil them.[13]

Of all the types of bread made with grains other than wheat, [this variety] is Andalusis' favorite; they find it delicious and unusual and eat a good deal of it during the yield season of the grain in their country.[14]

13 In the margin of the Berlin MS next to this text, fol. 3r, the copyist jotted down the word *māzza* (مازّة), which was undoubtedly meant to be descriptive of the grains *banīj*. They are low in gluten, hard to knead, and need to be baked immediately. See al-Zabīdī, *Tāj al-ʿarūs*, s.v. مزز.

14 (لاستطرافه عند الاندلسيين وكثرة استعمالهم له في فصل غلته ببلادهم). The reference to al-Andalus and Andalusis as 'they' and 'their country' evidently show that al-Andalus was no longer al-Tujībī's country of residence when he wrote the book. This comment is not included in the Madrid MS, fol. 5v.

CHAPTER I.2

Part One, Chapter Two: On *Tharāyid*[1]

I.2.1 *Tharīda* with Calves' Heads

Take the head of a fat male or female calf (*ʿijl*). Put water in a copper pot (*burma nuḥās*);[2] let the amount be enough to cover the head. When the water boils, place the head in it, and set it aside for an hour. Test it by pulling some of the hair by hand; if it comes off easily, quickly take it out of the water and pull off the hair. If any of the hair remains, return the head to the hot water [and repeat] until no hair remains. If scalding the head in water is not an option, then singe it on the fire.

Next, put it in a large vessel with enough water to cover it and leave it there to soften [the skin],[3] and then rinse it and scrape it to get rid of any of the singeing odors. After disjointing the head, wash the pieces and put them in a large pot, adding salt, olive oil (*zayt*), black pepper, coriander seeds (*kuzbara yābisa*), and an onion, either cut into pieces or pounded [in a mortar]. Pour water, more than enough to cover everything in the pot, and then place it on the fire and let it cook until done.

Break leavened bread into the tiniest pieces possible [and put it in a large bowl]. Ladle off the pot fat (*wadak*) and set it aside in a vessel, and then soak the bread with the broth and set it aside for a short while. Check on it to see if it has had enough of the broth; if not, then add more as needed, but add it carefully lest the *tharīd* dish should get too liquid-like. Pour the reserved fat all over the bread, place the head pieces on top, sprinkle the dish with Ceylon cinnamon (*qirfa*), and eat it salubriously, God willing.

For those who want to use the twice-kneaded bread (*khubz muʿād al-ʿajn*), let them knead the semolina flour as described earlier [in the previous chapter], let it rise, and then knead it again. Portion it into thin discs (*aqrāṣ ruqāq*), poke holes in them, and wipe their faces (**103r**) with water. After they bake in the *furn* (brick oven) or *tannūr* (clay oven), break them into small pieces and drench them with the broth as described above. For those who want to make

1 Sg. *tharīda*. It is a dish of bread sopped in rich broth and meat.

2 Originally, *burma* designated a soapstone pot.

3 Based on one of the meanings given in Corriente's *Dictionary of Andalusi Arabic*, s.v. *d-b-gh*; otherwise, the word is more commonly associated with tanning leather.

 | DOI:10.1163/9789004469488_005

tharīd with *muwarraqāt al-isfanj*,[4] let them break the breads into large pieces and drench them with plenty of the broth, more than they could absorb.

I.2.2 *Tharīda* with Heads and Other Parts of Sheep of Sacrifice (*ghanam al-aḍāḥī*)[5]

Take the heads and scald them with the trotters (*akāriʿ*) in boiling water, as mentioned earlier. If scalding is not an option, then singe them on the fire to get rid of the hair. Put them in a vessel with enough water to submerge them to soften their skins (*yudbagh*) thoroughly,[6] and then scrape them with a knife and rub them very well by hand to clean them of all impurities. Strike their nostrils on a stone so that the maggots (*dūd*) that bred inside their noses fall out.[7] Cut them at the joints into pieces and put them in a large pot after you wash them with water thoroughly.

Take the tripe (*karsh*) and [par]boil it and then take it out and scrape it with a knife until it looks white and clean [and cut it into pieces]. Take the caul fat, which is called *minsaj* and *ridāʾ*,[8] from inside the belly of the ram (*kabsh*)[9] and cut it into pieces. Fold them around the tripe pieces and tie them with intestines (*muṣrān*), which have been very well cleaned of whatever was inside them. Wind the intestines all around the tripe pieces to make *ʿuṣb* with them.[10] Put them in a pot with the heads [and trotters]; add salt, olive oil (*zayt*), coriander seeds (*kuzbara yābisa*), black pepper, and a small amount of cut onions. Add water—enough to more than just cover them. Cook the pot in the *furn* (brick oven) or at home [on the stove] until it is done.

---

4 This bread's name might sound self-contradictory; based on the recipes in the book, *muwarraqa* is a soft and thin-layered bread (see recipe i.4.17 below), whereas *isfanj* is a fritter that is spongy in texture. Still, we have a clue in Ibn Zuhr, *Kitāb al-Aghdhiya* 76, where a type of bread called *isfanj al-rukhām* is described as being baked on a heated smooth marble slab. We may assume that it was a thin variety. Based on this, *muwarraqāt al-isfanj* would have been more like the *qaṭāyif* pancakes of al-Mashriq, which, though thin, are spongy in texture.

5 Following one of the Muslim rituals, large numbers of sheep are slaughtered annually in celebration of the end of the Hajj ceremonies.

6 See n. 3 above.

7 Also called larvae of the nasal bot flies (*Oestrus ovis*), which grow in the noses of sheep.

8 Literally 'woven garment' and 'mantle,' respectively. In the eastern region of al-Mashriq, it was called *tharb*.

9 The recipe is being more specific here because rams were the most commonly used sheep for cooking. See, for instance, chapter ii.2 below.

10 Sg. *ʿaṣīb*. *ʿUṣbān* is another plural for this type of food. See glossary 5, s.v. *ʿuṣb*.

Break [bread called] *muwarraqāt al-isfanj*[11] into large pieces in a *tharīd* bowl (*mithrada*) and pour broth all over them, add more than they could absorb. Sprinkle Ceylon cinnamon (*qirfa*) on the dish, and eat it salubriously. The dish may also be made with unleavened (*faṭīr*) or leavened (*mukhtamir*) bread, as was described earlier, for those who wish to use them, with the help of God Almighty.

i.2.3 *Tharīda* with Heads of Kids that Are Still Small (*ṣighār al-jidāʾ*, sg. *jadī*)

Take the heads, wash and clean them, and put them in a pot. Add salt, olive oil (*zayt*), black pepper, coriander seeds (*kuzbara yābisa*), and a small amount of pounded onion (*baṣal madqūq*). Pour enough water to cover them and set the pot on the fire. When it is almost done, clean some spinach (*isfanākh*), wash it thoroughly, chop it, add it to the pot, and let it boil twice.[12]

Remove the pot from the fire and add strained boiled butter to it. Break bread into tiny pieces, any kind will do, [put them in a large bowl,] and drench them in broth. Test it with your finger to make sure it has had enough of the liquid. Take the heads out of the pot and place them on the *tharīd*, with the vegetables put under and all around them, and eat the dish salubriously, God Almighty willing.

i.2.4 *Tharīda* with Meat from Unpastured Cows (*baqar maʿlūf*)[13] and Winter Cabbages (*ukrunb shatawī*)[14]

Take the tastiest cuts of beef, such as briskets (*ṣudūr*, sg. *ṣadr*) and shanks (*amlāj*, sg. *mulj*).[15] Also take honeycomb tripe (*sudsiyya*) and rumen tripe (*ghalīẓ al-karsh*), which have been washed in hot water and scraped until they

---

11 See n. 4 above.

12 For more on this boiling technique, see glossary 9.2, s.v. *yaghlī*.

13 They are fed barley grains in restricted areas for speedy fattening, see Ibn Zuhr, *Kitāb al-Aghdhiya* 135.

14 This is a variant of what was more commonly called *kurunb*. Al-Ishbīlī, *ʿUmdat al-ṭabīb* i 313–5, praises the winter cabbage variety over the summer one. See *kurunbiyya* recipe ii.2.3 below, where winter cabbage is said to be milder in taste than summer cabbage with its sharp and pungent flavor (*shiddat ḥarāfa*). See glossary 12.

15 Based on Corriente, *Dictionary of Andalusi Arabic*, s.v. *m-l-j/m-l-ch*, *mulj* designates the calf of the human leg, which, in a quadruped, would be its shank.

are white and clean.[16] Now, wash and clean all of them and put them (103v) in a large pot with salt, olive oil, black pepper, coriander seeds (*kuzbara yābisa*), and a small amount of onion cut into pieces. Add water, more than enough to cover them all, and set the pot on the fire.

Take the hearts of large heads of cabbage and divide each into four sections; also choose the most tender of the rest of the leaves and add them to the cabbage hearts. Put them all in a separate pot with some water and let them boil three times.[17] Check on the cabbage; if it is almost cooked and all its bad unhealthy properties are gone,[18] take it out, rinse it in hot water, and add it to the meat pot.

[In a large bowl,] break into small pieces whatever kind of bread you prefer [and set it aside]. As soon as the meat and cabbage are cooked, pound a few tender tips of cilantro stalks[19] and add them to the pot. Let the pot boil only once (*ghalya wāḥida*), and then remove it from the fire and let it rest on embers (*ghaḍā*) for a short while to allow the fat (*wadak*) to accumulate on top. When this happens, ladle off the fat that has gathered [and set it aside,] and pour the broth all over the bread. Once enough is added, take out the meat and cabbage pieces and spread them all over the *tharīd*. Pour the [set aside] fat all over it, sprinkle it with Ceylon cinnamon (*qirfa*) and ginger (*zanjabīl*), and eat it salubriously, God Almighty willing.

This dish may also be cooked with fatty mutton (*laḥm ghanamī*) for those who wish to use it.

I.2.5 *Tharīda* with Meat of Unpastured Cows (*baqar maʿlūf*),[20] Gourds (*qarʿ*), and Eggplants (*bādhinjān*)

Take the tastiest cuts of beef as well as bones, such as hip bones and the like. Cut the meat, clean the bones, and put them all in a large pot. Add olive oil (*zayt*),

---

16 *Sudsiyya*, literally 'hexagonal,' is the second chamber of the cow's stomach, the reticulum, which is the most desirable part of the tripe. The rumen tripe is the first compartment of the stomach, which is large, smooth, and flat in texture.

17 The expression used is *thalāth ghalyāt*, see glossary 9.2, s.v. *ghalya* for how this was conducted.

18 Boiling cabbage before adding it to the dishes was believed to balance its excessively hot and dry properties. See glossary 11, s.v. *mizāj*; and 12, s.v. *kurunb*.

19 Cilantro is called *kuzbara khaḍrāʾ*, literally 'green coriander.' I here followed the BL MS, fol. 103v, where it is correctly copied as دق 'pound.' Otherwise, it is erroneously copied as دون in the Berlin MS, fol. 4r; and erroneously 'amended' as ذوب 'melt' in the edited Arabic text, p. 41.

20 See n. 13 above.

salt, black pepper, ginger (*zanjabīl*), coriander seeds (*kuzbara yābisa*), cumin, an onion cut into pieces, a whole head of garlic with the skin on, soaked white chickpeas,[21] leaves of citron (*utrujj*), and sprigs of herb fennel (*ʿūd basbās*).[22] Pour water, more than enough to cover them all, and put the pot on the fire.

Peel the eggplants and slit them into quarters [lengthwise] without separating them. Boil them in another pot in salted water to get rid of their bad, unhealthy properties.[23] When they are almost done, take them out of the pot, rinse them in hot water, and set them aside to drain. Scrape the outer skins of the gourds and clean out their insides; cut them into three-finger-wide pieces and put them with the eggplants in one vessel. Put saffron in a *mihrās* [to crush it],[24] and color the eggplants and gourds with it. Add both to the meat pot. When everything is cooked, add the desired amount of fine-tasting vinegar to it.

Now [get the bread ready]; break as much as you choose of leavened bread [into a large bowl], making the pieces as tiny as possible.

When the pot is completely cooked, remove it from the fire and leave it on embers (*ghaḍā*) until the fat gathers on top. Ladle the fat off [and set it aside], pour the broth on the bread, and test it with the finger to make sure it has had enough of it. Do this after you discard the citron leaves, fennel sprigs, and the head of garlic. (**104r**) [Arrange the meat and bones on top of it,] pour the [reserved] fat all over the *tharīd* bowl (*mithrad*), and sprinkle ginger and Ceylon cinnamon all over it.

Once eating commences, take out the bones in the middle of the *tharīd* bowl and empty their marrow all over it. [To extract the remainder,] strike the bones hard at the base of a mortar[25] and blow their fatty marrow [on the *tharīd* in the bowl]. Repeat with the vigorous striking and blowing of each bone until all the marrow inside comes out, all the while turning the *tharīd* bowl around so that each of its sides receives its share of it, and eat the dish salubriously, God Almighty willing.

---

21 *Ḥimmaṣ abyaḍ*. They are the common tan chickpeas, deemed the best of the chickpea varieties, see glossary 12.

22 *Basbās* is the Andalusi variant of what was more commonly called *rāzyānaj* and *shamar*/*shamār* in the eastern region. Herb fennel is used for its fronds as an herb, both fresh and dried, and the seeds. Bulb fennel, the vegetable, is also called *basbās*, and sometimes *basbās akhḍar* 'fresh fennel.'

23 With its excessively hot and dry properties, eggplant was believed to cause ailments like cancer and melasma if not pretreated before cooking it. See glossary 11, s.v. *mizāj*; and 12, s.v. *bādhinjān*.

24 *Mihrās* is a mortar made of a large, hollowed-out long stone or hardwood. See glossary 9.1.

25 *Miḥwal qāʿ al-mihrās* is the concave bottom of the hollowed-out hardwood, usually used to pound spices and moist ingredients.

I.2.6 *Tharīda* Called *mardūda* (Returned)[26]

Take fatty mutton (*laḥm ghanamī*) and cut it into large chunks, which you then clean and put in a large pot. Add salt, black pepper, coriander seeds (*kuzbara yābisa*), a chopped or ground onion, and plenty of olive oil (*zayt*). Let it fry for an hour until the meat looks white and releases all its juices. Pour in hot water and let it cook until done.

Now [to the bread:] take the dough that has been made with fresh yeast (*khamīr*) and set it aside until it is almost fully fermented. Knead it again with a small amount of flour, and knead it well. Portion [and flatten] it into thin discs (*aqrāṣ ruqāq*). Poke them with holes and bake them in the *furn* (brick oven) or *tannūr* (clay oven). Break the bread into the tiniest pieces possible.

When the meat is done cooking, add a bit of saffron to color it, and then take it out [and set it aside]. Strain the remaining broth and return it to the pot—but not the meat. Add the bread to the broth along with strained fresh butter (*zubd ṭarī*) or fine-tasting ghee (*samn*). When the bread is fully cooked, empty it into a large bowl (*mithrad*) and arrange the meat pieces all over it; or use *mislān*, as is the custom among the city dwellers and peasants.[27] Sprinkle Ceylon cinnamon (*qirfa*) and black pepper on top and serve it, God Almighty willing.

I.2.7 *Tharīda* with Mutton (*laḥm ghanamī*) and Milk (*laban ḥalīb*)[28]

Take a fat young male lamb (*kharūf fatī*) and disjoint it into large chunks. Put them in a large pot along with black pepper, salt, coriander seeds, a cut onion,

---

26 This is the name as given in both the BL MS, fol. 104r, and the Madrid MS, fol. 9v; apparently called so because the bread is kneaded and fermented twice. See the option given in recipe 1.2.1 for preparing twice-kneaded bread (*al-khubz al-muʿād al-ʿajn*). Additionally, bread for the *tharīd* is not just moistened in broth when served; it is returned to the pot to cook in the broth before serving it.

The Berlin MS gives it the name *maqbūla* 'accepted,' perhaps playing on the name *mardūda*, which also means 'rejected.' Interestingly, a divorced woman was called *mardūda* because she was sent back to her parents' home.

27 *Ahl al-bilād aw al-bādiya.* According to Corriente, *Dictionary of Andalusi Arabic*, s.v. *b-l-d*, *balda* designates a town. In al-Andalus, *ahl al-bādiya*, called *al-badawiyyūn*, designated the general populace in rural areas, see Yaḥyā b. ʿUmar, *Kitāb Aḥkām al-sūq* 136, n. 1. This interesting remark is included only in the Madrid MS, fol. 9v. *Mislān* is the entire hip section of the sheep, cooked and served in one piece. It is still a very traditional festive dish in North Africa.

28 The recipe's name gives the generic term for sheep (*ghanam*), see glossary 10; but the recipe itself specifies a male lamb (*kharūf*), which is less than a year old.

and enough water and put it on the fire. Take the meat out once it is done, [put it in a vessel,] and cover it with a sieve or anything that allows steam to escape.

Strain the broth to remove any unwanted particles (*thufl*). Wash the pot and return the strained broth to it. Break unleavened bread into tiny pieces and stir them into the broth. Let the pot cook on low heat, stirring the mix with the handle of a ladle (*dhanb al-mighrafa*) to prevent the bread from sticking to the bottom of the pot [while it is slowly cooking]. Pour milk slowly into the pot until enough is added [and let it cook for a while]. Ladle it into a *tharīda* bowl (*mithrad*), spread the meat all over it, and pour strained fresh butter on it.

For those who prefer to use fat chickens or capons (*khiṣyān*) instead, they can do so, and the bread may be cooked in their broth with the milk, but more butter needs to be used.

Sprinkle the dish with sugar, (**104v**) and eat it salubriously, God Almighty willing.

1.2.8 *Tharīda* Called *shāshiyyat ibn al-waḍīʿ* (the [Tasseled] Cap of the Lowborn Son)[29]

Take the tastiest parts of a fat young male lamb (*kharūf fatī*) or a suckling kid (*jadī raḍīʿ*). Cut them into pieces, clean them, and put them in a large pot, adding salt, olive oil (*zayt*), black pepper, coriander seeds (*kuzbara*), and a bit of chopped onion. Add water, more than enough to cover them all, and set the pot on the fire.

When the meat is almost cooked, take lettuce, fresh bulb fennel (*basbās*), fresh fava beans (*fūl akhḍar*), desert truffles (*kamʾa*), and a small amount of

---

29 *Shāshiyya* was an Andalusi cap-like, rounded piece of headgear, some of which were tasseled (as the one suggested in the recipe, see n. 32 below). *Ibn al-waḍīʿ* occurs in the BL MS, fol. 104v, the Madrid MS, fol. 10r, and the anonymous *Anwāʿ al-ṣaydala* 160, where a similar recipe is given and is said to be the specialty of Bijāya, a port city in Ifrīqiya (now in Algeria). Although it differs from al-Tujībī's version in some details, more importantly, it gives a reason for comparing the dish to a *shāshiyya*, see n. 32 below. Moreover, from verses in praise of the dish by Muslim jurist Abū ʿAbdallāh b. al-Azraq al-Andalusi (d. 1491), we learn that despite its name, *shāshiyyat al-faqīr* 'the poor man's cap'—as it is called here—was favored by all, high and low. See al-Maqqarī, *Nafḥ al-ṭīb* iii 298–303.

The Berlin MS, fol. 5r is the only source that gives the dish an elevated name by calling it *shāshiyyat ibn al-rafīʿ* 'cap of the highborn son.'

cilantro (*kuzbara khaḍrāʾ*). Clean them separately and choose the tender parts (*rakhṣ*) only. Remove the outer peels [i.e., jackets] of the fava beans, peel the truffles and cut them into pieces, and wash all the vegetables and add them to the meat pot.

When all is cooked, break bread—any kind will do—into the tiniest pieces possible [and put them in a large bowl].[30] Remove the pot from the fire and let it rest on embers (*ghaḍā*). Cut fresh cheese into pieces, add them to the pot, and immediately[31] start pouring broth on the bread until enough is added. Boil fresh butter in an earthenware pan (*ṭājin fakhkhār*) and strain it. Take the vegetables out of the pot and spread them on the entire face of the *tharīd*, along with the meat and cheese. Pour butter all over the face of the *tharīd*,[32] sprinkle it with Ceylon cinnamon (*qirfa*), and eat it salubriously, God Almighty willing.

I.2.9 *Tharīda* with Unleavened Bread (*faṭīr*), Cooked with Chicken

Take fat chickens and capons (*khiṣyān*), slaughter them, scald them in hot water [to pluck the feathers], open their bellies to take out the insides, and disjoint them. Put them in a large pot after you clean them, adding salt, olive oil, black pepper, coriander seeds, and … [The rest of the recipe is a repetition of the previous one, starting with "a bit of chopped onion." The following is the complete recipe].[33]

---

30 The Madrid MS, fol. 10v, specifies leavened bread.

31 I here amended the edited text by replacing the redundant في الجبن 'in the cheese' with في الحين 'immediately,' based on the BL MS, fol. 104v.

32 The anonymous author of *Anwāʿ al-ṣaydala* 161 explains why the dish is given this name. After *tharīd* bread is drenched in broth, and meat, vegetables, and green fava beans are all arranged above it in a dome-like fashion, chunks of butter are arranged around the top. The heat of the dish will cause the butter to melt down, with the green vegetables showing in between the falling streams of butter. The anonymous author says,

> This is how the dish got the name *shāshiyyat ibn al-waḍīʿ*: the falling white butter is like the cotton threads of the [tassel of the] *shāshiyya* dangling all around it,
> كأن في ذلك الزبد الابيض قطن شاشية يتدلى من كل جهة.

See also n. 29 above.

33 This must have been a copyist's oversight, which happens in the Berlin MS, fol. 5r, and the BL MS. The Madrid MS has only the one that follows.

I.2.10 *Tharīda* with Unleavened Bread (*faṭīr*), Cooked with Chicken

Take fat chickens and capons (*khiṣyān*), slaughter them, scald them in hot water [to pluck the feathers], open their bellies to take out the insides, and disjoint them. Put them in a large pot after you clean them, (**105r**) adding salt, olive oil, black pepper, coriander seeds, onions split into quarters and halves, and soaked chickpeas. Start cooking the pot on the fire.

Now [to the bread:] take semolina flour (*samīd*), moisten it with water, add salt to it [and set it aside for a while].[34] Knead it with a small amount of water vigorously and thoroughly. Take an iron pan (*ṭājin ḥadīd*) or an unglazed earthenware plate (*malla fakhkhār dūn muzajjaj*)[35] and place it on a moderate, gently burning fire (*layyina muʿtadila*). When the plate is heated, take the [portioned] dough, one piece at a time: add some ghee (*samn*) to it and press and rub it with the hand,[36] and then flatten it with a rolling pin (*shawbak*), fold it, add more ghee to it, and roll it out as thinly as possible. Put it on the *ṭājin* until it looks white and completely dry. Take it and strike it between both hands to separate the layers.[37] Cut it into medium pieces and put them in a *tharīd* bowl. Take another piece and do the same thing with it until all are finished. Take what you have accumulated of this bread, put them in a *kuskusū* pot,[38] and fit it on top of the chicken pot. Seal them together with a piece of dough all around the edges and cover the top of the *kuskusū* pot with a piece of cloth to keep the steam in. Let the bread cook with the steam coming up from the lower pot through the holes of the *kuskusū* pot.

Description of *shawbak*: it is a wooden cylinder that is thick in the middle and tapers towards both ends.

For those who prefer to portion the dough into small pieces and stack each three in a pile with ghee [between them], flatten them with a rolling pin as described above and dry them out on the *ṭājin*, and then finish cooking them in the *kuskusū* pot as mentioned; they can go ahead and do so.

[Back to the chicken:] Once the chicken is done, check the fat on top; there should be a good deal of it; if not, then add fine-tasting ghee and fresh butter and let it boil. Take the pot from the fire and leave it on embers until its fat gathers on top, which is then ladled out into a vessel and set aside.

---

34 This procedure is described in detail in recipe i.1.1 above.

35 See also recipe i.1.3 above, for making bread using these baking tools.

36 The verb used is *ʿarraka*, see glossary 9.2.

37 The Madrid MS, fol. 8r, compares this bread to *musammana*. See, for instance, recipe i.4.17 below.

38 This pot has a perforated bottom. See glossary 9.1, s.v. *qidr al-kuskusū*.

Pour broth on the *faṭīr* bread, [put in a *tharīd* bowl,] but be careful not to put too much; otherwise the bread disintegrates and spoils. Take out the chicken pieces, onions, and chickpeas and spread them on the bread in the middle of the *tharīd* bowl. Garnish all around the bowl's edges with boiled eggs, fine-tasting cured olives, and pickled lemons (*līm muṣayyar*). Pour the [set aside] fat in the vessel all over the dish, sprinkle it with Ceylon cinnamon (*qirfa*) and ginger (*zanjabīl*), and eat it salubriously, God Almighty willing.

This [*tharīd* of] *faṭīr* bread is exclusively made by people of Ifrīqiya, especially the urbanites of Tunis (*ḥaḍar ahl Tūnis*).[39] They often cook the dish for their celebrations and take pride in offering it for their feasts.

I.2.11 *Tharīda* with Unleavened Bread Called *shabāt*[40]

Take fat chickens and fattened capons (*khiṣyān*); also add whatever you choose of squabs (*firākh al-ḥamām*), partridges (*ḥajal*), and sparrows (*ʿaṣāfīr*). Put them all in a pot with salt, (105v) olive oil (*zayt*), black pepper, coriander seeds, and chopped onion; do this after slaughtering, cleaning, and cutting the birds open from their chests [to flatten them?].

Put the pot on a gently burning fire (*nār layyina*), and after the birds fry, pour in enough water to cover them and cook them until almost done. Take them out of the pot and thread them securely onto skewers (*safāfīd*, sg, *saffūd*). Prepare sauce (*maraq*) of vinegar, *murrī* (liquid fermented sauce), and olive oil. Sprinkle it on the birds and grill them on a moderate coal fire (*jamr muʿtadil*) until they brown.

[Now to the bread:] make thin discs of bread with very-well kneaded [unleavened] semolina dough[41] and pierce holes in them with a thin stick so that they bake well in the *furn* (brick oven) or *tannūr* (clay oven). Take them out and break them into [relatively] large pieces, the size of a *dīnār* coin each.[42]

---

39 In medieval times, Ifrīqiya constituted the coastal regions of what today are western Libya, Tunisia, and eastern Algeria. It is interesting that he should mention this Tunisian specialty; he lived in Tunis for more than 30 years, see introduction i.2, p. 17.

40 As it is copied in the BL MS; otherwise, it occurs as سبات *sabāt* in the Berlin MS, fol. 6r; and the Madrid MS, fol. 8v. A similar recipe in the anonymous Andalusi *Anwāʿ al-ṣaydala* 166 calls this dish *al-lamtūniyya*, adding that it was made in al-Andalus and North Africa. The name associates the dish with the Amazigh tribe Lamtūna, which was a branch of the Ṣinhāja tribe. See glossary 2, for more on *shabāt* bread.

41 Rolling out the bread into thin discs *raghāʾif riqāq* is mentioned in the Madrid MS, fol 8v.

42 The dinar was a gold coin about 0.75 of an inch in diameter. See, for instance, https://www.qantara-med.org/public/show_document.php?do_id=634&lang=en, accessed March 20, 2020.

Grate fine-tasting hard cheese (*jubn yābis*) with an *iskarbāj* (grater) and add enough of it to the broth [in the pot where the birds were boiled]; also add pounded garlic, enough to give it a garlicky flavor. When the pot boils, pour broth over the broken pieces of unleavened bread [that were put in a large bowl] until enough is added. Disjoint the [grilled] birds and arrange them all over the bread. Garnish the dish (*yunajjam*) with boiled eggs cut into halves with a thread; scatter skinned almonds all over it along with walnuts, [brined] green olives (*zaytūn akhḍar*) and oil-cured black olives (*zaytūn mutammar*),[43] and grated cheese. Sprinkle Ceylon cinnamon (*qirfa*) and spikenard (*sunbul*) all over it, and serve it, with the help of God Almighty and His power.

I.2.12 *Tharīda* with Chicken, Wonderful[44]

Take chickens, clean them, and disjoint them as was mentioned above. Put them in a large pot with salt, plenty of olive oil, black pepper, coriander seeds, cumin, a small amount of chopped or pounded onion, soaked white chickpeas,[45] boiled almonds,[46] leaves of citron (*utrujj*), sprigs of herb fennel (*ʿūd basbās*),[47] and a head of garlic with the skin on. Put the pot on the fire [and start cooking].

[Now to the bread:] take fine flour (*daqīq*) or semolina flour (*samīd*) and knead it with water, salt, and some sour fermented dough (*khamīr*).[48] Set it aside so that it ferments in the kneading bowl (*miʿjana*). As soon as it ferments, knead it vigorously again, and then portion it into medium discs (*aqrāṣ*), neither too big nor too small. Pierce holes in them, wipe their faces with water, and bake them in the *furn* (brick oven). [When taken out,] wipe them [to remove ashes that might have stuck to them] and break them into the smallest pieces possible.

---

43 *Mutammar* designates cured foods, such as meat and olives, as used here; see Ibn Manẓūr, *Lisān al-ʿArab*, s.v. تمر. For a recipe on curing olives, see x.2.4 below.

44 *ʿAjība*, as described in the Madrid MS, fol. 11v.

45 *Ḥimmaṣ abyaḍ*; they are the common tan chickpeas, deemed the best of the chickpea varieties. See glossary 12.

46 The purpose of boiling the almonds is not to cook them but facilitate removing their skins. In the Madrid MS, fol. 12r, the text occurs as 'skinned almonds.'

47 See n. 22 above.

48 This would be a piece of the previous day's dough; kept in a bowl to be used as a leavening agent.

When the chickens are almost done, dissolve enough saffron in cold water—careful not to use too much of it, otherwise it will spoil the dish. Add it to the pot and stir so that it colors all its contents. Set it aside for a short while, and then add the amount you like of fine-tasting vinegar and let it boil only once (*ghalya*).

Take eggs, [which you estimate to be] enough for *takhmīr*.[49] Break them in a wide, shallow bowl (*ṣaḥfa*); add salt, black pepper, ginger, and Ceylon cinnamon (*qirfa*). Beat them with a ladle (*mighrafa*) to combine, adding enough dissolved saffron to color them. Add the eggs to the pot and stir it gently (*yuḥarrak*), and then leave it on a gently burning fire (*nār layyina*).

[For garnishes,] boil eggs and divide them into quarters with a thread and put them aside in a vessel. Crush the gizzards (*qawāniṣ*) and livers (*akbād*) until they are as smooth as bone marrow (*mukhkh*). Add salt and whatever is available of aromatic spices (*afāwīh*) to them, along with the white of an egg. Shape the mix into discs, (**106r**) which you then fry in a skillet in sweet olive oil (*zayt ʿadhb*) until they brown. Cut them into long slices and put them with the split [boiled] eggs. Next, fry 4 egg yolks in sweet olive oil until they brown and add them to the split eggs.

Now [back to the pot,] ladle the fat (*wadak*), which has gathered on top, and set it aside. Pour broth on the bread until enough is added. Spread the meat [i.e., chicken pieces] all over it and garnish the dish with the split eggs, the above-mentioned yolks, and pieces made with the gizzards [and livers]. Pour the [set aside] fat all over them and sprinkle the dish with Ceylon cinnamon (*qirfa*) and ginger, and eat it salubriously, God Almighty willing.

Those who prefer to make the dish with [un]leavened bread, they can use it to prepare the dish as described above.[50]

---

49 The expression used here is *takhmīr al-qidr*, i.e., 'coating' or topping the food cooking in the pot with a layer of eggs beaten with other ingredients, such as seasonings and breadcrumbs. *Takhmīr* is added in the last stage of cooking the dish. This was a typically Andalusi-Maghribi cooking technique, usually done with dishes that have little sauce in them. With a dish that uses a good amount of liquid, and with the direction in the following statement to gently stir the pot after adding the beaten eggs, the egg mix will set in scrambled form. See glossary 9.2, s.v. *takhmīr*.

50 Unleavened bread must have been intended in this last statement; otherwise, it would be redundant because the bread used in the recipe is leavened.

1.2.13 *Tharīda* Called *mukarrara* (Refined)[51]

Take fattened young adult chickens. Clean them after disjointing them and put them in a pot with olive oil, black pepper, ginger, coriander seeds, and onion juice. After they fry, add plenty of water to the pot, and cook them until they disintegrate and fall off the bones.[52] [Discard the chicken] and strain the broth and cook other chickens in it until they also fall off the bones. [Discard the chickens] and strain the broth again. Cook other chickens in this broth with as much as you like of the spices usually used with them. Let them cook until they are fairly done.[53] Take them out of the pot [and set them aside].

Now take [fresh] bread, which has been crushed by rubbing it between the hands (*fatāt maḥkūk bi-l-yad*). Put them in a wide, shallow earthenware bowl (*ṣaḥfa fakhkhār*) and pour enough of the broth on them. Disjoint the set-aside chickens and arrange the pieces on the bread. [Put the bowl on a gentle fire] to heat up the dish until the bread particles combine into one mass. Sprinkle it with Ceylon cinnamon, black pepper, and spikenard and garnish it with eggs (*tunajjam*).

This *tharīd* is highly recommended for increasing the blood and reviving the strength of the emaciated.

1.2.14 *Tharīda*, Which Invigorates Coitus (*tuzīd fī l-bāh*), Wonderful[54]

Take fat young adult chickens, clean and disjoint them, and put them in a new pot with olive oil, salt, Ceylon cinnamon (*qirfa*), and coriander seeds. After the pot comes to a boil, add white chickpeas,[55] which have been soaked from early in the night before; add the soaking liquid as well. Add a suitable amount of onion juice extracted by pounding it and squeezing out the juice. Also add ghee (*samn*). When all this is done, add egg yolks [to poach in the heat of the pot].

Pour the broth on crumbs of *khubz al-ḥuwwārā*[56] and sprinkle the dish with spikenard (*sunbul*), cloves (*qaranful*), ginger (*zanjabīl*), black pepper (*fulful*),

---

51 The recipe gets its name from the broth that is refined by cooking and straining it twice.

52 The following details on straining and cooking the broth twice are mentioned in the Madrid MS only, fols. 12v–13r; the Berlin MS, which the edited Arabic text uses, does not include it, neither does the BL MS.

53 The word the recipe uses here is *muʿtadilan*, i.e., not overcooked like the previous ones.

54 *ʿAjība*, as described in the Madrid MS, fol. 13r.

55 They are the common tan chickpeas, deemed the best of the chickpea varieties. See glossary 12, s.v. *ḥimmaṣ*.

56 This is fine bread made with white bran-free flour, called *ḥuwwārā*, see glossary 2. The ref-

and Ceylon cinnamon (*qirfa*). Cover the bowl for a short while to allow it to absorb the liquid.

It would even be better if sparrows (*ʿaṣāfīr*) are used instead of chicken;[57] or both. It might also be cooked with carrots, as much as it can take, and it will be absolutely delicious and beneficial.[58]

I.2.15 *Tharīda* Called *shāqūma*,[59] Which Some of the Berbers Cook, Quite Delicious[60]

Cook medium-size pieces of mutton (*laḥm ghanamī*) with salt, olive oil, black pepper, coriander seeds, and a good deal of onion cut into halves and quarters, with enough water to make *tharīd* with it; [add the water] after frying the meat.

[To make the bread,] knead fine flour (*daqīq*) or semolina flour (*samīd*), which has been moistened with milk, (106v) and make it into thin discs. Bake them in *malla* (earthenware plate placed on the fire) and then break them into the tiniest pieces possible.

When the pot boils and the meat is done, pour broth on the bread and arrange the meat pieces over it. Pour strained [heated] fresh butter all over it—use plenty of it—and serve the dish, God Almighty willing.

erence to bread as *ḥuwwārā* points to the eastern origin of this recipe. Its counterpart in the Muslim West, is *darmak*.

57 Sparrows were believed to be highly aphrodisiac, see glossary 10.

58 *Wa-l-manfaʿa* is added in the Madrid MS, fol. 13r.

59 The meaning of the dish escapes me, unless it is related to *shaqam*, which is a dark variety of dates (al-Zabīdī, *Tāj al-ʿarūs*, s.v. شقم); probably similar to the delicious *ʿajwa*, the Prophet's favorite variety of dates. It was common to compare moist and delectable foods to fully ripe dates. Kneading the bread with milk and pouring a profuse amount of fresh butter all over this dish would indeed make it worthy of the analogy.

60 يستعملها بعض البربر لذيذة, addition from the BL and Madrid MSS, fols. 106r and 13r, respectively. This comment is not found in the Berlin MS, which the editor follows.

i.2.16 *Tharīda* with *qaṭāʾif* (Pancakes), Which Are Called *mushahhada*;[61] It Is an Eastern Dish (*Sharqiyya*)

Take a fat young adult chicken, open its belly to take out the entrails, but leave it whole. Pass the ends of its legs through its anal vent (*makhraj*) and clean it. Put it in a big pot with salt, a good deal of olive oil, black pepper, coriander seeds, and lots of onion—leave them whole if small, otherwise, cut them into pieces. Put the pot on the fire [and start cooking]. Pound the breast meat of another chicken and make small meatballs (*banādiq*) with it, with the addition of spices (*abzār*) and egg whites. Add them to the chicken pot.

When the chicken is cooked, take it out of the pot, put it in an earthenware pan (*ṭājin fakhkhār*), and send it to the *furn* (communal brick oven) for an hour or so until it browns; or fry it [at home] in a skillet in fine-tasting ghee (*samn*).

Next, poach 3 eggs in the broth,[62] and boil 3 more eggs and split them into quarters [with a thread]. Pound [red] meat and mix it with salt, black pepper, ginger, Ceylon cinnamon (*qirfa*), cloves (*qaranful*), almonds that have been boiled [to remove skins], and 3 eggs. Stuff a [long] piece of the large intestine (*mibʿar*) with this meat; and stuff it with [whole] cooked egg yolks as well.[63] Tie [both] of its ends with a thread and place it in a wide pot.[64] Put it on the fire, adding water, salt, olive oil, and a bit of *murrī* (liquid fermented sauce). Once [the sausage] is cooked, take it out and place it in an earthenware pan (*ṭājin fakhkhār*), adding to it a small amount of the liquid in which it was boiled after straining it. Send it to cook in the *furn* (communal brick oven), turning and moving it about several times to brown it on all sides.

Take *qaṭāʾif* (pancakes) and fold them—let the side with holes be inside.[65] Arrange them on a griddle (*mafrash ḥadīd*) placed on a moderately low fire and turn them repeatedly until they toast (*yaḥmarr*). When you put them in

---

61 The Madrid MS, fol. 13v, just calls them *qaṭāṭīf*. *Mushahhada* 'looking like honeycombs' was its general name in al-Andalus and al-Maghrib. In Ifrīqiya (the coastal regions of what today are western Libya, Tunisia, and eastern Algeria), it was also given the name *muṭanfasa* 'like carpets with smooth pile,' see Dozy, *Takmilat al-maʿājim* viii 327, s.v. *qaṭāʾif*. This kind of pastry is characterized by having holes on one side, which also gave it the name *muthaqqaba* 'having holes,' see anonymous Andalusi cookbook, *Anwāʿ al-ṣaydala* 184.

62 The verb used is *tukhammar*. Since the recipe does not mention beating them, we may assume that they were left to poach in the heat of the broth. Cf. n. 49 above.

63 I followed here the Madrid MS version, fol. 14r, which mentions using the intestine to stuff the meat mix (ويحشى مبعر); otherwise, the other two MSS make no mention of this important detail, which obscures the text. The intestine used is that of a quadruped.

64 *Qidr wāsiʿ*. A wide pot is used here because the long, stuffed intestine needs to be coiled in it in one layer.

65 See n. 61 above. See recipe i.4.15 below for instructions to make the *qaṭāʾif* batter.

the *mithrad* (large and wide *tharīd* bowl), unfold them, and let the side with holes be up so that they absorb the broth when poured.

Pour broth all over the pancakes until they are all drenched, flatten the surface, and put the [cooked] onions, chicken, and meatballs on top of them. Arrange the poached eggs all around, along with the quartered eggs. Cut the cooked intestines (*mibʿar*) into pieces and scatter them on top of the dish and all around it. Sprinkle it with Ceylon cinnamon, black pepper, and ginger and eat it salubriously, God Almighty willing.

I.2.17 *Tharīda Sharqiyya*,[66] Called *al-falyāṭil* (Made with Bread Composed of Stacked Thin Sheets)[67]

Slaughter a fat large chicken, and with the feathers still on, blow it hard [from the neck] until the skin separates from the meat of the entire body. Tie its neck with a thread and pluck the feathers [by dipping the chicken] in hot water. Scrape the skin with a scraper (*miḥakka*) and salt until it is clean.[68] Untie the thread, cut off the neck and remove the crop (*ḥawṣala*),[69] and debone the wings from underneath the skin, but leave their tips untouched. Do likewise with the thighs. Remove all chest bones from underneath the skin but leave the chicken's rear end (*zimikkā*) attached to the skin. (107r) Thus, all the bones and meat are gently and carefully taken out from underneath the skin.

Remove all bones from the meat and pound it along with meat taken from another chicken until it has the consistency of bone marrow (*mukhkh*). Add

---

66 That is, originally from/inspired by the eastern region, and yet it is given an Andalusi name.

67 Here I followed the Madrid MS, fol. 14v, rather than the BL and Berlin MSS, fols. 106v and 7v, respectively, where it occurs as *fayāṭil*, which could be a miscopy or a variant on the name. At any rate, in recipe i.2.24 below, it is copied as *falyāṭil* in all three MSS.

In search for a meaning for *falyāṭil*, I consulted Steingass' *Dictionary* first, where *filāṭa* (فلاطة) is described as 'a species of sweet cake made with sheep's milk,' which corresponds with recipe i.2.24 below. Given our two *falyāṭil* recipes in this chapter, the emphasis should be placed on the way the bread is made rather than the type of milk used. I found a credible root for *filāṭa* in Donkin, *Etymological Dictionary of Romance Languages*, where 'fila' designates 'a row.' Now, in both *falyāṭil* recipes, bread is prepared the same way: dough is flattened into very thin discs, which are then stacked in rows to assemble what would look like one whole bread, which Steingass calls 'cake' in his description. In light of the above, *falyāṭil* is highly likely to be a term coined in the Andalusi Romance ('Ajamiyyat al-Andalus).

68 *Miḥakka* is mentioned only in the Madrid MS, fol. 14v.

69 The following instructions describe how to debone the chicken, leaving the skin in one piece and free of any holes.

black pepper, ginger, Ceylon cinnamon (*qirfa*), spikenard (*sunbul*), cloves (*qaranful*), caraway (*karāwiya*), salt, olive oil, juices extracted from cilantro and mint (*naʿnaʿ*), and a bit of onion juice. Do not add too much of the cloves and spikenard. Mix them all with 8 eggs. Add boiled egg yolks to them, along with skinned almonds and meatballs (*banādiq*).[70]

Now examine the chicken's skin, sew up the torn places if any, and stuff it with the meat mixed with the [juices of the] herb leaves (*waraq*), and distribute the egg yolks and meatballs in the stuffing. The thighs, the wings, the rear end area, and the belly ought to be stuffed so that the chicken looks full and as it was before. Sew up the neck area with a thread and put the chicken in a pot.

Take 2 squabs (*firākh ḥamām*) and stuff their bellies and between the meat and the skin with the pounded meat of other squabs mixed with eggs. Sew up their bellies and the places where the stuffing was inserted through their skins and put them in the pot with the chicken.

Add salt to the pot, along with lots of olive oil, black pepper, coriander seeds, a chopped small onion, soaked chickpeas, skinned almonds, and 2 ladlefuls (1 cup) of fine-tasting vinegar. Set the pot on the fire and pour in enough water to moisten the *tharīd* [when you make it later]. [And start cooking the pot.]

[To make the bread:] moisten semolina flour (*samīd*) and then knead it with a small amount of water without using any leaven. Portion the dough and shape it into extremely thin discs; grease each one of them with ghee (*samn*) and stack them in one pile on an earthenware plate (*malla fakhkhār*). Put them in the *furn* (brick oven) as they are [i.e., stacked on the plate], but do not let them fully bake. Break them into medium pieces in a *tharīd* bowl [and set them aside].

Color the chicken and squabs with saffron [after they are cooked,] and [take them out of the pot and] put them in an earthenware pan (*ṭājin fakhkhār*) with a small amount of the broth. Send the pan to the *furn* (communal brick oven) and let the birds be turned over several times so that they brown [on all sides].

[Now back to the pot with the broth:] break enough eggs. Separate their yolks, mix them with pounded fresh cheese (*jubn ṭarī*) and skinned almonds, and add them to the pot. Stir the whites lightly (*yuḥarrak*) with salt, Ceylon cinnamon (*qirfa*), black pepper, ginger, spikenard, and juices of cilantro and mint, and color them with saffron and pour them into the pot.[71] Remove it from the fire and let it rest on embers (*ghaḍā*).

Chop the gizzards and livers and pound them [in a mortar]; add salt and whatever is available of aromatic spices (*afāwīh*), along with the white of an

70 The previous recipe explains how to make them.

71 When poured into the pot this way, the two egg mixes will poach in the hot broth. Later in the recipe, they will be called *takhmīr* used to garnish the *tharīd*, see also n. 49 above.

egg. Mix them all by hand until they bind and shape them into an *isfāriyya* disc.[72] Heat olive oil in a skillet and put the disc in it, turning it gently until it browns [on both sides]. Slice it into strips, which you then put in a vessel with boiled eggs split into quarters [with a thread] and 3 fried egg yolks. When you finish doing these things, ask for the pan to be brought back from the oven.

Start pouring broth [that is in the pot] on the bread little by little until enough is added. Place the chicken and squabs on top of the *tharīd*, remove the threads, (107v) and arrange [the following] all over and around them: the *takhmīr* that is in the pot,[73] the meatballs (*banādiq*), chickpeas, almonds, split eggs, fried egg yolks, and *isfāriyya* pieces. Sprinkle the dish with whatever is available of the aromatic spices (*afāwīh*), and eat it salubriously, God Almighty willing.

I.2.18 A Wonderful Stuffed *tharīda*, with Chicken

Take a fat and tender chicken, open its belly, and clean it. Chop all its meat as fine as possible. Add salt, black pepper, the two corianders—the dry [i.e., seeds] and the fresh herb [i.e., cilantro]—and a small amount of chopped onion.

Now knead semolina flour (*samīd*) or fine white flour (*darmak*) with water, salt, melted fresh butter, and 3 eggs to make a rich, soft dough. Mix the dough with the meat [prepared above], adding salt and black pepper as needed.

Pour melted butter into a new pot and move it around to coat it on all sides, with some extra remaining in its bottom. Make a large disc from another batch of dough and line the bottom and sides of the pot with it. Spread the dough with meat on the dough in the pot and cover it with the dough [by pulling it from the sides] so that the dough with meat does not stick to the sides of the pot [when baking]. Pour plenty of butter into the pot, enough to cover the dough, and let it be baked in the *furn* (communal brick oven), placed at a distance from the fire, until it is done.

Grill another fat and tender chicken on a skewer on a [coal] fire, which should be all around the chicken and not underneath it. Start grilling the chicken before making the [above] so that by the time the pot arrives from the *furn* the chicken will be grilled and ready. Empty the contents of the pot into a *tharīd* bowl [in one piece?], arrange the disjointed grilled chicken over it, and eat it salubriously, God Almighty willing.

72 They are thin and smooth meat patties. See recipe ii.6.3 below for more on them.

73 See n. 71 above.

1.2.19 Stuffed *tharīda,* with Squabs (*firākh al-ḥamām*)

Clean the squabs and cut their bellies open [and gut them]. Chop chicken gizzards (*qawāniṣ*) into small pieces and mix them with salt, the two corianders—the dry (seeds) and the fresh herb (cilantro)—black pepper, a small amount of pounded onion, a bit of *murrī* (liquid fermented sauce), and 2 eggs. Stuff the bellies of the squabs and underneath their skins with the mix. Sew up their bellies and put them in a wide pot with 2 ladlefuls (1 cup) of fine-tasting vinegar, a ladleful of olive oil, a bit of black pepper, coriander seeds, a small amount of chopped onion, and enough salt. Cook the pot on the fire.

Pound the breast of a chicken, adding Ceylon cinnamon (*qirfa*), ginger, black pepper, and 2 egg whites. Make them into meatballs (*banādiq*) and add them to the squabs' pot. When the squabs are cooked, color them with saffron and add 5 eggs to the pot.[74]

Crumble [the inside of] leavened bread (*khubz mukhtamir*) into very fine pieces and put them in a *tharīd* bowl.[75] Boil the breast of another chicken in water and salt only; and when cooked, pound it and mix it with the crumbled bread in the bowl. Pour enough of the broth that is in the squabs' pot all over them; pour melted fresh butter as well. Arrange the squabs and the meatballs on top of the *tharīd,* along with some split boiled eggs [and the *takhmīr*].[76] (**108r**) Sprinkle it with black pepper and Ceylon cinnamon (*qirfa*), and eat it salubriously, God Almighty willing.

1.2.20 *Tharīda* with Squabs (*firākh ḥamām*)[77]

Take squabs, cut their bellies open, and clean them. Put them in a pot with salt, olive oil, black pepper, coriander seeds, a bit of cumin, 2 ladlefuls (1 cup) of fine-tasting vinegar, and enough water.[78] Cook the pot and when it starts boiling, pour in some onion juice and let it cook until the squabs are done. Add 3 eggs to the pot.[79]

---

74 Usually referred to in the recipes as *takhmīr*. We may assume that the eggs are lightly beaten and added. See n. 49 above.

75 As we will next learn, it is the inside of the fermented bread, called *lubāb*, that is being used here.

76 See n. 74 above.

77 In the Madrid MS, fol. 16v, it is described as *Sharqiyya* 'eastern.' I used this version to fill in some small gaps in the text of the other two MSS.

78 Adding water at this stage is mentioned in the Madrid MS only, fol. 16v; otherwise, the edited text mentions it later, which is rather confusing.

79 The verb used here is *khammirhā*, from which we may assume that the eggs are lightly beaten and added. See n. 49 above.

Crumble unleavened bread into the smallest pieces possible and put them in a *tharīd* bowl (*mithrad*). Place a frying pan (*miqlāt*)[80] made of iron or glazed earthenware (*fakhkhār muzajjaj*) on the fire with oil in it. Once the oil boils, break 6 eggs and beat them with some salt until the whites are mixed with the yolks. Let the mix fry and brown on both sides in the pan (*ṭājin*) as one whole disc and then take it out in one piece and set it aside.

Take some of the broth, mix it with a small amount of fine-tasting honey with its beeswax (*shahd*), and pour it all over the crumbled bread put in the bowl (*thurda*). Take the squabs out of the pot [and set them aside]. Pour the remaining broth over the bread until enough is added[81] and give it a sprinkle of black pepper. Place the egg disc on top, and on top of the eggs, arrange the squabs. Sprinkle them with black pepper, and eat the dish salubriously, God Almighty willing.

I.2.21 *Tharīda* Made with Milk Only

Dissolve a piece of dough (*ʿajīn*) in water and put it in a large pot on low heat, stirring it constantly with a ladle. Strain fresh milk (*laban ḥalīb ṭarī*) and add it to the pot, stirring it gently; and as soon as it starts to thicken,[82] add crumbs of leavened or unleavened bread to it and stir it gently. Add more milk whenever it looks dry and continue doing this until it cooks. Remove the pot from the fire, empty it into a *mithrad* (large and wide *tharīd* bowl), sprinkle it with sugar, and eat it.

For those who prefer to eat it with honey (*ʿasal*), let them put it in a glass or an earthenware vessel, place it in the middle of the *tharīd* bowl, and eat it with small ladles (*maghārif ṣighār*).[83]

For those who want to have it with unbaked bread (*khubz ghayr maṭbūkh*), let them make well-kneaded firm dough using semolina flour (*samīd*), without any leaven, using a small amount of water, as this will result in firm dough. Small and very thin discs are made with it, which are then spread on a sieve

---

80 As it is called in the Madrid MS, fol. 17r; otherwise, in the other two MSS, the word occurs as *juzʾ* (part), irrelevant in context; but soon it will be called *ṭājin*.

81 We may assume that the *takhmīr* eggs, which have been added to the broth, see n. 79 above, are poured into the bowl with it.

82 This detail, and mentioning that breadcrumbs are added while the milk is cooking, are included only in the Madrid MS, fol. 17r–v.

83 They must have looked like today's round-bowled soup spoons, which can hold liquids efficiently.

to dry out in the sun.[84] When the milk starts boiling,[85] break the [sun-dried] discs into pieces and add them to it. Stir the pot gently with the handle of a ladle while pouring more milk repeatedly until enough is added. Empty it into a *tharīd* bowl, pour [melted] fresh butter all over it, sprinkle it with sugar, and eat it salubriously, God Almighty willing.

I.2.22 Another *tharīda* with Milk

Take fresh milk, put it in a pot on low heat, and stir it gently. Once it boils, add bread made with well-kneaded unleavened bread, which has been crumbled into very small pieces. Add milk to the pot repeatedly until the bread cooks; there should be more milk in the pot than the bread can absorb. [Empty it into a *tharīd* bowl and] sprinkle it with sugar and Ceylon cinnamon (*qirfa*), with a bowl filled with fresh butter put in the middle—it would be the utmost elegance to eat it with small ladles (*maghārif ṣighār*).[86] And eat it salubriously, God Almighty willing.

I.2.23 (108v) *Tharīda* with Milk, Baked in the *furn* (Brick Oven)

Take 2 *raṭl*s (2 pounds) of semolina flour (*samīd*) or fine white flour (*darmak*), [make dough with it, and] knead it very well. Roll it out into very thin discs, which you then bake slightly in the brick oven.

Take 2½ *qadaḥ*s (approx. 5½ pints/11 cups) of milk, stir it with 8 eggs and a small amount of flour, and cook it on a moderate fire [until it thickens into light custard].

Now take a new earthenware pan (*ṭājin fakhkhār*) and put a layer of butter and [the prepared] milk; spread one of the bread discs on it, followed by another layer of butter and milk, and another layer of bread. Continue doing this until all the bread discs and butter and milk are used. Spread a thick disc of bread on them to cover them well.

Send the *ṭājin* to the *furn* (communal brick oven). Let it bake for a while and then take it out, pour some milk all over it, and return it to the oven; do this one or two more times until enough milk is added. Once it is fully baked, [take

---

84 This will make it somewhat like pasta.

85 As explained in the Madrid MS, fol. 17v.

86 ومن تمام الظرف فيه أكله بالمغارف الصغار. This interesting suggestion is mentioned only in the Madrid MS, fol. 18r. See n. 83 above.

it out] and break the pan gently. The layered bread will come out all bound and in one piece. Slice it with a knife and cut it into pieces, and eat it salubriously, sprinkled with sugar, God Almighty willing.

I.2.24 *Tharīd* of *falyāṭil* (Made with Bread Composed of Stacked Thin Sheets)[87]

Make dough with semolina flour (*samīd*), water, and salt; knead it thoroughly and shape it into thin discs. Grease the face of each disc with ghee and then stack them in an earthenware plate (*malla*) so that they look like they are one piece. Send the plate to the *furn* (communal brick oven) and let it be taken out take when the bread is almost done; do not let it fully bake.

Meanwhile, take milk, strain it, and put it in a pot set on low heat; stir it constantly until it thickens. Break the bread into medium pieces, [put them in a *tharīd* bowl,] and pour [the thickened] milk all over them; use enough to saturate them. Pour whatever remains of this milk on top of the dish followed by melted butter. Sprinkle it with sugar, and eat it salubriously, God Almighty willing.

I.2.25 Making *tharīda* of *muthawwama* (with Garlic), for the Nayrūz Day,[88] Wonderful[89]

Take fat chickens and capons (*khiṣyān*), open their bellies, and take out the insides after plucking their feathers and washing them with water and salt. Clean them from the inside and the outside and insert the ends of their legs through their anal vents (*makhārij*, sg. *makhraj*). Put them on the fire in a pot with water and salt only.

But before doing this, shell fine walnuts and put them in hot water to soften their skins and facilitate removing them.[90] Remove the skins so that the walnuts look white and then wash them in cold water. Skin cloves of garlic and

---

87 See n. 67 above. The Madrid MS describes it as *Sharqiyya* 'eastern.'

88 Also written as Nawrūz in other sources. It is the Christian New Year festival celebrated in January, see introduction ii.6, p. 68.

89 As described in the Madrid MS, fol. 19r.

90 The verb used for this action is *yudbagh*, which is more commonly used in terms of tanning leather in liquids to soften it. See Corriente, *Dictionary of Andalusi Arabic*, s.v. *d-b-gh*. The editor of the Arabic text unjustifiably replaces this interesting usage of the verb with the generic *yūḍaʿ* 'put.'

FIGURE 41
Garlic, Dioscorides, *Kitāb al-Ḥashā'ish fī hāyūlā al-ʿilāj al-ṭibbī*, Arabic translation by Ḥunayn b. Isḥāq, Or. 289, fol. 93r, detail
UNIVERSITAIRE BIBLIOTHEKEN LEIDEN, HTTP://HDL.HANDLE.NET/1887.1/ITEM:1578266

cook them to remove their [garlicky] odor. Grate hard cheese (*jubn yābis*) with the special iron [cheese] grater (*iskarfāj*)[91] so that it looks like dust. As for the remaining cheese, add it to the walnuts and garlic without grating it and pound them all thoroughly. This is to be prepared in advance.

Before preparing the above, make dough with semolina flour (*samīd*), water, and salt; no yeast is used. Knead it [again] very well with a small amount of water,[92] shape it into thin discs, wipe their faces with water, pierce holes in them, (**109r**) and bake them to medium doneness.

When the chickens are almost done, take them out of the pot, wipe them thoroughly with olive oil, and send them to the *furn* (communal brick oven) in glazed earthenware pans (*ṭawājin fakhkhār muzajjaja*).[93] Let them be turned over and moved about several times to ensure they brown well on all sides, but care should be taken to not let them burn.

---

91 The word was earlier copied as *iskarbāj* in recipe i.2.11.

92 The verb used for the second kneading is *yuʿarrak*, which involves a more vigorous way of kneading mostly done by pressing and rubbing the dough with heels of hands.

93 Sg. *ṭājin*, see glossary 9.1.

So, while the chickens are in the oven, work on what was mentioned earlier of pounding garlic with the leftover ungrated cheese and walnuts until they became as smooth as bone narrow (*mukhkh*). Dissolve [some of] this mix in hot water in a large bowl (*miʿjana*),[94] adding plenty of olive oil. As soon as the chickens are out of the oven, disjoint them and put them in this sauce.[95]

Break the [prepared] bread into medium pieces—larger rather than smaller is better. Spread some of the cheese grated [earlier] in the bottom of a *tharīd* bowl and cover it with some of the broken bread; spread on them some more of the grated cheese [and spread bread on it]; continue doing this until the *tharīd* bowl is full.

Next, take the remaining pounded mix [of walnuts, garlic, and cheese]; if it does not have enough cheese, add some of the grated cheese to it so that it looks thick and white due to the amount of cheese added to it. Pour this mix all over the face of the *tharīd* that is in the bowl and pour fine, sweet olive oil all over it.[96] Little by little, pour the broth in which chickens were cooked on the *tharīd* after boiling it until enough is added and broth can be seen in the bottom of the bowl. If the broth is not enough, use boiling water, which has been kept boiling and ready in case it is needed. While adding the broth, bread must be folded from bottom to top until enough is added.

Sprinkle the *tharīd* with finely grated cheese; take the chicken pieces out of the bowl and spread them all over the *tharīd*. Sprinkle the dish with grated cheese, pour olive oil all over it, and eat it salubriously, God Almighty willing.[97]

This *muthawwama* is mostly consumed by Andalusis during the Nayrūz days as is the custom in their country. Some people prefer to grill the chickens on skewers instead of roasting them in the brick oven,[98] while others cook the dish with European wild rabbits (*qunilyāt*),[99] hares (*arānib*),[100] and

94 This kind of bowl is usually used for kneading bread dough.

95 The recipe refers to it as *maḥlūl* because the pounded mix was dissolved and thinned down with water and olive oil.

96 *Zayt ṭayyib ḥulw*. This olive oil is mellow in taste because it is pressed from fully ripe olives. See glossary 6, s.v. *zayt*.

97 The following concluding paragraph is from the Madrid MS, fol. 20r.

98 For grilling on an open fire, the word *shawī* is commonly used. For roasting and baking in ovens, the term is *ṭabkh*, a generic term that applies to cooking in liquids and otherwise.

99 Copied as *qulinyāt* at this place in the MSS. The name of this rabbit species is derived from the Spanish *conejo* (*Oryctolagus cuniculus*); it is smaller than the hare, *arnab*. See glossary 10. In the anonymous Andalusī cookbook *Anwāʿ al-ṣaydala* 38, 39, it occurs as *qunayna*.

100 Sg. *arnab*. Unlike the western region al-Maghrib, in the eastern region both the hare and the rabbit were called *arnab*. The former, however, was often more specifically described as *barrī* 'wild.' See Viré, "Hare," 97–100.

partridges (*ḥajal*) instead of chicken. *Qunilyāt* are seldom found in regions other than al-Andalus.[101]

i.2.26 *Tharīda* of *jināniyya*,[102] Made with All Kinds of Summer Vegetables

Take tender gourds (*qarʿ*), clean them from the inside and the outside,[103] and dice them into small pieces. Peel small eggplants and slit them into quarters [lengthwise] but keep them intact; stuff them with salt and set them aside to allow their unwholesome liquids to leach out.[104] Rinse them in fresh water (*māʾ ʿadhb*) and put them with the chopped gourd in a big pot with salt, plenty of olive oil, black pepper, coriander seeds, a chopped onion, and enough water to cover them all and more. Put the pot on the fire [and start cooking].

Take whatever vegetables (*buqūl*) are in season, as well as the young shoots of vines (*ghazl*) of grapes, snake cucumbers (*qiththā*), common cucumbers (*khiyār*), and gourds. Discard the inedible parts and chop them into very small pieces and wash them. When the gourds and eggplants are almost cooked, (**109v**) add these shoots (*buqūl*) [and continue cooking].

Make discs of bread with dough, which has been fermenting in a dough bowl (*miʿjana*). Bake them in the *furn* (brick oven) or *tannūr* (clay oven) and break them into pieces [in a *tharīda* bowl].

Take fine-tasting hard cheese (*jubn yābis*), chop [some of] it into pieces and add them to the pot, and grate some on the grater (*iskarbāj*).[105] Pound together fresh mint, cilantro (*kuzbara khaḍrāʾ*), and a clove of garlic (*ḥabbat thūm*) and add them to the pot. When the pot boils, pour [enough] broth over the bread. Take out the eggplants, gourds, and the rest of the vegetables from the pot and spread them on top of the *tharīd*. Sprinkle grated cheese all over it, and eat it salubriously, God Almighty willing.

---

101 The scarcity of these wild rabbits outside al-Andalus, i.e., in North Africa, is mentioned only in the Madrid MS. fol. 20r. That these wild rabbits were hard to find in places other than al-Andalus will be indicated again, also only in the Madrid MS, fol. 70.vb, in recipe ii.5.7 below.

102 I amended the name of the recipe, which erroneously occurs as *ḥamāma* (pigeon) in the BL and Berlin MSS. Only the Madrid MS, fol. 20r, copies it correctly as *jināniyya* (cooked with orchard produce). The recipe is for a vegetarian *tharīd*. For another *jināniyya* dish, see recipe vii.9 below.

103 The pithy inside of the gourd along with the seeds needs to be removed and the outer skin scraped.

104 See n. 23 above.

105 Also copied as *iskarfāj* at other places, see recipe i.2.25 above.

I.2.27 *Tharīda* of *baysār* (Dried Fava Beans),[106] which Is *fūl*[107]

Take crushed (*maṭḥūn*) dried fava beans,[108] rinse them in hot water once, rub them with olive oil, and put them in a pot. Pour enough fresh water (*māʾ ʿadhb*) to cover them. Add a head of garlic (*raʾs thūm*) and place the pot on the fire.

Take the innards (*baṭn*) of a fat young adult ram (*kabsh fatī*). Boil the tripe (*karsh*) in hot water and then scrape it with a knife until it looks white; clean the small intestine (*duwwāra*) and cut it into pieces along with the fatty *minsaj* (caul fat), which is called *ridāʾ*.[109] Make small rolls of wrapped tripe (*ʿuṣb*) with them.[110] Put them in another pot with salt, lots of olive oil, black pepper, coriander seeds, cumin, a chopped onion, and enough water to cover them all and more. Put the pot on the fire.

Break leavened bread into the smallest pieces possible [and set it aside]. Take the tripe rolls out once they cook and put them in a vessel [and set them aside]. Strain the broth in which they were cooked.

Once the fava beans are cooked, discard the head of garlic and stir the beans in the pot with a large ladle until they mash and look as smooth as bone marrow (*mukhkh*). Add hot water to it, enough to moisten the *tharīd*. Once the pot comes to a boil, start adding the crumbled bread bit by bit while stirring the pot. Gradually pour in the [strained] broth in which the tripe rolls were cooked until enough is added. Season it with salt as needed, add the [set aside] tripe rolls to it, and stir it briefly.

Immediately empty the pot into a *tharīd* bowl, scatter some fine-tasting olives all over its face, and eat it salubriously, God Almighty willing.

This dish needs to be cooked on a moderate to low fire, and caution is to be taken when cooking it, lest it should burn. Those who prefer to prepare it without the tripe rolls, they can do so; and those who want to put ghee, butter, or olive oil in the middle of the *tharīd* dish, along with radishes and onions when eating it, they can also go ahead and do so.

---

106 *Baysār* is the North African name for dried fava beans. Nowadays, the name is more commonly encountered in that region and Egypt in a dish called *biṣāra* 'porridge of dried fava beans.' This book's recipes that use fresh fava beans call it *fūl akhḍar* (green fava beans), see, for instance, recipe i.2.8 above and ii.2.32 below.

107 I used the Madrid MS, 20v–21v, to add some small details in the recipe not found in the other two MSS.

108 The dried fava beans must have been crushed coarsely because they will be further mashed after boiling them.

109 Literally 'garment.' See glossary 10.

110 Sg. *ʿaṣīb*. It is made by wrapping a piece of tripe in caul fat and tying it with a piece of the intestine wound all around it.

I have also heard that when crumbled bread is added to the cooked and mashed fava beans, milk is gradually poured into the pot until enough is added. After emptying it [into a *tharīd* bowl], it would be sprinkled with sugar, with bowls of honey (*ʿasal*) offered to eat with the *tharīd*. I personally have neither cooked it this way nor eaten it, but let those who wish to try it do so, (**110r**) with the help of God Almighty.

What I have mentioned of the varieties of *tharīd* dishes above should be sufficient, God Almighty willing. Still, even though most of them might hardly ever get to be cooked and tried, including them will indeed rarely fail to please with their novelty and exquisiteness. This is also true of most of the other chapters in the book.[111]

111 Apart from the first sentence of this paragraph, this concluding statement is found only in the Madrid MS, fol. 21v.

Part One, Chapter Three: On Soups (*Aḥsā'*) and Porridges[1]

I.3.1 Breadcrumb Soup (*ḥasū al-fatāt*) Cooked with Chicken Broth (*maraq al-dajāj*)

Take a fat and tender chicken or a young chicken (*farrūj*). Open its belly and clean it from the inside and the outside. Pound it lightly (*yuraḍḍ*), but leave it whole, and then put it in a new pot with salt, olive oil, a stick of Ceylon cinnamon (*ʿūd qirfa*), a small lump of mastic (*maṣṭakā*), ginger, coriander seeds, a small piece of onion, and enough water. Cook the pot on the fire.

Take [fresh] crumbs of leavened bread made with semolina (*samīd*) or fine white flour (*darmak*); rub and crush them between your hands little by little until they are all finely crushed. Sift them in a sieve, rub the [remaining] coarse particles, and sift them again until all the bread turns into fine crumbs. Set them aside in a covered vessel.

As soon as the meat in the pot is done, take it out [and use it for something else]. Strain the broth with a tightly woven piece of cloth (*khirqa ṣafīqa*), clean the pot, and return the broth to it. When it comes to a boil, sprinkle the breadcrumbs bit by bit with one hand while stirring the pot constantly with the other. Do this until all the breadcrumbs are added. Continue stirring the pot until the soup looks smooth and cooks well.

Take the pot from the fire and empty it into a glazed bowl (*ghaḍāra*), sprinkle it with cinnamon or drizzle it with a small amount of preserved juice of unripe grapes (*khall al-ḥiṣrim*),[2] and eat it salubriously, God Almighty willing.

1 Here written as *jashāyish*, sg. *jashīsh*. We notice that all the recipes in this chapter demand use of a new pot, which is undoubtedly due to the delicate and simple taste of these dishes.

2 See recipes x.7.12–4 below for making it. Note that in the two surviving Andalusi cookbooks, this one and anonymous *Anwāʿ al-ṣaydala*, *khall* not only designates regular 'vinegar' produced by fermentation but also, in a looser sense, unfermented, preserved 'sour juice,' and even freshly pressed out lemon juice. See glossary 8, s.v. *khall*.

 | DOI:10.1163/9789004469488_006

1.3.2 Another Breadcrumb Soup

Take a new pot and pour enough fresh water and olive oil in it. Wrap salt, ginger, a stick of Ceylon cinnamon (*ʿūd qirfa*), a lump of mastic (*maṣṭakā*), and a chopped side of an onion (*ṭaraf baṣala*) in a clean piece of cloth [and add it to the pot]. Put the pot on the fire [and start boiling it].

Take crumbs of leavened bread (*fatāt khubz mukhtamir*) and do with them as described above—such as rubbing them by hand and so forth. When the pot boils twice,[3] take out the cloth bundle and add breadcrumb as in the previous recipe. Remove the pot from the fire when it is done cooking. Break an egg in a wide, shallow bowl (*ṣaḥfa*) and whip it to mix the yolk with the white. When you ladle the soup into a glazed bowl (*ghaḍāra*), pour in the whipped egg and stir the soup until the egg binds with it. Sprinkle it with Ceylon cinnamon (*qirfa*), and eat it salubriously, God Almighty willing.

This soup might also be made without the egg. For those who like to cook it with cilantro and mint, (110v) let them lightly pound the tender tips of their sprigs and press out their juice into the soup—that is, if they want to use their juice only—otherwise, they may chop them finely with a knife and add them to the pot when it is almost done. Additionally, some people add fennel seeds (*nāfiʿ*), aniseeds (*anīsūn*), and ghee (*samn*) when the pot is first put on the fire, so know this.

1.3.3 Another Soup Made with Flour (*daqīq*)

Take a new pot, put enough water and salt in it, and put it the fire. Take wheat flour and put it in a *mithrad* (large *tharīd* bowl), moisten it with water, and stir it with a ladle until it dissolves and no lumps remain.

When the pot boils, pour the dissolved flour into it and stir it gently to prevent it from sticking to the bottom of the pot. Continue cooking until it is almost thick. Remove the pot from the fire, and once the boiling subsides, ladle the soup into a glazed bowl (*ghaḍāra*) and serve it.

For those who want to add breadcrumbs as well, let them take bread, split it with a knife, place it on the fire, and as soon as it browns, crumble it finely, drench it with olive oil, and use it.

---

3 For details on how this was conducted, see glossary 9.2, s.v. *ghalā*.

I.3.4 Soup Made with Fresh Yeast (*khamīr*)

Take a new pot and put enough water and salt in it, along with a bit of fennel seeds (*nāfiʿ*), aniseeds (*anīsūn*), and an unskinned clove of garlic. Put the pot on the fire.

Take the needed amount of very well fermented fresh yeast, and using a ladle, dissolve it in a *mithrad* (large *tharīd* bowl) with hot water. When the garlic is almost cooked, pour in the dissolved yeast and stir the pot constantly with a ladle until it is just done; do not keep it boiling for long because with this kind soup it is better to keep it thin. Empty it into a glazed bowl (*ghaḍāra*) and serve it. For those who prefer to discard the garlic clove, they may do so; and those who like to eat it may keep it.

I.3.5 Soup with Almonds and Wheat Bran (*nukhāla*)

Take coarsely crushed wheat bran, add plenty of hot water to it, and rub it and press it vigorously by hand until it releases all its essence [into the water]. Press out the bran and strain the liquid with a piece of cloth. Pour off any dusty-looking liquid (*māʾ mughbarr*) that might appear on top of the strained liquid.

Take a new pot (**111r**) and pour the strained liquid into it; add more water if needed. Finely pound skinned almonds until they look like bone marrow (*mukhkh*) and then dissolve them in water and strain the liquid. Add this [almond liquid] to the bran's strained liquid, and stir the pot continuously [while cooking] until the soup binds and thickens. Ladle it [into a bowl] and serve it, God Almighty willing.

I.3.6 Soup with Flour and Milk, Which Andalusis Call *lakhṭaj* (Silty)[4]

Dissolve flour in water and put it in a new pot on a medium fire. Strain milk and add it to the dissolved flour in the pot. Stir the pot until the soup becomes thick in consistency and then empty it into a bowl and serve it, God Almighty willing.

---

4 In Dozy, *Takmilat al-maʿājim* ix 223, *lakhṭaj* is said to be a Hebrew term designating 'silt.' As suggested by Corriente, *Dictionary of Andalusi Arabic*, s.v. *l-kh-ṭ-j*, it may be descriptive of 'slime.' He further adds that the name might have been derived from *lac* 'milk' with a pejorative suffix. Whether 'silt' or 'slime,' the soup will no doubt be thick and slippery in its finished form.

i.3.7 Soup, Which Andalusis Call *zabzīn*,[5] and Is Called *barkūs* by ahl al-ʿUdwa[6]

Put flour in a dough bowl (*miʿjana*) and sprinkle it with salted water. Gently move the flour around by hand until it binds and granulates (*yataḥabbab*) and then roll it between your palms to bind the granules into small chickpea-like balls. Sift them through a light sieve to get rid of whatever is left of [loose] flour and then allow them to dry spread out on a tray (*ṭabaq*).

Pour enough water in a new pot, adding salt, olive oil, coriander seeds, and a chopped side of an onion (*ṭaraf baṣala*). Put the pot on the fire, and as soon as it starts to boil vigorously, gently add what is in the tray. Stir the pot [and continue cooking] until the liquid starts to dry out and the ingredients come together. Chop fine-tasting hard cheese into small pieces and add them to the pot, along with finely chopped cilantro (*kuzbara khaḍrāʾ*). Once the pot comes to a boil, empty it [into a bowl] and serve it, God Almighty willing.

i.3.8 Soup with *banij* Flour[7]

Thoroughly dissolve *banij* flour with water in a wide, shallow bowl (*ṣaḥfa*). Put a new pot with enough water and salt in it on the fire. When it starts to boil, gently pour in the dissolved flour, and stir it constantly with a ladle until it is no longer liquidy and starts to thicken. Empty it [into a bowl] and serve it, God Almighty willing.

---

5 As the recipe clearly shows, it is a sort of couscous shaped like small balls. Its name may also be pronounced as *zebezín*, see Corriente, *Dictionary of Andalusi Arabic*, s.v. *z-b-z-n*. See also recipe i.5.8 below for *muḥammaṣ* (small balls of couscous), where it is also mentioned.

6 It is copied as *barkūkash* in the Madrid MS, fol. 21v. The reference here is to people of al-Maghrib, which, to the Andalusis, was on the other side of the Mediterranean. This soup is still cooked in present-day Morocco, where it is called *barkūkash* (according to a comment by Bin Shaqrūn, editor of the Arabic text, p. 60, n. 2). It seemed to have been a humble dish, not fit for the guests' table, judging from the Andalusi saying (أش دخل بركوكش في الضيافة) "What has *barkūkash* to do with hospitality?" See al-Zajjālī, *Amthāl al-ʿawām* ii 25.

7 Also copied as *banīj* in recipe i.1.5 above. It is a wild variety of millet, known as proso millet, *Panicum miliaceum*. See glossary 2.

I.3.9 Porridge of Coarsely Crushed Wheat (*jashīsh al-qamḥ*)

Pick over fine-quality wheat berries and crush them coarsely. Sift them to separate the crushed grains from the flour (*daqīq*) and bran (*nukhāla*). (**111v**) Wash the wheat and put it in a new pot with one-eighth of its weight fenugreek seeds (*ḥulba*), which have been soaked in water.[8] Pour in plenty of water and cook the pot. When it is done cooking, empty it into a glazed bowl (*ghaḍāra*), sprinkle it lightly with [dried] water mint (*ghubayrā*),[9] which has been crushed by hand, and serve it.

For those who prefer to cook it with milk (*laban ḥalīb*), they should not add fenugreek seeds. Additionally, the amount of water should be reduced and replaced with milk, which is added while the *jashīsh* is cooking until enough is used.

I.3.10 Porridge of Coarsely Crushed Barley (*jashīsh al-shaʿīr*)

Pound fine-quality barley grains with a large wooden or stone mortar (*mihrās*) to separate the husks (*qishr*) from the grains and then sift them. Coarsely crush the barley and sift it to remove the bran (*nukhāla*) and flour (*daqīq*).

Rinse the coarsely crushed barley, put it in new pot, and fill three-quarters of it with water. Let the pot cook in the *furn* (brick oven) all night long until the liquid turns brownish.[10] Ladle out the liquid (*ṣafwū*) only and serve it. It is what people with fevers (*maḥmūmūn*) and those having an excess in hot properties (*maḥrūrūn*) use to cool down.[11] For those who would like to have the liquid with the crushed barley, they can do so. For those who want to add fennel seeds (*nāfiʿ*) and aniseeds (*anīsūn*) to it to make it less cold in properties,[12] they can also go ahead and do so.

---

8 The verb used is *madbūgha*, see also recipe i.2.1, n. 3 above. To my knowledge, the only medieval source that mentions treating fenugreek seeds before using them is the anonymous *Kanz al-fawāʾid*, English trans., *Treasure Trove*, recipe 596, where the seeds are soaked in water for a couple of days to soften them and eliminate their bitterness.

9 غبيرا *ghubayrā*, as it is clearly copied in the BL MS, fol. 111v, and the Madrid MS, fol. 23v. It is water mint, *Mentha aquatica*, valued for its strong properties, which help with the bloating effects of food. In the Berlin MS, fol. 12v and the edited text that follows it, it is erroneously copied as عبير *ʿabīr*.

10 The word used is *yaḥmarr*, literally 'turn red.' Due to the lack of a word for brown in medieval times, red was used to also designate the color brown.

11 See glossary 11 for more on these medical terms.

12 See glossary 11, s.v. *mizāj*.

FIGURE 42 Rice, Dioscorides, *Fī Hayūlā al-ṭibb*, translation by Ḥunayn b. Isḥāq, fol. 94r, detail
FROM THE NEW YORK PUBLIC LIBRARY, SPENCER COLLECTION: HTTPS://DIGITALCOLLECTIONS.NYPL.ORG/ITEMS/5E66B3E8-B698-D471-E040-E00A180654D7

1.3.11 Porridge of Coarsely Crushed Rice (*jashīsh al-aruzz*)

This *jashīsh* is rarely cooked outside my hometown Mursiya,[13] and Balansiya,[14] may God return it [to the Muslims], because, of all the other Andalusi regions, they are the only places where rice is grown and cultivated abundantly.

When rice grains are pounded to husk them, some of them break, which is the *jashīsh* [used here]. These broken grains are taken out of the husked rice, sifted in a tight sieve [to separate them from the flour], and are stored and used as needed.

The way to cook this rice is to rinse it thoroughly in fresh water (*māʾ ʿadhb*) and put it in new pot with water—for each *raṭl* (1 pound) of coarsely crushed rice use 6 *raṭl*s (12 cups) water. Let the pot cook on moderate fire until it is done and then add the needed amount of finely crushed salt and [stir it and] serve it, God Almighty willing.

13 Murcia region in southeast Spain. This allusion and the following one offer clues for when al-Tujībī might have written his book. See the introduction, section i.2. This personal statement is not included in the Madrid MS.

14 Valencia is on the east coast of Spain; it is now famous for its paella rice dishes. It fell to the Christians in 1238, who were led by King James I of Aragon.

Part One, Chapter Four: On Pastries[1], *Mujabbanāt*, and *Isfanj*

1.4.1 (112r) Making *kaʿk* (Ring Cookies) Stuffed with Sugar and Almonds

Moisten fine white flour (*daqīq darmak*) with olive oil (*zayt*), rub it between the hands, and then knead it thoroughly with water, salt, and a small amount of fresh yeast (*khamīr*). Do not use too much water; work it in little by little until enough is added. You can tell by pulling a piece of the dough: if it stretches without breaking then it is done.

Next, finely pound sugar and a similar amount of skinned almonds in a copper mortar (*mihrās nuḥās*)—pound them separately and then combine them. If the mix tastes too sweet, add more of the almonds to balance the taste. Add rosewater, ginger, spikenard (*sunbul*), Ceylon cinnamon (*qirfa*), cloves (*qaranful*), black pepper, and a small amount of camphor (*kāfūr*) and knead them [with the sugar and almonds] until they bind. Roll the mix into cylinders by hand: make them like fingers in diameter and length, or a bit thinner and longer than fingers depending on how thin or how large or small you want them to be.

Set a clean table (*māʾida*) or a board (*lawḥ*) and roll out a piece of the dough [into a rectangle]. Place one of the filling cylinders along its longer side; [it should be long enough] to cover it all. Fold the dough over the filling and roll it by hand on the table until it is rolled well and is as long and as thin as you would like it to be. Curve the roll to form a ring cookie (*kaʿka*, pl. *kaʿk*) and combine the ends very well. Decorate it with a pair of copper tweezers (*minqāsh*) specially used for this purpose. Roll out another piece in a similar manner and continue doing this one after the other until all the dough and stuffing are used up.

Arrange the pieces on a board, which has been lightly dusted with flour, and bake them in the *furn* (brick oven). Care should be taken when baking them; also when transferring them one piece after the other from the board [when the baking is done]. Wipe them with a clean piece of cloth [after they are baked], and sprinkle them with rosewater [in which] a small lump of mastic [has been

---

1 In this book, they are collectively called *ṭaʿām al-khubz* 'bread-like foods.'

 | DOI:10.1163/9789004469488_007

dissolved]. Scent a vessel with the smoke of fine Indian aloeswood (*ʿūd Hindī*)[2] after sprinkling it with rosewater and put the cookies in it right away [while it is still damp]. Cover the vessel and set it aside until it is time to serve the cookies, God Almighty willing.

I.4.2 Another Kind [of *kaʿk*], Stuffed with Honey

Take the needed amount of honey (*ʿasal*) and let it boil on a moderate fire after you skim its rising froth (*raghwa*). Pound as much as is available of unstuffed *kaʿk* cookies with skinned almonds, and add them to the honey with rosewater and the needed amounts of aromatic spices (*afāwīh*).[3] Continue boiling the honey until it thickens (*yaʿqud*) and then remove the pot from the fire and set it aside until it cools. Oil your hands with olive oil and make cylinders (*fatāʾil*) with the honey and put them in a wide, shallow bowl (*ṣaḥfa*).

Knead the dough as mentioned above [in the previous recipe], roll out a piece on the table, stuff it with one of the abovementioned [honey] cylinders, and shape the piece into a ring cookie (*kaʿka*) as was done above. (**112v**)

For those who want to stuff them with dates instead of honey, let them pound the dried dates (*tamr*) called *shadānaj* until they are as smooth as bone marrow (*mukhkh*)[4] after cleaning them and removing their stones. The same spices are added to them, and the rest is the same as mentioned above. In fact, this is what most people use.[5]

I.4.3 Another Kind [of *kaʿk*] Made Plain without Any Stuffing (*sādhaj*)

Take fine white flour (*daqīq darmak*), rub it with olive oil first and then add fennel seeds (*nāfiʿ*) to it, and knead it with hot water, in which salt has been dissolved, and a bit of fresh yeast (*khamīr*). Knead it vigorously and thoroughly. Divide the dough into pieces; size depends on how large, small, thick, or thin you want them to be.

---

2 BL MS, fol. 112r, calls it *ʿūd Mandalī*, see glossary 8.

3 See the previous recipe for the familiar spices used with these cookies.

4 The name of the dates designates hematite, also known as bloodstone, which must have resembled the color of the dates called after it. The editor of the Arabic text describes this date variety as being soft and thick fleshed and says it is a favored variety today in Marrakesh and southern Morocco (p. 68, n. 1). See glossary 7, s.v. *tamr*.

5 وهذا ما يعمله اكثر الناس, mentioned only in the Madrid MS, fol. 25r. The expression used to designate the dates in this MS is *shidakh al-tamr* 'crushed dates.'

Roll the pieces one after the other on a table, curve them to make *kaʿk* (ring cookies), and decorate them with the *minqāsh* as mentioned above. Put them on a board lightly dusted with flour and bake them. Wipe them [with a piece of clean cloth when they come out of the oven] and store them away in a vessel until they are served, God Almighty willing.

I.4.4 Making *kaʿb al-ghazāl* (the Gazelle's Ankle Bone)[6]

Moisten flour with a small amount of olive oil,[7] and knead it very well with hot water in which salt—but not yeast—is dissolved. Add fennel seeds (*nāfiʿ*), aniseeds (*anīsūn*), black pepper (*fulful*), and ginger (*zanjabīl*) to the dough.

Thoroughly pound sugar and almonds together until they bind. Put them in a large bowl (*mithrad*), add rosewater and the usual aromatic spices,[8] and then knead them to combine the ingredients. Grease your hands with olive oil and roll the mix into very thin cylinders.

Roll out [a piece of] dough on the table, place a filling cylinder along it, and fold it to enclose the filling. Roll it into a cylinder as was done with the *kaʿk*, but leave it as a long cylinder; do not curve it into a circle. Place it on a *malla* (earthenware plate) and slice it with a knife crosswise into small pieces; make them the size of a fava bean each, and keep them close to each other.[9] [Repeat with the rest of the dough].

Bake them as they are in the *malla* in which they were sliced. [After the baking is done,] separate the pieces and store them in a clean vessel until they are served.

The kind of cookies mentioned here are indeed a novelty (*mustaṭraf*). Some of the ingenious cooks would add pounded skinned pine nuts (*ḥabb al-ṣanawbar*) to the filling, and when they slice the cylinders, they would insert a whole skinned pine nut inside each one of the cookies. But this would require patience and precision.

For those who prefer the cookies without the filling, let them add the [filling's] known spices to the dough itself while kneading it and then shape it into the abovementioned cylinders, [and slice them,] so know this.

---

6 The small cookies are compared to the gazelle's talus bone, also called astragalus. These cubic bones were and still are used as dice in traditional games.

7 The Madid MS, fol. 25r, does mention amount of oil used.

8 See the first recipe in this chapter for the filling spices.

9 The fava bean comparison is found only in the Madrid MS, fol. 25r.

i.4.5 Making Stuffed *qanāniṭ* (Mock Reed Tubes)[10]

Thoroughly knead fine white flour (*daqīq darmak*) with water; without yeast. [Roll out the dough] and wrap it around reed joints (*jiʿāb min qaṣab*) to completely cover them.[11] Roll them on the table with open hands to even up the dough on the reed joints. (**113r**) Slice the dough only and make [mock] small reed joints (*jiʿāb*) with them; separate them from each other and let them dry out on the reeds as they are.

Put honey (*ʿasal*) in a cauldron (*ṭinjīr*), [boil it,] and remove its froth (*raghwa*). Mix it with pounded fine-tasting walnuts, which have been shelled and their skins removed.[12] Also add as much as needed of the aromatic spices usually used [with cookies, see first recipe], and if any of the dough that dried on the reeds [accidentally] breaks, pound it and mix it with the honey. Let the honey boil until it thickens (*yaʿqud*).

Take the dough off the reed joints; do this gently. Fry them in an earthenware cauldron (*ṭinjīr fakhkhār*) with sweet olive oil (*zayt ṭayyib*) until they brown. Stuff them with the abovementioned filling and stick skinned almonds on both ends of each joint. Sprinkle them with Ceylon cinnamon (*qirfa*) and sugar, and serve them, with the help of God Almighty.

i.4.6 Making *luqam al-qāḍī* (Judge's Morsels)

Thoroughly pound sugar with three times more of its amount of skinned almonds, and add the usual aromatic spices [as in the first recipe]. Make dough similar to that of *kaʿk* [see the first recipe], roll out [the pieces of] dough into rectangles, and stuff them with the filling. Shape them into walnut-like pastries, fry them in sweet olive oil (*zayt ʿadhb*), sprinkle them with sugar, and serve them, God Almighty willing.

---

10 Sg. *qannūṭ*/*qannūd* is a reed tube, see recipe i.4.24 below, where an actual reed tube is used. The resulting delicate pastries are the predecessors of the Italian cannoli. A similar recipe, which predates this by more than three centuries, is found in al-Warrāq, *Kitāb al-Ṭabīkh*, English trans., *Annals*, 425, where it is called *ḥalāqīm* (tubes). In the fourteenth-century Egyptian cookbook *Kanz al-Fawāʾid*, English trans., *Treasure Trove*, recipes 285 and 308, a comparable recipe is called Zaynab's fingers.

11 Sg. *jaʿb*, occurs as *kaʿb* in Ibn Manẓūr, *Lisān al-ʿArab*, s.v. كعب, where it is said to be a reed joint, i.e., part of the stalk between two nodes (*ʿuqad*, sg. *ʿuqda*). See glossary 9.1, s.v. *qaṣab*.

12 The skins are removed by soaking the shelled walnuts in hot water, as directed in recipe i.2.25 above.

I.4.7 Making *ādhān maḥshuwwa* (Stuffed Ears)

Knead fine white flour (*daqīq darmak*) as mentioned above [recipe i.4.5]; roll it out, [and divide it into portions, which you then] fold to make them resemble ears.[13] Fry them in a skillet (*miqlāt*) with sweet olive oil (*zayt ṭayyib*), and as soon as you take them out of the skillet, stuff them with the same filling used for the abovementioned reed joints [recipe i.4.5]. Sprinkle them with sugar and Ceylon cinnamon, and serve them once they cool, God Almighty willing.

I.4.8 Making a Variety of *ṭaʿām al-khubz* (Pastry)

Pound sugar and almonds as was done before [recipe i.4.1] and knead them with the usual aromatic spices. Knead fine white flour (*daqīq darmak*) and make dough similar to that of *kaʿk* [recipe i.4.1]. Shape it into forms like walnuts, almonds, pine nuts (*ṣanawbar*), and the like; large and small, all stuffed with the usual filling.

Fry whatever you have made of these in a cauldron (*ṭinjīr*) oil enough oil to submerge them—handle them with care and move them with the ladle gently until they brown. Put the finished ones in large and wide glazed bowls (*ṣiḥāf muzajjaja*) and pour all over them honey, which has been skimmed and boiled with rosewater until it thickens. Season them with aromatic spices and musk (*misk*), and serve them once they cool, God Almighty willing.

I.4.9 *Muqawwara maḥshuwwa* (Cored Out and Stuffed Pastries)[14]

Knead 1½ *raṭl*s (1½ pounds) fine white flour (*daqīq darmak*) with the yolks of 15 eggs, a bit of fresh yeast (*khamīr*), and enough milk to make a firm dough—not soft. Shape it into thin discs, and set them aside to ferment.

Put a skillet on the fire with sweet olive oil (*zayt ʿadhb*). Once it boils, put the discs in it, turning them several times until they slightly brown—be careful not

---

13 The recipe does not give instructions here. In the anonymous Andalusi *Anwāʿ al-ṣaydala* 78, a recipe for making ears describes how to do this: a piece of the dough is flattened thinly into a disc—the size of a hand or larger—and it is then folded twice. The folds are pressed a little, but the edge is kept open while frying with the help of a thin stick. An anecdote in al-Maqqarī, *Nafḥ al-ṭīb* iv 138, mentions pastries called *ādhān al-qāḍī* 'judge's ears,' which could be another name for the 'stuffed ears' in this recipe.

14 A copy of this recipe can also be found in the anonymous *Anwāʿ al-ṣaydala* 71. I used it to add some missing details in this version.

to fry them any longer. (113v) Take them out of the skillet and core them out as is done with *muqawwara*.[15]

Take out the crumbs inside the pastries and rub them very well between the hands. [Separately] pound sugar and shelled and skinned walnuts and almonds, mix the nuts [only]. Spread some of the nut mix inside the *muqawwara* followed by some of the crumbs, repeat until the cavity is full. [Note that] sugar is sprinkled after each of the two layers [of crumbs and nuts]. Sprinkle rosewater while layering.

Boil ghee (*samn*) and honey (*ʿasal*) and pour them on the *muqawwarāt* until they are well moistened. Return the [cut-out] covers, which have been taken from their tops, pour some more of the honey and ghee on the covers,[16] sprinkle them with sugar, and serve them, God Almighty willing.

i.4.10 Making *aqrāṣ maḥshuwwa* (Stuffed Discs of Pastry)

Knead 2 *raṭl*s (2 pounds) fine white flour (*daqīq darmak*) with water, fresh yeast (*khamīr*), and salt to make a rather moist dough. Prepare the filling with sugar and almonds as was done earlier (recipe i.4.1).

Roll out half the dough and spread half the filling on it. [Join the edges of the dough to enclose the filling] and flatten it into a disc by repeatedly pressing it with an open hand (*yulṭam*) with some olive oil. Set it aside to ferment, and then put it in an iron pan (*ṭājin ḥadīd*),[17] which has been greased with olive oil, and bake it in the *furn* (brick oven). As soon as it browns, put it in a glazed bowl (*ghaḍāra*) and pour hot honey (*ʿasal sukhn*) all over it after poking holes in it with your finger so that it absorbs enough of it. Scatter pine nuts (*ḥabb ṣanawbar*) on it and scent it with musk (*misk*).[18]

Make small discs with the other half of the dough and stuff them with the remaining filling. Fry them in sweet olive oil (*zayt ʿadhb*) and put them

---

15 The recipe assumes common knowledge of how such hollowed-out dishes are made. Luckily, we learn from the corresponding recipe, mentioned in the above note, how this was done: a wide circle is cut out from the top crust first; later to be used as a cover for the finished *muqawwara*.

16 The details related to the covers are from the corresponding recipe mentioned in the above note.

17 In the Madrid MS, fol. 27r, it occurs as *ṭājin jadīd fakhkhār muzajjaj* 'a new glazed earthenware pan.'

18 The recipe does not explain how musk was used to impart its essence; most probably it was crushed and dissolved in some of the heated honey or rosewater.

in [another] glazed bowl; pour boiled honey (*ʿasal maghlī*) on them, sprinkle them with pounded walnuts, scent them with musk, and serve all [the *aqrāṣ*] together, God Almighty willing.

I.4.11 Making Another Variety Called *mithradat al-amīr* (the Prince's *tharīd* Bowls)[19]

Thoroughly knead fine white flour (*daqīq darmak*) with water, salt, fresh yeast (*khamīr*), and a bit of olive oil. Make 4 thin discs with a portion of the dough. Fry them in a skillet with lots of sweet olive oil (*zayt ʿadhb*) until they turn deep brown[20] and then crush them into very fine crumbs.

With the rest of the dough, make small pastries similar to *mujabbanāt*:[21] shape them like [small pie] shells and make lids for them. Lightly fry the shells and their lids in sweet olive oil.

Finely pound sugar, shelled and skinned almonds (*lawz*), pine nuts (*ṣanawbur*), and pistachios (*fustuq*). Season them with aromatic spices (*afāwīh*) and rosewater[22] and mix them with the crushed crumbs. Fill the abovementioned *mujabbanāt*-like shells with this filling and cover them with the lids. The lids need to be securely put so that they do not scatter all around.

Arrange the pastries in a wide, shallow bowl (*ṣaḥfa*) and put the rest of the filling between the pieces. Drizzle rosewater on them, sprinkle them with crushed sugar, and moisten them with thick honey-rosewater syrup.[23]

---

19 In the Madrid MS, fol. 27r, the word occurs as *thurda*, which is a variant on the name of the dish, *tharīd*; it corresponds with a similar recipe in the anonymous *Anwāʿ al-ṣaydala* 71. In the case of *mithrada*, the filled, small pie-like pastries would resemble miniature *tharīd* bowls.

20 The expression used is *tashtaddu ḥumratuhā*, literally 'looks very red.' Due to lack of a name for the color brown in medieval Arabic, it was often expressed in terms of red.

21 *Mujabbanāt* recipes are given below, i.4.33–9. However, none of them are made into filled, pie-like shells as described here. We may have our clue in one of the *mujabbanāt* recipes provided in the thirteenth-century augmented copy of al-Warrāq's tenth-century Baghdadi *Kitāb al-Ṭabīkh*, Istanbul MS, fol. 234v, where *mujabbana* dough is shaped into small pot-like shells with lids (برمة مصنوعة من العجين).

22 See, for instance, the first recipe in this chapter for the kind of spices used in sweet pastries.

23 The recipe calls it *sharāb jullāb ʿasalī*. Its thick consistency is described as *qawī al-ʿaqd*. For drinking purposes, such syrups were usually made medium in consistency and used as needed, diluted with water, see glossary 1.

I.4.12 Making *jawzīnaq* (Walnut-Filled Pinwheels)[24]

Pound fine-tasting walnuts in a wooden mortar vigorously until they look like bone marrow (*mukhkh*). Sprinkle them with some hot water and rub them by hand to separate the oil.[25] Strain the oil and mix it with fine-tasting honey with its beeswax (*shahd*). [Set aside.]

Take another amount of walnuts, soak them in hot water, and peel off their skins. (**114r**) Cool them in cold water, wipe them [dry] with a clean piece of cloth, and pound them vigorously in a wooden mortar. Mix them with suitable amounts of pounded sugar and black pepper.[26] [This will be the filling; set it aside.]

Knead fine white flour (*daqīq darmak*) with water to make a thin dough. Mix egg whites with it—as needed. Put a *kunāfa* pan on the fire,[27] and when it is hot enough, wipe its surface with beeswax (*shamʿ*) and then wipe it clean with a piece of cloth; this will prevent the discs from sticking to the pan. Pour some of the batter into the pan and move it around to spread the dough and let it cover its base. If the batter looks a bit thick, thin it down with a small amount of water, and if the bread disc sticks to the pan, grease it with some more beeswax and then wipe it. Make more of these bread discs until you are left with some of the batter. Mix the egg yolks with this remaining batter and make more bread discs with it as was done with the first batch.

Take all the finished bread discs, [and one by one] sprinkle a wide path-like line of the abovementioned filling along the folding line [*ṭayy*, i.e., middle] of each disc;[28] and fold it in half first, and then fold it two more times (to make a log). Slice them into round pieces (*qiṭaʿ mudawwara*). Arrange them in a wide and shallow glazed bowl (*ṣaḥfa muzajjaja*) and drench them with the [walnut] oil, which has been mixed with honey (*ʿasal*).[29] Crushed sugar needs to be sprinkled underneath and on top of the pastry pieces, and serve them, God Almighty willing.

---

24 The text of the opening section about extracting walnut oil in the BL MS, fol. 113v, and the Berlin MS, fol. 14v, is a bit confused. Here I used the Madrid MS, fol. 27v, which offers a better text. Cf. another *jawzīnaq* recipe, ix.4.1 below, which is a confection.

25 See below, recipe x.10, for more details on extracting such oils.

26 According to the Madrid MS version, the sugar should be equal in weight to the walnuts, or a little bit more.

27 It is called *miqlāt al-kunāfa* in the BL and Berlin MSS and *mallat al-kunāfa* in the Madrid MS, fol. 28r. See below, recipe i.4.14, for more on this type of pan and the *kunāfa* crepes.

28 I followed the Madrid MS, fol. 28r, and replaced طرف مستقيلة with the more coherent طريق مستطيلة.

29 The beginning of the recipe mentions *shahd* to be mixed with the oil, but now it is referred

I.4.13 Making *lawzīnaq* (Almond-Filled Pinwheels)[30]

Make these the same way *jawzīnaq* is made, [just replace walnuts with almonds,] only black pepper is not used with it, so know this.

I.4.14 Making *kunāfa* (Crepes)

Moisten 2 *raṭl*s (2 pounds) of excellent quality semolina (*samīd*) with hot water. Set it aside, covered, to allow it to soften, and then knead it relentlessly.

Next, pour water on the dough and work it with the hand as is done when making a starchy thin batter (*talbīna*) used for starching clothes. Do this until all its starch is extracted. Strain the liquid with a tightly woven piece of cloth so that none of the semolina particles stay in it. [Allow the liquid to settle and then] pour off the clear water on top, leaving the settled starchy sediment like a [disc of] bread in the bottom of the vessel. Add enough water to make it neither thin nor thick in consistency.

Put the mirror (*mirʾāt*) used for making *kunāfa* on a flameless coal fire.[31] Once it heats up, wipe it with a clean piece of cloth that has been dipped in sweet olive oil (*zayt ʿadhb*) and then pour some of the [prepared] *talbīna* (thin starchy batter); enough to cover it [in a thin layer]. Let it cook for a short while until it becomes a *ruqāqa* (thin sheet of bread, a crepe); remove it and put it in a wide, shallow bowl (*ṣaḥfa*). Repeat with the rest of the *talbīna*, wiping the pan with a cloth dipped in oil before baking each one and scraping the sides of the pan with a knife to prevent the bread sheets from sticking, which will spoil them.

Melt ¼ *raṭl* (4 ounces) butter (*zubd*) or ghee (*samn*) on the fire, add 2 *raṭl*s (2 pounds) honey, and stir them. Black pepper may also be added if wished. Spread the *kunāfa* crepes [on a platter], drench them in the melted butter and honey, and eat them while still hot. Ghee is preferred to butter [in this dish].

For those who want to keep *kunāfa* for later use: thinly cut the crepes with a pair of scissors.[32] (**114v**) Put a new pot on the fire with enough honey, and when

---

to as *ʿasal*. More precisely, *shahd* is honey with its beeswax, and hence, it is thicker than regular honey. See glossary 4.

30 See below, recipe ix.4.2, for another *lawzīnaq*, which is almond brittle.

31 It is a round metal pan called *mirʾāt Hindiyya* 'Indian mirror' in the anonymous *Anwāʿ al-ṣaydala* 176. It is referred to as *miqlāt al-kunāfa* and *mallat al-kunāfa* in recipe i.4.12, see n. 27 above. See glossary 2, s.v. *kunāfa*; and 9.1, s.v. *mirʾāt al-kunāfa*.

32 They are more efficiently cut into long shreds by oiling the surfaces of several crepes, stack-

it comes to a boil, skim off the froth (*raghwa*). Add the [shredded] crepes and let them cook until the mix has almost thickened. Start pouring ghee or olive oil and continue adding it so long as the mix absorbs it; stop when enough is added.[33] Remove the pot from the fire and store the *kunāfa* in its pot until needed. It may be eaten cold or heated up, sprinkled with sugar and Ceylon cinnamon (*qirfa*) at the time of serving it, God willing.

Ghee is more suitable for these crepes than butter; and for those who want to use sweet olive oil (*zayt ṭayyib*) instead of butter or ghee, they can do so, which is what most people use in cooking it anyway.[34]

i.4.14b[35] Another Kind of *kunāfa* (Crepes)

Moisten fine-quality semolina flour (*samīd*) with hot water, set it aside for an hour, and then knead it with fresh yeast made with white flour,[36] salt, and ½ *raṭl* (½ pound) fine white flour (*daqīq darmak*). When all the ingredients mix and become one cohesive dough, pour hot water on it slowly while moving it with the hand until it thins down and resembles *ḥarīra* in consistency.[37] Put it in a new pot and set it aside to ferment. It will be fully fermented when separated liquid and holes appear on its surface.

Put a tinned skillet (*miqlāt muqaṣdara*) on the fire and let it heat up. Wrap some crushed salt in a clean piece of cloth, dip it in olive oil, and wipe the pan with it several times. Pour enough of the batter into the skillet and turn it right and left until it evens up and becomes like a thin sheet of *khabīṣ* [see recipe i.4.19 below]. Let it cook well but take care not to brown it; pull it out (*tuqlaʿ*) and spread it on a board (*lawḥ*) or table (*māʾida*). Make other crepes similarly until the batter is finished, wiping the pan with the cloth bundle with salt in it after each one is done.

Put all the crepes in a large, wide bowl (*jafna*) in one pile and slit them with a knife [all way through] in intersecting lines (*mutaqāṭiʿ*). Pour honey, which has

---

ing them, and then rolling them and slicing them thinly, as explained in the anonymous fourteenth-century Egyptian cookbook *Kanz al-fawāʾid*, English trans., *Treasure Trove*, recipe 298.

33 The sign is when the ghee or oil starts to separate from the honey mix.

34 This addition is from the Madrid MS, fol. 29r.

35 To avoid confusion, I followed the editor's numbering of the recipe in the Arabic edition here. The 'b' must have been added to rectify the unintentional repetition of no. 14.

36 *Khamīr darmak* is sour leavened dough made with fine white flour.

37 *Ḥarīra* is a thin, flour-based, silky smooth soup with a flowing consistency.

been boiled with butter or ghee, sprinkle them with Ceylon cinnamon (*qirfa*), and serve them, God Almighty willing.

I.4.15 Making *qaṭāʾif* (Pancakes), Which Is *mushahhada*[38]

Sift semolina flour (*samīd*) in a fine-meshed sieve (*ghirbāl ṣafīq*). Thoroughly dissolve fresh yeast (*khamīr*) and salt in hot water and [gradually] pour it on the flour while stirring it by hand until it becomes somewhat thick (*khāthir*). [Gradually] add fresh milk (*laban ḥalīb ṭarī*) to it while stirring it by hand until it starts to stick to the hand, but take care not to let it be too thin. Put the batter in a clean pot and place it close to a portable stove (*kānūn al-nār*), where it gets some of its heat without being touched by the fire. Leave it there until it ferments.

Take the special pan (*ṭājin*) used for making *qaṭāyif*,[39] whose bottom is textured with blind holes. Heat it on the fire and then wipe it with a clean piece of cloth in which salt is wrapped and dipped in fine-tasting ghee (*samn*). Pour the batter in small amounts to make small discs—as *qaṭāyif* are usually made. Once they develop holes [on top], take them out and make some more.

[After the first batch is done,] the batter needs to be tested [by tasting a pancake]; if it turns out to be a bit too sour, (**115r**) add semolina flour, salt, and milk—as needed—and stir the mix. Continue making *qaṭāyif* until you have what you need. Put them in a large, wide bowl (*jafna*) and drench them in boiled honey mixed with melted butter or ghee. Sprinkle them with black pepper, Ceylon cinnamon (*qirfa*), and sugar, and serve them, God Almighty willing.

---

38 *Mushahhada* 'looking like honeycombs' was its name in al-Andalus and al-Maghrib; in Ifrīqiya (the coastal regions of what today are western Libya, Tunisia, and eastern Algeria) it was also called *muṭanfasa* 'like carpets with smooth luxurious pile.' See Dozy, *Takmilat al-maʿājim* viii 327, s.v. *qaṭāʾif*. This kind of pastry is characterized by having holes on one side, which gave it the name *muthaqqaba* 'having holes,' see anonymous Andalusi cookbook *Anwāʿ al-ṣaydala* 184. See recipe i.2.16 above, where such pancakes are used in a *tharīd* dish.

39 The Madrid MS, fol. 30r, adds that it is made of glazed earthenware (*fakhkhār muzajjaj*).

1.4.16 Making *qaṭāʾif ʿAbbāsiyya* (Stuffed Pancakes Abbasid Style)[40]

Stir semolina flour (*samīd*) in hot water with salt and fresh yeast (*khamīr*) as was done in the previous recipe. Pound sugar and skinned almonds as was described [in previous recipes]; season them with the usual aromatic spices [see first recipe in this chapter] and a small amount of rosewater.

When the *qaṭāyif* are cooked in the usual manner [as in the previous recipe], dissolve wheat starch (*nashā*) in water. Next, take each piece of *qaṭāyif*, turn it [so that the smooth side is up], put some of the pounded stuffing in the middle, fold it in half, and press the edges—thus the side with holes will be on the outside. Dip the edges in the dissolved starch [to seal them] and fry them in a skillet (*miqlāt*) with sweet olive oil (*zayt ʿadhb*) to seal them quickly. Take them out of the skillet gently. Arrange them in a wide, shallow bowl (*ṣaḥfa*); sprinkle them with sugar, Ceylon cinnamon (*qirfa*), spikenard (*sunbul*), and a bit of almond oil. If frying them in almond oil is a possible alternative, that would be the best.

Alternatively, the almonds [in the stuffing] may be pounded and then dried so that they look like semolina,[41] and then they are pounded [once again] with white sugar, cloves (*qaranful*), and spikenard (*sunbul*). Once the *qaṭāyif* are fried in the *ṭājin* as mentioned earlier,[42] sprinkle each piece with the filling and then fold it on what is inside it so that it looks like half a circle. Bind the edges with dough, which has been thinned down with rosewater, and then fry the pieces in sweet olive oil until they brown. Drain them to get rid of the frying fat and then submerge them in rose-petal syrup (*sharāb ward*), rosewater syrup (*sharāb jullāb*), or mastic-infused syrup (*sharāb maṣṭakā*)[43] and serve.

Or, put every pair of pancakes together with some of the filling between them; bind their edges with batter [as above], fry them in a pan until they brown, and serve them, God Almighty willing.

---

40 A recipe by this name also occurs in the anonymous *Anwāʿ al-ṣaydala* 196–7. It describes a similar recipe but differs stylistically at several places.

41 The reference here is to semolina that is sandy in texture and not semolina flour. See glossary 2.

42 *Miqlāt* and *ṭājin* are used synonymously in this recipe.

43 See glossary 1 for more on these syrups.

I.4.17 Making *muwarraqa* (Laminated Pastry), Which Is *musammana* (Layered with Ghee)[44]

Knead semolina flour (*samīd*) or fine white flour (*daqīq darmak*) with water and salt. Let the kneading be vigorous by rubbing and pressing it.[45] Melt ghee (*samn*) and use it to flatten very thinly a piece of the dough that is in the kneading bowl (*miʿjana*). Grease its surface with ghee and fold it upon itself. Flatten it again, [grease it with *samn*, and fold it again].[46] Flatten the piece by repeatedly pressing it with open hands (*tulṭam*), and put it in a [heated] skillet (*miqlāt*) or an earthenware plate (*malla*) set on the fire after greasing it with a bit of ghee so that the bread does not burn.

Take the bread from the skillet [or the plate] and strike it by hand to loosen and separate the layers. Put it in a large, wide bowl (*mithrad*), cover it with a piece of cloth, (**115v**) and repeat with the other pieces of dough until they are all done. Drench them in hot honey, sprinkle them with Ceylon cinnamon (*qirfa*) and sugar, and serve them, God Almighty willing.

For those who choose to make them by dividing the dough into small discs, greasing each one of them with ghee and stacking them in piles, and then rolling each stack into a very thin disc with a rolling pin or by hand, and serving them drenched in honey after baking them in the *malla* as mentioned above, they can go ahead and do so. So know this.

I.4.18 Another Kind of *muwarraqa*, Wonderful[47]

Knead fine white flour (*daqīq darmak*) into moist dough [by adding enough water]. Then knead in olive oil to make it really moist. Use yeast (*khamīr*) in making it.

---

44 The first name of this pastry describes its texture, whereas the second derives from the ingredient used for the layering.

45 The verb used is *yuʿarrak*, which is done more effectively with the heel of the hand; cf. *yuʿjan*, which is a more general term for kneading, used at the beginning of the recipe. The corresponding recipe in the anonymous *Anwāʿ al-ṣaydala* 179 confirms that no yeast is used. It also describes the well-kneaded dough as being soft and elastic in texture; you have to be able to pull a piece of it without it breaking.

46 In the corresponding recipe in the anonymous *Anwāʿ al-ṣaydala*, the dough is handled a bit differently: a piece of dough is flattened thinly on a board, greased with ghee, and then rolled like a rug (*ḥaṣīr*), which is then coiled and flattened until it turns into a thin disc.

47 *ʿAjība*, as described in the Madrid MS, fol. 31r.

Roll the dough out into a disc with thin edges. Fold it upon itself, blow into it, and twist the edges to trap the blown air in.[48] Do this several times, rotating the direction of the fold.[49] Shape it into a thick disc; put it in an earthenware pan (*ṭājin fakhkhār*) with olive oil poured in it. Press the disc with the finger at several places to make hollows (*madāhin*, sg. *mudhun*) and pour some olive oil all over it. Bake it in the *furn* (brick oven) until it browns and then take it out. Pour hot honey all over it, sprinkle it with Ceylon cinnamon (*qirfa*), and serve it.

For those who want to prepare it with rendered suet (*shaḥm mudhāb*), let them knead and roll out the dough with it and follow what was earlier mentioned of blowing and baking it. Honey poured on it should be boiling hot (*maghlī*) to keep the suet from solidifying, so know this with God's help and might.

I.4.19 Making *khabīṣ* (Thick Pudding with Crushed Starch Bread)

Clean coarsely crushed wheat (*jashīsh al-qamḥ*). Keep it soaked in water for a couple days and then vigorously rub the grains between the hands on the third day until the liquid looks white and is thicker in consistency. Strain it repeatedly until nothing remains [of the crushed grains] but the strained starchy liquid,[50] which has the consistency of yogurt (*rāyib*).[51]

Put a tinned iron skillet (*miqlāt ḥadīd muqaṣdara*) on the fire; remove it once it gets hot and then grease it with a bit of beeswax (*shamʿ*) and wipe it with a piece of new cloth. Return it to the fire and pour in some of the wheat starch liquid—add enough to cover its base. Once it sets into a white sheet and looks dry, peel it away gently and immediately spread it on a clean sieve in a sunny place. Wipe the skillet with beeswax and make other pieces until all the wheat liquid is used up.

Wiping the skillet with beeswax two or three times is necessary before baking a piece. Additionally, they need to be protected from dust or ash. If you want them yellow, then color the wheat starch liquid with saffron.

---

48 My guess is that at least three-quarters of the edge would have been twisted, and then it is blown and immediately twisted all the way. This would indeed trap the blown air more effectively.

49 Based on a detail given towards the end of this recipe, in the process of rolling out the dough and folding it, melted ghee (*samn*) is first spread on the dough before folding it, as was also done in the previous recipe.

50 The resulting liquid is referred to here as صفو الجشيش ولبابه 'starchy strained liquid from the coarsely crushed wheat,' see glossary 2, s.v. *lubāb*.

51 See below, chapter VI.2, for *rāyib* recipes.

When all the discs are finished, dry them in the sun spread on a sieve, which is set on a cage-like basket (*maḥbas*)[52] placed on a mat (*ḥaṣīr*). When they are completely dry,[53] [and to make sure that they are completely dry,] boil enough ghee (*samn*) in a pan and put one of the bread discs in it. If it floats to the surface immediately, this would be an indication that it is dry, (**116r**) but if it sinks to the bottom, it is not dry enough yet, and in this case, the bread discs are to be dried by exposing them to the heat of the fire provided it does not spoil them. [Once they are all dry,] fry them in the boiling ghee until they turn white. Put them in a clean large kneading bowl (*miʿjana*)[54] and turn them gently to let the excess frying fat they absorbed drip down.

Next, rub the bread discs between the hands [to crush them] and sift them through a sieve made of woven esparto grass (*ghirbāl ḥalfā*) into a clean large and wide bowl (*jafna*). Whatever remains in the sieve, rub it again between the hands and sift it. Do this until none of the bread particles remain. If the sieve holes get blocked, strike it by hand to unblock them. Cover the bowl to keep the crushed bread clean of dirt.[55]

Put strained honey with its beeswax (*shahd muṣaffā*) in a tinned copper pot; use the needed amount for making *khabīṣ* pudding. Do not use honey that is too reddish brown. Add the needed amount of egg whites (*raqīq al-bayḍ*); whip them together until the mix starts to look white. Put the pot on a low fire and continue stirring until the mix cooks and thickens. Add the *khabīṣ* [crushed bread] along with black pepper and continue stirring the pot on the fire for about an hour. Remove it from the fire when the ghee starts to [separate and] becomes visible.[56] Push the pudding to one side of the pot with the ladle [to separate it from the fat], ladle it out into a clean vessel, and put it away until it is time to serve it, God Almighty willing.

---

52 According to Dozy, *Takmilat al-maʿājim* iii 45, s.v. حبس, *maḥbas* is another name for *qafaṣ*.

53 The Madrid MS, fol. 32r, offers a better version in what follows than that of the BL and Berlin MSS. I used it to amend the text.

54 It is usually used for making bread dough.

55 This crushed bread will be referred to as *khabīṣ* in the following steps.

56 Since no additional ghee is added while it is boiling, we may assume that this would have been the fat that the *khabīṣ* discs absorbed when they were fried earlier.

i.4.20 Another Kind of *khabīṣ*, Well Recommended (*mustaḥsan*)[57]

Make thin sheets of bread (*ruqāq*) using wheat starch (*nashā*), which has been dissolved in water until it has the consistency of yogurt (*rāyib*),[58] as is done with the thin sheets for *jūdhāba*.[59] Set them aside to dry and then crush them to resemble fine breadcrumbs.[60]

Boil sweet olive oil (*zayt ʿadhb*) in a skillet and fry the *khabīṣ* [crumbs] in it, stirring quickly all the time lest they should burn. Strain them in a sieve to drain the oil and then throw them into thickened honey, which has been cooked in a separate pot on low heat. Leave the pot on the remaining heat so that it stays soft (*māʾiʿ*). Every time you fry an amount of the crumbs and drain them, immediately, and while still hot, throw them into the honey. Stir the mix with a ladle and vigorously combine the ingredients until they completely blend. Do this until all the crumbs are added.

[Skinned] almonds may be added to it; it may also be colored with saffron after the cooking is done so that it has reddish spots, if that is the desired look. Also, making the thin sheets of bread (*ruqāq*) using starch (*lubāb*), which has been freshly extracted from strained semolina (*samīd muṣaffā*),[61] would be much better than using [dried] wheat starch (*nashā*),[62] which is easily susceptible to mold (*ʿafan*) and goes bad and sour (*khamaj*).

i.4.21 Another Kind of *khabīṣ*, Exotic (*mustaṭraf*)[63]

Take one part fine-tasting honey and three parts water; put them in a cauldron (*ṭinjīr*) set on moderate heat until the froth appears [and discard it]. Color it with saffron and add equal amounts of Ceylon cinnamon (*qirfa*) and black pep-

57 As described in the Madrid MS, fol. 32v.

58 See below, chapter vi.2, for *rāyib* recipes.

59 The reference here is to *jūdhāba* recipe iii.2.31 below, where directions for making *ruqāq* are indeed promised but not given. Go to above recipes i.4.14 and 19 for *ruqāq*-making details. From the several references we have in this book and the anonymous Andalusi *Anwāʿ al-ṣaydala*, it is clear that the thin sheets of bread, called *ruqāq*, made for *khabīṣ*, *kunāfa*, and *jūdhāba* are prepared the same way and can be used interchangeably. See glossary 2, s.v. *ruqāq*.

60 I here followed the Madrid MS, fol. 32v, where the expression occurs as وتهشم كالفتات الدق, rather than the confused ويهشم بالفتاة الدق in the other two MSS.

61 As was done earlier in recipe i.4.14.

62 It is the kind of starch that is stored and used as needed. See glossary 2.

63 As described in the Madrid MS, fol. 33r. I used this MS to amend the text at several places.

per, as well as spikenard—one-sixth of their [combined] amounts. Feed the fire with wood and let the pot boil until some of the water evaporates and the honey cooks well.

[Away from the fire,] throw into the honey good-quality, coarsely crushed semolina (*samīd khashin*), which has been sifted to remove its flour (*daqīq*) and bran (*nukhāla*). Add it bit by bit while stirring the pot until it resembles thick, cereal-based soup (*ḥasū*) in consistency.[64] [Return the pot to the fire and] add olive oil; do this three times until the *khabīṣ* can no longer absorb it. (**116v**). Remove the pot from the fire and serve it after it cools, God Almighty willing.

Know that for each *qādūs* (6 pounds) of semolina,[65] 2 *dirhams* (6 grams) of saffron and 3 *raṭls* (3 pounds) of honey are used.

i.4.22 Making Good-Quality[66] *ruqāq al-khabīṣ* (Thin Sheets of Starch Bread)

Take the needed amount of wheat starch (*nashā*), dissolve it in cold water, enough to make it look like melted beeswax in consistency. Put a *mirʾāt al-kunāfa* (round metal plate) on low heat,[67] wipe it with olive oil using a clean piece of cloth, and pour the dissolved starch to make thin sheets of bread as was done with *kunāfa* [recipe i.4.14]. Hang all the finished ones on a clean rope to air-dry and then store them away and use as needed, with the help of God Almighty and His power.

i.4.23 Making *fālūdhaj* (Starch-Based Thick Pudding)

Clean coarsely crushed wheat grains and thoroughly winnow them (*yunfaḍ*). Put them in a large earthenware tub (*qaṣriyya*) and rinse them five to six times until the water comes out clean. Soak them in enough water to submerge them, and let them stay there for a long while, and then pour off the water without disturbing the grains. Next, rub the grains by hand against the sides of the tub; pour water on them again and rub them between the hands. Put a hair sieve (*ghirbāl shaʿr*) on another sieve, which is placed above another tub. Pour the

---

64 See *ḥasū* recipes in chapter i.3 above.

65 *Qādūs* is an earthenware vessel, also used as a capacity measure, which equals 3 *mudds* (each *mudd* equals approx. 2 *raṭls*/pounds). See glossary 9.1 for *qādūs* the vessel.

66 *Jayyida*, as described in the Madrid MS, fol. 33v.

67 See n. 31 for more on this tool.

contents [of the first tub] over the sieves so that no water remains with the grains [that have accumulated in the sieves]. Return the drained grains to the [first] tub, add water, and then rub the grains between the hands and strain them as above. Do this three times.[68]

Wash the sieves and the [first] tub very well and resume the process of rubbing the grains with water and straining them [into the second tub]. Do this three more times. [Allow the strained liquid in the second tub to settle and then] pour off the [clear] water so that nothing remains but a starchy solution (*lubāb*), which is pure and thick. Color it with saffron and stir it; add a bit of salt to it.

Put fine-tasting honey with its beeswax (*shahd*) in a tinned copper cauldron (*ṭinjīr nuḥās muqaṣdar*) and boil it on the fire until the froth is skimmed off and the honey almost thickens. Add plenty of fine-tasting ghee (*samn*); let it boil once with honey and then add the starch solution—double the amount of honey. Let the pot cook gently on low heat; stir it all the time, reaching the bottom of the pot while doing this so that it does not burn.

When it has almost reached the desired thickness and looks smooth, remove the pot from the fire and put it on embers (*ghaḍā*). Stir the pot with a ladle as is done with *ʿaṣīda* (smooth and dense flour-based soup). If it looks like it is thickening too much, pour in a bit of hot water; if it does not look fatty enough, add more ghee (*samn*) and return the pot to the fire so that the fat cooks and mixes with it, (117r) but take care not to let it burn. Season it with black pepper, and put it in a clean bowl (*ṣaḥfa*), and eat it salubriously, God Almighty willing.

I.4.24 Making *ra's maymūn* (Blessed Head)[69]

Moisten semolina flour with hot water and knead it very well after adding a bit of fine white flour (*daqīq darmak*), fresh yeast (*khamīr*), and salt. Add water

---

68 The aim of this process is to collect the strained liquid in the second tub.

69 *Maymūn* could be a man's name; it is also a generic name that designates 'slave' and 'monkey.' I chose to interpret it this way because the recipe clearly explains that it is supposed to look like a human head, and *maymūn*, as an adjective, means 'blessed,' 'prosperous,' etc. Marks, *Encyclopedia of Jewish Food*, s.v. *mimouna*, 407–8, suggests that it is a man's name that was associated with Jews. Another possibility, which he connects to medieval North African folklore, is that Mimouna was a female demon or goddess, who was regarded as Lady Luck, and her husband is another demon, whose name was Mimoun.

A copy of this recipe is also included in the anonymous Andalusi *Anwāʿ al-ṣaydala* 69. I used it here to slightly amend the edited text. I also used the Madrid MS, fol. 34v, for the same purpose. See the below recipe for another *ra's maymūn*, this time stuffed with squabs; and recipe ii.2.44, cooked with mutton.

little by little and knead it to a medium consistency. Mix it with ghee (*samn*) and 4 eggs for each *raṭl* (pound) [of semolina used]. Continue beating it with water and ghee until it thins down.

Take a new glazed earthenware pot that has a rounded body and a neck. Pour some ghee and olive oil into it [and move it around] to coat its interior. Pour the dough to fill the pot up to its lower neck and insert in the middle of the dough a reed tube (*qannūṭ*) that is open from one end to the other [i.e., hollow][70] after greasing it with ghee. Set the pot aside to let the dough ferment.

Once holes can be seen on the face of the dough, which is a sign that it has fermented, send the pot to the *furn* (communal brick oven) and let it bake at a distance from the fire until it is done. When taken out of the oven, shake the pot gently to loosen the [baked] dough from the sides and then break it carefully bit by bit so that it comes out in one piece. For the places where it does not separate, pour a bit of ghee on them and gently try with them so that it comes out unbroken. [This is important] because the main purpose of this pastry is to make it look like a human head (*ra's insān*). Take out the reed and fill the hole it made with ghee and honey or butter and honey.

Put the head as it is in a wide, shallow bowl (*ṣaḥfa*); stick cleaned pine nuts (*ṣanawbar*), pistachios, and almonds in it. Pour ghee melted in [hot] honey all over it, and sprinkle it with fine sugar, and serve it, God Almighty willing.

I.4.25 Another Kind of *ra's maymūn*, Stuffed [with a Squab][71]

Knead 1 *raṭl* (1 pound) of fine white flour (*daqīq darmak*) [with water] until it is somewhat moist. Knead it again with ½ *raṭl* ghee (*samn*), water, and 10 eggs. Beat them all until the dough becomes moist and soft.

Clean a squab (*farkh ḥamām*); remove its entrails [and set it aside]. Next, take breadcrumbs (*fatāt khubz*) and skinned almonds and mix them with 5 eggs; add black pepper, cassia (*dār Ṣīnī*), spikenard (*sunbul*), juices of cilantro and mint, a bit of pounded onion, and salt as needed. Chop the gizzard and liver of the squab and stuff the squab's cavity with all these ingredients [after

70 I replaced the irrelevant *munfarid* in the BL MS, fol. 117r, and Berlin MS, fol. 18r, with *manfūdh al-ṭarafayn* (open from one end to the other, like a tube), as it is copied in the Madrid MS, fol. 34v.

71 The anonymous Andalusi *Anwāʿ al-ṣaydala* 72 has a similar recipe, but this one is more complete.

mixing them]. Insert a boiled egg inside the stuffing in the cavity. Put the squab in a wide pot with water, salt, olive oil, coriander seeds, and chopped onion and cook the pot on the fire [until done].

Take another [glazed earthenware] pot with a rounded body and neck, pour olive oil into it [and move it around] to grease its interior. [First] pour some of the dough, then place the squab on it, and then pour the rest of the dough on the squab. Set the pot aside to ferment for an hour and then send it to the *furn* (communal brick oven) to bake. When it is done, gently break the pot after shaking it gently to loosen it from the walls of the pot. (117v)

Put the entire bread as it is in a wide, shallow bowl (*ṣaḥfa*), pour ghee mixed with boiled honey (*ʿasal maghlī*) all over it. Garnish it with toasted pine nuts (*ṣanawbar muḥammaṣ*), and sprinkle it with sugar, and serve it, God Almighty willing.

It may also be made in another way:
Chop the squab into small pieces, which you then put in a pot on the fire with salt, olive oil, black pepper, coriander seeds, and a bit of chopped onion. Once the meat has cooked, take it out of the pot and put it in a clean skillet, adding juices of cilantro and mint with 8 eggs, salt, black pepper, Ceylon cinnamon (*qirfa*), cassia (*dār Ṣīnī*), spikenard (*sunbul*), cloves (*qaranful*), and *murrī* (liquid fermented sauce). Mix them all with the meat [and set aside].

In another skillet, put the strained broth of the cooked squab with a small amount of olive oil. Once they boil, add them to the meat-eggs mix and stir the skillet until they brown and the eggs set, but be careful not to let them burn.[72]

Next, pound skinned almonds with pistachios and sugar until they all blend; knead them with rosewater and the spices mentioned in the above recipe. Prepare the dough as mentioned above.

[Now start layering the ingredients:][73] put [one-third] of the dough in the bottom of the [abovementioned glazed earthenware]. Put half the amount of the meat-egg mix on top of it; followed with [half] the sugar-nut mix. Once again, put [one-third of the] dough, followed by the rest of the meat-egg mix and then the rest of the sugar-nut mix. The last layer to be added is the rest of the dough. But do not forget to first pour olive oil or ghee into the pot to grease its interior, as this would prevent the dough from sticking to it.

72 The Madrid MS, fol. 36r, clearly instructs that the boiled broth is to be added to the meat-egg skillet, and not vice versa, as is mentioned in the other two MSS. This would indeed justify using two skillets.

73 I followed the Madrid MS because it is more lucid here than the text in the other two MSS.

Take the pot to the *furn* (communal brick oven) [and let it be put] at a distance from the fire until it bakes and browns. [Take it out,] break it gently, and do with it as was mentioned above. Pour ghee melted in [hot] honey all over it, sprinkle it with sugar, and eat it salubriously, God Almighty willing.

I.4.26 Making *murakkaba* (Assembled Crepes)[74]

Knead fine-tasting semolina flour with hot water into a hard dough and continue kneading, adding water with salt and a bit of fresh yeast (*khamīr*); continue adding water [in small amounts] and kneading the dough for a while until it becomes thin in consistency. Knead it again after adding egg whites—for each *raṭl* (pound) of semolina use the whites of 4 eggs—until the whites blend with the dough.

Put a wide unglazed earthenware pan (*ṭājin fakhkhār ghayr muzajjaj*) on the fire. As soon as it gets hot, wipe it with a piece of cloth in which salt is tied and then dipped in olive oil or melted ghee. Pour some of the dough into the pan to make a flat, thin sheet of bread (*raghīf raqīq*);[75] once it looks white, spread some more of the dough to coat it and flip the two together. Repeat with the rest of the dough—coating the top layer and flipping them together. When finished, all the layered discs of bread will look as if they were one piece, whereas in reality it is made of many layers assembled on top of each other.

Once finished, put it in a wide vessel (**118r**) and pour [heated] honey and ghee to cover it. Sprinkle it with Ceylon cinnamon (*qirfa*), and eat it salubriously, God Almighty willing.

---

74 A corresponding recipe in the anonymous Andalusi *Anwāʿ al-ṣaydala* 184 describes it as specialty of Qusanṭīna (Constantine), where it is called *Kutāmiyya*, derived from Kutām/Kutāma, a major Amazigh tribe in north Algeria. Constantine is a region in northeast Algeria.

This pastry must have been the prototype of today's Moroccan *maflūta* 'flipped,' made at the end of Passover on the Moroccan Jewish festival of Maymūna. Thin layers of leavened dough are fried and served with butter and honey. The etymological connection lies in the traditional way this pastry is prepared: when one layer is fried, another disc of the flattened dough is spread on top of it and flipped; then, another disc is put on top and the whole structure is flipped again; and so on until one ends up with a pile assembled of fried layers of crepes that are stuck to each other.

75 I used the corresponding recipe in *Anwāʿ al-ṣaydala* to provide several missing details.

i.4.27 Making *maqrūḍ* (Stuffed Cookie Bars), Fantastic[76]

Do with semolina flour (*samīd*) as was mentioned earlier[77] and then knead it very well with fresh yeast (*khamīr*) and a small amount of water. Prepare a filling of sugar and almonds as was mentioned earlier [in recipe i.4.1].

Roll out the dough into a square (*murabbaʿ*), put the filling along the middle part, [fold and seal the two sides of the square to enclose the filling,] and roll the strip as is usually done with *kaʿk*. Gently flatten the roll by repeatedly pressing it with an open hand (*yulṭam*) and slice it with a thin-bladed knife (*sikkīn murhaf*) into pieces, one finger long each and as wide as two fingers put together [approx. 4 inches by 1½ inches].

Fry the pieces in a skillet with olive oil until golden. Put them in a vessel [to drain them] until they look dry and then put them in a glass platter (*ṭabaq zujāj*); sprinkle them with sugar and serve them, God willing.

For those who want to fill the cookies with dates (*tamr*), let them prepare the filling exactly as was done with the *kaʿk* [date] filling mentioned earlier [recipe i.4.2]; and then they are fried as mentioned above, so know this, with the help of God Almighty.

i.4.28 Making *mushāsh Zubayda* (Zubayda's Ribs)[78]

Grind fine-tasting semolina flour (*samīd*) until it becomes [as fine as] *darmak* (fine white flour). Knead it with [water and] fresh yeast (*khamīr*) very thor-

---

76 As described in the Madrid MS, fol. 36v, which I used here to amend the text at several places. The name of this cookie derives from *q-r-ḍ* 'cut'; called so because they are not free-form pastries but cut into bars.

77 The recipe suggests here that the dough for these cookies is similar to that of *kaʿk* in recipe i.4.1 above, where semolina flour is first moistened and rubbed with olive oil and then kneaded.

78 *Mushāsh* generally designates the cartilaginous ends of bones that are soft and can be gnawed and sucked, such as the ends of chicken legs. The name of the recipe and the instructions given suggest that the resulting puffed pastries will look like breastbones (sternums) with the costal rib cartilages attached to them, called *mushāsh al-zūr* in medieval Arabic, see Ibn Manẓūr, *Lisān al-ʿArab*, s.v. مشش; nowadays called *al-ghuḍrūf al-ḍilʿī*. Reference to Zubayda, a girl's name, is obscure.

The anonymous *Anwāʿ al-ṣaydala* has three *mushāsh* recipes, with no reference to Zubayda, and they are different in details from this one. What they all have in common, however, is that the pastries are delicate and brittle. The *mushāsh* we encounter in the fourteenth-century, anonymous Egyptian cookbook, *Kanz al-fawāʾid*, English trans., *Trea-*

oughly. Take fine, fresh kidney fat (*shaḥm al-kilā*) and trim off the sinews (*ʿurūq*) and outer skin. Pound it in a mortar (*mihrās*) until it becomes as smooth as bone marrow (*mukhkh*).

Spread the dough into thin round sheets, smear each one with some of the pounded fat, and roll it the way a piece of paper is rolled.[79] Cut each roll into three pieces; bring together both ends of each piece and flatten it out with a rolling pin (*jawbak*). Using a knife, make cuts [on both sides] (*tushaqq*); four of them or whatever the size of the piece will allow.

Fry the pieces in a cauldron (*ṭinjīr*) with plenty of olive oil; pour some more oil if needed to keep them submerged in it while frying. Once they cook and puff, take them out of the oil and place them on sticks or a sieve put on a bowl until they look dry. Spread them in a vessel in one layer and drench them in honey, which has been boiled and its froth removed. Shell and skin walnuts and almonds, pound them coarsely, and scatter them on the pastries. Sprinkle them as well with black pepper, ginger (*zanjabīl*), Ceylon cinnamon (*qirfa*), hulled and unhulled sesame seeds (*simsim*), and sugar, and eat them salubriously, God Almighty willing.

I.4.29 Making *zalābiya* (Fried Latticed Fritters Dipped in Honey), Amazing[80]

Take a large piece of sour fermented dough (*khamīr*), dissolve it in water until it has the consistency of thickish yogurt (*laban khāthir*), strain it into a pot, and add sifted fine white flour (*daqīq darmak*) to it. (118v) Stir the mix, and when it dissolves, add more of the flour [gradually] until the mix looks smooth and neither thick nor thin in consistency.[81]

---

sure Trove, recipe 284, are lollipops, in which case the other meaning of *mushāsh* 'soft ends of bones that can be sucked and chewed' applies.

I used the Madrid MS, fol. 37r–v, to fill in details not found in the other two MSS.

79 تدرج درج اسجل, theMadrid MS explains.

80 As described in the Madrid MS, fol. 37v.

81 The recipe in *Anwāʿ al-ṣaydala* 199 also suggests coloring the dough differently: a portion of it may be colored red with *baqqam* 'sapanwood' (*Caesalpinia sappan*), from which red dye is obtained, *lukk*, which is the sweet-smelling deep red secretion of lac insects, especially the species *Kerria lacca*, or *fuwwa* 'madder.' Another portion may be colored golden yellow with saffron; and green with the juice of fresh fennel (*rāzyānaj akhḍar ṭarī*) and *ʿinab al-thaʿlab* 'black nightshade' (*Solanum nigrum*).

Pour some of the batter into a drinking vessel (*qadaḥ*), which has a hole in its bottom as wide as the little finger. You should have ready on the fire a skillet with lots of olive oil in it.[82] Close the hole with your finger, position the vessel exactly above the skillet, and then remove the finger from the hole and let the batter flow while moving the vessel to make discs with latticework and other designs.[83]

As soon as the pieces rise up to the surface (*intaṣaba*),[84] take them out immediately, [hold them briefly to] let the [extra] oil drip, and then immerse them in honey, which has been boiled and its foam skimmed. Keep them there until they absorb enough honey and then take them out and place them on a board (*lawḥ*) or a lattice of reeds (*shubbāk min qaṣab*), and keep them there until they look dry.

If the batter turns out to be thin, add more flour to it, [mix it,] and set it aside to ferment, and then make [*zalābiya*] pieces with it; and serve them, God Almighty willing.

1.4.30 Making *isfanj* (Yeasted Fritters, *buñuelos*), Good and Tasty[85]

Moisten fine-tasting semolina flour (*samīd*) with hot water, adding salt and fresh yeast (*khamīr*). Set it aside to soften and then knead it into hard dough. Start adding water to it little by little while kneading it for some time until it becomes soft in consistency. While thus kneading it, [every now and then] lift all the dough by hand and quickly return it to the kneading bowl (*miʿjana*) to incorporate air into it. Set it aside until it rises.

Put a clean tinned copper or iron skillet on the fire with the needed amount of olive oil;[86] as soon it boils, take a portion of the dough with your left hand and press it with your palm so that some of it comes out through the thumb and

---

82 The text misses an important detail regarding the oil used, which is included in the corresponding recipe in *Anwāʿ al-ṣaydala*. It stresses the importance of frying with plenty of very hot oil; otherwise, too little oil or not hot enough will cause the batter to stick to the pan.

83 The word used for latticeworks is *sarājīb*, sg. *sarjab*, which is the dialectal pronunciation of *sharjab* 'lattice window.' See Corriente, *Dictionary of Andalusi Arabic*, s.v. *sh-j-b*.

84 This would be a sign of doneness. The sign of doneness in the Madrid MS, fol. 37v, is when a piece turns white.

85 *Jayyid malīḥ*, as described in the Madrid MS, fol. 37v.

86 According to an *isfanj* recipe in the anonymous Andalusi *Anwāʿ al-ṣaydala* 112, the frying pan is to be filled with oil.

index fingers—the size depends whether you want to make it large or small; cut it off and put it in the skillet. Repeat until there are enough pieces frying in the oil.

To make the big ones, which are called *aqṣād*,[87] do not cover them with oil; instead, let it come to the level of their lower halves only, which will turn golden brown (*aḥmar*), whereas the upper halves will stay white. Move them gently until they are done and take them out and serve them.

To make the small ones, which are called *mughdir*,[88] put plenty of fat in the frying pan and cut the dough by squeezing it through the palm of the hand as previously mentioned; make the pieces as small as desired.

When the pan is full of the frying *isfanj* pieces and they start to brown, take them out and put them in a vessel. Start filling the pan with another batch of the *isfanj* pieces. When these start to brown, return the first batch to the pan and stir them all until they all cook and crisp.

Take them out of the pan and put them in a wooden vessel (*wiʿāʾ min ʿūd*), that is, after putting them first in another vessel to drain off their fat, and eat them, God willing.[89]

To test the dough before frying, shape a piece like a ring cookie (*kaʿk*) and drop it into the fat. If it keeps its shape while frying and rises to the surface once it is done, and its inside gets filled with holes, this is a sign that the dough is fully fermented; otherwise, leave it for a while to fully ferment, with the help of God Almighty.

I.4.31 Making Light and Airy Yeasted Fritters (*isfanj al-rīḥ*)[90]

(**119r**) Knead fine white flour (*daqīq darmak*) with water, salt, fresh yeast (*khamīr*), and sweet olive oil. Continue kneading it while adding water bit by bit until the dough becomes almost soft in consistency. Set it aside to ferment.

Put a skillet on the fire with plenty of olive oil. Make a piece with the fingers [as was done in the previous recipe], throw it into the oil, and continue until all

87 The name must have been derived from *qaṣd* 'breaking something in half,' Ibn Manẓūr, *Lisān al-ʿArab*, s.v. قصد. The finished fritters would look as if they were cut in half.

88 The dark color of the pieces, due to the thorough browning, must have inspired the name. In Ibn Manẓūr, *Lisān al-ʿArab*, s.v. غدر, *mughdir* designates a 'dark night.'

89 They were usually served as a sweet pastry, either sprinkled with sugar or drizzled with honey, as clearly explained in one of the *isfanj* recipes in the anonymous Andalusi *Anwāʿ al-ṣaydala* 62.

90 Literally *rīḥ* is 'air' and 'wind.'

the dough is used up. For those who want to make them puffed, let them knead the dough with eggs and continue as above.

i.4.32 Making *isfanj al-qulla* (Sponge Pastry Baked in an Earthenware Jar)[91]

Knead semolina flour (*samīd*) or fine white flour (*darmak*) into a soft and light dough as was mentioned earlier [in the above recipes].

Take a new earthenware jar (*qulla*) and pour plenty of olive oil in it, enough to flow on its inner walls so that they absorb it and some of it remains in the bottom. As soon as the dough ferments, fill the jar with it almost to its neck. In the middle of the dough insert the stem of a stripped date palm frond (*jarīdat nakhl*) or a hollowed reed after greasing it with oil.[92]

Take the jar to the *furn* (communal brick oven) and let it be put at a distance from the fire until it bakes. Take it out, shake it gently, and remove the reed. Pour honey and ghee or butter into the hole made by the reed, leave it for a short while, and then gently break the jar so that the pastry inside it does not break. Sprinkle it with Ceylon cinnamon (*qirfa*), pour ghee [melted] in [hot] honey all over it, and eat it, God Almighty willing.

Making cheese pastries (*mujabbanāt*)[93]

i.4.33 Making Fried [Cheese-Filled] *mujabbana*

Moisten semolina flour (*samīd*) with cold water in the summer and hot water in winter and then knead it as was done with the dough prepared for *isfanj* [in the previous recipes] and set it aside [to ferment].

Now take fresh cheese (*jubn ṭarī*);[94] if it is soft and moist (*raṭb*), then wash it with water only, put it in a large kneading bowl (*miʿjana*), and rub it between your palms until it is as smooth as bone marrow (*mukhkh*). If it is solid and dry

91 This type of *isfanj* was called *furniyya* in the eastern region, as in al-Warrāq's tenth-century *Kitāb al-Ṭabīkh*, English trans., *Annals* 416.

92 The reed is described as *qaṣaba manfūdhat al-ʿuqad*, i.e., it has been hollowed all through the joints.

93 The following seven recipes (i.4.33–9) all deal with varieties of this type of pastry, which was very popular in al-Andalus, see introduction ii.5.2.

94 The anonymous Andalusi *Anwāʿ al-ṣaydala* 180–1 provides useful information on the

(*jāf*) and somewhat salty, cut it into pieces, and let it stay in water to soften and get rid of its salt. Once it softens, wash it with water and then rub it between the palms until it is as smooth as bone marrow. Taste the cheese; if it lacks salt, add a bit of it; if it is too dry, moisten it with milk or hot water if milk is not available. For each *raṭl* (pound) of the [prepared] cheese, use a quarter of its amount of the dough. Mix them with aniseeds (*anīsūn*) and juices of fresh mint and cilantro. Mix them very well until they bind. [This would be the cheese stuffing.]

Put a tinned skillet (*miqlāt muqaṣdara*) on the fire with plenty of olive oil in it. Once it boils, [start forming the pastries:] wash your hands first with water; take a piece of the dough and spread it on your left hand; take a piece of the cheese with your right hand (**119v**) and put it in the middle of the dough and gather its edges on it. Now, encase and press this *mujabbana* in your left hand; do this tightly so that it comes out through the thumb and index fingers. Cut away the surplus dough [by pressing it tightly with the thumb and index fingers], flatten the *mujabbana* [which is now] on top of the thumb [and index fingers] with the back of the right hand,[95] press a single hole in the middle,[96] and put it in the skillet.

Put the pieces in the oil as they are done until the pan is full. Move the pieces around and flip them with an iron hook (*mikhṭāf*) until they cook and brown. If you see that one of them has already risen to the surface [before it is done,] put another piece that has already cooked on it so that they all cook at the same

---

cheese used for making the well-made *mujabbanāt* in Cordova, Seville, and Jerez in western al-Andalus, and in other parts in North Africa:

> Know that *mujabbana* is not prepared with one kind of cheese but with two cheeses, I mean cow cheese (*jubn baqarī*) and sheep cheese (*jubn ghanamī*). The reason is, if it is made with sheep cheese alone, the pastry will break open, and the cheese will seep out of it; and if it is made with cow cheese only, the cheese will bind and become one solid mass. The way to do it properly is to combine both cheeses—use one quarter of the amount cow cheese and three quarters of it sheep cheese; combine both cheeses and when fried, the cheese will have a medium texture, it will be firm enough not to seep into the pan.
>
> If the cheese needs some moisture, add milk that has just been drawn. The cheese should not be very fresh and soft but firm, unsalted, and dry. This is how our people make *mujabbana* in the western region of al-Andalus, in cities like Cordova, Seville, and Jerez (Sharīsh), and in other parts of North Africa (Bilād al-Maghrib).

Anwāʿ al-ṣaydala includes five recipes for *mujabbana* (62, 180–2), four of which share names and details with those in this book. I used them here to add some missing details.

95 The only practical reason for using the back of the right hand is because it is clean, unlike the hand itself, which has been handling the cheese mix. Thus, the surface of the fried pies will not look unattractively spotty.

96 This will make the *mujabbana* look somewhat like a doughnut.

time. Take them out and set them aside in a vessel for an hour and then transfer them to a large bowl (*mithrad*). Drench them in strained fresh butter melted in [hot] honey, sprinkle them with sugar and Ceylon cinnamon (*qirfa*), and eat them salubriously, God Almighty willing.

For those who want to serve *mujabbanāt* the way Andalusis do, [i.e.,] plain, without drenching them in honey, then let them put the pieces in a platter (*ṭayfūr*)[97] and sprinkle them with Ceylon cinnamon, pounded aniseeds, and sugar. Put a vessel filled with honey in the middle of the platter and eat the [*mujabbanāt*] bit by bit with the honey [by repeatedly dipping a piece in it after each bite]. In addition, using eggs with semolina flour [for the dough]—7 or 8 of them for each *raṭl* (pound) of flour—will make it even more delicious.

I.4.34 Making *mujabbana* Called *makhāriq* (Pastries with Holes in the Middle),[98] Also Called *muthallatha* (Made with Three Main Ingredients)[99]

Knead as much as needed of the semolina flour (*samīd*) with milk and a small amount of rosewater. Take an equal amount of fresh cheese and a similar amount of fresh butter.

Rub the cheese [between the hands] well and mix it with the butter. In case the cheese used tends to be dry and salty, soak it in water for a whole day. Add the cheese and butter to the dough and knead them all thoroughly; set the dough aside in the kneading bowl (*miʿjana*).

Put a skillet (*miqlāt*) on the fire with enough olive oil to cover the frying pieces. Cut the dough into small discs, pierce a hole in the middle of each, put them in the skillet until it is full, and turn them [as needed] with an iron hook (*mikhṭāf*). Once they cook and brown, take them out and put them in fine-tasting honey for about an hour, and then take them out and put them in a glazed earthenware vessel (*ināʾ fakhkhār muzajjaj*). Sprinkle them with sugar and Ceylon cinnamon (*qirfa*), and eat them salubriously, God Almighty willing.

---

97 Pl. *ṭayāfīr*, used for serving food at the table, see glossary 9.1 for more on this vessel. Etymologically, the Spanish *ataifor* is derived from it.

98 Like doughnuts; sg. *mukharraqa*. See Ibn Manẓūr, *Lisān al-ʿArab*, s.v. خرق, for instance, where a sheep having ears pierced with round holes is described as *kharqāʾ*.

99 The three ingredients are equal amounts of semolina flour, cheese, and butter. The BL and the Berlin MSS, fols. 119v and 20v, respectively, add a third name, *muwarraqa* (layered pastry), which is not applicable to the recipe described. The Madrid MS, fols. 39v–40r, mentions the first two names only.

I.4.35 Making Oven-Baked *mujabbana* with Milk, Called *qayjāṭa*[100]

Knead fine white flour (*daqīq darmak*) with water, salt, and a bit of fresh yeast (*khamīr*).[101] Knead it well and make very thin discs of bread with [some of it] after it ferments a little. Bake them in the brick oven; keep them at a distance from the flames of the fire and do not let them brown. (**120r**) [After they bake, take them out and] wipe them clean of the oven's dust and ashes.

Rub the cheese [between the hands] thoroughly and add juices of mint and cilantro, black pepper, and cloves (*qaranful*). If the cheese is somewhat dry, add milk to it after you heat it up a little.

Now, make a thick disc (*raghīf khashin*) with some of the dough and spread it uncooked in the bottom of a new pan (*ṭājin*);[102] spread enough cheese to cover it and then spread one of the baked thin bread discs on top of it; cover it with cheese and spread another thin bread on it. Continue doing this until all the bread discs and cheese are used up.[103] Pour heated-up milk on the [layered bread discs] and cover them all with a thick disc of dough [similar to the one on the bottom]. Send the pan to the oven to bake. Watch it carefully and check on it every now and then while baking. If you notice that it has absorbed the milk, pour some more, and continue doing this until enough is added.[104] Let it bake some more until the thick upper bread starts to look overbaked.

Take it out of the oven and remove [and discard] its cover, which is the thick bread on top. Pour honey, which has been heated and mixed with black pepper and cassia (*dār Ṣīnī*), all over the *mujabbana* after cutting it into crisscross

---

100 قيجاطة, copied as such in the Madrid MS, fol. 40r; and قيحاطة *qayḥāṭa*, in the Berlin and BL MSS, fols. 20r and 119v, respectively. Qayjāṭa/Qayshāṭa is also name of an Andalusi city in southern Spain, Quesada. Possibly, the recipe is associating this variety of *mujabbana* with the city itself. Etymologically, both the city and the *qayjāṭa* cheese pastry are ultimately derived from the Spanish *queso* 'cheese,' and *quesito* for fresh cheese. According to Corriente, *Dictionary of Andalusi Arabic*, s.v. *q-y-j-ṭ*, *qayjāṭ* is 'curd of milk,' which is fresh cheese.

In the corresponding recipe in the anonymous *Anwāʿ al-ṣaydala* 183, a second name is also given to it, *sabʿ buṭūn*, literally 'seven bellies.' Apparently, it was called so because the pastry was made with seven layers of thin bread, as described in Corriente, *Dictionary of Andalusi Arabic* cited above. For more on *qayjāṭa*, see glossary 2, s.v. *mujabbanāt*.

101 The Madrid MS, fol. 40r–v, mentions adding yeast. I used this MS here and at several other places in the recipe to amend the text.

102 In the anonymous *Anwāʿ al-ṣaydala* 183, the *ṭājin* used is a deep, green-glazed pan (*ḥantam*).

103 The anonymous *Anwāʿ al-ṣaydala* 183 gives the direction to fill the pan, up to two-thirds or three-quarters of it.

104 The sign is when the bread and cheese stop absorbing the milk.

lines (*mutaqāṭiʿ*). Keep it set aside, covered, for about an hour, until it cools a bit and has time to absorb the honey, and serve it. It is the most delicious food.

For those who prefer to fry the thin bread discs in olive oil [instead of baking them] they can do so, but they should avoid over frying them; and prepare the *mujabbana* as was done above.

These *mujabbanāt* may also be made plain and simple (*sādhaj*) without cheese by preparing the bread discs as mentioned earlier and layering them in the *ṭājin* one after the other without using cheese in between; and then milk is poured on them. A thick disc of bread is put on top, and it is sent to the oven and given milk as needed, repeatedly, until it fully bakes. It is then taken out of the oven, drenched in honey, and served as previously mentioned.

1.4.36 Making Another Kind of *mujabbana* [Oven-Baked, with Milk]

Knead the needed amount of fine white flour (*daqīq darmak*), first with water and then with olive oil and fresh yeast (*khamīr*). Thin the dough down with milk until it has the consistency of *isfanj* dough [i.e., almost soft]. Set it aside until it has visibly fermented.

Grease a large, new earthenware pan (*ṭājin*) with olive oil, spread a piece of the dough in its bottom, and cover it with cheese. Continue with the layering until all the dough and cheese are used up. Cover them with a disc from another dough,[105] as was done with the previous *mujabbana*, and bake the *ṭājin* as was previously mentioned. [When done and taken out of the oven,] drench it in honey, sprinkle it with Ceylon cinnamon (*qirfa*) and black pepper, and serve it, God Almighty willing.

1.4.37 (120v) Making Another Kind of *mujabbana* [of Fried Discs]

Take 1 *raṭl* (1 pound) fine white flour (*daqīq darmak*) and ½ *raṭl* fresh cheese; knead them by pressing and rubbing them together (*yuʿarrak*) until they combine. Knead them with 5 eggs, enough salt, and water if needed. Shape the dough into very thin discs and fry them in a skillet with lots of olive oil; do not let them change color.

105 بخبز 'with a bread dough disc,' as it occurs in the BL MS, is erroneously copied as بجبن 'with cheese' in the Berlin MS, fol. 21r.

Boil pounded walnuts with honey and pour them on the fried *mujabbanāt*. Chop pine nuts (*ṣanawbar*) and pistachios, sprinkle them on the pastries with sugar, and serve them, God Almighty willing.

I.4.38 Making Another Kind, Called *mujabbanat al-furn* (Oven-Baked Cheese Pastries)[106]

Knead fine white flour (*daqīq darmak*) with water, salt, and olive oil to make a medium dough. Rub fresh cheese between the hands until it has the consistency of bone marrow (*mukhkh*), using three-quarters the amount of flour. Mix aniseeds (*anīsūn*) and juices of mint and cilantro with the cheese.

Portion the dough to make large thin discs with it after greasing them with olive oil or ghee and rolling them out [several times to make them layered like *musammana*].[107] Put some cheese in the middle of each disc and fold the disc over it from all sides to cover the cheese, leaving an opening in the middle the size of a *dīnār* coin.[108] Gently press the pieces with an open hand (*yulṭam*) to flatten them, but not much, and be careful not to let the cheese come out of the dough. Make all the pieces the same way and bake them in the brick oven at a distance from the fire until they are fairly cooked and almost brown; be careful with them [lest they should overbake].

Clean the baked pieces of any dust and ashes [that might have clung to them while baking] and put them in a large and wide wooden or earthenware serving bowl.[109] Drench the pastries with heated honey mixed with strained melted butter, sprinkle them with Ceylon cinnamon (*qirfa*), sugar, and whatever is available of the aromatic spices usually added,[110] and eat them salubriously, God Almighty willing.

---

106 A comparable recipe, albeit much shorter, in *Anwāʿ al-ṣaydala* 182, calls it *mujabbana furniyya* (baked in the brick oven), and the anonymous author says that in his country, al-Andalus, it is called *Ṭulayṭuliyya* 'specialty of Toledo.'

107 'Like *musammana*' is an addition from *Anwāʿ al-ṣaydala*, see the note above. For a *musammana* recipe, see i.4.17 above.

108 The dinar was a gold coin about 0.75 inch in diameter. See, for instance, https://www.qantara-med.org/public/show_document.php?do_id=634&lang=en, accessed Jan. 18, 2020.

109 Called *makhfiyya* and vocalized as such in the BL MS; otherwise, it is given as *mukhfiyya* in sources like Corriente, *Dictionary of Andalusi Arabic*, s.v. *kh-f-w*, and explained as a glazed bowl or basin; and Dozy, *Takmilat al-maʿājim* iv 154, s.v. خفى. See glossary 9.1 for more on this vessel.

110 Such as black pepper, ginger, and cloves.

FIGURE 43 A wide and shallow flat-based serving bowl with inscriptions in pseudo-Arabic script, ca. fifteenth-century Valencia, Spain
THE WALTERS ART MUSEUM, 48. 1013

If fresh cheese is not available, (**121r**) replace it with cheese that has started to dry out and harden. In this case, it must be moistened as mentioned earlier [by adding warmed up milk or water], with the help of God and His might.

I.4.39 Making *mujabbana* Called *Ṭulayṭuliyya* (Specialty of Toledo)[111]

Knead fine white flour (*daqīq darmak*) with water, salt, and olive oil, as mentioned in *mujabbanat al-furn* [above]. Rub cheese between the hands [to crush it], using three-quarters the amount of flour used. Mix aniseeds and juices of mint and cilantro with the cheese, as mentioned above.

111 See also the above recipe, n. 106.

Roll out the dough into discs using a rolling pin (*shawbak*) and put enough of the crushed cheese in the middle of each. Fold the edges of the disc all over the cheese and gently press the discs repeatedly with an open hand (*tulṭam*) to flatten them, as mentioned above. Put the pieces in a copper or earthenware plate (*malla*) and bake them in the *kawsha* (baking chamber of the brick oven), which has been prepared for baking *kaʿk* (ring cookies) and the like.[112]

As soon as the pastries start to brown, take them out of the oven and put them on top of each other in a *mukhfiyya* made of earthenware or wood.[113] Drench them in melted and strained fresh butter and honey. Sprinkle them with sugar and Ceylon cinnamon (*qirfa*), and eat them salubriously, God Almighty willing.

I.4.40 Making *khubz maḥshū* (Double-Crusted Pie) Stuffed with Red Meat (*laḥm*), Squabs (*firākh*), Sparrows (*ʿaṣāfīr*), Starlings (*zarāzīr*), Fresh Cheese, or Fish (*ḥūt*)[114]

Take any kind of the mentioned meats and cook it the way you prefer. Next, make dough with flour, water, salt, and fresh yeast (*khamīr*); knead it into a firm dough. When it is almost fully fermented, make a disc with [part of it, large enough] to raise its sides to contain the stuffing [when assembling the pie]. Take the meat you chose to cook and add eggs mixed with aromatic spices (*afāwīh*) to it. Color it with saffron or juice of cilantro and spread it on the dough disc.

Make another disc with the dough, smaller than the first one, and cover it with it. Twist together the edges of the bottom layer with those of the top layer to seal them well and keep the stuffing in. Bake it in the *furn* (brick oven) and take it out when it is thoroughly cooked, and serve it, God Almighty willing.

---

112 كوشة معدة لطبخ الكعك او ما يكون مثلها, as it correctly occurs in the Madrid MS, fol. 42r; otherwise, it is erroneously copied as كرشة 'tripe' in the BL and Berlin MSS, fols. 121r and 21v, respectively. The editor of the Arabic text chose the latter reading, which is 'tripe,' clearly based on his inaccurate reading of the following word معدة *muʿadda* 'prepared for' as *maʿida* 'stomach.'

Such delicate pastries were baked in low-heat ovens, usually after the baker was done baking bread. Alternatively, they were put at the farthest section of the oven's floor away from the burning fire, for moderate-heat baking, as in the previous recipe. For more details on *kawsha*, see glossary 9.1, s.v. *furn*.

113 As it is called in the Madrid MS, fol. 42r, see n. 109 above. In the Berlin and BL MSS, fols. 21v and 121r, respectively, the bowl is just given the generic term *wiʿāʾ* 'vessel.'

114 In the anonymous Andalusi cookbook *Anwāʿ al-ṣaydala* 26, a somewhat similar double-crusted pie recipe, called *Barmakiyya*, recommends this dish as a victual for travelers.

Regarding the ones stuffed with cheese, crumble it into fine pieces, adding the needed amounts of egg, juices of fresh mint and cilantro, and whatever is available of the known aromatic spices. Mix them all, put them on the first dough disc, cover them with the other disc, as mentioned above, and bake it. So know this with the help of God Almighty.

Part One, Chapter Five: On All Kinds of Dishes That Are Sopped in Broth Like *Tharīd*; and Those Cooked in Ways Similar to Soup

I.5.1 (121v) Making *kuskusū* (Couscous)

Take fine-tasting semolina flour (*samīd*),[1] put it in a large kneading bowl (*miʿjana*), and sprinkle it with water in which a small amount of salt has been dissolved.[2] Stir it with your fingertips so that the particles stick to each other and then rub them between your palms gently until they look like ants' heads. Toss them in a fine mesh sieve (*ghirbāl khafīf*) to get rid of the remaining flour and keep them aerated [while loosely] covered.

To cook [a couscous dish], take the tastiest parts of the meat of fat young adult cows (*baqar fatī*) and their big bones. Put them in a large pot with salt, olive oil, black pepper, coriander seeds (*kuzbara yābisa*), a small amount of chopped onion, and enough water to cover them all and more.

Put the pot on the fire. When the meat is almost done, add whatever is available of vegetables for the season, such as cabbages (*ukrunb*), turnips (*lift*), carrots (*jazar*), lettuce (*khass*), fresh bulb fennel (*basbās*), fresh fava beans (*fūl akhḍar*), gourds (*qarʿ*), and eggplants (*bādhinjān*).

Once the meat and vegetables are done, take the special couscous pot, which has a perforated bottom, and gently fill it with the [prepared] *kuskusū* [grains]. Place it on top of the large meat and vegetable pot. Seal them together with dough all around the space between them to prevent any steam from escaping through it. Tie the top of the *kuskusū* pot with a thick towel (*minshaf ghalīẓ*) so that steam stays in, which will help it cook well. The test for its doneness is the vigorous velocity of steam emitting upwards and a rebounding sound when the couscous pot is struck by hand.

Empty the cooked couscous into a large kneading bowl (*miʿjana*) and rub it between the hands with fine-tasting ghee, [crushed] mastic (*maṣṭakā*), and

---

1 The editor of the Arabic text erroneously replaces *ṭayyib* 'fine-tasting,' as it is clearly copied in the Berlin MS, fol. 22r, and the BL MS, with *raṭb* 'moist,' which is irrelevant at this initial stage.

2 From recipe i.5.5 below, we understand that flour is added to semolina when making couscous grains, as it helps the semolina particles stick to each other.

 | DOI:10.1163/9789004469488_008

spikenard (*sunbul*) to separate the clumping grains. Put it in a large, wide bowl (*mithrad*); but do not fill it with it because you need to make room for the broth, which will be added to it.

Go and check on the meat broth in the pot and see if it is enough [to moisten the couscous]. If it turns out to be deficient, add more water and let it boil. Once it boils, take it from the fire and set it aside until the boiling abates. Pour the broth, in moderation, on the couscous; start first in the middle and then all around the sides. Set the bowl aside, covered, for an hour to give it time to absorb the broth. Test it with your finger to see if it was given enough of the broth; if not, pour some more as needed.

Take the bones out of the pot and stick them upright in the middle of the bowl; spread meat and vegetables all over the top; sprinkle it with Ceylon cinnamon (*qirfa*), black pepper, and ginger; and eat it salubriously, God Almighty willing.

For those who want to prepare the dish with mutton (*laḥm ghanamī*) or chicken, let them do so as described above, with the help of God and His power.

1.5.2 Another Kind Called *kuskusū jawzī* (Couscous with Walnuts), Tastes Delicious (*ladhīdh al-ṭaʿm*)

(122r) Take as much as needed of the tastiest cuts of beef (*laḥm baqarī*), mutton (*laḥm ghanamī*), or fattened chicken and cook them with the known spices (*abzār*) as mentioned earlier [in the above recipe]. Add eggplants, which have been peeled but left whole and boiled in salted water and rinsed and drained.

When the meat and vegetables [i.e., eggplants] are almost done, cook couscous in a pot as described earlier [in the above recipe]. Then, empty it [into a large bowl] and rub it between the hands with pounded walnut kernels, as well as Ceylon cinnamon (*qirfa*), spikenard (*sunbul*), and a small amount of [crushed] mastic (*maṣṭakā*). [Put the couscous in a serving bowl and] pour enough of the broth on it gradually. Arrange the meat pieces and vegetables all over it, sprinkle it with Ceylon cinnamon and spikenard, and serve it, God Almighty willing.

1.5.3 *Kuskusū* Cooked in Ways Other Than Having It Sopped in Broth (*min ghayr saqī*)

Take meat and vegetables out of the pot after they are done. Strain the broth to remove all bones and other impurities; add couscous to the pot and leave it until it absorbs all the liquid. Empty it into a large and wide serving bowl (*jafna*), arrange the meat pieces and vegetables all over it, and serve it. This variety is called *al-ghassānī*.[3]

[Alternatively,] couscous grains may be moistened with the broth of meat that has been cooked with vinegar and saffron as is done when making *tharīd al-khall*.[4] The vegetables used for this dish are eggplants and gourds.

[Another way of cooking it is to] crush crumbs of fine white flour bread (*khubz al-ḥuwwārā*)[5] into fine particles. Roll them between your hands with a small amount of water [to make them look like couscous grains] and then cook them in the pot specially prepared for such dishes [see recipe i.5.1]. Once their steam comes out and they cook well, empty them into [a large bowl] and rub them between the hands with some ghee (*samn*) or fat of the cooked meat.[6] Moisten it with the broth as is usually done [with couscous, see recipe i.5.1].

i.5.4 Another Kind of Couscous [Stuffed in a Roasted Lamb], Truly Scrumptious (*ladhīdh jiddan*)

Take a fat lamb (*kharūf*), [slaughter it,] skin it, open up its belly, and take out the entrails. Clean it and smear it from the inside with suet (*shaḥm*) pounded with the spices used for making meatballs (*banādiq*).[7]

Once the couscous is done cooking, rub it between the hands with ghee (*samn*), spikenard (*sunbul*), Ceylon cinnamon (*qirfa*), and a small amount of

3 Based on the medieval lexicons, it may be translated as 'gorgeous.' See, for instance, Ibn Manẓūr, *Lisān al-ʿArab*, s.v. غسن, where a fair-skinned, handsome man is called *ghassānī*. Judging from *ghassānī* recipes (see also recipe ix.1.2 below), the name may also be attributed to its fair color, and thus the attribution might have been linked to the fair-skinned Ghassanids of the Arab kingdom in the Levant, who were allies of the Byzantines before the advent of Islam. In the anonymous Andalusi *Anwāʿ al-ṣaydala* 158, this couscous dish is said to have been called *al-fityānī* in Marrakesh.

4 It is a dish of bread sopped in the broth of a sour vinegar stew called *sikbāj*. For *sikbāj* recipes, see, for instance, chapter 49 in al-Warrāq, *Kitāb al-Ṭabīkh*, English trans., *Annals* 248–55. The anonymous *Anwāʿ al-ṣaydala* 159 provides a recipe for this type of *tharīd*. Meat is cooked with salt, an onion, black pepper, saffron, cumin, garlic, sour vinegar, and plenty of olive oil. Once the meat cooks, vegetables are added, such as eggplants, gourds, and turnips. The recipe says that couscous may be sopped in its broth, as is done with bread.

5 This was its name in the eastern region; otherwise, it was more commonly called *khubz darmak* in the Muslim West, as in this book.

6 *Dasam al-laḥm*, also called *wadak*. The fat is usually skimmed off the top of the meat broth.

7 See, for instance, recipe ii.6.1 below.

[crushed] mastic (*maṣṭakā*); stuff the lamb's cavity with it. Sew up the belly and the upper part of the chest (*naḥr*) of the lamb, put it in the *tannūr* (clay oven), and roast it until it fully cooks.

[To serve it, take out the couscous stuffing and] put it in a large, wide bowl (*mithrad*); shred the lamb by hand (*yumazzaq*) and arrange it on top; sprinkle it with Ceylon cinnamon and spikenard; and eat it, God Almighty willing.

i.5.5 Another Kind of Couscous Cooked with *baysār* (Dried Fava Beans)[8]

Roll semolina with flour between the hands (*yuftal*) to make couscous grains and cook it as mentioned earlier [recipe i.5.1 above].

Take crushed dried fava beans (*fūl yābis*) and cook them in a new pot with enough water to cover them—use fresh water (*māʾ ʿadhb*) or rainwater; do not add salt. Before cooking the crushed beans, rinse them in hot water several times and rub them with fine-tasting olive oil (*zayt ʿadhb*).

When the fava beans are cooked and softened, use a large ladle to mash them by pressing them against the walls of the pot into a smooth and bone-marrow-like consistency. (**122v**) Add enough hot water [for the couscous that will be added next] and a suitable amount of salt that has been pounded and dissolved [in some water].

Once the beans' pot starts to boil, rub couscous grains between the hands with fine-tasting ghee—use a good deal of it. Add couscous to the pot and leave it there until it blends with the beans and absorbs enough liquid. Ladle the dish [into a large, wide bowl], and serve it, God Almighty willing.

For those who want to make it with *ʿuṣb*,[9] let them be cooked with the known spices in another pot, and when the time comes to add couscous to the beans, add the broth of the *ʿuṣb* to the beans' pot [instead of plain hot water]. When all is cooked, and the couscous is ladled into a large, wide bowl (*mithrad*), the *ʿuṣb* are arranged all over the top, with [a small bowl filled with] heated up fine-tasting ghee or butter or sweet green olive oil (*zayt ḥulw akhḍar*)[10] put in the middle, and eat the dish salubriously, God Almighty willing.

---

8 It is the regional North African name for dried fava beans. Nowadays more commonly encountered in that region and Egypt in a dish called *biṣāra* 'porridge of dried fava beans.' In recipes using fresh fava beans, they are called *fūl akhḍar* 'green fava beans.'

9 Based on the above recipe i.2.2, they are pieces of tripe tied with cleaned intestines wrapped all around them. Sg. *ʿaṣīb*. *ʿUṣbān* is another plural for this type of food. See glossary 5, s.v. *ʿuṣb*.

10 Also known as *zayt al-māʾ*, literally 'water olive oil,' because it was refined by treating it with water. See glossary 6, s.v. *zayt*.

I.5.6 Making *fidāwush* (Orzo)[11]

Knead ¼ *raṭl* (4 ounces) semolina flour (*samīd*) with water and salt to make a firm dough; knead it vigorously by pressing and rubbing it (*yuʿarrak*). Put the dough in a covered vessel and [start] rolling small pieces between the fingers to make them as long as wheat grains; thin with tapered ends.[12] Put whatever you finish in a tray placed close to your hands, and when the dough is finished, dry the rolled pieces in the sun. Make another batch of the dough and do with it as before, and continue doing this until you get the needed amount.

Whenever you need to cook the dish, take the tastiest cuts of the meat of a fat sheep, such as the breasts (*ṣadr*), sides (*ajnāb*), rumps (*adhnāb*), and other parts. Cut them into medium pieces, clean them, and put them in a large pot with lots of water; add salt, olive oil, black pepper, coriander seeds, and a small amount of cut onion. Put the pot on the fire [and let it boil].

Take the meat out when it is cooked and keep it covered in a large, wide bowl (*mithrad*). Strain the broth, wash the pot, and return the broth to it. If the liquid is enough, start cooking the *fidāwush*; otherwise, add more water. Bring the pot to a boil, add the *fidāwush* gently, and let them cook on moderate heat until done. While the pot is cooking, attach a small pot (*qudayra*) filled with hot water to its top to keep it hot.[13] If the liquid dries out while the *fidāwush* is cooking, add a bit of water in the small pot [as needed]. Once the *fidāwush* cooks, add fresh butter or ghee to it while it is still in the pot and keep it for an hour. Fold it gently with the handle of a ladle to avoid breaking the pasta pieces.

---

11 فداوش, as it is copied in the BL and Berlin MSS, fols. 122v and 23r, respectively; copied as *fudūsh* (فدوش) in the Madrid MS, fol. 44v. The pasta pieces are rolled to resemble wheat grains. A comparable type of pasta in the anonymous fourteenth-century Egyptian cookbook *Kanz al-fawāʾid*, English trans., *Treasure Trove*, recipe 117, is called *shaʿīriyya* because it is shaped like barley grains.

Note that in the anonymous Andalusi *Anwāʿ al-ṣaydala* 161, besides *fudūsh* (فدوش), as copied in the BnF MS Arabe 7009, fol. 58r, it also occurs as *fadāwīsh* (فداويش) in the Rabat MS M54, fol. 42v. All variants of the name are suggestive of a plural form.

Also note that in the Andalusi *Anwāʿ al-ṣaydala* 161–2, *fudūsh* is by implication a generic term for pasta made with semolina dough, of which there are three kinds:

1) The ones shaped like wheat grains, similar to the ones being prepared in this recipe, no specific name is given.
2) Balls, each the size of a coriander seed, called *ḥamīṣ* in Bijāya and the surrounding regions in Ifrīqiya.
3) Paper-thin pieces of pasta said to be women's food (*aṭʿimat al-nisāʾ*).

12 Cf. the barley-like pasta, orzo, made in recipe 117 in the anonymous fourteenth-century *Kanz al-fawāʾid*, English trans., *Treasure Trove*.

13 The small pot might have had some sort of a curved handle to attach it to the rim of the cooking pot to keep water hot with its steam.

Meanwhile, using butter or ghee, fry the meat pieces in a pan (*ṭājin*) until they brown. Empty the cooked *fidāwush* into a large, wide bowl (*mithrad*), arrange the meat pieces all over it, sprinkle it with Ceylon cinnamon (*qirfa*) and ginger (*zanjabīl*), and eat it, God willing.

For those who want to have the dish with fat chickens, let them cook the dish as mentioned above, with the help of God. (123r)

1.5.7 Making *muḥammaṣ* (Small Balls of Pasta)[14]

Knead semolina flour (*samīd*) the same way *fidāwush* dough was made [in the above recipe]. Roll it between the fingers into small balls that resemble peppercorns. Dry them in the sun and cook them the same way *fidāwush* was cooked—using beef, mutton, or chicken—and serve it.

For those who want to make them quickly, they may roll them into small balls all together in the kneading bowl itself (*miʿjana*), the way *zabzīn* is done [recipe i.3.7 above].

1.5.8 Making and Cooking *iṭriya* (Dried Thin Noodles)

Cook *iṭriya* as mentioned above using whatever you choose of meat cuts, with more suet (*shaḥm*). Those who want to fry the meat [after boiling it], they can go ahead and fry it; otherwise, it may be left unfried.

For those who do not already have the *iṭriya*,[15] let them make dough with semolina flour (*samīd*) or flour (*daqīq*),[16] with water and a bit of salt. The dough is kneaded vigorously into a firm consistency, and then it is rolled out on a table (*māʾida*) or a rectangular wooden board (*lawḥ mustaṭīl*) [into thin strings, which are cut into pieces and then] are hand rolled to make the *iṭriya* as thin as possible. They are to be dried in the sun and then cooked as mentioned above.

---

14 See n. 11 above.

15 This type of noodle was usually stored dried and used as needed. See glossary 2.

16 *Samīd* designates semolina flour from durum wheat, *Triticum durum*, which is yellowish in hue and sandy in texture. *Daqīq* here is a reference to *darmak* flour (called *ḥuwwārā* in the eastern region), which is fine white flour from bread wheat, *Triticum aestivum*. See glossary 2 for more on the types of flour.

I.5.9 Making *aruzz bi-l-laban al-ḥalīb* (Rice Porridge with Milk)[17]

Rinse white rice (*aruzz abyaḍ*) in hot water repeatedly until the water comes out clear and clean, and then put it in a large, wide bowl (*mithrad*) and push it all around its edges to allow the grains to drain.

Strain sheep's milk (*laban al-ḍaʾn*) through a tightly woven piece of cloth; it is the best milk for cooking this dish; cow's milk (*laban al-baqar*) comes next; and if neither is available then use goat's milk (*laban maʿz*). The needed amount of milk is 6 *raṭl*s (12 cups) for each *raṭl* (pound) of rice.

Put the rice in a large pot with a small amount of hot water and pour the entire amount of milk if the pot is large enough. [Otherwise, add it gradually as it is absorbed by the rice] Leave the pot on the fire until the milk gets hot; then remove the fire from underneath it and leave it on embers (*ghaḍā*) or low heat, just enough to keep it warm. Cover the pot with a clean piece of cloth (*mindīl*) and check on it repeatedly; if the heat is too low, add more of the embers; if the rice looks dry, add more milk. Continue doing this until the rice is fully cooked.

Season it with salt that has been washed,[18] pounded in a wooden mortar (*mihrās ʿūd*), and then dissolved in a small amount of milk or water. Alternatively, it may be added just finely crushed.[19] Stir the pot gently with the handle of a ladle (**123v**) to mix the salt with the rice to season it.

Empty the rice into a large, wide bowl (*mithrad*) and put a small bowlful of honey in the middle. Sprinkle it with sugar for those who want to have it with the dish, and eat it salubriously with clean boxwood spoons (*malāʿiq al-baqs*), with the help of God Almighty.

For those who want to cook it with mutton (*laḥm ghanamī*) or chicken (*dajāj*), let them cook the rice porridge with water only.[20] When it is done, add ghee or butter and leave the pot [on embers] for an hour or so.[21]

For those who want to cook it with water only [without the meat] and eat it with honey, they can do so. *Jashīsha* is cooked similarly [see recipe i.3.11 above], so know this.

---

17 It is also called *aruzziyya* in cookbooks of the eastern region.

18 To wash the salt, it is first dissolved in water and then strained and boiled until it recrystallizes.

19 As fine as dust '*ghubār*.'

20 We assume that the meat is first boiled until cooked, the broth is strained, and then the meat pieces are returned to the pot, after which rice is added.

21 As detailed in the Madrid MS, fol. 45v. In the BL MS, fol. 123v, and the Berlin MS, fol. 24r, the recipe's instruction is to let the porridge boil twice (*ghalyatayn*), see glossary 9.2, s.v. *ghalya*.

i.5.10 Making *muʿallaka* Called *bāzīn* (Cone-Shaped)[22]

Knead semolina flour (*samīd*) with water, salt, and fresh yeast (*khamīr*); set it aside to ferment in a kneading bowl (*miʿjana*).

Take whatever you have chosen of beef or mutton and put it in a clean pot with water, black pepper, salt, olive oil, coriander seeds, and a small amount of cut onion. Put the pot on the fire, and while the meat cooks, add vegetables to it, whatever is in season, such as cabbages (*ukrunb*), turnips (*lift*), gourds (*qarʿ*), or others, and let them cook with the meat.

Now [back to the dough:] make discs of bread with half of it; bake them in the *furn* (brick oven) until they are half done or a little bit more. Make balls of dough with the other half. Take the meat [and vegetables] out of the pot and throw the dough balls into it after straining the broth.

Once the balls cook and come up to the surface, break the baked bread discs in a large and wide serving bowl (*jafna*), pour enough broth to submerge them, and mash and press them (*yuʿallak*) with a large ladle until they fall apart. Next, add the cooked dough balls and mash and press them with the ladle after each addition until the bread and balls become one cohesive mass. If the mix looks dry while doing this, add broth bit by bit as needed, but avoid making it thin in consistency.

When you finish working on the bread mix, shape it into a large *jumjuma*,[23] put it in the middle of a large, wide bowl (*mithrada*), and arrange the meat and vegetables all around it. Make a hole or two in the middle of the *jumjuma*; fill one with sweet olive oil (*zayt ʿadhb*) and the other with [melted] butter or ghee. Sprinkle it with black pepper and Ceylon cinnamon (*qirfa*), and eat it salubriously, God Almighty willing.

---

22 The dish is called after its final shape when presented at the table. Etymologically, *bāzīn* 'cone-shaped' is of Amazigh origin, see http://www.tawalt.com/?p=8596, accessed Jan. 15, 2020. Most likely, it would be like a cone with a cut-off, rounded top, firstly because when served, one or two holes are made on its top, and secondly, in recipe ii.2.44 below, *jamājim* (sg. *jumjuma*) are formed by using vessels with narrow bases and broad rims.

The other name of the dish, *muʿallaka*, is descriptive of the way the cooked ingredients are mashed and beaten together until they become one cohesive mass. A recipe in al-Warrāq's Istanbul MS, fols. 230v–231r, explains the difference between the two terms *masqī*, which is a *tharīd* dish moistened by pouring the broth on the crumbled bread, and *muʿallak*, which is a variant on *tharīd* made by combining the bread and other ingredients into one smooth mass, which is chewy in texture.

23 Based on the name *bāzīn*, it is expected to be shaped like a cone, see the above note. Literally *jumjuma* (pl. *jamājim*) is a 'skull,' but generally it was also used to designate a round or conical solid mass, such as that of sugar. See also recipe ii.2.44 below.

FIGURE 44 Barley, Dioscorides, *Ajzāʾ min risāla fī l-nabātāt*, fol. 23r, detail
BNF, DEPARTMENT OF MANUSCRIPTS, ARAB 4947. SOURCE: GALLICA.BNF.FR/BNF

I.5.11 Making [a Dish with] *marmaz*, Which Is Coarsely Crushed Young Barley[24]

Take barley [spikes], which are still young and green (*farīk*), and beat them with a stick so that the grains scatter out of them. Parch the grains in an earthenware pan (*ṭājin fakhkhār*) to dry out some of their moisture.[25] Rub the grains between the hands (*yuḥakk*) to remove their husk (*safā*)[26] and then let them [completely] dry out in the sun. Coarsely crush the grains, sift them, [and store them].

Whenever you need to cook the dish, take as much as required of the meat of fat young adult cows (*laḥm baqar fatī*) or fat sheep (*ghanamī*) and cut it into pieces, which you then wash and put in a large pot with lots of water. Add olive oil, salt, black pepper, coriander seeds, half an onion, and whole aniseeds (*ḥubūb anīsūn*). Put the pot on the fire, and when the meat pieces are cooked, take them out and fry them in butter or ghee.

---

24 The grains are harvested when they are still green, soft, and full of moisture. The recipe also refers to them as *farīk*, see glossary 2.

25 The verb *yuqlā* is more generally used to designate frying in fat, but it may also imply dry toasting, as in this recipe.

26 The verb more commonly used for rubbing the grains thus is *yufrak*, from which *farīk* is derived.

Rinse the *marmaz* [prepared above] and add it to the pot with the meat broth in it [after straining it]. (**124r**) When it is cooked, add fresh butter; let it boil with it just once and empty it [into a serving bowl]. If while boiling the broth seems to be deficient, replenish it with hot water. When the cooked barley is emptied [into the serving bowl], spread the meat pieces over it, pour some more [melted] butter all over its face, sprinkle it with Ceylon cinnamon (*qirfa*) and ginger (*zanjabīl*), and eat it salubriously, God Almighty willing.

For those who want to cook it with milk and meat broth, or even without meat, let them do so. When prepared without meat, it has to be cooked like rice [as in recipe i.3.11 above], so know this.

i.5.12 Making *taltīn*[27]

Knead fine white flour (*daqīq*) with water, salt, and a small amount of fresh yeast (*khamīr*) to make a firm dough. Roll it out on a table (*māʾida*) into a very thin sheet and cut it with a knife into squares, two fingers wide (1½ × 1½ inches). Dry them in the sun [and store them].

When you need to cook them in wintertime, clean cabbage heads (*ukrunb*) of the outer layers of leaves[28] and finely chop the tender leaves and their hearts. Wash them and put them in a large pot and pour enough water [to cover them], adding salt, olive oil, black pepper, coriander seeds, and a side of an onion (*ṭaraf baṣala*) [that is] chopped.

Once the cabbage and onion are cooked, gently add the *taltīn* pieces to the pot while stirring them with the handle of a ladle so that they do not stick to each other. Let them cook in the pot until they are done and then add ghee or butter. [When you ladle the dish into a serving bowl,] pour [some more melted] butter or ghee, and eat it salubriously, God Almighty willing.

When making the dish in the summer or fall, remove the insides of gourds and scrape their outer skins. Chop them into small pieces and cook

---

27 Copied as *talūtīn* in Ibn Khalṣūn, *Kitāb al-Aghdhiya* 82. It is a dish cooked with a variety of pasta of very thin sheets cut into 1½-inch squares. In the thirteenth-century anonymous cookbook *Anwāʿ al-ṣaydala* 161–2, it is said to be a variety of *fidāwush*, esteemed as a delicacy cooked and eaten by women (*aṭʿimat al-nisāʾ*). The counterpart of this type of pasta in the medieval eastern region was *ṭuṭmāj*/*tuṭmāj*, also called *lakhsha*. See glossary 2.

28 The word used is *qāriḥ*, which, based on Ibn Manẓūr, *Lisān al-ʿArab*, s.v. قرح, is the first of things or whatever came earlier. The first layers of the leaves are usually discarded because they are tough.

them the same way the cabbages [above] were cooked, with the same spices and other stuff.

For those who want to cook the dish with milk, only salt and a small amount of water are used [at first]. Add the *taltīn* pieces to the pot with hot water and leave them in it long enough to moisten them. Pour milk into the pot next and continue adding it gradually so long as the pasta can absorb it. Once enough milk is added and the dish is cooked well, remove the pot from the fire and ladle the dish into a large, wide bowl (*mithrad*). Sprinkle it with sugar, pour [melted] fresh butter all over it, and eat it salubriously, God Almighty willing.

I.5.13 Making [Meatless] *harīsat al-qamḥ* (Wheat Porridge)

Thoroughly soak sifted, good-quality wheat grains in water for an hour and then [drain and] pound them in a large stone or wooden mortar (*mihrās*) to separate the husk (*qishr*) from the grains. Sift the grains again and winnow them (*yunfuḍ*) and then put them in a large pot. Pour water, much more than enough to cover them, (**124v**) and let the pot stay overnight in the *furn* (brick oven).

When you take the pot out the following morning you will see that the grains have cooked. Put a ladle in the pot and start stirring it vigorously until the grains fall apart and bind with the water. Stir in the needed amount of pounded salt and empty the dish into a large, wide bowl (*mithrad*). Place a bowlful of honey in the middle and eat it with boxwood spoons (*malāʿiq baqs*), God Almighty willing.

I.5.14 Making Porridge of Coarsely Crushed White Sorghum (*qiṭniyya bayḍāʾ*)[29]

Pound white sorghum in a wooden mortar (*mihrās ʿūd*) to separate the husk. Sift the grains, and then pick them over and crush them coarsely to make *jashīsh*. Sift the *jashīsh* and rinse it in several changes of water until it comes out clear.

---

29 According to Ibn Manẓūr, *Lisān al-ʿArab*, s.v. قطن, *qiṭniyya* is a collective noun for pulses as well as grains other than wheat and barley. They were planted in the summer and harvested at the end of it. Based on this recipe, it seems that the name specifically designates *dhura bayḍāʾ*, a white variety of sorghum, *Sorghum bicolor*. According to Ibn al-Bayṭār, *al-Jāmiʿ* ii 415, the white variety with heavy grains was deemed the best.

FIGURE 45 Boxwood, al-ʿUmarī, *Masālik al-abṣār*, fol. 262v, detail
BNF, DEPARTMENT OF MANUSCRIPTS, ARAB 2771. SOURCE: GALLICA.BNF.FR/BNF

Put the *jashīsh* in boiling water in a large pot and let it cook. When it is done and the liquid is absorbed, ladle it into a large, wide bowl (*mithrad*) and pour [heated up] butter all over it. Put a bowl in the middle filled with honey or sweet grape syrup (*rubb ʿinab ḥulw*),[30] and eat it salubriously.

30 It is made by boiling the juice of sweet grapes into a thick syrup, with no sugar added. See glossary 4.

For those who wish to put [in the middle of the dish, bowls of] grated hard cheese and mashed cooked garlic with sweet olive oil (*zayt ʿadhb*), or use the cheese dissolved with the cooked garlic in hot water instead, they can go ahead and do so, God Almighty willing.

PART 2

القسم الثاني في أصناف لحوم ذوات الأربع ويشتمل على ستة فصول

On Meats of Quadrupeds, and It Has Six Chapters

CHAPTER II.1

Part Two, Chapter One: On Beef (*Luḥūm Baqariyya*)

II.1.1 A Dish Called *jumlī* (All-In-One Dish)[1]

Take the tastiest cuts of beef, rumen tripe (*ghalīẓ al-karsh*), and the like;[2] cut them into medium pieces and clean them.

Pour sweet olive oil (*zayt ʿadhb*) in a new pot; put the meat in it along with salt, black pepper, coriander seeds, cumin, a small amount of chopped onion, soaked white chickpeas,[3] [skinned] boiled almonds, citron leaves (*waraq utrujj*), sprigs of herb fennel (*ʿūd basbās*),[4] garlic cloves, and *murrī naqīʿ* (sun-fermented liquid sauce);[5] use the amounts needed of these ingredients.

Stir the pot by hand to mix the meat with the spices (*abzār*) and all the other mentioned ingredients. Put it on the fire and stir it with a ladle repeatedly until [the meat] releases its moisture and it starts to turn white. Pour in hot water from the small pot,[6] but not too much. Stir the pot and let it cook on the fire.

Take [other] meat from the thigh (*fakhdh*), remove the veins and sinews (*ʿurūq*),[7] and thoroughly pound it in a wooden mortar (*mihrās ʿūd*). (**125r**) Add salt, black pepper, ginger, Ceylon cinnamon, spikenard, cloves, and the white of an egg. Mix and knead them well and shape them into meatballs (*banādiq*). Add them to the meat pot on the fire; also add 3 or 4 egg yolks [to poach]. Once the meat is cooked, color it with a bit of saffron, which has been pounded in a

---

1 I based the meaning of the dish on the assumption that it is derived from *jumla* 'complete,' 'total,' see Dozy, *Takmilat al-maʿājim* ii 290, s.v. جمل. The dish includes all cuts of meat, including offal, and judging from this recipe and the ones in the anonymous Andalusi *Anwāʿ al-ṣaydala* 6, 92, 95, 120, 151, all *jumlī* dishes contain vinegar and the fermented sauce called *murrī*, with lots of olive oil. The finished dish has little sauce left in it. From the last recipe in this chapter, we learn that it was usually offered as a large festive dish (*ṭaʿām kabīr*).

2 Rumen tripe is the first compartment of the stomach, which is large, smooth, and flat in texture.

3 *Ḥimmaṣ abyaḍ*, they are the common tan chickpeas, deemed the best of the chickpea varieties, see glossary 12.

4 *Basbās* is the Andalusi variant of what was more commonly called *rāzyānaj* and *shamar/shamār* in the eastern region.

5 For *murrī* recipes, see chapter x.8 below.

6 Judging from previous recipes, as in i.5.6, the small pot might have had some sort of curved handle to attach it to the rim of the cooking pot to keep water in it hot with the rising steam.

7 When making meatballs, such chewy particles are usually removed because they do not grind as well as meat does, which will spoil the meatballs' texture.

FIGURE 46 A cow, Dioscorides, *Fī Hayūlā al-ṭibb*, translation by Ḥunayn b. Isḥāq, fol. 79r, detail
FROM THE NEW YORK PUBLIC LIBRARY, SPENCER COLLECTION: HTTPS://DIGITALCOLLECTIONS.NYPL.ORG/ITEMS/5E66B3E8-C92D-D471-E040-E00A180654D7

copper mortar (*mihrās nuḥās*) and dissolved in water. After the pot cooks for a short while, add fine-tasting vinegar, just enough to season it.

Now, take enough eggs to top the food in the pot[8] and break them in a large bowl (*mithrad*). Add salt, pounded saffron, and spices; stir them all with a ladle to mix them. Remove the pot from the fire, pour the stirred eggs all over it, [and keep it on embers until the eggs set].

Boil 2 eggs in water and split each one into 4 sections [with a thread]. Once the pot cooks and the meat binds with the set eggs, ladle the dish into a glazed bowl (*ghaḍāra*), discarding the citron leaves, fennel sprigs, and garlic cloves. Let the meatballs and egg yolks show through the surface and garnish the dish with the split eggs and tender tips of mint sprigs (*ʿuyūn al-naʿnaʿ*). Sprinkle it with Ceylon cinnamon, ginger, and black pepper, and eat it salubriously, God Almighty willing.

---

8 The practice of topping the surface with a layer of seasoned beaten eggs, characteristic of Andalusi cuisine at the time, is called *takhmīr*, literally 'covering.'

11.1.2 Another Dish, Called *Burāniyya* [Fried Eggplants Layered with Meat][9]

Take meat similar to what was used [in the recipe] above and do with it as was done of cleaning and boiling tripe in hot water until it looks white, adding spices (*abāzīr*), egg yolks, meatballs with the rest of other things and cooking the pot on the fire.[10]

Take large eggplants and slice them into discs of medium thickness, neither too thick nor too thin. Put them on a board one above the other with salt sprinkled on each one. Weigh them with something heavy to pull out their black water and rid them of their bad, unhealthy properties.[11] Wash them in fresh water (*māʾ ʿadhb*), set them aside to drain, and then fry them in a pan in plenty of olive oil until they brown (*taḥmarr*), taking care not to let them tear up.

When the meat is cooked, cover it with enough eggs (*tukhammar*), as mentioned above [in the previous recipe]. Remove the fire from underneath the pot and let it stay [on embers] for about an hour. When the eggs thicken and set, and the fat in the pot gathers on top, line a glazed bowl (*ghaḍāra*) with fresh and tender leaves of citron (*utrujj*), arrange the eggplant slices all over them, and cover them with a layer of the cooked meat; add another layer of the eggplant slices over the meat. Garnish the dish with egg yolks, meatballs, split eggs, and tender tips of mint. Sprinkle the dish with Ceylon cinnamon and ginger, and eat it salubriously, God Almighty willing.

[Variations:]

Some additional steps may be taken to turn it into another dish:[12]
[1] Take eggplants, peel them, cut them into discs, put them in a pot with salted water, and let them cook until they are almost done. Take the pieces out, wash them in heated-up fresh water, and set them aside to drain.

Take another amount of meat, pound it in a mortar (*mihrās*), (**125v**) and add spices similar to those used with the meatballs [above] and 1 egg white. Knead

9 The name is an Andalusi variant on *Būrāniyya*, a dish of fried eggplants, named after Būrān, wife of Abbasid Caliph al-Maʾmūn (d. 833).

10 See the previous recipe for directions. Details for cleaning tripe, however, were not mentioned there.

11 See glossary 12, s.v. *bādhinjān*.

12 This sentence is found only in the Madrid MS, fol. 48r, which I also used to straighten the text at several places.

the mix very well to bind it. Now take a skillet, put it on the fire, and put olive oil in it. When the oil boils, throw in the eggplant pieces; turn them gently and do not let them fully fry. Take them out.

Now take the pounded meat and cover each disc of the eggplant with it; handle with oiled hands. Let their surfaces be smooth and totally covered with the meat. Return these pieces to the skillet and fry them and turn them gently until they brown. Do with these as was done [above] with the plain [fried] eggplant discs, [i.e., layering them] with meat to make a *Burāniyya* dish.

[2] If wished, you can take the eggplant pieces after boiling and rinsing them, pound them in a mortar into a smooth consistency, like bone marrow (*mukhkh*), and thoroughly mix them with meat that was pounded with spices. Wipe your hands with olive oil and shape the mix into thin discs. Fry them and do with them as was done with the eggplant pieces earlier [in the basic recipe], so know this.

[3] For those who want to use mutton (*laḥm ghanamī*) or chicken instead, they are cooked the same way.

[4] For those who want to use an earthenware pan (*ṭājin*) to cook the meat and eggplants, they may spread the [fried discs of] eggplant underneath the meat, as well as in the middle and on top of it. Send the *ṭājin* to the *furn* (communal brick oven) already topped with the seasoned beaten eggs (*mukhammar*) and let it bake until it sets and thickens (*yaʿqud*). Alternatively, it can be cooked at home [on direct heat] by covering the pan with another *ṭājin* in which burning coals are put. Wait until the dish sets and thickens and browns on top. For those who wish to ladle it into a green-glazed [serving] bowl (*ghaḍāra*), they have to do this with utmost care [to keep the layering intact], so know this.

[5] For those who want to make another variety with it, let them take the eggplants, split them in halves, core out their flesh after boiling them, and then replace the flesh with pounded meat seasoned with spices and mixed with an egg white.[13] The pieces are next dusted with fine white flour (*daqīq darmak*) and fried in sweet olive oil until they cook and brown, and then make *Burāniyya* with them [as in the basic recipe].

---

13 *Mufawwah* is derived from *afāwīh* 'spices,' see glossary 8.

11.1.3 Another Dish, Called *muthallath* (Made with Three Main Ingredients)[14]

Take whatever you choose of beef and cut it into pieces. Wash the meat, [put it in a pot,] and add salt to it, along with spices as was done in the above recipes, and olive oil and *murrī* (liquid fermented sauce) and such [as in the above recipes]. Put the pot on the fire and let the meat cook [without adding any liquid, stirring it frequently] until it looks almost white. Add heated-up water, enough [to cover], and let it cook.

Take fresh and tender turnips (*lift*), peel them, and cut them into fingers. Rinse them in water, color them very well with pounded saffron, and throw them into the pot. Also throw in some saffron dissolved in water. Once it boils, add fine-tasting vinegar, just enough to season it. Meatballs may also be added if wished. Take some eggs, break them into a large, wide bowl (*mithrad*), and add salt, black pepper, ginger, and a small amount of pounded saffron. Beat them with a ladle vigorously to mix the eggs with the spices. (**126r**)

Now take a look at the meat; if it is done and the turnips look nice and cooked, pour the eggs all over it (*tukhammar*),[15] remove the fire from underneath the pot, and leave it [on embers] until the eggs are thick enough to cover the top. Empty the dish into a glazed bowl (*ghaḍāra*) and put split [boiled] eggs and tender tips of mint sprigs all over it. Sprinkle it with Ceylon cinnamon and ginger, and eat it salubriously, God Almighty willing.

For those who want to use mutton instead, they can do so, God Almighty willing.

11.1.4 Another Dish, Called *murūziyya* (Plum Stew, Seasoned and Colored with Vinegar and Saffron)[16]

Take as much as needed of the tastiest cuts of the meat of a fat young adult cow and cut it into pieces. Wash the meat and put it in a new pot, adding salt, olive

14 According to the anonymous Andalusi *Anwāʿ al-ṣaydala* 204, meat dishes cooked with saffron, vinegar, and a kind of vegetable, such as turnips, eggplants, gourds, carrots, or lettuce stems stripped of their leaves, are called *muthallath*. From the last recipe in this chapter, we learn that it was usually offered as a large festive dish (*ṭaʿām kabīr*).

15 Madrid MS, fol. 48v, mentions adding the eggs at this point.

16 The name of the dish is thus vocalized in the BL MS, fol. 126r; but also as *marwaziyya*, fol. 151v. In the anonymous Andalusi *Anwāʿ al-ṣaydala* 19, it is said to be the food of Egyptians and people of Ifrīqiya (the coastal regions of what today are western Libya, Tunisia, and eastern Algeria) أطعمة إفريقية والبلاد المصرية. See glossary 5 for more on this dish.

FIGURE 47 A plum tree, *ijjāṣ*, Dioscorides, *Ajzāʾ min risāla fī l-nabātāt*, fol. 18v, detail
BNF, DEPARTMENT OF MANUSCRIPTS, ARAB 4947. SOURCE: GALLICA.BNF.FR/BNF

oil, black pepper, coriander seeds, cumin, soaked chickpeas, skinned almonds, whole garlic cloves, a small amount of onion, leaves of citron (*utrujj*), and sprigs of herb fennel (*ʿūd basbās*). Put the pot on the fire and let it cook without adding any water, stirring repeatedly until the meat releases its juices and looks white. Add hot water, enough to cover it, and let it cook.

Now, take a small, glazed earthenware pot (*ṭājin fakhkhār muzajjaj*) and put fine-tasting vinegar in it. Add [dried] *ihlīlaj* imported from Byzantium[17]—may

17 The implication here is that *ihlīlaj* imported from Byzantium (*Bilād al-Rūm*) designate a variety of *ʿayn al-baqar*, which is a generic name for plums (*Prunus subg. Prunus*), called

God destroy it[18]—which are plums (*ʿayn al-baqar*).[19] Take as much as needed; clean and wash them before adding them. Also take fine-tasting red raisins (*zabīb aḥmar*), wash them to get rid of sand, and put them in the small pot with the plums (*ʿayn*).[20] Put this pot on top of the cooking pot to heat up the vinegar and moisten the raisins and plums. Taste them; if you can detect the flavor of vinegar in them, pour the vinegar with the plums and raisins into the meat pot and let them cook. Do not add them until you have already thrown some saffron into the pot; use just enough to color it. Now taste the meat; the flavor of vinegar should be pronounced; if not, add some more as needed.

Once the meat is cooked, leave the pot on low heat for an hour so that it may simmer and allow the flavors to nicely blend (*yatajammar*).[21] Ladle the dish into a glazed bowl (*ghaḍāra*), sprinkle it with Ceylon cinnamon and ginger, and eat it salubriously, God Almighty willing.

11.1.5 Another [*murūziyya*] Dish, Cooked with Plums (*ʿayn al-baqar*) and Onions[22]

Take whatever you prefer of the tastiest cuts of beef; chop them, wash them, and put them in a pot. Add salt, plenty of olive oil, black pepper, coriander seeds, cumin, plenty of chopped onion, and fine-tasting *murrī* (liquid fermented sauce)—just the needed amount (*bi-miqdār*).

(**126v**) Put the pot on the fire [and let it cook] without adding any water, stirring it repeatedly until the meat heats up and releases its juices. Add hot water

---

ijjāṣ in the eastern region of al-Mashriq. The name *ijjāṣ* in al-Andalus, however, designated pears (*kummathrā*).

Thirteenth-century Ibn al-Ḥashshāʾ, *Mufīd al-ʿulūm* 129–30, rightly associates *ihlīlaj* with *ʿayn al-baqar/ijjāṣ*. Context in our recipe here obviously designates *ihlīlaj* as a variety of plum, which was no other than myrobalan plum/cherry plum (*Prunus cerasifera*). In medieval Egypt, it was called *qarāṣiyā*, also used for preparing a *marwaziyya* dish in the fourteenth-century Egyptian *Kanz al-fawāʾid*, English trans., *Treasure Trove*, recipe 65.

18 *Dammarahā Allāh*, this addition is found only in the BL MS, fol. 126r.

19 It also occurs as *ʿanbaqar*, *ʿabqar*, and *ʿayn*. See n. 17 above.

20 The name of *ʿayn al-baqar* is often shortened thus.

21 In the Berlin MS, fol. 26v, and the BL MS, fol. 126r, the word is clearly copied as يتجمر. I ruled out the possibility that it might have been يتحمر 'browned' since nothing is being fried or roasted here; or يتخمر 'to be covered with' since no eggs are mentioned. One of the meanings of جمر, given in Ibn Manẓūr, *Lisān al-ʿArab*, s.v. جمر, is 'combine' and 'integrate,' which applies to context here.

22 See the previous recipe, nn. 17 and 19 above.

to the pot, enough to just cover the meat—do not add more than is needed [and let it cook].

Now, take [dried myrobalan] plums (*ʿayn*), wash them, and put them in a small [glazed] earthenware pot (*ṭājin*) along with vinegar. Place this pot on top of the [cooking] meat pot and leave it there until the vinegar heats up and the plums moisten.

Take saffron, pound it in a mortar (*mihrās*), dissolve it in some water, and add it to the pot to color the meat and onions; use it sparingly. When the [meat] pot boils, add the plums and vinegar, but only after you inspect the onions and make sure that they have fully cooked; if done, then you may add the vinegar; if not, let them cook until done and only then add the vinegar. Now, taste the dish; if you find it delicious and to your taste, do not do anything. If it lacks [acidity], add some more vinegar.

Leave the pot on low heat so that it may simmer and allow the flavors to nicely blend (*yatajammar*).[23] Once the fat gathers on top, ladle the dish into a glazed bowl (*ghaḍāra*), and eat it salubriously, God Almighty willing.

If you want to make the dish with plums only, and without onions, then use skinned almonds, soaked chickpeas, and whole garlic cloves. Cook it as mentioned above with the spices, saffron, and vinegar. So know this, and cook it accordingly, God Almighty willing.

II.1.6 Another Dish, Called *arnabī*[24]

Take as much as needed of the tastiest cuts of beef. Dice the meat into small pieces, clean and wash it, and put it in a large, glazed earthenware pot (*ṭājin fakhkhār muzajjaj*). Add the needed amounts of water, salt, plenty of olive oil, black pepper, coriander seeds, cumin, a small amount of chopped onion, garlic—both crushed and whole—[dried] thyme (*ṣaʿtar*) crushed by hand, soaked chickpeas, skinned almonds, leaves of citron (*utrujj*), sprigs of herb fennel (*ʿūd basbās*), and the needed amount of *murrī* (liquid fermented sauce).

Put the pot on the fire [and let it cook] until it is done. At this point color it with pounded saffron, followed by fine-tasting vinegar, to taste. Let the pot cook until most of its liquid evaporates and only the fat remains. Remove the pot from the fire, set it aside until its heat subsides, and then ladle it into a glazed bowl (*ghaḍāra*), and eat it salubriously, God Almighty willing.

---

23 See n. 21 above.

24 This moist dish of fried meat, seasoned with vinegar and fermented sauce of *murrī*, is named so because its color resembles that of the brownish fur of a rabbit (*arnab*).

11.1.7 Another Dish, Called *rāhibī* (Cooked by Christian Monks)[25]

Take the tastiest cuts of fatty beef, such as the brisket (*ṣadr*), rumen tripe (*ghalīẓ al-karsh*), honeycomb tripe (*sudsiyya*),[26] shanks (*amlāj*, sg. *mulj*),[27] and the like. Cut them into medium pieces and wash them; and boil the tripe in hot water to clean it. (127r)

Put the meat in a new pot, adding salt, plenty of olive oil, black pepper, coriander seeds, leaves of citron (*utrujj*), sprigs of herb fennel (*ʿūd basbās*), and a small amount of *murrī* (liquid fermented sauce). Put the pot on the fire and let it cook [without adding any water], stirring it repeatedly until the meat releases its juices and starts to turn white.

Add hot water to the pot, but not much, just enough to cover the meat. Take onions, remove their outer skins, and chop them into small pieces. Rinse them in fresh water (*māʾ ʿadhb*) and set them aside. Now have a look at the meat, if it is almost done, add the onions, and when they are cooked, color them and the meat with saffron, which has been pounded and dissolved in a bit of water (*maḥlūl*). Also add fine-tasting honey or rose-petal honey jam (*murabbā al-ward al-ʿasalī*),[28] enough to give it a sweet taste. For those who want to replace the honey with very sour vinegar (*khall ḥādhiq*), they can go ahead and do so.

Take the pot to the *furn* (communal brick oven) and let it bake until the meat browns and the liquids evaporate and then take it out. Do the same thing if it is baked in the *tannūr* (clay oven). If you want to cook it in the house [on the stove], empty the contents of the pot into a glazed earthenware pan (*ṭājin muzajjaj*) and put it on moderate heat. Take another pan, made of iron or glazed earthenware, put strongly burning coals in it, and place it directly on top of the first pan. Check on it periodically until the top browns and the liquid evaporates. Take it from the fire and set it aside until it is no longer hot, and serve

---

25 What characterizes this dish is baking it in the *furn* (brick oven), which is the last stage of cooking it. There are five recipes for *rāhibī* in the Andalusi thirteenth-century anonymous cookbook *Anwāʿ al-ṣaydala* 136–8, which follow the same method. The reason given in *Anwāʿ al-ṣaydala* is that meat does not cook well and does not develop an appetizing aroma unless it is baked in the oven.

26 *Sudsiyya* literally means 'hexagonal.' It is the second chamber of the stomach, the reticulum, the most desirable part of the tripe. The rumen tripe is the first compartment of the stomach. It is large, smooth, and flat in texture.

27 In Corriente, *Dictionary of Andalusi Arabic*, s.v. *m-l-j*, *mulj* is said to designate the calf of the human leg, which is equivalent to the upper leg in quadrupeds.

28 The editor of the Arabic text, p. 100, misreads مربا *murabbā* 'jam' as مري *murrī*, the fermented sauce.

it, God Almighty willing. After you take the pot from the *furn* or whatever was used, sprinkle the dish with sweet-smelling rosewater, which will make the dish taste delicious and smell wonderful.

If you want to cook the meat in onion liquid (*māʾ baṣal*), in which case the dish would be called ***mufarrij*** (comforting) and ***shuʿāʿ al-shams*** (sunbeams), take the onions, chop and rinse them, and then cook them in a separate pot. Once done, press them hard to extract all their juice, which you then strain and add to the meat. Color the meat with saffron as soon as it cooks and add honey or rose-petal honey jam to it; put enough to give the dish a sweet taste. Cook the dish as was done with the first one; and use rosewater.

For those who want to cook these two dishes [of *rāhibī*] with mutton (*laḥm ghanamī*) or any kind of edible bird, they can do so, God Almighty willing.

II.1.8 Another Dish [of Beef], Fried with *murrī* (Liquid Fermented Sauce) and Garlic

Take beef, as much as needed, cut it into pieces, put it in a clean pot, and add water, salt, plenty of olive oil, black pepper, coriander seeds, fine-tasting *murrī*, and garlic cloves with the skins on. Put the pot on the fire until the meat cooks and then fries and browns after all the liquids evaporate.

Remove the pot from the fire and season it (*yuftaq*)[29] with preserved lemon juice (*khall laymūnī*) or that of Damascus citron (*khall al-zunbūʿ*)[30] or unripe grapes (*khall al-ḥiṣrim*),[31] and eat it salubriously, God Almighty willing.

---

29 I read the word as *yuftaq* يفتق, commonly used in medieval cookbooks to convey this sense, and not *yuʿattaq* يعتق 'to age,' as in the text. It must have been the copyist's misreading of the original word.

30 Kharna sour orange hybrid, *Citrus aurantium var. khatta*. Based on Dozy, *Takmilat al-maʿājim* v 364, زنبوع, the name *zunbūʿ* is of Amazigh origin. It is more commonly known as *kabbād* in the eastern region. For vinegar recipes, see chapter x.7 below.

31 See recipes x.7.12–4 for making preserved juice of unripe grapes; and recipe x.7.15 for preserved lemon juice. No recipes are given for preserved juice of *zunbūʿ*.

Note that in the two surviving Andalusi cookbooks, this one and anonymous *Anwāʿ al-ṣaydala*, *khall* not only designates regular 'vinegar,' produced by fermentation, but also, in a looser sense, unfermented, preserved 'sour juice,' and even freshly pressed out lemon juice. See glossary 8, s.v. *khall*.

II.1.9 (127v) Another Dish, [Pot Roast with a Dipping Sauce Called *jalja*]

Take [beef] pieces from the thighs (*afkhādh*, sg. *fakhdh*) and loins (middle back, *sinsin*); take their meat only, removing the suet (*shaḥm*). Cut it into large chunks, which you then wash and put in a clean pot with water—just the needed amount [to cover them]—along with black pepper and coriander seeds. Set the pot on the fire to cook.

[To prepare the sauce,] take garlic cloves and boil them in a separate pot; the amount depends on how much heat you want it to impart.[32] Once the garlic cloves are cooked, remove their skins and pound them in a mortar (*mihrās*)—use a wooden mortar; and put them in a glazed bowl (*ghaḍāra*). Next, take fresh cilantro (*kuzbara khaḍrā'*) and Macedonian parsley (*maqdūnis*), which is called *būshīn* in al-ʿAjamiyya (Andalusi Romance).[33] Pound them both and press out their juices into the garlic. Add a good deal of black pepper and fresh juice of unripe grapes (*khall ḥiṣrim ṭarī*).[34] Beat them all and mix them well to make a sauce (*marqa*) with them; set it aside.[35] If you cannot find vinegar of unripe grapes, use fine-tasting, very sour vinegar (*khall thaqīf*) instead.[36]

When all is ready and the meat is cooked, take it out of the pot; cut it into small pieces with a knife and put it in a separate glazed bowl. Strain its broth (*marqa*) and offer everything on the table [i.e., meat, garlic sauce, and strained meat broth].

The dish is eaten by dipping pieces of bread or meat in whichever you choose of the two sauces.[37] The cut meat can be thrown into the *jalja*, which is a

32 Heat in this context does not refer to physical temperature but to the innate properties (*mizāj*) of the garlic. Based on the Galenic theory of the humors, garlic is hot and dry in properties, and as such, it was believed to aid digestion, dispelling flatulence and breaking down coarse foods. See glossary 11, s.v. *mizāj*.

33 Marín, "Words for Cooking" 41, rightly comments that the word should have been *barshīn*; see Corriente, *Dictionary of Andalusi Arabic*, s.v. *p-r-sh-l/n*, of which the original was *perrixín*. She suggests the possibility of *būshīn* being a copyist's mistake. There is also the possibility that the word represented an already corrupted form of the word; both the Berlin MS, fol. 27v, and the BL MS, fol. 127v, copy it as *būshīn*. The Madrid MS does not include this bit of information.

34 See recipe x.7.14, which describes how the juice is extracted. See also n. 31 above.

35 This statement is found in the Madrid MS, fol. 51v. It refers to the prepared sauce as *marqa*, later in the recipe called *jalja*. In the cookbooks of the eastern region, such sauces are called *ṣalṣa*, see n. 38 below.

36 See vinegar recipes in chapter x.7 below.

37 *Fī iḥdā al-marqatayn*, as stated in the Madrid MS, fol. 50r. The verb 'dip' in the BL and Berlin MSS, fols. 127v and 27v, respectively, is *yuṣbagh*, derived from *ṣibāgh* 'dipping sauce.' The Madrid MS uses the verb *yughaṭṭas* 'dip.'

FIGURE 48
Serving meat with *jalja*, al-Ḥarīrī, *al-Maqāmāt*, fol. 120r, detail
BNF, DEPARTMENT OF MANUSCRIPTS, ARAB 3929. SOURCE: GALLICA.BNF.FR/BNF

sauce [*marqa*];[38] or if wished, you may dip the meat pieces in the sauce one by one, and eat them salubriously, God Almighty willing. The Byzantines (al-Rūm)[39] frequently use [such sauces] with roasted chickens, roasted and boiled red meat, or fish because this sauce (*marqa*), which is called *jalja*—written with the dotted letter *jīm* (*j*)—is one of their most venerable foods by virtue of its innate heat.[40] So know this and follow whatever suits you, God Almighty willing.

II.1.10 Recipe for Preparing a Pot of Garnishes (*qidr al-farsh*), Used with Large Festive Dishes (*ṭaʿām kabīr*)[41]

Take a large pot and put in it boiled rumen tripe (*ghalīẓ al-karsh*), small intestines (*duwwāra*), and large intestines (*maṣārīn khashna*) after cleaning

38 *Jalja* also occurs as *shalsha* in fish recipe v.1.5 below. It is no other than *ṣalṣa*/*ṣulṣ*, the table sauces we encounter in contemporary cookbooks from the eastern region, such as chapter 16 in the anonymous fourteenth-century Egyptian cookbook *Kanz al-fawāʾid*, English trans., *Treasure Trove*. *Jalja* and *shalsha* must have been the Andalusi dialectal pronunciation.

39 In the Madrid MS, fol. 50r, *al-Rūm* is replaced with *al-Naṣārā* 'Christians.'

40 See n. 32 above.

41 I followed here the Madrid MS, fol. 50v, because it offers a more meaningful reading of the

them and cutting them into pieces to your liking.[42] Such meats will be used to garnish dishes colored with saffron and cooked with vinegar.

So, when you put these meats in the pot, add with them skinned almonds and spices (*abāzīr*), as was done with the *jumlī* dish mentioned first [recipe ii.1.1]. Let the pot cook until all is done. Add a good number of meatballs (*banādiq*), many egg yolks [to poach whole in the broth], and pounded fresh suet (*shaḥm ṭarī*). Color all the ingredients with saffron to give them an intense [yellow] color.

When the cooking is done, [and it is time to serve a meal], put this pot next to you, and when you ladle the [main] dishes into the [serving] bowls (*ṣiḥāf*, sg. *ṣaḥfa*), such as *jumlī*, *muthallath* (recipe ii.1.3), and *ra's maymūn* (recipe ii.2.44), take some of it in a large ladle and scatter the pieces all over the faces of the bowls. Further garnish the dishes with split eggs and sprinkle spices [such as Ceylon cinnamon and ginger] all over them, the Exalted and Majestic God willing. (**128r**)

text. According to Corriente, *Dictionary of Andalusi Arabic*, s.v. *f-r-sh*, *farsh* is 'garniture of food.'

42 The rumen tripe is the first compartment of the stomach; it is large, smooth, and flat in texture.

CHAPTER II.2

Part Two, Chapter Two: On Mutton (*Luḥūm Ḍa'n*)[1]

II.2.1 A Dish Called *tafāyā bayḍā'* (Simple White Stew)[2]

Take meat from a yearling ram (*kabsh thanī*), whatever you choose of brisket (*ṣadr*), foreshanks (*yadayn*), and racks (*ajnāb*, sg. *janb*). Cut them into pieces, clean them, and put them in new pot, adding water and olive oil. Take a piece of new cloth and put ginger, washed salt (*milḥ maghsūl*),[3] coriander seeds, and a small amount of chopped onion in it. Tie the cloth and throw it into the pot, and as soon as you know that all the ingredients in it have imparted their essences into the pot,[4] take it out lest it should spoil the [whiteness of the] stew.

Let the meat cook until it is done. For those who wish to add meatballs (*banādiq*), let them do so. When the meat is done cooking, let the pot simmer to allow the flavors to nicely blend (*yataǰammar*),[5] and once the fat (*wadak*) gathers on top, ladle the dish and serve it, God Almighty willing.

If you want to cook it with the meat of a suckling kid (*jadī raḍī'*), young chickens (*farārīj*), or chickens (*dajāj*), follow the instructions above, with the help of God Almighty.

1 Mutton was also called *laḥm ghanamī* in al-Tujībī's list of chapters, see p. 111, n. 37 above. The abundance of mutton recipes in this chapter (a total of 46 recipes) clearly demonstrates the dominance of mutton over other meats in the medieval Andalusi and Maghribi cooking.

2 *Tafāyā* is one of the dishes that was served first in a meal, as mentioned in the Andalusi anonymous *Anwā' al-ṣaydala* 58. In a white *tafāyā* recipe, in the same source, p. 59, the dish is described as *sādhaja* (plain, neither sweet nor sour); it is also given its other name *isfīdbāja* (*isfīd* 'white' + *bā*[*j*] 'broth'), as it was called in the eastern region (it also occurs as *isfidhbāj* and *isbīdāj*). See, for instance, al-Warrāq, *Kitāb al-Ṭabīkh*, English trans., *Annals*, chapter 59.

In the anonymous Andalusi *Anwā' al-ṣaydala* 58, this dish is categorized as feminine (*mu'annatha*), praised for its balanced properties, and recommended for weak stomachs. In medieval Arabic sources, such as Ibn Ḥayyān, *al-Sifr al-thānī* 322, the name of the famous singer Ziryāb was associated with *tafāyā*, see introduction ii.5, pp. 48–50.

3 Salt was cleansed and purified by dissolving it into brine first to get rid of all the sand and other impurities and then boiling it until crystalized.

4 The editor of the Arabic text erroneously 'corrects' the comprehensive قوة ما فيها خرج في القدر to قوة ماء فيها خرج من القدر (?!).

5 See above, recipe ii.1.4, n. 21.

FIGURE 49 A ram, *kabsh*, Dioscorides, *Fī Hayūlā al-ṭibb*, translation by Ḥunayn b. Isḥāq, fol. 77r, detail
FROM THE NEW YORK PUBLIC LIBRARY, SPENCER COLLECTION: HTTPS://DIGITALCOLLECTIONS.NYPL.ORG/ITEMS/5E66B3E8-E8B5-D471-E040-E00A180654D7

II.2.2 Another Dish, Called *tafāyā khaḍrāʾ* (Simple Green Stew)[6]

Take meat from a yearling ram (*kabsh thanī*); whatever you choose of the tastiest parts mentioned [above]. Cut them into pieces, wash and clean them, and put them in a new pot after pouring olive oil in it—put enough to coat the pot plus an extra amount to cook the meat.[7] Add salt, black pepper, coriander seeds, skinned almonds, and a small amount of chopped onion.

6 See n. 2 above. Apparently, green *tafāyā* cooked with coriander juice was popularized by Ziryāb, see introduction ii.5, pp. 48–50.

7 The verb used, *tusqā* 'allow to absorb,' suggests that the new pot needs to be generously oiled first by pouring oil and turning it around to let all its sides be coated with it.

Put the pot on the fire and attach to its rim a small pot filled with fresh water so that it stays hot with its steam. [Let the meat cook] until it releases its juices and is about to turn white. Add some of the hot water [in the small pot]—enough to cover it—and let it cook until it is done.

Now take [other] meat and pound it in a mortar (*mihrās*); add salt, Ceylon cinnamon, ginger, black pepper, spikenard, and cloves (*qaranful*) as needed. Add egg whites as well. Knead the mix very well until the ingredients combine and bind and make it into meatballs (*banādiq*), which you then throw into the [meat] pot.

Take fresh cilantro, pound it in a wooden mortar (*mihrās ʿūd*), press out its juice by hand, and put it in a glazed bowl (*ghaḍāra*) and set it aside. If chard (*silq*) is available, take its green leaves, pound them, press out their juice, and add it to the cilantro juice [and set aside]. Also, take eggs, break them in a large, wide, and shallow bowl (*ṣaḥfa kabīra*), adding juice of fresh cilantro and juice of mint, as well as salt and aromatic spices (*afāwīh*). Beat them all vigorously [and set them aside for *takhmīr*]. (**128v**)

Take a look at the meat; if it is cooked, add the [set aside] juices of cilantro and chard. Take fresh suet (*shaḥm ṭarī*), remove the veins and sinews (*ʿurūq*), and pound it along with tender tips of sprigs of fresh cilantro and mint until the suet looks green. Add it to the pot.

Throw 3 or 4 egg yolks into the pot [to poach in the broth]. Top the surface with [the set-aside beaten eggs].[8] Remove the fire from underneath the pot and leave it on embers (*ghaḍā*) until the eggs thicken and set (*yaʿqud*) and the ingredients simmer and flavors nicely blend (*tatajammar*).

Take 2 eggs, boil them in water, and shell and split them into quarters [with a thread]. When all is done, ladle the dish into a glazed bowl (*ghaḍāra*)—let the egg yolks and the meatballs be visible. Arrange the egg quarters on top of the meat. You can fry the egg yolks in a pan if wished [instead of poaching them in the broth]. Sprinkle the dish with Ceylon cinnamon and ginger when served, and invoke the name of God Almighty and eat it salubriously,[9] God Almighty willing.

If you want to make this dish with eggplants, take as many as needed of small eggplants; peel them and split them into quarters up to their calyxes (*qaṭāmīr*, sg. *qiṭmīr*)—do not separate them. Take the eggplants and put them in a pot with salted water; put it on the fire and let the eggplants cook until they are done. Take them out, rinse them in hot water, press them gently [by hand

8 The verb used for this action is *yukhammar* (n. *takhmīr*).

9 وسمّ الله تعالى. This is a clear indication that *tafāyā* dishes were the first to be served in a meal, see also n. 2 above.

to get rid of excess moisture], and add them to the meat; and continue cooking until all is done. Add nothing to the pot aside from the juices of fresh cilantro, mint, and chard and the suet pounded with tips of cilantro and mint sprigs. Leave out the egg [yolks] and *takhmīr* (egg topping), there is no need for them.

This dish may also be made with the meat of young calves (*ʿajājīl ṣighār*), in which case it may be cooked either way. It may also be prepared with the meat of a suckling kid (*jadī raḍīʿ*) and fat chickens (*dajāj simān*), but they can only be done following the first method. These [varieties of meat] need to be prepared accordingly, God Almighty willing.

11.2.3 Another Dish, Called *kurunbiyya* (Cooked with Cabbages)[10]

Take whatever you choose of the tastiest cuts of meat from a fat young ram (*kabsh*). Cut them into pieces, wash and clean them, and put them in a new pot after pouring olive oil in it—put enough to coat the pot plus an extra amount to cook the meat.[11] Add salt, black pepper, coriander seeds, and a small amount of chopped onion.

Put the pot on the fire and attach to its rim a small pot filled with fresh water [to heat it up with its steam]. Stir the pot repeatedly until the meat releases its juices and starts to turn white. Add water from the small pot, just enough to cover the meat; do not put too much.

Take winter cabbages (*kurunb shatawī*)[12] and clean them meticulously, discarding the unwanted parts [e.g., outer leaves] but leaving their hearts whole with the small leaves attached to them. Chop the tender midribs (*aḍlāʿ*) after peeling them.[13] Put them in a pot with salted water and boil them on the fire; this would be a better and more effective way to get rid of their bad, unhealthy

10 Dishes cooked with vegetables were categorized as *baqliyyāt*, sg. *baqliyya* (from *baql* 'vegetables'). The anonymous thirteenth-century Andalusi cookbook *Anwāʿ al-ṣaydala* 134–5 calls a somewhat similar meat dish cooked with cabbages *baqliyyat Ziryāb*, see introduction ii.5, p. 50.

11 See n. 7 above.

12 Al-Ishbīlī, *ʿUmdat al-ṭabīb* i 313–5, praises winter cabbages over summer ones because they are sweeter, milder, and less pungent. In al-Ṭighnarī, *Zahrat al-bustān* 500, the summer variety is described as being excessively pungent (*shadīd al-ḥarāfa*), salty, and bitterish.

13 According to al-Ṭighnarī, *Zahrat al-bustān* 500, winter cabbages grow loosely packed heads with green leaves. In this recipe, the parts used are their tender hearts and the leaves closer to them, as well as the midribs of the larger leaves. In a recipe for white *kurunbiyya* in the anonymous *Anwāʿ al-ṣaydala* 205, the green parts of the large leaves are trimmed off, leaving only the midribs and looking like white turnip.

properties.[14] [Add them to the meat.] For those who prefer to just wash them in hot water and add them to the meat, they can do so.

When all is cooked, (**129r**) take a small amount of suet (*shaḥm*), pound it with tender tips of cilantro sprigs, and add it to the pot. Take a small amount of caraway seeds (*karāwiya*), lightly pound them in a mortar, and add them to the pot after it is done cooking. Leave it [on embers] for an hour until the boiling abates and the fat gathers on top.[15]

Ladle the dish into a glazed bowl and eat it, God Almighty willing.

If you want to make the dish with summer cabbages (*kurunb ṣayfī*), peel and clean them [as was done above], and always boil them due to their excessive pungency (*ḥarāfa*).[16] Once they boil, rinse them in heated-up fresh water and add them to the meat pot.

Next, take [other] meat, pound it, and discard the veins and sinews (*ʿurūq*); add the needed amounts of salt, black pepper, ginger, coriander seeds, Ceylon cinnamon, cloves (*qaranful*), and spikenard (*sunbul*); also add egg whites. Knead them all thoroughly until they combine and then make meatballs (*banādiq*) and throw them into the meat pot.

Take eggs, break them, and add salt, aromatic spices (*afāwīh*), and juice of fresh cilantro. Beat them very well so that they mix and set them aside. Next, take suet (*shaḥm*) and pound it with tender tips of sprigs of fresh cilantro and mint—enough to color the suet green—and add it to the pot. As soon as it boils, put the beaten eggs (*takhmīr*) all over the top and gently move and tilt the pot [to spread the eggs to cover the surface].[17] Remove the fire from underneath the pot and leave it on embers (*ghaḍā*) until the eggs set and thicken (*taʿqud*). You may also add egg yolks and skinned almonds [to the pot while still cooking].

When the pot is fully done, ladle the dish [into bowls], garnish it with split [boiled] eggs, and sprinkle it with Ceylon cinnamon and ginger, and eat it, God Almighty willing.

---

14 Cabbages were believed to be pungent, salty, and bitterish. They were blamed for bloating the digestive system, causing gurgles and phlegmatic vapors (*bukhār sawdāwī*).

15 The expression used here is '*tujammar al-qidr*,' which suggests the process of keeping the pot on embers so that it may nicely simmer and the flavors blend.

16 As described in al-Ṭighnarī, *Zahrat al-bustān* 500, summer cabbages have compacted leaves (called *kurunb maghlūq* 'tightly closed heads' in the anonymous *Anwāʿ al-ṣaydala* 206) with white tender stalks. They were generally believed to be more pungent than winter cabbages, see n. 12 above. For more on this vegetable, see glossary 12, s.v. *kurunb*.

17 That the pot is being moved and not the eggs in the pot is apparent in the instruction given in the following recipe for turnip stew, where the expression used is *yuḥarrak bi-l-yad* 'moved by hand.' Otherwise, food inside the pot itself will indeed be too hot to be stirred by hand.

You can also cook both varieties of this dish using veal by following the above instructions.

11.2.4 Another Dish, Called *liftiyya* (Cooked with Turnips)

Take whatever you choose of the tastiest cuts of meat from a fat young ram (*kabsh*), cut it into pieces, wash and clean it, and put it in a new pot after pouring in olive oil. Add salt, black pepper, coriander seeds—some people like to add cumin as well—and a small amount of chopped onion.

Put the pot on the fire to cook. Take a small pot filled with fresh water and attach it to its rim [so that it heats up with its steam]. Stir the pot repeatedly until the meat releases its juices and starts to turn white. Add water from the small pot to it, just enough to cover it, and continue cooking the pot.

Take turnips, peel them, wash them, and add them [whole] to the meat pot. When everything is cooked, remove the fire from underneath the pot and leave it for a short while [on embers] until the flavors blend and it is good to eat (*taʿtadil*). Ladle it into a glazed bowl (*ghaḍāra*), sprinkle it with Ceylon cinnamon, and eat it salubriously, God Almighty willing.

If you want (129v) to make the dish with summer turnips (*lift ṣayfī*),[18] cut deeply into their skins when you peel them, slice them into discs, wash them, and add them to the meat pot to cook. Next, take [other] meat, pound it, and remove its veins and sinews (*ʿurūq*). Add the needed amounts of salt, black pepper, ginger, Ceylon cinnamon, spikenard, cloves, and egg whites. Knead them well, make them into meatballs (*banādiq*), and throw them into the meat pot. Also take suet (*shaḥm*), pound it with tender tips of cilantro and mint sprigs, and add it to the pot.

Once the pot boils, take eggs and break them into a wide, shallow bowl (*ṣaḥfa*), adding cilantro juice and aromatic spices (*afāwīh*) as mentioned earlier.[19] Beat them all vigorously with a ladle so that they mix well. Now have a look at the meat and whatever there is in the pot. If you find that all is cooked and done, pour the eggs into the pot and move and tilt it by hand [to spread the eggs over the entire surface].[20]

Remove the fire from underneath the pot and leave it on embers (*ghaḍā*) until [the eggs] thicken and set and coat the cooked food (*taʿqud wa tatakham-*

18 Unlike winter turnips, they are said to be pungent, dry, and not so tender. See al-Ṭighnarī, *Zahrat al-bustān* 442; and Ibn al-ʿAwwām, *al-Filāḥa al-Andalusiyya* iv 307.

19 The spices often used are black pepper, ginger, and crushed saffron.

20 See n. 17 above.

FIGURE 50 Turnips, *Kitāb al-Diryāq*, fol. NP, detail
BNF, DEPARTMENT OF MANUSCRIPTS, ARAB 2964. SOURCE: GALLICA.BNF.FR/BNF

mar). Lade the dish into a glazed bowl (*ghaḍāra*), garnish it with split [boiled] eggs, sprinkle it with Ceylon cinnamon and ginger, and eat it salubriously, God Almighty willing.

If you want to add a small amount of juice of fresh cilantro to the pot before topping it with the eggs (*takhmīr*), go ahead and do so. You can also make both varieties with veal (*laḥm ʿijl*).

11.2.5 Another Dish, Called *qunnabīṭiyya* (Cooked with Cauliflower)

Take whatever you choose of the tastiest cuts of meat from a fat young ram (*kabsh*) and cut them into pieces. Wash and clean them and put them in a new pot, adding salt, plenty of olive oil, and black pepper. Also add coriander seeds and a small amount of chopped onion. Put the pot on the fire and attach a small pot with fresh water to its rim [so that it heats up with its steam]. Stir the pot, and when the meat releases its juices and is about to turn white, add water to it from the small pot, enough to cover it.

Take fresh and tender cauliflower and cut its head [into florets] by hand—leave out the stem (*ʿuslūj*)—and clean and wash them well. Now have a look at the meat; if it looks cooked, add the cauliflower and continue cooking until all is done. Take the fire from underneath the pot and leave it on embers (*ghaḍā*) so that the ingredients may simmer and flavors nicely blend (*tatajammar wa taʿtadil*). Ladle the dish into a glazed bowl (*ghaḍāra*), sprinkle it with Ceylon cinnamon and ginger, and eat it salubriously, God Almighty willing.

11.2.6 Another Dish, Called *silqiyya* (Cooked with Chard)

Take whatever you choose of the tastiest cuts of meat from a fat young ram (*kabsh*); cut them into pieces, wash and clean them, (130r) and put them in a new pot. Add salt, a good amount of olive oil, black pepper, coriander seeds, a small amount of chopped onion, soaked chickpeas, and skinned almonds. Put the pot on the fire and attach a small pot with fresh water to its rim [to keep it hot]. This water will be added to the meat, just enough to cover it, [that is, after it is stirred in the pot until it has released its juices and almost turned white]. After you add water, let the pot cook.

Now take fresh and tender chard and trim off the leafy parts from the midribs (*aḍlāʿ*) of the leaves. Cut the midribs into pieces, put them in a clean pot with water and salt, cook them to get rid of their brackish properties (*būraqiyya*),[21] and then take them out. Have a look at the meat; if it is almost done, add them to it.

When all is cooked, remove the fire from underneath the pot and leave it on embers (*ghaḍā*) so that the ingredients may simmer and flavors nicely blend (*tatajammar wa taʿtadil*). Ladle the dish into a glazed bowl (*ghaḍāra*), and eat it salubriously, God Almighty willing.

---

21 The brackish mineral in chard is sodium bicarbonate, *būraq* in Arabic.

FIGURE 51
Chard, *silq*, Dioscorides, *Kitāb al-Ḥashāʾish fī hāyūlā al-ʿilāj al-ṭibbī*, Arabic translation by Ḥunayn b. Isḥāq, Or. 289, fol. 84r, detail
UNIVERSITAIRE BIBLIOTHEKEN LEIDEN, HTTP://HDL.HANDLE.NET/1887.1/ITEM:1578266

II.2.7 Another Dish, Called *basbāsiyya* (Cooked with Fresh Bulb Fennel)[22]

Take as much as needed of meat from a fat young ram (*kabsh*), cut it, wash it, and put it in a new pot with salt, olive oil, black pepper, coriander seeds, and a small amount of chopped onion. Put the pot on the fire and let it cook while stirring it until it releases its juices and almost turns white. Add hot water to it as mentioned previously [in the recipes above]; add just enough to cover the meat.

Take fresh and tender fennel (*basbās ṭarī rakhṣ*) and discard the unwanted sections, choosing only the tender parts. Chop them finely; as fine as possible. For those who wish to pound them [in a mortar], they can do so. Wash the fennel and take a look at the meat; if it is done, add it to the pot and continue cooking.

Next, take suet (*shaḥm*) and pound it [in a mortar] with tender tips of fresh cilantro sprigs and those of fennel and add it to the pot. Also add a small amount of fresh cilantro juice. When the pot is fully cooked, leave it on a low fire to simmer and allow the flavors to nicely blend (*yatajammar*). Ladle the dish into a glazed bowl (*ghaḍāra*), and eat it salubriously, God Almighty willing.

22 This vegetable was known as *shamar*/*shamār* and *rāzyānaj* in the eastern region.

For those who want to have it topped with eggs (*takhmīr*), they may prepare it as was mentioned earlier in the green *tafāyā* dish (recipe ii.2.2), but [in this case] there needs to be a little sauce [in the pot].[23]

ii.2.8 Another Dish, Called *naʿnaʿiyya* (Cooked with Mint)

Take whatever you choose of the tastiest cuts of meat from a fat young ram (*kabsh*), cut it, wash and clean it, and put it in a new pot. Add salt, olive oil, black pepper, coriander seeds, and a small amount of chopped onion. Put the pot on the fire and attach to its rim a small pot filled with fresh water to heat it up with its steam. Stir the pot repeatedly until the meat releases its juices and almost turns white. Add enough of the heated-up water to cover it—but not too much.

Take fresh and tender mint, pick only the leaves and tender tips of the sprigs, (130v) and wash them to remove the sand and dust that might have clung to them. Put them in a clean pot with fresh water and cook them. Take them out when they are almost done and drain the liquid. If wished, this liquid may be used instead of the heated-up water [in cooking the meat], which indeed would be much better and more beneficial [than plain water].

Take the cooked mint, pound it [in a mortar] until it looks like paste, and add it to the meat pot. Also take suet (*shaḥm*), pound it with tender tips of cilantro and mint sprigs, and add it to the pot with a small amount of cilantro juice.

Let the pot cook until it is done, remove the fire from underneath it, and leave it on embers (*ghaḍā*) so that the ingredients may simmer and flavors nicely blend (*taʿtadil wa tatajammar*). Ladle the dish into a glazed bowl (*ghaḍāra*), and eat it salubriously, God Almighty willing.

ii.2.9 Another Dish, Called *turunjāniyya* (Cooked with Lemon Balm)[24]

It is made exactly like in the previous recipe [only replacing mint with lemon balm], neither a step more nor a step less, so know this.

---

23 The last suggestion is given in the Madrid MS, fol. 52r, only. Having little sauce in the pot if they are to be topped with *takhmīr* provides an important clue on the consistency of dishes it was used with.

24 The herb used is *turunjān, Melissa officinalis*, also called balm mint, whose leaves have a gentle citrusy scent. See glossary 8.

FIGURE 52 Borage, *lisān al-thawr*, Dioscorides, *Kitāb Dīsqūrīdis fī mawādd al-ʿilāj*, fol. 151r, detail
BRITISH LIBRARY: ORIENTAL MANUSCRIPTS, OR 3366, IN QATAR DIGITAL LIBRARY HTTPS://WWW.QDL.QA/ARCHIVE/81055/VDC_100022531380.0X000001

II.2.10 Another Dish, Cooked with *abū khuraysh*, Which Is *lisān al-thawr* (Borage)

Take meat from a fat young ram (*kabsh*), cut it, wash it, and put it in a new pot with salt, olive oil, black pepper, coriander seeds, and a small amount of chopped onion. Put the pot on the fire, stirring it repeatedly until the meat releases its juices and is about to turn white. Add hot water, just enough [to cover the meat],[25] and continue cooking the pot.

Take borage, remove the unwanted parts, and then chop it, wash it, put it in a clean pot with water and a bit of salt, and let it cook on the fire. Take it out, put it on a board, and strike it with the back of a knife's blade (*ẓahr al-sikkīn*) [repeatedly] until it is torn to shreds and becomes one mass.

Now have a look at the meat; if it is cooked, add the crushed herb. Also, take suet (*shaḥm*) and pound it with tender tips of cilantro sprigs and add it to the pot with a small amount of cilantro juice. Leave the pot for a short while on a low fire so that the ingredients may simmer and flavors nicely blend (*taʿtadil*

---

25 See recipe ii.2.2, for instance, for directions on how to prepare this hot water.

FIGURE 53 Orach, *qaṭaf*, Dioscorides, *Kitāb al-Ḥashā'ish fī hāyūlā al-ʿilāj al-ṭibbī*, Arabic translation by Ḥunayn b. Isḥāq, Or. 289, fol. 83r, detail
UNIVERSITAIRE BIBLIOTHEKEN LEIDEN, HTTP://HDL.HANDLE.NET/1887.1/ITEM:1578266

wa tatajammar). Ladle the dish into a glazed bowl (*ghaḍāra*), and eat it salubriously, God Almighty willing.

11.2.11 Another Dish, Cooked with Spinach (*isfanākh*)

Take as much as needed of the tastiest cuts of meat from a fat young ram (*kabsh*), cut it, wash and clean it, and put it in a new pot, adding salt, olive oil, black pepper, coriander seeds, and a small amount of chopped onion. (**137r**) Put it on the fire and let it cook, stirring it repeatedly until the meat

FIGURE 54 Blite, *yarbūz*, Dioscorides, *Kitāb al-Ḥashāʾish fī hāyūlā al-ʿilāj al-ṭibbī*, Arabic translation by Ḥunayn b. Isḥāq, Or. 289, fol. 82v, detail
UNIVERSITAIRE BIBLIOTHEKEN LEIDEN, HTTP://HDL.HANDLE.NET/1887.1/ITEM:1578266

releases its juices and is about to turn white. Add hot water, just enough to cover the meat.[26]

Now take spinach and clean it; take the tender leaves only. Put them in a clean pot with water and cook them on the fire. Take them out, put them on a board, and strike them with the back of a knife's blade (*ẓahr al-sikkīn*) until they are torn to shreds and become doughy in texture.

Take a look at the meat; if it is done, add the vegetable to it. Also, take suet (*shaḥm*) and pound it with the tender tips of cilantro and mint sprigs and add it to the meat; add cilantro juice as well. Leave the pot on a very low fire for a short while lest the vegetable should turn yellow. Ladle the dish into a glazed bowl (*ghaḍāra*) and eat it. When presented as a large dish in feasts, let it be offered garnished with fresh cheese, God Almighty willing.

If you want to use kid's meat (*laḥm jadī*), which would indeed go quite well with this dish, go ahead and cook it with it. Also, if you want to use meat of a yearling ram (*kabsh thanī*) with orach (*qaṭaf*) and blite (*yarbūz*),[27] prepare them as was done with the spinach dish, so, know this, God Almighty willing.

II.2.12 Another Dish, Cooked with Lettuce Heads (*ruʾūs al-khass*)

Take whatever you choose of the tastiest cuts of meat from a fat young ram (*kabsh*), cut it, wash and clean it, put it in a new pot, and add salt, olive oil, black pepper, coriander seeds, and a small amount of chopped onion. Put the pot on the fire and let it cook, stirring it repeatedly until the meat releases its juices and is about to turn white. Add hot water, just enough to cover the meat—do not add too much.[28]

Take lettuce [heads], remove all the green leaves, and peel and chop the stems, and then put them in a clean pot with water. Put it on the fire, and when the lettuce pieces are cooked, take them out and pound them in a wooden mortar (*mihrās ʿūd*) until they disintegrate and look like bone marrow (*mukhkh*).

Now take a look at the meat; if it is cooked, add the lettuce to it, and let it boil once or twice.[29] Next, top the surface with eggs, as was previously described.[30]

26 See the above note.

27 Leaves of wild amaranth, also known as *baqla Yamāniyya* 'Yemeni vegetable.' See glossary 12 for more on these leafy vegetables.

28 The editor of the Arabic text erroneously reads لا يكثر 'not to put too much' as لا يترك 'not to leave.'

29 See glossary 9.2, s.v. *ghalya*, for more on this cooking technique.

30 Covering the dish with a layer of eggs is called *takhmīr*; see, for instance, recipe ii.2.4 above.

Remove the fire from underneath the pot and leave it on embers (*ghaḍā*) to simmer and allow the flavors to blend well (*taʿtadil*). Ladle the dish [into a bowl], and eat it salubriously, God Almighty willing.

If you want to cook it like *qarʿiyya* (gourd stew), then take the meat and prepare and cook it as above, adding exactly the same ingredients. Now take lettuce, peel off the skins of their stems thoroughly, and slice them into very thin discs. Also take the tips of lettuce heads with their small leaves and split them into halves.[31] Wash them all and add them to the meat pot. (137v) Once it is cooked, [remove the fire from underneath the pot,] add [dried] thyme (*ṣaʿtar*) crushed between the hands, and leave the pot to simmer on low heat and allow the flavors to nicely blend (*yatajammar*). Ladle the dish into a glazed bowl (*ghaḍāra*), and eat it salubriously, God Almighty willing.

If you want, cook it with the meat of a suckling kid (*jadī raḍīʿ*). This will indeed go very well with it, with the help of God Almighty.

II.2.13 Another Dish, Called *rijliyya* (Cooked with Purslane)[32]

Take the needed amount of meat from yearling rams and do with it as was done in the previous recipes. After you put the pot on the fire, take fresh and young purslane that has not seeded yet. Chop it finely, the finest possible, and wash away the mucilaginous substance (*luʿāb*) in it by rubbing it gently between the hands with some salt. Add it to the meat pot [and continue cooking].

When all is cooked, take eggs, break them, and add what was previously mentioned in other places [in this book].[33] Beat them very well and pour them into the pot. Gently move it [i.e., the pot, to evenly spread the eggs]; and leave it on embers (*ghaḍā*) until the flavors nicely blend and the eggs set and thicken (*taʿtadil wa taʿqud*). Ladle the dish into a glazed bowl (*ghaḍāra*), and eat it, God Almighty willing.

---

31 The large green leaves are not used.

32 *Rijla* is also known as *baqla ḥamqāʾ*, see glossary 12.

33 Based on some of the previous recipes, salt, black pepper, ginger, saffron, and sometimes cilantro juice may be added.

FIGURE 55 Asparagus, *isfarāj*, al-Ghāfiqī, *Kitāb al-Adwiya al-mufrada*, MS 7508, fol. 138v, detail
REPRODUCED BY PERMISSION OF THE OSLER LIBRARY OF THE HISTORY OF MEDICINE, MCGILL UNIVERSITY

II.2.14 Another Dish, Cooked with Asparagus (*isfarāj*)[34]

Take as much as needed of meat from a fat young ram (*kabsh*); cut it, wash and clean it, put it in a pot, and add lots of olive oil, salt, black pepper, coriander seeds, and a small amount of chopped onion. Put it on the fire and stir it as was done in previous dishes. Add hot water, just enough to cover the meat.[35]

Take asparagus spears and remove the unwanted parts; take the tender ones only. Put them in a clean pot with water and salt, and cook them on the fire until they are done. Drain the liquid and taste the asparagus. If you find that they are no longer bitter, then all is set, but if they still are, add hot water to them and boil them once more to get rid of their bitterness. Take them out, rinse them in hot water, and let them drain completely in a sieve (*ghirbāl*).

Now take a look at the meat; if it is done, add the asparagus to finish cooking them. Next, take suet (*shaḥm*) and pound it with tender tips of cilantro and mint; add it to the pot along with juice of cilantro, and let it boil once or twice.[36] Next, take eggs, break them and mix [and beat] them with spices and cilantro juice as was done in previous recipes, and pour them all over the top (*tukhammar*). Remove the fire from underneath the pot and leave it on embers (*ghaḍā*) until the eggs set and thicken (*taʿqud*) and the flavors nicely blend (*taʿtadil*). Ladle the dish into a glazed bowl (*ghaḍāra*), garnish it with split boiled eggs as was done with the previous dishes, (**138r**) sprinkle it with Ceylon cinnamon and ginger, and eat it, God Almighty willing.

If you want to cook the asparagus with vinegar and color it with saffron,[37] add cumin to the spices, as well as garlic cloves, a small amount of *murrī* (liquid fermented sauce), and leaves of citron (*utrujj*). Once you put the meat pot on the fire to cook, take the asparagus, discard the unwanted parts, and boil them as mentioned above to get rid of bitterness, and then rinse and drain them and cut them into medium pieces.

Now have a look at the meat; if you find it is done or almost so, add the asparagus and continue cooking until all is done. Take saffron, pound it, dissolve it in some water, and add it to the pot; add just enough to color the meat

---

34 This was one of the foods that the famous singer Ziryāb popularized in al-Andalus. See introduction ii.5, p. 48. See also glossary 12, s.v. *isfarāj*. The anonymous Andalusi *Anwāʿ al-ṣaydala* 117–8 calls the vegetable by its Mashriqi name, *hilyawn*.

35 See above, recipe ii.2.2, for instance, for directions on how to prepare this hot water.

36 See glossary 9.2, s.v. *ghalya*, for more on this cooking technique.

37 According to the anonymous Andalusi *Anwāʿ al-ṣaydala* 204, meat dishes cooked with saffron, vinegar, and a vegetable are called *muthallath* (three-ingredient dish).

and asparagus—do not use too much of it. Once the pot comes to a boil, add fine-tasting vinegar, just enough to give it a nice flavor.

Take eggs, as many as needed, break them, and season them with aromatic spices (*afāwīh*), as was mentioned earlier, in addition to a small amount of saffron. Beat them all thoroughly and add them to the pot to cover the surface (*yukhammar*). Remove the fire from underneath the pot and leave it on embers (*ghaḍā*) until the eggs set and thicken (*taʿqud*) and the flavors nicely blend (*taʿtadil*). Ladle the dish into a glazed bowl (*ghaḍāra*), garnish it with split boiled eggs, sprinkle it with Ceylon cinnamon and ginger, and eat it, God Almighty willing.

If you want to cook it as a casserole dish (*muṭajjan*), take whatever you like of the abovementioned meat, chop it into small pieces, wash and clean it, and put it in a new pot. Add salt, plenty of olive oil, black pepper, coriander seeds, cumin, a small amount of [chopped] onion, a few cloves of garlic, leaves of citron (*utrujj*), sprigs of herb fennel (*ʿūd basbās*), and fine-tasting *murrī* (liquid fermented sauce)—add just the needed amount. Put the pot on the fire, stir it as was mentioned earlier, and then add hot water—just enough to cover the meat.[38]

Now take the asparagus and do with it as before, but leave the spears whole, do not cut them. Boil them [and set them aside]. Take saffron, pound it, dissolve it in some water, and add it to the meat pot. Once it boils, take some fine-tasting vinegar and add it to the meat—add just enough to give a nice flavor. Cover it with beaten eggs (*tukhammar*), as was mentioned above, and leave it on [very low] heat, as was mentioned above, but do not let the eggs set and thicken.

Take a glazed earthenware pan (*ṭājin muzajjaj*), put olive oil in it, and put it on the fire. When the oil heats up, take as many eggs as needed, break them in a wide, shallow bowl (*ṣaḥfa*) and beat them with a small amount of aromatic spices, and pour them into the pan to cover its bottom in an even layer. Now take some of the asparagus spears, gently press them between your hands [to get rid of excess moisture], and layer them on top of the eggs, followed by a layer of the meat; continue layering the asparagus spears and the meat until they are used up.

Take the broth in which meat was cooked, strain it, and pour it into the *ṭājin*. Break some more eggs and beat them with some aromatic spices and a small amount of saffron. Spread them on the face of the pan. Put some [whole] egg yolks as well.

38 See above, recipe ii.2.2, for instance, for directions on how to cook the meat and prepare the hot water for it.

Send the pan to the *furn* (communal brick oven), (138v) [and let it bake] until the eggs set and thicken—be careful not to let it burn. [You can serve it in the pan itself; or] if you want to take it out of the pan [and serve it,] garnished with split boiled eggs and sprinkled with Ceylon cinnamon and ginger, you can go ahead and do so, and eat it salubriously, God Almighty willing.

II.2.15 Another Dish, Cooked with Tender Spring Garlic (*farīk al-thūm*)[39]

Take the tastiest cuts from the meat of a fat ram (*kabsh*), such as the brisket (*ṣadr*) and racks (*ajnāb*, sg. *janb*). Cut them into pieces, clean them, and put them in a new pot. Add salt, plenty of olive oil, black pepper, coriander seeds, cumin, soaked chickpeas, a small amount of [chopped] onion, leaves of citron (*utrujj*), sprigs of herb fennel (*ʿūd basbās*), and *murrī* (liquid fermented sauce). Put the pot on the fire and do with it as was done in earlier recipes, [i.e.,] stirring it and adding the liquid.

Take [spring] garlic, remove the outer skins, and chop the green parts along with the stalks. As for the white heads, leave them whole; just slit them and color them with pounded saffron. Add them to the meat pot to cook. Add saffron as well.

Have a look at the meat; if it is almost done, add fine-tasting vinegar, as much as you see fit, seal the rim of the pot with a piece of dough or moistened paper (*kāghad*),[40] and send it to the *furn* (communal brick oven) to bake. Take it out when all the moisture is gone and it looks good.

If you want to cook the dish at home [on the stove], empty the cooked pot into a glazed earthenware pan (*ṭājin muzajjaj*), level the surface, and add some of the strained broth [in which meat and garlic were cooked]; put the pan on the fire. Now take another earthenware pan—an unglazed one—put strongly burning coals in it, and place it right above the meat pan. Keep checking on it until it is fully cooked to your satisfaction. Remove the pot from the fire, set it aside until its heat subsides, and serve it and eat salubriously, God Almighty willing.

---

39 According to the anonymous Andalusi *Anwāʿ al-ṣaydala* 204, a dish like this would be called *muthallath*, as it contains saffron, vinegar, and a vegetable, in this case spring garlic.

40 It is made from the fiber of the hemp plant. Cf. *qirṭās*, which is made from *bardī* 'Cyprus papyrus.' See glossary 9.1.

This dish may also be prepared with the meat of calves (*ʿujūl*, sg. *ʿijl*) and the meat of adult female goats (*ʿanz*) and young goats (*māʿiz*).[41]

II.2.16 Another Dish, Cooked with Fresh Green Almonds (*farīk al-lawz al-akhḍar*)[42]

Take the tastiest cuts from the meat of a fat ram (*kabsh samīn*), cut them into pieces, wash and clean them, and put them in a new pot with salt, olive oil, black pepper, coriander seeds, cumin, *murrī* (liquid fermented sauce)—but not much—a small amount of chopped onion, a few cloves of garlic, leaves of citron (*utrujj*), sprigs of herb fennel (*ʿūd basbās*), and soaked chickpeas. Put the pot on the fire and let it cook, stirring it repeatedly until the meat releases its juices and it is almost white. Add hot water, just enough to cover the meat, (**139r**) and leave the pot on the fire to finish cooking.

Now take fresh green almonds, remove their outer skins, and discard the unwanted parts; wash them and add them to the meat pot to cook with it. When they are almost done, color them with saffron, as mentioned earlier [in previous recipes]. Also add a ladleful of fine-tasting vinegar to give the dish a delicious flavor. Leave the pot on a low fire so that the ingredients may simmer and flavors nicely blend (*tatajammar*).

For those who want to top the dish with eggs (*yukhammar*),[43] they can go ahead and do so. Ladle the dish into a glazed bowl (*ghaḍāra*), sprinkle it with ginger, and eat it salubriously, God Almighty willing. For those who want to cook it with veal (*laḥm ʿijl*), they can do so, with the help of God.

II.2.17 Another Dish, Called *narjisiyya* (Looking Like Narcissus Flowers)[44]

Take meat from a fat young [ram] and cut it into pieces. Wash them and put them in a pot with salt, olive oil, black pepper, and coriander seeds. Cook the meat [in its released juices and the oil] until it is half done.

---

41 This addition is only given in the BL MS, fol. 138v.

42 A dish like this would be called *muthallath*, as it contains saffron, vinegar, and a vegetable, in this case the fresh green almonds—not really a vegetable but used as such. See also nn. 37 and 39 above.

43 See, for instance, recipe ii.2.2; see also glossary 9.2., s.v. *takhmīr*.

44 This recipe is identical with a *narjisiyya* found in the anonymous Andalusi *Anwāʿ al-ṣaydala* 136, where it is called *narjisiyya bi-l-jazar* (with carrots).

Cut scraped, fine-tasting carrots (*jazar*) into pencil-like strips,[45] the length of half a finger each. Add them to the meat pot with a small amount of water, vinegar, and saffron. Sprinkle in a small amount of washed rice grains (*aruzz*).[46]

When all is cooked, spread eggs beaten with saffron all over the surface, [and leave it on embers long] enough for the eggs to set and thicken (*yaʿqud*). Allow it to cool and then cut it with a knife into pieces, which will look like narcissus flowers.[47] [After adding the eggs,] the pot may also be cooked in the *furn* (brick oven), God Almighty willing.

II.2.18 Another Dish, Cooked with *ḥarshaf* (Cardoon), [of the Variety] Called *afzan*[48]

Take as much as needed of meat from a fat ram (*kabsh samīn*), cut it, wash and clean it, and put it in a new pot. Add whatever was added in the previous dishes to it; put the pot on the fire and do with it whatever was done in the previous dishes.

Now take cardoons and remove all their prickles (*shawk*) and all other unwanted parts. Boil them in water until they cook. Take them out, rinse them in hot water, chop them into small pieces, and add them to the meat pot. [Continue cooking] until all is done. Add saffron and vinegar as was done with the previous dishes. If you want it to be topped with eggs (*mukhammara*), follow what was done in the previous recipes, and leave the pot [on embers] until the eggs set and thicken. Ladle the dish into a glazed bowl (*ghaḍāra*), and eat it salubriously, God Almighty willing.

Laṣīf (gundelia) and *qannāriyya* (cultivated cardoon) are cooked the same way.[49]

If wished, all these [varieties] may be cooked as *Burāniyya*;[50] use them cut into discs, and add meatballs (*banādiq*) to them. *Ḥarshaf*[51] and *qannāriyya*

---

45 *Majrūd* (adj.), *j-r-d* (v.), designates the action of scraping the skins of carrots with a knife.

46 This is one of the few recipes that calls for rice.

47 The resemblance is in the resulting colors of yellow (carrot) and white (rice grains).

48 *Ḥarshaf* occurs as *khurshuf* in the Madrid MS, fol. 67r; it is the generic name for cardoons. *Afzan*/*afzān* is the name Maghribi Amazigh gave to wild cardoons (*ḥarshaf barrī*). See Ibn al-Bayṭār, *al-Jāmiʿ* ii 271, s.v. *ḥarshaf*; see also chapter vii.6 below.

49 *Laṣīf* (*Gundelia tournefortii*) is more commonly known as *ʿakkūb* in al-Mashriq. *Qannāriyya* is the Andalusi name for *ḥarshaf bustānī* 'cultivated cardoon' (*Cynara cardunculus var. altilis* DC). See glossary 12, s.v. *ḥarshaf*, for varieties of the plant.

50 The name is an Andalusi variant on *Būrāniyya*, see glossary 5. Cf. *Burāniyya* in recipe ii.1.2 above.

51 It occurs as *khurshūf* in the Madrid MS, fol. 67v. The reference here must be to the wild variety, *afzan*/*afzān*, used earlier in the recipe.

FIGURE 56 Cardoon, *qannāriyya*, called *kankar* in al-Mashriq, Dioscorides, *Kitāb al-Ḥashā'ish fī hāyūlā al-ʿilāj al-ṭibbī*, Arabic translation by Ḥunayn b. Isḥāq, Or. 289, fol. 111v, detail
UNIVERSITAIRE BIBLIOTHEKEN LEIDEN, HTTP://HDL.HANDLE.NET/1887.1/ITEM:1578266

are fried after boiling them. Additionally, all these cardoon varieties can be cooked with veal (*laḥm al-ʿujūl*), so know this and prepare them accordingly, God Almighty willing.

II.2.19 (139v) Another Dish, Cooked with *kam'a* (Desert Truffles), Which Are Called *tirfās*[52]

Take meat from a fat yearling ram (*kabsh thanī*), cut it into pieces, wash it, and put it in a new pot. Add salt, olive oil, black pepper, coriander seeds, and *murrī* (liquid fermented sauce)—but not much. Put the pot on the fire and stir it until the meat releases its juices and it almost looks white. Add hot water, just enough [to cover the meat], do not add too much.

Now take truffles and peel them after you wash them to remove any sand and similar stuff that might have stuck to them. Break them into pieces by hand, do not use a knife,[53] add them to the meat pot, and let them cook until done.

Remove the fire from underneath the pot and leave it on embers (*ghaḍā*) so that the ingredients may simmer and flavors nicely blend (*tatajammar*). Ladle the dish into a glazed bowl (*ghaḍāra*), sprinkle it with black pepper and ginger, and eat it salubriously, God Almighty willing.

II.2.20 Another Dish, Called *qarʿiyya* (Cooked with Gourds)[54]

Take meat from a fat yearling ram (*kabsh thanī*), such as its brisket (*ṣadr*) and racks (*ajnāb*). Cut it into pieces, wash it, and put it in a new pot. Add salt, a good amount of olive oil, black pepper, coriander seeds, and a small amount of chopped onion. Put the pot on the fire and do with it as was done in the previous recipes.

Now take a fresh and tender gourd,[55] scrape its outer skin, clean out the inside seeds (*zarīʿa*) and pith (*shaḥm*), and cut it into cubes. Wash the pieces and add them to the pot to cook with the meat. When all is done, add a few sprigs of *shaṭriyya* (thyme-leaved savory).[56] If *shaṭriyya* is not available, replace it with [dried] thyme (*ṣaʿtar*) crushed by hand; use it sparingly.

---

52 The name is of Amazigh origin. It occurs as *tirfāsh* in Ibn al-Bayṭār, *al-Jāmiʿ* i 188. *Kam'a* is the truffle's name in the eastern region. See glossary 12.

53 To my knowledge, such an instruction is found only in al-Tujībī's cookbook. Given the insipid flavor of desert truffles, my guess is that, compared with the knife-cut even pieces, the irregularly shaped truffle pieces broken by hand into chunks create many uneven edges that would absorb much more of the flavors of the liquids in which they are being cooked.

54 In the anonymous Andalusi *Anwāʿ al-ṣaydala* 204–3, a gourd dish cooked in a similar manner is categorized as *sādhaja* 'plain.' The word was descriptive of dishes that were neither sweet nor sour, which were thought of as being female dishes *mu'annatha*.

55 The gourd must have been large because only one is called for in the recipe.

56 *Satureja thymbra*, a variety of savory with long leaves that have a thyme-like flavor. See glossary 8.

Leave the pot on low heat so that the ingredients may simmer and flavors nicely blend (*tatajammar*). Ladle the dish into a glazed bowl (*ghaḍāra*), and eat it salubriously, God Almighty willing.

This dish may also be cooked with veal if wished.

11.2.21 Another Dish, Cooked with Apples, Both Sour-Sweet (*muzz*) and Sweet (*ḥulw*)

Take as much as needed of meat from a fat yearling ram (*kabsh thanī*). Cut it into pieces and wash and clean it. (**140r**) Put it in a new pot with salt, olive oil, black pepper, coriander seeds, a bit of cumin, and a small amount of onion. Put the pot on the fire and stir the meat until it releases its juices and it almost turns white. Add hot water to it, just enough to cover the meat [and cook it until almost done].

Now take some apples, peel them, and clean out their cores, removing the seeds (*zarīʿa*) and all. Cut them into pieces the way you like, add them to the meat pot, and let it cook until all is done. Add a small amount of saffron, followed by fine-tasting vinegar. Use only a small amount of vinegar if the apples are sour; but a ladleful of it with sweet apples, or whatever suits you.

Leave the pot [on embers] to allow the ingredients to simmer and flavors nicely blend (*tatajammar*). Ladle the dish into a glazed bowl (*ghaḍāra*), sprinkle it with Ceylon cinnamon and ginger, and eat it salubriously, God Almighty willing.

If wished, infuse the dish (*yuftaq*) with musk (*misk*), ambergris (*ʿanbar*), rosewater (*māʾ ward*), and camphor (*kāfūr*). Doing this will indeed endow it with qualities that would boost the psyche (*muqawwī lil-nafs*) and exhilarate the heart (*mufarriḥ*).

11.2.22 Another Dish, Cooked with Quinces (*safarjal*)

It is cooked exactly like the above, adding neither less nor more of the enhancing seasonings (*taftīq*) mentioned in the *tuffāḥiyya* dish,[57] so know this, and prepare it accordingly, God Almighty willing.

---

57 I.e., musk, ambergris, rosewater, and camphor.

FIGURE 57 Apples, Dioscorides, *Fī Hayūlā al-ṭibb*, translation by Ḥunayn b. Isḥāq, fol. 62r, detail
FROM THE NEW YORK PUBLIC LIBRARY, SPENCER COLLECTION: HTTPS://DIGITALCOLLECTIONS.NYPL.ORG/ITEMS/5E66B3E9-0539-D471-E040-E00A180654D7

FIGURE 58 A quince tree, Dioscorides, *Fī Hayūlā al-ṭibb*, translation by Ḥunayn b. Isḥāq, fol. 62v, detail
FROM THE NEW YORK PUBLIC LIBRARY, SPENCER COLLECTION: HTTPS://DIGITALCOLLECTIONS.NYPL.ORG/ITEMS/5E66B3E8-D881-D471-E040-E00A180654D7

II.2.23 Another Dish, Called *faḥṣī* (the Countryside Dish)[58]

It is cooked with pickled lemons (*līm muṣayyar*)[59] and whole pieces of Ceylon cinnamon. Take whatever you choose of meat and suet (*shaḥm*) from a fat ram (*kabsh samīn*), cut them into pieces, wash them, and put them in a new pot. Add salt, plenty of olive oil, black pepper, coriander seeds, a small amount of [chopped] onion, and sticks of Ceylon cinnamon. Put the pot on the fire and stir it repeatedly until the meat releases its juices and it almost looks white. Add hot water, just enough to cover the meat, not too much. Continue cooking the pot until the meat is almost done.

Now take pickled lemons (*līm muṣayyar*), as many as needed—but not too many. The best to use are the ones that have been preserved in lemon juice only.[60] Add them [whole] to the pot and continue cooking on a moderate fire until the lemons are done and no liquid remains in the pot except that of olive oil and the melted fat of the meat (*wadak*). Ladle the dish into a glazed bowl (*ghaḍāra*), sprinkle it with Ceylon cinnamon, and eat it salubriously, God Almighty willing.

This dish may also be cooked with the meat of fat chickens or veal, with the help of God Almighty.

II.2.24 Another [Mutton] Dish, Pot Fried (*maqlī fī l-qidr*)

(140v) Take as much as you like of meat and suet (*shaḥm*) from a fat ram (*kabsh samīn*), cut them into pieces, clean them, and put them in a new pot. Add salt, olive oil, black pepper, ginger, coriander seeds, a small amount of [chopped] onion, and small amounts of water and *murrī* (liquid fermented sauce).

Put the pot on the fire and let it cook gently until the water evaporates. Continue cooking while stirring the pot constantly until it browns. Remove the pot from the fire and ladle it into a glazed bowl (*ghaḍāra*). Add to it some preserved lemon juice (*khall līm*),[61] or that of Damascus citron (*khall*

58 The adj. *faḥṣī* is derived from *faḥṣ*, which designates plains, fields, and the countryside surrounding the inhabited areas in al-Andalus (Corriente, *Dictionary of Andalusi Arabic*, s.v. *f-ḥ-ṣ*). The dish was perhaps named so on account of its attractively speckled look, what with the unbroken cinnamon sticks and whole preserved lemons.

59 For recipes, see chapter x.3 below.

60 See chapter x.3 for preserving lemons, where mixing lemon juice with brine or even using brine alone are given as options.

61 See the note above.

zunbūʿ)[62] or fresh juice of unripe grapes (*khall ḥiṣrim ṭarī*),[63] and eat it salubriously, God Almighty willing.

II.2.25 Another Dish, Cooked with *murrī naqīʿ* (Sun-Fermented Liquid Sauce)[64]

Take as much as needed of meat from a fat ram (*kabsh samīn*), chop it into small pieces, clean it, and put it in a new pot. Add salt, olive oil, black pepper, coriander seeds, and a small amount of chopped onion. Also add *murrī*—just the needed amount—and a good amount of water.

Put the pot on the fire and let it cook until the meat is done. Leave it [on embers] to let it simmer and the flavors nicely blend (*tatajammar*). Empty the dish into a glazed bowl (*ghaḍāra*), pour whatever you choose of the previously mentioned vinegars [in the above recipe] on it, and eat it salubriously, God Almighty willing.

II.2.26 Another Dish, Called *shawā qidr* (Pot Roast)

Take as much as needed of the tastiest cuts of meat from a fat yearling ram (*kabsh thanī*); also take pieces from the places where there is the most fat, as well as choice pieces from the small and large intestines. Chop the meat into small pieces, clean it, but do not wash it; put it in a new pot. Take the small intestine, split it open, wash the inside, and clean it; chop it into small pieces and add it to the meat pot. Now take the large intestine, turn it inside out, scrape the inside to clean it, and then wash it, cut it into pieces, and add it to the meat.

Seal the pot, with its lid on, with some dough, or use paper (*kāghad*),[65] and take it to the *furn* (communal brick oven) to cook. Check on it and stir it fre-

---

62 Kharna sour orange hybrid, *Citrus aurantium var. khatta*. Based on Dozy, *Takmilat al-maʿājim* v 364, s.v. زنبوع, the name of this fruit is of Amazigh origin. It is more commonly known as *kabbād* in the eastern region, al-Mashriq. Al-Tujībī does not include recipes for making *khall zunbūʿ*.

63 See below, recipe x.7.14, for directions on extracting the juice. Note that in the two surviving Andalusi cookbooks, this one and anonymous *Anwāʿ al-ṣaydala*, *khall* not only designates regular 'vinegar' produced by fermentation but also, in a looser sense, unfermented, preserved 'sour juice,' and even freshly pressed out lemon juice or sour unripe grapes. See glossary 8, s.v. *khall*.

64 For *murrī* recipes, see chapter x.8 below.

65 It is made from the fiber of the hemp plant. Cf. *qirṭās*, which is made from *bardī* 'Cyprus

quently, and take it out when you know that it has cooked well. You should have ready with you some pounded Ceylon cinnamon, black pepper, ginger, and salt. Open the pot and add the spices and salt, only the needed amounts, do not put too much. Stir the pot to mix the meat with the salt and spices.

Ladle the dish into a glazed bowl (*ghaḍāra*) and sprinkle it with ginger and Ceylon cinnamon. If you like to use a small amount of any of the kinds of vinegar [mentioned in recipe ii.2.24] with it, go ahead and do so, (**141r**) and eat it salubriously, God Almighty willing.

II.2.27 **Another Dish, Called *lawziyya* (Cooked with Almonds)**

Take as much as needed of meat and suet (*shaḥm*) from a fat yearling ram (*kabsh thanī*). Cut them into pieces, wash and clean them, and put them in a new pot. Put clean salt, plenty of ginger, coriander seeds, and a small amount of onion in a piece of new cloth (*khirqa*); tie it and throw it into the pot along with plenty of olive oil. Put the pot on the fire and stir it repeatedly until the meat releases its juices and almost turns white. Add hot water, just enough to cover the meat, do not add too much, and continue cooking the pot.

Now take sweet almonds that have been skinned, washed in cold water, dried in a piece of cloth (*mindīl*), and pounded in a clean wooden mortar (*mihrās ʿūd*) until they have the consistency of bone marrow (*mukhkh*) and their oil (*duhn*) separates. Take them out and put them in a covered vessel to keep dust away.

Take the pot and empty it into a wide, shallow bowl (*ṣaḥfa*); transfer the meat pieces one by one into a separate vessel (*wiʿāʾ*). Strain the broth with a clean piece of cloth (*khirqa*) and wash the pot to remove whatever stuck to it. Put it back on the fire; return the strained broth and meat piece to it. Once it heats up, add the pounded almonds, and stir gently to help the almonds dissolve into the broth. Continue cooking until all the fats (*wadak*) in the pot separate and rise to the surface.

Remove the fire from underneath the pot and leave it on embers (*ghaḍā*) so that the ingredients may simmer and flavors nicely blend (*tatajammar*). Ladle the dish into a glazed bowl (*ghaḍāra*), and eat it salubriously, God Almighty willing.

If you want to add meatballs (*banādiq*) to the dish, you can do so. Additionally, if you want to cook it with lemon juice (*māʾ līm*), add it to the pot after

---

papyrus.' See glossary 9.1. The detail concerning covering the pot is mentioned only in the Madrid MS, fol. 54v.

the almonds are cooked; bring the pot to one or two boils, let it simmer [as described above], and ladle it, and eat it salubriously, God Almighty willing.

ii.2.28 Another Dish, from al-Mashriq (the Eastern Region),[66] Cooked with Taros (*qulqāṣ*)

It is cooked exactly like meat with turnips [recipe ii.2.4 above]. Choose only young and tender taros; peel them, slice them into discs, boil them in salted water, and then rinse them and add them to the meat. After the meat cooks with the taros, (141v) add a small amount of lemon juice (*mā' līm*)—it will make it taste more delicious—and eat it salubriously, God Almighty willing.

ii.2.29 Another Dish from al-Mashriq, Called *ṭabāhijiyya* (Succulent Fried Meat)

Take meat from a fat ram (*kabsh samīn*), cut it into finger-like strips, which you then cut into small pieces, separating the lean ones from the fatty ones. Spread the fatty pieces in the bottom of a pot and let them boil until they release their juices and their suet dissolves. Spread the lean meat pieces on top of these and let the pot boil without stirring it. When it comes to a boil, add salt, black pepper, caraway (*karāwiya*), and coriander seeds. Stir the pot, cover it with its lid, [and continue cooking it]; it will be done in no time.

If you want the dish to be sour, add the juice of sour pomegranate seeds, and eat it salubriously, God Almighty willing.

ii.2.30 Another Dish from al-Mashriq, Called *ṭabāhijiyya ṭibā'iyya* (Succulent Fried Meat, Which Has Agreeable Humoral Properties)[67]

Take meat [similar to the above] and cut it into small, thin slices (*sharā'iḥ*); put them in a wide, shallow bowl (*ṣaḥfa*), add vinegar, and leave them in it for an

---

66 Dishes cooked with taros were indeed quite popular in al-Mashriq, especially in Egypt, where it was one of the important crops grown in the region. See, for instance, anonymous fourteenth-century *Kanz al-fawā'id*, English trans., *Treasure Trove*, recipes 88 and 89 for *sitt shanā'* and *Mutawakkiliyya*, respectively. Note that *qulqāṣ* also occurs as *qulqās*, as in al-Tujībī's own list of the book's sections, p. 113.

67 The adj. *ṭibā'iyya* is derived from *ṭab'*, also called *mizāj*, associated with the properties of

hour to absorb it. Take them out and press them very well by hand to drain the vinegar. Take a soapstone pot (*burma*), put olive oil in it, and put it on the fire. When the oil boils, add the meat slices and let them fry in it until they brown.

Now take a wide, shallow bowl (*ṣaḥfa*) and put vinegar, *murrī* (liquid fermented sauce), coriander seeds, thyme (*ṣaʿtar*), and saffron in it. Set it aside for an hour and then strain the mix and take the resulting liquid.[68] Add it to the meat pot [gradually] while stirring it gently until enough liquid (*maraq*) is added. Remove the pot from the fire, and eat the dish, God Almighty willing.

II.2.31 Another Dish from al-Mashriq, Called *ṭabāhijiyya maghmūma* (Succulent Meat Fry Cooked in a Lidded Pot), Wonderful[69]

Take the meat of a fat ram (*kabsh samīn*). Cut the lean parts (*laḥm aḥmar*) into medium slices and those with suet in them into small slices. Put them in new pot with a large amount of olive oil by first spreading the fatty slices in its bottom followed by a layer of the lean slices spread all over them. Sprinkle them with salt, black pepper, coriander seeds, and caraway, along with fine-tasting vinegar and a small amount of *murrī* (liquid fermented sauce). Chop hard cheese (*jubn yābis*) into small pieces and spread it all over the meat. Cover the pot with a lid and let it cook, without stirring it, until the meat is done, and eat it salubriously, God Almighty willing.

II.2.32 (142r) Another Dish, Cooked with Fresh Fava Beans (*fūl akhḍar*), Called *fustuqiyya* (Pistachio Green)[70]

Take whatever you choose of the tastiest cuts of meat and suet from a fat yearling ram (*kabsh thanī*). Cut them into pieces, wash and clean them, and put them in a new pot. Add salt, olive oil, coriander seeds, small amounts of cumin, and [chopped] onion. Put the pot on the fire, stirring it [repeatedly] until the meat releases its juices and it almost turns white. Add hot water, just enough to cover the meat, and let it cook.

---

the four humors that are based on the Galenic theory. Physicians were sometimes referred to as *ahl al-ṭabāʾiʿ*, see, for instance, al-Ṭighnarī, *Zahrat al-bustān* 229. They were called so because they based their practices on the tenets of this theory. See glossary 11, s.v. *mizāj*.

68 This should be ready by the time the meat browns in the oil.

69 *ʿAjība*, as described in the Madrid MS, fol. 56v.

70 Described as *jayyida* 'good,' in the Madrid MS, fol. 56v.

Now take fresh and tender fava beans, peel and wash them, and put them in a clean pot with fresh water (*mā' ʿadhb*). Put the pot on the fire and cook the beans until done. Attach a small pot with water in it to the rim of the pot [so that it heats up with the steam of the cooking beans]. If the liquid dries out before the fava beans are done, add some of this heated-up water (*musakhkhan*) so that they have enough liquid to cook in. Once the fava beans are done, remove the pot from the fire and stir them vigorously with a large ladle until they disintegrate and have the consistency of bone marrow (*mukhkh*); set them aside.

Now have a look at the meat; if it is done, take the fava beans and add them to it, and stir the pot gently. Remove the fire from underneath the pot and [finish the cooking] on a gently burning fire (*nār layyina*). Take fresh suet and pound it with the tender tips of sprigs of cilantro or mint and add it to the meat and fava beans. Also add cilantro juice. Let the pot boil first and then simmer [on embers] so that its flavors may nicely blend (*tatajammar*). Ladle the dish into a glazed bowl (*ghaḍāra*), and eat it salubriously, God Almighty willing.

II.2.33 Another Dish, Cooked with Crushed Dried Fava Beans (*fūl yābis maṭḥūn*), Which is Called *baysār*[71]

Take meat from a fat yearling ram (*kabsh thanī*), as well as suet (*shaḥm*) and the choice pieces from the small intestine (*ʿuyūn al-duwwāra*). Cut them all into pieces, clean them, and put them in a new pot. Add salt, olive oil, black pepper, coriander seeds, cumin, and a chopped onion. Put the pot on the fire and let it cook, stirring it repeatedly until the meat releases its juices and it almost turns white. Add hot water, just enough to cover the meat, and continue cooking the pot.

Take [crushed dried] fava beans,[72] wash them several times in hot water, [drain them,] rub them with olive oil, and put them in a new pot, which has been greased with olive oil. Add hot water to the pot, with a whole onion, a head of garlic—leave it whole[73]—cumin, and fennel seeds (*basbās*). Put the

71 This was its North African name. Nowadays the name is more frequently encountered there, as well as in Egypt, as a dish called *biṣāra* 'porridge of crushed dried fava beans.' When referring to the fresh fava beans in this book, they are called *fūl akhḍar* (green fava beans), as in the previous recipe.

72 Called *fūl* here, and *baysār* in the Madrid MS, fol. 57r. The fava beans, described as *maṭḥūn* (crushed) at the beginning of the recipe, must have been crushed coarsely because they are washed several times, and later they will be further mashed after boiling them.

73 Adding the onion and garlic head whole will make discarding them after the beans are cooked easier.

pot on the fire and let it cook without stirring it until the beans cook.[74] If the liquid dries out before the beans are cooked, add some more hot water to it, and continue until they are done. Remove the onion and garlic from the pot.[75]

Now take some salt (**142v**) and put it in a wide, shallow bowl (*ṣaḥfa*) [and put it next to you]. Hold a ladle and insert it in the pot to stir the beans with it, adding some salt while stirring it; continue doing this until the beans disintegrate and look smooth and enough salt is added. Set the pot aside.

Have a look at the meat. If it looks cooked, start adding the fava beans little by little until they combine with the meat. Leave the pot on embers (*ghaḍā*) for an hour until it starts to lose its heat. Ladle the dish into a glazed bowl (*ghaḍāra*), and eat it salubriously, God Almighty willing.

II.2.34 Another Dish, Cooked with Crushed Chickpeas (*ḥimmaṣ maṭḥūn*)

Take cuts of meat from a yearling ram, such as the rump (*dhanb*), tail fat (*alya*), and brisket (*ṣadr*). Cut them into pieces, wash them, and put them in a new pot. Take chickpeas, crush them, sift out their skins, and add them to the meat pot. Add hot water, along with lots of olive oil, salt, black pepper, and a pounded onion.

Put the pot on the fire to cook. As soon as it comes to a boil, reduce the heat, and leave it to cook on a slow-burning fire until the chickpeas fall apart. Take out the meat pieces, stir the chickpeas in the pot to mash them, and then return the meat to the pot. Add fine-tasting vinegar—the amount depends on one's preference—and leave the pot on embers for an hour. Ladle the dish into a glazed bowl (*ghaḍāra*), and eat it, God Almighty willing.

II.2.35 Another Dish, from al-Mashriq, Called *ṭafshīla*[76]

Take cuts from a yearling ram, similar to the ones used in the previous recipe. Cut them into small pieces and put them in a new pot with salt, plenty of

---

74 Cooking the crushed beans without stirring them was believed to make them less bloating, as explained in al-Ghassānī, *Ḥadīqat al-azhār* 54.

75 This detail is included only in the Madrid MS, fol. 57v.

76 Copied as *mishliyya* in the Madrid MS, fol. 57v; possibly, a corrupted form of the dish's name, or a copyist's error. This recipe uses chickpeas only. However, based on the extant Mashriqi recipes for *ṭafshīl*, the dish is usually cooked with more than one kind of pulse

olive oil, black pepper, coriander seeds, and a chopped onion. Put the pot on the fire and stir it repeatedly until the meat releases its juices and it is almost white. Add a moderate amount of hot water (*wasaṭ*) and continue cooking the pot.

Take chickpeas and pound them until they are as fine as fine white flour (*darmak*). Sift them in a fine-meshed sieve.[77] Take the meat out of the pot piece by piece, put them in a glazed bowl (*ghaḍāra*)—keep it covered—and strain the broth with a clean piece of cloth.

Wash the pot and return it to the fire. Return the strained broth and the meat to it. Add saffron that has been pounded and dissolved in water. Also add pounded Ceylon cinnamon and fine-tasting vinegar—the amount depends on one's preference.

When all is cooked, take the ladle, put it in the pot, and start sprinkling chickpea flour (*daqīq al-ḥimmaṣ*) little by little while stirring the pot. Continue doing this until enough is added and the broth starts to thicken. Give all your attention to it [while doing this] lest it should burn and spoil. Remove the pot from the fire, ladle it in a glazed bowl (*ghaḍāra*), and eat it salubriously, God Almighty willing.

11.2.36 [143r] Another Dish, Called *al-ʿArabī* [Mutton Cooked with Whole Chickpeas][78]

Take as much as needed of the meat of a fat ram. Cut it into pieces, wash and clean it, and then put it in a new pot with salt, olive oil, black pepper, coriander seeds, a bit of cumin, plenty of soaked chickpeas, skinned almonds, a moderate amount (*wasaṭ*) of *murrī* (liquid fermented sauce), a chopped onion, leaves of citron (*utrujj*), and sprigs of herb fennel (*ʿūd basbās*).

---

and grain, such as lentils, chickpeas, beans, mung beans, and rice, all in one dish. See, for instance, al-Warrāq, *Kitāb al-Ṭabīkh*, English trans., *Annals*, chapter 66; and al-Warrāq's Istanbul MS, fols. 218r–221r. They all include vinegar.

The *ṭafshīla* dish seems to have been cooked from ancient times. Even the name itself is said to be of Hebrew origin (see al-Marzubānī, *Nūr al-qabas* 138). I have even found out that the Hebrew name can be traced back to the much older Akkadian root verb *ṭapāshu* 'to be fat.' Interestingly, a couple of medieval poems associate *ṭafshīla* with gaining weight.

77 *Ghirbāl shaʿr*, woven with animal hair.

78 Described as *jayyid* 'good' in the Madrid MS, fol. 57v. It is a simple dish of meat with lots of chickpeas, used whole. Judging from the last statement in the recipe, it seems to have been a simple staple in the Arab communities, offered in wedding festivities.

Put the pot on the fire and stir it [frequently] until the meat releases its juices and it looks almost white. Add hot water to the pot, just enough to cover the meat, and continue cooking until all is done.

Once the meat and the chickpeas are done, take saffron, pound it in a copper mortar (*mihrās nuḥās*), and add it to the pot; use enough of it to give the meat and chickpeas an intense color. Remove the fire from underneath the pot and leave it on embers (*ghaḍā*) so that the ingredients may simmer and flavors nicely blend (*tatajammar*). Ladle the dish [into a bowl], and eat it salubriously, God Almighty willing.

If you want to use veal instead, you can do so. When cooked for wedding festivities (*walāʾim*, sg. *walīma*), this dish is offered garnished with *farsh* and split [boiled] eggs,[79] so know this.

II.2.37 Another Dish, Called *ṣinābī* (Cooked with Mustard Sauce)[80]

It benefits weak and cold stomachs.

Take meat from a fat young [ram], clean it, cut it into pieces, and put it in a clean pot with salt, olive oil, coriander seeds, black pepper, a bit of cultivated rue (*sadhāb bustānī*),[81] a small amount of [chopped] onion, and a ladleful of vinegar. Put the pot on a slow-burning fire, and once the meat fries, add enough water and cook it until done.

Take the insides (*lubāb*) of leavened bread made with fine white flour (*darmak*) and lightly grate them.[82] Beat them with eggs and 2 ladlefuls of well-made mustard sauce (*ṣināb*). Cover the meat with this mix (*yukhammar*), and leave it for an hour [on embers] until the eggs thicken and set. Remove the pot from the coals and set it aside until its fat (*wadak*) rises to the surface, and eat it salubriously, God Almighty willing.

---

79 Recipe ii.1.10 above describes how to prepare such garnishes.

80 *Ṣināb*, also known as *khardal*, refers to the seeds themselves as well as sauces/condiments made with them. For mustard sauce recipes, see chapter x.1 below. See glossary 5 and 8, s.v. *ṣināb*, for mustard condiments and the seeds, respectively. Mustard, with its hot and dry properties, was used to cure cold-related maladies and aid digestion. See glossary 11, s.v. *mizāj*.

81 It was called *fayjan* in the Muslim West. See Ibn al-Jazzār, *al-Iʿtimād* 882.

82 *Maḥkūk yasīran* is an addition from the anonymous *Anwāʿ al-ṣaydala* 5, which is almost identical with this one. It also suggests replacing the breadcrumbs with pounded skinned almonds.

II.2.38 Another Dish [of Roasted or Grilled Side of Mutton][83]

Take a whole side (*janb*) of a yearling ram (*kabsh thanī*) with the chest part attached. Use a cleaver (*sāṭūr*) to break the ribs from the top to the bottom of the side; [just break the ribs,] the outside should look uncut. Break the ribs at three [parallel] places.[84] Rub the side with salt and black pepper thoroughly, lay it flat in a large, glazed earthenware pan (*ṭājin muzajjaj*), and let it be carried to the *furn* (communal brick oven) and placed at a distance from the fire until the meat cooks and browns. It must be turned on the other side until it browns [as well]. Take it out and serve it, (**143v**) God Almighty willing. If you want to add one of the vinegar varieties mentioned earlier before roasting it, you can do so.[85] Alternatively, you can eat it with mustard sauce (*ṣināb*).[86]

If you want to grill the meat,[87] thread the side on a [large] iron or wooden skewer (*saffūd*) and suspend it on a burning fire placed all around it [but not underneath it]. Let it grill gently and slowly until the meat is done. It has to be left in one piece, but you can divide it into pieces if you wish: after breaking the ribs with a cleaver [as shown above], cut it lengthwise [along the broken places], thread them on skewers, and grill them after rubbing them gently with salt and black pepper. Let them grill until done, and eat them salubriously, God Almighty willing.

II.2.39 Another Dish [of Grilled Mutton Strips and *tannūr*-Roasted Ram]

Take meat from the thighs (*afkhādh*) and loin (middle back, *sinsin*) of a fat ram—keep the suet on them. Slice the meat with a knife into thin strips (*sharāyiḥ riqāq*). Sprinkle them with pounded salt and thyme—but not too much—and black pepper. Fold the meat strips so that they all get coated with salt and spices.

Now take an iron griddle (*mafrash ḥadīd*) specially made for grilling meat strips. Put it on a flameless and smokeless medium fire and spread the meat strips on it. Once they brown, turn them on the other side to cook and brown. Remove them from the griddle and spread more of the strips until they are all

---

83 This recipe and the following three deal with ways to roast and grill meat.

84 The aim of breaking the ribs in this way is to be able to lay it flat in the roasting pan.

85 The varieties are mentioned in recipe ii.2.24 above.

86 Vinegar and mustard sauces were believed to aid the digestion of grilled meats. For mustard sauce recipes, see chapter x.1 below.

87 The term *shiwā'* is used here to designate grilling meat on an open fire.

done. Cover only the finished ones with something that allows steam to escape. When the time comes to serve the dish, put them on the table (*māʾida*) along with two bowls—one with *murrī naqīʿ* (sun-fermented liquid sauce) and one with *ṣināb* (mustard sauce). Dip the meat slices in whichever you choose of the sauces, and eat them salubriously, God Almighty willing.

If you want to roast a yearling ram in the *tannūr* (clay oven), insert a wooden skewer (*saffūd ʿūd*) through the buttocks (*dhanb*) and all the way through the neck. Cut off its forelegs right below the joints; also cut off the hind legs at the hock joints (*ʿurqūb*). Cut off its rump (*dhanb*), fatty tail (*alya*), and the meat on both haunches (*wirkayn*) as well. Take the tripe (*karsh*), intestines (*maṣārīn*), and heart (*fuʾād*); clean them all, cut them into pieces, and make a skewered *ʿuṣbāna* with them.[88] Wrap them well with a piece of caul fat (*minsaj*) and then wind a piece of the intestines all around them. Now take a skewer and pass it through both of the ram's sirloins (lower back, *khāṣiratayn*, sg. *khāṣira*); also insert with it the rump and the two pieces [i.e., fatty tail and haunches].[89] Put the cut off parts of the fore and hind legs inside the cavity.

[Light a fire in the *tannūr*] and heat it up until [its inner walls] look white. Once it is hot, put an earthenware pan (*ṭājin fakhkhār*) in its bottom and lower the ram in it, putting the lower end of the skewer inside the *ṭājin*. Do likewise with the skewer of the intestine roll (*ʿuṣba*).[90] Put a lid on the [top opening of the] *tannūr*; seal it with mud to prevent steam from escaping. Do likewise with any other openings.[91] Leave the *tannūr* closed like this until [according to your estimation] you know that the ram is done. Open it, take out the ram, and lay it on whatever you choose of leaves of mint (*naʿnaʿ*), herb-fennel fronds (*bas-bās*), myrtle leaves (*rayḥān*),[92] and the like. It may also be sprinkled with [a

88 Copied as *ʿaṣṣāba* in the Berlin MS, fol. 36v. Later in the recipe, it will be called *ʿuṣba* (pl. *ʿuṣbān*). Pieces of the tripe and the heart are threaded on a skewer, secured by wrapping them in caul fat; all to be wrapped with a piece of the intestine wound all around them. Cf. an earlier recipe, i.2.2, where similar rolls are made. Grilled rolls such as these are still made today in countries like Turkey, where they are called *kokorec*. See glossary 10, s.v. *ʿuṣb*.

89 The word referring to the two pieces is incoherently copied as والبيتين in the Berlin MS, fol. 36v, and the BL MS, fol. 143v. The Madrid MS, fol. 61r, does not include this detail. The editor of the Arabic text improvised and edited it as الاليتان 'two fatty tails,' but rams do not happen to have two tails. The word might have been a misreading of والشيئين 'the two things/parts.'

90 See n. 88 above.

91 See glossary 9.1, s.v. *tannūr* for a description of this type of oven.

92 Although *rayḥān* can be any sweet-smelling plant, it was particularly used to designate *ās* 'myrtle' in the western region, whereas in Iraq and the Levant it designated basil, variously called *ḥabaq*/*ḥawak* and *bādharūj*; as explained in Ibn Qayyim al-Jawziyya, *al-Ṭibb al-nabawī* 241.

sauce of] vinegar mixed with [chopped] mint, for those who prefer to have it like this. [To serve,] sprinkle it with some ground spices [such as cinnamon and ginger], with pounded salt [in small vessels] put close to it on the table, and eat it salubriously, God Almighty willing.

11.2.40 (144r) Another Dish, Called *al-kāmil* (Complete), Wonderful[93]

Take a fat yearling ram, slaughter it, skin it, and make a small opening in its belly from between the thighs—it should be just big enough for the hand to get in. Take out all that there is inside its cavity, wash it to remove the blood, and clean it and put it aside.

Take as many as needed of fat young adult chickens, as well as squabs (*firākh ḥamām*), fat turtledoves (*yamām*), and fat sparrows (*ʿaṣāfīr*). Cook them any way you prefer. Make a soupy mix (*ḥasū*) with the grated crumbs of bread (*lubāb al-khubz al-maḥkūk*) beaten with egg whites and all kinds of spices and herbs. Stuff the bird cavities with this mix and then take them one by one and insert them into the cavity of the ram until it is full. Pour what remains of the soupy stuffing into the cavity and add the usual [boiled] egg yolks, meatballs (*banādiq*), pickled lemons (*līm muṣayyar*), and olives. Completely sew up the opening with a strong thread.

Lay the ram flat (*yumadd*) as it is in the [heated] *tannūr* (clay oven); close its opening and seal it with clay.[94] Leave it there for a short while and then take it out.[95] Rub the entire ram with a mixture of vinegar, *murrī naqīʿ* (sun-fermented liquid sauce), a small amount of saffron, black pepper, and thyme (*ṣaʿtar*)—you should also have sprinkled the entire inside of the ram with this sauce before filling it. Now return the ram to the *tannūr*, reseal it tightly with clay,[96] and leave it there until it is fully done. Take it out and serve it, God Almighty willing.

---

93 *ʿAjīb*, as described in the Madrid MS, fol. 59v. A similar recipe is given in the anonymous Andalusi *Anwāʿ al-ṣaydala* 10, with some stylistic differences and minor additions and omissions of some details. It also offers another *kāmil* dish, p. 157, assembled with crumbled bread as *tharīd*, offered to kings, viziers, and the elite.

Al-kāmil was a favorite all-in-one festive dish, which rendered offering other dishes with it unnecessary, as we learn from an Andalusi saying, which mocked people who exaggerate in pleasing others: يعمل الكامل بزايد لون, "He makes *al-kāmil* and an extra dish with it." See al-Zajjālī, *Amthāl al-ʿawām* ii 482.

94 Laying the stuffed ram flat and sealing the oven with clay are mentioned only in the Madrid MS, fol. 59r. For such purposes, the bottom of the *tannūr* would have been lined with big flat bricks called *ājur* or *qirmīd*. See, for instance, al-Warrāq, *Kitab al-Ṭabīkh*, English trans., *Annals* 176.

95 The purpose for this initial brief roasting is to give the soupy filling some time to set.

96 Addition from Madrid MS, fol. 59r, see n. 94 above.

II.2.41 Another Dish, Called *aknāf* (Enclosed)[97]

Take a yearling ram (*kabsh thanī*), disjoint it [into large chunks], and divide the rib section into pieces, three ribs each (*thalāthan thalāthan*). Dig a pit in the ground; put lighted coals in it.[98] Put the neck piece first (*ʿunq*) and then start layering the other pieces on top of each other.

Now take a large pan (*ṭājin*)[99] and cover the meat in the pit with it. Push earth into the edges of the pan to lock in the steam of the [roasting] meat. Put firewood on the pan and all around it, light the fire, and leave it until, in your estimation, the top of the meat has browned. Push the fire aside, remove the pan, and turn the meat pieces, moving what was on the bottom to the top and what was on the top to the bottom. Cover the meat with the pan again, put back the burning firewood as it was before, and leave it for a while (literally, an hour) until, in your estimation, the meat has roasted and browned.

Push aside the firewood, remove the pan, and put the meat in a vessel. Sprinkle it with salt and black pepper, and eat it salubriously, God Almighty willing.

II.2.42 Another Dish, Cooked with Honey, Called *muʿassal*

(**144v**) Take meat cuts from a fat ram, such as the rump (*dhayl*), brisket (*ṣadr*), and similar pieces with a good deal of suet in them; also take suet from the kidneys. Dice them into small pieces, clean them, and put them in a new pot with salt, plenty of olive oil, coriander seeds, and enough water [to cover the meat]. Put the pot on the fire to cook.

Take fine-tasting honey, enough for what is cooking in the pot and put it in a cauldron (*ṭinjīr*) to clean it by skimming its froth.[100] Take the meat

---

97 Meat in this recipe is roasted while enclosed inside a prepared pit, and hence the name. The Madrid MS, fol. 58v, simply calls it *kabāb* (grilled chunks of meat). In the eastern region, it was more commonly known as *mallīn*, which is derived from *malla* 'baking by burying in sand.' In the anonymous Andalusi *Anwāʿ al-ṣaydala* 51, it is described as the preferred dish for weddings in the Levant. Today in Jordan, it is a traditional Bedouin dish, called *zarb*, which is derived from *ḍarb*, literally 'beating,' originally used to reflect the custom of beating *malla* bread to get rid of sand grains that adhered to it while buried.

98 *Nār al-jamr* is mentioned in the Madrid MS, fol. 58v, only. Heating up the base of the pit before arranging the meat in it is required in this roasting technique. See al-Warrāq, *Kitāb al-Ṭabīkh*, English trans., *Annals* 335–6. Once the pit heats up, all the coals or burnt firewood are usually removed before adding the meat.

99 This would most probably be made of iron, *ṭājin ḥadīd*.

100 This is done by mixing honey with some water and boiling it until the water evaporates and the resulting froth is skimmed off. See glossary 4, s.v. *ʿasal*.

out of the pot and set it aside. Strain the broth and set it aside. Wash the pot and then return it to the fire. Add the honey, followed by the meat and broth.

Now take wheat starch (*nashā*), 1½ *ūqiyyas* (1½ ounces) for each *raṭl* (pound) of honey used. Dissolve it with some water, strain it, and pour it slowly into the pot while stirring it constantly to prevent starch lumps. Color it with a bit of saffron. [Remove the fire from underneath the pot] and let it simmer [on embers] to allow the flavors to nicely blend (*yatajammar*). Once the fat gathers on top, you may eat the dish salubriously, God Almighty willing.

II.2.43 Another Dish [of Meat Sweetened with Honey], Called *ghassāniyya*[101]

Take meat similar to what was used in the previous recipe. Clean it and put it in a new pot with water, salt, plenty of olive oil, coriander seeds, and honey that has been boiled and skimmed of its froth.[102] Put it on the fire and let it cook until the meat is done.

Now take [coarse] semolina (*samīd*) and rinse it in hot water several times.[103] Add it to the meat pot bit by bit while stirring until all of it is used. Taste the dish: if it is not sweet enough, add some more honey; if it is thin in consistency, add some more semolina; do this until it tastes good. Keep on stirring the pot until its fat comes up to the surface; if it does not, then add more olive oil and continue cooking until the semolina is done. Put the pot at a distance from the fire, color it with a bit of saffron, leave it for a short while,[104] and then take it down [from the stove], ladle it, and eat it salubriously, God Almighty willing.

---

101 This is a variation on the previous *mu'assal* recipe. These sweet meat dishes were served among other courses that constituted the main meal. Other *mu'assal* and *ghassānī* recipes will be given later in the book (chapter ix.1), prepared as confections and served at the end of meals. See recipe i.5.3 above for another variety of *ghassānī*.

102 See n. 100 above.

103 Since the semolina particles are rinsed several times in hot water, I assumed it cannot be in the form of flour used in making bread.

104 Detail only in the Madrid MS, fol. 59v.

II.2.44 Another Dish, Called *ra's maymūn* (Blessed Head)[105]

Take meat from the sirloins (lower back, *khawāṣir*, sg. *khāṣira*) of a fat ram and choice sections from the small intestine (*ʿuyūn al-duwwāra*). Chop them into very small pieces, clean them, and put them in a new pot. Add salt, plenty of olive oil, black pepper, coriander seeds, cumin, a small amount of chopped onion, skinned almonds, soaked chickpeas, a ladleful of *murrī* (liquid fermented sauce), a few cloves of garlic, leaves of citron (*utrujj*), and sprigs of herb fennel (*ʿūd basbās*). Put the pot on the fire and stir it [repeatedly] until the meat releases its juices and almost turns white. Add hot water and let it cook until done. Now take saffron, pound it in a copper mortar, dissolve it in fresh water (*māʾ ʿadhb*), and add it to the meat pot to color it. (**145r**) Add fine-tasting vinegar to taste.

Take eggs, which you estimate to be enough [for the dish], and break them into a wide, shallow bowl (*ṣaḥfa*). Take some of the yolks and add them to the pot [to poach], and to the rest of the eggs, add salt, black pepper, ginger, Ceylon cinnamon, and a small amount of pounded saffron [and set it aside].

Take the meat out of the pot once it is done cooking and put it aside in a *ṣaḥfa* [along with the chickpeas, almonds, and poached egg yolks].[106] Strain the broth, discarding the citron leaves, fennel sprigs [and onion and garlic], and any cooking dregs (*thufl*).

Take the green-glazed earthenware vessels that are specially made with small bases and wide rims for cooking the dish.[107] Put them on the fire and add 2 *ūqiyyas* (2 ounces) olive oil to each.[108] Once the oil heats up, take the meat and whatever was with it of the chickpeas and almonds and mix them with the [set aside] eggs. Put 1 poached egg yolk in the bottom of each vessel and then fill it with the meat mix—but not all the way up to the rim. Take the fat (*wadak*) of the strained broth and add it to the olive oil in the vessel[109] [and start cooking them].

105 From above, recipe ii.1.10, we learn that *ra's maymūn* was customarily offered as a large festive dish (*ṭaʿām kabīr*). See other *ra's maymūn* recipes, i.4.24–5, prepared as pastries.

106 In the following instructions we will learn that these should have been kept aside with the meat.

107 A comparable recipe in the anonymous Andalusi *Anwāʿ al-ṣaydala*, and another one made with meatballs, 73–4, call this vessel *qādūs* and name the dish after it.

108 In the *qādūs* recipes—see above note, this earthenware vessel is not put directly on the fire; rather, it is buried in embers, *al-ghaḍā* (الغضا), which is erroneously copied in the edited Arabic text as الغطاء *al-ghiṭāʾ* 'lid.'

109 I assume that some of the boiled oil in the vessel will come up to the surface when the meat mix is added.

When the eggs thicken and set, and the fats are almost all absorbed, remove the vessels from the fire and leave them on heated stones (*raḍf*).[110] [When ready to serve,] turn each vessel over onto the middle of a glazed bowl (*ghaḍāra*); it will look like a rounded mass of white sugar (*jumjumat al-sukkar*).[111] Take a ladleful from the garnish pot previously mentioned [*qidr al-farsh*, recipe ii.1.10 above] and [scatter its contents] all over [each one of] them. Garnish the dish with split eggs, sprinkle it with spices [such as Ceylon cinnamon and ginger], and serve it, God Almighty willing.

II.2.45 Another Dish, Called *balāja*[112]

Take the lungs' windpipe (*qaṣabat al-ri'a*) of a fat ram with all the organs attached to it [i.e., lungs, heart, and liver], but not the spleen (*ṭiḥāl*). Cut them into large pieces and wash them. Also take the small intestine (*duwwāra*), remove what needs to be discarded, and wash it and cut it into pieces. Put them all in a new pot and add water, salt, olive oil, black pepper, coriander seeds, and as many as you want of onions split in halves. Put the pot on the fire and let it cook until the [organ] meats are almost done. Take them out of the pot, put them on a wooden board (*lawḥ*), and dice them very finely.[113] [Strain the broth and set it aside.]

Take the needed amount of eggs and break them in a wide, shallow bowl (*ṣaḥfa*); add salt, a good amount of black pepper, Ceylon cinnamon, and ginger. If ginger is not available, replace it with pellitory (*ʿāqir qarḥā*).[114] Add saffron

---

110 This direction is found only in the Madrid MS, fol. 60r. This is important, ensuring that the molds set well and come out in one piece.

111 Pl. *jamājim al-sukkar*. The reference here is to the molded white sugar cones, which in the eastern region were more commonly called *sukkar ublūj* or *ṭabarzad*. See glossary 4.

112 Probably the name of the dish derived from *balaj* 'merriment' and 'delight'; see al-Zabīdī, *Tāj al-ʿarūs*, s.v. بلج. The Madrid MS, fol. 60r–v, calls it *al-baljiyya al-Asadiyya*, probably named after the Andalusi Arab tribe of Banū Asad. *Balāja* was a popular Andalusi dish sold in the food markets. See glossary 5.

There seems to have been regional variations on the dish. In the anonymous Andalusi *Anwāʿ al-ṣaydala* 27, the dish is prepared somewhat differently: the meat pieces are fried and no breadcrumbs are used. The author/compiler says that this was the way it was made in the western region, like Cordova and Marrakesh and in between.

113 The Madrid MS, fol. 60v, suggests using a pair of scissors to do this.

114 *Anacyclus pyrethrum*. Its Amazigh name is *tāghandasat*. It is an exclusively Moroccan plant used mostly for its roots, which are intensely hot and sharp in properties, believed to boost sexual activities. See Ibn al-Bayṭār, *al-Jāmiʿ* iii 157–8.

and the crumbs of leavened bread (*fatāt khubz mukhtamir*) as well.[115] Beat all these ingredients well with a ladle. Now take the resulting fat of the strained broth (*ṣafwū al-marqa*), along with the chopped heart and the rest of the meats, and add them all to the egg [mixture].

Take a glazed earthenware pan (*ṭājin fakhkhār muzajjaj*) and pour olive oil in it, followed by the eggs with whatever was mixed with them.[116] Spread [poached] egg yolks and [skinned] almonds over its face (*yunajjam*) and drizzle it with fat scooped from the strained broth (*wadak*). Send it to the *furn* (communal brick oven) to be placed at a distance from the fire. It is to be left there until it cooks and browns, and then taken and set aside to cool, after which it may be served, God Almighty willing.

If you want to make the dish with meat, take pieces from the thighs (*afkhādh*) and loins (middle back, *sinsin*);[117] put them in a new pot—without cutting them—(**145v**) add water and salt, and let them cook until they fall apart (*yataharra'*). Take the meat out of the pot and shred it by hand until it looks like meat prepared for porridge (*harīsa*).[118] Put it in a glazed earthenware pan with the eggs beaten with spices and saffron as mentioned earlier. Pour plenty of sweet olive oil (*zayt ṭayyib*) on it and then put it in the *furn* to bake and brown. Let black pepper, ginger, and pellitory [added to the egg mixture] be plentiful. And serve the dish, God Almighty willing.

II.2.46 Another Dish, Which Andalusis Call *qaliyya* (Moist Fries)

Take the lungs' windpipe [with the organs attached to it] as mentioned above; and the small intestine (*duwwāra*) and tripe (*karsh*) as well. Boil the tripe in hot water until it looks white, and clean the intestine and split it open. Chop into small pieces the [organs attached to the] windpipe, along with the tripe and intestine, and put them all in an earthenware or iron pan (*ṭājin*). Add water, salt, olive oil, black pepper, coriander seeds, a small ladleful of *murrī naqī*ʿ (sun-fermented liquid sauce), cumin, and a chopped onion.

---

115 Apparently, the crumbs were added sparingly to this type of dish. The Andalusi market inspector al-Saqaṭī, *Fī Ādāb al-ḥisba* 39, criticizes marketplace cooks who beef up the *balāja* they cook with lots of breadcrumbs.

116 Based on al-Saqaṭī, *Fī Ādāb al-ḥisba* 39, when put in the pan to bake, the well-made *balāja* mix should not be higher than the width of two fingers put together.

117 As suggested in the Madrid MS, fol. 60v.

118 I.e., thread-like shreds.

Put the pan on the fire and let it cook until all is done. At this point, add fine-tasting vinegar, as much as needed, and leave the *ṭājin* on the fire so that it may boil once or twice.[119] Take the pan from the fire, and eat the dish salubriously, God Almighty willing.

119 See glossary 9.2, s.v. *ghalya*, for more on this cooking technique.

Part Two, Chapter Three: On Lamb (*Luḥūm Khirfān*)[1]

II.3.1 A Dish Called *badīʿī* (Unique)[2]

Take cuts from a lamb (*kharūf*), such as brisket (*ṣadr*), racks (*ajnāb*, sg. *janb*), and rump (*dhanb*). Cut them into small- to medium-size pieces, put them in a new pot, and add salt, water, plenty of olive oil, black pepper, coriander seeds, and a small amount of chopped onion. Put the pot on the fire to cook.

When the pot is almost done, take fresh cheese, which has been made two or three days before,[3] wash it in fresh water (*māʾ ʿadhb*),[4] and then slice it into thin, palm-size squares. Take as many eggs as you choose, break them into a large, wide bowl (*mithrad*), but put aside 5 or more of their yolks. Add salt and black pepper to the eggs, along with ginger, Ceylon cinnamon, saffron, and juices of cilantro and mint. Beat them all until they mix well. (**146r**) Take the cheese [slices], dip them in the [egg mix in the] bowl, move them in it so that they get colored with the saffron, [and take them out and put them aside].

Add saffron to the [cooking meat], but not much, [and continue cooking it]. Then, have a look at it; if it is done, take it out and set it aside [in a vessel]. Strain the broth and set it aside.

Take a large, glazed earthenware pan (*ṭājin muzajjaj*), put olive oil in it, and then line its bottom with cheese [slices]; put a level layer of the meat on top of it followed by another layer of cheese; [and continue layering] until all the

1 Sg. *kharūf*, a male sheep less than a year old.

2 Generally, it is a casserole dish made with diced meat and sliced cheese drenched in beaten eggs. This must have been one of the signature dishes in the medieval Muslim West. A recipe in the thirteenth-century Aleppan cookbook by Ibn al-ʿAdīm, *al-Wuṣla ilā-l-ḥabīb* ii 609–10; English trans., *Scents* 137–9, includes *badīʿiyya* and describes it as *min aṭʿimat al-Maghāriba*, i.e., of North Africa. It uses the three characteristic ingredients of meat, cheese, and eggs, with some adaptations to the Eastern Mediterranean ways of cooking. The other Andalusi cookbook *Anwāʿ al-ṣaydala*, 11, 25–6, includes three *badīʿī* recipes, which cook the same dish but differ in many details. Al-Tujībī's version is the longest and most detailed.

3 In the anonymous *Anwāʿ al-ṣaydala* 25, the reason for not using very fresh cheese is because it falls apart (*yanḥall*).

4 This is preceded by *wa yakūn ḥārr* 'let it be hot,' which I take to be a misplaced reference to the water used for washing the cheese, as this indeed would facilitate cutting it into thin slices without breaking it.

 | DOI:10.1163/9789004469488_011

FIGURE 59 A lamb, *kharūf*, Ibn al-Muqaffaʿ, *Kalīla wa Dimana*, fol. 101r, detail
BNF, DEPARTMENT OF MANUSCRIPTS, ARAB 3465. SOURCE: GALLICA.BNF.FR/BNF

meat and cheese are used up. Take the fat (*wadak*) in the broth—do this gently [so that it does not mix with the broth]—and pour it over the pan. Take the [remaining] beaten eggs [prepared above] and pour them to cover the meat and cheese. Spread the [set aside] egg yolks and skinned almonds on the face of the pan as garnish (*yunajjam*), drizzle a bit more of the strained broth [all over it], and sprinkle it with whatever you choose of aromatic spices (*afāwīh*).

Send the pan to the *furn* (communal brick oven) and let it bake at a distance from the fire until it cooks and browns. Once it browns and all the moisture evaporates, it is to be taken out[5] and set aside to cool, after which it may be eaten salubriously, God Almighty willing.

5 Both the Berlin and BL MSS erroneously copied فيخرج 'taken out' as فيحرك 'stirred.' In the Madrid MS, fol. 62r, it occurs as أُخرج 'taken out.'

This dish is made the same way with meat of a suckling kid (*jadī raḍīʿ*) or fat chickens, so know this, and follow the instructions accordingly to cook it the way you like.

II.3.2 Another Dish, [Shepherds' Fare] Called *muʿallak*[6]

Take a whole fat suckling lamb (*kharūf raḍīʿ*); but leave out its head, heart, tripe, and intestines.[7] Cut it from one joint to the other,[8] and after cleaning the pieces, put them in a large earthenware or iron cauldron (*ibrīm*).[9] [Put the pot on the fire and let the meat cook,] while stirring it,[10] until it releases its juices and cooks.

Take fresh cheese made around three days earlier, clean it, cut it into pieces, and add it to the meat [in the pot]. Stir them both with a ladle, and continue doing this until the meat and cheese combine into one mass.

If the meat happens to be fatty enough and releases a good deal of melted suet (*wadak*), which renders using additional olive oil or butter unnecessary, that will be fine and well. Otherwise, you need to add olive oil, but butter would be more suitable for it. Add either one [gradually] until the dish cooks and is about to brown. At this point, stop adding butter, [or olive oil if used,] and finish the cooking on a medium fire.

Ladle the dish into a large, wide bowl (*mithrad*), and serve it, God Almighty willing. Sprinkle it with Ceylon cinnamon and black pepper, if these are available, because this kind of food is mostly cooked [by shepherds] in the sheepfolds (*marāḥil al-ghanam*),[11] so know this.

---

6 The name is descriptive of the way meat and cheese are mixed together until they become one cohesive mass. Cf. another *muʿallak* recipe, i.5.10 above. In the anonymous Andalusi *Anwāʿ al-ṣaydala* 167, it is said to be one of the two dishes (the other one being *maqlū*, which is chopped fatty lamb cooked and bound with milk, fresh cheese, and lots of butter) that were common fare among shepherds in the steppes of Cordova (*bādiyat Qurṭuba*). They are described as being dense foods that are slow to digest, but very nutritious.

7 I.e., the innards, as clearly directed in the Madrid MS, fol. 62r.

8 According to this direction, the lamb would be in three pieces, being cut horizontally across the upper fore-leg joints and the upper rear-leg joints.

9 *Ibrīm* must have been a regional variation on what was more commonly known as *burma*. *Burma* (pl. *birām*) specifically designated a soapstone pot, but it was also used as a generic name for a pot, in this case a cauldron. In the anonymous Andalusi *Anwāʿ al-ṣaydala*, which is contemporaneous with al-Tujībī's cookbook, a similar large cauldron is called *burma* when cooking a comparable *muʿallak* dish, which differs in detail, p. 167; and in a rice pudding recipe, p. 162.

10 Based on internal evidence, I consider يحك 'scrape' a copyist's misreading of يحرك 'stir.'

11 See n. 6 above for more on this kind of pastoral food.

11.3.3 Another Dish [of Lamb Roast]

Take as much as you like of the tastiest cuts of lamb, clean them, and put them in an iron pan (*ṭājin ḥadīd*). Add water, salt, olive oil, black pepper, coriander seeds, a chopped piece of an onion, and as much as you like of *murrī naqīʿ* (sun-fermented liquid sauce). Put the pan on the fire, and when the meat is almost done, you can color it with saffron if you want to color the dish.

Take the pan to the *furn* (communal brick oven) (**146v**) to finish cooking and browning. When it comes out, set it aside to cool slightly, and eat it salubriously, God Almighty willing.

If you want to replace *murrī naqīʿ* with *murrī al-ḥūt* (fermented fish sauce), you can do so; it goes well with it.[12]

11.3.4 Another Dish [of Lamb with Desert Truffles]

Take as much as you like of the tastiest cuts of lamb, cut them into pieces, clean them, and put them in a new pot. Add salt, olive oil, black pepper, coriander seeds, a small amount of chopped onion, and *murrī naqīʿ* (sun-fermented liquid sauce). Put the pot on the fire, and when the meat releases its juices and it is almost cooked, add hot water [and continue cooking].

Take desert truffles (*tirfās*), wash them, peel them, break them into pieces by hand,[13] and add them to the meat pot [and let them cook] until they are done. Leave the pot on embers (*ghaḍā*) to simmer and allow the flavors to nicely blend (*yatajammar*), and eat the dish salubriously, God Almighty willing.

If you want to boil the truffles in salted water first and then add them to the pot, you can do so; this indeed would be a better way to do it. If you want to use *murrī al-ḥūt* (fermented fish sauce) instead of *murrī naqīʿ*, you can also do so.

11.3.5 Another Dish [of Stewed Leg of Lamb]

Take a leg of lamb (*fakhdh kharūf*) and cut deep slits all over it (*yusharraḥ*).[14] Put it in a new pot and add salt, black pepper, coriander seeds, 2 ladlefuls of

---

12 For *murrī* recipes, see chapter x.8. below.

13 To my knowledge, such an instruction is found only in al-Tujībī's cookbook. Given the insipid flavor of desert truffles, my guess is that compared with the evenly cut pieces done with a knife, the irregularly shaped truffle pieces broken by hand into chunks create many uneven edges that would absorb much more of the flavors of the liquids in which they are being cooked.

14 References to the leg in the recipe indicate that it is meant to be kept in one piece.

vinegar, half a ladleful of *murrī* (liquid fermented sauce), and a ladleful of olive oil. Put the pot on the fire to cook, and when it is nicely done, take the leg out of the pot and fry it in olive oil in an iron or glazed earthenware pan (*ṭājin*). [Strain the broth and set it aside.]

Take 5 eggs, a small amount of flour, and breadcrumbs (*fatāt khubz*); beat them all together. Return the leg of lamb to the pot with a small amount of the broth and the egg mixture; let them cook until done. Return rest of the broth to the pot and leave it [on embers] to simmer and allow the flavors to nicely blend (*yatajammar*). Ladle the dish into a glazed bowl (*ghaḍāra*), and eat it salubriously, God Almighty willing.

11.3.6 Another Dish [of Leg of Lamb Stewed with Almonds]

Take a leg of lamb and cut deep slits all over it, but keep it in one piece (*tusharraḥ ṣaḥīḥa*). Put it in a pot, adding salt, olive oil, black pepper, coriander seeds, and pounded almonds dissolved in water. Put the pot on the fire to cook. Once it is done, top it with a layer of eggs beaten with breadcrumbs.[15] Leave the pot on embers (*ghaḍā*) so that it simmers and cooks well, and eat it salubriously, God Almighty willing.

11.3.7 (147r) Another Dish [of a Stuffed Rack of Lamb]

Take the rack (*janb*) of a fat lamb and insert a knife between the meat and ribs to separate them gently, but keep the rack in one piece. Sprinkle salt on it and set it aside.

[To prepare the stuffing:] take meat from the legs and other parts, pound it,[16] and add a ladleful of olive oil, half a ladleful of *murrī naqīʿ* (sun-fermented liquid sauce), skinned almonds, a ladleful of cilantro juice, black pepper, eggs, and breadcrumbs (*futātat khubz*). Break the eggs first and then mix them with the spices, crumbs, and the rest of the ingredients. Take an earthenware or iron skillet (*miqlāt*) and put olive oil in it. As soon as it boils, take the pounded meat, which has been combined with the eggs and other ingredients, and put it in the skillet on a medium fire until the stuffing (*ḥashū*) is done—do not overcook it.

---

15 This culinary practice, characteristic of Andalusi cuisine, is called *takhmīr*, see glossary 9.2.

16 At this point in the recipe, pounding the meat is mentioned only in the Madrid MS, fol. 62v. Later in the recipe all the MSS will describe this meat as pounded (*madrūs*).

Stuff the area between the meat and ribs of the rack [with the prepared meat mix]; do this gently. Rub the rack with *murrī* and then place it in a pan (*ṭājin*) and take it to the *furn* (communal brick oven) to bake.

If you want to cook the lamb rack at home [on the stove], put it in a wide-rimmed pot. Wash the vessel used for combining the stuffing with water and place it on the rack in the pot.[17] The way to position the rack in the pot is to let the ribs face upwards and the stuffed part downwards. Let it cook [on a medium fire] until it is all done, and eat it salubriously, God Almighty willing.

II.3.8 Another Dish [of Sweetened Lamb]

Take whatever you like of meat from a fat lamb, cut it into pieces, wash it, and put it in a new pot. Add sugar, fine-tasting honey, rosewater, almonds—pounded and whole ones—and hulled sesame seeds (*juljulān*). Put the pot on a moderate fire and let it cook while stirring it constantly until the meat is done.

Now take 2 pieces of *ka'k* (dry ring cookies),[18] pound them finely, and add the resulting meal (*daqīq*) to the pot, which by now should have been placed on embers (*ghaḍā*); stir the pot with a ladle until it thickens, God Almighty willing, and eat it salubriously with the help of God Almighty.

II.3.9 Another Dish [of a Roasted Whole Lamb]

Take a fat and tender lamb, open its belly, but leave it whole. Clean it and rub it with olive oil, salt, black pepper, and coriander seeds. Set it aside briefly.

Take fresh cheese and rub and mash it with your hands until it disintegrates. Add cilantro juice to it, along with black pepper, Ceylon cinnamon, mint juice and the tips of mint sprigs, sweet olive oil (*zayt 'adhb*), and salt. Beat them all together very well and use this mix to stuff the lamb's cavity, including the area between the thighs and under the racks.

Take a small amount of water and dissolve some cheese in it [by pressing and rubbing]. Add eggs and spices and beat them all. Put the lamb in a large pan (*ṭājin kabīr*) and pour the cheese-egg mix all over it. Take it to the *furn* (communal brick oven) to bake at a distance from the fire, and take it out when it is cooked and browned.

You need to sew up the cavity after stuffing the lamb, so know this.

---

17 The vessel could have been a large and wide earthenware bowl, such as a *ṣaḥfa*.

18 To make such cookies, see recipe i.4.3 above.

II.3.10 Another Dish [of a Whole Lamb Stuffed with Birds and Roasted]

Take a fat lamb, slaughter it, skin it, and make a small opening in its belly. Take out whatever is inside, and clean the lamb and set it aside.

Now take fat sparrows (*ʿaṣāfīr*), fat starlings (*zarāzīr*), fat turtledoves (*yamām*), (**147v**) and squabs (*afrākh ḥamām*). Boil the turtledoves and squabs.[19] [Prepare the stuffing by mixing breadcrumbs and egg whites beaten together with all kinds of spice and herbs] and stuff the birds' cavities with it. Insert them in the cavity of the lamb and sew up the opening. Rub the lamb with *murrī naqīʿ* (sun-fermented liquid sauce) in which saffron and black pepper have been dissolved.

Put the lamb in a pan (*ṭājin*) large enough to contain it. Sprinkle it all with a sauce (*marqa*) made by combining olive oil, *murrī* (liquid fermented sauce), the juice of 1 onion, cilantro juice, black pepper, coriander seeds, and saffron. Also put in what was left of the stuffing.

Put the pan in the *furn* (brick oven) and leave it there until it cooks and browns on all sides. Take it out and serve it, God Almighty willing. A young male goat (*jadī*) may be cooked the same way if you want to use it.

II.3.11 Another Dish [of Rack of Lamb, Stuffed and Roasted]

Take the rack of a fat lamb and salt it after separating the meat from the ribs in the middle section only. Take some more meat, pound it, and mix with it pounded almonds, breadcrumbs (*fatāt khubz*), a ladleful of fresh bulb fennel juice (*māʾ basbās akhḍar*), and an egg. Beat them all with black pepper, ginger, salt, and Ceylon cinnamon, and then stuff the space between the meat and ribs with this mix.

Take some pounded meat, thin it down with water, and beat it with 2 egg yolks.[20] Put the rack in an earthenware pan (*ṭājin fakhkhār*), spread the meat mix all over it, and send it to the *furn* (communal brick oven). It must first be partially cooked at home [on the stove] and then sent to the *furn*. When it completely cooks and browns, take it out and serve it, God Almighty willing.

---

19 The MSS mentions a stuffing but the directions for making it are missing. The added text in brackets is based on recipe ii.2.40 above, which also uses similar birds to fill the cavity of a ram.

20 The two egg yolks are referred to here as *faṣṣayn* (sg. *faṣṣ*, pl. *fuṣūṣ*). See Corriente, *Dictionary of Andalusi Arabic*, s.v. *f-ṣ-ṣ*.

11.3.12 Another Dish [of Roasted Stuffed Rack of Lamb, with Chopped Intestines]

Take the rack (*janb*) and brisket (*ṣadr*) of a lamb [in one piece]. Insert a knife between the meat and bones to separate them, but keep them as they are in one piece. Take some more meat and pound it with almonds, breadcrumbs (*futātat khubz*), mint juice, salt, and black pepper; and use it to stuff between the meat and ribs. Put the rack in a glazed earthenware pan (*ṭājin muzajjaj*).

Take the small and large intestines,[21] wash them, and chop them into small pieces. Add egg yolks and spices to them and beat them together [and set them aside]. Put the *ṭājin* on the fire and pour liquid (*maraq*) over it made of water, olive oil, black pepper, coriander seeds, a small amount of [chopped onion], and a ladleful of *murrī naqīʿ* (sun-fermented liquid sauce). Once the meat cooks, spread the [prepared] eggs and chopped intestines all over it; keep the broth (*maraq*) in the pan.

Take the pan to the *furn* (communal brick oven) and put it at a distance from the fire. When all is cooked, the broth has evaporated and the meat has browned, take the pan out of the oven, leave it to slightly cool, and then eat it salubriously, God Almighty willing.

11.3.13 Another Dish [of a Roasted Whole Lamb, with *ʿuṣba* 'Intestine Roll']

Take a whole fat lamb [with the head]. Also take whatever is inside the belly [i.e., organs, tripe, and intestines], wash them all and clean them, and make *ʿuṣba* with them.[22]

Take a large *ṭājin* (earthenware pan) or a small *qaṣriyya* (earthenware tub).[23] Put the lamb and intestine roll in it; carry it to the *furn* (brick oven) and place it at a distance from the fire until the meat roasts and browns. Take the pan out, (148r) gently turn the lamb over so that its other side browns with the head

---

21 Called *duwwāra* and *maṣārīn*, respectively.

22 Pieces of tripe and organs are wrapped in caul fat in one roll and then wrapped with a piece of intestine wound all around it. Cf. an earlier recipe, i.2.2, where smaller individual rolls are made. When roasted in the *tannūr* (clay oven) they are threaded onto a long skewer first; see above, recipe ii.2.39, for a comparable *ʿuṣba* roll. Grilled rolls such as these are still made today in countries like Turkey, where they are called *kokorec*. See glossary 10, s.v. *ʿuṣb*.

23 *Qaṣriyya* is typically a large tub.

[and the intestine roll]. As soon as it browns, take it out, sprinkle it with whatever spices you prefer, put [a small bowl of] pounded salt close to it, and eat it salubriously, God Almighty willing.

If you want to use the *tannūr* (clay oven), skewer the lamb with an iron or wooden rod (*saffūd*) and put it in the *tannūr* together with the intestine roll (*ʿuṣba*), which has been likewise skewered. Let the lower tips of the skewers be in a pan (*ṭājin*), which has been placed in the bottom of the *tannūr* with some water in it to receive the dripping melted fat (*wadak*) of the lamb and *ʿuṣba*. [Close the openings of the *tannūr* to seal in the heat and humidity.] Open the *tannūr* when they are cooked and browned, and take them out and serve them [as above], God Almighty willing.

II.3.14 Another Dish, Mashriqi Called *maḍīra* (Lamb Stew with Milk)[24]

Take the head (*ra's*), brisket (*ṣadr*), rump (*dhanb*), loin (middle back, *sinsin*), and the lowest two ribs (*quṣrayayn*, sg. *quṣrā*)[25] of a fat lamb. Put them in a large new pot and add water and salt, enough to cook them. Once they cook, take them out and put them in a wide, shallow bowl (*ṣaḥfa*).

Take skinned almonds and pound them well until they look like bone marrow [and set them aside]. Now take fresh milk (*laban ḥalīb ṭarī*) that has just been drawn; strain it and put it in a new pot. Pound a couple of onions and add them to the milk pot. Put it on the fire and add the meat pieces to it when the milk comes to a boil. Let them boil together. Next, take the pounded almonds and add them to the milk [pot and stir]. Top the surface (*yukhammar*) with a couple of eggs, which have been gently stirred [just enough to mingle whites with yolks].[26] When you ladle the meat with its milk [sauce], sprinkle it with black pepper, and eat it salubriously, God Almighty willing.

---

24 It is one of the favorite dishes in the eastern region, touted as the healer of all maladies. This white dish was attractively served in blue bowls.

25 Copied as *quṣayrā* (قصيرى) in the Madrid MS, fol. 64r.

26 We understand from the Madrid MS, fol. 64r, that the dish is further cooked to allow the eggs to set. Based on the previous recipes, this would be done on embers after the fire is taken from underneath the pot.

II.3.15 Another Mashriqi Dish, Also Called *maḍīra* (Lamb Stew with Yogurt),[27] Wonderful[28]

Take the head (*ra's*), brisket (*ṣadr*), loin (middle back, *sinsin*), rump (*dhanb*), fore shanks (*yad*), and the lowest two ribs (*quṣayrā*) of a fat lamb. Cut them all into medium pieces and put them in a new pot, adding butter and whole onions. Keep the pot on the fire until the meat cooks and boils in the butter.

Take buttermilk (*laban makhīḍ*) that was made earlier and left to thicken and sour;[29] add it to the meat pot and let it cook gently on a moderate fire until it comes to a boil. At this point, cover the surface (*yukhammar*) with some yeast dough (*khamīrat al-ʿajīn*) and [chopped] cilantro.[30] Leave the pot [on embers after removing the fire from underneath the pot, to let it simmer and the flavors nicely blend].[31] Ladle the dish, sprinkle it with black pepper, and eat it salubriously, God Almighty willing.

II.3.16 Another Mashriqi Dish Called *mulabbaqa* (Lamb with Crumbled Bread Softened with Fat)[32]

(**148v**) Take the tastiest cuts from a fat lamb as mentioned above, but not the head. Clean the meat and put it in a new pot, adding salt, 3 [whole] onions, and a good deal of strained butter. Put the pot on the fire, and when the meat is cooked, add fresh milk (*laban ḥalīb ṭarī*) after you strain it. Stir the pot on a low fire until it boils.

Now take 1 [fresh loaf of] semolina bread (*khubz samīd*) or any amount that would be enough for the milky broth used. Crumble it into the finest particles

---

27 See n. 24 above.

28 As described in the Madrid MS, fol. 64r.

29 See glossary 3 for more on this dairy product.

30 I assume that yeast would have first been thinned down with water, and perhaps some cilantro juice, before spreading it on top.

31 'Leave the pot' is added only in the Madrid MS, fol. 64r.

32 The name of this dish, ملبقة, was inaccurately copied as مبلقة in the BL MS, fol. 148r, and the Berlin MS, fol. 41r; and ملقية in the Madrid MS, fol. 64r. This was most probably due to the copyists' unfamiliarity with this eastern dish. In the eastern region, *mulabbaqa* was a variety of *tharīd* (see chapter i.2 for such dishes). It was esteemed as a delicacy, valued for its soft texture and rich buttery flavor. To my knowledge, only one *mulabbaqa* recipe survived, it can be found in chapter 83 in al-Warrāq's tenth-century Baghdadi cookbook *Kitāb al-Ṭabīkh*, English trans., *Annals* 340.

possible and sift it in a sieve made of esparto grass (*ḥalfā*).[33] Put the crumbs in a clean wide-mouthed pot, pour the milky broth into it, and pour butter gradually [while stirring] until enough is added and the bread cannot soak up anymore. Ladle it into a large, wide bowl (*mithrad*),[34] arrange the cooked meat pieces all over it, and eat it salubriously, God Almighty willing.

If you want to cook the lamb as a green or white *tafāyā*; or with spinach (*isfanākh*), blite (*yarbūz*),[35] lettuce (*khass*), or purslane (*rijla*): prepare it as was described earlier [in the previous chapter ii.2 on mutton, recipes 1, 2, 11, 12, and 13], God Almighty willing.

33 Also known as halfah grass, *Lygeum spartinum*, native to southern Europe and North Africa.

34 This bowl is usually used for serving *tharīd* dishes (recipes in chapter i.2).

35 Leaves of wild amaranth, also known as *baqla Yamāniyya* 'Yemeni vegetable.' See glossary 12 for more on this leaf vegetable.

CHAPTER II.4

Part Two, Chapter Four: On Young Goat Meat (*Luḥūm al-Jidāʾ*)[1]

II.4.1 A Dish [of Oven-Braised Kid's Meat]

Take whatever parts you like of a fat suckling kid (*jadī raḍīʿ*), clean the meat, and put it in a glazed earthenware pan (*ṭājin fakhkhār muzajjaj*). Add water, salt, olive oil, coriander seeds, and *murrī naqīʿ* (sun-fermented liquid sauce)—but not much.

Put the pot on the fire, and when the meat cooks, add a bit of saffron, which has been pounded and dissolved in water—if you choose to add it, otherwise, just leave it as it is. Send the *ṭājin* to the *furn* (communal brick oven) and let it cook until the meat browns and the broth somewhat reduces. Take it out and serve it, God Almighty willing.

If you want to cook the meat of a suckling kid as white or green *tafāyā*[2]—or cook it with mint (*naʿnaʿ*),[3] balm mint (*turunjān*),[4] fresh bulb fennel (*basbās*),[5] spinach (*isfanākh*), blite (*yarbūz*),[6] lettuce (*khass*),[7] or purslane (*rijla*);[8] or cook it with fresh cheese (*jubn ṭarī*) and desert truffles (*tirfās*) as a *badīʿī* dish;[9] or with fresh fava beans (*fūl akhḍar*) as a *fustuqiyya* dish[10]—then follow the instructions I gave you in the previous two chapters, God Almighty willing.

If you want to roast the kid in one piece in the *furn* (brick oven) or *tannūr* (clay oven), then prepare it exactly as you previously did with lamb [recipe ii.3.10 and 13 above], God Almighty willing.

---

1 Sg. *jadī*, it is a male goat, a kid, less than a year old.

2 See recipes ii.2.1–2 above.

3 See recipe ii.2.8 above.

4 It is also called lemon balm, whose leaves have a gentle scent of citrus, see glossary 8. See recipe ii.2.9 above.

5 See recipe ii.2.7 above.

6 Leaves of wild amaranth, also known as *baqla Yamāniyya* 'Yemeni vegetable.' See glossary 12 for more on this leaf vegetable. For spinach and *yarbūz* recipes, see ii.2.11 above.

7 See recipe ii.2.12 above.

8 See recipe ii.2.13 above.

9 For a *badīʿī* dish, see recipe ii.3.1 above. The editor of the Arabic text mis-amended the perfectly coherent text او بالجبن الطري وبالترفاس بديعي to the confusing او بالجبن الطري او بالترفاس البديعي.

10 See recipe ii.2.32 above.

FIGURE 60 A young goat with its mother, Ibn al-Muqaffaʿ, *Kalīla wa Dimana*, fol. 110r, detail
BNF, DEPARTMENT OF MANUSCRIPTS, ARAB 3465. SOURCE: GALLICA.BNF.FR /BNF

Part Two, Chapter Five: On Wild Meat (*Luḥūm al-Waḥsh*)

II.5.1 (131r) A Dish [of Braised Wild Meat]

Take meat from a deer (*ayyal*), oryx (*baqar al-waḥsh*), ass (ḥimār),[1] ibex (*waʿl*), or gazelle (*ghazāl*). Use whichever is available of the ones I mention to you here; take their briskets, ribs, foreleg shanks (*yadayn*, sg. *yad*), and places containing the most suet (*shaḥm*).

Cut the meat into pieces, wash and clean it, and put it in a large pan (*ṭājin*). Add water, salt, olive oil, black pepper, coriander seeds, cumin, a small amount of chopped onion, garlic—both pounded and whole cloves—thyme (*ṣaʿtar*), soaked chickpeas, skinned almonds, leaves of citron (*utrujj*),[2] sprigs of herb fennel (*ʿūd basbās*), and a ladleful of fine-tasting *murrī* (liquid fermented sauce).

Put the *ṭājin* on the fire and let it cook until the meat is done, and then add saffron, which has been [pounded and] dissolved [in water]. When the pot boils [with the saffron in it], add as much as you like of fine-tasting vinegar, and leave the *ṭājin* on a moderate fire until part of the broth reduces and its fat (*wadak*) shows on top. At this point, remove it from the fire and set it aside until it loses some of its heat, and eat it salubriously, God Almighty willing.

The hare (*arnab*),[3] European wild rabbit (*qunilya*),[4] and hedgehog (*qunfudh*)[5] are cooked the same way, so know this and prepare them accordingly,[6] God Almighty willing.

---

1 It would most certainly have been meat of a wild ass (*ḥimār al-waḥsh*), as meat of the domesticated donkey was not consumed.

2 At two places (after 'thyme' and after 'skinned almonds') in this list of ingredients, the editor of the Arabic text misreads و 'and' as او 'or.'

3 Unlike the western region al-Maghrib, in the eastern region both the hare and the rabbit were called *arnab*. The former, however, was often more specifically described as *barrī* 'wild.' See Viré, "Hare," 97–100.

4 The name of this rabbit species is derived from the Spanish *conejo* (*Oryctolagus cuniculus*), it is smaller than the hare, *arnab*. The name is copied as *qunayna* in the Madrid MS, fol. 65r, and the anonymous *Anwāʿ al-ṣaydala* 38, 39.

5 It is called *qunfūdh* in the Madrid MS, fol. 65r.

6 For more on these animals, see glossary 10.

 | DOI:10.1163/9789004469488_013

FIGURE 61 A stag, *ayyal*, al-Qazwīnī, *ʿAjāʾib al-makhlūqāt wa-gharāʾib al-mawjūdāt*, fol. 107r, detail
BRITISH LIBRARY: ORIENTAL MANUSCRIPTS, OR 14140, IN *QATAR DIGITAL LIBRARY* HTTPS://WWW.QDL.QA/ARCHIVE/81055/VDC_100023586788.0X000001

II.5.2 Another Dish [of Thin Meat Patties, Called *aḥrash*, with Vinegar Sauce][7]

Take whatever is available of [wild] meat from the thighs (*fakhdh*), foreleg shanks (*yadayn*, sg. *yad*), loin (middle back, *sinsin*), and sirloins (lower back, *khawāṣir*, sg. *khāṣira*). [Remove the bones,] slice the meat into thin pieces, and beat them on a wooden block (*ṭalya min ʿūd*)[8] with the iron rod (*qaḍīb ḥadīd*) specially used for making *aḥrash* (thin meat patties) and *mirkās* (small sausages);[9] or use a cleaver (*sāṭūr*). Pound the meat until it is torn and looks like dough. If suet is available, also add it and beat it with the meat.

Add salt, black pepper, coriander seeds, cumin, and vinegar—all as needed. Take garlic cloves and a small amount of onion, pound them, add water to them, and then strain the liquid and add it to the *aḥrash* [mix] in a large kneading

7 For more on similar meat patties, see recipes ii.6.3, 7 below.

8 It is usually used as a chopping board. See Corriente, *Dictionary of Andalusi Arabic*, s.v. *ṭ-l-y*, where the word is said to have been derived from late Latin *taleare* 'to cut.'

9 It also occurs as *mirqās* in recipe ii.6.4 below.

bowl (*mi'jana*). Thoroughly mix the meat with the spices and whatever else is used. Put a small piece of it on the fire to grill and taste it. If you are totally satisfied with it, well and good; otherwise, add more of what is lacking until it is perfectly delicious.

Take a clean skillet and put it on the fire with olive oil in it. When the oil boils, grease your hands with some olive oil, take a piece of the meat, and shape it into a round [thin] disc; make it as small or as big as you want it to be. Place it in the skillet, let it fry, and then turn it. Take it out once it cooks and browns and put it in a vessel.

When you are done [frying them all], take a small earthenware pan (*ṭājin*), put pounded garlic and a small amount of water in it, [put it on the fire] and while the garlic cooks, add fine-tasting vinegar as needed. Once they boil, take some of the *aḥrash*, put them in a glazed bowl (*ghaḍāra*), and pour the boiled vinegar [as a sauce] over them.[10] If you like, put *murrī naqī'* (sun-fermented liquid sauce) on some of them; and leave some without adding anything to them. (131v)

The meat of wild animals (*waḥsh*) and that of the hare (*arnab*)[11] and European wild rabbit (*qunilya*)[12] are all cooked as above, so know this.

11.5.3 Another Dish [of Roasted or Grilled Wild Meat]

Take thighs (*afkhādh*) and loin (middle back, *sinsin*) of any kind of wild meat. Slice it any way you choose and season it with pounded salt, thyme, and black pepper.[13]

If you want to roast it in the *tannūr* (clay oven), heat it up until [its inner wall] looks white and then stick the meat slices to it. Close the upper opening of the *tannūr*, and when [according to your estimation] you know that the meat slices have cooked and browned, remove the lid and take them out. However, [this should be done] after you have already prepared a glazed bowl (*ghaḍāra*) filled with [a sauce of] sweet olive oil (*zayt 'adhb*) mixed with cooked and pounded garlic. So, when you take the meat out of the oven, immediately

---

10 Dipping sauces eaten with fried and grilled meats are mostly referred to as *marga* in this book. Dipping sauces were called *ṣibāgh* in the eastern region. See, for instance, *ṣibāgh* chapters 32 and 35 in al-Warrāq, *Kitāb al-Ṭabīkh*, English trans., *Annals*.

11 See n. 3 above.

12 See n. 4 above.

13 The editor of the Arabic text misreads و 'and' as او 'or.'

cut it into smaller pieces, and put it in the [prepared] bowl of olive oil and garlic [sauce]. Once this is done, you may eat the dish salubriously, God Almighty willing.

If you want to roast the meat in the *furn* (brick oven), put the slices in an earthenware pan (*ṭājin fakhkhār*) after salting them, add olive oil and pounded garlic, and send it to the oven. As soon as the slices cook and brown, take them out, cut them into pieces in a glazed bowl (*ghaḍāra*), and pour the olive oil and garlic [sauce, as prepared above,] all over them, and eat the dish salubriously, God Almighty willing.

If you want to add a small amount of preserved lemon juice (*khall līm*), or that of Damascus citron (*khall zunbūʿ*),[14] or of unripe grapes (*khall ḥiṣrim*) to the meat,[15] you can go ahead and do so.

If you want to grill the meat on an iron griddle (*mafrash ḥadīd*), spread the fire [of burning coals] first and then put the griddle on top of it. Spread the slices on the griddle, turning them as needed until they grill and brown. Remove them from the griddle and put them in the bowl of olive oil and garlic [sauce, prepared above]. When all is done, you may eat it salubriously, God Almighty willing.

If you want to grill the meat on skewers, after slicing it, further cut it into smaller pieces, which you then thread on skewers and grill suspended on the fire. Take a wide, shallow bowl (*ṣaḥfa*) and put vinegar, olive oil, *murrī* (liquid fermented sauce), pounded garlic, black pepper, and Ceylon cinnamon in it. Also take a feather from a chicken's wing, wash it, dip it in the bowl, and brush the skewered meat pieces with it [while grilling]. Do this repeatedly until the meat grills and browns and it has had enough of the feather brushing. Take the meat pieces off the skewers, put them in a glazed bowl (*ghaḍāra*), and eat the dish salubriously, God Almighty willing.

If you want to grill the meat directly on burning coals (*jamr*), light a fire, and once it burns, remove [the ones causing] smoke and flames, also remove any ashes on top of the coals. Spread the meat slices on the coals and keep an eye on them, [turning them as needed and] removing any ashes that might have stuck to them. Once they cook and brown, cut them into smaller pieces, which you then put in a *ghaḍāra* with the garlic and olive oil [sauce, prepared above]. Once all this is done, you may eat it salubriously, God Almighty willing.

---

14 Kharna sour orange hybrid, *Citrus aurantium var. khatta*. Based on Dozy, *Takmilat al-maʿājim* v 364, s.v. زنبوع, the name of this fruit is of Amazigh origin. It is more commonly known as *kabbād* in the eastern region.

15 See recipes x.7.12–3 for making preserved juice of unripe grapes; recipe x.7.15 for preserved lemon juice. No recipes are given for *khall zunbūʿ*.

FIGURE 62 Rabbit, *arnab*, al-Qazwīnī, *ʿAjāʾib al-makhlūqāt wa-gharāʾib al-mawjūdāt*, fol. 96r, detail
THE WALTERS ART MUSEUM, W. 659

ii.5.4 Another Dish [with Hare], Called *mughaffar* (Clad)[16]

(132r) Take the [slaughtered] hare (*arnab*),[17] wash and clean it, and then cut it at the joints. Take the pieces and remove the meat from the bones. Take the bones and put them in new pot (*qidr*); add a good amount of water, salt, olive oil, black pepper, coriander seeds, soaked chickpeas, a small amount of [chopped] onion, several cloves of garlic, cumin, a ladleful of *murrī* (liquid fermented sauce), 2 ladlefuls of fine-tasting vinegar, and a small amount of saffron [which has been pounded and] dissolved in water. Put the pot on the fire to cook.

Now take the meat, pound it in a mortar (*mihrās*) very well; add a bit of salt, black pepper, Ceylon cinnamon, and ginger and a small amount of pounded saffron, coriander seeds, cumin, and egg whites. Thoroughly knead the meat with the spices to mix them well.[18] Take out the bones from the pot and coat them with the [pounded] meat so that they look as they were before.

Take an earthenware pan (*ṭājin fakhkhār*), pour some of the broth from the [bones'] pot into it, and let it boil. Next, take the [clad] joints one by one and gently place them in the *ṭājin*; [let them cook] until they firm up and are almost done.

---

16 The name of the dish, as given in the Madrid MS, fol. 66v, is descriptive of the way rabbit meat is being prepared here. My interpretation of the name is based on Ibn Manẓūr, *Lisān al-ʿArab*, s.v. غفر, where *mighfar* is described as a garment that covers the body or a piece of headgear worn underneath the helmet. Cf. other *mughaffar* recipes, iii.2.8 and vii.2.15 below.

17 See n. 3 above.

18 The following, up until "an earthenware pan," was inadvertently left out in the edited Arabic text, which resulted in an obscure text. I filled in the missing words using the BL MS, fol. 132r, and the Berlin MS, fol. 42v.

Take an iron or earthenware skillet (*miqlāt*), put olive oil in it, and once it boils, take the joints one by one and let them fry gently in the pan until they brown. Take them out and put them in a glazed bowl (*ghaḍāra*).

Take the broth [remaining in the bones' pot], strain it, and return it to the pot (*qidr*). Take eggs, break them, and add salt, aromatic spices (*afāwīh*), and saffron to them; [beat them] and add them to the pot. Also add the egg yolks (*muḥāḥ al-bayḍ*).[19] Take [other] egg yolks and fry them; also take an egg or two, boil them in water, shell them, and split them into quarters. If any of the pounded meat was leftover, make meatballs (*banādiq*) with it, and cook them [in the pot].

When all these are done, take the bowl with the fried pieces in it and pour some of the strained broth on them, along with what was in the pot of the chickpeas, [skinned] almonds, the [scrambled] eggs, and the [poached] egg yolks. Put the fried egg yolks and the shelled [boiled and split] eggs in as well. Sprinkle black pepper, ginger, and Ceylon cinnamon all over the dish, and eat it salubriously, God Almighty willing.

If you want to use a European wild rabbit (*qunilya*) when making this dish,[20] you can cook it the same way.

II.5.5 Another Dish [of Oven-Braised Hare]

Take a [slaughtered] hare (*arnab*),[21] wash it and clean it, cut it into pieces at the joints, and put them in a glazed earthenware pan (*ṭājin fakhkhār muzajjaj*). Add water, salt, olive oil, black pepper, coriander seeds, cumin, and *murrī naqīʿ* (sun-fermented liquid sauce), and color it with saffron. Put the pan on the fire to cook, and once it is done, add a ladleful of fine-tasting vinegar to it and send it to the *furn* (communal brick oven). Take it out as soon as the meat browns and the liquid evaporates and set it aside to cool a bit, and eat the dish salubriously, God Almighty willing.

If you want to use a European wild rabbit (*qunilya*) when making this dish,[22] prepare it the same way, God Almighty willing.

19 Sg. *muḥḥ*. These must be the egg yolks remaining after using their whites in the pounded meat mixture. Apparently, they are left whole to poach in the pot.

20 See n. 4 above.

21 See n. 3 above.

22 See n. 4 above.

11.5.6 Another Dish [of Fried Hare with Sauce]

(**132v**) Take a [slaughtered] hare (*arnab*)[23] and cut it into pieces, which you then wash and clean and put in a new pot with water, salt, olive oil, black pepper, coriander seeds, and a small amount of chopped onion. Put the pot on the fire [to cook] and take out the meat when it is done.

Take a tinned iron skillet, put olive oil in it, and put it on the fire. Once the oil boils, put [some of] the meat pieces in it, turning them gently until they brown. Take them out and put them in a glazed bowl (*ghaḍāra*); continue frying until all the pieces are done.

Take a pan (*ṭājin*) and put a small amount of water in it. Pound some garlic cloves and add them to the pan to cook. When the garlic is cooked and all the moisture is evaporated, add vinegar to it. Take the tastiest part of the strained broth,[24] add it to vinegar, and let them boil. Sprinkle black pepper on the [fried pieces of] meat, pour the vinegar mix all over them, and eat the dish salubriously, God Almighty willing.

If you want to prepare [the sauce] with hard cheese (*jubn yābis*), then pound it first with the cooked garlic and then thin them down with the strained broth. Pour it all over the fried meat in the bowl, and eat the dish salubriously, God Almighty willing.

11.5.7 Another Dish of Grilled [Hare], Wonderful[25]

Take a [slaughtered] hare (*arnab*),[26] wash and clean it, and thread it whole onto an iron or wooden skewer. Grill it on moderate heat at a distance from the fire. There should be a wide, shallow bowl (*ṣaḥfa*) next to you in which you have put [a mix of] salt dissolved in rosewater, along with pounded garlic, black pepper, Ceylon cinnamon, and *murrī naqīʿ* (sun-fermented liquid sauce). Put a feather in it and use it to glaze the [grilling] hare repeatedly until it grills and browns. Take it off the skewer, cut it into pieces, discard their bones, and put them in a glazed bowl (*ghaḍāra*), which has olive oil and [cooked and pounded] garlic in it.

If you want, baste the [grilling] hare with fresh butter, as this will keep it moist. Additionally, you can replace the olive oil and garlic [sauce] with [one

23 See n. 3 above.
24 This would be the top, which is mostly fat and oil.
25 *Mashwī ʿajīb*, as described in the Madrid MS, fol. 69r.
26 See n. 3 above.

FIGURE 63 A decorated plate, fifteenth-century Seville, Spain
MET NY—ROGERS FUND, 1930, ACCESSION NUMBER: 30.53.2

made with] *murrī naqīʿ* (sun-fermented liquid sauce), [dried] crushed thyme (*ṣaʿtar maḥkūk*), and olive oil.

If you want to use another sauce (*marqa*), take hard cheese (*jubn yābis*), grate it with a grater (*iskarfāj*), dissolve it in hot water, and then add it to the pounded cooked garlic and olive oil [sauce], and put the [grilled] meat in it.

If you want to make another sauce, take juices of fresh cilantro and Macedonian parsley (*maqdūnis*)[27] and add pounded [cooked] garlic, black pepper,

27 The Madrid MS, fol. 69r, calls this type of parsley *bakdūnis*, which must have been a local variant on the name. See glossary 8.

and vinegar to them. All these are to be put in a wide, shallow bowl (*ṣaḥfa*), and the [grilled] meat is dipped in them.[28]

Whatever dishes you prepare with the hare (*arnab*) you can make with the European wild rabbit (*qunilya*),[29] so know this, and prepare them accordingly.

If you want to roast the *qunilya* in the *furn* (brick oven), and it will still come out moist and tender (*raṭība*), then put it whole in a clean pot—do not cut it into pieces—add plenty of olive oil to it along with garlic [and let it roast in the oven]. Take it out when done, cut it into pieces in a glazed bowl (*ghaḍāra*), and pour whatever liquids remained in the pot all over it. Add one of the vinegars previously mentioned as well,[30] for it will make it smell good and taste delicious, and eat it salubriously, God Almighty willing. (**133r**)

---

28 Unlike the generic term *yūḍaʿ* 'is put' in the Berlin MS, fol. 43r, the BL MS, fol. 132v, and the Madrid MS, fol. 69r, use the more specific term *yuṣbagh* 'to be dipped,' from which *ṣibāgh* 'dipping sauce' is derived (see glossary 9.2, s.v. *yuṣbagh*). A similar sauce is given in recipe ii.1.9 above, where it is called *jalja* and is said to be a popular Byzantine dipping sauce. See recipe v.1.5 below, where it is referred to as *shalsha*. See also n. 10 above.

29 The Madrid MS, fol. 70vb, adds *idhā wujidat* 'if available' and does not include any further details provided in the Berlin and BL MSS.

30 See recipe ii.2.24 above.

CHAPTER II.6

Part Two, Chapter Six: On Foods Incorporated into Dishes Cooked with Meat of Quadrupeds, and Which Are Akin to Making Meatballs (*Banādiq*)[1]

II.6.1 Meatballs (*banādiq*)[2]

Take meat from the thighs (*afkhādh*) and loins (middle back, *sinsin*); remove the veins and sinews (*ʿurūq*) and pound it in a wooden mortar (*mihrās ʿūd*) until it looks doughy. Put it in a wide, shallow bowl (*ṣaḥfa*); add salt—just the needed amount—black pepper, ginger, Ceylon cinnamon, a bit of mastic (*maṣṭakā*), spikenard, cloves—just a bit of it—and egg whites. Knead them all until they mix well and combine into one mass.[3]

If a big amount of food is being prepared, such as in wedding festivities (*walāʾim*, sg. *walīma*) and the like, take a new pot and put water, olive oil, coriander seeds, and a small amount of chopped onion in it. Put it on the fire, and when it comes to a boil, grease your hands with olive oil, take a piece of the meat and shape it into a ball—as big or as small you want it to be—using a *muʿakʿik*,[4] and throw it into the boiling water in the pot. [Continue doing this] until they are all done. Let the meatballs cook in the pot until all the water evaporates and then fry in the pot's olive oil and fat (*wadak*) until they brown. Leave the pot on embers (*ghaḍā*) until the time comes to use them to garnish the bowls being served in wedding feasts.[5]

---

1 The wording of this chapter's heading is somewhat different from the version given in the parts/chapters list given in al-Tujībī's introduction. In addition, except for the chapter's last recipe, it is not specified here what sort of red meat is being used.

2 I here followed the Madrid MS, fol. 53v, which gives the dish its specific name, which is *banādiq*.

3 This detail is from the Madrid MS.

4 I failed to find references to this tool in any other sources. It could not have been a mold of some sort because the recipe gives the option of making the meatballs any size desired. My guess is that it was a sort of rounded bowl in which the piece of meat was put and then shaken around to give it a ball-like form. The name could have been a term derived from *ʿukka*, which is a small, rounded vessel made of leather used to keep ghee in it, see Ibn Manẓūr, *Lisān al-ʿArab*, s.v. عكك. In the Madrid MS, fol. 53v, the recipe simply instructs the cook to shape the meat into hazelnut-size balls by rolling them between the palms.

5 This addition is from the Madrid MS, fol. 53v.

 | DOI:10.1163/9789004469488_014

In case the food being cooked is not much, such as only one or two pots, then put the meatballs in the cooking pot itself [directly after rolling them]. When you ladle food into the glazed serving bowls (*aghḍira*, sg. *ghaḍāra*), let the meatballs show on their surfaces, God Almighty willing.

ii.6.2 A Dish of Meatballs,[6] Which Offers Good Nourishment (*ḥasan al-ghidhā'*)

Take fatty meat and pound it as mentioned [above]; add spices as mentioned above, in addition to *murrī naqīʿ* (sun-fermented liquid sauce), a small amount of onion juice (*mā' baṣal*), caraway, and egg whites. Form the mix into large balls to make them resemble round chunks of meat.

In a clean pot, put *murrī*, vinegar, olive oil, juice of an onion, saffron, and skinned almonds. Once the liquid (*marqa*) comes to a boil throw in the meatballs. After they are fully cooked, cover them with eggs beaten with spices (*yukhammar*),[7] and leave the pot on embers (*ghaḍā*) until it is time to serve them.

ii.6.3 (133v) Making *isfiriyya* (Thin and Smooth Meat Patties)[8]

Take meat similar to what was mentioned in the recipe before the one above [i.e., first recipe], remove the veins and sinews (*ʿurūq*), and beat it on a wooden block (*ṭalya khashab*)[9] with the iron rod usually used for pounding meat.[10] When the pounding is done and all the veins and sinews have been removed,

---

6 *Banādiq*, as given in the Madrid MS, fol. 53v.

7 I followed the Madrid MS, fol. 54r, here and for the rest of the recipe because it offers a more accurate text. Topping the dish thus with seasoned eggs is called *takhmīr*, literally 'covering.' See glossary 9.2.

8 إسفرية. See also recipe i.2.17 above, where it is called *isfāriyya* إسفارية. It also occurs as *isfiryā* إسفريا and *isfīriyya* إسفيرية in recipe iii.1.1 below, and the anonymous Andalusi *Anwāʿ al-ṣaydala*, 3, 4, 91, 110, 146, where it is made in several different ways, including meatless ones. See glossary 5, s.v. *isfiriyya*.

9 It is usually used as a chopping board. See Corriente, *Dictionary of Andalusi Arabic*, s.v. *ṭ-l-y*, where the word is said to have been derived from the late Latin *taleare* 'to cut.'

10 The difference in terminology between *ḍarb* 'beating' and *dars* 'pounding' indicates that the iron rod is to beat the meat horizontally on the board as opposed to the vertical pounding of meat in a mortar. The recipe's version in the Madrid MS, fol. 54r, uses an iron rod, called *ʿamūd ḥadīd*, or the back of a cleaver (*sāṭūr*) to beat the meat on a wooden board (*khashaba*).

put the meat in a large, wide bowl (*mithrad*); add salt, black pepper, Ceylon cinnamon, a small amount of mastic (*maṣṭakā*), spikenard (*sunbul*), cloves (*qaranful*) as needed, and egg whites. Knead them all until the mix looks like bone marrow (*mukhkh*). If it still needs to be further pounded, pound it in a wooden mortar (*mihrās ʿūd*) with the spices and the egg whites in it.

Now take a skillet (*miqlāt*), grease it with olive oil, and heat it up slightly. Once it gets slightly hot, take the meat and put it in the skillet, flatten and smoothen it with your hands,[11] and rub the surface with olive oil. [When one side is cooked,] gently flip the disc.[12] The aim is to make the disc thin and smooth.

[When the disc is done frying,] put it on a board (*lawḥ*) and cut it lengthwise into slices, which you keep in a glazed bowl (*ghaḍāra*) and use to garnish foods when they are ladled into the glazed serving bowls, God Almighty willing, by spreading them on their surfaces along with split [boiled] eggs, God Almighty willing.

II.6.4 Making *mirqās* (Small Sausage Links)[13]

Take meat from the thighs (*afkhādh*), loins (middle back, *sinsin*), and similar cuts. Beat it on a wooden block (*ṭalya khashab*)[14] with the iron rod mentioned above; beat it vigorously until it falls apart, and then remove the veins and sinews (*ʿurūq*). When you finish beating it, put it in a large kneading bowl (*miʿjana*).[15] Take fresh suet (*shaḥm ṭarī*), what equals one-third the amount of meat or a little bit more,[16] remove all the veins and sinews, chop it with a knife into the smallest pieces possible, and add it to the meat, in which you have already put salt, black pepper, ginger, Ceylon cinnamon, a small amount of mastic (*maṣṭakā*), spikenard, cloves, slightly pounded aniseeds (*anīsūn*), and cumin. Take a small amount of onion and a clove or two of garlic, pound them, mix them with water, and strain them; add the resulting liquid to the meat. Also

11 Smoothening the surface by hand is the Madrid MS addition, fol. 54r.

12 I follow here the Madrid MS, which reads *tuḥawwal* 'flipped over' rather than the generic *tujʿal* 'put.'

13 Copied as *mirqāsh* in the Madrid MS, fol. 54r. It occurs as *mirkās* in recipe ii.5.2 above, and in the anonymous Andalusi *Anwāʿ al-ṣaydala*, 1, 4, 145. According to the recipe, they are hung to dry in the sun, or smoked.

14 See n. 9 above.

15 This kind of bowl is usually used for kneading bread dough.

16 Using an amount of suet that equals one-third the amount of meat was the standard ratio, as we learn from the market inspector al-Saqaṭī, *Fī Ādāb al-ḥisba* 36.

add *murrī naqīʿ* (sun-fermented liquid sauce) and vinegar—just the needed amounts—as well as rosewater and chopped mint leaves. Knead all the ingredients in the bowl until they mix very well. Beat the meat again with the suet in it.

Take a piece of the meat and grill it on the fire and taste it. If you like it, well and good; (**134r**) but if you find it deficient in salt or other [spices], add what is lacking, and set it aside.

Now take intestines (*maṣārīn*); let them be taken from a large grown female goat (*ʿanz*) or a large ram (*kabsh*) because their intestines will be larger and stronger [than those of the smaller ones]. Take a [metal] ring (*ḥalqa*), bend it [until almost doubled], and pass the intestine through its gap to scrape it [from the inside and outside][17] to remove its meaty [outer layer], and it becomes clean [from the inside].[18] Put the [scraped] intestine in a wide, shallow bowl (*ṣaḥfa*) filled with water.[19]

Take one of the ends of the intestine and push it into the stem of a funnel (*qimʿ*) until most of it is inserted.[20] Now hold the funnel with the help of your left thumb and push the meat mix into the funnel with your right thumb so that the intestine moves out of the funnel with the meat in it. If you find the meat mix a bit too dense [to push], add some water to moisten it. Continue doing this until it is done [i.e., filled]. Once you have a filled intestine, take it, clean it [from the outside], and make sausages (*mirqās*) as big or as small you want them. [To do this,] divide one piece from the other by removing the meat between them [done by squeezing the dividing place] and twisting the intestine. Fold the entire intestine and hang it to expose it to sun or smoke.

A recipe for cooking *mirqās* for wedding feasts (*walāʾim*):
Separate [the sausage links] and put them in a pot. Add a moderate amount of water and a little bit of salt and put the pot on the fire. Stir it constantly until the sausages release their juices and fat. Remove the strong fire and let them cook on low heat until they fry and brown.

---

17 The verb used in the Berlin MS, fol. 44r, is *taḥnūhu* (تحنوه), which means 'peel' or 'scrape,' see Ibn Manẓūr, *Lisān al-ʿArab*, s.v. حنى.

18 Scraping the intestine thus would also remove the inner mucous lining.

19 The Madrid MS, fol. 54v, recommends that the intestines are to be drained on a tray of woven esparto grass (*ḥalfā*).

20 I followed the copy of Madrid MS, fol. 54v, حتى يتحصل عليه اكثره as it makes more sense than حتى يكون كثيراً 'until there is plenty of it' in the other two MSS. The Madrid MS adds that the funnel is to be greased with olive oil from the inside before using it.

For wedding feasts, the amount used for each serving bowl (*ghaḍāra*) is about 10 sausages. And if you are cooking the *mirqās* in your own house, then you may cook them with spring garlic (*farīk thūm*),[21] or with onions as *rāhibī*,[22] or *jumlī* topped with eggs (*mukhammar*).[23] Indeed, this is the way *mirqās* would be prepared for wedding feasts in al-ʿUdwa.[24]

Alternatively, you may fill a pan (*ṭājin*) with them and bake them in the *furn* (brick oven),[25] or fry them with the addition of vinegar or mustard sauce (*ṣināb*).[26] Or grill them skewered, but in this case they need to be eaten while still hot because they contain suet. So, you need to know and understand these things, and cook them however you wish.

If you want to store the sausages away, cook them until you are sure that all the moisture in them has evaporated and then put them in a new pot. Render fresh, fine-tasting suet with salt, and make sure all the moisture in it has evaporated. Pour it all over the *mirqās*; enough to cover them all. Store the pot in a dry place, and whenever you want to serve them, take out the amount you wish to use and heat them up [in a pan] on the fire; add a suitable amount of vinegar, and eat them salubriously, God Almighty willing.

If you want to use eggplants with meat and suet [in stuffing the sausages], take fresh and tender eggplants, peel them, and boil them in water until they cook. Pound them until they disintegrate, mix them with some eggs [and the meat mixture], and stuff them [into the intestines]. These sausages are well recommended (*mustaḥsan*), God Almighty willing.

II.6.5 Another Dish [of Meat Pancakes Drenched in Sauce]

(**134v**) Take meat and all the other ingredients I previously mentioned to you,[27] adding a small amount of fine white flour (*daqīq darmak*) and fresh yeast (*khamīr*). Thin down the meat mix with water until it looks like *talbīna* (thin starchy batter).[28]

---

21 As in recipe ii.2.15 above.

22 As in recipe ii.1.7 above.

23 As in recipe ii.1.1 above.

24 That is the North African region, which is on the other side of the Mediterranean.

25 The adj. *maḥshū* 'filled' suggests that sausage links would have been coiled to fill the entire pan.

26 *Ṣināb*, also known as *khardal*, designates the seeds themselves, as well as sauces/condiments made with them. For sauce recipes, see chapter x.1 below. See also glossary 5 for the mustard condiment/sauce; and glossary 8 for the seeds.

27 See the first recipe in this chapter.

28 See recipe i.4.14 above for more on *talbīna*.

Put the skillet on the fire with a small amount of olive oil, and once it heats up, spread some of the pounded meat mixture in it; put enough to fill the [base of the] pan. When you see that it has started to brown, take it out, and replace it with another one after you replenish the olive oil [in the pan]. Continue doing this until you finish them all.

Prepare a sauce (*maraq*) made with vinegar, *murrī naqīʿ* (sun-fermented liquid sauce), and mustard sauce (*ṣināb*).[29] Drench [the meat pancakes] with it, and eat the dish salubriously, God Almighty willing.

ii.6.6 Making *laqāniq* (Large Sausages)[30]

These are made exactly like *mirqās* (recipe ii.6.4 above), except that no *murrī* (liquid fermented sauce) is added to them, and a pounded onion and cilantro are used in them. Moreover, *laqāniq* are made larger than *mirqās*, and the intestine used should be wider, so choose accordingly. Once you finish making them, boil them very briefly in water, and then take them out and hang them in a ventilated place [to dry].

Whenever you want to eat sausages, take them one by one and cut them into pieces. Then, put them in an earthenware skillet (*miqlāt fakhkhār*) or an earthenware pan (*ṭājin*) on a moderate fire without using any olive oil. Stir the pieces [frequently] until they release their fat. Add vinegar to them if wished, and eat them salubriously, God Almighty willing.

If you want to cook them with other dishes as was mentioned in the *mirkās* [above],[31] go ahead and do so, with the help of God Almighty.

ii.6.7 Making *aḥrash* (Thin Meat Patties)[32]

They are made with the same meat and spices (*abāzīr*) used in *mirkās*;[33] and the meat is beaten the same way, to the letter.

29 See n. 26 above. An uncooked sauce, such as the one prepared here, is called *jalja* and *shalsha* in other recipes (ii.1.9, v.1.5). See glossary 5, s.v. *jalja*.

30 In other sources, we may also come across other variants on the name, such as *maqāniq* and *naqāniq*, or *dakānik*, as in the anonymous Andalusi *Anwāʿ al-ṣaydala*. Cf. *laqāniq* recipes in al-Warrāq, *Kitāb al-Ṭabīkh*, English trans., *Annals*, chapter 36.

31 The text alternates between *mirqās* and *mirkās*, even in the same recipe.

32 This is how the name of these patties is clearly vocalized in the BL MS, fol. 134v. Another *aḥrash* recipe is given in ii.5.2 above, made with the meat of wild animals. Others are made with gourd, recipe vii.1.4; and eggplant, recipe vii.2.5.

33 See n. 31 above.

If you want to make it without suet (*shaḥm*), break some eggs on the meat and whip all the ingredients until they mix and totally blend. Now take a skillet made of tinned iron (*ḥadīd muqazdar*) or glazed earthenware (*fakhkhār muzajjaj*), put olive oil in it, and place it on the fire. Take the meat mix and shape it [like] small flat bread discs (*khubayzāt*). Put them in the oil when it starts boiling, and turn them gently. Take them out as soon as they brown, put them in a glazed bowl (*ghaḍāra*), and pour *murrī naqīʿ* (sun-fermented liquid sauce) or heated-up vinegar all over them.

If you want to prepare them another way, take two small skillets and put one [of them close to] your hands.[34] Take a piece of the meat and shape it into a small *kaʿka* [i.e., like a ring cookie], and put it in the middle [of this skillet]. Next, take some of the meat and mix it with fine white flour—as fine as powder (*ghubār daqīq al-darmak*)[35]—and egg whites. Shape it into meatballs (*banādiq*), which you then stick next to each other all around the meat ring so that the entire piece looks like a bread disc (*raghīf*). Put the skillet on a low fire and put olive oil in it. When you know that the [bottom] of the disc has browned, turn it into the second skillet along with the oil in it, (**135r**) [and let it fry on low heat]. Start assembling meat in the [first] skillet once again, and continue doing this—turning the [assembled meat discs] from one pan to the other. Put the finished ones that have browned on both sides in a glazed bowl (*ghaḍāra*), and when all the pieces are done, pour *murrī naqīʿ* or boiled vinegar all over them, and eat them salubriously, God Almighty willing.

If you want to make them with suet (*shaḥm*): take fine-tasting fresh suet, half the amount of the meat used, and chop it into the finest pieces possible. Put it with the meat in a large kneading bowl (*miʿjana*) and mix them thoroughly. Take an iron skillet (*miqlāt ḥadīd*), put it on the fire, and put a small amount of olive oil in it. Once the oil heats up, take the mixed meat, shape it into discs like small, flat bread (*khubayzāt*), and put them in the skillet, turning them gently [as needed] until they cook and brown. Take them out and put them in a glazed bowl (*ghaḍāra*), and eat them salubriously, God Almighty willing. They are most delicious eaten when still hot due to the suet they contain.

If you want to make sauce for it with vinegar, olive oil, and garlic cooked together, you can do so.

---

34 Based on context, I am filling in a lacuna here in the BL MS, fol. 134v; the same lacuna is found in the Berlin MS, fol. 45r. The Madrid MS does not include this recipe.

35 This powdery flour is a by-product of milling wheat grains in a quern (*raḥā*) or the larger grinder (*ṭāḥūna*), which produces fine powder that falls all over the place. It was collected and used in making glues, dusting foods with it before frying, or as in this recipe. See Ibn Waḥshiyya, *al-Filāḥa al-Nabaṭiyya* i 421.

If you want to store them and use them as needed (*yurfaʿ*), follow the same method used for *mirkās*.[36]

II.6.8 Making *qubā* (Stuffed Omasum Tripe)[37]

Take the omasum tripe, turn it inside out, wash it with vinegar and salt, and clean it very well. Take fine-tasting meat from the thighs and the like, pound it in a wooden mortar very well, and add salt, black pepper, coriander seeds, Ceylon cinnamon, ginger, spikenard, cloves, a small amount of mastic (*maṣṭakā*), a ladleful of *murrī* (liquid fermented sauce), juices of fresh cilantro and mint, skinned almonds, pine nuts (*ṣanawbar*), and a small amount of chopped suet. Take some eggs as well, break them on the meat, and beat the mix very well. Also take cooked egg yolks and a whole egg—boiled and shelled.

Put [half of] the meat mix inside the omasum tripe, positioning [some of] the egg yolks at various places in the stuffing. The whole egg should be placed in the middle of it. Then, stuff the rest of the meat and what is left of the egg yolks. Tie the two openings of the omasum tripe, put it in an earthenware cauldron (*ṭinjīr fakhkhār*) or a large pot (*qidr*), and add water, salt, olive oil, black pepper, coriander seeds, and a chopped small onion.

Put the pot on the fire to cook, and when the *qubā* is almost done, take it out and put it in a large earthenware pan (*ṭājin*), color it with pounded saffron, and take all the fatty broth (*wadak*) you find in [whichever pot you used,] *qidr* or *ṭinjīr*, and add it to the pan along with a small amount of lemon juice (*māʾ līm*). Send it to the *furn* (communal brick oven), and let there be someone available to turn it [several times while cooking] until it browns on all sides and then it is taken out of the oven.

Cut it open with a knife however you like when served, (**135v**) and eat it salubriously, God Almighty willing.

---

36 See recipe above, ii.6.4, p. 286, where the sausages are preserved in salted rendered suet.

37 Omasum is the third chamber in the stomach of a ruminant. The word is clearly vocalized as قُبا in the Berlin and BL MSS, fol. 46v and 135r, respectively. The only other extant recipe for stuffed omasum tripe, a version of haggis, is found in al-Warrāq, *Kitāb al-Ṭabīkh*, English trans., *Annals*, chapter 48, p. 245, where it is copied as *qibba* (قِبّة). *Qubā* must have been a regional dialectal variant.

II.6.9 Making Stuffing for *mibʿar* (Fresh Sausages Encased in Large Intestines)

It is made exactly like the [*qubā*] above, but the cooked egg yolks need to be cut in half since the *mibʿar* (large intestine) is not large enough for whole ones. Keep them whole if the *mibʿar* is wide enough; and [in this case] use boiled eggs as well, so understand this and prepare them accordingly, God Almighty willing.

II.6.10 Making *harīsa* (Wheat Porridge with Meat)[38]

Take as much as you want of meat from the thigh of a fat young cow (*baqar fatī*); put it in an unglazed earthenware pot (*qidr fakhkhār dūn muzajjaja*). Add wheat berries, which have been soaked and pounded in a mortar to get rid of their outer husks. Let them be a third of the amount of meat.

Add plenty of water to the pot, and take it to the *furn* (communal brick oven) to [cook slowly] all night long. Take it out the following morning and put it on the house [stove] fire to cook until the remaining water evaporates. Take a large knife or an iron skewer and hold it upright in the pot and stir the meat with it so that it shreds and disintegrates.

Take some flour, dissolve it in water, and pour it into the middle of the pot with the meat [and wheat] in it. Insert a ladle into the pot and beat its contents vigorously until they all blend and it becomes chewy in texture (*yataʿallak*).

Take fresh suet (*shaḥm*), pound it, remove all the unwanted parts [such as the sinews and veins], and render it in an earthenware pan (*ṭājin fakhkhār*). Once it renders, ladle the *harīsa* into a glazed bowl (*ghaḍāra*) and drizzle it with it.

If you want, take some of the [finished] *harīsa* and fry it in olive oil in a pan used for frying yeasted fritters (*miqlāt al-isfanj*).[39] Spread it on the face of [the *harīsa* ladled in the] bowl. Add [cooked] egg yolks, fried sparrows (*ʿaṣāfīr*), and sprinkle it with Ceylon cinnamon as well.

If you want to cook it at home [on the stove], you can do so but take care not to let it burn. **Also, if you want**, you can cook it with mutton (*laḥm ghanamī*) or chicken (*dajāj*) [instead of beef]; and you may use rice (*aruzz*) instead of wheat (*qamḥ*),[40] so know this.

---

38 For a meatless variety, see recipe i.5.13 above.

39 Such frying pans are made of tinned copper or iron, see recipes i.4.30–1 above.

40 Unfortunately, the editor of the Arabic text confused its sense by mis-amending the Berlin MS, fol. 46r, changing the copy's legibly written أو رزّا 'or rice' to أو بالإوز 'or with geese.'

PART 3

القسم الثالث

في أصناف لحوم الطير ويشتمل على سبعة فصول

On Dishes with Various Types of Poultry, and It Has Seven Chapters (136r)

Part Three, Chapter One: On Meat of Geese (*Iwazz*)[1]

III.1.1 A Dish [of Oven-Browned Stuffed Goose]

Take a tender and fat goose, slaughter it, and before removing the feathers, blow into it [through the neck] to separate the skin from meat, and find a way to work through the hard-to-get sections.[2] Next, tie its neck with a thread, pluck the feathers by [dipping it first in] hot water, and clean the bird. Open up its belly and take out the entrails; wash the bird thoroughly, put it in a vessel, and keep it aside.

Take another goose, slaughter it, pluck its feathers, open up its belly, take out the entrails, and then debone the meat and pound it in a wooden mortar (*mihrās ʿūd*) until it disintegrates. When you are done with this, add salt, black pepper, coriander seeds, ginger, Ceylon cinnamon, cloves, spikenard, and breadcrumbs (*fatāt*) of semolina bread (*khubz samīd*). Break eggs on the meat, as many as needed to bind it. Also add *murrī naqīʿ* (sun-fermented liquid sauce) and skinned almonds. Knead all the ingredients by hand thoroughly to mix them; also add a small amount of saffron.

Stuff the cavity of the goose, as well as between the skin and meat; and sew up the belly. You need to keep aside some of the stuffing without breadcrumbs to make meatballs (*banādiq*) with it [and set them aside].

Take a large cauldron (*ṭinjīr*), pour in fresh water (*māʾ ʿadhb*), plenty of olive oil, salt, black pepper, coriander seeds, and a chopped half of an onion. Put the pot on the fire, and when it almost comes to a boil, gently take the goose—you should have already tied the skin of its neck with a thread—and lower it into the pot; check on it all the time by turning it gently. To prevent the bird's skin from rupturing while boiling in the pot, let there be with you a large needle ready to prick the skin; thus, any steam [forming underneath it] will find a way to escape without breaking it.

---

1 Apparently, in this cookbook only geese are used; there is no mention of ducks, called *burak* in the Muslim West (more commonly called *baṭṭ* in other regions). There is also the possibility that ducks are indeed used in the recipes because ducks in the western region were also called *iwazz al-qurṭ*. For more on these aquatic birds, see glossary 10, s.v. *iwazz*.

2 A skewer may be used in such cases, as we learn from a stuffed chicken recipe in Ibn al-ʿAdīm, *al-Wuṣla ilā-l-ḥabīb* ii 525–6; English trans., *Scents* 51.

 | DOI:10.1163/9789004469488_015

FIGURE 64 A goose, al-Qazwīnī, *ʿAjāʾib al-makhlūqāt wa-gharāʾib al-mawjūdāt*, fol. 115r, detail
BRITISH LIBRARY: ORIENTAL MANUSCRIPTS, OR 14140, IN *QATAR DIGITAL LIBRARY* HTTPS://WWW.QDL.QA/ARCHIVE/81055/VDC_100023586788.0X000001

When the bird looks cooked, remove the pot from the fire; take the bird out gently and put it in a large earthenware pan (*ṭājin*). Color it with saffron, and take some of the strained broth with all its fats and oils and add it to the *ṭājin*. Let it be carried to the *furn* (communal brick oven) to brown at a distance from the fire. Give directions to have it gently turned over to brown the underside.

[**Preparing garnishes for the goose**:] Take what remains of the strained broth and put it in a clean pot, adding olive oil, black pepper, and a small amount of *murrī* (liquid fermented sauce); [set this aside].

Take 10 eggs or more and break them in a wide, shallow bowl (*ṣaḥfa*). Add salt, black pepper, Ceylon cinnamon, ginger, and a small amount of saffron. Beat them with a ladle vigorously to mix the spices [with the eggs] and let the whites mingle with the yolks. (**136v**) Take 5 egg yolks and put them in the pot [to poach] with the meatballs [prepared earlier].[3] Once they cook, add fine-tasting vinegar to the pot—just the needed amount—and when it comes to a boil add the beaten eggs and lightly move the pot [so that the eggs spread on the entire surface]. Remove the fire from underneath the pot and keep it on

3 Adding the meatballs at this stage is mentioned in the Madrid MS, fol. 70rc, only.

embers (*ghaḍā*) until the eggs set and just a small amount of sauce remains in the pot.[4] [Set this aside.]

[To prepare an *isfīriyya* 'smooth and thin patties':[5]] take the gizzards (*qawāniṣ*) and livers (*kubūd*) and pound them in a mortar thoroughly. Add salt and aromatic spices (*afāwīh*) and knead them with the egg whites. Take a skillet and put it on the fire with olive oil. Shape the pounded mix into a thin disc, put it in the skillet, and turn it to brown on the other side. Carefully take it out of the pan, put it on a wooden board (*lawḥ*), and cut it into strips with a knife. Get them ready along with split boiled eggs and fried egg yolks. [Set them aside.]

[**Now back to the goose:**] Send someone to check on the *ṭājin* in the *furn*; if it looks cooked and browned, let it be taken out; otherwise, it is to be left until it browns.

Transfer the goose into a wide plate and drizzle the strained broth [prepared above] all over it. Spread on it the [poached] egg yolks, *takhmīr*,[6] and the meatballs. Garnish it with the *isfīriyya* strips, split boiled eggs, and fried egg yolks. Sprinkle it with Ceylon cinnamon and ginger, and serve it, God Almighty willing. Garnish it with tender tips of mint sprigs (*ʿuyūn naʿnaʿ*) as well.

III.1.2 Another Dish [of a Goose, Grilled Rotisserie Fashion or Oven Roasted, with Sauces]

Take a tender and fat goose, slaughter it, and pluck its feathers.[7] Open up its cavity, wash it, and thread it onto an iron or wooden skewer. Now prepare the fire by putting it on both sides of the goose, and not underneath it, with the skewer suspended at a higher level by resting both its ends on rocks; this way the goose will not have contact with dust on the ground.

Turn the skewer by hand constantly, and watch the fire all the time and keep it going.[8] There should be right next to you a wide, shallow bowl (*ṣaḥfa*) with water, salt, a bit of olive oil, pounded garlic, and aromatic spices (*afāwīh*). Take

4 This is called *takhmīr*, see glossary 9.2. Dishes that have little sauce in them were often served with a topping of eggs, which have been whipped, poured to cover the surface, and left to set on low heat.

5 The name also occurs as *isfiriyya* and *isfāriyya*, see recipe ii.6.3 above.

6 See n. 4 above.

7 The editor of the Arabic text needlessly 'amended' the perfectly legible تنتفها *tantufuhā* 'pluck its feathers,' in all the MSS, to تنقيها *tunaqīhā* 'clean it.'

8 In the eastern region, meat grilled this way was called *kardanāj*. See, for instance, al-Warrāq, *Kitāb al-Ṭabīkh*, English trans., *Annals*, chapter 90. A special skewer with a handle was used to facilitate the rotating.

a goose feather, wash it, dip it in the bowl, and baste the [grilling] goose with it whenever it looks dry. Let the goose grill very well until it browns and is fully done, which in the long days [of summer] will happen only if the grilling lasts from early morning to around noontime; but patience pays off.

To test for doneness, hold a leg or a wing and pull it towards you, it should come off easily. Also, if you shake [either one], their meat will fall off easily, or you can easily pull it off the bone. These are signs that the meat is fully cooked.

[**To make the sauce,**] take hard cheese (*jubn yābis*) and finely grate it on the grater (*iskarfāj*) into dust-like particles. Also take garlic and cook it in any pot you want and then pound it well. Now take hot water and dissolve the cheese and garlic in it. (**149r**) Put the mix in a glazed bowl (*ghaḍāra*), adding fine-tasting olive oil to it. Next, take the goose meat, break it into pieces by hand, and put them in the bowl. Stir the pieces by hand so that they mix with the cheese, garlic, and olive oil, and eat the dish salubriously, God Almighty willing. If you want, use only olive oil and garlic [for the sauce]; or, it can be *murrī naqīʿ* (sun-fermented liquid sauce) [mixed with] crushed [dried] thyme (*ṣaʿtar*) and olive oil. Do it whichever way you like.

If you want to roast the goose in the *furn* (brick oven), then salt it, put it in a large earthenware pan (*ṭājin*), along with olive oil and pounded garlic, and give it a sprinkle of black pepper. Send the pan to the oven and let it be put at a distance from the fire. The goose is to be turned over [several times] until it cooks and browns. Once cooked, it is cut into pieces and served,[9] God Almighty willing.

If you want, you may cook the goose as *jumlī* or *rāhibī* as I mentioned to you in the first chapter of the second part,[10] God Almighty willing.

9 The roasting juices seasoned with the added garlic, olive oil, salt, and black pepper will serve as its sauce.

10 See recipes ii.1.1 and ii.1.7 above. *Jumlī* is a succulent meat dish seasoned with *murrī* (liquid fermented sauce) and vinegar. *Rāhibī* is an oven-braised meat dish, cooked with onions and sweetened with honey or rose-petal jam and the like.

CHAPTER III.2

Part Three, Chapter Two: On Chicken (*Dajāj*)

III.2.1 A Dish of *tafāyā bayḍā'* (Simple White Stew)[1]

Take a fattened young adult chicken (*dajāja musammana fatiyya*), and after slaughtering it and plucking its feathers [by dipping it first] in hot water, rub its outside skin with salt, and clean its cavity. You may disjoint it however you like; or leave it in one piece if wished, just cut off its neck and insert the ends of its legs through its anal vent (*makhraj*).

Put the chicken in a new pot along with water and olive oil.[2] Pound ginger and coriander seeds and put them in a piece of new cloth with a stick of Ceylon cinnamon (*qirfa*), a lump of mastic (*maṣṭakā*), washed salt (*milḥ maghsūl*),[3] and a small amount of chopped onion. Tie the cloth [into a bundle] with a thread and put it in the pot. Let the pot cook on the fire, and as soon as you know that the spices have released all their aromas and flavors into the liquid, take the bundle out so that the liquid does not get discolored.

If you want to take the breast of another chicken, pound it, season it with aromatic spices (*afāwīh*), add egg whites to it, and make meatballs with it, [and add them to the pot], go ahead and do so. If you want to add egg yolks [to poach in the broth], you can also do so. If you want to top it with a mix of egg whites and breadcrumbs (*fatāt*), do so by all means.[4]

Now have a look at the chicken; if you find that it is done, remove the fire from underneath the pot and leave it on embers (*ghaḍā*) to simmer (*tatajammar*).[5] Empty it into a glazed bowl (*ghaḍāra*), sprinkle it with pounded Ceylon

---

1 As it is named in the Madrid MS, fol. 71v. The BL MS, fol. 149r, and the Berlin MS, fol. 47v, give its name at the very end of the recipe. In the eastern region, the dish was called *isfidhbāj* and *isbīdāj*. See, for instance, al-Warrāq, *Kitāb al-Ṭabīkh*, English trans., *Annals*, chapter 59. In the Andalusi anonymous *Anwāʿ al-ṣaydala* 59, this dish is categorized as feminine (*mu'annatha*), praised for its balanced properties, and recommended for weak stomachs. See also above, recipe ii.2.1, n. 2, for more on the name of the dish.

2 I used the Madrid MS version of the recipe, fol. 72r–v to fill in some missing details in the other two MSS.

3 Salt was cleansed and purified by first dissolving it into brine to get rid of all the sand and other impurities and then boiling it until crystalized.

4 Covering the top of the dish with such a layer is called *takhmīr*; see glossary 9.2.

5 See glossary 9.2 for more on this cooking expression.

DOI:10.1163/9789004469488_016

FIGURE 65 A chicken, al-Qazwīnī, *'Ajā'ib al-makhlūqāt wa ghārā'ib al-mawjūdāt*, fol. 187r, detail
BNF, DEPARTMENT OF MANUSCRIPTS, ARAB 221.
SOURCE: GALLICA.BNF.FR/BNF

cinnamon, or the tender ends of mint sprigs if you wish, and eat the dish salubriously, God Almighty willing.

This dish is called *tafāyā bayḍā'*; it has been mentioned earlier in the second chapter of the second part of this book.[6]

III.2.2 Another Dish, Called *tafāyā khaḍrā'* (Green Simple Stew)

(149v) Making this dish has been described earlier in the chapter referred to above [in the previous recipe].[7]

III.2.3 Another Dish, Called *lawziyya* (Cooked with Almonds)

It has been mentioned earlier in the chapter referred to above [in the first recipe].[8]

6 See *tafāyā* recipe ii.2.1 above, cooked with mutton.
7 See recipe ii.2.2 above, cooked with mutton.
8 See recipe ii.2.27 above, cooked with mutton.

III.2.4 Another Dish, Called *kāfūriyya* (Flavored with Camphor)[9]

It is made exactly like *lawziyya*; except that when the almonds—of which you should have used 4 *ūqiyyas* (4 ounces) for a single chicken—have cooked, add fine-tasting lemon juice (*mā' līm*) to the pot—amount to taste. Let the pot cook until it boils with the lemon juice in it, [add enough camphor to flavor it,[10]] and then remove the fire from underneath the pot and let it simmer (*tatajammar*).[11] Empty the dish into a glazed bowl (*ghaḍāra*), and eat it salubriously, God Almighty willing.

III.2.5 Another Dish, Called *zīrbājiyya muḥallāt* (Mildly Sour Golden Stew, Sweetened)[12]

Take a fat young adult chicken that is large in size, slaughter it, and do with it as you did earlier [in the first recipe], such as cleaning it and the like. Keep the chicken whole but cut off its neck and insert the ends of its legs through its anal vent (*makhraj*).

Put the chicken in a large new pot, adding salt, sweet olive oil (*zayt ʿadhb*), black pepper, coriander seeds, small amounts of cumin and chopped onion, citron leaves, and the needed amount of fresh water (*mā' ʿadhb*). Put the pot on the fire and let it cook. When it is almost done, color it with a small amount of saffron, which has been pounded and dissolved in water. Next, add fine-tasting vinegar to taste.

Now take 4 *ūqiyyas* (4 ounces) almonds, which have been shelled and skinned, and pound them in a mortar (*mihrās*) until they look pasty. Have a look at the chicken; if you see that it has cooked well, add the pounded almonds to the pot and stir until they dissolve into the liquid. Let the pot cook on a medium fire until it comes to a boil or two.[13]

---

9 The recipe does not mention adding camphor, but judging from a *kāfūriyya* recipe in the anonymous Andalusi *Anwāʿ al-ṣaydala* 18, camphor is indeed to be added to flavor the dish, after which it is named. I amended the recipe based on this book and the Madrid MS, fol. 72r.

10 The Madrid MS clearly shows that the dish is to be flavored: يوضع في القدر ما يفتقه من, followed by a lacuna, which should have been الكافور 'camphor.' See the above note.

11 See glossary 9.2 for more on this cooking expression.

12 A similar recipe, albeit shorter, is also found in the anonymous Andalusi *Anwāʿ al-ṣaydala* 17–8.

13 See glossary 9.2, s.v. *ghalya* for more on this boiling technique.

Next, take fine-tasting sugar, as much as the almonds, dissolve it in rosewater or fresh water, strain it, and add it to the pot. Have a taste: if you find the liquid too sweet, add more vinegar; if it is not sweet enough, add more sugar until you approve of its taste. [Remove the fire from underneath the pot] and leave it on embers [to simmer] and allow the flavors to nicely blend (*taʿtadil*). Ladle the dish into a glazed bowl (*ghaḍāra*), top it with split [boiled] eggs if you want to, and eat it salubriously, God Almighty willing.

III.2.6 Another Dish, Called *mukhallal* (Soured with Vinegar)[14]

Take a fat young adult chicken, slaughter it, and do with it as you did earlier [in the first recipe], such as cleaning it and the like. Put it in a new pot, adding water, salt, olive oil, black pepper, coriander seeds, caraway, a small amount of chopped onion, a few cloves of garlic, skinned almonds, soaked chickpeas, a bit of *murrī naqīʿ* (sun-fermented liquid sauce), (150r) citron leaves, and sprigs of herb fennel (*ʿūd basbās*). Put the pot on the fire to cook, and when it is almost done, take saffron, pound it, dissolve it in water, and add it to the chicken pot; use enough to color it. Next, add fine-tasting vinegar (*khall ṭayyib*)—amount to your liking.

Now take a small pot (*qudayra*); also take coriander seeds and black pepper and the breast of [another] chicken. Pound the breast in a mortar (*mihrās*) and make it into meatballs [with the coriander and black pepper] following the directions given in the sixth chapter of the second part of this book.[15] Put the meatballs in the small pot along with [whole] egg yolks. Take some [more] eggs and break them in a wide, shallow bowl (*ṣaḥfa*), adding salt, spices (*abāzīr*), and saffron. Beat them well with a ladle to mix them, pour them into the small pot, and let them cook on a low fire until they set. Now take an egg or two, boil them in water, and then shell them and split them into quarters.

Check on the chicken, if you see that it has cooked well, ladle it into a glazed bowl (*ghaḍāra*) and put whatever is in the small pot all over it. Garnish it with split eggs and tender tips of mint sprigs (*ʿuyūn al-naʿnaʿ*). Sprinkle the dish with Ceylon cinnamon and ginger, and eat it salubriously, God Almighty willing.

---

14 In the eastern region, such dishes were more commonly known as *sikbāj*.

15 See recipes ii.6.1–2 above.

III.2.7 Another Dish, Called *al-mufattit* (the Crumbler)[16]

Take a chicken as described above, slaughter it, and then cut it into pieces at the joints the way you like after washing and cleaning it. Put it in a new pot and add whatever was previously mentioned [in the recipe above]. Put the pot on the fire to cook after adding water as needed.

Now take the meat of another chicken; pound it, season it, and make meatballs (*banādiq*) with it as was described [in the recipe] above. When the chicken in the pot is almost cooked, add these meatballs to it.

Next, take the chicken's gizzard (*qāniṣa*) and liver (*kabd*); pound them and shape them into a flat disc (*raghīf*), which you fry in a pan with a small amount of olive oil and then cut it on a board [into stripes], as was earlier described in making *isfīriyya* [recipe ii.6.3 above]. Put the cut pieces in a glazed bowl (*ghaḍāra*) and set it aside.

Take 10 eggs and break them in a wide, shallow bowl (*ṣaḥfa*), but take 3 of the egg yolks [keep them whole] and set them aside. Add salt, all the aromatic spices [usually used], and a bit of pounded saffron; beat them with a ladle until they mix very well. Next, take a small, glazed earthenware pan (*ṭājin fakhkhār muzajjaj*), put the needed amounts of water, vinegar, *murrī* (liquid fermented sauce), and olive oil in it, and put it on the fire and let it boil. Once it boils, take the beaten eggs and add them to it. Stir the pan and let it cook until the eggs are a hard scramble.

Next, fry the set-aside egg yolks with olive oil in a pan until they brown and add them to the *isfīriyya* [strips in the bowl]. (150v) Also, boil an egg or two, shell them, split them into quarters, and add them to the *isfīriyya* bowl along with the [fried] egg yolks.

Now have a look at the chicken [in the pot], if you find that it has cooked, take it out, and fry it in sweet olive oil (*zayt ṭayyib*), but do not let it brown.[17]

[To serve the dish:] Take a large glazed bowl (*ghaḍāra*) and line it with fresh citron leaves. Spread some of the scrambled eggs over them. Next, arrange the chicken pieces [with the meatballs] on top of them, and spread the rest of the scrambled eggs in between the pieces. Let the meatballs show. On top of the

16 In the Berlin and BL MSS, fols. 48v and 150r, respectively, the name of the dish is clearly vocalized as *al-mufattit*, i.e., the agent that does the crumbling. Possibly, the dish is recommended here as being good for crumbling kidneys and bladder stones. In al-Bustānī's *Muḥīṭ al-Muḥīṭ*, s.v. فت, *al-mufattit* is mentioned as a curative agent, recommended by physicians. An example given on such a *mufattit* is *ḥajar Yahūdī* (حجر يهودي) 'Jew's stone,' *Lapis judaicus*.

17 The expression used is *niṣf qalī* 'half fried.'

chicken, scatter the fried egg yolks, *isfīriyya* pieces, the split [boiled] eggs, and a small amount of strained chicken broth. Sprinkle the dish with Ceylon cinnamon and ginger, and eat it salubriously, God Almighty willing.

III.2.8 Another Dish, Called *mughaffar* (Clad)[18]

Take two chickens of the kind mentioned [in the above recipes] and slaughter them and clean and wash them as you did earlier [in the first recipe]. Cut them at the joints and then remove the meat from around the bones, but leave the skins attached to the pieces. Take the meat and pound it thoroughly in a wooden mortar, removing all that there is of the veins and sinews (*ʿurūq*).

Take the bones [with skins attached] and put them in a new pot (*qidr*) with salt, water, plenty of olive oil, black pepper, coriander seeds, and a good amount of cumin. Also add pounded onion, a few cloves of garlic, skinned almonds, soaked chickpeas, half a ladleful of *murrī* (liquid fermented sauce), and 1 ladleful of fine-tasting vinegar. Put the pot on the fire to cook.

Next, take the pounded meat and add salt, black pepper, ginger, coriander seeds, Ceylon cinnamon, a small amount of *murrī naqīʿ* (sun-fermented liquid sauce), and egg whites. Beat them all together and mix them by hand until they all blend very well.

Take the [cooked] chicken bones one by one and reconstruct them with the [pounded mix of] meat[19] until they are all done. If possible, return the skins to the pieces, as this would make them look perfect. Now take some of the broth, put it in a large pan (*ṭājin*), and set it on the fire. Gently transfer the chicken pieces to the pan and let them cook on a low fire until the meat holds and sets. Once they are done, take them out and put them in a clean skillet set on a medium fire and let them fry. Fold them gently so that they brown on all sides.

Before you start frying the pieces, take whatever remains of the pounded meat [mix] and make meatballs with it, which you then cook in the broth that is still in the pot until they are done. Also, take the gizzards and livers,

---

18 In Ibn Manẓūr, *Lisān al-ʿArab*, s.v. غفر, *mighfar* is a garment that covers the body or a piece of headgear worn underneath the helmet. Cf. another *mughaffar* dish prepared with rabbit meat, recipe ii.5.4 above. In both cases, the cut joints are reconstructed with their own meat after pounding and seasoning it. See also recipe vii.2.15 below, prepared with eggplant.

19 This is better expressed in the Madrid MS, fol. 73v, as وتنشأ به أعضاؤه 'and reconstruct the pieces with it'; cf. the general term وتجعل 'and put' in the other two MSS.

pound them, add aromatic spices (*afāwīh*) and egg whites to them, and make an *isfīriyya* (thin and smooth patty) with the mix as described earlier [in the previous recipe]. Along with these, prepare split [boiled] eggs and fried egg yolks. (151r) Discard the remaining bones in the pot. Break about 5 eggs and beat them with some aromatic spices. Strain the broth, clean the pot, and then return to it only the best [i.e., the clearest and richest] of the strained broth (*ṣafwū al-ṣafwa*) in both the pot and the *ṭājin* in which the [reconstructed] pieces were [initially] cooked. Also return to the pot the meatballs, almonds, and chickpeas [that were cooked in it]. Cover all these with the [beaten] eggs and let the pot cook on a low fire.[20]

So, when you finish preparing all these things, take a glazed bowl (*ghaḍāra*) and line it with fresh citron leaves and a few of bay laurel (*rand*). Arrange the [fried] pieces on the leaves and scatter all that there is in the pot over them. On top of these, scatter the *isfīriyya* pieces, the split boiled eggs,[21] and the fried egg yolks. Sprinkle the dish with Ceylon cinnamon and ginger, [garnish it] with tender tips of mint sprigs (*ʿuyūn naʿnaʿ*), and eat it salubriously, God Almighty willing.

If wished, you can cook [the whole] chicken halfway and then take it out and remove the meat on its chest and the two thighs. Pound it and mix it with spikenard, Ceylon cinnamon, black pepper, coriander seeds, and egg whites; and then spread it on the chest and thigh bones [to reconstruct it]. Fry the chicken and return it to the broth pot to cook. It will also be splendid if a pan (*ṭājin*) is used to cook the [prepared] chicken in the *furn* (brick oven) without frying it.

III.2.9 Another Dish, Called *ḥūtiyya* (Cooked Like Fish)[22]

Take a chicken of the kind described [in the recipes above], slaughter it, and follow what you did to it previously [in the first recipe]. Cut it into pieces if you want to; otherwise, keep it whole. Put it in a new pot and add water, salt, olive oil, black pepper, coriander seeds, and a small amount of chopped onion. Put the pot on the fire to cook.

---

20 This cooking technique is called *takhmīr*, see glossary 9.2. We assume that at this point the cook can now start frying the reconstructed joints.

21 According to the Madrid MS, fol. 74r, the eggs are split in halves.

22 The only resemblance I have been able to establish between this chicken dish and fish is that after frying, the chicken, like fish, is submerged in a vinegar-garlic based sauce, as in recipe V.1.8 below for fried fish.

When the chicken is done, take it out, put it in a clean skillet (*miqlāt*) with a small amount of olive oil, and let it fry gently on a low fire until it browns; do this whether it is cut into pieces or kept whole.

[**To make the sauce,**] take an earthenware pan (*ṭājin fakhkhār*) and put 3 pounded cloves of garlic in it. Strain the [chicken] broth and take its fat (*wadak*) and add it to the pan, which you then place on the fire to cook the garlic. Add as much as you desire of fine-tasting vinegar and taste it. If it is too strong, add more of the broth until it tastes good to you, but if the taste somewhat lacks acidity (*fātir*), add some more of the vinegar.

Put the chicken in a glazed bowl (*ghaḍāra*), sprinkle it with black pepper, and pour the vinegar, garlic, and broth that were cooked together all over it, and eat it salubriously, God Almighty willing. You may also garnish the dish with split [boiled] eggs and tender tips of mint sprigs. This would indeed be the recommended way to serve it especially for wedding festivities (*walāʾim*, sg. *walīma*), in which case the chickens (**151v**) are served whole, so know this.

III.2.10 Another Dish, Called *Jaʿfariyya* (Gold Yellow)[23]

Take a chicken of the kind described earlier [in the above recipes] and follow what you did to it previously [in the first recipe]. Put it in a new pot and add water, salt, plenty of olive oil, black pepper, coriander seeds, and a bit of cumin. Also add onion, skinned almonds, soaked chickpeas, a few cloves of garlic, *murrī naqīʿ* (sun-fermented liquid sauce)—just the needed amount—citron leaves, and sprigs of herb fennel (*ʿūd basbās*). Put the pot on the fire to cook.

Once the chicken cooks, add a ladleful of fine-tasting vinegar after coloring the broth with saffron.[24] Let the pot come to a boil and then remove it. Gently take the chicken out of the pot and put it in a glazed earthenware pan (*ṭājin muzajjaj*). Add some of the strained broth (*ṣafwū al-marqa*) and only the almonds and chickpeas. Put the *ṭājin* in the *furn* (brick oven) to [further] cook it, and take it out once it is completely done: the chicken has completely

23 A simpler version of this *Jaʿfariyya* chicken dish is included in the anonymous Andalusi *Anwāʿ al-ṣaydala* 19, where the author gives two possibilities for the dish's name:
1) Due to the large amount of saffron used, it is compared to *dhahab Jaʿfarī*, which is the name of the finest kind of gold.
2) It is named after the person who invented it, whose name was Jaʿfar.
See glossary 5 for more on this dish.

24 Apparently, plenty of saffron was added, see the above note.

browned on all sides and all the liquid has evaporated, leaving nothing but olive oil and the melted fat (*wadak*) of the chicken. Put it in a glazed bowl (*ghaḍāra*), garnish it with split [boiled] eggs and tips of mint sprigs, and eat the dish salubriously, God Almighty willing.

If you want, take the partially cooked chicken out of the pot,[25] fry it in a skillet (*miqlāt*) until it browns on all sides, and then return it to the pot after cleaning it, along with the broth in which it was cooked with its fats and oils.[26] Also add a ladleful of vinegar and another one of *murrī* (liquid fermented sauce), olive oil, meatballs, soaked chickpeas, black pepper, saffron, ginger, and citron leaves. Let it cook on the fire until it is done [and most of the liquid has evaporated]. Top it (*tukhammar*) with eggs beaten with spices and leave it on heated stones (*raḍf*) until its fat separates and comes up to the surface.

III.2.11 Another Dish, Called *murūziyya* (Plum Stew, Seasoned and Colored with Vinegar and Saffron)

Take a chicken of the kind described [in the recipes above], slaughter it, and follow what you did to it previously [in the first recipe]. Cook it as described in the first chapter of the second part of this book [recipes ii.1.4–5], God Almighty willing.

III.2.12 Another Dish, Called *rāhibī* (Monk's Food)

Take a chicken of the kind described [in the recipes above], slaughter it, and follow what you did to it previously [in the first recipe]. (**152r**) Cook it as described in the [corresponding] recipe in the first chapter [of the second part of this book, recipe ii.1.7].

25 I here followed the text of the Madrid MS, fol. 74v, because it makes more sense culinarily; otherwise, the other two MSS fry the fully cooked chicken.

26 The Madrid MS (see the above note) mentions that the broth also is returned to the pot, which will indeed facilitate cooking the soaked chickpeas added at this stage.

III.2.13 Another Dish, Called *mufarrij* (Comforting), Also Called *shuʿāʿ al-shams* (Sunbeams)

Take a chicken of the kind described [in the above recipes], slaughter it, and follow what you did to it previously [in the first recipe]. Cook it as described in the [corresponding] recipe in the first chapter [of the second part] mentioned above [recipe ii.1.7].

III.2.14 Another Dish, Called *faḥṣī* (the Countryside Dish)

Take a chicken of the kind described [in the above recipes], slaughter it, and follow what you did to it previously [in the first recipe]. Cook it as described in the second chapter of the second part of this book [recipe ii.2.23].

III.2.15 Another Dish, Called *naʿnaʿiyya* (Cooked with Mint)

Take a chicken of the kind described [in the above recipes], slaughter it, and follow what you did to it previously [in the first recipe]. Cook it as described in the second chapter of the second part [recipe ii.2.8]. Also cook it with lemon balm (*turunjān*) exactly the same way, neither a step more nor a step less.

III.2.16 Another Dish, Called *qarʿiyya* (Cooked with Gourd)

Take a young adult chicken (*dajāja fatiyya*) or small young chickens (*farārīj ṣighār*), slaughter them, and follow what you did previously [in the first recipe]. Cook them as described in the second chapter of the second part of this book [recipes ii.2.12 and ii.2.20].

III.2.17 Another Dish, Called *ḥiṣrimiyya* (Cooked with the Juice of Sour Unripe Grapes)

Take a fat young adult chicken, slaughter it, and wash and clean it. Keep it whole, just cut off its neck; or divide it into pieces if wished. Put it in a new pot and add water, salt, olive oil, black pepper, coriander seeds, and a small amount of chopped onion. Put the pot on the fire to cook.

Once it is done, add strained fresh juice of unripe grapes (*mā' ḥiṣrim ṭarī*);[27] or you may use a high-quality sun-cooked variety;[28] add it to taste. Leave the pot on a low fire to simmer and the flavors nicely blend (*taʿtadil*). Ladle the chicken into a glazed bowl (*ghaḍāra*), and eat it salubriously, God Almighty willing.

III.2.18 Another Dish, Called *summāqiyya* (Cooked with Sumac)

(152v) Take a chicken as described [in the recipes] above, slaughter it, and do with it as was done earlier [in the first recipe]. Put it in a new pot with water, salt, a good amount of olive oil, black pepper, coriander seeds, and a small amount of [chopped] onion. Put it on the fire to cook.

When the chicken is almost done, take fine quality sumac that is free of any mold (*ʿafan*). Clean it and then pound it and put it in a clean piece of cloth; tie it and put it in the chicken pot to [further] cook. Taste the broth; if the flavor of sumac is distinct, take the bundle out of the pot and leave it on a low fire to simmer and the flavors nicely blend (*yaʿtadil*). Empty the pot into a glazed bowl (*ghaḍāra*), and eat the dish salubriously, God Almighty willing.

III.2.19 Another Dish, Mashriqi (Eastern)

Take a chicken of the kind mentioned [in the recipes above], slaughter it, and wash and clean it as you did earlier [in the first recipe]. Cut it into pieces however you choose; put it in a new pot with water, salt, olive oil, black pepper, coriander seeds, and a small amount of chopped onion. Put the pot on the fire to cook.

While the chicken cooks, take 40 fine-tasting raisins (*zabīb*), wash them in water to remove all that might have stuck to them of sand grains, and then pound them into a marrow-like consistency. Next, take cilantro (*kuzbara khaḍrā'*) and pound it and extract its juice. Now take this juice and dissolve the [pounded] raisins in it.[29] Strain this liquid and add it to the chicken pot; add half a ladleful of vinegar as well.

---

27 In the above recipes, II.1.9 and II.2.24, it is called *khall ḥiṣrim ṭarī*. See recipe X.7.14 for how to make it.

28 *Maʿmūl lil-shams*. For recipes on preserving the juice of unripe grapes, see X.7.12–4 below. See also recipes in the fourteenth-century anonymous Egyptian cookbook *Kanz al-fawāʾid*, English trans., *Treasure Trove*, recipes 152–4.

29 The editor of the Arabic text inadvertently reads *zabīb* (زبيب) 'raisins' as *zayt* (زيت) 'olive oil.'

Next, take 4 eggs, break them in a wide, shallow bowl (*ṣaḥfa*), and add salt, black pepper, ginger, and juices of cilantro and mint. Beat them well with a ladle, and pour them on the food in the pot to cover it (*tukhammar*). Remove the fire from underneath the pot and leave it on embers (*ghaḍā*) so that it simmers and the flavors blend (*taʿtadil*). Ladle the dish into a glazed bowl (*ghaḍāra*), sprinkle some Ceylon cinnamon on it, and eat it salubriously, God Almighty willing.

III.2.20 Another Mashriqi Dish, Called *dajājat ʿumrūs* (the Chubby Boy's Chicken)[30]

Take a chicken of the kind mentioned [in the recipes above], slaughter it, and follow what you earlier did to it [in the first recipe]. It should be grilled whole. (153r) Thread it onto a skewer—any kind will do, and grill it as was described earlier [in recipe iii.1.2 above] by placing it at a distance from the fire. When it is almost done, take it off the skewer and chop its meat as fine as possible. Put the meat in a new pot; add salt, olive oil, coriander seeds, a small amount of [chopped] onion, and all kinds of spices.[31] [Put the pot on the fire to cook, with some water].

When the chicken is completely cooked and the pot boils,[32] take milk (*laban ḥalīb*), strain it, put it in a wide, shallow bowl (*ṣaḥfa*), break eggs in it, and add some fresh yeast (*khamīr*). Whip them all thoroughly until they mix very well. Add this mix to the chicken pot and stir it slowly on a low fire. Remove the fire from underneath the pot and leave it on embers (*ghaḍā*) for a short while to allow flavors to blend (*taʿtadil*), and eat it salubriously, God Almighty willing.

---

30 In al-Fayrūzābādī, *al-Qāmūs al-Muḥīṭ*, s.v. عمرس, *ʿumrūs* is descriptive of a chubby boy; it is also a name for a lamb. My guess is that this luscious chicken dish, with its custard-like fluffy consistency, would indeed be a delight to eat, especially by a *ʿumrūs*. Alternatively, the dish might simply have been named after a ʿAmrūs, an Arabized version of the Spanish Ambrosio, in which case the dish's name should be read as *dajājat ʿAmrūs*. I owe this detail on the alternative name to the anonymous reviewer of this book.

31 As added in the Madrid MS, fol. 75v.

32 This indicates that some liquid should have also been added.

III.2.21 Another Dish [Called *Yahūdiyya* 'Jewish'][33]

Take a large young adult chicken, slaughter it, and clean and wash it as you did earlier [in the first recipe]. Leave the chicken whole.

Take eggs and boil them until soft.[34] Take breadcrumbs (*fatāt khubz*), put them in a wide, shallow bowl (*ṣaḥfa*), and add the eggs to them, as well as salt, ginger, black pepper, Ceylon cinnamon, and coriander seeds. Knead them all very well, adding a bit of saffron, skinned almonds, chopped mint leaves, cooked egg yolks, and half a ladleful of olive oil. Stuff the chicken's cavity and its sides with this mix,[35] and sew it up.

Gently put the chicken in a new pot that is large and wide. Add water, salt, olive oil, black pepper, coriander seeds, and a small amount of chopped onion; put it on the fire to cook. When the water comes to a boil, [repeatedly] move the chicken from one side of the pot to the other with the tip of a ladle so that it does not get stuck in one corner of the pot. You should have with you a large needle, which is used to pierce the skin to allow steam to escape and keep it from tearing.

Remove the pot from the fire when the chicken is cooked; color it with saffron, but not much. Now put it in a pan (*ṭājin*), along with some of the pot's strained broth (*ṣafwū al-maraq*) and its fat (*wadak*). Put it in the *furn* (brick oven) and let it brown at a distance from the fire, gently turning it so that the other side browns as well.

Take the chicken out of the *ṭājin* and put it in a glazed bowl (*ghaḍāra*) along with any fat remaining in the pan. Garnish it with split [boiled] eggs and tender tips of sprigs of mint. Sprinkle Ceylon cinnamon and ginger all over it, and eat it salubriously, God Almighty willing.

This dish is called *al-Yahūdiyya*.

---

33 As it is called in the Madrid MS, fol. 75v. The BL MS, fol. 153r, will mention this name at the end of the recipe, whereas the Berlin MS, fol. 51r, does not make any such reference.

34 Half-boiled, as instructed in the Madrid MS, fol. 75v.

35 The stuffing was put between the meat and the skin in the breast area, as was done in recipe iii.1.1 above.

FIGURE 66
A young chicken, *farrūj*, al-Qazwīnī, *ʿAjāʾib al-makhlūqāt wa gharāʾib al-mawjūdāt*, fol. 345r, detail
FROM THE NEW YORK PUBLIC LIBRARY, SPENCER COLLECTION: HTTPS://DIGITALCOLLECTIONS.NYPL.ORG/ITEMS/A43B28C0-28EC-0138-FE1C-276765519E25

III.2.22 Another Dish, Called *Turkiyya* (Turkish)[36]

Take a large chicken, and prepare it exactly as above, adding to the stuffing fine-tasting olives—slit (*mashqūq*) or unslit ones—and fine-tasting pickled lemons (*līm muṣayyar*).[37] (153v) Use 2 lemons and 10 or less olives. So, know this and prepare it accordingly with the help of God Almighty.

III.2.23 Another Dish [of Stuffed Chicken]

Take a large young adult chicken, slaughter it, and follow what you did to it previously [in the first recipe]. Blow it from the neck to separate the skin from the meat; make a slit from the neck down to the lower chest. Push the skin from the thighs, rear end (*zimikkā*), and wings. Remove the meat carefully, but leave the bones as they are—intact.

Take another adult chicken or large young chickens (*farrūj kabīr*), and take the meat of whichever you have chosen. Pound it with the meat of the first chicken in a mortar (*mihrās*) until it becomes doughy in texture; remove the veins and sinews (*ʿurūq*). Add salt, black pepper, Ceylon cinnamon, a lump of mastic, and coriander seeds, and break about 6 eggs on them. Knead them

36 Based on the recipe, it is the addition of olives and preserved lemons that give it a Turkish character.

37 For ways to preserve olives and lemons, see chapters x.2 and x.3 below, respectively.

together by hand until they mix well. Stuff the cavity of the chicken with it and put a lemon preserved in salt and 5 olives in the middle. Also, cover the bones by putting meat on the thighs, breasts, and rear end area. Carefully return the skin [to cover the meat] and sew it up so that it looks as it was before;[38] also sew up the neck.

Put the chicken in a large, wide pot (*qidr*), and add water, salt, olive oil, black pepper, coriander seeds, and a small amount of chopped onion. Put the pot on the fire to cook, [and while cooking,] turn the chicken repeatedly until it is done.

Once the chicken cooks, take it out of the pot and put it in a large pan (*ṭājin*). Color it with saffron and add a small amount of the strained broth to it. Send the *ṭājin* to the *furn* (communal brick oven) along with someone to check on it [while in the oven] and turn it until it browns on all sides. Take it out and put it in a glazed bowl (*ghaḍāra*) along with any liquid remaining in the pan. Garnish it with split [boiled] eggs and tender tips of mint sprigs, and eat it salubriously, God Almighty willing.

III.2.24 Another Dish [of Stuffed Chicken]

Take a young adult chicken that is large and fat; slaughter it, and with the feathers still on, blow it from the neck to separate the skin from the meat. Tie its neck and carefully pluck its feathers [by dipping it first] in hot water. Rub its skin with salt by hand to get rid of all the dirt. Open up its belly and remove its entrails and red lungs.[39] Clean the chicken by washing it with water.

Take the gizzard, (**154r**) wash it very well, chop it into tiny pieces, and put it in a wide, shallow bowl (*ṣaḥfa*). Break 3 eggs on it and add a small amount of breadcrumbs (*fatāt*), salt, black pepper, and coriander seeds, a small amount of pounded onion, juices of cilantro and mint, and a small amount of *murrī naqīʿ* (sun-fermented liquid sauce). Stuff the chicken's cavity with this mix and sew it up.

Take the breast of another chicken and chop it into tiny pieces, which you then salt and fry in an earthenware skillet (*miqlāt fakhkhār*) with olive oil until it cooks and browns. Empty it into a wide, shallow bowl (*ṣaḥfa*) and add coriander seeds, chopped cilantro, black pepper, a small amount of pounded onion,

38 This detail is from the Madrid MS, fol. 76r.

39 The Berlin MS وزيتها 'its oil,' irrelevant to the context, is clearly copied as وريتها 'its lungs' in the BL MS, fol. 153v.

a bit of *murrī*, and 3 eggs. Beat them all together until they mix and stuff them into one side of the chicken between the skin and meat.

Next, take meat from any of the tender parts in the chicken [used above],[40] pound it in a mortar (*mihrās*), and mix with it what was already used above. Stuff the mix into the other side of the chicken [between the skin and meat] as well as the neck, which you then tie with a thread.

Put the chicken in a pan (*ṭājin*) and let it be placed in the *furn* (brick oven) at a distance from the fire to roast. There should be someone to turn the chicken from time to time until it cooks and browns.

Take a small pot (*qudayra*) and put vinegar and *murrī* in it. Also add black pepper, coriander seeds, cilantro juice, a bit of pounded onion, olive oil, and the needed amount of water. Place it on the fire to cook. Next, take the breast of a chicken, pound its meat in a mortar (*mihrās*), remove any veins and sinews (*ʿurūq*), and make meatballs with it following the directions given earlier.[41] Shape the meat into well-rounded balls and add them to the small pot to cook. Top the meatballs and liquid in the pot with 3 eggs beaten with cilantro juice, salt, and the familiar spices [usually used] for *takhmīr*.[42]

Now have a look at the chicken in the oven; if you see that it has cooked and browned, take it out and put it in a glazed bowl (*ghaḍāra*). Arrange the meatballs on it, with all that there is in the small pot. Garnish it with split [boiled] eggs and tender tips of mint sprigs. Sprinkle it with whatever you wish [of Ceylon cinnamon or ginger], and eat it salubriously, God Almighty willing.

III.2.25 Recipe for *narjisiyya* (Looking Like Narcissus Flowers)[43]

Take a fat chicken, slaughter it, clean it, and then cut it into pieces: 2 thighs, 2 breasts, and 2 wings. Put them in a pot with salt, olive oil, *murrī* (liquid fermented sauce), black pepper, coriander seeds, and thyme (*ṣaʿtar*). Let the pieces fry, without adding any water, until they brown.

---

40 In this step and the following ones, I amended the text following the Madrid MS, fol. 77r, which offers a more coherent reading of the recipe. Unfortunately, the editor of the Arabic text follows the Berlin MS only, which omits some steps in this section, and obscures the sense of the recipe.

41 See, for instance, recipe ii.6.1 above.

42 A pot thus topped with eggs is usually left on embers to set. See glossary 9.2 for more on this cooking technique.

43 *Narjisiyya* dishes were called so because they were made to resemble narcissus flowers (white/green/yellow). See, for instance, recipe ii.2.17 above. In this dish, we have white chicken, green cilantro juice, and yellow eggs.

Take onions and fresh cilantro, pound them together, and press out their juices into the pot; let there be enough to cover the chicken. Boil the pot for an hour. Now take a small amount of the inside of leavened bread (*lubāb khubz mukhtamir*),[44] grate it, and beat it with 2 or 3 eggs, along with black pepper and saffron. Top the pot with this mix (*tukhammar*) and leave it on heated stones[45] until its fat separates and gathers on top, and serve it.

III.2.26 Recipe for *Qurashiyya*[46] [Fried Chicken Pieces, Simmered in Saffroned Sauce]

(154v) Take a cleaned fat chicken and cut it into pieces as mentioned earlier [in the recipe above]. Put the pieces in a pot with salt, olive oil, a small amount of chopped onion, black pepper, and a small amount of water. Bring the pot to a good boil and then take the chicken pieces out and fry them in a pan with olive oil until they brown on both sides.

Take a clean pot and put 2 ladlefuls of *murrī* (liquid fermented sauce) and olive oil in it, along with coriander seeds, saffron, cumin, and a bit of thyme (*ṣaʿtar*). Put it on the fire, and when it comes to a boil, add the chicken pieces to it and top them (*tukhammar*) with 6 eggs beaten with saffron. Once the eggs set [on embers], remove the pot, and serve the dish.

III.2.27 A Dish Called *jalīdiyya* (Frosty)[47]

It is made with a chicken (*dajāja*), goose (*iwazza*), or capon (*khaṣiyy*). Clean whichever is available of these birds after slaughtering it and put it in a pot. Take 2 *raṭl*s (2 pounds) raisins, pound them thoroughly, add water to them, and press and mash them (*yumras*) to release all their sweetness. Strain them and

44 *Lubāb* usually designates the soft white crumb inside thick and crusty bread.

45 The editor of the Arabic text follows the miscopied, irrelevant *waṣf* (وصف) 'description' in the Berlin MS, fol. 52r, instead of the more obvious *raḍf* (رضف) as copied in the Madrid MS, fol. 77r. The BL MS copies the word correctly as *raḍf*.

46 The dish was most probably named after one of the Arab tribes in al-Andalus, who claimed descendant from the Quraysh, the Prophet's tribe. It is distinguished by the use of saffron in the sauce itself as well as with the beaten eggs that top it.

47 This recipe is identical with a *jalīdiyya* in the anonymous Andalusi *Anwāʿ al-ṣaydala* 23–4. Another *jalīdiyya* in that cookbook, p. 126, is topped with a layer of beaten egg whites, which indeed would give it the semblance of frost (*jalīd*), after which this chicken dish might have originally been named.

put the strained liquid in the pot. Also add enough vinegar,[48] 2 ladlefuls of olive oil, black pepper, coriander seeds, a chopped half of an onion, and salt. Let it cook until the sauce thickens.[49]

Take pounded skinned almonds and walnuts, as well as the grated inside of bread (*lubāb khubz maḥkūk*),[50] and black pepper; beat them with 6 eggs. Top the pot with this mix (*tukhammar*) after everything is cooked and scatter whole egg yolks (*muḥāḥ bayḍ ṣiḥāḥ*) all over it.[51] Leave the pot on heated stones (*raḍf*)[52] until its fat (*wadak*) rises to the surface, and serve the dish.

III.2.28 Recipe for *thūmiyya* (Chicken Braised with Garlic)[53]

Take a fat chicken, remove the entrails, and wash them [with the chicken] and set them aside. Take 4 *ūqiyyas* (4 ounces) skinned garlic cloves and pound them until they have the consistency of bone marrow (*mukhkh*); mix them with all that was taken from the inside of the chicken. Fry them in olive oil—put enough to cover them—until the garlicky odor disappears. Put them in a pot with the chicken, along with salt, black pepper, spikenard, black cardamom (*qāqulla*), Ceylon cinnamon, ginger, cloves, saffron, skinned blanched almonds (*lawz masmūṭ*)—both pounded and whole—a good amount of olive oil, and a small amount of water to prevent the pot from burning. [Cover the pot and] seal it with dough; put it in the *furn* (brick oven) until it is done, and serve it.

III.2.29 (155r) A Chicken Recipe Called *al-badawiyya* (Peasants' Dish)[54]

Take a cleaned fat chicken, disjoint it, and [and put it] in a pot with olive oil, salt, black pepper, coriander seeds, and vinegar. Let it cook halfway and then

48 In the corresponding recipe mentioned in the above note, 3 ladlefuls are called for.

49 I followed here the corresponding recipe mentioned in n. 47 above, where the word occurs as تخثّر 'thicken' rather than تحمّر 'redden,' as copied in the three MSS.

50 See n. 44 above.

51 The verb used is *tunajjam* 'garnish'; literally 'stud with stars.'

52 See n. 45 above.

53 This recipe is almost identical with *thūmiyya* in the anonymous Andalusi cookbook *Anwāʿ al-ṣaydala* 24, with the addition that the served dish would emit a pleasant aroma that would permeate the dining area. It also adds that it was the favorite dish of Sayyid Abū al-Ḥasan. He was Ibn Abī al-Ḥafṣ, governor of Marrakesh during the time of the twelfth-century Almohads.

54 In al-Andalus, *ahl al-bādiya* and *badawiyyūn* designated the general populace in rural areas, see al-Andalusī *Kitāb Aḥkām al-sūq* 136, n. 1.

take it out, fry it in a pan to brown, and return it to the sauce in the pot. Add juice of fresh cilantro and juice of a white onion (*baṣala bayḍāʾ*). After it has fully cooked, top it (*tukhammar*) with 8 eggs [beaten], and scatter whole egg yolks (*muḥāḥ bayḍ ṣiḥāḥ*) over it. Keep the pot on heated stones (*raḍf*)[55] until its fat (*wadak*) rises to the surface, and serve the dish.

III.2.30 Recipe for *Ibrāhīmiyya*[56] [Sweet and Sour Chicken]

Take a chicken or lamb. Clean the chicken and cut it into smaller pieces—2 pieces of each part.[57] Put them in a pot and pour a ladleful of olive oil, a ladleful of very sour vinegar (*khall thaqīf*), and 5 ladlefuls of sugar syrup infused with rose petals (*sharāb ward sukkarī*).[58] Also add black pepper, saffron, coriander seeds, salt, and a small amount of onion. Put the pot on the fire to cook until done and then sprinkle it with split skinned almonds, pistachios, spikenard, and cloves.

In a wide and shallow bowl (*ṣaḥfa*), dissolve a bit of very fine white flour (*ghubār al-ḥuwwārā*) in rosewater;[59] you might also enhance its flavor (*yuftaq*) with a small amount of camphor (*kāfūr*) dissolved in rosewater. Beat this mixture with 4 eggs and top the pot with it (*yukhammar*), which you then leave on heated stones (*raḍf*)[60] until the fat separates [and gathers on top], and serve it, God Almighty willing.

III.2.31 Recipe for Making *jūdhāba* [Bastilla!][61]

Choose fattened young adult chickens (*dajāj musammana fatiyya*), clean them, and cut open their chests [to flatten them]. Put them in a pot as they are, whole; and add sweet olive oil (*zayt ʿadhb*), salt, black pepper, Ceylon cinnamon, spike-

55 See n. 45 above.
56 This sweet and aromatic dish is named after the famous Abbasid gourmet Prince Ibrāhīm b. al-Mahdī (d. 839), half-brother of Hārūn al-Rashīd. See introduction ii.5, p. 46.
57 I.e., 2 thighs, 2 breast pieces, and 2 wings, as in recipe iii.2.25 above.
58 See glossary 1.
59 See glossary 2, s.v. *ḥuwwārā*.
60 See n. 45 above.
61 This recipe is the precursor of what is in modern Moroccan cuisine called بسطيلة *basṭīla* 'bastilla,' the savory-sweet bird pie.

The anonymous Andalusi *Anwāʿ al-ṣaydala* 175–7 includes a recipe similar to this one, except that it reverses the order of preparations, beginning with the bread part before

nard, and black cardamom (*qāqulla*). Put the pot on the fire to cook, using [a small amount of] fine-tasting rosewater instead of water. [The finished pot] should not have sauce left in it.

Once the chickens cook, take a couple of thin sheets of bread (*ruqāq*), to be mentioned later,[62] and spread them in the bottom of a pot—either of stone (*ḥijāra*) or earthenware (*fakhkhār*). The pot's bottom and sides should be smeared with tallow taken from the kidneys [of sheep] after cleaning and pounding it into a marrow-like consistency. Let the bread sheets hang down from the sides to use them [later] to cover other sheets.

On the bread spread in the bottom, sprinkle sugar, [skinned] almonds—both split and pounded—cloves, and spikenard; a scoop (*gharfa*) [of them]. Drizzle a good amount of sweet olive oil over them and sprinkle them with sugar and rosewater, in which small amounts of camphor and musk have been dissolved—let it be enough to moisten the sugar. Next, spread (155v) 1 or 2 more sheets of the *ruqāq*; sprinkle them with sugar, almonds, the spices (*ʿaqāqīr*), and olive oil; drizzle them with rosewater as was done earlier; and then spread another sheet of *ruqāq*, and continue doing this until half the pot is full.

Take the prepared chickens,[63] which should have been rubbed with saffron dissolved in rosewater, and arrange them in the middle of the pot. Cover them with *ruqāq* sheets and sprinkle them with sugar and almonds [and the other ingredients] as was done earlier; cover them with some more *ruqāq*; [and continue] until the pot is full and the chickens are buried in the middle.[64]

When all is done, sprinkle it with lots of sugar, drizzle a good amount of olive oil and rosewater all over it, and cover it all with the *ruqāq* sheets hanging from

---

giving directions for cooking the chicken. In that cookbook, it is called *jūdhābat Umm al-Faraj* and described as an Eastern dish (*ṭaʿām Mashriqī*). Indeed, *jūdhāba* recipes are found in all the extant Arabic medieval cookbooks from al-Mashriq, essentially prepared as a sweet bread pudding, generally composed of very thin sheets of bread layered and baked in the *tannūr* (clay oven) with a roasting chunk of meat suspended above it.

62 *Al-madhkūra baʿdu*; while the BL and Berlin MSS make no further mention of directions for making *ruqāq*, the Madrid MS, fol. 79v, does indeed later mention them briefly:

> As for *ruqāq*, making them is well known; semolina flour is first moistened and then thoroughly kneaded with salt and a small amount of water, and then flattened into the needed amount of *ruqāq*s (thin sheets of bread). For those who want to prepare it more elegantly using fine white flour kneaded with butter and the like, they can do so.

More detailed instructions were given earlier in recipes i.4.14 and 19 above, which are more or less similar to what the anonymous *Anwāʿ al-ṣaydala* 175–6 describes in its *jūdhāba* recipe, see the above note.

63 The editor of the Arabic text incorrectly 'corrects' the MS text by changing the plural *dajāj* 'chickens' to the singular *dajāja*.

64 See the above note.

the pot's sides. Cover the pot with a tight lid, seal it with dough, and put it in a moderately hot *furn* (brick oven). Leave it there for the same amount of time that it takes meat to cook in a pot.

When you take the pot out and break its seal, it will emit a fragrant aroma.[65] Discard the layers of *ruqāq* that have been covering it if they are burnt by the fire; also discard whatever has stuck to the sides of the pot. Turn it onto a *ṣaḥfa* (wide, shallow bowl) as it is in one piece, and present it thus. This dish is excellent, remarkably delicious, and exotic; it is indeed of the kings' foods. It generates good humors,[66] provides good nutrition, and its properties are well balanced.

[**Baklava-like *Jūdhāba*:**][67] This *jūdhāba* dish may be prepared without chicken or meat by alternating layers of *ruqāq* with layers of almonds—split and pounded—along with sugar, Indian spices,[68] and saffron. It is then moistened with rosewater and sweet olive oil (*zayt ʿadhb*) [and baked]. When done [baking], it is put in a *ṣaḥfa* and eaten with sugar syrup infused with rose petals (*sharāb ward sukkarī*) and fresh butter; or have it without syrup. Serve it whichever way you like.

III.2.32 A Recipe for a Dish Called *maghmūm* (Covered)

It is made with a chicken (*dajāja*), a goose (*iwazza*), squabs (*firākh ḥamām*) or turtledoves (*yamām*).

Take a cleaned chicken and put it in a pot as it is, whole, with the chest cut open.[69] Add salt, olive oil, black pepper, coriander seeds, and a small amount of onion. Half-cook the chicken and then take it out and put it in another pot, adding the fat [from the first pot], *murrī naqīʿ* (sun-fermented liquid sauce), saffron, spikenard, thyme (*ṣaʿtar*), and citron leaves. Stuff a whole lemon (*līma*) in

---

65 I read the copied فتمّ 'it is completed' (irrelevant in the given context) in the MSS as فغمّ 'emits a pleasant-smelling aroma' based on context. See Ibn Manẓūr, *Lisān al-ʿArab*, s.v. فغم.

66 *Jayyid al-khulūṭ* (sg. *khalṭ*). See glossary 11, s.v. *mizāj*.

67 The corresponding recipe in the anonymous *Anwāʿ al-ṣaydala* (mentioned above, n. 61) calls it *sādhaja* (plain and simple). It describes it in a more detailed manner, with the addition of beaten eggs while layering the dish.

68 Called *ʿaqāqīr Hindiyya* in the recipe, referring to spikenard and cloves used in the principal recipe above.

69 It seems that the aim of cutting the chest open is to be able to flatten it slightly; later in the recipe a lemon is said to be put in the cavity.

its cavity, sprinkle [skinned] split almonds all over it, and cover the top of the pot with [flattened] dough. Put it in the *furn* (brick oven) until it is done, and serve it.

III.2.33 Another Dish [of Rotisserie Stuffed Chicken, smothered in Sauce]

Take a chicken as described earlier; slaughter it and do with it as you did previously.[70] Now take its gizzard, clean it, chop it into fine pieces, and add salt, black pepper, coriander seeds, chopped cilantro, a bit of *murrī* (liquid fermented sauce), and 3 broken eggs. Mix them all, stuff the chicken cavity with them, and sew it up.

Take the breast of another chicken and pound it in a mortar (*mihrās*) with skinned almonds, a small amount of coarse semolina (*samīd ghalīẓ*), and ghee (*samn*). Add to these black pepper, coriander seeds, **(156r)** *murrī*, a small amount of [chopped] onion, juices of fresh cilantro and mint, and broken eggs. Beat them together to mix them well and use them to stuff the areas between the skin and meat.

Salt the chicken from the outside, carefully thread it onto a skewer (*saffūd*), and grill it suspended above the fire. Rotate it [constantly],[71] and [while grilling,] repeatedly smear it with salt and olive oil until it cooks and browns.

[To prepare the sauce,] take a small pot and put water, as needed, in it. Also add salt, vinegar, *murrī*—just the needed amount—a bit of sugar, [chopped] cilantro and coriander seeds, black pepper, sausages (*laqāniq*) cut into pieces,[72] and meatballs made with the breast of another chicken. When all is cooked, top them with a mix of 5 eggs [beaten with] pounded skinned almonds as was

---

70 The recipe seems to be referring to recipes like iii.2.23–4 above, where the skin is separated from the meat by blowing into its neck. In the Madrid MS, fol. 80r, the following details are given:

> Take a large fat chicken and slaughter it but leave the feathers on. Blow it from the neck to separate the skin from the meat, and tie its neck with a thread. Pluck the feathers gently [by dipping the chicken first] in hot water and then rub it with salt to clean it. Open up the cavity and take out the entrails and the lungs and clean it inside and outside.

71 Once again, the editor incorrectly 'corrects' the MSS text by replacing وتديرها 'and rotate it' with the redundant وتذرها 'and sprinkle it.' Obviously, the chicken is being grilled by constantly rotating it on an open fire; a grilling technique, which in the eastern region, was called *kardanāj*, see glossary 9.2.

72 They are a large type of sausage, see recipe ii.6.6 above.

described earlier [in the recipes above].[73] Let the fire burn underneath the pot [for a while] and then leave it on embers (*ghaḍā*).

Take a look at the chicken; if you find that it has cooked and browned, remove it carefully from the skewer and put it in a glazed bowl (*ghaḍāra*). Pour all the contents of the pot over it, sprinkle it with Ceylon cinnamon, and eat it salubriously, God Almighty willing.

III.2.34 Another Dish, Mashriqi [of Rotisserie Stuffed Chicken with Sauce]

Take a chicken as described earlier and do with it as you did previously.[74] Now take its gizzard, chop it into fine pieces after you clean it, and add sweet olive oil (*zayt ʿadhb*), black pepper, coriander seeds, chopped cilantro, salt, a small amount of chopped onion, skinned almonds chopped into fine pieces, and 3 eggs. Beat them all and stuff the chicken's cavity with the mix. Sew up its opening and skewer it and grill it suspended on low heat.[75]

While the chicken cooks and browns, take vinegar, *murrī* (liquid fermented sauce), coriander seeds, caraway (*karāwiyā*), juice of fresh cilantro, and thyme (*ṣaʿtar*) and combine them. Next, remove the chicken from the skewer and put it in a glazed bowl (*ghaḍāra*). Pour the sauce (*marqa*) all over it if wished; alternatively, you can put it aside [in a bowl] so that you may dip [morsels of] bread and chicken in it, and eat it salubriously, God Almighty willing.

III.2.35 (156v) Another Mashriqi Dish [of a Succulent Oven-Roasted Chicken]

Take a chicken as described earlier and do with it as you did previously.[76] Next, take its gizzard, chop it finely, and add spices (*abāzīr*) and eggs to it. Stuff the chicken's cavity with the mix and sew up the opening.

Take the gizzard of a goose (*iwazza*), put it in a pot, and add salt, *murrī* (liquid fermented sauce), vinegar, black pepper, and caraway and coriander seeds.

---

73 Such as recipes iii.2.27 and 30 in this chapter. Covering the cooked food in the pot with beaten eggs is called *takhmīr*, see glossary 9.2.

74 See n. 70 above.

75 Following the directions in the above recipe, the skewered chicken is to be rotated constantly on an open fire. In the eastern region this grilling technique was called *kardanāj*, see glossary 9.2.

76 See n. 70 above.

Place the chicken in this pot and put it in the *furn* (brick oven); let someone be available to check on the pot and turn over the chicken occasionally. Meanwhile, have a taste of the liquid [in the pot]: if you like it fine and well; otherwise, add what is lacking. Take care not to let the pot burn. When the chicken is cooked and browned, take it out and put it in a glazed bowl (*ghaḍāra*), drizzle any liquid [remaining in the pot] all over it, and eat it salubriously, God Almighty willing.

III.2.36 Another Mashriqi Dish [of Roast Chicken Variously Stuffed]

Take a chicken as described earlier and do with it as you did previously—cleaning and blowing it.[77] Next, take its gizzard, chop it finely, and add salt, olive oil, coriander seeds, chopped cilantro, black pepper, a bit of chopped onion, and 3 eggs. Mix them all, stuff them into the chicken's cavity, and sew up the opening.

Take another chicken, debone the meat, pound it well in a mortar (*mihrās*), and add salt, black pepper, Ceylon cinnamon, a bit of spikenard, juice of fresh cilantro, and 3 eggs. Beat them all together to mix them and stuff one side of the chicken with them between the skin and meat.

Next, take the breast of another chicken, chop it finely, salt it, and fry it in olive oil in a pan (*miqlāt*) until it cooks. Remove the pan from the fire and add *murrī* (liquid fermented sauce), black pepper, and 2 eggs. Beat them to mix and stuff the other side of the chicken with them [also between the skin and meat].

Tie the chicken's neck [with a thread,] put it in a pan (*ṭājin*), and send it to the *furn* (communal brick oven) to roast at a distance from the fire. Let it be turned over [occasionally] until it cooks and browns.

[To prepare the sauce,] take 3 eggs and boil them in water, and when they are cooked, take them out, shell them, and take out their cooked yolks. Take fresh cilantro, chop it, and pound it with the yolks to a marrow-like consistency. Add vinegar, *murrī*, black pepper, caraway and coriander seeds, and olive oil. Stir to mix them. (157r)

Put the [cooked] chicken in a glazed bowl, drizzle the sauce (*maraq*) all over it, and eat it salubriously, God Almighty willing.

---

77 See n. 70 above.

III.2.37 Another Mashriqi Dish [of Stewed Chicken Variously Stuffed]

Take a chicken as described earlier and do with it as you did previously.[78] Next, take the gizzard, chop it into small pieces, and add salt, black pepper, fresh cilantro, coriander seeds, *murrī* (liquid fermented sauce), a small amount of chopped onion, and pounded tender red meat. Break 2 eggs on these and beat them until they mix well. Stuff the cavity of the chicken with this mix and sew it up.

Take large sausages (*laqāniq*),[79] cut them into strips lengthwise, and add juice of fresh cilantro, coriander seeds, olive oil, *murrī*, black pepper, and 3 beaten egg yolks. Mix them all with the sausages and stuff one side of the chicken [between the skin and meat] with them.

Next, take the breast of another chicken, pound it in a mortar, and add coriander seeds, chopped fresh cilantro, black pepper, olive oil, the pounded kernels of 2 walnuts, *murrī*, and 2 eggs. Beat them all and stuff the other side of the chicken with them [also between the skin and meat].

Take tender red meat, pound it, and add spices (*abāzīr*) to it as was done above. Stuff the neck of the chicken with it and sew it up.

When you finish doing all these things, take the chicken and put it in a wide-rimmed pot or a cauldron (*ṭinjīr*). Add vinegar and *murrī*—let vinegar dominate the flavor—olive oil, whole sausages (*laqāniq*), *isfīriyya*,[80] meatballs (*banādiq*), salt, black pepper, coriander seeds, and a small amount of chopped onion. Color the chicken with saffron, add water enough to cook the chicken, and put it on the fire.

Gently turn the chicken over while cooking, taking care not to break the skin. Once it cooks, take it out of the pot, put it in a pan (*ṭājin*) with the remaining liquid (*marqa*), and top it with eggs [beaten with] pounded walnuts.[81] Send it to the *furn* (communal brick oven) to brown its face and to cook the egg topping (*takhmīr*). Once it browns, take it out of the oven, put it in a glazed bowl (*ghaḍāra*), and arrange some split eggs on it. [Sprinkle it with] whatever you like of aromatic spices (*afāwīh*), and eat it salubriously, God Almighty willing.

---

78 See n. 70 above.

79 They are a large type of sausage, see recipe ii.6.6 above.

80 They are smooth and thin meat patties, see recipe ii.6.3 above. For the meatballs, see, for instance, recipe ii.6.1 above.

81 This cooking technique is called *takhmīr*, see glossary 9.2.

III.2.38 Another Mashriqi Dish [of Stewed Stuffed Chicken]

Take a chicken as described earlier and clean it from the inside and the outside.[82] Take its gizzard after cleaning it, chop it finely, and add salt to it with chopped fresh cilantro, coriander seeds, black pepper, (157v) a small amount of chopped onion, and 2 eggs. Beat them all to mix and stuff the cavity of the chicken with them. Sew the cavity up and tie the neck with a thread. Put the chicken in a wide pot (*qidr wāsiʿa*) with salt [and water] and put it on the fire to cook. When done, take it out, put it in a green-glazed bowel (*ghaḍāra*), and arrange split eggs on it.

Now take the yolks of 3 [boiled] eggs and put them in a wide, shallow bowl (*ṣaḥfa*). Add some of the broth (*marqa*) in which the chicken was cooked and rub them by hand until they disintegrate and the broth looks yellow. Pour it all on the chicken after removing the threads from the cavity and neck. Take out the chicken's stuffing and mix it with the yellow broth [in the bowl]. Sprinkle the dish with black pepper and Ceylon cinnamon, and eat it salubriously, God Almighty willing.

III.2.39 Another Mashriqi Dish [of Stewed Stuffed Chicken]

Take a fat chicken as described earlier and do with it as you previously did.[83] Take its gizzard, chop it into small pieces, and mix it with the breast of [another] chicken, which has been cut into fine pieces. Add salt, black pepper, coriander seeds, chopped fresh cilantro, a small amount of pounded onion, and 2 eggs. Beat them until they mix well, stuff them into the chicken's cavity, and sew it up. Put the chicken in a wide pot, add water and salt as needed, and put the pot on the fire to cook.

Next, take boiled eggs and the cooked liver and pound them in a mortar (*mihrās*), adding tender tips of fresh cilantro, a bit of rue (*sadhāb*), and a clove of garlic; pound them all thoroughly [and set aside]. Take the yolks of boiled eggs as well and pound them separately, add mild and gentle vinegar (*khall ḥulw*, literally sweet vinegar) to them, with *murrī* (liquid fermented sauce), black pepper, coriander seeds, and caraway, and stir them [and set aside].

Now have a look at the chicken; if it is done, take it out and put it in a glazed bowl (*ghaḍāra*). Put the eggs pounded with the liver and the rest of the of abovementioned things all over the chicken, and eat it salubriously, God Almighty willing.

---

82 See n. 70 above.

83 See n. 70 above.

III.2.40 Another Mashriqi Dish [of Stuffed Skins of Chicken and Squabs]

Take a large fat chicken, slaughter it, and separate its skin from its meat by blowing it through the neck with its feathers still on. For areas that did not separate, gently work them with your fingers or whatever may be used to do this. Now tie its neck [with a thread] while it is thus puffed (**158r**) and pluck its feathers by [dipping it in] hot water, taking care not to break the skin. Cut open the skin at the neck and take out all the meat and bones gently. Leave the skin attached to the tip of the rear end (*zimikkā*); also leave it attached to the [lowest] halves of the legs [i.e., drumsticks] and the tips of the wings at the joints.

Remove any bones from the meat and pound it thoroughly with the meat of another chicken in a mortar (*mihrās*), discarding all the veins and sinews (*ʿurūq*). After you are done with the pounding, add salt, black pepper, ginger, Ceylon cinnamon, coriander seeds, and juices of fresh cilantro and mint,[84] a small amount of pounded onion, sweet olive oil (*zayt ʿadhb*), and *murrī naqīʿ* (sun-fermented liquid sauce). Now take 6 eggs and boil them in water; and when cooked, shell them, pound them in a mortar until they disintegrate, and mix them with the meat. Also take the yolks of 4 boiled eggs and a whole boiled egg. Stuff the chicken's skin with the meat-spice mix and the eggs.[85] Reshape the skin to give it the semblance of a chicken, sew up the neck and any torn places in the skin, and place it in a new wide pot.

Next, take 2 squabs and do with them as was done with the chicken [and put them in the pot with the chicken]. Add water, salt, olive oil, black pepper, coriander seeds, a small amount of chopped onion, vinegar, and just the needed amount of *murrī*. Now take the chicken and squab gizzards, chop them finely, and add them to the pot. Also add small sausages (*mirqās*) cut in half.[86] Let the water added to the pot be enough to cook the birds.

Put the pot on the fire to cook and turn the birds carefully and gently. Once they are done, color the broth with saffron—use it sparingly; and when the pot boils once with saffron, remove it from the fire. Put the chicken in a large wide and shallow bowl (*ṣaḥfa*) along with the squabs; pour the strained broth all over them and [garnish them with] split boiled eggs and tender tips of mint sprigs. Sprinkle the dish with whatever you wish of spices, and eat it salubriously, God Almighty willing.

---

84 In all the MSS, و 'and' is clearly written to indicate that both juices are used. The editor of the Arabic text incorrectly 'corrects' it to أو 'or,' p. 173.

85 Judging from previous recipes, boiled egg yolks are interspersed in the meat mix while stuffing, and the whole egg is put in the middle of it.

86 For making these sausages, see recipe ii.6.4 above.

If you want to send the pot to the *furn* (communal brick oven) to brown [after it is done cooking on the fire], go ahead and do so. [Whichever way the dish is cooked,] the aim is to keep the birds in perfect shape with untorn skins when offered in the bowl, [that is] until you split it and serve it, with the help of God Almighty and His power.

III.2.41 Another Mashriqi Dish [of Stewed Stuffed Chicken Topped with Quince]

Take a chicken like the one described above and clean it thoroughly. Take its gizzard after washing it, chop it into fine pieces, (**158v**) and add salt, black pepper, coriander seeds, pounded fresh cilantro, *murrī* (liquid fermented sauce), a small amount of chopped onion, olive oil, pounded meat taken from another chicken, and 3 broken eggs. Beat them all until they mix well, stuff them into the chicken's cavity, and sew it up.

Put the chicken in a wide pot and add fine-tasting vinegar (*khall ṭayyib*), *murrī*—just the needed amount—olive oil, whatever remained of the stuffing, and caraway. Put the pot on the fire to cook in a good amount of water [added to the ingredients above]. Move the chicken occasionally and take care not to let it be stuck in one area. Add juices of fresh cilantro and onion as well.[87]

Take 2 quinces, free of mold (*ʿafan*) and worms (*sūs*), discard the unwanted parts from the inside and outside,[88] and put them in the pot to cook with the chicken. Once they cook, take them out, pound them in a mortar (*mihrās*), and mix them with pounded fresh cilantro, breadcrumbs (*fatāt khubz*), 3 eggs, and pounded chicken. Add the needed amount of spices (*abāzīr*) and beat them all with the eggs until they mix well. Take some of the pot's broth, strain it, stir it with the quince mix to thin its consistency,[89] and then spread it all over the dish as a topping (*khamīra*).[90] Remove the fire from underneath the pot to let it simmer and allow the flavors to nicely blend (*tatajammar*) [on embers].

Empty the dish into a glazed bowl (*ghaḍāra*), and eat it salubriously, God Almighty willing.

---

87 In all the MSS, و 'and' is clearly written to indicate that both juices are used. The editor of the Arabic text incorrectly 'corrects' it to أو 'or,' p. 174.

88 I.e., they are cored and peeled.

89 In both BL MS, fol. 158v, and the Berlin MS, fol. 56r, the word is clearly meant to be يخف 'becomes thin in consistency,' and not يجف 'dries' as occurs in the edited Arabic text.

90 See glossary 9.2, s.v. *takhmīr*.

III.2.42 Another Dish [of a Chicken Casserole Layered with Beaten Eggs]

Take whatever you like of fattened chickens and capons (*makhāṣī*),[91] slaughter them, pluck their feathers, and clean them meticulously. Cut them into pieces: 2 from the breast; and the same from the rear end (*zimikkā*) and thighs. Put them all in a new wide pot, adding water, salt, plenty of olive oil, black pepper, coriander seeds, a small amount of chopped onion, skinned almonds, and pine nuts (*ḥabb ṣanawbar*). Put the pot on the fire to cook, and when done, add pounded saffron, which has been dissolved [in liquid]—add just enough to color it, no more.

Next, take a good number of eggs—about 20 for each bird used—break them into a large, wide bowl (*mithrad*), adding salt, black pepper, ginger, Ceylon cinnamon, cloves, just the needed amount of spikenard, a small amount of [chopped] onion, mastic (*maṣṭakā*), juices of fresh cilantro and mint, and a small amount of saffron. Put aside as many as you wish of egg yolks [keep them whole] and beat the rest to combine them.

Take a large pan (*ṭājin*) and put some of the strained broth and its fat in it. Take the chicken pot and empty it into another large bowl (*mithrad*). Take the [cooked] chicken pieces, dip them in the beaten eggs, and arrange them in the bottom of the pan. Cover them with [a layer] of the beaten eggs. You should have already spread [another] layer of the eggs in the bottom of the pan [before layering the chicken pieces]. Spread more of the chicken pieces in another layer, (**159r**) and spread the remaining beaten eggs all over—there should be enough to submerge them.

Dot the face of the pan with the [reserved] egg yolks and the almonds and pine nuts [that were cooked in the pot]. Pour in the remaining fat (*wadak*) extracted from the broth—take the fat only. Sprinkle the top of the pan with Ceylon cinnamon and ginger and put it in the *furn* (brick oven) to set and brown at a distance from the fire. Take it out and use it, God Almighty willing. It will taste better if you let it slightly cool.

III.2.43 Another Dish [of Fried Chicken Pieces Enveloped in Eggs][92]

Take whatever you like of fattened chickens and capons (*makhāṣī*) and do with them as you did above—cleaning and cutting them into pieces. Put them in a

---

91 The plural also occurs as *khiṣyān*, as in recipe i.2.25 above; the singular is *khaṣiyy*, as in recipe iii.2.27 above.

92 In recipe iii.5.7 below we will learn that such dishes are called *maḥshī*.

large new pot and add water, salt, plenty of olive oil, black pepper, coriander seeds, a small amount of chopped onion, skinned almonds, pine nuts (*ḥabb ṣanawbar*), freshly harvested acorns (*ballūṭ*) and chestnuts (*qasṭal ṭarī*), and walnuts, which have been shelled and blanched to remove their skins. Put the pot on the fire to cook.

Take eggs—30 for each bird—and add salt to them after breaking them [in a large bowl (*mithrad*)]. Also add black pepper, ginger, Ceylon cinnamon, spikenard, cloves, and saffron—just the needed amount. Thoroughly beat the eggs with a ladle after setting aside about 10 of the yolks [leave them whole]. Continue doing this until the eggs mix with the spices.

Now have a look at the chicken pieces; if you find that they are cooked, empty the pot into another large bowl (*mithrad*). Take a large tinned skillet (*miqlāt muqaṣdara*), put it on the fire with olive oil and some of the pot's broth after straining it [to heat it up], and then remove it from the fire. Pour some of the eggs [prepared above] in it [as a layer], arrange the chicken pieces [in one layer] on it, and then add enough of the eggs to cover them; put as much as the skillet can hold.

Put the skillet on low heat, and when you see that the egg mix is about set, take a knife and separate the chicken pieces with whatever was stuck on them of the egg mix. Let the pieces fry by turning them gently until they cook and brown. Be careful not to let them burn. When the pieces are done frying, arrange them in a glazed bowl (*ghaḍāra*). Also add the remaining egg mix,[93] which did not stick to the chicken pieces, after coagulating it by frying. Put more of the chicken pieces and the egg mix in the skillet [and fry them as was done above]; continue until all the pieces are done, God Almighty willing.

Take the [set aside] egg yolks and fry them; and if you want to pound the livers and make *isfīriyya* with them as described earlier,[94] go ahead and do so. You may also make meatballs (*banādiq*). Garnish the chicken pieces, which have been arranged in one layer in bowls,[95] with [fried] egg yolks, *isfīriyya* [strips], split [boiled] eggs, and meatballs. Drizzle whatever fat (*wadak*) remained [in the pot] all over it and sprinkle it with whatever you like (**159v**) of aromatic spices.

---

93 The recipe calls the egg mix used to envelope the chicken pieces *ḥashū*, which generally designates food that is being stuffed.

94 They are smooth and thin meat patties, see recipe ii.6.3 above.

95 *Aghḍira*, sg. *ghaḍāra*. Several bowls are needed here because the chicken pieces are spread in single layers.

[Note:] The almonds, walnuts, acorns, and chestnuts [that were in the chicken pot] should have been added to the beaten eggs when they were poured into the skillet. Some people may also add fine-tasting hard cheese chopped into small pieces to the egg mix.[96]

Eat the dish salubriously, God Almighty willing.

III.2.44 Another Dish [of Chicken Variously Roasted and Grilled][97]

Take a fat young adult chicken, clean it thoroughly, and salt it inside and out. Insert it on an iron or wooden skewer and let it grill suspended above a fire that is only burning around it; do not put any fire underneath it. Continue turning and basting it with a mix of olive oil, *murrī* (liquid fermented sauce), and pounded garlic while grilling until it cooks and browns.[98]

[For the sauce,] take black pepper, caraway and coriander seeds, thyme, vinegar, *murrī*—just the needed amount—and olive oil. Put them all in a small pot (*qudayra*) and put it on the fire to cook. When it comes to a boil, have a taste of it; if you like the flavor, add 4 [raw, unbroken] whole eggs to the pot. Once the eggs cook, remove it from the fire. Cut the chicken into pieces in a wide, shallow bowl (*ṣaḥfa*), and pour the sauce (*maraq*) all over them, along with the eggs after shelling them.

If you like, replace this sauce with a mixture of olive oil and boiled and pounded garlic. Cut the chicken into pieces while still hot and add them to the olive oil and garlic. Alternatively, you may add pounded garlic to the sauce mentioned first and let them cook with it. And eat it salubriously, God Almighty willing.

If you want to use [an uncooked] sauce made with olive oil, *murrī naqīʿ*, and dried thyme crushed by hand, then go ahead and do this.

If you want, take fine-tasting hard cheese (*jubn yābis*) and grate it into dust-like particles with an *iskarfāj* (grater). Take garlic cloves, boil them in water, and then pound them and put them in a glazed bowl (*ghaḍāra*). Dissolve the finely grated cheese in some hot water and mix it with the garlic. Cut the chicken into pieces, mix them well with the cheese and garlic [sauce], and then pour olive oil on them.

---

96 The egg mix used to pad/envelop the chicken piece is referred to as محشى *miḥshā* in the BL MS, fol. 159v, and the Berlin MS, fol. 57v; and حشو *ḥashū* in the Madrid MS, fol. 83v.

97 The Madrid MS, fol. 83v, calls this dish محشو *maḥshū*, which is descriptive of the way the chickens are dressed in sauces after grilling or roasting them. See glossary 9.2.

98 I followed here the Madrid MS, fol. 83v, because it provides key words on positioning the fire and turning the chicken while grilling.

If you want to replace the cheese [mentioned above] with *shīrāz* (very thick drained yogurt) or thick yogurt (*rāyib khāthir*),[99] you may do so. This would be particularly good with small young chickens (*farārīj ṣighār*), which have been roasted in the *tannūr* (clay oven).

If you want to roast the chicken in the *tannūr*, thread it onto a skewer and then light the *tannūr* [with a strong fire until its inner walls heat up and] look white.[100] Put the skewer inside the *tannūr* [vertically]; but first, put a pan (*ṭājin*) with water and olive oil in it on the floor of the *tannūr* and then put the lower end of the skewer in it. Cover the opening of the *tannūr* and seal it with mud. When you know that [according to your estimation] the chicken is done, take it out, and cut it into pieces (**160r**) in a wide, shallow bowl (*ṣaḥfa*). Dress it with any of the [sauces] I mentioned to you.

If you want to roast the chicken in a pot (*qidr*) in the *furn* (brick oven), take the chicken and thread it on a small skewer. The skewer should stand inside the pot after you rub the chicken with salt,[101] and there should be olive oil and pounded garlic in the pot itself. Cover the pot, seal it with dough, and then put it in the *furn* at a distance from the fire until [according to your estimation] you know that it is done. Take it out and use it however you like.

If you want to roast the chicken in a pan (*ṭājin*) in the *furn*, first rub the chicken with olive oil and salt and then put it in the pan along with olive oil and pounded garlic. Put the pan in the *furn* at a distance from the fire; there should be someone available to turn the chicken periodically until it cooks and browns. Take it out when done and use it, God Almighty willing.

III.2.45 Another Dish [of Chicken Roasted and Glazed with Egg Yolks][102]

Take a fat young adult chicken, clean it thoroughly, and leave it whole. Salt it and baste it with a mix of olive oil, *murrī naqīʿ* (sun-fermented liquid sauce), black pepper, and thyme. Put it in a pan (*ṭājin*) with a small amount of water and send it to the *furn* (communal brick oven) to roast and brown.

---

99 For yogurt recipes, see VI.1.2 and VI.2.2 below, respectively.

100 See glossary 9.1. See also recipe I.1.2, where more details are given on how to light the *tannūr*.

101 I followed here the Madrid MS, fol. 84r, which clearly copies 'let the skewer stand inside the pot' as ويوقف السفود في داخل القدر, to replace the Berlin MS, fol. 57v, وتوقعها في القدر 'and let it fall into the pot,' most probably a copyist's misreading of وتوقفها 'let it stand.' In this position, the chicken does not have to be turned over while roasting, which explains the absence of such instructions here.

102 It is described as مشوي 'roasted' in the Madrid MS, fol. 84v.

Take about 6 [raw] egg yolks and add black pepper, Ceylon cinnamon, and ginger to them. Now have a look at the chicken. If you find that it has cooked, take it out and baste it with the yolks after mixing them well with the spices. Baste the chicken thoroughly; it should be entirely coated. Return the pan to the oven to let the eggs coagulate—while turning the chicken so that it browns on all sides—but be careful not to let it burn. When the chicken is fully done, take it out and use it, God Almighty willing.

III.2.46 Another Dish [of Chicken Simmered in Rosewater and Honey, Served as *tharīd*]

Take a fat young adult chicken, clean it thoroughly, and put it whole in a new pot. Add 2 ladlefuls of honey dissolved in rosewater, 3 ladlefuls of olive oil, salt—just the needed amount—black pepper, skinned almonds, and a small amount of water. Put the pot on low heat to cook.

[To make the bread,] take fine white flour (*daqīq darmak*) and knead it with some sour fermented dough (*khamīr*) and a small amount of water. Roll it out with a rolling pin (*jawbak*) into thin discs (*ruqāq*)—the thinnest you can get them. Put them in a pan (*ṭājin*) one above the other; (160v) grease each one with olive oil while layering. Continue doing this until the dough is finished. Drape the layered *ruqāq* with a thick disc (*raghīf ghalīẓ*) made with another kind of dough.[103]

Take the pan to the *furn* (communal brick oven) and let it bake at a distance from the fire; take it out when you see that the coarse bread [on top] has browned. Now take the cooked chicken and put it in a glazed bowl (*ghaḍāra*). Break the *ruqāq* bread into pieces and put them on the chicken. Pour broth all over them, sprinkle the dish with crushed sugar, and eat it salubriously, God Almighty willing.

III.2.47 Another Dish [of Young Chickens Simmered in Rosewater and Sugar, Served as *tharīd*]

Take young chickens (*farārīj*), clean them thoroughly, but leave them whole. Put them in a new pot with 3 *ūqiyyas* (approx. ⅓ cup) rosewater that has 3

---

103 It would be made with a less fine flour, such as whole wheat, because it is used as a protective layer that will be discarded.

ūqiyyas (3 ounces) sugar dissolved in it. Also add black pepper, pine nuts (*ḥabb ṣanawbar*), skinned almonds, 2 ladlefuls of fine-tasting olive oil, and a small amount of water. Put the pot on the fire to cook.

Now take thin *khabīṣ* sheets, the making of which has been described in the first part of this book [recipe i.4.22]. Fry them in a clean skillet in olive oil until they brown. Take them out, break them into pieces, and add them to the pot with the young chickens. Leave the pot on low heat until it thickens and cooks. Empty the young chickens and whatever there is in the pot into a wide, shallow bowl (*ṣaḥfa*), sprinkle it with crushed sugar and Ceylon cinnamon, and eat it salubriously, God Almighty willing.

This dish may also be cooked with squabs (*firākh al-ḥamām*), with the help of God and His power.

III.2.48 Another Dish, Mashriqi, [Made with Chicken Meatballs and Chestnuts]

Take a chicken breast, pound it very well, and make meatballs (*banādiq*) with it as described earlier [in recipes ii.6.1–2 above], adding juice of fresh cilantro as well. [Shape them and] put them aside in a wide, shallow bowl (*ṣaḥfa*). Now, take freshly harvested chestnuts (*qasṭal ṭarī*) if available. In case they are not fresh, boil them until they cook and soften [and set them aside].

Take a small pot and put water in it along with salt, coriander seeds, black pepper, juices of onion and cilantro, and olive oil. Put it on the fire, and when it comes to a boil, add the [prepared] meatballs and let them cook.

Next, take the [set aside] chestnuts, pound them, and add them to the meatballs [in the pot] with a small amount of vinegar. Top the pot with beaten eggs (*tukhammar*) as was done in earlier dishes,[104] [leave it on embers,] and when it nicely simmers and sets (*iʿtadala*), eat it salubriously, God Almighty willing.

---

104 The recipe calls this *takhmīr* 'coating' or 'topping,' see glossary 9.2. Dishes that have little sauce in them were often served with a topping of eggs beaten with spices and left to set while on low heat. See, for instance, close to the end of recipes iii.2.19, 26, and 33 in this chapter.

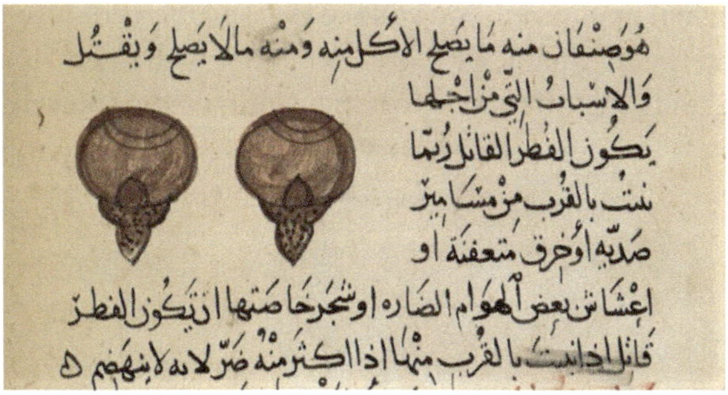

FIGURE 67 Mushrooms, *fuṭr*, Dioscorides, *Kitāb Dīsqūrīdis fī mawādd al-ʿilāj*, fol. 140v, detail
BRITISH LIBRARY: ORIENTAL MANUSCRIPTS, OR 3366, IN QATAR DIGITAL LIBRARY HTTPS://WWW.QDL.QA/ARCHIVE/81055/VDC_100022531380.0X000001

III.2.49 (161r) Another Mashriqi Dish, [Made with Diced Chicken and Mushrooms]

Take a chicken breast and dice it; also dice some *fuṭr* (mushrooms), which is *faqʿ*.[105] Everything should be washed very well [before dicing], and do not use too much meat.

Put them in a pot, adding water, salt, olive oil or butter, a chopped onion, juice of fresh cilantro, and black pepper. Put the pot on the fire to cook, and when it is done, add a small amount of *murrī* (liquid fermented sauce) and top the dish (*tukhammar*) with a couple of eggs, as was described earlier.[106] Ladle it into a glazed bowl (*ghaḍāra*), sprinkle it with black pepper, and eat it salubriously, God Almighty willing.

Chicken, roasted (*mashwī*)[107]

Clean several fat chickens and put them in a pot (*qidr*) in which they are raised from its base by means of sticks arranged in its bottom. Cover the pot, seal it (*yuṭayyan*),[108] and put it in the *furn* (brick oven) as it is, at a distance from the fire, until the chickens are done roasting.

---

105 Since the recipe is from the eastern region, where mushrooms were more commonly known as *fuṭr*, al-Tujībī provides its common name in the Muslim West, which is *faqʿ*. On the other hand, *faqʿ* in the eastern region designated a white variety of desert truffles also known as *kamʾa*.

106 See n. 104 above.

107 This dish is found only in the Madrid MS, fol. 85v.

108 Literally 'sealed with clay', but judging from previous recipes, dough was used to seal the pots in such cases.

Take the pot out, and [when uncovered, you will see that] all the [dripping] fat (*wadak*) has gathered in the bottom of the pot. Mix this fat with salt, black pepper, Ceylon cinnamon, and ginger pounded together. Sprinkle the chickens with it and serve them.

Part Three, Chapter Three: On Meat of Partridges (*Ḥajal*)

III.3.1 A dish [of Oven-Browned partridge], Fantastic[1]

Take a partridge, discard its skin, and clean and wash it thoroughly. Put it in a new pot with water, salt, olive oil, black pepper, coriander seeds, a small amount of chopped onion, skinned almonds, a ladleful of *murrī* (liquid fermented sauce), and a bit of vinegar. Put it on the fire to cook.

When the partridge is done cooking, take it out and put it in a pan (*ṭājin*), adding the strained broth (*ṣafwū*) in which it was cooked. Put it in the *furn* (brick oven) to brown and then take it out and serve it, God Almighty willing.

III.3.2 Another Dish, [Stewed with Meatballs,] Fantastic[2]

Take a partridge, discard its skin, wash it from the inside and the outside, and put it in a pot with water, salt, black pepper, coriander seeds, cumin, a small amount of chopped onion, a few cloves of garlic, soaked chickpeas, skinned almonds, leaves of citron (*utrujj*), sprigs of herb fennel (*ʿūd basbās*),[3] and a small amount of *murrī* (liquid fermented sauce). Put the pot on the fire to cook.

When the pot is almost done, take the meat of the breast from another partridge, pound it very well, and make meatballs with it, as was described earlier;[4] add them to the pot. Color the partridge with saffron and then add as much as you prefer of fine-tasting vinegar.

Now take eggs, break them in a wide, shallow bowl (*ṣaḥfa*), add a bit of saffron, salt, and aromatic spices, as was described to you earlier,[5] (**161v**) and top the pot with them. Remove the fire from underneath the pot and leave

1 *ʿAjīb*, as described in the Madrid MS, fol. 86r.

2 See the above note.

3 *Basbās* is the Andalusi variant of what was more commonly called *rāzyānaj* and *shamar/shamār* in the eastern region.

4 See, for instance, recipe ii.6.1 above.

5 See, for instance, close to end of recipes iii.2.19, 26, and 33 in the previous chapter. This egg mix is used as a topping called *takhmīr*, see glossary 9.2 for more on this cooking technique.

 | DOI:10.1163/9789004469488_017

FIGURE 68
Partridges, *ḥajal*, Anonymous, *Kitāb Naʿt al-ḥayawān*, fol. 9r, detail
BRITISH LIBRARY: ORIENTAL MANUSCRIPTS, OR 2784, IN QATAR DIGITAL LIBRARY HTTPS://WWW.QDL.QA/ARCHIVE/81055/VDC_100023556967.0X000001

it on embers (*ghaḍā*) to allow the topping to set. Put the contents of the pot in a glazed bowl (*ghaḍāra*), spread [boiled] split eggs all over it, sprinkle it with Ceylon cinnamon and ginger, and eat it salubriously, God Almighty willing.

III.3.3 Another Dish [of Stuffed Partridge][6]

Take a partridge, clean and wash it, but leave the skin on. However, before plucking the feathers, the bird has to be blown [through the neck].[7]

[For the stuffing:] Take the meat of another partridge or lamb, pound it in a mortar (*mihrās*) very well, and add skinned almonds—some pounded and some left whole—pine nuts (*ṣanawbar*), breadcrumbs, black pepper, ginger, salt, and Ceylon cinnamon. Take 2 boiled eggs, [shell them,] crush them by hand, and add them to the meat. Also take uncooked egg yolks and knead and press them with the meat and the crushed eggs until they are all well combined.

6 A recipe in the Andalusi *Anwāʿ al-ṣaydala* 42 that bears similarities to this one calls this dish *ḥajala Yahūdiyya* 'a Jewish partridge.' It seems that such elaborate stuffed birds were a Jewish specialty. See also recipe iii.2.21 above.

7 See, for instance, recipe iii.2.24 above, where a chicken is prepared similarly.

Stuff the partridge [with the above] between the skin and meat, and in its cavity as well. Sew it up and put it in a pan (*ṭājin*). Add water, salt, olive oil, black pepper, and coriander and put it on the fire to cook. When the partridge is almost done, color it with saffron, add a ladleful of *murrī naqīʿ* (sun-fermented liquid sauce) to the pan, and put it in the *furn* (brick oven). Take the pan out of the oven when the partridge is browned, set it aside to slightly cool, and eat it salubriously, God Almighty willing.

III.3.4 Another Dish [of Stewed Partridge], good[8]

Take a partridge, discard its skin, and wash and clean it very well; leave it whole. Put it in a new pot with water, salt, black pepper, coriander seeds, olive oil, and a ladleful of white vinegar.

Take the breast of another partridge and pound it well. Take half of it and make *isfīriyya* (flat and smooth patties) with it as described in the sixth chapter of the second part of this book [recipe ii.6.3 above]; set them aside. Take the other half of the meat and pound skinned almonds with it; thin them down with water and add them to the partridge pot.

Once the partridge cooks, top it with a mix of egg whites [beaten] with a small amount of flour and breadcrumbs.[9] [Remove the fire from underneath the pot] and leave it on embers (*ghaḍā*) so that the topping may set, ingredients simmer, and flavors nicely blend (*tatajammar*).

Empty the pot into a glazed bowl (*ghaḍāra*), arrange the cut pieces of *isfīriyya* on top, sprinkle it with ginger, and eat it salubriously, God Almighty willing.

III.3.5 (162r) Another Dish [of Rotisserie Partridge, with Sauce]

Take a partridge, discard its skin, and pass it through an iron or wooden skewer. Suspend it above a fire burning on both sides of it. Rotate [the skewer constantly] by hand until it is cooked and browned, basting it periodically with a mix of olive oil, salt, *murrī* (liquid fermented sauce), and pounded garlic.

When the partridge is cooked and browned, take it off the skewer and cut it into pieces in a wide and shallow earthenware bowl (*ṣaḥfa fakhkhār*). Cover

---

8 *Jayyid*, as described in the Madrid MS, fol. 86v.

9 This is usually referred to as *takhmīr*, see n. 5 above.

the pieces with any of the sauces (*marqa*) I mentioned to you in the second chapter of the third part of this book,[10] and eat it salubriously, God Almighty willing.

10 The cross reference here is to the previous chapter on chicken. See, for instance, sauce recipes in iii.2.34 and 44.

CHAPTER III.4

Part Three, Chapter Four: On Meat of Squabs (*Firākh Ḥamām*)

III.4.1 A Dish [of Browned Squabs]

Take a squab, slaughter it, and gently pluck its feathers. Open its cavity and take out the entrails. Wash and clean it and then put it in a new pot. Add a small amount of water, salt, plenty of olive oil, black pepper, coriander seeds, a few cloves of garlic, and small amounts of chopped onion and fine-tasting *murrī* (liquid fermented sauce). Put the pot on the fire to cook.

When the squab is cooked and all the water has evaporated, leave the pot on low heat while moving the squab around in the pot until it fries and browns in the oil. Remove the pot from the fire and put the squab in a wide, shallow bowl (*ṣaḥfa*), and eat it salubriously, God Almighty willing.

This is how you also cook them when you have a couple or more of them; adjust the amounts [of the other ingredients] depending on how few or how many are being cooked, with the help of Almighty God.

III.4.2 Another Dish [of Oven-Browned Squabs]

Take squabs, clean them thoroughly, and put them in a glazed earthenware pan (*ṭājin muzajjaj*). Add water, salt, olive oil, black pepper, coriander seeds, a small amount of cumin, a few cloves of garlic, skinned almonds, a ladleful of fine-tasting *murrī* (liquid fermented sauce), and half a ladleful of vinegar. Put the pan on the fire to cook.

When the squabs are done, (**162v**) take the pan to the brick oven [and let it bake] until some of its liquid evaporates and the squabs brown. Take the pan out, set it aside to cool a little, and then eat it salubriously, God Almighty willing.

III.4.3 Another Dish, Called *rāhibī* (Monks' Food)

Take squabs, clean them very well, and cook them as was described in the [corresponding] recipe in the first chapter of the second part of this book [recipe ii.1.7 above].

 | DOI:10.1163/9789004469488_018

III.4.4 Another dish, Called *mufarrij* (Comforting)

Take squabs and do with them as was done above. Cook them as was described in the [corresponding] recipe in the first chapter of the second part of this book [recipe ii.1.7 above].

III.4.5 Another Dish, Called *qarʿiyya* (Cooked with Gourd)

Take squabs and do with them as was done above. Cook them as was described in the [corresponding] recipe in the second chapter of the second part of this book [recipe ii.2.20 above].

III.4.6 Another Dish [of Fried Squabs, with Garlic Sauce]

Take squabs,[1] clean them thoroughly, and put them in a new pot. Add water, salt, black pepper, coriander seeds, a small amount of chopped onion, and olive oil. Put the pot on the fire to cook.

When the pot boils and the birds are done, take a clean skillet (*miqlāt*) and put it on the fire with fine-tasting olive oil. When the oil boils, take the birds out of the pot and put them in the skillet to fry. Turn them gently [while frying] to brown them.

[**To make the sauce,**] take a small earthenware pan (*ṭājin fakhkhār*) and take a few cloves of garlic. Pound the garlic, add it to the pan with some of the strained broth from the pot, and put it on the fire. When the garlic cooks, add fine-tasting vinegar, and once it comes to a boil, pour it all over the squabs, and eat the dish salubriously, God Almighty willing.

III.4.7 Another Dish [of Oven-Browned Squabs]

(**163r**) Take squabs, clean them thoroughly, and put them in a new pot. Add water, salt, olive oil, black pepper, coriander seeds, a small amount of chopped onion, and skinned almonds. Color the squabs with saffron and put the pot on the fire to cook.

---

1 I amended the text here following the Madrid MS, fol. 87v, which has *firākh* written rather than *ḥamām*, as copied in the BL and Berlin MSS. At any rate, the directions that follow will refer to them as *firākh*.

Now take eggs—about 5 or 6 for each bird used. Break them in a large bowl (*mithrad*) and add breadcrumbs, salt, black pepper, Ceylon cinnamon, ginger, and juices of fresh cilantro and mint. Beat them all with a ladle or by hand to combine them, but you should have taken away as many as you want of [whole] egg yolks before beating the mix.

Take a look at the birds, if you see that they have cooked, take them out and arrange them in a large pan (*ṭājin*) with their breasts facing upwards. Now pour [the egg mix] all over them;[2] let it be enough to submerge them. Also pour all the broth's fat (*wadak*) and dot its face (*tunajjam*) with the [reserved] egg yolks and the almonds [from the pot]. Sprinkle the pan with Ceylon cinnamon and ginger and take it to the *furn* (communal brick oven). Let it be put at a distance from the fire [and let it bake] until it sets and browns and the liquid evaporates. Take the pan out, set it aside to cool a bit, and eat the dish salubriously, God Almighty willing.

III.4.8 Another Dish [of Stuffed Squabs]

Take squabs and clean them thoroughly. Take the meat of some of them with the gizzards and livers and pound them in a mortar very well. Add salt, black pepper, ginger, Ceylon cinnamon, coriander seeds, and a bit of pounded onion. Break 3 eggs on them, add skinned almonds, and mix them all.

Stuff the meat mix into the cavities of the birds and between their skins and meat. Sew them up and put them in a new pot with water, salt, olive oil, black pepper, coriander seeds, and a small amount of chopped onion. Put the pot on the fire to cook.

When the squabs are done, take them out and put them in a large pan (*ṭājin*). Color them with saffron and add some of the strained broth (*ṣafwū al-marqa*) to the pan. Take it to the *furn* (communal brick oven) and let it be put at a distance from the fire until the birds brown on all sides. Take the pan out and put the birds in a glazed bowl (*ghaḍāra*). Garnish them with [boiled] split eggs and tender tips of mint sprigs. Sprinkle Ceylon cinnamon and ginger all over the dish, and eat it salubriously, God Almighty willing.

---

2 In the BL MS, fol. 163r, and the Madrid MS, fol. 87v, the eggs are said to be poured: وثم تجعل عليها البيض 'and put the eggs on them,' and ويصب عليها البيض 'and the eggs are poured over them,' respectively. In the Berlin MS, fol. 60r, it is copied as وتجعل عليها 'and it is put on them,' the 'it' obviously refers to the eggs, but the editor incorrectly 'amends' it by adding ماء 'water' in square brackets, which distorts the meaning the of the text.

III.4.9 Another Dish (of Stuffed Deboned Squabs)

Take squabs, and after slaughtering them, blow hard [into their necks] until their skins are separated from the meat. Tie their necks [with a thread] and pluck their feathers [by dipping them first] in hot water. Clean the birds, open their cavities, [take out the entrails,] and wash them thoroughly. Next, make a slit in the neck of each squab, cut off the neck and remove it, and do your best to gently remove the [rest of the] bones [with the meat]. However, keep (**163v**) the tip of the rear end (*zimikkā*), the [lower] halves of the legs [i.e., drumsticks], and the tips of the wings attached to the skin.

Pound the [removed] meat with some more from other squabs, and do with it exactly as was described in the second chapter of the third part of this book [recipe iii.2.40 above], God Almighty willing.

III.4.10 Another Dish [of Squabs], Grilled (*mashwī*)[3]

Take whatever is available of squabs, clean them very well, and thread them onto an iron skewer. Grill them as was mentioned earlier [e.g., recipes iii.2.44 and iii.3.5]. When fully done, take them off the skewer and cut them into pieces in a glazed bowl (*ghaḍāra*). Drench them with [a sauce of] thick yogurt (*laban khāthir*),[4] cooked and pounded garlic,[5] and fine-tasting olive oil, all mixed well, and eat the dish salubriously, God Almighty willing.

3 As described in the Madrid MS, fol. 88r.

4 Also called *rāyib khāthir* in recipe iii.2.44 above. For yogurt recipes, see chapter vi.2 below.

5 The edited Arabic text overlooks mentioning garlic, which is clearly copied in all the MSS.

CHAPTER III.5

Part Three, Chapter Five: On Meat of Fat Turtledoves (*Yamām Musmina*)[1]

III.5.1 A Dish [of Browned Turtledoves]

Take as many fat turtledoves as you want, slaughter them and clean them, and then open their cavities and wash and clean them thoroughly. Put them in a new pot with water, salt, plenty of olive oil, black pepper, coriander seeds, a small amount of chopped onion, and a few cloves of garlic—leave them unskinned. Put the pot on the fire to cook.

When the liquid evaporates and the turtledoves are cooked, leave the pot on low heat, moving the birds around gently until they brown. Remove the pot from the fire and put the turtledoves in a glazed bowl (*ghaḍāra*). Sprinkle them with Ceylon cinnamon and ginger, and eat them salubriously, God Almighty willing.

III.5.2 Another Dish, Called *mufarrij* (Comforting)

Take as many as you want of fat turtledoves and do with them as was done above. Cook them as was described in the [corresponding] recipe in the first chapter of the second part of this book [recipe ii.1.7 above], with the help of God Almighty.

III.5.3 Another Dish, Called *naʿnaʿiyya* (Cooked with Mint)

Take as many as you want of fat turtledoves and do with them as was done above. Cook them as was described in the [corresponding] recipe in the second

1 *Musmina* is addition from the Madrid MS, fol. 88v, where it is clearly vocalized as such. According to Ibn Manẓūr, *Lisān al-ʿArab*, s.v. سمن, any creature that is naturally built to be fat is described as *musmin*. *Yamām* is the commoners' name for *shifnīn*, which is an undomesticated migratory variety of pigeon, described as being smaller than the domesticated pigeon (*ḥamām baladī*).

 | DOI:10.1163/9789004469488_019

FIGURE 69 Turtledoves, folio from a Persian *Manāfiʿ al-ḥayawān* of Ibn Bakhtīshūʿ, (recto), c. 1300, detail
CLEVELAND MUSEUM OF ART: HTTPS://WWW.CLEVELANDART.ORG/ART/1945.382

chapter of the second part [recipe ii.2.8 above], God Almighty willing. (**164r**) It is cooked exactly the same way with lemon balm (*turunjān*).[2]

2 Also called balm mint, *Melissa officinalis*, see glossary 8.

III.5.4 Another Dish [of Fried Turtledoves, with Garlic Sauce]

Take as many as you want of fat turtledoves and do with them as was done above. Put them in a new pot with water, salt, olive oil, black pepper, coriander seeds, and a small amount of chopped onion. Put the pot on the fire to cook.

Once the turtledoves cook, take a clean skillet and put it on the fire with olive oil. As soon as the oil boils, take the turtledoves from the pot and fry them in the pan, moving them around while frying until they brown. Take them out and put them in a glazed bowl (*ghaḍāra*).

[**For the sauce,**] take pounded garlic and put it in a skillet with some of the strained broth. When the garlic has cooked in the liquid, pour it along with the liquid all over the turtledoves, and eat them salubriously, God Almighty willing.

III.5.5 Another Dish [of Pot-Roasted Turtledoves]

Take as many as you want of fat turtledoves, clean them from the outside, and remove their crops (*ḥawāṣil*, sg. *ḥawṣala*), but do not open their cavities. Take garlic cloves, skin them, and insert one in the nostril (*minkhar*) and one in the anal vent (*makhraj*) of each turtledove.[3]

Now take an iron skewer as thin as a large needle (*misalla*),[4] thread the turtledoves onto it from their beaks, and put it in a large pot after you line its bottom with the crust of a [large] bread.[5] Find a way to make [two] holes in the upper part of the pot so that the turtledoves dangle in the air [from the horizontally positioned skewer]. Cover the pot, seal it with dough, and send it to the *furn* (communal brick oven) to be put at a distance from the fire.

When the dough turns black or almost so, take the pot out of the oven. Take the turtledoves out with the bread crust, [put them in a serving dish,] sprinkle them with ginger, black pepper, and Ceylon cinnamon, and eat them salubriously, God Almighty willing.

[Note:] Before you thread the turtledoves onto the skewer, you should rub them with [a mix of] salt, olive oil, *murrī* (liquid fermented sauce), black pepper, and Ceylon cinnamon, and then put them in the pot, with the help of God Almighty.

---

3 Regarding the nostrils of the turtledoves (also called nares), I assume that the garlic clove would have been inserted under the operculum membrane, which is like a lid or flap covering the nostrils.

4 As added in the Madrid MS, fol. 89r, في رقة المسلة.

5 My guess is that the cut side would face upwards to absorb the falling juices of the roasting turtledoves.

III.5.6 Another Dish [of Turtledoves, Salt Crusted and Roasted], *mashwī*[6]

Take as many as you want of fat turtledoves and do with them whatever you did earlier [to clean and wash them].

Take fine-tasting pounded salt and an earthenware pan, glazed or unglazed, and spread the salt in the pan's base. Take the turtledoves, arrange them in the pan [in one layer] with their backs downwards, and cover them entirely with salt. Send the pan to the *furn* (communal brick oven) and leave it [to bake] until the salt sets and solidifies. At this point, take the pan out and remove the salt [crust] from the turtledoves with a knife. [Put the turtledoves in a serving vessel,] sprinkle them with Ceylon cinnamon and ginger, and eat them salubriously, God Almighty willing.

If you want to make this dish with squabs (*firākh ḥamām*), you can go ahead and do so.

III.5.7 (164v) Another Dish, Called *maḥshī*[7]

Take as many fat turtledoves as you want; open their cavities, clean them thoroughly, and cook them as described in the second chapter of the third part of this book [recipe iii.2.43], but for each turtledove use 4 eggs,[8] so know this.

III.5.8 Another Dish, *mashwī* (Grilled)[9]

Take as many fat turtledoves as you want and clean them thoroughly, it is up to you whether you want to open their cavities [and remove the entrails] or not, and then thread them on an iron skewer. Take a vessel (*āniya*) and put in it salt dissolved in water, olive oil, *murrī naqīʿ* (sun-fermented liquid sauce), pounded garlic, black pepper, ginger, and Ceylon cinnamon. [This would be the basting sauce.] Take a chicken feather, wash it, and put it in the vessel.

Place the lighted fire on both sides [of the grilling birds] and not the middle. Let both ends of the skewer rest on rocks [to suspend it above ground lev-

---

6 As described in the Madrid MS, fol. 89r.

7 According to the recipe's instructions, pieces of turtledoves are enveloped in an egg mix and fried. See glossary 9.2, s.v. *maḥshī*, for more on this term.

8 By comparison, 30 eggs were used per large chicken in the recipe referenced here.

9 As described in the Madrid MS, fol. 89r. The turtledoves are grilled by rotating them rotisserie style.

el].[10] While rotating the skewer by hand, repeatedly baste the turtledoves with the feather. Continue doing this until they grill well and brown. Take them off the skewer, and eat them salubriously, God Almighty willing.

If you want to use any of the sauces (*marqa*) mentioned in the second chapter of the third part of this book,[11] go ahead and do so with the help of God Almighty.

10 The rocks are mentioned only in the Madrid MS, fol. 89r. In the BL MS and the Berlin MS, fol. 61r, the instruction is to 'put the skewer on something high.'

11 See, for instance, recipes iii.2.34 and iii.2.44.

Part Three, Chapter Six: On Meat of Starlings (*Zarāzīr*)[1]

FIGURE 70 A starling, *zurzūr*, al-Qazwīnī, *ʿAjāʾib al-makhlūqāt wa-gharāʾib al-mawjūdāt*, fol. 120r, detail
BRITISH LIBRARY: ORIENTAL MANUSCRIPTS, OR 14140, IN *QATAR DIGITAL LIBRARY* HTTPS://WWW.QDL.QA/ARCHIVE/81055/VDC_100023586788.0X000001

III.6.1 A Dish [of Fried Starlings, with Sauce]

Take fat white starlings, pluck their feathers, clean them, open their cavities, and wash them. Put them in a new pot with water, salt, olive oil, black pepper, coriander seeds, and a small amount of [chopped] onion. Put the pot on the fire to cook.

While the starlings cook, take a clean tinned skillet (*miqlāt muqaṣdara*) and put olive oil in it; once it boils, take the starlings out of the pot and put them in it to fry. Move them about gently until they all brown.

[**For the sauce,**] take garlic, pound it, and put it in the skillet after all the starlings are taken out. Add some of the strained broth from the pot and let the garlic cook in the liquid and then pour it all over the starlings, and eat them salubriously.

1 This chapter and the following one are missing from the Madrid MS.

 | DOI:10.1163/9789004469488_020

Whatever dishes were cooked with turtledoves [in the previous chapter] may also be cooked with starlings.[2] Additionally, if you want to make *rāhibī* or *jumlī* with them, follow the [corresponding] recipes given in the first chapter of the second part of this book [recipes ii.1.1 and ii.1.7 above]. (**165r**)

2 The following is added only in the BL MS, fol. 164v.

Part Three, Chapter Seven: On Meat Of Sparrows (*ʿAṣāfīr*)[1]

III.7.1 A Dish [of Fried Sparrows, with Sauce]

Take as many as you want of sparrows, open their cavities, and clean and wash them thoroughly. Put them in a new pot with water, salt, olive oil, black pepper, coriander seeds, and a small amount of [chopped] onion. Put the pot on the fire to cook. Once the sparrows are done, take a clean skillet and put olive oil in it, and as soon as it boils, take the sparrows out of the pot and put them in the skillet and let them fry.

Next, take pounded garlic and add it to the skillet with the sparrows still in it. Add strained broth (*ṣafwū al-marqa*) as well. Leave the skillet on the fire until the garlic cooks and [most of] the broth evaporates. Ladle the sparrows and whatever remains of the sauce (*marqa*) and garlic [into a bowl], and eat them salubriously, God Almighty willing.

III.7.2 Another Dish [of Browned Sparrows, Soured with Vinegar]

Take as many as you want of sparrows, clean and wash them, and put them in a new pot with water, salt, olive oil, black pepper, coriander seeds, a small amount of chopped onion, and fine-tasting *murrī* (liquid fermented sauce)—just the needed amount. Put the pot on the fire to cook.

When the pot liquid is reduced, leave it on low heat, and continue moving the sparrows around until [the liquid evaporates and] the sparrows brown. Ladle them into a glazed bowl (*ghaḍāra*), pour some preserved juice of unripe grapes (*khall al-ḥiṣrim*) or preserved lemon juice (*khall al-līm*) all over,[2] and eat them salubriously, God Almighty willing.

---

1 This chapter is missing from the Madrid MS.

2 See below, recipes X.7.12, 13, and 15, for directions on how to make them. Note that in the two surviving Andalusi cookbooks, this one and anonymous *Anwāʿ al-ṣaydala*, *khall* not only designates regular 'vinegar' produced by fermentation but also, in a looser sense, unfermented preserved 'sour juice,' and even freshly pressed out lemon juice. See glossary 8, s.v. *khall*.

 | DOI:10.1163/9789004469488_021

FIGURE 71
Sparrows, Anonymous, *Kitāb Naʿt al-ḥayawān*, fol. 22v, detail
BRITISH LIBRARY: ORIENTAL MANUSCRIPTS, OR 2784, IN QATAR DIGITAL LIBRARY HTTPS://WWW.QDL.QA/ARCHIVE/81055/VDC_100023556967.0X000001

III.7.3 Another Dish, Called *maḥshī*; Baked in the Brick Oven in a Pan (*ṭājin*)

Take as many sparrows as you want, clean them thoroughly, and cook them as was described in the second chapter of the third part of this book [recipe iii.2.43 above]. Use as many eggs as sparrows, God Almighty willing.[3]

III.7.4 Another Dish [of Grilled Sparrows]

Take fat sparrows, clean them, and skewer them on a stick. [Grill them and] baste them with the basting mix (*dihān*) mentioned in the fifth chapter of the third part of this book [recipe iii.5.8 above], God Almighty willing.

3 Whereas in the referenced recipe the chicken pieces are coated with a thick layer of eggs and fried, using as many as 30 eggs for each chicken, only 1 egg is used here per sparrow. The dish is going to be baked in the oven in a pan, casserole style: a layer of the beaten eggs is topped with a layer of the sparrows, which are then drenched in the rest of the eggs.

PART 4

القسم الرابع وهو ثلاثة فصول

في طبخ اللون المسمى بالصنهاجي والكرش المحشوة واللسان الصنهاجي

And It Has Three Chapters: On a Dish Called Ṣinhājī,[1] *Stuffed Tripe, and* Ṣinhājī *Tongue*

∴

1 It must have been the specialty of Ṣinhāj, one of the largest Amazigh tribes in North Africa.

Part Four, Chapter One: On Cooking a Dish Called *Ṣinhājī*[1]

(165v) Take a glazed earthenware pan (*ṭājin muzajjaj*)—the largest possible—and put in it the tastiest cuts of beef (*laḥm baqarī*), mutton (*laḥm ghanamī*), a suckling kid (*jadī raḍīʿ*), whatever is available of wild meat (*laḥm al-waḥsh*), hares (*arānib*)[2] and European wild ones (*qunilyāt*),[3] chickens (*dajāj*), geese (*iwazz*), partridges (*ḥajal*), squabs (*firākh ḥamām*), fat turtledoves (*yamām*), fat white starlings (*zarāzīr bīḍ*), and fat sparrows (*ʿaṣāfīr*).

Whatever needs to be cut, cut it into medium pieces, and leave whole the ones that do not need to be cut. Also add small sausages (*mirqās*), large sausages (*laqāniq*), thin meat patties (*aḥrash*), lemons and olives preserved in salt (*muṣayyar*), skinned almonds, soaked chickpeas, citron leaves (*waraq utrujj*), and sprigs of herb fennel (*ʿūd basbās*). Add water, salt, olive oil, black pepper, coriander seeds, chopped fresh cilantro, mint leaves, several cloves of garlic,[4] a chopped half of an onion, and a ladleful of *murrī* (liquid fermented sauce). Color the meats with saffron, and put the *ṭājin* on the fire to cook.

Next, take fine-tasting tender cabbages (*kurunb*), turnips (*lift*), eggplants (*bādhinjān*), fresh bulb fennel (*basbās*), and carrots (*jazar*) when in season.

---

1 The anonymous Andalusi cookbook *Anwāʿ al-ṣaydala* provides two recipes for this dish: one is said to be the commoners' *Ṣinhājī* (pp. 138–9), made more or less like this one. The recipe concludes by recommending it as a fit-for-all dish, regardless of the eaters' ages or humoral properties, which is attributed to the inclusion of all varieties of meat and vegetables, as well as vinegar, fermented sauce, spices, and the like added to it. The other one (p. 4) is called *Ṣinhājī mulūkī*, a royal dish enjoyed by the elite, made in a much simpler way with less varieties of meat and no vegetables.

It seems to me that a dish like *Ṣinhājī* could well have been the origin of the Spanish festive dish *olla podrida*, famously described by Cervantes in *Don Quixote*, part ii, chapter 20, at the wedding of Camacho. For a very interesting discussion of *olla podrida*, See Nadeau, "Spanish Culinary History of Cervantes' 'Bodas de Camacho.'"

2 Unlike the western region al-Maghrib, in the eastern region both the hare and the rabbit were called *arnab*. The former, however, was often more specifically described as *barrī* 'wild.' See Viré, "Hare," 97–100.

3 The name of this rabbit species is derived from the Spanish *Conejo* (*Oryctolagus cuniculus*). They are smaller than the hares. See glossary 10.

4 Garlic is missing from the Berlin MS but mentioned in the BL MS, fol. 165v, and the Madrid MS, fol. 90v.

 | DOI:10.1163/9789004469488_022

Remove all the unwanted parts, wash them, color them with saffron, and add them to the *ṭājin*. When all is cooked, add apples and quinces, which have been cut into pieces [after] they are cleaned of [their cores, seeds, and] peels.

Add fine-tasting vinegar to suit your taste, and let the *ṭājin* boil with the vinegar once or twice. Remove the pot from the fire and transfer it to a slow-burning fire until it loses some of its heat,[5] and eat it salubriously, God Almighty willing.

5 In the Madrid MS, fol. 90v, the pot is kept on low heat until it is time to serve it.

Part Four, Chapter Two: On Making Stuffed Tripe (*Karsh Maḥshuwwa*), Wonderful[1]

Take tripe (*karsh*) from a fat ram (*kabsh*), boil it in hot water, and scrape it with a knife until it looks white and clean. Leave it in one piece and do not split it open; just cut off the omasum.[2]

Take fine-tasting meat, pound it very well, and set it aside. Take a tender chicken and stuff it as was earlier mentioned in the second chapter of the third part.[3] Also take a couple of stuffed squabs [recipe ii.4.8], small sausages [recipe ii.6.4], meatballs [recipe ii.6.1], *isfiriyya* [recipe ii.6.3], and cooked [whole] egg yolks. [Set all these aside.]

Next, take meat from a young ram (*kabsh fatī*), such as its brisket (*ṣadr*) and rump (*dhanb*), cut it into medium pieces, and put them in a new pot. Add water, salt, olive oil, black pepper, coriander seeds, and a small amount of chopped onion. Put the pot on the fire to cook. (**166r**) Now take fresh and tender cabbages and clean them; take their inner leaves (*qulūb ukrunb*) and add them to the [cooking] meat pot. Add tender leaves of chard (*ʿuyūn silq*) as well.[4]

Now take the [stuffed] chicken and squabs and put them in [another] pot. Add water, salt, olive oil, black pepper, coriander seeds, and a small amount of pounded onion. Put the pot on the fire to cook.

Next, take a small pot and put the sausages and meatballs in it with the addition of a small amount of water and olive oil. Put this pot on the fire to cook and leave it there until the water evaporates, and gently fry [the sausages and meatballs] in the remaining oil. Remove the pot from the fire.

Have a look at the meat pot. If the meat is cooked, add juice of fresh cilantro, and remove it from the fire. Do likewise with the pot of chicken and squabs.

Next, take the set-aside pounded meat, mentioned earlier, and mix it with salt, black pepper, Ceylon cinnamon, ginger, a bit of mastic, spikenard, and cloves, which have been blended in a small amount of water before adding

1 *ʿAjība*, addition from the Madrid MS, fol. 90r.

2 It is called *rummāna* here, literally 'pomegranate'; and *qubā* in recipe ii.6.8 above. It is the third compartment of the ruminant stomach, which looks like a ball.

3 There are many recipes for stuffed chicken, see, for instance, recipes iii.2.21 and iii.2.39 above.

4 Th addition of chard at this point is mentioned in the Madrid MS, fol. 90r, only. The recipe will later mention the chard.

 | DOI:10.1163/9789004469488_023

them to the meat. Take 10 eggs and a small amount of grated breadcrumbs (*futāta maḥkūka*) and knead them with the meat and spices.

Take the tripe and stuff it with [a layer of] some of the meat-egg mix, followed by [half] the meat cooked with cabbages and chard. Then add 1 squab, followed by the chicken, and then the other squab, followed by the [rest of the] meat and vegetables. [Scatter on them] a good amount of skinned almonds and pine nuts (*ḥabb ṣanawbar*). Next, add the egg yolks, sausages, meatballs, and *isfīriyya* after frying it.[5] These you scatter in between all the layers of the stuffing. Now take what remains of the [meat-egg] stuffing, mix it with some of the strained broth of the meat and the chicken and squabs, and add it to the tripe.

Tie the tripe with a strong thread, put it in a large pan (*ṭājin*), and add the remaining broth and water, enough to submerge it. Put it on the fire to cook, and when it is done, take it out of the pan and pour off the broth [into a vessel]. Wash the pan and return only the fat (*wadak*) of the broth to it. Put the [cooked] tripe back in it and send it to the *furn* (communal brick oven) to brown. Add a small amount of *murrī naqīʿ* (sun-fermented liquid sauce) to it [before sending it to the oven]. Take it out when it browns and put it in a glazed bowl (*ghaḍāra*). Split it open [with a knife], sprinkle it with Ceylon cinnamon, and eat it salubriously, God Almighty willing.

5 The name also occurs as *isfāriyya* and *isfiryā* in al-Tujībī's recipes, see glossary 5. *Isfīriyya* was usually cut into strips after frying it.

Part Four, Chapter Three: On Making [*Ṣinhājī*] Tongue[1]

Take meat from a ram's thighs and loin (middle back, *sinsin*) and beat it on a board with an iron rod (*qaḍīb ḥadīd*). Discard the veins and sinews (*ʿurūq*), and then pound it well in a mortar (*mihrās*). (**166v**) Add salt to it, as well as black pepper, coriander seeds, juices of fresh cilantro and mint, a small amount of onion juice, and a bit of fine-tasting *murrī* (liquid fermented sauce). Beat them all until they combine, then break in a couple of eggs on them, and mix them very well.

Now take caul fat (*minsaj*)[2] and spread it on a board. Take the pounded meat, place it on the caul fat and roll it around it, shaping it into a rectangle (*mustaṭīl*),[3] and then place it on a sieve to dry. [To cook it,] take a skewer and pass it though the meat; grill it as I mentioned earlier to you.[4] Let it grill and brown and then take it off the skewer, and eat it salubriously, God Almighty willing.

1 The recipe is for making a mock tongue. A mixture of pounded meat is flattened into a rectangle to mimic the tongue's shape. The dish was described as *Ṣinhājī* in the main heading to this part. It must have been the specialty of Ṣinhāj, one of the largest Amazigh tribes that played an important role in the history of North Africa and the Sahara.

2 The Madrid MS, fol. 92r, explains it as fat inside the ram's belly. See glossary 10.

3 This is done to make it look like a tongue.

4 The Madrid MS, fol. 92r, mentions that the skewer is suspended at a distance from the fire, as was described in the grilling recipes. See, for instance, the first part of recipe iii.2.44 above.

 | DOI:10.1163/9789004469488_024

PART 5

القسم الخامس

في أنواع الحيتان وضروب البيض ويشتمل على فصلين إثنين

On Varieties of Dishes with Fish and Eggs, and It Has Two Chapters

CHAPTER V.1

Part Five, Chapter One: On [Dishes with] Various Types of Fish

Know that all kinds of fish, especially the large ones, must be scaled, [lightly] boiled in water,[1] and then taken out and washed and left to drain. After this, they can be fully cooked, with the help of God Almighty.[2]

V.1.1 A Dish [of Braised Fish]

Take large fish like *shūlī* (sturgeon), *shābil* (allis shad), *mannānī* (grouper), *kammūn*,[3] and large *būrī* (flathead grey mullet).[4] Clean them from the outside by scaling them and open their bellies and clean and wash them. Boil them [lightly] in water and then cut them into medium pieces.

Now take a glazed earthenware pan (*ṭājin fakhkhār muzajjaj*) and add plenty of olive oil to it, along with vinegar, *murrī* (liquid fermented sauce), and a few cloves of garlic. Then, take a wide, shallow bowl (*ṣaḥfa*) and put black pepper, coriander seeds, a bit of cumin, pounded saffron, and a bit of mastic in it. Dissolve and mix them all with the addition of a small amount of water and add them to the *ṭājin*.

Take the fish pieces one after the other, roll them in the *ṭājin*'s marinade,[5] and let them be saturated in it to absorb the flavors of the spices and the other

---

1 As we understand from the below recipes, v.1.9, 12, and 15, with the instruction to give fish *salqa khafīfa* 'a light boil,' the fish is not meant to fully cook in this preparatory step.

2 I slightly amended this opening statement using the Madrid MS, fol. 92r, and the corresponding passage in the anonymous *Anwāʿ al-ṣaydala* 149.

3 I failed to find any reference to this fish, كمون . The Madrid MS does not mention it. The name might have been a modified form or a copyist's misreading of القبطون, which is a large fish mentioned only in the anonymous *Anwāʿ al-ṣaydala* 150 and 154. In Corriente, *Dictionary of Andalusi Arabic*, s.v. *q-b-ṭ*, it is said to perhaps be a gilthead bream. It was not unusual to turn *q* to *t*, and *ṭ* to *t*, resulting in الكبتون for instance.

4 النوري الجبليل, as it occurs in the BL MS, fol. 166v, and the Berlin MS, fol. 63r, is clearly a copyist's misreading of البوري الجليل. In the Madrid MS, fol. 92r, it correctly occurs as البوري الكبير.

5 The expression used in the BL MS, fol. 166v, and the Berlin MS, fol. 63r, is تمرقها بالمرقة, *tamruqihā bi-l-marqa*, literally 'soak them in the liquid.' Cf. the Madrid MS, fol. 92v, where the expression is تمرغها, *tumarrighuhā*, which suggests rolling the pieces to soak and saturate them.

 | DOI:10.1163/9789004469488_025

FIGURE 72 Fishing by net, al-Qazwīnī, *ʿAjāʾib al-makhlūqāt wa gharāʾib al-mawjūdāt*, fol. 125v, detail FROM THE NEW YORK PUBLIC LIBRARY, SPENCER COLLECTION: HTTPS://DIGITALCOLLECTIONS.NYPL.ORG/ITEMS/BF251690-28EB-0138-5426-7FFB54E3F087

ingredients. When all the pieces are finished, spread them in the *ṭājin* in one layer, pour in a small amount of water, and put it on the fire to cook.

When the cooking is done, take it to the *furn* (communal brick oven) to brown the top. [Alternatively,] if you want to do this at home [on the stove], take an unglazed earthenware pan (*ṭājin turāb dūn muzajjaj*) and place it on (**167r**) top of the *ṭājin* that has the fish in it. Put strongly burning fire in it—strong enough to reach the fish pieces to brown them and evaporate the liquids in the pan. Once the dish is cooked, remove the pan from the fire, let it cool, and eat it salubriously, God Almighty willing.

You can also make it with juice of fresh cilantro, in which case use all the ingredients mentioned except for vinegar and *murrī*. It is at its best when eaten cold. *Jarrāfa* fish (gilthead bream)[6] is cooked similarly, with the addition of walnuts, either pounded or left whole.[7]

V.1.2 Another Dish [of Braised Fish, Cooked] with *jarrāfa* (Gilthead Bream) and *būrī* (Flathead Grey Mullet)

Take whichever is available of these fish, clean them from the outside and the inside, wash them thoroughly after [lightly] boiling them in water, and then cut them into medium pieces. Put them in a glazed earthenware pan (*ṭājin muzajjaj*) and add salt to them with plenty of olive oil, black pepper, coriander seeds,

6 As suggested in Corriente, *Dictionary of Andalusi Arabic*, s.v. *j-r-f*.
7 I amended the edited text slightly here using the Madrid MS, fol. 92r.

a bit of cumin, a lump of mastic, a small amount of *murrī naqīʿ* (sun-fermented liquid sauce), a small amount of water, and citron leaves. Add some pounded saffron and roll the fish pieces in the spice mix to saturate them with its flavors and color. [Put it on the fire to cook.]

Next, take onions, clean them, cut them into medium pieces, and then put them in a pot with a small amount of water. Put the pot on the fire, and once the onions cook, take them out and add them to the *ṭājin* after you color them with saffron. [Reserve the remaining boiling liquid.]

Check on the liquid in the *ṭājin*. If only a small amount of it remains while the fish is still not cooked yet, add some of the boiling onion liquid. Once the fish cooks, add some honey or cooked grape syrup (*rubb ʿinab maṭbūkh*)[8] and take it to the *furn* (communal brick oven) to brown. If you want to do the browning at home [on the stove], do as described in the above recipe. Allow the *ṭājin* to cool, and eat the dish salubriously, God Almighty willing.

V.1.3 Another Dish, Called *murawwaj* (Quick and Easy)[9]

Take whatever is available of fish, be they big or small, scaleless (*muls*) or with scales (*ḥarish*); scrape them from the outside and open their cavities and clean them. After [lightly] boiling them in water, wash them, cut them into small pieces, salt them, and set them aside.

Take a pan (*ṭājin*) and add vinegar, *murrī* (liquid fermented sauce),[10] a good amount of olive oil, black pepper, coriander seeds, a bit of cumin, a few cloves of garlic, and a bit of thyme (*ṣaʿtar*). Put the pan on the fire and add the fish pieces once it starts to boil vigorously. Cover the pan with a wide, shallow bowl (*ṣaḥfa*) and let the fish cook until done, which will go fast.[11] Take the pan from the fire, and eat the dish salubriously, God Almighty willing.

---

8 It is grape juice cooked down to a syrup consistency, with no sugar added. See glossary 4.

9 In the eastern region, the term commonly used for similar fast-cooked dishes was *mulahwaj*; see, for instance, al-Warrāq, *Kitāb al-Ṭabīkh*, English trans., *Annals*, chapter 75. See Ibn Manẓūr, *Lisān al-ʿArab*, s.v. روج and لهج. Another *murawwaj* recipe is found in the anonymous Andalusi *Anwāʿ al-ṣaydala* 152–3, which differs stylistically and in some details from al-Tujībī's and is said to be the way fish was cooked in Sabta 'Ceuta' and western al-Andalus.

10 According to the corresponding Andalusi recipe mentioned in the above note, for two parts of vinegar, less than a part of *murrī* is used.

11 The expression used is ويكون ذلك مسرعا *wa yakūnu dhālika musraʿan*, which is a key description of the way this dish is meant to cook.

This dish may also be made with small sardines (*sardīn*) and anchovies (*shuṭūn*),[12] in which case they should be cooked with juice of fresh cilantro, some skinned cloves of garlic, and a small (**167v**) amount of vinegar, so know this.

V.1.4 Another Dish [of Fish Patties and Balls]

Take whatever kind you find of large thick-fleshed fish (*ḥītān ghalīẓa*), scale them, [lightly] boil them in water, and then skin them. Take the meat, remove the bones and spines (*shawk*), and pound it in a mortar (*mihrās*), discarding any sinewy particles.[13]

After thoroughly grinding the meat, put it in a wide, shallow bowl (*ṣaḥfa*) and add salt, black pepper, Ceylon cinnamon, ginger, a pounded lump of mastic, a bit of cumin, saffron, coriander seeds, a small amount of onion juice, garlic, mint juice, *murrī naqīʿ* (sun-fermented liquid sauce), and olive oil. Knead the mix very well.[14]

Now take a clean skillet (*miqlāt*) and put olive oil in it. Once it heats up, [start] shaping the pounded meat into large and small patties (*quraṣ*) and balls (*banādiq*). Put them in the pan to fry, turning them gently to brown on all sides. Once done, take them out, and put some more of them in to fry; continue until they are all done.

If you want to add egg whites and very fine wheat flour (*ghubār al-darmak*) to the ground [fish] and mix them with it, you may go ahead and do so. Also, when you put them [i.e., the fried patties and balls] in a glazed bowl (*ghaḍāra*),[15] you may put lemon juice (*māʾ līm*) or *murrī naqīʿ* (sun-fermented liquid sauce). Or[16] use sauce (*marqa*) made with vinegar, lots of olive oil, *murrī naqīʿ*, and pounded garlic—all boiled in a glazed earthenware pan (*ṭājin fakhkhār muzajjaj*). Choose whichever you want, and eat the dish salubriously, God Almighty willing.

---

12 A regional fish name for what was known as *balam* or *absāriyya* in Egypt. See glossary 10.

13 The word used is *ʿurūq*, which specifically designates veins but may generally include sinews as well. They are all elastic in nature and do not grind well.

14 The scribe of the Berlin MS, fol. 64r, adds the following suggestion: "If you want to add egg whites and very fine wheat flour (*ghubār al-darmak*) to the ground [fish] and mix them with it, you may go ahead and do so;" in the BL MS, fol. 167v, it is later added in the options given at the end of the recipe. The edited Arabic text overlooks mentioning it.

15 The Berlin MS, fol. 64r, misreads حين 'when,' as it is clearly copied in the BL MS, fol. 167v, as جبن 'cheese.'

16 The editor of the Arabic text inaccurately reads it as و 'and.'

V.1.5 Another Dish [of Grilled Fish]

Take whatever is available of any kind of large thick-fleshed fish (*ḥītān ghalīẓa*), scale them, clean their cavities, and [lightly] boil them in water. Cut them into medium pieces, salt them, and set them aside.

Now take a vessel and put dissolved salt in it, along with *murrī* (liquid fermented sauce), olive oil, black pepper, Ceylon cinnamon, pounded garlic, and ginger. Put a washed feather in the vessel [and set it aside].

Take the fish pieces, thread them on an iron skewer, and set it on the fire, which has been placed on both sides of the skewer [but not directly underneath it]. Rest both ends of the skewer on rocks to raise it above the ground, [constantly] rotating it by hand and basting the fish all the while with the feather.[17] Continue doing this until the fish cooks and browns.

Take a glazed bowl (*ghaḍāra*) and put olive oil in it with pounded cooked garlic. Take the fish pieces off the skewer, cut them into small pieces, mix them with the olive oil and garlic, and eat the dish salubriously, God Almighty willing.

If you want to, grill small fish directly on coals as is done with *sardīn* (sardines), which appear in May (Māya) or October (Uktūbar), or *jarkam*,[18] which appear in September (Shatanbar), or any other kinds of fatty fish at the beginning of their season. After lighting the fire, spread it, and let all its flames and smoke dissipate. Sprinkle the fish with salt if they have not been salted, spread them on the fire, and turn them until they cook and brown. You can dip them in garlic and olive oil [sauce, mentioned above,] or have them just by themselves; (**168r**) do whatever you like, and eat them salubriously.

If you want to bake *shābil* (*shad*) and the like, take a new large and flat tile (*qirmida*), spread it with a layer of salt, put the fish on it, coat them with salt, and enter the brick into the *furn* (brick oven). When you see that the salt has solidified or is about to turn brown, take the tile out and remove the salt. You should have ready a wide, shallow bowl (*ṣaḥfa*) with salt, black pepper, ginger, Ceylon cinnamon, and other similar spices. Also have ready: a bowl with olive oil and [pounded cooked] garlic; a bowl with *murrī naqīʿ* (sun-fermented liquid sauce); and a bowl with *shalsha*, made as described earlier in the fifth chapter of the second part of this book.[19]

---

17 See above, recipe iii.5.8, where turtledoves are grilled similarly. In the eastern region, meat grilled this way was called *kardanāj*. See glossary 5.

18 I have failed to find references to this fish other than here, where it is clearly described as a small fatty variety of fish. Even in Corriente, *Dictionary of Andalusi Arabic*, s.v. *j-r-k-m*, the description is based on this text.

19 This is a reference to a dipping sauce in the above recipe ii.5.7e, made by combining juices

Also, if you want to bake and brown sardines or any other small varieties in the *furn* (brick oven), put them in an earthenware plate (*malla fakhkhār*) and let them bake and brown. [When done,] take the *malla* out and serve the fish however you like, with the help of God Almighty.

V.1.6 Another Dish [of Sardines Baked with Vegetables]

Take small sardines, clean and wash them, and then salt them. Take fresh cilantro, mint, fresh bulb fennel (*basbās*), and onion; chop these vegetables as fine as possible, and rinse them. Spread a layer of these vegetables in the bottom of a pan (*ṭājin*), followed by a layer of sardines, another one of vegetables, and another of sardines. Do this until the *ṭājin* is full. Sprinkle it with Ceylon cinnamon, ginger, and a bit of mastic. Take the *ṭājin* to the *furn* (communal brick oven) to cook and brown, and then take it out and serve it, God Almighty willing.

V.1.7 Another Dish [with Scaleless Fishes]

Take whatever is available of *sarda* (Atlantic bonito), *ṭardanas* (plaice),[20] and the like and clean and skin them. Take the meat—but leave the spines intact—and pound it very well. Add breadcrumbs and salt if the fish has not been salted. Also add black pepper, ginger, Ceylon cinnamon, spikenard, cloves, mastic—but not much—pounded saffron, coriander seeds, a bit of cumin, and eggs—not too many, add just enough to combine the meat.

Spread the meat mix on the spines to shape them as fish, as they were before, and arrange them in a pan (*ṭājin*) one next to the other. Take the remaining

---

of cilantro and Macedonian parsley, pounded cooked garlic, lots of black pepper, and vinegar. In that recipe, it is given the generic name *marqa* 'sauce.' In recipe ii.1.9 above, it is more specifically referred to as *jalja*, called *shalsha* here.

20 The fish names are السردة والطردنس, as clearly copied in the Madrid MS, fol. 94r; erroneously copied as السرذة الظرذانس in the Berlin and BL MSS, fols. 64v and 168r, respectively, and the edited Arabic text.

Ṭardanas is mentioned in other sources: 1) In the anonymous Andalusi *Anwāʿ al-ṣaydala* 151, a recipe describes *ṭardanas* as a good variety of fish (*ḥūt maḥmūd*); 2) In Ibn al-Zayyāt, *al-Tashawwuf ilā rijāl al-taṣawwuf* 160, *ṭardanas* is praised as high-quality fish. The identification of the fish as plaice is based on the French *tardineau* given in 1926 dictionary on fishing by H. de la Blanchère, cited by the editor of Ibn al-Zayyāt, *al-Tashawwif* 160, n. 284. The recipe itself describes it as scaleless fish (*ḥūt amlas*).

meat and make meatballs with some of it, adding skinned almonds and pine nuts. Add juice of fresh cilantro to the rest of the meat to thin it down[21] and put it in between the fish [along with the meatballs]. Pour in plenty of olive oil and put the pan in the *furn* (brick oven) to cook and brown [until all moisture evaporates and] only the olive oil remains.[22] Take it out and serve it, God Almighty willing.

If you want to bake this type of scaleless fish (*ḥūt amlas*) in a pan (*ṭājin*), then take the fish, cut them open from the back, take out their spines, (**168v**) and discard their heads, but leave the rest whole, do not cut them into pieces; and wash them.

Put a small amount of water in a *ṭājin* along with olive oil, black pepper, coriander seeds, cumin, [dried] crumbled thyme (*ṣaʿtar maḥkūk*), garlic—some left whole and some pounded—saffron, *murrī* (liquid fermented sauce), and vinegar [to make a sauce with them]. Put the fish in this sauce (*marqa*) and turn them so that they are all coated with it. The fish will be baked in this same *ṭājin*. Pour plenty of olive oil all over them and put the *ṭājin* in the *furn* (brick oven). Place it at a distance from the fire until it cooks and browns and all the moisture evaporates. Take it out, set it aside to slightly cool, and eat it salubriously, God Almighty willing.

V.1.8 Another Dish, Fried (*maqlī*)

Take any kind of fish—large or small, with scales or scaleless—clean and wash it, and then [lightly] boil it in already boiling water (*māʾ maghlī*). Wash it, cut the large ones among them into pieces, and leave the small ones whole. Salt them, if they have not been salted, and leave them on a sieve (*ghirbāl*) to drain.[23]

Now take a clean skillet and add olive oil—the amount depends on how fatty or lean the fish is. Once the oil boils, put the fish pieces in it and let them fry, gently turning them over. If you see that the flesh of the fish has started to split, dust the pieces with flour first and then put them in the pan to fry. In addition, if the fish is big, split the pieces to extract the spine and then fry them. The fire

21 تخفف 'thin down,' as it is copied in the BL MS, fol. 168r, and the Madrid MS, fol. 94r; erroneously copied as تحبب (?) in the Berlin MS, fol. 64v.

22 The expression used is يجف الزيت, literally 'the olive oil dries.'

23 The editor of the Arabic text inadvertently left out the word تترك 'leave it,' which obscures the sense of the sentence.

has to be moderate. When the pieces have fried and browned, take them out and put them in a glazed bowl (*ghaḍāra*).

[**Preparing dipping sauces for fried fish:**]

If the [fried pieces are of] fish that has scales (*ḥūt aḥrash*), take an earthenware pan (*ṭājin fakhkhār*), put pounded garlic in it, and let it cook [with some water]. Add vinegar, bring the pan to a boil, and then pour [this sauce] all over fish in the glazed bowl.

Alternatively, you may take the tender tips of sprigs of the variety of parsley (*karafs*) called *maqdūnis* (Macedonian parsley), as well as those of mint (*naʿnaʿ*) and cultivated rue (*fayjan*).[24] Pound them all with garlic, put them in a pan (*ṭājin*) with vinegar, and let them boil on the fire. Pour this sauce (*marqa*) all over the fish pieces, set them aside so that they may cool and absorb [the sauce flavors], and then eat the dish salubriously, God Almighty willing.

If the [fried pieces are of] scaleless fish (*ḥūt amlas*), boil pounded garlic with olive oil and water in a skillet and let them cook until all the water evaporates. Pour the [remaining] garlic and olive oil all over the fish.

If the fish used is of the kind called *mull* (red mullet),[25] then add coarsely pounded walnuts to the vinegar-garlic sauce [given above].

V.1.9 A Dish of Large Fish [Braised in the Oven]

Take whatever is available of this fish, scale and clean it, and boil it lightly. Cut it into pieces, sprinkle them with lots of salt, and set them aside for an hour, after which you wash them with boiling water thoroughly and leave them [on a sieve] to drain all the moisture.

Now take large onions, pound them in a wooden mortar, and press out the juice by means of a piece of cloth. Put the resulting juice in a glazed earthenware pan (*ṭājin muzajjaj*)—put enough to submerge the fish pieces.[26] Add *murrī naqīʿ* (sun-fermented liquid sauce) to it, (**169r**) along with lots of olive oil, black pepper, ginger, coriander seeds, cumin, saffron, a small amount of vinegar, some mastic (*maṣṭakā*), spikenard, Ceylon cinnamon, black cardamom (*qāqulla*), galangal (*khūlanjān*), and thyme (*ṣaʿtar*). Arrange the fish pieces in

---

24 The edited text misreads the و 'and' as it occurs in the MSS, as أو 'or.' *Fayjan* was the herb's name in the Muslim West; it was called *sadhāb bustānī* in the eastern region.

25 المل (*Mullus barbatus*). According to Ibn al-Bayṭār, *al-Jāmiʿ* iii 137, *mull* is the indigenous Andalusi name ('Ajamiyyat al-Andalus) for what is otherwise called *ṭarastūj*/*tarastūj*.

26 The editor of the Arabic text neglected to add the word حوت 'fish,' as it is clearly copied in the MSS.

this sauce (*marqa*) after rolling them in it first [to coat them completely with it]. Put the *ṭājin* in the *furn* (brick oven) and leave it there [to cook] until the fish browns, all the liquid evaporates, and nothing remains but oil. Take it out and serve it.

v.1.10 Another Dish, Called *rāhibī* (Monks' Food), Wonderful[27]

Take a fresh fish (*ḥūt ṭarī*), scale it, sprinkle it with salt, and let it stay weighed down with stones overnight. Wash it and boil it until it looks white, and then wash it in cold water and let it boil in a pan (*ṭājin*) with the addition of lots of olive oil—for each *raṭl* (1 pound) of fish use 4 *ūqiyyas* (½ cup) oil. Add *murrī naqīʿ* (sun-fermented liquid sauce), thyme, sprigs of herb fennel (*ʿīdān basbās*), citron leaves, black pepper, saffron, spikenard, ginger, and a bit of mastic as well. Also add enough chopped onion after boiling it in salted water—for each *raṭl* of fish use ⅓ *raṭl* onion. Put the *ṭājin* in the oven and keep it there until the liquids evaporate and the fish browns on top. Take it out and serve it.

Another Dish, Cooked as [White] *tafāyā* Made with Large Fish Varieties[28]

[Lightly] boil a big fish after cleaning and scaling it and then cut it into pieces. Wash them and put them in a pot with salt, plenty of olive oil, spices (*abzār*), galangal (*khūlanjān*), a bit of mastic, and juice of a pounded onion. Pound shelled almonds, walnuts, and pine nuts to a marrow consistency (*mukhkh*); dissolve them in water and pour the solution all over the fish pieces. Also add the tender tips of fresh herb fennel (*ʿuyūn al-basbās*). Meatballs are essential in this dish; make them with fish meat the same way they are made with mutton [as in recipe ii.6.1] and let the pot cook in the *furn* (brick oven). That is it (*intahā*).

---

27 *ʿAjīb*, as described in the Madrid MS, fol. 95r. Cf. another *rāhibī* dish, cooked with beef, recipe ii.1.7 above.

28 This recipe is given only in the Madrid MS, fol. 95v. It is for the white variety of *tafāyā* stew; cf. recipes ii.2.1–2 above, where it is cooked with mutton. The following recipe (v.1.11), which is called white *tafāyā* in the BL MS, fol. 169r, and the Berlin MS, fol. 65v, is in fact a recipe for green *tafāyā*. I changed its name to green *tafāyā* following the Madrid MS, fol. 95v.

V.1.11 A Dish of Green *tafāyā*[29]

Take a large fish, scale it, wash it, and then cut it into pieces and [lightly] boil them in salted water, as was done in the previous recipes. Put the fish pieces in a pan (*ṭājin*) and submerge them in juices of fresh mint and cilantro, as well as lots of olive oil, a small amount of juice extracted from a pounded onion, black pepper, coriander seeds, ginger, salt, a bit of mastic, and the tender parts of fresh bulb fennel (*ʿuyūn basbās*). Put the pan in the *furn* (brick oven) until it cooks and browns and the liquids evaporate, and take it out and serve it.

V.1.12 Another Dish, Called *basbāsiyya* (Cooked with the Juice of Fresh Bulb Fennel), Wonderful[30]

Take a large fish, scale it and wash it, and then cut it into pieces, which you then boil lightly in salted water. Take them out and put them in a pan (*ṭājin*). Pound fresh bulb fennel (*basbās akhḍar*) and press out its juice all over the fish—let there be enough to submerge the fish. Also add plenty of olive oil, black pepper, coriander seeds, ginger, salt, juice of an onion, and a bit of mastic. Put the pan in the *furn* (brick oven) until it browns on top and the liquids evaporate. Take it out and serve it.

V.1.13 Another Dish, Cooked as *jumlī*[31]

(169v) Take large fish, scale them, and keep them salted and weighed down [with stones] overnight. Wash them, [lightly] boil them in salted water, and then wash and drain them and arrange them in a pan (*ṭājin*). Pour 2 ladlefuls of vinegar and 1 ladleful of *murrī naqīʿ* (sun-fermented liquid sauce) all over them, adding black pepper, saffron, ginger, cumin, mastic, celery seeds (*bazr karafs*), citron leaves, bay leaves (*waraq rand*), sprigs of herb fennel (*ʿīdān basbās*), thyme, garlic, and lots of olive oil. Put the pan in the *furn* (brick oven) until the liquids evaporate and take it out as soon as it browns on top.

---

29 See the note above.

30 As described in the Madrid MS, fol. 95v.

31 It is a succulent dish seasoned with *murrī* (liquid fermented sauce) and vinegar. Cf. recipe ii.1.1 above, where the dish is cooked with beef.

V.1.14 Another Dish [of Baked Fish]

Take large fish, scale them, and do with them as explained above. Arrange them in a pan (*ṭājin*) and add enough vinegar and *murrī naqīʿ* (sun-fermented liquid sauce). Also add garlic cloves, which have been inserted in [dried] sprigs of thyme, and lots of olive oil, along with saffron, citron leaves, split [skinned] almonds, black pepper, coriander seeds, a bit of salt if needed, a bit of mastic, spikenard, and black cardamom (*qāqulla*). Put the pan in the *furn* (brick oven) until the liquids evaporate and it browns on top, and serve it.

V.1.15 Another Dish [of Baked Slices of Fish]

Take fine-tasting varieties of fish, scale them, and cut them into pieces if they are big, or slice them into strips (*yusharraḥ*). Sprinkle them with salt, boil them lightly, and then wash them. Put them in a pan (*ṭājin*) after giving them a rub with a mix of saffron and salt to color them.[32] Pour plenty of olive oil on them and submerge them in fresh juices of cilantro and mint. Throw in some of the tips of their sprigs as well. Also add black pepper, coriander seeds, ginger, Ceylon cinnamon, and a bit of mastic. Put the *ṭājin* in the brick oven [to cook] until all the moisture evaporates and the top browns, and serve it, God Almighty willing.

V.1.16 Another Dish [of Formed Sardines][33]

Take sardines or any similar fish, scale them, and then clean them and [lightly] boil them in salted water. Put them in a wide, shallow bowl (*ṣaḥfa*), remove their spines, and collect their meat only, which you then finely pound the way you do when making meatballs (*banādiq*). Add black pepper to it, along with coriander seeds, Ceylon cinnamon, ginger, and spikenard. Squeeze juices of fresh cilantro and mint on it and sprinkle it with fine white flour (*daqīq darmak*). Beat all the ingredients [to bind them] and then form (*yunashsha*ʾ) the mix into sardines to make them look as they initially were, or any preferred shape.

---

32 The editor of the Arabic text erroneously read the word حتى ينصبغ 'to color them' in the MSS as حتى ينضج 'to cook them,' which obscures the text.

33 A comparable recipe in the anonymous Andalusi *Anwāʿ al-ṣaydala* 152 is called *al-munashshā* 'formed/shaped.' The verb *yunashsha*ʾ is used within the recipe itself. Both words are derived from the Arabic root نشا 'shape/form.'

Dust the pieces with flour and fry them in olive oil in a skillet (*miqlāt*) until they cook. Prepare for them a sauce (*marqa*) made with vinegar, olive oil, and pounded garlic. Boil these ingredients in an earthenware pan (*ṭājin fakhkhār*) and pour it all over the fish, and serve.

V.1.17 Another Dish, Cooked as *maḥshī* (Stuffed)[34]

Choose fine-tasting varieties of fish, scale them, and [lightly] boil them in salted water after cutting them into pieces. (203r) If the fish is large, split it in half lengthwise [first and then cut it into pieces]. Discard the spines and bones and then fry the pieces in olive oil in a skillet (*miqlāt*) until they brown.

Take a pan (*ṭājin*), break some eggs in it, and add crumbs of grated bread (*fatāt khubz maḥkūk*), black pepper, saffron, Ceylon cinnamon, spikenard, ginger, coriander seeds, plenty of olive oil, and a small amount of *murrī naqīʿ* (sun-fermented liquid sauce). Sprinkle split skinned almonds on them and beat them all [to combine].

Bury (*tadfun*) the prepared fish pieces in the egg mix. Put the pan in the *furn* (brick oven) and keep it there until the dish sets and browns on top. Take it out and serve it. It is splendid (*ʿajīb*).

V.1.18 Another Dish, Called *mughaffar* (Coated)[35]

Take whatever is available of fine-tasting varieties of fish, scale them, and then [lightly] boil them in salted water.[36] Cut them lengthwise into long slices and remove all the bones.

In a large, wide earthenware tub (*jafna*), beat eggs with very fine white flour (*ghubār darmak*)[37] or crumbs of grated bread, along with black pepper, Ceylon

---

34 It is a dish of fish pieces stuffed/buried in eggs. The edited Arabic text here erroneously includes the word *jumlī* in the name of the dish. In the Berlin MS, which the editor follows, the word *jumlī* is clearly crossed out and replaced with *maḥshī*. It is correctly copied in the BL MS, fol. 169v, and the Madrid MS, fol. 96v.

35 See recipes ii.5.4 and iii.2.8 above for preparing the dish with other meats; and recipe vii.2.15 below, prepared with eggplants. In this recipe, slices of fish are coated with a seasoned mix of eggs and breadcrumbs and then fried.

36 I followed here the Madrid MS, fol. 97r, where the fish is said to be boiled يصلق, as is done in the rest of the fish recipes, and not washed يغسل, as copied in the other two MSS.

37 See glossary 2 for more on this super fine flour.

cinnamon, ginger, saffron, coriander seeds, and *murrī naqīʿ* (sun-fermented liquid sauce). Dip the fish pieces in the egg mix and fry them in olive oil in a skillet (*miqlāt*) until they brown.

Make sauce (*marqa*) for them by mixing vinegar, *murrī*, and olive oil. Boil them first and then pour them all over the fish, and serve.

If you want to cook the fish as *burāniyya* or *muthallath*, you can do so by preparing them as you do with red meat.[38] In this case, however, they must be cooked in the *furn* (brick oven) in earthenware pans (*ṭawājin*, sg. *ṭājin*), as is done in the previous [fish recipes], God Almighty willing.

V.1.19 Another Dish [of Boiled Fish, with Sauce]

Take any kind of large thick-fleshed fish (*ḥūt ghalīẓ*), clean it, wash it, and cut it into large pieces. Take a large pot with water; add salt if the fish has not already been salted. Put it on the fire and add the fish pieces once the water starts to boil vigorously. Keep watching the fish; if you see that it has turned white and meat is about to split, take the pieces out and put them in a glazed bowl (*ghaḍāra*). Prepare whatever you like of sauce (*marqa*) for the fish, using any spices you like, and eat it salubriously, God Almighty willing.

V.1.20 Another Dish [of Fried Stuffed Fish]

Take fish of the kind known as *kaḥla* (red sea bream),[39] clean it inside and outside, wash it, and then gently pull off the skin, starting with the head and leaving it attached to the tail. Take away its meat and discard the backbone.

Now take the meat, pound it very well, and mix it with salt, black pepper, coriander seeds, cumin, Ceylon cinnamon, ginger, spikenard, cloves, a bit of mastic, and egg whites. Stuff the skin with the meat mix and put it put back the way it was. Fry it in olive oil in a skillet (*miqlāt*) until (**203v**) it cooks and browns. [While frying,] turn over the fish gently so that the skin does not break. Put it in a glazed bowl (*ghaḍāra*), and eat it salubriously, God Almighty willing.

---

38 See recipes ii.1.2–3 above.

39 Copied as *kaḥlāʾ* in the Madrid MS, fol. 97r; also known in English as blackspot seabream, *Pagellus bogaraveo*. In Ghālib, *Mawsūʿa*, its other name is given as *jarbīdī*.

V.1.21 Another Dish [of Fried Fish with Stuffing][40]

Take a fish (*samaka*), clean and wash it, and then salt it and set it aside. Take the meat of another fish after you clean it and remove its bones and pound it very well in a mortar (*mihrās*). Add vinegar to it, along with *murrī* (liquid fermented sauce), coriander seeds, Ceylon cinnamon, juice of an onion, breadcrumbs, and broken eggs. Gently blend the ingredients [to make the stuffing]. Put a skillet with olive oil in it on the fire and put the stuffing (*ḥashū*) in it. Stir it and fold it until it cooks.

Now take the [set aside] whole fish and fry it in the pan until it browns. If the fish is large, cut it into pieces to make frying it easier. Put the fish in a shallow, wide bowl (*ṣaḥfa*), top it with the stuffing, and serve it, God Almighty willing.

V.1.22 Another Dish [of Fish with Stuffing, Simmered in a Pot]

Take a fish (*samaka*), clean it, scale it, and then salt it [and set it aside]. Take skinned almonds, pine nuts, and the meat of another fish, which has been pounded [in a mortar], along with pounded garlic,[41] breadcrumbs, olive oil, cooked egg yolks (*fuṣūṣ bayḍ*), and salt; mix them all.[42] Now, spread the mix in a pot and place the [set-aside] fish in it.[43] Put the pot on low heat to cook, God Almighty willing.

V.1.23 Another Dish [of Fish with Stuffing, Baked in the Brick Oven]

Take a fish (*samaka*), clean it, scale it, and then salt it [and set is aside]. Take almonds and pine nuts—some left whole and some pounded. Also take olive oil, breadcrumbs, and eggs. Beat all the ingredients to combine[44] and then spread them in a pan (*ṭājin*).

---

40 The stuffing in this recipe is cooked and used to cover already fried fish. Interestingly, this recipe and the three following ones use the standard word for fish, which is *samak*, rather than the indigenous North African *ḥūt*. Possibly, the recipes were Mashriqi 'Eastern' in origin.

41 Both *madqūq*, for the fish meat, and *madrūs*, for the garlic, are used synonymously here to designate ingredients being pounded in a mortar.

42 This mix of ingredients is called *ḥashū* 'stuffing,' although fish would be placed either in it, or underneath it, as in the previous recipe.

43 The editor of the Arabic text, p. 206, leaves out the prepositional phrase *fīhā* 'in it,' which obscures the text.

44 It will soon be referred to as *ḥashū* 'stuffing' in the recipe. See n. 42 above.

Now take the fish and put it in the middle of the pan.[45] Put some cooked egg yolks (*fuṣūṣ bayḍ*) and olive oil on it and send it to the *furn* (communal brick oven); let it be placed at a distance from the fire so that it does not burn. Once the stuffing (*ḥashū*) sets and cooks and the fish is done, take the pan out of the oven, set it aside until it loses some of its heat, and eat it salubriously, God Almighty willing.

v.1.24 Another Dish [of Fried Fish with Fishballs]

Take a fatty fish (*samaka samīna*), clean it, salt it, [and set it aside]. Now take the meat of another fish and pound it very well; add a fistful of very fine white flour (*ghubār darmak*),[46] salt, and black pepper and (**204r**) beat them into a fine mix [and set it aside].

Now take a new pot and put olive oil in it, along with black pepper, coriander seeds, and a couple ladlefuls of juice of fresh cilantro. Also add thyme (*ṣaʿtar*), a few pounded cloves of garlic, and a [cooked and shelled] egg. Put the pot on the fire to cook.

Take the pounded meat [mix] and make meatballs with it, as was described in the sixth chapter of the second part of this book [recipe ii.6.1]. Put them in the pot to cook and then top them (*tukhammar*) with a mix of breadcrumbs and eggs.[47] Egg yolks must be added to the pot as well [before topping it with the egg mix].

Take the salted fish and fry it in a skillet (*miqlāt*) with olive oil. Turn it while frying so it browns on all sides. Put it in a wide, shallow bowl (*ṣaḥfa*), add to it whatever there is in the pot, and eat it salubriously, God Almighty willing.

v.1.25 Another Dish [Made with Eels]

Take whatever you like of thick-fleshed or medium *silbāḥ* (pl. *salābīḥ*, common eel), which is [also] known as *anqala* and *sillawr*.[48] Rub their tails with ashes [to

45 *Wasṭ* 'in the middle' is mentioned only in the BL MS, fol. 203v.

46 See glossary 2 on this kind of fine flour.

47 In the Madrid MS, fol. 97v, only egg whites are used. This cooking technique is called *takhmīr*. See glossary 9.2.

48 *Anqala* must have been a variation on *anqalīs*. *Silbāḥ* was the regional name for the eel in the Muslim West, and *mārmāhīj*/*marmāhīj* and *sillawr* were the fish's most common

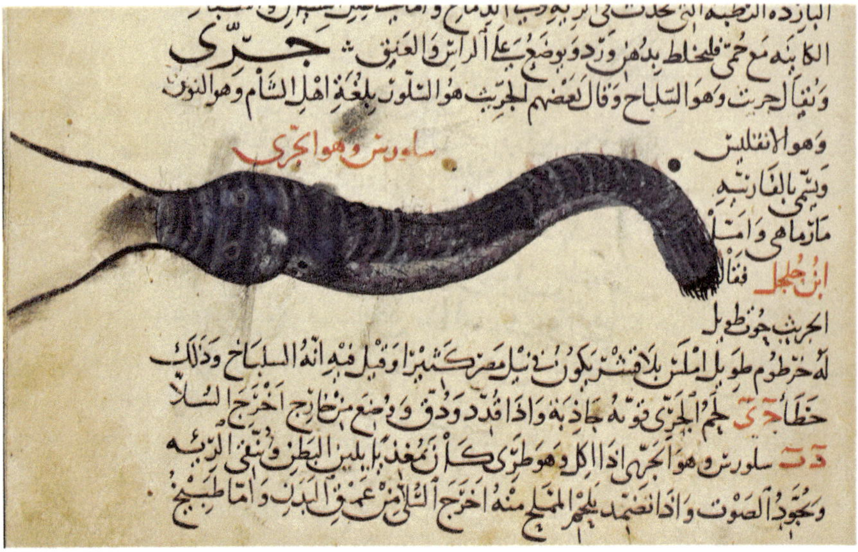

FIGURE 73 An eel, al-Ghāfiqī, *Kitāb al-Adwiya al-mufrada*, MS 7508, fol. 111r, detail
REPRODUCED BY PERMISSION OF THE OSLER LIBRARY OF THE HISTORY OF MEDICINE, MCGILL UNIVERSITY

be able] to strip their skins from the tails and then pull off the entire skins all the way from the tails. After cutting off their heads, cut them into medium pieces. Wash them thoroughly so that the blackness is removed and then put them in a glazed earthenware pan (*ṭājin muzajjaj*). Add salt, plenty of olive oil, black pepper, coriander seeds, cumin, pounded saffron, *murrī* (liquid fermented sauce), vinegar, and whole cloves of garlic. Put the pan on the fire to cook by adding a small amount of water. When the water has almost all evaporated, put the pan in the *furn* (brick oven) and let it brown on top.

If you want to [brown them] at home [on the stove], then do with them as was described earlier [in recipe v.1.1].

If you want to cook the dish in a skillet with olive oil and garlic, take the eel, peel off its skin, and clean it and salt it. Take a clean skillet, put it on the fire, and add olive oil to it. Once it boils, take the eel after you cut it into medium pieces and put it in the pan, folding the pieces gently while frying. Take them out as soon as they cook and brown on all sides.

---

names in the eastern region. Al-Arbūlī, *al-Kalām ʿalā al-aghdhiya* 152, includes an entry on *silbāḥ*, in which the recommendation is to skin it and cook it in the brick oven with olive oil and *murrī* (liquid fermented sauce).

Now take garlic, pound it, and put it in the skillet to cook,[49] and once it is done, add some more olive oil and return the fried pieces to the pan so that they absorb enough of the garlic flavor. Remove the pan from the fire and empty whatever there is in it into a large, shallow bowl (*ṣaḥfa*), and eat the dish salubriously, God Almighty willing.

v.1.26 Another Dish [of Baked Fresh Tuna][50]

Take a fresh tuna (*tunn*), choose a small one if available, slit it open from the back, and remove its backbone (*shawka*). Put it in a large earthenware tub (*qaṣriyya*), submerge it in vinegar mixed with pounded cumin (204v) and pounded garlic, and let it steep in the mix overnight. Take it out the following morning, wash it very well, and cut it into medium pieces.

Now take a glazed earthenware pan (*ṭājin muzajjaj*) and put salt, black pepper, coriander seeds, cumin, saffron, *murrī* (liquid fermented sauce), and vinegar in it. Stir all the ingredients to combine [into a sauce][51] and then take the tuna pieces one by one, put them in the pan, and rub them by hand with the sauce (*marqa*) so that they absorb the flavors of the spices. Layer the pieces in the pan, pour plenty of olive oil on them, and add sour *ihlīlaj* (myrobalan plums)[52] or sour apples, with citron leaves and several cloves of garlic. Take the pan to the *furn* (communal brick oven), and once the fish is done and the plums are cooked, take it out and serve it, God Almighty willing.

[Note:] The tuna pieces used here are taken from the back loin (*khāṣira*) and belly loin (*surra* 'navel').[53]

---

49 Based on recipe v.1.29 below, garlic is fried in the remaining oil.

50 This recipe and the following four call for tuna (تن *tunn*, *Thunnus thynnus*, Atlantic bluefin tuna), both fresh, salt-cured and, air-dried, *mushamma*ʿ 'mojama.' See glossary 10, s.v. *tunn*.

51 The editor of the Arabic text misreads وتحلّ 'and dissolve' in the Berlin MS, fol. 67v (copied similarly in the BL MS, fol. 204v) as وتحر (no meaning). The word might have originally been a misreading of وتحرك 'and stir.'

52 It is a variety of *ʿayn al-baqar* (plums), also used in recipe ii.1.4 above.

53 I follow here the Madrid MS, fol. 98v, which separates the two cuts with the conjunction 'and' و, which is missing in the other two MSS.

V.1.27 Another Dish [of Fried Fresh Tuna]

Take any parts of [fresh] tuna other than the back loin (*khāṣira*).[54] Cut them into pieces and wash and salt them.

Take a clean skillet (*miqlāt*), put it on the fire, and add olive oil to it. Once the oil boils, take the pieces and put them in the skillet, turning them gently so that they brown on all sides. Take them out, put them in a glazed bowl (*ghaḍāra*), and eat them salubriously, God Almighty willing.

If you want to dress the fish with [a sauce of] vinegar, pounded garlic, and caraway, then put vinegar and garlic [with the caraway] in a small pan (*ṭājin ṣaghīr*). Put it on the fire to boil, and pour it on the fried pieces in the bowl, and eat it salubriously, God Almighty willing.

For those who wish to fry pieces from the back loin (*khāṣira*) and the belly loin (*surra* 'navel'), they need to be patient so that they may fry well.[55]

V.1.28 Another [Fresh Tuna] Dish, Grilled (*mashwī*)[56]

Take as much as you want of tuna fish, slice it into strips (*sharā'iḥ*), and salt it.[57] Thread the strips onto an iron skewer and grill them as I have mentioned to you earlier [in recipe V.1.5 above]. While grilling, baste the pieces with salt, which has been dissolved in olive oil, *murrī naqīʿ* (sun-fermented liquid sauce), pounded garlic, black pepper, and Ceylon cinnamon. Do this until the fish browns, and eat it like this [i.e., without sauce].

If you want to dip [the grilled] pieces in [a sauce of] olive oil mixed with pounded cooked garlic, go ahead and do as you wish, and eat it salubriously, God Almighty willing.

V.1.29 Another Dish, Made with Dried Tuna (*tunn yābis*), Which Is Called *mushammaʿ*[58]

(170r) Take as much as you want of this kind of tuna and cut it into very thin long strips. Put them in an earthenware pan (*ṭājin fakhkhār*), add water, and

---

54 Tuna loins are thick and better suited for slow baking, as in the above recipe.

55 This statement is only included in the Madrid MS, fol. 98v. The cuts from the loins will take longer to fry inside and out because they are thick.

56 I followed here the Madrid MS, fol. 98v, where the dish is described as such.

57 Addition from the Madrid MS.

58 The word is derived from *shamʿ* 'beeswax,' and *mushammaʿ* suggests a waxy texture. It is

put it on the fire. When it comes to a vigorous boil, take the pieces out, remove whatever has stuck to them of sand and salt, and then wash them until they are clean.

Now take a clean skillet (*miqlāt*) and add olive oil to it. Once the oil boils, put the tuna pieces in it to fry, turning them gently until they brown. Take the tuna out and put pounded garlic in the skillet to fry in the [remaining] oil. Add more oil and return the fried tuna pieces to it so that they absorb the flavor of the garlic. Empty the skillet into a glazed bowl (*ghaḍāra*) and drizzle the tuna with fresh lemon juice (*khall līm ṭarī*), preserved juice of Damascus citron (*khall zunbūʿ*),[59] or preserved juice of unripe grapes (*khall ḥiṣrim*),[60] and eat the dish salubriously, God Almighty willing.

If you want to dress the tuna with vinegar and pounded garlic, then put vinegar and garlic in a small pan (*ṭājin ṣaghīr*), and after they cook, pour them on the [fried] tuna. You can also put the fried tuna in this *ṭājin* and let it boil [in the sauce] to moisten and absorb the garlic flavor, with the help and power of God Almighty.

v.1.30 Another [Dried Tuna] Dish, Called *rāhibī* (Monks' Food)[61]

Take as much as you like of dried tuna (*tunn yābis*)[62] and do with it as was done in the above recipe [i.e., slicing, boiling, and cleaning them]. Cook the pieces in a pan (*ṭājin*) with onions following the *rāhibī* recipe in the first chapter of the second part of this book [recipe ii.1.7]. Use plenty of olive oil in cooking it.[63] **If wished**, replace the honey used [in making *rāhibī*] with grape syrup (*rubb ʿinab*).[64] Finish cooking it in the brick oven as was mentioned [in that recipe].

---

salt-cured and air-dried tuna, which came to be known as *mojama* in Spanish. See glossary 10, s.v. *tunn*.

59 Kharna sour orange hybrid, *Citrus aurantium var. khatta*. Based on Dozy, *Takmilat al-maʿājim* v 364, s.v. زنبوع, the name of this fruit is of Amazigh origin. It is more commonly known as *kabbād* in the eastern region. Al-Tujībī gives no recipes for making *khall zunbūʿ*.

60 See recipes x.7.12–3 for making preserved juice of unripe grapes; and recipe x.7.15 for making preserved lemon juice. Note that in the two surviving Andalusi cookbooks, this one and anonymous *Anwāʿ al-ṣaydala*, *khall* not only designates regular 'vinegar' produced by fermentation but also, in a looser sense, unfermented preserved 'sour juice,' and even freshly pressed out lemon juice. See glossary 8, s.v. *khall*.

61 Cf. another *rāhibī* fish dish in this chapter, recipe v.1.10; and recipe ii.1.7 above, cooked with beef.

62 For this type of tuna, see the above recipe, n. 58.

63 The rest of the recipe is found only in the BL MS, fol. 170r, and the Madrid MS, fol. 99r.

64 It is grape juice cooked down to a syrup consistency, with no sugar added. See glossary 4.

And once done, take it out and serve it, God Almighty willing.

[The BL MS, fols. 170r–171r, and the Madrid MS, fols. 99r–100r, add recipes that are not found in the Berlin MS, and hence not to be found in the edited Arabic text, which follows it. They are included here, and enclosed in curly brackets.]

{Another [dried tuna] dish, called *arnabī*

Cook the dried tuna (*tunn yābis*) as was done in the *arnabī* dish described in the first chapter of the abovementioned part [i.e., the second part, see recipe ii.1.6].[65]

Another dish [of dried tuna baked in a casserole]

Wash the dried tuna (*tunn yābis*) as was mentioned earlier [in recipe v.1.29], clean it, and chop it as fine as possible. Put it in a clean skillet with a small amount of olive oil and put it on the fire. Let the tuna fry lightly while gently [stirring it] until some of its moisture dries out.

Take a pan (*ṭājin*), put olive oil in it, [and set it aside]. Take a large bowl (*mithrad*) and put a small amount of moistened breadcrumbs in it, along with black pepper, Ceylon cinnamon, ginger, spikenard, cloves, a bit of mastic, pounded saffron, coriander seeds, and beaten eggs—set some of the egg yolks aside. Beat together all the ingredients to combine them well, (170v) add the tuna, and mix it with them.

Put the tuna mix in the [prepared] pan (*ṭājin*), dot its face with the [set aside] egg yolks (*tunajjam*), pour a good amount of olive oil all over, and sprinkle it with Ceylon cinnamon and ginger. Take the pan to the *furn* (communal brick oven) and let it bake at a distance from the fire until it cooks and browns on top. Let it cool slightly, and eat it salubriously, God Almighty willing.

Another dish [of dried tuna with eggplants]

Wash the dried tuna (*tunn yābis*) as mentioned above [recipe v.1.29], cut it into medium pieces, and fry them lightly. Peel some eggplants, cut off their calyxes (*qaṭāmīr*, sg. *qiṭmīr*), split them into halves lengthwise, and boil them in salted water so that [at least] some of their bad, unhealthy properties leach out.[66] Let the eggplants fully cook and then take them out and rinse them in hot water.

---

65 The BL MS inadvertently merges this recipe with the following one.

66 With its excessively hot and dry properties, eggplant was believed to cause ailments like cancer and melasma if not pretreated before cooking it. See glossary 11, s.v. *mizāj*; and glossary 12, s.v. *bādhinjān*.

Next, chop onions, boil them in a pot until they cook, and take them out and put them a pan (*ṭājin*) with the eggplants and tuna. Add plenty of olive oil, black pepper, coriander seeds, and cumin. If you are not using onions, you may also add unskinned garlic cloves, *murrī naqīʿ* (sun-fermented liquid sauce), and vinegar. If onions are used, then use the liquid in which they were boiled to replace the garlic, vinegar, and *murrī*.

Put the pan on the fire to cook at home first, and when all is done, finish cooking it in the *furn* (brick oven) to brown on top. Leave it aside to slightly cool, and eat it salubriously, God Almighty willing.

For those who want to cook tuna that has been pickled in an earthenware jar (*tunn muṣayyar fī jarra*):[67] using [thick] pieces from the back loin (*khāṣira*) and belly loin (*ṣurra*),[68] let them cook it in a pan (*ṭājin*), either with onions [and its boiling liquid] or with vinegar with *murrī* and saffron, as was mentioned previously [in the above recipe]. This should be done after soaking the tuna in water to soften it (*yudbagh*) and then rinsing it in water to get rid of its initial saltiness. Likewise is done with salt-cured sardines (*sardīn mumallaḥ*) [before using them in recipes like the following].

For those who want to fry salt-cured sardines (*sardīn muṣayyar mumallaḥ*),[69] let them boil them in water first to get rid of their saltiness [and then fry them].

For those who want to fry salt-cured sardines (*sardīn muṣayyar mumallaḥ*), again, let them boil them first in water, and then after frying them, drench them with a boiled [sauce of] pounded garlic, vinegar, and caraway. Likewise is done with pickled tuna (*tunn muṣayyar*),[70] God Almighty willing.

Salt-cured sardines (*sardīn mumallaḥ*) may be cooked as *rāhibī* with onions after frying them, the same way beef *rāhibī* is made in its given chapter [recipe ii.1.7]. More of the spices and olive oil are used for this one.}[71]

---

67 For pickling large fish, see recipe x.6.1 below, where the fish is preserved in a salt-vinegar solution and kept in jars. In the Madrid MS version, the vessel is named *jarra* (earthenware jar); in the BL MS, fol. 170v, the jar is given the unusual name *raqqūja*, which, to my knowledge, is found nowhere else. My guess is that the word was an indigenous variant for *riqq/riqāq*, which were jars made with thin, molded and dried sheets of leather and used to store water, milk, yoghurt, and wine, and as we learn here, pickled fish.

68 In the above recipes, v.1.26–7, the word was copied as *surra*.

69 For salt-curing small fish, see recipe x.6.2 below.

70 See n. 67 above.

71 Here end the recipes included only in the BL and Madrid MSS; see my note on p. 380.

FIGURE 74 Fish, al-Ḥarīrī, *al-Maqāmāt*, fol. 61r, copied and illustrated by al-Wāsiṭī, detail
BNF, DEPARTMENT OF MANUSCRIPTS, ARAB 5847. SOURCE: GALLICA.BNF.FR/BNF

[The following concluding paragraph is found in all three MSS:][72]
Know that all kinds of fish are bad for people with moist and cold humors.[73] Fish changes the elemental properties of the digesting food into bad, unhealthy ones quickly if it does not digest properly.[74] After eating fish, one has to drink undiluted wine (*sharāb ṣirf*), or a [drink of diluted] grape syrup (*rubb ʿinab*), or a drink of [diluted] aromatic honeyed syrup (*sharāb ʿasal mufawwah*).[75] One may also take a sip of *murrī naqīʿ* (sun-fermented liquid sauce) or vinegar flavored with squills (*khall al-ʿunṣul*).[76] Fish should not be eaten after exhaustingly intensive physical activities, nor should exhausting activities be performed after eating it. In addition, one should not drink too much water when eating fish. In cases of intense thirst, water should be taken mixed with any of the drinks mentioned above, (**171r**) God Almighty willing.

72 The anonymous Andalusi *Anwāʿ al-ṣaydala* 155 concludes its section on fish recipes with a passage on the nature of fish as food and how to avert its harms that is largely similar to the following, which points to the possibility that both were drawing their material from similar sources.

73 The entire passage is an application of the Galenic theory of the humors. People possessing such humors were described as phlegmatic, and fish does not agree with them because it is cold and moist in properties. The anonymous Andalusi *Anwāʿ al-ṣaydala* 155 adds that fish agrees more with people who have hot and dry humors. See glossary 11, s.v. *mizāj*.

74 See glossary, s.v. *istiḥāla*.

75 See glossary 1, for more on these drinks.

76 Squill, *Drimia maritima*, is a variety of wild onion valued for its strong medicinal properties. For a recipe, see x.7.11 below. See also glossary 8 for *baṣal al-ʿunṣul* and *khall al-ʿunṣul*.

Part Five, Chapter Two: On Varieties of Egg Dishes

V.2.1 A Dish of *isfīriyya* (Thin Omelets)[1]

Take as many eggs as you want and break them in a large, wide bowl (*mithrad*). Add salt, black pepper, coriander seeds, juice of fresh cilantro,[2] juice of mint, a bit of saffron, a small amount of fermented dough (*ʿajīn mukhtamir*), cumin, pounded garlic, and Ceylon cinnamon. Beat them all by hand vigorously until they mix well.

Take a clean skillet (*miqlāt*) and put some olive oil in it. Once the oil boils, pour in the egg mix, letting it spread and cover the entire skillet [in a thin layer]. When the eggs set, fold the disc so that it looks like a reed tube (*qannūṭ*). Slice it into pieces, whatever size you like, and let them fry gently on low heat, turning them as needed to brown on all sides. If the skillet gets too crowded with the pieces, take some of them out to make more room for the rest to fry easily. As soon as some are finished, take them out and put them in a glazed bowl (*ghaḍāra*); [continue doing this] until all the pieces are done.

Do not pour too much of the egg mix into the skillet as this would not result in well-folded egg rolls.[3] [After they are done,] you may, if you want, pour some boiled vinegar on them,[4] and eat them salubriously, God Almighty willing.

If you want to make the *isfīriyya* in another way, add *murrī naqīʿ* (sun-fermented liquid sauce) and vinegar to the broken eggs to replace the fresh juices of cilantro and mint; also, leave out the fermented dough. Beat the eggs by hand with the addition of pounded saffron, a good amount of black pepper, ginger, Ceylon cinnamon, spikenard, cloves, a bit of mastic, pounded garlic, coriander seeds, and cumin. Set them aside for an hour.

Now take a skillet and put it on the fire with olive oil—but not much. Once the oil boils, pour the eggs [to cover the entire pan in a thin layer]. Then, take a

1 Name is added in the Madrid MS, fol. 100r.

2 The editor of the Arabic text inadvertently replaces the correctly copied خضرا 'fresh' in all MSS with يابسة 'dry.'

3 This is an additional remark found only in the Madrid MS, fol. 100v.

4 I followed here the Madrid MS, fol. 100v, which uses the verb يصب 'pour.' The BL MS, fol. 171r, and the Berlin MS, fol. 68v, use the generic verb تجعل 'put.'

 | DOI:10.1163/9789004469488_026

FIGURE 75
A hen sitting on eggs, Dioscorides, *Fī Hayūlā al-ṭibb*, translation by Ḥunayn b. Isḥāq, fol. 80r, detail
FROM THE NEW YORK PUBLIC LIBRARY, SPENCER COLLECTION: HTTPS://DIGITALCOLLECTIONS.NYPL.ORG/ITEMS/5E66B3E8-B1C8-D471-E040-E00A180654D7

ladle and use it to pull the egg [disc] away from the edges of the skillet. Fold the egg [disc], three times only if too much of the egg mix was added, as this will make it too thick for you[5] to fry. Therefore, fold them according to how thick or thin they are.[6] When you are thus done with the folding, slice them into pieces, as large or as small as you like them to be, [and fry them]. If the skillet gets too crowded with the pieces, take some out to make more room for the rest to fry easily. Turn the pieces over gently to avoid breaking them.

Once they fry and brown on all sides, (**171v**) take them out and put them in a glazed bowl (*ghaḍāra*) in one layer; and continue frying the rest of the pieces. Pour some boiled vinegar on them,[7] or use vinegar mixed with cooked [and pounded] garlic, or just leave them without adding anything;[8] choose whichever way you like, and eat it salubriously, God Almighty willing.

---

5 At this point, the editor of the Arabic text inadvertently skipped about a dozen words, which I provided based on the Berlin and BL MSS, fols. 68v and 171r, respectively.

6 The thin ones are rolled like reed tubes, as described in the first part of the recipe.

7 See n. 4 above.

8 The Madrid MS, fol. 100v, calls this plain variety *sādhaja*. In the edited Arabic text, أو 'or,' as it is clearly copied in all the MSS, is replaced with و 'and,' which confuses the text.

V.2.2 Another Dish [of Fried Eggs], Fantastic[9]

Take as many eggs as you want, and take a clean tinned skillet (*miqlāt muqazdara*).[10] Put it on the fire and add olive oil—but not much. Once the oil boils, take the eggs and break them one at a time, adding salt and black pepper if wished. Fold the white of the egg over its yolk to make it look like a disc (*qurṣa*) and turn it gently to brown on all sides. Meanwhile, break another egg [and do the same with it] until you finish them all. Every time you fry one, take it out and put it in a glazed bowl (*ghaḍāra*), [and do this] until you are done with all of them.

If wished, pour boiled vinegar on the eggs, or vinegar with garlic as mentioned above. Alternatively, you may use *murrī naqīʿ* (sun-fermented liquid sauce), or do not add anything; do it the way you like, and eat it salubriously, God Almighty willing.

V.2.3 Another Dish [of Stuffed Eggs, Used as Garnishes][11]

Take as many eggs as you want and put them in a pot filled with water only. Put them on the fire until they cook and harden. Take them out and put them in cold water to cool, and then shell them and set them aside.

Using a thread, cut the eggs in the middle crosswise into halves, gently take out their yolks, and put them in a wide, shallow bowl (*ṣaḥfa*). Add pounded salt—but not much—black pepper, ginger, Ceylon cinnamon, cloves, spikenard, and a bit of mastic. If you want to add a small amount of juices of fresh cilantro and mint, you can do so; and if you want, replace these with a small amount of *murrī* (liquid fermented sauce); do it whichever way you want. Mix the yolks with the spices, knead them very well by hand, and then shape them into yolk-like balls.

Put the yolk balls back to where they were inside the white [halves]. Tie the halves with clean thread so that they do not separate; or use a thin sprig of [fresh] thyme. Glaze the eggs with egg white and dust them with very fine white

---

9 *ʿAjīb*, as described in the Madrid MS, fol. 100v.

10 مقزدرة, as it is copied in the BL and Berlin MSS, fols. 171v and 69r, respectively; otherwise, generally copied as *muqaṣdara* (مقصدرة).

11 There is a similar recipe in the anonymous fourteenth-century Egyptian cookbook *Kanz al-fawāʾid*, English trans., *Treasure Trove*, recipe 172, where it is called *bayḍ maḥshī* 'stuffed eggs.'

flour (*ghubār daqīq al-darmak*).[12] When you are done with these, take a clean skillet and put in some sweet olive oil (*zayt ṭayyib*). Once the oil boils, (**172r**) dip the eggs in it and be careful not to let the halves separate. Fry them and turn them [until they are] browned, and then take them out and [garnish] whatever dishes you like with them, sprinkled with Ceylon cinnamon, God Almighty willing.

V.2.4 A Dish Called *nīmbarisht* (Poached Eggs)[13]

Take as many eggs as you wish. Take a small pot with salted water in it and put it on the fire. When it starts to boil vigorously, take an egg and break it into the water. As soon as it sets, but not too much, take it out with a ladle; do this gently to avoid making a crack through which the yolk might seep. Put it in a wide, shallow bowl (*ṣaḥfa*) with vinegar and olive oil in it. Break another egg, as was done earlier, and continue doing this until the eggs are finished, and eat them salubriously, God Almighty willing.

V.2.5 Another Dish [of Eggs Sunny-Side Up]

Take a glazed earthenware pan (*ṭājin muzajjaj*) and put olive oil in it, with vinegar, *murrī* (liquid fermented sauce), black pepper, coriander seeds, cumin, a pounded clove of garlic, and salt. Beat them all with a ladle to mix them well.

Now take as many eggs as you want and break them in the pan one after the other [keeping them intact] until all the eggs are used. Take the pan to the *furn* (communal brick oven) and put it at a distance from the fire until the eggs set and brown and the liquids evaporate. Take the pan out and serve it, God Almighty willing.

If you want to cook it at home [on the stove], take the pan and put in it whatever you put [in it from] above, [that is, liquids and spices,] and cook it on the fire. Once it starts to boil vigorously, take the eggs and break them one after the other [and keep them whole], making sure not to let them touch one another. Remove the pan from the fire when the eggs set and the liquids evaporate, and eat them salubriously, God Almighty willing.

---

12 It is a by-product of milled wheat, as fine as dust. See glossary 2 on this kind of fine flour.

13 Copied as *numayrashāt* نميرشات in the Madrid MS, fol. 101r; and *naymarasht* نيمرشت in the BL MS, fol. 142r. See glossary 5.

V.2.6 Another Dish [of Scrambled Eggs]

Take a pan (*ṭājin*) and put olive oil, fresh butter (*zubd ṭarī*), or ghee (*samn*) in it—use whichever you want. Add salt, black pepper, and coriander seeds, and put the pan on the fire.

Take as many eggs as needed and break them into a wide, shallow bowl (*ṣaḥfa*), beat them by hand to mix them well, (**172v**) and pour them into the pan on the fire. Stir them with the egg ladle (*mighrafat al-bayḍ*)[14] to break and separate them until they set and cook and all the moisture evaporates. Remove the pan from the fire, sprinkle the eggs with Ceylon cinnamon, and eat the dish salubriously, God Almighty willing.

V.2.7 Another Dish [of Boiled Eggs]

Take as many eggs as you want and put them in a pot filled with water only; put the pot on the fire. If you want to have the eggs very lightly boiled for the purpose of slurping them,[15] then let them come to a single boil and take them out and have them with salt and black pepper. If you want them firm, let them further boil until their liquidy insides coagulate;[16] and the eggs tend to float to the surface. Take them out and shell them. Serve them with bread, season them with salt and black pepper,[17] and eat them salubriously, God Almighty willing.

V.2.8 Another Dish [of Omelet][18]

Take as many eggs as you want, break them in a wide, shallow bowl (*ṣaḥfa*), and add a good amount of fresh cilantro juice, with breadcrumbs, pounded almonds and walnuts, salt, and black pepper. Beat them all very well.

---

14 This would have been more like a spatula to stir and break the scrambling eggs.

15 The phrase used here is للشرب, literally 'for drinking.' The expression is still used today everywhere in Arab-speaking regions to designate eggs left in boiling water just long enough to heat them up, and they are still runny in texture and are good for slurping right from the eggshell.

16 The word used is تجف, literally 'become dry.'

17 The expression used for seasoning here is *taṣbughuhā*, derived from *ṣibāgh*, which is generally used to designate dipping sauces.

18 This is a tasty omelet with breadcrumbs and nuts. In the eastern region, such dishes were more commonly known as *ʿujaj*, sg. *ʿujja*.

Put a skillet (*miqlāt*) on the fire with lots of olive oil and pour in the eggs. [While cooking,] continue adding oil whenever it decreases until [the omelet] is done; gently turn it so that it browns on all sides. Remove it from the fire, put it in a wide and shallow bowl (*ṣaḥfa*), and eat it salubriously, God Almighty willing.

V.2.9 Another Dish [of Poached Eggs]

Take a small pot (*qudayra ṣaghīra*) and put water in it, along with vinegar, olive oil, *murrī* (liquid fermented sauce), black pepper, coriander seeds, cilantro, and salt. Put the pot on the fire and let it boil many times.[19]

Take as many eggs as you wish and break them gently into the pot; keep them whole[20] and let them cook on low heat. Once you see that the eggs have cooked, top the surface (*tukhammar*) with a mix of eggs beaten with very fine white flour (*ghubār daqīq*).[21] Leave the pot on low heat until the topping thickens (*taʿqud*), ingredients simmer, and flavors nicely blend (*tatajammar*). Empty the dish [into a serving vessel], and eat it salubriously, God Almighty willing.

V.2.10 Another Dish [of Eggs Scrambled with Chickpeas]

Take a small pot (*qudayra ṣaghīra*) and put water in it with black pepper, olive oil, coriander seeds, juice of fresh cilantro, soaked chickpeas, and a small amount of chopped onion. Put the pot on the fire to cook.

As soon as the chickpeas cook, take as many eggs as you want and break them in a wide, shallow bowl (*ṣaḥfa*). (173r) Add a bit of salt to them,[22] with black pepper and fresh juices of cilantro and mint. Beat them all vigorously to mix them well and put them in the [chickpea] pot on low heat. Stir the pot constantly with a ladle until the eggs cook. Empty the dish into a *ṣaḥfa*, sprinkle it with Ceylon cinnamon, and eat it salubriously, God Almighty willing.

If you want to make this dish with vinegar and saffron, then you need to add cumin to the spices and replace the juices of cilantro and mint with vinegar and *murrī naqīʿ* (sun-fermented liquid sauce). Also add a few cloves of garlic

---

19 On how this was conducted, see glossary 9.2, s.v. *ghalā*.
20 This addition is in the Madrid MS, fol. 102r, only.
21 See n. 12 above.
22 A slight damage in text here in the Berlin MS, fol. 70r, reads as وتجعل عليها قليلا in the BL MS, fol. 173r.

and a bit of pounded saffron to the pot. Saffron should also be added to the eggs when you break and beat them. Do with the dish as was done above, and eat it salubriously, God Almighty willing.[23]

V.2.11 Another Dish [of Cooking Eggs in Hot Ashes]

Take as many eggs as you want and bury them in ashes (*ramād*) where they can get some heat from the fire. If you want them to be liquidy enough to slurp,[24] turn them frequently to heat them up from all sides, and then have them with salt and black pepper, God Almighty willing.

If you want the eggs to completely coagulate, let them stay in the ashes while you frequently turn them on all sides until [according to your estimation] you know that they are done. Put them in cold water, shell them, and eat them with salt, black pepper, and Ceylon cinnamon, God Almighty willing.

23 The Madrid MS, concludes the chapter with this recipe, leaving out the last one, with this comment: الى غير ذلك من انواع كثيرة تركتها "There are many other varieties, which I did not include."

24 See n. 15 above.

PART 6

القسم السادس في الألبان وكل ما يكون منها

ويشتمل على ثلاثة فصول

On Dairy Foods (Albān), *and It Has Three Chapters*

Part Six, Chapter One: A Recipe for Rennet-Curdled Milk (*ʿAqīd al-Laban al-Ḥalīb*) and What Is Made with It

Curdling milk with rennet (*ʿaqd al-ḥalīb*)[1]

Take milk (*laban ḥalīb*) that has just been drawn from sheep (*ḍaʾn*), cows (*baqar*), or goats (*maʿz*, sg. *miʿza*). Strain it into an earthenware vessel and keep it close to the fire so that it catches some of its heat. Take the amount needed of rennet (*infaḥa*)[2] from lambs or kids. Put it in a clean piece of cloth, which you hold and dip into the vessel while pressing and rubbing it by hand until all of it dissolves [into the milk]. Leave the milk for an hour to curdle (*yanʿaqid*).[3]

VI.1.1 A Recipe for Making Cheese (*jubn*)[4]

Take a fan (*mirwaḥa*) made of [woven] esparto grass (*ḥalfā*),[5] similar to the ones used for fanning the fire, and make a ring of [woven] esparto in its middle; like a ring cookie (*kaʿka*). (173v) Sew it to the fan so that it does not move. Make the ring small, the size of the palm; [the strip of woven esparto used is] 2 spans long or more (approx. 15 inches) so that you make a circle with it on the fan.[6]

Cut through the rennet-curdled milk (*ʿaqīd*) in the vessel where it was made, [take some of it, put it in the prepared mold, and] press it with your hand to drain it. Add some more [and do the same] until the mold is full. Take another fan, similar to the first one used [but without the sewed ring], place it on the

1 Only the Madrid MS, fol. 102v, provides this subtitle.

2 A variant on *minfaḥa*; it is the fourth stomach of the suckling lambs, kids, or calves. See glossary 3.

3 Madrid MS, fol. 102v, adds that alternatively, milk can be curdled with blossoms (*nawār*) of a variety of cardoon (*khurshūf* [sic]), which is called *laṣīf* (gundelia). This will be later mentioned in recipe vi.1.4 below. See glossary 12, s.v. *ḥarshaf*, for varieties of the plant.

4 This recipe is for fresh cheese (*jubn ṭarī*). Instructions for hard cheese (*jubn yābis*) will be given in the third chapter of this part.

5 Also called halfah grass, see glossary 9.1.

6 The recipe here describes making the esparto cheese mold, which will be called *miqdār* later in the recipe.

 | DOI:10.1163/9789004469488_027

curdled milk in the mold (*miqdār*), and press it further with your hand until all the liquid drains. Put it aside, make another mold, and do with it as you did with the first one. Continue doing this until you make the amount of cheese you want. Set them aside to drain all day long if they have been made in the morning (*ghudwa*); or all night long if they were made in the evening (*ʿashāʾ*).

Remove the top fans and undo the sewing of the small rings and remove them. Put the cheese discs [on their faces] on a wooden board (*lawḥ*) and then remove the bottom fan. Sprinkle the cheese with salt [to drain it further] if you want to keep it for later. Do not salt it if you want [to use it fresh] to make *mujabbana* [recipes i.4.33–9 above] or *badīʿiyya* [recipe ii.3.1 above] with it.

[Recipes with fresh cheese:]

If you want to make a casserole (*ṭājin*) of cheese and eggs, take as much [fresh] cheese as you want, wash it, and crumble it in a wide, shallow bowl (*ṣaḥfa*). Add broken eggs, enough for the amount of cheese used, add salt as well, if the cheese is unsalted, and pounded saffron, black pepper, coriander seeds, fresh juices of cilantro and mint, and Ceylon cinnamon. Beat them all by hand to mix them well.

Take a glazed earthenware pan (*ṭājin muzajjaj*) and put a small amount of olive oil in it. Pour in the cheese and egg mixture and level the surface by hand. Garnish it with [raw] whole egg yolks,[7] add enough olive oil to cover the top, and sprinkle it with Ceylon cinnamon. Take the pan to the *furn* (communal brick oven) and let it be put at a distance from the fire until it sets and browns. Take it out and leave to lose some of its heat, and eat it salubriously, God Almighty willing.

If you want this dish to be fried in a skillet, do not let the mix be as thin [as the above]. Take a clean skillet (*miqlāt*) and put a moderate amount of olive oil in it.[8] Once it boils, make small discs with the cheese-egg mix and fry them in the skillet, turning them gently until they cook and brown. If you notice that they are breaking [while frying], add a piece of dough to the mix and combine them well, so know this and act accordingly.

If you want to fry the cheese without eggs, take cheese that was curdled five or so days ago and that is salted and completely drained, wash it to get rid of the excess salt, and slice it into strips, about three-fingers wide.

Take a skillet and put a small amount of olive oil in it. Once it heats up,[9] take the cheese [pieces] and fry them until they cook and brown. Turn them gently

7 Based on the Madrid MS, fol. 103r, where the instruction is *yunajjam bi-fuṣūṣ bayḍ*.

8 The expression used here is *zayt wasaṭ* 'neither too much nor too little.'

9 The verb generally used is *ghalā* literally 'boil'; even in this case when the amount is little.

[while frying] to brown them on all sides. Take them out, (**179r**) put them in a glazed bowl (*ghaḍāra*), sprinkle them with black pepper and Ceylon cinnamon, and eat them salubriously, God Almighty willing.

If you want to eat this fresh cheese (*jubn ṭarī*) with honey or figs (*tīn*), slice it into fingers, which you then dip in honey, and eat salubriously, God Almighty willing.[10] It is a well-loved food.[11]

VI.1.2 Recipe for Making *shīrāz* (Very Thick Drained Yogurt)

Take the amount you want of the rennet-curdled milk (*ʿaqīd*),[12] put it in a *quffa* (large round basket) woven of esparto grass (*ḥalfā*),[13] and cover it. Hang the basket until all the liquid drains and then take it down and press the [thickened yogurt] through a hair sieve (*ghirbāl shaʿr*) by hand until all of it passes into a big bowl (*mithrad*) put underneath it. Add some salt and stir it with a ladle to mix it with the *shīrāz*. Put it in a clean earthenware pot that has not been touched by water and put it away until needed.

Whenever you want to eat *shīrāz*, take some out with a ladle and put it in a wide, shallow bowl (*ṣaḥfa*). Level the surface with the ladle and let the *shīrāz* fill the bowl to its rim. Garnish it with olives and [pickled] young caper berries (*faqqūṣ al-kabar*) arranged all around the rim,[14] with a pickled lemon (*līma muṣayyara*) put in the middle.[15] Give the dish a light sprinkle of nigella seeds (*shūnīz*) and a drizzle of sweet olive oil (*zayt ʿadhb*).

This kind [of dairy food] does not keep well for long, and it is most delicious eaten before it sours, so know this. Green onions (*baṣal akhḍar*) are served with it.[16]

The way to eat the dish is to take some tender green onions, discard the outer layer of each one, wash them in salted water first and then in water only, and set them aside. When it is time to eat it, hold an onion with your hand and pick up some *shīrāz* with it—just what amounts to a mouthful—and eat it salubriously, God Almighty willing.

---

10 The recipe does not specify whether the figs are fresh or dried.

11 فهو شئ مستطاب, addition from the Madrid MS, fol. 103r.

12 See the opening passage in this chapter.

13 Also called halfah grass, see glossary 9.1.

14 The berries are at the stage where they are not fully grown, and the seeds inside them have not fully developed yet. See chapter x.4 below on pickling capers.

15 See below, chapter x.3, for ways to pickle lemons.

16 The following passage is found only in the BL MS.

VI.1.3 Recipe for Making *khilāṭ* (Condiment of Very Thick Drained Yogurt Infused with Chopped Vegetables)[17]

It is made exactly like *shīrāz* [above]; but the difference is that you take salt-preserved tender shoots of capers (*ʿasālīj al-kabar*),[18] wash them, chop them finely, and mix them with the drained curdled milk. [To serve it,] spread it in a wide, shallow bowl (*ṣaḥfa*), level the surface with a ladle, garnish it with olives and [pickled?] lemons, drizzle it with olive oil [as described above], and eat it salubriously, God Almighty willing.

VI.1.4 Making Rennet-Curdled Milk [Sweetened] with Honey (*ʿaqīd bi-l-ʿasal*)

(179v) Take milk, strain it, and curdle it as described earlier.[19] If wished, you can curdle the milk with blossoms (*nawār*) of a variety of cardoon (*ḥarshaf*) called *laṣīf* (gundelia),[20] which would indeed be suitable for it. When curdling the milk, add honey dissolved in milk—amount depends on how sweet you want it to be. Put it aside to set, and use it however you like, God Almighty willing. It can be eaten with eggs, which is a delicious way to have it.[21]

ʿAqīd made without honey[22] can be eaten with fine-tasting figs.

---

17 Pl. *akhlāṭ*. The chopped vegetables in this recipe are pickled tender stems of capers. Cf. other recipes in al-Warrāq, *Kitāb al-Ṭabīkh*, English trans., *Annals* 199–200; and anonymous *Kanz al-fawāʾid*, English trans., *Treasure Trove*, recipes 509 and 510.

18 See below, chapter X.4, for ways to preserve them.

19 See the opening passage in this chapter.

20 See n. 3 above.

21 Addition from the Madrid MS, fol. 103v.

22 In both MSS, Berlin and BL, the phrase occurs as دون عمل. Possibly, this was simply a copyist's misreading of دون عسل 'without honey,' which is appropriate in the given context. See also the last statement in recipe VI.1.1 above, where figs and honey are given as alternative choices. Madrid MS, fol. 103v, replaces this last statement with "*ʿaqīd* may be eaten with eggs, which is a delicious way to have it."

Part Six, Chapter Two: On Making *Rāyib* (Yogurt) and Extracting Butter

VI.2.1 Recipe for Making Sieve-Strained Rennet Yogurt (*rāyib mugharbal*)

Take the amount you want of rennet-curdled milk (*ʿaqīd*) mentioned earlier [in the opening passage in vi.1 above], keep it in an esparto vessel, and suspend it (*yuʿallaq*) to drain most of its liquid.[1] Now take a hair sieve (*ghirbāl shaʿr*) and place it on a large, wide, and shallow bowl (*ṣaḥfa kabīra*) or an earthenware tub (*maḥbas fakhkhār*).[2] Put the curdled milk in the sieve and rub and press it by hand so that it all passes down to the vessel underneath it. Add salt—just the needed amount—and beat them to mix. Put it away in an earthenware vessel, and use it whenever you wish, God Almighty willing.

This is made like *shīrāz*, except that *shīrāz* is completely drained of liquid, whereas for this one, some of it is kept.[3]

VI.2.2 Recipe for Making Yogurt without Rennet in a Leather Vessel (*rāyib al-qirba*)[4]

Take a tanned leather vessel (*qirba madbūgha*), put some of the drained liquid of yogurt called *mays*[5] (whey) in it to rinse it;[6] do this several times to

1 Suspending the vessel is mentioned in the Madrid MS, fol. 103v only. Whereas in the earlier recipe, vi.1.2 for making *shīrāz*, the liquid of the curdled milk is completely drained, resulting in a cream cheese-like consistency, this one is just thickened yogurt, similar to what nowadays is called *labneh* and Greek yogurt. See also the concluding remark in this recipe.

2 See glossary 9.1 for more on this vessel.

3 This remark given at the end of the recipe in found only in the Madrid MS, fols. 103v–104r.

4 All three extant MSS consistently copy the word for yogurt as *rāyib*, which the editor of the Arabic text changes to the more orthographically correct *rāʾib* in this recipe. The *qirba* vessel was and still is made from the entire skin of a young goat or lamb. See glossary 9.1.

5 Copied as *mayṣ* in the Madrid MS, fol. 104r.

6 The verb used here for rinsing leather using a sour solution is *taqṣuruhā*, see glossary 9.2, s.v. *qaṣr*.

 | DOI:10.1163/9789004469488_028

remove any traces of tanning smells (*ṭīb al-dibāgh*).[7] Next, wash it with water to clean it, and then squeeze out the water and fill it with strained milk (*laban ḥalīb*).

Put the vessel in a wooden box (*naqīr khashab*) with a lid.[8] Make a hole in it with an affixed spout (*mīzāb*) to allow the water used to wash the vessel to run out of it. Put the box in a place that is always shaded from the sun; or close to the *sāqiya* (animal-driven waterwheel).[9] Put fresh grape leaves (*waraq dāliya*), willow leaves (*waraq ṣafṣāf*), or any other similar ones all over the *qirba* vessel.

Every morning [for three consecutive days] wash the *qirba* from the outside and scrape it with the back of a knife's blade (*qafā al-sikkīn*) or with a wooden spoon made specially for this task. This must only be done by a clean person (*ṭāhir*), be it man or woman.[10] Change the position of the vessel in the box and clean it, wash the box, replace the leaves with new ones, and put the cover back.

After three days you will see that the milk has coagulated and turned into yogurt (*rāyib*). Take the amount you want and replace it (174r) with milk. If you want the yogurt to be very thick, leave it longer, until it solidifies. It is in this thickened yogurt (*rāyib khāthir*), mixed with olive oil and garlic, that you dip grilled squabs, young chickens, or gourd.[11] If you take out this thick yogurt, you must leave some of it in the vessel to be used as a yogurt starter (*khamīr*), so understand this. And be careful not to neglect cleaning and washing the vessel [as described above] because milk spoils quite fast.

Rāyib that is thin in consistency (*khafīf*) is consumed as a drink and eaten with bread, but *rāyib* that is dense in consistency (*ṣafīq*) is used as mentioned above. Additionally, the same things made with *shīrāz* (recipe vi.1.2) and *khilāṭ* (recipe vi.1.3) can be made with it, and eat it salubriously, God Almighty willing.

vi.2.3 Recipe for Extracting Butter (*istikhrāj al-zubd*)

Take milk (*laban ḥalīb*) immediately after it has been drawn, strain it, put it in an earthenware vessel (*wiʿāʾ fakhkhār*), and set it aside for a day and a night [i.e.,

---

7 The smell would not necessarily have been unpleasant because the word used here is *ṭīb* 'scent.' See glossary 9.2, s.v. *dibāgh*.

8 This is one of the meanings given in Dozy, *Takmilat al-maʿājim* x 288, s.v. نقر.

9 The waterwheel could have been used at an irrigation well, or to haul river water. Besides these, *sāqiya* could have also referred to an irrigation ditch or an orchard with irrigating channels. See Dozy, *Takmilat al-Maʿājim* vi 99, s.v. سقى.

10 A menstruating woman is thought of as being unclean, and both men and women who have not had a bath after intercourse are also said to be unclean.

11 See above, recipe iii.2.44, for the birds and below, recipe vii.1.8, for the gourd.

24 hours, to ferment]. Next, empty it into a churning vessel (*shakwa*),[12] which you then attach to a tripod (*ḥammāla*).

Churn the vessel vigorously to mix the milk well, and as soon as it loosens and separates (*inḥalla*) and butter starts to congeal, take fresh water and add it to the milk in the *shakwa*. Continue churning even more strenuously until the butter clumps. Enter your hand into the *shakwa* to take it out, and drink the milk remaining in it,[13] with the help of God Almighty.

If you want to turn ghee (*samn*) back into fresh butter (*zubd*) because you happen to need it [and do not have it], take ghee[14] and wash it [and melt it] in hot water once or twice. Then, put it in cold water and stir it repeatedly [until it congeals again]. Pick it up by hand, put it in a vessel, and use it [as butter], God Almighty willing.

12 The vessel is made with the skin of a kid or a lamb.

13 This milk was called *makhīḍ* 'buttermilk.'

14 See glossary 3, s.v. *samn*, for how it was made from butter.

CHAPTER VI.3

Part Six, Chapter Three: On Ripening[1] Hard Cheese in a Jar (*Khābiya*)[2] and Ways For Cooking It; and Remedying Butter and Milk[3]

VI.3.1 Recipe for Making [Cured Hard Cheese]

Take cheese that has been made in the second half of March (Māris) or in April (Ibrīl), salt it, and arrange [the pieces] on a wooden board placed above the ground at a location touched by the breeze but not the sun. Regularly wipe the pieces with a woolen cloth, followed by a rub with olive oil and salt; do this until you know that they have been salted enough and that they have lost all their moisture, which would be in May (Māya).

Take a *khābiya*,[4] which has previously been used to keep olive oil, and clean it by wiping it; do not wash it with water. Rub the cheese pieces with olive oil and arrange them in the jar tightly next to each other; there should be no spaces between them. Continue doing this until the jar is filled. Cover it and tightly seal it (**174v**) with clay to cover the entire lid.

Set the jar aside for 15 days, after which open it and reposition the cheese pieces by putting the ones on top in the bottom and the ones in the bottom on top. Cover the jar and seal it with clay [as it was]. Leave it for ten more days and then reposition the cheese pieces once again.

Continue doing this until the cheese moistens, and when you open the jar, you will see that their insides have developed holes filled with oil. At this point it can be used, served with fine bread and sweet grapes all autumn long, God Almighty willing.

1 The word for ripening cheese used here is *tarbiya* (as it occurs in the Berlin and BL MSS, fols. 72r and 174r, respectively), which the editor of the Arabic text changes to *tahyi'a* 'preparing.' The Madrid MS, fol. 104r, does not provide this detail.

2 It is a large cylindrical earthenware jar with a tapered rounded bottom. See glossary 9.1.

3 The editor inadvertently changes إصلاح 'remedying' (as it is correctly copied in all MSS) to استخراج 'extracting,' irrelevant to the chapter.

4 See glossary 9.1 for more on this vessel.

VI.3.2 A Dish Made with a Hard Cheese [Dipping Sauce with Garlic and Olive Oil]

Take the amount of cheese you want, peel off the rind (*qishr*), and grate it with an *iskarfāj* (grater) until it becomes as fine as dust. Take garlic cloves, boil them in water until they cook, and then take them out and pound them in a wooden mortar (*mihrās khashab*). Add a bit of salt to it.

Now take hot water and mix it with the cheese 'dust' and garlic until they dissolve in it. Add sweet olive oil (*zayt ṭayyib*) to it, and eat it salubriously, God Almighty willing. If you want to add skinned and pounded walnuts to the cheese and garlic, you can go ahead and do so, with the help of God Almighty.

VI.3.3 Another Dish [of Fried Cheese Slices]

Take the abovementioned cheese [recipe VI.3.1], soak it in water to soften (*yadbugh*),[5] and then clean it and cut it into thin squares. Take a clean skillet and put olive oil in it—but not much. Put the cheese pieces in it and turn them gently to brown on all sides. Take them out, put them in a wide, shallow bowl (*ṣaḥfa*), and eat them salubriously, God Almighty willing.

Use sesame oil (*zayt al-simsim*) for frying, if you can get it,[6] because it goes very well with the cheese. It has been remarked that cheese thus fried can help get rid of garlic and onion breath if eaten [after having them], God Almighty willing.

VI.3.4 Another Dish [of Grilled Cheese]

Take the abovementioned cheese, peel off its rind, and cut it into small pieces, which you then thread onto a thin stick. Grill the cheese until it browns on all sides, and eat it salubriously, God Almighty willing.

---

5 The word is more commonly used in terms of tanning leather in liquids to soften it. See Corriente, *Dictionary of Andalusi Arabic*, s.v. *d-b-gh*. The Madrid MS, fol. 105v, uses the verb *yarṭub* 'moisten.'

6 Sesame oil was more commonly known as *shayraj* in the eastern region, where it was more abundant. This recipe clearly indicates that in the Muslim West, it was not as available as olive oil was. See glossary 6, s.v. *zayt al-simsim*; and glossary 8, s.v. *simsim*.

VI.3.5 How to Remedy Butter When It Goes Rancid

(175r) Take the strained liquid in which a rockrose shrub (*shajar al-astab*) has been boiled[7] and boil the butter in it. It will taste as fresh and delicious as it was, God Almighty willing.

VI.3.6 Recipe for Keeping Milk from Souring Quickly

To keep milk from souring quickly, take a piece of fresh cheese (*jubn ṭarī*) and drop it into the milk vessel; it will not let it sour [quickly].

---

7 The edited Arabic text followed the Berlin MS, fol. 72v, where it is erroneously copied as الاسيت; it similarly occurs in the BL MS, fol. 175r. There is no such plant, to my knowledge. In the Madrid MS, fol. 105v, it is clearly copied as الاستب (*astab*, from Spanish *estepa*), which is rockrose, also called halimium, *Halimium halimifolium*. It is a flowering shrub native to the Mediterranean Basin. See Corriente, *Dictionary of Andalusi Arabic*, s.v. *ʾ-s-t-p*; see also glossary 8.

PART 7

القسم السابع في البقول وما اليها

ويشتمل على عشرة فصول

On Vegetables (Buqūl) *and the Like, and It Has Ten Chapters*[1]

∴

1 With the exception of a few instances, this entire part is about meatless dishes, which in the eastern region were called *bawārid al-buqūl* 'cold vegetable dishes' and *muzawwarāt al-buqūl* 'simulated vegetarian dishes,' which Christians would eat during Lent and physicians prescribe for the sick because they were deemed lighter and easier to digest. See, for instance, the anonymous Egyptian cookbook *Kanz al-fawā'id*, English trans., *Treasure Trove*, chapter 8; and al-Warrāq's tenth-century cookbook *Kitāb al-Ṭabīkh*, English trans., *Annals*, chapters 45 and 46.

Part Seven, Chapter One: On Dishes Made with Gourd (*Qarʿ*)

VII.1.1 A Dish [of Fried Gourd Topped with Almonds]

Take gourds (*qarʿ*), scrape their skins [with a knife], remove their [pithy] centers,[1] and boil them in salted water.[2] Take them out when done and set them aside on a board to drain. Put a clean skillet on the fire with olive oil. Once it boils, take the gourd pieces, dust them with flour, and put them in the skillet to fry, turning them [to brown on both sides]. When cooked and browned, put them in a glazed bowl.[3]

Take a small pot and put vinegar in it with black pepper, salt, olive oil, and a small amount of water. Put it on the fire to boil and then add a ladleful of fresh cilantro juice and let it boil. Take the fried gourds, cut them into medium pieces, and put them in the small pot.

Next, take pounded skinned almonds, breadcrumbs, and an egg yolk (*faṣṣ bayḍa*). Mix them well, and then take some of the liquid in the small pot and stir it into the breadcrumbs, almonds, and the yolk. Spread this mix on the gourd pieces in the small pot,[4] remove the fire from underneath it, and leave it on embers (*ghaḍā*) so that it simmers and the flavors nicely blend (*taʿtadil wa tatajammar*). Empty the dish into a glazed bowl (*ghaḍāra*), and eat it salubriously, God Almighty willing.

VII.1.2 Another Recipe [of Gourd Simmered with Walnuts]

Take as many gourds as you want, scrape them from the outside, clean their insides, and cut them into medium pieces. Put them in a pot with water and salt, put it on the fire to cook, and then take out the gourd pieces.

---

1 They also contain seeds, see glossary 12, s.v. *qarʿ*.

2 Judging from later instructions, the gourds are perhaps just cut into large slices at this stage.

3 The edited Arabic text contains several repeated instructions—an editorial mishap no doubt.

4 The egg topping is usually referred to as *takhmīr* in this book. See glossary 9.2, for more on this cooking technique.

 | DOI:10.1163/9789004469488_030

FIGURE 76 Gourds on the vine, Dioscorides, *Fī Hayūlā al-ṭibb*, translation by Ḥunayn b. Isḥāq, fol. 103v, detail
FROM THE NEW YORK PUBLIC LIBRARY, SPENCER COLLECTION: HTTPS://DIGITALCOLLECTIONS.NYPL.ORG/ITEMS/5E66B3E8-7EC4-D471-E040-E00A180654D7

Take a clean pot and put a small amount of water in it, along with olive oil, black pepper, coriander seeds, vinegar, *murrī* (liquid fermented sauce), a sprig of fresh thyme (*ghuṣn ṣaʿtar*), a few cloves of garlic, and a small amount of onion. Put it on the fire to cook, and once it boils, take the gourd, cut it into smaller pieces, and add them to it.

Next, take shelled walnuts,[5] pound them in a mortar (*mihrās*), and mix them with breadcrumbs and [raw] eggs. Add salt, black pepper—not much—and a bit of pounded saffron. Beat them all with some of the liquid in the pot until they mix well and then add them to the gourd pot. Remove the fire from (**175v**) underneath the pot and leave it on embers (*ghaḍā*); give the pot a stir.[6] Put some egg yolks (*fuṣūṣ bayḍ*) in it [to poach] and leave it until the sauce thickens and the flavors nicely blend (*taʿqud wa taʿtadil*). Empty the dish into a glazed bowl (*ghaḍāra*), and eat it salubriously, God Almighty willing.

---

5 جوزا مقشورا, as it is clearly copied in the BL MS, fol. 146r; walnuts are also mentioned in the Madrid MS, fol. 106r. This place in the text of the Berlin MS, fol. 73v, is damaged. The editor's guess was that it was almonds, perhaps based on the previous recipe. However, we notice that the first three recipes add variety to the dishes' flavors by using different kinds of nuts: almonds in the first, walnuts here, and pine nuts in the next.

6 By stirring the pot, the walnut mix is meant to combine with the rest of the ingredients and not be a topping.

VII.1.3 Another Recipe [of Gourd Topped with Pine Nuts]

Take as many gourds as you want and do with them as above [i.e., cleaning and boiling]. Take a clean pot and put water in it with salt, olive oil, coriander seeds, black pepper, and a small amount of chopped onion. Put it on the fire, and once it boils, add the gourd; also add egg yolks [to poach].

Take pine nuts and breadcrumbs, pound them in a mortar (*mihrās*), add juice of fresh cilantro, egg whites, salt, and black pepper to them, and beat them all. Stir some of the liquid in the pot with the nut mix well and then add it to the pot.[7] Remove the fire from underneath the pot and leave it on embers (*ghaḍā*) until it nicely cooks (*taʿtadil*). Ladle it into a glazed bowl (*ghaḍāra*), and eat it salubriously, God Almighty willing.

VII.1.4 Another Recipe [of Gourd Patties]

Take as many gourds as you want and do with them as was previously done [i.e., cleaning and boiling]. After they boil, take them out and press them [by hand] to remove excess moisture. Next, pound them thoroughly in a mortar (*mihrās*) until they become one mass. Add salt—just the needed amount—black pepper, and breadcrumbs. Break some eggs on these and beat them all. Do not let the mix be on the thin side.

Now take a clean skillet, put it on the fire, and pour in some olive oil. Once it boils, take the pounded gourd mix and make small discs with it, similar to the *aḥrash* patties.[8] Put them in the skillet to fry, gently turning them to brown on all sides, and put the done ones in a glazed bowl (*ghaḍāra*). Continue with the frying until you finish them all, and eat the dish salubriously, God Almighty willing.

VII.1.5 Another Recipe [of Gourd Topped with Almonds]

Take as many gourds as you want and do with them as was previously done [i.e., cleaning and boiling]. Take a new pot and put water in it, along with salt,

---

7 Since there are no instructions to stir the pot after adding the egg mix, we may assume that it is to be spread as a topping, called *takhmīr*, see glossary 9.2.

8 *Aḥrash* are usually made with meat; see, for instance, recipes ii.5.2 and ii.6.7 above. See also *aḥrash* made with eggplant, recipe vii.2.5 below.

coriander seeds, black pepper, and a small amount of chopped onion. Put it on the fire to allow the spices to cook and then add the gourd after chopping it. Next, take skinned almonds and pound them in a mortar (*mihrās*) with breadcrumbs, an egg, and juice of fresh mint; stir them all to mix and add them to the pot.[9] Put it on low heat until it cooks and the flavors nicely blend (*yuṭbakh wa yaʿtadil*). Empty the dish into a glazed bowl, and eat it salubriously, God Almighty willing.

VII.1.6 Another Recipe [of Chopped Gourd Simmered with Milk]

(**176r**) Take as many gourds as you want and scrape and clean them as was done previously. Dice them and put them in a clean pot with salt, coriander seeds, black pepper, caraway, and a chopped onion. Put it on the fire and stir gently until all the moisture evaporates.

Now take milk, stir it with a small amount of fine white flour (*daqīq darmak*), and pour it into the pot. Add ghee (*samn*) as well. Let the pot cook on low heat, stirring it gently until it cooks. Empty the dish into a large glazed bowl (*ghaḍāra kabīra*), sprinkle it with crushed sugar (*sukkar masḥūq*), and eat it salubriously, God Almighty willing.

VII.1.7 Another Recipe [of Mashed Gourd Simmered with Milk]

Take as many gourds as you want and do with them as was done previously [i.e., cleaning and boiling]. After they are done boiling, take them out and pound them in a mortar (*mihrās*) until the mass becomes doughy in texture. Add black pepper, coriander seeds, and juice of fresh cilantro.

Put the gourd in a clean pot, adding fine-tasting ghee, milk, and a small amount of *murrī* (liquid fermented sauce). Put the pot on medium heat and let it cook gently, stirring it constantly to prevent it from burning. Once it cooks, empty it into a glazed bowl (*ghaḍāra*), sprinkle it with Ceylon cinnamon and black pepper, and eat it salubriously, God Almighty willing.

---

9 See n. 7 above.

VII.1.8 Another Recipe [of Mashed Gourd with Thick Yogurt][10]

Take as many gourds as you want and do with them as was done previously—scraping, cleaning, and washing. Cut them into pieces, put them in a clean pot with water and salt, and put them on the fire to cook. Once the gourds are done, take them out, press out their moisture, and grate them [while pressing] on a fine-meshed sieve woven with hair or esparto grass (*ḥalfā*).[11] Set it on a large bowl (*mithrad*) so that the grated gourd falls into it.

Now take thick yogurt like *shīrāz* or *rāyib al-qirba* [recipes vii.1.2 and vii.2.2 above], add boiled and pounded garlic to it—amount to taste—and mix them well with the gourd in the bowl. Spread the mix in a glazed bowl (*ghaḍāra*), drizzle some sweet olive oil (*zayt ṭayyib*) all over it, and eat it salubriously, God Almighty willing.

VII.1.9 Another Recipe (of Fried Gourd Slices, Coated with Eggs)

Take as many gourds as you want and do with them as was done previously [i.e., cleaning and washing]. Slice them into long pieces, boil them until they cook, and then take them out and spread them on a sieve or a board to drain.

Take eggs, break them in a wide, shallow bowl (*ṣaḥfa*), and add black pepper, coriander seeds, caraway, and a small amount of flour. Beat them vigorously to mix them well. Next, take a clean skillet, put it on a moderate fire, and put a small amount of olive oil in it. As soon as it heats up, put the gourd pieces in it, and turn them to brown on all sides. Take them out, (**176v**) one after the other, and dip them in the eggs to coat them, and return them to the skillet. Do this repeatedly with each piece until the gourd looks completely hidden inside the egg coating.

Once the pieces are all done and browned, take them out of the skillet and put them in a glazed bowl (*ghaḍāra*). Sprinkle them with a bit of *murrī* (liquid fermented sauce), scatter them with chopped fresh cilantro, and eat the dish salubriously, God Almighty willing.

---

10 A dish of mashed gourd mixed with thick yogurt and seasoned with garlic is also found in the cookery books hailing from Abbasid Baghdad. See, for instance, tenth-century al-Warrāq, *Kitāb al-Ṭabīkh*, English trans., *Annals* 231.

11 Also known as halfah grass, *Lygeum spartinum*, native to southern Europe and North Africa. See glossary 9.1, s.vv. *ghirbāl* and *ḥalfā*.

VII.1.10 Another Recipe (of Boiled Gourd in Vinegar and Olive Oil Sauce)

Take as many gourds as you want and do with them as was done previously [i.e., cleaning and washing]. Cut them into long slices, put them in a clean pot with water and salt, and cook them on the fire. Take the slices out as soon as they are done and spread them on a board to drain. Next, take a glazed bowl (*ghaḍāra*) and put vinegar and olive oil in it, add the gourd slices, and eat the dish salubriously, God Almighty willing.

If you want to add pounded garlic to [the sauce], you need to boil it with the vinegar first and then make the sauce, with the help of God Almighty.

VII.1.11 Making a thick pudding of gourd (*fālūdhaj al-qarʿ*);[12] it softens the bowels[13]

Take honey that has been skimmed of its froth,[14] put it in a clean pot, and cook it on the fire. Once it boils,[15] take as many gourds as you want, scrape them from the outside, and clean their insides, removing the white pith (*shaḥm*) and seeds (*zarīʿa*). Clean them and dice them into small pieces, and then put them in a clean pot with water and cook them on the fire.

Once the gourd is done, take it out, rinse it in cold water, and press out the extra moisture by hand. Pound it in a wooden mortar (*mihrās*) until it becomes doughy in texture. Next, take a large bowl (*mithrad*) and set a fine-meshed sieve woven with hair on top of it. Put the gourd in the sieve and grate it by hand against the mesh so that it falls into the bowl. Color it with a bit of saffron and put it in a pot with [boiled] honey. Stir the pot to mix them and let it cook on moderate heat. (177r)

As soon as you see that the honey is about to thicken, start adding fine-tasting ghee (*samn ṭayyib*) or olive oil; do this repeatedly so long as it is being absorbed by the gourd mix. As soon as enough fat is added and it can no longer

12 Generally, *fālūdhaj* is a thick starch-based pudding, see recipe i.4.23 above.

13 The three extant MSS at our disposal mention that it has the benefit of softening the bowels. In the Madrid MS, fol. 107r, وهو مما يلين البطن; in the BL MS, fol. 144v, and the Berlin MS, fol. 74r, وهو يلين الطبيعة. It is not clear how this text came to be edited as ويسمى الطلبية 'and it is called *al-ṭalabiyya*' in the edited Arabic text, p. 226. To my knowledge, no such dish name ever existed.

14 See glossary 4, s.v. *ʿasal*, for details on how and why this was done.

15 The Madrid MS more logically begins with preparing the gourds and then boiling the honey, as the former would take a while to finish.

be absorbed, remove it from the fire while it is still soft and thin. Ladle it into a glazed bowl (*ghaḍāra*), sprinkle it with black pepper, and eat it salubriously, God Almighty willing.

Part Seven, Chapter Two: On Dishes with Eggplants (*Bādhinjān*)

VII.2.1 A Dish [of Fried Eggplant Slices Simmered in Sauce and Topped with Eggs][1]

Take as many eggplants as you want, peel them, slice them into thin discs,[2] and stack them on a board—there should be pounded salt between the pieces. Once you finish doing this, weigh them down with stones or any other [heavy] objects to help draw their black water out.[3]

Alternatively, if you want to boil the eggplant slices in water and salt, put them in a clean pot and let them cook until the pieces are almost done. Take them out, rinse them in hot water, and set them aside to drain.

[To prepare the sauce,] take a clean pot and put vinegar in it with juice of fresh cilantro, olive oil, black pepper, unskinned cloves of garlic, skinned almonds, soaked chickpeas, a small amount of chopped onion, a fresh sprig of thyme (*ghuṣn ṣaʿtar*), and a citron leaf. Put the pot on the fire to cook all these ingredients.

Take a clean skillet and put it on moderate heat. Put a small amount of olive oil in it if the eggplant pieces were boiled; otherwise, add plenty of it if they were not. Once the oil boils, put the eggplant pieces in the skillet and let them fry well. When you are done frying, add them to the sauce (*marqa*) in the pot, along with [raw] whole egg yolks (*fuṣūṣ bayḍ*), and let them set.

Next, take eggs, break them, and add salt and pepper to them with ginger and a bit of pounded saffron. Beat them to mix and pour them all over the dish.[4] Remove the fire from underneath the pot and leave it on embers (*ghaḍāra*) so

1 This dish is a vegetarian variation on *Burāniyya*, usually cooked with meat. Cf. recipe ii.1.2 above.

2 As specified in the Madrid MS, fol. 110r.

3 Eggplant was believed to have an unhealthy and excessive amount of hot and dry properties. It was suspected of causing ailments like cancer and melasma if not pretreated before incorporating it into dishes. See glossary 11, s.v. *mizāj*; and 12, s.v. *bādhinjān*.

4 The Madrid MS, fol. 110v, correctly adds the verb *yukhammar*, which was a familiar cooking technique in the Muslim West, see glossary 9.2, s.v. *takhmīr*.

 | DOI:10.1163/9789004469488_031

FIGURE 77 Eggplants, al-Ghāfiqī, *Kitāb al-Adwiya al-mufrada*, MS 7508, fol. 73r, detail
REPRODUCED BY PERMISSION OF THE OSLER LIBRARY OF THE HISTORY OF MEDICINE, MCGILL UNIVERSITY

that it cooks well and the flavors nicely blend (*taʿtadil*). Empty the pot into a glazed bowl (*ghaḍāra*), and eat the dish salubriously, God Almighty willing.

VII.2.2 Another Dish [of Mashed Eggplants, Seasoned and Topped with Eggs]

Take as many eggplants as you want and put them in a clean pot after peeling them. Place the pot on the fire to cook, and when the eggplants are done, take them out, press out the excess moisture [by hand], and pound them in a wooden mortar very well. Put them in (177v) a wide, shallow bowl (*ṣaḥfa*) and set them aside.

Now take a new pot and put olive oil in it with *murrī* (liquid fermented sauce), salt, and a small amount of water. Put the pot on the fire, and when it boils, add the eggplant and stir the pot gently. As soon as it cooks, add [raw] whole egg yolks (*fuṣūṣ bayḍ*) and let them set.

Take egg whites beaten with breadcrumbs, black pepper, and ginger and pour them all over the dish.[5] Remove the fire from underneath the pot and

5 The expression used is *tukhammir bihi al-qidr*. See the above note.

leave it on embers (*ghaḍā*) to cook well and the flavors nicely blend (*taʿtadil*). Empty the pot into a glazed bowl (*ghaḍāra*), sprinkle Ceylon cinnamon all over the dish, and eat it salubriously, God Almighty willing.

VII.2.3 Another Dish [of Fried Eggplant Slices, Simmered in Sauce and Topped with Eggs]

Take as many eggplants as you want, peel them, slice them into discs, and put them in a pot with water and salt. Put the pot on the fire to cook, and when the eggplant is done, take the pieces out and spread them on a sieve or a board [to drain].

[To prepare the sauce,] take a clean pot and put a small amount of water in it along with salt, olive oil, *murrī* (liquid fermented sauce), vinegar, black pepper, coriander seeds, a bit of cumin, thyme, a few cloves of garlic, and a small amount of chopped onion. Put the pot on the fire until it boils and whatever there is in it cooks.

Take a clean skillet and put olive oil in it—but not much. Once it heats up, add the eggplant pieces and fry them, turning them over until they cook and brown. Take them out and add them to the sauce (*marqa*) in the pot after discarding the garlic cloves and onion pieces and let them cook in it. Add [raw] whole egg yolks (*fuṣūṣ bayḍ*), and when they set, take eggs beaten with breadcrumbs and aromatic spices (*afāwīh*) and pour them into the pot to cover the top.[6] Remove the fire from underneath the pot and leave it on embers (*ghaḍā*) until it cooks well and the flavors nicely blend (*taʿtadil*). Empty the pot into a glazed bowl (*ghaḍāra*), sprinkle black pepper and Ceylon cinnamon all over the dish, and eat it salubriously, God Almighty willing.

VII.2.4 Another Dish [of Whole Eggplants, Simmered in Sauce and Topped with Eggs]

Take as many eggplants as you want, split each in half [lengthwise] up to its calyx (*qiṭmīr*), [keep them attached,] stuff them with salt, soak them in water long enough to help pull their black water out, and then wash and clean them and press them [by hand] to get rid of the excess moisture.

6 See n. 4 above.

Take a clean skillet, put olive oil in it, and put it on the fire. Once the oil boils, take the whole eggplants and put them in the skillet to fry, turning them repeatedly until they fry well (**178r**) and are completely cooked; remove them from the fire.

Take a clean pot and put vinegar, black pepper, and coriander seeds in it. Put it on the fire, and once it boils, add the eggplants and leave them there until they boil. Top the pot (*yukhammar*) with a mix of egg whites beaten with breadcrumbs and spices.[7] Remove the fire from underneath the pot and leave it on embers (*ghaḍā*) to simmer and the flavors nicely blend (*taʿtadil*). Empty the pot into a glazed bowl (*ghaḍāra*), and eat the dish salubriously, God Almighty willing.

VII.2.5 Another Dish [of Eggplant Patties]

Take as many eggplants as you want, peel them, and boil them in salted water. Take them out once they cook, rinse them in hot water, and press out the excess moisture. Pound them [in a mortar] thoroughly, clean them of any unwanted parts, and put them in a wide, shallow bowl (*ṣaḥfa*). Add salt, black pepper, Ceylon cinnamon, ginger, olive oil, *murrī* (liquid fermented sauce)—but not much—and break eggs on them—enough to bind them; add breadcrumbs as well, and beat them all vigorously. Do not let the mix be thin in consistency.[8]

Now take a clean skillet, add olive oil, and put it on the fire. Once the oil heats up, make small patties with the eggplant mix, similar to an *uḥayrish* [each].[9] Fry them in the skillet and turn them to brown on all sides. If you want to make it [i.e., the entire amount] as a single disc, spread all the eggplant mix in the skillet and let it fry gently on moderate heat; wait until it fries completely [on one side] and then turn it carefully. Once it cooks and browns, put it in glazed bowl (*ghaḍāra*), sprinkle it with Ceylon cinnamon and black pepper, and eat it salubriously, God Almighty willing.

---

7 See n. 5 above.

8 Apparently, the editor of the Arabic text failed to notice لا 'do not' copied in the margin of the Berlin MS, fol. 75v. The BL MS copies the complete sentence.

9 الأحيرش, as copied in the Berlin and BL MSS, fols. 75v and 179r, respectively; and الاحرش in the Madrid MS, fol. 110v. The former must have been a variant on the latter; it also occurs in this form in al-Ishbīlī's *ʿUmdat al-ṭabīb* i 45. Cf. other *aḥrash* recipes, ii.5.2, ii.6.7, and vii.1.4 above.

VII.2.6 Another Dish [of an Eggplant Condiment]

Take as many eggplants as you want, peel them, and boil them in salted water. Take them out, rinse them in hot water, and press out the excess moisture. Pound them [in a mortar] very well, discarding the unwanted parts. Put them in a wide, shallow bowl (*ṣaḥfa*) and add vinegar and olive oil to them along with garlic, which has been boiled and pounded. Those who prefer to add caraway as well, they can do so, and eat the dish salubriously,[10] God Almighty willing.

VII.2.7 Another Dish, [Mock Stuffed Eggplants][11]

Take as many eggplants as you want, peel them, and split them into quarters [lengthwise] but keep them attached by leaving the calyxes (*qaṭāmīr*, sg. *qiṭmīr*) intact. Stuff the eggplants with salt to draw out their black water and then rinse them and put them in a clean pot with water and salt. Put the pot on the fire, (178v) and when the eggplants are well done, take them out and press out the excess moisture. Take the eggplants but set their calyxes aside [after cutting them off].[12]

Put the eggplants in a large kneading bowl (*miʿjana*)[13] and rub them by hand until they become doughy in texture. If some of them still need to be pounded,[14] go ahead and [use a mortar] to pound them. Now take a clean skillet or a glazed earthenware pan (*ṭājin fakhkhār muzajjaj*), put olive oil in it along with the [mashed] eggplants, and stir them constantly until all the moisture evaporates. If you wish, you may just leave them without frying.

Next, take breadcrumbs and put them in a large bowl (*mithrad*);[15] add fresh juice of mint and break eggs on them—enough for the amount of eggplants used. Set aside some of the yolks to garnish [*tunajjim*] the dish's top with them.

---

10 Such dishes were usually offered as dips scooped with bread.

11 *Maḥshū* 'stuffed,' as described in the Madrid MS, fol. 111r. I used this MS version at several places in the recipe to amend the text. The dish is giving the illusion of eggplants being stuffed by arranging the calyxes on the face of the casserole.

12 The recipe uses an unusual term to designate the eggplant flesh: *ṭaʿm*, literally 'flavor' or 'taste'; this must have been a regional usage of the word.

13 The bowl is usually used for kneading dough, *ʿajīn*.

14 The Berlin and the BL MSS, fols. 75v and 178r, respectively, misread, *al-dars* 'pounding,' as it occurs in the Madrid MS, fol. 111r, as *al-ruʾūs* 'heads,' which is irrelevant in the given context.

15 Such large bowls were customarily used to serve *tharīda* dishes, as those prepared in chapter i.2.

Add salt and black pepper to the breadcrumbs and eggs, along with ginger, Ceylon cinnamon, coriander seeds, and a bit of pounded saffron. Beat them all by hand until they mix well; add the [mashed] eggplants and stir them all until they become one mass.

Empty the mix into a large glazed pan (*ṭājin muzajjaj*) after you put a small amount of olive oil in it. Level the surface with your hand and garnish it with the [set aside raw egg yolks]. Additionally, spread the [set aside] calyxes, put upright, all over the surface;[16] underneath each one of them, put a whole cooked clove of garlic and a piece of fine-tasting hard cheese.[17] Pour plenty of olive oil all over its face, sprinkle it with black pepper and Ceylon cinnamon, and take it to the *furn* (communal brick oven). Let the pan bake at a distance from the fire until it all sets and browns. Take it and set it aside to lose some of its heat, and eat it salubriously, God Almighty willing.

VII.2.8 Another Dish, Called *tūma* (Looking Like Ostrich Eggs)[18]

Take as many eggplants as you want and do with them as was done above. Set them aside after rubbing and pressing them by hand until they become doughy in texture.

Now take hard cheese (*jubn yābis*), peel off its rind, and grate it into dust-like particles with a steel grater (*iskarfāj maṣnūʿ*).[19] Take garlic cloves as well and cook them in water to full doneness and then pound them with what remained of the cheese after grating it. Add them to the eggplants along with the grated cheese; add olive oil as well. Combine them all by hand very well and then spread the mix in a glazed bowl. Arrange the eggplant calyxes, standing upright, over its face; coat the top with finely grated cheese—amount to taste—and pour olive oil all over it, and eat it salubriously,[20] God Almighty

16 I here amended the text with the help of the Madrid MS, fol. 111r, which provides this detail about what gave it the name *maḥshū*:
وتوقف قطامير الباذنجان على وجه الطاجن.

17 The Berlin MS, which the editor of the Arabic text used, is a little damaged at this place. The editor's guess, which was 'egg white,' turns out to be *ṭayyib* 'fine-tasting,' as copied in the BL MS, fol. 179v.

18 As called in the Madrid MS, fol. 111r. *Tūma* designates pearls or ostrich eggs, see Ibn Manẓūr, *Lisān al-ʿArab*, s.v. توم. The dish must have acquired this name by virtue of the domed eggplant calyxes arranged on its surface, which are coated with a thorough dusting of finely grated white cheese.

19 The full name of this alloy is *fūlādh maṣnūʿ*, as mentioned in Ibn Sīnā, *al-Qānūn* i 491.

20 The Madrid ms, fol. 111v, adds pounded walnuts to the mix. It also instructs the cook

willing. [While eating it,] replenish the finely grated cheese and olive oil whenever they look depleted.

VII.2.9 Another Dish [of Eggplant Casserole][21]

Take as many eggplants as you want, peel them, and cut them lengthwise into thin slices from bottom to top, including the calyxes—each slice the width of the eggplant itself. Put the slices in a clean pot with water and salt and put them on the fire. Once they cook well, (180r) take them out and spread them on a sieve (*ghirbāl*) to drain the excess moisture.

Take a large, wide, and shallow bowl (*ṣaḥfa*) and put vinegar and *murrī* (liquid fermented sauce) in it, along with black pepper, coriander seeds, cumin, dried thyme crushed between the fingers (*ṣaʿtar maḥkūk*), and garlic—both pounded and whole.

Taste the eggplants; if too salty, rinse the pieces in water to remove the excess salt and then gently press them between your hands. Dip them piece by piece in the [above] sauce (*marqa*), pushing them down while doing so to absorb enough of it.

Next, take an earthenware pan (*ṭājin fakhkhār*) and put olive oil in it. Take the eggplant pieces, spread them in the pan, and pour the remaining sauce all over them along with lots of olive oil. Take the pan to the *furn* (communal brick oven) to bake at a distance from the fire. When all the moisture evaporates and only oil remains, take the pan out and leave it to cool, and invoke the name of God and eat it salubriously,[22] God Almighty willing.

VII.2.10 Another Dish [of a Casserole with Small Eggplants][23]

Take small eggplants, as many as you want, peel them, and slit them lengthwise into quarters but do not separate them. Stuff them with salt and soak

---

to use lots of olive oil on its face. The dish must have been served as a condiment scooped with bread.

21 The Madrid MS, fol. 111v, gives a shorter and stylistically different version, see recipe vii.2.19 below, where it is called *arnabiyya*.

22 That is, say *Bism Allāh* (بسم الله). This is an indication that such cold vegetable dishes were the first to be eaten—before the main hot ones.

23 The Madrid MS, fols. 111v–112r, gives a shorter and stylistically different version, see recipe vii.2.20 below.

them in a wide and shallow bowl (*ṣaḥfa*) with a small amount of water to help pull out their black water.[24]

Next, rinse the eggplants in fresh water and then put them in a clean pot with water in it and put it on the fire. Take them out once they boil and spread them on a sieve to drain the excess moisture. Put them in a clean pot, adding water, olive oil, salt if needed, black pepper, coriander seeds, and a bit of cumin. Put it on the fire to cook, and once the eggplants are done, add *murrī naqīʿ* (sun-fermented liquid sauce)—just as needed—and as much as you prefer of fine-tasting vinegar. Once the pot boils, take the eggplants out gently so that they do not break and pack them in a pan (*ṭājin*) next to each other, standing,[25] with their calyxes showing on top.

Take breadcrumbs, blend them with a small amount of water, and break some eggs on them, enough for the amount of eggplant used. Add black pepper, Ceylon cinnamon, ginger, coriander seeds, and pounded saffron; beat them all very well to combine them. Take this mix and gently pour it all over the eggplants until they are totally submerged and nothing shows but the tips of the calyxes. Garnish the top with [raw] whole egg yolks (*fuṣūṣ bayḍ*) and pour some of the strained liquid [from the pot where the eggplants cooked] and some olive oil [on it].

Take the pan to the *furn* (communal brick oven) to bake at a distance from the fire until it is completely done—[eggs] set, liquid evaporates, and top browns. Take it out of the oven, set it aside to cool, and eat it salubriously, God Almighty willing.

If you want to prepare the dish with fresh juices of cilantro and mint, then leave out the cumin, saffron, vinegar, and *murrī*; and cook it [as above,] with the help of God Almighty and His power.

VII.2.11 Another Dish [of Simmered Small Eggplants]

Take small eggplants, as many as you want, and do with them as above. Take them and put them in a clean pot (180v) with water, lots of olive oil, black pepper, coriander seeds, a bit of cumin, fine-tasting *murrī* (liquid fermented sauce), unskinned garlic cloves, and a small amount of chopped onion. Put the

---

24 See n. 3 above.

25 The word used in the Berlin and BL MSS, fols. 76v and 180r, respectively, to express the idea of packing the eggplants thus is *muṣaṭṭaba* 'making a bench-like formation'; and *marṣūṣa* 'packed next to each other,' in the Madrid MS, fol. 111v.

pot on the fire to cook, and when the eggplants are done, taste them for salt; add more if needed. Empty the pot into a glazed bowl (*ghaḍāra*), pour some lime juice (*māʾ līm akhḍar*) all over,[26] and eat the dish salubriously, God Almighty willing.

VII.2.12 Another Dish [of Simmered Diced Eggplants][27]

Take as many eggplants as you want, and after peeling and dicing them, add plenty of salt to them. Keep them soaked in a wide, shallow pan (*ṣaḥfa*) with a small amount of water to pull out their black water,[28] and then rinse them in hot water to clean them and remove the salt.

Now take a good amount of onions, chop them finely, wash them in salted water, and then rinse them to get rid of the salt. Put them in a clean pot along with the eggplants and add a small amount of water to them along with lots of olive oil, black pepper, coriander seeds, a bit of cumin, and a small amount of *murrī naqīʿ* (sun-fermented liquid sauce). Put the pot on the fire to cook, and once the eggplants and onions are done, empty the dish into a glazed bowl (*ghaḍāra*), and eat it salubriously, God Almighty willing.

If you want, add [chopped] suet (*shaḥm*), or cook it with cured meat (*qadīd*).

VII.2.13 Another Dish [of Stuffed Whole Eggplants][29]

Take nice-looking eggplants, remove their calyxes carefully to keep their original looks, [and set them aside]. With a sharp knife, gently hollow out the insides of the unpeeled eggplants from the calyx side.

Take the hollowed-out flesh and boil it in salted water until it cooks; throw out the water. Knead and mash the flesh in a pan (*ṭājin*), as was mentioned earlier [in recipe vii.2.7 above], with crumbs of grated bread, eggs, and spices.

---

26 Describing lemon as *akhḍar* 'green' is an indication that lime is being used here. See glossary 7, s.v. *līm*.

27 The Madrid MS, fol. 112r, gives a shorter and stylistically different version, see recipe vii.2.21 below.

28 See n. 3 above.

29 The Madrid MS, fol. 112r–v, gives a longer and stylistically different version, see recipe vii.2.22 below. A comparable dish is found in the anonymous Andalusi cookbook *Anwāʿ al-ṣaydala* 144, where it is aptly called *maḥshī* 'stuffed.'

Fill the eggplant shells with this mix, put the calyxes back in their places, tie them with a thread, pack them in the pan one next to the other, spread what remained of the stuffing all over, and pour olive oil on them. Put the pan in the *furn* (brick oven) until it sets and cooks.

This dish may also be made with pounded meat, sparrows—stewed or fried—and boiled egg yolks. The eggplants are stuffed with these along with the rest of the stuffing.[30] The dish will look beautiful with the eggplants in the dish perfectly shaped as if nothing has been done to them; delicious and exotic, indeed.

If wished, the dish may be made green with juices of fresh cilantro and mint; or it can be left without them.

VII.2.14 Another Dish [of Stuffed Eggplant Halves][31]

(**181r**) Take [large] eggplants that are free of bitterness; do not peel them. Split them in halves lengthwise and boil them in salted water until they are done. Throw out the water, and scoop out the flesh of the eggplant halves, taking care to keep intact the shape of the shells themselves.

Take the eggplant [flesh] and mash and mix it with meat that is already pounded and cooked, as described above.[32] Beat them all with eggs and spices, as was mentioned in the *maḥshī* recipe.[33] Fill the cored-out eggplant halves with this stuffing, dust their surfaces with fine white flour (*darmak*), and fry them in olive oil in a skillet; care must be taken to preserve their shapes. Keep them until they brown and then serve them by themselves or make a sauce (*marqa*) for them like the one prepared in the recipe for fried eggplants [see recipe vii.2.18 below]. The sauce may also be made with meat broth, vinegar, *murrī naqīʿ* (sun-fermented liquid sauce), and saffron, and topped

---

30 The following details are found only in the BL MS, fol. 180v; the Berlin MS copy of the recipe, fol. 77r, does not include it.

31 A comparable dish is found in the anonymous Andalusi cookbook *Anwāʿ al-ṣaydala* 144–5, which I used to amend the text.

32 'As described above' is out of place here simply because this book does not contain the recipe originally included in the manual from which al-Tujībī chose his collection of eggplant recipes for the chapter. We know this because the anonymous Andalusi cookbook, mentioned in n. 29 above, which shares some of the eggplant recipes in this chapter, precedes this recipe with another one using pounded cooked meat, and the dish is specifically called *maḥshī* 'stuffed.'

33 See the note above.

with beaten eggs (*tukhammar*) the way the *Burāniyya* dish is prepared.[34] It will be wonderful indeed.

VII.2.15 Another Dish, Prepared as *mughaffar* (Coated)[35]

Take eggplants that are free of bitterness and cut them into thin rectangular slices (*alwāḥ*, sg. *lawḥ*), lengthwise and crosswise. Boil them in a pot with salted water and then throw out the water and set the pieces aside to drain.[36] Now take fine white flour (*daqīq darmak*), and in a wide, shallow bowl (*ṣaḥfa*), beat it with eggs, black pepper, saffron, coriander seeds, juice of fresh cilantro, and a small amount of *murrī naqīʿ* (sun-fermented liquid sauce); let the mix have the consistency of thick soup (*ḥasū khāthir*). Dip the eggplant slices in it and fry them in olive oil in a skillet until they brown. If wished, make a sauce (*marqa*) for them as was mentioned in the above [recipe], or just serve them as they are.[37]

VII.2.16 Recipe for Eggplant Omelet (*ʿujja*)

Choose eggplants that are free of bitterness, peel them, and boil them in salted water until they cook well and fall apart (*yanḥall*).[38] Take them out of the water and mash and press them (*yuʿarrak*) in a wide, shallow bowl (*ṣaḥfa*) with crumbs of grated bread, eggs, olive oil,[39] *murrī naqīʿ* (sun-fermented liquid sauce), black pepper, coriander seeds, and Ceylon cinnamon. Beat them until the mix looks even in texture and then fry it [the mix] in thin discs (*rughaf*, sg. *raghīf*) in a skillet in olive oil until they cook and brown. Make a sauce (*marqa*) for them with vinegar, *murrī*, and pounded garlic boiled together; pour it on the omelets and serve.

---

34 See, for instance, the first recipe in this chapter, which is indeed a *Burāniyya* dish, although is not specifically called so. See also above, recipe ii.1.2, cooked with meat.

35 Cf. other *mughaffar* recipes, ii.5.4, iii.2.8, and v.1.18.

36 Addition from the corresponding recipe in the anonymous Andalusi *Anwāʿ al-ṣaydala* 145.

37 The edited Arabic text replaces *aw* 'or,' as it is clearly copied in the BL MS, fol. 181r, with *wa* 'and,' which obscures the text.

38 The editor's close guess of the word in the damaged part of the Berlin MS, fol. 77v, as *wa yustaḥkam* 'and thoroughly cooks' turns out to be *wa yanḥall* 'and it falls apart,' as copied in the BL MS, fol. 181r.

39 The BL MS, fol. 181r, helps fill in a few words missing from a damaged part in the Berlin MS, fol. 77v.

VII.2.17 Recipe for Eggplant-Filled *mirqās* (Small Sausages)[40]

Choose eggplants that are free of bitterness, as many as you want, peel and boil them, and pound them with chopped suet along with a small amount of *murrī naqīʿ* (sun-fermented liquid sauce) and all the spices and other ingredients used for making meat sausages. Stuff the intestines (*muṣrān*) with this mix as was described earlier [see *mirqās* recipe ii.6.4 above]. Eggs, however, must be added to the stuffing because it is only by adding them that the filling binds and stays inside.[41]

VII.2.18 Another Dish [of Fried Eggplants]

Take as many eggplants as you want, peel them, and slice them into discs. Sprinkle them with salt and weigh them down with a stone or any other [heavy] object to pull out their black water.[42] [Leave them aside for a while, and then] take them and put them in hot water for a short while. Rinse them very well to get rid of the salted water [and set them aside to drain the excess moisture].

Now take a clean skillet and put olive oil in it. Once it boils, add the eggplant pieces and let them fry until they cook and brown. (**181v**) Take them out and put them in a glazed bowl (*ghaḍāra*) and serve them.

If you want to pour [a sauce of] boiled vinegar and pounded cooked garlic on them, you can do so. You may also mix finely grated hard cheese (*ghubār jubn*) with the garlic and vinegar [sauce], along with a small amount of sweet olive oil (*zayt maṭbūkh*).[43] Do whichever you like, and eat the dish salubriously, God Almighty willing.[44]

---

40 This recipe is uncharacteristically brief; it does not even mention that the eggplant is to be pounded with the suet. I used the Madrid MS, fol. 113v, to fill this in. A similar recipe with more details is found in the anonymous Andalusi *Anwāʿ al-ṣaydala* 145, according to which, the seasoning ingredients used in the filling include black pepper, Ceylon cinnamon, spikenard, onion juice, and coriander seeds.

41 In *Anwāʿ al-ṣaydala*, mentioned in the above note, the sausages are fried in olive oil and eaten hot, with or without sauce (*marqa*).

42 See n. 3 above.

43 *Zayt maṭbūkh*, literally 'cooked oil,' is another name used in this book besides *zayt ṭayyib*, *zayt ʿadhb*, and *zayt ḥulw*, to designate a mild and sweet variety of olive oil used throughout the book for cooking purposes. According to al-Anṭākī, *Tadhkira* 200, it is produced by boiling pulp of fully ripe olives and then pressing their oil out. See glossary 6, s.v. *zayt*.

44 This is the last eggplant recipe in the Berlin MS, fol. 77v; and after three lines, which begin

[The BL MS, fol. 181v, concludes the eggplant chapter with the following recipe on grilling it; the Berlin MS does not include it; and the Madrid MS, fols. 113v–114r, gives a very brief version of it.[45]]

Another dish [on eggplants, showing ways for grilling them]
Take as many eggplants as you want and put them in hot ashes (*ramād sukhn*); cover them with ashes as well. Light a fire over them and all around, and keep them there to bake until [according to your estimation] you know that they have cooked well. Take them out and cut them into [large] pieces.

Put olive oil and pounded cooked garlic in a wide, shallow bowl (*ṣaḥfa*). Take the eggplants, discard their skins, leave them for a while [to drain their black juices], and then chop them and mix them with the olive oil and garlic. Sprinkle them with salt and black pepper, fold them to mix well, and eat the dish salubriously, God Almighty willing.

If you want to bake the eggplants in the *tannūr* (clay oven), place them in the middle of its embers (*ghaḍā*). If you want to use the *furn* (brick oven) instead, put the eggplants in an unglazed pan (*ṭājin ghayr muzajjaj*) and put it in the oven until they fully bake; use them as described above, God Almighty willing.

Do not eat too many eggplants prepared this way because they can agitate black bile (*muhayyij lil-sawdāʾ*).[46]

[The following are the versions the Madrid MS gives (fols. 111v–112v) of the above BL and Berlin MSS recipes vii.2.9, 10, 12, and 13]:[47]

---

with chapter vii.3 on carrots, the manuscript ends, which obviously is due to the unfortunate loss of folios. We are lucky that the BL MS survived; it is a complete copy of this manuscript. From this point forth, I will be using the Madrid and BL MSS; I will also use them to check the edited Arabic text.

45 Here is the Madrid MS version: **Grilled dish (*al-mashwī*):**

> Bury the eggplants in the embers of a clay oven (*ghaḍā al-tannūr*) or any other [fire]; or bake them in an unglazed pan in the *furn* (brick oven) until done. Peel them, press out their juices, and mash them (*yuhashsham*, literally 'smash').

46 This will cause illnesses related to an excess in black bile. Grilling eggplants was not believed to be a healthy way to consuming them. See glossary 11, s.v. *mizāj*, for more on the humors (*akhlāṭ*).

47 The editor of the Arabic text **does not** alert the readers to this issue and numbers them as if they were a continuation of the primary Berlin manuscript he is following. I kept the editor's numbering to avoid confusion but moved the recipes to the end of the chapter.

VII.2.19 A Dish Called *arnabiyya*[48]

Peel the eggplants, cut them into halves [lengthwise] with their calyxes, and boil them in salted water until they cook, and then [take them out] and press them [to get rid of the excess moisture].[49] In a wide and shallow pan (*ṣaḥfa*), put vinegar, *murrī* (liquid fermented sauce), black pepper, coriander seeds, cumin, dried thyme crushed by hand (*maḥkūk*), and pounded and whole garlic cloves. [Dip the eggplant pieces in this sauce] after checking their saltiness.[50] Take them out and spread them in a pan (*ṭājin*) that has been greased with olive oil. Pour the rest of the sauce all over them along with plenty of olive oil. Let it cook in the *furn* (brick oven) at a distance from the fire until all the moisture evaporates.

VII.2.20 Another Dish [of Eggplant Casserole][51]

Peel[52] small eggplants, scrape their calyxes, and slit them into quarters lengthwise without separating the pieces. Boil them [in salted water] or stuff them with salt, weigh them [with a heavy object for some time, and then] wash them and [set them aside to] drain the excess moisture. Cook the eggplants in a pot with water, salt—if needed—olive oil, spices (*abzār*), cumin,[53] vinegar, and *murrī* (liquid fermented sauce). [After they cook,] take them out and pack them next to each other standing upright in a pan (*ṭājin*) with the calyxes pointing upwards.

---

48 Cf. recipe vii.2.9 above. The editor's guess of the dish's name as *al-azaliyya* (الأزلية), literally 'the everlasting one,' was based on the Madrid MS, fol. 111v, where it is copied as الارلية (?), which turns out to be a misreading of *al-arnabiyya* الارنبية 'like a rabbit' (feminine form of the masculine *arnabī*). We know this due to the presence of a comparable recipe named *arnabī* in the anonymous Andalusi *Anwāʿ al-ṣaydala* 143. Cf. another *arnabī* recipe, ii.1.6 above, prepared with meat. The dish acquired its name from the seasonings used, mainly vinegar and *murrī*, which give it a rabbit-like brownish hue.

49 I filled in the missing directions in the recipe based on recipe vii.2.9 above and the counterpart recipe in the anonymous *Anwāʿ al-ṣaydala*, mentioned in the above note.

50 The editor of the Arabic text misreads *yukhtabar* 'check for' as *yunzaʿ* 'take off,' irrelevant in this context. In the similar recipe above, vii.2.9, the eggplant slices are to be rinsed to get rid of excessive saltiness.

51 Cf. recipe vii.2.10 above.

52 The editor of the Arabic text misreads *yuqashshar* 'peel' as *yushaqq* 'slit.'

53 Although cumin is a spice, which could have been implied in the generic term *abzār* that precedes it, it is nonetheless mentioned because, in the option given at the end of the recipe, the cook will be instructed to leave out cumin.

Blend breadcrumbs with water and break enough eggs [on them] to cover the eggplants; all beaten with spices and saffron. Gently and cautiously pour this mix all over the pan to cover the eggplants; let only the calyxes show. Garnish the top with [raw] whole egg yolks (*fuṣūṣ bayḍ*)[54] and pour the strained broth [of the cooked eggplants] and a small amount of olive oil all over the top. Let the pan bake in the *furn* (brick oven) until it fully cooks and [the sauce] thickens.

For those who want to prepare it with fresh juices of cilantro and mint, let them leave out the vinegar, saffron, cumin, and *murrī*.

VII.2.21 Another Dish [of Simmered Diced Eggplants][55]

Peel eggplants and dice them, and then either salt them and weigh them down [with a heavy object,] or[56] salt them profusely and soak them in a small amount of water in a wide, shallow bowl (*ṣaḥfa*), or boil them [in salted water]. Rinse the eggplants [and let them drain].

Finely chop a good amount of onions, wash them twice, and cook them with the eggplants in a pot with a small amount of water, lots of olive oil, black pepper, coriander seeds, a bit of cumin, and *murrī* (liquid fermented sauce). Let the pot cook until all is done and then empty it into a wide, shallow bowl (*ṣaḥfa*).

This dish may also be cooked with fresh or cured (*qadīd*) meat.

VII.2.22 Another Dish [of Stuffed Whole Eggplants][57]

Take a large, well-proportioned eggplant; leave it whole with the skin on.[58] Gently remove its calyx so that it keeps its shape intact and then core it out carefully with a thin-bladed knife (*sikkīn raqīq*), removing all its flesh from the calyx opening.

Cook the eggplant flesh in salted water until well done and then throw out the water and mash and press the eggplant with crumbs of grated bread and

---

54 The editor of the Arabic text erroneously reads *tunajjam* 'garnish' as *tatajammar* 'simmer and nicely blend.'

55 Cf. recipe vii.2.12 above.

56 The editor of the Arabic text erroneously read أو 'or' as و 'and.'

57 Cf. recipe vii.2.13 above.

58 The editor of the Arabic text misread *fa-tutrak* 'to be left' as *fa-tunazzal*, irrelevant in the context.

an egg beaten with all the spices (*abāzīr*), as mentioned in previous recipes. Return all this to the eggplant cavity—there should be enough to fill it. Return the calyx to where it was and tie it with a strong thread.

Do the same thing with other eggplants until you have the needed amount. Put them all packed in one pan (*ṭājin*), [spread] the remaining stuffing on them, and pour olive oil all over. Let the pan cook in the *furn* (brick oven) until [the sauce] thickens and [the stuffing] sets.

For those who want to mix the pounded meat of a ram and the like with the eggplant [stuffing], or stewed sparrows or fried ones, with boiled egg yolks, and stuff the eggplants with them, they can go ahead and do so. Also, if wished, [the stuffing] can be colored green with fresh juices of cilantro and mint.

The most important thing [in this recipe] is to keep the shape of the eggplants intact, for this indeed is the novelty of it (*mustaṭraf*).[59]

59 Interestingly, the corresponding recipe in the anonymous Andalusi *Anwāʿ al-ṣaydala* 144 ends with this instruction: "Put the [cooked] eggplants as they are, whole, in a wide shallow bowl, as if nothing has been done with them." See also the ending comments in recipe vii.2.13 above.

Part Seven, Chapter Three: On Dishes with Carrots (*Jazar*)

A dish [of carrots in sauce]

Take large fine-tasting carrots, lightly scrape their skins, cut them in half lengthwise, and then split each half into two pieces;[1] discard their inner cores. Wash the pieces thoroughly and then take a clean pot, put the carrots in it with the addition of water and salt, and put it on the fire to cook.

Once the carrot pieces cook, take them out gently and spread them on a sieve (*ghirbāl*) or a board (*lawḥ*) to drain the excess moisture. Now take a clean skillet, put sweet olive oil (*zayt ʿadhb*) in it, and place it on the fire. Once the oil boils, put the carrot pieces in it to fry and brown. Take them out and put them in a glazed bowl (*ghaḍāra*). Pour [a mix of] boiled vinegar, pounded cooked garlic, (**182r**) and caraway all over them, and eat them salubriously, God Almighty willing.

If you want, skip frying the carrot pieces. You may also use them to garnish *kawāmil* dishes[2] after frying the pieces and dipping them only in mustard sauce (*ṣināb*).[3]

---

1 Note that here ends the Berlin MS, fol. 77v, after which the editor of the Arabic text had to resort to the Madrid MS, which somewhat differs stylistically from the Berlin MS and tends to give fewer instructions. The edited Arabic text, which now follows the Madrid MS, fol. 114r, is flawed at some places and misses some words due to the inability of the editor to read them.
However, I continue to follow the BL MS for my translation to the very end of the text, which indeed helps maintain the stylistic consistencies throughout.

2 Sg. *al-kāmil*, it was a favorite festive all-in-one dish, see recipe ii.2.40 above.

3 *Ṣināb*, also known as *khardal*, designates the seeds themselves as well as sauces/condiments made with them. For recipes, see chapter x.1 below. See also glossary 5 for mustard condiment/sauce; and glossary 8 for the seeds.

 | DOI:10.1163/9789004469488_032

FIGURE 78 Last folio, 77v, in the Berlin MS
STAATSBIBLIOTHEK ZU BERLIN—PREUSSISCHER KULTURBESITZ, ORIENTABTEILUNG, MS WETZSTEIN II 1207

FIGURE 79 Carrots, al-Ghāfiqī, *Kitāb al-Adwiya al-mufrada*, MS, fol. 113r, detail
REPRODUCED BY PERMISSION OF THE OSLER LIBRARY OF THE HISTORY OF MEDICINE, MCGILL UNIVERSITY

Part Seven, Chapter Four: On Dishes Made with Desert Truffles (*Kamʾa*)[1]

VII.4.1 A Dish [of a Casserole of Desert Truffles and Cheese]

Take whatever you want of *kamʾa*, which is called *tirfās*,[2] wash them thoroughly, and then peel them and cut them into small pieces—do this by hand, do not use a knife.[3] Put the truffles in a clean pot with water and put it on the fire to cook. Let them boil once or twice[4] and then empty them into a wide, shallow bowl (*ṣaḥfa*); rinse them once in hot water (*yushṭaf*).

Next, take fresh cheese, crumble it in a large bowl (*mithrad*), and add broken eggs to it, enough for the cheese and truffles used. Set aside some of the egg yolks, [keep them whole,] and add salt and black pepper to the eggs, along with ginger, Ceylon cinnamon, coriander seeds, fresh juices of cilantro and mint, and a bit of saffron. Beat all these vigorously by hand or with a ladle to mix them well and then combine them with the truffles.

Take a glazed pan (*ṭājin muzajjaj*) and put some olive oil in it. Spread the egg-cheese-truffle mix in it. Level the surface and garnish it with the [whole] egg yolks. Sprinkle its face with black pepper and Ceylon cinnamon and drizzle it with some more olive oil. Take the pan to the *furn* (communal brick oven) and let it set and brown at a distance from the fire. Take it out and leave it aside until it is no longer hot, and invoke the name of God and eat it salubriously,[5] God Almighty willing.

---

1 Note that this chapter is missing from the Madrid MS and the edited Arabic text that follows it. Only the BL MS has it.

2 The name is of Amazigh origin. *Kamʾa* is the truffle's name in the eastern region. See glossary 12.

3 To my knowledge, this is mentioned only in al-Tujībī's cookbook. Given the insipid flavor of desert truffles, my guess is that, compared with the evenly cut pieces using a knife, the irregularly shaped truffle pieces broken by hand create many uneven edges that would absorb much more of the flavors of liquids in which they are being cooked.

4 See glossary 9.2, s.v. *ghalya*, for how this was conducted.

5 That is, say *Bism Allāh* (بسم الله). This is an indication that such cold vegetable dishes were the first eaten, before the main hot ones.

 | DOI:10.1163/9789004469488_033

FIGURE 80 A desert truffle, *kam'a*, al-Ghāfiqī, *Kitāb al-Adwiya al-mufrada*, MS 7508, fol. 250r, detail

VII.4.2 Another Dish [of Boiled Desert Truffles]

Take as many desert truffles as you want and do with them as was done above [i.e., cleaning, peeling, boiling, and rinsing]. When they are cooked [and ready to use], add some of the [boiling] liquid to them, sprinkle them with salt, black pepper, and ginger, give them a quick stir to mix, and eat them salubriously, God Almighty willing.

VII.4.3 Another Dish [of Desert Truffles Simmered with Butter]

Take as many desert truffles as you want and do with them as was done above. Put them in new pot, adding butter that has been heated up and strained. Let the pot cook on the fire until all is done and then empty the dish into a glazed bowl (*ghaḍāra*). Sprinkle it with salt and black pepper—but not much—and eat it salubriously, God Almighty willing.

VII.4.4 Another Dish [of Roasted Desert Truffles]

Take the largest desert truffles you can find, scrape them from the outside, and wash them well until they are cleaned of whatever has adhered to them of sand and the like. Dry them with a piece of cloth (*mindīl*).

Now take a piece of tow linen (*mushāqat al-kattān*) and moisten it with water. Take the truffles, put them in its middle, and wrap it around them. Put this bundle in embers (*ghaḍā*) until, according to your estimation, they have roasted. Take the bundle out (**182v**) and remove the cloth. Cut the truffles into quarters by hand, sprinkle them with salt, black pepper, and ginger—but not much—and eat them salubriously, God Almighty willing.

The best ovens for roasting truffles are those used in distilling rosewater,[6] if available, so know this.

6 Distilling ovens are being recommended here because they are usually lighted with slow-burning coals, which produce moderately low heat. See, for instance, al-Kindī, *al-Taraffuq fī l-ʿiṭr* 92.

Part Seven, Chapter Five:[1] On Cooking Asparagus (*Isfarāj*),[2] and It Has One Dish

Take as much asparagus as you want and discard the unwanted parts. Take the tender spears only, put them in a clean pot with water in it, and place it on the fire. Take another pot with water only and put it on the fire as well. Once the asparagus boils three times or so,[3] pour off the liquid and replenish it with hot water from the other pot; resume the boiling. Do this several times until the asparagus is no longer bitter. Rinse them in hot water, press out the excess moisture, and put them in a glazed bowl (*ghaḍāra*). Pour olive oil and vinegar all over them, also put split boiled eggs on top, and eat the dish salubriously, God Almighty willing.

---

1 Note that this chapter is missing from the Madrid MS and the edited Arabic text that follows it. Only the BL MS has it.

2 This was the name of this vegetable in the Muslim West; in the eastern region it was known as *hilyawn*.

3 *Thalāth ghalyāt*, see glossary 9.2, s.v. *ghalya*, for more on how this was conducted.

 | DOI:10.1163/9789004469488_034

FIGURE 81 Asparagus, *isfarāj*, al-Ghāfiqī, *Kitāb al-Adwiya al-mufrada*, MS 7508, fol. 138v, detail
REPRODUCED BY PERMISSION OF THE OSLER LIBRARY OF THE HISTORY OF MEDICINE, MCGILL UNIVERSITY

Part Seven, Chapter Six: On *Ḥarshaf*, Which Are *Qannāriyya* and *Afzan*[1]

Afzan is the best for cooking.

VII.6.1 A Dish for [Mashed *afzan* Cooked with Milk]

Take cardoons of the kind called *afzan* (wild cardoon), remove their thistles and all the unwanted parts, put them in a clean pot with water, and put it on the fire. Take them out of the pot as soon as they boil once or twice,[2] rinse them in hot water, and set them aside.

Take another pot and put finely chopped onion in it with a small amount of water, salt, coriander seeds, and black pepper. Put it on the fire to cook. Once the onion is done, take milk (*laban ḥalīb*) with a piece of butter in it and add it to the pot. Keep it on the fire until it boils.

Now take the [boiled] cardoons (*ḥarshaf*), pound them in a mortar very well, and add them the pot of milk and onion [and mix them all]. Immediately remove the pot from the fire, empty it [into a bowl], and eat the dish salubriously, God Almighty willing.

VII.6.2 Another Dish [of Cardoons Simmered in Oil]

Take cardoons (*ḥarshaf*), whichever variety is available to you, clean them of the unwanted parts [including thistles], and boil them in salted water after cutting them into round pieces. [Take them out of the water,] rinse them, and put them in a pan (*ṭājin*) with lots of olive oil, fine clear vinegar (*khall naqī*), black

1 Note that this chapter is missing from the Madrid MS and the edited Arabic text that follows it. Only the BL MS has it. The chapter's title is significant as it helps us identify the varieties of cardoon used and their names. Based on it, *ḥarshaf* is a generic name for cardoons (*Cynara carduncululus*). *Qannāriyya* and *afzan*/*afzān* are two types of this plant: *qannāriyya* is cultivated cardoon (*Cynara carduncululus var. altilis* DC) and *afzan* is wild cardoon (*Cynara carduncululus var. sylvestris L*). See glossary 12, s.v. *ḥarshaf*.

2 See glossary 9.2, s.v. *ghalya*, for more on how this was conducted.

 | DOI:10.1163/9789004469488_035

FIGURE 82
Cultivated cardoon, *kankar*, Dioscorides, *Kitāb Dīsqūrīdis fī mawādd al-ʿilāj*, fol. 12v, detail
BRITISH LIBRARY: ORIENTAL MANUSCRIPTS, OR 3366, IN QATAR DIGITAL LIBRARY HTTPS://WWW.QDL.QA/ARCHIVE/81055/VDC_100022531380.0X000001

pepper, coriander seeds, cumin, garlic—both pounded and whole ones—dried thyme, which has been crushed between your hands, and citron leaves.

Put the pot on the fire to cook, and once the cardoons are done and all the water has evaporated and nothing remains but the oil, remove the pot from the fire. Leave it to cool slightly, and invoke the name of God and eat them salubriously,[3] God Almighty willing.

VII.6.3 Another Dish [of Fried Cardoons]

(183r) Take cardoons (*ḥarshaf*), whichever variety is available to you, and do with them as was done in the above recipe. Take a clean frying pan, put olive oil in it, and put it on the fire. Once the oil boils, fry the cardoon pieces in it, turning them to brown on all sides. Put them in a glazed bowl (*ghaḍāra*) and dress them with vinegar and garlic, which has been first cooked in water and then pounded and boiled with the vinegar, and eat them salubriously, God Almighty willing.

3 That is, say *Bism Allāh* (بسم الله). This is an indication that such cold vegetable dishes were the first to eat before the main hot ones.

CHAPTER VII.7

Part Seven, Chapter Seven: On Cooking Mushrooms (*Fuṭr*),[1] and It Has One Dish

FIGURE 83 Mushrooms, Dioscorides, *Fī Hayūlā al-ṭibb*, translation by Ḥunayn b. Isḥāq, fol. 206v, detail
FROM THE NEW YORK PUBLIC LIBRARY, SPENCER COLLECTION: HTTPS://DIGITALCOLLECTIONS.NYPL.ORG/ITEMS/5E66B3E8-93BB-D471-E040-E00A180654D7

Take as much as you want of *fuṭr*, which is *fuqqāʿ*. Wash them thoroughly and dice them into small pieces. Put them in a new pot with a small amount of water, salt, olive oil, coriander seeds, chopped fresh cilantro, chopped onion, and black pepper.

Put the pot on the fire to cook. As soon as the mushrooms are done, add small amounts of vinegar and *murrī* (liquid fermented sauce) and top them (*tukhammar*) with a couple of eggs [beaten with] some flour—as is usually done with *takhmīr*.[2] Leave the pot on embers (*ghaḍā*) until it sets and thickens, and invoke the name of God and eat it,[3] God Almighty willing.

1 Note that this chapter is missing from the Madrid MS and the edited Arabic text that follows it. Only the BL MS has it. The name of the mushrooms also occurs as *faqʿ*, as in recipe iii.2.49 above.

2 Topping dishes with a layer of beaten eggs was a familiar last stage in preparing dishes with little sauce in them, like this one. See glossary 9.2, s.v. *takhmīr*.

3 That is, say *Bism Allāh* (بسم الله). This is an indication that such cold vegetable dishes were the first ones eaten.

 | DOI:10.1163/9789004469488_036

Part Seven, Chapter Eight:[1] On Cooking with Spinach (*Isfānākh*), Blite (*Yarbūz*),[2] Lettuce (*Khass*), and the Like[3]

VII.8.1 A Dish [of Boiled Leafy Vegetables, Mashed and Seasoned]

Take whichever is available of the vegetables (*buqūl*) I mentioned above; clean them, remove the unwanted parts, and put them in a clean pot with water to cook on the fire. As soon as they boil once or twice,[4] put them on a board (*lawḥ*) and beat them with the back of a knife's blade (*qafā al-sikkīn*) until they become doughy in texture. Take them and put them in a new pot with salt, sweet olive oil (*zayt ʿadhb*), black pepper, coriander seeds, a small amount of chopped onion, and a small amount of water. Put the pot on the fire, let it cook until it boils and the vegetables cook, and then remove it. Prolonged boiling should be avoided because the vegetables will turn yellow and spoil.

If you want to use skinned almonds as well, pound them lightly and add them to the vegetables. Egg yolks and fresh butter can be added, too. Once the dish is done, empty it into a glazed bowl (*ghaḍāra*), and eat it salubriously, God Almighty willing.

VII.8.2 Another Dish [of Boiled and Seasoned Leafy Vegetables]

Take whichever is available of the vegetables I mentioned to you, clean them, and remove the unwanted parts. With spinach, cut off the roots only and keep the leaves whole; do likewise with blite. As for lettuce, take only their tender hearts and the tender leaves closer to them. Put whatever you chose of these vegetables in a clean pot with water and salt and put it on the fire to cook.

---

1 The editor of the Arabic text erroneously reports this chapter as missing from the Madrid MS (see his note in the Arabic edition, p. 237). In reality it does exist in the Madrid MS, fol. 107r–v, where it is complete, minus the chapter's title, which appears on a different page (fol. 114r). I used the Madrid MS here to fill in a few details missing in the BL MS.

2 Leaves of wild amaranth, also known as *baqla Yamāniyya* 'Yemeni vegetable,' See glossary 12 for more on this leaf vegetable.

3 The vegetables called for in this chapter are all leafy ones.

4 See glossary 9.2, s.v. *ghalya*, for more on how this was conducted.

 | DOI:10.1163/9789004469488_037

FIGURE 84 Blite, *yarbūz*, also known as *baqla Yamāniyya*, Dioscorides, *Fī Hayūlā al-ṭibb*, translation by Ḥunayn b. Isḥāq, fol. 100v, detail
FROM THE NEW YORK PUBLIC LIBRARY, SPENCER COLLECTION: HTTPS://DIGITALCOLLECTIONS.NYPL.ORG/ITEMS/5E66B3E8-FDDD-D471-E040-E00A180654D7

As soon as the vegetables cook, take them out, press out the excess moisture, (**183v**) put them in a glazed bowl (*ghaḍāra*), pour olive oil and vinegar all over them, and eat them salubriously, God Almighty willing.

Do the same thing with cabbages (*kurunb*) and turnips (*lift*) and their leaves. If you want to add vinegar mixed with pounded cooked garlic to the cabbages, go ahead and do so, with the help of God and His Might.

Part Seven, Chapter Nine:[1] On Cooking *Jināniyya*[2]

Take a fresh and tender gourd (*qarʿa*), scrape its outer skin, and remove the inside [seeds and pith]. Dice it into very small pieces and then wash it and set it aside.

Take fresh and tender small eggplants (*bādhinjān*), scrape off the calyxes, peel off their black skins, and slit them [lengthwise] into quarters but not all the way, keep them attached. Put them in a pot with water and salt and put it on the fire to cook. Let the eggplants boil three times[3] and then take them out and rinse them in hot water. [Put them] in a new pot along with the gourd, add water—but not much—salt, plenty of olive oil, black pepper, coriander seeds, and a small amount of chopped onion. Put the pot on the fire to cook.

Next, take blite (*yarbūz*), purslane (*rijla*), and whatever is available of other [leaf] vegetables (*buqūl*).[4] Also take budding snake cucumbers (*ʿuyūn qiththāʾ*) and the young shoots of their vines (*ghazl*); and budding common cucumbers (*ʿuyūn khiyār*) and the young shoots of their vines.[5] Also take young shoots of gourd vine, fresh cilantro, and tender tips of mint sprigs (*ʿuyūn naʿnaʿ*). Clean them all carefully, removing all the unwanted parts, wash them, chop them finely—the finest you can get them—put them in another clean pot with water in it, and let them cook. As soon as they boil once or twice,[6] remove the pot from the fire, strain the vegetables, and discard the liquid. Give them a rinse in hot water, press out the excess moisture, and add them to the gourd and eggplant pot and let it boil.

---

1 This chapter is not missing from the Madrid MS as the editor of the Arabic text proclaims in his note, p. 237. It is incomprehensible how the editor could have missed it, as it occurs immediately before the tenth chapter. Note that chapters in the Madrid MS are not numbered. The BL MS, which I followed here, gives its appropriate number.
I used the Madrid MS, fols. 107v–108r, to fill in a few details missing in the BL MS.

2 The dish derives its name from *junayna* (orchard), called so because it incorporates orchard produce. As we are told in the anonymous Andalusi *Anwāʿ al-ṣaydala* 148, it was the custom to cook such dishes in orchards, picnic style, preferably in the summer and fall. In the eastern region, such a dish was called *bustāniyya* (derived from *bustān* 'orchard'), as in al-Warrāq's tenth-century *Kitāb al-Ṭabīkh*, English trans., *Annals* 290.

3 See glossary 9.2, s.v. *ghalya*, for more on how this was conducted.

4 See the previous chapter on leafy vegetables.

5 These are two kinds of cucumbers, *Cucumis melo var. flexuosus* and *Cucumis sativus*, respectively. See glossary 12.

6 See glossary 9.2, s.v. *ghalya*, for more on how this was conducted.

 | DOI:10.1163/9789004469488_038

Next, take fresh cilantro, clean it, and then pound it in a mortar (*mihrās*) with one or two cloves of garlic; add them to the gourd and eggplant pot. Now have a look at the gourds and eggplants; if you see that they are done, take small pieces of fine-tasting hard cheese and add them to the pot. Take another amount of cheese, grate it with the *iskarfāj* (grater) until it is as fine as dust, and set it aside.

Take the pot and empty it into a large glazed bowl (*ghaḍāra*). Sprinkle the dish with the [set aside] grated cheese, pour plenty of olive oil all over it, and eat it salubriously, God Almighty willing. [While eating it] sprinkle more grated cheese as needed.

It has been mentioned that this dish may also be cooked with mutton from young adult sheep and that the meat should be very fresh, used right after the sheep has been slaughtered. It can also be cooked with all kinds of vegetables [and not only the ones mentioned here], so know this.

Part Seven, Chapter Ten: On Cooking Taros (*Qulqāṣ*),[1] and It Has One Dish[2]

(**184r**) Take sweet taros that are young and tender (*fatī*). Wash off the soil, peel them, and cut them into thin slices lengthwise. Boil them in salted water briefly and then take them out of the pot and set them aside to dry. Fry them in olive oil or [rendered] suet (*shaḥm*). Once they brown, take them out and put them in a glazed bowl (*ghaḍāra*), give them a light sprinkle of lemon juice (*khall līm*),[3] and eat them salubriously, God Almighty willing.

1 It also occurs as *qulqās*, as in al-Tujībī's own list of the book's sections, p. 113.

2 Note that the whole chapter is also included in the Madrid MS and the edited Arabic text that follows it.

3 In the two surviving Andalusi cookbooks, this one and anonymous *Anwāʿ al-ṣaydala*, *khall* not only designates regular 'vinegar' produced by fermentation but also, in a looser sense, unfermented preserved 'sour juice,' and even freshly pressed out lemon juice. See glossary 8, s.v. *khall*. In light of this, the lemon juice used here could be fresh or preserved.

 | DOI:10.1163/9789004469488_039

PART 8

القسم الثامن في الفول والحمص وما أشبههما

وهو يشتمل على ثلاثة فصول

On Fava Beans (Fūl), *Chickpeas* (Ḥimmaṣ), *and the Like. It Has Three Chapters*

Part Eight, Chapter One: On Fresh and Dried Fava Beans (*Fūl*)[1]

VIII.1.1 A Dish Called *fustuqiyya* (Pistachio Green)[2]

Take as much as you want of fresh and tender fava beans [in the pod], shell their two peels,[3] wash them in fresh water (*māʾ ʿadhb*), rub them with olive oil, and put them in a new pot that has been greased with olive oil. Add water and olive oil, a chopped onion, and coriander seeds to them, and put the pot on the fire to cook.

Once the beans are done, pick out [and discard] whatever is visible of the chopped onion, enter the ladle in the pot, and start beating the beans and pressing them until they mash and blend. Take clean and pure salt, pound it [in a mortar], and start adding it to the pot bit by bit while stirring the pot, and continue tasting it until enough salt is added.

Take fresh cilantro, pound it in a mortar (*mihrās*), press out the juice, pour it into the pot of beans, and let it cook on low heat until it boils and thickens. Empty the pot into a glazed bowl (*ghaḍāra*), sprinkle it with cumin with a drizzle of sweet olive oil (*zayt ʿadhb*),[4] and eat it salubriously, God Almighty willing.

If you want to cook the dish with fresh suet (*shaḥm ṭarī*), then pound it first and add it [to the pot] with the fresh cilantro [juice],[5] so understand this and do accordingly, with the help of God Almighty.

---

1 The BL MS I used here as a basic text offers a longer version comprised of eight recipes, compared to the four recipes given in the Madrid MS, which the editor of the Arabic text used. I will still refer to the latter whenever it introduces food names or terms not used in the BL MS.

2 The name of the dish is given only in the Madrid MS, fol. 108r.

3 The Arabic expression is تقشره من قشريه, the two peels being the jacket and the outer skin of each bean.

4 Adding olive oil is mentioned only in the Madrid MS, fol. 108v.

5 The Madrid MS recipe also suggests using very finely and thinly chopped suet from around the small intestine (*duwwāra*).

FIGURE 85 Green fava beans, Dioscorides, *Fī Hayūlā al-ṭibb*, translation by Ḥunayn b. Isḥāq, fol. 96r, detail
FROM THE NEW YORK PUBLIC LIBRARY, SPENCER COLLECTION: HTTPS://DIGITALCOLLECTIONS.NYPL.ORG/ITEMS/5E66B3E9-1480-D471-E040-E00A180654D7

VIII.1.2 Another Dish [of Fried Fresh Fava Beans]

Take as much as you want of fresh fava beans [in the pod], shell their outer peels [i.e., the jackets], and then wash them and put them in a clean pot with fresh water. Put it on the fire to cook. When the beans are done, add salt, bring the pot to a boil, and then remove it from the fire and drain the liquid [but save some of it].

Take a clean skillet and put it on the fire with olive oil; add the beans as soon as the oil boils. Let them fry gently while stirring them, and take them out of the skillet once they brown.

Now take garlic, pound it, and add it to the skillet with some of the liquid in which the beans were cooked. Once the garlic cooks and all the moisture evaporates, add olive oil. Return the beans to the skillet and stir them with garlic and oil until the oil boils. Empty them into a glazed bowl (*ghaḍāra*), sprinkle them (**184v**) with black pepper, and eat them salubriously, God Almighty willing.

If you want, replace the garlic and olive oil with *murrī naqīʿ* (sun-fermented liquid sauce) and thyme, and eat it salubriously, God Almighty willing.

Also, if you want, take the beans after boiling them and fry them lightly. Take a small pot and put a small amount of water in it with black pepper, coriander seeds, *murrī naqīʿ*, pounded garlic, a small amount of chopped onion, and plenty of olive oil. Put the pot on the fire, and when it boils, add the beans and let them cook until some of the liquid (*marqa*) evaporates and the beans cook well. Empty them [into a bowl] and serve them, God Almighty willing.

In addition, if you want to cook both of the previous dishes with *musammakh* [dried] fava beans, which are *manbūt* (sprouted),[6] you can go ahead and do so, God Almighty willing.

VIII.1.3 Another Dish [of Fresh Fava Beans Simmered with Spring Garlic]

Take as much as you want of fresh fava beans [in the pod] and shell their outer peels [i.e., the jackets]. Also take the tender stems of young green garlic (*ʿasālīj thūm akhḍar*);[7] cut off their leaves and discard them. Put the beans with the [cut] garlic stems in a new pot.[8] Add plenty of olive oil to them with a small amount of water. Keep the pot on the fire until both the beans and garlic cook, all the liquid evaporates, and only the oil remains. Empty the pot into a glazed bowl (*ghaḍāra*), sprinkle the dish with black pepper and salt, and eat it salubriously, God Almighty willing.

VIII.1.4 Another Dish [of Boiled Fresh Fava Beans]

Take fresh fava beans [in the pod], shell their outer peels [i.e., the jackets], wash them, and put them in a clean pot with fresh water. Put it on the fire to cook, and once beans are done, add salt and let them boil. Drain the liquid and put the beans in a glazed bowl (*ghaḍāra*) with some salt and black pepper sprinkled on them, and eat them salubriously, God Almighty willing.

If you want to put vinegar and olive oil as well, which would be their sauce (*marqa*), do go ahead and put them, and eat the dish salubriously, God Almighty willing.

---

6 The term *musammakh* occurs in the BL MS, fol. 184v only. That al-Tujībī needed to explain what it was is testimony to its regional uniqueness. I have seen similar usage of the word related to sprouting unhusked rice grains before planting them in Ibn ʿAwwām, *al-Filāḥa al-Andalusiyya* iv 100. In al-Zabīdī, *Tāj al-ʿArūs*, s.v. سمخ, it is used to designate a seedling.

7 In the Madrid MS, fol. 108v, this part is called *aʿnāq thūm akhḍar*, literally 'necks of green garlic.' Garlic is used while still young, before their bulbs fully form.

8 Cutting them is mentioned in the Madrid MS.

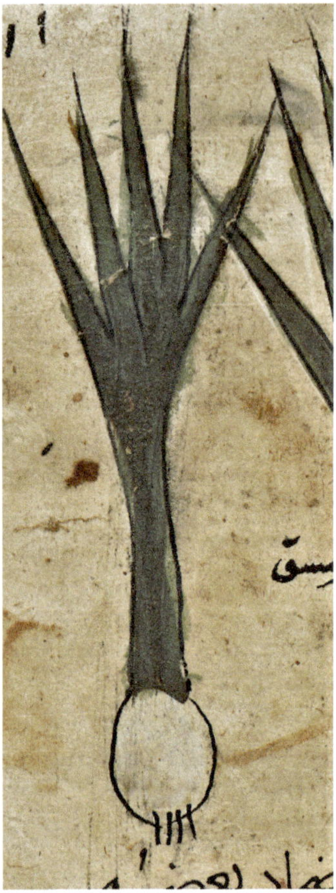

FIGURE 86
Spring garlic, Dioscorides, *Kitāb al-Ḥashāʾish fī hāyūlā al-ʿilāj al-ṭibbī*, Arabic translation by Ḥunayn b. Isḥāq, Or. 289, fol. 93r, detail
UNIVERSITAIRE BIBLIOTHEKEN LEIDEN, HTTP://HDL.HANDLE.NET/1887.1/ITEM:1578266

VIII.1.5 Another Dish [of Boiled Fresh Fava Beans in the Pod]

Take fine-tasting fresh and tender fava beans and leave them with their outer peels. Put them in a large pot with fresh water and put it on the fire to cook. As soon as beans are done [take them out of the water and put them in a bowl]. Pound salt and black pepper,[9] and eat the beans salubriously, God Almighty willing.

9 The following repeated recipe will describe how to use salt and pepper with the dish.

VIII.1.6 Another Dish [of Boiled Fresh Fava Beans in the Pod]

[The above recipe is repeated here, with the addition of how the beans are eaten:]

Take fine-tasting fresh and tender fava beans and leave them with their outer peels. Put them in a large pot with fresh water and put it on the fire to cook. As soon as beans are done, pound salt and black pepper and put them in a vessel next to you. Empty the beans into a large, wide, and shallow bowl (*ṣaḥfa*) and eat them by dipping each first in black pepper and salt—after cleansing it [i.e., the salt] of any impurities,[10] God Almighty willing.

VIII.1.7 Another Dish [with Sprouted Dried Fava Beans]

Take sprouted fava beans (*fūl musammakh*),[11] wash them, and put them in new pot with fresh water. Put the pot on the fire to cook, and once the beans are done, drain the liquid and empty the beans (**185r**) into a glazed bowl (*ghaḍāra*). Take salt and cultivated rue (*fayjan*),[12] pound them together very well, add them to the beans, mix them well, and eat the dish salubriously, God Almighty willing.

If you want to add pounded cumin as well, do so. Also, it would be lovely (*ḥasanun*) if you take the beans after sprouting them (*tasmīkh*), peel and wash them in fresh water, and then fry them in a skillet in sweet olive oil (*zayt ʿadhb*) on a low fire until they brown. Season them with salt, black pepper, Ceylon cinnamon, and whatever other spices you like, and offer them with other foods consumed as *naql*.[13] It would not hurt either to keep the [skinned] beans soaked for an hour in the water in which they were sprouted (*māʾ zarʿihi*) before frying them; they will even taste better.[14]

[The following text enclosed in curly brackets is an addition from the Madrid MS, fol. 109r]

---

10 Salt was cleaned of impurities by dissolving it first in water and then straining it and boiling it until all the water had evaporated and the salt recrystallized.

11 See n. 6 above.

12 More commonly known as *sadhāb* in the eastern region. See glossary 8.

13 ما يتنقل به. The expression is closely associated with drinking occasions, when imbibing wine alternated with nibbling on small dishes, called *naql*. It was also used generally to designate snack foods. See glossary 5.

14 Frying fava beans as described here was called *Ziryābī* in medieval times because it was from the renowned singer Ziryāb that Andalusis learnt how to cook them to perfection. See introduction ii.5, p. 51.

{Of the quick dishes prepared with fresh fava beans:[15]
Boil the shelled fava beans in water alone and then drain them. Sprinkle them with black pepper and salt; or make sauce of vinegar and olive oil for them.

You may also cut off both ends of the fava beans themselves with a knife and then fry them in olive oil and sprinkle them with black pepper, Ceylon cinnamon, and a bit of salt. This is called *rās barṭāl* (sparrow's head).[16] The sprouted beans (*fūl manbūt*) can be prepared similarly.

The fava beans may also be boiled in their pods, using water only, and then they are peeled and eaten with pounded black pepper and salt.

The sprouted beans may be peeled and split in halves and then fried in olive oil and sprinkled with spices and salt. These are also called *rās barṭāl* (sparrow's head).[17] Additionally, after frying them, they can be dipped in rosewater.

Cooking sprouted beans in water is well-known. They must be boiled in water alone, and the boiling water is thrown out. Salt and cultivated rue (*fayjāl*)[18] are pounded and eaten with them. Cumin may also be added, which would indeed be the best way to eat them.}

VIII.1.8 Another Dish (Made with Dried Fava Beans)[19]

Take as much as you want of crushed dried fava beans (*fūl yābis*), pick them over, and wash them in hot water several times until the liquid comes out clear. Rub them with olive oil and put them in a new pot that has been greased with olive oil. Add fresh water, an onion that has been sectioned into quarters but left in one piece, a whole head of garlic, coriander seeds, and fennel seeds (*basbās*).[20]

---

15 *Min al-anwāʿ al-mukhtaṣara fī ṭabkh al-fūl al-akhḍar* (من الانواع المختصرة في طبخ الفول الاخضر).

16 *Barṭāl* is the Andalusi Arabized form (ʿAjamiyyat al-Andalus) of the Spanish *pardal* for 'sparrow.' See Corriente, *Dictionary of Andalusi Arabic*, s.v. *p-r-ṭ-l*, where the word's Latin origin is given as *pardālus*. The bird's tiny size inspired several Andalusi sayings, such as: (أش برطال؟ اواش مراق) "What is *barṭāl* good for? And what sort of stew can one make with it?"; or (إش في برطال ما يقدد؟) "What is the value of *barṭāl*, which is not even worth curing?" See al-Zajjālī, *Amthāl al-ʿawām* ii 28.

17 See the above note.

18 It occurs as *fayjan* in the BL MS; see, for instance, recipe v.1.8 and recipe viii.1.7 in this chapter.

19 In this recipe, the Madrid MS, fol. 109r calls the dried fava beans *faysār*. Otherwise, they are more commonly called *baysār* in the book. For another *baysār* recipe, see i.2.27 above.

20 *Basbās* is the Andalusi name of what was more commonly called *rāzyānaj* and *shamar*/*shamār* in the eastern region.

Put the pot on the fire to cook, and as soon as the beans are done, take the onion and garlic out of the pot.[21] Insert a ladle in the middle and continue stirring [and pressing] the beans until they disintegrate and blend. If it turns out to be very thick, add a small amount of hot water—but do this after you salt the pot bit by bit until enough is added.

Let the pot cook on low heat until all the moisture evaporates, and then remove it from the fire and ladle it into a glazed bowl (*ghaḍāra*). Sprinkle cumin and a small amount of olive oil on this *baysār* dish, let it slightly cool, and eat it salubriously, God Almighty willing.

If wished, this dish may be eaten with onions, radishes, or olives.[22]

21 Detail mentioned in the Madrid MS, fol. 109v.

22 This addition is from the Madrid MS, fol. 109v.

Part Eight, Chapter Two: On Dishes with Chickpeas (*Ḥimmaṣ*)[1]

VIII.2.1 A Dish [of Fried Fresh Green Chickpeas]

Take as much as you want of fresh green chickpeas (*ḥimmaṣ akhḍar*), shell their outer peels [i.e., jackets], and snip off the chickpeas pointed ends.[2] Take a clean skillet and put olive oil in it—but not much—and put it on the fire. As soon as the oil boils, put the chickpeas in it and let them fry gently while stirring them until they cook and brown.

Remove the skillet from the fire and put the chickpeas in a small glazed bowl (*ghaḍāra ṣaghīra*). Sprinkle them with *murrī naqīʿ* (sun-fermented liquid sauce), black pepper, and coriander seeds, and eat them salubriously, God Almighty willing.

VIII.2.2 Another Dish [of Boiled and Seasoned Dried Chickpeas]

Take dried chickpeas (*ḥimmaṣ yābis*) and soak them in fresh water after rinsing them; put them in a new pot once they soften (*yarṭub*), along with the soaking water. (185v) Add chopped onion, black pepper, coriander seeds, and a bit of pounded saffron.

Put the pot on the fire to cook, and as soon as the chickpeas are done, add a small amount of *murrī naqīʿ* (sun-fermented liquid sauce) and a ladleful of fine-tasting vinegar. Remove the pot from the fire when the vinegar boils, empty it into a glazed bowl (*ghaḍāra*), and eat the dish salubriously, God Almighty willing.

If you want to cook the chickpeas without onion and vinegar, go ahead and do so. Once they are in the serving bowl (*ghaḍāra*), pour freshly pressed lemon juice (*khall līm ṭarī*) all over them,[3] and serve them with the help of God Almighty.

---

1 Note that the whole chapter is also included in the Madrid MS and the edited Arabic text that follows it.

2 The Madrid MS, fol. 109v, compares the pointed end to a harmful prickle (*shawka*).

3 Note that in the two surviving Andalusi cookbooks, this one and the anonymous *Anwāʿ al-*

 | DOI:10.1163/9789004469488_041

FIGURE 87 Fresh chickpeas, al-Ghāfiqī, *Kitāb al-Adwiya al-mufrada*, MS 7508, fol. 185r, detail
REPRODUCED BY PERMISSION OF THE OSLER LIBRARY OF THE HISTORY OF MEDICINE, MCGILL UNIVERSITY

VIII.2.3 Another Dish [of Boiled Dried White and Black Chickpeas][4]

Take as much as you want of white and black chickpeas, rinse them, and put them in a new pot with fresh water, let it be plenty—much more than enough to submerge them. Set them aside for the entire day to let them moisten and

---

ṣaydala, *khall* not only designates regular 'vinegar' produced by fermentation but also, in a looser sense, unfermented preserved 'sour juice,' and even freshly pressed out lemon juice, as it is used here. See glossary 8, s.v. *khall*. For preserved lemon juice, see recipe X.7.15 below.

4 White chickpeas, *ḥimmaṣ abyaḍ*, are the common tan variety, deemed the best. Black chickpeas, *ḥimmaṣ aswad*, are second best, but they are also said to have the strongest properties.

release all their goodness into the water.[5] Put the pot on the fire with the soaking water, and when the chickpeas are cooked, add salt, ginger, and black pepper. Pour off the broth into a glazed bowl and drink it, for all the goodness is in it, especially the broth of black chickpeas.[6] For those who want to eat the chickpeas as well, they can do so.

Eating chickpeas regularly can help in gaining weight. Indeed, their benefits are many, especially the black ones; so know this, and may God aid our efforts.[7]

5 Addition from the Madrid MS, fol. 109v.

6 The Madrid MS adds that the broth is taken for its well-known benefits. Chickpeas, particularly their broth, were believed to have aphrodisiac properties. See glossary 12, s.v. *ḥimmaṣ*.

7 The Madrid MS. fol. 109v, adds that eating chickpeas may help soften the bowels (*yulayyin al-ṭabīʿa*).

CHAPTER VIII.3

Part Eight, Chapter Three: On Cooking All Kinds of Lentils (*ʿAdas*), and It Has One Dish[1]

FIGURE 88 Lentil plant, Dioscorides, *Kitāb al-Ḥashāʾish fī hāyūlā al-ʿilāj al-ṭibbī*, Arabic translation by Ḥunayn b. Isḥāq, Or. 289, fol. 78v, detail
UNIVERSITAIRE BIBLIOTHEKEN LEIDEN, HTTP://HDL.HANDLE.NET/1887.1/ITEM:1578266

Take whatever kind of lentils are available to you, wash them, and put them in a new pot with fresh water, olive oil, black pepper, coriander seeds, and chopped onion. Put the pot on the fire to cook.

As soon as the lentils are done, add salt—but not much—a bit of pounded saffron, and as much as you like of fine-tasting vinegar. Break 3 eggs into the pot, and as soon as they set and the vinegar boils, remove the pot from the fire, empty it into a glazed bowl (*ghaḍāra*), and eat the dish salubriously, God Almighty willing.

If you want to cook the lentils without onions, you may do so, with the help of God Almighty. As for those who want to cook them with taros (*qulqāṣ*),[2] they can do so after boiling and chopping them into small pieces.[3]

1 Note that the whole chapter is also included in the Madrid MS and the edited Arabic text that follows it.
2 It also occurs as *qulqās*, as in al-Tujībī's own list of the book's sections, p. 113.
3 Here ends the BL MS recipe. The following text is from the Madrid MS, fol. 110r.

 DOI:10.1163/9789004469488_042

Lentils may also be cooked with [the addition of] sour fermented dough (*khamīr*),[4] which has been dissolved [in water first] and then cooked with the lentils on low heat. Once the dish starts to thicken, add fine-tasting ghee (*samn*) or sweet olive oil (*zayt ʿadhb*) little by little; continue adding it so long as the lentils can absorb it. Remove the pot from the fire when it has cooked well and can no longer absorb any more fat. [Ladle it into a bowl] and sprinkle it with the needed amounts of vinegar and finely pounded black pepper (*sakhātat fulful*).[5]

4 The editor of the Arabic text misreads it as *jamīr* (meaningless in this context).

5 This unusual word must have been derived from *sikhtīt*, which designates anything that is powdery in texture. See Ibn Manẓūr, *Lisān al-ʿArab*, s.v. سخت. The editor of the Arabic text chose not to include it in the recipe.

PART 9

في المعسلات وأنواع الحلواء وما يتنوع من ذلك كله من العسل والسكر

ويشتمل على سبعة فصول

On Muʿassalāt[1] *and All Sorts of Confectionary* (Ḥalwāʾ), *with All Kinds of Variations,* (186r) *Made with Honey and Sugar. It Has Seven Chapters*

∵

1 Sg. *muʿassal.* It is a thickened starch-based pudding, sweetened with honey. It was known as *fālūdhaj* in the eastern region. See glossary 4.

Part Nine, Chapter One:[1] On Making *Muʿassal*[2] and *Ghassānī*[3]

IX.1.1 Making *muʿassal*[4]

Take as many *raṭl*s (pounds) as you want of fine-tasting honey. Put it in an earthenware cauldron (*ṭinjīr fakhkhār*)[5] and let it cook on the fire to soften and then strain it with a piece of woolen cloth or any other fabric. Wash the cauldron well and return the honey to it.

Take fine-tasting dry wheat starch (*nashā*), pick it over, put it in a large bowl (*mithrad*), [and dissolve it in liquid].[6] The amount should be 2 *ūqiyya*s (2 ounces) of starch for each *raṭl* of honey.[7] [Set it aside.] Add skinned and split almonds to the honey, as well as saffron—use only enough of it to color it because too much of it will affect the taste.

Put the cauldron with honey in it on the fire, and as soon as it starts to heat up, pour in what is in the bowl little by little while stirring the pot to avoid forming lumps. Continue stirring the pot until it mixes well and begins to thicken. [At this point] add a small amount of olive oil while stirring until it is all absorbed; add more of the oil while constantly stirring. Do this repeatedly so long as it is being absorbed. The sign that *muʿassal* has cooked is when it can no longer absorb the oil. Remove it from the fire and set it aside in the same vessel it was cooked in [until needed].

---

1 Note that the whole chapter is also included in the Madrid MS and the edited Arabic text that follows it.

2 See n. 1 on the title page of this part above.

3 It is like *muʿassal* but made with white honey and no saffron is used. Based on medieval lexicons, it may be translated as 'gorgeous.' See, for instance, Ibn Manẓūr, *Lisān al-ʿArab*, s.v. غسن, where a handsome fair-skinned man is called *ghassānī*. Judging from *ghassānī* recipes (see also recipe ii.2.43 above), the name may also be attributed to its fair color.

4 A similar *muʿassal* recipe can also be found in the anonymous Andalusi *Anwāʿ al-ṣaydala* 198. I used it here to provide a few missing steps in this recipe.

5 Typically, they are large round-bottomed pots made of metal, soapstone, or earthenware. The other name for this pot is *dast*. The Madrid MS, fol. 114r, uses a *ṭājin* (pan).

6 Such as plain water as is done in the following recipe, or rosewater as suggested in anonymous, *Anwāʿ al-ṣaydala* 198.

7 The anonymous *Anwāʿ al-ṣaydala* calls for 4 *ūqiyya*s of the starch. Additionally, it instructs the cook to dissolve it in rosewater before adding it, which explains why in this recipe it is put in a large bowl. The liquid used can also be fresh water, as directed in the following recipe.

 | DOI:10.1163/9789004469488_043

To serve it in glazed bowls, let the ladle be greased first with the oil in the *mu'assal* vessel and then ladle it out into the bowls; take as much—or as little—as you want, level it in the bowls, and garnish it (*yunajjam*) with pieces of *fānīdh* (pulled sugar taffy)[8] and crushed sugar.

This is usually the last dish served to end a meal,[9] God Almighty willing.

IX.1.2 Making *ghassānī*[10]

Take as many pounds as you want of fine-tasting white honey (*'asal abyaḍ*),[11] and do with it as was done above [of boiling and straining]. Next, return it to the cooking vessel (*wi'ā'*),[12] where it is going to be cooked and thickened. Also take hulled white sesame seeds (*juljulān abyaḍ maqshūr*), 3 *ūqiyyas* (3 ounces) for each *raṭl* (pound) of honey used, and a similar amount of skinned and split almonds. Take fine-tasting dry wheat starch (*nashā*), as much as was used above [i.e. 2 *ūqiyyas* starch per *raṭl* of honey], and dissolve it in fresh water [in a bowl].

Put the honey vessel on the fire, with the almonds and sesame seeds. As soon as you see that it has started to boil, add the starch [solution] little by little while constantly stirring. If while stirring it you see that it is about to thicken, start adding the olive oil, as was mentioned above, until enough is added. Once it stops absorbing the oil, remove the vessel from the fire and leave [the *ghassānī* pudding] in it. Whenever you want to serve it, do as was done above, God Almighty willing. (186v)

8 *Aṭrāf al-fānīdh*, as it occurs in the Madrid MS, 114v. For a *fānīdh* recipe, see ix.6.1 below.

9 يستعمل في آخر الاطعمة as copied in the BL MS, fol. 186r. In the anonymous Andalusi *Anwā' al-ṣaydala*, the expression مستعمل عندنا عقب الالوان 'offered in our region after having the main dishes,' suggests that it was a typical Andalusi tradition.

10 See n. 3 above. Unlike the Madrid MS version, fol. 114v, the BL MS, fol. 186r, offers the complete text.

11 It is a light-colored variety of honey, preferred for making fair-colored candies and sweets.

12 The kind of vessel usually used is *ṭinjīr*; see, for instance, the previous recipe.

Part Nine, Chapter Two: On Making Varieties of Confectionary (*Ḥalwā*ʾ)[1]

IX.2.1 Making Soft and White *ḥalwā*ʾ,[2] Absolutely Wonderful

Take as much as you want of fine-tasting honey, put it in a clean cauldron (*ṭinjīr*) set it on low heat, and stir it constantly with a giant fennel stalk (*kalkha*)[3] or a reed (*qaṣaba*) with a copper ring attached to its end. When the honey heats up to the degree that your finger [dipped in it] cannot stand its heat, remove it from the fire and continue stirring the pot constantly while it is on the ground until it cools a bit. Add egg whites as they are [i.e., without whipping]—4 whites for each *raṭl* (pound) of honey used. Beat them until they look homogenous and the egg whites can no longer be discerned.

Return the pot to low heat and constantly stir it until the honey turns very white. If at this point you would like to throw in some shelled walnuts or almonds, go ahead and do so, God Almighty willing.

IX.2.2 Making *ḥalwā*ʾ *al-fālūdhaj* (Starch-Based Confection)[4]

Take as much as you want of fine-tasting honey and put it in a clean tinned cauldron (*ṭinjīr muqaṣdar*). Put it on the fire and keep it there until the honey softens and then strain it in a piece of woolen cloth or any other fabric.

Clean the cauldron by washing it and then return the honey to it. Take fine-tasting dry wheat starch (*nashā yābis*)—1½ or 2 *ūqiyya*s (1½ or 2 ounces) per

---

1 Note that the whole chapter is also included in the Madrid MS and the edited Arabic text that follows it.

2 *Bayḍā*ʾ 'white' is mentioned in the Madrid MS, fol. 114v. The resulting confection will be like soft nougat.

3 *Ferula communis*, a plant with a long, straight, and sturdy hollow stalk. See glossary 9.1.

4 Ordinary *fālūdhaj* is like a thick pudding served in bowls. The variety of *fālūdhaj* described here is further thickened and spread on a slab and divided into smaller pieces, like halva. Here I used a similar recipe in the anonymous Andalusi *Anwāʿ al-ṣaydala* 207–8 to add a few instructions missing from this recipe. This type of *fālūdhaj* is comparable to what was called *fālūdhaj muʿallak* (chewy textured) in al-Warrāq's tenth-century Baghdadi cookbook *Kitāb al-Ṭabīkh*, English trans., *Annals*, chapter 93.

 | DOI:10.1163/9789004469488_044

raṭl (pound) of honey—and a bit of saffron. Dissolve the starch in fresh water and add it to the honey.[5] As soon as it starts to thicken, add olive oil—4 *ūqiyyas* per *raṭl* of honey. Also add as ½ *ūqiyya* yellow beeswax (*shamʿ aṣfar*) per 1½ *raṭls* of honey.[6]

When the oil starts to ooze out (*yarshaḥ*) and separate, spoon it out; the more taken out of it, the drier the confection will be, otherwise it will remain moist.[7] Add as much as you want of skinned almonds and continue cooking the pot on low heat until it cooks [and thickens]. Add as much as you like of hulled sesame seeds (*simsim*). Remove the pot from the fire and spread the mix on a marble slab (*rukhāma*) or a smooth board (*lawḥ*) [and form it into large or small discs or any other shapes you like,][8] God Almighty willing.

IX.2.3 Another Kind of *fālūdhaj* (Starch-Based Confection)[9]

Take as much as you want of fine-tasting honey and put it in a clean cauldron (*ṭinjīr*). Put it on the fire on low heat until the honey softens and then strain it in a piece of woolen cloth. Wash the cauldron and put the honey back in it.

Now take dry wheat starch (*nashā yābis*)[10]—2½ *ūqiyyas* (2½ ounces) per *raṭl* (pound) of honey—1 *dirham* (3 grams) crushed saffron, and olive oil—4 *ūqiyyas* per *raṭl* of honey. [Add all these to the cauldron and] put it on low heat, stirring it [constantly] with the reed (*qaṣaba*).[11] Once it thickens, add ½ *raṭl* skinned almonds. Remove the cauldron from the fire and pour the mix on a marble slab (*rukhāma*). Wait until it is lukewarm and then knead and press it by hand until its oil oozes out. Shape it into thin discs by striking pieces of it [on the marble], (187r) and serve them, God Almighty willing.

If you want to add sesame seeds (*simsim*), take as much as the mix can take of unhulled sesame and add them when the *fālūdhaj* is done cooking and thickening. Remove it from the fire and spread it on the marble slab as was mentioned above, with the help of God Almighty.

---

5 Based on previous recipes, it has to be added gradually with constant stirring of the pot.

6 Addition from anonymous *Anwāʿ al-ṣaydala* 208, mentioned in n. 4 above. The yellow beeswax used here to thicken the confection was deemed the best for cooking purposes. See glossary 8.

7 Addition from anonymous *Anwāʿ al-ṣaydala* 208, mentioned in n. 4 above.

8 Addition from anonymous *Anwāʿ al-ṣaydala* 208, mentioned in n. 4 above.

9 See n. 4 above.

10 Based on previous recipes, starch will have to be dissolved in water before adding it.

11 Described in the first recipe in this chapter.

IX.2.4 White *juljulāniyya* (Nougat with Sesame Seeds)

Take as much as you want of fine-tasting honey and put it in a cauldron (*ṭinjīr*). Put it on a fire on low heat until the honey softens and then strain it in a piece of woolen cloth. Return the honey to the cauldron and let it cook on low heat, stirring and doing the finger test.[12] If the honey no longer sticks to it, remove it from the fire, and stir it until it is lukewarm.

Beat the whites of 5 eggs for each *raṭl* [of honey] if red honey (*ʿasal aḥmar*) is used;[13] otherwise, use 4 whites if it is white honey.[14] [Put the whites in a big bowl] and whip them by hand until they are foamy. Add them to the lukewarm honey [in the cauldron] and beat them for a good while, and then put the cauldron on low heat and continue stirring it with the reed (*qaṣaba*)[15] until it turns white and thickens.

Take hulled sesame seeds (*simsim maqshūr*)—enough for the amount of the [confection]—and add them to the honey pot. Stir the mix until it thickens and remove it from the fire. Spread it on a marble slab (*rukhāma*) and make it into discs, whatever size you wish.[16]

IX.2.5 Making *qubbayṭ majbūdh* (Pulled Honey Taffy)[17]

Take as much as you want of fine-tasting white honey,[18] put it in a clean cauldron (*ṭinjīr*), and set it on the fire on medium heat until the honey softens and then strain it in a piece of woolen cloth. Wash the cauldron and put the honey back in it and put it on the fire, stirring it constantly with the reed

12 A drop of it was put between the tips of the forefinger and thumb to feel its stickiness. We learn this from a recipe in the fourteenth-century Egyptian cookbook *Kanz al-fawāʾid*, English trans., *Treasure Trove*, recipe 437.

13 It is a reddish-brown variety of honey. The extra egg white used is to help give the nougat a lighter color.

14 It is light-colored honey, preferred for making fair-colored candies and sweets.

15 See the first recipe in this chapter.

16 In a comparable recipe in the anonymous Andalusi *Anwāʿ al-ṣaydala* 209, it is suggested that the discs are divided into strips with a knife, which are to be separated when the candy cools.

17 *Majbūdh* is derived from the verb *j-b-dh*, a variant on *j-dh-b* 'pull,' see Ibn Manẓūr, *Lisān al-ʿArab*, s.v. جبذ. Ibn Khalṣūn, *Kitāb al-Aghdhiya* 102, gives an alternative name for *qubbayṭ*, which is *nāṭif*. Al-Warrāq, *Kitāb al-Ṭabīkh*, English trans., *Annals* 389, calls a similar candy *nāṭif ʿasal ʿalā al-mismār* 'nail-pulled honey taffy.'

18 See n. 14 above.

(*qaṣaba*)[19] until it thickens. Test it [by dropping a small amount] on a marble slab (*rukhāma*); if it thickens and sets fast,[20] remove the pot from the fire and pour the honey on the marble slab.

Now take a large iron nail with an upward-bent head and nail it to the wall. Take the thickened honey, thread it into the nail, and pull it; and then fold it, thread its end onto the nail again, and pull it. Do this repeatedly. If the honey cools, take it closer to the fire to heat it up and resume pulling it repeatedly until it turns white. Form it into rings like *kaʿk*, each the size of the palm of the hand. Put them away in a vessel of glass (*zujāj*) or wood (*ūd*), and use them however you like.[21]

They do not stay good for more than a day. Therefore, they would be at their best when eaten while still fresh (*ṭarī*) with plain ring cookies (*kaʿk sādhaj*),[22] so know this, and do accordingly, God Almighty willing.

IX.2.6 Making *ḥalwāʾ mukhammara* (Rosy-Colored Confection)[23]

(187v) Take as much as you want of fine-tasting white honey,[24] put it in a cauldron (*ṭinjīr*), set it on the fire on medium heat until it softens, and then strain it in a piece of woolen cloth. Clean the cauldron by washing it, then return the honey to it and put it on a medium fire. Stir it [constantly] to prevent it from burning, using a thick reed with a tip of brass (*ṣufr*).

Take the whites of 6 eggs for each *raṭl* (pound) of honey if it is *shahd* (honey with its beeswax), and 10 whites if it is not *shahd*. Whip the whites by hand until a foam rises, [meanwhile] let the honey cool to lukewarm by stirring it, and then throw in the egg whites. Return the cauldron to the fire, constantly stirring it with the reed (*qaṣaba*)[25] until the honey turns very white. Remove it from the fire.

---

19 Described in the first recipe in this chapter.

20 I suspect the word في ساعة ʻin an hour' (!) in the BL MS, fol. 187r, to be a misreading of ساعته في ʻthe moment it is put,' which indeed is closer to سريعا ʻquickly,' in the Madrid MS, fol. 115v.

21 The following remark is provided in the BL MS only.

22 See above recipe i.4.3 for plain *kaʿk*.

23 The confection got its name from *khumra*. Based on Ibn Manẓūr, *Lisān al-ʿArab*, s.v. خمر, *khumra* was *wars* (Ceylon cornel) and other substances, which women applied to their faces to make their complexions look rosy. The verb used for this action is *takhammarat*. *Wars* was also used to extract a red dye. For the identification of *wars*, see Ghālib, *Mawsūʿa*, s.v. ورس. The crushed and lightly fried *khabīṣ* is the coloring agent in this recipe.

24 See n. 14 above.

25 See the first recipe in this chapter.

Clean a large skillet or a tinned pot (*qidr muqaṣdara*), fill it with sweet olive oil (*zayt ʿadhb*), let it heat up well, and throw in *khabīṣ*.[26] Let them fry briefly and then take them out with a perforated ladle (*mighrafa muthaqqaba*). If the thin sheets of *khabīṣ* are used whole, fry them one by one; take them out as they fry and put them on a wooden board (*lawḥ*) to cool.

Once the fried *khabīṣ* [pieces] cool, crush them into a flour-like consistency and throw the thickened honey on them. Stir them until the mix looks homogenous.[27] For each *raṭl* of honey, use 2 *raṭl*s of the *khabīṣ* flour. Set it aside to cool completely and thicken well (*yataṣaffaq*) before using it.

Another way for cooking this confection:[28] Take sesame seeds (*simsim*), hull them, lightly toast them (*taḥmisuhu*), and use them instead of *khabīṣ*. [In this case,] the honey needs to be thickened with a good amount of egg whites, like 20 or even more, God Almighty willing.

IX.2.7 Making *ḥalwāʾ al-khabīṣ* (Confection Made with Thin Sheets of Wheat Starch Bread)

Take 4 *raṭl*s (4 pounds) of fine-tasting white honey,[29] put it in a cauldron (*ṭinjīr*), set it on low heat until it softens, and then strain it in a piece of woolen cloth. Clean the cauldron by washing it, return the honey to it, and put it on the fire, stirring it constantly until it thickens.

Now take a clean skillet, pour lots of olive oil in it, and put it on the fire. As soon as it boils, take 1 *raṭl* of *khabīṣ* (thin sheets of wheat starch bread),[30] break them into pieces, and add them to the skillet in batches; keep them until they turn malleable and moist. Take them out quickly and add them to the thickened honey while they are still very hot. Stir the pot very well to mix them all, and serve it, God Almighty willing.

---

26 They are delicate thin sheets of bread made with wheat starch. See above recipes i.4.19 and 22.

27 Addition is from the Madrid MS, fol. 116r.

28 This phrase is included in the Madrid MS, fol. 116r only; otherwise, the BL MS, fol. 187v continues with the recipe, which causes some confusion in the text.

29 See n. 14 above.

30 See n. 26 above.

IX.2.8 Recipe for *ḥalāwiyya*[31] *sukkariyya* (Sugar-Sweetened Confection)

Take 1 *raṭl* (1 pound) sugar and pound it. Also take ⅔ *raṭl* of the inside crumb of fine white bread (*lubāb khubz darmak*) and grate it until it looks like semolina (*samīd*); [also take] the whipped whites of 6 eggs.[32]

Heat up 1 *raṭl* of olive oil in a cauldron (*ṭinjīr*), and as soon as it boils, add the sugar, breadcrumbs, and egg whites. Stir the pot constantly on low heat until the sweet cooks and thickens and then set it aside to cool. [Spread it in vessels and] sprinkle pounded sugar and spikenard all over it.

IX.2.9 Making Chewy Candy (*muʿqad*)[33] with Sugar and Almonds

Take one *raṭl* (1 pound) sugar, put it in a glazed earthenware pan (*ṭājin fakhkhār muzajjaj*), and pour enough rosewater and water to submerge it. Put the pan on the fire until the sugar dissolves and then strain it with a hair sieve (*ghirbāl shaʿr*).

Clean the pan by washing it, return (**188r**) the sugar [solution] to it, and resume cooking on medium heat. Check for doneness by spooning some of it and dropping it on a large marble slab (*ṣallāya rukhām*); wait for it to cool. If [the dropped syrup] thickens quickly and forms a mass that produces a ringing sound when thrown on the marble slab, you know that it is done. And you will have already taken ¼ *raṭl* almonds and skinned and then chopped them, or coarsely crushed them in a mortar, which would be a better way to do them.

When the sugar is cooked and you have already taken the ¼ *raṭl* of almonds [and worked on them], add them to the sugar [syrup] and beat them with a ladle to mix well. Next, grease a marble slab with sweet olive oil (*zayt ʿadhb*) or freshy extracted oil from sweet almonds. Empty the thickened syrup (*al-muʿqad*) onto the slab, and [while still warm,] take one piece at a time, spread it by hand, and shape it into discs (*aqrāṣ mudawwara*).[34]

It is made the same way with pine nuts or pistachios. Really delicious, God Almighty willing.

---

31 Copied as *ḥalwāʾ* in the Madrid MS, fol. 116v.

32 Whipping the whites is an addition from the Madrid MS, fol. 116v.

33 As it occurs in the BL MS; *maʿqūd* and *ʿaqīd* are variants on the name, as they occur in the anonymous Andalusi *Anwāʿ al-ṣaydala* 211, and the anonymous Egyptian *Kanz al-fawāʾid*, English trans., *Treasure Trove*, recipes 348 and 371.

34 A comparable recipe in the anonymous Andalusi *Anwāʿ al-ṣaydala* 211 suggests forming the candies into any shape fancied, such as dates stuffed with almonds, figs, grapes, and raisins.

IX.2.10 Another [*muʿqad*] Variety

Take 1 *raṭl* (1 pound) sugar and mix it with 2 *raṭl*s (2 pints/4 cups) sweet-smelling rosewater. Cook them [in a *ṭājin*] on low heat until the sugar dissolves and then strain it with a piece of woolen cloth. Clean the pan (*ṭājin*) by washing it, return the [dissolved] sugar to it, and put it on the fire, constantly stirring until it cooks very well. Remove it from the fire and continue stirring until it becomes lukewarm.

Take the whites of 12 eggs and whip them by hand vigorously until foamy. Add them to the sugar [pot] and return it to the fire, continuously stirring it with the confection reed (*qaṣabat al-ḥalwāʾ*)[35] until it turns white with the consistency of *ʿaṣīda* (smooth and dense flour-based soup).

Remove the pot from the fire and stir in ½ *raṭl* pistachios if available;[36] otherwise, use a similar amount of split skinned almonds. Do with it as was done in the previous recipe, God Almighty willing.

IX.2.11 Making *rukhāmiyya* (Marble-Smooth Chewy Candy)

Take fine-tasting white sugar (*sukkar abyaḍ*), dissolve it in a small amount of water, put it on a low fire [to boil], and skim its froth. Take almonds that have been skinned, pounded, and dried until they look like semolina (*samīdh*). When the sugar is about to thicken, throw in the almonds—use ⅔ the amount of sugar. Add the almonds after you add a small amount of camphor (*kāfūr*) [that has been] dissolved in rosewater with spikenard and cloves.

Continue stirring the pot until the sugar thickens and then pour it onto a greased marble slab (*rukhāma*) [and spread it into a disc]. Press the top with a greased smooth board to make the surface look even and smooth, and cut it with a knife into thin strips (*aqlām*) or any other shapes you fancy. Leave them to cool (188v) and then put them away.

IX.2.12 Making Chewy Candy with Honey (*muʿqad al-ʿasal*)[37]

Take as much as you want of fine-tasting honey; put it in a clean cauldron (*ṭinjīr*), put it on the fire until it softens, and then strain it with a tightly woven piece

35 See the first recipe in this chapter, where it is described.

36 *In amkana*, only added in the BL MS, fol. 188r, is suggestive of the availability or affordability of almonds over pistachios.

37 As it occurs in both the BL MS, fol. 188v, and the Madrid MS, fol. 117r. See also n. 33 above.

of cloth (*mindīl ṣafīq*). Clean the cauldron by washing it, return the honey to it, and put it on the fire to cook until it thickens well.[38]

Now take the whites of 5 eggs per *raṭl* (pound) of honey that does not contain beeswax (*ghayr shahd*); otherwise, use 4 egg whites with *shahd* (honey with its beeswax). Whip the whites well, until foamy, and add them to the honey, whipping both vigorously to mix them well. Put the cauldron on low heat, continuously stirring it with the confection reed (*qaṣabat al-ḥalwā'*);[39] be patient with it until it turns very white and thickens. Stir in 1 *raṭl* of coarsely crushed shelled walnuts, and use it,[40] God Almighty willing.

38 In the Madrid MS, the recipe suggests doing the finger test, see recipe ix.2.4 above.

39 See the first recipe in this chapter, where it is described.

40 As in the above *mu'qad* recipes ix.2.9–10.

Part Nine, Chapter Three: On Making *Qāhiriyya* (Delicate Cairene Ring Cookies) and *Sanbūsak* (Marzipan)[1]

IX.3.1 A Variety [of *Qāhiriyya*, Fried][2]

Take as much as you want of fine-tasting sugar and an equal amount of skinned sweet almonds. Pound them both in a mortar (*mihrās*) until they become doughy in texture. Put them in a large bowl (*mithrad*); add rosewater, Ceylon cinnamon, cloves, spikenard, black pepper, ginger, nutmeg (*jawzat al-ṭīb*), galangal (*khūlanjān*)—but not much—and a bit of camphor if wished. Knead them all very well until they mix and blend and form a rather stiff dough. Shape the mix into small rings to resemble *kaʿk* (ring cookies).

Next, take fine white flour (*daqīq darmak*), enough for the amounts of sugar and almonds used. Knead it with fresh yeast (*khamīr*) and a bit of salt [and water]; let the mix be rather thin in consistency. Set it aside to ferment. Take some wheat starch (*nashā*), pound it, and then stir it into the batter.

Take a clean skillet and pour in sweet olive oil (*zayt ʿadhb*); but oil of sweet almonds (*duhn lawz ḥulw*) would be better. As soon as it boils, take the almond rings one by one, dip each in the batter to completely coat it, and then put it in the skillet to fry. As soon as a cookie starts to turn golden brown, quickly take it out and put it in a wide, shallow bowl (*ṣaḥfa*), arranging them in a pretty fashion.

[When the frying is done,] pour fine-tasting honey, whose foam has been skimmed [after boiling it], all over them; or use well-thickened rosewater-

1 In both the Madrid and BL MSS, chapters three to seven follow the same sequence of their respective recipes. However, the editor of the Arabic text inexplicably jumbled their sequence; and what adds more to the chaos, is that the recipes themselves are similarly mixed up. Due to the extensive disruptions caused by the editor, it would indeed be futile on my part to comment on discrepancies between these two MSS and the edited Arabic text within the chapters themselves.

2 They are delicate Cairene cookies, evidently popular not just in Cairo. An identical recipe is found in the anonymous Andalusi *Anwāʿ al-ṣaydala* 67–8. The most detailed recipe is found in the anonymous Egyptian *Kanz al-Fawāʾid*, English trans., *Treasure Trove*, recipe 322.

 | DOI:10.1163/9789004469488_045

honey syrup (*sharāb jullāb ʿasalī*).[3] Sprinkle them with crushed sugar, and eat them salubriously, God Almighty willing.

IX.3.2 Another Variety [of *Qāhiriyya*, Baked]

Take sugar and almonds, as much as you want, and do with them as you did in the previous recipe—the pounding, kneading, and the rest. (**189r**) Shape it into rings, smaller than the ones above. Take whatever amount you want of wheat starch (*nashā*) and sift it [and set it aside].

Now, take the rings one by one and sprinkle them with starch, enough to coat them on all sides. Arrange them in an earthenware plate (*malla fakhkhār*) or an iron plate (*malla ḥadīd*) and take it to the *furn* (communal brick oven). Let it bake at a distance from the fire until the rings set and are about to brown. Take them out immediately, allow them to cool, and serve them, God Almighty willing.

If *malla* is not available, use a board (*lawḥ*); grease it with olive oil and arrange the pieces on it after dusting them with starch or fine white flour (*daqīq darmak*).

IX.3.3 Another Variety of *Qāhiriyya* [Fried]

Take 2 *raṭl*s (2 pounds) fine-tasting sugar and mix it with fresh water or rosewater. Boil them in a cauldron (*ṭinjīr*) on low heat, skimming the froth [as needed], until they turn into a thick syrup.[4] Throw in 2 *raṭl*s finely pounded skinned almonds; also add ¼ *raṭl* very fine wheat flour (*ghubār darmak*).[5] Knead them all well until they become one thick homogenous mass and the almonds release their oil (*duhn*). At this point, add spikenard and cloves, which have been dissolved in rosewater, and a bit of camphor, as desired. Knead them all well and shape the mix into large and small rings, like *kaʿk* (ring cookies), and set them aside to slightly dry.

---

3 The thick consistency of the syrup is described as *mashdūd al-ʿaqd*. Otherwise, such syrups were usually boiled to medium consistency, referred to as *qiwām al-ashriba*, and used in a diluted form as drinks. See glossary 1.

4 The expression used here is *ḥattā tatajallab* 'until it becomes *jullāb*.' In the Madrid MS, fol. 117v, the thickening of the syrup is conveyed by the verb *yaltaff*. For more on *jullāb*, see glossary 4.

5 It is a by-product of crushed wheat, as fine as dust. See glossary 2.

Dip the rings in wheat starch that has been dissolved in water into a thick batter in a wide, shallow bowl (*ṣaḥfa*) and colored with saffron or left white without saffron. Take the rings out of it, leave them aside briefly [to slightly dry], and then put them in a skillet with boiling olive oil—the oil should be enough for the rings to be inserted in it (*tanghariz*).[6] Let them fry briefly and take them out quickly before they start to brown. Douse them in syrup infused with rose petals (*sharāb ward*), rosewater syrup (*jullāb*), or syrup infused with mastic (*sharāb maṣṭakā*).[7] Put them away, and serve them [as needed], God Almighty willing.

IX.3.4 Making *sanbūsak* (*marzipan*)[8]

Take fine-tasting sugar, dissolve it in rosewater, and add almonds, which have been thoroughly pounded until they turn doughy in texture. [Put them in a pot on the fire and] gently stir them on low heat until the mix thickens and combines into one mass (*yaltaff*), similar to the *Qāhiriyya* stuffing [in the above recipes].

Remove the pot from the fire, and when it is lukewarm, add [skinned] split almonds,[9] spikenard, cloves, a bit of mastic, and ginger—but not much. All these spices (*ʿaqāqīr*) are to be crushed and added after dissolving them in rosewater, in which a bit of camphor (*kāfūr*) and musk (*misk*) have been dissolved. Beat and rub all these ingredients until they blend and then shape the mix into hand-size discs that are thick and rounded.[10]

---

6 That is, just enough to barely cover the rings. Too much oil will let them move about and spoil their shapes.

7 For more on these syrups, see glossary 1, s.v. *sharāb* 1.

8 This confection is unlike *sanbūsak* we encounter in the medieval cookbooks from the eastern region, where they are made as fried pastries, typically shaped into triangles of thin sheets of dough and filled with a sweet stuffing of nuts and sugar, or savory with meat. See al-Warrāq, *Kitāb al-Ṭabīkh*, English trans., *Annals* 190–2; and anonymous *Kanz al-fawāʾid*, English trans., *Treasure Trove*, recipes 115, 116, 127.

A similar marzipan recipe is included in the anonymous Andalusi *Anwāʿ al-ṣaydala* 196, where it is said to have been made for Almohad Caliph Abū Yūsuf al-Manṣūr (d. 1199). It is called, the recipe adds, *sanbūsak al-mulūk* 'fit for kings.'

9 In the Madrid MS, fol. 118r, the almonds are coarsely crushed (*mahshūm*).

10 The corresponding recipe in the anonymous *Anwāʿ al-ṣaydala* 196 also suggests shaping the marzipan pieces as oranges, apples, and plums. It also mentions that this delicious food is offered as *naql*. *Naql* is snack food closely associated with drinking sessions, when imbibing wine alternated with nibbling on small dishes. See glossary 5, s.v. *naql*.

This is the true *sanbūsak*. As for what people of Ifrīqiya make of *sanbūsak* stuffed with pounded meat, it is, to be sure, devoid of any flavor, and far from being delicious.[11]

11 (ليس فيه طعم ولا لذاذة). In medieval times, Ifrīqiya included the coastal regions of what today are western Libya, Tunisia, and eastern Algeria. Al-Tujībī's prejudice against this type of *sanbūsak* must have been based on his personal experience in these regions, where he spent more than half of his lifetime, see introduction i.2. Here is how the Madrid MS, fol. 118r, expresses this prejudice against the meat-stuffed *sanbūsak* of Ifrīqiya: "Look at the *sanbūsak* they make! ... It is neither commendable nor relished" (أنظر الذي يصنعه اهل افريقية ... فليس بمستحسن ولا مستطاب).

The anonymous *Anwāʿ al-ṣaydala* 196 does indeed provide a recipe for savory *sanbūsak* pastries stuffed with meat, but he calls this variety "the commoners' *sanbūsak*."

Part Nine, Chapter Four:[1] On Making *Jawzīnaq* and *Lawzīnaj*[2] (Walnut and Almond Confections)

IX.4.1 (189v) Making *jawzīnaq* (Walnut Confection)[3]

Take as much as you want of a new crop walnuts, which are free of mold (*ʿafan*), and crack them, discard the outer shells, and clean them. Take half the kernels, put them [in a vessel] and pour boiling water on them—enough to soak them—and then remove the skins. Dry them in a piece of cloth (*mindīl*) and set them aside. Now take the other half and pound it very well to facilitate extracting their oil, as I describe to you in another part in this book [chapter x.10 below]. Put the extracted oil (*duhn*) in a vessel and stow it away.

Take the set-aside walnuts and pound them very well and then put them on a wide stone slab (*ṣallāya*)[4] and crush them until they resemble [the smooth texture of] the brain (*damāgh*). Now take 3 parts fine-tasting sugar and 2 parts of the crushed walnuts; pound them together very well [until they become one mass] and have a taste. If the mix is sweet enough, well and good; otherwise, add more sugar.[5]

Take some of the extracted oil, grease the stone slab with it, and put the sugar-walnut mix on it. Strike and press the mix with your hands [to flatten it] and cut it into pieces. Sprinkle them with sugar, black pepper, Ceylon cinnamon (*qirfa*), and cassia (*dār Ṣīnī*), and serve them, God Almighty willing.

If you want to make it with honey, take fine-tasting honey, put it in a cauldron (*ṭinjīr*), [let it boil, and] skim off its froth after straining it.[6] Stir it on the fire [constantly] until it thickens and then add the pounded walnuts to it. Stir the pot to mix them [until they become one doughy mass]. Put the mix on the stone slab (*ṣallāya*), which has been greased with the extracted walnut oil (*duhn jawz*), and spread it into a thin layer with your hands. Cut it into pieces,

---

1 See my comment on the edited Arabic text in chapter ix.3, n. 1 above.

2 It is copied as *lawzīnaq* in the Madrid MS, fol. 118r.

3 A similar confection, which uses pistachios instead of walnuts, is found in al-Warrāq's tenth-century Baghdadi cookbook, *Kitāb al-Ṭabīkh*, English trans., *Annals* 401, where it is called *khabīṣ yābis maftūt* (dry and crumbly confection).

4 It is used with a large stone, called an *fihr*, to crush ingredients like spices and aromatics.

5 Addition from the Madrid MS, fol. 118v.

6 See, for instance, recipe ix.2.2 above on how honey was strained.

 | DOI:10.1163/9789004469488_046

which you then sprinkle with the spices mentioned above. You can also add camphor, if wished, which indeed will be the perfect way to make it.

IX.4.2 Making *lawzīnaj* (Almond Brittle)

Take fine-tasting sugar, as much as you want, and dissolve it in sweet-smelling rosewater and fresh water. Put the solution in a cauldron (*ṭinjīr*) and let it boil and then strain it. Add honey to it—1 *ūqiyya* (1 ounce) per 1 *raṭl* (1 pound) of sugar.

Now take skinned sweet almonds, pound them thoroughly, and keep them aside in a vessel. Resume cooking the sugar [solution] on low heat, constantly stirring it, until it cooks and thickens. Remove it from the fire and add the [pounded] almonds—10½ *ūqiyya*s per 1 *raṭl* of sugar. Stir the cauldron vigorously until the mix blends and becomes one mass. Put it on a stone slab (*ṣallāya*) after greasing it with almond oil (*duhn lawz*), [spread it into a thin layer with your hand,][7] cut it into pieces, and sprinkle them with sugar.

7 As was done in the first recipe.

Part Nine, Chapter Five: On Making *Qaṣab Ḥulw* (Reeds of Candy)[1]

Take 4 *raṭl*s (4 pints) milk, strain it, and add it to 2 *raṭl*s (2 pounds) (**190r**) sugar. [Stir them to] dissolve the sugar and then strain them.

Put the mix in a new glazed earthenware pan (*ṭājin fakhkhār muzajjaj*) or a tinned cauldron (*ṭinjīr muqaṣdar*). Put the pot on a medium fire and gently stir the pot all the time until the mix thickens and begins to leave furrows behind when stirred (*yatasharrak*).[2]

Empty the mix onto a wide stone slab (*ṣallāya*). Wait until it is lukewarm, and then take pieces of it and flatten them into four-finger-wide rectangular sheets. Roll them on sifted fine white flour (*daqīq darmak*) to make them look like reed tubes. Trim off both ends of each piece with a knife so that they look even. Arrange them on plates and use them, God Almighty willing.

1 See my comment on the edited Arabic text in chapter ix.3, n. 1 above. A similar recipe is found in the anonymous Andalusi *Anwāʿ al-ṣaydala* 70.

2 In Ibn Manẓūr, *Lisān al-ʿArab*, s.v. شرك, *sharak* are said to be grooves and furrows seen on roads. This was the only meaning of the word I found that fits into our culinary situation here.

 | DOI:10.1163/9789004469488_047

CHAPTER IX.6

Part Nine, Chapter Six:[1] On Making *Fānīdh* (Pulled Sugar Taffy) and *Ishqāqūl* (Rings of Solomon)[2]

IX.6.1 Making *fānīdh* (Pulled Sugar Taffy)

Take 5 *raṭl*s (5 pounds) fine-tasting sugar, put it in a tinned cauldron (*ṭinjīr muqaṣdar*), add fresh water—enough to dissolve it—and put the pot on a moderate fire. As soon as it boils and its foam rises, skim all of it until nothing remains. Continue cooking until the sugar is done. To test for doneness: insert an iron spoon (*milʿaqa ḥadīd*) in it and take it out; you will see that some syrup has stuck to it; and if you throw a hardened piece of this syrup, you will hear a ringing sound.

Take a wide marble slab (*ṣallāya rukhām*) and grease it with sweet olive oil (*zayt ʿadhb*) or oil of sweet almonds (*duhn lawz ḥulw*). Empty the cooked sugar onto it and sprinkle it with finely crushed mastic—but not much. Roll the sugar, pass [one of its ends] through a nail (*mismār*), and pull it repeatedly until it turns very white.[3] Roll it in wheat starch (*nashā*) and spread it on the marble slab. With a pair of scissors, cut it into pieces, as big or as small as you want them,[4] and keep them in a glass vessel (*wiʿāʾ zujāj*) or a wooden bowl (*makhfiyya min ʿūd*),[5] and use them however you wish.

---

1 See my comment on the edited Arabic text in chapter ix.3, n. 1 above.

2 اشقاقول, as it is clearly copied in both the BL and Madrid MSS, fols. 190r and 119r, respectively, in Maghribi script style, with its distinct *fāʾ* ف and *qāf* ق letters, using a dot beneath the letter for the former and one dot above the letter for the latter. The confection is inaccurately edited as اشفافول *ishfāfūl* in the Arabic text edition.

As to what *ishqāqūl* might mean, Dozy, *Takmilat al-maʿājim* vi 332, s.v. شقاقل, offers a valuable hint—it might be related to *rayç chicâquil*, which is said to be the Italian *sceau de Salomon* 'ring of Solomon.' In al-Warrāq's tenth-century Baghdadi cookbook, *Kitāb al-Ṭabīkh*, English trans., *Annals* 412, 413, and 601–2, there are references to a hard sugar candy called *sukkar Sulaymānī*. Typically, the pieces were shaped into small and delicate rings, similar to today's Lifesavers candy, but they also took other forms, like fingers and drops, as in our recipe here.

3 For details on using the nail and pulling the sugar, see recipe ix.2.5 above.

4 A similar recipe in the anonymous Andalusi *Anwāʿ al-ṣaydala* 213 suggests forming the candy into other shapes: rings, discs, twists, and bracelets. It also recommends spreading them on a wooden board to cool and dry before storing them. Cf. a *fānīdh* recipe in the anonymous Egyptian *Kanz al-fawāʾid*, English trans., *Treasure Trove*, recipe 265.

5 As it is clearly vocalized in the BL MS; pl. *makhāfī*. It is a large and wide serving bowl, and as

 | DOI:10.1163/9789004469488_048

IX.6.2 Making *ishqāqūl* [Drops of Hard Sugar Candy][6]

Take as much as you want of sugar and do with it as was done in the previous recipe until it cooks [and thickens]. Mix it with black pepper, Ceylon cinnamon, ginger, and a small amount of pounded mastic.[7] Grease a marble slab (*ṣallāya*) and drop the syrup on it in small amounts to make the drops (*quraṣ*), make them as large or as small as you want them. Once they cool, keep them in a vessel of glass (*zujāj*) or wood (*ʿūd*), and use them, God Almighty willing.

If you want, add juice of fresh and tender lemons (*māʾ al-līm al-ghaḍḍ*) to the cooking syrup after it thickens. [The way to eat these lemon drops is to] keep a drop in your mouth and suck it slowly;[8] it will sweeten breath (*yuṭayyib al-nakha*) and aid digestion. (190v)

described here and in the above recipe i.4.38, it was made of wood or glazed earthenware. The name of this bowl is given as *mukhfiyya* in sources like Corriente, *Dictionary of Andalusi Arabic*, s.v. *kh-f-w*, and Dozy, *Takmilat al-maʿājim* iv 154, s.v. خفى.

6 See n. 2 above for the pronunciation and meaning of this candy. A compatible recipe in the anonymous *Anwāʿ al-ṣaydala* 212–3 is simply called *qurṣ al-sukkar* 'sugar rounds.'

7 Unlike the above recipe, sugar is not pulled here but immediately made into drops (*quraṣ*/*aqrāṣ*).

8 In Arabic, this whole sentence is expressed in one word, *tumsikuhu*, literally 'keep it,' included only in the BL MS.

Part Nine, Chapter Seven: On Varieties of Desserts from the Eastern Region (*Sharqiyya*)[1]

IX.7.1 A Variety Called *damāgh al-Wāthiq* (al-Wāthiq's Brain)[2]

Take 4 *raṭl*s (4 pounds) fine-tasting honey and put it in a cauldron (*ṭinjīr*), which you then set on the fire until the honey softens. Strain it[3] and return it to the cauldron after cleaning it. Add mastic and spikenard after crushing them, ½ *dirham* (1½ grams) of each.

Now take wheat starch (*nashā*)—half the amount of the honey—pound it, [dissolve it in a small amount of water,] and add it to the cauldron little by little, while stirring it continuously until the mix thickens and looks homogenous but thinner than *fālūdhaj* in consistency.

Add ¼ *mudd* (½ pound) hulled sesame seeds (*juljulān maqshūr*)[4] and 2 *ūqiyya*s (2 ounces) shelled and skinned almonds. Also add sweet olive oil (*zayt ʿadhb*) so that it does not stick to the sides of the cauldron. Continue stirring until the mix thickens to *fālūdhaj* consistency. Remove the pot from the fire and empty it into a vessel of glass (*zujāj*) or glazed earthenware (*fakhkhār muzajjaj*).

Whenever you need to serve it, take out the needed amount and put it in a glazed bowl (*ghaḍāra*). Sprinkle it with crushed sugar and pounded almonds, walnuts, or pistachios, and eat it salubriously, God Almighty willing.

---

1 See my comment on the edited Arabic text in chapter ix.3, n. 1. *Sharqiyya* desserts here are not substantially different from the ones offered in chapter ix.2 above.

2 In the Madrid MS, fol. 119v, it is called *damāgh al-Mutawakkil*. Abbasid Caliphs al-Wāthiq (d. 847) and al-Mutawakkil (d. 862) were sons of al-Muʿtaṣim and grandsons of Hārūn al-Rashīd; under their patronage learning and the pursuit of the sciences flourished.

This dessert is indeed a variety of *fālūdhaj* (see recipe ix.2.2 above), which was popular in the eastern region. It was deemed a highly nutritious, delicious food, which, above all, was believed to benefit the brain, literally 'increase it' *yuzīd fi-l-damāgh*. To my knowledge, no such name as *damāgh al-Wāthiq* or *damāgh al-Mutawakkil* existed in al-Mashriq. It must have been the Andalusis' playful rendition of the famous *fālūdhaj*.

3 See above recipe ix.2.2 for directions on straining honey.

4 A *mudd* equals 2 pounds. It is said to be a capacity measure of what both hands put together would hold.

 | DOI:10.1163/9789004469488_049

IX.7.2 Another Variety Called *zumurrudī* (Emerald Green)

Take honey—the same amount used in the previous recipe—and do with it as you did above. After straining it, add Ceylon cinnamon, spikenard, and cloves after crushing them—½ *dirham* (1½ grams) of each.

Take crumbs of cold bread made with fine white flour (*khubz darmak*)—1 *raṭl* (1 pound). Rub them between your hands until they look like semolina (*samīdh*) and add ½ *dirham* each of saffron and crushed indigo (*nīlaj*) to them.[5] Sprinkle the crumbs with a small amount of water and rub them between your hands with the saffron and indigo until they turn green. [Set them aside.]

After the honey starts to boil in the cauldron, throw in 4 *ūqiyyas* (4 ounces) wheat starch dissolved in a small amount of water while stirring the pot continuously. Once the honey thickens, throw in the [set aside] colored crumbs and continue stirring until the mix looks homogenous.

While stirring the pot, start adding sweet olive oil (*zayt ʿadhb*) [little by little] until the mix can absorb no more of it and it thickens to *fālūdhaj* consistency. Remove it from the fire and empty it into a vessel. Sprinkle coarsely crushed sugar and pistachios on it, or use shelled and skinned almonds or walnuts after coarsely crushing them, and eat it salubriously, God Almighty willing.

IX.7.3 Another Variety Called *ḥalwāʾ al-qaṭāyif* (Thick Pudding with Minced Pancakes)

(**191r**) Take fine-tasting honey as was mentioned in the previous recipes and do with it as you did above. After straining it, add Ceylon cinnamon, black pepper, and spikenard after crushing them—½ *dirham* (1½ grams) of each;[6] also take ¾ *dirham* (2¼ grams) crushed saffron.

When the honey comes to a boil, add 4 *ūqiyyas* (4 ounces) dry wheat starch that has been dissolved [in water]. Take one *raṭl* (1 pound) of already cooked *qaṭāyif* pancakes,[7] cut them into the tiniest pieces possible, and add them to the honey pot.[8] Stir the pot constantly until the *qaṭāyif* disintegrates into the honey and the mix looks homogenous.

---

5 It is a plant valued for its blue dye, see glossary 8. The combination of saffron and indigo will color the dessert green.

6 At this point in the Madrid MS, 119v (and the edited Arabic text that follows it), unrelated text begins, which belongs to a recipe dealing with olives. Luckily, the BL MS, copies it correctly, giving us the complete recipe.

7 For the *qaṭāyif* recipe, see i.4.15 above.

8 I deleted here a repeated mention of adding the starch.

Add sweet olive oil (*zayt ʿadhb*) while stirring; add it gradually [in small amounts] so long as it absorbs it. Once it can no longer do this, and it thickens to *fālūdhaj* consistency, remove it from the fire and empty it into a vessel of glass or glazed earthenware. Sprinkle it with sugar when served, as was described above, and eat it salubriously, God Almighty willing.

PART 10

القسم العاشر

في الكوامخ وما ينضاف اليها من عمل الخلول وعمل المري على اختلاف انواعه

واصلاح الزيت واستخراجه ان عدم من حبوب أخر واستخراج الادهان

المحتاج اليها في الطبخ

وما يصلح الاطعمة من كثرة الملح ونتن اللحم وما اشبه ذلك

ويشتمل على اثني عشر فصلا

On Pickles and Condiments (Kawāmikh)[1] *and Other Related Preparations for Varieties of Vinegar and* Murrī (*Fermented Liquid Sauce*)*; Remedying Olive Oil and Replacing It With Other Oils When Not Available; Remedying Overly Salty Foods and Raw Meat That Does Not Smell Fresh; and the Like. It Has Twelve Chapters*

∴

1 Evidently, calling pickled foods and condiments like mustard sauce *kawāmikh* must have been an Andalusi usage of the term. We encounter the same terminology in the fourteenth-century *al-Kalām ʿalā l-aghdhiya* by the Andalusi scholar al-Arbūlī, 146. Cf. the eastern region al-Mashriq, where *kawāmikh* specifically designated dairy-based fermented condiments; see, for instance, recipes in al-Warrāq's tenth-century Baghdadi cookbook, *Kitāb al-Ṭabīkh*, English trans., *Annals*, chapter 40.

Part Ten, Chapter One: On Making *Ṣināb* (Mustard Sauce)[1]

X.1.1 A Variety [of Mustard Sauce, Made with Almonds][2]

Take recently dried mustard of the small-seed variety, the kind imported from Bilād al-Rūm (Byzantium)—it is the best. Take as much as you need of them, wash them repeatedly in water to remove all dirt that is in them—use hot water—and then put them in a large bowl (*mithrad*). Now take skinned almonds, twice the amount of mustard seeds, and mix them with the seeds.

Take a large mortar (*mihrās*) made of wood, which would be the best, or stone, or copper (*nuḥās*), which is inferior to the other two but can be used if nothing else is available. Take [some of] the mustard mix, put it in the mortar, and pound it gently until the almonds disintegrate. While doing this, let there be next to you a wide, shallow bowl (*ṣaḥfa*) with vinegar and a bit of salt in it. Dip the pestle (*yad al-mihrās*) repeatedly in the vinegar (**191v**) while pounding. Continue doing this until the almonds completely disintegrate. Take the mix out of the mortar with a ladle and put it in a vessel, which needs to be kept covered to prevent dust from getting into it and spoiling it. Now put another amount of the [seed-almond] mix into the mortar and do with it as above until you finish the entire mix.

Take the amount you want of the pounded mix and return it to the mortar, adding to it very sour white vinegar while stirring it with the pestle to help release the almonds' moisture. Add the vinegar little by little, and avoid putting more than is needed, otherwise the sauce will be thin in consistency. Take a fine-meshed hair sieve (*ghirbāl shaʿr ṣafīq*) set on a vessel of glazed earthenware or glass. Take the mustard mix out of the mortar and put it in the sieve [and press and rub it through the mesh to let the sauce drip down into the vessel]. Transfer the resulting sauce into a separate vessel. This will make the first sauce (*al-awwal*).

---

1 Note that the entire chapter is missing from the Madrid MS and the edited Arabic text that follows it.

2 *Ṣināb*, also known as *khardal*, designates the seeds themselves as well as sauces/condiments made with them. See glossary 5 for the mustard condiment/sauce; and glossary 8 for the seeds.

 | DOI:10.1163/9789004469488_050

FIGURE 89 Mustard plant, Dioscorides, *Ajzāʾ min risāla fī l-nabātāt*, fol. 42r, detail
BNF, DEPARTMENT OF MANUSCRIPTS, ARAB 4947. SOURCE: GALLICA.BNF.FR/BNF

Repeat what you did with the first batch using the mustard mix [remaining in the sieve]: Return it to the mortar, pound it lightly while adding vinegar, and then rub and press it through the mesh, as described above. [This will make the second sauce.]

Do this a third time, and even a fourth time if possible. Also, if you want to mix the first sauce with the second, and it will still be good to use for the purpose intended, you can go ahead and do so. If wished, you may leave each sauce separate and serve them [in small bowls] at the table (*māʾida*) when you serve the dishes, God Almighty willing.

X.1.2 Another Variety [of Mustard Sauce, Made with Defatted Mustard Seeds][3]

Take as much as you want of the abovementioned mustard seeds, wash them several times in water, then dry them and pound them vigorously in a mortar (*mihrās*),[4] and then sift them in a hair sieve (*ghirbāl shaʿr*). Now take shelled and skinned almonds, pound them, and then mix them with the mustard seeds. Pound them together and press them out to extract their oils.[5]

Now take crumbs of bread made with fine white flour (*darmak*) and put them in cold water. Knead them with the [above defatted] mustard mix by adding them little by little. Next, add fine-tasting, very sour white vinegar, in which the needed amount of salt has been dissolved; put enough of it to thin the mustard mix to your liking. Strain the mix thoroughly with a clean piece of cloth, adding a small amount of honey to it to get rid of any bitterness.

All these [sauces] are good, God Almighty willing.

3 A similar recipe is included in the anonymous Andalusi *Anwāʿ al-ṣaydala* 32. Our cookbook here offers a more accurate reading of the text.

4 In the anonymous Andalusi *Anwāʿ al-ṣaydala* mentioned in the above note, the pounded mustard seeds are said to be as fine as kohl.

5 The extracted oil will be used for other purposes. Judging from today's practices, defatting mustard seeds before using them for making sauces was needed because the oxidation of the oil will cause the sauce to deteriorate fast. See, for instance, Taniguchi, "Preparation of Defatted Mustard" 413.

CHAPTER X.2

Part Ten, Chapter Two: On Curing Olives (*Zaytūn*)[1]

X.2.1 A Variety [of Brined Green Olives, Called *zaytūn musharraḥ*][2]

Take as much as you want of large green olives, the harvest of the month of September (Shatanbar), but they must be gently picked by hand; otherwise, they will smash and spoil. Wash them to get rid of dust and then score them with a small thin knife (*sikkīn daqīq*), but do not go deep to the stones (*ʿaẓm*).[3] Also, there should be four (**192r**) or three slits in an olive, depending on their size.[4] Now, put the olives in a vessel of glazed earthenware or glass, submerge them in fresh water without adding any salt, and set them aside as was described above.[5]

[To prepare brine,] take white salt (*milḥ abyaḍ*),[6] pound it, put it in a large bowl (*mithrad*), and pour fresh water in it, enough [in your estimation] to submerge the olives—let it be moderately salty. [Pour off the water in which the olives were kept and] replace it with the brine. Keep the vessel covered for three days and then taste the olives: if you like them, well and good; otherwise, add more salt or more water if needed and then use them. They are truly delicious, God Almighty willing.

If you want to pour off the brine after the olives are done and replace it with olive oil, you can do so.

---

1 Note that in the Madrid MS (and the edited Arabic text that follows it), only the last two recipes in this chapter are included.

2 Olives preserved in brine are also called *zaytūn al-māʾ*, literally 'water olives.' The first three recipes in this chapter follow this method. Cf. recipes for preserving olives in the anonymous Egyptian *Kanz al-Fawāʾid*, English trans., *Treasure Trove*, recipes 557–68.

3 Literally *ʿaẓm* is 'bone'; using it to designate the olive pit is a regional dialect usage.

4 Scoring olives this way gave them the name *zaytūn musharraḥ*, as we learn from Ibn al-ʿAwwām, *al-Filāḥa al-Andalusiyya* iii 528.

5 Obviously, this chapter was taken from a source where other olive recipes preceded this one. Based on al-Ṭighnarī, *Zahrat al-Bustān* 196–7, olives preserved in a similar manner are called *zaytūn Miṣrī* (Egyptian-style olives) and are kept in water for a whole month.

6 It designates salt obtained by the solar evaporation of saline waterbodies; also called *milḥ sabkhī*. See glossary 8, s.v. *milḥ*.

 | DOI:10.1163/9789004469488_051

FIGURE 90 Olives, al-ʿUmarī, *Masālik al-abṣār*, fol. 171v, detail
BNF, DEPARTMENT OF MANUSCRIPTS, ARAB 2771. SOURCE: GALLICA.BNF.FR/BNF

X.2.2 Another Variety [of Brined Green Olives, Called *zaytūn maksūr*][7]

Take medium olives, the harvest of the month of October (Uktūbar), before they ripen. Crack them on a board so that the flesh breaks but does not separate from the stone. Put the olives in fresh water as you did in the above recipe; but you need to change the water once. Next, put them in the brine and leave them until they are done [as in the recipe above].

Whenever you want to use the olives, take the amount [needed] and put them in a small, wide, and shallow bowl (*ṣaḥfa*), add some crushed [dried]

7 As called by Ibn al-ʿAwwām, *al-Filāḥa al-Andalusiyya* iii 528; or *mukassar*, as in al-Ṭighnarī, *Zahrat al-bustān* 197. See also n. 2 above.

thyme (*ṣaʿtar*), and lightly drizzle them with olive oil. Stir them by hand to mix them well, and eat them salubriously, God Almighty willing.

If you want to keep the olives whole [without cracking them], take a clean pitched earthenware jar (*khābiya muzaffata*),[8] put the olives in it, and add enough water to submerge them. Add a suitable amount of salt and taste it, adjusting the salt until you like it. [Put the lid on,] seal it tightly [with clay], and leave it for ten days, after which you open the jar and taste the olives. If you find that they are not salty enough, add more salt and return the lid to the jar and seal it tightly with clay so that no air will deter the curing of the olives. Leave them there until, in your estimation, they are done.

Whenever you want to use them, open up the jar, take the amount you want, and put the jar back as it was [i.e., with the lid on and sealed]. Take the olives and either crack them and add thyme and olive oil to them or leave them whole; do whatever you wish, God Almighty willing.

X.2.3 Another Variety [of Brined Green Olives][9]

(192v) Take olives, the harvest of the months of October (Uktūbar) and November (Nawnabar), any kind and any size will do; wash them to clean them of dust. Take a new pitched earthenware jar (*khābiya muzaffata*)[10] that has been rinsed (*quṣirat*) with water until the smell of pitch (*zift*) is gone.[11]

Fill the jar with alternating layers of olives and a variety of *ṣaʿtar* (thyme) called *shardhūn*[12] and then fill it with enough fresh water to more than submerge the olives. Cover it [with its lid], seal it tightly with clay, and leave it as it is for days, after which open it and check on its water. If you find it lacking, replenish it. And taste it: if it is not salty enough, add some more. Seal it with clay and leave it as it is until you need to use the olives. Serve them whichever way you like, God Almighty willing.

If you want to crack them before packing them in the jar, you can do so.

---

8 *Khābiya* is a large cylindrical jar with a tapered rounded bottom. For pitch, see glossary 9.1, s.v. *zift*.

9 See n. 2 above.

10 See n. 8 above.

11 In the Madrid MS, fol. 120r, the jar is said to be coated with olive oil *muzayyat*, or it has previously been used to store olive oil.

12 Conehead thyme, a Mediterranean wild variety, *Thymus capitatus*. In *ʿUmdat al-ṭabīb* ii 407–8, al-Ishbīlī describes *shardhūn* as a variety of wild thyme, called *ṣaʿtar al-zaytūn* 'thyme used with olives.' See glossary 8, s.v. *ṣaʿtar*.

X.2.4 Another Variety [of Oil-Cured Black Olives, Called *zaytūn mutammar*][13]

Take the amount you want of fully ripe olives,[14] small or large, wash them to get rid of dust, and set them aside to dry. Take a wooden board (*lawḥ*) and position it between your hands. Take the olives one by one, put them on the board, and strike them [lightly] with another board[15] or a wooden pestle to crack the olives; do not let their flesh separate from the stones. Alternatively, you may press them between your fingers [one by one] to flatten them (*yufʿaṣ*).[16] Once you are done, take them and put them in a *quffa* (large round basket) woven of esparto grass (*ḥalfā*), which you then sew up or tie with a rope and weigh down with stones and the like to let the olives moisture seep out.

Leave the basket until the olives lose all their moisture and shrivel[17] and then open the basket, take the olives out, and put them in a very large bowl (*miʿjana kabīra*).[18] Add pounded salt, pounded fine-tasting thyme (*ṣaʿtar*), and olive oil. Mix them all vigorously to combine the salt and thyme with the olives. Put them in vessels of glazed earthenware or glass and then submerge them in sweet olive oil (*zayt ṭayyib*) [and store them until needed]. Whenever you want to use the olives, take some out with a small ladle (*mighrafa ṣaghīra*).

Care should be taken to not let the oil be at a lower level than the olives [at any time], as this will expose them to air and cause them to rot and putrefy fast.[19] So keep this in mind. You must also know that nobody, whether man or woman, who is unclean (*najis*),[20] should get near these olives or cure them. This also applies to what will be described in the following [chapters on preserving foods]. So know this, and may God be our guide in doing the right thing. (**193r**)

13 As called by Ibn al-ʿAwwām, *al-Filāḥa al-Andalusiyya* iii 531; and al-Ṭighnarī, *Zahrat al-bustān* 198–200. See recipe i.2.11 where such cured olives are used.

14 In the Madrid MS, fol. 120r, they are described as *akḥal* 'black.'

15 In al-Ṭighnarī, *Zahrat al-bustān* 197, the striking board is described as small, with a handle by which to hold it. He strongly disapproves of using stones for this task.

16 يفعص, an interesting verb, used in the Madrid MS, fol. 120r. The BL MS, fol. 192v, uses the verb *yuʿjan* (kneaded).

17 According to Ibn al-ʿAwwām, *al-Filāḥa al-Andalusiyya* iii 531, this will take about a week.

18 This must be a very large bowl, because an ordinary *miʿjana*, usually used to knead dough, is already big.

19 The thing to do is to replenish the oil whenever it decreases.

20 Such as menstruating women and men and women who have not bathed after intercourse.

CHAPTER X.3

Part Ten, Chapter Three:[1] On Pickling Lemons (*Taṣyīr al-Līm*)[2]

X.3.1 A Variety [of Pickled Lemons Stuffed with Salt]

Take fresh and tender fully ripe lemons (*līm ṭarī mutanāhī*) at the end of their ripening season; take as many as you want. Wash them, dry them, and then cut them into quarters lengthwise but not all the way [keep them intact]. Put the lemons in a large bowl (*mithrad*) as you slit them until they are all finished. Take pure salt and pound it very well. Once you are done with this, take the lemons one by one, stuff them with salt, and pack them neatly in a glass vessel (*wiʿāʾ zujāj*) until it is full.

Now take [other] lemons, cut them in halves and press out their juice into a large bowl (*mithrad*)—the amount should be enough to submerge lemons in the [glass] vessel. Strain the juice through a piece of cloth and pour it on the lemons until they are submerged with it.[3]

Cover the vessel and put it in a sunny place for three days or so, after which taste the liquid; if it is not salty enough, add some more salt. Seal the top completely with honey mixed with pounded gum tragacanth (*kathīrā*),[4] which would be the best thing to do, but olive oil can also prevent lemons from going bad (*khamaj*). Remove the vessel from the sun and store it in a dry, well-ventilated place.

If you want to mix the [lemon] juice (*khall*) with water and salt,[5] you can do so. You may also replace it with water and salt: Take fresh water, add enough

1 Note that this chapter is also included in the Madrid MS, fols. 120v–121r, but the BL MS, which I followed here, offers more detailed versions with interesting comments, such as how to take the lemons out of the jar and how to serve them. In addition, the editor of the Arabic text, who follows the Madrid MS, inaccurately read the text in several places.

2 Lemon is more commonly called *laymūn* in the eastern region, and the word for pickling, *taṣyīr*, occurs as *takhlīl* in Ibn al-ʿAwwām, *al-Filāḥa al-Andalusiyya* iii 533.

3 The Madrid MS, fol. 120v, calls this lemon juice *khall al-līm*, literally 'lemon vinegar.' Note that in the two surviving Andalusi cookbooks, this one and anonymous *Anwāʿ al-ṣaydala, khall* not only designates regular 'vinegar' produced by fermentation but also, in a looser sense, unfermented preserved 'sour juice,' and even freshly pressed out lemon juice, as it is used here. See glossary 8, s.v. *khall*.

4 The verb used to convey this action is *taṭbaʿuhu* 'seal it.' The edible white variety of tragacanth is used here as a thickener. See glossary 8.

5 See n. 3 above.

 | DOI:10.1163/9789004469488_052

FIGURE 91 Fully ripe lemons, al-ʿUmarī, *Masālik al-abṣār*, fol. 202v, detail
BNF, DEPARTMENT OF MANUSCRIPTS, ARAB 2771. SOURCE: GALLICA.BNF.FR/BNF

salt to it, and taste it; if you find it pronouncedly salty, fine and well; otherwise, add more salt until it is so and then pour it on the lemons—add enough to submerge them.

If you want to add honey to speed up their maturation, you can do so. Keeping the jar in a sunny place for a while will do the same, and when you see that the lemons are about done, remove them from the sun; otherwise, they will go bad.

In addition,[6] some people may make them in another way: They would first keep lemons soaked in water for several days and then drain them and discard the [soaking] liquid. Next, they would slit and stuff them with salt, as was mentioned earlier, and pack them tightly in a glazed vessel one by one until it is full.

---

6 The following simple and basic method is found only in the Madrid MS, fol. 121r.

Then, they would seal[7] the jar as it is without adding any further liquid. The lemons will mature easier and faster if some of them are sectioned (*yufaṣṣ*).[8] This would indeed be the easiest method to pickle lemons. So know this and do as directed, God Almighty willing.

X.3.2 Another Variety [of Pickled Lemons, Stuffed with Sugar and Spices]

Take large, fresh, and tender lemons that have fully ripened (*līm mutanāhī ṭarī jalīl*); wash and dry them as described above. Take fine-tasting sugar, pound it, and add Ceylon cinnamon to it along with spikenard, ginger, black pepper, cloves, a bit of mastic (*maṣṭakā*), and galangal (*khūlanjān*). Stuff the lemons with the mix and put them in a rectangular glass jar (*zīr mustaṭīl min zujāj*),[9] big enough for 50 lemons. Pack the lemons tightly in the jar as you stuff them one after the other until it is full.

Take other lemons, cut them in halves, and press out their juice into a large bowl (*mithrad*) until you have enough for the lemons in the jar. Strain the juice, add salt to it—amount to your liking—(**193v**) and pour it on the lemons—enough to submerge them.

Put the jar at a sunny place for a day or two, depending on how strong the sun is, and then remove it, seal its top with sweet olive oil (*zayt ʿadhb*), and store it in a dry, well-ventilated place. Whenever you need, take some out with a small spoon (*milʿaqa ṣaghīra*), and offer them [with the meal] at the table (*māʾida*); or use them in cooking, God willing.

But be careful not to let the unclean (*najis*) handle them [at any stage of making them],[10] and may God aid our efforts.

7 I here amended the Madrid text by replacing *yaṭmaʿ* (يطمع), unrelated to the given text and an obvious copyist's misreading of *yuṭbaʿ* (يطبع) 'to be sealed.'

8 They would have been peeled and their skins and membranes removed, leaving only the juicy chunks. Citrus sections thus prepared were called *fuṣūṣ*, sg. *fuṣṣ*.

9 Usually, *zīr* is a large earthenware jar with a round and wide top.

10 Such as menstruating women and men and women who have not bathed after intercourse.

CHAPTER X.4

Part Ten, Chapter Four: On Various Ways for Pickling Capers (*Taṣyīr al-Kabar*)[1]

X.4.1 [A Variety of Pickled Caper Shoots, *ʿasālīj al-kabar*]

Take the tops and tender parts of shoots of the caper plant (*ʿasālīj*),[2] clean them, discarding the unwanted parts, and thoroughly wash them with water. Take salt and clean it; and take a new glazed earthenware jar (*khābiya*)[3] that has been well rinsed with water (*quṣirat*). Fill the jar with alternating layers of salt and capers.

Take vinegar and fresh water—⅓ water to ⅔ vinegar. Put them in a large earthenware tub (*qaṣriyya*), beat them by hand to mix them well, and pour the mix on capers in the jar. Put enough to submerge them and fill the jar. Cover it and set it aside and then open it after three days. If you see that the liquid (*marqa*) has decreased, add some more, using one-third to two-thirds as described above. Likewise with the salt [i.e., add more if needed].

Cover the jar and seal it with clay and set it aside for about 30 days, after which, open it to check on [the caper shoots], adding to it what is needed [of liquid or salt]. Seal the jar again and set it aside until the caper shoots are good to eat, and serve them God willing.

[**Ways to serve them:**] They are usually eaten mixed with vinegar and olive oil. You can also chop the pickled caper shoots and mix them with thick yogurt (*laban khāthir*) or *shīrāz* (very thick drained yogurt),[4] as I described to you in the first chapter of the sixth part of this book.[5]

As for caper buds (*nawār al-kabar*), which have not opened yet, and the young caper berries (*faqqūṣ*), which are not fully grown and whose seeds (*zarīʿa*) are still small, these are pickled the same way as above. So know this.

---

1 Note that this chapter is also included in the Madrid MS, fols. 121r–122r, and the edited Arabic text that follows it. However, the BL MS text, which is being followed here, is longer and offers more details and explanations.

2 Sg. *ʿaslūj*; see glossary 5, s.v. *kabar*, for the pickles; and glossary 7 for the plant.

3 *Khābiya* is a large cylindrical jar with a tapered rounded bottom.

4 See recipe vi.1.2 for *shīrāz*; and recipe vi.2.1–2 for thick yogurt.

5 The reference here is to *khilāṭ*, recipe vi.1.3.

FIGURE 92 Capers, al-Ghāfiqī, *Kitāb al-Adwiya al-mufrada*, MS 7508, fol. 274r, detail

X.4.2 Another Variety [of Pickled Capers] If You Want Them Made with Several Changes of Water (*maqṣūr*)

Take caper shoots (*ʿasālīj*) as described above, clean them, and put them in a large earthenware tub (*qaṣriyya*). (194r) Submerge them with fresh water, which you need to change twice a day—in the morning and in the evening. Do this until the capers are no longer bitter, which will take about three days or even more. You also need to taste them every day until you find that they are no longer bitter.

Take the caper shoots out of the tub, wash them thoroughly, and then put them in a large kneading bowl (*miʿjana*). Now take salt, sprinkle it all over them, and stir them to allow them to absorb it. Set them aside for an hour without adding any water.

Next, take a new earthenware jar (*khābiya*),[6] as was mentioned in the previous recipe, and put the capers in it. Take vinegar and water,[7] mix them in a large tub (*qaṣriyya*), and pour them on the capers in the *khābiya* jar—there should be enough to submerge them. Check on the capers frequently in case the liquid has decreased, in which case you must add more of it. If you prefer the flavor of vinegar to be dominant, then use more of it.

Whenever you want to use the caper shoots, wash them well and mix them with olive oil and vinegar, and eat them salubriously, God Almighty willing.

Caper buds (*nawār*) and young caper berries (*faqqūṣ*) are pickled the same way caper shoots are done. So understand this, and may God with His help and might guide us to do the right thing.

---

6 See n. 3 above.

7 Two thirds vinegar to one-third water, as in the recipe above.

Part Ten, Chapter Five: On Pickling (*Taṣyīr*) Eggplants (*Bādhinjān*), Onions (*Baṣal*), and Turnips (*Lift*)[1]

X.5.1 Making Eggplant [Pickles]

Take fresh eggplants and peel them, remove their calyxes (*qaṭāmīr*, sg. *qiṭmīr*), and slit them lengthwise, but not all the way; slit the large ones into sixths or eighths, and the small ones into fourths, fifths, or thirds; or just cut them [crosswise] into rounds.

Put the eggplants in a large pot with fresh water and salt, put it on the fire, and then remove it after it boils once or twice.[2] Take the eggplants out of the pot and spread them on a sieve (*ghirbāl*) or a raised wooden board to drain.

Take a pitched earthenware vessel (*wiʿāʾ fakhkhār muzaffat*),[3] or use one that is glazed from the inside and outside (*muzajjaj min dākhilihi wa khārijihi*). Put the eggplants in it and taste them; if they are not salty enough, add salt. Pour in vinegar and fresh water as was described above.[4] [After three days,] check on them; if you find that the liquid has decreased, add more of it, and then cover the vessel and seal it with clay.

Whenever you want to use the [pickled] eggplants in cooking dishes like *ḥarīsh*[5] and *Burāniyya*,[6] or any dishes cooked with vinegar, (**194v**) take some out, wash them, and cook with them whatever you want, God Almighty willing.

---

1 Note that the Madrid MS—and the edited Arabic text that follows it—contains the first recipe only, and it is not even complete. More confusingly, it is merged with unrelated recipes on chicken and other dishes that belong to earlier parts of the book. In the chapter heading itself, the editor of the Arabic text only mentions pickling the eggplants and disregards the rest, which includes pickling onions and turnips.

2 See glossary 9.2, s.v. *ghalya*, for more on this cooking technique.

3 For pitch, see glossary 9.1, s.v. *zift*.

4 The ratio of vinegar to water is 2 to 1, as stated in recipe X.4.1 above. The liquid should be enough to submerge the eggplants, and as in the previous recipes, the jar is to be left for three days and then checked.

5 It could be a variant on *aḥrash*, which are fried thin patties. For eggplant patties, see above, recipe vii.2.5. In the Madrid MS, fol. 122r, the two dishes are incoherently copied as الجزيرة اواليوانية.

6 It is a famous eggplant dish, see, for instance, recipe ii.1.2 above.

 | DOI:10.1163/9789004469488_054

FIGURE 93 Onions, Dioscorides, *Kitāb al-Ḥashā'ish fī hāyūlā al-ʿilāj al-ṭibbī*, Arabic translation by Ḥunayn b. Isḥāq, Or. 289, fol. 92v, detail

UNIVERSITAIRE BIBLIOTHEKEN LEIDEN, HTTP://HDL.HANDLE.NET/1887.1/ITEM:1578266

If you want, after boiling the eggplants, stuff one of the slits in each eggplant with pounded fresh and tender parsley (*karafs*) [of the variety] called *maqdūnis* (Macedonian parsley);[7] and stuff the other slit with pounded fresh mint. This will give them a deliciously fragrant aroma.

X.5.2 Making Onion [Pickles]

Choose fine and sweet onions that have not been touched by rain. Clean off the roots by hand and discard their thin outer skins. Take fine-tasting honey—enough for the amount of onions used—and put it in a large kneading bowl (*miʿjana*). Take vinegar and water—same ratios as those mentioned above.[8] Whip them all [i.e., with the honey] to mix them well and have a taste. If it is pronouncedly sweet, add more vinegar—but not much. Take nigella seeds (*shūnīz*), pick them over, and add them to the pickling liquid (*marqa*)—amount to taste. Also add salt.

Take an earthenware vessel (*wiʿāʾ fakhkhār*), either pitched (*muzaffat*)[9] or glazed (*muzajjaj*), and put the onions in it and pour in the pickling liquid; put enough to submerge them. Cover the jar (*khābiya*),[10] and tie its mouth with something that does not allow air to get in.[11] Set it aside for three days and then open it. If you find that the liquid has decreased, add more; and if when you taste it you find it lacking in honey, vinegar, or salt, add more of whatever is deficient.

Seal the jar with clay and leave it until you need to use the pickles. Take the amount you want and then tie it again, God Almighty willing.

X.5.3 Making Turnip [Pickles]

Take fresh and tender turnips, clean them, peel them completely, and then cut them into long pieces, medium in size. Take a large pot (*qidr*) or cauldron (*ṭinjīr*), put water in it, and place it on the fire; add salt and pounded safflower

7 At this point, the Madrid MS abruptly shifts to other recipes (fols. 122v–126r), all repeated from chapter iii.2 on chicken and chapter ii.6 on dishes with ground meat.

8 The ratio of vinegar to water is 2 to 1, as stated in recipe x.4.1 above.

9 For pitch, see glossary 9.1, s.v. *zift*.

10 So, the vessel mentioned is a *khābiya*, which is a large cylindrical jar with a tapered rounded bottom.

11 Thin sheets of leather, called *riqq*, were usually used for such purposes.

FIGURE 94 Turnips, Dioscorides, *Fī Hayūlā al-ṭibb*, translation by Ḥunayn b. Isḥāq, fol. 98v, detail
FROM THE NEW YORK PUBLIC LIBRARY, SPENCER COLLECTION: HTTPS://DIGITALCOLLECTIONS.NYPL.ORG/ITEMS/5E66B3E9-1DDC-D471-E040-E00A180654D7

(*ʿuṣfur*). When the water starts to boil vigorously, add the turnips and let them boil once or twice,[12] after which you take them out and put them in a large kneading bowl (*miʿjana*). Add pounded saffron and move the turnip pieces around until they are all colored well with it. Next, take mustard seeds (*ṣināb*), pound them very well, and then add them to the turnips and rub them between your hands. When you are done with this, cover the bowl with a wooden board (*lawḥ*) and leave the turnips to cool. Remove the board once they cool, have a look at them, and rub a piece [between your fingers]; if the mustard seeds used turn out not to be enough, add some more.

Next, take fine-tasting sweet raisins (*zabīb ḥulw*), pick them over, pound them very well, and then knead them thoroughly with fine-tasting vinegar—the mix should be neither too thin nor too thick. Take a clean tub (*qaṣriyya*) and put a fine-meshed sieve (*ghirbāl ṣafīq*) on top of it. Put the raisin mix in the sieve and rub and press it by hand so that all the liquid (*marqa*) passes into the tub. Now take a hair sieve (*ghirbāl shaʿr*) and strain the liquid once or twice.

Take the turnips from the bowl and put them in an earthenware vessel, **(195r)** either pitched (*muzaffat*)[13] or glazed (*muzajjaj*) from the inside and outside.

12 See glossary 9.2, s.v. *ghalya*, for more on this cooking technique.
13 For pitch, see glossary 9.1, s.v. *zift*.

Add the [strained] liquid and stir them together by hand or with a ladle—let the liquid submerge the turnips. Cover the vessel and leave it for 3 days, after which open it and taste the liquid. If the mustard seeds turn out to be lacking, add more of them after pounding and sifting them. Do likewise with saffron. If saffron is not available, use safflower instead. [Cover and seal the jar until the turnips are done.]

Use these turnips in cooking dishes that have them; or serve them [as pickles] after drizzling them with olive oil, and eat them salubriously, God Almighty willing.

Part Ten, Chapter Six: On Pickling Fish (*Taṣyīr al-Ḥūt*)[1]

x.6.1 A Variety [of Pickled Fish][2]

Take any kind of large or medium fish available to you, clean them, slit them open from their backs and remove their spines and whatever there is in their cavities. Boil them lightly in heated water with salt and then wash them thoroughly with cold water. Cut the big ones into [medium] pieces and leave the medium ones whole. Clean them of unwanted parts in their cavities and gills and then salt them.

Take fine-tasting vinegar; if it is too sour (*ḥādhiq*), dilute it with water—just enough to make it moderately sour; add pounded thyme (*ṣaʿtar*) and nigella seeds (*shūnīz*) to it.

Put the fish pieces in a clean vessel, sprinkle them with salt, and pour the [above] liquid (*marqa*) on them—add more than enough to submerge them. Tie the opening of the vessel and check on it every now and then to make sure that the liquid has not decreased.

Whenever you want to use the fish, take out the amount you need and the pieces you wish to use, God Almighty willing.

x.6.2 Another Variety [of Preserved Fish], from Which Fermented Fish Sauce (*murrī al-ḥūt*) Is Made. It Is Called *ṣīr* (Salt-Cured Small Fish)[3]

Take as many as you want of very small fish, put them in an earthenware jar (*jarra*) after washing them—but do not do anything else to them. Add salt—half the fish weight; thus you will have three portions (*athlāth*) [: two of fish and one of salt].

---

1 Note that this chapter with its two recipes is altogether missing from the Madrid MS and the edited Arabic text that follows it.

2 In the eastern region, fish preserved in similar ways was called *mamqūr*. See, for instance, chapter 37 in al-Warrāq, *Kitāb al-Ṭabīkh*, English trans., *Annals* 194–5.

3 Small fish used for making such preparation were usually anchovies; but other small fishes were also used, as in this recipe. Salt-cured fish prepared here will be needed in recipe x.8.13 below. See glossary 10, s.v. *ṣīr*.

 DOI:10.1163/9789004469488_055

FIGURE 95 Salt-cured fish, Dioscorides, *Fī Hayūlā al-ṭibb*, translation by Ḥunayn b. Isḥāq, fol. 76v, detail
FROM THE NEW YORK PUBLIC LIBRARY, SPENCER COLLECTION: HTTPS://DIGITALCOLLECTIONS.NYPL.ORG/ITEMS/5E66B3E9-0D19-D471-E040-E00A180654D7

Put the jar in a sunny place and put a [long] reed (*qaṣaba*) in it. Stir it three times a day [with the reed] until the fish and salt disintegrate and become one doughy mass that no longer smells of fish and starts to turn brownish. Remove jar from the sun and store it in a dry, ventilated place.

Whenever you want to make *murrī* [fish sauce] with them, [take out what you need,] and add thyme, the kind that is called *shardhūn*,[4] also known as

4 Conehead thyme, a Mediterranean wild variety, *Thymus capitatus*. See glossary 8, s.v. *ṣaʿtar*.

murkīra;[5] use a good amount of it. Stir this *ṣīr* mix very well, [adding more thyme as needed,] until you like the way it tastes. Use it [to make *murrī*] as I will later mention to you in the proper place in this book [recipe x.8.13 below], God Almighty willing.

5 This other name for the *shardhūn* variety of thyme is nowhere else to be found. See glossary 8, s.v. *ṣaʿtar*.

Part Ten, Chapter Seven: On Making Varieties of Vinegar[1]

X.7.1 Making *khall al-ʿinab* (Grape Vinegar), Here Is a Variety of It

Take fine-tasting fully ripe grapes. Fill a clean jar with the bunches and set it aside for three days, after which add more bunches to fill it.[2] Take other grapes, press out their juice in a press (*miʿṣara*), and pour it into the jar to fill it. If you want the vinegar to be white, use white grapes; (**195v**) and for red vinegar use black grapes. Add about 5 *raṭl*s (5 pints) of fresh water to the jar and then close its opening with something that prevents animals [or insects] from falling into it but can still allow rising vapors [of fermentation] to escape the jar.

Once the vinegar is ready to use, take out the amount needed and replace it with hot water. If you want, take the grape bunches out of the jar, press out their juice in a press, and divide the resulting juice between two jars, adding heated up fresh water—a quarter of the amount of the juice. This will still make delicious vinegar, with the help of God Almighty.

X.7.2 Another Variety [of Vinegar, Made with Figs]

If you cannot get grapes, use fresh or dried figs (*tīn*) instead, and fill half of a clean earthenware jar (*jarra*) with them. Add very hot water to fill the jar and put it at a warm place where it can get some heat. Keep it until the figs rot and sour and then strain the liquid, which will be pure vinegar with the help of God Almighty.

1 Note that of the 16 recipes in this chapter as copied in the BL MS, only the last two—recipe X.7.15 for lemon vinegar and recipe X.7.16 for vinegar infused with mint—are included in the Madrid MS, fol. 261, and the edited Arabic text that follows it.

2 More space will be made in the jar as the grapes shrivel during these three days.

 | DOI:10.1163/9789004469488_056

FIGURE 96 Grapes, al-ʿUmarī, *Masālik al-abṣār*, fol. 186r, detail
BNF, DEPARTMENT OF MANUSCRIPTS, ARAB 2771. SOURCE: GALLICA.BNF.FR/BNF

FIGURE 97 A fig tree, Dioscorides, *Fī Hayūlā al-ṭibb*, translation by Ḥunayn b. Isḥāq, fol. 69r, detail
FROM THE NEW YORK PUBLIC LIBRARY, SPENCER COLLECTION: HTTPS://DIGITALCOLLECTIONS.NYPL.ORG/ITEMS/5E66B3E8-74F2-D471-E040-E00A180654D7

FIGURE 98 Black pepper plant, *fulful aswad*, Dioscorides, *Ajzāʾ min risāla fī l-nabātāt*, fol. 41r, detail
BNF, DEPARTMENT OF MANUSCRIPTS, ARAB 4947. SOURCE: GALLICA.BNF.FR/BNF

X.7.3 Another Variety [of Vinegar, Sweet and Sour]

If you want vinegar to taste sweet and sour (*ḥulw ḥāmiḍ*), take as much as you want of fine-tasting vinegar and add sweet grape juice that has just been pressed—the amount used depends on how sweet you want the vinegar to be. Put the mix in one vessel, seal its opening with bitumen (*qār*),[3] and set it aside for a whole month. When you open the jar, you will find that the vinegar has turned sweet and sour, and it will stay as such until it is all consumed, with the help of God Almighty.

[**Another method:**] If you take 1 jarful of [grape] juice and 2 jarfuls of fine-tasting vinegar; empty them into a clean cauldron (*ṭinjīr*) or a large earthenware pot, which would be the best to use. Put the pot on the fire to boil until one-third of it is reduced and then strain it and put it in a clean vessel, pitched (*muzaffat*)[4] or oiled (*muzayyat*). Close and tie its opening, leave it for 20 days, and then use it. You will find that the vinegar has turned sweet and sour, with the help of God Almighty.

[**Another method:**] If you take 1 jarful of vinegar and mix it with 2 jarfuls of [grape] juice and 3 jarfuls of water, and then let them boil on the fire in an

3 It is mineral pitch that seeps naturally from the ground.
4 For *zift*, see glossary 9.1.

earthenware vessel until one-third of it is reduced, and then strain it, put it in jars as was mentioned above, and leave it for 20 days, and use it, you will find that it has turned sweet and sour, with the help of God Almighty.

X.7.4 Another Variety Called *khall al-fulful* (Vinegar Infused with Black Pepper), It Aids Digestion (*haḍūm*) and Is Very Aromatic[5]

Take 25 *raṭl*s (25 pints) vinegar, let it be fine tasting and very sour (*ḥādhiq*),[6] [and put it in a vessel.] Take 2 *ūqiyya*s (2 ounces) fine black pepper, tie it in a cloth bundle, and hang it in the vinegar vessel so that it dangles and dips in the vinegar itself. Seal the vessel with clay, and when you open it after eight days, you will find that the vinegar tastes of black pepper. Use it whichever way you like, with the help of God Almighty.

X.7.5 Remedying Vinegar when Its Acidity Weakens (*fatara*)

Take grape pomace (*thufl*),[7] dry it, [and use it as needed]. Take 4 *raṭl*s (4 pounds) of it, as well as 3 bunches of grapes. Put them in the jar of vinegar that has weakened (*khall fātir*) and seal its mouth with clay. When opened after three days, you will find that the vinegar has become good and very sour (*thaqīf*),[8] (**196r**) with the help of God Almighty.

X.7.6 Another Way [to Revive Weak Vinegar]

Take the [weak] vinegar and divide it among 3 jars. Take 2 of the jars and boil their vinegar until a third of it is reduced. Add this to the jar containing one-third of the [weak] vinegar that has not been cooked, and seal it with clay. When you open it after eight days, you will find that the vinegar has become good and very sour (*thaqīf*), with the help of God Almighty.

5 This method was also used to remedy vinegar that does not smell appetizing, as we learn from al-Ṭighnarī, *Zahrat al-bustān* 155.

6 In the degrees of sourness of vinegar, while *thaqīf* designates very sour vinegar, *ḥādhiq* designates even a more intense level of sourness.

7 It is the pulpy substance left after pressing the juice from the grapes.

8 See n. 6 above.

x.7.7 Another Way [to Revive Weak Vinegar]

Take chickpeas, cook them in fresh water until they are done, and then strain them [and use the boiling liquid]. Take one part of the chickpea liquid and add it to ten parts of the [weak] vinegar. It will become good and turn very sour (*thaqīf*),[9] God Almighty willing.

x.7.8 Another Way [to Help Vinegar Keep Its Acidity][10]

Take one part water that is comparable in intensity to acidity, such as sea water, and mix it with one part fine-tasting vinegar (*khall ṭayyib*). Also take barley grains—but not much—soak them in water for three days, and then drain them and add them to the vinegar. Also add a small amount of parched barley seeds (*shaʿīr maqlū*). This will keep the vinegar as good as it was [when first made] in taste and acidity, with the help of God Almighty.

x.7.9 Making *khamīr al-khall* (Vinegar Base)

Take 1 *raṭl* (1 pound) fine-tasting raisins (*zabīb*), remove the seeds, and pound them very well until they look like paste. Add 1 *raṭl* honey to them, along with 2 *raṭl*s (2 pints) fine-tasting vinegar and 1 *raṭl* preserved juice of unripe grapes (*khall ḥiṣrim*).[11] Mix them all thoroughly, put them in a glazed earthenware vessel (*wiʿāʾ muzajjaj*), and tightly seal its opening with clay to prevent any air from getting in.

Set the vessel aside in the sun, for ten days in hot regions and 40 days in moderate ones. Once the specified time has elapsed, and it is time to open the vessel, move it away from the sun and leave it for several days, after which you can open it. Do this by somehow protecting your face from the heat emitting from the jar. [This will be the vinegar base, *khamīr*.]

---

9 We assume that vinegar was sealed in a jar and left for a period of time, as described in the above methods.

10 This recipe shows how to prevent already good-quality vinegar from changing over time.

11 See below, recipes x.7.12 and 13, for ways to make it. Note that in the two surviving Andalusi cookbooks, this one and anonymous *Anwāʿ al-ṣaydala*, *khall* not only designates regular 'vinegar' produced by fermentation but also, in a looser sense, unfermented preserved 'sour juice,' and even freshly pressed out lemon juice. See glossary 8, s.v. *khall*.

FIGURE 99 A squill, *baṣal al-ʿunṣul*, Dioscorides, *Ajzāʾ min risāla fī l-nabātāt*, fol. 45r, detail
BNF, DEPARTMENT OF MANUSCRIPTS, ARAB 4947. SOURCE: GALLICA.BNF.FR/BNF

Whenever you want to make vinegar, take a pound of this *khamīr*, dissolve it in 10 *raṭl*s of hot water [in a pot] and whip the mix while it is on the fire. As soon as it gets colored, remove it, and then strain it after it cools and use it [as vinegar],[12] God Almighty willing.

12 According to al-Jawbarī, *al-Mukhtār fī kashf al-asrār* 118, a thirteenth-century book on revealing the secrets of swindlers, this type of vinegar is adulterated because it is artificially made. Nevertheless, to al-Tujībī and makers of such vinegars, it must have been a convenient and acceptable way to obtain vinegar when the 'natural' stuff was not available, or when traveling.

X.7.10 How to Test Vinegar to Find Out If It Has Been Adulterated by Diluting It with Water or Not

Take the suspected vinegar, [put it in a vessel,] and add *būraq al-khubz* (sodium bicarbonate), which is *naṭrūn* (natron).[13] If the vinegar starts to bubble and froth (*ghalā wa azbada*), then it pure. If it only bubbles and does not froth, then it is diluted with water. This is how vinegar is tested, so know this.

X.7.11 Making *khall al-ʿunṣul* (Vinegar Flavored with Squills)[14]

Take an earthenware vessel that has been glazed from the outside. In its inside there should be a ledge (*ifrīz*) around its middle, which has been affixed while it was being made.

Take squills (*baṣal al-ʿunṣul*), clean them of all molded parts and whatever is inedible and slit each with a [sharp] piece of wood—do not use iron utensils. Take each onion, discard its outer layer, and cut each subsequent layer into large wide pieces; pass them through a thread using a wooden needle. When you finish doing this, take very sour vinegar (*khall thaqīf*) and pour it into the vessel; let it be just one finger width below the inside ledge.

The amount of vinegar in the vessels used should be the same, which by weight is 4 *raṭls* (4 pounds).[15] (**196v**) Use ⅓ *raṭl* (approx. 5 ounces) squills with each *qafīz* (60 pounds) of vinegar. For those who want to give the vinegar stronger properties, let them add ½ *ūqiyya* (approx. 15 grams) of chopped cores of the squills to the vinegar in the vessel. [But care should be taken because] adding too much of this will make the vinegar taste bitter.

Take the thin top sections of the stems of date palm fronds (*jarīd al-nakhl*), divide them into smaller pieces, and arrange them on the ledge like a lattice. [In layers,] spread on them [leaves of] lemon balm (*turunjān*), mint (*naʿnaʿ*), marjoram (*marzanjūsh*), and water mint (*ghubayrā*),[16] and ending with [lay-

13 See glossary 8, s.vv. *būraq* and *naṭrūn*.

14 *ʿUnṣul* (*Drimia maritima*) is a variety of wild onion, full of thick juice that is bitter and acrid in taste. It is principally used for medicinal purposes. See glossary 8, s.vv. *baṣal al-ʿunṣul* and *khall*, for *khall al-ʿunṣul*. See also the last paragraph in the fish chapter v.1, where this vinegar is used to ward off the harms of eating fish.

15 Therefore, the size of the jars should accommodate this, i.e., the 4 pints should come up to the level where vinegar is one finger width below the ledge.

16 Also occurs as *ghubayra* (غبيرة), not to be confused with *ghubayrāʾ*, which is the tree of the sorbus fruit.

ers] of *fulāyū* (pennyroyal) and mother of thyme (*nammām*).[17] Now take the threaded onion pieces and spread them on these herbs (*aḥbāq*, sg. *ḥabaq*) in one layer; and layer on top of them more of the herbs [as was done above].

Cover the vessel with a wide and shallow earthenware bowl (*ṣaḥfa*) and seal the opening tightly with clay so that no air can get into it. Leave the vessel in a sunny place for 40 days. If after 20 days have elapsed you want to replace the herbs with fresher ones, you can do so.

At the end of the abovementioned period of time, open the vessel carefully and take out the herbs, squill, and the stem pieces. Strain the vinegar in a large basket of esparto grass (*quffa min ḥalfā*) after rinsing it in water repeatedly to get rid of the esparto grass smell. Put the strained vinegar in small vessels of glazed earthenware (*fakhkhār muzajjaj*) or glass (*zujāj*) and use it in cooking dishes like those of eggplant and fish; or use it however you want. Seal the vessels' tops with olive oil to protect the vinegar from contact with air, God Almighty willing.

X.7.12 Making *khall al-ḥiṣrim* (Preserved Juice of Unripe Grapes),[18] Here Is a Variety

Take any amount you want of unripe grapes (*ḥiṣrim*) and pound them very well in a mortar of wood (*ʿūd*) or glazed earthenware (*muzajjaj*). Press out their juice, and after straining it, put it in glass vessels.

Leave the vessels in the sun, and every three days filter (*turawwiq*)[19] the juice through a tightly woven piece of cloth. Add a small amount of fine-tasting salt to it and continue filtering it until you no longer see any sort of cloudiness (*ṭakhā*) at the bottom of the vessels.[20]

---

17 See glossary 8 for more on these herbs. Arranging the leaves and herbs in layers is suggested by the expression used: وتنهي بالفلايوا والنمام.

18 This recipe describes how to make a clear filtered variety, which is left in the sun to 'cook.' In recipe iii.2.17, al-Tujībī describes it as *khall maʿmūl lil-shams* 'made to be left in the sun' and deems it a high-quality variety.

Note that in the two surviving Andalusi cookbooks, this one and anonymous *Anwāʿ al-ṣaydala*, *khall* not only designates regular 'vinegar' produced by fermentation but also, in a looser sense, unfermented preserved 'sour juice,' and even freshly pressed out lemon juice. See glossary 8, s.v. *khall*.

19 *Tarwīq* 'filtering' aims at making liquids clear; cf. *taṣfiya* 'straining,' which is less thorough.

20 *Ṭakhā'* literally designates high thin clouds and the haziness of the moon. See Ibn Manẓūr, *Lisān al-ʿArab*, s.v. طخا.

The duration of keeping the juice to 'cook' in the sun is 40 days, after which seal the vessels' tops with olive oil and store them in ventilated places, God Almighty willing.

x.7.13 Another Variety [of Preserved Juice of Unripe Grapes,[21] Cooked and Reduced]

Take as much as you want of juicy unripe grapes and do with them as above [i.e., pounding and pressing]. Strain the juice and put it in a large glazed earthenware pot. Let it boil on a medium fire until about a quarter of the juice has reduced and then remove it from the fire. Strain the juice after it cools, empty it into glass vessels, and seal their tops with olive oil, God Almighty willing.

x.7.14 Another Variety [with Freshly Extracted Juice of Unripe Grapes];[22] Used by Those Who Need It When It Is Still Early in the Season [for the Sun-Cooked Variety]

Take bunches of unripe grapes and put them in a clean pot; add water enough to submerge them and put it on the fire. As soon as it boils three times or so,[23] remove it from the fire. [Take out the bunches,] press them to extract the juice, and then strain it. Use the resulting liquid when cooking meat dishes,[24] God Almighty willing.

x.7.15 Making *khall al-līm* (Preserved Lemon Juice)[25]

Take fine-tasting lemons that have fully ripened,[26] wash them to remove dust and other impurities, and cut them lengthwise into halves.[27] Press out their

---

21 Although called *khall* 'vinegar,' juice here is preserved without fermentation, see n. 18 above.

22 Called *khall ḥiṣrim ṭarī* in recipes ii.1.9 and ii.2.24; and *mā' al-ḥiṣrim al-ṭarī* in recipe iii.2.17. See n. 18 above.

23 *Thalāth ghalyāt*, see glossary 9.2, s.v. *ghalya*, for more on this cooking technique.

24 As in recipes ii.1.9, ii.2.24, ii.5.3, and iii.2.17; see also n. 22 above.

25 This recipe and the following one are the only ones included in the Madrid MS, see n. 1 above. See also n. 18 on usage of the term *khall* 'vinegar.'

26 In the Madrid MS, fol. 126r, the lemons are mentioned as *līm akhḍar* (limes). Describing lemons as green is an indication that lime is being used here; see a similar usage in recipe vii.2.11 above and in glossary 7, s.v. *līm*.

27 Interestingly, the recipe recommends cutting the lemons lengthwise, and not crosswise,

FIGURE 100
Mint, *naʿnaʿ*, Dioscorides, *Ajzāʾ min risāla fī l-nabātāt*, fol. 56v, detail
BNF, DEPARTMENT OF MANUSCRIPTS, ARAB 4947. SOURCE: GALLICA.BNF.FR/BNF

juice into a large bowl (*mithrad*) until you collect the amount you need. Strain it through a light piece of cloth (*khirqa khafīfa*), pour it into glass vessels, and add salt—but not much. Leave the vessels in a place the sun reaches (**197r**)[28] and then strain the juice [which is now vinegar] once or twice. [Store it in vessels] sealed with olive oil, and use it however you want, God Almighty willing.

x.7.16 Making *khall al-naʿnaʿ* (Distilled Vinegar Infused with Mint)

Take as many as you want of fresh and tender green leaves of mint[29] and wash them in fresh water to remove all dirt and other impurities attached to them. After chopping them, put them in a large kneading bowl (*miʿjana*) with an equal amount by weight of fine-tasting white vinegar. Let them steep for an hour and then put them in the cucurbit (*qādūs al-taqṭīr*),[30] which is used for distilling rosewater and the like. Fasten the alembic (*inbīq*) into the head of the *qādūs*, light a fire underneath it, and leave it until the liquid is distilled and the

as we are used to doing nowadays. Interestingly, I did come across online discussions that recommend the lengthwise method, as it is believed to yield more juice, such as this one: https://lifehacker.com/cut-lemons-lengthwise-to-get-more-juice-507786943, accessed March 22, 2020.

28 We may assume that the duration of keeping the lemon juice 'cooking' in the sun would be around 40 days, as mentioned, for instance, in recipe x.7.12 above.

29 Note that only the leaves are being used here. In the anonymous fourteenth-century Egyptian cookbook, *Kanz al-fawāʾid*, English trans., *Treasure Trove*, recipe 157, mint leaves are used in a similar manner.

30 More commonly called *qarʿa* in the eastern region.

vinegar [in the *qādūs*] dries out. Take the distilled vinegar, clean the *qādūs* by washing it, and then put in another batch [of mint and vinegar], and do with them as you did [above].

Strain the resulting vinegar, store it in glass vessels, and use it in dishes of grilled meat, fish dishes, and the like, God Almighty willing.

Vinegar infused with balm mint (*khall al-turunjān*) is done the same way.[31]

31 *Turunjān* (*Melissa officinalis*) is also called lemon balm. Its leaves have a gentle scent of citrus.

Part Ten, Chapter Eight: On Making Sun-Fermented Liquid Sauce (*Murrī Naqīʿ*), Cooked Liquid Sauce (*Murrī Maṭbūkh*), and Other Kinds[1]

x.8.1 Making *murrī naqīʿ* (Sun-Fermented Liquid Sauce)[2]

Take fine-tasting whole barley grains at the end of March (Māris), pick them over and sift them, and after leaving them in the sun for a whole day, crush them. Sift off the bran (*nukhāla*), [set it aside,] and knead the flour thoroughly without adding any salt to the dough. Form it into small conical pieces like those of sugar (*jamājim al-sukkar*)[3] and press a hole in the middle of each one with the tip of a ladle's handle (*dhanb mighrafa*).[4] When all the pieces are done—the dough should be very firm in consistency—take a large board, raise it a couple of spans above the ground,[5] and sprinkle it with the [set aside] bran.

Now take the dough pieces and wrap each one with a leaf of the caprifig tree (*dhukār*),[6] let it cover the entire piece, and stuff the edges of the leaf inside the hole. Arrange them on the board in rows, sprinkle them with the rest of the bran, and cover them all with the leaves of the caprifig tree. Place the board in an airy spot that the sun does not reach. Leave them like this for 20 days and then turn them, cover them with more leaves if needed, and leave them for 20 more days.

Once the 40 days have elapsed, remove the leaves and bran. You will find that the dough pieces have dried and are all coated with green mold (*ʿafan*)

---

1 Note that the entire chapter is included in the Madrid MS and the edited Arabic text that follows it.

2 A *murrī* recipe comparable to this one is found in al-Ṭighnarī, *Zahrat al-bustān* 139–43. I used it to add some details that are missing in al-Tujībī's version. Al-Ṭighnarī mentions that the famous physician Abū al-Ḥasan Shihāb al-Muʿayṭī himself copied this recipe for him. A *murrī* recipe found in the anonymous fourteenth-century *Kanz al-fawāʾid*, English trans., *Treasure Trove* 162–3 largely follows the same method. It must have been a popular recipe.

3 Al-Ṭighnarī gives an additional name, *qand*, which is crystallized sugar, usually formed into cones. For *jamājim al-sukkar*, see glossary 4, s.v. *sukkar*.

4 In the Madrid MS, fol. 126r, the hole is made with one's finger.

5 A span, *shibr*, is the distance between the stretched little finger and thumb, approx. 9 inches.

6 *Ficus carica sylvestris* (S) is the male pollen-bearing wild variety of the common fig, used to pollinate the edible fig. See glossary 7, s.v. *tīn*.

 | DOI:10.1163/9789004469488_057

tinged with redness. These [dough pieces] are [now] called *būdhaq*.[7] Scrape them with a knife thoroughly until nothing of the rotten parts or anything else remains on them. Break them, pound them into flour, and sift them. Whatever has not passed through the sieve, pound it and sift it again, and repeat until it all passes through it.

Take the amount you want to use of this [*būdhaq*] flour and weigh it. Take an equal amount of wheat flour whose bran has been sifted out, take half its amount of pounded pure salt, and take what equals their amounts together of fresh water. Put them all in a large kneading bowl (*miʿjana*) in one, two, or more batches, depending on how large the bowl is, and dissolve them with the water.[8] As you finish a batch, put it in a clean, sweet-smelling earthenware jar (*khābiya*),[9] which has been used only for keeping olive oil. Do this in the evening, filling it only to below its neck, to make room for fermentation and stirring.

When the jar is filled, add 4 *ūqiyyas* (4 ounces) each of aniseeds (*anīsūn*), fennel seeds (*rāzyānaj*), coarsely crushed coriander seeds (*kuzbara yābisa*), and nigella seeds (*shūnīz*). Also add ½ *raṭl* (½ pound) common thyme (*ṣaʿtar*)—the leaves only—a fistful (**197v**) of *ṣaʿtar mulūkī*[10]—take the entire sprigs—citron leaves, chopped herb fennel (*basbās*), tender tips of the caprifig tree branches, and a pinecone (*jumjuma min ṣanawbar*), which has been emptied of its seeds. All the above amounts would be enough for each *rubʿ* (8 ¾ pounds) used of the barley flour called *būdhaq* [prepared earlier].[11] Adjust their amounts according to how much more or less you are using.

Add olive oil to the jar, a little bit more than enough to cover the dissolved flour. Take a stick from the caprifig with three tines at its end, called *rūṭabāl*,[12] to be used for stirring the mix, and put it in the jar. Tie the mouth of the jar with

---

7 Addition from the Madrid MS, fol. 126v. It is the base for making fermented sauces. See glossary 8, s.v. *murrī*.

8 Based on al-Ṭighnarī, 141, see n. 2 above, the consistency should resemble that of *ḥasāʾ*, which is soup of medium thickness. See, for instance, *ḥasū* recipes in chapter i.3 above.

9 According to al-Ṭighnarī, 141, see n. 2 above, it has to be nonporous. *Khābiya* is a large cylindrical jar with a tapered rounded bottom.

10 Erroneously edited as *al-lūlī* in the Arabic edition, p. 262. *Ṣaʿtar mulūkī* is literally 'royal thyme.' Possibly, it is another name for another type of thyme, called *nammām al-malik* 'the king's thyme,' which is a wild variety called mother of thyme, *Thymus glaber*. See glossary 8, s.v. *nammām*.

11 See glossary 13 for the weight called *rubʿ*, literally 'quarter.'

12 The name is given only in the Madrid MS, fol. 126v. It is inaccurately read as *dūṭabāl* in the edited Arabic text, p. 263. As described in the recipe, it looks like a three-tine cultivator; cf. Corriente, *Dictionary of Andalusi Arabic*, s.v. *r-ṭ-b-l*, where it is said to be related to the Latin *rutabellu* 'rake.' In "Words for Cooking" 45, n. 30, Manuela Marín, who must have

a clean piece of cloth and cover it with a sheet of leather taken from a leather container (*ẓarf*), which has been used for storing olive oil—let the hair side of the leather be next to the cloth and its inner side exposed to the air. Put the jar at a place where the sun shines and sets, and stir it three times a day for 20 days.

[After these 20 days,] take wheat flour sifted of its bran, half the amount that was used earlier—which by now should be sixth of all that was used before [i.e., *būdhaq*, wheat flour, and salt]. Divide it into three parts. Take the first part and knead it with [water] and fresh yeast (*khamīr*)—but no salt. Leave it for a while to ferment and then shape it into thin discs. Pierce their faces with holes and put them in the *furn* (brick oven) until they firm up; do not let them bake completely, and take them out while still soft. Immediately cut them into small pieces and throw them into the jar; cover its mouth with the cloth and leather right away to prevent steam from escaping the jar. Keep it like this for a day and night, after which open the jar, put your hand in it, and start pressing and mashing the bread very well until it disintegrates and becomes indistinguishable from the rest of the jar's contents. For seven days,[13] continue stirring the jar [three times a day] as was done earlier.

On the eighth day from when you put the [first part of] bread in the jar, take the second part of the wheat flour and do with it exactly as you did with the first part. Take the third part of the flour on the eighth day from when you put the second part, and do the same with it. Thus, the duration of putting the bread three times will be 21 days. Leave the jar for three more days, stirring it [three times a day] as usual.

Take a vessel made of woven esparto grass (*ḥalfā*) with a three-finger-wide base and about 3 spans (approx. 27 inches) wide on top, with three or four loops (*maʿālīq*) attached to it, and suspend it from a piece of wood[14] with a large kneading bowl (*miʿjana*) put underneath it. Empty the contents of the jar into this vessel. Wait until all the liquid strains [and drips into the bowl] and nothing remains in the esparto vessel but the dregs (*thufl*).[15]

Take the strained liquid and distribute it among small bowls. Expose them to the sun all day and cover them during the night. [Continue doing this] until you see that the salt has started to form a crust on top of the bowls, which is a sign that they have 'cooked' well. Gently remove the salt crusts—do this either

been consulting the edited text only, is right to suspect the edited word to be Corriente's *rūṭabāl*.

13 The number of days at this point is mentioned in the Madrid MS, fol. 127r.

14 I added here a few details from the Madrid MS, fol. 127r, where this dripping device is called *maṣṣāl*.

15 Addition from the Madrid MS, fol. 127r.

FIGURE 101 Two physicians filtering a medicinal preparation with a suspended straining vessel put on top of a large bowl, the same way *murrī* would have been strained, Arabic version of Dioscorides, *De Materia Medica*, fol. W. 675r, detail
THE WALTERS ART MUSEUM, W. 675

in the morning or in the evening. Strain the *murrī* and put it in earthenware vessels glazed from the inside and the outside. Tie their mouths [with pieces of cloth] and leave them in a sunny place during the day but take them inside during the night. Do this for five days and then store the vessels away. This would be the first *murrī* (*al-awwal*).[16]

Now take the dregs, return them to the jar, add hot water, and stir them three times a day for ten days or more. Next, add the baked bread twice within ten

16 *Al-murrī al-awwal* is deemed a prime quality sauce, good enough to serve as a table sauce. The Madrid MS, fol. 127v, also calls it *ra's al-murrī* 'the best.'

more days, but this time the bread has to be baked well, until it browns, (**198r**) and then take it out of the oven, pound it in a mortar until it is as fine as dust (*ghubār*), and add it to the jar.

After a couple of days, empty the jar into the esparto vessel as was mentioned above and divide [the strained liquid] among small bowls. When salt crusts appear on top of the bowls, remove the salt and strain the *murrī*, which you then put it in glazed earthenware vessels. Leave them in the sun until they 'cook' well and then store them away, God Almighty willing. This would be the second *murrī* (*al-thānī*).[17]

If you want, put some of the first *murrī* in a small jar (*khābiya ṣaghīra*) lined with olive oil (*muzayyata*)[18] and add honey and pounded carob (*kharnūb*).[19] It will be exceedingly good in taste and aroma (*binna*), especially for those who put it at the table [as a condiment] while eating, and not cooked in dishes, so know this.

If you want to use linen (*kattān*) to make the strainer (*muṣaffī*), you can do so. When using the esparto grass strainer, do not put *murrī* in it before rinsing it repeatedly and drying it in the sun until all the odors of what was used to soften the esparto grass is gone,[20] so know this. Even the slightest negligence, haste, or slackness will put to waste all the work done. And beware of letting any unclean person (*najis*) deal with it from start to finish,[21] not even transferring it from one place to the other, so know this and act accordingly, and may God with His help and might be our guide.

x.8.2 Another Variety of [*murrī naqīʿ* 'Sun-Fermented Liquid Sauce']

Take as much as you want of fine-tasting barley grains, crush them, sift their bran, [and set it aside]. Make stiff dough with the flour [and water], but do not use any salt. Shape it into discs, ¼ *raṭl* (4 ounces) each, and make them two and a half fingers thick. Pierce three holes in the middle of each.

Take a wooden board, raise it above the ground, and spread [the set-aside] barley bran all over its surface. Spread a layer of caprifig leaves on it[22] and

17 Al-Ṭighnarī, *Zahrat al-bustān* 143, comments that the remaining dregs after obtaining the second *murrī* are only good enough for fuel. See n. 2 above.

18 In the Madrid MS, fol. 127v, it is *muzaffata* 'pitched.'

19 *Ceratonia siliqua*, of which the pulp of the pods is used. See glossary 7.

20 In Ibn al-Bayṭār, *al-Jāmiʿ* ii 408, it is mentioned that esparto grass is softened with cows' dung (*arwāth baqar*).

21 Such as menstruating women and men and women who have not bathed after intercourse.

22 See n. 6 above.

arrange the discs of dough all over them. Cover them all with [more] caprifig leaves and another layer of barley bran. Put the board in an airy place that the sun does not reach at all. Leave them until the bread pieces are dry and then remove the bran and leaves. Turn the bread discs over and return the leaves all over them again. Leave them until they dry out and then move the leaves covering them to the sides.

Once the bread discs are completely and thoroughly dry, scrape them with a knife very well to remove whatever was stuck to them of bran and leaves, as well as the rotten parts (*khamaj*). Do this meticulously with the knife so that nothing remains of them. Set them aside for three days so that not a trace of moisture remains in them. Break them with a wooden *mayjam*[23] into chickpea-size pieces and then crush and sift them until they turn to flour. This is the base (*aṣl*) for making *murrī*, and it is called *būdhaq*.

Now take the amount you need of this [*būdhaq*] flour and take an equal amount of wheat flour sifted from its bran; also take crushed salt, half the amount of the wheat flour used, which will be a fifth of the entire amounts used.

Take a large jar (*khābiya*),[24] which has been used for storing olive oil and smells good, and put it at a high place where the sun rises and sets. Take the [two] flours and the salt, put them on a leather spread (*naṭʿ*), and mix them; (**198v**) and then put them all in the jar—do this in the evening. Add fresh water to them, enough to give the mix the consistency of *ḥarīra*.[25] Whip them by hand to mix them well and dissolve all lumps. Add olive oil enough to cover the mix. Also add a fistful (*qabḍa*) of thyme (*ṣaʿtar*), citron leaves, ½ *ūqiyya* (approx. 15 grams) fennel seeds (*bazr basbās*) and herb fennel sprigs (*ʿīdān basbās*), 2 pinecones, and 2 *ūqiyyas* (2 ounces) nigella seeds (*shūnīz*).

Now take a stick from the caprifig tree with three tines at its end[26] and stir the jar with it twice a day—once in the morning and once in the evening—for seven consecutive days. [When not being stirred,] the jar should always be

---

23 It is more accurately copied as *minjam* in the Madrid MS, fol. 128r. In Ibn Manẓūr, *Lisān al-ʿArab*, s.v. نجم, *minjam* is said to be something used to hammer down the tent's post (*watad*), which could be a rounded stone or a piece of iron, etc. The word *mayjam* must have been a common misnomer, which was discussed and corrected in ʿAbd al-Tawwāb, *Manāhij taḥqīq al-turāth* 248. *Mayjam* is still used in Morocco to designate a wooden mallet; see for instance, https://www.ward2u.com/showthread.php?t=10379&pp=40, accessed Jan. 15, 2020.

24 See n. 9 above.

25 It is a flour-based silky-smooth soup with a flowing consistency, which is rather thinner than *ḥasāʾ*, see n. 8 above.

26 See n. 12 above.

covered with a tightly woven piece of cloth tied to its mouth and topped with a sheet of leather taken from a pleasant-smelling vessel (*ẓarf*) that has been used to store olive oil. The flour and water mix should be below the neck of the jar to leave room for fermentation [and stirring], so know this.

On the eighth day, take fine-tasting wheat flour, which has been sifted of its bran—let it be half the amount used first—and divide it into three parts. Take the first part and make it into dough, without salt and unleavened (*faṭīr*); shape it into medium discs, which you then put in the *furn* (brick oven). Take them out when they firm up and are almost baked. Immediately break them into pieces and throw them into the jar, which you then cover to trap in steam. On the fourth day [of putting bread in the jar], open it, put your hand in, and start pressing and mashing it vigorously, rubbing it against the walls of the jar until it all disintegrates and looks indistinguishable from the rest of the mix.

On that same fourth day, take the second part of the wheat flour and do with it exactly as you did with the first part. Leave the jar for three more days and then take the third part and do with it exactly as you did with the previous two parts. Then, resume stirring the jar, once in the morning and once in the evening, for 40 days.

When this period has elapsed, take wheat flour, which has been sifted from its bran, the same amount as above, which is half the amount of wheat flour first used, divide it into two parts, and make it into dough without salt and without yeast. Shape it into discs, each weighing about ½ *raṭl* (½ pound). Pierce small holes all over their faces and take them to the *furn* (communal brick oven) to bake very well and turn intensely brown, as this will determine the sauce's color. Take them out, break them into pieces, and then either pound them [in a mortar] or crush them until they turn into flour. Add this flour to the jar and stir it vigorously. Continue stirring the jar—once in the morning and once in the evening—until 20 days have elapsed.

Take the second part of the wheat flour and knead it as was done before and then bake the bread discs in the oven until they brown. If you want the *murrī* to be intensely dark [literally *aswad* 'black'], then bake them until they look dark [but not burnt]. If you want the *murrī* to look brownish red (*ashqar*),[27] let the bread pieces bake until they turn brown [*aḥmar*, literally 'red'], then crush them and add them to the jar and stir it. Continue stirring the jar, once in the morning and once in the evening, until the end of autumn.

27 In the medieval lexicons, *ashqar* is associated with the rusty red or chestnut red of cattle, and a human's ruddy complexion.

When it is time to use the sauce, take a strainer (*miṣfā*) made of esparto (*ḥalfā*),[28] wash and rinse it thoroughly to get rid of the odors of what was used to soften the esparto,[29] and hang it as I described to you [in the previous recipe]. Empty the contents of the jar into it and let the liquid drip into a vessel put underneath it until nothing remains in it but the dregs (*thufl*).[30] Take all the *murrī* that has accumulated in it, strain it, and divide it among earthenware vessels that are glazed from the inside and outside. (**199r**) Add sweet olive oil (*zayt ʿadhb*) to seal the vessels' tops; it can be taken with the *murrī* when you serve it, God Almighty willing. [This would be the first *murrī*.]

Take the dregs and return them to the jar. Add hot water, and stir it three times a day for eight days. Add bread baked as was done above, and leave the *murrī* jar for eight more days. Meanwhile, you should continue stirring it [three times a day]. Strain the *murrī* and use it for cooking purposes, God Almighty willing.

x.8.3 A Variety of *murrī maṭbūkh* (Nonfermented Cooked Liquid Sauce)

Take wheat flour, barley flour, and crushed salt; 1 *mudd* (2 pounds) of each. Also take coarsely crushed coriander seeds, nigella seeds (*shūnīz*), aniseeds (*anīsūn*), and fennel seeds (*rāzyānaj*); ¼ *ūqiyya* (approx. 8 grams) of each. Combine the spices with the flours and salt, knead them (with water), and make two discs of bread with them. Take them to the *furn* (communal brick oven) to bake very well until they turn intensely brown (*yaḥmarr ḥumra shadīda*), and take them out. Break them into pieces and crush them until they turn into flour.

Put this flour in a new pot with ¾ *rubʿ* (6½ pints) fresh water,[31] a pinecone (*jumjumat ṣanawbar*) emptied of its seeds, 2 *raṭl*s (2 pounds) apples, 2 *raṭl*s quinces that have been peeled and chopped, and 2 *raṭl*s honey that has been strained and its froth skimmed.[32] Keep the pot in the *furn* (brick oven) overnight [to slowly cook in the remaining heat of the oven]. Take it out in the morning, press and mash [its contents] vigorously, and then set it aside for a

28 In the Madrid MS, fol. 129r, this draining device is called *maṣṣāl*, from *m-ṣ-l* 'drip.'

29 See n. 20 above.

30 As added in the Madrid MS, fol. 129r.

31 The edited Arabic text confusingly leaves out the measure *rubʿ*, which clearly occurs as ثلاثة ارباع الربع 'three-quarters of the *rubʿ* measure,' in the Madrid MS, fol. 129r, which the editor follows.

32 Honey was strained by softening it on the fire with some water and then letting it boil until the water evaporates and the froth is skimmed off.

couple hours. Strain the mix with a clean cloth and put [the resulting *murrī*] in a glazed earthenware vessel. This would be the first *murrī* (*al-awwal*).

Next, take the remaining dregs, [put them back in the pot,] and return them to the oven with fresh water—half the amount first used. Keep it in the oven overnight and then take it out and press and mash the mix vigorously. Set it aside for an hour and then strain it [to get the liquid, which would be the second *murrī*], and use it, God Almighty willing.

x.8.4 Another Variety [of *murrī maṭbūkh*]

Take flours of wheat and barley with their bran and crushed salt; one *mudd* (2 pounds) of each. Weighing them is better [i.e., more accurate] than measuring them by bulk. Also, take coarsely crushed coriander seeds, nigella seeds (*shūnīz*), fennel seeds (*basbās*), and aniseeds (*anīsūn*); ½ *ūqiyya* (approx. 15 grams) of each.

Mix all the ingredients and knead them thoroughly with a small amount of water. Shape them into a couple of bread discs, take them to the *furn* (communal brick oven), and let them bake very well until they turn intensely brown. Take one of them out and leave the other one to bake more until it almost turns black. Break them into pieces and crush them until they turn into flour.

Put the flour mix in a new pot, along with 1¼ *raṭls* (1¼ pounds) fine-tasting honey and ¾ *rubʿ* (6½ pints) fresh water. Cover the pot, seal it with mud, and keep it in the *furn* (brick oven) overnight. Take it out in the morning and press and mash its contents very well. Set it aside until the dregs settle and then strain the liquid and store it away in glazed earthenware vessels. [This would be the first *murrī*.]

Next, take the dregs, [put them in a pot,] and return them to the *furn* after adding fresh water—half the amount of water used the first [time]. Keep the pot overnight in the oven and then take it out [in the morning], strain the liquid, and use it, God Almighty willing. [This would be the second *murrī*.]

If you want to color the first *murrī* with 1½ *dirhams* (4½ grams) crushed saffron, go ahead and do so, with the help of God Almighty.

x.8.5 Another Variety [of *murrī maṭbūkh*][33]

Take 2 *mudds* (4 pounds) of fine-tasting flour, 1 *mudd* salt, a handful (*kaff*) of nigella seeds (*shūnīz*), and as much of each of fennel seeds (*basbās*), aniseeds (*anīsūn*), and coarsely crushed coriander seeds (*kuzbara yābisa*).

Knead them into a stiff dough, (**199v**) which you then make into medium-sized discs of bread. Keep them in the *furn* (brick oven) overnight. When you take them out in the morning, they will look musk colored (*miskī*).[34] Pound them until they are the size of fava beans or chickpeas. Take them with whatever was crushed with them and put them in a glazed earthenware pot (*qidr fakhkhār*). Pour fresh water on them; let it be much more than enough to submerge them. Add 1 *raṭl* (1 pound) honey, as well as citron leaves and sprigs of herb fennel (*ʿīdān basbās*) and thyme (*ṣaʿtar*). Set it aside for a day and then take it to the *furn* (communal brick oven) and let it cook until it thickens and changes color.

Take the pot out, press and mash its contents, and then strain it with a piece of cloth (*mindīl*). Have a taste of [the strained liquid]; add some salt if there is not enough of it, and color it with 1 *dirham* (3 grams) crushed saffron. This is the first *murrī* (*al-awwal*). Store it away.

If you choose to cook the pot at home [on the stove, instead of in the *furn*], put [the bread mix] in a tinned cauldron (*ṭinjīr muqaṣdar*) or a tinned pot (*qidr muqaṣdar*) [and let it cook on the fire] until it thickens as was done above. Strain it and store it away.

Return the dregs to the pot and add water to them—two-thirds of the water used first. Cover the pot, seal it with clay, keep it in the *furn* overnight, and then take it out the following morning and strain it. This would be the second *murrī* (*al-thānī*).

If you wish to extract a third *murrī* (*thālith*), return the dregs to the pot and add water to them—half the amount of water used for the second *murrī*. Keep the pot overnight in the *furn* and take it out the following morning. Strain it and mix [this resulting third *murrī*] with the second. Return the mix to the pot and boil it until it thickens. Alternatively, put the mix in glazed bowls (*aghḍira*, sg. *ghaḍāra*) and leave them in the sun until the liquid thickens and salt appears on the surface. Strain it and store it away, God Almighty willing.

---

33 This BL MS version of the recipe offers more details than the Madrid MS text, fols. 129v–130r.

34 I.e., dark reddish brown.

x.8.6 Another Variety [of *murrī maṭbūkh*]

Take 3 *raṭl*s (3 pounds) wheat flour and 1 *raṭl* salt and knead them [with water] into stiff dough, which you then shape into bread discs. Take them to the *furn* (communal brick oven) and let them bake until they turn intensely dark (literally *aswad* 'black'). Take them out, pound them very well until they turn into flour, and put them in a new pot. Add 20 *raṭl*s (20 pints) fresh water and 1 *raṭl* fine-tasting honey. Also add, nigella seeds (*shūnīz*), fennel seeds (*basbās*), and coarsely crushed coriander seeds, 1 *ūqiyya* (1 ounce) of each; tie each of these spices in a piece of cloth separately and then add them to the pot.

Cover the pot, seal its lid with clay, and then keep it in the *furn* (brick oven) overnight. Take it out in the morning, [discard the spice bundles,] and press and mash all that there is in it vigorously. Set it aside for an hour and then strain it and store it away. [This would be the first *murrī*.]

Return the dregs to the pot, adding 10 *raṭl*s water, ½ *raṭl* honey, and half the amounts of the spices. Add some salt. Keep the pot in the *furn* overnight, take it out in the morning, do with it as you first did, and store it away, God Almighty willing.

x.8.7 Making [Nonfermented] *murrī* with Sweet *muṣṭār* (Juice of Sweet Grapes)[35]

Take 6 *raṭl*s (6 pounds) barley flour sifted of its bran (*mugharbal*), add a third of its amount salt, and knead them with water into dough. Shape it into discs, which you then bake in the *furn* (brick oven) until they look musk colored (*miskī*).[36]

Take 4 *raṭl*s wheat flour, add a third of its amount of salt, and knead them [with water] into stiff dough. [Shape it into discs,] which you then bake as you did with the first flour.

When the bread discs get cold, break them into medium pieces first and then put them all in a large new pot. Pour juice of sweet grapes, which is called *muṣ-*

---

35 Copied as *mustār* in the Madrid MS, fol. 130r. It is freshly pressed juice of sweet grapes, which is the initial stage for wine making.

36 That is, dark reddish brown. *Miskī* is copied as *washakī* in the Madrid MS, fol. 130r. The latter is an adjective derived from *washak*, more commonly known as *washaq* and *ushshaq*. It is the aromatic resin gum ammoniac extracted from the stem of *Dorema ammoniacum*, a perennial herb. It is similar in color to musk. See glossary 9.2, s.v. *washakī*.

ṭār, on them; add enough to cover the bread by ⅔ span (approx. 6 inches).[37] Also add (200r) 10 leaves of citron, carobs (*kharnūb*), quinces, and apples.[38] Also add pinecone (*jumjumat ṣanawbar*) and sprigs of herb fennel (*ūd basbās*). Leave an empty space—⅔ span—between the grape juice in the pot and its lid so that there may be enough room for boiling without spilling over. Seal the pot tightly with clay, but leave a hole to allow the pot to exhale.[39] Let it cook overnight in the *furn* at a distance from the fire. Take it out in the morning, strain it, and store away the [resulting *murrī*].

Now take the dregs, return them to the pot, and add another amount of the sweet grape juice (*muṣṭār*) to them, as was mentioned above. Keep the pot in the oven overnight, take it out in the morning, and strain the *murrī*. If it turns out to be thin, cook it again at home [on the stove] until it gets thicker. Store it away in a glazed earthenware vessel and top it completely with plenty of sweet olive oil. This will keep it from molding. Whenever you want to add it [to cooking foods], do your best to remove the oil if what it is being used with it are dishes with pure and clear liquids (*nuqakh*) and the like,[40] God Almighty willing.

x.8.8 Another Variety [of *murrī* with *muṣṭār*]

Take 3 *raṭl*s (3 pounds) wheat flour, knead it [with water] into stiff dough, and shape it into discs. Bake them in the *furn* (brick oven) until they turn intensely dark (literally *aswad* 'black'); take them out, pound then coarsely, and put them in a new pot.

For the 3 *raṭl*s of wheat flour used, add 1 *qadaḥ* (approx. 2¼ pints) *muṣṭār* and 1 *raṭl* minus a quarter [i.e., ¾ *raṭl*] salt. Cover the pot with a lid that has a hole in it [and seal it with clay]. Let there also be added with the *muṣṭār* quinces,[41] fennel seeds (*bazr basbās*), nigella seeds (*shūnīz*), a fistful of thyme (*ṣaʿtar*), citron leaves, and a small amount of honey for those who like the *murrī* to be sweeter.

Keep the pot overnight in the *furn* and take it out in the morning. Strain the *murrī* with a piece of woolen cloth and store it away. This would be top-

37 A span is approx. 9 inches long. See glossary 13, s.v. *shibr*.
38 It is my assumption that they are peeled and cut before adding them.
39 Last detail is from the Madrid MS, fol. 130r.
40 Based on Ibn Manẓūr, *Lisān al-ʿArab*, s.v. نقخ, *nuqākh* (pl. *nuqakh*) is clear and pure water.
41 They must have been peeled and cut.

quality *murrī* (*al-ra's*).[42] Taste it; if turns out to be lacking in salt, add some more. If you see that it is rather thin in consistency (*raqīq*), put it in wide shallow, bowls (*ṣiḥāf*, sg. *ṣaḥfa*) and expose them to the sun until you are satisfied with the consistency; or cook it on the fire to reduce it. It is then put in a glazed earthenware vessel and stored.

Take the dregs and return them to the pot, adding more salt and water.[43] Keep the pot overnight in the *furn*, take it out in the morning, and then strain it and use it right away.[44]

x.8.9 Another Variety [of *murrī* with *muṣṭār*]

Take 3 *mudds* (6 pounds) flour—half barley and half wheat—and 1½ *mudds* salt and knead them all [with water] to make stiff dough, which you then shape into discs and bake in the *furn* (brick oven) until they are intensely brown. Pound them until they are as fine as flour.

Put this flour in a large new pot and add 25 *raṭls* (25 pints) sweet *muṣṭār*—[adjust] depending on how much it can take. Add a fistful of thyme, sprigs of herb fennel (*ūd basbās*), and citron leaves. Also add fennel seeds (*zarīʿat basbās*), coarsely crushed coriander seeds, and nigella seeds (*shūnīz*)—of these three seeds, use ¼ *raṭl* (¼ pound)—one-third of each.

Now put the pot on the fire to boil until half of the *muṣṭār* has evaporated and then remove it. Mash and press whatever there is in it of the spices with the flour and then strain it with a tightly woven piece of cloth (*mindīl ṣafīq*). Store away the strained *murrī* in a glazed earthenware vessel;[45] and use it after three months, God Almighty willing.

x.8.10 Making Fast [Nonfermented] Sauce (*murrī muʿajjal*), which May Replace the Sun-Fermented Sauce (*murrī naqīʿ*)

Take 1 *raṭl* (1 pound) flour of wheat or barley and put it in an earthenware pan (*ṭājin fakhkhār*). Put it on the fire and stir the flour in it [constantly] until it

42 Also called *al-awwal* 'the first.'
43 Adding water is addition from the Madrid MS, fol. 130v.
44 The implication here is that this second *murrī* is not good enough for storing.
45 As described in other recipes, the stored *murrī* has to be kept covered with olive oil to protect it from molding.

turns musk colored (*miskī*)[46] and then remove it (200v) from the fire. [Immediately] add 2 *ūqiyyas* (2 ounces) pounded salt to it; add fresh water to them—enough to give the mix a rather thin consistency. Set it aside to cool and then press and mash it vigorously by hand. Strain it and set [the resulting liquid] aside.

Next, take a small amount of honey, put it in a small glazed earthenware pan (*ṭājin muzajjaj*) and let it boil until it turns intensely dark. Strain it into the liquid prepared earlier. Add fennel seeds (*basbās*), nigella seeds (*shūnīz*), aniseeds (*anīsūn*), coarsely crushed coriander seeds (*kuzbara yābisa*), and thyme (*ṣaʿtar*)—all tied in a piece of cloth and added. Use this *murrī* right away, God Almighty willing.

x.8.11 Making Another [Fast] Variety of *murrī* [with Honey][47]

Take 1 *raṭl* (1 pound) honey, a similar amount of chopped onion, and another similar amount of pounded salt. Dissolve them in water, the amount of which should equal twice the amount of all the ingredients [i.e., 6 pints]. Put them in a new pot, keep it overnight in the *furn* (brick oven), and take it out in the morning. Press and mash the ingredients vigorously and then strain the mix and use the [resulting strained *murrī*] right away, God Almighty willing.

If the sauce turns out to be thin (*khafīf*), put it in glazed bowls (*aghḍira*, sg. *ghaḍāra*) and keep them in the sun until you like its consistency. So know this and do accordingly, God Almighty willing.

x.8.12 Another *murrī* Variety, Ready to Use in a Day [Made with Burnt Bread][48]

Knead 2 *raṭls* (2 pounds) wheat flour with ½ *raṭl* salt [and water, form the dough into a disc], and bake it [in the *furn*] until it browns (*taḥmarr*). Also knead 1 *raṭl* barley flour with ½ *raṭl* salt [and water], and bake the bread disc [you make with it] until it burns (*yaḥtariq*). Break them into pieces and soak them in hot

---

46 I.e., dark reddish brown.

47 The text in the Madrid MS, fol. 131r, is shorter than that of the BL MS. In addition, instead of 1 pound per each ingredient, the Madrid MS gives the total of 3 pounds equally divided among the three ingredients. Furthermore, the editor of the Arabic text misread several words in the Madrid MS text, which confused the sense of the recipe.

48 This recipe is found only in the Madrid MS, fol. 131r.

water—enough to submerge them. Set them aside for a day and a night (*yawm wa layla*, i.e., 24 hours) and then strain them [and reserve the resulting liquid].

Take 1 *raṭl* raisins (*zabīb*) and a similar amount of carob (*kharrūb*). Also take nigella seeds (*shūnīz*), fennel seeds (*rāzyānaj*), sesame seeds (*simsim*), and aniseeds (*anīsūn*)—1 *ūqiyya* (1 ounce) of each. Also take a fistful (*qabḍa*) of sprigs of herb fennel (*ʿūd basbās*), a few citron leaves, pine nuts (*lubb ṣanawbar*),[49] and a few scales of pinecones (*ʿūd ṣanawbar*). Cook them all in fresh water, enough to submerge them all, to allow all the spices (*adwiya*) to release their properties (*qiwā*) into the water. Strain the liquid (*māʾ*, literally 'water') and add it to the liquid that was strained first. Put them in a pot and boil them on low heat until it reduces and thickens (*yaltaff*) to your liking.

x.8.13 Making *murrī al-ḥūt* (Fermented Fish Sauce)

Take 1 *raṭl* (1 pound) of *ṣīr* (salt-cured small fish), mentioned in the sixth chapter of the tenth part of this book [recipe x.6.2],[50] and put them in a sieve (*ghirbāl*) fitted on a large earthenware tub (*qaṣriyya*).[51] Use 5 *raṭl*s (5 pints) of sweet *muṣṭār* (juice of sweet grapes) with them; pour it little by little while moving and stirring the fish about.

Continue doing this until all the liquid is extracted and nothing remains in the sieve but the dregs (*thufl*).[52] Remove the sediment from the sieve, add another batch of *ṣīr* with another amount of *muṣṭār* poured on them, [and do as above] until you get the needed amount [of *murrī*]. Make sure that thyme [of the variety] called *shardhūn* was already added to the *ṣīr* [when it was salt cured].[53]

Put the extracted *murrī* in a clean earthenware jar (*jarra*)[54] previously used for storing olive oil. Add chopped pieces of quince to it, as well as onions, which have been slit into sections but not separated. Set the jar aside to give it time

---

49 In the edited text, it inaccurately reads as '*laban ṣanawbar*' (pine milk).

50 In the Madrid MS, fol. 131v, no such citation is given simply because the entire chapter is nonexistent there. Still, the user of the edited Arabic text would have made sense of the recipe were صير *ṣīr* not incorrectly and misleadingly edited as the irrelevant صبر *ṣabr* 'aloe.' See glossary 10, s.v. *ṣīr*.

51 The tub detail is an addition from the Madrid MS, fol. 131v.

52 The extracted liquid will be the *murrī* being made in this recipe.

53 *Shardhūn* is conehead thyme, a Mediterranean wild variety, *Thymus capitatus*. It was indeed added in the above *ṣīr* recipe, x.6.2.

54 The editor of the Arabic text leaves out several details mentioned in the Madrid MS, fol. 131v, which unfortunately obscures the method being used here to ferment the sauce.

to ferment (*yaghlī*).[55] Meanwhile, skim off any impurities you see daily, once in the morning and once in the evening, until the liquid stops fermenting and dregs settle in the bottom of the jar.

If you want to transfer *murrī* into other jars, which were also used to store olive oil, go ahead and do so. Cover their tops with olive oil [to prevent molding] and seal the jars' mouths with clay until it is time to use the sauce in the winter.

The way to serve this sauce is to put some of it in a glazed bowl (*ghaḍāra*) with olive oil; chopped onion may also be added for those who want to have it; and put fried eggs in it, or fried fish, and olives.[56] So know this.

In addition, if you want the fish sauce to look red, let the grape juice (*muṣṭār*) be taken from black grapes (*ʿinab akḥal*); and light-colored sauce [literally 'white'] is made with white grapes, so know this. You can use grape wine (*khamr*) if *muṣṭār* is not available, following the same method above. [It will still be permissible because] fermentation of the sauce will totally destroy the [intoxicating] effect of wine,[57] so know this.

x.8.14 Ways to Remedy Sun-Fermented Liquid Sauce (*murrī naqīʿ*)

If the *murrī* tastes sourish due to a lack of enough exposure to the sun and not enough stirring [while fermenting], take walnuts, shell them, pound the kernels (*ṭaʿm*) finely, and add them to the *murrī*. Stir the vessel [several times a day?] for days, and the *murrī* will no longer be sourish, God willing.

If the *murrī* turns out to be too salty, take wheat flour, [knead it with water] without salt, and make a disc of bread with it. Bake it in the *furn* (brick oven) until it is overbaked (*ṭabkh balīgh*), break it into pieces, pound it until it looks like flour, knead it with honey—add just enough to moisten it—and combine it into one mass. Put [the flour mass] in the *murrī* and leave it there for three days and then strain it. It will no longer be overly salty, with the help of God and His might.

55 The same word, *yaghlī*, is used to designate boiling on the fire and fermentation.
56 Adding fish and olives is an addition from the Madrid MS, fol. 131v.
57 The Arabic expression occurs as ويبطل فعل الخمر بالجملة.

Part Ten, Chapter Nine: On Making Oil (*Zayt*) with Ingredients Other Than Olives When They Are Not Available; and Remedying Olive Oil When It Spoils and Its Flavor or Aroma Deteriorates[1]

x.9.1 (201r) Making Oil (*zayt*) Using Ingredients Other Than Olives[2]

Take equal amounts of *ḥabb al-buṭm* (berries of the terebinth tree), which are called *al-ḥabba al-khaḍrā'*,[3] shelled walnuts, skinned almonds, and sesame seeds (*simsim*). Boil them and then press out the oil,[4] which you can use instead of olive oil after straining it. The remaining sediment can be fed to cows, God Almighty willing.

x.9.2 Ways to Remedy Olive Oil[5]

[1] Take salt and *būraq* (sodium bicarbonate),[6] crush them thoroughly, and add them to a jar of cold-pressed olive oil that has just been extracted;[7] use just the needed amount. This will improve the oil's flavor and aroma.

---

1 Note that this chapter and the following ones, to the end of the book, are also included in the Madrid MS, and in the edited Arabic text that follows it.

2 *Zayt* specifically designates oil from olives; oil extracted from other ingredients is generally referred to as *duhn*. The recipe describes how to make oil from ingredients other than olives, and it can still be used as a substitute for olive oil.

3 Literally 'green berries,' *Pistacia terebinthus*, see glossary 7.

4 There must be a missing instruction here; otherwise, no oil can be obtained by just boiling these ingredients. See the following chapter, x.10, for more details on how to extract similar oils with hot water. Additionally, based on a more or less similar recipe in Qusṭā Ibn Lūqā, *al-Filāḥa al-Rūmiyya* 315, the ingredients are to be crushed or pounded first and then pressed to extract the oil. Instead of cows, Qusṭa's version recommends feeding sheep with the resulting dregs to fatten them.

5 There are similarities between remedies offered here and those in Qusṭā Ibn Lūqā, *al-Filāḥa al-Rūmiyya* 318–9, 320; and, to some extent, the Andalusi al-Ṭighnarī, *Zahrat al-bustān* 208–9, who copied from Qusṭā.

6 See glossary 8.

7 The Arabic expression is *zayt ṭarī ḥīna ʿamalihi* (زيت طري حين عمله). For cold-pressed olive oil, see glossary 6, s.v. *zayt ṭarī*.

 | DOI:10.1163/9789004469488_058

FIGURE 102 *Buṭm*, al-Ghāfiqī, *Kitāb al-Adwiya al-mufrada*, MS 7508, fol. 68r, detail
REPRODUCED BY PERMISSION OF THE OSLER LIBRARY OF THE HISTORY OF MEDICINE, MCGILL UNIVERSITY

[2] You may also take 8 parts juice of sweet grapes (*ʿaṣīr al-ʿinab al-ḥulw*)[8] and add it to 20 parts olive oil; add a small amount of licorice root (*ʿūd al-sūs*) as well.[9] Seal the vessels' tops with clay, leave them for ten days, and when you open them, you will find that the olive oil tastes good. As for the grape juice, you will find that it has separated from the oil and turned into good wine, for those who imbibe it.[10]

[3] You can also take citron roots (*ʿurūq utrujj*), fry them, and add them to olive oil that has clouded (*zayt ʿakir*). They will clarify it and improve its flavor.

8 This was called *muṣṭār* in the previous chapter.

9 *Glycyrrhiza glabra*, the dried roots look like twigs (*ʿūd*). See glossary 8.

10 In the BL MS, wine is called شراب *sharāb*, which though literally means 'drink' was usually used to designate intoxicating drinks. Qusṭā Ibn Lūqā, *al-Filāḥa al-Rūmiyya* 319, calls it *sharāb ṣirf* (undiluted wine). Cf. the Madrid MS, fol. 132r, which calls it what it is, خمر *khamr* (intoxicating drink). In the edited Arabic text, which follows the Madrid MS, the editor misreads خمرا as حمرا (?) and adds a footnote that the text is incomplete, which it is not if read correctly.

[4] Additionally, you can take a burnt brick (*ājura*), put it on the fire until it reddens, and then break it and immediately throw it into the jar of unpleasant-smelling olive oil. It will remove the bad smell, improve its quality, and clarify it.

[5] You may also take one part dry barley bread and a similar amount of parched salt grains, pound them together, and tie them in a piece of linen cloth (*khirqa kattān*), which you then dip in the vessel of olive oil that went bad. This will remedy it.[11]

[6] Moreover, take the outer layers of bark (*liḥā'*) of an olive tree, and take some of its leaves as well. Pound them together very well, adding a small amount of parched salt grains. Tie them all in a piece of linen, which you then hang in the olive oil vessel—let it be immersed in the oil. Leave the jar for three days. When you take out the bundle, you will find that the oil is no longer cloudy, and its taste has improved, with the help of God Almighty.

[7] Also, if cumin and bark of the olive tree were [tied in a bundle as above] and put in the jar of unsavory (*muntin*) olive oil, the odor will go and the oil will taste good,[12] with the help of God Almighty and His power.

11 According to Qusṭā Ibn Lūqā, *al-Filāḥa al-Rūmiyya* 320, this will help remove unpleasant odors of oil.

12 Interestingly, in a short chapter dealing with ways to improve the quality and odor of olive oil in Qusṭā Ibn Lūqā's *al-Filāḥa al-Rūmiyya* 321, this treatment was suggested if a rat (*juradh*) or other creatures happened to fall into the jar and died there and stunk the oil.

Part Ten, Chapter Ten: On Extracting Oils (*Adhān*)[1] When Needed For Some Dishes

Oil of sweet almonds (*duhn al-lawz al-ḥulw*)

Take shelled sweet almonds that have been recently dried (*ṭarī*) and pound them [with their brown skins] in a mortar (*mihrās*) until they are smooth in consistency, like a brain (*damāgh*). Also take fresh water and heat it up in a clean glazed earthenware vessel.

To each *raṭl* (pound) of pounded almonds add 1 *ūqiyya* (1 ounce) very hot water. Press and mash the almonds vigorously until you start to see their oil coming out between your fingers. Put them in a tightly woven piece of cloth (*khirqa ṣafīqa*) and gently press out the oil until it is all extracted.

Pound the dregs again, add a small amount of hot water to them, and set them aside until they absorb the water. Press and mash them again until whatever remained of the oil is extracted. The amount of oil extracted from 1 *raṭl* [of almonds] is about a fourth or a third of the almonds [weight]—depending on the expertise of the person doing it, so know this.

Oils of walnuts, hazelnuts, pistachios, pine nuts, and sesame seeds (**201v**) are all extracted the same way. All these oils must always be freshly extracted when used in dishes. They should not be extracted earlier than that because they spoil fast [and go rancid]. So avoid doing this, may God with His Grace guide us to the right path.

---

1 Sg. *duhn*. It is commonly used to designate oil extracted from nuts and seeds other than olives. Generally, various types of olive oil are used throughout the book, unless otherwise specified.

 | DOI:10.1163/9789004469488_059

FIGURE 103 A sweet almond tree, Dioscorides, *Fī Hayūlā al-ṭibb*, translation by Ḥunayn b. Isḥāq, fol. 66r, detail
FROM THE NEW YORK PUBLIC LIBRARY, SPENCER COLLECTION: HTTPS://DIGITALCOLLECTIONS.NYPL.ORG/ITEMS/5E66B3E8-A9D2-D471-E040-E00A18064D7

Part Ten, Chapter Eleven: On Making Cured Meat (*Qadīd*)[1]

Take any kind of meat you like and cut it into thin long slices—the thinnest and longest you can get them. Take a large kneading bowl (*miʿjana*) and add intensely sour vinegar (*khall ḥādhiq*) and pounded salt—but not much.[2] Add the meat and stir it with them every now and then so that it may absorb enough of vinegar and salt; do this from morning till noon prayer time.

Take the meat out and add *murrī naqīʿ* (sun-fermented liquid sauce) to it, along with coriander seeds, black pepper, cumin, and caraway. Mix and fold meat with the spices until it absorbs enough of their flavors. Have a taste; if you find that some of the spices are lacking, add some more of them, and likewise with the salt.

Keep the meat with the spices for a whole day [i.e., till noon of the following day][3] so it will taste good with all the spices it has absorbed. Hang the pieces [on a rope] at a sunny location until the afternoon (*ʿaṣr*). Take them from the rope, put them in a sieve (*ghirbāl*), and cover them with something light. In the following day, return them to the rope at the sunny location; continue doing this for days until the meat completely dries. Store it in a vessel kept in a dry, ventilated place away from the sun.

Cook with this meat whatever you like of dishes, as you would with fresh meat, God Almighty willing. So know this. The meat may also be made with just salt and water, and then it is left in the sun to dry [as was done above], so know this.

I have also come across a variety of cured meat in *Kitāb Tafsīr al-adwiya* (Book on explaining medicinal drugs) by Ibn Janāḥ, which he called *namaksūd*.[4] It is meat cured with crushed salt. The difference between *namaksūd* and *qadīd* is that *namaksūd* is made with the meat of a ram (*kabsh*), either left

1 Cf. *qadīd* recipe in al-Warrāq, *Kitāb al-Ṭabīkh*, English trans., *Annals* 370, where the sliced cured meat is dried in the oven and formed into interesting spirals. The resulting texture is described as being brittle and crumbly to the bite.

2 According to al-Rāzī, *Manāfiʿ al-aghdhiya* 113, preparing *qadīd* with vinegar, as is being done here, would help improve its overly hot properties and its digestibility.

3 I followed here the text in the Madrid MS, fol. 132v, to amend the BL text, where the timing for hanging the meat to dry is somewhat confused.

4 He is eleventh-century Abū al-Walīd Marwān b. Janāḥ al-Qurṭubī, and the actual title of his

 | DOI:10.1163/9789004469488_060

whole or split in half. Meat [thus prepared] would remain moist and smooth and fatty (*dasim*), your hands would get greasy when you touch it, and when you cut it, the knife would go though it as easily as it does with fresh meat. Furthermore, *namaksūd* is not cut into pieces the way *qadīd* is.[5] You can make it and try it for yourself, and may God with His Grace guide us to the right path.

book is *Kitāb al-Talkhīṣ*. See introduction i.3 for more on this source, and see glossary 5, s.v. *namaksūd*, for more on this food.

5 Cf. the description of *namaksūd* in al-Ḥuṣrī, *Jamʿ al-jawāhir* 239, where it is described as meat cut into blocks and then salted, spread on boards, and left in an airy place until it is dry. Preserved thus it can be used as travelers' provisions by soaking it in water before using it.

Part Ten, Chapter Twelve: On Ways To Remedy Food

X.12.1 Remedying Salty Food

Take flour and knead it into dough [with water] without adding salt. Leave it in the cooking pot with the meat for about an hour and then take it out. It will make the dish less salty, God Almighty willing.

X.12.2 A Way to Remedy Unsavory [Raw] Meat[1]

Take the meat and use it in any dish you want to cook, and when you put the pot on the fire, add an almond or a walnut, unshelled, with a hole pierced through it from top to bottom, and with the kernel (*ṭaʿm*) inside it. Take it out [and discard it] when the meat is cooked and the dish is done. The meat will no longer smell bad,[2] with the help of God and His might.

1 The Arabic word designating an 'unpleasant smell' is *natn*, adj. *muntin*.

2 Using nuts to get rid of the unpleasant odors of meat must have been a trustworthy method; similarly recommended by al-Warrāq, *Kitāb al-Ṭabīkh*, English trans., *Annals* 96; and anonymous *Kanz al-fawāʾid*, English trans., *Treasure Trove* 75.

 | DOI:10.1163/9789004469488_061

PART 11[1]

القسم الحادي عشر في طبخ الجراد والقمرون وأغلال

On Cooking Jarād (*Locusts*), Qumrūn (*Freshwater Shrimps*), *and* Aghlāl (*Edible Land Snails*)

∵

1 The BL MS, fol. 201v, mistakenly copies it as chapter 13. The Madrid MS, fol. 133r copies it correctly.

FIGURE 104 A locust, al-Qazwīnī, *ʿAjāʾib al-makhlūqāt wa ghārāʾib al-mawjūdāt*, fol. 359v, detail
FROM THE NEW YORK PUBLIC LIBRARY, SPENCER COLLECTION: HTTPS://DIGITALCOLLECTIONS.NYPL.ORG/ITEMS/BC77C080-28EC-0138-6020-2F60FE3841DF

XI.1 Cooking Locusts (*jarād*),[1] [Fried]

Take as many as needed of the large locusts, (**202r**) called *al-ʿArabī*,[2] when they arrive to the region.[3] Put them in a pot with hot water, boil them once or

1 Cf. another recipe in al-Warrāq, *Kitāb al-Ṭabīkh*, English trans., *Annals* 208, for locusts pickled in brine. See glossary 10 for more on locusts as food.

2 In the eastern region they were more commonly called *jarād Aʿrābī*, i.e., desert locusts, *Shistocerca gregaria*. In his *al-Ḥayawān* v 565, al-Jāḥiẓ is in favor of the fat *Aʿrābī* locusts; they are delicious eaten cold and hot, either grilled, boiled, or threaded on strings and baked buried in the heated sand as *malla*.

3 In the Madrid MS, fol. 133r الذي يهب في بعض السنين 'which are blown our way some of the years,' i.e., the migratory locusts. Ibn Zuhr, *Kitāb al-Aghdhiya* 29–30, describes them as red, large, and agile. He says the ones in al-Andalus, i.e., the nonmigratory grasshoppers, are not known as a source of food, they might even be harmful.

twice,[4] and take them out. Discard their wings and legs and fry them in a clean skillet with olive oil until they brown and are totally dry. Take them out and put them in a small glazed bowl (*ghaḍāra*).[5] Add *murrī naqīʿ* (sun-fermented liquid sauce) and Ceylon cinnamon (*qirfa*), and serve them, God Almighty willing.

Although what follows [i.e., shrimps] is regarded as bad-quality fish that is abhorrent to eat,[6] I am including them here because most people do not find them so and look forward to their season. They are said to be crustaceous fish (*qishrat ḥūt*).[7]

XI.2 Cooking Freshwater Shrimps (*qumrūn*),[8] [Boiled and Fried]

Take as many as you want, put them in a pot with water, and on low heat, let them boil three times.[9] Remove the pot from the fire and pour off the liquid. [Put the shrimps in a small bowl,] add pounded salt and thyme (*ṣaʿtar*), and serve.

You may also fry them in a clean skillet with olive oil until they brown and dry out. Put them in a small glazed bowl (*ghaḍāra*),[10] add *murrī naqīʿ* (sun-fermented liquid sauce), along with thyme, black pepper, Ceylon cinnamon, and salt, and serve the dish, God Almighty willing. They are more delicious prepared this way.

Qumrūn are mostly found in some big rivers, especially in the Guadalquivir in Seville (*Wādī Ishbīliya*).[11] They are also found in the valley river of Bijāya.[12]

---

4 See glossary 9.2., s.v. *ghalya*, for more on this boiling technique.

5 Note that this would be a small dish, eaten as *naql* (mezza) and *idām*, which is a small dish eaten with bread as an appetizer, as al-Jāḥiẓ explains in *al-Ḥayawān* v 566.

6 Ibn Zuhr, *Kitāb al-Aghdhiya* 33, challenges this negative opinion of the shrimps that stems from the fact that they do not have blood, or very little of it. In their defense, he says, unlike the common fish, they are moderately hot and do not have mucilaginous properties (*luzūja*).

7 This interesting commentary on shrimps is found only in the Madrid MS, fol. 133r. The edited Arabic text, which follows it, neglects to include it.

8 القُمرون is clearly vocalized as such in the BL MS, fol. 202r. Ibn Zuhr, *Kitāb al-Aghdhiya* 33, identifies them as the highly aphrodisiac fish species with many legs, called *rabīthāʾ*. Also known as *rūbyān*, *arbiyān*, and *jarād al-baḥr* (locusts of the sea). In al-Warrāq, *Kitāb al-Ṭabīkh*, English trans., *Annals* 207, a condiment, called *ṣaḥnāt*, is made with them.

9 See n. 4 above.

10 See n. 5 above.

11 The editor of the Arabic text inaccurately read *wādī* 'valley river' as *bilād* 'region.'

12 A Mediterranean port city in Ifrīqiya (now in Algeria). According to al-Ḥimyarī, *al-Rawḍ al-miʿṭār* 81, the river was about two miles long, and it was surrounded with recreational

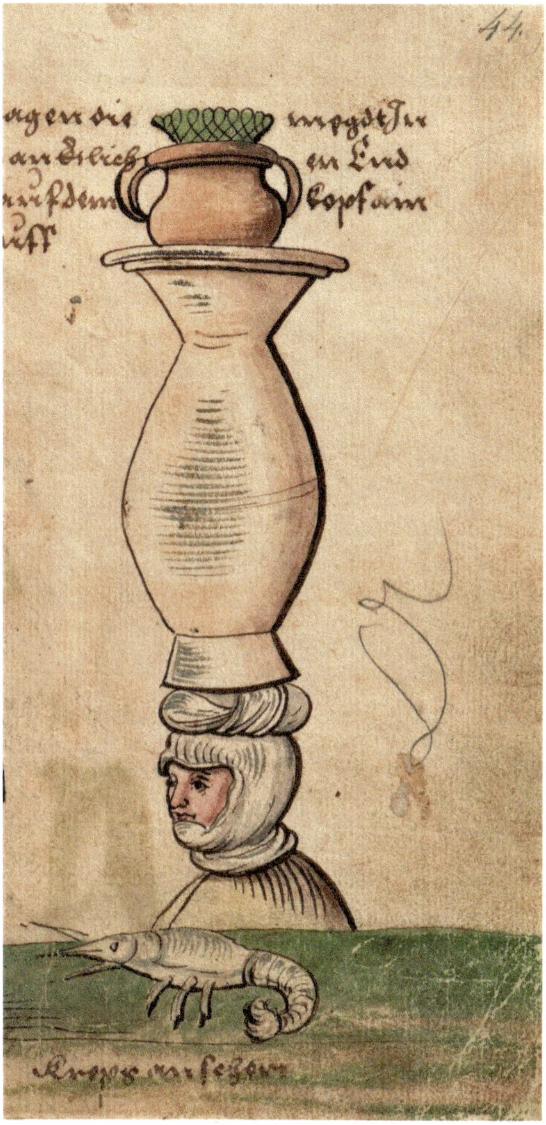

FIGURE 105
A fifteenth-century Morisca peddler carrying on her head what looks like a pot of simmering freshwater shrimps on a small portable stove. A stove would explain the thick piece of cloth put directly on her head to insulate her from the heat, Christoph Weiditz, *Trachtenbuch* 'Costume book,' ca. 1530, p. 44, detail
GERMANISCHES NATIONALMUSEUM, HS. 22474

It is said that they are particularly beneficial in breaking down [urinary tract] stones (*ḥaṣā*).

---

parks and orchards watered by waterwheels. It is interesting that al-Tujībī should mention it; he spent about eight years in this place before he settled in Tunis, see introduction i.2.

Only the Madrid MS, fol. 133r–v, mentions the locations where the *qumrūn* were mostly found.

FIGURE 106
A citron tree branch showing the thorns, used in picking out cooked snails from shells. Dioscorides, *Fī Hayūlā al-ṭibb*, translation by Ḥunayn b. Isḥāq, fol. 63v, detail
FROM THE NEW YORK PUBLIC LIBRARY, SPENCER COLLECTION: HTTPS://DIGITALCOLLECTIONS.NYPL.ORG/ITEMS/5E66B3E8-B21D-D471-E040-E00A180654D7

XI.3 Cooking *aghlāl* (Edible Land Snails),[13] Which Andalusis Call *qawqan*[14]

Take the amount you need of these, wash them in cold water repeatedly to get rid of all their viscidity (*laʿbiyya*), followed by a last wash with salt and water, and then a final rinse with just water. Put them in a large pot with cold water

---

13 Called *escargot* in French. Today in Morocco, such edible snails are still known by the name *ghlāl*, sg. *ghlāla*, and are popular street food.

14 Dozy, *Takmilat al-Maʿājim* viii 413, s.v. قوقن, explains that *qawqan* is a corruption of the Latin word for conch, which at first was used to designate the solid shell but later was used to include the entire creature.

FIGURE 107 A land snail, Dioscorides, *Kitāb al-Ḥashāʾish fī hāyūlā al-ʿilāj al-ṭibbī*, Arabic translation by Ḥunayn b. Isḥāq, Or. 289, fol. 59v, detail
UNIVERSITAIRE BIBLIOTHEKEN LEIDEN, HTTP://HDL.HANDLE.NET/1887.1/ITEM:1578266

and put it on the fire. When they come to a boil, add *ḍawmarān* (river mint)[15] and citron leaves.

Add salt—just the needed amount—when the snails are fully cooked.[16] Empty them into a large vessel and eat them with bread. Use the thorns of the citron tree (*shawk al-utrujj*) or similar objects to pick them out [from the shells], God Almighty willing.

[17][Like shrimps,] snails, too, are an abhorrent food to eat; still, most people eat them. They do not find them repugnant because snails feed on a great deal of greens and herbs growing in springtime.

15 *Mentha acquatica*. Its other names include *ḥabaq al-māʾ* and *fūdhanaj nahrī*. See glossary 8.

16 The following remark on how to serve and eat the snails is given only in the BL MS, fol. 202r.

17 The following observation is given only in the Madrid MS, fol. 133v.

PART 12

القسم الثاني عشر في الغاسولات وهو فصل واحد

On Handwashing Preparations (Ghāsūlāt), *and It Has One Chapter*[1]

∵

1 I was delighted to discover that, except for minor changes (and the addition of "God Almighty willing" at the end of each recipe, characteristic of the BL MS), the entire chapter, excluding the last recipe (xii.8), was taken from Ibn al-Jazzār, *Kitāb fī Funūn al-ṭīb wa-l-ʿiṭr* 117–20. I have used it to amend the text at several places. Abū Jaʿfar Aḥmad b. al-Jazzār al-Qayrawānī (Latinized as Algizar) was a famous tenth-century physician who was born and died in al-Qayrawān (898–980). Ibn al-Jazzār claims the recipes to be of his own making. Note that whereas in the Madrid MS, fols. 133v–134r, the text is complete with the bonus recipe at the end; in the BL MS, the concluding folio is missing. The last folio we have ends with the incomplete sixth recipe (xii.6). The edited Arabic text suffers a great deal from the editor's frequent textual misreadings.

XII.1 Recipe for *ushnān* (Handwashing Compound)[1]

Wash and cleanse your hands with it; it will also perfume them. It is beneficial to the mouth and gums; and removes odors of overly greasy foods (*ghimr*) [from the hands].

Its components (*akhlāṭ*):

Take 100 *dirhams* (10½ ounces) good-quality *bunk*.[2] Also take dried petals of red roses, citronella blossoms (*fuqqāḥ al-idhkhir*), dried marjoram (*marzanjūsh*), cyperus (*suʿdā*),[3] sandalwood (*ṣandal*), dried citron leaves, and dried laurel leaves (*waraq rand*)—take 10 *dirhams* (1 ounce) of each. Also, take fine *sukk* (aromatic pastilles),[4] aloeswood that has not been coated with aromatics (*ʿūd ghayr muṭarrā*),[5] cloves (*qaranful*), nutmeg (*jawz bawwa*), Indian spikenard (*sunbul Hindī*),[6] and aloeswood fruit (*harnuwa*)[7]—take 3 *dirhams* (9 grams) of each.

Pound all the ingredients very well and then knead them with rosewater. Leave the mix aside for a day and a night and then put it on a wide stone slab (*ṣallāya*) and crush it.[8] Continue doing this until the mix dries out and then store it away. Use it to wash the hands; it is aromatic and its benefits are manifold, God Almighty willing.

1 Note that none of the handwashing preparations, called *ushnān* in this chapter, use the ingredient *ushnān* (potash), after which the handwashing compounds came to be called. See glossary 11, s.v. *ushnān* 1 and 2. Al-Tamīmī, *Ṭīb al-ʿarūs* 253, calls such cleansing preparations *ushnān bidūn* (without) *ushnān*.

Ibn al-Jazzār, who is al-Tujībī's source for this chapter, says that he concocted this recipe for the upper classes (*ashrāf*).

2 بنك, as it is lucidly copied in the BL and Madrid MSS, is erroneously read as نبك *nabak* in the edited Arabic text in all the recipes where it occurs. This most probably is due to the editor's unfamiliarity with the ingredient. In Marín, "Words for Cooking" 44, the same error is repeated, which led to mistaking it for *nabk*/*nabq*, the fruit of the *sidr* 'lotus jujube tree,' which it is not. The editor in Ibn al-Jazzār's Arabic edition misread بنك as سك.

Of all the other extant medieval cookbooks, *bunk* recipes are only found in al-Warrāq, *Kitāb al-Ṭabīkh*, English trans., *Annals*, in chapter 129 on handwashing preparations. See the first appendix for a possible identification of this ingredient.

3 Copied as *suʿd* in Ibn al-Jazzār's version (mentioned in n. 1 on this part's title page above). See glossary 8, s.v. *suʿdā*.

4 See glossary 8 for more on this aromatic compound.

5 Aloeswood chips smeared with ambergris, musk, and camphor were usually used as incense (*bakhūr*). Aloeswood that had not been treated this way was described as *nayʾ* or *khām* 'raw.'

6 Also called *sunbul al-ṭīb*, and *sunbul ʿaṣāfīrī*, see glossary 8, s.v. *sunbul*.

7 Also called *fulayfula*, they look like black peppercorns but smaller, see glossary 8.

8 A rounded stone, called a *fihr*, was usually used for this task.

FIGURE 108 A tenth-century ivory pyxis from the time of Umayyad Caliph ʿAbd al-Raḥmān III, used for keeping handwashing preparations, *ushnān*
MET NY—THE CLOISTERS COLLECTION, 1970

XII.2 Another Recipe for *ushnān*,[9] Superior to the Previous One

Take 20 *mithqāls* (3 ounces) *bunk*;[10] also take dried melon peels (*qushūr al-biṭṭīkh*),[11] dried peels of apples and citrons, dried marjoram (*marzanjūsh*), and

9 See n. 1 above.

10 See n. 2 above. The editor of Ibn al-Jazzār's Arabic edition misread بنك 'bunk' here as مسك 'musk.'

11 *Biṭṭīkh* was used to designate watermelon and muskmelon. The recipe does not specify

dry storax resin (*mayʿa yābisa*)[12]—10 *mithqāl*s of each—cyperus (*suʿdā*), sandalwood (*ṣandal*), sweet costus (*qusṭ ḥulw*), and shelled *maḥlab*[13]—4 *mithqāl*s (18 grams) of each—mace (*basbāsa*), black cardamom (*qāqulla*), cubeb (*kabāba*), cloves (*qaranful*), and aloeswood (*ʿūd*) (202v)—2 *mithqāl*s of each—and 1 *mithqāl* (4½ grams) camphor (*kāfūr*).

Pound all the ingredients [but not the camphor], sift them, knead them with high-quality red wine (*sharāb aḥmar*), and shape them into a disc (*qurṣ*). Let it dry in a shaded place and then crush it on a wide stone slab (*ṣallāya*) with a *fihr* (rounded stone), adding 2 *mithqāl*s high-quality *sukk* (aromatic pastilles).[14] Once you are done with this, infuse the mix with camphor;[15] you may also add a bit of musk (*misk*). It is splendid for the mouth and gums, and tastes good as well, God Almighty willing.

XII.3 Recipe for *ushnān*, Which Kings Use

Take 30 *dirhams* (3 ounces) *bunk*;[16] also take fine aloeswood (*ūd*), yellow sandalwood (*ṣandal aṣfar*), aloeswood fruit (*harnuwa*),[17] cloves (*qaranful*), and nutmeg (*jawz bawwa*)—3 *mithqāl*s (13½ grams) of each. Pound them all and sift them.

Now take 5 *mithqāl*s (22½ grams) *sukk*,[18] 3 *mithqāl*s *lakhlakha*,[19] and ½ *dirham* (1½ grams) musk (*misk*). Crush the musk with the *sukk* and then add rosewater to them. Add them, with the *lakhlakha*, to the rest of the ingredients [mentioned above]. Knead them all together and set them aside overnight. In the following morning, put the mix on a wide stone slab (*ṣallāya*), crush it very well,[20] and then store the mix away and use it [as needed], God Almighty willing.

---

which one is being used here. Judging from an *ushnān* preparation in al-Tamīmī, *Ṭīb al-ʿarūs*, recipe 266, it is more likely to be muskmelon.

12 See glossary 8 for more on this ingredient.

13 The aromatic kernels of pits of a variety of small black cherries, *Prunus mahaleb*.

14 See glossary 8 for more on the aromatic compound.

15 The expression used to convey infusing is *yuftaq bi-kāfūr*. See glossary 9.2, s.v. *yuftaq*.

16 See n. 2 above.

17 See n. 7 above.

18 See glossary 8 for more on the aromatic compound.

19 It is an aromatic compound principally used as potpourri, but also to perfume the body. It also had some medicinal benefits. We learn this from Ibn al-Jazzār's chapter on such preparations in *Kitāb fī Funūn al-ṭīb* 94–107. It is kept stored in powder form or a moist thick blend to be diluted and used as needed. See glossary 11.

20 See n. 8 above.

XII.4 Recipe for a Compound (*akhlāṭ*) That May Be Used instead of *ushnān*

It freshens and sweetens the breath (*tuṭayyib al-nakha*) and does no harm if swallowed [by accident], it removes unpleasant greasy odors, and it is beneficial to teeth. It is what kings use to wash their hands after meals.

Its components (*akhlāṭ*):

Take Ceylon cinnamon (*qirfa*) and camphor (*kāfūr*)—3 *dirhams* (9 grams) of each; 2 *dirhams* cloves (*qaranful*), frankincense (*kundur*),[21] dry storax resin (*mayʿa yābisa*),[22] and citronella roots (*uṣūl al-idhkhir*)—5 *dirhams* of each; white sandalwood (*ṣandal abyaḍ*)[23] and cyperus (*suʿdā*)—10 *dirhams* of each; and 30 *dirhams jawz ḥamām* (a variety of usnea).[24]

Pound all the ingredients, sift them, and use them. You may also mix in 15 *dirhams* Armenian clay (*ṭīn Armanī*) that has been parched (*maqlū*) and slightly crushed. This is a well-known tried and true recipe, God Almighty willing.

XII.5 Recipe for Sweet-Smelling *ushnān*, Remarkably Beneficial

It is used to wash the hands safely, clearing melasma (*kalaf*) and freckles (*namash*) and moisturizing them [i.e., the hands].

Its components (*akhlāṭ*):

Take barley flour, lentil flour, and fava bean flour—30 *mithqāls* (4¾ ounces) of each. Also take dried myrtle leaves (*waraq ās*), dried petals of red roses, *bunk*,[25] and dried marjoram (*marzanjūsh*)—10 *mithqāls* (approx. 1½ ounces)

---

21 Also known as *lubān*, see glossary 8.

22 I replaced *mayʿa sāyila*, which is the moist storax resin with a honey-like consistency, mentioned in the BL MS, fol. 202v, with *mayʿa yābisa* (dry storax resin) as it occurs in the Madrid MS, fol. 134r, and Ibn al-Jazzār, *Kitāb fī Funūn al-ṭīb* 119. See glossary 8 for more on this ingredient.

23 It is a sweet-smelling variety of sandalwood, see glossary 8, s.v. *ṣandal*.

24 As it occurs in the BL MS. It is a lightweight variety of usnea mingled with clay. The name is copied as *khurʾ ḥamām*, literally 'pigeons' droppings,' in the Madrid MS, fol. 134r. Otherwise, it occurs as *jawz bawwa* 'nutmeg' in Ibn al-Jazzār, *Kitāb fī Funūn al-ṭīb* 119, which is the source for these recipes.

In the medieval books on botany, the name as it occurs in al-Tujībī's MSS, *khurʾ ḥamām* and *jawz ḥamām*, is alternatively called *jawz jundum*, a Persian loan word. As we gather from Ibn Sīnā, *al-Qānūn* i 525, it is a variety of *ushna* 'usnea.' See glossary 8, s.v. *khurʾ ḥamām*, for more on this ingredient.

25 See n. 2 above. I replaced سك *sukk* in the BL MS, fol. 202v, with بنك *bunk*, as it occurs in

of each. Also take sweet costus (*qusṭ ḥulw*) and grated sandalwood (*ṣandal*)—5 *mithqāls* (22½ grams) of each; and *sukk*,[26] cloves (*qaranful*), and black cardamom (*qāqulla*)—2 *mithqāls* (9 grams) of each.

Pound the ingredients (*adwiya*), sift them, and knead them with the white part of the melon rind (*shaḥm al-biṭṭīkh*).[27] Shape the mix into discs and let them dry in a shaded place. Pound them thoroughly and infuse them with a bit of camphor if available (*in amkana*).[28] If this is not possible, then infuse the mix with the aromatic smoke of incense (*yubakhkhar*) before drying them, using *nidd* or *muthallatha*.[29]

Use it for washing the hands; it is wonderful.

XII.6 *Ushnān* Recipe

It perfumes the hands,[30] sweetens the breath, and firms up the gums (*yashudd al-laththa*). It is what kings use for washing their hands.

Take dried apple peels, dried citron peels, and dried marjoram (*marzanjūsh*)—20 *mithqāls* (approx. 3 ounces) of each.[31] (**Madrid MS 134v**) Also take cyperus (*suʿdā*), *bunk*,[32] citronella blossoms (*fuqqāḥ al-idhkhir*), and [dried] petals of red roses—10 *mithqāls* (approx. 1½ ounces) of each. Also take mace (*basbāsa*), black cardamom (*qāqulla*), cubeb (*kabāba*), aloeswood fruit (*harnuwa*),[33] cloves (*qaranful*), *salīkha* (bark similar to cassia), fagara (*fāghira*),[34]

---

the Madrid MS, fol. 134r, and Ibn al-Jazzār, *Kitāb fī Funūn al-ṭīb* 119. *Sukk* will be mentioned later in the recipe.

26 See glossary 8 for more on the aromatic compound.

27 *Shaḥm*, literally 'suet.' The reference here must be to watermelon rind.

28 The expression used to convey infusing is *yuftaq bi-kāfūr*. See glossary 9.2, s.v. *yuftaq*.

29 *Nidd* designates an incense compound containing ambergris, aloeswood, and musk. *Muthallatha* is the best variety of this incense compound, as it is composed of equal parts of these three ingredients. See glossary 11.

30 The editor of the Arabic text erroneously read *al-yadayn* (اليدين) 'the two hands,' as it correctly occurs in both MSS, as *al-badan* (البدن) 'the body.' *Ushnān* is certainly not used with parts other than the hands and mouth.

31 These are the last words in fol. 202v of the BL MS, which is an indication of a missing folio to conclude al-Tujībī's cookbook. To finish this recipe and the following one, I based the rest of the text on the last page in the Madrid MS, fol. 134v; and Ibn al-Jazzār's chapter in *Kitāb fī Funūn al-ṭīb* 120.

32 See n. 2 above.

33 See n. 7 above.

34 *Zanthoxylum fagara*, also known as the toothache tree, and lime prickly ash; and *kabāba Ṣīnī* 'Chinese cubeb.' See glossary 8. Instead of *salīkha* and *fāghira*, Ibn al-Jazzār's recipe, *Kitāb fī Funūn al-ṭīb* 120, uses *falanja*, which is a small variety of Chinese cubeb.

cassia (*dār Ṣīnī*), and grated sandalwood (*ṣandal*)—2 *mithqāls* (9 grams) of each; and aloeswood (*ʿūd*) and camphor (*kāfūr*)—1 *mithqāl* of each.

After pounding and sifting all the ingredients, they can be used to wash the hands. It is what kings and high-rank people wash their hands with after eating.

XII.7 *Ghāsūl* (Washing Preparation), Which Cleanses the Hands and Removes Greasy Odors

Take 4 *mithqāls* (18 grams) cloves (*qaranful*), 1 *ūqiyya* (1 ounce) sodium carbonate (*naṭrūn*), and 3 *ūqiyyas* fava bean flour (*daqīq fūl*). Crush them all very well and wash the hands with them. It tastes good, and it is quite beneficial.[35]

XII.8 Another [*ghāsūl*][36]

Crush chickpeas and then sift them and use [the resulting powder] to wash the hands after eating; it will do the job. This is the *ushnān* that people would usually use.

35 Here ends Ibn al-Jazzār's text on which this chapter drew.

36 A very simple recipe added by al-Tujībī himself.

[Final Bonus Recipe][1]

Making *muṣannab* (juice of sweet grapes preserved with mustard seeds)[2]
{Take 1 *raṭl* (1 pound) fine-tasting mustard seeds for each 20 *rub*ʿs (83 liters) of sweet grape juice.[3]} Crush 1 *raṭl* of fine-tasting mustard seeds and then sift them and knead them with fine-tasting honey {using enough to combine the seeds into paste}.

Rinse a new [earthenware] vessel with water (*yuqṣar*) several times for two to three days, after which pour off the water and let the vessel dry out for a day and a night. Next, smear its bottom and inner sides with [a moderate layer of] the mustard kneaded with honey; and set it aside to dry out, also for a day and a night, to give it time to draw in the mustard's moisture and its flavor [into its pores].

---

1 This last recipe in the Madrid MS, fol. 134v, is not related in subject to part xii, which deals exclusively with handwashing preparations. In the Madrid MS it is written by the same hand, and there is no way to tell whether it was in the original manuscript or added in subsequent copies. It is more like a bonus recipe tossed in for the readers' general benefit. Cf., for instance, the last recipe in the Gotha MS of *Kanz al-fawāʾid*, English trans., *Treasure Trove* 248–9, which deals with making ghee directly from milk and concludes a chapter on desserts.

2 The editor of the Arabic edition misreads the text at many places, beginning with the title, which he reads as صنعة من صناب 'A recipe for mustard sauce,' whereas in the Madrid MS it clearly occurs as صنعة مصنب 'making *muṣannab*.' The difficulties the editor faced in deciphering the recipe led him to the unjustifiable conclusion that the text is "extremely confused."

But some details are indeed missing. Luckily, I came across a similar recipe in eleventh-century agronomist Ibn Baṣṣāl, *Kitāb al-Filāḥa* 181. The same recipe is also found in twelfth-century Ibn al-ʿAwwām, *al-Filāḥa al-Andalusiyya*, Madrid 1802 edition, ii 418–9, where he cites his source as Ibn Baṣṣāl's *Kitāb al-Qaṣd wa-l-bayān* (*Kitāb al-Filāḥa* mentioned above). Some stylistic variations and slight differences in details do exist between the two. Al-Tujībī, or whoever added this recipe, could have used either one for his source.

Whereas in Ibn Baṣṣāl's book the recipe occurs at the very end of the book, as it is in al-Tujībī's, in Ibn al-ʿAwwām's, it is included in a chapter dealing with ways to preserve sweet grape juice so as to prevent it from fermenting and turning into wine. This recipe in particular comes highly recommended by Ibn al-ʿAwwām because it preserves grape juice for a long time without developing alcohol, and, in the process, intensifies its sweetness. He says that it is a proven Sicilian method (وهكذا يعمل في صقلية وهي نسخة صحيحة), which Ibn Baṣṣāl is in favor of, and quotes him saying that he has never seen anything like it (لم أر مثلها في هذا النوع). This might indeed have justified its bonus status as an impressive finale in al-Tujībī's book.

Note that text in the recipe enclosed between curly brackets is from Ibn al-ʿAwwām's and Ibn Baṣṣāl's books. They fill in the missing parts in the recipe.

3 Each *rub*ʿ equals 8¾ pounds/pints.

FIGURE 109
Andalusi jar, by Diego Sánchez Sarabia, 1762
COLLECTION OF ROYAL ACADEMY OF FINE ARTS OF SAN FERNANDO

Pour 20 *rubʿ*s of strained sweet grape juice[4] {gently} into the vessel. If the juice used is meant to fill the vessel, then the mustard paste should coat the entire interior of the vessel up to its mouth. Otherwise, the mustard paste should be flush with the level of the juice.

This juice will make a delicious, sweet drink. Its flavor will never degenerate,[5] neither will it taste of mustard. It is a tried-and-true recipe (*shayʾ mujarrab*).

The book is finished.
May God bless our Master Muhammad,
and his family and companions.

4 This juice was earlier called *muṣṭār*, see recipe x.8.7 above.

5 The word used here is *faḍāʿa* 'appalling quality,' which by implication suggests that the grape juice will not generate any alcohol, and hence it will not intoxicate.

Glossary

The information in the following sections is mainly based on medieval Arabic sources, especially those on botany, dietetics, agronomy, and horticulture, mostly hailing from the western region of the Arabo-Muslim world.

Contents

1. Beverages

Al-Tujībī's *Fiḍālat al-khiwān* does not include a chapter on beverages. The only beverage recipe in the book is for *muṣannab*, which is on preserving grape juice with mustard seeds to keep it sweet and unfermented.

ʿaṣīr ʿinab ḥulw (عصير عنب حلو) sweet grape juice, also called *musṭār*, entry below.
khamr (خمر) wine, see *sharāb* 2 below.
māʾ (ماء) water. Drinking water is mentioned only once, at the end of chapter v.1, where the eaters are cautioned against drinking too much of it after eating fish.
muṣannab (مصنّب) sweet grape juice preserved with mustard seeds, see the last recipe in the book; see also *musṭār* below.
musṭār (مسطار), ***muṣṭār*** (مصطار) also called *ʿaṣīr ʿinab ḥulw*. It is the fresh juice of sweet grapes, obtained by pressing the grapes and then straining them to get rid of the skins, stems, and seeds.

In the medieval Arabic lexicons, *musṭār* is said to be name of wine that has recently been pressed (i.e., not fermented yet); it is also used to designate soured wine. The name was said to be a Levantine word of Byzantine origin.[1] In al-Tujībī's cookbook, however, *musṭār* clearly designates fresh juice of sweet grapes. It is used in recipes x.8.7–9 and 13 to make *murrī* sauce; and in recipe x.9.2 to remedy olive oil, and in the process, it turns into fermented wine. The last recipe in the book deals with *muṣannab*, which is preserved *musṭār* that stays sweet and unfermented by using mustard seeds.

sharāb 1 (شراب), pl. *ashriba* (أشربة) generally designates beverages, such as wine (see *sharāb* 2 below) and nonalcoholic drinks.

qiwām al-sharāb (قوام الشراب) is a term that describes the consistency of syrups used for making sweet drinks after diluting them with water. The standard proportions of sugar and fruit juice were 10 *raṭl*s (10 pounds) sugar and 3⅓ *raṭl*s fruit juice.[2] Sugar is first mixed with water and boiled, and then fruit juice is added and the boiling resumes until it becomes syrup of medium consistency. In this state, syrups were stored and used as needed.

These sweetened drinks were consumed for their refreshing properties; and more importantly, they were also offered at the end of meals as an aid to digestion. With

1 See Ibn Manẓūr, *Lisān al-ʿArab*, s.v. سطر.
2 As specified in Ibn al-Ukhuwwa, *Maʿālim al-qurba* 115.

DOI:10.1163/9789004469488_066

FIGURE 110
A pitcher, ca. fifteenth-century Spain
MET NY—THE CLOISTERS COLLECTION, 1956, ACCESSION NUMBER: 56.171.146

the addition of spices and herbs, they were also recommended by physicians as tonic drinks with curative properties. The following are the syrups mentioned in al-Tujībī's cookbook:

sharāb ʿasal mufawwah (شراب عسل مفوّه) spiced honeyed syrup. It is one of the recommended drinks that may replace wine after having fish (see end of chapter v.1). A recipe for such a drink is given in the pamphlet dealing with medicinal drinks, stomachics, and electuaries that is appended to the Andalusi cookbook *Anwāʿ al-ṣaydala*.[3] The pamphlet calls it *sharāb al-ʿasal*. It is composed of 15 *raṭls* (15 pints) water and 5 *raṭls* (5 pounds) honey boiled down to a syrup

3 See Huici Miranda (ed.), *Kitāb al-Ṭabīkh* 235–56; for the syrup, see p. 238.

FIGURE 111 A physician ladling from a *sharāb* cauldron, folio from an Arabic translation of the *Materia Medica* of Dioscorides, 1224, detail
CLEVELAND MUSEUM OF ART: HTTPS://CLEVELANDART.ORG/ART/1977.91

of medium consistency. More than 20 spices, such as Ceylon cinnamon, ginger, mastic, nutmeg, cassia, Chinese *rāwand* 'dried rhubarb,' spikenard, and green and black cardamom, are crushed, tied in a piece of cloth, and thrown into the boiling syrup. The syrup is used diluted in water and valued for its hot properties. It is said to be good for a weak liver and stomach and has the power to break up bodily phlegm and soften the bowels.

sharāb al-jullāb (شراب الجلاّب) syrup made with rosewater and sugar but also with honey at times, as in *sharāb al-jullāb al-ʿasalī* below. There are many ways to make the syrup: Ibn Sīnā, *al-Qānūn* iii 465, provides a recipe in which 2 pounds of sugar are first gently boiled with ½ cup water, and then, just before the pot is removed from the fire, ¼ cup rosewater is added. He also gives an alternative recipe, according to which 1 *kayl* (a volume measure) of sugar is used with 3 *kayl*s pure rosewater; both are boiled gently until one-third remains. Al-Anṭākī, *Tadhkira* 118, recommends boiling sugar with an equal amount or more, by weight, of rosewater.

The resulting syrup was usually consumed diluted with water, sometimes chilled with ice, and served as a refreshing drink, and more significantly, as a curative beverage believed to benefit the stomach, chest, and lungs. In addition, it was believed to be very effective in softening the bowels.[4] With its moderate properties leaning more towards coldness, it was valued for its cooling effects that quench thirst, alleviate fevers, and cure hangover symptoms.[5]

In al-Tujībī's cookbook, this syrup is further boiled to a thicker consistency and used to douse pastries instead of honey, see recipes i.4.11, and 16.

sharāb al-jullāb al-ʿasalī (شراب الجلاب العسلي) rosewater-honey syrup, made by gently boiling honey with rosewater down to a medium syrup consistency. In al-Tujībī's cookbook, this syrup is further boiled to a thicker consistency and used to douse pastries in recipes i.4.11 and 16; and recipe ix.3.1.

sharāb maṣṭakā (شراب مصطكى) syrup infused with mastic. A recipe for such a drink is given in the pamphlet dealing with medicinal drinks, stomachics, and electuaries that is appended to the Andalusi cookbook *Anwāʿ al-ṣaydala*.[6] Three *ūqiyya*s (approx. 3½ ounces) of mastic, crushed and tied in a bundle, are cooked with 3 *raṭl*s (3 pounds) of sugar or honey and the strained liquid of a *raṭl* of fresh mint that has been boiled in enough water to cover it. Used diluted in water, it was highly recommended as a digestive. In al-Tujībī's cookbook, a similar syrup, most probably cooked with plain water, is further boiled to a thicker consistency and used to douse pastries in recipes i.4.16 and ix.3.3.

sharāb rubb al-ʿinab (شراب ربّ العنب) grape syrup or molasses, also called *ʿaqīd* and *rubb*, consumed as a drink by diluting it with water. It is recommended after having fish, as mentioned in the last paragraph of chapter v.1. See glossary 4, s.v. *rubb ʿinab*, for more on this sweetener.

sharāb ward (شراب ورد) syrup infused with rose petals. In the pamphlet appended to the Andalusi cookbook *Anwāʿ al-ṣaydala* dealing with medicinal drinks, stomachics, and electuaries,[7] two recipes are given: one with fresh

---

4 See ibid., 239.
5 Al-Malik al-Muẓaffar, *al-Muʿtamad* 102–3.
6 See Huici Miranda (ed.), *Kitāb al-Ṭabīkh* 239.
7 See ibid., 241.

FIGURE 112
Stacked wine jars, al-Ḥarīrī, *al-Maqāmāt*, fol. 33r, copied and illustrated by al-Wāsiṭī, detail
BNF, DEPARTMENT OF MANUSCRIPTS, ARAB 5847. SOURCE: GALLICA.BNF.FR/BNF

rose petals and the other with dried petals. One *raṭl* (1 pound) of fresh rose petals are first steeped in boiling water and set aside for a day. The petals are then rubbed with the water they were steeped in, and strained. One *raṭl* of sugar is added to the strained liquid and boiled to syrup of medium consistency. When used dried, 1 *raṭl* of the petals are steeped in 3 *raṭl*s boiled water and then mashed and drained. The resulting liquid is boiled down to a syrup with 2 *raṭls* white sugar.

A drink made with this syrup was said to excite the appetite, fortify the internal organs, and gently soften the bowls. In al-Tujībī's cookbook, this syrup is further boiled to a thicker consistency and used to douse pastries in recipes i.4.16, and ix.3.3.

sharāb ward sukkarī (شراب ورد سكري) sugar syrup infused with rose petals, see above entry. In al-Tujībī's cookbook this syrup is used in a sweet and sour chicken stew, recipe iii.2.30, and served at the table along with a *jūdhāba* dish, recipe iii.2.31.

sharāb* 2** (شراب), also called ***khamr (خمر) wine. It is produced as a by-product in recipe x.9.2 for remedying olive oil and is said to be a good-quality wine for those who imbibe it. In recipe x.8.13, it is used in a preparation for *murrī al-ḥūt* 'fermented fish sauce.'

sharāb aḥmar (شراب أحمر) red wine, used in recipe xii.2 for making a handwashing preparation.

sharāb ṣirf (شراب صرف) undiluted wine, recommended after having fish; see final paragraph in chapter v.1.

2. Bread, Grains, Pasta, Noodles, and Sweet and Savory Pastries

ādhān maḥshuwwa (آذان محشوة) pastries shaped like ears and stuffed with nuts, see recipe i.4.7.
ʿajīn (عجين) dough.

ʿajīn raṭb (عجين رطب) wet and soft dough.
ʿajīn yakūn lil-khiffa (عجين يكون للخفة) dough that is rather soft in consistency.
ʿajīn yamīl ilā al-shidda (عجين يميل الى الشدة) dough that is rather stiff in consistency.
yumadd (يمد) v. said of dough to be flattened with a rolling pin.
yuqarraṣ (يقرص) v. said of dough to be portioned before baking.

aqrāṣ (اقراص), sg. ***qurṣ*** (قرص) discs of bread or pastry.
aqrāṣ maḥshuwwa (اقراص محشوة) stuffed discs of pastry, see recipe i.4.10.
aqrāṣ ruqāq (اقراص رقاق) thin discs of bread and pastry.
aruzz (ارز) rice. Al-Ghassānī, *Ḥadīqat al-azhār* 33, mentions that it was pronounced *rawz* (روْز) in Fez and *rūz* (روز) in Amazigh. We learn from al-Tujībī that growing rice was mostly restricted to the eastern and southeastern coasts of Spain, which indeed explains the limited number of rice dishes in his cookbook, see *jashīsh al-aruzz* below. This information is verified in *Kitāb al-Aghdhiya* 196 by the Andalusi al-Rundī,[1] who mentions that rice was used in Bilād al-Andalus, particularly in its eastern region, where it was an important grain that was grown abundantly there and consumed frequently. The rest of al-Andalus, he writes, imported it from them. They used it in cooking a variety of dishes, except for making bread, due to its high price there; to them, wheat grain was superior to it, adding that they were not used to eating rice bread anyway. Rice was more valued by their physicians, who recommended it to cure some ailments.

aruzz abyaḍ (ارز ابيض) white rice, mentioned once in al-Tujībī's cookbook, recipe i.5.9, for making a delicate rice pudding with milk.
jashīsh al-aruzz (جشيش الارز) broken grains of rice that result from pounding the grains to separate them from the husk. The broken rice pieces are taken out of the husked rice, sifted in a tight sieve to separate them from the rice flour,

1 Based on his name, he must have been based in the city of Runda (Ronda) in southern Spain.

 | DOI:10.1163/9789004469488_067

FIGURE 113 A table with folded discs of bread arranged all around it, al-Ḥarīrī, *al-Maqāmāt*, fol. 120r, detail
BNF, DEPARTMENT OF MANUSCRIPTS, ARAB 3929. SOURCE: GALLICA.BNF.FR/BNF

and stored and used as needed, as in recipe i.3.11. We learn from al-Tujībī that this dish was rarely cooked outside Mursiya (Murcia) and Balansiya (Valencia) in southeast Spain. Both cities are still famous today for their paella rice dishes.

In terms of its properties, rice was said to be closer to moderation, leaning more towards heat and dryness. It is slightly constipating and bloating. Red rice (*ruzz aḥmar*) (i.e., unhusked brown rice) was believed to have more power to control bowel movements (*yaʿqil al-baṭn*).[2] To remedy rice, the recommended way was to eat it cooked with fat, milk, and sugar. Eaten thus, it was said to provide a good deal of nourishment and increase semen production.[3] Due to its bloating and blocking effects in the system, the recommendation was to eat it with purging foods, such as salty condiments, and meat cooked with the fermented sauce called *murrī*, chard that has been seasoned with *murrī*, or capers and vinegar.[4]

---

2 See Ibn Wāfid, *al-Adwiya al-mufrada* 43; al-Ṭighnarī, *Zahrat al-bustān* 438–40.
3 Al-Arbūlī, *al-Kalām ʿalā al-aghdhiya* 120.
4 See al-Rundī, *Kitāb al-Aghdhiya* 188.

FIGURE 114 Rice, *aruzz*, Dioscorides, *Ajzāʾ min risāla fī l-nabātāt*, fol. 24r, detail
BNF, DEPARTMENT OF MANUSCRIPTS, ARAB 4947. SOURCE: GALLICA.BNF.FR/BNF

banīj (بنيج), ***banij*** (بنج) proso millet, *Panicum miliaceum*.[5] Al-Ishbīlī calls it *jāwars* (جاورس) and considers it a wild variety of *dukhn* (دخن) millet, the grains of which are small and whitish. He gives its indigenous Andalusi (ʿAjamiyya) name as *banijja* (بنّجة) and *banjāyin* (بنجاين), and *āmzaqūr* (آمزقور) as its Amazigh name.[6] In the margin of the Berlin MS next to the relevant text, fol. 3r, millet grain is described as *māzza* (مازّة) 'low in gluten.' It undoubtedly was supposed to designate the grains, which were known for being low in gluten and hence hard to knead, see al-Zabīdī, *Tāj al-ʿarūs*, s.v. مزز.

daqīq al-banīj (دقيق البنيج) flour of proso millet.

ḥasū daqīq al-banīj (حسو دقيق البنيج) soup made with flour of proso millet, recipe i.3.8.

khubz al-banīj (خبز البنيج) bread made with proso millet, recipe i.1.5. The grain was known for being low in gluten. As such, its dough was not easy to knead, and bread made with it needed to be baked immediately after it was shaped. This bread seems to have been a favorite among Andalusis, as the recipe clearly states. In addition, physicians in the Muslim West gave it their seal of approval, such as Ibn Zuhr, *Kitāb al-Aghdhiya* 12, where he mentions that it was deemed most delicious after those made with wheat and barley, adding that it agrees with the digestive system (*taʾlafuhu al-ṭabīʿa*).

---

5 As identified in Corriente, *Dictionary of Andalusi Arabic*, s.v. *p-n-ĉ-(y-n)*.

6 Al-Ishbīlī, *ʿUmdat al-ṭabīb* i 128, s.v. *jāwars*; and i 241, s.v. *dhura*.

bāzīn (بازين), see *muʿallaka* below.

būdhaq (بوذق) bread rotted and used as a base, *khamīra*, for making the fermented sauce called *murrī naqīʿ*. See glossary 8, s.v. *murrī*.

daqīq (دقيق) flour or anything pounded finely. When *daqīq* by itself occurs in recipes, it is meant to generally designate finely milled wheat flour.

daqīq al-banīj (دقيق البنيج) flour of proso millet, see *banīj* above.

daqīq al-darmak (دقيق الدرمك) fine bran-free white flour, see *darmak* below.

daqīq al-ḥuwwārā (دقيق الحوارى) fine bran-free white flour, see *ḥuwwārā* below.

daqīq al-shaʿīr (دقيق الشعير) barley flour.

darmak (درمك) fine bran-free white flour, as it was explicitly described by the fourteenth-century Andalusi scholar al-Arbūlī, *al-Kalām ʿalā l-aghdhiya* 124. The name is descriptive of its consistency: etymologically, *darmak* designates anything that is pounded finely, even fine dust is called *darmak*. It was the name generally used in the Muslim West; its eastern Mashriqi counterpart was *ḥuwwārā*, see the entry below. It was the type of flour used in making fine breads and pastries. See also *qamḥ* below.

ghubār daqīq al-darmak (غبار دقيق الدرمك) powdery flour, fine as dust in texture, see *ghubār al-ḥuwwārā*, s.v. *ḥuwwārā* below. It is used in recipes like ii.6.7 for meat patties of *aḥrash* and for coating fish pieces before frying them, as in recipe v.1.4.

fatāt khubz (فتات خبز), ***futātat khubz*** (فتاتة خبز) breadcrumbs.

fatāt maḥkūk bi-l-yad (فتات محكوك باليد) breadcrumbs that have been crumbled by rubbing them between the hands.

fidāwush (فداوش) small pieces of pasta shaped like grains; made with *samīd* 'semolina flour' in recipe i.5.6. A comparable type of pasta in the anonymous fourteenth-century Egyptian cookbook *Kanz al-fawāʾid*, English trans., *Treasure Trove*, recipe 117, is called *shaʿīriyya* because the pieces are shaped like barley grains.

In the anonymous Andalusi *Anwāʿ al-ṣaydala* 161–2, *fidāwush* is by implication a generic term for pasta 'semolina dough,' of which there are three kinds:

1. Pasta shaped like wheat grains (no specific name given).
2. Pasta balls, the size of a coriander seed each, called *ḥamīṣ* in Bijāya and the surrounding regions in Ifrīqiya.
3. Paper-thin pieces of pasta said to be women's food (*aṭʿimat al-nisāʾ*).

Based on al-Arbūlī, *al-Kalām ʿalā al-aghdhiya* 127, this type of pasta is very nourishing, especially when cooked with meat. Eating it regularly is said to cause blockages in the bowels.

harīsa (هريسة) wheat porridge cooked with meat, as in recipe ii.6.10; and meatless, as in recipe i.5.13, where the suggestion is to serve it in a large dish, with a small bowl filled with honey put in the middle, and eaten with boxwood spoons (*malāʿiq baqs*).

ḥuwwārā (حوارى) fine bran-free flour of the common wheat (*Triticum aestivum*); the name designates its white color. The term is mostly used in the eastern region of al-Mashriq; its counterpart in the western region is *darmak*, see above. Because of the high level of gluten it contains, it was deemed suitable for making good chewy bread. As described by al-Harawī, *Baḥr al-jawāhir* 137, *ḥuwwārā* bread is made with wheat that has been husked, washed repeatedly to whiten it, dried in the shade, and then crushed into flour.

In al-Tujībī's cookbook, the Western name *darmak* is largely used. Calling flour by its Mashriqi name of *ḥuwwārā* points to the possibility of the recipe's eastern origin; see recipes iii.2.30 for an *Ibrāhīmiyya* chicken dish, as well as recipes i.2.14 and i.5.3.

ghubār al-ḥuwwārā (غبار الحوارى) powdery flour, a by-product of milling wheat grains in a quern (*raḥā*) or the larger grinder (*ṭāḥūna*). The grinding process produces powder, as fine as dust, which falls all over the place.[7] It was collected and used to make glue and to coat foods with it before frying them. It was called *ghubār al-darmak* in the Muslim West.

isfanj (اسفنج), literally 'sponge,' are yeasted fritters, *buñuelos*; fried puffed pastries, light and spongy in texture, made with semolina flour (*samīd*) or fine white flour (*darmak*), see recipes i.4.30–2.

aqṣād (اقصاد) fritters that look as if they were split in half.
isfanj al-qulla (اسفنج القلة) spongy pastry baked in an earthenware jar.
isfanj al-rīḥ (اسفنج الريح) light and airy yeasted fritters.
mughdir (مغدر) dark-colored fritters.

iṭriya (اطرية) dried thin noodles, usually stored and used as needed. Recipe i.5.8 describes how to make them from scratch with semolina flour (*samīd*) or fine flour (*daqīq*) when dried noodles are not available.

According to Ibn Khalṣūn, *Kitāb al-Aghdhiya* 81, *iṭriya* is very nourishing, but due to its density, it is slow to pass through the digestive system and causes blockages in the liver. It is suitable for people who exert rigorous physical activities. The best, he adds, is *iṭriya*, which has been made with semolina flour and rolled out into thin noodles.

---

7 See Ibn Waḥshiyya, *al-Filāḥa al-Nabaṭiyya* i 421.

jashīsh (جشيش) coarsely crushed grains and pulses used in making porridges, see recipes i.3.9–11 and i.5.14; see also glossary 5.

jawzīnaq (جوزينق) walnut pinwheel cookies, recipe i.4.12. There is another variety of *jawzīnaq*, recipe ix.4.1, which is a confection, see glossary 4.

kaʿb al-ghazāl (كعب الغزال) small cookies made to resemble the gazelle's ankle bone, also called talus bone and astragalus. See recipe i.4.4.

kaʿk (كعك) ring cookies, made *sādhaj* 'plain,' with no sugar and unstuffed, and *maḥshū* 'stuffed'; see recipes i.4.1–3.

khabīṣ (خبيص), ***waraq al-khabīṣ*** (ورق الخبيص) thin sheets of bread made with wheat starch, see recipe i.4.9. It is used to make a thick pudding of *khabīṣ*.

khamīr (خمير) fresh yeast, obtained by setting aside a piece of fermented dough for the following day's baking. When this is not available, Ibn al-Bayṭār, *al-Jāmiʿ* iii 341, describes how to make it from scratch. Flour is kneaded with some olive oil and water and left overnight, during which time it will sour and ferment and will be ready to use in the morning. Of its medicinal uses, soup made with it can check diarrhea.

khamīrat al-ʿajīn (خميرة العجين) yeast used in fermenting dough.

khamīr mutanāhī fī l-ikhtimār (خمير متناهي في الاختمار) fresh yeast, which is very well fermented and soured.

khubz (خبز) bread, collectively. An individual bread was commonly referred to as *raghīf* (pl. *raghāyif*, *rughfān*). See recipes in chapter i.1 for making different types of bread; and chapter i.2 on *tharāyid*, which are dishes of bread sopped in rich broth and meat.

The following are the types of bread mentioned in al-Tujībī's recipes:

khubz al-banīj (خبز البنيج) bread made with proso millet, see *banīj* above.

khubz faṭīr (خبز فطير) unfermented bread, made by flattening dough into a thin disc and pricking it with a stick all over its face before baking. It was regarded as a nourishing type of bread, albeit slow to digest on account of its density. Therefore, it was said to be fit for physically active people. Adding fennel and nigella seeds to it was said to facilitate its digestion.[8]

khubz al-furn (خبز الفرن) bread baked in the *furn* (brick oven), usually thicker and fluffier than the clay oven bread. Apparently, this type of bread stayed fresh longer than the clay oven bread; the recipe says to keep it in a vessel and use it as needed. See recipe i.1.1.

---

8 See Ibn Khalṣūn, *Kitāb al-Aghdhiya* 80.

khubz ghayr maṭbūkh (خبز غير مطبوخ) unbaked bread. In recipe i.2.21 it is specifically made for a milk *tharīd*. A well-kneaded, firm dough is made with semolina flour (*samīd*) and a small amount of water, with no leaven. It is then shaped into small and very thin discs, which are spread on a sieve to dry out in the sun. This will result in what looks like pasta.

khubz al-ḥuwwārā (خبز الحوارى) bread made with fine bran-free white flour, see *ḥuwwārā* above.

khubz al-malla (خبزالملة) thin flat bread, baked in a flat wide plate on a direct source of heat, as in recipe i.1.3. See also *malla*, in glossary 9.1. It is said to be a dense variety of bread that is slow to digest; only people with strong stomachs can digest it well.[9]

khubz mu'ād al-'ajn (خبز معاد العجن) twice-kneaded and twice-risen bread, see recipe i.2.1.

khubz mukhtamir (خبز مختمر) fermented bread, which was deemed the best of breads on account of its balanced properties and ease of its digestion. In the description of Ibn Khalṣūn, *Kitāb al-Aghdhiya* 80, yeasted dough had to be soft and moist and kneaded thoroughly so that the baked bread comes out as light and porous as a sea sponge.

khubz samīd (خبز سميد) bread made with semolina flour, see *samīd* below.

khubz al-tannūr (خبز التنور) bread baked in the clay oven, recipe i.1.2. It was said to be the best on account of the oven's moderate heat, which allows the bread to bake well from the inside and outside.

raghīf khashin (رغيف خشن) a thick disc of bread, used in recipe i.4.35 as a protective layer on top of a cheese casserole baked in the brick oven (*furn*).

khubz maḥshū (خبز محشو) a luxurious double-crusted pie stuffed with meat, birds, or fish, see recipe i.4.40. In the anonymous Andalusi cookbook *Anwā' al-ṣaydala* 26, a somewhat similar double-crusted pie recipe, called *Barmakiyya*, is recommended as a victual for travelers.

kunāfa (كنافة) crepes made with starchy thin batter. They are eaten fresh with butter and honey poured all over them; or kept for later use by cutting them into thin shreds with scissors and boiling them in honey. See recipes i.4.14–14b.

kuskusū (كسكسو) couscous made with semolina flour (*samīd*); see recipe i.5.1, which describes how it is made and cooked; see also recipes i.5.2–5 for a variety of tasty ways to cook it. In the medieval eastern region, couscous was known and cooked. The thirteenth-century Aleppan cookbook *al-Wuṣla ilā l-ḥabīb* includes a recipe,

---

9 Al-Arbūlī, *al-Kalām 'alā al-aghdhiya* 125.

described as *kuskusū al-Maghāriba* (i.e., people of North Africa).[10] It is similarly included in the anonymous fourteenth-century Egyptian cookbook *Kanz al-fawā'id*.[11]

Couscous is generally believed to be of Amazigh origin of ancient roots. Couscous utensils similar to the ones we are familiar with were excavated in tombs that date back to the second century BC, during the reign of an Amazigh king who "unified the ancient Kingdom of Numidia by bringing together the northern part of modern Algeria, as well as Tunisia and Libya." Additionally, couscous utensils that date back to the ninth century were also excavated in a region southwest of the Algerian capital.[12]

In the opinion of al-Arbūlī, *al-Kalām ʿalā al-aghdhiya* 127, couscous is quite nourishing when completely digested, but this was not always the case because it leaves the stomach very fast due to its heavy nature. This led to the belief that it caused blockages in the bowels.

lawzīnaq (لوزينق) almond pinwheel cookies, recipe i.4.13; see also *jawzīnaq* above.

lubāb (لباب) freshly extracted liquid wheat starch; see, for instance, recipe i.4.19. Cf. *nashā* (entry below), which is dried wheat starch.

lubāb al-khubz (لباب الخبز) the soft inside of crusty leavened bread; crumbs.

lubāb khubz mukhtamir (لباب خبز مختمر) inside crumbs of fermented bread.

luqam al-qāḍī (لقم القاضي), literally 'judge's morsels'; walnut-like pastries sprinkled with sugar, see recipe i.4.6.

maqrūḍ (مقروض) stuffed cookie bars, fried and sprinkled with sugar, see recipe i.4.27.

marmaz (مرمز) coarsely crushed young barley. The grains are harvested when they are still green, soft, and full of moisture, see recipe i.5.11, where they are also called *farīk*.

mithradat al-amīr (مثردة الامير), literally 'the prince's *tharīd* bowls'; filled small, pie-like pastries made to resemble miniature *tharīd* bowls, see recipe i.4.11.

muʿallaka (معلكة), also called ***bāzīn*** (بازين), a savory dish cooked with meat in which bread is served as a conical mass surrounded by the cooked meat and vegetables. See recipe i.5.10.

muḥammaṣ (محمص) small balls of pasta, resembling peppercorns, made with semolina flour. See recipe i.5.7.

mujabbanāt (مجبنات), sg. ***mujabbana*** (مجبنة) cheese pastries, which were a popular snack food in al-Andalus and beyond; as well as in North Africa and Egypt.[13] See introduction ii.5.2, pp. 55-6 for more on the cultural history of this pastry.

---

10 By Ibn al-ʿAdīm, ii 608, English trans., *Scents* 137.

11 English trans., *Treasure Trove*, recipe 123.

12 "If Couscous be the Food of Love," https://www.france24.com/en/20180123-unesco-couscous-algeria-morocco-rivalry-unity, accessed May 4, 2020; cited in Gaul, "Light Enough to Travel: Couscous" 110. See also Wright, *Mediterranean Feast* 660–4.

13 A thirteenth-century augmented version of al-Warrāq's *Kitāb al-Ṭabīkh*, which was written

Al-Tujībī dedicates a whole section in his chapter on pastries to *mujabbanāt*, see recipes i.4.33–9. When fried, cheese is either mixed with the dough or stuffed in it, or both. Some of them are made with holes in the middle like doughnuts. The baked ones are made by layering thin sheets of dough with cheese.

The *mujabbana* varieties included in al-Tujībī's cookbook are:

mujabbanāt al-furn (مجبنات الفرن) oven-baked cheese pastries, also called *Ṭulayṭuliyya*, entry below.

makhāriq (مخارق), sg. ***mukharraqa*** (مخرقة) fried doughnut-like cheese pastries, made by kneading three equal parts of semolina dough, butter, and grated cheese. They are shaped into small discs with holes in the middle, and hence the name *makhāriq*, see recipe i.4.34.[14]

muthallatha (مثلثة) fried doughnut-like cheese pastries, made by kneading three equal parts of semolina dough, butter, and grated cheese. They are also called *makhāriq*, see above.

qayjāṭa (قيجاطة), ***qayjāṭiyya*** (قيجاطية) oven-baked cheese pastry, made by layering very thin discs of bread with cheese in a pan and gradually moistening the casserole with milk while baking. It can also be made without cheese as the recipe suggests, see i.4.35. Qayjāṭa/Qayshāṭa is also the name of an Andalusi city located in the province of Jaén in southern Spain, Quesada. That the two designations were recognized by Andalusis back then is evident from an amusing anecdote related by Ibn ʿĀṣim, *Ḥadāʾiq al-azāhir* 131. It was about a man who told an interpreter of dreams that he saw himself eating *mujabbana*. The interpreter's answer was, "You are going to be taken a prisoner of war in Qayjāṭa, God willing, based on the saying *qayjaṭlī nijabbin lak*."[15]

Etymologically, both the city and the *qayjāṭa* cheese pastry are related to the Spanish *queso* 'cheese,' and *quesito* for fresh cheese.[16] According to Corriente, *Dictionary of Andalusi Arabic*, s.v. *q-y-j-ṭ*, *qayjāṭ* is 'curd of milk,' and *qayjāṭa* is a kind of 'cheesecake,' which he describes as cheese pastry made with seven layers of thin bread. He got the number of the bread layers from the corresponding recipe in the anonymous *Anwāʿ al-ṣaydala* 183, which gives

---

in Egypt, includes five *mujabbanāt* recipes in a pastry chapter, Istanbul MS, fols. 233r–234v. The name survived in the Spanish *almojábana*.

14 In Tunisia today, *makhāriq* are made without cheese.

15 (قيجطلي نجبن لك) "If you make *qayjāṭa* for me, I will bring you fresh cheese," said of the benefit of coöperation and exchange of favors. Qayjāṭa, the city, fell to the Christians in 1225.

16 In addition, we read in the following link that as a surname, Quesada designates one who came from Quesada, as well as one who made cheese or cheesecakes: http://surnames.meaning-of-names.com/quesada/.

the pastry another name, *sabʿ buṭūn*, literally 'seven bellies.' Corriente plausibly relates the name *qayjāṭa* to the Latin adj. *caceata*, which means 'mixed with cheese.'

Ṭulayṭuliyya (طليطلية) oven-baked cheese pastries, specialty of Toledo, a city in the west of al-Andalus. It is made by filling thin discs of dough with grated cheese and folding their sides to cover it, see recipes i.4.38–9.

muqawwara maḥshuwwa (مقورة محشوة) pastries cored out and stuffed with a mix of nuts and sugar along with the crumbled cored-out crumbs, recipe i.4.9.

murakkaba (مركبة) assembled crepes, recipe i.4.26. A corresponding recipe in the anonymous Andalusi *Anwāʿ al-ṣaydala* 184 describes it as specialty of Qusanṭīna, a region in northeastern Algeria, where it was called *Kutāmiyya*, derived from Kutām/Kutāma, a major Amazigh tribe in northern Algeria.

This pastry must have been the prototype of today's Moroccan *maflūta* (the flipped), made at the end of Passover on the Moroccan Jewish festival of Maymūna. Thin layers of yeasted dough are fried and served with butter and honey. The etymological connection lies in the traditional way this pastry is prepared: when one layer is fried, another disc of the flattened dough is spread on top of it and flipped; then another disc is put on top and the whole thing is flipped again; and so on until one ends up with a pile of fried layers stuck to each other, and hence the name *maflūta*.

musammana (مسمنة) discs of layered bread made by flattening dough, spreading it with melted ghee (*samn*), and folding it several times, see recipes i.4.17–8. Also called *muwarraqa*, entry below.

mushahhada (مشهدة) pancakes, see *qaṭāʾif* below.

mushāsh Zubayda (مشاش زبيدة) puff pastries. The name of the recipe and the instructions given suggest that the resulting pastries would look like breast bones with four or more of the costal rib cartilages attached to them, see recipe i.4.28 for more on this pastry.

muwarraqa (مورقة) laminated pastries, whose name is descriptive of its layered texture, see recipes 1.4.17–8. Another name for it is *musammana*, on account of *samn* (ghee) used in layering the dough.

nashā (نشا) dry wheat starch; good quality starch is described as *yābis ṭayyib*, thoroughly dry and tastes good and not sour. To obtain *nashā*, wheat grains are first soaked in clear water and then washed, and the water drained is and replaced. This would be repeated five times a day, and preferably continued during the night. Once the grains soften, water is drained slowly without agitating it. The wheat grains are then stomped by feet, some water is poured over them, and whatever husk floats on the surface is removed with a strainer. The resulting starchy solution is strained and spread on large flat tiles under the scorching heat of the sun.

FIGURE 115 Wheat, the green head in the middle is used to make *farīk*, Dioscorides, *Ajzā' min risāla fī l-nabātāt*, fol. 22v, detail
BNF, DEPARTMENT OF MANUSCRIPTS, ARAB 4947. SOURCE: GALLICA.BNF.FR/BNF

Starch that does not completely dry would turn sour, that is why the recommendation is to make it in summer.

nashā maḥlūl (نشا محلول) starch that has been dissolved in liquid.
nashā yābis (نشا يابس) dried starch.

nukhāla (نخالة) bran of grains; usually sifted out of crushed grains. See the *murrī* recipes in chapter x.8, which have their uses for the bran; and recipe i.3.5 for making soup with it.

nukhāla khashna (نخالة خشنة) coarsely crushed bran.

qamḥ (قمح) wheat, *Triticum*. This was its common name in the Levant, Egypt, and the Muslim West. In Iraq, the preferred term was *ḥinṭa* (حنطة). *Burr* (بُرّ) was a purer Arabic term.[17] Based on al-Ṭighnarī, *Zahrat al-bustān* 401–2, the season for growing wheat in al-Andalus was from the middle of October to January, when the lands were dependent on rainfall. Such lands, al-Ṭighnarī adds, produced the best of wheat varieties, and fine delicious bread was made with its milled flour.

Several varieties were grown in the Muslim West; they come under two main categories:

1. Hard wheat (*ṣulb*): the grains are heavy, fat, full, hard, and not easy to crush. They look waxy (*shamʿī*) and glistening (*barrāq*) from the outside, are smooth in texture, and are almost transparent. Such grains are high in starch content, low in bran and husk, and are more suitable for making fine varieties of flour. They are said to be nourishing but slow to digest. Tenth-century Ibn Ḥawqal, *Ṣūrat al-arḍ* 90, describes hard wheat growing in al-Maghrib in the Sijilmasa region in the northern edge of the Sahara as grains that are fine tasting and hard to break (*ṣulb al-maksar, ladhīdh al-ṭaʿm*).
2. Soft wheat (*rakhū*): the grains are light in weight (*sakhīf*), brittle in texture (*mutakhalkhil*), easy to break, and opaque. Such grains are high in bran and husk content and lower in starch than hard wheat. They are more suitable for making whole wheat flour (*khushkār*).[18]

Al-Ghassānī, *Ḥadīqat al-azhār* 123–4, names and describes the best and most prevalent variety of wheat from which *darmak* and *samīd* are milled (see entries in this section). He describes its grains as being golden yellow (the color of the sun); they are fat, full, and dense, and convex in shape. In Fez, he adds, this variety is known as *ṣadr bāz* 'hawk's breast.' Al-Ishbīlī, *ʿUmdat al-ṭabīb* i 185, calls this wheat variety *laṭrijāl* (لطرجال).

The type of wheat described above is amber durum wheat (also known as pasta wheat, *Triticum durum*), which is hard to mill, high in protein, and lower in gluten than common wheat/bread wheat, *Triticum aestivum*.[19] Whereas durum wheat is plastic in texture, common wheat is elastic on account of its gluten content.[20] This renders the former suitable for making pasta and the latter more conducive for making bread.

---

17 As explained in Ibn Manẓūr, *Lisān al-ʿArab*, s.v. برر.

18 Al-Isrāʾīlī, *Kitāb al-Aghdhiya* ii 3–5.

19 In medieval sources, wheat low in gluten content was described as *ghayr ʿalik*, i.e., it does not make bread chewy in texture.

20 This variety of wheat was described as *ʿalik*, i.e., gives bread made with it the desirable chewy texture.

Al-Ishbīlī, *ʿUmdat al-ṭabīb* i 185, mentions a red wheat variety, called *zayyūn* (زيون), named for the red color of the grains. He says the grains are similar to *laṭrījāl* (the durum wheat variety mentioned above), but unlike them, they can be milled easily.[21] According to Ibn Rushd, *al-Kulliyyāt* 395, dense and heavy wheat grains that are full and glistening are the best to make bread with.

Thirteenth-century Andalusi physician Ibn Khalṣūn, *Kitāb al-Aghdhiya* 79–80, categorizes milled wheat varieties and the bread made with them as follows:

al-darmak (الدرمك) fine bran-free white flour; moist and hot in properties. Bread made with it is said to be very nourishing but slow to digest and purge from the digestive system. This can be remedied by kneading it well, using the needed amounts of salt and yeast, and baking it well.

al-madhūn (المدهون) fine white flour that contains some bran, and it is the best and most balanced in properties. It is less moist than *al-darmak* (above) and not as dry as *al-aḥmar* (below). It is the best bread to eat.[22]

al-aḥmar (الاحمر) brown flour, literally 'red.' It is whole wheat flour, from which nothing is removed. It is also known as *khushkār* (خشكار) and *daqīq ḥinṭī* (دقيق حنطة). It is hot and dry in properties; less nourishing than the above two, but it digests faster and is easily purged from the digestive system.

al-samīd (السميد) semolina flour, similar in properties to *al-madhūn* (above) in that it is moderately moist and hot. Bread and *kuskusū* are made with it. Due to its sandy texture, *samīd* used for making bread is sprinkled with water to moisten and soften it and then kneaded an hour later; the kneading has to be long and vigorous to release its gluten.

Wheat was highly praised by physicians for its moderately hot and moist properties. It was esteemed as the most suitable of grains for human consumption.[23]

qanāniṭ maḥshuwwa (قنانيط محشوة) mock reed tubes, stuffed with nuts and honey, see recipe i.4.5.

qaṭāʾif (قطائف) pancakes, served drenched in honey mixed with butter or ghee and sprinkled with sugar, cinnamon, and black pepper. *Mushahhada* 'looking like hon-

21 This variety is comparable to today's hard red winter wheat, with its strong flavor and high protein and gluten content. Flour milled from its grains is suitable for baking bread and pastries.

22 That was the physicians' opinion of it. Otherwise, people generally preferred the first type, which is finer and whiter, despite the fact that it is not easy to digest.

23 See, for instance, Ibn Rushd *al-Kulliyyāt* 395, who maintains that doctors unanimously agree that it is the most suitable nonmeat food for people with normally balanced properties (*nās ṭabīʿiyyīn*), who are dwellers in the fifth and fourth zones, i.e., the Mediterranean basin.

eycombs' was its name in al-Andalus and al-Maghrib. In Ifrīqiya,[24] it was also called *muṭanfasa* 'like carpets with smooth luxurious pile.'[25] This kind of pastry is characterized by having holes on one side, which gave it the name *muthaqqaba* 'having holes,' see the anonymous Andalusi cookbook *Anwāʿ al-ṣaydala* 184.

The pancakes are baked in a special pan, called *ṭājin al-qaṭāʾif*, made of glazed earthenware with a base textured with blind holes. See *qaṭāʾif* recipes i.4.15–16; and i.2.16, where such pancakes are used in a *tharīda* dish to replace bread.

qaṭāʾif ʿAbbāsiyya (قطائف عباسية) pancakes, stuffed and fried, as in recipe i.4.16; and as the name suggests, they are made after the Abbasid style.

qayjāṭa (قيجاطة) a variety of *mujabbanāt* cheese pastries, oven baked. See entry for *mujabbanāt* in this section.

qishr (قشر), also ***safā*** (سفا) husk, such as that of rice, wheat, and barley grains.

qiṭniyya bayḍāʾ (قطنية بيضاء) a white variety of sorghum, *Sorghum bicolor*.[26] According to Ibn al-Bayṭār, *al-Jāmiʿ* ii 415, the white variety with heavy grains was deemed the best. In *al-Iḥāṭa* i 143, Ibn al-Khaṭīb called it *dhura ʿArabiyya* (Arabian sorghum) and described it as the finest of the good-tasting varieties of *qaṭānī*. He added that it was the staple food of peasants and workers in wintertime in Granada. Quoting Ibn Waḥshiyya, *al-Filāḥa al-Nabaṭiyya*, Ibn al-ʿAwwām, *al-Filāḥa al-Andalusiyya* iv 137–42, describes how to make bread with it, with the recommendation that it must be eaten with fat and sweet substances to facilitate its digestion. Porridge made with it in al-Tujībī's recipe i.5.14 is drenched with heated butter and served with a bowlful of honey or sweet grape molasses.

raghīf (رغيف), pl. ***rughaf*** (رغف) disc of bread.

raghīf raqīq (رغيف رقيق) thin disc of bread, commonly baked in the *tannūr* (clay oven).

raghīf ghalīẓ (رغيف غليظ), ***raghīf khashin*** (رغيف خشن) thick disc of bread, commonly baked in the *furn* (brick oven).

raʾs maymūn (رأس ميمون), literally 'the blessed head,' pastry shaped like a human head, recipes i.4.24–5. See glossary 5 for another variety cooked with mutton. *Maymūn* could be a man's name; it is also a generic name given to designate 'slave' and 'monkey.' I chose to interpret the pastry this way because the recipe clearly explains that it is supposed to look like a human head, and *maymūn*, as an adjective, means 'blessed,'

---

24 The coastal regions of what today are western Libya, Tunisia, and eastern Algeria.

25 See Dozy, *Takmilat al-maʿājim* viii 327, s.v. *qaṭāʾif*.

26 *Qaṭānī* (pl.) in general collectively designates pulses as well as grains other than wheat and barley; called so because they were planted in the summer and harvested at the end of it. See Ibn Manẓūr, *Lisān al-ʿArab*, s.v. قطن.

'prosperous,' etc. Marks, *Encyclopedia of Jewish Food*, s.v. *Mimouna*, 407–8, suggests that it is a Jewish man's name. Another possibility, which he connects to medieval North African folklore, is that Mimouna was a female demon or goddess, who was regarded as Lady Luck, and her husband was another demon, whose name was Mimoun.

ruqāq (رقاق) thin discs of bread.

sabāt (سبات) see *shabāt* below.

samīd (سميد) semolina flour, sandy in texture. It is a product of durum wheat, *Triticum durum*, the hardest of all varieties of wheat. See also *qamḥ* above. As instructed in al-Tujībī's recipes, *samīd* flour has to be kept moistened with water for an hour before kneading it to make bread and pastries.

> ***samīd khashin*** (سميد خشن), ***samīd ghalīẓ*** (سميد غليظ) coarsely crushed semolina, used in recipe i.4.21, for instance, for making a thick pudding (*khabīṣ*), and recipe iii.2.33 in a chicken stuffing mix.

shabāt (شبات), ***sabāt*** (سبات) a variety of delicate thin bread, which al-Tujībī's recipe i.2.11 describes as *raghā'if riqāq* (i.e., thin sheets of bread), made unleavened (*faṭīr*) and baked and cut into pieces for a *tharīda* dish named after it. The anonymous *Anwāʿ al-ṣaydala* offers two more *shabāt* dishes:

> ***tharīd al-shabāt***, p. 172, which uses yeasted dough made into thin *shabāt* breads and baked on a heated plate (*malla*) or in the *tannūr* 'clay oven.'
>
> ***shabāt bi-shaḥm***, p. 180, which are thin sheets of leavened bread kneaded with suet and fried in it and served with honey. Apparently, *shabāt* prepared this way was associated with a leisurely life and fine cuisine. In an Andalusi saying criticizing the indifference of the affluent to the needs of the common people, the ruler's daughter asks a poor petitioner if he intends to make *shabāt* with suet,[27] sounding much like Queen Marie Antoinette and her "let them eat brioche."

In the *Dictionary of Andalusi Arabic*, the etymological link that Corriente establishes between *shabāt*/*sabāt* and the Hispanic Romance *sópa* 'soup' (s.vv. *sh-p-p* and *s-b-t*) is unconvincing because it fails to consider that *shabāt*, as the recipes clearly indicate, is indeed the name of the bread rather than the name of the sop/sopa dish (*tharīd*) it is served with. It is equally unconvincing that the name of this bread and

27 (سمعت بنت السلطان الساعي يسعى، قالت كتعمل شبات بشحم؟), al-Zajjālī, *Amthāl al-ʿawām* ii 421.

the *tharīd* dish made with it are associated with the Sabbath,[28] simply because the bread was made with suet and the *tharīd* combined chicken and cheese, both practices not considered kosher by Jews.

Possibly, and by way of suggestion, the bread's name, *shabāt*, could have originally evolved as a coined Andalusi term for thin flat bread that was typically baked on heated plates. In the culinary sources available to us, such heated plates are called by their Arabic names *malla* and *ṭājin ḥadīd*.[29] For a clue about the unusual nomenclature of the *shabāt* bread we may have to go all the way to countries like Argentina and Brazil, where today a staple flat bread is called *pan de chapa* 'hotplate bread.' *Chapa*, the hot plate, bears witness to the survival of a medieval tradition that the immigrant Arabs and Jews took with them after their expulsion from Spain. In the Spanish culinary contexts, *chapa* must have designated a heated plate, which was not any different from the *malla* and *ṭājin ḥadīd* mentioned above, and the bread associated with it metamorphosed to *shabāt* in al-ʿAjamiyya (Andalusi Romance).

shaʿīr (شعير) barley. It had many uses for the Andalusi cook, as revealed in al-Tujībī's cookbook. It is used in a couple of porridge recipes, i.3.10 and i.5.11; and recipes for making the fermented condiment *murrī*, x.8.1–4, 7, 9, 10. Parched barley grains are used to revive weak vinegar, recipe x.7.8; and it is one of the components of a hand-washing preparation called *ushnān*, recipe xii.5.

jashīsh al-shaʿīr (جشيش الشعير) coarsely crushed barley grains, used in making porridge, as in recipe i.3.10.

marmaz (مرمز) coarsely crushed young barley, also known as *farīk*. See recipe i.5.11.

nukhālat shaʿīr (نخالة شعير) barley bran.

shaʿīr maqlū (شعير مقلو) parched barley grains, literally 'fried'; used along with soaked barley grains in recipe x.7.8 to help vinegar keep its acidity.

Barley is closer to moderation in its properties, leaning more towards coldness and dryness. It is said to be less nourishing than wheat but easier and faster to digest because it has less gluten and more bran. Using it in spring and summer was recommended because it was said to alleviate heat-related ailments and quench thirst.[30] It was also said to cause bloating in people suffering from cold-related ailments and colic pains.

28 As in Zaouali, *Medieval Cuisine* 75.

29 See al-Tujībī's recipe i.1.3, and glossary 9.1, s.v. *malla*.

30 Al-Arbūlī, *al-Kalām ʿalā al-aghdhiya* 128–9; al-Ṭighnarī, *Zahrat al-bustān* 407; and al-Isrāʾīlī, *Kitāb al-Aghdhiya* ii 62–1.

FIGURE 116 Barley heads, in varying degrees of ripeness, Dioscorides, *Fī Hayūlā al-ṭibb*, translation by Ḥunayn b. Isḥāq, fol. 92v, detail
FROM THE NEW YORK PUBLIC LIBRARY, SPENCER COLLECTION: HTTPS://DIGITALCOLLECTIONS.NYPL.ORG/ITEMS/5E66B3E8-E9BB-D471-E040-E00A180654D7

ṭaʿām al-khubz (طعام الخبز), literally 'bread-like foods,' a general term for pastries.

talbīna (تلبينة) a thin starchy batter made by dissolving wheat starch in water. It is synonymous with *nashā maḥlūl* 'dissolved wheat starch.' Recipe i.4.14 describes how starch is extracted from semolina dough.

taltīn (تلتين), copied as *talūtīn* (تلوتين) in Ibn Khalṣūn, *Kitāb al-Aghdhiya* 82. In Dozy, *Takmilat al-maʿājim* ii 57, s.v. تلتل, it occurs as *tulaytlī* (?) تليتلي and *tlitslī* تلتسلي. It is made into thin sheets cut into 1½-inch squares, see recipe i.5.12. The anonymous thirteenth-century cookbook *Anwāʿ al-ṣaydala* 161–2 does not give it a specific name, it is only described as a paper-thin (*fī riqqat al-kāghīd*) variety of *fidāwush*, esteemed as a delicacy cooked and eaten by women (*aṭʿimat al-nisāʾ*). The counterpart of this type of pasta in the medieval eastern region was *ṭuṭmāj/tuṭmāj*, also called *lakhsha*, literally 'slippery.'[31]

Ibn Khalṣūn, *Kitāb al-Aghdhiya* 82, describes it as having dense humors, even denser and slower to digest than *zabzīn*, mentioned below.

zabzīn (زبزين), also pronounced *zebezīn*, as suggested in Corriente, *Dictionary of Andalusi Arabic*, s.v. *z-b-z-n*. It is a variety of pasta shaped like small chickpeas, see recipe i.3.7. Dozy, *Takmilat al-maʿājim* v 284–5, s.v. زبزين, describes it as food of al-Maghrib, where it was also called *bazīn* or *bazīna*. Al-Tujībī explains that Ahl al-ʿUdwa call it *barkūs*.[32] This dish is still cooked in present-day Morocco.

Ibn Khalṣūn, *Kitāb al-Aghdhiya* 82, describes *zabzīn* as being dense in humors and slow to digest, causing colic pain. Only people who exert strenuous physical activities should eat it.

zalābiya (زلابية) latticed fritters dipped in honey, see recipe i.4.29. In the anonymous Andalusi *Anwāʿ al-ṣaydala* 199, it is called *shubbākiyya* 'latticed' as well. *Zalābiya* was a popular street food throughout the medieval Arabo-Muslim world. The following are verses on a *zalābiya* fryer by the ninth-century Baghdadi poet Ibn al-Rūmī:

> I saw him at the crack of dawn frying *zalābiya*,
> Looking like tubes of reed, delicate and thin.
> The oil I saw boiling in his pan was like the hitherto elusive alchemy.
> The batter he threw into the pan looking like silver,
> Would instantly transform into lattices of gold.[33]

---

31 The dish's name survives in today's Algerian cuisine as *tlītlī*, prepared with chicken and orzo-like pasta pieces.

32 It is copied as *barkūkash* in the Madrid MS, fol. 21v. Ahl al-ʿUdwa is a reference to people of al-Maghrib, which, to the Andalusis, was on the other side of the Mediterranean.

33 In al-Ṣafadī, *al-Wāfī bi-l-wafayāt* xvii 121.

The earliest extant *zalābiya* recipe comes from al-Warrāq's tenth-century Baghdadi cookbook *Kitāb al-Ṭabīkh*, English trans., *Annals* 414–5, where the batter is slowly poured into the boiling oil through a hole made in a coconut shell. In al-Tujībī's recipe, a large drinking vessel (*qadaḥ*) with a hole in its bottom is used instead.

In the medieval medical opinion, *zalābiya*, with its hot properties, was believed to be lighter than *qaṭāyif* pastries (pancakes) and faster to digest. It was also believed to be beneficial to coughs and phlegmatic ailments in the chest and lungs.[34]

34 Ibn al-Bayṭār, *al-Jāmiʿ* ii 473.

3. Dairy

albān (البان) a general term for dairy foods.

ʿaqīd (عقيد) rennet-curdled milk, which may be eaten with honey or fresh figs, as in recipe vi.1.4. It may also be used to make cheese, as in recipe vi.1.1. *ʿAqīd* may be curdled with blossoms of a variety of cardoon (*ḥarshaf*) called *laṣīf* (gundelia), see recipe vi.1.4 and glossary 12, s.v. *ḥarshaf*, for more on the varieties of the plant.

In terms of properties related to coldness and density, it was said to be in between milk and fresh cheese, and more nourishing than them. On account of its density, it was blamed for causing blockages but can be remedied by having honey after eating it.[1]

infaḥa (انفحة), ***minfaḥa*** (منفحة) rennet, obtained from the fourth stomach of suckling lambs, kids, or calves.

jubn (جبن) cheese, see recipe vi.1.1 for making fresh cheese, with suggested ways to consume it; and recipe vi.3.1 for ripening and curing hard cheese, with ways to cook it.

Fresh cheese was said to be cold and moist in properties, which generate dense humors. Still, it was believed to be better than hard cheese because it was more nourishing. It also digests faster than hard cheese due to its moisture content. Hard cheese, on the other hand, offered meagre nourishment, caused constipation, and was said to be putrefying. On the other hand, it had the benefit of exciting the appetite.[2]

ghubār al-jubn (غبار الجبن) finely grated hard cheese.

jubn baqarī (جبن بقري) cow cheese, which is said to bind into one solid mass when exposed to heat, see n. 94 for recipe i.4.33.

jubn ghanamī (جبن غنمي) sheep cheese, which is said to melt when exposed to heat, see n. 94 for recipe i.4.33.

jubn maḥkūk (جبن محكوك) cheese grated with a grater called *iskarfāj*, see glossary 9.1.

jubn ṭarī (جبن طري) fresh cheese; when very fresh and still soft and moist, it is said to be *raṭb*. When kept for a while in brine, turning rather solid and dry, it is described as *jāf*, see *mujabbana* recipe i.4.33. Fresh cheese is eaten sliced into fingers and dipped in honey. In addition, it is served fried and as a casserole with eggs, see recipes on p. 394.

jubn yābis (جبن يابس) hard cheese. Recipe vi.3.1 describes how to ripen it in a large jar called *khābiya*, see glossary 9.1. For recipes with hard cheese, see vi.3.2–4.

---

1 Al-Arbūlī, *al-Kalām ʿalā al-aghdhiya* 157.

2 Ibid.; Ibn Zuhr, *Kitāb al-Aghdhiya* 30.

 | DOI:10.1163/9789004469488_068

qishr al-jubn (قشر الجبن) rind of hard cheese, usually peeled off before grating the cheese, as in recipes vi.3.2, 4, and 8.

tarbiyat al-jubn (تربية الجبن) ripening hard cheese to cure it, see recipe vi.3.1.

khamīr (خمير) yogurt starter.

khilāṭ (خلاط), pl. *akhlāṭ* (اخلاط) a dairy condiment made with very thick drained yogurt, which has been mixed with chopped vegetables. In the *khilāṭ* recipe vi.1.3, the vegetable used is salt-preserved tender stems of capers.[3] Ibn Khalṣūn, *Kitāb al-Aghdhiya* 31, strongly discourages eating it. He says it is the most harmful of foods and has to be avoided because it causes putridity in the body.[4]

laban (لبن) may designate milk and yogurt. Often, milk is referred to as *laban ḥalīb* and yogurt as *laban ḥāmiḍ* 'sour milk.' Of milk varieties used in al-Tujībī's cookbook, sheep's milk, *laban ḍa'n*, is the most preferred, next is cow's milk, *laban baqar*. Goat's milk, *laban mā'iz*, is used when the first two are not available, see recipe i.5.9.

laban ḥalīb (لبن حليب) milk, see *laban* above.

laban ḥalīb ṭarī (لبن حليب طري) fresh milk.

laban khāthir (لبن خاثر), also called *rāyib khāthir* (رايب خاثر), thick yogurt, obtained by draining some of its whey, see recipe vi.2.2.

laban makhīḍ (لبن مخيض) buttermilk. It is milk remaining in the churning vessel after its butter has been extracted. It can either be consumed directly or left for a period of time to allow it to thicken and sour, as explained in *maḍīra* recipe ii.3.15. See recipe vi.2.3 for extracting butter from churned milk. With its cold and dry properties, buttermilk was said to quench thirst in the summertime.[5]

laban rāyib (لبن رايب) yogurt, see *rāyib* below.

mays (ميس), *mayṣ* (ميص) whey extracted by draining yogurt.

rāyib (رايب) yogurt, see recipes vi.2.1–2 for ways to make it. With its cold and dry properties, yogurt was generally believed to agree with the young and those having excess heat and yellow bile in their humors; otherwise, it was harmful to old and phlegmatic people.[6]

---

3 Cf. other *khilāṭ* recipes in al-Warrāq, *Kitāb al-Ṭabīkh*, English trans., *Annals* 199–200; and anonymous, *Kanz al-fawā'id*, English trans., *Treasure Trove*, recipes 509 and 510.

4 Ibn Khalṣūn must have been referring to some *khilāṭ*s that after adding the vegetables, were left for several days before consuming them, as is the case in *Kanz al-fawā'id* recipes mentioned in the note above. In al-Tujībī's recipe, it is served immediately.

5 Ibn Khalṣūn, *Kitāb al-Aghdhiya* 90.

6 Ibid., 89.

rāyib khafīf (رايب خفيف) yogurt, thin in consistency.

rāyib khāthir (رايب خاثر) thick yogurt; recipes vi.2.1–2 describe how to thicken yogurt: in the first recipe, some of the liquid is drained; and in the second recipe, yogurt is left longer to thicken.

rāyib mugharbal (رايب مغربل) sieve-strained yogurt made with rennet, see recipe vi.2.1. It is similar to what we encounter in the fourteenth-century Egyptian cookbook *Kanz al-fawāʾid*, English trans., *Treasure Trove*, recipe 508, where it is called *qanbarīs*.

rāyib al-qirba (رايب القربة) yogurt made in a leather vessel called a *qirba*, without any rennet or yogurt starter; see recipe vi.2.2.

rāyib ṣafīq (رايب صفيق) thick yogurt.

samn (سمن) ghee, obtained by boiling butter until all the moisture evaporates and nothing remains but its fat. The best was said to be ghee from cows' milk, and next was ghee from sheep's milk. With its hot and moist properties, it was believed to be nourishing and good for coughs and dryness in the mouth and throat. As a facial cream, it was said to give the complexion luster and glow.[7]

shīrāz (شيراز) very thick yogurt obtained by draining all the whey, resulting in a cream-cheese-like consistency. Due to its density, it was eaten with olive oil or butter to remedy it.[8] It was described as being dry in properties and the least cold among yogurt varieties. The recommendation was to avoid it, or at least not to have it in excess, as it was believed to be harmful to the brain and the nervous system.[9] On the other hand, we read in Andalusi al-Rundī, *Kitāb al-Aghdhiya* 188, that *shīrāz* was used as an appetizer (*mushahhī lil-akl*), particularly when made with preserved capers, which would make it good for the stomach and spleen. See al-Tujībī's recipe vi.1.2 for making *shīrāz* and for ways to serve it.

zubd (زبد) butter. Recipe vi.2.3 describes how to separate it from milk using a vessel made with the skin of a kid or a lamb, called a *shakwa*, see glossary 9.1. Butter was believed to be good for coughs and clearing the lungs of phlegm.[10] Interestingly, al-Tujībī provides a method for reconstructing butter from ghee, see recipe vi.2.3.

zubd maghlī (زبد مغلي) boiled butter, strained and drizzled on dishes just before serving.

zubd muṣaffā (زبد مصفى) butter that has been strained after melting it.

zubd ṭarī (زبد طري) fresh butter.

---

7 Al-Anṭākī, *Tadhkira* 218–9.

8 Al-Arbūlī, *al-Kalām ʿalā al-aghdhiya* 157.

9 Ibn Khalṣūn, *Kitāb al-Aghdhiya* 90; Ibn Zuhr, *Kitāb al-Aghdhiya* 31.

10 Ibn Khalṣūn, *Kitāb al-Aghdhiya* 90; Ibn Zuhr, *Kitāb al-Aghdhiya* 31.

4. Desserts and Sweeteners

ʿaqīd al-ʿinab (عقيد العنب) grape juice concentrate, see *rubb al-ʿinab* below.

ʿasal (عسل) bees' honey, used in recipes as a sweetening agent after boiling it, skimming its froth, and straining it with a woolen piece of cloth. It is the principal sweetening agent used in al-Tujībī's recipes—rather than sugar. This seems to have been the general preference of people in the Muslim West. In his account of al-Maghrib, in *Ṣubḥ al-aʿshā* v 176, al-Qalqashandī makes a similar observation. He says that although sugarcane grew in the region and excellent qualities of sugar were produced there, people did not care much for it and preferred to use honey, of which they had plenty. According to Ibn Zuhr, *Kitāb al-Aghdhiya* 69, honey at its best should be clear, neither thick nor thin in consistency, and emanate a pleasant fragrance. See also *shahd* below.

ʿasal abyaḍ (عسل ابيض), literally 'white honey,' is fair-colored honey, which is the preferred variety for making candies and sweets, as those made in chapter ix.2. Ibn Zuhr, *Kitāb al-Aghdhiya* 69, recommends it for making syrups infused with rose petals and rosewater, which were used diluted with water for making cold drinks.

ʿasal aḥmar (عسل احمر), literally 'red honey,' it is a reddish-brown variety of honey, sometimes called *yāqūtī* (i.e., like cornelian).[1] Ibn Zuhr, *Kitāb al-Aghdhiya* 69, recommends it for making syrups for hot drinks, as color would not be an issue for these drinks. It is mentioned only once in al-Tujībī's cookbook, in recipe ix.2.4, for making nougat. The recipe instructs the cook to use 5 egg whites; only 4 are needed if white honey is used.

ʿasal maghlī (عسل مغلي) boiled honey. In al-Tujībī's recipes, it is usually skimmed and strained with a woolen piece of cloth before it is poured on pastries and sweets.

ʿasal manzūʿ al-raghwa (عسل منزوع الرغوة) honey, which has been boiled and skimmed of its froth.

ʿasal muṣaffā (عسل مصفى) strained honey, usually done with a piece of woolen cloth.

ʿasal sukhn (عسل سخن) honey that is heated, not boiled, as in recipe i.4.10.

Honey was esteemed as a good source of food that generated good blood, strengthened the stomach, and kept the body in good health. It was recommended as a

1 Al-Bīrūnī, *al-Ṣaydana* 264.

 | DOI:10.1163/9789004469488_069

cure for cold-related illnesses. It was also deemed a highly aphrodisiac food that boosted erections and increased semen. In virtue of its preservative properties and delicious taste, it was also used as a medium for combining medicinal herbs and spices. Although sugar was similarly used, in cases when these medicinal preparations needed to be more effective in purging (*jalāʾ*) and breaking down densities (*taqṭīʿ*), honey was the preferred medium, as sugar was weaker in this respect.[2] Also due to its high nutritional value and excessively hot properties, it was deemed fit for the elderly and phlegmatic.[3]

damāgh al-Wāthiq (دماغ الواثق), literally 'al-Wāthiq's brain,' recipe ix.7.1; also called *damāgh al-Mutawakkil*. Abbasid Caliphs al-Wāthiq (d. 847) and al-Mutawakkil (d. 862) were sons of al-Muʿtaṣim and grandsons of Hārūn al-Rashīd. Under their patronage, learning and the pursuit of the sciences flourished.

This dessert is a variety of *fālūdhaj*, see recipe ix.2.2, which was well-liked in the eastern region. It was deemed a highly nutritious, delicious food, which, above all, was believed to benefit the brain, literally 'increase it' *yuzīd fi-l-damāgh*. A joke is told about a Bedouin who once paid a visit to Umayyad Caliph ʿAbd al-Malik b. Marwān (d. 705) while he was devouring *fālūdhaj*. The caliph offered it to the Bedouin, encouraging him to try it by saying that it increases the brain, to which the Bedouin replied, "If it were true what the Commander of the Faithful is saying, then his head would be as large as that of a mule."[4] To my knowledge, no such name as *damāgh al-Wāthiq* or *damāgh al-Mutawakkil* existed in al-Mashriq. It must have been the Andalusis' playful rendition of the famous *fālūdhaj*.

fālūdhaj (فالوذج) thick starch-based pudding, see recipes i.4.23 and ix.2.2. In the eastern region, it was very popular, believed to benefit the brain; literally, they said, "it increases the brain," *yuzīd fi-l-damāgh*. See *damāgh al-Wāthiq* above.

fālūdhaj al-qarʿ (فالوذج القرع) thick pudding made with honey and mashed gourd, recipe vii.1.11. The recipe recommends it for softening the bowels.

fānīdh (فانيذ) pulled sugar taffy, see recipe ix.6.1 for making it. In recipe ix.1.1, pieces of it are used to garnish *muʿassal* (entry below), which is a variety of thickened pudding.

ghassānī (غساني) thick pudding made with honey and wheat starch, see recipe ix.1.2. It is similar to *muʿassal*, mentioned below, but made with white honey and no saffron.[5] See also the savory *ghassānī* recipes in glossary 5.

---

2 See Ibn Rushd, *al-Kulliyyāt* 430.

3 Al-Rāzī, *Manāfiʿ al-aghdhiya* 240; al-Malik al-Muẓaffar, *al-Muʿtamad* 377–9; Ibn al-Bayṭār, *al-Jāmiʿ* iii 165–7.

4 Ibn Manẓūr, *Mukhtaṣar Tārīkh Dimashq* xv 229.

5 Based on the medieval lexicons, it may be translated to 'gorgeous.' Judging from the *ghassānī* recipes, the name may also be attributed to its fair color. See, for instance, Ibn Manẓūr, *Lisān al-ʿArab*, s.v. غسن, where a fair-skinned handsome man is called *ghassānī*.

ḥalwā' (حلواء) general term for a confection.

ḥalwā' al-fālūdhaj (حلواء الفالوذج) starch-based confection, recipe ix.2.2. Ordinary *fālūdhaj*, see entry above, is like a thick pudding served in bowls. This variety of *fālūdhaj* is further thickened and spread on a slab and divided into smaller pieces, like halva. It is comparable to what was called *fālūdhaj muʿallak* (chewy textured) in al-Warrāq's tenth-century Baghdadi cookbook, *Kitāb al-Ṭabīkh*, English trans., *Annals*, chapter 93.

ḥalwā' al-khabīṣ (حلواء الخبيص) confection made with thin sheets of wheat-starch bread, recipe ix.2.7.

ḥalwā' mukhammara (حلواء مخمرة) 'rosy-colored confection,' recipe ix.2.6. It got its name from *khumra*. Based on Ibn Manẓūr, *Lisān al-ʿArab*, s.v. خمر, *khumra* was *wars* (Ceylon cornel) and other substances, which women applied to their faces to make their complexions look rosy. The verb used for this action is *takhammarat*. *Wars* was also used to extract a red dye.[6] The crushed, lightly fried *khabīṣ* (thin sheets of wheat-starch bread) are what give the confection its rosy hue.

ḥalwā' al-qaṭāyif (حلواء القطايف) halwa with minced pancakes, recipe ix.7.3.

ḥalāwiyya sukkariyya (حلاوية سكرية) confection sweetened with sugar, recipe ix.2.8.

ishqāqūl (اشقاقول) rings of Solomon, a variety of hard sugar candy, see recipe ix.6.2, and n. 2 related to it, for more on this type of candy.

jawzīnaq (جوزينق) walnut confection, recipe ix.4.1. A similar confection, which uses pistachios instead of walnuts, is found in al-Warrāq's tenth-century Baghdadi cookbook, *Kitāb al-Ṭabīkh*, English trans., *Annals* 401, where it is called *khabīṣ yābis maftūt* 'dry and crumbly confection.' *Jawzīnaq* is also the name given to pinwheel cookies in the pastry chapter, recipe i.4.12.

jullāb (جلاب) syrup made with rosewater and sugar, but also with honey at times, see *sharāb al-jullāb al-ʿasalī* below. Such syrups were usually consumed as drinks diluted with water. For more on this syrup, see glossary 1, s.v. *sharāb* 1, for *sharāb al-jullāb*. In al-Tujībī's cookbook, this syrup is further boiled to a thicker consistency and used to douse pastries instead of honey in recipes i.4.11 and 16.

juljulāniyya (جلجلانية) nougat made with honey, egg whites, and hulled sesame seeds, see recipe ix.2.4.

lawzīnaj (لوزينج) almond brittle, made with sugar, honey, rosewater, and ponded almonds, see recipe ix.4.2.

muʿassal (معسل) thickened starch-based pudding, sweetened with honey, see recipe ix.1.1. It was more commonly known as *fālūdhaj* in the eastern region.

muʿqad (معقد), ***maʿqūd*** (معقود), ***ʿaqīd*** (عقيد) chewy candy, made with sugar, rosewater, and almonds, see recipe ix.2.9.

6 For the identification of *wars*, see Ghālib, *Mawsūʿa*, s.v. ورس.

FIGURE 117 Ceylon cornel, *wars*, al-Ghāfiqī, *Kitāb al-Adwiya al-mufrada*, MS, fol. 149r, detail
REPRODUCED BY PERMISSION OF THE OSLER LIBRARY OF THE HISTORY OF MEDICINE, MCGILL UNIVERSITY

muʿqad al-ʿasal (معقود العسل) chewy candy, made with honey and egg whites, see recipe ix.2.12.

murabbā al-ward al-ʿasalī (مربا الورد العسلي) rose-petal and honey jam, which is the only type of conserve mentioned in al-Tujībī's cookbook. It is used as a sweetening agent in a braised-meat dish called *rāhibī*, see recipe ii.1.7.

Qāhiriyya (قاهرية) delicate ring cookies, fried and baked, named after the city of Cairo, see recipes ix.3.1–3.

qaṣab ḥulw (قصب حلو) reeds of candy made with sugar and milk, see recipe ix.5.

qubbayṭ majbūdh (قبيط مجبوذ) pulled honey taffy,[7] see recipe ix.2.5, where the suggestion is to eat it freshly made with plain ring cookies, *kaʿk*. Ibn Khalṣūn, *Kitāb*

7 *Majbūdh* is derived from the verb *j-b-dh*, a variant on *j-dh-b* 'pull.' See Ibn Manẓūr, *Lisān al-ʿArab*, s.v. جبذ.

al-Aghdhiya 102, gives *nāṭif* as an alternative name for *qubbayṭ*. Al-Warrāq, *Kitāb al-Ṭabīkh*, English trans., *Annals* 389, calls a similar candy *nāṭif ʿasal ʿalā al-mismār* 'nail-pulled honey taffy.'

rubb ʿinab (ربّ عنب) grape juice concentrate, made by boiling the juice down to a thick consistency without adding any sugar. Also referred to as *rubb ʿinab maṭbūkh* (entry below) in al-Tujībī's cookbook.

rubb ʿinab ḥulw (ربّ عنب حلو) syrup made by boiling the juice of sweet grapes down to a thick consistency. It is offered in a small bowl in recipe i.5.14 as a condiment consumed with a porridge dish to replace honey. See also the following entry.

rubb ʿinab maṭbūkh (ربّ عنب مطبوخ) grape juice cooked down to a syrup consistency. The juice is reduced by boiling it down to a third of its original amount, without adding any sugar. In al-Tujībī's cookbook, it is used in recipes v.1.2 and 30 as a seasoning agent in fish dishes instead of honey. It is also recommended as a diluted drink to facilitate digestion after having fish; see the last paragraph in chapter v.1. Its other names include: *ṭilāʾ*, *ʿaqīd al-ʿinab*, *dibs al-ʿinab*, *maṭbūkh*, and *maybakhtaj*.[8]

rukhāmiyya (رخامية) marble-smooth chewy candy, made with sugar and crushed almonds, see recipe ix.2.11.

sanbūsak (سنبوسك) marzipan made with sugar, almonds, rosewater, and aromatic spices, see recipe ix.3.4. This confection is unlike the *sanbūsak* we encounter in the medieval cookbooks from the eastern region, where they are fried pastries, typically shaped into triangles of thin sheets of dough filled with a sweet stuffing of nuts and sugar or made savory with meat, as in al-Warrāq, *Kitāb al-Ṭabīkh*, English trans., *Annals* 190–2; and the anonymous *Kanz al-fawāʾid*, English trans., *Treasure Trove*, recipes 115, 116, 127. A similar marzipan recipe is included in the anonymous Andalusi *Anwāʿ al-ṣaydala* 196, where it is said to have been made for Almohad Caliph Abū Yūsuf al-Manṣūr (d. 1199). It was called *sanbūsak al-mulūk* 'fit for kings.' According to al-Tujībī, this is the true *sanbūsak*. We also learn from the anonymous Andalusi cookbook that marzipan was shaped into oranges, apples, and plums, which were offered as delicious, sweet nibbles for *naql*. *Naql* was a snack food closely associated with drinking sessions, when imbibing alcohol alternated with nibbling on small dishes.

shahd (شهد) honey with its beeswax. Because it is thicker in consistency than regular honey, less egg whites are needed in recipe ix.2.6 than with honey.

shahd muṣaffā (شهد مصفى) strained honey with its wax.

sharāb (شراب), pl. ***ashriba*** (اشربة) are commonly syrups of medium consistency used diluted as refreshing and rejuvenating drinks, see glossary 1. In al-Tujībī's cookbook,

8 See Ibn al-Bayṭār, *al-Jāmiʿ* iii 142, s.v. *ṭilāʾ*.

the following designate syrups of a rather thick consistency used to douse fried and baked pastries:

sharāb al-jullāb (شراب الجلاب) rosewater syrup, see *jullāb* above.

sharāb al-jullāb al-ʿasalī (شراب الجلاب العسلي) rosewater-honey syrup, made by gently boiling honey with rosewater down to a medium syrup consistency. In al-Tujībī's cookbook, this syrup is further boiled to a thicker consistency and used in recipes i.4.11 and 16 and ix.3.1.

sharāb maṣṭakā (شراب مصطكى) mastic-infused syrup, see glossary 1, s.v. *sharāb* 1. In al-Tujībī's recipes i.4.16, and ix.3.3, this syrup is further boiled down to a thicker consistency.

sharāb ward (شراب ورد) syrup infused with rose petals, see glossary 1, s.v. *sharāb* 1. In al-Tujībī's recipes i.4.16 and ix.3.3, it is further boiled down to a thicker consistency.

sharāb ward sukkarī (شراب ورد سكري) sugar syrup infused with rose petals, see glossary 1, s.v. *sharāb* 1. In al-Tujībī's cookbook, it is used in a sweet and sour chicken stew, recipe iii.2.30; and served at the table along with a *jūdhāba* dish in recipe iii.2.31.

sukkar (سكر) sugar obtained from sugarcane, *qaṣab al-sukkar*. In al-Tujībī's cookbook, sugar is used mostly sprinkled on some finished savory dishes cooked with milk, such as recipes i.2.7, 22–4, and 27; and some chicken dishes, as in the *basṭīla*-like *jūdhāba* dish, recipe iii.2.31. It is also the basic sweetener in fillings used in making cookies, as in chapter i.4, and some confections in chapter ix.4. However, with thick puddings and for dousing pastries after baking or frying them, honey that has been boiled and skimmed of its froth is used; see the recipes in chapter i.4. For honey, see *ʿasal* above.

In his account about the Muslim West, al-Qalqashandī, *Ṣubḥ al-aʿshā* v 176, points out that although sugar was produced and processed in al-Maghrib, people there did not care for it because they preferred honey, of which they had plenty. It was even said that in their region only foreigners and the sick used sugar. The quality of sugar produced in al-Maghrib, especially in places like Sous (Sūs), Marrakesh, Salé (Salā), and Alegria, was highly praised, especially refined sugar (*mukarrar*), and said to be comparable to that of Egypt. It was described as intensely white, solid, and fine tasting. It was exported to the entire Muslim West.[9]

Sugar was described as having hot properties, but moderately so in comparison with bee honey. It was also said to be moist, unlike honey, which was dry.

9 See Mūsā, *al-Nashāṭ al-iqtiṣādī fī l-Maghrib al-Islāmī* 240.

As described by Ibn Wāfid, *al-Adwiya al-mufrada* 74, sugar has the power to open obstructions in the system and cleanse it; and unlike honey, it causes neither thirst nor does harm to the stomach.

jamājim al-sukkar (جماجم السكر) molded white sugar cones, more commonly called *sukkar ublūj* or *ṭabarzad* in the eastern region. It was refined white sugar processed in conical pottery molds with three holes in the bottom to allow the remaining molasses and impurities to drip down, leaving behind molded fine white sugar. In al-Tujībī's cookbook, the molded cones of sugar are mentioned only for the analogy, see recipe x.8.1, where pieces of bread are formed into a similar shape.

sukkar abyaḍ (سكر ابيض) refined white sugar. It is used only in two recipes: i.4.16, for Abbasid-style stuffed *qaṭāyif*; and ix.2.11, for a chewy candy.

sukkar masḥūq (سكر مسحوق) crushed sugar used for garnishing dishes, as in recipes i.4.11, iii.2.46, vii.1.6, and ix.3.1.

zumurrudī (زمردي) thick emerald-green pudding, see recipe ix.7.2. The green color is obtained by adding saffron and indigo, *nīlaj*, to the cooking pudding.

5. Dishes and Prepared Foods: Main and Side Dishes, Snacks, Condiments, Pickles, Dips, and Table Sauces

aḥrash (احرش) thin meat patties fried in oil, see recipes ii.5.2 and ii.6.7. Of the varieties made with vegetables, see vii.1.4 with gourd and vii.2.5 with eggplant. The consistency of the prepared *aḥrash* is made just firm enough to be shaped into a thin disc by hand. Cf. *isfīriyya* (entry below), another sort of thin patty, whose consistency is batter-like.

aḥsā' (احساء) soups, see *ḥasū* below.

arnabī (ارنبي), f. ***arnabiyya*** (ارنبية) a moist dish of fried beef, as in recipe ii.1.6; and an eggplant dish, as in recipe vii.2.19. In both cases, both vinegar and the fermented sauce called *murrī* are used to season the dish. Although such dishes have no rabbit (*arnab*) meat in them, they are called so because their color resembles that of its brownish fur.

ʿaṣīda (عصيدة) smooth and dense flour-based soup.

badawiyya (بدوية) 'peasants' dish,' a simple preparation of fried chicken, seasoned with fresh cilantro and onion juice, see recipe iii.2.29.

bādhinjān (باذنجان) eggplant. Al-Tujībī's cookbook offers a generous number of eggplant dishes, such as *Būrāniyya*, recipe ii.1.2; and recipes, i.5.2, ii.1.6, and ii.3.1. It is cooked with dried tuna, pp. 380–1. All of chapter vii.2 deals with meatless eggplant dishes, such as: *arnabiyya*, recipe vii.2.19; stuffed *maḥshū*, recipe vii.2.14; an omelet, *ʿujja*, recipe vii.2.16; stuffed *mirqās* sausages, recipe vii.2.17; eggplant slices dipped in batter and fried, called *mughaffar*, recipe vii.2.15; and many more. Eggplants are also pickled in recipe x.5.1 for *muṣayyar al-bādhinjān*.

badīʿī (بديعي), literally 'unique.' It is a casserole dish made with diced meat and sliced cheese drenched in beaten eggs. This must have been one of the signature dishes in medieval North Africa. A recipe in the thirteenth-century Aleppan cookbook by Ibn al-ʿAdīm includes *badīʿiyya* and describes it as the specialty of the North Africans *min aṭʿimat al-Maghāriba*.[1] It uses the three characteristic ingredients, meat, cheese, and eggs, with some adaptations to the Eastern Mediterranean ways of cooking. The other Andalusi cookbook, *Anwāʿ al-ṣaydala* 11, 25–6, includes three *badīʿī* recipes, which cook the same dish but they differ in many details. Al-Tujībī's version is the longest and most detailed, see recipe ii.3.1.

---

1 Ibn al-ʿAdīm, *Al-Wuṣla ilā-l-ḥabīb* ii 609–10, English trans., *Scents* 137–9.

 | DOI:10.1163/9789004469488_070

FIGURE 118 Dishes spread on *khiwāns*, al-Ḥarīrī, *al-Maqāmāt*, fol. 47v, copied and illustrated by al-Wāsiṭī, detail
BNF, DEPARTMENT OF MANUSCRIPTS, ARAB 5847. SOURCE: GALLICA.BNF.FR/BNF

balāja (بلاجة) a popular Andalusi dish sold in the food markets, see recipe ii.2.45. Probably its name is derived from *balaj* 'merriment' and 'delight,' see al-Zabīdī, *Tāj al-ʿarūs*, s.v. بلج. The Madrid MS, fol. 60r–v, calls it *al-baljiyya al-Asadiyya*, probably named after the Andalusi Arab tribe of Banī Asad.

There seems to have been regional variations on the dish. In the anonymous Andalusi *Anwāʿ al-ṣaydala* 27, the dish is prepared somewhat differently: the meat pieces are fried and no breadcrumbs are used. The author/compiler says that this is the way it was made in the western region, in Cordova, Marrakesh, and in between. Even when breadcrumbs are added, as in al-Tujībī's recipe, it had to be used sparingly, as we learn from the Andalusi market inspector, al-Saqaṭī, *Fī Ādāb al-ḥisba* 39, who criticizes marketplace cooks who beef up the *balāja* they cook with lots of breadcrumbs. Also, according to him, the well-made *balāja* should not be higher than the width of two fingers put together when it is spread in the pan to bake.

banādiq (بنادق) meatballs, which are incorporated into many dishes to supplement the meat that is already cooking in the pot. Recipe ii.6.1 describes how to make them using meat cuts from the thighs (*afkhādh*) and loins (middle back, *sinsin*). *Banādiq* are also made with fish, as in recipe v.1.24.

baqliyyāt (بقليات), sg. ***baqliyya*** (بقلية) vegetable dishes. They were either cooked with meat, as in some of the recipes in chapter ii.2, using cabbages, turnips, chard, and the like, or cooked meatless as in part vii. Such dishes were categorized as feminine (*mu'annatha*), in that they were seasoned plainly, neither sweet nor sour, *sādhaj*, and were served first in a given meal, as they were believed to naturally soften the bowels and ease the digestion of the subsequent dishes.[2]

In the eastern region, meatless *baqliyyāt*, like the ones given in al-Tujībī's part vii, were more commonly called *bawārid al-buqūl* 'cold vegetable dishes' and *muza-*

---

2 See al-Tujībī's introduction, p. 110; and the anonymous thirteenth-century Andalusi cookbook, *Anwāʿ al-ṣaydala* 58.

wwarāt al-buqūl 'simulated vegetarian dishes,' which Christians would eat during Lent, and physicians prescribed them for the sick because they were deemed lighter and easier to digest. See, for instance, the anonymous Egyptian cookbook *Kanz al-fawāʾid*, English trans., *Treasure Trove*, chapter 8; and al-Warrāq's tenth-century cookbook *Kitāb al-Ṭabīkh*, English trans., *Annals*, chapters 45–6.

barkūkas (بركوكس), ***barkūkash*** (بركوكش), also called ***zabzīn*** (زبزين), a variety of soup (*ḥasū*) made with couscous balls the size of a small chickpea each, see recipe i.3.7. This couscous variety is similar to what is called *muḥammaṣ* in recipe i.5.8. It seemed to have been a humble dish not fit for the guests' table, judging from the Andalusi saying (أش دخل بركوكش في الضيافة) "What has *barkūkash* to do with hospitality?"[3]

basbāsiyya (بسباسية) stew of fresh bulb fennel, chopped and cooked with meat, as in recipe ii.2.7. In another recipe, v.1.12, fish is baked in its extracted juice.

bayḍ khifāf li-l-shurb (بيض خفاف للشرب) runny boiled eggs to slurp, see recipe v.2.7, where the eggs are boiled only once and then seasoned with salt and black pepper before having them.

Burāniyya (بورانية) an eggplant dish named after Būrān (d. 883), the wife of Abbasid Caliph al-Maʾmūn, see recipe ii.1.2.

dajāj (دجاج) chicken, the favorite meat to cook in all of al-Andalus. Al-Tujībī's chapter iii.2 abounds with an impressively wide variety of chicken recipes, 49 in all. A good number of them are said to be of Mashriqi origin (i.e., from the eastern region, such as Baghdad, Egypt, and the Levant). Of particular interest are: recipe iii.2.21, described as *Yahūdiyya* 'Jewish,' in which a large chicken is stuffed in the cavity and underneath the skin; *dajājat ʿumrūs* 'the chubby boy's chicken,' recipe iii.2.20, which is a luscious chicken pudding; the elaborate *jūdhāba* dish, reminiscent of today's bastilla, recipe iii.2.31; and many more.

faḥṣī (فحصي), 'the countryside dish,' cooked with diced fatty mutton and suet, with unbroken cinnamon sticks and whole preserved lemons, see recipe ii.2.23.

falyāṭil (فلياطل) *tharīda* made with bread composed of stacked thin discs of dough, see recipes i.2.17 and 24, and n. 67 in the chapter regarding the dish's name.

fustuqiyya (فستقية) pistachio-green meat stew, which gets its color from fresh fava beans, see recipe ii.2.32.

ghassānī (غساني), ***ghassāniyya*** (غسانية) a meat dish sweetened with honey, see recipe ii.2.43. It is a variation on a *muʿassal* dish, recipe ii.2.42. These sweet meat dishes were served within the courses of the main meal. Other *muʿassal* and *ghassānī* recipes are also given in chapter ix.1, prepared as confections and served at the end of the meal. See also recipe i.5.3, for another variety of *ghassānī* cooked as a couscous dish.

---

3 See al-Zajjālī, *Amthāl al-ʿawām* ii 25.

ḥarīra (حريرة) silky-smooth flour-based soup that is flowing in consistency. It is rather thinner than *ḥasū* (entry below). Al-Tujībī's cookbook does not give a *ḥarīra* recipe, only its consistency is mentioned.

harīsa (هريسة) wheat porridge made with meat, recipe ii.6.10, and eaten drizzled with rendered suet. It is also made meatless in recipe i.5.13 and eaten with honey.

ḥasū (حسو), pl. ***aḥsāʾ*** (احساء) soup; it is medium in consistency generally, see recipes i.3.1–8.

> ***ḥasū khāthir*** (حسو خاثر) thickened soup.
> ***ḥasū ṣafīq*** (حسو صفيق) soup dense in consistency.

ḥiṣrimiyya (حصرمية) chicken dish soured with the juice of unripe grapes, *ḥiṣrim*, see recipe iii.2.17.

ḥūt (حوت) fish, which was more commonly called *samak* in the eastern region. See chapter v.1 for an impressive variety of fish dishes.

ḥūt muṣayyar (حوت مصير) pickled fish, preserved in a salt-vinegar solution and kept in jars, see recipe x.6.1. In the eastern region, fish preserved in similar ways were called *mamqūr*. See, for instance, chapter 37 in al-Warrāq, *Kitāb al-Ṭabīkh*, English trans., *Annals* 194–5.

idām (إدام) a general term for condiments, dips, and sauces that were eaten with bread before the main meal to whet the appetite.

isfiriyya (إسفرية), also occurs as *isfāriyya* (إسفارية), *isfiryā* (إسفريا), and *isfīriyya* (إسفيرية) in al-Tujībī's recipes. They are thin and smooth patties, see recipes i.2.17, ii.6.3, and iii.1.1. In the anonymous Andalusi *Anwāʿ al-ṣaydala* 3, 4, 91, 110, and 146, other recipes are found that are made in several different ways. However they are made, what they all have in common is their consistency, which has to be batter-like (i.e., thin enough to be ladled into the skillet and then spread and smoothened into a large disc to fry in a small amount of oil). Cf. another sort of patty, called *aḥrash* (entry above), whose consistency is made just firm enough to be shaped into thin discs by hand.

Jaʿfariyya (جعفرية) a golden-yellow chicken dish. The anonymous author of the Andalusi *Anwāʿ al-ṣaydala* 19, where a simple version of the dish is given, offers a couple of possibilities for the dish's name:

1. Due to the large amount of saffron used, it is compared to *dhahab Jaʿfarī*, the name for the finest kind of gold.[4]
2. It is named after the person who invented it, whose name was *Jaʿfar*.

There is also the possibility that it was named after Jaʿfar b. ʿUthmān al-Muṣḥafī (d. 982), chamberlain of Andalusi Umayyad Caliph al-Ḥakam al-Mustanṣir Billāh (d. 976). It is said that the famous Jaʿfarī gold *dīnār* was minted in his time.[5]

---

4 According to Steingass's *Dictionary* this fine gold was named after a famous alchemist.

5 See Ibn Saʿīd, *al-Mughrib* i 18.

jalīdiyya (جليدية) a 'frosty' bird dish. For a possible explanation of the dish's name, see recipe, iii.2.27, n. 47.

jalja (جلجة) table sauce, dipping sauce, see recipe ii.1.9; the name also occurs as *shalsha* in fish recipe v.1.5. It is similar to the *ṣalṣa*/*ṣulṣ* we encounter in contemporary cookbooks from the eastern region, such as in chapter 16 in the anonymous fourteenth-century Egyptian cookbook *Kanz al-fawāʾid*, English trans., *Treasure Trove*, which offers a variety of 15 recipes. *Jalja* and *shalsha* were the Andalusi dialectal pronunciation (ʿAjamiyya). It is an uncooked dipping sauce that is generally vinegar based; only the garlic it contains is cooked before adding it to the sauce mix to get rid of its strong smell. It is usually served in small bowls, in which the eaters dip their morsels of food.

jashīsh (جشيش), pl. ***jashāʾish*** (جشائش) porridge of coarsely crushed grains and pulses, see recipes i.3.9–11 and i.5.14.

jashīsh aruzz (جشيش ارز) porridge of broken grains of rice, recipe i.3.11.

jashīsh qamḥ (جشيش قمح) porridge of coarsely crushed wheat berries, recipe i.3.9.

jashīsh qiṭniyya bayḍāʾ (جشيش قطنية بيضاء) porridge of a coarsely crushed white variety of sorghum, *Sorghum bicolor*, see recipe i.5.14.

jashīsh shaʿīr (جشيش شعير) porridge of coarsely crushed barley grains, recipe i.3.10.

jināniyya (جنانية) a dish cooked with orchard produce, see recipe vii.9. In recipe i.2.26, *jināniyya* is a vegetarian variety of *tharīd*, which uses all kinds of vegetables.

The dish derives its name from *junayna* (orchard), called so because it incorporates orchard produce. As we are told in the anonymous Andalusi *Anwāʿ al-ṣaydala* 148, it was the custom to cook such dishes in the orchards, picnic style, preferably in summer and fall. In the eastern region, such a dish was called *bustāniyya*; the name is derived from *bustān* 'orchard.' See al-Warrāq's tenth-century *Kitāb al-Ṭabīkh*, English trans., *Annals* 290.

jūdhāba (جوذابة) a sweet and savory chicken dish, a precursor of what in modern Moroccan cuisine is called *basṭīla* (بسطيلة), more commonly called pastilla. See recipe iii.2.31.

The anonymous Andalusi *Anwāʿ al-ṣaydala* 175–7 includes a recipe, which is more or less similar to al-Tujībī's, called *jūdhābat Umm al-Faraj*, and describes it as an Eastern dish (*ṭaʿām Mashriqi*). Indeed, *jūdhāba* recipes are found in all the extant Arabic medieval cookbooks from al-Mashriq; essentially prepared as a sweet and savory dish composed of a sweet pudding of layered thin sheets of bread baked in the *tannūr* (domed clay oven) underneath a roasting chunk of meat suspended above them. See, for instance, al-Warrāq, *Kitāb al-Ṭabīkh*, English trans., *Annals*, chapter 92; and anonymous *Kanz al-fawāʾid*, English trans., *Treasure Trove*, recipes 131, 132, 269, 274, and 294.

In al-Tujībī's recipe, the dish is cooked in an earthenware pan. Layers of thinly rolled out discs of bread alternate with layers of spiced sugar and crushed and split almonds, and they are sprinkled with rosewater enhanced with camphor. Cooked chicken is buried in the middle of the layers. The whole casserole is baked in the brick oven and turned over in one piece when served. Al-Tujībī commends it for its flavor and benefits.

It is also prepared in a baklava-like fashion, without chicken, by alternating layers of *ruqāq* bread with layers of almonds—split and pounded along with sugar, spices, and saffron. The dish would then be moistened with rosewater and sweet olive oil and baked. When done, it is turned over in one piece and eaten with sugar syrup infused with rose petals (*sharāb ward sukkarī*) and fresh butter.

jumlī (جملي) an 'all-in-one dish,'[6] a succulent beef dish that incorporates all cuts of meat, including offal. Judging from this recipe and the ones included in the anonymous Andalusi *Anwāʿ al-ṣaydala* 6, 92, 95, 120, and 151, all *jumlī* dishes contained vinegar and the fermented sauce *murrī*, with a good deal of olive oil. The finished dish would have little sauce left in it. See recipe ii.1.1. It was usually offered as a large festive dish (*ṭaʿām kabīr*). *Jumlī* is also cooked with fish, as in recipe v.1.13, using the same combination of vinegar, *murrī*, and olive oil, with a variety of spices and herbs.

kabar (كبر) capers, see chapter x.4 for ways to preserve them; and recipes vi.1.2–3, where they are used to garnish the dishes.

ʿasālīj al-kabar (عساليج الكبر) caper shoots. The tops and tender sections of the shoots are used in pickling the plant, as shown in chapter x.4. Also to be pickled similarly are:

faqqūṣ al-kabar (فقوص الكبر) young caper berries, which are not fully grown and whose seeds (*zarīʿa*) are still small.

nawār al-kabar (نوار الكبر) caper buds, which have not opened yet, as al-Tujībī explains in recipe x.4.1.

al-kāmil (الكامل) 'the complete dish'; a favorite festive dish that renders offering other dishes with it unnecessary. See recipe ii.2.40 and n. 93 for more details.

karsh maḥshuwwa (كرش محشوة) an elaborate dish of stuffed tripe, see recipe iv.2.

kawāmikh (كوامخ) pickled foods and condiments, see chapters x.1–6 for making mustard sauces, curing olives, pickling lemons, capers, eggplants, onions, turnips, and fish; and making varieties of vinegar and *murrī* sauce.

---

6 I based the meaning of the dish on the assumption that it derived its name from *jumla* 'complete,' 'total,' see Dozy, *Takmilat al-maʿājim* ii 290, s.v. جمل.

Evidently, calling such foods *kawāmikh* was an Andalusi usage of the term. We encounter the same terminology in the fourteenth-century Andalusi scholar al-Arbūlī, *al-Kalām ʿalā l-aghdhiya* 146. Likewise, Ibn al-Ḥashshā', *Mufīd al-ʿulūm* 65, mentions that they are used while eating (بين يدي الطعام) to whet the appetite. In the eastern region, *kawāmikh* specifically designated dairy-based fermented condiments. See, for instance, recipes in al-Warrāq's tenth-century Baghdadi cookbook *Kitāb al-Ṭabīkh*, English trans., *Annals*, chapter 40.

kurunbiyya (كرنبية) cabbage stew cooked with mutton, see recipe ii.2.3.

kuskusū (كسكسو) couscous dishes, recipes i.5.1–5 offer an interesting variety of couscous dishes. We are also given details on how to make couscous grains from scratch and the special pot used in steaming them. For *kuskusū*, the grain, see glossary 2.

lakhṭaj (لخطج) 'silty' soup, thick and slippery in texture, made with flour and milk, see recipe i.3.6.[7]

laqāniq (لقانق) large sausages, see recipe ii.6.6. In other sources, we also come across other variants on the name, such as *maqāniq* and *naqāniq*, or *dakānik*, as in the anonymous Andalusi *Anwāʿ al-ṣaydala*.[8]

lawziyya (لوزية) a dish of mutton simmered in almond sauce, see recipe ii.2.27.

līm muṣayyar (ليم مصير) pickled lemons, see the recipes in chapter x.3 for ways to preserve them. They were used as a table condiment and incorporated into the cooked dishes. In al-Tujībī's cookbook, they are used in dishes as a garnish, as in *tharīd* recipe i.2.10 and yogurt condiment recipe vi.1.2. They are added whole to a dish called *faḥṣī*, recipe ii.2.23; and used in stuffing sheep and birds, as in recipes ii.2.40 and iii.2.22.

Writing in eleventh-century Granada, al-Ṭighnarī, *Zahrat al-bustān* 290, says that pickled lemons were particularly favored by people of the eastern region (*ahl al-Mashriq*). They made them annually, he adds, and stored them in glass containers. He seems to have been implying that in his region at the time they were not as popular. Apparently, by al-Tujībī's time, pickled lemons had already been well-established as a familiar condiment in the western region.[9]

lisān Ṣinhājī (لسان صنهاجي) 'mock tongue,' made with a mixture of pounded meat and flattened into a rectangle to mimic the tongue's shape. Al-Tujībī describes it as *Ṣin-*

---

7 In Dozy, *Takmilat al-maʿājim* ix 223, s.v. لخطج, *lakhṭaj* is said to be a Hebrew term designating 'silt.' And as suggested by Corriente, *Dictionary of Andalusi Arabic*, s.v. *l-kh-ṭ-j*, it may be descriptive of 'slime.' He further adds that the name might have been derived from *lac* 'milk' with a pejorative suffix.

8 Cf. *laqāniq* recipes in al-Warrāq, *Kitāb al-Ṭabīkh*, English trans., *Annals*, chapter 36.

9 Also mentioned by the fourteenth-century Maghribi traveler Ibn Baṭṭūṭa, *Tuḥfat al-nuẓẓār* ii 12. Sixteenth-century al-Ghassānī, *Ḥadīqat al-azhār* 21, uses the term *tābil* 'spicing and seasoning agent' when referring to this condiment and says that commoners in Fez call it *līm musayyar* (ليم مسير).

hājī. It must have been the specialty of Ṣinhāj, one of the largest Amazigh tribes in North Africa.

maḍīra (مضيرة) lamb stew with milk or yogurt, see recipes ii.3.14–5. It was one of the favorite dishes in the eastern region, touted as the healer of all maladies. This white dish was usually served in blue bowls for an aesthetic effect.

maghmūm (مغموم), literally 'covered,' a seasoned chicken dish that is cooked in the *furn* (brick oven) in a pot sealed with flattened dough, see recipe iii.2.32.

maraq (مرق) may generally refer to the liquid in a dish. It is also used in al-Tujībī's cookbook to designate pickle juice and sauce. The latter is a concocted dipping condiment served with the dish; see, for instance, the sauce prepared in recipe ii.6.5, made by combining vinegar, *murrī naqīʿ* (sun-fermented liquid sauce), and mustard sauce. The sauces suggested in recipe iii.2.44 are served with grilled chicken. These sauces were comparable to what was prepared in the eastern region, where they were more commonly called *ṣibāgh*, as in al-Warrāq, *Kitāb al-Ṭabīkh*, English trans., *Annals*, chapters 24, 34, and 35. In addition, the term *maraq*, designating sauce, is also used interchangeably with *jalja* and *shalsha*, as in recipes ii.1.9 and v.1.5, respectively, see *jalja* above.

mardūda (مردودة), literally 'returned,' a *tharīda* dish cooked with mutton, see recipe i.2.6. Apparently, the dish got its name from the twice-fermented bread used in it. Additionally, the bread is not just moistened in the broth when served; it is returned to the pot to further cook in the broth before serving it.

mibʿar (مبعر), pl. *mabāʿir* (مباعر) fresh sausages made with the large intestine, see recipe ii.6.9.

mirqās (مرقاس), ***mirqāsh*** (مرقاش) small sausage links, see recipe ii.6.4. According to the recipe, after the intestines are filled, they are hung to dry in the sun, or smoked.

mislān (مسلان) the entire hip section of the sheep, cooked and served in one piece on top of a *tharīd* dish, see recipe i.2.6. The recipe mentions that serving *tharīd* this way was the custom among city dwellers and peasants in North Africa. *Mislān* is still a traditional festive dish in the region.

muʿallak (معلك), literally 'chewy,' descriptive of the way ingredients, such as bread in recipe i.5.10 or meat and cheese in recipe ii.3.2, are mixed until they become one cohesive mass.

muʿassal (معسل) a meat dish sweetened with honey (*ʿasal*), see recipe ii.2.42. See also *ghassānī* above, which is a variation on *muʿassal*. These sweet meat dishes were served among other courses that constituted the main meal. Other *muʿassal* and *ghassānī* recipes are given in chapter ix.1, where they are prepared as confections and served at the end of the meal.

Ibn Zuhr, *Kitāb al-Aghdhiya* 139, did not approve of the way cooks usually prepared this type of sweet meat dish, which tasted good but caused the meat to toughen in the process. His solution was to cook *muʿassal* the usual way and then discard the meat and replace it with meat already cooked in a simple stew, called *tafāyā bayḍā'* (entry below). The pot would then be allowed to simmer for a short while so that the meat could absorb the stew's flavors.

mufarrij (مفرج) 'comforting dish' of meat braised in the oven with the strained liquid of boiled onions. It is delicately sweet and perfumed with rosewater. *Shuʿāʿ al-shams* 'sunbeams' is cooked the same way. Both of them are variations on the *rāhibī* dish 'monk's food,' cooked with chopped onions, see recipe ii.1.7.

mufattit (مفتت), literally 'the crumbler,' a chicken dish, recipe iii.2.7. As the name suggests, the dish must have been recommended as being good for crumbling stones in the kidneys and bladder. In al-Bustānī, *Muḥīṭ al-Muḥīṭ*, s.v. فت, *al-mufattit* is mentioned as a curative agent recommended by physicians.[10]

mughaffar (مغفر), literally 'clad.' Several recipes in al-Tujībī's cookbook are named thus. See recipe ii.5.4, with rabbit meat; iii.2.8, with chicken; v.1.18, with fish; and vii.2.15, with eggplant. All are cut into pieces and fried after coating or dipping them in batter.

mukhallal (مخلل) a chicken dish soured with vinegar, see recipe iii.2.6. Such dishes were more commonly called *sikbāj* in the eastern region.

mulabbaqa (ملبقة) a variety of *tharīd* made with lamb and crumbled bread, which has been cooked and softened with milk and butter, see recipe ii.3.16. In the eastern region, *mulabbaqa* was regarded as a delicacy valued for its soft texture and rich buttery flavor. Only one *mulabbaqa* recipe survived from there, found in chapter 83 in al-Warrāq's tenth-century Baghdadi cookbook *Kitāb al-Ṭabīkh*, English trans., *Annals* 340.

murawwaj (مروج) a quick and easy fish dish, see recipe v.1.3. In the eastern region, the term commonly used for similar fast cooked dishes was *mulahwaj*; see, for instance, al-Warrāq, *Kitāb al-Ṭabīkh*, English trans., *Annals*, chapter 75.[11] Another *murawwaj* recipe is found in the anonymous Andalusi *Anwāʿ al-ṣaydala* 152–3, where it is said to be the way fish was cooked in Sabta 'Ceuta' and western al-Andalus.

murrī (مري) liquid fermented sauce, which in al-Tujībī's cookbook served as a seasoning ingredient as well as a table sauce offered with cooked foods. Its frequent use in the cookbook points to its ubiquity in the Andalusi cuisine. For *murrī* as a seasoning agent, see glossary 8.

Chapter x.8 in al-Tujībī's cookbook is dedicated to recipes for varieties of *murrī*, fermented and nonfermented. Often, the sauce variety in the recipes is not specified, but it is almost certain that the sun-fermented *murrī naqīʿ* would have been the preferred choice.

---

10 An example given of such a *mufattit* is *ḥajar Yahūdī* (حجر يهودي) 'Jew's stone,' *Lapis judaicus*.

11 For the meaning of the word, see Ibn Manẓūr, *Lisān al-ʿArab*, s.vv. روج and لهج.

The following are *murrī* varieties mentioned as table sauces in al-Tujībī's recipes:

murrī al-ḥūt (مري الحوت) fermented fish sauce, see recipe x.8.13, which describes how to make it and suggests a way for serving it: fish sauce and olive oil are put in a bowl, to which are added chopped onion, fried eggs or fried fish, and olives. See also glossary 8, s.v. *murrī*.

murrī naqīʿ (مري نقيع) sun-fermented liquid sauce, a laborious preparation that takes months to process, see recipes x.8.1–2. In al-Tujībī's cookbook it is incorporated into the cooking dishes as a seasoning agent or made into a sauce by mixing it with other ingredients. It is also used as a table condiment by itself. In recipe ii.2.39, for instance, it is served in small bowls, in which grilled thin strips of mutton are dipped and then eaten. In recipes ii.5.2 and ii.6.7, it is poured over meat patties before serving them.

murūziyya, marwaziyya (مروزية) a sour plum stew seasoned and colored with vinegar and saffron. See recipes ii.1.4–5, where it is cooked with beef, and recipe iii.2.11, with chicken. From Dozy, *Takmilat al-maʿājim* x 51, s.v. مروزيا, we learn that the dish was called *al-ʿāṣimī* in Granada. It must have acquired this name after the plums used in making it. The Andalusi Ibn Luyūn (d. 1349) did indeed mention *al-ʿāṣimī* fruit in his agricultural handbook in verse, *Kitāb Ibdāʾ al-malāḥa*, fol. 29r, pointing out that it was what physicians called *ijjāṣ* 'plums'; it must have been another regional Andalusi plum name besides *ʿayn l-baqar*.

As suggested by Corriente, *Dictionary of Andalusi Arabic*, s.v. *m-r-z*, the name of the dish could have been related to Marū 'Merv' in Central Asia. The dish was in effect the western version of the well-known eastern *sikbāj* and *zīrbāj* dishes typically cooked with vinegar and saffron, and often with a small amount of a sweet agent to balance the flavor.

muṭajjan (مطجن) a casserole dish assembled in an earthenware pan, called a *ṭājin*, and baked in the brick oven (*furn*), as in recipe ii.2.14.

muthallath (مثلث) a meat dish typically cooked with saffron, vinegar, and a kind of vegetable, see al-Tujībī's recipe ii.1.3, which uses turnips.[12] It was offered as a large, elaborately garnished festive dish, *ṭaʿām kabīr*, as described in recipe ii.1.10.

namaksūd (نمكسود) a variety of cured meat, preserved with crushed salt; but unlike *qadīd* (entry below), *namaksūd* is made with ram meat (*kabsh*), either left whole or split in half. The preserved meat remains moist, soft, and greasy; and like fresh meat, it can easily be cut with a knife, see recipe x.11.

12 The anonymous Andalusi *Anwāʿ al-ṣaydala* 204 defines the dish as such, and the vegetables suggested in the definition include turnips, eggplants, gourds, carrots, or lettuce stems stripped of their leaves.

In al-Ḥuṣrī, *Jamʿ al-jawāhir* 239, *namaksūd* is described as meat cut into blocks and then salted, spread on boards, and left in an airy place until it is no longer moist. Preserved thus it can be used as travelers' provisions by soaking it in water before using it.

In *Manāfiʿ al-aghdhiya* 113–5, al-Rāzī describes cured meats like *namaksūd* and *qadīd* as being dry and hot in properties, slow to digest, and offering little nourishment. To drive away the harms of *namaksūd*, al-Rāzī recommends the prolonged soaking of the meat in water first and then cooking it with viscous leafy vegetables like spinach, orach, and chard, along with a good deal of oil and suet.

naql (نقل) snack foods, served as appetizers and mezza offerings. The term is closely associated with drinking sessions, when imbibing alternated with nibbling on small dishes, as in recipe viii.1.7 for fried fava beans that have been sprouted and skinned and recipe ix.3.4 for a marzipan confection called *sanbūsak*.

narjisiyya (نرجسية) a dish that is made to look like narcissus flowers, with their white, green, and yellow colors, see recipes ii.2.17 and iii.2.25.

nīmbarisht (نيمبرشت), *numayrashāt* (نميرشات), *naymarasht* (نيمرشت) poached eggs, see recipe v.2.4. It was deemed the most healthful way to consume eggs.

qadīd (قديد) cured meat, made by cutting meat into thin strips, seasoning it, and then hanging it on ropes in sunny and airy places to dry, as described in recipe x.11.[13] See also *namaksūd* above.

In *Manāfiʿ al-aghdhiya* 113–5, al-Rāzī describes *qadīd* as being dry and hot in properties, slow to digest, and offering little nourishment. We also learn from his book that it was the perfect snack food to have in small amounts to satisfy the fake pangs of hunger that drunkards often experience. He also recommends it for people who wish to push their main meal until later.

qaliyya (قلية) an Andalusi name for a simple dish of fried chopped organ meat and innards, see recipe ii.2.46.

qidr al-farsh (قدر الفرش) a pot of prepared garnishes, see recipe ii.1.10. A large pot is cooked with pieces of tripe and intestines, along with meatballs, egg yolks, and many more, all brightly colored yellow with saffron. They are spread on top of dishes served at festive occasions.

rāhibī (راهبي) 'monks' food,' a dish of meat and chopped onions, braised in the oven in its last cooking stage, see recipe ii.1.7. According to the thirteenth-century anonymous Andalusi cookbook, *Anwāʿ al-ṣaydala* 136–8, baking it in the oven would cook the meat well and give it an appetizing aroma. The dish is delicately sweetened with honey or rose petal jam and perfumed with rosewater. Variations on *rāhibī* are

---

13 Cf. *qadīd* recipe in al-Warrāq, *Kitāb al-Ṭabīkh*, English trans., *Annals* 370, where the cured meat is slowly dried in low-heat oven and formed into interesting spirals. The resulting texture is described as brittle and crumbly to the bite.

mufarrij (comforting) and *shuʿāʿ al-shams* (sunbeams), which are cooked with the strained boiled liquid of the onions rather than the onions themselves. *Rāhibī* is also made with dried tuna (*tunn yābis*), see recipe v.1.30.

ra's maymūn (رأس ميمون) 'blessed head,' a mutton dish in recipe ii.2.44, which is molded to resemble a head using a special earthenware vessel. See also glossary 2 for other varieties prepared as pastries.

Maymūn could be a man's name; it is also a generic name given to designate 'slave' and 'monkey.' I chose to interpret it as 'blessed head' because *maymūn*, as an adjective, means 'blessed' and 'prosperous.' Marks, in *Encyclopedia of Jewish Food*, s.v. *mimouna*, 407–8, suggests that it is a Jewish man's name. Another possibility, which he connects to medieval North African folklore, is that Mimouna was a female demon or goddess, who was regarded as Lady Luck, and her husband is another demon, whose name was Mimoun.

sanbūsak (سنبوسك) a favorite snack food in the medieval eastern region. However, according to al-Tujībī, true *sanbūsak* is a marzipan confection, as in recipe ix.3.4. He had a very low opinion of the type of *sanbūsak* that people of Ifrīqiya made. They stuff them with pounded meat, which to him was utterly tasteless and not at all delicious. The anonymous author of *Anwāʿ al-ṣaydala* 196 does indeed provide a recipe for savory *sanbūsak* pastries stuffed with meat, which he labels as "commoners' *sanbūsak*."

sardīn muṣayyar mumallaḥ (سردين مصير مملح) salt-cured sardines, see recipe, p. 381. For salt-curing small fish, see recipe x.6.2.

shāqūma (شاقومة) a simple *tharīda* dish of cooked mutton with bread sopped in its broth and drizzled with plenty of melted butter. See recipe i.2.15, where it is described as a delicious Amazigh dish.

shāshiyyat ibn al-waḍīʿ (شاشية ابن الوضيع), literally 'cap of the lowborn son,' a delicious variety of *tharīda*, which despite its name was said to please all, high and low, see recipe i.2.8 with its related footnotes for more on the dish. The word *shāshiyya* in the name of the dish was an Andalusi piece of rounded cap-like headgear, some of which were tasseled.[14]

shawā qidr (شوا قدر) pot roast, cooked with beef, recipe ii.1.9; and mutton, recipe ii.2.26. The sealed pot, with chopped meat in it, is cooked in the brick oven.

shuʿāʿ al-shams (شعاع الشمس), literally 'sunbeams,' a dish of braised meat, see *al-mufarrij* and *rāhibī* above.

---

14 Al-Andalus used to export this type of headgear to North Africa. However, after the fall of Granada in 1492, the expelled Moriscos established an enduring *shāshiyya*-making industry in Tunisia. In North Africa today, this originally Andalusi *shāshiyya*, the soft cap-like headgear, is not to be confused with *shāshiyya Istanbūlī* or *Majīdī* (Ottoman style), which is the fez (*ṭarbūsh*).

ṣināb (صناب) mustard sauce, as it was called in the Muslim West. *Khardal* was its common name in the eastern region. Mustard sauce was valued for its hot and dry properties believed to aid digestion. In al-Tujībī's cookbook, it is offered at the table with grilled meat in recipe ii.2.39; and used as a seasoning ingredient in a dish called *ṣinābī*, recipe ii.2.37. Recipes x.1.1–2 describe how to make mustard sauce. For mustard seeds, see glossary 8, s.v. *ṣināb*.

ṣinābī (صنابي) a mutton dish, seasoned with mustard sauce, see recipe ii.2.37; it is recommended for people with weak and cold stomachs.

Ṣinhājī (صنهاجي) meat and vegetable dish, which must have been the specialty of Ṣinhāj, one of the largest Amazigh tribes in North Africa. The dish is cooked in a very large glazed pot to accommodate the wide variety of meats and vegetables, sausages, meatballs, etc. used in making it, see recipe iv.1. The anonymous Andalusi cookbook *Anwāʿ al-ṣaydala* provides two recipes for this dish:

1. Commoners' *Ṣinhājī* (pp. 138–9), made more or less like al-Tujībī's version. The recipe concludes by recommending it as a fit-for-all dish, regardless of the eaters' ages or humoral properties, which is attributed to the inclusion of the myriad meats and vegetables, as well as vinegar, fermented sauce, spices, and much more.
2. *Ṣinhājī mulūkī* (p. 4), a royal dish enjoyed by the elite, made in a much simpler way with less varieties of meat and no vegetables.

It seems to me that a dish like *Ṣinhājī* could well have been the origin of the Spanish festive dish *olla podrida*, famously described by Cervantes in *Don Quixote*, part ii, chapter 20, at the wedding of Camacho.[15]

summāqiyya (سماقية) a chicken dish seasoned and soured with sumac, recipe iii.2.18. It is the only recipe in the book that uses this spice. Sumac did not seem to be as ubiquitous as it was in the eastern region. For sumac, the ingredient, see glossary 8.

ṭaʿām kabīr (طعام كبير) large festive dishes, like *jumlī*, recipe ii.1.1; *muthallath*, recipe ii.1.3; and *ra's maymūn*, recipe ii.2.44. They were elaborately garnished, as described in recipe ii.1.10.

ṭaʿām al-walāʾim (طعام الولائم) festive dishes offered in wedding celebrations. In al-Tujībī's cookbook, dishes prepared for such events are served on large platters, impressively and elaborately garnished, as suggested in recipes ii.2.36 and iii.2.9. Meatballs called *banādiq* and small sausage links called *mirqās* were favorite garnishes, see recipes ii.6.1 and 4, respectively, for making them.

ṭabāhijiyya (طباهجية) a succulent meat fry, see recipes ii.2.29–31, where it is said to be a Mashriqi dish (i.e., of eastern origin).

---

15 For a very interesting discussion of *olla podrida*, See Nadeau, "Spanish Culinary History of Cervantes' 'Bodas de Camacho.'"

tafāyā bayḍā' (تفايا بيضاء) a simple white stew, whose eastern counterpart was *isfīdbāja*. See, for instance, al-Warrāq, *Kitāb al-Ṭabīkh*, English trans., *Annals*, chapter 59. In the anonymous Andalusi *Anwāʿ al-ṣaydala* 58, this dish is categorized as feminine (*mu'annatha*), praised for its balanced properties, and recommended for weak stomachs. In the opinion of the Andalusi polymath Ibn Rushd, *al-Kulliyyāt* 399, it is the simplest way to cook meat and the most balanced in properties.

In medieval Arabic sources, such as Ibn Ḥayyān, *al-Sifr al-Thānī* 322, the name of the famous singer Ziryāb was associated with this dish, see the introduction, section ii.5. For *tafāyā* recipes, see ii.2.1, cooked with mutton; iii.2.1, with chicken; and with fish, p. 369.

tafāyā khaḍrā' (تفايا خضراء) simple green stew, which gets its color from fresh cilantro juice, as in recipe ii.2.2 cooked with mutton; recipe iii.2.2, cooked chicken; and recipe v.1.11, with fish. See *tafāyā bayḍā'* for more on this type of dish.

ṭafshīla (طفشيلة) a porridge-like dish of mutton and crushed pulses, said to be of Mashriqi origin, see al-Tujībī's recipe ii.2.35, where only chickpeas are used. Based on the extant Mashriqi recipes of *ṭafshīl*, the dish is usually cooked with more than one kind of pulse and grain, such as lentils, chickpeas, beans, mung beans, and rice, all in one dish. See, for instance, al-Warrāq, *Kitāb al-Ṭabīkh*, English trans., *Annals*, chapter 66; and al-Warrāq's Istanbul MS, fols. 218r–221r.

tharīda (ثريدة), ***thurda*** (ثردة), pl. ***tharāyid*** (ثرايد) a dish of bread sopped in meat broth. Chapter i.2, with its 27 recipes, offers an impressive variety of such dishes, a testimony to the dish's popularity. *Tharīda* dishes given specific names are discussed in this section, entered alphabetically.

tharīda muthawwama (ثريدة مثومة) *tharīda* made with chicken and cooked with garlic. It was especially made for the Christian Nayrūz, which was celebrated at the beginning of January. See recipe i.2.25.

tharīdat al-qaṭā'if (ثريدة القطائف) *tharīda* cooked with chicken, and it uses *qaṭā'if* pancakes for its bread. See recipe i.2.16.

thūmiyya (ثومية) chicken dish braised with garlic, described as aromatic, see recipe iii.2.28.

tunn muṣayyar fī jarra (تن مصير في جرة) tuna that has been pickled in an earthenware jar, see recipes p. 381. For pickling large fish, see recipe x.6.1, where fish is preserved in a salt-vinegar solution and kept in jars.

turunjāniyya (ترنجانية) stew cooked with mutton and leaves of *turunjān*, which is lemon balm, also called balm mint. This herb has a gentle scent of citrus. For the ingredient, see glossary 8; for the dish, see recipe ii.2.9.

ʿujja (عجة) an omelet dish, of which we are given only two varieties in the book of *Fiḍāla*: in recipe v.2.8, the eggs are whipped with cilantro juice, breadcrumbs, and nuts. In recipe vii.2.16, they are mixed with mashed boiled eggplants, breadcrumbs, and seasonings.

ʿ*uṣb* (عصب), ʿ*uṣbān* (عصبان), sg. ʿ*uṣba* (عصبة), ʿ*aṣīb* (عصيب), and ʿ*aṣṣāba* (عصّابة). Generally, they are strips of meat wrapped in caul fat, tied with intestines, and roasted. Based on recipe i.2.2, they are pieces of tripe tied with cleaned intestines wrapped all around them and boiled. In recipe ii.2.39, they are pieces of sheep's tripe and heart threaded through a skewer, secured by wrapping them in caul fat, and then the entire thing is wrapped with a piece of the intestine wound all around them and grilled. Grilled rolls such as these are still made today in countries like Turkey, where they are called *kokorec*.

Yahūdiyya (يهودية) a Jewish dish of a simmered chicken, which has been stuffed in the cavity and underneath the skin with a seasoned mix of boiled eggs and breadcrumbs, see recipe iii.2.21.

zabzīn (زبزين) a variety of soup (*ḥasū*), also called *barkūkash*, see the entry above.

zaytūn (زيتون) cured table olives. Unripe green olives (*zaytūn akhḍar*) and those that have just turned black (*zaytūn aswad*) were cured by brining. Table olives were also made with fully ripe black olives by salt-curing them. In this edible form, olives were served as a table condiment along with other dishes, and as an ingredient in cooking the dishes. In al-Tujībī's recipes, olives are often used to garnish the ready to serve dishes.

Olives were cured in several ways. The following are the varieties included in al-Tujībī's chapter x.2:

zaytūn musharraḥ (زيتون مشرح) brined green olives, which have been scored at several places, see recipe x.2.1.

zaytūn maksūr (زيتون مكسور) brined green olives, which have been cracked, see recipe x.2.2.

zaytūn mutammar (زيتون متمر) fully ripe black olives, which have been cured by bruising them first and then putting a heavy weight on them to drain their moisture. They are stored in jars submerged in olive oil. See recipe x.2.4.

Cured olives were believed to strengthen the stomach and open blockages. They also had the power to stimulate the appetite, provided they were eaten in the middle of the meal, so that they might prevent digesting food from lingering in the stomach. Otherwise, olives were not regarded as a significant source of nutrition.

zīrbājiyya muḥallāt (زيرباجية محلاة) golden chicken stew, mildly soured and sweetened, recipe iii.2.5.

6. Fats and Oils

alya (الية) sheep tail fat, mentioned only twice in al-Tujībī's cookbook, recipes ii.2.34 and ii.2.39, for a dish of mutton with crushed chickpeas and grilling a yearling ram, respectively. Based on al-Tujībī's corpus of recipes, suet (*shaḥm*) was the preferred solid fat in Andalusi cuisine. This may be attributed to the sheep breeds indigenous to North Africa and southern Spain, which were thin tailed, unlike the sheep of the eastern region, with their impressively large fatty tails.

duhn (دهن), pl. *adhān* (ادهان) commonly used to designate oil extracted from nuts and seeds rather than olives. Olive oil is called *zayt* (entry below).

duhn al-bunduq (دهن البندق) hazelnut oil, see recipe x.10 for ways to extract it.

duhn al-fustuq (دهن الفستق) pistachio oil, see recipe x.10 for ways to extract it.

duhn al-jawz (دهن الجوز) walnut oil. It is used in making pastries, as in recipe i.4.12, for *jawzīnaq* (walnut pinwheel cookies), and recipe ix.4.1 for another *jawzīnaq*, which is a walnut confection.

duhn al-lawz al-ḥulw (دهن اللوز الحلو) oil of sweet almonds, see recipe x.10 for ways to extract it. The same method can be used to extract the oils of walnuts, hazelnuts, pistachios, pine nuts, and sesame seeds. The recipe recommends using these oils while still fresh, as they get rancid quite fast. Almond oil is recommended for frying the delicate ring cookies *Qāhiriyya* in recipes ix.3.1 and 3; and in a *lawzīnaj* recipe (almond brittle) ix.4.2; and recipe ix.6.1 for *fānīdh* (pulled sugar taffy).

duhn al-ṣanawbar (دهن الصنوبر) oil of pine nuts, see recipe x.10 for ways to extract it.

duhn al-simsim (دهن السمسم), ***zayt al-simsim*** (زيت السمسم) sesame oil; more commonly called *shayraj* in the eastern region. It was an insignificant food item in al-Andalus and al-Maghrib, where olive oil was dominant. According to al-Qalqashandī, *Ṣubḥ al-aʿshā* v 175, sesame production was scant in the region, and they did not bother to extract *shayraj* 'sesame oil' from it because they had olive oil, which was used even in making the *muzawwarāt* 'meatless dishes' for the sick. Sesame oil, he adds, was used for medicinal purposes mainly, and for anything else, olive oil was the preferred fat, even in making desserts.

In al-Tujībī's cookbook, only once is it suggested that sesame oil is favored to olive oil, in recipe vi.3.3 for fried cheese, and even there, its use was dependent on its availability. *Wa in amkana* 'if possible'—the expression al-Tujībī uses in the recipe—does give the impression that its production was not abundant. Additionally, the disadvantage of sesame oil, which rendered it unsuitable for a wider usage, was the belief

FIGURE 119 A fat-tailed sheep, al-Qazwīnī, *ʿAjāʾib al-makhlūqāt wa gharāʾib al-mawjūdāt*, fol. 364r, detail
FROM THE NEW YORK PUBLIC LIBRARY, SPENCER COLLECTION: HTTPS://DIGITALCOLLECTIONS.NYPL.ORG/ITEMS/C39478C0-28EC-0138-CFB8-1D225A876C35

that it went rancid and deteriorated quite fast, and hence had to be used fresh only, as cautioned in al-Tujībī's recipe x.10. The seeds themselves were equally insignificant as a culinary ingredient, see glossary 8, s.v. *simsim*.

samn (سمن) ghee, a common ingredient in al-Tujībī's cookbook; sometimes used interchangeably with butter, especially in *tharīd* dishes and pastries. It is frequently used in making pastries and desserts; it is boiled with honey and drizzled on rich breads and pastries and rubbed into couscous and pasta grains to moisten them. For frying purposes, it is used in dishes that do not require prolonged cooking, as with scrambled eggs. In an interesting segment in recipe vi.2.3, there are instructions for turning ghee into fresh butter when the latter is not available.

samn ṭayyib (سمن طيب) fine-tasting ghee.

shaḥm (شحم) suet, used when still very fresh (*ṭarī*) for optimum flavor. It is frequently used in dishes with meat to moisten them, added either in chunks, diced, or pounded into bone-marrow consistency. In a dish of roasted lamb stuffed with couscous, recipe i.5.4 for instance, it is pounded with spices and used to smear the inside of the lamb with it before stuffing it.

shaḥm al-kilā (شحم الكلى) kidney fat, used in recipe i.4.28 for layering puff pastry after pounding it into bone-marrow consistency.
shaḥm mudhāb (شحم مذاب) rendered suet, used in recipe i.4.18 for a layered type of pastry.
shaḥm ṭarī (شحم طري) fresh suet.

wadak (ودك) melted fat of meat resulting from cooking it in liquid. In al-Tujībī's cookbook, it is collected, strained, and returned to the dish, especially in the last stage of browning it in the brick oven, which is frequently done in recipes.
zayt (زيت) olive oil, the most frequently used fat in al-Tujībī's recipes for savory and sweet dishes alike; and used for frying. Although it is mentioned as just *zayt* at many places in al-Tujībī's cookbook, it occurs even more often specified as *zayt ʿadhb* (زيت عذب), *zayt ḥulw* (زيت حلو), and *zayt ṭayyib* (زيت طيب), which are descriptive of fine-tasting sweet and mellow olive oil extracted from fully ripe olives and often refined, resulting in olive oil that is free of astringency and acidity.

Based on the thirteenth-century Maghribi historian al-Marrākushī (d. 1250),[1] three olive oil varieties were commercially produced:

1. ***zayt al-yadd*** (زيت اليد) 'hand-pressed,' also called *zayt al-miʿṣara* (زيت المعصرة) 'extracted with a press.' This was the untreated cold-pressed olive oil, described as green (*akhḍar*). Good quality oil of this sort was said to be freshly extracted (*ṭarī*), clear (*ṣāfī*), and fine tasting (*ṭayyib*). It was the equivalent of today's extra virgin olive oil.

   Al-Ṭighnarī, *Zahrat al-bustān* 204–5, calls similar extra virgin olive oil *zayt al-nuqṭa* (زيت النقطة) (i.e., olive oil that oozes drop by drop); it was deemed the best as it was extracted without resorting to water or heat. According to his method, recently gathered fine olives are gently crushed (to avoid breaking the stones) in the evening, and then they are put in a large vessel and thoroughly pressed by feet until oil starts to come out of the olives. The crushed olives are then kept suspended above tubs overnight to receive the dripping oil, which is strained and stored in jars.

1 Al-Marrākushī, *Wathāʾiq al-Murābiṭīn wa-l-Muwaḥḥidīn*, 288–91, 458–9.

2. ***zayt al-mā'*** (زيت الماء), literally 'water olive oil', called so because it was treated with water. This variety was described as green, clear, pure (*naqī*), sweet (*'adhb*), and fine tasting (*ṭayyib*). From al-Marrākushī we learn it was a more desirable commodity and higher in price than *zayt al-yadd* because it was thinner in consistency and clearer.

   In the eastern region of al-Mashriq, this variety of olive oil was called *zayt maghsūl* (زيت مغسول), literally 'washed olive oil.' Olives were first crushed with a small amount of salt (1/20 of their weight) and pressed between wooden blocks. Then, the resulting pressed oil was mixed and beaten (*yuḍrab*) with fresh water (*mā' 'adhb*); this was done several times (*duf'āt*). In the last change of water, the vessel would be left for a while until the oil separated and came up to the surface, and then it was collected.[2] This was believed to improve the oil's properties and purify it, eliminating its acidity and astringency.

   This would have been the kind of refined olive oil predominantly used in al-Tujībī's recipes, described as fine-tasting sweet and mellow olive oil. Also, it is called ***zayt ḥulw akhḍar*** (زيت حلو أخضر) sweet green olive oil once, in recipe i.5.5, where it is offered as a condiment in a small bowl to be eaten with couscous.

3. ***zayt maṭbūkh*** (زيت مطبوخ), literally 'cooked olive oil,' called so because it was treated with heat. It was another variety of refined olive oil, described as clear (*ṣāfī*) and fine tasting (*ṭayyib*), but not green. Al-Anṭākī, *Tadhkira* 200, describes the process of extracting oil from olives by cooking them: The fully ripe olives are first crushed, then cooked (*yuṭbakh*) on the fire, and their oil is pressed out in the oil presses. The resulting oil, he says, is called *zayt 'adhb* 'sweet olive oil,' whose properties are moderately hot and dry. In al-Tujībī's cookbook, olive oil is given the name *zayt maṭbūkh* only once, recipe vii.2.18, where it is incorporated into a vinegar-based sauce for fried eggplants.

   We also learn from the twelfth-century Andalusi agronomist al-Ṭighnarī, *Zahrat al-bustān* 210–1, of a way to remove the characteristic odor of olive oil and prevent it from solidifying in winter by 'cooking' it in a double boiler, which he calls *inā' muḍā'af*. A large pot made of copper or earthenware is filled with water and a smaller glazed pot is filled with olive oil and suspended in the larger one from its handles; three-quarters of it must be immersed in the water. Fire is lighted underneath the big pot and the cooking goes on until the

2 As explained in anonymous, *Taṣānīf al-aṭ'ima*, fols. 57v–58r. It is a medieval volume on dietetics, 65 folios long, frequently supplemented with recipes, Wellcome Library MS Arabic 57. Although the script is Maghribi, it clearly originated in the eastern region, al-Mashriq, judging from the culinary content.

FIGURE 120 Olives, al-Qazwīnī, *ʿAjāʾib al-makhlūqāt wa gharāʾib al-mawjūdāt*, fol. 164v, detail
FROM THE NEW YORK PUBLIC LIBRARY, SPENCER COLLECTION: HTTPS://DIGITALCOLLECTIONS.NYPL.ORG/ITEMS/DAF7EAB0-28EB-0138-4299-0CDA5977DCD5

olive oil heats up and starts to bubble. Water in the large pot should be replenished with hot water whenever it decreases. Al-Ṭighnarī says the resulting oil is called *zayt shārij* (heat-treated olive oil),[3] and he says it is quite delicious when used with all sorts of dishes, especially *tharīda* (bread sopped in meat broth, see al-Tujībī's chapter i.2).

In al-Tujībī's cookbook, olive oil is further described in the following terms:

zayt ʿakir (زيت عكر) cloudy olive oil, which can be remedied as instructed in recipe x.9.2.
zayt muntin (زيت منتن) unsavory olive oil, see recipe x.9.2 for ways to remedy it.
zayt ṭarī (زيت طري) fresh, recently pressed olive oil.

3 Al-Ṭighnarī is our only source for treating olive oil with heat generated by means of a double boiler to improve its flavor. Interestingly, sesame oil extracted by grinding the seeds first and then kneading them with hot water to extract the oil was called *shayraj*.

Ibn Rushd, *al-Kulliyyāt* 399, highly praises olive oil for its nutritious benefits and balanced properties, which slightly lean towards heat. In his opinion, olive oil is greatly suited to human consumption. That is why, he says, all meats are cooked with it in his country, al-Andalus.

zayt al-simsim (زيت السمسم) sesame oil, more commonly called *duhn al-simsim* (entry above).

zubd (زبد) butter, used frequently in al-Tujībī's recipes by incorporating it into the cooking dishes or generously drizzling it all over the ladled ones just before serving them and after heating it up and straining it. It is also mixed with honey and drizzled all over fried and baked pastries. Recipe vi.2.3 describes how it is extracted from milk, and how to reconstruct it from ghee.

zubd ṭarī (زبد طري) fresh butter.

7. Fruits and Nuts

ʿayn al-baqar (عين البقر), *ʿanbaqar* (عنبقر), *ʿabqar* (عبقر), and *ʿayn* (عين) generic name for plums, *Prunus subg. Prunus*. This was the fruit's name in al-Andalus; it was more commonly known as *ijjāṣ* in the eastern region.[1] Al-Ishbīlī, *ʿUmdat al-ṭabīb* ii 419, says that *ʿayn al-baqar* was what their physicians referred to as *ijjāṣ* and adds that it was called so because of its resemblance to the pupil of the cow's eye in size and shape. He also mentions many prune varieties, ranging in color from red to yellow, black, and white, and those that were the size of big olives and others as big as chicken eggs. The latter variety is called *shāhlūk* (شاهلوك), it is greenish white, with a hint of bitterness. It is sweet but dense in texture and not so juicy, which causes it to lack the laxative property for which plums are known.[2]

Of the kinds that were brought to al-Andalus in dried form (*muzabbab*) and stored in jars, al-Ishbīlī mentions:

ijjāṣ Armīnī (إجاص أرميني) cherry plums, also known as myrobalan plums, *Prunus cerasifera*; called *ihlīlaj* in al-Tujībī's recipes. See also the *ihlīlaj* entry in this section.

ijjāṣ Dimashqī (إجاص دمشقي) damson plums, *Prunus domestica subsp. insititia*, said to be similar in shape to pigeons' eggs.

According to al-Ishbīlī, the best of the dried varieties were the ones imported from Asia Minor, especially in the areas close to Pergamon, Galen's city. The Byzantine variety of dried plums used in al-Tujībī's beef recipes ii.1.4–5 for *murūziyya* must have been the Armenian plums mentioned above. In the recipes it is specifically called *ihlīlaj* (entry below); and in a fresh tuna dish, recipe v.1.26, sour *ihlīlaj* in particular is used.

ballūṭ (بلوط) acorns, fruits of the *ballūṭ* tree, *Quercus*, used once in al-Tujībī's cookbook in recipe iii.2.43 for chicken. Al-Ghassānī, *Ḥadīqat al-azhār* 57, says that it is a well-known food and that there were two main types of it, the rounded and the oblong. Chestnuts (*shāhballūṭ*), he says, are a variety of acorn, see *qasṭal* below.

With their cold and dry properties, acorns were believed to have the power to control bowel and bladder movements.[3]

---

1 As confirmed in Andalusi books on botany and horticulture, such as al-Ṭighnarī, *Zahrat al-bustān* 229; and al-Ghāfiqī, *Kitāb fi-l-Adwiya al-mufrada*, fols. 10v–11r. Note that the name *ijjāṣ* in al-Andalus designated pears (*kummathrā*).

2 See also al-Bīrūnī, *al-Ṣaydana* 24–6.

3 See Ibn al-Bayṭār, *al-Jāmiʿ* i 151.

 | DOI:10.1163/9789004469488_072

FIGURE 121 A plum tree, *ijjāṣ*, Dioscorides, *Fī Hayūlā al-ṭibb*, translation by Ḥunayn b. Isḥāq, fol. 92v, detail
FROM THE NEW YORK PUBLIC LIBRARY, SPENCER COLLECTION: HTTPS://DIGITALCOLLECTIONS.NYPL.ORG/ITEMS/5E66B3E8-E0D2-D471-E040-E00A180654D7

FIGURE 122 Acorns, al-ʿUmarī, *Masālik al-abṣār*, fol. 149v, detail
BNF, DEPARTMENT OF MANUSCRIPTS, ARAB 2771. SOURCE: GALLICA.BNF.FR/BNF

biṭṭīkh (بطيخ) designates both watermelon (*Citrullus lanatus*/*vulgaris*) and muskmelon (common melon, *Cucumis melo*). Often, it is hard to tell which variety is being referred to in the medieval recipes, for instance, especially when contextual clues are lacking. In al-Tujībī's chapter on handwashing preparations, two recipes use melon peels: in xii.2, they are just mentioned as *qushūr al-biṭṭīkh*, which could be either one; recipe xii.5 specifically mentions the white part of the melon rind, *shaḥm al-biṭṭīkh*, which points to watermelon.

More detailed accounts of melon varieties may be found in some of the medieval Andalusi books on botany and horticulture. From these we learn the following:[4]

1. ***biṭṭīkh*** (بطيخ) muskmelons, common melons, *Cucumis melo*, of which there were many types, such as:

biṭṭīkh sukkarī (بطيخ سكري), called so because it is sweet; also called *miʿnāq* because it has a long neck; *biṭṭīkh ʿuqābī* because its neck is curved like the eagle's beak; and al-*miʿnāq* because its neck is long. It is described as a large variety of muskmelon, rough skinned and pleasant smelling, with sweet yellow flesh.

biṭṭīkh ijjāṣī (بطيخ اجاصي) which looks like a large pear, with a wide base and no neck on top, like a cone (*makhrūṭ*). It has a rough skin and dense flesh.

biṭṭīkh baṭṭī (بطيخ بطي) a small variety that looks like a duck with its short and curved neck.

biṭṭīkh Jazīrī (بطيخ جزيري) called so because it grew abundantly in al-Jazīra al-Khaḍrāʾ (Algeciras, in southern Spain).

al-biṭṭīkh al-Mursī (البطيخ المرسي) was grown in Murcia in southeast Spain. It is described as a large variety of muskmelon, with cracking, rough dusty-yellow skin, it has a good deal of flesh, but not so sweet.

biṭṭīkh Armīnī (بطيخ ارميني) 'Armenian muskmelon,' grown abundantly in Valencia and Egypt. In the Levant, it was called *dastubawayh* (دستبويه), *luffāḥ* (لفاح) in Egypt, and *Khurāsānī* (خراساني) and *shammām* (شمام) in Iraq. It is *Cucumis dudaim*, called Queen Ann's pocket melon in English. This variety of muskmelon is round and small with a thin skin. It is fleshy, but the flesh is soft; it is extraordinarily aromatic, but not so sweet. Its skin is yellow with reddish stripes. Because of these stripes, it was also called *biṭṭīkh ʿitābī* (بطيخ عتابي) after the fashionable striped cloth of *al-ʿitābiyya* at the time.

2. ***dullāʿ*** (دلاع) watermelon, *Citrullus lanatus/vulgaris*. This was its name in the Muslim West. Its Amazigh name was *Aflasṭīn* (أفلسطين). In the eastern region, it was called *biṭṭīkh Filasṭīnī* (بطيخ فلسطيني) 'watermelon of Palestine'; *biṭṭīkh Hindī* and *Sindī* (بطيخ هندي, بطيخ سندي) 'Indian watermelon'; and *biṭṭīkh Shāmī* (بطيخ شامي) 'Levantine watermelon.' It is a striped type of watermelon (*muṭarraq*), with a good deal of flesh that is profusely juicy. Its varieties include: watermelon with an intensely green skin and black seeds, and watermelon with yellowish-green skin and dark brown seeds.

With their cold and moist properties, all varieties of melon, albeit in varying degrees, were believed to cleanse the stomach, kidneys, and bladder. They were also recom-

4 Sources used here are Ibn al-ʿAwwām, *al-Filāḥa al-Andalusiyya* iv 375–7, 387; al-Ishbīlī, *ʿUmdat al-ṭabīb* i 86; and Ibn al-Bayṭār, *al-Jāmiʿ* i 135.

FIGURE 123
Hazelnuts, *bunduq*, al-ʿUmarī, *Masālik al-abṣār*, fol. 255r, detail
BNF, DEPARTMENT OF MANUSCRIPTS, ARAB 2771. SOURCE: GALLICA.BNF.FR/BNF

mended as a diuretic and were good for fevers. Their peels were used dried and crushed to cleanse and exfoliate the skin and to remove greasy odors from hands and the mouth.[5]

qushūr al-biṭṭīkh (قشور البطيخ) melon peels, used in a handwashing preparation, *ushnān*, in recipe xii.2. The recipe does not specify which variety of melon is to be used. However, judging from an *ushnān* recipe in al-Tamīmī, *Ṭīb al-ʿarūs*, recipe 266, it is more likely to be muskmelon.

shaḥm al-biṭṭīkh (شحم البطيخ) white part of the watermelon rind, used in a handwashing preparation, *ushnān*, in recipe xii.5.

bunduq (بندق) hazelnuts, *Corylus avellana*. Al-Ghassānī, who lived in sixteenth-century Fez, says that hazelnut trees grew in al-Andalus and gives *jillawz* (جلّوز) as their name in North Africa.[6] According to Ibn al-ʿAwwām, *al-Filāḥa al-Andalusiyya* ii 351–5, the varieties available were the rounded hazelnuts and the elongated ones.

As reflected in al-Tujībī's recipes, their culinary use was negligible; they are mentioned only once in recipe x.10, along with other nuts, on ways to extract their oil, but they must have been consumed as a snack food. Their properties were said to be moderately hot and dry, and based on al-Anṭākī, *Tadhkira* 92, having them with pepper would arouse coitus, and consuming them mixed with sugar was said to cure

5 Ibn al-Bayṭār, *al-Jāmiʿ* i 136.
6 See al-Ghassānī, *Ḥadīqat al-azhār* 66–7.

coughs. On the hand, they were said to be the densest of all nuts and the least nourishing, slowing digestion and causing dense winds.

dhukār (ذكار) caprifig, the male, pollen-bearing wild variety of the common fig tree, used to pollinate the edible fig, see *tīn* below.

fustuq (فستق) pistachios, *Pistacia vera*. They are used sparingly in al-Tujībī's recipes; often mixed with other nuts. Two recipes that bear the name *fustuqiyya*, ii.2.32 and viii.1.1, are called so not because pistachios are used in making them but because they are pistachio green. This was due to the limited access to this sort of nut. Based on the account of al-Qalqashandī on al-Maghrib, neither pistachio nor hazelnut trees grew there; what they had was all imported from the land of the Franks (Bilād al-Faranj).[7] In a recipe for a chewy candy, ix.2.10, pistachios are said to be used if available *in amkana*;[8] otherwise, almonds may be used as a substitute for them. Indeed, we do read in al-Ishbīlī, *ʿUmdat al-ṭabīb* 482–3, that the best were imported from the Levant, where they grew abundantly; as for the varieties grown in al-Andalus, he mentions three: *mufallaq*, *imlīs*, and *birjīn*, of which there were male and female trees. Al-Ṭighnarī, *Zahrat al-bustān* 307, mentions that the female pistachio tree would stop producing if the male next to it was cut off.[9]

In books on dietetics and botany, pistachios are described as having much hotter properties than those of almonds and walnuts; they are dry, somewhat astringent, and bitter. They were said to be good for the stomach and liver due to their astringency and pleasant aroma and were also said to be best eaten after meals. They sweeten the breath, stop palpitations, and generate good blood; they invigorate coitus, nourish the brain, and improve memory and mental faculties.[10] Pistachios were also included in foods believed to bring joy to the heart (*mufarriḥ*).[11] Interestingly, pistachios were also used in aromatic preparations: In a recipe for *ghāliya*, a perfume compound, the parched kernels are crushed and mixed with other aromatics.[12] In al-Zahrāwī, *Kitāb al-Taṣrīf* 274, charred pistachio shells (قشور الفستق المحرقة) were included in his list of ingredients used in making aromatic compounds.

ḥabb al-buṭm (حب البطم) berries of the terebinth tree (*shajarat al-buṭm*), *Pistacia terebinthus*; they are called *al-ḥabba al-khaḍrā*ʾ, literally 'the green berries.' They are

7 Al-Qalqashandī, *Ṣubḥ al-aʿshā* v 176.

8 This addition is found only in the BL MS, fol. 188r.

9 See also al-Ghassānī, *Ḥadīqat al-azhār* 228.

10 See Ibn Waḥshiyya, *al-Filāḥa al-Nabaṭiyya* ii 1182; Ibn al-Bayṭār, *al-Jāmiʿ* iii 222; Ibn Wāfid, *al-Adwiya al-mufrada* 80; Ibn Jazla, *Minhāj al-bayān*, fol. 157v.

11 See, for instance, Ibn Qāḍī Baʿalbak, *Mufarriḥ al-nafs* 98.

12 Al-Kindī, *al-Taraffuq fī l-ʿiṭr* 70.

FIGURE 124 A pistachio tree, Dioscorides, *Fī Hayūlā al-ṭibb*, translation by Ḥunayn b. Isḥāq, fol. 66r, detail
FROM THE NEW YORK PUBLIC LIBRARY, SPENCER COLLECTION: HTTPS://DIGITALCOLLECTIONS.NYPL.ORG/ITEMS/5E66B3E8-A9D2-D471-E040-E00A180654D7

FIGURE 125 Terebinth trees, Dioscorides, *Fī Hayūlā al-ṭibb*, translation by Ḥunayn b. Isḥāq, fol. 42r, detail
FROM THE NEW YORK PUBLIC LIBRARY, SPENCER COLLECTION: HTTPS://DIGITALCOLLECTIONS.NYPL.ORG/ITEMS/5E66B3E9-2573-D471-E040-E00A180654D7

small oblate berries, which grow in bunches and are left to dry on the trees. In their dried from, they are like nuts, with green and oily shriveled skins, hard shells, and oily kernels that taste somewhat like pistachios.

Terebinth seeds were valued for their oil, and they were believed to invigorate coitus and help with weight gain. However, they were said to be bad for the stomach. The tree's aromatic resin was highly regarded as an aid to digestion when chewed regularly. It was deemed even better than mastic gum. The entire plant is astringent, and with its hot and dry properties, it was believed to dispel winds and aid menstruation.[13] The seeds are used in al-Tujībī's recipe x.9.1, in combination with other seeds, to make oil, which can be used when olive oil is not available.

al-ḥabba al-khaḍrā' (الحبة الخضراء) terebinth berries, see *ḥabb al-buṭm* above.

ḥiṣrim (حصرم) unripe grapes, see *ʿinab* below.

ihlīlaj (اهليلج) myrobalan plums, also known as cherry plums, *Prunus cerasifera*, a plum variety. In al-Andalus, the plum was generically called *ʿayn al-baqar* (entry above). In the eastern region, al-Mashriq, it was called *ijjāṣ*.

In al-Tujībī's recipe ii.1.4 for *murūziyya*, *ihlīlaj* is said to be a variety of *ʿayn al-baqar*. The recipe further explains that these plums are imported from Byzantium (Bilād al-Rūm), from which we may deduce that they were transported and stored in dried form. This type of plum was called *qarāṣiyā* in medieval Egypt, where it was similarly used in a *marwaziyya* dish in the fourteenth-century Egyptian *Kanz al-fawā'id*, English trans., *Treasure Trove*, recipe 65.

The Byzantine plums used in al-Tujībī's abovementioned recipe are called *ijjāṣ Armīnī* (إجاص أرميني) in al-Ishbīlī, *ʿUmdat al-ṭabīb* ii 419. According to him, they were the best of the plum varieties that were dried (*tuzabbab*) and transported from Asia Minor, especially from the areas close to Pergamon, Galen's city.

ihlīlaj ḥāmiḍ (اهليلج حامض) sour myrobalan plums, used in recipe v.1.26 for a dish of baked fresh tuna.

Note that the *ihlīlaj*/*halīlaj* 'myrobalan' we encounter in the medieval books on dietetics in the eastern region were only valued for their medicinal benefits and were not enjoyed as food due to their unpleasant bitter and astringent taste. See, for instance, Ibn al-Bayṭār, *al-Jāmiʿ* iv 502, s.v. *halīlaj*. This indeed must have necessitated al-Tujībī's explanation that the *ihlīlaj* being used in recipe ii.1.4 for *murūziyya* is the cooking myrobalan, a variety of *ʿayn al-baqar*, the table-fruit plum.

ʿinab (عنب) grapes, grown plentifully in al-Andalus. They were consumed as a fruit, and the juice was taken as a drink, either fresh or made into wine. The juice was also boiled into a syrup consistency, called *rubb* and *ʿaqīd*, which was used as a sweetening agent, like honey; or diluted and taken as a nonalcoholic drink, as mentioned in glossary 1. It was also preserved in an unfermented state in jars treated with mustard seeds, as described in the last recipe in the book.

ḥiṣrim (حصرم) sour unripe grapes, the best are said to be the ones that have no trace of sweetness in them. With their cold and dry properties, they were

13 See Ibn Wāfid, *al-Adwiya al-mufrada* 137–8; Ibn al-Bayṭār, *al-Jāmiʿ* i 134–6; and al-Anṭākī, *Tadhkira* 84.

believed to curb an excess in yellow bile, cure vertigo, and relieve thirst. Drinks made with it were said to strengthen the stomachs of pregnant women and prevent fetuses from aborting. They were also said to control bowel movements, strengthen the liver, and excite the appetite. On the other hand, *ḥiṣrim* can generate winds and cause colic.[14]

In al-Tujībī's *Fiḍāla*, fresh juice of *ḥiṣrim* is used in a chicken recipe, iii.2.17; *ḥiṣrim* juice preserved by 'cooking' it under the sun's heat (*maʿmūl lil-shams*) is given as an alternative. For *khall ḥiṣrim*, see glossary 8, s.v. *khall*.

ghazl al-karm (غزل الكرم) young shoots of grape vines; chopped and added as a vegetable to a summer *jināniyya* dish in al-Tujībī's recipe i.2.26.

ʿinab akḥal (عنب اكحل) black grapes. *Akḥal* is a western dialectal term for *aswad* 'black.'

ʿinab ḥulw (عنب حلو) sweet grapes.

musṭār (مسطار) juice of recently pressed grapes, see entry in glossary 1.

thufl al-ʿinab (ثفل العنب) grape pomace, which is the pulpy substance left after pressing juice from grapes. It is used in recipe x.7.5, along with grapes to remedy vinegar that has weakened in acidity.

ʿunqūd ʿinab (عنقود عنب) a bunch of grapes.

waraq dāliya (ورق دالية), ***waraq karm*** (ورق كرم) grape leaves, used fresh and wetted in recipe i.1.2 to give a gloss to baking breads; and to protect a jar of fermenting milk in recipe vi.2.2.

jawz (جوز) walnuts; they grew abundantly in the Muslim West and were widely known and used for culinary purposes. Andalusi horticultural sources mention two walnut types:

barjīl (برجيل) with small kernels enclosed in hard shells.[15]

imlīsī (امليسي) with large kernels enclosed in thin shells.

If fresh walnuts are needed, Ibn al-ʿAwwām, *al-Filāḥa al-Andalusiyya* ii 219, suggests soaking the kernels in lukewarm water to soften. He also recommends walnuts to remove greasy odors in a cooking pot and adding a small amount of it pounded and mixed with honey to the pot to save overly salted food.

In al-Tujībī's recipes, walnuts are used in a variety of dishes and pastries: recipe i.4.12 for pinwheel cookies; with couscous in recipe i.5.2; added to vinegar-garlic dipping sauces in recipe v.1.8; a *jawzīnaq* confection in recipe ix.4.1; and many more.

---

14 See Ibn al-Bayṭār, *al-Jāmiʿ* ii 277–8; and al-Anṭākī, *Tadhkira* 136.

15 See Ibn al-ʿAwwām, *al-Filāḥa al-Andalusiyya* ii 215; and al-Ishbīlī, *ʿUmdat al-ṭabīb* i 144.

FIGURE 126 A walnut tree, Dioscorides, *Fī Hayūlā al-ṭibb*, translation by Ḥunayn b. Isḥāq, fol. 66v, detail
FROM THE NEW YORK PUBLIC LIBRARY, SPENCER COLLECTION: HTTPS://DIGITALCOLLECTIONS.NYPL.ORG/ITEMS/5E66B3E9-0C0D-D471-E040-E00A180654D7

jawz maqshūr (جوز مقشور) shelled walnuts.

jawz maqshūr min qishrayhi (جوز مقشور من قشريه) walnuts, whose outer shells and the thin brown skins adhering to the kernels have been removed. The thin brown skins were removed by soaking the shelled walnuts first in hot water and then peeling them off, as described in recipe i.4.12 for pinwheel cookies. Another method for removing the thin brown skins is described in Ibn al-Bayṭār, *al-Jāmiʿ* i 240: Shelled walnuts are put in a pan with fine flour and are allowed to parch slowly on low heat; in the process, the flour particles will burn the skins.

ṭaʿm al-jawz (طعم الجوز) walnut kernels; *ṭaʿm* used in this sense must have been a regional variant in the Muslim West of what was more commonly called *lubb* in the eastern region.

With their moderately hot and somewhat humid properties, walnuts were said to be beneficial to cold kidneys and colic; they dissipate winds and expel intestinal worms. Eating walnuts was also said to remove bad breath.[16]

kabar (كبر), also known as *kubbār* (كبّار), *qubbār* (قبّار), *aṣaf* (اصف), and *laṣaf* (لصف) capers. They are said to have little nutritional value, but consuming them pickled would help revive the appetite. They were best eaten at the beginning of the meal.[17]

ʿasālīj al-kabar (عساليج الكبر), sg. *ʿaslūj* (عسلوج) are the tender parts of shoots of the caper plant, consumed pickled, as in chapter x.4, and used in a yogurt condiment called *khilāṭ* in recipe vi.1.3.

faqqūṣ al-kabar (فقوص الكبر) young caper berries, at the stage when they are still not fully grown and the seeds (*zarīʿa*) inside them have not fully developed yet. They are used pickled in recipe vi.1.2 to garnish a condiment of drained yogurt.

kabar maqṣūr (كبر مقصور) pickled capers made with several changes of water, see recipe x.4.2. See also chapter x.4 for ways to pickle them.

nawār al-kabar (نوار الكبر) caper buds that have not opened yet, see chapter x.4 for ways to pickle them.

kharnūb (خرنوب), ***kharrūb*** (خروب) carob, *Ceratonia siliqua*. It is also called *qarāṭiyā* (قراطيا), and commoners in Fez call it *tāsilqū* (تاسلقو).[18] *Kharrūb*, which etymologically is the origin of the Spanish *algarroba* and the French and English *caroube/carobe*/carob, may ultimately be traced back to the ancient Akkadian *kharuba*.[19]

---

16 See al-Anṭākī, *Tadhkira* 120; and Ibn al-ʿAwwām, *al-Filāḥa al-Andalusiyya* ii 219.

17 Al-Anṭākī, *Tadhkira* 294.

18 Al-Ghassānī, *Ḥadīqat al-Azhār* 310.

19 See, for instance, *The Akkadian Dictionary*: http://www.assyrianlanguages.org/akkadian/dosearch.php?searchkey=1409&language=id, accessed Jan. 25, 2020.

FIGURE 127 Capers, *kabar*, Dioscorides, *Kitāb al-Ḥashā'ish fī hāyūlā al-ʿilāj al-ṭibbī*, Arabic translation by Ḥunayn b. Isḥāq, Or. 289, fol. 99v, detail
UNIVERSITAIRE BIBLIOTHEKEN LEIDEN, HTTP://HDL.HANDLE.NET/1887.1/ITEM:1578266

Carob is an evergreen tree of the mountains, of which the pulp of its pods is used. Its other name, *shajarat Sulaymān* (شجرة سليمان) 'Solomon's tree,' goes back to an Islamic folklore story, which tells how a new tree used to grow in King Solomon's temple daily. When he first saw the carob tree, it told him its name was *kharrūb*, to which he responded, *"Al-kharrūb kharāb,"* predicting the destruction (*kharāb*) of his kingdom, which took place shortly after.[20]

Based on al-Ishbīlī,[21] the variety available in al-Andalus was *kharrūb Shāmī* (Levantine carob), which he says was a well-known fruit.[22] In the Levant and Egypt, a confection (*ḥalwā*) was made with its molasses (*rubb al-kharrūb*). According to

20 Al-Ishbīlī, *ʿUmdat al-ṭabīb* i 207.
21 Ibid.
22 The Levant was the major source for carob even in ancient times. Galen, who did not

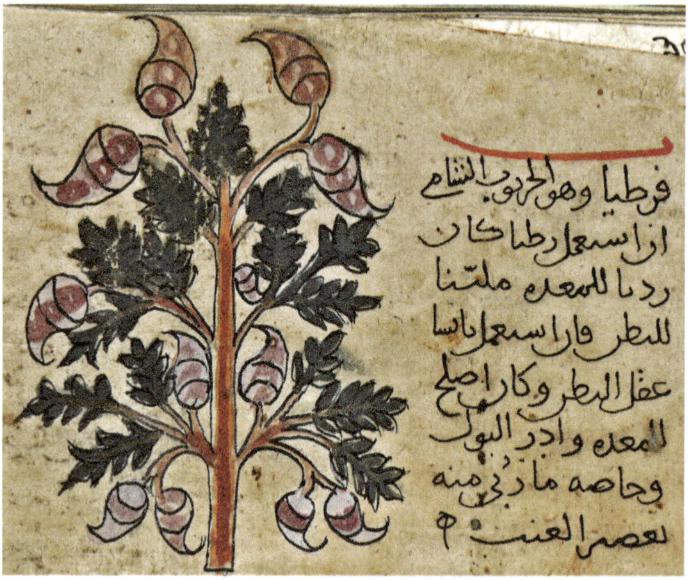

FIGURE 128 A carob tree, Dioscorides, *Kitāb al-Ḥashaʾish fī hayulā al-ʿilāj al-ṭibbī*, Arabic translation by Ḥunayn b. Isḥāq, Or. 289, fol. 46v, detail
UNIVERSITAIRE BIBLIOTHEKEN LEIDEN, HTTP://HDL.HANDLE.NET/1887.1/ITEM:1578266

him, the Levantine carob tree produces large and long pods, valued for their high sugar content; indeed, so much so that the fully ripe pods drip their honey-like juice on the ground. They are also called *ṣandalī* because they are as brown as sandalwood.

Eating carob when still fresh was believed to cause diarrhea; but dried carob had the advantage of curbing bowel movements. It is said to nourish the body and generate good humors when well digested. It is also said to excite the appetite.

Al-Anṭākī, *Tadhkira* 150, mentions that the unripe pods were used to ferment milk and make delicious cheese, similar to *qarīsha*, a kind of cottage cheese. In al-Tujībī's cookbook, it is used as one of the flavoring agents in three preparations for *murrī*, the liquid fermented sauce, recipes x.8.1, 7, and 12.

lawz (لوز) almonds, *Prunus dulcis*, of which there were two varieties: large and sweet almonds (*lawz ḥulw*); and small and bitter ones (*lawz murr*).[23] In al-Tujībī's cookbook skinned almonds are used extensively in savory and sweet dishes.

---

approve of this fruit because it does not get purged from the system fast, said, "It would be better for us not even to import them from the eastern region where they are produced." See Powel, *Galen* 95.

23 See Ibn al-ʿAwwām, *al-Filāḥa al-Andalusiyya* ii 189.

farīk al-lawz al-akhḍar (فريك اللوز الاخضر) fresh green almonds, used in recipe ii.2.16.

lawz maqshūr (لوز مقشور) skinned almonds. This was easily done by lightly boiling them first.

lawz masmūṭ (لوز مسموط) almonds that have been blanched in order to skin them.

For medicinal purposes, bitter almonds were preferred for their hot and dry properties. With their hot and moist properties, sweet almonds were valued as food and medicine. They were recommended for opening blockages in the liver and spleen; also used to help purge phlegm from the chest and lungs, improve eyesight, and purge dense winds in the colon. Having five bitter almonds was believed to delay intoxication, and sweet almonds were said to help with weight gain.[24]

līm (ليم) a general name for the citrus fruit lemon in the Muslim West, more commonly called *laymūn* (ليمون) in the eastern region, al-Mashriq.[25] Although *līm* and *laymūn* were specifically mentioned as varieties of the lemon fruit in contemporary books on botany and agriculture in the western region (discussed below), in al-Tujībī's cookbook, they seem to be used synonymously. Preserved lemon juice, for instance, is generally called *khall līm*, but it also occurs once as *khall laymūnī*, in recipe ii.1.8. When recipes particularly ask for limes, they would be called *līm akhḍar* (green lemons).

That *līm* and *laymūn* were indeed recognized as two varieties of the lemon fruit in the western region is evident, for instance, in fourteenth-century Ibn Baṭṭūṭa's description of mangos grown in India, and how when still green, they would be preserved in salt (*yuṣayyar*), "as we do in our country with *līm* and *laymūn*," he explains.[26] Additionally, based on other contemporary sources in the region, several lemon varieties were mentioned. Al-Ishbīlī,[27] for instance, describes the following varieties he knew of:

24 See Ibn al-Jazzār, *al-Iʿtimād* 572–3; and al-Ghassānī, *Ḥadīqat al-azhār* 164.

25 In al-Tujībī's cookbook, lemon is called *līmū*, sometimes described as *akhḍar* 'green,' which designates lime. In al-Ishbīlī, *ʿUmdat al-ṭabīb* i 44, the name occurs as *līm*, *laymūn*, and *lamūn* (لمون). Ibn al-ʿAwwām, *al-Filāḥa al-Andalusiyya* ii 283, calls it *lāmūn* (لامون).

26 Ibn Baṭṭūṭa, *Riḥla* iii 94. Its Moroccan editor identifies *līm* as the small lime variety, which are called *laymūn doqq* 'small lemons' in Morocco today, and adds that they are still pickled in salt as *muṣayyar*. See variety no. 3, discussed in this entry.

27 Al-Ishbīlī, *ʿUmdat al-ṭabīb* i 44.

FIGURE 129 Green almonds, al-ʿUmarī, *Masālik al-abṣār*, fol. 201r, detail
BNF, DEPARTMENT OF MANUSCRIPTS, ARAB 2771. SOURCE: GALLICA.BNF.FR/BNF

FIGURE 130 Limes growing on a tree, al-Qazwīnī, *ʿAjāʾib al-makhlūqāt wa gharāʾib al-mawjūdāt*, fol. 174v, detail
FROM THE NEW YORK PUBLIC LIBRARY, SPENCER COLLECTION: HTTPS://DIGITALCOLLECTIONS.NYPL.ORG/ITEMS/EE80F6F0-28EB-0138-F849-23627D2C85E1

1. Lemons that look like *utrunj* 'citron'[28] but are intensely acidic. To this, al-Ṭighnarī, *Zahrat al-bustān* 290, adds that *laymūn* is smaller than citron and has pointed ends; they are not so juicy, and the pulp segments adhere to the peel. Ibn al-ʿAwwām, *al-Filāḥa al-Andalusiyya* 265, describes them as yellow and calls them ***lāmūn*** (لامون). Obviously, what is being described here is the common yellow lemon, *Citrus limon.*
2. Lemons that look like citrons in size and color, albeit shorter and rounder, and each lemon has an end with a growth, which is like a sizable knobble, looking like a herniated belly button.[29] They are very acidic. To this description, al-Ghassānī, *Ḥadīqat al-azhār* 21, adds that these lemons are intensely yellow and specifically calls them ***laymūn*** (ليمون).

Evidently, a domestic variety of the common yellow lemon *Citrus limon* is being described here. It might well be the ancestor of what today is known as the Moroccan lemon, *Citrus limon* (*L.*) *Burm.* In Morocco today, this kind is called *bouserra* (بو سرة) 'having a navel'; also described as *beldī* 'domestic.' It is used for making preserved lemon.[30]

3. Lemons that are smaller than *nāranj* 'sour oranges'; and their trees are thorny. They are yellow, rounded, and a little bit oval, like chicken and pigeon eggs in size and shape. To these descriptions, al-Ghassānī, *Ḥadīqat al-azhār* 21, adds that their peels are thin, they are quite juicy, and are intensely acidic. Al-Ghassānī, who lived in Fez and wrote his book in 1585, specifically calls these lemons ***līm*** (ليم), and, more significantly, adds that it was these lemons that were used to make the preserved lemons called *līm musayyar*.[31]

Clearly, what is being described here is a domestic variety of lime, which today in Morocco is called ***doqq*** (دُقّ),[32] literally 'small,' *Citrus limonum Risso var.*

---

28 *Utrunj* is a variant of *utrujj.*

29 In his observations on Egyptian lemons, ʿAbd al-Laṭīf al-Baghdādī, *Riḥla* 75, mentions a variety similar to the one being described here; he calls it *laymūn mukhattam* (ليمون مختّم) 'as if pressed with a ring.' He says it is round, oblate, with a depression at each end. *Mukhattam* is suggestive of a ring-like depression around the knobble. This indeed corresponds with today's local Moroccan lemon, called *bouserra*; see, for instance, the following website where lemon is described in a similar manner: https://citrusvariety.ucr.edu/citrus/marrakech.html, accessed Feb. 1, 2020.

30 Paula Wolfert mentions this lemon in her seminal *Couscous and Other Good Food from Morocco* 30–1.

31 مسيّر [sic], which must have been a dialectal variant on مصيّر *muṣayyar*, as it occurs in al-Tujībī's cookbook and many other sources.

32 Also mentioned by Wolfert, see n. 30 above.

pusilla R; also described as *beldī* 'domestic.' This **lime variety** must have been a descendant of the lime associated with Persia, *Citrus latifolia*. Tenth-century Ibn Waḥshiyya, *al-Filāḥa al-Nabaṭiyya* i 334, calls the Persian limes *līmū* (ليمو), adding that the tree was originally Indian. He describes the edible grown lime as round and green, which eventually turns yellow.[33] It has sour pulp and a pleasant scent.[34]

The following are lemon-related descriptions and expressions as they occur in al-Tujībī's cookbook:

khall līm (خل ليم), also called ***khall laymūnī*** (خل ليموني) in recipe ii.1.8. It is preserved lemon juice, used in several recipes sprinkled on fried dishes or vegetable dishes before serving them. It may also designate freshly pressed lemon juice; for more on this, see glossary 8, s.v. *khall*.

līm ghaḍḍ (ليم غض) tender young lemons.

līm muṣayyar (ليم مصير) pickled lemons, entry in glossary 5.

līm mutanāhī (ليم متناهي) fully ripe lemons.

līm mutanāhī ṭarī jalīl (ليم متناهي طري جليل) large fresh and tender lemons that have fully ripened.

līm ṭarī (ليم طري) fresh lemons.

mā' līm (ماء ليم) fresh lemon juice, used in small amounts, or to taste, in several recipes (ii.2.27–8, ii.5.3, iii.2.4, and v.1.4). Another name given to lemon juice, which can be a reference to fresh or preserved lemon juice, is *khall al-līm* (خل الليم).[35]

We learn from eleventh-century al-Ṭighnarī, *Zahrat al-bustān* 290–1, that lemon juice was not as familiar of a beverage in the western region as it was in the eastern side, al-Mashriq.[36] He tells his readers that an anecdote he read

33 In both stages, the green and the yellow, limes are juicy and edible and may be used for all purposes. This is what distinguishes them from the rest of citrus fruit, including the common yellow lemons, which need to ripen to their yellow stage before using them.

34 The domestic Egyptian variety of lime, *Citrus limonum pusilla*, is called *laymūn baladī* (native lemons) and *laymūn Miṣrī* (Egyptian). They are the Persian *līmū* and *banzahīr*. Al-Anṭākī, *Tadhkira* 316, similarly describes this variety as round and small and having a very thin peel. See also Viré, "Orange," 194.

35 Note that in the two surviving Andalusi cookbooks, this one and anonymous *Anwāʿ al-ṣaydala*, *khall* not only designates regular 'vinegar' produced by fermentation but also, in a looser sense, unfermented preserved 'sour juice,' and even freshly pressed out lemon juice. See glossary 8, s.v. *khall*.

36 In the eastern region, it was mostly consumed as a sweetened beverage, *sharāb al-laymūn*.

in a Mashriqi book proves that lemon juice was indeed a good thing to have, as it had the power to combat deadly poisons.[37]

mā' līm akhḍar (ماء ليم اخضر) juice of fresh limes (literally, 'green lemons'), used for instance in an eggplant dish, recipe vii.2.11. Depending on context, *akhḍar* may designate the color 'green' and 'freshness.' I chose to interpret it as a reference to the green lemons we call limes, because nowhere in the two extant Andalusi cookbooks do we come across *līm yābis* (dried lemons) being used to justify calling the fresh ones *akhḍar* 'fresh.'[38] Additionally, al-Tujībī's recipes use other terms to convey freshness, as in some of the above entries.

In al-Tujībī's recipes, lemon juice as a souring agent does not feature as prominently as it does in the fourteenth-century anonymous Egyptian cookbook *Kanz al-Fawā'id*, English trans., *Treasure Trove*. *Murrī* and varieties of vinegar-based sauces show up more frequently in the recipes. This must have been largely due to the different natures of land and air in the two regions. In the opinion of the eleventh-century Egyptian physician Ibn Riḍwān, Egypt's air is putrid, humid, and hot.[39] Lemon and other acidic fruits and their juices, with their cold and dry properties, were thought of as being more conducive to such conditions. Al-Andalus, on the other hand, enjoys more temperate and cooler weather. *Murrī*, for instance, with its hot and dry properties, was more suitable for the western region. As shown in al-Tujībī's cookbook, lemons were mostly used as pickles and preserved juice.

Besides its culinary uses in the kitchen and on the dining tables as a condiment, lemon was also deemed beneficial medicinally. It was valuable as a breath freshener and was recommended for a weak stomach, and as an aid to digesting coarse foods. It was said to have the power to cleanse the digestive system after eating fatty and rich foods. In addition, it was used to treat nausea, headaches, and vertigo, and to curb the unhealthy cravings of pregnant women. It was believed to excite the appetite and combat hangovers.[40]

qasṭal (قسطل), also called ***shāhballūṭ*** (شاهبلوط), literally 'king of acorns.' They are chestnuts, *Castanea*, said to be a sweeter species of acorn. The Moroccan physician al-Ghassānī, *Ḥadīqat al-azhār* 57, who lived in Fez, mentions that chestnuts were not

37 His reference must have been to al-Qāḍī al-Tanūkhī, *al-Faraj ba'd al-shidda* iv 158–9.

38 On the other hand, references to fresh apricots as *akhḍar* as opposed to *yābis* 'dried' is justifiable because apricots in their edible stage are indeed yellow, in which case *akhḍar* would designate 'freshness' beyond any doubt. See, for instance, apricot stew recipes 120 and 121 in the anonymous fourteenth-century Egyptian cookbook *Kanz al-fawā'id*, English trans., *Treasure Trove*.

39 Dols, *Medieval Islamic Medicine*, Ibn Riḍwān Arabic text 27.

40 Ibn al-Bayṭār, *al-Jāmi'* iv 395–400; al-Ṭighnarī, *Zahrat al-bustān* 291.

native to his region; rather, they grew in al-Andalus (*ʿUdwat al-Andalus*) and were imported from there. In al-Tujībī's cookbook, chestnuts are used in two chicken recipes, iii.2.43 and iii.2.48, where they are mashed and mixed with meat to make meatballs.

> ***qasṭal ṭarī*** (قسطل طري) freshly harvested chestnuts. Because they rot very fast, the way to store them was to take them while still fresh and tender, as soon as they had been harvested, and bury them in pits, called *maṭāmīr*, with bases lined with sand. The pits were then completely covered to prevent contact with air. To revive these dried chestnuts and make them taste as if they were fresh, after taking them out of the pit, they were spread on a clean and wet piece of ground and lightly sprinkled with sand. They were sprinkled with fresh water once daily for eight consecutive days, after which they were washed and used like fresh chestnuts.[41]

With their cold and dry properties, chestnuts were believed to be astringent and constipating. Nevertheless, compared with *ballūṭ* 'acorn,' they were said to be less cold due to their sweetness. They are described as slow to digest, but once digested, they can be nourishing. The recommended way to have them was with sugar.[42]

rummān (رمان) pomegranates, of which there were many varieties, some sweet (*ḥulw*), some sour-sweet (*muzz*), and some sour (*ḥāmiḍ*); there were the juicy ones (*māʾī*) and the dry ones (*ʿaẓmī*). The preferred pomegranates were the large juicy ones with intensely red smooth peels. Of the varieties available in the western region, *al-Safarī* (السفري) was deemed the best on account of its smooth, sweet taste. It grew to huge sizes, with quadrangular seeds that had fleshy and juicy arils and very tiny seeds.[43] Writing in sixteenth-century Fez, al-Ghassānī, *Ḥadīqat al-azhār* 253, says that the best pomegranates growing there were the impressively huge *maymūna* type; as for Marrakesh, he adds, all their pomegranates were good because they grew nothing but the *Safarī* kind.

---

41 As directed in Ibn al-ʿAwwām, *al-Filāḥa al-Andalusiyya* iii 512–3.

42 Ibn al-Bayṭār, *al-Jāmiʿ* i 152.

43 This variety was introduced to al-Andalus when one of the sisters of Emir ʿAbd al-Raḥmān I (d. 788), founder of the Andalusi Emirate of Cordova, sent him a large amount of choice pomegranates from al-Mashriq. One of the versions of the story tells that ʿAbd al-Raḥmān distributed them among his courtiers; one of them, whose name was Safar b. ʿUbayd, planted the seeds in his estate in Rayya (Malaga) and took care of the plant and manipulated it until it produced a wonderful pomegranate variety that was called after his name. See al-Ṭighnarī, *Zahrat al-bustān* 212; Ibn al-ʿAwwām, *al-Filāḥa al-Andalusiyya* ii 172; al-Ishbīlī, *ʿUmdat al-ṭabīb* i 256–7. *Safarī* is the Arabic origin for the Spanish *zafari*.

FIGURE 131 A chestnut tree, Dioscorides, *Fī Hayūlā al-ṭibb*, translation by Ḥunayn b. Isḥāq, fol. 58r, detail
FROM THE NEW YORK PUBLIC LIBRARY, SPENCER COLLECTION: HTTPS://DIGITALCOLLECTIONS.NYPL.ORG/ITEMS/5E66B3E8-F1D6-D471-E040-E00A180654D7

FIGURE 132 A pinecone tree, Dioscorides, *Fī Hayūlā al-ṭibb*, translation by Ḥunayn b. Isḥāq, fol. 41r, detail
FROM THE NEW YORK PUBLIC LIBRARY, SPENCER COLLECTION: HTTPS://DIGITALCOLLECTIONS.NYPL.ORG/ITEMS/5E66B3E9-1EEB-D471-E040-E00A180654D7

Cooking with pomegranate juice does not seem to have been common in Andalusi cuisine. It is used only once in al-Tujībī's cookbook, in a *ṭabāhijiyya*, recipe ii.2.29, for a succulent fried meat dish soured with the juice of pomegranates; and it is said to have come from the eastern region, where pomegranates were much more ubiquitous culinarily. Pomegranates, however, were valued as a table fruit; they were also believed to have some medicinal benefits. The sour variety was said to stimulate the appetite and curb yellow bile. Sweet pomegranate was deemed beneficial for fevers and coughs, and as an aid to coitus.

safarjal (سفرجل) quinces, *Cydonia oblonga*. As al-Ishbīlī describes them in *'Umdat al-ṭabīb* ii 553–4, many varieties were known and grown, ranging from the sweet and acidic to the oblong and rounded: Of the **oblong ones**, there were two varieties, the sweet and the sour-sweet (*muzz*). These were known as Fāsī quinces (i.e., from Fez); also called *minahhad* (منهّد) because the fruits look like virgins' breasts, and the knobbles at their stem ends look like nipples. They taste sweet and sour, are sweet smelling, and quite juicy. Of the well-known **round varieties**, there were two kinds: the sweet ones and the sour-sweet ones. They grew into very large quinces, with smooth peels and a good deal of seeds.

Recipes in al-Tujībī's cookbook show limited interest in this fruit. They are used in two savory dishes: recipe ii.2.20, cooked with mutton, and recipe iii.2.41, cooked with chicken. They are also combined with apples in a *Ṣinhājī* dish, recipe iv.1; and in preparations for the liquid sauce *murrī* in recipes x.8.3, 7, and 13, most probably to enhance their color and aroma.

Quinces were believed to excite the appetite, energize the body, and gladden the soul even by just smelling them. Having the fruit with alcoholic drinks was said to prevent hangovers. It was also believed that if a pregnant woman started eating quince regularly from the third month of pregnancy, she would give birth to a beautiful, smart child. Sharp steel knives were better avoided in cutting it, as they were believed to cause it to lose its juice fast.[44]

ṣanawbar (صنوبر), also occurs as ***ḥabb ṣanawbar*** (حب صنوبر) and ***lubb ṣanawbar*** (لب صنوبر).[45] They are pine nuts harvested from the female stone pine, *Pinus pines*.[46]

Pine nuts are used in al-Tujībī's recipes as a filling along with other nuts for pastries, as in recipes i.4.4 and 11, and in some savory dishes, as in recipe ii.6.8 for stuffing tripe. They are also toasted and sprinkled on the finished dishes as a garnish.

44 Al-'Umarī, *Masālik* xx 201; al-Anṭākī, *Tadhkira* 208.

45 Also called *ḥabb al-mulūk* 'seed of kings.'

46 In today's lexicons, the tree is identified as *al-ṣanawbar al-thamarī*. The tree is native to the Mediterranean region.

jumjumat ṣanawbar (جمجمة صنوبر) a whole pinecone. In recipes for *murrī* preparations of fermented liquid sauces, an entire cone, emptied of its seeds, would be added; see recipes x.8.1, 2, 3, and 7. Pine was valued for its preservative properties.

ʿūd ṣanawbar (عود صنوبر) scales of the pinecone, used in *murrī* recipe x.8.12.

With their hot and humid properties, pine nuts were said to be good for chronic coughs. They were also deemed beneficial to the elderly and people with cold properties, who can snack on them while imbibing alcoholic drinks. It was also believed to excite the two appetites (sex and food), but was said to be slow to digest.[47]

tamr (تمر) dates. It may generally refer to the fruit of the date palm, *Phoenix dactylifera*; but also more specifically designates dates in their last stage of ripening, when they turn sweet and soft and contain the least amount of moisture and can be safely stored as dried fruit.

Al-Tujībī's cookbook makes minimal use of this fruit; only to stuff cookies in recipes i.4.2 and 27. The date palm that was brought by the Arabs to Iberia did not successfully acclimatize to the colder and less humid areas over there, and as a result, dates were not as important as they have always been in the eastern region of al-Mashriq. In his chapter on grafting trees, al-Ṭighnarī, *Zahrat al-bustān* 363, attributes the unpalatable taste of dates grown in al-Andalus to insufficient heat and humidity, which are essential to produce sweet dates. In *al-Filāḥa al-Andalusiyya* ii 348, Ibn al-ʿAwwām has a remedy for the Andalusi dates known for being unpalatably astringent (*ʿafiṣ*). His recommendation is to boil the fully ripe dates in fresh water to help them release their astringency; after this, the water is discarded and the dates are left to dry. They will taste good, he assures the reader.

From the Andalusi al-Rundī, *Kitāb al-Aghdhiya* 196,[48] we learn that dates were imported to his region of Bilād al-Andalus and the areas closer to it from the al-Maghribi shore, Barr al-ʿUdwa, adding that palms growing in al-Andalus did not produce palatable dates. Of their nutritional properties, he says they are slow to digest due to their density and cause headaches. However, when fully digested, they can be impressively nourishing, even more so than figs. He recommends eating them with sugar candy, almonds, or pine nuts for curing coughs, but cautions against eating them when unripe.

47 See al-Anṭākī, *Tadhkira* 245; and al-Ghassānī, *Ḥadīqat al-azhār* 192–3.

48 Based on his name, he must have been based in the city of Runda (Ronda) in southern Spain.

FIGURE 133 Male and female date palms, Dioscorides, *Fī Hayūlā al-ṭibb*, translation by Ḥunayn b. Isḥāq, fol. 59v, detail
FROM THE NEW YORK PUBLIC LIBRARY, SPENCER COLLECTION: HTTPS://DIGITALCOLLECTIONS.NYPL.ORG/ITEMS/5E66B3E8-776E-D471-E040-E00A180654D7

shadānaj (شدانج) a variety of dried dates, mentioned in recipe i.4.2. The word is more commonly written as *shādanaj*/*shādhanaj*/*shādhana* in other sources, as in al-Bīrūnī, *al-Ṣaydana* 385. The word itself designates hematite, also known as bloodstone, which must have resembled the color of the dates named after it. In the Arabic edition of al-Tujībī's *Fiḍālat al-khiwān*, the editor Bin Shaqrūn (p. 68, n. 1), explains that this date variety, which is soft and thick fleshed, is a favored variety today in Marrakesh and southern Morocco.

tīn (تين) figs, *Ficus carica*, of which many varieties were mentioned in medieval books on botany and horticulture in the Muslim West. There were white figs, red figs, and black figs; some of these produced *bākūr* figs, which ripened at the beginning of the season, usually without pollination, followed later in the season by the regularly pollinated figs.[49]

In *al-Filāḥa al-Andalusiyya* iii 302, Ibn al-ʿAwwām gives a detailed description on the pollination process. The caprifig *dhukār*, *Ficus carica sylvestris*, which is the male, pollen-bearing wild variety of the common fig tree, is used to pollinate the cultivated edible fig. Several of these caprifigs are hung close to the edible immature figs to let the fig wasp (*Blastophaga psenes*) transfer pollen to the female flowers inside them. He compares these wasps to the insect *baʿūḍ* 'mosquito.'

Figs, fresh and dried, were enjoyed as fruit by themselves; or paired with other foods, such as in al-Tujībī's recipe vi.1.1, where they are eaten with a variety of fresh cheese. Figs are also used in making vinegar, as in recipe x.7.2.

Besides the figs, other parts of the fig tree had their culinary uses. Adding fresh or dry sticks from the fig tree to meat in a pot was believed to hasten its cooking, and even tenderize it if it proved to be tough. Adding three fully ripe figs to a meat pot had the same effect. Stirring heated milk with a fig stick was believed to curdle it into yogurt, but generally, cooks were cautioned against using fig wood for grilling and baking purposes due to its sappiness.[50]

dhukār (ذكار) caprifig, *Ficus carica sylvestris*, which is the male, pollen-bearing wild variety of the common fig tree, used to pollinate the cultivated edible fig, see *tīn* above.

tīn jāff (تين جاف), ***tīn yābis*** (تين يابس) dried figs.

tīn ṭarī (تين طري) fresh figs.

ʿūd dhukār (عود ذكار) sticks from the caprifig tree, see *dhukār* above. They are used to stir the large jars of *murrī* sauce daily while fermenting in the sun over a period of time, see recipes x.8.1–2.

waraq dhukār (ورق ذكار) leaves of the caprifig tree, see *dhukār* above. Fig leaves in general have antiseptic properties. In al-Tujībī's cookbook, they are used to cover bread pieces while molding in preparations for the sun-fermented liquid sauces of *murrī*, recipes x.8.1–2.

According to medieval medical opinion, figs were deemed the best among fruits, the least harmful and the most beneficial. The recommendation was to eat them

49 Al-Ghassānī, *Ḥadīqat al-azhār* 296.

50 Ibn al-ʿAwwām, *al-Filāḥa al-Andalusiyya* ii 232.

peeled because their skins were said to be hard on the digestion. Additionally, eating figs while imbibing wine was strongly discouraged, as this was thought to cause sicknesses.[51]

tuffāḥ (تفاح) apples, of which many varieties grew in al-Andalus, ranging from the sweet (*ḥulw*) and sour-sweet (*muzz*) to the sour (*ḥāmiḍ*) and insipid (*tafih*), and in varying sizes, textures, and colors. In addition, the shapes of apples were also manipulated with the help of molds (*qawālib*, sg. *qālab*). We are told that before the apples fully matured, they would be caged in differently shaped molds and kept there until they grew larger and took the shape of whatever the mold was. Something similar was done with fruits like pears, pomegranates, citron, and the like.[52]

The Andalusi varieties mentioned are:

baqsī (بقسي) oblate in shape, with firm sweet pulp, aromatic, and as yellow as *baqs* 'boxwood.'

khazāʾinī (خزائني) a variety that matures in winter. It is red, with a dense flesh, and very aromatic. It was this variety that was kept in storage, to be served to dignitaries, guests, and the sick.

munahhad (منهّد) 'breast-shaped,' said to be extremely aromatic, with a very smooth red peel.

qulaybī (قليبي) rounded, with smooth and bright yellow peel; sweet, very juicy, and wonderfully aromatic.

rukhāmī (رخامي) said to be large, sweet, with soft pulp and a green peel.

shuʿaybī (شعيبي) oblong, with soft flesh and yellow skin. It is seedless.

ʿulwī (علوي), of which there was the sweet variety and the sour-sweet one; described as red with yellow striping and very aromatic. These grew abundantly in Granada, Toledo, and Zaragoza.[53]

With their moderate properties, apples were said to be both food and medicine. Especially beneficial were the sweet ripe ones, and the large aromatic varieties with crisp flesh and thin skins. They were praised for having the power to strengthen and gladden the heart, and when enclosed in dough and baked, they were said to excite poor appetites. Sniffing aromatic apples was also believed to fortify the heart and brain.[54] In al-Tujībī's cookbook, apple is used just a few times in dishes. It is cooked

51 See al-Ṭighnarī, *Zahrat al-bustān* 187–8; Ibn al-ʿAwwām, *al-Filāḥa al-Andalusiyya* ii 231.

52 See al-Ṭighnarī, *Zahrat al-bustān* 246–7.

53 See al-Ishbīlī, *ʿUmdat al-ṭabīb* i 118–9; Ibn al-ʿAwwām, *al-Filāḥa al-Andalusiyya* ii 303.

54 Ibn Sīnā, *al-Qānūn* i 691.

FIGURE 134
Citrons at different stages of ripeness, Dioscorides, *Fī Hayūlā al-ṭibb*, translation by Ḥunayn b. Isḥāq, fol. 63v, detail
FROM THE NEW YORK PUBLIC LIBRARY, SPENCER COLLECTION: HTTPS://DIGITALCOLLECTIONS.NYPL.ORG/ITEMS/5E66B3E8-B21D-D471-E040-E00A180654D7

with mutton in recipe ii.2.21, and with tuna in recipe v.2.26, using the sour variety. It is also used with quinces in preparing *murrī* sauces in recipes x.8.3 and 7 to enhance their aroma and color.

qushūr tuffāḥ (قشور تفاح) apple peels, used in al-Tujībī's cookbook in handwashing preparations, *ushnān*, recipes xii.2 and 6, to enhance their aroma.
tuffāḥ ḥulw (تفاح حلو) sweet apples.
tuffāḥ muzz (تفاح مزّ) sour-sweet apples.

utrujj (اترجّ), ***turunj*** (ترنج) true citron, *Citrus medica*. See also *zunbūʿ* below. With a few exceptions, only the aromatic leaves, fresh and dried, are used in al-Tujībī's recipes. Medicinally, all parts of *utrujj* were highly valued for their restorative and digestive properties, especially the leaves. It was said to strengthen the stomach and stimulate the appetite. It was also recommended for palpitations and alleviating thirst and hangovers.

qishr utrujj (قشراترجّ) citron peel, used dried only in a couple recipes for handwashing preparations, recipes xii.2 and 6.

shawk utrujj (شوك اترجّ) thorns of the citron tree, used to pick out cooked snails from their shells in recipe xi.3.

ʿurūq utrujj (عروق اترجّ) citron roots, used in recipe x.9.2 to remedy olive oil by clarifying and improving its flavor.

waraq utrujj (ورق اترجّ) citron leaves. This is the part of the citron plant most frequently used, fresh and dried, in al-Tujībī's recipes for savory dishes, *murrī* preparations, and in a handwashing compound, recipe xii.1.

zabīb (زبيب) raisins, which are dried, seeded grapes. In al-Tujībī's cookbook, they are used in a few recipes, mostly soaked and mashed, and their juice is strained. The raisins the book mentions are:

zabīb aḥmar (زبيب احمر) red raisins, praised for their sweetness and moderate properties. They are specifically called for in recipes ii.1.4 and iii.2.11 for *marwaziyya* stews.

zabīb ḥulw (زبيب حلو) sweet raisins, used in a turnip pickling recipe, x.5.3, and a vinegar recipe, x.7.9.

Al-Ṭighnarī, *Zahrat al-bustān* 159–62, mentions two methods for drying grapes followed in al-Andalus:

zabīb shamsī (زبيب شمسي) 'sun-dried raisins,' said to be very sweet, delicious, and smell much better than *zabīb al-aghshiya*. He criticized farmers of his time who spread the grapes on the ground without protecting them from dust and rainwater. He recommends covering the ground with a layer of gravel or fragmented bricks, or whole sprigs of wormwood (*shīḥ*),[55] to keep the grapes clean and dry.

---

55 The variety most likely to have been prevalent in al-Andalus was *shīḥ Armīnī* 'Armenian wormwood,' *Artemisia pontica* (S), also called small absinthe. Honey produced by bees that have fed on its blossoms was said to be as white as camphor. With its hot and dry

zabīb al-aghshiya (زبيب الاغشية) 'raisins processed in baskets,' recommended for cold zones where the grapes ripen late in the season and more rain falls. Grapes were put in esparto grass baskets, dipped very briefly in a boiling liquid of water treated with ash and fine olive oil, and then raised above the water to let them drain. The grapes were then spread on ground covered with fragmented bricks or wormwood, as mentioned in *zabīb shamsī* above.

The best raisins were the large, thin-skinned, fleshy ones; and removing the seeds before eating them was recommended. With their moderately hot properties, sweet raisins were said to be good for chest pains and phlegmatic coughs. They were also believed to sweeten the breath and help with gaining weight and fortifying the flesh. According to Muslim tradition, those who eat 21 red raisins first thing in the morning will never get sick.[56]

zaytūn (زيتون) olives, *Olea europaea*, of which many varieties grew in the Muslim West. Al-Ishbīlī, *ʿUmdat al-ṭabīb* i 280, for instance, mentions the following types:

al-aḥmar (الاحمر) a red variety.
al-lajin (اللجن) small and not fleshy.
al-mansāl (المنسال) rounded and the size of a large grape.
al-mulyān (المليان) a large olive, as big as the thumb's first phalanx (*unmula*), wide and oblong with a slight curve.
al-murqīr (المرقير) similar in shape to *al-ṭaral* (mentioned below), but larger, with more flesh and a smaller pit. It is my speculation that these olives were of the purple variety. Based on Dozy, *Takmilat al-maʿājim* x 47, s.v. مرقيرة, the word can be traced back to the Latin adj. *muricarius*, designating the color purple, extracted from the Mediterranean sea snails murex; adopted in Arabic as *murrīq* (مرّيق).
al-ṭaral (الطرل) short and not curved; it is said to be the best.
al-warkaṭ (الوركط) oval and larger than a pigeon's egg.

The olive-related terms and varieties mentioned in al-Tujībī's cookbook are:

ʿaẓm al-zaytūn (عظم الزيتون) olive stone or pit. The term must have been a dialectal usage in the Muslim West for what was called *nawāt* in the eastern region. For smaller seeds, such as those of capers, apples, gourds, and fennel, the term *zarīʿa* was used.

---

properties, it was used to expel parasitic intestinal worms and relieve flatulence. See al-Ghassānī, *Ḥadīqat al-azhār* 338–9.

56 See Ibn al-Bayṭār, *al-Jāmiʿ* ii 454; and Ibn al-ʿAwwām, *al-Filāḥa al-Andalusiyya* iii 493–9.

laḥm al-zaytūn (لحم الزيتون) flesh of the olives.

liḥāʾ (لحاء) outer layers of the olive tree barks, used with other ingredients in al-Tujībī's recipe x.9.2 to remedy olive oil that has turned cloudy.

waraq zaytūn (ورق زيتون) leaves of the olive tree, used with the abovementioned olive tree bark for the same purpose.

zaytūn akhḍar (زيتون اخضر) green olives that are not yet ripe.

zaytūn akhḍar jalīl (زيتون اخضر جليل) large green olives.

zaytūn aswad (زيتون اسود) black olives that are fully ripe. Olives that are in the ripening stage between green and black are called *zaytūn yāqūtī* (زيتون ياقوتي) ruby-colored olives.

zaytūn wasaṭ (زيتون وسط) medium-sized olives.

For table olives, see glossary 5, s.v. *zaytūn*; and for olive oil extracted from the fruit, see glossary 6, s.v. *zayt*.

zunbūʿ (زنبوع) Damascus citron.[57] In the eastern region, al-Mashriq, it was more commonly known as *kabbād* (كبّاد).[58] Based on Dozy, *Takmilat al-maʿājim* v 364, *zunbūʿ* is the Amazigh name for this fruit. Al-Ghassānī, *Ḥadīqat al-azhār* 21, describes it as a nice-looking fruit, larger than a *nāranj* 'sour orange,' with a bumpy skin that is orange in color. Al-Anṭākī, *Tadhkira* 50, explains that *zunbūʿ* is called *astabūn* in Persian[59] and that it is the fruit of a *nāranj* tree (sour orange, *Citrus aurantium*),[60] which has been grafted with the true citron *utrujj* (see entry above).

In al-Tujībī's cookbook, *zunbūʿ* is used only in the form of preserved juice. For *khall al-zunbūʿ*, see glossary 8, s.v. *khall*. However, judging from the fourteenth-century anonymous Egyptian cookbook *Kanz al-fawāʾid*, English trans., *Treasure Trove*, this variety of citron seems to have been more commonly used in daily prepa-

57 Categorized as a Kharna sour orange hybrid, *Citrus aurantium var. khatta*. For more on this variety, see: http://www.citrusvariety.ucr.edu/citrus/kharna.html, accessed Feb. 2, 2020. The Latin name was first suggested in 1888 by Bonavia, *The Cultivated Oranges and Lemons* 17. He says it makes "a good sweet jelly, and also a good marmalade." It is not to be confused with the sour orange *nāranj*, *Citrus aurantium*.

In the modern western sources, *kabbād* was described in detail for the first time in 1963 by Chapot, "Le cedrat kabbad," where it was said to be a hybrid between true citron and orange, and that it originated in Damascus.

58 See al-Qalqashandī, *Ṣubḥ al-aʿshā* v 176, where he mentions *zunbūʿ* as one the trees growing in the western region and explains that its name was *kabbād* in Egypt and the Levant.

59 In Ibn al-ʿAwwām, *al-Filāḥa al-Andalusiyya* 265, the name occurs as *bastanbūr*, which might well have been a regional variant on the name, or simply a copyist's misreading of the word.

60 *Nāranj* is not used in any of al-Tujībī's recipes, see introduction ii.4, p. 30.

rations of dishes than *utrujj* (*Citrus medica*) because it has more juice than *utrujj*. *Utrujj*, on the other hand, with its stronger properties, was mostly reserved for medicinal purposes and in digestive and rejuvenating preparations.

8. Ingredients Used in Dishes and Other Preparations: Herbs, Spices, Aromatics, Minerals, Food Colors, and Seasoning Sauces

abāzīr (اباززير) ***abzār*** (ابزار) seasoning spices in general, although the term more particularly designates spice seeds.

abū khuraysh (ابو خريش) borage, *Anchusa azurea.* This was the herb's name in Ifrīqiya;[1] in al-Andalus, it was called *kaḥlā'* (كحلاء).[2] Otherwise, it was generally known as *lisān al-thawr* (لسان الثور) in the eastern region, which is the name by which it was mostly recognized. This would explain why al-Tujībī provided it alongside the indigenous one, see recipe ii.2.10, where it is cooked with mutton.

The plant, with its leaves that look like cows' tongues, is not exceptionally aromatic, but was believed to generate a euphoric effect when cooked in dishes or mixed with drinks. It was also believed to counteract black bile.[3]

adwiya (ادوية) spices in general.

afāwīh (افاويه) spices in general, especially the aromatic ones. The Andalusi cookbook contemporary with al-Tujībī's, the anonymous *Anwāʿ al-ṣaydala* 67, gives examples of *afāwīh rafīʿa* 'fine aromatic spices' used in making delicate cookies: *qirfa* (cinnamon), *dār Ṣīnī* (cassia), *sunbul* (spikenard), *fulful* (black pepper), *khūlanjān* (galangal), and *jawz al-ṭīb* (nutmeg). In addition, al-Maqqarī, *Nafḥ al-ṭīb* i 199, on the authority of al-Masʿūdī, *Murūj al-dhahab*, mentions that there were 25 varieties of *afāwīh*; the examples he gives are: *sunbul* (spikenard), *qaranful* (cloves), *ṣandal* (sandalwood), *qirfa* (Ceylon cinnamon), and *qaṣab al-dharīra* (sweet flag). He also mentions the five basic varieties of aromatic spices (*uṣūl al-ṭīb*): musk, camphor, aloeswood, ambergris, and saffron, adding that they were all from India, but saffron and ambergris were also obtained from al-Andalus.

aḥbāq (احباق), sg. *ḥabaq* (حبق) aromatic herbs in general, although *ḥabaq* was more particularly a generic name for mint.

ʿanbar (عنبر) ambergris, *Ambra grisea*, is the substance located in the intestines of the sperm whale (*Bilaenopetra musculus*), valued for its aroma. According to Ibn al-Jazzār, *al-Iʿtimād* 384, it is described as something that a sea creature, which looked like a cow, disgorged out of its stomach. The best, he says, was rich and chewy

1 In medieval times, Ifrīqiya constituted the coastal regions of what today are western Libya, Tunisia, and eastern Algeria.

2 According to Ibn al-Ḥashshā', *Mufīd al-ʿulūm* 69.

3 See, for instance, al-Malik al-Muẓaffar, *al-Muʿtamad* 525; and Ibn Jazla, *Minhāj al-bayān*, fol. 195v.

 DOI:10.1163/9789004469488_073

FIGURE 135 Borage, *abū khuraysh*, also called *lisān al-thawr*, Dioscorides, *Kitāb Dīsqūrīdis fī mawādd al-ʿilāj*, fol. 151r, detail
BRITISH LIBRARY: ORIENTAL MANUSCRIPTS, OR 3366, IN QATAR DIGITAL LIBRARY HTTPS://WWW.QDL.QA/ARCHIVE/81055/VDC_100022531380.0X000001

in texture, and bluish in hue. Based on al-Ḥimyarī, *al-Rawḍ al-miʿṭār* 339, the best of ambergris collected from the western zone (*al-ʿanbar al-gharbī*) came from the coasts of Shadhūna (Medina-Sidonia) in southern Spain.

In al-Tujībī's cookbook, it is only used once, in recipe ii.2.21, in combination with musk (*misk*), rosewater (*māʾ ward*), and camphor (*kāfūr*), to give the dish qualities that would boost the psyche (*muqawwī lil-nafs*) and exhilarate the heart (*mufarriḥ*). In the handwashing preparation in part xii, its use is implied in the ingredient *nidd*, called for in recipe xii.5.

With its hot and dry properties, it was recommended for the elderly to heat up their bodies. Additionally, inhaling its fumes was believed to break down dense winds and phlegm in the head. It was generally believed to benefit the entire nervous system, and drinking it repeatedly with honey drinks was believed to restore the sexual appetite lost in old age. Also, adding a small piece of it to one's wine was said to induce fast intoxication.[4]

4 Al-Anṭākī, *Tadhkira* 263; and al-Malik al-Muẓaffar, *al-Muʿtamad* 395.

FIGURE 136
A cylindrical jar for keeping dried herbs and spices, decorated with a band of pseudo-Kufic letters, commonly used in spice stores and hospital pharmacies, fourteenth-century Valencia
CLEVELAND MUSEUM OF ART: HTTPS://WWW.CLEVELANDART.ORG/ART/1945.28

anīsūn (انيسون) aniseeds, *Pimpinella anisum*, also called *ḥabba ḥulwa* 'sweet seed,' *basbās Rūmī* 'Byzantine fennel,' and *rāzyānaj Shāmī* 'Levantine fennel.' The seeds are said to be similar to caraway, but a bit smaller, with a sweet taste tinged with sharpness and a slight bitterness. They were valued for soothing cold-related ailments, strengthening the stomach, and helping with flatulence.[5]

5 Al-Ishbīlī, *ʿUmdat al-ṭabīb* i 63–4, 155; and Ibn al-Bayṭār, *al-Jāmiʿ* i 82.

FIGURE 137 Aniseed plant, *anīsūn*, *Kitāb al-Diryāq*, fol. NP, detail (BnF, Department of manuscripts, Arab 2964)
SOURCE: GALLICA.BNF.FR/BNF

ḥubūb anīsūn (حبوب انيسون) whole aniseeds, used when the recipe does not require the seeds to be crushed, as in recipe i.5.11.

ʿaqāqīr (عقاقير) spices in general.

ʿaqāqīr Hindiyya (عقاقير هندية) Indian spices, such as spikenard, Ceylon cinnamon, cloves, and galangal.

ʿāqir qarḥā (عاقر قرحا) pellitory, also known as Spanish chamomile, *Anacyclus pyrethrum*. Its Amazigh name is *tāghandasat*. The plant is said to be indigenous to the Muslim West and the best is found in Ifrīqiya.[6] The part most used was the roots, which were in demand due to their many medicinal benefits. They were described as being intensely hot and sharp in properties and were believed to be capable of purging and cleansing the digestive system and breaking down foods to facilitate digestion. It was also said to boost the sexual activities of people with cold humoral properties.[7]

In recipe ii.2.45 for *balāja*, it is given as a substitute for ginger in case the latter is not available, which points to its availability and affordability over imported ginger.

baṣal (بصل) onions, *Allium cepa*, of which many types were available for the Andalusi cook, and they all differed in their properties and pungency depending on their shape and color. The white ones were generally less pungent than the red ones; the dried ones were more pungent than the fresh ones; and the raw ones were more pungent than the cooked ones.

Of the white onions, the following were grown at several locations in al-Andalus, such as Qalʿat Ayyūb 'Calatayud,' and Ṭurṭūsha 'Tortosa,' in the northeastern region of Catalonia:

1. White egg-shaped onions (*abyaḍ mudaḥraj*).
2. *Zubdī* onions that were butter yellow, quite large, oblate in shape (*mufarṭaḥ*), and slightly pungent.
3. Another variety of white onions, which were huge and oblate; a single onion would cover a pot. They were sweet and mellow.

Of the red onions, the following grew abundantly at places like Bāja 'Beja' and al-Jazīra al-Khaḍrā' 'Algeciras' in southern al-Andalus:

1. Small, red egg-shaped onions.
2. Red oblong onions, which were the most pungent and moist of all varieties.
3. Huge flattish red onions, called *baṣal Rūmī* (Byzantine onions), which looked like discs and were large enough to cover a pot.[8]

The following are the terms and varieties of onion used in al-Tujībī's cookbook:

baṣal abyaḍ (بصل ابيض) white onions, their juice is extracted and used in recipe iii.2.29 for a chicken dish.

baṣal akhḍar (بصل اخضر) green onions, used in recipe vi.1.2 to be eaten with a yogurt condiment.

6 See n. 1 above.
7 Ibn al-Bayṭār, *al-Jāmiʿ* iii 157–8; Ibn al-Jazzār, *al-Iʿtimād* 815–6; and al-Anṭākī, *Tadhkira* 258.
8 All information on onions and their varieties is from al-Ishbīlī, *ʿUmdat al-ṭabīb* i 93–4.

FIGURE 138 Pellitory, Dioscorides, *Fī Hayūlā al-ṭibb*, translation by Ḥunayn b. Isḥāq, fol. 147r, detail
FROM THE NEW YORK PUBLIC LIBRARY, SPENCER COLLECTION: HTTPS://DIGITALCOLLECTIONS.NYPL.ORG/ITEMS/5E66B3E8-EDAB-D471-E040-E00A180654D7

FIGURE 139 Onions, Dioscorides, *Fī Hayūlā al-ṭibb*, translation by Ḥunayn b. Isḥāq, fol. 107v, detail
FROM THE NEW YORK PUBLIC LIBRARY, SPENCER COLLECTION: HTTPS://DIGITALCOLLECTIONS.NYPL.ORG/ITEMS/5E66B3E8-9D1C-D471-E040-E00A18065 4D7

baṣal kabīr (بصل كبير) large onions, used mainly for their juice. In recipe v.1.9 they are pounded in a wooden mortar to extract juice and use it in a fish dish.

baṣala maqṭūʿa (بصلة مقطوعة) a chopped onion.

baṣala mashqūqa (بصلة مشقوقة) an onion that has been split into sections but left in one piece.

baṣal ṣaghīr (بصل صغير) small onions, used for chopping purposes, as in recipes i.2.17 and ii.6.8.

ṭaraf baṣala (طرف بصلة) a cut-off piece of an onion (more literally, a cut-off tip or side of an onion); sometimes referred to as *qiṭʿa min baṣala* 'a piece of an onion.'

With their hot and dry properties, onions were believed to open blockages and excite the appetite when eaten pickled or raw. If eaten raw, the recommendation was to rinse them first with salt and wine vinegar. They were said to generate winds and induce thirst. Eating a roasted onion for four consecutive days was believed to have the power to stimulate coitus, and eating onions first thing in the morning was said to increase semen. Cooking them with meat dishes was believed to have the benefit of eliminating the unpleasant odors of cooking meat.[9]

baṣal al-ʿunṣul (بصل العنصل) squills, *Drimia maritima*, a wild variety of onions called *baṣal barrī*, also called *ishqīl* (اشقيل). The onions with their large bulbs grow in a rocky coastal habitat, very common in the Mediterranean region. They are full of thick juice, bitter, and acrid in taste. Despite their intense bitterness, mice eat them readily only to succumb to their toxic scilliroside; that is why they were popular as a rodenticide, which gave them the name *baṣal al-faʾr* (بصل الفأر) 'onions for mice.' They were principally used for medicinal purposes in small amounts due to their strong hot and dry properties, which were believed to have rarefying powers that break up and thin down dense humors.[10]

In al-Tujībī's cookbook, squills are only used as vinegar infused with their properties, see recipe x.7.11. This vinegar is mentioned at the end of the fish chapter v.1 as one of the ways resorted to after eating fish to ward off its harms.

basbās (بسباس) herb fennel, *Foeniculum vulgare*, used for its fronds, fresh and dried, as an herb, and the seeds, which are the most commonly used part of the herb fennel.

Basbās was the plant's most common name in al-Andalus. Additionally, fennel seeds in al-Andalus were also called by another name, ***nāfiʿ*** (نافع), literally 'beneficial.' Al-Ishbīlī, *ʿUmdat al-ṭabīb* i 107 and 246, explains that this was its name among commoners in recognition of its blessed benefits for curing many ailments. In the eastern region, fennel was more commonly known as ***rāzyānaj*** (رازيانج) and ***shamar*** (شمر).

In al-Tujībī's cookbook, fennel is referred to in the following terms:

basbās (بسباس) fennel seeds. When fresh fennel, the vegetable, is called for in the recipe, it is always qualified with *akhḍar* 'green.'

basbās akhḍar (بسباس اخضر), literally 'green fennel,' it is bulb fennel, used fresh as a vegetable, see glossary 12.

bazr basbās (بزر بسباس) fennel seeds.

nāfiʿ (نافع) fennel seeds.

ʿūd basbās (عود بسباس) sprigs of herb-fennel fronds, used in al-Tujībī's recipes fresh and dried.

ʿuyūn al-basbās (عيون البسباس) tender tips of the herb fennel.

zarīʿat basbās (زريعة بسباس) fennel seeds.

---

9 Al-Ṭighnarī, edited by García Sánchez, *Zahrat al-bustān* 480; and Ibn al-Bayṭār, *al-Jāmiʿ* i 133.

10 See al-Anṭākī, *Tadhkira* 83.

FIGURE 140 A squill, Dioscorides, *Fī Hayūlā al-ṭibb*, translation by Ḥunayn b. Isḥāq, fol. 114v, detail
FROM THE NEW YORK PUBLIC LIBRARY, SPENCER COLLECTION: HTTPS://DIGITALCOLLECTIONS.NYPL.ORG/ITEMS/5E66B3E8-EC62-D471-E040-E00A180654D7

FIGURE 141 Herb fennel, *basbās*, Dioscorides, *Kitāb al-Ḥashā'ish fī hāyūlā al-ʿilāj al-ṭibbī*, Arabic translation by Ḥunayn b. Isḥāq, Or. 289, fol. 126r, detail
UNIVERSITAIRE BIBLIOTHEKEN LEIDEN, HTTP://HDL.HANDLE.NET/1887.1/ITEM:1578266

With their hot and dry properties, fennel seeds were used to open blockages in the liver and bladder and to drive out bloating winds. It was also said to encourage milk production in lactating mothers and sharpen eyesight. On the other hand, it was believed to be slow to digest and nutritionally insignificant.[11]

basbāsa (بسباسة) mace, the lacy skin covering nutmeg, see *jawzat al-ṭīb* below. Its properties and benefits are more or less like those of nutmeg. In al-Tujībī's cookbook, it is used only twice in handwashing preparations, recipes xii.2 and 6.

bazr kattān (بزر كتّان) linseeds, used in desserts, the way sesame seeds are used. They are not an ingredient used in al-Tujībī's recipes; they are only mentioned in his introductory section dealing with dietary regulations, p. 110.

Linseeds are said to cause bloating even when used already toasted. The best seeds are the newly harvested ones, heavy for their size, and soft due to the amount of oil they contain. With their hot and dry properties, they were said to improve the color of the complexion, were deemed good for the hair, and increased semen; having them mixed with honey and black pepper was said to invigorate coitus.[12]

bunk (بنك) an indeterminate aromatic ingredient used in hand cleansing and aromatic preparations in medieval Arabic sources, including cookbooks, medicinal and dietary books, and those dealing with botany and perfumes and other scented preparations. In al-Tujībī's cookbook, it is used in most of the handwashing preparations, *ghāsūlāt*, given in part xii. His source for this part was tenth-century Ibn al-Jazzār's book on perfumes and aromatics, *Kitāb fī Funūn al-ṭīb wa-l-ʿiṭr* 117–20.[13] For more on *bunk*, see Appendix 1.

būraq (بورق) a natural mineral, of which several varieties were known in medieval times. A major variety was the Armenian sodium borate, called *būraq Armanī*, said to be the purest. It was described as white, light, and brittle, and as having the strongest properties. Although it was said to be bad for the stomach, it was used in very small amounts medicinally, such as to relieve colic. With its hot, dry, and purging properties, it was used to cleanse the body and improve the color of the complexion. This was not the kind of *būraq* to be used for cooking purposes and ingested with foods.

Ibn al-Bayṭār, *al-Jāmiʿ* i 171, says that Armenian *būraq* was not available in his region, al-Andalus, adding that what they had was ***būraq Miṣrī*** (بورق مصري), which was sodium bicarbonate imported from Egypt,[14] of which there were two kinds:

---

11 Ibn al-Bayṭār, *al-Jāmiʿ* ii 428–30; and Ibn al-Jazzār, *al-Iʿtimād* 529–30.
12 Ibn Wāfid, *al-Adwiya al-mufrada* 49; and al-Anṭākī, *Tadhkira* 80.
13 Ibn al-Jazzār was a famous physician from al-Qayrawān (in Tunisia today) in the Maghreb.
14 It was obtained from the saline oases in western Egypt (Wādī Naṭrūn).

naṭrūn (نطرون), which was reddish in hue and tasted salty and sour with a trace of bitterness.

būraq al-khubz (بورق الخبز), which looked like white flour and tasted salty and sour, but not bitter. It was used as a leavening agent in making bread. We also learn from Ibn al-Bayṭār that the Egyptian bakers used to dissolve it in water and wipe the already shaped pieces of bread with its solution to make them look bright and glossy.

Naṭrūn and *būraq al-khubz* are similar due to their chemical component sodium bicarbonate. Both have hot, dry, and purging properties, but *naṭrūn* was said to be stronger in this respect; still, they were used interchangeably. For instance, in al-Tujībī's recipe x.7.10 for testing vinegar for adulteration, *būraq al-khubz*, which is used in the test, is said to be the same as *naṭrūn*. In another recipe, x.9.2, the flavor of olive oil is improved with the addition of *būraq* and salt.

When we come to the handwashing preparations, the ingredient *naṭrūn* is used in recipe xii.7. In this instance I translated it as borax, which is sodium borate, following Ibn al-Bayṭār, *al-Jāmiʿ* i 171, who says that in al-Andalus, true natron was not the abovementioned natural product of *būraq Miṣrī*. Rather, it was a variety of *būraq maṣnūʿ* (i.e., it was 'made'), resulting from cooking glass, potash, and other ingredients together. He described it as crystalized salt, with strong properties that had the power to break down densities and purge impurities. It was used in baths to wash off dirt and heal pruritus (*ḥakka*) and to improve the color of the complexion.[15]

būshīn (بوشين)[16] Macedonian parsley, *Petroselinum macedonicum*, more commonly known as *maqdūnis*. *Būshīn* was its name in al-ʿAjamiyya (Andalusi Romance), as al-Tujībī explains in recipe ii.1.9. See *karafs* and *maqdūnis* below.

dār Ṣīnī (دارصيني) cassia, *Cinnamomum cassia*, which literally means 'the Chinese tree.'[17] It is used only four times in al-Tujībī's cookbook,[18] unlike Ceylon cinnamon, *qirfa* (entry below), which is extensively used.

---

15 See also Ibn al-Jazzār, *al-Iʿtimād* 906–9.

16 Marín, "Words for Cooking" 41, rightly comments that the word should have been *barshīn*; see Corriente, *Dictionary of Andalusi Arabic*, s.v. p-r-sh-l/n, of which the original was *perrixín*. She suggests the possibility of *būshīn* being a copyist's mistake. There is also the possibility that the word represented an already corrupted form of the word; both the Berlin MS, fol. 27v, and the BL MS, fol. 127v, copy it as such. The Madrid MS does not include this bit of information.

17 According to al-Ghāfiqī, *Kitab fī l-Adwiya al-mufrada*, fol. 122r, this is the tree's name in Persian.

18 It is found in *ra's maymūn* recipe i.4.25, which uses squabs in preparing it; recipe i.4.35 for making *mujabbana*, recipe ix.4.1 for a walnut confection; and recipe xii.6 for a handwashing preparation.

FIGURE 142
Cassia, *Kitāb al-Diryāq*, fol. NP, detail
BNF, DEPARTMENT OF MANUSCRIPTS, ARAB 2964. SOURCE: GALLICA.BNF.FR/BNF

In medieval books on botany, four varieties of cinnamon were recognized:

dār Ṣīnī (دار صيني) cassia, true Chinese cinnamon imported from China, sometimes called *dār Ṣīnī al-Ṣīn*. It has thick, heavy, and brittle bark that is not so sweet, rather bitter and astringent, with an aroma closer to that of *qirfa* 'Ceylon cinnamon.'

dār ṣūṣ (دار صوص), which is inferior to true Chinese cinnamon. It is like true *qirfa* 'Ceylon cinnamon,' albeit browner and less brittle. It smells like true *qirfa* and is as fragrant and as sharp in taste, but it is less sweet than true *qirfa*, and hotter and dryer in properties.

qirfa (قرفة) true Ceylon cinnamon. It is intensely aromatic, sweetish, and somewhat sharp and pungent, but compared with cassia, *dār Ṣīnī* (see the first variety above), its hot and dry properties are weaker.

qirfat al-qaranful (قرفة القرنفل) combines the names of *qirfa* and *qaranful* (cloves). It is a thick bark that looks like *qirfa*, albeit darker and not as brittle, and tastes and smells like true cloves, but weaker in properties.[19]

In all its varieties, cinnamon is hot and dry in properties, albeit in varying degrees. It was believed to be good for the stomach by heating it up, aiding digestion, opening its blockages, and drying up phlegm. It was also believed to energize the brain, induce a state of euphoria, and arouse coitus. Cassia, the strongest among them, was extensively used in medicinal preparations, digestives, and aromatic compounds. It was believed to be good for the stomach.

ḍawmarān (ضومران) river mint, *Mentha acquatica*. Ibn al-Bayṭār, *al-Jāmiʿ* iii 127, points out that this was its name in al-Andalus; otherwise, *ḍaymarān* was its most common pronunciation. Its other names are: *ḥabaq al-māʾ* and *fūdhanaj nahrī*. It is a variety of wild mint, said to be the strongest in properties in heat and dryness. It was the mint variety to eat with bloating foods, such as lentils and fava beans.[20] It is used only once in al-Tujībī's cookbook, recipe xi.3 for boiled snails *aghlāl*. See also *ghubayrā* below.

fāghira (فاغرة) fagara, *Zanthoxylum fagara*, also called *kabāba Ṣīnī* 'Chinese cubeb.' It is a chickpea-like berry with a black seed inside. It was hot and dry in properties, mostly included in cures for the ailing stomach. It was also used as a mouth freshener and incorporated into perfumed compounds. It is used once in a handwashing preparations in al-Tujībī's recipe xii.6.[21]

fayjan (فيجن), ***fayjāl*** (فيجال) rue of the cultivated variety, *Ruta graveolens*. This was the herb's name in the Muslim West. It was more commonly called *sadhāb bustānī* in the eastern region, where it was more widely used in small amounts to garnish dishes. In al-Tujībī's cookbook, however, it is used only a few times in sauces, fish dishes, and with fava beans, added in small amounts.

---

19 See, for instance, al-Malik al-Muẓaffar, *al-Muʿtamad* 185–7; al-Ghāfiqī, *Kitab fī l-Adwiya al-mufrada*, fols. 122r–123v.

20 Ibn Jazla, *Minhāj al-bayān*, fol. 67r.

21 See Ibn Wāfid, *al-Adwiya al-mufrada* 168.

FIGURE 143 Cultivated rue, *fayjan*, Dioscorides, *Fī Hayūlā al-ṭibb*, translation by Ḥunayn b. Isḥāq, fol. 137v, detail
FROM THE NEW YORK PUBLIC LIBRARY, SPENCER COLLECTION: HTTPS://DIGITALCOLLECTIONS.NYPL.ORG/ITEMS/5E66B3E8-B7F0-D471-E040-E00A180654D7

Regardless of its bitter and acrid taste and unpleasant smell, rue was valued for its power to deflate flatulence and wind and remove garlic and onion odors when chewed after a meal. It was used as a contraceptive and abortive when inhaled. It was believed to work as an antidote to poison. Small quantities were recommended because having an excess of it was believed to dull the mind and heart and weaken the eyes.[22]

---

22 See Ibn al-Jazzār, *Kitāb fī Funūn al-ṭīb* 882–4.

fulāyū (فلايو), also occurs in other sources as ***fulayyā*** (فليا) and ***fulayya*** (فلية), pennyroyal, *Mentha pulegium*. It is a variety of wild mint, which Ibn al-Jazzār, *al-Iʿtimād* 741–7, says is of the mountain variety (*jabalī*), which has the strongest properties of dryness and heat among the other mint varieties. He describes the plant as having thin stalks with dusty-looking rounded leaves that emit a powerful aroma.

Pennyroyal was believed to excite the appetite, stimulate digestion, help purge dense and mucilaginous humors through the lungs and chest, and function as a diuretic. It was also believed to have the power to dislodge the placenta and abort fetuses.[23]

In al-Tujībī's cookbook, pennyroyal is used only once, in recipe x.7.11 for making vinegar flavored with squills (*khall al-ʿunṣul*), see the entry below.

fulful aswad (فلفل اسود) black peppercorns, *Piper nigrum*, ubiquitous in al-Tujībī's cookbook. The intense heat of black pepper was highly valued as an aid to digestion, expelling dense winds and opening blockages in the system. It was believed to excite the appetite and invigorate coitus. It was also said to be harmful to the kidneys, which can be remedied with honey.

ghubayrā (غبيرا), ***ghubayra*** (غبيرة) water mint, *Mentha aquatica*;[24] identified as ***fūdhanaj nahrī*** (فوذنج نهري), literally 'river mint,' in al-Ishbīlī, *ʿUmdat al-ṭabīb* ii 462 *Fūdhanaj nahrī* is a wild variety of mint said to grow along the banks of rivers and streams and is described as having leaves larger than those of the cultivated mint *naʿnaʿ*, with a strong, sharp aroma. With its hot and dry properties, it was said to help with bloating when eaten with gaseous foods, like fava beans and lentils. Smelling it was said to revive the fainted, and chewing it was believed to remove the odor of garlic.[25]

It is used twice in al-Tujībī's cookbook: recipe i.3.9 for coarsely crushed wheat (*jashīsh al-qamḥ*) and recipe x.7.11 for vinegar flavored with squills (*khall al-ʿunṣul*). See also *ḍawmarān* above.

harnuwa (هرنوة), also called ***fulayfula*** (فليفلة), fruits of the aloeswood tree of the species *Aquilaria*. They look like peppercorns, but smaller and tannish in color; their aroma resembles that of aloeswood. Physicians recommended them for strengthening the stomach and improving digestion. It was also said to refresh and gladden the soul, especially when chewed. Al-Bīrūnī, *al-Ṣaydana* 375–6, mentions that it was one of the ingredients used for making women's perfumes (*ṭīb al-nisāʾ*).[26]

---

23 Al-Anṭākī, *Tadhkira* 432–3.

24 This is not to be confused with *ghubayrāʾ* غبيراء, the sorbus fruit tree, *Sorbus domestica*.

25 Ibn al-Jazzār, *al-Iʿtimād* 741–7; al-Anṭākī, *Tadhkira* 278; and al-Malik al-Muẓaffar, *al-Muʿtamad* 434.

26 See also, al-Malik al-Muẓaffar, *al-Muʿtamad* 607; and al-Anṭākī, *Tadhkira* 365.

FIGURE 144 Black pepper, Dioscorides, *Fī Hayūlā al-ṭibb*, translation by Ḥunayn b. Isḥāq, fol. 110v, detail
FROM THE NEW YORK PUBLIC LIBRARY, SPENCER COLLECTION: HTTPS://DIGITALCOLLECTIONS.NYPL.ORG/ITEMS/5E66B3E8-C9F6-D471-E040-E00A180654D7

In al-Tujībī's cookbook, it is used in three of the handwashing preparations, recipes xii.1, 3, and 6.

ḥulba (حلبة) fenugreek, *Trigonella foenum-graecum*. The parts used of the plant are its seeds and leaves, and with their hot and dry properties, they were said to be beneficial for coughs and asthma, and for stimulating the appetite and coitus. The plant, however, was blamed for causing nausea and headaches when consumed in excess. It was also believed to foul the breath, perspiration, and urine.[27] In al-Tujībī's cookbook, it is used only once—the seeds, in recipe i.3.9 for wheat porridge.

27 Al-Malik al-Muẓaffar, *al-Muʿtamad* 133.

FIGURE 145 Fenugreek, *ḥulba*, al-Ghāfiqī, *Kitāb al-Adwiya al-mufrada*, MS, fol. 184r, detail
REPRODUCED BY PERMISSION OF THE OSLER LIBRARY OF THE HISTORY OF MEDICINE, MCGILL UNIVERSITY

ḥulba madbūgha (حلبة مدبوغة) fenugreek seeds that have been soaked in water, as mentioned in al-Tujībī's recipe i.3.9. From the anonymous *Kanz al-fawāʾid*, English trans., *Treasure Trove*, recipe 596, we learn that the seeds were kept soaked for two days to get rid of their bitterness.

idhkhir (اذخر) citronella, *Cymbopogon*, a sweet-smelling reed-like rush with small thin stems that sway with the wind. It has aromatic blossoms, which look like fluffed cotton, with roots that are black from the outside with a white inside. The roots and the blossoms are the parts used in al-Tujībī's recipes on handwashing preparations, recipes xii.1, 4, and 6.

FIGURE 146 *Idhkhir*, *Kitāb al-Diryāq*, fol. NP, detail
BNF, DEPARTMENT OF MANUSCRIPTS, ARAB 2964.
SOURCE: GALLICA.BNF.FR/BNF

fuqqāḥ al-idhkhir (فقاح الاذخر) the aromatic blossoms of citronella, which look like fluffed cotton.

uṣūl al-idhkhir (اصول الاذخر) citronella roots, black from the outside with a white inside; bitter in taste.

With its astringent properties, the plant was also used internally in medicinal preparations to help stop bleeding. An overdose was said to induce sleep. The fine stems themselves were used as toothpicks, called *khilāl ma'mūnī* (i.e., 'safe-to-use toothpicks'). They were also used in making brooms and baskets. The plant was said to be at its best when recently obtained; reddish with a good deal of blossoms. The plant's aroma was said to be akin to that of roses.[28]

jawzat al-ṭīb (جوزة الطيب), also called ***jawz bawwa*** (جوز بوة) nutmeg, *Myristica fragrans*, brought from India. According to al-Ghāfiqī, *Kitāb fī l-Adwiya al-mufrada* fol. 106v, good nutmeg was heavy and reddish brown. Light and dry black ones were bad quality. With its hot and dry properties, it was beneficial in sweetening the breath, aiding digestion, and dispelling winds.

In al-Tujībī's cookbook it is sparingly used: once in recipe ix.3.1 for delicate ring cookies; and in handwashing preparations, recipes xii.1, 3, and 4.

juljulān (جلجلان) sesame seeds, as they were more commonly called in the Muslim West. See *simsim* below.

juljulān abyaḍ maqshūr (جلجلان ابيض مقشور) hulled white sesame seeds, used in recipe ix.1.2 for a thickened starch-based pudding. Unhulled sesame is described as *ghayr maqshūr*.

kabāba (كبابة) cubeb, *Piper cubeba*, used in al-Tujībī's cookbook only in a couple handwashing preparations, recipes xii.2 and 6. Another name for it is *ḥabb al-ʿarūs* (حب العروس) 'the bride's seeds,' called so because the saliva of the groom who has chewed cubeb would pleasure his bride while having sex, as Ibn Sīnā explains in *al-Qānūn* i 520.

Kabāba are dark brown berries of the pepper family. They are aromatic, and their taste is tinged with bitterness. They were said to give a pleasant odor to the breath, mouth, and stomach and were believed to be good for gum diseases, which explains their inclusion in the cleansing *ushnān* compounds.[29]

kāfūr (كافور) camphor. It is the white and aromatic crystalline resinous sap of the camphor tree (*Cinnamomum camphora*), native to India and China. The tree was described as being so huge that its shade was enough to accommodate a hundred men. Several such fantastical stories also tell how the tree was often frequented and protected by tigers (called *bubūr*, sg. *babr*). Camphor gatherers had access to the trees for only a month, when tigers were in heat, and as a result of which they would get sick, and both males and females would head to the seashores to cure themselves with seawater.[30]

---

28 Ibn al-Bayṭār, *al-Jāmiʿ* i 21; Ibn al-Jazzār, *al-Iʿtimād* 675–7; Ibn Wāfid, *al-Adwiya al-mufrada* 47–8; al-Bīrūnī, *al-Ṣaydana* 27–8; and Ibn Jazla, *Minhāj al-bayān*, fol. 20r.

29 Ibn al-Jazzār, *al-Iʿtimād* 220; and Ibn al-Bayṭār, al-*Jāmiʿ* iv 303–4.

30 Al-Nuwayrī, *Nihāyat al-arab* xi 195–7.

FIGURE 147 A camphor tree being protected by a tiger, al-Qazwīnī, *ʿAjāʾib al-makhlūqāt wa ghārāʾib al-mawjūdāt*, fol. 171v, detail

FROM THE NEW YORK PUBLIC LIBRARY, SPENCER COLLECTION: HTTPS://DIGITALCOLLECTIONS.NYPL.ORG/ITEMS/EA052830-28EB-0138-9209-2D6DAE5BDED6

Two kinds of camphor were available depending on how they were obtained:

kāfūr makhlūq (كافور مخلوق), which was naturally extracted by slitting the tree and collecting the seeping resin.

kāfūr maʿmūl (كافور معمول), which was extracted from the cut wood by boiling it so that it released the remaining resin.

With its cold and dry properties, camphor was medicinally used to treat headaches and heat-related ailments. It was also believed to boost the psyche (*muqawwī lil-nafs*) and exhilarate the heart (*mufarriḥ*), as we are told in al-Tujībī's recipe ii.2.21, where it has to be used in combination with musk and ambergris. This was necessary to counterbalance the camphor's cold properties and counteract its negative effects on the libido.[31]

In al-Tujībī's cookbook camphor is incorporated into some of the handwashing compounds given in part 12 and added to savory dishes in very small amounts, as in recipe iii.2.30 for *Ibrāhīmiyya* and recipe iii.2.31 for *Jūdhāba*. There is even a dish called *kāfūriyya*, recipe iii.2.4, made to resemble camphor with its fair color and seasoned with a bit of camphor. It is also used in the dried cookies called *kaʿk* and several sweets. It did not seem to be a readily available or affordable flavoring item; in *ushnān* recipe xii.5, the instruction is to use camphor if available (*in amkana*).

kammūn (كمون) cumin seeds, *Cuminum cyminum*, of which many varieties are known, but no particular kind is demanded in any of al-Tujībī's recipes. The most commonly used cumin was the tan-colored variety, called *kammūn abyaḍ* 'white cumin.'

With its hot and dry properties, cumin was believed to have the power to dissipate gastric winds, aid digestion, and warm the cold liver. As a seasoning spice, it is repeatedly used in al-Tujībī's recipes for savory dishes prepared with all kinds of meat, but more frequently with fava beans and eggplant dishes.

karafs (كرفس). In the medieval Arabo-Muslim world, the name *karafs* designated:

1. Stalk celery, *Apium graveolens var. dulce*.
2. The herb parsley, *Petroselinum sativum*, of which two varieties were known:
   2.1. *karafs* (كرفس) common parsley, *Petroselinum crispum*.
   2.2. *maqdūnis* (مقدونس) Macedonian parsley, *Petroselinum macedonicum*, see the *maqdūnis* entry below for more on this type of parsley.

Maqdūnis was the variety used in al-Tujībī's cookbook. As for stalk celery, only the seeds (*bazr karafs*) were included in his book.

31 See Ibn al-Bayṭār, *al-Jāmiʿ* iv 296–7; al-Anṭākī, *Tadhkira* 293; and Ibn al-Jazzār, *al-Iʿtimād* 644–5.

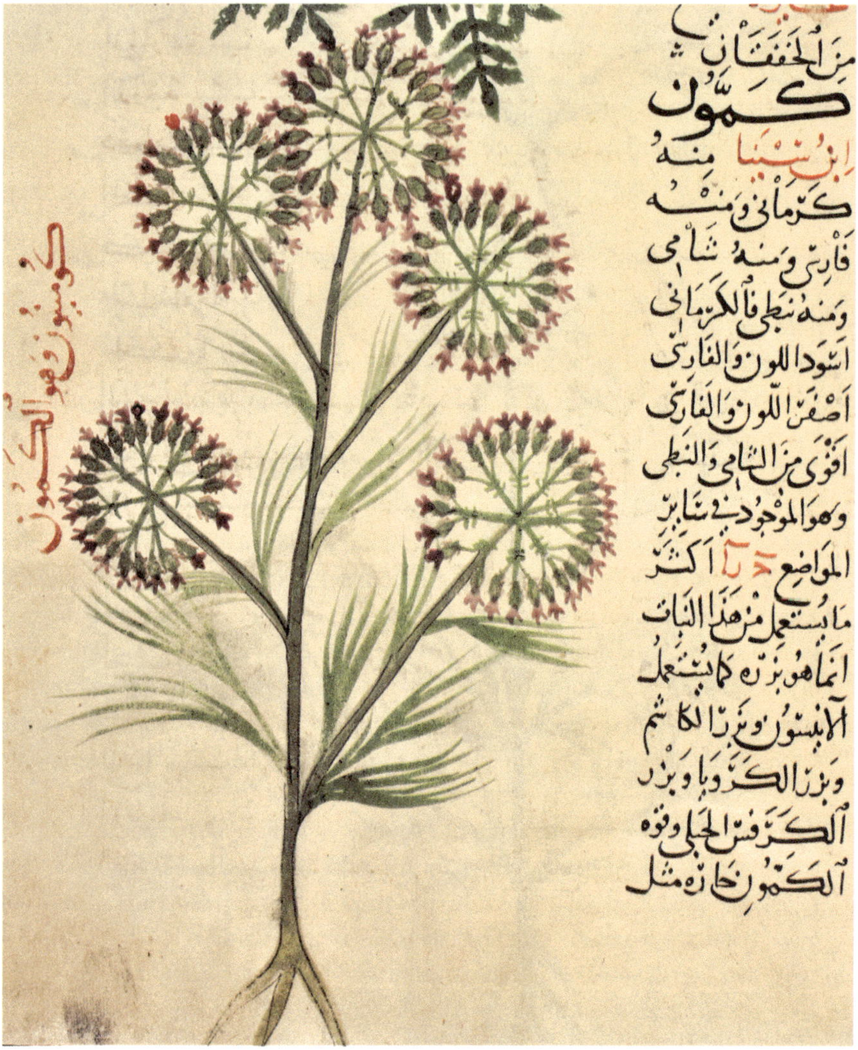

FIGURE 148 Cumin, al-Ghāfiqī, *Kitāb al-Adwiya al-mufrada*, MS, fol. 258r, detail
REPRODUCED BY PERMISSION OF THE OSLER LIBRARY OF THE HISTORY OF MEDICINE, MCGILL UNIVERSITY

bazr karafs (بزر كرفس) celery seeds, used only once in al-Tujībī's cookbook, in recipe v.1.13 for a fish dish. The seeds were believed to be beneficial to the stomach and to have the power to open liver blockages.[32]

32 Al-Rāzī, *al-Ḥāwī* vii 153.

FIGURE 149 Common parsley, Dioscorides, *Fī Hayūlā al-ṭibb*, translation by Ḥunayn b. Isḥāq, fol. 143v, detail
FROM THE NEW YORK PUBLIC LIBRARY, SPENCER COLLECTION: HTTPS://DIGITALCOLLECTIONS.NYPL.ORG/ITEMS/5E66B3E9-1AEE-D471-E040-E00A180654D7

FIGURE 150 Caraway, Dioscorides, *Ajzāʾ min risāla fī l-nabātāt*, fol. 63v, detail
BNF, DEPARTMENT OF MANUSCRIPTS, ARAB 4947. SOURCE: GALLICA.BNF.FR/BNF

With its hot and dry properties, parsley was said to excite the appetite, open blockages, and dissolve kidney stones. It was diuretic and had the power to drive out dense winds and freshen the breath. It was also believed to invigorate coitus in both men and women.[33]

karāwiya (كراوية) caraway, *Carum carvi*. The entire plant is aromatic, but the seeds are the most commonly used part. It is moderately used in al-Tujībī's cookbook in meat dishes and vegetable ones, especially those of eggplant and gourd. With its hot and dry properties, it was primarily used to aid digestion, relieve bloating, and purge the system of gastric winds.[34]

33 See al-Anṭākī, *Tadhkira* 298.

34 Ibn al-Jazzār, *al-Iʿtimād* 678; and al-Ṭighnarī, *Zahrat al-bustān* 464–5.

FIGURE 151 Tragacanth, *kathīrā'*, al-Ghāfiqī, *Kitāb al-Adwiya al-mufrada*, MS, fol. 256r, detail
REPRODUCED BY PERMISSION OF THE OSLER LIBRARY OF THE HISTORY OF MEDICINE, MCGILL UNIVERSITY

kathīrā (كثيرا) gum of the tragacanth tree, *Astragalus gummifer*. Its white variety was deemed the best for edible purposes. It is used once in al-Tujībī's cookbook, in recipe x.3.1 for pickled lemons. It is viscous, odorless, and tasteless; and with its moderate properties, it was deemed good for coughs and chest ailments. Gum arabic (*ṣamgh ʿArabī*) was often used as a substitute.[35]

khall (خل), pl. *khulūl* (خلول) vinegar. In al-Tujībī's cookbook, it is used for pickling vegetables, fruits, and fish, see chapters x.2–6. Recipes for making vinegar are given in chapter x.7. Vinegar is also a liquid spice, extensively used in savory dishes as a seasoning agent. In a chicken dish called *mukhallal*, recipe iii.2.6, it is the principal seasoning ingredient.

35 Ibn al-Jazzār, *al-Iʿtimād* 455–6.

Additionally, as reflected in the two extant Andalusi cookbooks, al-Tujībī's and the anonymous *Anwāʿ al-ṣaydala, khall* not only designates regular 'vinegar' produced by fermentation but also, in a looser sense, unfermented preserved 'sour juice,' and even freshly pressed out lemon juice and sour unripe grapes. See the relevant entries below.

With its cold and dry properties, vinegar was believed to have rarefying and drying effects on the body. It was deemed beneficial to the stomach and was believed to have the power to excite the appetite. In his introduction, al-Tujībī quotes the famous saying by the Prophet Muḥammad, *Niʿma al-idām al-khall* "vinegar is the best of appetizers."

khall abyaḍ (خل ابيض) white vinegar.

khall fātir (خل فاتر) vinegar that has weakened and is no longer acidic enough.

khall al-fulful (خل الفلفل) vinegar infused with black pepper; it is aromatic and digestive.

khall ḥādhiq (خل حاذق) very sour vinegar.[36]

khall ḥiṣrim (خل حصرم) unfermented preserved juice of unripe grapes. For recipes on preserving the juice, see recipe x.7.12 for the sun-cooked variety, *maʿmūl lil-shams* 'made to be left in the sun,' which al-Tujībī deems a high-quality variety. Recipe x.7.13 describes the fire-cooked variety, and recipe x.7.14 is for the freshly extracted juice.[37] For unripe grapes, see *ḥiṣrim* in glossary 8, s.v. *ʿinab*.

In al-Tujībī's cookbook, all the recipes that incorporate unripe grapes use it in this preserved form called *khall* 'vinegar.' For instance, it is used in sauces that are paired with roasted and fried meats, as in recipes ii.1.9 and iii.7.2, and recipe v.1.29 with tuna. Still, in three recipes, ii.1.9, ii.2.24, and iii.2.17, the so-called vinegar is just the sour juice of fresh unripe grapes, see the next entry.

khall ḥiṣrim ṭarī (خل حصرم طري) freshly extracted juice of sour grapes, used in recipes ii.1.9, ii.2.24, and iii.2.17. It is in fact no more than sour grape juice that is extracted by first boiling the fresh bunches to soften them and then pressing them, see recipe x.7.14. This would be prepared by those who needed this ingredient while it is still early in the season for the sun-cooked variety given in recipe x.7.12, and which al-Tujībī describes, in recipe iii.2.17, as *maʿmūl lil-shams* (معمول للشمس) 'made to be left in the sun' and deems it a high-quality variety.

36 In the degrees of sourness of vinegar, while *thaqīf* designates very sour vinegar, *ḥādhiq* designates even a more intense level of sourness.

37 Cf. three recipes for preserving the juice of unripe grapes in the anonymous fourteenth-century Egyptian cookbook *Kanz al-fawāʾid*, English trans., *Treasure Trove*, recipes 152–4.

khall ḥulw (خل حلو), literally 'sweet,' it is mild vinegar that is gentle in nature.

khall ḥulw ḥāmiḍ (خل حلو حامض) vinegar that is sour-sweet.

khall 'inab (خل عنب) grape vinegar, see recipe x.7.1 for making it.

khall līm (خل ليم), also called ***khall laymūnī*** (خل ليموني) in recipe ii.1.8. It is preserved lemon juice, see recipe x.7.15 for making it. It may also designate freshly pressed lemon juice, see *mā' al-līm* in glossary 7, s.v. *līm.*

khall līm ṭarī (خل ليم طري), although called 'vinegar,' it is in fact no more than extracted fresh lemon juice, as it is used in two recipes: 5.1.29, where it is drizzled on fried pieces of dried tuna before serving it; and x.3.1, where it is used to submerge salted lemons ready for pickling in a vessel. For the usage of the term *khall*, see the main entry above.

khall na'na' (خل نعنع) distilled vinegar infused with mint, see recipe x.7.16.

khall ṭayyib (خل طيب) fine tasting vinegar.

khall al-'unṣul (خل العنصل) vinegar flavored with squills (*baṣal al-'unṣul*), which is a variety of wild onion, *Drimia maritima*. See *baṣal al-'unṣul* in this section and recipe x.7.11 for making it.

khall zunbū' (خل زنبوع) preserved juice of Damascus citron.[38] Al-Tujībī includes no recipes for making it.

khamīr al-khall (خمير الخل) vinegar base, which has a paste-like consistency, made in recipe x.7.9, to be stored and used as needed. According to the instructions, whenever one wants to make vinegar, a pound of this *khamīr* is dissolved in hot water and then whipped and cooked on the fire until the mix looks like vinegar. The resulting vinegar was regarded by some as adulterated because it is artificially made.[39] To al-Tujībī and makers of such vinegars, it must have been a convenient and acceptable way for obtaining vinegar when the 'natural' stuff was not available, or when traveling.

khūlanjān (خولنجان) galangal, *Alpinia galangala*. It is a rhizome of the ginger family, said to be imported from China. It is used sparingly in al-Tujībī's cookbook: twice in dishes cooked with large fish, once in a Qāhiriyya cookie, and once in preserved lemons.

With its hot and dry properties, it was recommended for phlegmatic people and was used in cooking and in medicinal preparations as an aid to digestion and a breath freshener. It was especially recommended as an aphrodisiac. Holding a piece

---

38 It is more commonly known as *kabbād* in the eastern region al-Mashriq. See glossary 7 for more on this fruit.

39 See al-Jawbarī, *al-Mukhtār fī kashf al-asrār*, a thirteenth-century book on revealing swindlers' secrets.

of it in one's mouth was said to cause an intense erection, so says Ibn al-Jazzār, *al-I'timād* 673–4.

khur' ḥamām (خرء حمام), ***jawz ḥamām*** (جوز حمام) a variety of lightweight usnea mingled with mud. It is mentioned in one of al-Tujībī's handwashing preparations, recipe xii.4.

The name as it occurs in al-Tujībī's cookbook is alternatively called *jawz jundum*—a Persian loan word—in medieval books on botany, where it is compared to dried light-yellow and chickpea-like granulated clay.[40] Al-Anṭākī says it is something (*shay'*, for lack of a better definitive term) that is a cross between a plant and soil; clumped in granules like tan chickpeas. He further speculates that their moisture caused them to be lightly mixed with soil. Ibn Sīnā, *al-Qānūn* i. 525, s.v. كور كندم, is more specific in describing it as a lightweight variety of usnea (ushna) mingled with clay. The ingredient's Arabic name is variously given as:

khur' ḥamām 'pigeons' droppings,'[41] as it was called in Raqqa in the Levant; also described as *Raqqī*.

jawz ḥundum, as its name was in Baghdad.

turbat al-'asal, literally 'honey soil,' in al-Andalus, where it was said to have been imported from Zāb al-Qayrawān (now in Tunisia); described as *Barbarī* (Amazigh), with very strong properties. Its Andalusi name stems from the practice of using it to make strong honey wine, which was said to develop intoxicating levels of alcohol within one day. Bees were also said to feed on them, resulting in honey that was said to be more intoxicating than wine.

With the exception of al-Tujībī's recipe, none of the botanical sources mention its use in handwashing preparations; it was mainly touted as a strong sex enhancer, increasing semen and arousing coitus, but also as an aid for weight gain. Given its drying, cooling, and purging properties, as well as its power to check bleeding, it might have indeed been useful in such handwashing compounds.

kundur (كندر) frankincense, also known as *lubān*. It is the resinous gum of the olibanum tree, *Boswellia sacra*, of the Yemen region. Although generally used for incense, it is included in a handwashing preparation in recipe xii.4. With its hot and dry prop-

---

40 Al-Musta'īnī, *al-Mufradāt al-ṭibbiyya* 21; Ibn al-Jazzār, *al-I'timād* 234; Ibn al-Bayṭār, *al-Jāmi'* i 244; Ibn Wāfid, *al-Adwiya al-mufrada* 91; and al-Anṭākī, *Tadhkira* 122. It is inaccurately identified as a tree called mangosteen, *Garcinia mangostana*, in Ghālib, *Mawsū'a*, s.v. جوز كندم.

41 Cf. a variety of potash—mentioned in Mashriqi sources—called *khur' al-'aṣāfīr* 'sparrows droppings' due to its white-colored granules. See al-Warrāq, *Kitāb al-Ṭabīkh*, English trans., *Annals* 778–9.

FIGURE 152 Coriander plant, *kuzbara*, Dioscorides, *Kitāb al-Ḥashā'ish fī hāyūlā al-ʿilāj al-ṭibbī*, Arabic translation by Ḥunayn b. Isḥāq, Or. 289, fol. 134r, detail
UNIVERSITAIRE BIBLIOTHEKEN LEIDEN, HTTP://HDL.HANDLE.NET/1887.1/ITEM:1578266

erties, it was used to dry up phlegm in the chest and treat bronchitis. It was also believed to aid digestion and enhance memory.[42]

kuzbara (كزبرة) coriander, *Coriandrum sativum*. The word designates the seeds and the leaves, and a distinction is made by referring to the fresh cilantro leaves as ***kuzbara raṭba*** (كزبرة رطبة) and ***kuzbara khaḍrā'*** (كزبرة خضراء). When the recipe requires only

42 See Ibn al-Bayṭār, *al-Jāmiʿ* iv 348–52.

the tender tips of the cilantro stems, they would be called *ʿuyūn al-kuzbara al-khaḍrā*ʾ (عيون الكزبرة الخضراء). The seeds are referred to as ***kuzbara yābisa*** (كزبرة يابسة), and often just as *kuzbara*. Al-Maghribi physician, al-Ghassānī, *Ḥadīqat al-azhār* 139, says that commoners in his city of Fez called it *qaṣbūr* (قصبور).

The fragrant coriander seeds and leaves are extensively used in al-Tujībī's cookbook; they are present in almost all the savory dishes, which is comparable to the ubiquitous use of the plant in the extant Arabic medieval books hailing from the eastern region. By contrast, the herb parsley has limited uses in al-Tujībī's cookbook, see the *maqdūnis* entry below for more on this issue.

Fresh leaves of cilantro were said to improve digestion and induce sleep. It was believed that chewing the seeds or the fresh leaves would remove the unpleasant breath odors of onion and garlic. The advantage of the seeds was that they linger in the stomach with the food in it, thus giving it time to digest well. The seeds and the leaves were believed to strengthen the heart and delight the soul.[43]

maḥlab (محلب) aromatic kernels of pits of a variety of small black cherries, *Prunus mahaleb*, of a mountainous tree growing in Lebanon and Azerbaijan. Crushed *maḥlab* is used in one of al-Tujībī's handwashing preparations, recipe xii.2, as it was believed to have the power to remove the undesirable greasy odors of foods and bodily odors. Using it internally had the benefit of purifying the stomach and dissipating dense winds.[44]

māʾ līm (ماء ليم) fresh lemon juice, used in small amounts, or to taste, in several recipes. See *māʾ līm* in this section, s.v. *khall*.

māʾ līm akhḍar (ماء ليم اخضر) lime juice, used once in a meatless eggplant dish, recipe vii.2.11. For lemon, the fruit, see *līm* in glossary 7.

māʾ līm ghaḍḍ (ماء ليم غض) juice of fresh and tender lemons, mentioned once in recipe ix.6.2 for sugar candy.

māʾ maṭar (ماء مطر) rainwater, used as a substitute for fresh sweet water (*māʾ ʿadhb*) in recipe i.5.5. Rainwater was stored and used, as it was deemed an excellent quality water, especially when gathered during the summer and during thunderstorms. Water gathered during stormy weather was not approved of. The disadvantage of rainwater was that it got putrid fast due to lack of density in its properties. The remedy was to boil it before it putrefied.[45]

maqdūnis (مقدونس), ***bakdūnis*** (بكدونس), ***baqdūnis*** (بقدونس) Macedonian parsley, *Petroselinum macedonicum*, which is a variety of *karafs bustānī*, the cultivated herb

---

43 Ibn al-Bayṭār, *al-Jāmiʿ* iv 327–31; Ibn Wāfid, *al-Adwiya al-mufrada* 58–9; al-Malik al-Muẓaffar, *al-Muʿtamad* 488–9; and al-Anṭākī, *Tadhkira* 300–1.

44 See Ibn al-Jazzār, *al-Iʿtimād* 392–3; and al-Anṭākī, *Tadhkira* 322–3.

45 See Ibn al-Bayṭār, *al-Jāmiʿ* iv 409.

parsley, *Petroselinum sativum*, called ***būshīn*** (بوشين)[46] in al-ʿAjamiyya (Andalusi Romance), as al-Tujībī explains in recipe ii.1.9. It was also named *karafs Rūmī* 'Byzantine parsley' and *karafs jabalī* 'mountain parsley.' The other variety of the herb parsley is *karafs*, *Petroselinum crispum*, common parsley.

Of the two types of cultivated parsley (*karafs bustānī*), common parsley (*karafs*) and Macedonian parsley (*maqdūnis*), the latter is described as having smaller leaves, which are more aromatic and sharper in taste than the former.[47] It was also described as the greenest of all varieties of parsley.[48] Al-Ishbīlī, *ʿUmdat al-ṭabīb* i 315, says that it was plentiful in al-Andalus and describes it as being flavorful and pleasantly aromatic. In addition, the Moroccan physician al-Ghassānī, *Ḥadīqat al-azhār* 138, says that *karafs* was common and well-known in his city of Fez.

In al-Tujībī's cookbook, *maqdūnis* is used just a few times: it is incorporated into dipping sauces served with a pot roast, recipe ii.1.9; grilled rabbit, recipe ii.5.7; and fried fish, recipe v.1.8. In recipe x.5.1, eggplants prepared for pickling are slit and stuffed with sprigs of *maqdūnis* along with other slits stuffed with sprigs of mint. Lack of culinary interest in this herb cannot possibly be attributed to its scarcity in al-Andalus; as displayed in the previous paragraph, it grew abundantly there. It was as available and well-known in the Muslim West, as it was in the eastern region, al-Mashriq.[49]

Still, use of parsley in al-Tujībī's cookbook does not compare with that of the ubiquitous coriander plant (*kuzbara*)—both the fresh herb and the seeds. The abundant presence of coriander in Andalusi cuisine, as reflected in al-Tujībī's recipes, might be attributed to its much more pronounced flavor and fragrance than the timid parsley, whose seeds, besides, play an insignificant role in their daily cooking. Economically perhaps, propagating a plant like coriander, whose leaves and seeds were equally aromatic and bursting with flavor, cannot be underestimated, especially when in the general medicinal opinion of their physicians and herbalists, whatever worked with parsley would work equally well with coriander.[50]

marzanjūsh (مرزنجوش) marjoram, *Origanum majorana*; also called *mardaqūsh* (مردقوش) and *ādhān al-fār* (آذان الفار) 'mouse ears.' It is a very sweet-smelling herb with fuzzy leaves. In al-Tujībī's cookbook it is used several times as an ingredient

46 See n. 16 above.
47 As explained in Ibn al-Jazzār, *al-Iʿtimād* 776–8.
48 Ibn Waḥshiyya, *al-Filāḥa al-Nabaṭiyya* ii 781.
49 It is to be pointed out here that the argument offered in Marín, "Words for Cooking" 41–2, regarding the herb parsley is inexact. Marín's observation is that "scarce use of parsley" in al-Tujībī's cookbook "matches its absence in the Eastern cookbooks." Parsley, the herb and, to a much lesser extent, celery, were never absent in the eastern cookbooks; on the contrary, it was frequently used in the extant eastern recipes.
50 Ibn al-Bayṭār, *al-Jāmiʿ* iv 310.

FIGURE 153
Marjoram, *marzanjūsh*, Dioscorides, *Kitāb Dīsqūrīdis fī mawādd al-ʿilāj*, fol. 33r, detail
BRITISH LIBRARY: ORIENTAL MANUSCRIPTS, OR 3366, IN QATAR DIGITAL LIBRARY HTTPS://WWW.QDL.QA/ARCHIVE/81055/VDC_100022531380.0X000001

in handwashing preparations and once in a recipe for vinegar, x.7.11. With its hot and dry properties, it was recommended for treating cold-related ailments, such as nasal congestions and opening blockages. Its strong properties were said to hasten intoxication when sniffing it while drinking wine.[51]

maṣṭakā (مصطكا) mastic, which is resin obtained from the mastic tree, *Pistacia lentiscus*. Another name for it is *ʿilk Rūmī* (علك رومي) 'Byzantine gum.' It was said to have been brought from Cypris and the mastic island Khios. The best was described as bright white and sweet smelling.

ḥabbat maṣṭakā (حبة مصطكا) a lump of mastic.

Mastic was valued for its refreshing aroma and was believed to have medicinal benefits, such as thinning phlegm to facilitate its purging, heating the stomach, and exciting the appetite. It is chewed as gum and taken internally to freshen the breath and induce aromatic belching. It is also said that cooking rainwater with a bit of mastic would improve its taste and its digestibility. Ibn Rushd, *al-Kulliyyāt* 430, acknowledges its popularity in al-Andalus, saying that its benefits, especially in fortifying the stomach and all other organs, are so well-known in the region that he does not need to elaborate on the issue.

In al-Tujībī's cookbook it is repeatedly used in savory dishes, such as soups, stews, couscous, meatballs, fish balls, and meat patties, and chicken, fish, and egg dishes,

51 See Ibn al-Jazzār, *al-Iʿtimād* 657–9; and al-Malik al-Muẓaffar, *al-Muʿtamad* 557.

as it was believed to remove the unpleasant odors of the cooking meats (*zafar*) and aid their digestion. Mastic is also used in pickling lemons and to flavor sweets and the syrups in which they are drenched.

mā' ward (ماء ورد) distilled rosewater, used in cooking and aromatic preparations. Medicinally, it was valued for its moderately cold, dry, and astringent properties, used to cool the hot stomach and liver, strengthen the brain, and relieve hangover symptoms.[52]

In al-Tujībī's cookbook, it is used a few times, added in small amounts in savory dishes, as in a meat dish called *rāhibī*, recipe ii.1.7; sausages, recipe ii.6.4; and sauce served with a grilled rabbit, recipe ii.5.7. Still, it is more frequently used in sweet-savory dishes, as in a sweet lamb dish, recipe ii.3.8; some of the dishes borrowed from the eastern region, such as sweetened *zīrbājiyya*, recipe iii.2.5; and *tharīd* dishes of chicken stewed in sweetened broth, recipes iii.2.46 and 47. It is also used to flavor pastries and sweets.

may'a yābisa (ميعة يابسة) sweet-smelling dry storax resin, obtained from the bark of the storax tree, *Styrax*, also called the benzoin tree. *May'a* is generally available in three forms:

may'a sā'ila (ميعة سائلة), also called *isṭarak* (إصطرك). It is resin with a honey-like consistency extracted from the bark of the storax tree by boiling it and pressing out the resin.

may'a yābisa (ميعة يابسة) designates the bark after boiling it (see above) with the remaining resin attached to it.

lubnā (لبنى) is storax gum (*ṣamgh*), deemed the best among them.

All these varieties were valued for their aroma and antiseptic qualities when applied topically. The aromatic resin is used in perfumes and incense. Additionally, with its hot and dry properties, it was said to be medicinally effective in treating cold-related ailments, just by inhaling it.[53] It is used in two handwashing preparations in al-Tujībī's last part, recipes xii.2, 4.

milḥ (ملح) salt. It is always added to the dishes as needed, although not all the recipes mention it with the rest of the ingredients. For cooking purposes and in foods, the salt used was usually white (see *milḥ abyaḍ* below), added to foods already washed and cleaned (see *milḥ maghsūl* below).

Salt was valued as an aid for food preservation for its power to dry up moisture and combat putridity. In cooking meat dishes, its use was necessary to eliminate

52 See Ibn al-Jazzār, *al-I'timād* 136–7.

53 See ibid., 270–3; and Ibn Wāfid, *al-Adwiya al-mufrada* 71–2.

FIGURE 154 A storax tree, Dioscorides, *Fī Hayūlā al-ṭibb*, translation by Ḥunayn b. Isḥāq, fol. 39r, detail
FROM THE NEW YORK PUBLIC LIBRARY, SPENCER COLLECTION: HTTPS://DIGITALCOLLECTIONS.NYPL.ORG/ITEMS/5E66B3E8-EA79-D471-E040-E00A180654D7

the unpleasant greasy odors (*zafar*) of meat. It was believed to excite the appetite and aid digestion.[54]

Al-Tujībī's cookbook does not specify the kind of salt used, except in the following cases:

milḥ abyaḍ (ملح ابيض) white salt. Two varieties of edible white salt were common in medieval kitchens:

> ***milḥ Andarānī*** (ملح اندراني), also called *milḥ ṭabarzad* (طبرزد), rock salt; it was deemed of a fine quality, distinguished by its pure white color and translucent crystals.
>
> ***milḥ sabkhī*** (ملح سبخي) salt obtained by solar evaporation of saline waterbodies; also called *milḥ al-ʿajīn* (ملح العجين) and *milḥ al-khubz* (ملح الخبز); although literally it is 'salt for making bread,' it was used as an all-purpose salt.

White salt is called for in recipe x.2.1 for brine-cured green olives. Specifying the kind of salt in this case is necessary to ensure that the vibrant greenness of the olives would not be spoiled with impure salt.

milḥ maghsūl (ملح مغسول) washed salt, which was cleansed and purified by dissolving it into brine first to get rid of all the sand and other impurities by straining it and then boiling it until it crystalized. This clean and pure salt is specifically called for in two simple white stews (*tafāyā bayḍāʾ*), recipes ii.2.1 and iii.2.1, to preserve the whiteness of the dish.

milḥ maqlū (ملح مقلو) parched salt grains, used in recipe x.9.2, along with other ingredients, to remedy olive oil that has gone bad and to improve its taste. Heating up salt by parching it was believed to intensify its already hot and dry properties, which would have the power to draw out humidity and impurities.

misk (مسك) musk. It is a greasy secretion produced in a glandular sac beneath the skin of the abdomen, behind the navel of the male musk deer (*Moschus*), described as having two white span-long tusks that grow upwards. We are told that these deer were found in Tibet and China, but musk from the former was deemed superior because deer over there fed on aromatic plants like Indian spikenard (*sunbul al-ṭīb*) and other aromatics. Another factor that affected the quality of musk was that in Tibet, musk gatherers did not take the secretion directly from the sac (called *nāfija*, pl. *nawāfij*);[55] instead, they let it mature inside it and waited to gather the secretion

---

54 See Ibn al-Bayṭār, *al-Jāmiʿ* iv 455–8; Ibn al-Jazzār, *al-Iʿtimād* 897–901.

55 The full sac that is still attached to the deer is called *faʾrat al-misk* (فأرة المسك) because it looks like a mouse.

when the deer rubbed its sac on hot rocks to release it. And even if they did hunt the deer and cut off their sacs, they would leave the musk inside and trade them as such. Not so in China, where deer were hunted and their sacs cut off even before the musk inside them matured—much like fruit when picked before they ripen. Additionally, their musk was taken out of the sacs and traded; adulterating musk was easy when handled this way.[56]

With its hot and dry properties, musk was believed to be beneficial for the elderly and people with cold properties during winter. It was also said to induce euphoria and invigorate coitus.[57]

In al-Tujībī's cookbook, musk is used in two handwashing preparations, recipes xii.2–3. It is also internally ingested by incorporating it into several dishes in small quantities, for its aroma and medicinal benefits, as in recipes i.4.8 and 10, iii.2.31, and ix.3.4 for pastries and sweets. In recipe ii.2.21 for a meat dish with apples, the instruction is to spice it with musk (*misk*) along with other aromatics, like rosewater and camphor, if the intended effect is to boost the psyche (*muqawwī lil-nafs*) and exhilarate the heart (*mufarriḥ*).

murkīra (مركيرة) a variety of thyme, see *ṣaʿtar* below.

murrī (مري) liquid fermented sauce, used as a seasoning ingredient and a table sauce. For the latter, see the entry in glossary 5. *Murrī* as a seasoning agent is frequently used in al-Tujībī's recipes. Chapter x.8 provides an impressive variety of recipes for making *murrī*, ranging from the sun-fermented cereal-based and fish-based ones to the nonfermented ones, which are cooked on the fire. The recipes mentions two grades of *murrī*:[58]

al-murrī al-awwal (المري الاول) first *murrī*, obtained from the first round of straining the fermented or cooked sauce. It is deemed a prime quality sauce, good enough to serve as a table sauce. The Madrid MS, fol. 127v, also calls it *ra's al-murrī* 'the best.'

al-murrī al-thānī (المري الثاني) second *murrī*, obtained from the second round of straining the sauce. From recipe x.8.2 we learn that it is good enough for cooking purposes. The remaining dregs after the second round are only good enough for fuel.[59]

The *murrī* varieties included in al-Tujībī's cookbook are:

---

56 See Ibn Wāfid, *al-Adwiya al-mufrada* 156–7; and Ibn al-Jazzār, *al-Iʿtimād* 333.

57 See al-Bīrūnī, *al-Ṣaydana* 345–6; and al-Malik al-Muẓaffar, *al-Muʿtamad* 564–7.

58 For a good study of *murrī*, see Waines, "*Murrī*: The Tale of a Condiment."

59 As we learn from al-Ṭighnarī, *Zahrat al-bustān* 143.

murrī al-ḥūt (مري الحوت) fermented fish sauce, used in seasoning lamb in recipes ii.3.3–4. See also recipe x.8.13, which describes how to make it and serve it.

Fish-based fermented sauces were made all around the Mediterranean basin and the Near East from ancient times onward. The tenth-century physician al-Isrāʾīlī, *Kitāb al-Aghdhiya* iii 250, calls it *mānūn* 'fish juice.'[60] In terms of its properties, fish sauce was said to be colder and less powerful than barley-based varieties on account of fish's cold and moist properties. In passing, Ibn Manẓūr, *Lisān al-ʿArab*, s.v. ذبح, calls fish sauce *murrī nīnān* (مري نينان), made with a mixture of salt, fish, and wine and left in the sun to ferment. Wine is said to be permissible in this case because it changes its nature in the process. Al-Tujībī's recipe for fish sauce uses fresh sweet grape juice, with grape wine given as an acceptable option for the same reason Ibn Manẓūr gives.

murrī muʿajjal (مري معجل) a fast nonfermented sauce, used to replace the sun-fermented variety when not available. See recipes x.8.10–2 for ways to make it.

murrī al-musṭār (مري المسطار) nonfermented liquid sauce made with the sweet juice of grapes, called *musṭār*. See recipes x.8.7–9 for ways to make it.

murrī naqīʿ (مري نقيع) sun-fermented liquid sauce; a laborious preparation that takes months to process and uses rotted bread, called *būdhaq* (بوذق), as its base. See recipes x.8.1 and 2. According to Ibn al-Ḥashshāʾ, *Mufīd al-ʿulūm* 78, it was called *murrī Nabaṭī* (indigenous to Iraq) in the eastern region of al-Mashriq and was deemed the strongest in properties.

In al-Tujībī's cookbook it is mostly incorporated into the cooking dishes or made into a sauce by mixing it with other ingredients. It is also used as a table condiment by itself. In recipe ii.2.39, for instance, it is served in small bowls, in which thin grilled strips of mutton are dipped and eaten. In recipes ii.5.2 and ii.6.7, it is poured over meat patties before serving them.

nāfiʿ (نافع) fennel seeds, see *basbās* above.

nammām (نمام), also called *nammām al-malik* (نمام الملك), literally 'the king's thyme,' and *saysanbar* (سيسنبر). It is a variety of wild thyme, called mother of thyme, *Thymus glaber*.[61] It smells like marjoram, but stronger, so much so that the whole area becomes redolent with it, which gave it the name *nammām*, a gossiper who cannot keep a secret. With its hot and dry properties, it was used as a diuretic and antiseptic. It was also said to purge phlegm from the head, and promote menstruation.

60 *Nūn* is fish in Syriac, as al-Isrāʾīlī explains. *Mā* generally designates 'liquid.'

61 As identified in Ghālib, *Mawsūʿa*, s.v. *saʿtar amraṭ*.

FIGURE 155
Mother of thyme, *nammām*, Dioscorides, *Ajzāʾ min risāla fī l-nabātāt*, fol. 58v, detail
BNF, DEPARTMENT OF MANUSCRIPTS, ARAB 4947. SOURCE: GALLICA.BNF.FR/BNF

Having a drink with *nammām* steeped in it was said to stop hiccups.[62] In al-Tujībī's cookbook, it is used in recipe x.7.11 for making vinegar flavored with squills.

naʿnaʿ (نعنع) cultivated mint, grown in orchards, *Mentha*; also recognized as *fūdanaj bustānī* (فودنج بستاني) (i.e., the cultivated variety of *fūdanaj*), which is the generic name for the mint family. Ibn al-Jazzār, *al-Iʿtimād* 420–3, gives its Latin name, *minta* (منتة).

ʿuyūn al-naʿnaʿ (عيون النعنع) tender tips of mint sprigs, often used to garnish dishes before serving them.

Mint is used extensively in al-Tujībī's cookbook; and with the exception of recipes using it as the main ingredient, as in *naʿnaʿiyya* stews in recipes ii.2.8, iii.2.15 and iii.5.3, it is almost always used in combination with fresh cilantro, juiced, pounded, or chopped.

With its hot and dry properties and fine aroma, mint was said to aid digestion and encourage burping. It was also believed to prevent fresh milk from curdling if a few sprigs of it were steeped in it.

naṭrūn (نطرون) natron, sodium bicarbonate, see *būraq* above.

nīlaj (نيلج) indigo, *Indigofera tinctoria*; a plant valued for its blue dye, obtained from the variety cultivated in orchards (*bustānī*). It is used in recipe ix.7.2 for an emerald-green confection, to obtain a green colorant by mixing it with saffron.

62 See al-Malik al-Muẓaffar, *al-Muʿtamad* 300–1; and Ibn al-Jazzār, *al-Iʿtimād* 424–7.

qāqulla (قاقلّة) black cardamom, *Amomum subulatum*, greater cardamom, used in cooking and aromatics. It is a large variety of cardamom related to *hāl* (هال), which is green cardamom. Only the large variety, *qāqulla*, is used several times in al-Tujībī's recipes: iii.2.28 and 31 for a chicken dish braised with garlic and *jūdhāba*, respectively; a couple of fish dishes, recipes v.1.9 and 14; and in recipes xii.2.5–6 for handwashing preparations.

Qāqulla is the fruit of an Indian plant called *kakūlā* (ككولا) in Hindi, according to al-Bīrūnī, *al-Ṣaydana* 299. It might also have been named after Qāqula, which Ibn Baṭṭūṭa, *Tuḥfat al-nuẓẓār* ii 189, describes as a place somewhere around Java Island. It is a sweet-smelling spice with a hot taste. With its hot and dry properties, it was said to be medicinally beneficial for strengthening the stomach, aiding digestion, and combatting nausea and vomiting.[63]

qaranful (قرنفل) cloves, *Syzygium aromaticum*, unopened flower buds of a small evergreen tree indigenous to China and India. It has a bitingly hot and somewhat bitter taste. With its hot and dry properties, it was medicinally beneficial for the stomach and liver; it had the power to drive away winds and sweeten the breath. It was also believed to arouse coitus however it was taken.[64] It was a valued cooking spice in virtue of its pleasant aroma. In al-Tujībī's cookbook, it is relatively frequently used in savory dishes, some pastries and desserts, and in dishes with ground meat. It is in dishes with fish and eggs in chapters v.1 and v.2, where its use is noticeably more frequent, as well as the handwashing preparations in part xii, where it features in all the recipes.

qirfa (قرفة) Ceylon cinnamon, *Cinnamomum verum*. Al-Ishbīlī, *ʿUmdat al-ṭabīb* ii 503, says that it is one of the finest spices (*afāwīh rafīʿa*). It was the most commonly used cinnamon variety in al-Andalus and North Africa.[65] This is indeed reflected in al-Tujībī's cookbook, where it is used extensively in the dishes themselves as well as sprinkled on them when served. Cf. the other type of cinnamon, cassia *dār Ṣīnī*, which is used sparingly in al-Tujībī's cookbook, five times only, two of which are in combination with *qirfa*, recipes i.4.25 and ix.4.1.

This general preference for Ceylon cinnamon over cassia might well have been due to its sweet taste and intense aroma, which rendered it more conducive to the daily dishes, sweet and savory alike. Cassia, in comparison is less sweet and not as intensely fragrant as Ceylon cinnamon. However, for medicinal purposes, cassia was more valued for its hotter and dryer properties. Additionally, based on al-Anṭākī, *Tadhkira* 163, we gather that Ceylon cinnamon might have even been less costly than cassia, which was often adulterated with it. See also *dār Ṣīnī* above.

---

63 See Ibn al-Jazzār, *al-Iʿtimād* 177–9.

64 Ibid., 381.

65 Al-Ishbīlī says it is a familiar spice; and Ibn al-Jazzār, *al-Iʿtimād* 619, calls it *qirfat al-ʿāmma*, i.e., cinnamon of the general public.

FIGURE 156 Costus, *Kitāb al-Diryāq*, fol. NP, detail
BNF, DEPARTMENT OF MANUSCRIPTS, ARAB 2964. SOURCE: GALLICA.BNF.FR/BNF

ʿūd qirfa (عود قرفة) a stick of Ceylon cinnamon. Unground cinnamon is used a few times in al-Tujībī's cookbook in recipes for broths, for instance, that need to stay white and clear, in which cases the sticks would be discarded once the cooking is done, as in recipes i.3.1 and iii.2.1.

qusṭ ḥulw (قسط حلو) sweet costus, also known as *qusṭ baḥrī* (قسط بحري) sea costus and *qusṭ ʿArabī* (قسط عربي) Arabian costus, brought from Abyssinia.[66] It is described as

66 See al-Bīrūnī, *al-Ṣaydana* 307–8.

FIGURE 157 Myrtle, Dioscorides, *Kitāb al-Ḥashāʾish fī hāyūlā al-ʿilāj al-ṭibbī*, Arabic translation by Ḥunayn b. Isḥāq, Or. 289, fol. 45v, detail
UNIVERSITAIRE BIBLIOTHEKEN LEIDEN, HTTP://HDL.HANDLE.NET/1887.1/ITEM:1578266

white, lightweight, and strongly fragrant. It is said to be superior to the Indian costus because it is softer, sweeter, more fragrant, and hence better suited for aromatic preparations. It is this type of costus that is used in two of al-Tujībī's handwashing preparations, recipes xii.2 and 5.

All costus varieties have hot and dry properties, and as such, they were believed to dry phlegm in the head and remedy cold-related ailments when inhaled and taken internally. It is also said that it can excite coitus if mixed with a drink of wine and honey.[67]

67 See Ibn al-Jazzār, *al-Iʿtimād* 590–1.

FIGURE 158 *Salīkha*, Dioscorides, *Kitāb al-Ḥashā'ish fī hāyūlā al-ʿilāj al-ṭibbī*, Arabic translation by Ḥunayn b. Isḥāq, Or. 289, fol. 8v, detail
UNIVERSITAIRE BIBLIOTHEKEN LEIDEN, HTTP://HDL.HANDLE.NET/1887.1/ITEM:1578266

rayḥān (ريحان) myrtle, *Myrtus communis*, as it was commonly called in the Muslim West. Otherwise, *rayḥān* was said to be any sweet-smelling plant in the eastern region, except in Iraq and the Levant, where it designated basil, variously called *ḥabaq*/*ḥawak* and *bādharūj*.[68] Myrtle in the eastern region was called *ās*, see *waraq ās* below.

sadhāb (سذاب) rue; ***sadhāb bustānī*** (سذاب بستاني) cultivated rue, called ***fayjan*** in the Muslim West; see the entry above.

salīkha (سليخة) in the Arabic medieval books on botany is specified as the bark of an Indian tree and said to be a variety of cassia (*dār Ṣīnī* 'Chinese cinnamon'). The tree

68 See Ibn Qayyim al-Jawziyya, *al-Ṭibb al-nabawī* 241.

FIGURE 159
Thyme, *ṣaʿtar*, Dioscorides, *Ajzāʾ min risāla fī l-nabātāt*, fol. 58r, detail
BNF, DEPARTMENT OF MANUSCRIPTS, ARAB 4947. SOURCE: GALLICA.BNF.FR/BNF

is described as having a trunk with a thick bark, which is ruby red, sweet smelling, and forms into long tubes when dried. Its taste is said to be somewhat flavorful, tinged with saltiness, stickiness, and heat, with an aroma reminiscent of wine. From al-Ghassānī, *Ḥadīqat al-azhār* 279, we learn that it was available at the perfume and drug stores in his city of Fez, where it was called *qishr al-zalīkha*.

With its hot and dry properties, it was said to strengthen the stomach and all the important body organs and open obstructions by dissipating winds and dense humors. Apparently, it was stronger in properties than cassia; when cassia was used as a substitute for it, the recommendation was to double its amount.[69] It is used once in al-Tujībī's last part on handwashing preparations, recipe xii 6.

ṣandal (صندل) sandalwood, *Santalum*, an aromatic wood brought from regions of southern India, used in incense and other aromatic compounds and medicinal preparations. It is used in almost all the recipes in al-Tujībī's last part dealing with handwashing preparations. Two varieties are mentioned in particular:

ṣandal abyaḍ (صندل ابيض) white sandalwood, which is a sweet-smelling variety.
ṣandal aṣfar (صندل اصفر) yellow sandalwood; it smells good, but its aroma is not rich.

69 See Ibn al-Jazzār, *al-Iʿtimād* 627–30; al-Ishbīlī, *ʿUmdat al-ṭabīb* ii 542; and al-Ghassānī, *Ḥadīqat al-azhār* 279–80.

With its cold and dry properties, sandalwood was deemed beneficial for soothing headaches caused by excess heat. It was also used in baths as a rub to mask odors of depilatory *nūrā*.[70]

ṣaʿtar (صعتر) common thyme, *Thymus vulgarus*. In sources other than al-Tujībī, the name also occurs as *zaʿtar* (زعتر) and *saʿtar* (سعتر). It is a versatile herb, used frequently in al-Tujībī's recipes with stews, grilled meats, pickling olives and fish, and the fermented condiment *murrī*. It is used fresh and dried, chopped, and crumbled; and when a whole sprig is called for, it is referred to as *ghuṣn ṣaʿtar*.

Besides the common cultivated thyme used in al-Tujībī's recipes, the following varieties are also specifically required:

murkīra (مركيرة), another name given to *shardhūn*, which is conehead thyme, a Mediterranean wild variety (entry below). The BL MS of al-Tujībī's cookbook, fol. 195r, recipe x.6.2 for pickling fish, is our only source for this term. The name could have been a dialectal variant of *murqīra*. Now, we know from al-Ishbīlī, *ʿUmdat al-ṭabīb* i 280, that *murqīr* is a variety of olives; we also know from the same source, ii 407–8, that *shardhūn* is called *ṣaʿtar al-zaytūn*, which implies that it was the thyme variety used in curing olives. Based on this, the name *murkīra*, which al-Tujībī's recipe gives as a synonym for *shardhūn*, must have derived from the *murqīr* olive mentioned by al-Ishbīlī. See also *murqīr*, in glossary 7, s.v. *zaytūn*.

ṣaʿtar mulūkī (صعتر ملوكي), literally, 'royal thyme,' used in recipe x.8.1. It is possibly another name for another type of thyme, called *nammām al-malik* 'the king's thyme,' which is a wild variety called mother of thyme, *Thymus glaber*. See *nammām* above.

shardhūn (شرذون), ***shardūn*** (شردون) conehead thyme, a Mediterranean wild variety, *Thymus capitatus*. In al-Ishbīlī, *ʿUmdat al-ṭabīb* ii 407–8, *shardhūn* is called *ṣaʿtar al-zaytūn* 'thyme used with olives.' Al-Tujībī's cookbook does indeed prove this practice to have been true, for *shardhūn* is used in recipe x.2.3 for curing olives.

According to al-Ishbīlī, *shardhūn* grew around rocks and on rugged mountains (*arḍ maḥṣaba*). He describes it as a short plant with very tiny leaves and small purple flowers growing at the ends of their stems; it is hot and slightly bitter in taste. He adds that the arborists of Seville call it *ṣaʿtar al-zaytūn*, and those of Toledo and Zaragoza call it *shardhūn*. He further identifies it as a variety of *ṣaʿtar Fārisī* 'Persian hyssob.' In al-Tujībī's cookbook, *shardhūn* is

70 Ibn al-Bayṭār, *al-Jāmiʿ* iv 340, s.v. *kils*.

specifically called for in recipe x.2.3 for brining olives and recipe x.6.2 for pickling fish. In the latter recipe, an alternative name for *shardhūn* is given, which is *murkīra* (entry above).

Thyme is hot and dry in properties, and as such, it was recommended to aid the digestion of dense foods and diffuse gastric winds. It was believed to soothe toothaches, heal gums, improve memory, and sharpen eyesight. In all these effects, the wild thyme varieties were said to be stronger in properties than the cultivated thyme, which was mainly used for culinary purposes.[71]

shajar al-astab (شجر الاستب) rockrose, also called halimium, *Halimium halimifolium*. It is a fragrant flowering shrub native to the Mediterranean Basin. *Astab* was its name in al-ʿAjamiyya (Andalusi Romance); in Spanish it was *estepa*, which is rockrose. *Astab* was also identified as *shaqwāṣ* (شقواص),[72] *shaqāṣ* (شقاص), and other variants, said to be the shrub of *lādhan Isbānī*, the Spanish variety of ladanum, which is a species of rockrose.[73] In al-Tujībī's recipe vi.3.5, water in which a branch of *astab* has been steeped is used to remedy rancid butter.

shamʿ (شمع) beeswax, used in recipes i.4.12 and 19 to grease a pan with it and then wipe it out before baking thin breads in it.

shamʿ aṣfar (شمع اصفر) yellow beeswax, another name for beeswax is *mūm* (موم). It was deemed an excellent variety used for cooking purposes, as in recipe ix.2.2, where the purpose is to thicken a starch-based confection with it. It was gathered from the honey cells themselves or from the walls of hives. It is yellowish in hue, lightweight, and sweet smelling; easy to knead and does not crumble. According to Ibn Wāfid, *al-Adwiya al-mufrada* 41, white wax was inferior to yellow beeswax.

shardhūn (شرذون) conehead thyme, a wild Mediterranean variety, see *ṣaʿtar* above.

shaṭriyya (شطرية) thyme-leaved savory, *Satureja/Satureia thymbra*,[74] a variety of savory with long leaves that have thyme-like flavor, which explains the association of this herb with thyme *ṣaʿtar* in the medieval books on botany. Ibn al-Bayṭār, *al-Jāmiʿ* iii 111, says *shaṭriyya* is a name given to a variety of thyme with long leaves and adds that it was grown in Egypt, just as it was in his country, al-Andalus.

---

71 See Ibn al-Jazzār, *al-Iʿtimād* 669–72.

72 See https://ar.wikipedia.org/wiki/%D8%B4%D9%82%D9%88%D8%A7%D8%B5, accessed March 26, 2020. See also Corriente, *Dictionary of Andalusi Arabic*, s.v. *ʾ-s-t-p*; and Roberts, *Comprehensive Etymological Dictionary* i, s.v. *estepa*.

73 Ibn al-Bayṭār, *al-Jāmiʿ* iii 359; and al-Ishbīlī, *ʿUmdat al-ṭabīb* i 72–3.

74 In Ghālib, *Mawsūʿa*, s.v. ندغ, it is called *nadgh ṣaʿtarī* (ندغ صعتري).

FIGURE 160 *Shaṭriyya*, Dioscorides, *Fī Hayūlā al-ṭibb*, translation by Ḥunayn b. Isḥāq, fol. 134r, detail
FROM THE NEW YORK PUBLIC LIBRARY, SPENCER COLLECTION: HTTPS://DIGITALCOLLECTIONS.NYPL.ORG/ITEMS/5E66B3E8-FC06-D471-E040-E00A180654D7

In al-Ishbīlī, *ʿUmdat al-ṭabīb* ii 406–7, *shaṭriyya*, also called *ṣaʿtar al-Ṣaqāliba* 'thyme of the Slavs,' is said to be a type of the Persian variety of thyme (*ṣaʿtar Fārisī*). Al-Ishbīlī describes the cultivated variety (*bustānī*), which grows in the summer, and the wild variety (*barrī*), as having dark green leaves that have a strong taste—hot and sharp, with blue flowers growing at the tips of stems. He says both of them were well-known in al-Andalus and were commonly used—fresh and dried—in boiled dishes (*masālīq*). Another name al-Ishbīlī gives for it is *nadgh* (ندْغ),[75] which designates savory.

Shaṭriyya is used once in recipe ii.2.20 for gourd stew. The instruction is to use it sparingly, which must have been due to the herb's strong flavor.

shūnīz (شونيز) nigella seeds, *Nigella sativa*, also known as *ḥabba sawdāʾ* (حبة سوداء) 'black seed' and *kammūn aswad* 'black cumin.' With its hot and dry properties, it was said to be beneficial in dealing with bloating and dissipating winds in the digestive system. Its smoke was used as an insect repellant.[76]

75 See the above note.
76 See Ibn al-Jazzār, *al-Iʿtimād* 719; and al-Bīrūnī, *al-Ṣaydana* 421–2.

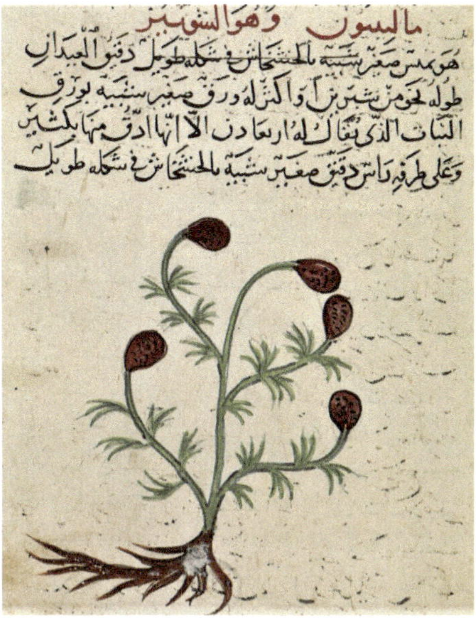

FIGURE 161
Nigella plant, Dioscorides, *Kitāb Dīsqūrīdis fī mawādd al-ʿilāj*, fol. 62r, detail
BRITISH LIBRARY: ORIENTAL MANUSCRIPTS, OR 3366, IN QATAR DIGITAL LIBRARY HTTPS://WWW.QDL.QA/ARCHIVE/81055/VDC_100022531380.0X000001

In al-Tujībī's cookbook, nigella is consistently called *shūnīz* and is infrequently used. In recipe vi.1.2, for instance, it is sprinkled on a dish of drained yogurt; it is incorporated into pickles, in chapters x.5 and 6, and in the fermented sauces called *murrī* in chapter x.8.

simsim (سمسم) sesame seeds, more commonly called *juljulān* in the Muslim West, where they did not seem to be a significant culinary ingredient. Judging from al-Tujībī's cookbook, neither the seeds nor oil were used much. For sesame oil, see *duhn al-simsim*, glossary 6. In al-Tujībī's recipes, the seeds are used sprinkled on bread and pastries, as in recipes i.1.5 and i.4.28; or incorporated into dishes, as in a sweet lamb dish, recipe ii.3.8; and in desserts, recipes ix.1.2, ix.2.2–4, and ix.2.6.

The seeds, with their hot and humid properties, were believed to be bad for the stomach, cause bad breath when they stay trapped between the teeth, and induce vomiting. Toasting the seeds was said to remedy them.

According to the Andalusi horticultural books, the sesame plant, which was brought to the region with the Arab rule, was weak, and its cultivation was said to be better if delayed until warmer weather.[77] This would translate to a shorter growing season and might explain its limited availability compared with the ubiquitous olives.

77 See Ibn al-ʿAwwām, *al-Filāḥa al-Andalusiyya* iv 49–50; and al-Ṭighnarī, *Zahrat al-Bustān* 448–9.

FIGURE 162 Varieties of Cyperus, *suʿd*, Dioscorides, *Fī Hayūlā al-ṭibb*, translation by Ḥunayn b. Isḥāq, fol. 21v, detail
FROM THE NEW YORK PUBLIC LIBRARY, SPENCER COLLECTION: HTTPS://DIGITALCOLLECTIONS.NYPL.ORG/ITEMS/5E66B3E8-881F-D471-E040-E00A180654D7

ṣināb (صناب) mustard seeds, *Brassica*. This was their name in the Muslim West; as for the eastern region, they were commonly known as *khardal*. Good-quality seeds were described as light in color, large and plump, and when pounded, the insides should look yellow and feel somewhat moist. The hot and dry properties of the seeds were valued as an aid to digestion; they were also said to have the power to break down and dissipate moisture in the head and stomach. An unusual benefit of the seeds was that they were said to help with forgetfulness when they were applied to the head after shaving it.[78]

The seeds are infrequently used in al-Tujībī's cookbook; as in making mustard sauce, called *ṣināb* (entry below). They are also used in recipe x.5.3 for making pickled turnips, and in the last recipe in the book for preserving sweet grape juice.

ṣināb (صناب) mustard sauce, valued for its hot and dry properties that were believed to aid digestion. It was offered at the table, for instance, with grilled meat in recipe

78 See Ibn al-Bayṭār, *al-Jāmiʿ* ii 318–9; and Ibn al-Jazzār, *al-Iʿtimād* 866–7.

ii.2.39; and used as a seasoning ingredient in a dish called *ṣinābī*, recipe ii.2.37. For the seeds, see the above entry.

suʿdā (سعدى),[79] ***suʿd*** (سعد) cyperus, *Cyperus esculentus*, also called tigernut. It is a grass-like aquatic plant, of which only the tubers are edible. The good ones were said to resemble olive pits, dense and heavy, hard to bruise, and sweet smelling. In al-Tujībī's cookbook, it is used only in the handwashing preparations in part xii. With its hot and dry properties, *suʿd* was also deemed medicinally beneficial. Its astringency was believed to have a tannic effect on the stomach. It was used to treat hemorrhoids, strengthen a weak stomach and liver, dissolve kidney stones, and remove bad odors in the mouth and nose.[80]

sukk (سك) aromatic pastilles, used a few times in al-Tujībī's part xii for handwashing preparations. In other sources, *sukk* was also used to flavor foods and drinks; it was used in aromatic and restorative preparations, such as incense, breath fresheners, and stomachics. See, for instance, the anonymous fourteenth-century Egyptian *Kanz al-Fawāʾid*, English trans., *Treasure Trove*, recipes 379, 456, 661, and 673. It was valued for its medicinal benefits, such as fortifying internal organs and curbing bowel movements.

Its basic component is a preparation called *rāmak* (رامك). *Rāmak* is a dark-colored mix of *ʿafṣ* 'gall' and *umluj*, which is emblic myrobalan.[81] Fresh dates can be substituted for the latter. In a complex and time-consuming operation, *rāmak* is made into small discs of dough, threaded, set aside to dry, and used as needed in making *sukk*.[82]

The best variety is said to be *sukk miskī*, made with musk. *Rāmak* is first pounded and kneaded with water and set aside overnight. It is then mixed with crushed musk. The mix is kneaded well and then shaped into discs, which are left on the back of a sieve to dry for about a year. Ibn Wāfid, *al-Adwiya al-mufrada* 77, says that the longer it is kept the more aromatic it gets and the stronger its properties become; he recommends it as the *sukk* to use.[83]

sunbul (سنبل) spikenard, *Nardostachys jatamansi*; also called *nārdīn* (ناردين). Its sweet-smelling amber-colored rhizomes are the most used part. They are oblong and woody, with many hairy minor roots entangled all around them, and tufted fibers crown them. The spikenard rhizomes are sometimes referred to as *ʿaṣāfīr*, literally 'sparrows.' Before using them, the dried rhizomes are cleaned of the dry mud attached to them. This sweet-smelling mud was said to be good for washing the hands.[84]

79 According to al-Bīrūnī, *al-Ṣaydana* 220, this variant of the name is of Syriac origin.
80 See Ibn al-Jazzār, *Kitab al-Iʿtimād* 498; and al-Anṭākī, *Tadhkira* 206–7.
81 Also known as Indian gooseberry, *Phyllanthus emblica*.
82 As described by al-Nuwayrī, *Nihāyat al-arab* xii 40–2.
83 See also Ibn al-Bayṭār, *al-Jāmiʿ* iii 32–3; and Ibn Sīnā, *al-Qānūn* i 664.
84 See Ibn Wāfid, *al-Adwiya al-mufrada* 75.

FIGURE 163 Varieties of spikenard, *Kitāb al-Diryāq*, fol. NP, detail
BNF, DEPARTMENT OF MANUSCRIPTS, ARAB 2964. SOURCE: GALLICA.BNF.FR/BNF

Spikenard is frequently used in al-Tujībī's recipes for pastries, savory dishes of red meat, chicken and fish, pickles, vinegar, and desserts. True to al-Bīrūnī's remark that spikenard was rarely used without coupling it with cloves (*qaranful*),[85] the recipes almost always include cloves wherever spikenard is used. This was most probably done to enhance its properties and benefits, which they share.

Medicinally, spikenard was believed to be good for the stomach, liver, and spleen. It was said to have the power to dispel winds in the stomach, bring pleasure to the soul, and boost memory and sexual appetites.[86]

sunbul Hindī (سنبل هندي) Indian spikenard, also called *sunbul al-ṭīb* (سنبل الطيب) and *sunbul ʿaṣāfīrī* (سنبل عصافيري), called so because the rhizomes look like sparrows. This variety is darker and shorter than the rest of the varieties, and it has the most aroma and the strongest properties. It is used once, in al-Tujībī's recipe xii.1 for a handwashing compound; otherwise, for cooking purposes the variety of spikenard is not specified in the recipes.

tābil (تابل) a general term for seasoning spices. The anonymous thirteenth-century *Anwāʿ al-ṣaydala* 87 gives a basic combination of these spices: one part black pepper, two parts caraway seeds, and three parts coriander seeds; all pounded and sifted.

---

85 Al-Bīrūnī, *al-Ṣaydana* 236–7.
86 Ibn al-Bayṭār, *al-Jāmiʿ* iii 48–51; and al-Ishbīlī, *ʿUmdat al-ṭabīb* ii 528–9.

FIGURE 164 Garlic, Dioscorides, *Ajzāʾ min risāla fī l-nabātāt*, fol. 44v, detail
BNF, DEPARTMENT OF MANUSCRIPTS, ARAB 4947. SOURCE: GALLICA.BNF.FR/BNF

thūm (ثوم) garlic; the most commonly used is *thūm bustānī* (ثوم بستاني), the common cultivated garlic, *Allium sativum*. According to al-Anṭākī, *Tadhkira* 110, the best garlic has large cloves, which are easy to separate and skin; in taste it is not too sharp, and when cut, it feels somewhat sticky, like honey. Garlic is frequently used in al-Tujībī's cookbook, always cooked, as this was believed to neutralize its powerful odor. This liberal use of garlic must have been encouraged by the dominant medical belief that garlic was beneficial to people living in cold regions and during cold winters, which in fact applies to the conditions in al-Andalus more than to a hot and humid region like Egypt, where garlic was sparingly used.[87]

87 Judging from the surviving anonymous fourteenth-century Egyptian cookbook *Kanz al-fawāʾid*, English trans., *Treasure Trove*.

With its hot and dry properties, garlic was believed to help dispel flatulence and thin the blood. It was used to cure the bites of rabid dogs and stop persistent chronic coughs. Some physicians called it the antidote of rural folks, *tiryāq ahl al-barr*. It was also deemed beneficial for amnesia and for the elderly with humors that were dominantly cold. People with hot humors may safely eat it pickled.[88]

ʿasālīj thūm akhḍar (عساليج ثوم اخضر) tender stems of young garlic; also occurs as *aʿnāq thūm akhḍar* (اعناق ثوم اخضر), literally 'necks of green garlic.' It is spring garlic used while still young before the bulbs fully form, see recipe viii.1.3.

farīk al-thūm (فريك الثوم) fresh and tender young spring garlic, used in recipes ii.2.15, and ii.6.4, p. 286.

ḥabbat thūm (حبة ثوم) a clove of garlic.

ra's thūm (رأس ثوم) a head of garlic.

ṭīn Armanī (طين ارمني) dry blackish-red clay brought from Armenia,[89] described as having a good aroma and a dust-like taste. When crushed finely, no stones or sand can be seen in it. It is used in al-Tujībī's last part on handwashing preparations, recipe xii.4, on account of its tremendous drying powers and smooth and clinging texture. Medicinally, with its cold and dry properties, it was said to be good for diarrhea and bleeding, as well as setting broken bones.[90]

turunjān (ترنجان) lemon balm, balm mint, *Melissa officinalis*, also recognized as *bādharanjawayh* (باذرنجويه) by physicians and botanists. It is an herb valued for its aromatic leaves, which smell like citron; described as the herb that brings joy to the heart (*mufarriḥ al-qalb*). It is good for ailments related to an excess in phlegm and black bile; it sweetens the breath and aids the digestion of dense foods. In al-Tujībī's cookbook, it is used in a mutton dish called *turunjāniyya*, recipe ii.2.9, and used in making vinegar, as in recipe x.7.11.[91]

ʿūd (عود) aloeswood, the sweet-smelling dark resinous heartwood of *Aquilaria* and *Gyrinops* trees in Southeast Asia. The best wood is described as blackish, heavy, bright, bitter, and aromatic.

In al-Tujībī's cookbook it is used in part xii dealing with handwashing preparations. Due to its bitterness and acridity, it was mostly beneficial as an incense to perfume the body and in dentifrice compounds (*sanūnāt*) to cleanse the teeth and

---

88 Ibn al-Jazzār, *al-Iʿtimād* 854–5; al-Anṭākī, *Tadhkira* 110; and Ibn al-Bayṭār, *al-Jāmiʿ* i 208–10.

89 Ibn al-Bayṭār, *al-Jāmiʿ* iii 151; and al-Anṭākī, *Tadhkira* 256, describe its color as being yellowish and golden.

90 Ibn al-Bayṭār, *al-Jāmiʿ* iii 151; and Ibn al-Jazzār, *al-Iʿtimād* 318–9.

91 Al-Bīrūnī, *al-Ṣaydana* 113; Ibn al-Jazzār, *al-Iʿtimād* 218–9; and Ibn Wāfid, *al-Adwiya al-mufrada* 50–1.

FIGURE 165 Licorice, *Kitāb al-Diryāq*, fol. NP, detail
BNF, DEPARTMENT OF MANUSCRIPTS, ARAB 2964.
SOURCE: GALLICA.BNF.FR/BNF

sweeten the breath. In the kitchen, its aromatic smoke was used to infuse foods and cooking and serving utensils, as in recipe i.4.1.

With its dry and hot properties, it was rendered effective in medicinal preparations for aiding digestion, curbing an excess in phlegm, expelling winds, relieving asthma symptoms, and improving coitus.[92] Related varieties and terms used in al-Tujībī's cookbook are:

92 Al-Anṭākī, *Tadhkira* 265; Ibn Wāfid, *al-Adwiya al-mufrada* 166–7; and Ibn al-Jazzār, *al-Iʿtimād* 350.

ʿūd ghayr muṭarrā (عود غير مطرّا) aloeswood chips that have not been smeared with ambergris, musk, and camphor; also called *ʿūd nay*ʾ or *ʿūd khām* 'raw aloeswood.' They are used in recipe xii.1 for a handwashing preparation. Aloeswood chips that were smeared with these aromatics were called *ʿūd muṭarrā* and were usually used as incense (*bakhūr*), as explained in Ibn al-Ḥashshāʾ, *Mufīd al-ʿulūm* 166.

ʿūd Hindī (عود هندي), also called *ʿūd Mandalī* (عود مندلي), Indian aloeswood. It is said to be the best of all varieties and the most expensive. It is black and moist and heavy enough to sink when put in water to test it.[93] In al-Tujībī's cookbook, it is used once in a *kaʿk* recipe, i.4.1, to infuse a cookie container with its fine smoke.

ʿūd al-sūs (عود السوس) dried licorice roots, *Glycyrrhiza glabra*, which look like twigs. They are sweet and moderately hot and medicinally beneficial for the chest and coughs. They are used only once, along with other ingredients, in recipe x.9.2 to improve the flavor and aroma of freshly pressed olive oil.

ʿuṣfur (عصفر) safflower, *Carthamus tinctorius*. They are the flowers of a plant whose seeds are called *qurṭum*; used only once in al-Tujībī's cookbook, in recipe x.5.3 for pickling turnips, as a substitute for saffron. The abundance of saffron in al-Andalus certainly rendered resorting to safflower as a substitute unnecessary. Still, based on al-Anṭākī, *Tadhkira* 261, safflower was useful as it improved the aroma and taste of foods and shortened their cooking time.

ushnān (اشنان) potash, see glossary 11, s.v. *ushnān* 2.

waraq ās (ورق آس) leaves of myrtle, *Myrtus communis*, also called *rayḥān* in the Muslim West. They are used in recipe ii.2.39 for grilled mutton and in recipe xii.5 for a handwashing preparation. The leaves were valued for their sweet smell, cold and dry properties, and astringency.

waraq rand (ورق رند), also known as *ghār* (غار), leaves of bay laurel, *Laurus nobilis*. They are sweet-smelling albeit bitter. Al-Anṭākī, *Tadhkira* 267, mentions that they are put between figs to enhance their aroma and prevent them from generating worms. Many superstitions were wound around them, such as carrying them would bring about prosperity and high status, and if spinsters fumigated with it before a Wednesday sunrise, they would definitely get married.

In al-Tujībī's recipes, the leaves are used only twice: for lining a bowl with them along with citron leaves to serve fried chicken joints in, recipe iii.2.8; and in recipe xii.1 for a handwashing preparation.

---

93 As explained in al-Nuwayrī, *Nihāyat al-arab* xii 17–8.

FIGURE 166 Bay laurel, *ghār*, Dioscorides, *Kitāb al-Ḥashā'ish fī hāyūlā al-ʿilāj al-ṭibbī*, Arabic translation by Ḥunayn b. Isḥāq, Or. 289, fol. 23r, detail
UNIVERSITAIRE BIBLIOTHEKEN LEIDEN, HTTP://HDL.HANDLE.NET/1887.1/ITEM:1578266

waraq utrujj (ورق اترج) leaves of true citron, *Citrus medica*, frequently mentioned in stew recipes. The fresh whole leaves are added as a flavoring agent.

waraq ward aḥmar (ورق ورد احمر) petals of red roses, used dried in part xii for hand-washing preparations. They were valued for their intense fragrance; their distilled water was said to be much more fragrant than that of the pink thorny roses usually used for distillation.[94]

zaʿfarān (زعفران) saffron, *Crocus sativus*, used extensively in al-Tujībī's recipes to enliven the color of cooking foods and for its subtle aroma. This liberal use of saffron was made possible by the fact that saffron, which was introduced by the Arabs, grew

94 See al-Ṭighnarī, *Zahrat al-bustān* 233.

FIGURE 167 Saffron, *Kitāb al-Diryāq*, fol. NP, detail
BNF, DEPARTMENT OF MANUSCRIPTS, ARAB 2964.
SOURCE: GALLICA.BNF.FR/BNF

successfully in southern Spain and the northern region of al-Maghrib. Al-Ghassānī, *Ḥadīqat al-azhār* 108, says that it grew abundantly in Toledo, Baza (Basṭa), and Marrakesh. According to al-Ishbīlī, *ʿUmdat al-ṭabīb* ii 277, the best saffron grew in Toledo, with stigmas that were thick and intensely red. The Andalusi agronomist al-Ṭighnarī, *Zahrat al-bustān* 487–90, includes a chapter on how to plant and harvest it. He says that once saffron flowers reach maturation, the stigmas are gathered, and either they are crushed in mortars or soaked in water to soften and stick together, after which they are formed into discs with oiled hands and left to dry and then stored

FIGURE 168 Ginger, Dioscorides, *Ajzāʾ min risāla fī l-nabātāt*, fol. 41v, detail
BNF, DEPARTMENT OF MANUSCRIPTS, ARAB 4947. SOURCE: GALLICA.BNF.FR/BNF

in earthenware vessels and used as needed.[95] In his treatise on market inspection and regulations, Ibn ʿAbdūn al-Ishbīlī, *Risāla fī l-Qaḍāʾ wa-l-ḥisba* 60, did not recommend selling saffron prepared this way because it could easily be adulterated; his preference was for selling it as loose threads.

With its hot and dry properties and light astringency, it was a valuable medicinal ingredient, believed to be good for the digestive and respiratory systems and opening blockages in the liver and veins. It was also said to have the power to stimulate coitus and ease labor. Adding it to alcoholic drinks would intensify their intoxicating effects and induce extreme joy, which was said to almost verge on manic euphoria. The advice was that one should use no more than 1 *dirham* (3 grams/½ teaspoon) because overdosing was fatal. To facilitate its grinding, the recommendation was to leave it for a while in the sun or a heated new earthenware pan while stirring it all the time.[96]

zanjabīl (زنجبيل) ginger, *Zingiber officinale*, used extensively in al-Tujībī's recipes, both in cooking the dishes and sprinkled on them when served, often with Ceylon cinnamon and black pepper. It was imported already dried from the Far East; the best was said to come from China. This was due to the fact that fresh ginger, with its moist properties, rotted fast; it was best preserved by drying and was revived by soaking it in water before using it.[97] We also learn from al-Anṭākī, *Tadhkira* 198, that some lesser varieties grew in India and in the south of the Arabian Peninsula.

With its hot properties, ginger was believed to aid digestion and expel winds in the system. It was also believed to be a great aid to coitus. Ginger preserved in brine or honey was especially beneficial in this respect.

95 See also Ibn al-ʿAwwām, *al-Filāḥa al-Andalusiyya* iv 206–10.

96 See Ibn Wāfid, *al-Adwiya al-mufrada* 146–7; Ibn al-Jazzār, *al-Iʿtimād* 402–3; al-Anṭākī, *Tadhkira* 196; and al-Malik al-Muẓaffar, *al-Muʿtamad* 247–9.

97 See Ibn al-Jazzār, *al-Iʿtimād* 602; and al-Ḥashshāʾ, *Mufīd al-ʿulūm* 59.

9.1. In the Kitchen: Cooking and Serving Implements and Utensils

ājur (آجر) big flat bricks, used in recipe x.9.2 to help get rid of the unpleasant smell of olive oil by adding it to the oil after heating it up and breaking it into small pieces.

awānī (اواني), sg. *āniya* (آنية) vessels, see also *inā'* and *wi'ā'*.

awānī dhahab (اواني ذهب) gold vessels.
awānī fakhkhār (اواني فخار) earthenware vessels.
awānī fiḍḍa (اواني فضة) silver vessels.
awānī ḥadīd (اواني حديد) iron vessels.
awānī ḥantam (اواني حنتم) green-glazed vessels.
awānī nuḥās (اواني نحاس) copper vessels.
awānī qaṣdīr (اواني قصدير) tin vessels.
awānī raṣāṣ (اواني رصاص) lead vessels.

burma (برمة), pl. *birām* (برام) soapstone or earthenware pot, see *ibrīm* below.

burma nuḥās (برمة نحاس) copper pot, used in precooking preparations, such as in recipe i.2.1, where it is filled with boiling water and the head of a calf is dipped in it for an hour to help remove its hair.

furn (فرن) brick oven, built with a front opening and a spacious flat and horizontal baking surface, called a *kawsha* (entry below), which is almost circular and domed. Fuel is lighted on the left side of the baking chamber, and when it is heated, the ashes are swept away and the baking begins.[1] Such descriptions specifically apply to the communal brick ovens in cities that served neighborhood customers. These ovens were built inside small shops, called *dukkān* (دكان) or *ḥānūt* (حانوت), which were also referred to as *furn*, whose operator was called a *farrān* (فرّان). Besides the oven itself, there was a kind of reception zone, where customers would buy bread and deposit and pick up their home-prepared casseroles (*ṭawājin*, sg. *ṭājin*) and baking trays. A third zone was allocated for storing firewood. It was mandatory for the brick ovens to be built with high roofs and large chimneys to drive out smoke.[2]

Services offered at the communal brick ovens were available in urban neighborhoods. It is also safe to assume that in rural areas brick ovens, *afrān*, albeit built

1 See Hassan and Hill, *Islamic Technology* 219.
2 See, for instance, Ibn al-Ukhuwwa, *Ma'ālim al-qurba* 91.

FIGURE 169 A shallow bowl, ca. fourteenth-century Spain
MET NY—ROGERS FUND, 1930, ACCESSION NUMBER: 30.53.1

smaller and simpler, were available to the cooks.[3] In addition, judging from al-Tujībī's recipes, we get the impression that in the households, urban and otherwise, domestic brick ovens built outside the living areas were mainly used for baking the daily bread and other simple tasks. Otherwise, the browning of casserole dishes and poultry and fish put in clay vessels, called *ṭājin*, are almost invariably sent to the neighborhood brick oven to be placed at a distance from the fire. Delicate varieties of bread and pastries are similarly baked.

3 Writing about the daily lives of Egyptian peasants, seventeenth-century al-Shirbīnī, *Hazz al-quḥūf* 194, mentions that the household *furn* was used for baking the daily bread and simmering pots of beans, as well as baking modest fish and pigeon *ṭājin*s.

FIGURE 170 A serving vessel, *ghaḍāra*, late thirteenth-century Málaga, Spain
MET NY—GIFT OF GEORGE BLUMENTHAL, 1941, ACCESSION NUMBER: 41.100.173

kawsha (كوشة) the rounded and domed baking chamber of the brick oven, called a *furn*, see above. It is the most important section in the bakehouse. The person who undertakes the task of baking the shaped bread dough and other baked foods by entering them into the oven and taking them out is called a *kawwāsh* (كوّاش).[4] The *kawsha* floor, where the baking takes place, is divided into three zones:

1. The left zone, called *mustawqad*, where the fire is lit with fuel wood.
2. The middle zone, the hottest place in the oven.
3. The right zone, where moderately low heat is maintained to bake delicate breads and cookies, for instance.[5]

furn (فرن) bakehouse, communal brick oven, see above.

furn taqṭīr mā' al-ward (فرن تقطير ماء الورد) ovens especially built for distilling rosewater. In al-Tujībī's recipe vii.4.4, they are said to be the best for roasting truffles because they are usually lighted with slow-burning coals to produce a moderately low heat.[6]

ghaḍā (غضا) embers on which pots are left to simmer.

ghaḍāra (غضارة) a glazed bowl. The large ones were frequently used as serving vessels in al-Tujībī's recipes. *Ghaḍāra* bowls were made with pure clay, called *ghaḍār* and *ṭīn ḥurr*, and then glazed.[7]

---

4 Both *kawsha* and *kawwāsh* are regional terms common even today in North Africa.

5 Information on *furn* and *kawsha* is based on the field research conducted on traditional bakeries in 2015 by Ḥakīma, *Afrān Tilimsān*, MA dissertation, University of Abū Bakr Bilqāyid, Algeria.

6 See, for instance, al-Kindī, *al-Taraffuq fī l-ʿiṭr* 92.

7 See, for instance, Ibn Manẓūr, *Lisān al-ʿArab*, s.v. غضر.

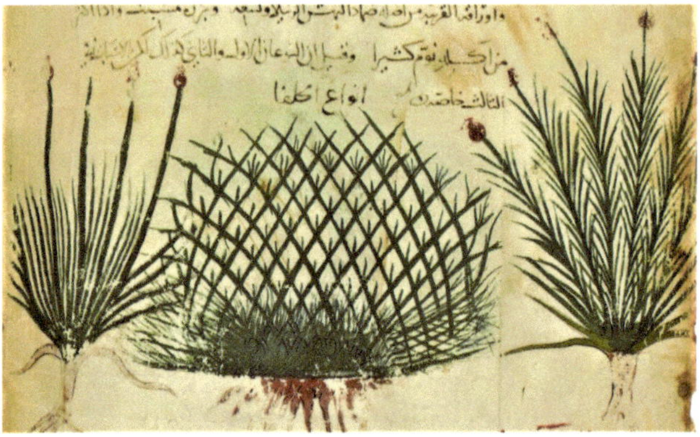

FIGURE 171 Esparto grass, *ḥalfā*, Dioscorides, *Ajzāʾ min risāla fī l-nabātāt*, fol. 88v, detail
BNF, DEPARTMENT OF MANUSCRIPTS, ARAB 4947. SOURCE: GALLICA.BNF.FR/BNF

ghaḍāra kabīra (غضارة كبيرة) a large glazed bowl.

ghaḍāra ṣaghīra (غضارة صغيرة) a small glazed bowl, used for serving small dishes, such as *naql* 'snack foods,' as in recipe viii.2.1 for fried fresh chickpeas, fried locusts in recipe xi.1, and recipe xi.2 for fried freshwater shrimps.

ghirbāl (غربال) sieve.

ghirbāl ḥalfā (غربال حلفا) sieve made with esparto grass, see *ḥalfā* below.

ghirbāl ṣafīq (غربال صفيق) fine-meshed sieve.

ghirbāl shaʿr (غربال شعر) fine-meshed sieve, usually made with coarse horse-hair.

ghiṭāʾ (غطاء) lid (of a pot).

ghiṭāʾ mathqūb (غطاء مثقوب) lid with a hole in it.

ḥalfā (حلفا) esparto grass, also known as halfah grass, *Lygeum spartinum*, a plant native to southern Europe and North Africa. It was used woven into various receptacles. In al-Tujībī's cookbook there is need for it to be used as a sieve (*munkhul*); as a tray to drain cleaned intestines prepared for sausages, recipe ii.6.4; a strainer (*muṣaffī*) to filter the prepared fermented sauce of *murrī*, recipe x.8.1; and a mold (*miqdār*) for making fresh cheese, recipe vi.1.1. Esparto has to be rinsed repeatedly and dried in the sun until all the odors of what was used to soften it are gone. From Ibn al-Bayṭār, *al-Jāmiʿ* ii 408, we learn that this was done with cows' dung (*arwāth baqar*).

FIGURE 172 *Jafna*, a large and wide serving bowl, fifteenth-century Valencia, Spain
MET NY—GIFT OF HENRY G. MARQUAND, 1894, ACCESSION NUMBER: 94.4.361

ḥaṣīr (حصير) mat made with woven reeds or date palm fronds.

ḥaṭab (حطب) firewood, used in recipe ii.2.41 to roast meat chunks enclosed inside a prepared pit, see the recipe for more details.

ibrīm (ابريم) large earthenware or iron cauldron, as used in recipe ii.3.2. *Ibrīm* is a possible regional variant on what was more commonly called *burma*, pl. *birām*, which originally was made of soapstone. As al-Tujībī's recipe suggests, it must have also been used as a generic name for a pot and, in this case, a cauldron. In the anonymous Andalusi *Anwāʿ al-ṣaydala* 162 and 167, which is contemporaneous with al-Tujībī's cookbook, a similar large cauldron is called a *burma*.

ināʾ (اناء) generic term for a vessel.

ināʾ muzaffat (اناء مزفت) a vessel coated from the inside with *zift* (see entry below), which is black resinous pitch.

iskarbāj (اسكرباج), ***iskarfāj*** (اسكرفاج) cheese grater.

> ***iskarfāj maṣnūʿ*** (اسكرفاج مصنوع) a grater made of steel, which is an alloy of iron and carbon and sometimes other elements. The full name of this alloy is *fūlādh maṣnūʿ*, as mentioned in Ibn Sīnā, *al-Qānūn* i 491. It is used in recipe vii.2.8 for grating hard cheese into dust-like particles.

jafna (جفنة) a serving bowl, large and wide. It was also used in the kitchen to whip eggs, for instance.

jarīd nakhl (جريد نخل) stems of stripped date palm fronds, used in recipe x.7 for making vinegar and recipe i.4.32 for a baked variety of pastries.

jarra (جرة) earthenware jar.

FIGURE 173 A server tending to fire burning in the stove, al-Ḥarīrī, *al-Maqāmāt*, fol. 140r, copied and illustrated by al-Wāsiṭī, detail
BNF, DEPARTMENT OF MANUSCRIPTS, ARAB 5847. SOURCE: GALLICA.BNF.FR/BNF

jawbak (جوبك), ***shawbak*** (شوبك) rolling pin. As al-Tujībī describes it in recipe i.2.10, it is a wooden cylinder which is thick in the middle and tapers towards both ends.

jild ḍa'n (جلد ضأن) sheep skin, used to keep fermenting dough warm, as in recipe i.1.1.

kāghad (كاغد) paper made from the fiber of the hemp plant *qinnab* (قنّب), *Cannabis sativa sativa*. It is not a narcotic like *Cannabis sativa indica* (*qinnab Hindī/ḥashīsha*), which is marijuana. Cf. *qirṭās*, which is made from *bardī* papyrus, *Cyprus papyrus*. It was used moistened to seal pots baked in the *furn* (brick oven), as in recipes ii.2.15 and 26.

kalkha (كلخة) giant fennel stalk, *Ferula communis*, a plant with a long and straight, sturdy hollow stalk. It is used in recipe ix.2.1 to stir nougat syrup.

kānūn al-nār (كانون النار) a small portable stove (*mawqid*) used for cooking and heating purposes. In al-Tujībī's cookbook, recipe i.4.15, it is only mentioned as a heat source to keep *qaṭāyif* batter warm and facilitate its fermentation.

kattān (كتّان) a piece of linen cloth; used in recipe i.1.1 to keep the portioned bread dough warm while fermenting; made into a strainer (*muṣaffī*) in recipe x.8.1 to strain *murrī* sauce; and wrapped around ingredients used to remedy olive oil that has gone bad in recipe x.9.2.

mushāqat al-kattān (مشاقة الكتّان) a piece of tow linen, moistened and used to wrap desert truffles to protect them while roasting.

kawsha (كوشة) the baking chamber of the brick oven, see *furn* above.

khābiya (خابية) large cylindrical earthenware jar with a tapered, rounded bottom, mostly used for pickling purposes and storing foods like cheese.

khābiya muzaffata (خابية مزفتة) large cylindrical earthenware jar coated with pitch from the inside, used for pickling purposes.

khābiya muzayyata (خابية مزيتة) large cylindrical earthenware jar coated with olive oil from the inside.

khābiya ṣaghīra (خابية صغيرة) a small earthenware jar, which may be used at the table to serve dipping sauces. Al-Tujībī's recipe x.8.1, p. 522, for instance, suggests filling it with good *murrī* sauce flavored with honey and pounded carob pulp.

khayṭ (خيط) thread, used in al-Tujībī's recipes to cut boiled eggs, sew up stuffed cavities of animals, and similar tasks.

khirqa (خرقة) piece of cloth with raw edges.

khirqa kattān (خرقة كتّان) piece of linen cloth, see *kattān* above.

khirqa khafīfa (خرقة خفيفة) light piece of cloth.

khirqa ṣafīqa (خرقة صفيقة) tightly woven piece of cloth.

lawḥ (لوح) wooden board used mostly for cutting purposes.

lawḥ mustaṭīl (لوح مستطيل) a rectangular wooden board, used for rolling out dough or pasta; a *māʾida* (table) was also used for the same purpose.

mafrash ḥadīd (مفرش حديد) iron griddle with a broad and flat surface, used for toasting *qaṭāʾif* pancakes in recipe i.2.16 and grilling meat strips, as in recipe ii.2.39.

maḥbas (محبس) cage-like basket, also called *qafaṣ*, used in recipe i.4.19 to dry *khabīṣ* sheets of pastry.

maḥbas fakhkhār (محبس فخار) a large, wide earthenware tub used in recipe vi.2.1 to strain yogurt.

māʾida (مائدة) table, used for serving food, as in recipes x.1.1 and x.3.2. It was also useful for cooks who used it to roll out dough when making pastries and pasta, as in chapters i.4 and i.5.

Although most medieval dictionaries draw the line between *māʾida* and *khiwān* by stating that the former designates a table already spread with the served foods, whereas the latter is the table itself as a piece of furniture, the usage in al-Tujībī's recipes shows no such distinctions. The only place where *khiwān* shows up in his book is its title.

malla (ملة) a flat wide plate used for baking flat thin bread on a direct source of heat, as in recipe i.1.3. Originally, *malla* was a pit in which flattened dough is baked in hot ashes and stones. The allusions to *malla* in al-Tujībī's cookbook suggest an earthenware or iron plate, which is heated by placing it on the fire. This must have been the Andalusi usage of the term. Ibn Khalṣūn, *Kitāb al-Aghdhiya* 92, explains that *khubz al-malla* is *khubz al-ṭabaq*. Now, *khubz al-ṭābaq* is flat bread baked on a wide plate, called *ṭābaq* in the eastern region of al-Mashriq. As for the genuine *malla* bread that is baked in pits, Ibn Khalṣūn calls it *khubz al-ramād* 'ash bread.'

malla fakhkhār (ملة فخار) earthenware plate.
malla fakhkhār dūn muzajjaj (ملة فخار دون مزجج) unglazed earthenware plate.
malla ḥadīd (ملة حديد) iron plate.
malla nuḥās (ملة نحاس) copper plate.

mallat al-kunāfa (ملة الكنافة) *kunāfa* pan, see *mir'āt al-kunāfa* below.
mighrafa (مغرفة), pl. *maghārif* (مغارف) ladle, its handle is referred to as *ṭaraf al-mighrafa*.

mighrafa kabīra (مغرفة كبيرة) large ladle.
mighrafa muthaqqaba (مغرفة مثقبة) perforated ladle, used to scoop pieces of fried thin bread out of the skillet in recipe ix.2.6.
mighrafa ṣaghīra (مغرفة صغيرة) small ladle, used in recipes for scooping small amounts, such as taking cured olives out of a vessel, recipe x.2.4. It may also designate what might have resembled today's round-bowled soup spoons, used in recipes i.2.21 and 22.
mighrafat al-bayḍ (مغرفة البيض) ladle, specially used for scrambling eggs, which would have been more like a spatula.

miḥakka (محكة) scraper, used with salt in recipe i.2.17 to scrape and clean the skin of a chicken.
mihrās (مهراس) mortar made of a large and heavy hollowed-out long stone or hardwood, see also the varieties below. The pestle used with it is called *yad al-mihrās*, literally 'the mortar's handle.'

mihrās ḥajar (مهراس حجر) stone mortar. A large one is used to crush barley and wheat grains, as in recipes i.3.10 and i.5.13. It is also used in recipe x.1.1 for crushing mustard seeds as a second best to a wooden mortar.
mihrās muzajjaj (مهراس مزجج) glazed earthenware mortar, specifically used in recipe x.7.12 for crushing the acidic unripe grapes (*ḥiṣrim*).
mihrās nuḥās (مهراس نحاس) copper mortar, used mainly to grind saffron threads. It is also used once in crushing almonds, in recipe i.4.1. If almonds need to be pounded until they release their oil, a wooden one is used.

FIGURE 174 Two physicians working on a medicinal preparation, using a large *miʿjana*, folio from an Arabic translation of the *Materia Medica* of Dioscorides, 1224, detail
CLEVELAND MUSEUM OF ART: HTTPS://CLEVELANDART.ORG/ART/1977.91

mihrās ʿūd (مهراس عود) wooden mortar, usually reserved for pounding wet ingredients, such as meat, boiled garlic, green herbs like cilantro and mint, gourd, eggplant, nuts, salt, and the like. Big wooden mortars are needed for coarsely crushing grains like wheat and barley, as in recipes i.3.10, and i.5.3.

miʿjana (معجنة) large kneading bowl. According to Ibn al-Ḥashshāʾ, *Mufīd al-ʿulūm* 8, *ijjāna* (اجّانة) was its name in the eastern region, where it was used for washing clothes and kneading dough.

miʿjana kabīra (معجنة كبيرة) this must have been a huge bowl because an ordinary *miʿjana* used to knead the dough is already large. It is used in recipe x.2.4 to prepare olives for curing.

mikhṭāf (مخطاف) iron hook, used in recipes i.4.33–4 to turn over cheese-filled pastries (*mujabbanāt*) while frying.

milʿaqa (ملعقة), pl. ***malāʿiq*** (ملاعق) spoon.

milʿaqa baqs (ملعقة بقس) boxwood spoon, used with porridges in recipes i.5.9 and 13, and *tharīd* with milk in recipe i.2.21. The boxwood tree is said to be similar to that of the myrtle, and its yellow wood is described as hard.[8] Al-Ḥimyarī, *Ṣifat Jazīrat al-Andalus* 124, mentions that boxwood trees grew abundantly in Ṭurṭūsha 'Tortosa' in the northeastern region of Catalonia.

milʿaqa ḥadīd (ملعقة حديد) iron spoon, used in recipe ix.6.1 to test the doneness of a thick sugar syrup.

milʿaqa ṣaghīra (ملعقة صغيرة) small spoon, used to take preserved lemons out of a jar in recipe x.3.2.

mindīl (منديل) clean piece of cloth with neat edges, similar to towels and napkins, used for different purposes depending on the cloth and size; cf. *khirqa*, which is just a snipped off piece of cloth with raw edges.

mindīl ghalīẓ (منديل غليظ) thick piece of cloth.

mindīl kattān (منديل كتّان) a piece of linen cloth.

mindīl ṣafīq (منديل صفيق) tightly woven piece of cloth used for straining liquids.

mindīl ṣūf (منديل صوف) a piece of woolen cloth used to strain heated honey.

minqāsh nuḥās (منقاش نحاس) decorating tweezers made of copper, used for making geometric impressions on pastries, as in *kaʿk* recipe i.4.1.

minshaf ghalīẓ (منشف غليظ) thick towel, used in couscous recipe i.5.1 to cover the top of the pot to keep the steam in.

miqdār (مقدار) cheese mold made of woven esparto grass; see recipe vi.1.1, which gives details on shaping it.

miqlāt (مقلاة) skillet.

miqlāt fakhkhār (مقلاة فخار) earthenware skillet.

miqlāt ḥadīd muqaṣdara (مقلاة حديد مقصدرة) tinned iron skillet.

miqlāt al-kunāfa (مقلاة الكنافة) *kunāfa* pan, see *mirʾāt al-kunāfa* below.

miqlāt muqaṣdara (مقلاة مقصدرة) tinned skillet; also occurs as ***miqlāt muqazdara*** (مقلاة مقزدرة) in recipe v.2.2.

miqlāt nuḥās muqaṣdara (مقلاة نحاس مقصدرة) tinned copper skillet.

---

8 See Ibn al-Bayṭār, *al-Jāmiʿ* i 141.

mir'āt al-kunāfa (مرآة الكنافة), also called ***mir'āt Hindiyya*** (مرآة هندية), a round metal pan set on a flameless coal fire, used for cooking the thin sheets of crepe-like pastry for *kunāfa*, see recipe i.4.14. It is also referred to as *miqlāt al-kunāfa* and *mallat al-kunāfa* in recipe i.4.12.

mirwaḥa (مروحة) fan made of woven esparto grass (*ḥalfā*), used for fanning the fire.

misalla (مسلة) large needle.

miʿṣara (معصرة) grape juice press used in recipe x.7.1 to press out grape juice for making vinegar.

mithrad (مثرد) large, wide bowl named after the *tharīd* dish in which is served in it, see entry in glossary 5. Based on al-Tujībī's recipes, it also served as an all-purpose bowl for cooks to use while preparing the dishes.

mukhfiyya (مخفية), pl. ***makhāfī*** (مخافي) a wide serving bowl, made of wood (*ʿūd*) or glazed earthenware, as it is used in al-Tujībī's recipes.[9] The name of the dish was adopted in Spanish as *almofia*. In Dozy, *Takmilat al-maʿājim* iv 153–4, s.v. خفي, its Moroccan synonym is given as *maṣīṣa*. According to the Arabic dictionary by Majmaʿ, *al-Muʿjam al-wasīṭ*, s.v. *m-ṣ-ṣ*, *maṣīṣa* is *qaṣʿa*, which is a large and wide serving bowl.

The name *mukhfiyya* might have been derived from *khafā*, which designates lightening when it shines faintly, as explained in Ibn Manẓūr, *Lisān al-ʿArab*, s.v. خفا. Based on this, *mukhfiyya* bowls were called so possibly due to their semi-glossy finish. In recipes i.4.38–9, a *mukhfiyya* is used for serving *mujabbanāt* cheese pastries; and in recipe ix.6.1, pieces of pulled taffy are kept in it.

munkhul (منخل) sieve.

muqaṣdar (مقصدر), ***muqazdar*** (مقزدر) coated with *qaṣdīr* (قصدير) tin, also called *raṣāṣ qalʿī* (رصاص قلعي) and *raṣāṣ abyaḍ* (رصاص ابيض), which was believed to be good-quality lead in medieval times.

naqīr khashab (نقير خشب) wooden box used in recipe vi.2.2 for making yogurt.

naṭʿ (نطع) leather spread.

qadaḥ (قدح) drinking vessel, available in different sizes, the smallest of which was said to be enough for two people. In wine-drinking contexts, it refers to an empty glass, whereas *ka's* is a filled one. A large *qadaḥ* was used for collecting drawn milk, and a small one was used as a cup. It was also used for keeping butter.[10] For *qadaḥ* as a weight measure, see glossary 13.

In recipe i.4.29, *qadaḥ* with a hole pierced in its base is used for allowing *zalābiya* batter to run through it into the boiling oil.

qaḍīb ḥadīd (قضيب حديد) iron rod used for crushing meat into paste in recipes ii.5.2 and iv.3.

---

9 Based on Corriente, *Dictionary of Andalusi Arabic*, s.v. *kh-f-w*, it is a glazed bowl or basin.

10 See Dozy, *Takmilat al-maʿājim* viii 192, s.v. قدح.

qaḍīb raqīq min ʿūd (قضيب رقيق من عود) thin wooden stick, used for grilling pieces of cheese.

qādūs (قادوس) an earthenware vessel with a round shape that is tapered inwards, used in food preparations and as a capacity measure, see glossary 13. The term also designates buckets attached to irrigating water wheels (*nāʿūra*), plant pots, and in recipe ii.2.44 as small earthenware cooking vessels.

qādūs al-taqṭīr (قادوس التقطير) distilling cucurbit; called *qarʿa* in the eastern region. The alembic is called *inbīq*.

qannūṭ (قنوط), ***qannūd*** (قنود), pl. ***qanānīṭ*** (قنانيط) reed tube; in the eastern region it is more commonly called *qanāt*, which designates canes, hollow reeds made into spears, as well as water canals because of the resemblance in shape. According to *The American Heritage Dictionary*, s.v *q-n-w*, the word is of Akkadian origin, *qanû*, from which is derived the Aramaic *qanyā*, Greek *kanna*, and Latin *canna*, all meaning 'reed.'[11] *Qannūṭ* of the western region must have been the Andalusi Romance of thc Late Latin *cannūtus*.[12]

qannūṭ qaṣab manfūdh al-ṭarafayn (قنوط قصب منفوذ الطرفين) reed tube that is open from one end to the other (i.e., hollow). It is inserted inside a variety of pastry just before putting it in the oven. The hole made with it would be filled with honey after the baking is done, as described in recipe i.4.24. See also *qaṣaba* below.

qār (قار) mineral pitch, bitumen, which seeps naturally from the ground. See also *zift* below. In recipe x.7.3 for making vinegar, a jar is sealed with it.

qaṣaba (قصبة) reed stalk, used in al-Tujībī's recipes mostly for stirring thickened puddings and syrups. It would most likely be the kind referred to as *qaṣab Fārisī*, which Ibn Wāfid, *al-Adwiya al-mufrada* 119, also called *qaṣab Andalusi*. It is identified in Dozy, *Takmilat al-maʿājim* viii 284, s.v. قصب, as *Arundo donax*, described as a solid reed variety; thick, long, and sturdy, used for making arrows.[13] See also *qannūṭ* above.

jiʿāb min qaṣab (جعاب من قصب) reed joints,[14] used in recipe i.4.5 to shape cannoli-like pieces of pastry.

---

11 See, https://ahdictionary.com/word/semitic.html#q%CA%BFd, accessed April 8, 2020.

12 In Spanish, *canuto*.

13 See Ibn Sīnā, *al-Qānūn* i 644.

14 Sg. *jaʿb*, occurs as *kaʿb* in Ibn Manẓūr, *Lisān al-ʿArab*, s.v. كعب, where it is said to be a reed joint, i.e., part of the stalk between two nodes (*ʿuqad*, sg. *ʿuqda*).

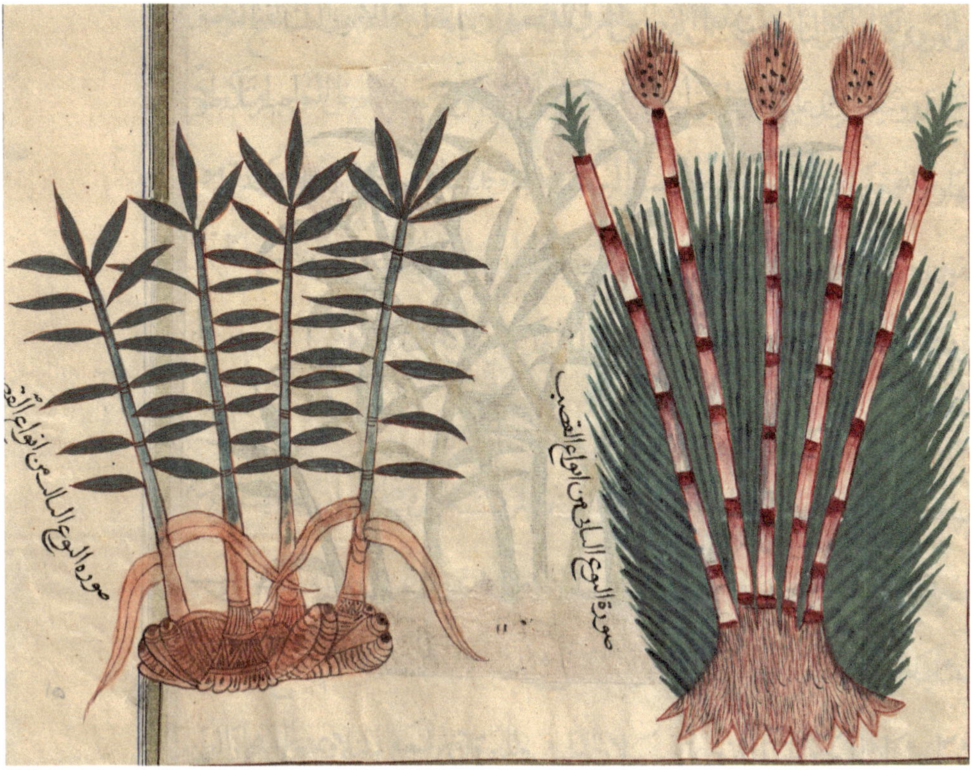

FIGURE 175 Varieties of reeds, Dioscorides, *Fī Hayūlā al-ṭibb*, translation by Ḥunayn b. Isḥāq, fol. 48r, detail
FROM THE NEW YORK PUBLIC LIBRARY, SPENCER COLLECTION: HTTPS://DIGITALCOLLECTIONS.NYPL.ORG/ITEMS/5E66B3E8-C5EA-D471-E040-E00A180654D7

qaṣabat al-ḥalwā (قصبة الحلوا) a reed stalk described in recipe ix.2.1 as having a ring of brass attached to its end, used in stirring desserts in chapter ix.2.

qaṣaba manfūdhat al-ʿuqad (قصبة منفوذة العقد) a reed that has been hollowed all through the joints. In recipe i.4.32 for a baked pastry, it is inserted in the batter just before baking it to create a hole in its middle, to be filled with honey when it is done baking.

shubbāk min qaṣab (شباك من قصب) a reed lattice, used in recipe i.4.29 to drain *zalābiya* fritters after dipping them in honey.

qaṣriyya (قصرية) large and wide earthenware tub, similar to *mirkan* and *ijjāna*, commonly used for washing clothes but are also useful in the kitchen.

qaṣriyya ṣaghīra (قصرية صغيرة) small earthenware tub.

qidr (قدر) pot; and ***fam al-qidr*** (فم القدر) is its rim; literally, its mouth.

qidr fakhkhār (قدر فخار) earthenware pot.
qidr fakhkhār dūn muzajjaja (قدر فخار دون مزججة) unglazed earthenware pot.
qidr ḥantam (قدر حنتم) green-glazed pot.
qidr ḥijāra (قدر حجارة) stone pot, used in recipe iii.2.31 for a bastilla-like *jūdhāba* casserole.
qidr jadīda (قدر جديدة) new pot, frequently called for in al-Tujībī's recipes, which would be necessary when using an earthenware pot (*qidr fakhkhār*)—not to be used more than once—or a glazed pot (*qidr ḥantam/muzajjaj*) to replace one that has already been used up to five times. Al-Tujībī provides these guidelines in his introduction, p. 109.

The rationale behind such practices, as given by al-Tujībī's source, Ibn Zuhr, *Kitāb al-Aghdhiya* 137, is that their porous surfaces, especially those of the unglazed ones, *fakhkhār*, are absorbent and food trapped in them would putrefy and mold; regular washing cannot efficiently get to them. If these pots are used again, the putrefied particles in the pores would contaminate the cooking food and cause harm to the body. The green-glazed ones, *ḥantam*, are less porous and can be used more often, up to five times.

qidr kabīra muzajjaja (قدر كبيرة مزججة) large glazed earthenware pot.
qidr al-kuskusū (قدر الكسكسو) couscoussier, described in detail in recipe i.5.1.
qidr naẓīf (قدر نظيف) clean pot.
qidr wāsiʿ (قدر واسع) large and wide pot.
qidr wāsiʿat al-fam (قدر واسعة الفم) wide-rimmed pot.

qimʿ (قمع) funnel, used in recipe ii.6.4 to facilitate filling sausage intestines.
qirba madbūgha (قربة مدبوغة) a vessel made of tanned leather, used in recipe vi.2.2 for making yogurt.
qirmida (قرمدة) large flat brick, used in recipe v.1.5 for baking salt-encrusted fish in the brick oven.
qudayra (قديرة) small pot, which had many uses, such as preparing sauces served with dishes and securing a small amount of hot water to be added to the cooking pot as needed. In recipe i.5.6, for instance, the cook is directed to attach a small pot filled with hot water to the top of the pot to keep it hot. The small pot might have had some sort of a curved handle to attach it to the rim of the cooking pot.
quffa min ḥalfā (قفة من حلفا) a large round basket woven of esparto grass. See also *ḥalfā* above.
qulla (قلة) earthenware jar, used in recipe i.4.32 for baking pastry.
raḍf (رضف) heated stones, used to keep a pot warm after the cooking is done.

ramād (رماد) ash, used heated to cook eggs by burying them in it, as in recipe v.2.11. In recipe v.1.25, the tails of eels are rubbed with it to help strip off their skins.

raqqūja (رقوجة) an unusual name for *jarra* 'jar,' found only in the BL MS, fol. 170v. The term must have been an indigenous variant for *riqq*/*riqāq*, which were jars made with thin molded sheets of leather, used to store water, milk, yogurt, wine, pickled fish, and the like.

rīsha (ريشة) a feather used for basting grilling birds.

rukhāma (رخامة) marble slab used in making confections, see *ṣallāya rukhām* below.

rūṭabāl (روطبال) a stick from the caprifig with three tines at its end, used for stirring fermenting *murrī* sauce in recipe x.8.1. It looks like a three-tine cultivator. In Corriente, *Dictionary of Andalusi Arabic*, s.v. *r-ṭ-b-l*, it is said to be related to the Latin *rutabellu* 'rake.'

saffūd ḥadīd (سفود حديد) iron skewer.

saffūd ʿūd (سفود عود) wooden skewer.

ṣaḥfa (صحفة) wide, shallow bowl, often used in al-Tujībī's recipes for mixing ingredients; cf. *ghaḍāra*, which is mentioned mostly as a serving bowl.

> ***ṣaḥfa fakhkhār*** (صحفة فخار) earthenware wide, shallow bowl.
>
> ***ṣaḥfa kabīra*** (صحفة كبيرة) large, wide, and shallow bowl.

ṣallāya (صلاية) stone slab used with a large rounded stone, called a *fihr*, to finely crush spices and aromatics.

ṣallāya rukhām (صلاية رخام) wide marble slab used in making confections, as in chapters ix.2 and 6. The recipes sometimes just refer it as *rukhāma*.

sāṭūr (ساطور) cleaver, used to break the ribs of a whole side of ram before grilling it, as in recipe ii.2.38; and to pound meat into paste consistency, as in recipe ii.5.2.

shakwa (شكوة) a churning vessel made with the skin of a kid or a lamb; its tripod is called *ḥammāla*. It is used to churn milk vigorously to extract its butter, as in recipe vi.2.3.

shawbak (شوبك), ***jawbak*** (جوبك) rolling pin, described in recipe i.2.10 as a wooden cylinder, thick in the middle and tapered towards both ends.

sikkīn (سكين) knife.

> ***qafā al-sikkīn*** (قفا السكين), ***ẓahr al-sikkīn*** (ظهر السكين) back of the knife's blade, used to give cooked leaf vegetables, such as spinach and borage, blunt strikes to mash them, as in recipes ii.2.10–1 and vii.8.1. This blunt side of the blade is also used in recipe vi.2.2 for scraping clean a leather container.
>
> ***sikkīn min ʿūd*** (سكين من عود) wooden knife, used to scrape clean a leather container in recipe vi.2.2.
>
> ***sikkīn murhaf*** (سكين مرهف) thin-bladed knife, used in recipe i.4.27 to cut delicate stuffed cookies.

sirbāl (سربال) apron.
ṣufr*/*ṣifr (صفر) brass, or white copper, also known as *isfaydhūr*.[15]
ṭabaq 1 (طبق) vessel, usually a tray or platter.

> ***ṭabaq ʿūd*** (طبق عود) wooden platter.
> ***ṭabaq zujāj*** (طبق زجاج) glass tray or platter.

ṭabaq 2 (طبق), variant on ***ṭābaq*** (طابق), iron or stone plate used for baking flat bread and grilling on a direct source of heat. Also called *malla*, see above.
ṭāḥūnat al-yad (طاحونة اليد) a small rotary hand-mill for grinding grains; mentioned only in the anonymous Andalusi cookbook, *Anwāʿ al-ṣaydala* 173, where it is used for coarsely crushing grains.
ṭājin (طاجن) pan; a versatile cooking vessel in the Andalusi kitchen. As used in al-Tujībī's recipes, it can be placed on direct heat, but it is more frequently used in the brick oven for baking and roasting purposes.

> ***ṭājin fakhkhār*** (طاجن فخار), ***ṭājin turābī*** (طاجن ترابي) earthenware pan.
> ***ṭājin fakhkhār muzajjaj*** (طاجن فخار مزجج) glazed earthenware pan.
> ***ṭājin ḥadīd*** (طاجن حديد) iron pan or plate.
> ***ṭājin kabīr*** (طاجن كبير) large pan.
> ***ṭājin muzajjaj*** (طاجن مزجج) glazed earthenware pan.
> ***ṭājin al-qaṭāyif*** (طاجن القطايف) special pan used for cooking *qaṭāyif* 'pancakes.' It is made of glazed earthenware with a bottom textured with blind holes, perhaps to create interesting surface textures on the cooking pancakes, see recipe i.4.15.
> ***ṭājin ṣaghīr*** (طاجن صغير) small pan.
> ***ṭājin wāsiʿ*** (طاجن واسع) wide pan.
> ***ṭājin wāsiʿ min fakhkhār ghayr muzajjaj*** (طاجن واسع من فخار غير مزجج) a wide unglazed earthenware pan with low sides. It is used in the oven and as a frying pan for dishes that require low heat.

ṭalya min ʿūd (طلية من عود), ***ṭalya khashab*** (طلية خشب) wooden block, usually used as a chopping board. It was also used in butchers' shops to cut meat for customers. Each night, at the end of the day's work, the butcher was required to sprinkle his meat board with salt to prevent maggots from breeding in it. He was also supposed to cover it with esparto grass and tie it to prevent dogs from licking it.[16] In Corriente,

---

15 See al-Bīrūnī, *al-Jamāhir* 431.
16 See al-Saqaṭī, *Fī Ādāb al-ḥisba* 33.

Dictionary of Andalusi Arabic, s.v. *ṭ-l-y*, *ṭalya* is said to have been derived from the Late Latin *taleare* 'to cut.'

tannūr (تنور) clay oven, an indispensable and versatile baking, roasting, and cooking fixture in the Andalusi households of al-Tujībī's time. It is bell shaped, with its main opening on top. This opening is referred to as *fam al-tannūr*, literally its mouth. It also has a smaller hole in the bottom, called a *rawwāj*, also referred to as *athqāb suflā* 'lower holes' in al-Tujībī's cookbook. It facilitates air circulation in the *tannūr*; also used to sweep out ashes of burnt wood. It was closed, along with the top opening, when a low fire was required for slow roasting; and kept open when stronger heat was needed to brown the baking foods. The best of *tannūr*s were those built with a large interior and walls of medium thickness, based on the specifications given in al-Warrāq's tenth-century cookbook.[17] It was built outside the living quarters and kitchen in an open space, which faced the opposite direction of the wind, as this would help blow smoke away from the house.

From al-Tujībī's references to *tannūr*, we learn that the Andalusi oven was not any different from the Mashriqi *tannūr*, and it had similar uses. For making *tannūr* bread, with instructions on how to light it and prepare it for baking, see al-Tujībī's recipe i.1.2. For roasting a whole lamb stuffed with couscous, see recipe i.5.4. Recipe ii.2.39 provides very interesting details on roasting a skewered yearling ram; and in recipe ii.2.40, a ram is roasted by laying it flat on large bricks arranged in its bottom.

ṭayfūr (طيفور), pl. ***ṭayāfīr*** (طيافير) a large deepish platter used for presenting food at the table, as in recipe i.4.33 for *mujabbanāt* cheese pastries.

Although *ṭayfūr* as a vessel is not to be found in the medieval lexicons,[18] we encounter it in several other medieval sources where it also occurs as *ṭayfūriyya* (طيفورية). In al-Warrāq's tenth-century cookbook *Kitāb al-Ṭabīkh*, English trans., *Annals*, it is frequently used for serving dishes; there we find the large ones, the wide and shallow ones, and the small ones for serving sauces. Ibn Baṭṭūṭa mentions it as a nice-looking serving bowl filled with dried fruits; also as a small tray of gold and as a large platter filled with sweets, draped with a piece of silk fabric, and offered as a gift.[19]

According to al-Maqrīzī's account of Egypt during Fatimid times, it was a tray of different sizes loaded with cookies, covered with a conical top (*muqawwara*) with a silken cloth draped on it, and carried on servers' heads and distributed on religious occasions. The largest loaded tray would weigh around 100 pounds. It was also used as a serving tray with bowls (*zabādī*) arranged in it. The large tray-like *ṭayfū-*

17 See al-Warrāq, *Kitāb al-Ṭabīkh*, English trans., *Annals* 88–9.

18 It is only said to be a man's name, and the name of a small bird, with no further details. In Ghālib, *Mawsūʿa*, it is identified as *Aeglalites* (S), which is the little ringed plover.

19 Ibn Baṭṭūṭa, *Tuḥfat al-nuẓẓār* i 255, and ii 104–5.

riyya, used for serving hot dishes, was called *qawāʾimiyya* (i.e., with legs, albeit short ones). Or they were set on silver stands (*marāfiʿ*) and carried to the dining caliphs and dignitaries.[20]

Additionally, Egyptian scholar al-Qalqashandī described how he and his group were served food in the sultans' courts in al-Maghrib. He said they were served *tharāʾid* in large bowls,[21] called *jifān* (sg. *jafna*), with a variety of serving bowls loaded with all kinds of foods arranged all around them. He called these bowls *ṭayāfīr*, explaining that they were the same as the wide serving bowls called *makhāfī* (sg. *mukhfiyya*, see entry above).[22]

Ṭayāfīr bowls were also made in small sizes for serving snack foods, such as salted pistachios, as we learn from these verses:

> Look at these small *ṭayāfīr* of salted pistachios.
> The nuts enclosed in cracked-open shells,
> Are like birds' tongues showing through their beaks.[23]

Etymologically, the Spanish *ataifor* is an adopted Arabic name. Although nowadays it designates a bowl, during the medieval Inquisition, it was often mentioned as a large communal platter in which couscous was served, see introduction iii.7, pp. 74–5, and iv, p. 97.

In today's traditional wedding ceremonies in Morocco, *ṭayfūr* is a large platter filled with gifts, covered with conical tops, and carried to the bride's wedding party. The small ones are offered with sweets on religious festivals and feasts. In Saudi Arabia today, *ṭawfariyya* (طوفرية) is a tray with low sides used to offer food and drinks to guests.

ṭinjīr (طنجير) cauldron, a large wide pot with a rounded base, made of metal, soapstone, or earthenware. The other name for this pot is *dast*. It is mostly used in cooking main dishes prepared in large quantities, as in stuffed tripe recipe ii.6.8, and desserts.

> ***ṭinjīr fakhkhār*** (طنجير فخار) earthenware cauldron.
> ***ṭinjīr nuḥās muqaṣdar*** (طنجير نحاس مقصدر) tinned copper cauldron.

ʿūd al-dhukār (عود الذكار) a stick from the caprifig tree, *Ficus carica sylvestris*, which is the male pollen fig tree bearing a wild variety of the common fig, used to pollinate the edible fig. See also *rūṭabāl* in this section.

20 See al-Maqrīzī, *al-Khiṭaṭ* 541, 597, 611.
21 Sg. *tharīda*, a staple dish of bread sopped in broth, see chapter i.2 for recipes.
22 See al-Qalqashandī, *Ṣubḥ al-aʿshā* v 205.
23 Al-Ṣafadī, *al-Wāfī bi-l-wafayāt* iii 21.

FIGURE 176 Pitch, *zift*, extracting it and cooking it down, Dioscorides, *Fī Hayūlā al-ṭibb*, translation by Ḥunayn b. Isḥāq, fol. 43v, detail
FROM THE NEW YORK PUBLIC LIBRARY, SPENCER COLLECTION: HTTPS://DIGITALCOLLECTIONS.NYPL.ORG/ITEMS/5E66B3E8-AB6B-D471-E040-E00A180654D7

waraq dhukār (ورق ذكار) leaves of the caprifig tree (see above entry), used in *murrī* preparations for fermented liquid sauce. They are valued for their antiseptic properties.

waraq karm (ورق كرم), ***waraq dāliya*** (ورق دالية) grape leaves used to give bread a shine in recipe i.1.2; and for covering a jar of curdling yogurt, recipe vi.2.2.

waraq ṣafṣāf (ورق صفصاف) willow leaves, used for covering a jar of curdling yogurt in recipe vi.2.2.

wiʿāʾ (وعاء) a general term for a vessel, see also *ināʾ* above.

- ***wiʿāʾ kabīr*** (وعاء كبير) large vessel.
- ***wiʿāʾ khazafī*** (وعاء خزفي) earthenware vessel.
- ***wiʿāʾ min ḥalfā*** (وعاء من حلفا) vessel made of woven esparto grass, see *ḥalfā* above.
- ***wiʿāʾ min ʿūd*** (وعاء من عود) wooden vessel.
- ***wiʿāʾ muzajjaj min dākhilihi wa khārijihi*** (وعاء مزجج من داخله وخارجه) a vessel that is glazed on the inside and the outside.

ẓarf (ظرف) general term for a container; in recipe x.8.1 it is mentioned as a leather vessel used for storing olive oil.

zift (زفت) black resinous pitch, from conifers, such as *arz* (male cedar trees) and *tannūb* (fir trees). The fresh moist resin was called *zift raṭb*. Dry pitch, called *zift yābis*, was obtained by boiling it until the pitch thickens and becomes very sticky. At room temperature, it becomes dry and brittle, and whenever needed, it is melted by heating it.

With its very hot, dry, and astringent properties, it was valued for its ability to fight putridity. It was used, for instance, to heal scabies in camels and kill lice and their eggs in humans. In the kitchen, it was smeared on the inside of jars used for storing liquids. Jars treated this way would be nonporous, and the pitch itself would help preserve the liquids kept in them. In al-Tujībī's recipes, such jars are used for storing vinegar.

zīr mustaṭīl min zujāj (زير مستطيل من زجاج) a rectangular glass jar, used in recipe x.3.2 for pickling lemons. It is said to be large enough for 50 lemons. The regular *zīr* is a large earthenware jar with a round wide top.

9.2. In the Kitchen: Culinary Techniques and Terms

abkhira (ابخرة), ***bukhār*** (بخار) steam.
ʿadhb (عذب) fresh (water), sweet (olive oil).
ʿafan (عفن) mold (in bread).
ʿalā al-māʾida (على المائدة) while eating at the table.
bayna yadayy al-ṭaʿām (بين يدي الطعام) said when serving (a condiment bowl, for instance) at the table to be eaten with the food.
bi-miqdār (بمقدار) just the needed amount.
daqīq (دقيق), see *duqāq* below.
dukhkhān (دخان) smoke.
duqāq (دقاق), ***daqīq*** (دقيق) fine, tiny, opposite of ***ghalīẓ*** (غليظ) large and thick.
farsha (فرشة) a layer.
fatāʾil (فتائل) small cylinders, as in *kaʿk* recipe i.4.2.
fātir (فاتر) lukewarm, as with water; insipid for not being sour enough, as with sauce and vinegar.
ghalīẓ (غليظ) large (e.g., head of cabbage, intestines); thick (e.g., disc of bread); thick and dense (e.g., soup); coarsely crushed (e.g., semolina).
ghalya (غلية) a boil. The cooking pot is briefly removed from the fire until boiling subsides, and then it is returned to resume boiling.[1] The number of boils was often used to measure cooking time. See also *yaghlī* in this section.

> ***ghalya laṭīfa*** (غلية لطيفة) a light boil, said of a pot that is allowed to boil gently and briefly.
> ***ghalya qawiyya*** (غلية قوية) a vigorous boil.
> ***ghalya wāḥida*** (غلية واحدة) a single boil, said of a pot when it comes to a first full boil.
> ***ghalyatayn*** (غليتين) two boils.
> ***thalāth ghalyāt*** (ثلاث غليات) three boils.

ḥarāfa (حرافة) pungency.
iltiʾām (التئام) binding, said of ingredients, for instance, when they bind and form dough.
iltifāf (التفاف), v. ***yaltaff*** (يلتف) bind together (e.g., ingredients).
iṣlāḥ (اصلاح) remedying, fixing, salvaging, as in chapter x.9 for remedying olives.
jamr muʿtadil (جمر معتدل) moderately hot coal fire.

1 See, for instance, al-Nābulusī, *ʿAlam al-malāḥa* 270, where he describes how to reduce syrups used for making drinks.

DOI:10.1163/9789004469488_075

FIGURE 177
Food preparations, folio from *Divan* of Jāmī, 52.20.4, detail
MET NY—PURCHASE, JOSEPH PULITZER BEQUEST, 1952

jumjuma (جمجمة), pl. *jamājim* (جماجم) a rounded mass.

> ***jumjumat al-sukkar*** (جمجمة السكر) rounded mass of a molded white sugar cone, which in the eastern region was more commonly called *sukkar ublūj* or *ṭabarzad.*

kardanāj (كردناج) grilling technique, according to which skewered whole birds are constantly kept rotating on an open fire.

khafīf (خفيف) thin in consistency (e.g., soup).

khamaj (خمج) n. rotting of bread; also descriptive of wheat starch that has turned bad and sour.

khāthir (خاثر) somewhat thick but still runny in consistency (e.g., a batter consistency).

laʿbiyya (لعبية) viscidity (of *aghlāl* 'snails').

lahab (لهب) flames of fire.

luʿāb (لعاب) mucilaginous substance, such as that of *rijla* 'purslane.'

madqūq (مدقوق) pounded in a mortar.

madrūs (مدروس) pounded in a mortar.

> ***dūna madrūs*** (دون مدروس) not pounded.

maḥlūl (محلول) dissolved in liquid.

maḥshū (محشو), ***maḥshī*** (محشي) descriptive of foods stuffed with other foods; the two words are used interchangeably. They also occur in contexts suggesting the state of being stuffed in or buried in something else, as in recipe v.1.17, where fish is buried in an egg mix. Or in recipe iii.2.44, where *maḥshū* is descriptive of the way chicken is dressed in different sauces after grilling or roasting it.

ḥashū (حشو) generally designates a stuffing. It also occurs in some recipes to designate what is being used to envelop the food, as in recipe iii.2.43, where an egg mix is applied to coat chicken pieces.

maqlī fī l-qidr (مقلي في القدر) fried in a pot rather than in a skillet, as in recipe ii.2.24 for mutton.

maraq (مرق), ***marqa*** (مرقة) liquid resulting from cooking, boiling, and baking and roasting food, such as broth, stew, and sauce. Dipping sauces prepared separately are similarly referred to in al-Tujībī's recipes.

marṣūṣ (مرصوص) arranged next to each other, packed tightly (e.g., lemons preserved in a jar).

masmūṭ (مسموط) adj. slaughtered sheep or chicken briefly scalded in boiling water to pluck their wool or feathers; almonds briefly boiled to remove their skins.

maṭbūkh (مطبوخ) stewed, cooked in liquid on the stove.

maṭbūkh fī l-furn (مطبوخ في الفرن) baked in the oven.

maṭḥūn (مطحون) crushed.

miskī (مسكي) musk colored, which is dark reddish brown.

mīzāb (ميزاب) spout.

mu'annak (مؤنك), also ***mubayyaḍ*** (مبيض) tin plated.

mufawwah (مفوه) food seasoned with spices, derived from *afāwīh* 'spices.'

mukhammar (مخمر) adj. derived from *takhmīr* 'covering,' which, in the Andalusi cooking context, designates topping food in its last stage of cooking with a layer of eggs beaten with other ingredients, such as seasonings and breadcrumbs. See *takhmīr* below. Additionally, in the case of recipe ix.2.6 for dessert, *mukhammar* is derived from *khumra*, which is *wars* (Ceylon cornel), used to extract a red dye.

muntin (منتن) adj. descriptive of meat that has an unpleasant odor.

musammakh (مسمخ) sprouted, used in recipe viii.1.2 in relation to sprouting fava beans. The term *musammakh* occurs only in the BL MS, fol. 184v. That al-Tujībī needed to explain what it was is testimony to its regional uniqueness. I have seen a similar usage of the word related to sprouting unhusked rice grains before planting them in Ibn ʿAwwām, *al-Filāḥa al-Andalusiyya* iv 100. In al-Zabīdī, *Tāj al-ʿArūs*, s.v. سمخ, it is used to designate seedlings.

muṣaṭṭab (مصطب) descriptive of eggplants packed together, making a bench-like formation, as in recipe vii.2.10.

mutaqāṭiʿ (متقاطع) intersecting, cut into a crisscross.

muzaffat (مزفت) designates a jar pitched with *zift*, which is resin of conifers; see *zift* in glossary 9.1. In al-Tujībī's cookbook, pitched jars are used for storing pickles and brined olives. Pitch was believed to have a preservative property.

muzayyat (مزيت) designates a jar that has been coated with olive oil, or it has previously been used to store oil.

nadī (ندي) damp (e.g., a vessel).

nār (نار) fire, always used in the recipes to designate a source of heat, supposedly in a stove, on which the vessels cook. Various degrees of heat are mentioned in the recipes to accommodate the cooking dishes:

> ***nār layyina*** (نار لينة) gently burning fire.
> ***nār layyina muʿtadila*** (نار لينة معتدلة) moderately gentle fire.
> ***nār muʿtadila*** (نار معتدلة) moderate fire.

In some recipes, the stove is also used in such a way that it enables the cook to use it to brown casseroles in lieu of the oven proper. In recipe ii.1.7 for a beef dish, the cook is instructed to put the glazed casserole pan on moderate heat; and another pan with strongly burning coals in it is placed directly on its rim. The pan is thus left to cook until the top browns and the liquid evaporates. This way of 'baking on the stove' was described in other sources as *al-ṭabkh bayn nārayn*, literally 'cooking between two fires.'[2]

qawī al-ʿaqd (قوي العقد) descriptive of syrup that has boiled and thickened.

qurṣ (قرص), pl. ***quraṣ*** (قرص) and ***aqrāṣ*** (أقراص) disc; round patty (e.g. of ground meat)

raghīf (رغيف) a flat disc (of bread).

raghwa (رغوة) froth (e.g., of boiling honey).

rakhṣ (رخص) tender (e.g., vegetables, chicken).

raqīq (رقيق) thin, opposite of ***thakhīn*** (ثخين) thick (e.g., of soup consistency).

al-ra's (الرأس) top quality, in reference to the fermented sauce *murrī*,[3] also called *al-awwal* 'the first.' See, for instance, *murrī* recipe x.8.1.

ṣada' (صدأ) rust.

sādhaj (ساذج) a plain dish that is neither sweet nor sour.

ṣafāqa (صفاقة) thickness (e.g., of soup consistency); opposite of *khiffa* (خفة) thinness.

ṣafwū al-marqa (صفو المرقة) the strained broth.

salqa khafīfa (سلقة خفيفة) a light boil.

samīk (سميك) thick.

samīn (سمين) fat; cf. ***musamman*** (مسمن) fattened.

saqī (سقي) drenching (e.g., bread or couscous) with liquid.

sarājīb (سراجيب) latticework designating shapes of fried *zalābiya*, see recipe i.4.29.

sarīʿ al-fasād (سريع الفساد) spoil very quickly (e.g., curdling milk).

sharāyiḥ riqāq (شرايح رقاق) thin strips (of meat).

---

2 See, for instance, recipe 111 in the anonymous fourteenth-century Egyptian cookbook *Kanz al-fawā'id*, English trans., *Treasure Trove*.

3 This brings to mind the modern-day usage of the term in Morocco, where a top-quality spice mix is called *rās al-ḥānūt* 'the best in the shop.'

shawī ʿalā al-jamr (شوي على الجمر) grilling directly on burning coals.

sukhn (سخن) hot; cf. ***maghlī*** (مغلي) boiled.

sulāfa (سلافة), also ***thufl*** (ثفل) pomace, pulpy material remaining after juice has been pressed from fruit (e.g., apples and grapes).

sūs (سوس) worms inside fruit; cf. ***dūd*** (دود) worms that breed inside the sheep's nose, mentioned in recipe i.2.2.

tabkhīr (تبخير) infusing and scenting a vessel with aromatic smoke, such as that of Indian aloeswood (*ʿūd Hindī*).

taḥmīr (تحمير) browning food by frying or baking.

tajmīr (تجمير) the process of leaving pots to simmer on embers to allow flavors to blend nicely and cooking liquids thicken. The expression often used is *tatajammar wa taʿtadil*.

ṭakhā (طخا)[4] cloudiness forming at the bottom of vinegar vessels, which needs to be filtered, see recipe x.7.12.

takhmīr (تخمير) the process of coating/topping dishes in their last stage of cooking with a layer of eggs beaten with other ingredients, such as seasonings and breadcrumbs. This was a typically Andalusi cooking technique, usually done with dishes that have little sauce in them.

ṭaʿm (طعم) kernels of nuts; flesh of eggplants.

ṭāqa (طاقة) layer.

taʿqud (تعقد) v. thicken (e.g., syrup).

tashwīṭ (تشويط) singeing (a sheep's head) on direct fire to burn the hairs.

taṣyīr (تصيير) pickling, more commonly referred to as *takhlīl* in the eastern region.

taṭyīb (تطييب) seasoning with aromatic spices.

thaqāfa (ثقافة), adj. *thaqīf* (ثقيف) acidity (e.g., vinegar).

thufl (ثفل) sediment, dregs.

ʿūd (عود) wood, more commonly called *khashab* in the eastern region.

walāʾim (ولائم), sg. *walīma* (وليمة) wedding festivities.

yadbugh (يدبغ) soften (e.g., cheese) by soaking it in water, as in recipe vi.3.1.[5]

yaftur (يفتر) become lukewarm *fātir*.

yaghlī (يغلي) boil; also, ferment (e.g., fish sauce, recipe x.8.13).

> ***yaghlī ghalya wāḥida*** (يغلي غلية واحدة) boil only once.
> ***yaghlī thalāth ghalyāt*** (يغلي ثلاث غليات) boil three times.
> ***yaghlī ghalayān kathīr*** (يغلي غليان كثير) boil many times.

---

4 *Ṭakhāʾ* literally designates high thin clouds and the haziness of the moon. See Ibn Manẓūr, *Lisān al-ʿArab*, s.v. طخا.

5 The word is more commonly used in terms of tanning leather in liquids to soften it. See Corriente, *Dictionary of Andalusi Arabic*, s.v. *d-b-gh*.

When the pot comes to a full boil, it is removed from the fire until the boiling subsides, and then it is returned to resume boiling. See also *ghalya* above.

yaḥmuḍ (يحمض) become sour, a desirable quality in vinegar.

yaḥtariq (يحترق) burn and spoil.

yaltaff (يلتف) mix ingredients until they combine into one mass; or when a boiling liquid thickens and reduces.

yanʿaqid (ينعقد) curdle (e.g., milk).

yarshaḥ (يرشح) exude, ooze (e.g., oil that separates from cooking and thickening *fālūdhaj*, recipe ix.2.2).

yarṭub (يرطب) become damp/hydrate (e.g., dough) with the addition of liquid.

yataʿaffan (يتعفن) v. rot.

yaʿtadil (يعتدل) descriptive of flavors blending nicely in a simmering pot.

yataḥabbab (يتحبب) granulate, such as when moistened flour is rolled between the hands to make couscous-like pasta, as in recipe i.3.7.

yataharraʾ (يتهرأ) disintegrate and fall apart.

yataṣaffaq (يتصفق) curdle and thicken (e.g., fermenting milk).

yatashurrak (يتشرك) thicken and begin to leave furrows behind when stirred, as in recipe ix.5 for making candy.

yaẓhar wadakuhā (يظهر ودكها) descriptive of fat (in a simmering pot) when it accumulates on top. This is a sign that the dish is done cooking.

yuʿarrak (يعرك) press and rub dough while kneading it vigorously.

yuball (يبل), also ***yuraṭṭab*** (يرطب) moisten, dampen (e.g., semolina flour).

yudhan (يدهن) baste (e.g., a chicken) with sauce while grilling it.

yudharr (يذر) sprinkle a small amount of ground cinnamon, sugar, etc. on a dish before serving it.

yudhbaḥ (يذبح) slaughter.

yuḍrab (يضرب) beat (eggs or batter).

yudras (يدرس) pound (meat); thresh or trample (wheat grains).

yufaṣṣ (يفص) section (lemons) by peeling them and removing skins and membranes, leaving only the juicy chunks. Citrus sections thus prepared were called *fuṣūṣ*, sg. *fuṣṣ*.

yuftal (يفتل) shape into small cylinders, *fatāʾil*; roll (*samīd* flour) between the hands to make couscous.

yuftaq (يفتق) season or infuse a dish (with aromatics like musk, ambergris, and the like) to enhance the flavor.

yughabbar (يغبر) dust (e.g., pieces of fish) with fine flour before frying.

yugharbal (يغربل) sift (e.g., grains to remove the husks).

yughsal (يغسل) wash, rinse.

yuḥakk (يحك) grate (e.g., hard cheese), usually done with an *iskarfāj* 'grater.'

yuḥakk bi-l-yad (يحك باليد) rub (e.g., fresh bread) into small particles between the hands.

yuḥammar (يحمر) brown (food) by frying or baking.
yuḥammaṣ (يحمص) parch/dry toast in a pan on direct heat, also occurs as *yuqlā*, a general term for frying.
yuḥarrak (يحرك) stir (food in a pot).

> ***yuḥarrak niʿman*** (يحرك نعما) gently stir (food in a pot).
> ***yuḥarrak al-qidr bi-l-yad*** (يحرك القدر باليد) hold the pot and move and shake it with the food inside it.

yujrad (يجرد), adj. *majrūd* (مجرود) scrape (e.g., carrots).
yukhammar (يخمر) see *takhmīr* above.
yulatt (يلتّ) coat, such as sprinkling dough with fine flour to coat it before portioning it to prevent it from sticking to the hands, as used in recipe i.1.1. Otherwise, *yulatt* generally designates rubbing and mixing fat into dry ingredients.
yulṭam (يلطم) flatten (dough) by repeatedly pressing it with an open hand.
yumassak (يمسك) flavor (food) with *misk* 'musk.'
yumazzaq (يمزق) shred (meat) by hand.
yumkhaḍ (يمخض) churn (milk) to make butter.
yunajjam (ينجم) garnish a dish.
yunaqqā (ينقى) clean (vegetables), discarding the inedible parts.
yuntaff (ينتف) pluck bird feathers.
yuqarraṣ (يقرص) shape (dough) into *aqrāṣ* 'discs.'
yuqlā (يقلى) fry in fat; dry toast in a skillet on the fire, also occurs as *yuḥammaṣ*.
yuqlaʿ (يقلع) pull out (e.g., a thin sheet of bread) from a pan, as in recipe i.4.14b.
yuqṣar (يقصر), n. ***qaṣr*** (قصر) rinse (a jar, a tanned leather vessel, or a esparto strainer) to get rid of unwanted odors.
yuraḍḍ (يرض) crush, bruise.
yurashsh (يرش) sprinkle.
yurawwaq (يروق) filter liquid through a tightly woven piece of cloth; cf. *yuṣaffā* (strain), which is less thorough.
yuṣabb (يصب) pour.
yuṣaffā (يصفى) strain using a strainer.
yusāṭ (يساط) whip (eggs).
yuṣbagh (يصبغ) dip food in *ṣibāgh* (dipping sauce).
yusḥaq (يسحق) crush.
yushaqq (يشق) cut in half.
yusharraḥ (يشرح) cut deep slits all around (a leg of lamb); also, cut (meat) into thin slices.
yushawwaṭ (يشوط) singe (e.g., a sheep's head) on the fire to burn the wool.
yushṭaf (يشطف) rinse in water.

FIGURE 178 A server filtering wine, al-Ḥarīrī, *al-Maqāmāt*, fol. 33r, copied and illustrated by al-Wāsiṭī, detail
BNF, DEPARTMENT OF MANUSCRIPTS, ARAB 5847. SOURCE: GALLICA.BNF.FR/BNF

yuslakh (يسلخ) skin (e.g., a slaughtered sheep or a fish).

yuṭayyab (يطيب) season with aromatic spices (*afāwīh*).

yuṭayyan (يطين) seal (e.g., a *tannūr* oven) with *ṭīn* 'mud.' The term is also used even when the sealing agent is dough, usually done with pots and casseroles.

yuṭbaʿ (يطبع), also ***yukhtam*** (يختم) seal (e.g., pickles) with a layer of olive oil to protect them from exposure to air.

yuṭbakh (يطبخ) cook (food on the stove); bake (food in the oven).
yuthrad (يثرد) break bread into small pieces and sop them in *tharīd* broth.
yuṭwā (يطوى) fold (e.g., rolled out dough).
wadak (ودك) fat accumulating on top of cooking meat.
wasaṭ (وسط) designates a moderate amount or a medium size.
washakī (وشكي) adj. descriptive of a dark reddish brown, used in recipe x.8.7 to designate the color of very well-baked bread. *Washakī* is derived from *washak*, more commonly known as *washaq* and *ushshaq*. It is the aromatic resin gum ammoniac extracted from the stem of Dorema ammoniacum, a perennial herb. Possibly, the *washakī* wine mentioned in Ibn Quzmān, *Iṣābat al-aghrāḍ* 28, was named after it on account of a similarity in color.
zahim (زهم) adj. having an unpleasant greasy odor.

10. Meats and Eggs

aghlāl (اغلال), called ***qawqan*** (قوقن) in al-Andalus. These are the edible land snails (*escargot* in French) that needed to be washed thoroughly before boiling them to get rid of their viscidity (*laʿbiyya*), as instructed in al-Tujībī's recipe xi.3. They were served in small bowls, enjoyed as a small dish offered with citron tree thorns to pick out the meat from the shells. Al-Tujībī says they were quite popular in al-Andalus because they fed on plenty of greens and herbs growing in springtime. Today, in Morocco these edible snails are still known by the name *ghlāl*, sg. *ghlāla*, and are a popular street food.

Regarding the Andalusi name *qawqan*, Dozy, *Takmilat al-Maʿājim* viii 413, s.v. قوقن, explains that *qawqan* is a corruption of the Latin *concha*, which at first was used to designate the solid shell, but later it was used to include the entire creature.

aḥshāʾ (احشاء) entrails (e.g., of birds or fish).

ukāriʿ (اكارع) trotters (e.g., of sheep); they are simmered with heads and tripe pieces in *tharīd* recipe i.2.2.

ʿanza (عنزة), pl. *ʿanz*, a grown female goat; cf. *tays*, which is a grown male goat. The general term for young goats is *māʿiz*; a young female is called *miʿza*, and the young male is called *jadī*.

arnab (ارنب), pl. ***arānib*** (ارانب) hares and rabbits;[1] recipes for cooking them are included in al-Tujībī's chapter ii.5. Their meat was said to be cold and dry in properties, generating blood dominated by acrid black bile. Meat of old hares and rabbits was dismissed as being hard to digest and bad-quality meat, while meat of the young ones was recommended. As for the immature ones, they were said to nourish the body quickly and invigorate coitus, especially when stewed with onions and chickpeas.[2] See also *qunilya* below.

ʿaṣāfīr (عصافير), sg. *ʿuṣfūr* (عصفور) sparrows, *Passer domesticus*; they are small wild birds known to live close to human habitats, in rural and urban areas, and hence the designation *ʿaṣāfīr ahliyya* (عصافيراهلية).[3] The best were said to be fat ones caught in winter, and young ones rather than old ones. Their meat, described as hot and

---

1 Unlike the western region al-Maghrib, in the eastern region both the hare and the rabbit were called *arnab*. The former, however, was often more specifically described as *barrī* 'wild.' See Viré, "Hare," 97–100.

2 Ibn Zuhr, *Kitāb al-Aghdhiya* 24.

3 In al-Andalus, another name for a sparrow was *barṭāl*, which was the Andalusi Arabized form of the Spanish pardal. See Corriente, *Dictionary of Andalusi Arabic*, s.v. *p-r-ṭ-l*.

FIGURE 179 Cooked snails at a food stall in Morocco
PHOTO BY ADAM JONES, PH.D./GLOBAL PHOTO ARCHIVE/WIKIMEDIA COMMONS (HTTPS://AR.WIKIPEDIA.ORG/WIKI/%D8%AD%D9%84%D8%B2%D9%88%D9%86_(%D8%B7%D8%B9%D8%A7%D9%85)#/MEDIA/%D9%85%D9%84%D9%81:SNAILS_FOR_SALE_-_DJERMAA_EL-FNA_(CENTRAL_SQUARE)_-_MEDINA_(OLD_CITY)_-_MARRAKESH_-_MOROCCO.JPG)

dry, was said to offer little nutrition to the body; nevertheless, they were said to be beneficial. They were especially good for cold-related illnesses such as hemiplegia (*fālaj*) and facial paralysis (*laqwa*). More importantly, they were believed to increase semen and excite the libido, especially when fried with eggs as an omelet. Because the cooked sparrows were eaten with the bones, the physicians' advice was to chew their meat very well; otherwise, bone splinters would scratch the esophagus and stomach.[4] Al-Tujībī's chapter iii.7 is all about cooking sparrows.

ʿaṣāfīr simān (عصافير سمان) fat sparrows, preferred for grilling purposes, as in recipe iii.7.4.

4 Al-Damīrī, *Ḥayāt al-ḥayawān* 487; al-Anṭākī, *Tadhkira* 261; and Ibn Zuhr, *Kitāb al-Aghdhiya* 15.

FIGURE 180 A male goat, *tays* (see *ʿanza*), al-Qazwīnī, *ʿAjāʾib al-makhlūqāt wa-gharāʾib al-mawjūdāt*, fol., detail
BRITISH LIBRARY: ORIENTAL MANUSCRIPTS, OR 14140, IN *QATAR DIGITAL LIBRARY* HTTPS://WWW.QDL.QA/ARCHIVE/81055/VDC_100023586788.0X000001

baqar (بقر) cows; for beef, see *laḥm baqar* below.

baqar maʿlūf (بقر معلوف) cows fed barley grains in restricted areas for speedy fattening.[5]

baqar fatī samīn (بقر فتي سمين) fat young cows.

bayḍ (بيض) eggs, unless otherwise mentioned, they are chicken eggs. It was believed that eggs that were not fertilized during their formation were poor in nutrition. The best were said to have been the fertilized ones obtained the day they were laid; some might contain two yolks. Egg yolk was preferred over egg white, which was believed to slow digestion and generate undercooked humors and a good deal of phlegm. Egg yolk, on the other hand, was favored for its nutritive properties, which generated wholesome humors.

In the book of *Fiḍāla*, eggs are used extravagantly as a garnish and as a binder in foods cooked with ground meat, such as meatballs, sausages, and meat patties. They are also whipped with spices, herbs, and breadcrumbs and poured over foods in their last stages of cooking, in a process called *takhmīr* (see glossary 9.2). Without doubt it was the abundance of chicken raised on a large scale in the countryside that allowed the Andalusi cooks to use eggs freely. Additionally, the Andalusi farmers had

5 See Ibn Zuhr, *Kitāb al-Aghdhiya* 135.

FIGURE 181
Rabbits, which look more like *arānib barriyya* 'hares' (see *arnab*), Anonymous, *Kitāb Naʿt al-ḥayawān*, fol. 167v, detail
BRITISH LIBRARY: ORIENTAL MANUSCRIPTS, OR 2784, IN QATAR DIGITAL LIBRARY HTTPS://WWW.QDL.QA/ARCHIVE/81055/VDC_100023556967.0X000001

their own ways of storing eggs and keeping them from spoiling. Ibn al-ʿAwwām, for instance, recommends storing them in vessels lined with a thick layer of bran or hay, soaking them in water, and keeping them in salt, or soaking them in brine for three or four hours and then storing them in hay.[6]

bayāḍ al-bayḍ (بياض البيض) egg whites; also called ***raqīq al-bayḍ*** (رقيق البيض).
bayḍ khifāf li-l-shurb (بيض خفاف للشرب) very lightly boiled eggs for the purpose of slurping them, *li-l-shurb*, literally 'for drinking' them; see recipe v.2.7. The expression is still used today everywhere in Arab-speaking regions to designate eggs left in boiling water just enough to heat them up so that they can be slurped from their shells.
bayḍ mashqūq (بيض مشقوق) split boiled eggs, often used as garnish. The splitting was done with a thin thread.
fuṣūṣ bayḍ (فصوص بيض) whole egg yolks, cooked and uncooked, depending on the context; also referred to as *muḥāḥ bayḍ ṣiḥāḥ* 'egg yolks left whole.'
muḥḥ bayḍ (مح بيض), pl. ***muḥāḥ bayḍ*** (محاح بيض) general term for egg yolk, usually uncooked; when boiled, they are referred to as *muḥāḥ bayḍ maṣlūqa*.
nīmbarisht (نيمبرشت), *numayrashāt* (نميرشات), *naymarasht* (نيمرشت) poached eggs, see recipe v.2.4. They were deemed the most healthful way to consume eggs.[7]

buṭūn (بطون), sg. *baṭn* (بطن) innards, organs, and bowels in the abdomen of a slaughtered animal. The parts used in al-Tujībī's cookbook related to quadrupeds are:

6 Ibn al-ʿAwwām, *al-Filāḥa al-Andalusiyya* vi 271.
7 See Ibn Zuhr, *Kitāb al-Aghdhiya* 19.

akbād (اكباد), *kubūd* (كبود), sg. *kabd* (كبد) livers.

duwwāra (دوارة), also called ***maṣīr al-duwwāra*** (مصير الدوارة), the coiled small intestine of sheep and cows, see *muṣrān* below.

ghalīẓ al-karsh (غليظ الكرش) rumen tripe of cows and sheep, see *karsh* below.

mibʿar (مبعر) large intestine of sheep and cows, see *muṣrān* below.

minsaj (منسج), also called ***ridāʾ*** (رداء), literally 'woven garment' and 'mantle,' respectively. It is caul fat, called *tharb* in the eastern region. Caul fat is used several times in the recipes to wrap around meat, as in i.2.27 for making tripe rolls and iv.3 for shaping minced meat mix like a cow's tongue.

maṣārīn (مصارين) intestines; see *muṣrān* below.

qubā (قبا) omasum tripe, see *karsh* below.

sudsiyya (سدسية) honeycomb tripe, see *karsh* below.

dajāj (دجاج), sg. *dajāja* (دجاجة) chicken; in Arabic, the term is not gender specific. Still, there is a specific name for the male chicken, which is *dīk* (ديك). When castrated, the male chicken is called *khaṣiyy*, see entry below. Most of al-Tujībī's chicken recipes call for young adult chickens that are large, fat, and tender.

The large number of chicken recipes in the book of *Fiḍāla* is testimony to their popularity and availability in al-Andalus. It was in the Andalusi countryside that chicken was raised on a large scale for meat and eggs. The farmers followed simple methods for propagating large numbers of chicks by means of artificial incubation. Ground dried chicken droppings were put in glass vessels, and eggs were arranged in them, with their pointed ends facing upwards. They would then be covered with chicken feathers and once again with ground chicken droppings. After regularly turning the eggs over twice a day for 20 days, they would hatch chicks.[8]

Terms associated with chickens that are used in al-Tujībī's cookbook:

afkhādh (افخاذ) thighs.

dajāja musammana fatiyya (دجاجة مسمنة فتية) fattened young adult chicken.

dajāja rakhṣa (دجاجة رخصة) a tender chicken.

dajāj simān (دجاج سمين) fat chickens.

farrūj (فروج) young chickens, see entry below.

ḥawṣala (حوصلة) crop.

janāḥ (جناح), pl. ***ajniḥa*** (اجنحة) wing.

jild (جلد) skin.

khaṣiyy (خصي) a capon, see entry below.

makhraj (مخرج) anal vent.

---

8 As detailed in Ibn al-ʿAwwām, *al-Filāḥa al-Andalusiyya* vi 265–6.

FIGURE 182
A sparrow (see *ʿaṣāfīr*), al-Qazwīnī, *ʿAjāʾib al-makhlūqāt wa-gharāʾib al-mawjūdāt*, fol. 121v, detail
BRITISH LIBRARY: ORIENTAL MANUSCRIPTS, OR 14140, IN *QATAR DIGITAL LIBRARY* HTTPS://WWW.QDL.QA/ARCHIVE/81055/VDC_100023586788.0X000001

FIGURE 183 A rooster, *dīk*, al-Qazwīnī, *ʿAjāʾib al-makhlūqāt wa-gharāʾib al-mawjūdāt*, fol. 127v, detail
THE WALTERS ART MUSEUM, W. 659

minkhar (منخر) nostril.
minqār (منقار) beak.
qāniṣa (قانصة), pl. ***qawāniṣ*** (قوانص) gizzard.
ṣadr (صدر) breast.
zimikkā (زمكّى) rear end.

With its moderately hot and moist properties, chicken meat, of both the male and female, was said to be the most suitable for all people any time in the year, especially the inactive ones among them leading leisurely lives. Good nutrition was said to be generated by meat of young adult chickens, which was also said to stimulate semen production, unlike the meat of old ones. Additionally, chicken was also said to be beneficial to convalescents, as it had the power to bring bodily humors back to balance. Its broth was said to cure leprosy (*judhām*), and the meat of young adult chickens and their brains were believed to increase brain mass and improve intellectual faculties.[9]

9 Al-Arbūlī, *al-Kalām ʿalā al-aghdhiya* 136–7; Ibn Khalṣūn, *Kitāb al-Aghdhiya* 84; Ibn Zuhr, *Kitāb al-Aghdhiya* 15.

FIGURE 184 A young chicken, *farrūj*, al-Qazwīnī, *ʿAjāʾib al-makhlūqāt wa-gharāʾib al-mawjūdāt*, fol. 128v, detail
THE WALTERS ART MUSEUM, W. 659

ḍaʾn (ضأن) adult sheep, whose meat is at its best when the animal is fat and no more than two years old, described as *fatī*. Mutton was deemed the most nourishing and most temperate of all meats, which best suited people with temperate humors. Generally, the younger the animal is, the moister and better its meat is. Meat of a sheep older than four years was not looked upon as top-quality mutton.[10]

A mature female sheep, the ewe, is called *shāt* (شاة), and a mature male sheep, the ram, is called *kabsh* (كبش). When they are still in their first year, the male lamb is called *kharūf* (خروف) or *ḥamal* (حمل), and the ewe lamb is called *kharūfa* (خروفة) or *naʿja* (نعجة).

When sheep reach their second year, and they have no more than two permanent incisors in each of their jaws, the young sheep (both the female 'maiden ewe' and the male 'hogget') is called *thanī* (ثني) 'yearling.'

farrūj (فروج), **farārīj** (فراريج) young chickens under one year old; females that have not started laying eggs. Males that have just started crowing were said to be at their best when eaten at this stage. Their meat was generally believed to digest easily and generate good blood. Their fat was deemed superior to that of adult chickens.[11] Ibn Khalṣūn, *Kitāb al-Aghdhiya* 87, recommends fat adolescent ones that are black.

farrūj kabīr (فروج كبير) large young chickens, used sometimes to replace a chicken (*dajāja*).

farārīj ṣighār (فراريج صغار) small young chickens, used roasted or stewed.

10 See al-Anṭākī, *Tadhkira* 247; and al-Malik al-Muẓaffar, *al-Muʿtamad* 347.

11 Ibn Jazla, *Minhāj al-bayān*, fol. 156v.

firākh ḥamām (فراخ حمام) squabs, young pigeons. In al-Tujībī's cookbook, when *firākh* by itself is used, it is to be understood that the reference is to young pigeons; this is because young chickens in Arabic are always specifically called *farrūj* and *farārīj*. Meat of fledglings (called *nawāhiḍ* نواهض and *zaghālīl* زغاليل), especially the fat ones, was said to be the best and lightest; it was believed to invigorate coitus. Al-Tujībī's recipes make frequent use of these birds, as in chapter iii.4, in addition to recipes dispersed in other chapters.

fuʾād (فؤاد) heart.

ghanam (غنم) generic name for sheep (*ḍaʾn*) and goat (*māʿiz*). In al-Tujībī's cookbook, *ghanam* generally designates sheep. See also *laḥm ghanamī* below.

> ***ghanam al-aḍāḥī*** (غنم الاضاحي) sheep of sacrifice. Following one of the Muslim rituals, large numbers of sheep are slaughtered annually in celebration of the end of the Hajj ceremonies. See *tharīd* recipe i.2.2, which uses their heads, trotters, and tripe.
>
> ***mislān*** (مسلان) entire hip section of a sheep, mentioned in recipe i.2.6, where it is cooked and served in one piece on top of a *tharīd* dish. From the recipe, we learn that was the custom among city dwellers and peasants. To this day, it is still a very traditional festive food in North Africa.

ḥajal (حجل) partridge, known as *qabaj* (قبج) in the eastern region. Its meat is used in ways comparable to those of chicken, except for their skins, which are always discarded, as demonstrated in al-Tujībī chapter iii.3. Obviously, it is too tough compared to the chicken's delicate skin. Al-Arbūlī, *al-Kalām ʿalā al-aghdhiya* 137, recommends consuming partridge and speculates that it could be a type of wild chicken. A popular way of catching them was by dazing them with wheat berries, which have been boiled with seeds of henbane (*binj*), thrown in their way.[12]

ḥamām (حمام), sg. *ḥamāma*, usually referred to as *ḥamām baladī* (حمام بلدي); they are domestic pigeons, *Columba livia domestica*,[13] of which there were two types:

> ***ḥamām ahlī*** (حمام اهلي), *ḥamām insī* (حمام إنسي) domesticated house pigeons, usually kept in cages.[14]
>
> ***ḥamām barī*** (حمام بري) feral pigeons. They were said to stay in cotes (*abrāj*) and the like, away from people.

---

12 As suggested in al-Andalusī, *Kitāb fī l-Filāḥa* 78.

13 They are a subspecies of pigeon (*ḥamām*). See also *yamām* below, which is another subspecies of pigeon.

14 Al-Damīrī, *Ḥayāt al-ḥayawān* ii 107; and Ibn al-ʿAwwām, *al-Filāḥa al-Andalusiyya* vi 239.

FIGURE 185 Partridges, *ḥajal*, al-Qazwīnī, *ʿAjāʾib al-makhlūqāt wa-gharāʾib al-mawjūdāt*, fol. 118v, detail
BRITISH LIBRARY: ORIENTAL MANUSCRIPTS, OR 14140, IN *QATAR DIGITAL LIBRARY* HTTPS://WWW.QDL.QA/ARCHIVE/81055/VDC_100023586788.0X000001

None of al-Tujībī's recipes use fully grown pigeons; only squabs (*firākh ḥamām*), see entry above.

ḥūt (حوت), pl. *ḥītān* (حيتان) fish, as it was commonly called in the Muslim West. Calling fish *samak* was more common in the eastern region. In four of al-Tujībī's fish recipes (v.1.21–4), however, fish is uncharacteristically called *samak*; a sure sign that they were borrowed Mashriqi dishes.

Fish-related terms used in al-Tujībī's cookbook:

ḥītān ghalīẓa (حيتان غليظة) thick-fleshed fish.
ḥītān ḥarish (حيتان حرش) fish with scales.
ḥītān kibār (حيتان كبار) big fish.
ḥītān muls (حيتان ملس) scaleless fish.
ḥūt muṣayyar (حوت مصير) pickled fish, which was called *mamqūr* in the eastern region. See for instance chapter 37 in al-Warrāq, *Kitāb al-Ṭabīkh*, English trans., *Annals* 194–5. For pickling large fish, see recipe x.6.1, where fish is preserved in a salt-vinegar solution and kept in jars.
ḥūt ṭarī (حوت طري) fresh fish.
ḥūt ṭayyib (حوت طيب) fine-tasting varieties of fish.
jild (جلد) skin.
khayāshīm (خياشيم) gills.

FIGURE 186 Pigeons, *ḥamām*, al-Qazwīnī, *ʿAjāʾib al-makhlūqāt wa-gharāʾib al-mawjūdāt*, fol. 117r, detail
BRITISH LIBRARY: ORIENTAL MANUSCRIPTS, OR 14140, IN *QATAR DIGITAL LIBRARY* HTTPS://WWW.QDL.QA/ARCHIVE/81055/VDC_100023586788.0X000001

qushūr (قشور) scales, *yuqashshar* v. scale.
samaka samīna (سمكة سمينة) fatty fish.
shawka (شوكة) backbone; may also refer to the prickly bones when used in the plural, *shawk*.

Al-Tujībī's chapter v.1 offers 33 recipes, dealing with many kinds of fish, cooked in a myriad of ways. Here are the fish varieties called for in the recipes:

al-būrī al-jalīl (البوري الجليل), ***al-būrī al-kabīr*** (البوري الكبير) large fish variety of flathead grey mullet, *Mugil cephalus*; cooked by cutting it into pieces and braising it, as in recipes v.1.1 and 2. According to Ibn Rushd, *al-Kulliyyāt* 397, it was the most preferred fish variety.
jarkam (جركم) I have failed to find references to this fish in places other than al-Tujībī's cookbook.[15] In recipe v.1.5, it is described as fatty small fish that appears in September.
jarrāfa (جرافة) gilt-head bream, *Sparus aurata*;[16] cooked by cutting it into pieces and braising it, as in recipes v.1.1–2.
kaḥla (كحلة), ***kaḥlāʾ*** (كحلاء) red sea bream, *Pagellus bogaraveo*; also known in English as blackspot seabream. In Ghālib, *Mawsūʿa*, its other name is given as *jarbīdī* (جربيدي). It is fried after stuffing it in its own skin in recipe v.1.20.

15 Even in Corriente, *Dictionary of Andalusi Arabic*, s.v. *j-r-k-m*, the description is based on al-Tujībī's text.
16 As suggested in Corriente, *Dictionary of Andalusi Arabic*, s.v. *j-r-f*.

kammūn (كمون) big-headed mullet (?). I failed to find any references to a fish by the name كمون . The Madrid MS does not mention it. The name might have been a modified form or a copyist's misreading of *al-qabṭūn* القبطون, which is a large fish mentioned only in the anonymous *Anwāʿ al-ṣaydala* 150, 154. In Corriente, *Dictionary of Andalusi Arabic*, s.v. *q-b-ṭ-n*, it is said to be big-headed mullet, which is grey mullet. It was not uncommon in dialectal Arabic to turn *q* to *t*, and ṭ to t, resulting in الكبتون, which might have been miscopied as الكمون. In recipe v.1.1, it is described as a large variety of fish, which is cut into pieces and braised.

mannānī (مناني) grouper, *Epinephelus marginatus*; described as a large variety of fish; cut into pieces and then marinated and braised in recipe v.1.1.

mull (مُلّ) red mullet, *Mullus barbatus*. According to Ibn al-Bayṭār, *al-Jāmiʿ* iii 137, *mull* is the indigenous Andalusi name (ʿAjamiyyat al-Andalus) for what was otherwise called *ṭarastūj*/*tarastūj* (ترستوج/طرستوج). In al-Arbūlī, *al-Kalām ʿalā al-aghdhiya* 151, the name occurs as *mūl* (مول), praised as a good variety of scaly fish that generates good nutrition, digests fast, and is the least viscid of fishes. Indeed, according to an Andalusi saying, "He who has eaten *mull* does not need to try any other fish" (من اكل الملّ, اكل الكل).[17] It is prepared fried in recipe v.1.8.

sarda (سردة) Atlantic bonito, *Sarda sarda*; large mackerel-like fish. It also occurs as *sardana* in the anonymous Andalusi *Anwāʿ al-ṣaydala* 151. Al-Tujībī's recipe v.1.7 indicates that it is a scaleless fish (*ḥūt amlas*). This is confirmed in al-Arbūlī, *al-Kalām ʿalā al-aghdhiya* 152, where it occurs as *sarāda* (سرادة) and described as a scaleless fish, which is viscid but very delicious; adding that blood this fish generates in the eater's body would not be bad when consumed fresh. It is cooked in a couple of ways in recipe v.1.7.

sardīn (سردين) sardines, *Clupea pilchardus*; described in recipe v.1.5 as a small variety of fish (*ḥūt ṣaghīr*) that is fatty. The recipe also recommends using them when they first appear in May and October. Small sardines (*sardīn ṣaghīr*) are used in recipe v.1.3 for *murawwaj* (a quick and easy dish); and v.1.6 for a casserole of sardines layered with chopped herbs and vegetables and baked in the *furn* (brick oven). Salt-cured sardines (*sardīn muṣayyar mumallaḥ*) are served fried after boiling them first to get rid of excess salt, see p. 381.

sardīn muṣayyar mumallaḥ (سردين مصير مملح), salt-cured sardines. Recipe x.6.2 also calls them *ṣīr* and describes how to preserve them.

shābil (شابل) allis shad, *Alosa alosa*. As described in al-Arbūlī, *al-Kalām ʿalā al-aghdhiya* 151, it is the type of fish that is born at sea and migrates to sweet-water

17 See al-Zajjālī, *Amthāl al-ʿawām* ii 342.

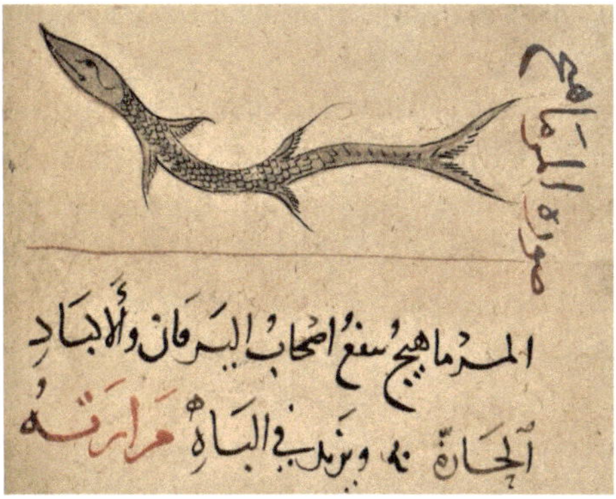

FIGURE 187
An eel, Anonymous, *Kitāb Naʿt al-ḥayawān*, fol. 28v, detail
BRITISH LIBRARY: ORIENTAL MANUSCRIPTS, OR 2784, IN QATAR DIGITAL LIBRARY HTTPS://WWW.QDL.QA/ARCHIVE/81055/VDC_100023556967.0X000001

rivers to spawn, like the Guadalquivir in Seville (*Wādī Ishbīliya*). It is praised as the most delicious of fishes and the best for generating good-quality humors. It is said to be good for healthy people, especially the young. Indeed, in an Andalusi saying, a *shābil* fish dish prepared with its appropriate spices is said to be too good to miss (شابل بأبزار).[18] Al-Tujībī's recipes include one to prepare it braised in v.1.1; and in v.1.5, it is encrusted in salt and baked in the oven on a flat tile and served with a variety of sauces.

shūlī (شولي) sturgeon, *Acipenser sturio*; al-Arbūlī, *al-Kalām ʿalā al-aghdhiya* 151, praises it in similar terms to *shābil*, see above. In recipe v.1.1, it is cut into pieces and braised.

shuṭūn (شطون) anchovies, *Engraulidae*. The name is a regional variant on what was known as *balam* and *absāriyya* in Egypt.

silbāḥ (سلباح), pl. *salābīḥ* (سلابيح) common eel, *Anguilla anguilla*. Its other names are *anqala* (انقلة) and *sillawr* (سلّور), as explained in recipe v.1.25. *Anqala* must have been a variant of *anqalīs*. *Silbāḥ* was the regional name for eel in the Muslim West, and *mārmāhīj*/*marmāhīj* and *sillawr* were its most common names in the eastern region. The slime layer on the eel, which makes it slippery, and its unattractive appearance gave rise to several sayings associating it with elusiveness, deviousness, and ugliness, as in the saying (سلباح لا شكل ولا ملاح) "as unattractive as an eel" or (بحل صلباح ما يموت حتى يذبح) "like an eel, which truly dies only when slaughtered."[19]

Al-Arbūlī, *al-Kalām ʿalā al-aghdhiya* 152, includes an entry on *silbāḥ*, in which the recommendation is to skin it and cook it in the brick oven with olive oil and *murrī* (liquid fermented sauce). In al-Tujībī's recipe v.1.25, it is braised.

18 Ibid., ii 437.
19 See ibid., ii 427 and 149, respectively.

ṣīr (صير) salt-cured sardines,[20] also called *sardīn muṣayyar mumallaḥ*, see entry above.

ṭardanas (طردنس) plaice, *Pleuronectes platessa*; cooked in al-Tujībī's recipe v.1.7 in a couple of interesting ways. The recipe describes it as smooth-skinned scaleless fish (*ḥūt amlas*). In the anonymous Andalusi *Anwāʿ al-ṣaydala* 151, a recipe describes *ṭardanas* as a good variety of fish, *ḥūt maḥmūd*. It is also highly praised in Ibn al-Zayyāt, *al-Tashawwuf ilā rijāl al-taṣawwuf* 160.[21]

tunn (تنّ) tuna fish, see entry below.

Fish was known to be cold and moist in properties, and freshwater fish was believed to be even more so. The best freshwater fish, called *samak ṣakhrī*, was found in running waters with pebbly beds. The best saltwater fish was found offshore. Fish types that have plenty of blood in them, with large rough scales on their skins, were believed to be good. The best part of a fish was said to be its tail because it moves a great deal, and the worst was its head. All kinds of fish were believed to be hard to digest. The recommendation was to choose the scaly medium-sized ones. To remedy fish, it has to be salted and left for an hour and then cooked with *murrī* (fermented sauce) and a great deal of olive oil. Having a few licks of honey after eating fish was also recommended.[22]

ʿijl (عجل) calf, whose meat was said to be easier to digest than beef. For veal, see *laḥm ʿijl* below.

ʿijl fatī (عجل فتي) young calf.

iwazz (اوز), sg. *iwazza* (اوزة) geese, *Anser*. In al-Tujībī's book of *Fiḍāla* only recipes for geese, tender and fatty ones, are given, in chapter iii.1.

Although there is no mention of ducks, *Anas*, called *baṭṭ* (بطّ) in Arabic, in al-Tujībī's book, there is the possibility that ducks are indeed used in the recipes because ducks in the Muslim West were also called *iwazz al-qurṭ*, besides their other name, *burak*.

Despite what we read in Ibn Manẓūr, *Lisān al-ʿArab*, s.v. بطط, that *baṭṭ* is another name for *iwazz*, the former being an Arabized word whereas the latter is Arabic,

20 Cf. *ṣīr* in medieval Egypt, where it was mostly made with anchovies. See anonymous Egyptian cookbook *Kanz al-fawāʾid*, English trans., *Treasure Trove* 617.

21 The identification of this fish as plaice is based on the French *tardineau* given in the 1926 dictionary on fishing by H. de la Blanchère, cited by the editor of Ibn al-Zayyāt, *al-Tashawwif* 160, n. 284.

22 Ibn Khalṣūn, *Kitāb al-Aghdhiya* 88; and al-Arbūlī, *al-Kalām ʿalā al-aghdhiya* 150–1. See also the concluding paragraph in al-Tujībī's chapter on fish, v.1.

this does not always seem to be the case in the culinary records we have from the medieval eastern and western regions. For instance, we do come across many texts where meat and eggs of both birds are mentioned separately. See, for instance, al-Rāzī, *Manāfiʿ al-aghdhiya* 169; and al-Warrāq, *Kitāb al-Ṭabīkh*, English trans., *Annals* 116; both hailed from the eastern region. Therefore, al-Damīrī's description in *Ḥayāt al-ḥayawān* i 414–5, seems to be more credible:

> ***iwazz*** (اوز) are the large birds (i.e., geese).
> ***baṭṭ*** (بط) are the smaller ones that do not fly (i.e., ducks).

As for the Muslim West, based on sources from that region other than al-Tujībī's cookbook, we gather the following:

1. Geese were called ***iwazz***, of which there were wild geese *iwazz barrī* (اوز بري) and domesticated geese *iwazz ahlī* (اوز اهلي); bred for their meat and eggs.
2. Ducks were called ***burak*** (بُرَك), sg. *burka* (بُركة), which was the indigenous name in the western region for what was more commonly known as *baṭṭ* (بط) in the eastern region. There were wild ducks *burak barrī* (برك بري) and domesticated ducks *burak ahlī* (برك اهلي) bred for their meat and eggs. They were also called *iwazz al-qurṭ* (اوز القرط) in the anonymous Andalusi cookbook *Anwāʿ al-ṣaydala* 16, where they are clearly identified as *baṭṭ* 'duck' and described as having flat bills and a darkish color. They are also said to be the best of the aquatic birds because they get fat very fast, and as such, they are most delicious when grilled.[23]

From Ibn al-ʿAwwām, *al-Filāḥa al-Andalusiyya* vi 255, we learn that *burak* 'ducks,' in particular, were fattened by feeding them with dough and soaked dried figs. To fatten their livers they were fed moistened pellets of ground, toasted sesame seeds. Meat of ducks and geese was said to be very hot and moist in properties, and blood they generate was believed to turn bad quickly, causing fevers. The recommendation was to use the fully grown ones.[24]

jadī (جدي), pl. *jidā* (جِدا) a kid, which is a young male goat less than one year old, see *laḥm jadī* below.

> ***jadī raḍīʿ*** (جدي رضيع) suckling kid.
> ***ṣighār al-jidāʾ*** (صغار الجدا) kids that are still small.

23 See al-Arbūlī, *al-Kalām ʿalā al-aghdhiya* 140; Ibn Zuhr, *Kitāb al-Aghdhiya* 16; and Ibn al-ʿAwwām, *al-Filāḥa al-Andalusiyya* vi 253–4.

24 Al-Arbūlī, *al-Kalām ʿalā al-aghdhiya* 140.

FIGURE 188
A duck and a goose (see *iwazz*), as described in the MS, Anonymous, *Kitāb Naʿt al-ḥayawān*, fol. 10v, detail
BRITISH LIBRARY: ORIENTAL MANUSCRIPTS, OR 2784, IN QATAR DIGITAL LIBRARY HTTPS://WWW.QDL.QA/ARCHIVE/81055/VDC_100023556967.0X000001

jarād (جراد) locusts, used in recipe xi.1, where they are fried and served in small bowls as a snack food. The only other locust recipe available to us from the medieval era is found in al-Warrāq, *Kitāb al-Ṭabīkh*, English trans., *Annals* 208, where they are pickled in brine.

Al-Tujībī's recipe specifically mentions the large locusts, called *jarād ʿArabī* (جراد عربي). In the eastern region, they were more commonly called *jarād Aʿrābī* (جراد اعرابي) (i.e., desert locusts), *Shistocerca gregaria*. They are migratory locusts that happen to blow westwards some years. Ibn Zuhr, *Kitāb al-Aghdhiya* 29–30, describes them as red, large, and agile. He says the ones in al-Andalus (i.e., the nonmigratory grasshoppers) were not known as a source of food, they might even be harmful.[25] Al-Jāḥiẓ, *al-Ḥayawān* v 565, praises the fat *Aʿrābī* locusts. He says they are delicious eaten cold and hot, grilled, boiled, and threaded on strings and baked buried in heated sand (*malla*), adding that they can be cooked fresh or dried and served as an appetizer with bread as *idām*, or as *naql*.[26]

kabsh (كبش) a ram, fat ones (*samīn*) were preferred. Judging from the large number of recipes in which their meat is used in al-Tujībī's chapter ii.2, mutton from young rams was the preferred meat at the time. See *laḥm kabsh* below.

25 In al-Ṭabarī, *Firdaws al-ḥikma* 437, they are called جراد البساتين 'orchard grasshoppers' and described as nonflying long-legged green insects.

26 *Naql* was a snack food closely associated with drinking sessions, when imbibing alcohol alternated with nibbling on small dishes.

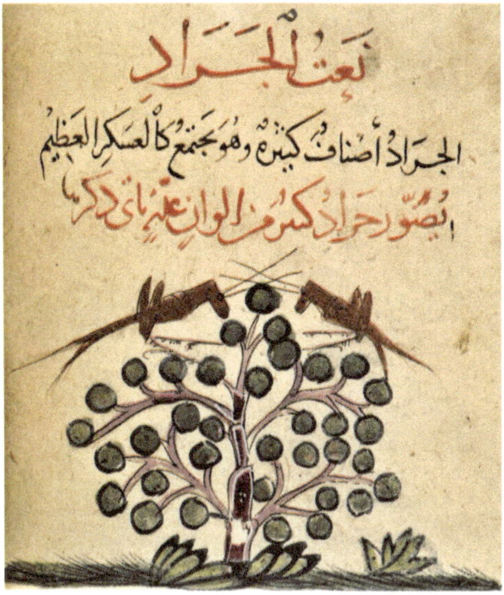

FIGURE 189
Locusts, Anonymous, *Kitāb Naʿt al-ḥayawān*, fol. 61v, detail
BRITISH LIBRARY: ORIENTAL MANUSCRIPTS, OR 2784, IN QATAR DIGITAL LIBRARY HTTPS://WWW.QDL.QA/ARCHIVE/81055/VDC_100023556967.0X000001

kabsh fatī samīn (كبش فتي سمين) fat young ram.

kabsh thanī (كبش ثني) a yearling ram; when the sheep reach their second year, and they have no more than two permanent incisors in each of their jaws.

kabsh thanī samīn (كبش ثني سمين) a fat yearling ram.

karsh (كرش), pl. *kurūsh* (كروش) tripe of ruminants. It has four compartments: 1) rumen, the first compartment; 2) honeycomb; 3) omasum; 4) abomasum, the true stomach where final digestion occurs. It is also the most active compartment in young ruminants, from which the milk-curdling enzyme, rennet, is taken.

Tripe was believed to have cold and dry properties, be slow to digest, and have little nutritional value. The recommendation was to cook it well and season it with vinegar.[27]

ghalīẓ al-karsh (غليظ الكرش) rumen tripe, the first compartment of the cow's stomach, which is large, smooth, and flat in texture. In recipes i.2.4 and ii.1.1, 7, and 10, it is used with other cuts of beef.

qubā (قبا) omasum tripe, third compartment of the ruminant stomach, which looks like a ball, also called *rummāna*, used in recipes iv.2 and ii.6.8. The only other extant recipe for stuffed omasum tripe, a version of haggis, is found in al-Warrāq, *Kitāb al-Ṭabīkh*, English trans., *Annals*, chapter 48, 245, where

27 Ibn Khalṣūn, *Kitāb al-Aghdhiya* 88.

FIGURE 190 A ram and a male lamb, *kabsh* and *ḥamal*, Dioscorides, *Fī Hayūlā al-ṭibb*, translation by Ḥunayn b. Isḥāq, fol. 77r, detail
FROM THE NEW YORK PUBLIC LIBRARY, SPENCER COLLECTION: HTTPS://DIGITALCOLLECTIONS.NYPL.ORG/ITEMS/5E66B3E8-E8B5-D471-E040-E00A180654D7

it is copied as *qibba* (قِبّة). *Qubā* must have been a regional dialectal variant.

rummāna (رمانة), literally 'pomegranate,' omasum tripe, see *qubā* above.

sudsiyya (سدسية) honeycomb tripe, literally 'hexagonal.' It is the second chamber of the cow's stomach, the reticulum, the most desirable part of the tripe, used with other cuts of beef in recipes i.2.4 and ii.1.7.

kharūf (خروف), pl. *khirfān* (خرفان) male lamb less than a year old. The fat ones were preferred. For lamb, the meat, see *laḥm kharūf* below.

kharūf fatī (خروف فتي) young male lamb.

kharūf fatī samīn (خروف فتي سمين) fat young male lamb.

kharūf raḍīʿ (خروف رضيع) suckling lamb, the fat ones were preferred; see recipe ii.3.2, where it is cooked by shepherds in the sheepfolds.

khaṣiyy (خصي), pl. ***khiṣyān*** (خصيان), ***makhāṣī*** (مخاصي) capon. Male chickens were castrated while still chicks, as this was believed to make their meat tender and fatty.

laḥm (لحم) general name for meat. The following are meat-related terms used in the recipes:

laḥm mahzūl (لحم مهزول) lean meat.
laḥm rakhṣ (لحم رخص) tender meat.
laḥm samīn (لحم سمين), also called ***laḥm mujazzaʿ*** (لحم مجزع) fatty meat.
luḥūm dhawāt al-arbaʿ (لحوم ذوات الاربع) meat of quadrupeds.

laḥm baqarī (لحم بقري) beef. Meat from grown cows was said to be dense and cold in properties, hard to digest, and generate black bile. It was said to be well-suited for people who are physically active. See chapter ii.1, with its ten beef recipes, for ways to cook it.

laḥm baqarī maʿlūf (لحم بقري معلوف) beef from unpastured cows, fed on grains.

The choice fatty cuts and parts of beef mentioned in the recipes:

afkhādh (افخاذ), sg. *fakhdh* (فخذ) thighs.
amlāj (املاج), sg. *mulj* (ملج) shanks.[28]
ʿaẓm al-wirk (عظم الورك) hip bone.
laḥm baqarī fatī samīn (لحم بقري فتي سمين) beef from a young fat cow.
ṣadr (صدر) brisket.
sinsin (سنسن) loin, the middle back ribs area.

laḥm ḍaʾn (لحم ضان) mutton, see *laḥm ghanamī* below.

laḥm ghanamī (لحم غنمي) mutton. Although *ghanam* is a generic name for sheep (*ḍaʾn*) and goat (*māʿiz*), it specifically designates the meat of adult sheep (*ḍaʾn*) in al-Tujībī's recipes. Ibn Zuhr, *Kitāb al-aghdhiya* 21, says mutton was what most people used for their cooking, which indeed is reflected in the large number of recipes, 46 of them, offered in chapter ii.2. Mutton is described as having hot and moist properties. The best meat was said to be taken from females and males, including the castrated ones, that were neither too old nor too young. Meat of yearling rams was said to be good-quality meat that did not need to be remedied in any way,[29] see *laḥm kabsh* below.

laḥm ghanamī samīn (لحم غنمي سمين) fatty mutton.

---

28 Based on Corriente, *Dictionary of Andalusi Arabic*, s.v. *m-l-j/m-l-ch*, *mulj* designates the calf of the human leg, which in a quadruped would be its shank.

29 Al-Arbūlī, *al-Kalām ʿalā al-aghdhiya* 130.

laḥm ʿijl (لحم عجل) veal, said to digest better than beef.

laḥm jadī (لحم جدي) meat of a kid, which is a young male goat less than one year old. Its meat was said to be almost balanced in its properties, generating temperate blood leaning towards dryness. The recommendation was to cook it with plenty of suet. Meat of suckling kids (*jadī raḍīʿ*) was praised as being perfect, delicious, and nourishing, generating good-balanced blood. It was the recommended food for convalescents.[30]

laḥm kabsh (لحم كبش) mutton from a male sheep; and fatty mutton from a yearling ram, *laḥm kabsh samīn*, was deemed the best. Almost all the recipes in chapter ii.2 use this meat, see also *laḥm ghanamī* above. The choice mutton cuts used in the recipes:

ajnāb (اجناب), sg. *janb* (جنب) whole sides, usually with the chests attached.
fakhdh (فخذ) thigh.
ṣadr (صدر) brisket.
sinsin (سنسن) loin, the middle back ribs area.
ʿunq (عنق) neck section.
yadayn (يدين) fore shanks.

For finely ground mutton, thighs and loins are used, as in a recipe for making a mock tongue in chapter iv.3.

laḥm kharūf (لحم خروف) lamb, preferably taken from fat lambs. Although delicious, it was believed to be too moist in properties. The recommendation was to have it grilled and roasted.[31] The choice parts and cuts mentioned in the recipes:

dhanb (ذنب) rump.
quṣrayayn (قصريين), sg. *quṣrā* (قصرى) and *quṣayrā* (قصيرى) the last two pairs of ribs, called 'floating ribs.'
ra's (راس) head.
ṣadr (صدر) brisket.
sinsin (سنسن) loin, the middle back rib area.
yad (يد) fore shank.

laḥm al-waḥsh (لحم الوحش), pl. *luḥūm waḥshiyya* (لحوم وحشية) wild meat, taken from a deer (*ayyal*), oryx (*baqar al-waḥsh*), ass (*ḥimār*),[32] ibex (*waʿl*), or gazelle

---

30 Ibid., 132–3.
31 Ibn Zuhr, *Kitāb al-Aghdhiya* 21.
32 It would most certainly have been meat of a wild ass (*ḥimār al-waḥsh*), as meat of the domesticated donkey was not consumed.

FIGURE 191
A wild ass, Anonymous, *Kitāb Naʿt al-ḥayawān*, fol. 152r, detail
BRITISH LIBRARY: ORIENTAL MANUSCRIPTS, OR 2784, IN QATAR DIGITAL LIBRARY HTTPS://WWW.QDL.QA/ARCHIVE/81055/VDC_100023556967.0X000001

(*ghazāl*). They were all said to be cold and dry in properties, dense, and hard to digest.

Choice cuts from these animals mentioned in the recipes:

aḍlāʿ (اضلاع) ribs.
fakhdh (فخذ), pl. *afkhādh* (افخاذ) thigh.
khawāṣir (خواصر), sg. *khāṣira* (خاصرة) sirloins, lower back.
mawāḍiʿ al-shaḥm (مواضع الشحم) places containing the most suet.
ṣadr (صدر) brisket.
sinsin (سنسن) loin, the middle back rib area.
yadayn (يدين), sg. *yad* (يد) fore shanks.

māʿiz (ماعز), pl. ***maʿz*** (معز) goat in general. A grown female is called *ʿanz* (عنز), and a young one is *miʿza* (معزة). A grown male goat is *tays* (تيس), and a young one is *jadī* (جدي). The meat of grown goats was best taken from castrated males. The meat of old goats was not favored because it was believed to generate disorders related to black bile. Goat meat in general was described as hard to digest due to its cold anddry properties. Cooking it with a good deal of suet (*shaḥm*), along with oil and hot spices, would remedy it.[33]

minsaj (منسج) caul fat, see *buṭūn* above.

mislān (مسلان) entire hip section of sheep, see *ghanam* above.

mukhkh (مخ) bone marrow, see recipe i.2.5, which describes how to get it out of the bones and serve it to diners.

33 Al-Arbūlī, *al-Kalām ʿalā al-aghdhiya* 132. Hot spices in medieval times referred to those possessing hot properties, such as black pepper, caraway, coriander seeds, and cassia.

FIGURE 192 A gazelle (see *laḥm al-waḥsh*), Ibn al-Muqaffaʿ, *Kalīla wa Dimana*, fol. 53v, detail
BNF, DEPARTMENT OF MANUSCRIPTS, ARAB 3465. SOURCE: GALLICA.BNF.FR/BNF

muṣrān (مصران), ***maṣārīn*** (مصارين), sg. ***maṣīr*** (مصير) intestines of quadrupeds. In al-Tujībī's cookbook, intestines of sheep and cows are stuffed to make sausages of different sizes and chopped and cooked in dishes, as in recipe ii.1.10.

duwwāra (دوارة) the small intestine, used chopped in dishes and as sausage casings in making *mirqās*, which are small sausages, recipe ii.6.4, and the somewhat larger *laqāniq*, recipe ii.6.6.

mibʿar (مبعر) the large intestine, also referred to as ***maṣārīn khashna*** (مصارين خشنة). They are chopped and used in dishes and used as casings for making large sausages; sometimes large enough to include whole boiled eggs in the stuffing, as in recipe ii.6.9.

ʿuyūn al-duwwāra wa-l-mibʿar (عيون الدوارة والمبعر) choice pieces from the small and large intestines.[34]

namaksūd (نمكسود) meat cured by salting a whole ram or a side with crushed salt. The resulting cured meat stays moist, and the knife goes through as if it were fresh meat, as al-Tujībī explains in chapter xi.11. Following the advice of al-Rāzī, *Manāfiʿ al-aghdhiya* 114, it has to be soaked in water for a while before cooking it with vegetables, like spinach and chard, with a good deal of fresh suet, ghee, almond oil, or sesame oil. See also the *namaksūd* entry in glossary 5.

qadīd (قديد) salt-cured meat, prepared by cutting it into thin long strips and then seasoning and hanging it on ropes until it loses all its moisture, as described in chapter xi.11. Based on al-Rāzī, *Manāfiʿ al-aghdhiya* 114–5, it was to be eaten in small amounts as a snack food before the meal, or to fool the appetite, especially while imbibing alcohol. See also the *qadīd* entry in glossary 5.

qawqan (قوقن) snails, also called *aghlāl* (entry above).

qishrat ḥūt (قشرة حوت) crustaceous fish, describing shrimps in part xi.

qumrūn (قمرون) freshwater shrimps, which, in al-Tujībī's recipe xi.2, are said to be mostly found in big rivers, especially in the Guadalquivir in Seville. Ibn Zuhr, *Kitab al-Aghdhiya* 33, rightly identifies them as the highly aphrodisiac fish species with many legs, called *rabīthāʾ*. Their other names include: *rūbyān*, *arbiyān*, and *jarād al-baḥr* (locusts of the sea). In al-Warrāq, *Kitāb al-Ṭabīkh*, English trans., *Annals* 207, a condiment called *ṣaḥnāt* is made with them. They were said to have moderately hot and moist properties, and not viscid like fish.

qunfudh (قنفذ) hedgehog, mentioned in recipe ii.5.1. Ibn Zuhr, *Kitāb al-Aghdhiya* 25, says that its meat is delicious and particularly recommends its fat as a sexual enhancer by rubbing it on the male organ.

qunilya (قنلية), pl. ***qunilyāt*** (قنليات) European wild rabbit, *Oryctolagus cuniculus*. The name of this rabbit species is derived from the Spanish *conejo*. They are smaller than the hares and were in demand for their flavorful meat and excellent fur that was worn by Andalusis, as al-Maqqarī reports.[35] Nets woven with hemp fibers were used to catch them.[36]

Ibn Khalṣūn, *Kitāb al-Aghdhiya* 86, describes its meat as cold and dry in properties. Due to its viscidity, it was believed to generate phlegm and winds. On the other hand, because it is somewhat aromatic, it was believed to generate less black bile than the meat of the hare (*arnab*). Young females are said to be the best; cooked

34 In today's Moroccan Arabic, *ʿayn al-duwwāra* designates caul fat, which is the thin membrane attached to the stomach and intestines and surrounds the organs.

35 Al-Maqqarī *Nafḥ al-ṭīb* i 198.

36 Al-Ishbīlī, *ʿUmdat al-ṭabīb* ii 512.

FIGURE 193 Hedgehogs (see *qunfudh*), Dioscorides, *Fī Hayūlā al-ṭibb*, translation by Ḥunayn b. Isḥāq, fol. 70r, detail
FROM THE NEW YORK PUBLIC LIBRARY, SPENCER COLLECTION: HTTPS://DIGITALCOLLECTIONS.NYPL.ORG/ITEMS/5E66B3E8-91CD-D471-E040-E00A180654D7

with vinegar, fermented *murrī* sauce, garlic, olive oil, onions, and spices. In al-Tujībī's chapter ii.5, both hares and *qunilyas* are cooked more or less the same way.

Qunilya rabbits did not seem to be readily available outside of Spain. As reported in al-Maqqarī, *Nafḥ al-ṭīb* i 198, they were not indigenous to the northwest side of al-Maghrib, Barr al-Barbar, only the ones brought to Sabta (Ceuta) from Spain and propagated there were to be found. See also *arnab* above.

ra's (راس), ***ru'ūs*** (رؤوس) heads of calves, lambs, and kids simmered in dishes served as *tharīda*, as in recipes i.2.1–3. Generally, heads were said to be dense and hard to digest, but quite nourishing.

rummāna (رمانة), literally 'pomegranate,' is the omasum tripe, see *qubā*, s.v. *karsh*, above.

tharb (ثرب) caul fat, see *minsaj*, s.v. *buṭūn* above.

tunn (تنّ) *Thunnus thynnus*, Atlantic bluefin tuna, which was available for catching in the Mediterranean Sea in May. Al-Tujībī's tuna recipes are the only ones that have come down to us from the entire medieval Arabo-Muslim world.[37] Both fresh and cured, tuna is used in an interesting variety of dishes.

37 The ten or so fish recipes in the other Andalusi cookbook, the anonymous *Anwāʿ al-ṣaydala*, do not use tuna.

FIGURE 194 Tuna fish, Dioscorides, *Fī Hayūlā al-ṭibb*, translation by Ḥunayn b. Isḥāq, fol. 79r, detail
FROM THE NEW YORK PUBLIC LIBRARY, SPENCER COLLECTION: HTTPS://DIGITALCOLLECTIONS.NYPL.ORG/ITEMS/5E66B3E8-C92D-D471-E040-E00A180654D7

Ibn al-Bayṭār, *al-Jāmiʿ* i 194, briefly discusses tuna, which the Levantines called *tunna* (تنّة). He mentions that when the grown tuna fish leave *al-Baḥr al-Muẓlim* 'the dark sea' (i.e., the Atlantic Ocean) and enter the Mediterranean Sea (which he calls Baḥr al-Shām 'Levantine sea'), they would be caught with nets. These large and fat fish, he adds, are preserved in salt and stored. In trade, dried tuna was a valuable commodity. Apparently, to Ibn al-Bayṭār's contemporaries, tuna fish and their mysterious migratory ways made for a fascinating conversation subject during their social gatherings.[38]

The coastal areas of Shadhūna (Medina-Sidonia) in southern Spain and Sabta (Ceuta) in North Africa were said to be the most active centers for catching tuna fish with nets and harpoons.[39] The spot where tuna fish were captured was called *al-maḍraba* (المضربة) in Arabic, adopted in Spanish as *almadraba*. The method itself of catching tuna, however, was an ancient one, going back to the times of the Carthaginians. See introduction ii.4.1, p. 38 for details on how they were caught.

The tuna-related terms used in al-Tujībī's recipes:

khāṣira (خاصرة) back loin.
mushammaʿ (مشمع), also called ***tunn yābis*** (تن يابس) 'dried tuna'; it is salt-cured air-dried tuna. Etymologically, the Spanish *mojama* is derived from *mush-*

38 The expression he uses is, ويتنادم به ذكره. We now know that tuna fish go there to reproduce.

39 Al-Ḥimyarī, *al-Rawḍ al-miʿṭār* 303, where he described the harpoons as long spears with wing-like heads and long ropes of hemp (*qinnab*) attached to their ends. Ibn al-Bayṭār, *al-Jāmiʿ* i 194, mentions that nets were used to catch them.

*amma*ʿ. The term is related to *sham*ʿ 'beeswax'; and *mushamma*ʿ is descriptive of its stiff waxy texture. See recipes v.1.29–30 and pp. 380–1 for ways to cook it.

sharāʾiḥ (شرائح) strips.

shawka (شوكة) backbone.

surra (سرة) 'navel,' belly loin.

tunn muṣayyar (تن مصير) tuna preserved by pickling it in a salt-vinegar solution, see p. 381 for ways to cook it.

tunn muṣayyar fī jarra (تن مصير في جرة) tuna pickled in an earthenware jar, see recipe x.6.1 for pickling large fish in a salt-vinegar solution.

tunn ṭarī (تن طري) fresh tuna, preferably the small ones, are used baked, fried, and grilled in al-Tujībī's recipes v.1.26–8.

tunn yābis (تن يابس), also called *mushamma*ʿ (see entry above). It is dried tuna that has been salt-cured and air-dried.

Tuna preserved in salt was said to be of little benefit to the body, especially when fried, in which case they spoil the humors by generating yellow bile and phlegm.[40]

ʿurqūb (عرقوب) lamb hock, small cut of meat directly above the foot; the hock joint.

ʿurūq (عروق) veins and sinews in meat. More specifically, the word *ʿurūq* designates veins. In the recipes it is used more loosely to include tough chewy sinews, *aʿṣāb*. Such chewy particles are usually removed when making foods with ground meat, such as meatballs, patties, and sausages. Because they do not grind well, they would prevent the meat mix from binding well.

ʿuṣb (عصب), *ʿuṣbān* (عصبان), sg. *ʿuṣba* (عصبة) grilled rolls made by first threading pieces of tripe and heart through a skewer, which are then secured by wrapping them in caul fat. They would then be wrapped with a piece of intestine wound all around them and grilled. See, for instance, recipe i.2.2. Grilled rolls such as these are still made today in countries like Turkey, where they are called *kokorec*.

yamām (يمام) turtledoves; a wild migratory variety of pigeons,[41] described as being smaller than the domesticated ones (*ḥamām baladī*). *Yamām* was said to be the name the commoners gave to *shifnīn barrī*, whose cooing was described as melancholic.

Turtledoves are game birds, whose meat was said to be dry and hot in properties, which can be remedied by cooking it in plenty of fat. Their meat was deemed most suitable, after squabs' meat, for the elderly and the convalescent. The recommendation was to eat them while still young and avoid ones older than one year, which were believed to be harmful.[42]

---

40 Ibn Khalṣūn, *Kitāb al-Aghdhiya* 88.

41 They are a subspecies of pigeons (*ḥamām*).

42 Ibn al-Bayṭār, *al-Jāmi*ʿ ii 85; and al-Damīrī, *Ḥayāt al-ḥayawān* ii 628.

FIGURE 195
Turtledoves, *yamām*, also called *shifnīn*. Anonymous, *Kitāb Naʿt al-ḥayawān*, fol. 20v, detail
BRITISH LIBRARY: ORIENTAL MANUSCRIPTS, OR 2784, IN QATAR DIGITAL LIBRARY HTTPS://WWW.QDL.QA/ARCHIVE/81055/VDC_100023556967.0X000001

Generally, their meat was said to be nourishing; it was believed to improve memory and other mental faculties, and having it cooked in olive oil with eggs was said to be particularly beneficial in boosting coitus.[43] Al-Tujībī's chapter iii.5 offers an interesting variety of ways for cooking them, such as roasting them while dangling, skewered through their beaks (iii.5.5) or oven-cooked encrusted in salt (iii.5.6).

yamām musmina (يمام مسمنة) fat turtledoves.[44]

zarāzīr (زرازير), sg. *zurzūr* (زرزور) starlings; also called *sūdāniyyāt* (سودانيات). Nets (*shirāk*) were the best way to catch them. Two varieties of the bird were consumed:

1. Black starlings, described as having hot and dry properties, especially at the beginning of their season. The properties of their meat was said to improve as they grew fatter with the cooler weather, which was when they started to feed on olives.
2. White starlings, which were preferred to the black ones. Their meat was said to be delicious, more nourishing, and colder and moister than that of the black ones, thus generating good blood.

Meat of starlings in general was not regarded as safe because they usually feed on grasshoppers and insects that could be poisonous. To remedy this, the recommendation was to catch them alive and keep them in house cages for two or three days to give their systems enough time to digest and purge the food they ate in the wild

43 See al-Arbūlī, *al-Kalām ʿalā al-aghdhiya* 137; and al-Damīrī, *Ḥayāt al-ḥayawān* ii 628.
44 According to Ibn Manẓūr, *Lisān al-ʿArab*, s.v. سمن, any creature that is naturally built to be fat is described as *musmin*.

before slaughtering them. Their meat was believed to invigorate coitus, but be bad for the brain. To avoid their harms, only the fat ones should be eaten, served with sauces if grilled; or stewed with a good deal of olive oil. Additionally, eating dried figs with walnuts after having them was also recommended.[45] In al-Tujībī's chapter on starlings, iii.6, only fat white ones are used.

45 Al-Damīrī, *Ḥayāt al-ḥayawān* ii 583; Ibn Khalṣūn, *Kitāb al-Aghdhiya* 86; and Ibn Zuhr, *Kitāb al-Aghdhiya* 17.

11. Medical Terms and Hygienic Preparations

akhlāṭ (اخلاط), sg. ***khalṭ*** (خلط), the four humoral fluids: *al-damm* (blood), *al-balgham* (phlegm), *al-ṣafrā'* (yellow bile), and *al-sawdā'* (black bile). See *mizāj* below.

akl/ṭa'ām ghalīẓ (اكل/طعام غليظ) dense food that may be dry or viscous in consistency.

'alīl manhūk (عليل منهوك) a fatigued and emaciated sick person.

amzija (امزجة) humoral fluids; sg. *mizāj*, see entry below.

amzija raṭba bārida (امزجة رطبة باردة) are humoral fluids that are moist and cold in properties.

aṣḥāb al-ḥaṣā (اصحاب الحصى) people suffering from kidney and bladder stones.

bāh (باه) coitus; ***tuzīd fī l-bāh*** (تزيد في الباه) is descriptive of foods that invigorate coitus, see recipe i.2.14 for a *tharīd* dish, the only dish in the entire book that professes such effects. Ingredients used in the recipe known to be aphrodisiacs are chicken and, to a greater extent, sparrows, chickpeas, and carrots.

haḍm (هضم) digestion.

haḍūm (هضوم) adj. is food that functions as a digestive, such as *khall al-fulful*, which is vinegar infused with black pepper, see recipe x.7.4.

ḥarāra (حرارة) heat, which in the Galenic vocabulary does not refer to physical temperature as much as the innate properties (*mizāj*) of food, as with garlic in recipe ii.1.9. Based on Galen's theory of the humors, garlic is hot and dry in properties, and as such, it was believed to aid digestion, dispel flatulence, and break down coarse foods. See also *mizāj* below.

ḥidda (حدة) and ***inḥirāf*** (انحراف), literally 'going off the straight line.' This is descriptive of the unbalanced humoral properties of certain foods, such as sausages and fried foods; and cooking utensils, such as those made of copper. Such notions were based on the Galenic theory of the humors, according to which fried foods are overly hot and moist in properties, and hence unbalanced. In this respect, they share the same nature with copper. See *mizāj* below.

ghāsūlāt (غاسولات) handwashing preparations, also called *ushnān* (entry below).

istiḥāla (استحالة) n. change that occurs to digesting food in the system and turns its elemental properties into harmful ones, as is the case with fish if it does not digest properly.

> ***sarī' al-istiḥāla ilā l-fasād*** (سريع الاستحالة الى الفساد) is descriptive of digesting food, whose elemental properties change into harmful ones quickly, as in the case of fish when it does not digest well, see the last paragraph in chapter v.1.

 | DOI:10.1163/9789004469488_077

FIGURE 196
A pharmacy jar decorated with stylized inscriptions of the Arabic word *al-ʿāfiya* (العافية) 'good health,' from which the Spanish *alafia* is derived, fifteenth-century Spain
MET NY—GIFT OF J. PIERPONT MORGAN, 1917

kalaf (كلف) melasma; see recipe xii.5 for a handwashing preparation that claims it can remove the brown spots.

khalṭ ṣafrāwī (خلط صفراوي) yellow bile, which is hot and dry in properties, see *mizāj* below.

lakhlakha (لخلخة) an aromatic compound principally used as a potpourri but also to perfume the body. It has some medicinal benefits as well. We learn this from Ibn al-Jazzār's chapter on such preparations in *Kitāb fī Funūn al-ṭīb* 94–107. It is kept stored in powder form or a moist thick blend to be diluted and used as needed.

maḥmūmūn (محمومون) people with fevers. Porridge of coarsely crushed barley, recipe i.3.10, is said to be good for them.

maḥrūrūn (محرورون) people having an excess of hot properties. Porridge of coarsely crushed barley, recipe i.3.10, is said to be good for them.

maʿida bārida (معدة باردة) a cold stomach, and hence weak because it lacks the heat necessary for good digestion.

maʿida ḍaʿīfa (معدة ضعيفة) a weak stomach. Foods like *tafāyā*, recipes ii.2.1–2 and iii.2.1–2, praised for their balanced properties, are recommended for such stomachs.

mizāj (مزاج) humoral temperament or property. Based on the Galenic theory of the humors, all objects in nature, animate and inanimate, are composed of four elements (*arkān*): fire, air, water, and earth. Each possesses its own innate quality, called a property, temperament, or nature; in Arabic, *mizāj* (pl. *amzija*) or *ṭabʿ* (pl. *ṭabāʾiʿ*). There are four basic types of properties: hot, cold, dry, and moist. And each entity in nature is composed of a blend of these elements.

In regard to the human body, these elements are described in terms of humors, or elemental fluids, called *akhlāṭ* or *ruṭūbāt khalṭiyya*, and there are four of them: blood (*damm*), hot and moist; phlegm (*balgham*), cold and moist; yellow bile (*ṣafrāʾ*), hot and dry; and black bile (*sawdāʾ*), cold and dry. All of them are generated by the digested food in the stomach and liver.

Each individual human body has its own combination of these humors, which in a healthy state is normal. For instance, some people are naturally prone to having an excess in phlegm, described as *aṣḥāb al-ruṭūbāt* or *aṣḥāb al-balgham*. To maintain health, they should eat foods that match their natures, that is, foods with moist and cold properties. People who are naturally prone to heat, *aṣḥāb al-amzāj al-ḥārra*, should eat foods with hot properties. People who are naturally prone to cold, *aṣḥāb al-amzāj al-bārida*, should eat foods with cold properties. People whose humors are balanced, *aṣḥāb al-amzāj al-muʿtadila*, should eat foods with balanced properties. Still, having balanced humors does not imply a perfect balance of the humors, which is more a theory than a real state. Rather, balance (*iʿtidāl*) may be within a wide range of proportions (leaning more or less towards it) that are still healthy.

Sometimes the normal, balanced state of the humors is altered, either to excess or deficiency, due to internal or external causes, such as sicknesses or being exposed to acute conditions of heat or cold. This imbalanced state in the innate elements is called *mizāj ghayr muʿtadil*. It is an unhealthy state, which can be corrected and brought back to health by manipulating the properties of foods consumed. A person suffering from a fever, and hence having an excess of hot properties, can be relieved by consuming foods with cold properties, such as gourd.[1]

Foods themselves are manipulated in the same manner. Coarse and dense ones, for instance, which are hard to digest, such as grain porridges, can be balanced by eating them with *murrī* (liquid fermented sauce), black pepper, and cinnamon. The hot and dry properties of these ingredients can break down the densities of these porridges and facilitate their digestion.[2]

mufarriḥ (مفرح), descriptive of food that exhilarates the heart, as in recipe ii.2.21, where adding musk, ambergris, rosewater, and camphor was said to give the dish such a property.

muhayyij li-l-sawdāʾ (مهيج للسوداء) foods that agitate black bile, such as eggplants, which cause illnesses related to an excess in black bile. See *mizāj* above.

muqawwī li-l-nafs (مقوي للنفس), descriptive of food that boosts the psyche, as in recipe ii.2.21, where adding musk, ambergris, rosewater, and camphor was said to give the dish such a property.

nakha (نكهة) breath odor.

namash (نمش) freckles; recipe xii.5 is for a handwashing preparation that claims it can remove them.

qiwā (قوى) inherent humoral powers of foods and medicine.

quwwa summiyya (قوة سمية) toxic humoral power of food.

radāʾa (رداءة) descriptive of humoral properties that are bad and not healthy.

ṭabʿ (طبع) humoral temperament or property, also called *mizāj* (entry above).

ṭabīʿa (طبيعة), literally 'nature,' a euphemistic term for the 'digestive system.'

taʾlafuhu al-ṭabīʿa (تألفه الطبيعة) is said of foods that agree with the digestive system; see recipe i.1.5, n. 7, on making bread with millet flour.

---

1 The basics of the Galenic humoral theory explained here are lucidly discussed in the thirteenth-century book by Ibn Khalṣūn, *Kitāb al-Aghdhiya* 43–5. Ibn Khalṣūn summarizes the concept as maintaining health with similars and curing with opposites (حفظ الصحة بالمثل وزوال المرض بالضد).

2 For a more detailed account of the Galenic theory of the humors, see al-Warrāq, English trans., *Annals* 55–64; Dols, *Medieval Islamic Medicine* 3–14; Waines, "Dietetics in Medieval Islam," 228–40; and Waines, "'Luxury Foods' in Medieval Islamic Societies," 571–80.

yulayyin al-baṭn (يلين البطن), *yulayyin al-ṭabīʿa* (يلين الطبيعة) is said of foods that soften the bowels, such as in recipe vii.1.11 for a gourd pudding and recipe viii.2.3 for a chickpea dish.

ushnān 1 (اشنان), also called *ghāsūlāt* (غاسولات). They are handwashing preparations ranging from elaborate and expensive compounds to cheap and simple ones. See part xii for recipes; and for the ingredients used in making them, see glossary 8.

Although none of the recipes use the ingredient potash, called *ushnān* (see the following entry), they are still called *ushnān*. In al-Tamīmī, *Ṭīb al-ʿarūs* 253, they are more accurately called *ushnān bidūn* (without) *ushnān*. We read in al-Ḥashshāʾ, *Mufīd al-ʿulūm* 110, that *ushnān* (potash) was not known in the Muslim West, which indeed explains the absence of this ingredient in the recipes.

ushnān 2 (اشنان) potash, made by first producing ashes from the *ushnān* plant, which is saltwort, *Salsola kali*. While still fresh, the branches are burnt to ashes and collected and then continuously sprinkled with water to allow them to leach. The solution of the ashes and water is put in a large pot and boiled until all the moisture evaporates and only a white residue is left, which becomes potash.

yajraʿ (يجرع) to take sips of a drink, as in the last paragraph of chapter v.1 on fish. After eating fish, one is advised to take a few sips of the liquid fermented sauce *murrī*, undiluted wine, or spiced honey drinks as digestives.

yahḍum al-ṭaʿām (يهضم الطعام) said of foods that aid digestion, as in recipe ix.6.2 for making the lemon-flavored hard sugar candy drops *ishqāqūl*. They are kept in the mouth and sucked slowly.

yashudd al-laththa (يشد اللثة) firm up the gums, as in recipe xii.6, where a handwashing preparation is said to do this.

yuraṭṭib al-aṭrāf (يرطب الاطراف) moisturize hands, as in recipe xii.5, where a handwashing preparation is said to do this.

yusammin (يسمن) help in gaining weight; see recipe viii.2.3, where chickpeas are said to do this.

yuṭayyib al-nakha (يطيب النكهة) sweeten the breath; recipes xii.4 and 6 for handwashing preparations claim they can do this.

12. Vegetables and Legumes

ʿadas (عدس) lentils, *Lens culinaris*. Good-quality lentils are said to be the heavy ones that cook fast and do not discolor their soaking water. They are at their best when newly harvested because they decay and get worm-eaten fast due to the amount of moisture they contain. In properties, they are said to lean more towards coldness, dryness, and astringency. They do not digest fast and generate gastric winds that do not dissipate fast. Medieval physicians disapproved of the way the affluent cooked it by adding sweetening agents; this caused densities and blockages in the liver and spleen, they claimed. Vinegar, on the other hand, was believed to break down its densities and facilitate its digestion; lentil recipes in al-Tujībī's *Fiḍāla*, viii.3, do indeed use it.

Lentils had some medicinal benefits; their broth was believed to soothe coughs, chest pains, and fevers. With their astringency and purging qualities, they were used in compounds to wash the body, exfoliate the complexion, and remove dark spots.[1] One of the ingredients in a handwashing recipe in al-Tujībī's *Fiḍāla*, xii.5, is lentil flour.

daqīq ʿadas (دقيق عدس) lentil flour. It is used, along with the flour of barley and fava beans, in recipe xii.5 for a handwashing compound.

afzān (افزان) wild cardoon, which Ibn al-Bayṭār identifies as the name the Moroccan Amazigh gave to *ḥarshaf barrī* 'wild cardoon' (*Cynara cardunculus var. sylvestris*).[2] See *ḥarshaf* below.

bādhinjān (باذنجان) eggplants, *Solanum melongena*, of which al-Ishbīlī, *ʿUmdat al-ṭabīb* i 79–80, says there were many kinds. Of these he mentions the black Andalusi variety (*Andalusi aswad*), which did not seem to have been of a good quality. According to his description, they were rounded in shape and thin skinned, with a hot, sharp flavor, a good deal of seeds and not much flesh, and small calyxes. The other variety, the Levantine white eggplants (*abyaḍ Shāmī*), were elongated in shape with large thorny calyxes and thin skins. They had a good deal of flesh, with few seeds, and a delicious flavor. There was also the Egyptian pinkish variety (*muwarrad Miṣrī*), which was exactly like the Levantine variety, except for their white and red variegated skins.

1 See, for instance, al-Isrāʾīlī, *Kitāb al-Aghdhiya* ii 100; al-Anṭākī, *Tadhkira* 258–9; and al-Ṭighnarī, *Zahrat al-bustān* 438.

2 See Ibn al-Bayṭār, *al-Jāmiʿ* ii 271, s.v. *ḥarshaf*.

 | DOI:10.1163/9789004469488_078

FIGURE 197 Lentils, Dioscorides, *Ajzāʾ min risāla fī l-nabātāt*, fol. 27v, detail
BNF, DEPARTMENT OF MANUSCRIPTS, ARAB 4947. SOURCE: GALLICA.BNF.FR/BNF

Eggplants are used frequently in al-Tujībī's cookbook, a testimony to their popularity in the western cooking, as it was indeed popular in the eastern region. They are fried, layered in meat casseroles, variously stuffed, and grilled; in addition to an entire chapter, vii.2, allotted to meatless dishes. The following are eggplant-related expressions and descriptions used in the book of *Fiḍāla*:

bādhinjān ḥasan al-shakl (باذنجان حسن الشكل) nice-looking eggplants, used in recipe vii.2.13 for stuffing them.
bādhinjān ḥulw (باذنجان حلو) eggplants that are free of bitterness, literally 'sweet.'
bādhinjān kabīr al-jirm (باذنجان كبير الجرم) large eggplants.
bādhinjān muʿtadil (باذنجان معتدل) evenly shaped eggplants.
bādhinjān ṣaghīr (باذنجان صغير) small eggplants.
māʾ al-bādhinjān (ماء الباذنجان) liquid of raw eggplants, which was said to be harmful and needed to be drawn out and discarded. This was done either by

FIGURE 198 Eggplants, al-Ghāfiqī, *Kitāb al-Adwiya al-mufrada*, MS 7508, fol. 73r, detail

giving eggplants an initial boil in salted water or by slicing and salting them and weighing them down with heavy objects. This was done especially before frying them, see, for instance, recipe ii.1.2.

qiṭmīr (قطمير), pl. ***qaṭāmīr*** (قطامير) eggplant calyxes, also occurs as *qimʿ* (قمع) in sources other than al-Tujībī.

ṭaʿām al-bādhinjān (طعام الباذنجان) eggplant flesh; sometimes called *laḥm*, literally 'meat.'

Eggplants were recommended for sweetening the odor of sweat and removing underarm odors (*ṣunān*). They were said to strengthen the stomach and dry up humidities not generated by the body itself.[3] They were, however, maligned by physicians on account of their bitterness and excessively hot and dry properties. Eggplants were believed to generate bad, unhealthy humors that caused ailments like cancer and melasma if not pretreated before cooking them, see *mā' al-bādhinjān* above. Cooking them with vinegar and a good deal of olive oil, for instance, was believed to be the best way to neutralize their bad properties.[4] Eating grilled eggplants was not recommended. A recipe for preparing them this way in al-Tujībī's eggplants chapter, p. 424, comes with a caveat: "Do not eat too many eggplants prepared this way because they agitate black bile" (*muhayyij lil-sawdā'*).

baql (بقل) fresh vegetables, also called *khuḍra*.

baqla Yamāniyya (بقلة يمانية) blite, called *yarbūz* in the Muslim West, entry below.

basbās (بسباس), also referred to as *basbās akhḍar* (بسباس اخضر) 'fresh/green fennel' and *nāfiʿ* (نافع) 'beneficial.' It is fresh bulb fennel, *Foeniculum vulgare var. azoricum*. In the eastern region, it was more commonly known as *rāzyānaj*, *shamar*, and *shamār*. See also glossary 8 for *basbās*, the herb fennel.

Al-Ishbīlī, *'Umdat al-ṭabīb* i 106, describes *basbās* as a vegetable that can be consumed raw by virtue of its tenderness and lusciousness (*min aḥrār al-buqūl*). He says it was a well-known cultivated variety of fennel (*bustānī*), distinguished by its wide and large stalks. In al-Tujībī's cookbook, fresh bulb fennel is used in meat dishes with other vegetables, as in recipes i.2.8 and i.5.1; or as the main vegetable in a dish, as in the *basbāsiyya* recipe ii.2.7. Bulb fennel also goes well with fish; it is used in three recipes in the fish chapter, v.1.6, 10, and 12.

basbās ṭarī rakhṣ (بسباس طري رخص) fresh and tender bulb fennel.

mā' al-basbās al-akhḍar (ماء البسباس الاخضر) juice extracted from fresh bulb fennel used in the stuffing of a roasted rack of lamb, recipe ii.3.11.

With its moderately hot and dry properties, fresh bulb fennel was said to strengthen the stomach and open blockages in the kidneys, liver, and bladder. Its fresh juice mixed with honey was deemed beneficial for persistent fevers.[5]

baysār (بيسار) dried fava beans, *Vicia faba*. This was their name in the Muslim West; otherwise, they were more commonly known as *fūl yābis* (فول يابس) in the eastern region. In al-Tujībī's cookbook, dried fava beans are always crushed (*maṭḥūn*) when added to the cooking pots. In this form, they are incorporated into meat dishes, as in recipes i.2.27, i.5.5, and ii.2.33; and in meatless ones, as in some of the recipes

3 Al-Anṭākī, *Tadhkira* 74.
4 See al-Ghassānī, *Ḥadīqat al-azhār* 55.
5 See Ibn al-Jazzār, *al-I'timād* 528–9.

in chapter viii.1. Additionally, they are used crushed finely into flour (*daqīq fūl*) in recipe xii.7 for a handwashing preparation, as they were believed to be effective in removing grease and food odors from hands with their cleansing and purging properties (*yajlū*).

faqʿ (فقع) mushrooms, as they were called in the Muslim West; more commonly known as *fuṭr* in the eastern region, see entry below.

fujl (فجل) radishes, *Raphanus sativus*, the best of which is said to be the tender cultivated variety. In al-Tujībī's cookbook, it is twice suggested to be offered raw with dishes cooked with dried fava beans, recipes i.2.27 and viii.1.8. The cultivated varieties that were available in the western region are:[6]

1. Big radishes, called *al-rukhāmī* 'marble-like,' whose edible roots are described as white, large, and densely textured, with thick peels and mild flavor. A broken root would look like white marble. Their leaves are wide and quite tender and juicy.
2. Small radishes, the most commonly consumed, called *baladī* (local). They are similar to the large ones but smaller and hotter in flavor.

Radishes are hot and dry in properties, and as such, having them raw with dense foods like fava beans was recommended, as they were believed to facilitate digestion, induce burping, and purge winds.[7]

fūl (فول) fava beans, also known as *bāqillāʾ* (باقلاء) and *bāqillā* (باقلى), *Vicia faba*. They were well-known and frequently used in the medieval kitchen. Three main varieties were recognized: the Egyptian, brown (literally red) and large; the Yemeni, black and large; and the Levantine, fair colored (literally white) and large.[8] When used fresh in al-Tujībī's cookbook, they are referred to as *fūl akhḍar* (see the following entry). For dried fava beans, see *baysār* above.

fūl akhḍar (فول أخضر) fresh fava beans, *Vicia faba*. They are used in al-Tujībī's cookbook, either with other vegetables or as the main ingredient, as in recipe ii.2.32 for *fustuqiyya* 'pistachio-green stew.' Chapter viii.1 is allotted to meatless fava beans dishes.

musammakh (مسمخ) sprouted fava beans, also called *manbūt* (منبوت). Only the BL MS, fol. 184v, uses the term. That al-Tujībī needed to explain what it was is testimony to its regional uniqueness.[9] See recipes viii.1.2 and 7.

qishr aʿlā (قشر اعلى) outer peel of beans, the jacket.

---

6 As described in al-Ishbīlī, *ʿUmdat al-ṭabīb* ii 470–1; and al-Ghassānī, *Ḥadīqat al-azhār* 215.

7 See al-Anṭākī, *Tadhkira* 273.

8 Ibn al-ʿAwwām, *al-Filāḥa al-Andalusiyya* iv 147.

9 I have seen similar usage of the word, related to sprouting unhusked rice grains before planting them, in Ibn ʿAwwām, *al-Filāḥa al-Andalusiyya* iv 100. In al-Zabīdī, *Tāj al-ʿArūs*, s.v. سمخ, it is used to designate a seedling.

FIGURE 199 Radishes, Dioscorides, *Kitāb al-Ḥashā'ish fī hāyūlā al-ʿilāj al-ṭibbī*, Arabic translation by Ḥunayn b. Isḥāq, Or. 289, fol. 80v, detail
UNIVERSITAIRE BIBLIOTHEKEN LEIDEN, HTTP://HDL.HANDLE.NET/1887.1/ITEM:1578266

Fava beans were said to be moderate in properties, which are also purging and cleansing (*yajlū*). They were good for expelling humidities from the lungs; their broth was said to be especially good for this purpose, as well as preventing kidney and bladder stones. On the negative side, they were considered the most bloating of all foods, inducing feelings of lethargy and laziness, and causing nightmares. To reduce their bloating effect, prolonged soaking and cooking were recommended to facilitate their digestion. Additionally, cooking them with black pepper, salt, thyme, caraway, rue, and olive oil was believed to help in this respect.[10]

10 Al-Ghāfiqī, *Kitāb fi-l-Adwiya al-mufrada*, fols. 70v–71r; al-Malik al-Muẓaffar, *al-Muʿtamad* 37–8; and al-Ghassānī, *Ḥadīqat al-azhār* 54.

FIGURE 200 Green fava beans, Dioscorides, *Fī Hayūlā al-ṭibb*, translation by Ḥunayn b. Isḥāq, fol. 96r, detail
FROM THE NEW YORK PUBLIC LIBRARY, SPENCER COLLECTION: HTTPS://DIGITALCOLLECTIONS.NYPL.ORG/ITEMS/5E66B3E9-1480-D471-E040-E00A180654D7

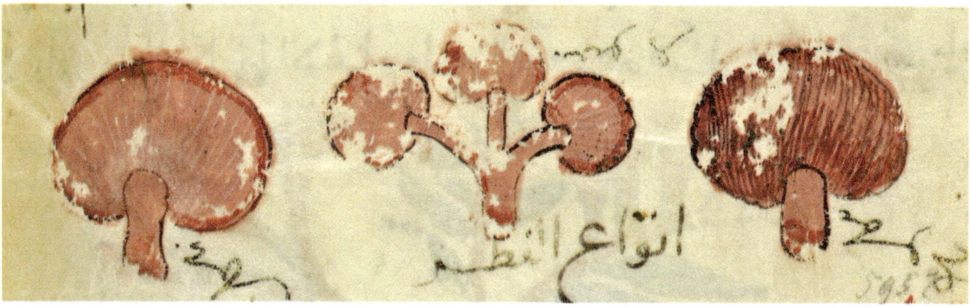

FIGURE 201 Mushrooms, Dioscorides, *Ajzāʾ min risāla fī l-nabātāt*, fol. 94v, detail
BNF, DEPARTMENT OF MANUSCRIPTS, ARAB 4947. SOURCE: GALLICA.BNF.FR/BNF

fuṭr (فطر) mushrooms, called *faqʿ* in the Muslim West. On the other hand, *faqʿ* in the eastern region designated a white variety of *kamʾa* 'truffles.'

Mushrooms were not a significant source of food; in al-Tujībī's cookbook, they show up in just a couple of recipes: iii.2.49, diced with chicken and topped with eggs; and recipe vii.7 for a simple meatless dish, also used diced, seasoned with fermented sauce of *murrī* and vinegar, and topped with eggs.

Medieval physicians and herbalists had a very low opinion of them, as not all of them were recognized as edible. In his entry on mushrooms, al-Malik al-Muẓaffar, *al-Muʿtamad* 425, for instance, says he cannot say anything good about them; while some varieties are deadly, even those that do not kill are hard to digest and generate dense, harmful humors with their cold properties. Dried mushrooms, on the other hand, were thought to be safer than the fresh ones because poisonous varieties were believed to rot before they dry out. The best mushrooms were the white ones that were rather dry and not slimy to the touch. Their taste was dismissed as being bland, and overindulgence was to be avoided.[11] All the above undoubtedly justifies the other name given to mushrooms, which is *al-turrahāt* (التّرّهات) 'the good-for-nothing frivolous food.'[12]

ghazl (غزل) young shoots of the vines of grapes, snake cucumbers (*qiththā*), common cucumbers (*khiyār*), and gourds. They are chopped and added as vegetables to a summer *jināniyya* dish in al-Tujībī's recipe i.2.26.

ḥarshaf (حرشف), ***khurshūf*** (خرشوف) cardoon, *Cynara cardunculus*, it is the generic name for the cardoon plant, of which the following are varieties:

afzan (افزن), also occurs as *afzān* (افزان), *Cynara cardunculus var. sylvestris L*, wild cardoons. Based on Ibn al-Bayṭār, *al-Jāmiʿ* ii 271, s.v. *ḥarshaf*, it is the name

11 See al-Bīrūnī, *al-Ṣaydana* 290–1; and al-Rāzī, *Manāfiʿ al-aghdhiya* 189.
12 Al-Ghassānī, *Ḥadīqat al-azhār* 218.

FIGURE 202 A vine of snake cucumbers, *qiththā'*, with young shoots, *ghazl*, al-Qazwīnī, *'Ajā'ib al-makhlūqāt wa ghārā'ib al-mawjūdāt*, fol. 200r, detail
FROM THE NEW YORK PUBLIC LIBRARY, SPENCER COLLECTION: HTTPS://DIGITALCOLLECTIONS.NYPL.ORG/ITEMS/17E2D480-28EC-0138-C573-0C13C7D5E313

Moroccan Amazigh gave to *ḥarshaf barrī* 'wild cardoons.' Al-Ghāfiqī, *Kitāb fi-l-Adwiya al-mufrada*, fol. 190r, describes them as having large heads with sharp thorns.

laṣīf (لصيف), also occurs as *laṣif* (لصف) gundelia, *Gundelia tournefortii*, which is another variety of wild cardoons, more commonly called *'akkūb* in the eastern region. Andalusis called them *qannāriyya barriyya* 'wild cardoon.' Al-Ghāfiqī, *Kitāb fi-l-Adwiya al-mufrada*, fol. 190r, compares them to thistles with long stems, many leaves, and thorny heads. Al-Ishbīlī, *'Umdat al-ṭabīb* 169, says they were a very popular vegetable in al-'Udwa (the North African side of the Mediterranean) but not as much in al-Andalus. They are cooked with meat in recipe ii.2.18, and their blossoms, *nawār*, are used to curdle milk into *'aqīd* in recipe vi.1.4.

qannāriyya (قنارية) *Cynara cardunculus var. altilis* DC, cultivated cardoons (*ḥarshaf bustānī*). *Qannāriyya* is the Andalusi Romance ('Ajamiyyat al-Andalus) for what was in the eastern region more commonly known as *kankar* and

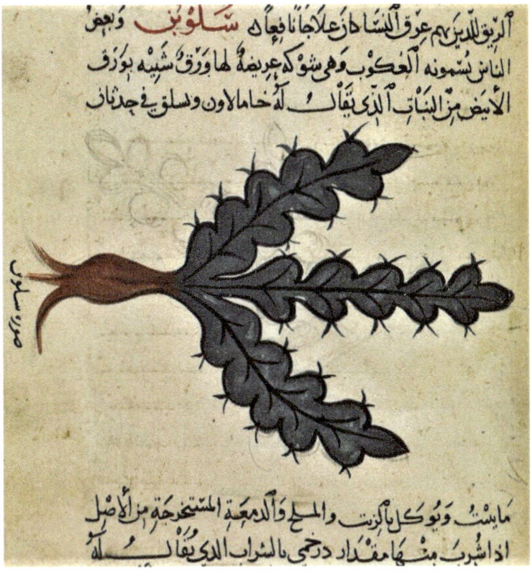

FIGURE 203
ʿAkkūb, a variety of wild cardoon, Dioscorides, *Kitāb Dīsqūrīdis fī mawādd al-ʿilāj*, fol. 161r, detail
BRITISH LIBRARY: ORIENTAL MANUSCRIPTS, OR 3366, IN QATAR DIGITAL LIBRARY HTTPS://WWW.QDL.QA/ARCHIVE/81055/VDC_100022531380.0X000001

kanjar. They are described as having the largest leaves and the least thorns.[13]

Cardoons are described as having dry and hot properties, and as such they had the power to excite the appetite and arouse coitus. They were said to be a diuretic and good for purging phlegm from the lungs. They were said to be most beneficial when eaten overcooked and overseasoned because they were slow to digest on account of their density. When still young and tender, cardoons, like asparagus, were eaten raw.[14] The heading in al-Tujībī's chapter vii.6 recommends *afzan* as the best variety to be used for cooking purposes. See recipe ii.2.18 for a meat dish, and chapter vii.6 for meatless ones. As Ibn Rushd explains, *al-Kulliyyāt* 436, cardoons, like eggplants, can absorb the flavor of the meat they are cooked with, which makes them taste quite delicious.

ḥimmaṣ (حمّص) chickpeas, *Cicer arietinum*. They are an indispensable ingredient in al-Tujībī's cookbook, used mostly dried; after soaking them for a while in water, they are used in soupy dishes like stews and *tharāyid* of bread broken into pieces and sopped in broth. They are also used in other interesting ways, such as cooking them with scrambled eggs, recipe v.2.10; crushed in a porridge-like meat dish, recipe ii.2.34;

---

13 Based on Ibn al-Bayṭār, *al-Jāmiʿ* iv 271–2; and al-Ghāfiqī, *Kitāb fi-l-Adwiya al-mufrada*, fol. 190r. See also, Ibn al-Ḥashshāʾ, *Mufīd al-ʿulūm* 66.

14 See al-Ghāfiqī, *Kitāb fi-l-Adwiya al-mufrada*, fol. 190v.

FIGURE 204 Cultivated cardoon, *kankar*, called *qannāriyya* in al-Andalus, al-Ghāfiqī, *Kitāb al-Adwiya al-mufrada*, MS, fol. 275v, detail

and several other meatless ones, where they are used fresh and dried as the main ingredient, as in chapter viii.2.

ḥimmaṣ abyaḍ (حمص ابيض), literally 'white,' they are the common tan chickpeas, deemed the best of the chickpea varieties.

ḥimmaṣ akhḍar (حمص اخضر) fresh green chickpeas in the pod, used as the main ingredient in recipe viii.2.1 for a meatless dish.

FIGURE 205 Fresh chickpeas, Dioscorides, *Ajzāʾ min risāla fī l-nabātāt*, fol. 26v, detail
BNF, DEPARTMENT OF MANUSCRIPTS, ARAB 4947. SOURCE: GALLICA.BNF.FR/BNF

ḥimmaṣ aswad (حمص اسود) black chickpeas, said to be closer in quality to the white ones, and among all the chickpea varieties, they were said to have the strongest properties, apparently so strong that drinking their broth was believed to abort fetuses.[15]

ḥimmaṣ mablūl (حمص مبلول) chickpeas that have been soaked in water for a while before using them.

ḥimmaṣ maṭḥūn (حمص مطحون) crushed dried chickpeas, used in a porridge-like recipe ii.2.34, cooked with meat.

ḥimmaṣ yābis (حمص يابس) dried chickpeas, generally used whole after soaking them in water for a while to soften them.

15 Al-Ṭighnarī, *Zahrat al-Bustān* 414.

Chickpeas were deemed the best of all pulses, but not easy on the digestion, and they caused bloating. The recommendation was to have them in the middle of the meal. With their hot and dry properties, they were said to be the best cure for cold-related headaches and chest ailments. They were used as a diuretic and were believed to open blockages in the liver and spleen and cleanse the kidneys and crumble their stones. A mixture of chickpea flour and yogurt was believed to clear melasma (*kalaf*). They were also said to stimulate milk in lactating mothers and increase semen production. Moreover, they were greatly esteemed for their aphrodisiac properties.[16] Curiously, according to the other Andalusi cookbook, anonymous *Anwāʿ al-ṣaydala* 55, it was only the broth resulting from boiling chickpeas that has the benefits; otherwise, the boiled chickpeas themselves were food fit only for peasants and the greedy.

ḥubūb (حبوب) general term for beans and grains.

isfānākh (اسفاناخ) spinach, *Spinacia oleracea*; a leaf vegetable used sparingly in al-Tujībī's cookbook, often with other leafy vegetables, like lettuce and blite (*yarbūz*);[17] with meat stews, as in recipes i.2.3 and ii.2.11; and in meatless dishes, as in chapter vii.8.

Al-Ishbīlī, *ʿUmdat al-ṭabīb* i 103 and 234, calls spinach *baqla dustiyya* (بقلة دستية) and *dustī* (دستي), explaining that they designated *isfānākh*. He also gives it the name *Tustarī* (تُستري) and attributed it to the Persian city of Tustar,[18] where it grew abundantly, adding that spinach growing in al-Andalus in his time originally started with spinach seeds imported from Tustar, hence the name.

Spinach was a winter leaf vegetable, esteemed for being the least harmful because it did not cause bloating or generate phlegm. With its balanced properties, it was regarded as a good source of food, raw and cooked, for the sick suffering from chest ailments. It was also said to be effective in softening the bowels and was valued for its purging and cleansing properties.[19] All the above do indeed justify Ibn al-ʿAwwām's description of it as *raʾīs al-buqūl* 'chief of vegetables.'[20]

isfarāj (إسفراج), *isfāranj* (إسفارنج) asparagus, *Asparagus officinalis*. This was one of the foods that the famous singer Ziryāb popularized in al-Andalus.[21] Asparagus was described as a spring vegetable of which these varieties were known:

16 See ibid.; and al-Ghassānī, *Ḥadīqat al-azhār* 124.
17 Leaves of wild amaranth.
18 Pronounced Shushtar in Persian. It is a city in southwestern Iran, close to the southern Iraqi borders. From ancient times on, Tustar was renowned for its agricultural produce.
19 Al-Anṭākī, *Tadhkira* 46; and al-Ghāfiqī, *Kitāb fi-l-Adwiya al-mufrada*, fol. 35r–v.
20 Ibn al-ʿAwwām, *al-Filāḥa al-Andalusiyya* iv 279.
21 See introduction ii.5, p. 48.

hilyawn barrī (هليون بري) asparagus found in the wild, with spears growing on prickly plants. Al-Ishbīlī, *ʿUmdat al-ṭabīb* ii 608, says that of the varieties that grew spears, they were purplish in color, with a tinge of bitterness; they were consumed boiled.

hilyawn bustānī (هليون بستاني) asparagus cultivated in orchards. The plant has no thorns and looks like that of dill. The spears of this variety, which was first propagated by transplanting wild plants into orchards, were described as being more delicious and tender than the wild ones. They were yellowish green and as thick as the index finger. Al-Ishbīlī, *ʿUmdat al-ṭabīb* ii 607, says that his description of cultivated asparagus was based on what he saw at the ruler's orchard, which was taken care of by Ibn Baṣṣāl.[22] The cultivated variety must have been held in high regard as, according to al-Ishbīlī, they were often gifted to kings and dignitaries and offered as treats to dining guests. This variety was said to be the most balanced in properties and the most nutritious because it digested well, benefitting the body more than any other vegetable and increasing semen production.[23]

hilyawn rīfī (هليون ريفي), ***hilyawn faḥṣī*** (هليون فحصي) asparagus growing wild in the countryside outside the cities. Al-Ishbīlī, *ʿUmdat al-ṭabīb* ii 608, says that the spears were similar to the *bustānī* ones, albeit thicker and not as dense in texture, with a sweet taste free of bitterness (*ʿadhbat al-madhāq*).

hilyawn ṣakhrī (هليون صخري) asparagus growing wildly in rocky mountains. Al-Ishbīlī, *ʿUmdat al-ṭabīb* ii 607–8, describes it as a prickly plant with spears as thin as the little finger; eaten boiled in the springtime.

Two recipes are given in al-Tujībī's cookbook. In recipe ii.2.14, asparagus is cooked with meat in various interesting ways, and in vii.5, it is boiled and served seasoned with olive oil and vinegar. Judging from al-Ishbīlī's remarks above, wild-growing asparagus was eaten boiled, which would rid it of bitterness. Al-Ghassānī, *Ḥadīqat al-azhār* 96, says that the spears were eaten in springtime, and people loved their taste. He adds that they grew abundantly in Fez where he lived. Still, we do learn from Ibn al-ʿAwwām, *al-Filāḥa al-Andalusiyya* v 153, that the orchard variety (*bustānī*) was much more delicious and far more tender than the wild ones (*barrī*).

---

22 He was a famous Andalusi horticulturalist, a contemporary of Ibn al-ʿAwwām. The reference to the garden here must have been to *Ḥāʾiṭ al-Sulṭān*, the botanical garden created by al-Muʿtamid b. ʿAbbād (d. 1095), ruler of Seville, where Ibn Baṣṣāl worked and experimented with plants.

23 Al-Ghāfiqī, *Kitāb al-Adwiya al-mufrada*, fols. 138v–139r.

FIGURE 206 Asparagus, Dioscorides, *Kitāb al-Ḥashā'ish fī hāyūlā al-ʿilāj al-ṭibbī*, Arabic translation by Ḥunayn b. Isḥāq, Or. 289, fol. 84v, detail
UNIVERSITAIRE BIBLIOTHEKEN LEIDEN, HTTP://HDL.HANDLE.NET/1887.1/ITEM:1578266

FIGURE 207
Carrots, cultivated (R) and wild (L), Dioscorides, *Ajzāʾ min risāla fī l-nabātāt*, fol. 61v, detail
BNF, DEPARTMENT OF MANUSCRIPTS, ARAB 4947. SOURCE: GALLICA.BNF.FR/BNF

For medicinal purposes, the wild varieties of asparagus, which were well-known in al-Andalus, where they grew abundantly, were said to be more beneficial due to their stronger properties. With its purging power, asparagus was used to open blockages in the liver and kidneys. It was also said to change the odor of urine, but it was highly esteemed for being effective in invigorating coitus. Asparagus was deemed more beneficial to the body when eaten at the end of the meal. Eating it boiled was said to be the best way to have it because having it raw would cause nausea and bad digestion.[24]

jazar (جزر) carrots, *Daucus carota subsp. sativus*, used infrequently in al-Tujībī's cookbook, mostly as a secondary ingredient used with other vegetables; except for a *narjisiyya* dish in recipe ii.2.17, where the carrots are deliberately cut into pencil-like strips so that the final dish might resemble narcissus flowers. Carrots are the main subject of a short chapter, vii.3, dealing with ways to prepare meatless dishes with them.

The cultivated varieties of carrots growing in al-Andalus were said to be weaker in properties than the wild-growing ones. Of the cultivated ones, several root colors were recognized: *abyaḍ* 'white,' which could have been a variety of parsnip; *aḥmar* 'red'; *aṣfar* 'yellow'; *aswad* 'black,' which might have been the dark-purple ones; and *mujazzāʿ* 'variegated.' With their hot and moist properties, carrots were highly esteemed for arousing sexual appetites and invigorating coitus, see recipe i.2.14.

kamʾa (كمأة) desert truffles. In the Muslim West it was called *tirfās* (entry below).

24 Ibid.

FIGURE 208 Cultivated lettuce, Dioscorides, *Kitāb al-Ḥashāʾish fī hāyūlā al-ʿilāj al-ṭibbī*, Arabic translation by Ḥunayn b. Isḥāq, Or. 289, fol. 88v, detail
UNIVERSITAIRE BIBLIOTHEKEN LEIDEN, HTTP://HDL.HANDLE.NET/1887.1/ITEM:1578266

khass (خس) lettuce, *Lactuca sativa*, of which several varieties were used in al-Andalus, eaten in winter and spring. According to al-Ishbīlī, *ʿUmdat al ṭabīb* 215–6, the most consumed lettuce variety was called *al-khass al-baladī* ʻindigenous lettuce.ʼ It grew large heads with long, pointed yellowish-green leaves, which looked as if they were oiled; they were juicy and insipid. Another variety was called *al-ḥāḥī* (الحاحي); it was the sweetest of all kinds to eat. Its leaves were also long but rounded and somewhat wrinkled; they were yellowish green and soft.

Lettuce is used sparingly in al-Tujībī's cookbook, either as a secondary ingredient with other vegetables or as the main vegetable in meat dishes, as in recipe ii.2.12, where only the stems are used. The book also offers ways to cook meatless dishes with lettuce and other leafy vegetables in chapter vii.8.

FIGURE 209 Unripe cucumbers, Dioscorides, *Fī Hayūlā al-ṭibb*, translation by Ḥunayn b. Isḥāq, fol. 103v, detail
FROM THE NEW YORK PUBLIC LIBRARY, SPENCER COLLECTION: HTTPS://DIGITALCOLLECTIONS.NYPL.ORG/ITEMS/5E66B3E8-7EC4-D471-E040-E00A180654D7

With its cold and moist properties, lettuce was believed to be good for relieving sunstrokes and delirium. It was said to benefit a hot stomach, quench thirst, excite the appetite, induce sleep, help stop wet dreams, and weaken coitus.[25]

khiyār (خيار) common cucumbers, *Cucumis sativus*. In al-Tujībī's cookbook, only the budding cucumbers and their young shoots are used in two *jināniyya* dishes, usually prepared and cooked on picnics in orchards, see recipes i.2.26 and vii.9.

25 Al-Ghassānī, *Ḥadīqat al-azhār* 306–7; and al-Malik al-Muẓaffar, *al-Muʿtamad* 163.

ghazl al-khiyār (غزل الخيار) young shoots of the common cucumber vines.
ʿuyūn al-khiyār (عيون الخيار) the budding common cucumber.

In the Andalusi books on botany and horticulture,[26] the common cucumber growing there was compared to the shape of the citron, in that they took the shape of elongated ovals,[27] unlike *qiththāʾ* 'snake cucumbers,' which were long and thin and densely fleshed. Their peels were whitish green, which turned yellow at maturation. Cucumbers were early summer produce.

khuḍra (خضرة) fresh vegetables in general, also called *baql.*

kurunb (كرنب), ***ukrunb*** (اكرنب) cabbages, *Brassica oleracea var. capitata*; also generally called *kurunb Nabaṭī* and *kurunb Andalusi.* In al-Tujībī's cookbook, cabbages are often used with other vegetables, as in recipes i.5.1, 10, 12, and iv.1–2. They are also the main vegetable cooked with meat in recipes i.2.4 and ii.2.3; and just boiled and served seasoned with olive oil and vinegar as a side dish in recipe vii.8.2.

aḍlāʿ al-kurunb (اضلاع الكرنب) midribs of cabbage leaves.
dhirāʿ al-kurunb (ذراع الكرنب) a whole cabbage leaf with its midrib.
ʿuyūn al-kurunb (عيون الكرنب) tender hearts of cabbage heads.

Cabbage was a well-known vegetable, of which many varieties are mentioned in the Andalusi books on botany and horticulture. Generally speaking, the cabbage plant was divided into two categories:

1. True cabbages, called ***multaff*** (ملتف), also ***malfūf*** (ملفوف), with their characteristic heads of leaves.
2. Cauliflower, called ***ghayr multaff*** (غير ملتف), it does not have an entire head of leaves, but it has leaves that surround a cauliflower head, which can be broken into smaller florets.[28] See *qunnabīṭ*, below.

In al-Tujībī's recipes, two kinds of cabbages are used:

kurunb shatawī (كرنب شتوي) winter cabbages. Based on al-Tujībī's recipe ii.2.3, they are described as having a milder and sweeter taste than cabbages grown in the summer. Al-Ishbīlī, *ʿUmdat al-ṭabīb* i 313–5, favors this less pungent vari-

---

26 See Ibn al-ʿAwwām, *al-Filāḥa al-Andalusiyya* iv 391; al-Ishbīlī, *ʿUmdat al-ṭabīb* i 220; and al-Ghassānī, *Ḥadīqat al-azhār* 308.

27 This variety of cucumbers was called *khiyār bādharank* (خيار باذرنك), i.e., 'looking like citron'; called so after the Syriac word *bādharank,* which designated citron, as explained in al-Bīrūnī, *al-Ṣaydana* 21, 300–1.

28 As described in al-Ṭighnarī, *Zahrat al-bustān* 458; and al-Anṭākī, *Tadhkira* 299.

ety to the summer variety. They are also said to grow large green leaves that form loosely packed heads.

kurunb ṣayfī (كرنب صيفي) summer cabbages, which, based on al-Tujībī's recipe ii.2.3, have a sharp and pungent flavor (*shiddat ḥarāfa*). This has been confirmed in other Andalusi sources, which describe it as being excessively sharp, salty, and bitterish. Of its physical appearance, the leaves were described as white and tender, forming a compacted head, which gave it the name *kurunb maghlūq* 'tightly closed cabbage.'[29]

Ibn Zuhr, *Kitāb al-Aghdhiya* 56, disapproves of cabbages on account of their hot and dry properties. He says people like to eat this vegetable, and they say good things about it, but in reality, it is the most harmful of all foods, causing black-bile related disorders, scabies, leprosy, and epilepsy; in this respect, it is similar to eggplants.

Generally, cabbages were believed to be pungent, salty, and bitterish. They were blamed for bloating the digestive system, causing gurgles and black-bile vapors (*bukhār sawdāwī*). Boiling them in salted water before adding them to the cooking dishes was believed to be the best way to remedy them. Physicians recommended them for cold-related ailments. They were believed to cure hangovers, and eating them before drinking wine was said to delay intoxication.[30]

laṣīf (لصيف) gundelia, *Gundelia tournefortii*, a variety of wild cardoons; more commonly known as *'akkūb* in al-Mashriq. See *ḥarshaf* above.

lift (لفت) turnips, *Brassica rapa*, variously called *saljam*, *shaljam*, and *shalgham* in the eastern region. Several cultivated varieties were available in al-Andalus:

lift Andalusi mudawwar (لفت اندلسي مدور), which were small, rounded bright-white turnips, they grew abundantly in Seville and Cordova.

lift Rūmī ṭawīl (لفت رومي طويل), which were Byzantine elongated turnips.[31]

lift ṣayfī (لفت صيفي) summer turnips, which were said to be pungent, dry, and not so tender, unlike winter turnips.[32]

lift Ṭulayṭulī (لفت طليطلي) turnips of Toledo, also called *abū shād*; they were small red turnips that caused bloating and offered little nutrition when eaten cooked. They were mostly used for pickling purposes.[33]

---

29 See, for instance, al-Ṭighnarī, ed. García Sánchez, *Zahrat al-bustān* 500–1.

30 Ibn al-Bayṭār, *al-Jāmiʿ* iv 215–9.

31 See al-Ishbīlī, *'Umdat al-ṭabīb* 7; and Ibn al-'Awwām, *al-Filāḥa al-Andalusiyya* iv 307.

32 Al-Ṭighnarī, *Zahrat al-bustān* 442; and Ibn al-'Awwām, *al-Filāḥa al-Andalusiyya* iv 307.

33 Ibn al-Bayṭār, *al-Jāmiʿ* iii 90.

FIGURE 210
Turnips, Dioscorides, *Ajzāʾ min risāla fī l-nabātāt*, fol. 29r, detail
BNF, DEPARTMENT OF MANUSCRIPTS, ARAB 4947. SOURCE: GALLICA.BNF.FR/BNF

In al-Tujībī's cookbook, turnips are used in several recipes, either as a secondary ingredient combined with other vegetables and meat, as in recipes i.5.1 and 10, or as the main vegetable in meat dishes, as in recipes ii.1.3 and ii.2.4. They are also prepared as a vegetable side dish seasoned with olive oil and vinegar in recipe vii.8.2; and preserved as pickles in recipe x.5.3. The preference was to use turnips when in season, which was winter, when they were tender and sweet. In the recipes we have, after peeling them, they are either added to the pot whole or cut into fingers. Before adding summer turnips to the pot, the cook is instructed to go deeper when peeling them and then dice them. See recipe ii.2.4 and *lift ṣayfī* above.

Turnips were said to be difficult to digest but offer good nutrition to the body and excite coitus. They were also believed to have purging properties that work as a diuretic and blockage opener. Pickled turnips were said to excite the appetite but have no significant nutritional value.[34]

qannāriyya (قنارية) cultivated cardoon, *Cynara cardunculus var. altilis* DC. This is the colloquial Andalusi name for *ḥarshaf bustānī*, see *ḥarshaf* above.

qarʿ (قرع) gourd, *Lagenaria*, of which several varieties were known in al-Andalus. Al-Ishbīlī, *ʿUmdat al-ṭabīb* ii 502–3, mentions the following:

Gharnāṭī (غرناطي) named after Granada, where it grew abundantly. It is the length of an arm, ridged, and conical in shape, in that one of its ends is wider than the other. It is very white, with a good deal of tasty, sweet flesh.

ʿinānī (عناني) gourd that is long, thin, and smooth; it grew abundantly in Seville and Cordova.

injāṣī (انجاصي) called so because the gourd looks like a pear.

jirārī (جراري) called so because the gourd looks like a jar.

miʿnāq (معناق) a round variety with a long thin neck.

34 Ibn al-Bayṭār, *al-Jāmiʿ* iii 89–90.

FIGURE 211 Gourd, *qarʿ*, al-Qazwīnī, *ʿAjāʾib al-makhlūqāt wa ghārāʾib al-mawjūdāt*, fol. 190v, detail

BNF, DEPARTMENT OF MANUSCRIPTS, ARAB 2173. SOURCE: GALLICA.BNF.FR/BNF

In al-Tujībī's cookbook, gourd is used as a secondary ingredient, as in recipes i.2.5, 26, and i.5.1, 3, 10. In some recipes it is the principal vegetable in a meat dish, as in recipes ii.2.12, 20. Recipes in chapter vii.1 all deal with meatless gourd dishes.

ghazl al-qarʿ (غزل القرع) young shoots of a gourd vine, chopped and cooked with other vegetables in two *jināniyya* recipes, i.2.26 and vii.9.

shaḥm (شحم) pith, which is the white fibrous center of the gourd, usually discarded.

zarīʿa (زريعة) seeds (of a gourd).

With its cold and moist properties and neutral flavor, *qarʿ* was deemed the perfect food for the sick, especially those with fevers. Oil extracted from its seeds was believed to induce sleep. A pudding made with it, called *fālūdhaj al-qarʿ* in recipe vii.1.11, is touted as a bowel softener.

qaṭaf (قطف) orach, a leaf vegetable of the amaranth family, *Atriplex hortensis*; also known as *sarmaq*, *baql al-Rūm*, and *al-baqla al-dhahabiyya*. It is used only once in al-Tujībī's cookbook, recipe ii.2.11, as an alternative for spinach. The leaves are described as tender and juicy, somewhat mucilaginous, like *mulūkhiyya* 'Jew's mallow,' and a bit salty. With its cold and moist properties, orach was recommended for soothing fevers.[35]

qiththā' (قثاء) snake cucumber, *Cucumis melo var. flexuosus.* In al-Tujībī's cookbook, only the budding snake cucumbers and their young shoots are used in two *jināniyya* dishes, which were prepared and cooked on picnics in orchards, recipes i.2.26 and vii.9.

ghazl al-qiththā' (غزل القثاء) young shoots of snake cucumbers.
'uyūn al qiththā' (عيون القثاء) budding snake cucumbers.

In *al-Filāḥa al-Andalusiyya* iv 361, Ibn al-'Awwām mentions four varieties of *qiththā'*:

1. Dark green, long, and ridged; they grew abundantly in Fez.
2. Yellowish green, long, and ridged; they grew abundantly in Seville.
3. A variety called *qinnabī,* described as speckled, green with black spots, long and thick, and sweet tasting (i.e., free of bitterness).
4. *'Unnāqī,* called so because the cucumber looks like a very long, thin neck; available in the 'Udwa, which is the North African region.

All types of cucumber were said to be weak plants that did not tolerate cold weather and rain.

qiṭniyya bayḍā' (قطنية بيضاء) is *dhura bayḍā',* a white variety of sorghum, *Sorghum bicolor,* also known as great millet. It is cooked as porridge in al-Tujībī's recipe i.5.14.

According to Ibn Manẓūr, *Lisān al-'Arab,* s.v. قطن, *qiṭniyya* is a collective noun for pulses as well as grains other than wheat and barley. Based on al-Tujībī's recipe, it seems that the name specifically designated a white variety of sorghum. According to Ibn al-Bayṭār, *al-Jāmi'* ii 415, the white variety with its heavy grains was deemed the best.

qulqās (قلقاس), *qulqāṣ* (قلقاص), and commoners in al-Andalus called it *qurqāṣ* (قرقاص) taro, *Colocasia esculenta.* It is a tuber described as resembling a coconut from the outside with a white interior. Al-Ghassānī, *Ḥadīqat al-azhār* 233–4, compares the tubers to large turnips, adding that the plant, with its impressively large and lusciously green leaves, was grown in orchards for their physical appeal. He also says that in autumn, the leaves were used for lining trays used in collecting figs picked from the trees.

Only three recipes use taro in al-Tujībī's cookbook; in recipe ii.2.28 it is cooked with meat; in chapter vii.10 it is fried and served as a meatless side dish; and in

35 See Ibn al-Bayṭār, *al-Jāmi'* iv 272.

recipe viii.3 it is cooked with lentils. Due to their slight astringency and considerably sharp taste, only the young tubers, sweet and tender, are used in the dishes; first they would be peeled and then either diced or cut into thin slices. Indeed, their taste is so sharp that al-Ishbīlī, *'Umdat al-ṭabīb* ii 508, warns they could cause swallowing in the mouth that might lead to death by asphyxiation. With their hot and moist properties, taros were deemed the best food taken to help gain weight and arouse coitus.

qunnabīṭ (قنّبيط) cauliflower, *Brassica oleracea var. Botrytis*; used only once in al-Tujībī's cookbook, recipe ii.2.5, where the florets are cooked with meat. The plant is also called *kurunb Shāmī* 'Levantine cabbage,' as it was recognized as a cabbage variety. The head of the cauliflower was said to grow in the middle of the leaves and was described as a round structure composed of a myriad of smaller heads tightly packed together, ranging from large yellow heads to light-yellow medium ones and yellowish-white ones.[36]

Al-Ghāfiqī, *Kitāb al-Adwiya al-mufrada*, fol. 249v, mentions a variety of cauliflower that he says was called *kurunb Mawṣilī* (كرنب موصلي) (i.e., a cabbage variety from the city of Mawṣil in northern Iraq). He gives its Persian name, *kalam* (كلم), which is kohlrabi, *Brassica oleracea*. He says only the bulbous stem (he incorrectly calls it *aṣl* 'root'), which looks like turnip, is eaten.

ra's al-qunnabīṭ (راس القنبيط) head of cauliflower florets, which are separated by hand to cook.

'uslūj al-qunnabīṭ (عسلوج القنبيط) stem or stalk of a cauliflower head.

zahr al-qunnabīṭ (زهر القنبيط), also called ***bayḍ*** (بيض) and ***jummār*** (جمار) florets of cauliflower.

Cauliflower was said to be denser and slower to digest than cabbages. Physicians recommended avoiding the plant altogether, as it was blamed for generating bad quality blood. Overindulgence was blamed for weak eyesight and having bad dreams. They also recommended eating it cooked with meat, or with olive oil or almond oil. The florets were said to generate bloating winds, which would invigorate coitus and facilitate intercourse.[37]

rijla (رجلة), also called *baqla ḥamqā'* (بقلة حمقاء) common purslane, *Portulaca oleracea*. It is a succulent sprawling plant with tiny fruit capsules filled with round seeds. Two cultivated varieties grew in the Muslim West: *rijla Andalusiyya* 'Andalusi purslane'

---

36 Ibn al-'Awwām, *al-Filāḥa al-Andalusiyya* iv 291, copying Ibn Waḥshiyya, *al-Filāḥa al-Nabaṭiyya*.

37 Al-Ghāfiqī, *Kitāb al-Adwiya al-mufrada*, fol. 249v.

FIGURE 212 Chard, Dioscorides, *Fī Hayūlā al-ṭibb*, translation by Ḥunayn b. Isḥāq, fol. 101v, detail
FROM THE NEW YORK PUBLIC LIBRARY, SPENCER COLLECTION: HTTPS://DIGITALCOLLECTIONS.NYPL.ORG/ITEMS/5E66B3E9-0452-D471-E040-E00A180654D7

and *rijla Miṣriyya* 'Egyptian purslane.' The latter was deemed the most delicious of all cultivated varieties.[38]

Purslane is used just a few times in al-Tujībī's cookbook; in recipes ii.2.13 and ii.4.1, as the main vegetable in meat dishes; and recipe vii.9, as a meatless dish with several other vegetables. In cooking the dishes, only fresh and young purslane that has not seeded yet is used.

luʿāb (لعاب) the mucilaginous substance in purslane leaves. After chopping purslane, cooks are instructed in recipe ii.2.13 to get rid of its mucilage by rubbing it gently between the hands with some salt.

With its cooling effect on the body, purslane and its seeds were believed to quench thirst and relieve fevers and headaches. Overindulgence was blamed for causing the loss of the two appetites (food and sex) and dimming vision.[39]

silq (سلق) chard, *Beta vulgaris subsp. vulgaris.* It was a well-known vegetable, of which there were several kinds distinguished by their size and color:

silq abyaḍ (سلق ابيض), literally 'white chard,' on account of its light-green leaves, which grew on long stems and were narrow and not wrinkled. It was a medium-sized variety.[40]

38 Al-Ṭighnarī, ed. García Sánchez, *Zahrat al-bustān* 494–5.
39 Al-Anṭākī, *Tadhkira* 86–7.
40 See Ibn al-ʿAwwām, *al-Filāḥa al-Andalusiyya* iv 297; and al-Ṭighnarī, ed. García Sánchez, *Zahrat al-bustān* 502.

silq aswad (سلق اسود), literally 'black chard,' called so on account of its dark-green leaves. Of this variety, there was chard characterized by its nice-looking leaves that were tender, large, and wide; there was also the small chard variety, with its small wrinkled leaves that were not as intensely green as the large ones.

Chard is used sparingly in al-Tujībī's cookbook. In a meat stew, recipe ii.2.6, only the midribs of the leaves are used, and before adding them to the cooking meat, they are cut and boiled in salted water first to get rid of their brackish properties (*būraqiyya*) as the recipe explains.[41] To color a *tafāyā* stew green, recipe ii.2.2, chard leaves are pounded and their juice is pressed out and used; and the tender inner leaves (*qulūb silq*) are used along with many other ingredients to stuff tripe in recipe iv.2.

aḍlāʿ al-silq (اضلاع السلق) midribs of chard leaves.

Chard was regarded as a good source of food when prepared the right way to get rid of its brackish properties, such as cooking it with oil, vinegar, mustard, and caraway seeds. Otherwise, chard would generate bad blood and cause bloating and gurgles.

tirfās (ترفاس) desert truffles, *Terfeziaceae*. Al-Ghassānī, *Ḥadīqat al-azhār* 144, says that this was its name among the commoners in the Muslim West; and its Amazigh origin was well recognized.[42] Otherwise, truffles were more commonly known by their Arabic name ***kam'a*** (كمأة) in the eastern region; physicians and botanists from both regions called it this.

Desert truffles grow naturally in arid and semiarid areas with hot climates and sandy soils, and they are collected in the springtime. In books on botany they were described as rounded roots,[43] with neither stem nor leaves, and were white, red, or black. They were also said to be high in moisture, with an insipid flavor (*tafih*).[44] Numerous varieties of the desert truffles were known but the most prized ones were the smooth fair-colored ones with a dense texture. The less dense ones that were soft and moist were said to be of bad quality.[45]

In al-Tujībī's cookbook, truffles are cooked with meat, such as in recipes i.2.8, ii.2.19, ii.3.4, and ii.4.1. In chapter vii.4, they are the main ingredient in meatless

---

41 The brackish mineral in chard is sodium bicarbonate, *būraq* in Arabic.

42 See, for instance, al-Ishbīlī, *ʿUmdat al-ṭabīb* i 324; and Ibn al-Bayṭār, *al-Jāmiʿ* i 188, who calls it *tirfāsh*.

43 We now know that a truffle is a fungus growing underground.

44 They have little flavor of their own compared to the pungent European truffles. Desert truffles absorb the flavors of the liquids used in preparing and cooking them.

45 Al-Ishbīlī, *ʿUmdat al-ṭabīb* 324–7, mentions many varieties in his entry on this plant.

FIGURE 213 Blite, *yarbūz*, Dioscorides, *Ajzāʾ min risāla fī l-nabātāt*, fol. 31r, detail
BNF, DEPARTMENT OF MANUSCRIPTS, ARAB 4947. SOURCE: GALLICA.BNF.FR/BNF

dishes; variously prepared. They are baked in a casserole, boiled, and roasted. Interestingly, in preparing them for the pot, after they are cleaned and washed well, the cook is instructed to break them into pieces by hand, not with a knife.[46]

With their cold and moist properties, truffles were said to cause heaviness in the stomach and were slow to digest. To remedy them, averting their harm and facilitating their digestion, they had to be cooked and eaten with a good deal of olive oil,

46 To my knowledge, this is mentioned only in al-Tujībī's cookbook. Given the insipid flavor of desert truffles, my guess is that compared with the evenly cut pieces using a knife, the irregularly shaped truffle pieces broken by hand create a lot of uneven edges that would absorb much more of the flavors of the liquids in which they are being cooked.

and seasoned with fermented sauce of *murrī*, mustard, and thyme; spices with hot properties, such as black pepper and cinnamon, were also recommended.[47]

Interestingly, from the twelfth-century Sevillian book on market inspection by Ibn ʿAbdūn, *Risāla fī l-Qaḍāʾ wa-l-ḥisba* 43, we get the impression that truffles did not seem to be an essential food item or even a respectable one. He describes it as frivolous food of the shameless and the licentious (*fākihat al-khullāʿ*), adding that they should not be served in the vicinity of a mosque. My guess is that truffles were possibly popular as one of the fun foods people had as snacks (*naql*) during drinking sessions, in the manner of what we call mezza today.

ukrunb (اكرنب) cabbages, see *kurunb* above.

yarbūz (يربوز) blite, which is a variety of wild amaranth, *Amaranthum blitum*. This was its regional name in the Muslim West. Otherwise, it was called *baqla Yamāniyya* (بقلة يمانية) 'Yemeni vegetable,' and *baqla ʿArabiyya* (بقلة عربية) in other regions. This summer leaf vegetable has a high liquid content, with no distinguished flavor of its own. In al-Tujībī's cookbook, it is cooked like any other leafy vegetable, such as spinach and lettuce, by incorporating it into meat dishes, as in recipes ii.2.11, ii.3.16, and ii.4.1; and meatless ones, as in chapter vii.8.

Consumed as food, *yarbūz* was said to generate good humors; and with its moist and cold properties, it was also useful in alleviating thirst and benefitting people with fevers. To relieve heatstrokes, its juice was mixed with oil infused with rose petals (*duhn al-ward*). It also worked as a laxative.[48]

47 See Ibn al-Bayṭār, *al-Jāmiʿ* iv 343–4.

48 See Ibn al-Bayṭār, *al-Jāmiʿ* i 142.

13. Weights and Measures

Weights and measures in al-Tujībī's book are sparingly used in recipes dealing with savory dishes, as opposed to desserts, where ratios of honey and starch, for instance, are needed to ensure the right consistency; or recipes dealing with more laborious and lengthy preparations, such as making vinegar and fermented sauce of *murrī*. The right measurements in such cases are critical, making or breaking them. In part xii for handwashing preparations, weights are given throughout as they deal with aromatic compounds that require specialized knowledge and practice, especially if we know that the chapter was copied from *Kitāb fī Funūn al-ṭīb wa-l-ʿiṭr* by the famous physician Ibn al-Jazzār, see introduction i.3, p. 22

Modern equivalents of medieval weights and measures are approximate. Some of the medieval weights had different values in different parts of the Islamic world. In giving modern equivalents, ounces and pounds are used. Small weights measuring less than an ounce are more conveniently given in grams. Liquid measurements are given in terms of a pint (= 2 cups) and a cup (= 16 tablespoons).

dirham (درهم) = 3 grams = ½ teaspoon
mithqāl (مثقال) = 4½ grams
ūqiyya (اوقية) = approx. 1 ounce

¼ ***ūqiyya*** = approx. 8 grams
½ ***ūqiyya*** = approx. 15 grams

raṭl (رطل) = approx. 1 pound
mudd (مد) = approx. 2 pounds[1]
qadaḥ (قدح) = 2¼ pounds or pints
rubʿ (ربع) = 8¾ pounds or pints[2]
qādūs (قادوس) an earthenware vessel, also used as a capacity measure that equals 3 *mudds* (each *mudd* equals approx. 2 *raṭl*s/pounds).
qafīz (قفيز) = 60 pounds

1 It is said to be a capacity measure of what both hands put together would hold. See, for instance, Abū al-ʿAbbās al-Sabtī, *Ḥaqīqat al-dīnār wa-l-dirham* 126.

2 Literally 'quarter,' calculated as a quarter of the weight measure *wayba* ويبة, which is 16 kilograms. Al-Suyūṭī, *Ḥusn al-muḥāḍara* ii 321, mentions that one *rubʿ* equals 4 qadaḥs and that each *qadaḥ* equals 232 *dirhams*.

 | DOI:10.1163/9789004469488_079

FIGURE 214 A pair of scales, al-Qazwīnī, *ʿAjāʾib al-makhlūqāt wa gharāʾib al-mawjūdāt*, fol. 28r, detail
BNF, DEPARTMENT OF MANUSCRIPTS, ARAB 2178. SOURCE: GALLICA.BNF.FR/BNF

Approximate Weight and Length Measures:

arbaʿat aṣābiʿ (اربعة اصابع) width of four fingers put together.
gharfa (غرفة) a scoop taken with a ladle or by hand.
ḥajm al-dīnār (حجم الدينار) size of a *dīnār*, which is a gold coin about 0.75 inch in diameter.[3] It is used in recipe i.2.11 to measure the approximate size of broken pieces of bread.
juzʾ (جزء), pl. ***ajzāʾ*** (اجزاء) parts given in ratios, as in recipe i.4.21, where the ratio of honey to water is 1 to 3; or recipe x.5.1, where the ratio of vinegar to water is 2 to 1.
kaff (كف) a handful, which is as much as the cupped hand would grasp or contain.
mighrafa (مغرفة) a ladleful, approx. ½ cup capacity.
mighrafa ṣaghīra (مغرفة صغيرة) a small ladleful.
qabḍa (قبضة) a fistful, which is the amount that a closed fist would hold.
shibr (شبر) a span, the distance between the stretched little finger and thumb, approx. 9 inches.
siʿat iṣabʿayn (سعة اصبعين) width of two fingers put together.
siʿat thalāthat aṣābiʿ (سعة ثلاثة اصابع) width of three fingers put together.

3 For dinar, the gold coin, see, for instance, https://www.qantara-med.org/public/show_document.php?do_id=634&lang=en, accessed Jan. 18, 2020.

APPENDIX 1

Bunk, the Mystery Ingredient

Bunk (بنك) is an indeterminate ingredient used in hand-cleansing and aromatic preparations in medieval Arabic sources, including cookbooks, medicinal and dietary books, and those dealing with botany and perfumes and other scented preparations.

In al-Tujībī's cookbook, it is used in most of the handwashing preparations, *ghāsūlāt*, given in part xii. His source for this chapter was Ibn al-Jazzār's tenth-century book on perfumes and aromatics, *Kitāb fī Funūn al-ṭīb wa-l-ʿiṭr* 117–20.[1] The only other extant medieval Arabic cookbook that has *bunk* recipes is the tenth-century text by al-Warrāq, *Kitāb al-Ṭabīkh*, English trans., *Annals*, with its four recipes in chapter 129 that deal with handwashing preparations, including *bunk muṭayyab*, which is *bunk* scented and enhanced by mixing it with other aromatics. In these recipes, good quality *bunk* is required, the preferred variety of which, according to al-Warrāq, is described as Iraqi, yellow, and lightweight (*bunk aṣfar khafīf ʿIrāqī*). In addition, al-Warrāq's recipes refer to the preparation as *bunk muḥammaṣ*, which is descriptive of slow parching or toasting ingredients on low heat while constantly stirring, a process with which we are familiar today as when roasting coffee beans, for instance.[2]

In al-Warrāq's recipes, the term *bunk* designates the ingredient as well as the preparation. In verses quoted in his chapter that are accredited to the famous Abbasid poet and gastronome, Kushājim (d. 961), a *bunk* preparation is described, from which we learn that it was musk colored (i.e., dark reddish brown) and silk smooth in texture:

> *Bunk* obliterates greasy smells of food on hands and whatever of sweets and fats.
> Whether traveling or at home, neglect not to wash your hands with it when the nimble server passes around with it.
> Nothing surpasses *bunk* to wash the hands after having a fragrant, scrumptious meal.
> Like musk in color,[3] and soft as silk on the hands and face.

---

1 Ibn al-Jazzār was a famous physician from al-Qayrawān (in Tunisia today) in the Maghreb.

2 Parching is generally recognized as a way to bring out the aromas of spices and other ingredients. In addition, that *bunk* was also supposed to be used already parched is confirmed in Ibn al-Jazzār's usage, *Kitāb fī Funūn al-ṭīb wa-l-ʿiṭr* 104; except he uses the term *maqlū*, which in this context means 'dry fried in a pan,' i.e., 'toasted,' 'parched.'

3 I.e., dark reddish brown.

 | DOI:10.1163/9789004469488_080

FIGURE 215
Umm ghaylān, al-ʿUmarī, *Masālik al-abṣār*, fol. 227v, detail
BNF, DEPARTMENT OF MANUSCRIPTS, ARAB 2771. SOURCE: GALLICA.BNF.FR/BNF

> I could not care less for *ushnān* if *bunk* is within reach; as for cyperus, I would wish it well in hell.[4]

From other books contemporary with al-Warrāq's, we learn that besides hand-cleansing preparations, *bunk* was incorporated into other compounds, like *dharīra* (perfumed and incensed body powder), *adhān* (body oils), *musūḥ* (ointments), and *lakhlakha* (potpourri).[5]

Now, as to what *bunk* might possibly be: while on the one hand it seems to have been a quite familiar ingredient in medieval preparations, on the other, nobody was quite clear as to what precisely it was. In the medieval lexicons, it is vocalized as بُنْك and frustratingly defined as a well-known aromatic ingredient *ṭīb maʿrūf*; some say it is a word of Arabic origin, while others see it as a loan word.[6] It is even mistakenly described as an Arabized rendition of *binj*, which is henbane.[7]

1. The following are citations and descriptions of *bunk*, which I garnered from the early medieval documents (chronologically enlisted):

4 *Ushnān* designates a handwashing compound made with potash, see entry in glossary 11. Cyperus (*suʿd*) are sweet-smelling astringent tubers also used in handwashing preparations, see entry in glossary 8.

5 As in Ibn al-Jazzār, *Kitāb fī Funūn al-ṭīb wa-l-ʿiṭr*; al-Tamīmī, *Ṭīb al-ʿarūs*; and al-Kindī, *al-Taraffuq fī l-ʿiṭr* 72 and 79.

6 Of the other meanings given to *bunk* in lexicons: 'base,' 'purest part' of a thing, 'origin,' 'a night hour,' and 'settle at a place.' All irrelevant to our ingredient.

7 See, for instance, al-Zabīdī, *Tāj al-ʿarūs*, s.v. بنك.

1.1. The description of *bunk* in the treatise on aromatic substances *Jawāhir al-ṭīb al-mufrada*, fols. 31v and 42r, by the Abbasid physician Ibn Māsawayh (d. 857), is perhaps one of the earliest surviving records we have where *bunk* is mentioned. In it, Ibn Māsawayh includes *bunk* in his list of secondary aromatics (*al-afāwīh*).[8] He describes it as follows,

> *Bunk* is a variety brought from Yemen. The best is yellow, light, and aromatic; white *bunk* is no good. It is said that it is wood of the tree *umm ghaylān* (ام غيلان) that falls there and gets worm-eaten and shreds. It comes from the trunk of the tree; it is used in making women's dry aromatic compounds; and it looks like the inside of the worm-damaged base of the date palm frond, *karab al-nakhl*.

1.2. Another contemporary of Ibn Māsawayh is Abū Ḥanīfa al-Dīnawarī (d. 895), founder of Arabic botany, who was frequently quoted by his successors. In his book on plants, *Kitāb al-Nabāt* 87, he mentions that *umm ghaylān* (ام غيلان) is the commoners' name for *ṭalḥ* (طلح), a variety of acacia, *Acacia gummifera*.
1.3. Al-Rāzī (d. 925), *al-Ḥāwī* vii 9, on the other hand, mentions only *bunk al-ās* (بنك الآس), which he describes as a kind of hand-shaped growth that appears on the trunk of the myrtle tree, adding that it is astringent in properties. In a separate entry, and without associating it with *bunk*, he mentions *umm ghaylān* as an astringent ingredient that can dry up humidities in the womb and in cases of hemoptysis (*nafth al-damm*). In his other book, *al-Manṣūrī*, fol. 45v, in a section on aromatics, he briefly mentions *bunk* as an ingredient that is hot and dry in properties and can check unpleasant odors of sweat and the depilatory *nūrā* 'quick lime.'[9]
1.4. Ibn Buklārish (d. 1107), in *al-Mustaʿīnī*, fol. 17r–v, follows al-Rāzī by identifying *bunk* as *bunk al-ās*, mentioned in the above point, claiming that the other physicians misidentified it.
1.5. Ibn al-Jazzār (d. 980) in his *Kitāb fī Funūn al-ṭīb wa-l-ʿiṭr*, from which al-Tujībī copied his chapter on handwashing preparations, frequently uses *bunk* in his recipes, which call for the yellow variety (*bunk aṣfar*); no further details are given. In one recipe, he refers to it as bunk *maqlū*, synonymous with *muḥammaṣ* 'parched,' which is an indication that it was used already parched, most probably to bring out its aroma.

---

8 The primary ingredients being musk, ambergris, aloeswood, camphor, and saffron. Ibn Māsawayh's treatise was translated into English by Martin Levey, *Ibn Māsawaih and His Treatise on Simple Aromatic Substances*.

9 Ibn al-Quff (d. 1286), *Jāmiʿ al-gharaḍ* 382–3, explains that this can be done by rubbing the skin with pounded *bunk*.

1.6. Al-Tamīmī (d. 1000), in *Ṭīb al-ʿarūs*, uses *bunk* in many of his preparations and refers to it as *aṣfar* 'yellow,' *ʿUthrī* 'Yemeni,' and *ṭawāmīr* 'paper-thin pieces,' with no further descriptions.

1.7. Andalusi physician al-Zahrāwī (d. after 1013), *Kitāb al-Taṣrīf* 274 and 279, includes *bunk* in his list of aromatic ingredients, the best of which is described as yellow and looks like shaved wood in that it is lightweight, brittle, and soft. Heavy *bunk* is said to be inferior.

1.8. Ibn Sīnā (d. 1037), in *al-Qānūn* i 394–5, offers some more interesting details, although those pertaining to its identity sound less assured than those on what it was used for and its effects:

> *Bunk* is something (شيء) brought from India and Yemen. Some say it is from the trunks of an *umm ghaylān* tree that got worm-eaten and fell. Yellow *bunk* that is lightweight and sweet smelling is the best. White and heavy *bunk* (*abyaḍ razīn*) is inferior. *Bunk* is hot and dry in properties, but some say it is cold. It invigorates the organs; it purifies the skin and dries up humidities underneath it. It sweetens body odors and checks odors of the depilatory *nūrā* 'quick lime'; it is also good for the stomach. It confuses the mind and intellect (يشوش الذهن والعقل).

1.9. Al-Bīrūnī (d. 1048), in *al-Ṣaydana* 99, while largely repeating the aforementioned information, adds some new tidbits: it is the Latin *nasqafthan*,[10] and *bunk* is its Persian name. *Bunk* brought from Yemen is called *ʿUmānī*, and it grows abundantly in the southern regions of the Arabian Peninsula. Choice *bunk* is brought from India, where it is said to be worm-eaten flakes that fall from sandalwood trees, *nakhr al-ṣandal* (نخر الصندل), the best of which are the yellow pieces that can be easily pierced.

1.10. Al-Ghāfiqī (d. 1165), in *Kitāb fī l-Adwiya al-mufrada*, fol. 68r, based his description of *bunk* on his predecessors' comments. His additions include: *bunk* looks like the bark of the mulberry tree;[11] it is burnt by itself as incense for its aromatic smoke, as well as incorporated with other ingredients to make incense compounds, *akhlāṭ al-dukhn al-murakkaba* (أخلاط الدخن المركبة). Women use it to fumigate their private parts, as this was believed to help contract the *fam al-riḥm* (فم الرحم) 'external os'[12] that has suffered dryness. Of its other medicinal benefits, it strengthens a cold stomach and the liver, whether used internally or externally in poultices.[13]

---

10 It could be a reference to the ancient drug nepenthe, mentioned in the *Odyssey* as a remedy for grief, something that eases the pain of sorrow; still unidentified.

11 The bark of the mulberry tree is flaky.

12 It is the uterine cervix's opening into the vagina.

13 Ibn al-Quff (d. 1286), *Jāmiʿ al-gharaḍ* 383, adds that consuming it can also mask the odors of garlic, onions, and alcoholic drinks.

FIGURE 216 *Bunk*, al-Ghāfiqī, *Kitāb al-Adwiya al-mufrada*, MS, fol. 58r, detail

In another entry in al-Ghāfiqī's book, fols. 228v–229r, quoting Abū Ḥanīfa al-Dīnawarī (mentioned in point 1.2 above) on a tree called *ṭalḥ, Umm ghaylān* (*Acacia gummifera*) is said to be another name for it. It is described as a large tree with a good deal of leaves; its spikes are not as large as those of other acacia varieties and are the least harmful, with sweet-smelling white blossoms. Its pods are large and look like those of fava beans; they are eaten by sheep and camels. The tree produces a good deal of thick gum resin that forms large lumps. Ropes are made with its fiber, and its wood is hard and of a good quality. He also adds that a sticky sweet-tasting and sweet-smelling substance forms between its sapwood and bark, which people love to suck on as a breath freshener. Additionally, on the bark there appears something sticking to it like gum, *ṣamgh* (soluble hardened sap), but it is not it. People dislodge it from the bark. They throw away the red substance they find in it and wash it and chew it; it makes the best chewing gum (*lubān*, also called *ʿilk*), the whitest and the most elastic.

FIGURE 217
Sanṭ tree, al-ʿUmarī, *Masālik al-abṣār*, fol. 275v, detail
BNF, DEPARTMENT OF MANUSCRIPTS, ARAB 2771. SOURCE: GALLICA.BNF.FR/BNF

1.11. Egyptian physician al-ʿAṭṭār al-Hārūnī (d. after 1260), in his *Kitāb Minhāj al-dukkān* 214, describes *bunk* with more confidence than the rest, as he assuredly tells us that he had it in his possession (وكان عندي) and describes it as follows based on his first-hand experience:

> It is wood that looks like brownish yellow sandalwood; it is an aromatic ingredient and is capable of absorbing others' aromas. It is brought from India, and although it is called *bunk Miṣrī* 'Egyptian,' it is not really from Egypt. It is called so because it is scented and enhanced by mixing it with other aromatics, *yuṭayyab*, in Egypt, and then used.

2. Clearly, the aforementioned allusions to *bunk* do not seem to be describing one ingredient in particular. While some describe it as having hot and dry properties, others say it is cold and dry; and while some describe it as wood shreds that are said (يقال) to be from *umm ghaylān* tree, others hint at the possibility that the sandalwood tree might be the source for these shreds; and still others claim it is a growth on the trunks of myrtle trees. In addition, the source for *bunk* is said to not only be Yemen but also India and Iraq. The best is said to be yellow and light, whereas white and heavy shreds are said to be of a bad quality. *Bunk* is also described as a kind of mind-altering substance, at least in the opinion of Ibn Sīnā. So what is *bunk*?

FIGURE 218
Samura tree, al-ʿUmarī, *Masālik al-abṣār*, fol. 241r, detail
BNF, DEPARTMENT OF MANUSCRIPTS, ARAB 2771. SOURCE: GALLICA.BNF.FR/BNF

Apparently, the name *bunk* was used as a kind of blanket term that covered more than one object, and accounts of it varied largely depending on where and who wrote them:

2.1. *Bunk* as shreds of acacia bark:

In the medieval botanical and medical records, *bunk* is associated with acacia. It is an ancient tree, valued for its timber, resin, leaves, and pods that fed their animals. Its bark, roots, and blossoms were used for medicinal purposes, as well as in aromatics and incense. Acacia is also known to contain psychoactive alkaloids (DMT) in varying degrees, depending on the species. This indeed confirms Ibn Sīnā's description of *bunk* as a mind-altering ingredient, mentioned in 1.8 above.

The medieval sources in particular associate *bunk* with *umm ghaylān*, a species of acacia. This association, however, does not seem to be based on first-hand knowledge; the expression usually used is *yuqāl annahu* (يقال انه) 'it is said to be'; the source is not specified. On the other hand, none of the *umm ghaylān* entries in these medieval sources connect it with *bunk*, even when both are included in the same book. My guess is that this was the case because *bunk* was obtained from several acacia sources:

> 2.1.1. *Bunk* obtained from *umm ghaylān* in Yemen: The tree frequently said to be the source for Yemeni *bunk* is *umm ghaylān*, which is a variety of acacia,[14] see al-Ghāfiqī, point 1.10 above. It is a wild variety of acacia, *sanṭ barrī* (سنط بري), also called *ṭalḥ* (طلح), *Acacia gummifera Wild.* Another Yemeni tree that is a variant of

14 Hundreds of acacia species grow throughout the world. The genus for acacia in Arabic is

umm ghaylān is *samur* (سمر), *Acacia tortilis*, with highly aromatic white blossoms, rough fissured bark, and good-quality aromatic and edible gum. It is also called the menstruating tree because the resin it oozes looks like blood.[15]

In the extant recipes incorporating *bunk*, the good quality variety is described as *aṣfar*, which generally designates 'yellow' but may also describe yellowish-black *aswad musharrab ṣufra*, which indeed is descriptive of the bark shreds of acacia trees.

2.1.2. *Bunk* obtained from Iraq, *bunk ʿIrāqī*, could be the acacia tree called *ṭalḥ ʿIrāqī* (طلح عراقي), *Acacia gerradii* (S). It grows sweet-smelling white blossoms and has darkish fissured bark. Based on al-Warrāq's *bunk* recipes, good-quality *bunk* is obtained from it.

2.1.3. *Bunk*, described as white, *bunk abyaḍ*, was said to be an inferior variety. Generally, *abyaḍ* designates whiteness, but it was also used to designate light hues. Possibly, white *bunk* was obtained from the acacia species *sanṭ abyaḍ* (سنط ابيض), *Acacia albida*, which is native to the Middle East and Africa. The tree has pale-colored branches and grey bark that fissure when the tree gets old. *Acacia albida* was mentioned by Pliny the Elder (d. 79 AD) in *Natural History* xiii, chapter 19. Comparing it with dark-wooded acacia species, he says the white variety "will rot very rapidly," which explains why using it for *bunk* in medieval times was not recommended.

2.1.4. *Bunk* from India is the acacia variety *Acacia nilotica*, called the gum arabic tree, thorn mimosa, and Egyptian acacia; in Arabic, *qaraẓ* (قرظ), *shawka Miṣriyya* (شوكة مصرية), and *sanṭ ʿArabī* (سنط عربي). In India, it is called *babool/babul* and the Indian gum arabic tree. The tree has a fissured dark brown bark, which exudes the edible gum arabic, and scented blossoms.[16]

2.2. *Bunk* is also said to be the worm-eaten flakes that fall from the sandalwood trees, *nakhr al-ṣandal*, in India, see al-Bīrūnī 1.9 above.

---

sanṭ (سنط), which is ultimately derived from the Akkadian 'samṭu,' see Thompson, *Assyrian Botany* 184. In ancient Egyptian, it was 'shndt,' see Manniche *Ancient Egyptian Herbal* 65.

15 Other varieties of acacia that have been growing in Yemen and are valued for their resin and timber are: *Acacia asak*, *ʿasaq* (عسق) in Arabic; and *Acacia mellifera*, also known as *A. seyal* or *A. Senegal*, called *sanṭ muʿassal* (سنط معسل) and *sanṭ sayyāl* (سنط سيال) in Arabic, commonly referred to as the 'gum tree' in English. Based on a private correspondence with Dr. Hanne Schönig, coeditor of *Herbal Medicine in Yemen*.

16 I managed to get hold of some babul to check for aroma and texture. The bark is indeed brittle and emits a faint aroma; parching produced a stronger aroma. Rubbing my hands with finely ground babul helped remove a garlicky smell and my skin felt smooth.

2.3. Moreover, we come across *bunk al-ās*, a kind of growth that appears on the trunks of myrtle trees, mentioned by al-Rāzī and al-Mustaʿīnī, as mentioned above in 1.3 and 1.4.

2.4. There is also the possibility that *bunk* obtained from Yemen could have been *qishr al-bunn* (قشر البن) husks of coffee beans:

In my previous translation of al-Warrāq's cookbook,[17] I presented *bunk* as parched shreds of coffee beans and husks; it was a guess inspired by William Ukers's discussion of the beginnings of coffee history.[18] Although hard evidence is not available to us today regarding the beginnings of the consumption of coffee as a hot brewed beverage in Yemen, called *qahwa*, prior to its spread in the fifteenth century,[19] it is not difficult to trace the availability of coffee beans, called *bunn* (بنّ) in that region. Archaeological findings in 2004 and 2005 by an American and French team have already established "an ancient botanical origin" in Bonga, the birthplace of Arabica coffee in southwestern Ethiopia.[20] As to how and when the coffee plant spread to Yemen, this must have happened in the sixth century when Ethiopia invaded the Himyarite Kingdom in Yemen.[21]

It is my assumption that the coffee plant *bunn*, with its hot and dry properties and astringency, though still unrecognizable outside Yemen at the time, was exported from there as shreds of husks, which passed for *bunk*, and was used for its medicinal benefits and pleasant aroma when parched and mixed with various other ingredients. One of the benefits of *bunk* as an ingredient in the prepared hand-cleansing compounds is that it has the capacity to absorb odors, as was pointed out by al-ʿAṭṭār al-Hārūnī, see 1.11 above. In light of what we now know about coffee, this observation holds true.[22] Additionally, the effects of coffee on the mind might also explain Ibn Sīnā's observation about the psychotic effect of *bunk*, describing it as *mushawwish* (see 1.8 above).

---

17 English trans., *Annals* 766–9. I have to point out here that I have been having second thoughts about the interpretation I suggested for a sixth-century line of verse (قهوة مرة بماء سخين) as "a hot bitter brew of coffee," which of course is perfectly acceptable if we are sure the *qahwa* being referred to here is indeed coffee. There is a possibility that the poet was referring to dark, bitter wine, also called *qahwa*, which was offered to him heated in the Roman style while he was visiting Damascus.

18 Ukers, *All About Coffee* 8.

19 Note that preparing coffee as a beverage with the roasted coffee beans themselves was a late development. In its early stages, what was called *qahwa* was brewed with the parched husks of coffee berries, called *qishr*. Here is a line of verse by the seventeenth-century Cairene scholar Zayn al-ʿĀbidīn al-Bakrī that describes coffee brewed this way, cited by al-Qāsimī *Risāla fī l-Shāi wa-l-qahwa* 25: "We boil the husk (*qishr*) and it comes out / As dark as ink, redolent with the aroma of musk."

20 See Koehler, *Where the Wild Coffee Grows* 49; and Fregulia, *A Rich and Tantalizing Brew* 48.

21 See Fregulia, *A Rich and Tantalizing Brew* 45.

22 People these days are using coffee grounds as a fridge deodorizer and an air freshener; they are also rubbing their hands with them to get rid of the odors of garlic, onion, fish,

In support of the possibility that coffee beans and husks might indeed have been one of the ingredients that passed for *bunk*, I mention here by way of analogy the early history of the beverage tea, *shāi*, which was only known late in the Arabo-Muslim world, even much later than coffee, but in reality, it was used much earlier for its medicinal properties. As early as the eleventh century, al-Bīrūnī, *al-Ṣaydana* 128–9, describes a plant he calls *chai* (چاي), which is its Chinese name he says. It is in fact tea, which was still a mysterious plant in the Arabo-Muslim world but was imported and used for its medicinal benefits. With its cold properties, it was believed to soothe headaches, as we learn from Ibn Jazla (d. 1100), *Minhāj al-bayān*, fol. 129r, who calls it *shāh Ṣīnī* (شاه صيني) because it came from China. Ibn al-Bayṭār (d. 1248) mentions that it was medicine imported to the region in the form of thin black sheets, which were used to treat headaches by taking it internally, and that it was used to treat heat-related swellings by applying it topically.[23] As late as the sixteenth century, and as described by al-Anṭākī, *Tadhkira* 226, tea was still used in similar ways, medicinally as a drink and topically as an emollient and body powder, *dharūr*.

In light of the above, associating *bunk* with coffee is not as outlandish an idea as some might make it sound.[24] Even the origin of the name of this elusive ingredient, *bunk*, hitherto unexplained, might originally have stemmed from the coffee tree and its beans back in the sixth century when the tree was transported to Yemen from Ethiopia, as mentioned earlier; from the southwestern region called Bonga. It is highly likely that

---

and the like. I tried it myself, and it works. I even had a pleasant experiment with the coffee husks. After parching them, I ground them finely and rubbed my hands with some of it after chopping garlic, and they felt smooth as silk and the odor disappeared.

23 Ibn al-Bayṭār, *al-Jāmiʿ* iii 64.

24 As in Charles Perry, "*Ushnān* and Perfuming the Banquet" 247, n. 19. In his article, Perry strongly rejects my coffee proposition,

"Nawal Nasrallah contends that *bunk* is the earlier form of *bunn* … and rewrites the *bunk* recipes to go with her vision of people washing themselves with coffee grounds …. [T]his identification is implausible for linguistic reasons and the descriptions of *bunk* do not at all accord with coffee beans."

"Washing themselves with coffee grounds" does not at all accurately reflect how *bunk*, be it coffee or acacia, was supposed to be used by the medieval handwashers. First of all, based on the extant recipes, *bunk* the ingredient is never used by itself; it is always mixed with a myriad of spices, herbs, and oils. Second, *bunk* compounds were not meant to replace soap or *ushnān*; rather, they were offered after using these, to further purify the hands by getting rid of all remaining greasy odors. Al-Warrāq, *Kitāb al-Ṭabīkh*, English trans., *Annals* 505, explains the proper way hands were supposed to be cleaned, beginning with *ushnān* to wash them, followed by a fresh amount of *ushnān* and *maḥlab* (an aromatic compound made with the kernels of pits of a variety of small black cherries) to wash the mouth, and then *bunk* was offered, sometimes with *suʿd* (cyperus), to remove food odors altogether.

the new coffee tree in Yemen was given the name *bunk*[25] after the region where it came from,[26] and the name persisted to cover other similar woodsy shreds of ingredients.

To sum up, depending on which plant is meant by *bunk*, it either has cold and dry properties, like acacia and *bunk* from the myrtle tree, or hot and dry ones, like the husks of coffee beans. They are all astringent. Besides using *bunk* in hand-cleansing compounds, it was also valued for its medicinal benefits and burnt as incense. The acacia plant is also known to contain some psychoactive alkaloids (DMT) in varying degrees, depending on the species, which supports Ibn Sīnā's description of *bunk* as a mind-altering substance. As for coffee, it does indeed have caffeine, which is a stimulant and a psychoactive substance that affects how one thinks and feels; causing agitation, irritability, and anxiety if consumed in excess.

25 Arabic does not have the *g* sound; it is usually converted to *k*.

26 In Ethiopic coffee beans are called *buno*/*buna*/*bunna*; cf. Arabic *bunn*.

APPENDIX 2

In the Kitchen with Ibn Razīn al-Tujībī: Modern Adaptations of Twenty-four Recipes from *Fiḍālat al-Khiwān*

(*Photography by Nawal Nasrallah*)

MENU:

Seasoning Condiments:

1. *Khall al-Ḥiṣrim* (preserved juice of unripe grapes), recipe x.7.14.
2. *Murrī Maṭbūkh* (nonfermented cooked liquid sauce), recipe x.8.6.

Snack Foods and Side Dishes:

3. *Shīrāz* (a dish of thick drained yogurt), recipe vi.1.2.
4. *Fūl Ziryābī*, also called *Rās Barṭāl* (sparrow's head), recipe viii.1.7.
5. *Fūl Akhḍar Maqlī* (fried fresh fava beans), recipe viii.1.2.
6. *Isfarāj Maṣlūq* (boiled asparagus), recipe vii.5.
7. *Isfanākh Maṭbūkh* (spinach cooked with almonds), recipe vii.8.1.
8. *Fuṭr Mukhammar* (mushrooms topped with eggs), recipe vii.7.
9. *Bādhinjān Muṭajjan* (oven-braised eggplant), recipe vii.2.9.
10. *Qarʿ* (skillet zucchini dish topped with almonds), recipe vii.1.1.
11. *Aqrāṣ Samak* (fish cakes), recipe v.1.4.

Main Dishes:

12. *Tafāyā Khaḍrāʾ* (green lamb stew), recipe ii.2.2.
13. *Kuskusū Min Ghayr Saqī*, called *Ghassānī* (couscous that is not drenched in broth), recipe i.5.3.
14. *Isfarāj Muṭajjan* (oven-baked asparagus with lamb), recipe ii.2.14.
15. *Tharīda Tuzīd fī l-Bāh* (chicken dish with bread for invigorating coitus), recipe i.2.14.
16. *Dajājat ʿUumrūs* (comforting chicken dish), recipe iii.2.20.
17. *Tharīda Min al-Laban al-Ḥalīb, Maṭbūkh fī l-Furn* (oven-baked bread dish with milk), recipe i.2.23.
18. *Ḥūt Muṭajjan* (oven-baked fish casserole), recipe v.1.14.

 | DOI:10.1163/9789004469488_081

Dessert:

19. *Muʿassal* (honey pudding), recipe ix.1.1.

Pastries:

20. *Mujabbanat al-Furn* (oven-baked cheese buns), recipe i.4.38.
21. *Mushāsh Zubayda* (Zubayda's crispy crunchy ribs), recipe i.4.28.
22. *Kaʿb al-Ghazāl* (small almond-stuffed cookies), recipe i.4.4.

Soup for the Indisposed:

23. *Ḥasū min Fatāt al-Khubz* (breadcrumb soup), recipe i.3.2.

Breath Freshener after Eating Garlic and Onion:

24. *Jubn Maqlī* (fried cheese, served with honey), recipes vi.1 and vi.3.3.

Mujabbana, recipe 20

1 *Khall al-Ḥiṣrim*

Preserved Juice of Unripe Grapes, recipe x.7.14
(Makes approx. 1 cup)

Although called vinegar, this souring agent is simply preserved juice without fermentation. It is mostly used to season meat dishes with little sauce in them before serving them, as in recipes ii.1.8 and iii.7.2; or lightly drizzle a bowl of chicken soup with it, as in recipe i.3.1.

To make it, use 2 pounds unripe grapes, either fresh or thawed frozen ones. Crush them in a food processor and then strain the juice into a medium pot. Let it boil on medium heat until a fourth of the juice has reduced, about 15 minutes. Strain the juice again after it cools, and store it in a glass container. I keep it in the refrigerator; if kept at room temperature, seal the top with a layer of olive oil, as was done in medieval times.

2 *Murrī Maṭbūkh*

Nonfermented Cooked Liquid Sauce, recipe x.8.6
(Makes about 2 cups)

This is the faster and less labor intensive *murrī* variety that al-Tujībī's cookbook offers in place of the traditional fermented ones, called *murrī naqīʿ*, that take months of care and waiting. While cooking, it fills the house with a pleasant aroma reminiscent of coffee beans being roasted. For recipes requiring the fermented variety, as most of them do, I used soy sauce as a replacement in the redacted recipes.

2 cups whole wheat flour
A scant ¼ cup (2 ounces) salt
1 cup water
6½ cups water
⅓ cup (2½ ounces) honey
½ ounce (3 teaspoons) of each of nigella seeds, fennel seeds, and coarsely crushed coriander seeds, all tied in a cloth bundle.

....

1. Make a medium-consistency dough with flour, salt, and water. Knead it briefly and flatten it into a disc, make it as thin as possible, and bake it on a cookie sheet in the oven that has been preheated to 400 °F. Keep it there until it is dark brown all over. Allow the bread to cool, then break it into small pieces by hand, and grind it in a food processor.

2. Sift the crushed bread and put it in a medium-sized heavy pot. Add the remaining ingredients and put the pot on medium heat to bring it to a gentle boil, and then leave it on very low heat for a couple of hours; it does not need to be stirred. Let it cool.

3. Discard the spice bundle, mash the contents of the pot by hand, and then strain it. Have a taste and see if you need to add some more honey to balance its saltiness. Store the resulting liquid in the refrigerator. Use it as a dipping sauce or a seasoning agent as required by the recipes.

3 *Shīrāz*

A Dish of Thick Drained Yogurt, recipe vi.1.2

A remarkable presentation of a yogurt dish. Instead of scooping it up with a piece of bread, as was usually done, the recipe's instruction is to serve washed tender green onions with it: hold an onion, pick up some *shiraz* with it, and eat.

To make this dish, you need drained yogurt, such as store-bought Greek yogurt, or drain it yourself. Spread it in a wide bowl, arrange olives and caperberries all around the edges, put a preserved lemon in the middle, lightly sprinkle it with nigella seeds, give it a generous drizzle of olive oil, and serve it with green onions.

4 *Fūl Ziryābī*, also called *Rās Barṭāl* (sparrow's head)

Fried and Salted Fava Beans à la Ziryāb, recipe viii.1.7
(Makes about 2 cups)

Although al-Tujībī does not give this snack food this name, medieval accounts on the life of Ziryāb in al-Andalus tell how Andalusis learnt how to fry their favorite snack food (*naql*) of dried fava beans, resulting in a crispy and brittle texture, from him; see introduction ii.5, p. 51. From al-Tujībī's cookbook we learn that fava beans prepared this way were called *rās barṭāl*, a name which in today's North African cooking designates dishes of fresh and tender fava bean pods sliced crosswise into small pieces and cooked.

½ pound dried fava beans
¼ cup olive oil
Salt, black pepper, and cinnamon for seasoning the beans

....

1. Wash the beans well and then soak them in plenty of water. Leave them for about 3 days to allow the beans to start sprouting. Take them out (do not throw out the soaking liquid yet), remove their skins, and split the beans in half. Return them to the soaking liquid and keep them there for about an hour, after which take them out and let them drain for a short while (now you can throw out the liquid).

2. Put the oil in a large heavy skillet, add the beans, and let them fry in it on low heat, stirring often, until the beans dry and turn golden brown. This will take about an hour, so perhaps it would be a good idea to fry the beans while you are in the kitchen doing some other cooking, as I did.

3. Once the beans are done, sprinkle them with good quality sea salt, black pepper, and cinnamon. Allow them to cool and serve them the way you would nuts.

5 *Fūl Akhḍar Maqlī*

Fried Fresh Fava Beans, recipe viii.1.2
(Makes 2 servings)

Small meatless dishes of fava beans were among the Andalusis' favorite snack foods and mezza-like small dishes, collectively called *naql*.

8 ounces fresh or frozen shelled fava beans, with skins on
2 tablespoons olive oil, divided
2 cloves of garlic, crushed

....

1. Boil the fava beans in salted water and then drain them. Set aside ¼ cup of the liquid they were boiled in.
2. Lightly fry the beans in a tablespoon of oil. Take them out and set them aside.
3. Add the crushed garlic to the pan, along with the set-aside liquid, and let the garlic cook until all the liquid evaporates. Add the other tablespoon of oil and let the garlic fry in it. Return the fava beans to the pan and stir them for a few seconds. Set the pan aside for an hour and then serve the dish in a bowl. Sprinkle the bowl of fava beans with black pepper. To eat the beans, squeeze out their pulp into your mouth and discard the skins.

6 *Isfarāj Maṣlūq*

A Simple Side Dish of Boiled Asparagus, recipe vii.5

Judging from al-Tujībī's recipe, the variety of asparagus available to the Andalusi cooks back then needed to be boiled in several changes of water on account of their bitterness. Luckily, today we need only boil them once. See the introduction, p. 48, on how Andalusis were introduced to this enticing vegetable.

To make the dish, take as many asparagus spears as you would like, discard the tough parts, and cook the spears in boiling salted water. Take them out, arrange them on a platter, give them generous drizzles of olive oil and vinegar, and garnish the dish with quartered eggs.

7 *Isfanākh Maṭbūkh*

A Meatless Dish of Spinach Cooked with Almonds, recipe vii.8.1
(Makes 2 servings)

An easy and tasty way to eat spinach. The crushed almonds cooked with this vegetable is a successful twist on an otherwise familiar dish.

8 ounces spinach leaves (I used baby spinach)
¼ medium onion, finely diced
2 tablespoons olive oil
¼ teaspoon of each of salt, black pepper, and crushed coriander seeds
2 heaping tablespoons coarsely crushed almonds
2 egg yolks
1 teaspoon butter (optional)

....

1. Blanch the spinach in boiling water for about a minute. Drain it in a colander and then put it on a cutting board and beat it with the back of a large knife to coarsely mash it.

2. In a medium-size heavy pot, fry the onion with the olive oil until it looks transparent. Stir in the salt, spices, and almonds.

3. Add the spinach with a small amount of water (2–4 tablespoons), and stir the mix on medium-low heat until the liquid evaporates.

4. Gently stir in the egg yolks (and butter if used) until they set. Remove the pot from the fire immediately and empty it into a plate. Garnish to taste. Serve it hot or at room temperature.

8 *Fuṭr Mukhammar*

A Meatless Dish of Mushrooms Topped with Eggs, recipe vii.7
(Makes 2 servings)

A mushroom dish packed with flavor that you will want to make again and again. In medieval times, such meatless vegetable dishes, called *baqliyyāt*, would have been served first because they were believed to have the benefit of softening the bowels. They were also enjoyed as snack foods.

8 ounces mushrooms, chopped
¼ cup olive oil
¼ cup chopped cilantro
¼ cup water
1 small onion, finely chopped
1 teaspoon crushed coriander
¼ teaspoon each of salt and black pepper
1 tablespoon each of vinegar and soy sauce
2 eggs
1 tablespoon wheat flour

....

1. Put the mushrooms in a medium-sized heavy skillet along with the olive oil, cilantro, water, onion, coriander, salt, and black pepper. Stir them frequently on moderately high heat for about 10 minutes, or until all the moisture evaporates.

2. Add the vinegar and soy sauce, stir for a couple of minutes, and then remove the skillet from the burner.

3. Beat the eggs with the flour and season them lightly with pinches of salt, black pepper, and crushed coriander. Pour the egg mix on top of the mushroom mix in an even layer. Put the skillet on low heat for about 10 minutes, or until the eggs set, and then serve.

9 *Bādhinjān Muṭajjan*

Oven-Braised Eggplant, recipe vii.2.9
(Makes 4 servings)

This is a luscious eggplant side dish served at room temperature. Although it requires a lot of oil, any surplus after baking may be spooned off.

One large eggplant, or two medium ones, about 1½ pounds
¼ cup vinegar
2 tablespoons soy sauce
¼ teaspoon black pepper
½ teaspoon each of coriander, cumin, and dried thyme, crushed between the hands
2 garlic cloves, mash one and slice the other
¼ cup, plus 2 tablespoons, olive oil

1. Peel the eggplant and then slice it lengthwise into ¼-inch thin slices. Lightly boil the slices in salted water and then take them out and spread them on a sieve to drain well.

2. Prepare the sauce in a shallow bowl by combining the rest of the ingredients, except for the oil.

3. Spread ¼ cup olive oil in the bottom of a casserole pan. Press the eggplant slices in the sauce on both sides one by one; arrange the coated eggplant slices next to each other in the pan. Pour any remaining sauce all over the eggplant slices and then drizzle with 2 tablespoons olive oil.

4. Bake the pan on the middle shelf in an oven preheated to 350 °F. Bake for 30–40 minutes, or until all the moisture evaporates and only the oil remains. Allow the dish to cool and serve it.

10 *Qar*ʿ

Skillet Zucchini Dish Topped with Almonds, recipe vii.1.1
(Makes 4 servings)

Another delicious vegetable side dish. This one is best eaten piping hot from the pan. Note that I use the New World variety zucchini. In medieval times what they had was gourd varieties of the *Lagenaria* genus, which belongs to the *Cucurbitaceae* family, the best known of which is the bottle gourd (*L. sinceraria*), also known as Opo. You can find it at Asian stores.

1 pound green zucchini
Flour for coating the zucchini pieces
Oil for frying
For the sauce:
¼ cup each of olive oil, vinegar, and water
½ cup cilantro juice, obtained by putting the herb in a food processor and then pressing it in a fine-meshed colander with a large spoon and collecting the juice in a bowl
½ teaspoon salt
¼ teaspoon black pepper
For the topping:
¼ cup crushed almonds
1 tablespoon breadcrumbs
1 egg

....

1. Peel and slice the zucchinis lengthwise into ⅓-inch thick pieces. Boil them in salted water, take them out while still firm, and arrange them on a sieve to drain well.

2. Lightly dust the zucchini slices with flour and fry them in ⅓-inch heated oil until they nicely brown. Set them aside.

3. In a medium skillet, combine all the sauce ingredients except for the cilantro juice. Bring it to a boil, add cilantro juice, and resume boiling for about 5 minutes. After this is done, arrange the set-aside fried zucchini slices in the skillet.

4. Add some of the sauce in the skillet to the topping ingredients and beat them well. Spread the mix all over the zucchini in the skillet. Let it simmer gently, covered, on low heat until the topping sets and cooks. Serve the dish immediately.

11 *Aqrāṣ Samak*

Fish Cakes, recipe v.1.4
(Makes about 12 2-inch-wide patties)

These flavorful fish cakes will make a nice lunch for a couple of people, in a sandwich or served with salad and warm bread. They can also be offered on a platter with their dipping sauce as a snack food.

Patty mix:
12 ounces raw fish
½ teaspoon each of salt and coriander
¼ teaspoon each of black pepper, cinnamon, and ginger
⅛ teaspoon cumin
1 to 2 lumps of mastic, crushed
A pinch of saffron, crushed
1 clove of garlic, crushed
2 tablespoons each of onion juice and mint juice
1 tablespoon each of soy sauce and olive oil
1 egg white, whipped
¼ cup white wheat flour
Oil for frying
For the dipping sauce: 3 tablespoons olive oil, 2 tablespoons vinegar, 1 tablespoon soy sauce, and 1 crushed clove of garlic

....

1. Lightly boil the fish for about 5 minutes and then take it out and put it in a colander to drain well and cool.

2. When ready to make the mix, press the extra moisture from the fish and flake it with your fingers into small pieces. The resulting amount should be enough to fill 1 cup, packed. You may skip this and use leftover cooked fish.

3. Mix the fish with the rest of the patty ingredients until they form a cohesive mass. Form the mix into small discs, about 2-inches wide, and form them and fry in ⅓ inch of hot oil. Turn them once to brown on both sides. When done, put them in a colander to drain the extra oil and help them remain crisp.

4. Prepare the dipping sauce by boiling the ingredients in a small pot for about 5 minutes on medium-low heat. Serve the sauce in a small bowl, and give it a whip before eating the dish, as the oil tends to separate. You may also serve the fishcakes simply drizzled with lemon juice, as the original recipe suggests.

12 *Tafāyā Khaḍrā'*

Green Lamb Stew, recipe ii.2.2
(Makes 4 servings)

Tafāyā, cooked either white or green, was an Andalusi signature dish that was praised for its balanced properties. The green variety in particular was said to have been inspired by the famous court singer Ziryāb, see introduction ii.5, pp. 48–50. This enticingly green dish is really tasty and well deserves the high regard in which it was held.

1 pound lamb on the bone
¼ cup olive oil
1 teaspoon salt
½ teaspoon black pepper
½ teaspoon coriander
¼ cup skinned and slivered almonds
¼ medium onion, chopped
For the meatballs: ½ pound ground meat; ½ teaspoon salt; ¼ teaspoon each of cinnamon, dried ginger, and black pepper; a dash of cloves, 2 egg whites, and 1 tablespoon flour
½ cup juice each of cilantro and chard, obtained by crushing them in a food processor and then pressing out the juice with a large spoon through a fine-meshed sieve.
For garnish: split boiled eggs and a sprinkling of cinnamon and ginger

....

1. Put the lamb and oil in a medium pot and cook them, stirring occasionally, until all the moisture evaporates. Add the salt, black pepper, coriander, almonds, and chopped

onion. Add boiling water, just enough to cover them, give the pot a stir, and continue cooking until almost done, about 45 minutes.

2. Meanwhile combine all the ingredients for the meatballs, shape the mix into balls the size of small walnuts. When the meat is almost done, drop in the meatballs, gently stir the pot, and let them cook.

3. Add the green juice of cilantro and chard during the last 10 minutes of cooking.

4. Ladle the dish into a deep and wide bowl, garnish it with the boiled eggs, and serve it with bread.

13 *Kuskusū Min Ghayr Saqī*, called *Ghassānī*

A Dish of Couscous That is Not Drenched in Broth, recipe i.5.3
(Makes 2 servings)

Unlike the other couscous dishes in al-Tujībī's cookbook, this one is left to steam in broth in a pot rather than having broth added to the steamed couscous bowl. In this respect, it is similar to rice dishes with separated grains, called *ruzz mufalfal* in the eastern region of the Muslim world. Al-Tujībī suggests that the dish may also be prepared with chicken.

1 pound lamb, preferably on the bone
¼ medium onion, chopped
2 tablespoons olive oil
¾ teaspoon salt
1 teaspoon coriander
½ teaspoon black pepper
1 medium carrot, cut into rather thick sticks
½ cup fresh or frozen fava beans, skinned
1 cup couscous

....

1. Put the meat, onion, olive oil, salt, coriander, and black pepper in a medium-sized heavy pot. Add enough water to more than cover the meat. Bring it to a quick boil, skimming as needed, and then let it simmer on low heat until the meat is done (about 1 hour). Add the carrots and fava beans to the pot about 10 minutes before the meat is done cooking.

2. To cook the couscous, take the meat and vegetables out of the pot and put them in a vessel. Strain the remaining broth. Return 1¼ cups of it to the pot (set aside any leftover broth). Bring it to a boil and then add the couscous to it. Gently stir the pot with a fork. Keep it covered on very low heat for about 5 minutes. Fluff the couscous grains a couple of times while it is steaming. Sprinkle it with some broth if needed.

3. Ladle the couscous into a large shallow bowl. Arrange the meat and vegetables all around it. Heat up the remaining broth, put it in a bowl, and serve it with the dish.

14 *Isfarāj Muṭajjan*

Oven-Baked Asparagus with Lamb, recipe ii.2.14
(Makes 4 servings)

Asparagus was cooked with meat in some elaborate ways, as in this dish. In my first attempt to cook it, the texture turned out to be rather soggy. Adding some flour to the egg mixture in my second attempt helped bind the ingredients.

½ pound lamb, cut into ½-inch cubes
¼ cup olive oil
½ teaspoon each of salt, coriander, and cumin
¼ teaspoon each of black pepper and crushed fennel seeds
¼ medium onion, chopped
2 whole cloves of garlic
2–3 citron leaves, if available
2 tablespoons soy sauce
1 tablespoon vinegar
¼ teaspoon saffron, steeped in 2 tablespoons hot water
24 asparagus spears, trimmed, boiled in salted water, and drained
6 eggs, divided

2 tablespoons cilantro juice, obtained by crushing it in a food processor and then pressing out the juice with a large spoon through a fine-meshed sieve.
3 tablespoons wheat flour, divided

……………………………

1. In a medium-sized heavy pot, put the meat, olive oil, salt, coriander, cumin, black pepper, fennel, onion, garlic, citron leaves, and soy sauce. Let the pot cook, stirring it occasionally, until the meat turns white. Add hot water, not much, just enough to cover the meat, and continue cooking until the meat is done and the sauce thickens, about 20 minutes. Stir in the vinegar and half of the saffron liquid and let the pot cook for about 5 more minutes. Discard the garlic cloves and citron leaves.

2. Meanwhile, whisk 2 of the eggs with 2 tablespoons cilantro juice, 1 tablespoon flour, and pinches of salt, coriander, and black pepper. Once the meat pot is done cooking, spread the egg mixture all over the top to cover it, and leave the pot on very low heat to allow the eggs to coagulate; do not let them fully set.

3. Now, take a casserole dish (I used a 7-inch × 7-inch glass pan), and grease it thoroughly. Whisk 2 of the eggs with 1 tablespoon of flour and pinches of salt, black pepper, and coriander. Spread the eggs in the bottom of the pan. Arrange one-third of the asparagus spears on top of it, followed by half of the meat mixture. Repeat the layering of asparagus and meat, followed by the last third of the asparagus.

4. Whisk two eggs with 1 tablespoon flour and pinches of salt, black pepper, and coriander, along with the remaining steeped saffron. Spread this mixture all over the top.

5. Bake the pan on the middle shelf of an oven preheated to 350 °F for about 10 minutes or so, until the top eggs set. Take it out and serve it.

15 *Tharīda Tuzīd fī l-Bāh*

A Chicken Dish with Bread for Invigorating Coitus, recipe i.2.14
(Makes two servings)

This recipe, the only one of its kind in al-Tujībī's cookbook, is packed with ingredients that were known in medieval times for their effectiveness in this regard, such as chickpeas along with their soaking liquid, egg yolks, hot spices like cloves and ginger, and carrots. Although chicken is used in the recipe, sparrows, we are told, would be even more beneficial.

½ cup dried chickpeas, washed and soaked in water
2 chicken thighs
2 tablespoons olive oil
¾ teaspoon salt
1 teaspoon coriander
½ cup onion juice, obtained by crushing a large onion and straining it
1 large carrot, sliced into ½-inch discs
2 tablespoons ghee, or substitute with butter
2 raw egg yolks, keep them whole
2 small discs of flat white bread, such as naan or pita
For sprinkling on the dish: dashes of cloves, dried ginger, black pepper, cinnamon, and spikenard, if available

....

1. Boil the chickpeas with the soaking water, adding more plain water as needed, until done.

2. Meanwhile, in a medium pot, put the chicken, oil, salt, and coriander. Add just enough water to cover them and start cooking the pot, first on high heat to bring it to a boil and then lower it to medium, skimming as needed.

3. Add the boiled chickpeas with about 1 cup of the boiling liquid. Also add the onion juice, carrots, and ghee. Continue cooking the pot until all is done. Turn off the heat and immediately add the egg yolks to the pot, keep them whole. Cover the pot to allow the yolks to set, about 3 minutes or so.

4. Meanwhile, break the bread into small pieces and put them in a deep and wide bowl. Drench them with the broth from the pot and then arrange the chicken pieces along with the rest of the ingredients all over the bread. Sprinkle the spices all over the dish and serve it.

16 *Dajājat ʿUumrūs*

A Comforting Chicken Dish, recipe iii.2.20
(Makes 4 servings)

A delightful way to prepare chicken. It is light and fluffy in texture on account of the custard-like sauce used when cooking it.

¼ cup olive oil
¼ medium onion, finely chopped
1 packed cup finely chopped grilled chicken (I used store-bought rotisserie chicken)
¾ teaspoon salt
1 teaspoon coriander
¼ teaspoon each of ginger, nutmeg, cloves, black pepper, and cinnamon
For the fermented dough: ⅓ cup white wheat flour, mixed with ⅓ cup warm water and ½ teaspoon dry yeast, and left to ferment for an hour.
2 cups milk
2 eggs

....

1. In a medium pot, stir the onion with oil until it softens, 1–2 minutes. Add chicken, salt, coriander, and the rest of the spices. Stir the pot on medium-low heat until the ingredients mix well and emit a pleasant aroma, about 3 minutes.

2. Thoroughly whisk the fermented dough with the milk and eggs (I used an electric mixer) and then pour the mix into the chicken pot. On medium heat, gently stir the pot until the milk sauce starts to thicken. Continue cooking on low heat until the mix looks like a thick pudding. Take it off the heat, and serve in bowls.

17 *Tharīda Min al-Laban al-Ḥalīb, Maṭbūkh fī l-Furn*

Oven-Baked Bread Dish with Milk, recipe i.2.23
(Makes 4 servings)

A unique *tharīd* dish, in which bread is not sopped in broth after the cooking is done but layered with a custard-like sauce and baked in the oven. It comes out bubbly and hot, ready to be enjoyed by itself, sprinkled with sugar, or served with grilled chicken. In the recipe, the *tharīd* is meant to be served in one piece after gently breaking the earthenware pan in which it was baked. For practical reasons, I used a nonstick 8-inch square pan. For the dish I used a thin sheet of bread variously called *ruqāq*, *marqūq*, *markūk*, *khubz sāj*, and *lawāsh* in Arab countries, more commonly sold as lavash bread in Western stores.

3 cups milk
2 eggs
¼ cup white wheat flour
A pinch of salt
1 large sheet of lavash bread
¼ cup butter, cut into small cubes
Sugar for sprinkling

1. In a medium pot, whisk together the milk, eggs, flour, and salt. Cook the mix on medium heat, stirring constantly, until it starts to thicken, about 10 minutes.

2. Grease an 8-inch nonstick square pan (or any shape of a comparable capacity). Spread some of the milk mix in the bottom of the pan, dot it with some of the butter cubes, and spread a layer of the bread to cover the surface. Continue with the layering until all the bread and milk are used up.

3. Bake the pan on the middle shelf in an oven preheated to 350 °F for about 30 minutes, or until the milk mix sets and the top looks golden at spots. Take it out of the oven, pass a knife all around the edges to release the stuck parts, and turn it over in one piece on a platter. Or you may simply cut it into four portions in the pan and take them out with a spatula. Sprinkle the pieces with sugar and serve them hot.

18 *Ḥūt Muṭajjan*

Oven-Baked Fish Casserole, recipe v.1.14
(Makes 2 servings)

This is one of the many fish dishes included in al-Tujībī's cookbook. It is seasoned with fermented sauce of *murrī* and baked in the *furn* (brick oven) with a good amount of olive oil. Cooking fish this way was recommended by the medieval physicians who thought of it as being hard to digest on account of its cold and moist properties. The dish is quite simple to make and flavorful; just do not let the fish overbake and toughen.

Two serving-size pieces of skinned fish filets, about 12 ounces
¼ cup vinegar
2 tablespoons soy sauce
2 cloves of skinned garlic, with a sprig of fresh thyme attached to each one through a small slit made at one of their ends
¼ cup olive oil
¼ cup slivered almonds
½ teaspoon crushed coriander seeds
¼ teaspoon black pepper
2 citron leaves, if available
A lump or two of mastic gum, crushed
A pinch of saffron

1 black cardamom pod (available at Indian stores, see glossary 8, s.v. *qāqulla*), use only the seeds after crushing them

....

Arrange the fish pieces in a casserole dish. Mix the rest of the ingredients and pour them over the fish. Bake the dish in an oven preheated to 400 °F for about 20 minutes, or until most of the liquid evaporates and the fish browns. For best results, choose a fatty type of fish, such as salmon. To cut down on the baking time and avoid overbaking the fish, I suggest that all the ingredients, minus the fish, should be first boiled in a small pot on medium heat until the liquid is reduced, and then pour it on the fish and bake as directed above for about 10 minutes. Broil the top for the last 2 or 3 minutes to brown it.

19 *Muʿassal*

Honey Pudding, recipe ix.1.1
(about 4–6 servings)

A luscious pudding to finish your meal with in emulation of Andalusi dining. The taste is reminiscent of today's confection *luqum* (also known as *rāḥat al-ḥulqūm*, *ḥulqūm*, *malban*, and *lokum*, and in English as Turkish delight), but with a pudding-like consistency. In the eastern region of the medieval Arabo-Muslim world, al-Mashriq, this dessert was more commonly called *fālūdhaj*, the earliest recipes of which were preserved in Ibn Sayyār al-Warrāq's tenth-century Baghdadi cookbook *Kitāb al-Ṭabīkh*.

1 ounce (3 level tablespoons) cornstarch (to replace the wheat starch used back then)
½ cup rosewater
1 cup water, at room temperature
6 ounces honey
¼ teaspoon saffron, steeped in 1 tablespoon hot water
½ cup slivered and lightly toasted almonds
¼ cup oil

....

1. In a medium bowl, whisk the starch with the rosewater and water until all the starch dissolves. Set aside.

2. Put the honey in a medium-sized heavy pot, and bring it to a gentle boil on medium heat, stirring occasionally, for about 4 minutes.

3. Gradually add the starch solution while constantly stirring the pot. Stir in the steeped saffron with the liquid. Also add the almonds. Continue cooking the pud-

ding on medium-low heat, constantly stirring, until the mix starts to thicken and looks glossy, 4 to 5 minutes.

4. Stir in a small amount of the oil first and then gradually add the rest of the oil until you notice that the pudding has stopped absorbing the oil. This will take about 5 minutes. Turn off the heat, and serve the pudding in small bowls.

20 *Mujabbanat al-Furn*

Oven-Baked Cheese Buns, recipe i.4.38
(Makes 9 pieces)

I followed al-Tujībī's direction and left an opening in the middle when filling and shaping the *mujabbana*, without a clue as to why that was to be done. I was pleasantly surprised to see that, while baking, the cheese filling puffed and beautifully domed out of the opening – seeing this the comparison between *mujabbanāt* and pregnant women in Andalusi verses started to make perfect sense; see introduction ii.5.2, p. 56.

The trick to keeping these domes from collapsing is to make sure that the cheese dome of each piece has developed a crust before taking it out of the oven. As I learnt, they do not all bake exactly at the same time, so take them out as they are done.

For the dough:
3 cups white wheat flour
½ teaspoon salt
⅓ cup oil
1 cup warm water
For the filling:
12 ounces fresh white cheese (such as Hispanic cheese *queso fresco*), mildly salty
1 teaspoon ground fennel or aniseeds
2 tablespoons each of mint and cilantro juice
For flattening the dough: approx. ⅓ cup melted butter

....

1. To make the dough, in a medium bowl mix the flour and salt, and then add the oil and work it into the flour by rubbing the mix between your hands until all lumps are gone. Add water and knead the mix into a somewhat soft dough. Lightly oil your hands while handing if the dough is a bit sticky. Set it aside to rest. Well-made dough should be elastic in texture; if you pull a piece it will stretch easily without breaking, as al-Tujībī comments.

2. Meanwhile, prepare the filling. Break cheese into smaller pieces and grind it in a food processor into very fine particles. Mix the cheese with the fennel and mint and cilantro juices.

3. To form the pastries, divide the dough into 27 walnut-size pieces and form them into balls. On a lightly floured surface, take one piece, flatten it with a rolling pin into about a 3-inch disc, and lightly brush it with butter. Take a second piece, flatten it the same way, lay it on the first disc, and brush it with butter. Take a third piece and do the same thing with it, but do not brush it with butter. Now, with a rolling pin, flatten the stacked three layers into a thin disc, 8½ inches in diameter. Spread a suitable amount of the cheese filling on the disc, leaving about an 1½–inch border that is clear of the filling. Gather the edges of the disc into the center, leaving about an inch opening. Put the finished piece on a large baking sheet and gently press it with the palm of your hand to flatten it a bit. Repeat with the rest of the pieces.

4. Lightly brush the *mujabbana* pastries with butter and bake them on the middle shelf of an oven preheated to 370 °F until the pieces brown at spots and the cheese filling has domed, set, and feels crusty when lightly pressed with the finger, about 30 minutes. Serve them right away, sprinkled with cinnamon and drizzled with honey heated up with some butter, or lightly sprinkle them with powdered sugar.

21 *Mushāsh Zubayda*

Zubayda's Crispy Crunchy Ribs, recipe i.4.28
(Makes 16 pieces)

This delicate pastry is lusciously crunchy to the bite. The name given to the recipe, and the way the dough is shaped, are indeed suggestive of breastbones (sternums), with the costal rib cartilages attached to them, called *mushāsh al-zūr* in medieval Arabic. Zubayda, whoever she was, must have been the cook's muse when creating this token of affection.

3 cups white wheat flour
½ teaspoon salt
1½ teaspoons dry yeast, dissolved in 1½ cups warm water
Oil or melted ghee, about ⅓ cup, for brushing the dough
Oil for frying
1 cup warmed up honey, or sugar syrup made with 1 cup sugar, 1 cup water, and 1 tablespoon each of honey, rosewater, and lemon juice, boiled to a medium-consistency syrup
For garnish: Coarsely crushed toasted almonds and walnut, sesame seeds, cinnamon, black pepper, and powdered sugar

....

1. To make the dough, mix the flour and salt, add the water with yeast, and knead the mix into a rather soft dough. Set it aside to ferment, covered, for about an hour.

2. Divide the dough into 16 walnut-size pieces and then shape them into balls. Take a ball and roll it out thinly into a disc on a lightly floured surface. Lightly brush the disc with ghee or oil (butter will not work because the liquid it contains might cause the oil to splatter when frying). Roll the piece into a log and fold it into two equal parts. Join the ends well and then lightly flatten the piece with a rolling pin or by hand. Using a sharp knife, make four scores on each side of the piece (these will be the ribs). Put the finished piece on a lightly floured tray, and repeat with the rest of the pieces.

3. Fry the pieces in 2-inches of oil (I used a smallish pot and fried three pieces at a time). They will sink in the oil first and then quickly rise to the top. Flip the pieces to let them cook on all sides. Take them out when they turn golden, in about 3 minutes or so, and put the finished ones in a colander to drain well.

4. When all the pieces are done, arrange them on a platter, drizzle them with honey or sugar syrup, and sprinkle them the nuts, sesame, black pepper, cinnamon, and powdered sugar. Delicious eaten warm, and any leftovers kept in the refrigerator should be warmed up before serving.

22 *Kaʿb al-Ghazāl*

The Gazelle's Ankle Bone, Small Almond-Stuffed Cookies, recipe i.4.4
(Makes about 150 small pieces)

The resulting cookies will be small, each the size of a fava bean, as the recipe directs. The cookies are compared to the gazelle's talus bone, also called the astragalus. These small cubic bones were, and still are, used as dice in traditional games.

From the recipe we learn that these fun-to-eat cookies were meant to be made to last; stored and eaten as needed. I expect them to have been the cookies to make as provisions to nibble on while on the road. In addition, spicy cookies like these, with their hot properties, would have indeed been beneficial as a digestive aid when consumed after a meal (more like digestive biscuits). Feel free to adjust the spice amounts to your liking.

3 cups white wheat flour
1 teaspoon each of aniseed and fennel seeds, ground
¼ teaspoon each of ginger and black pepper
⅔ cup oil
¾ cup warm water
½ teaspoon salt
For the filling:
1 cup sugar
2 cups (7 ounces) slivered almonds
½ teaspoon cinnamon

¼ teaspoon each of ginger, cloves, and black pepper
2 tablespoons rosewater

....

1. To make the dough, mix the flour with aniseed, fennel, ginger, and black pepper. Add the oil. Mix them together by rubbing the flour between the fingers until the lumps look like breadcrumbs. Dissolve salt in the warm water and knead the dough with it. Set it aside to rest while preparing the filling.

2. Put the sugar, almonds, cinnamon, ginger, cloves, and black pepper in a food processor and turn it on until the mix starts to bind (about 3 minutes). Add the rosewater through the spout while the food processor is working, and keep it on until the mix binds.

3. Take a piece of the dough, roll it into a log (like a thick pencil) between the hands, and then flatten it with a rolling pin into an approx. 2-inch-wide strip that is ⅛-inch thick. Take a piece of the filling and roll it between your fingers into a log, approx. ½-inch thick. Arrange these logs all along the middle of the flattened dough. Turn one side of the dough over the filling, and then roll it over again so that the sides meet to enclose the filling. Roll it gently by hand to smooth it and make sure nothing shows of the filling. Trim off both edges and press the openings. Carefully transfer the roll onto a cookie sheet, and continue working on the other rolls until all are finished. Keep space between the filled logs. Using a thin sharp knife, cut the logs into about 1-inch-long pieces (i.e., the size of a large fava bean). Do not move the pieces, keep them where they are.

4. Bake the cookies on the middle shelf of an oven preheated to 400 °F for about 25 minutes (move the cookies to the top shelf during the last 10 minutes of baking) until the bottom browns and the top starts to change color. Take the cookie sheet out, and using a thin spatula, immediately transfer the cookies to a wicker tray or basket (if kept on the sheet, some of the filling that might have seeped will stick to it). Wait until they firm up and cool and then recut them with a thin sharp knife. When completely cool, keep them in a storage container and use as needed.

23 *Ḥasū min Fatāt al-Khubz*

Breadcrumb Soup, recipe i.3.2
(Makes 2 servings)

This is a soothing soup worth trying. Given its simplicity, the smoothness of its texture, and the care taken to allow the spices used to just release their goodness, this soup must have been offered as a comfort food, perhaps to an ailing family member. Serving soup as an initial dish in the meal was customary neither in the eastern nor the western Arabo-Muslim regions.

3 cups plain water (you may substitute it with any broth of your choice)
1 tablespoon olive oil
Tie in a bundle: ¼ teaspoon each of salt, ginger, aniseed, and fennel seeds; a small piece of onion; a stick of cinnamon; a small lump of mastic gum
⅓ cup fine breadcrumbs
1 teaspoon each of finely chopped tender leaves of cilantro and mint

....

In a medium pot, on medium heat boil together the water, oil, and the spice bundle for 15 minutes or so. Remove the bundle, and then gradually add the breadcrumbs while stirring the pot. Let the mix boil gently, occasionally stirring, until the soup starts to slightly thicken, about 10 minutes. Stir in the chopped herbs, let the pot cook for a minute more, and serve.

24 *Jubn Maqlī*

Fried Cheese, Served with Honey, recipes vi.1 and vi.3.3

We learn from al-Tujībī that fried cheese can banish garlic and onion breath. Therefore, next time you have a meal enriched with raw garlic or onion, treat yourself to cheese sticks dipped in honey. Not all cheeses can be fried. Halloumi cheese and any Hispanic white frying cheese, like *queso para frier*, will work. However, if you want to have the fried cheese with honey, the former will not be suitable because it is overly salty.

To make this small dish, cut the cheese into fingers, wipe them with a paper towel if they look wet, this is to avoid splatter, and fry them in a small amount of oil heated up in a nonstick frying pan. Avoid overcrowding the pan.

Serve the cheese fingers stacked on a small platter. If wished, offer a small bowl of honey with them.

Works Cited

ʿAbd al-Laṭīf al-Baghdādī. *Riḥlat ʿAbd al-Laṭīf al-Baghdādī fī Miṣr*. Edited by ʿAbd al-Raḥmān al-Shaykh. Cairo, 1998.

ʿAbd al-Tawwāb, Ramaḍān. *Manāhij taḥqīq al-turāth bayna al-qudāmā wa-l-muḥdithīn*. Cairo, 1985.

Abū al-ʿAbbās al-Sabtī. *Ḥaqīqat al-dīnār wa-l-dirham wa-l-ṣāʿ wa-l-mudd*. Edited by Muḥammad al-Sharīf. Abū Dhabi, 1999.

Abū Ḥanīfa al-Dīnawarī. *Kitāb al-Nabāt*. Edited by Bernhard Lewin. Wiesbaden, 1974.

Abū Muṣṭafā, Kamāl. *Jawānib min al-ḥayāt al-ijtimāʿiyya wa-l-iqtiṣādiyya wa-l-dīniyya wa-l-ʿilmiyya fī al-Maghrib al-Islāmī*. Alexandria, 1996.

Ahlwardt, W. *Verzeichniss der arabischen Handschriften* v, 1893. MS no. 5473.

al-Andalusī, Abū al-Khayr. *Kitāb fī l-Filāḥa*. Edited by Muḥammad al-Rasmūkī. Fez, 1939.

Anonymous. *Anwāʿ al-ṣaydala fī alwān al-Aṭʿima*. MS M54, National Library of the Kingdom of Morocco, Rabat.

Anonymous. *Anwāʿ al-ṣaydala fī alwān al-Aṭʿima*. MS M54, National Library of the Kingdom of Morocco, Rabat. Edited by ʿAbd al-Ghanī Abū al-ʿAzm. Rabat, 2003.

Anonymous. [Title missing]. MS Arabe 7009,[1] Bibliothèque nationale de France, Paris.

Anonymous. [Title partially missing]. MS Arabe 7009, Bibliothèque nationale de France, Paris. Edited by Ambrosio Huici Miranda. *Kitāb al-Ṭabīkh fī l-Maghrib wa-l-Andalus fī ʿaṣr al-Muwaḥḥidīn li-muʾallif majhūl*. In *Ṣaḥīfat Maʿhad al-Dirāsāt al-Islāmiyya fī Madrīd*. Madrid, vols. 9 and 10 (1961–2): 21–256.

Anonymous. *The Book of Sent Soví: Medieval Recipes from Catalonia*. Edited by Joan Santanach, and English translation by Robin Vogelzang. Barcelona, 2014.

Anonymous. *Kanz al-fawāʾid fī tanwīʿ al-mawāʾid*. Edited by Manuela Marín and David Waines. Beirut, 1993. English translation by Nawal Nasrallah, *Treasure Trove of Benefits and Variety at the Table*. Leiden, 2018.

Anonymous. *Tārīkh al-Andalus* (also known as *Dhikr bilād al-Andalus*). Edited by ʿAbd al-Qādir Būbāya. Beirut, 2007.

Anonymous. *Taṣānīf al-aṭʿima*. MS Arabic 57, fols. 48r–112v, Wellcome Library, London. Online: https://wellcomelibrary.org/item/b20295017#?c=0&m=0&s=0&cv=0&z=-0.1256%2C-0.0392%2C1.2512%2C0.7849. Accessed May 20, 2020.

Anonymous. *Treasure Trove of Benefits and Variety at the Table: A Fourteenth-Century Egyptian Cookbook*. English translation by Nawal Nasrallah. Leiden, 2018.

al-Anṭākī, Dāwūd b. ʿUmar al-Baṣīr. *Tadhkirat ulī al-albāb al-jāmiʿ lil-ʿajab al-ʿujāb*. Beirut, n.d.

1 This is another MS copy of the MS mentioned above.

al-Arbūlī,[2] ʿAbd al-ʿAzīz. *Al-Kalām ʿalā al-aghdhiya*. Edited by Amador Diaz Garcia. Granada, 2000.

al-ʿAṭṭār al-Hārūnī, Abū al-Munā Dāwūd. *Kitāb Minhāj al-dukkān wa dustūr al-aʿyān fī aʿmal wa tarākīb al-adwiya al-nāfiʿa li-l-abdān*. No editor. Cairo, n.d.

al-Bakr, Khālid ʿAbd al-Karīm. *Amthāl ʿArabiyya min al-Andalus: Raṣd wa dirāsa*. Riyadh, 2018.

Bellahsen, Fabien, and Daniel Rouche. *Tunisia: Mediterranean Cuisine*. English translation by Vivien Groves. Potsdam, 2006.

Bin Sharīfa, Muḥammad. *al-Zajjālī: Amthāl al-ʿawām*. Vol. 1. Fez, 1971.

Bin Sharīfa, Muḥammad. *Ibn Razīn al-Tujībī: Ḥayātuhu wa āthāruhu*. Casablanca, 2009.

al-Bīrūnī, Abū al-Rayḥān. *Kitāb al-Ṣaydana*. Edited and translated in English by Ḥakīm Muḥammad Saʿīd, *Al-Biruni's Book on Pharmacy and Materia Medica*. Karachi, 1973.

al-Bīrūnī, Abū al-Rayḥān. *Al-Jamāhir fī maʿrifat al-jawāhir*. Edited by Yūsuf al-Hādī. Teheran, 1995.

Bos, Gerrit, et al. *Marwān ibn Janāḥ: On the Nomenclature of Medicinal Drugs (Kitāb al-Talkhīṣ)*. 2 vols. Leiden, 2020.

al-Bustānī, Buṭrus. *Muḥīṭ al-Muḥīṭ*. Beirut, 2008.

Chabrán, Rafael. "Medieval Spain." In *Food in Medieval Times*. Edited by Melitta Weiss Adamson, 125–53. London, 2004.

Chalmeta, Pedro. *El zoco medieval: Contribución al estudio de la historia del Mercado*. Almería, 2010.

Chapot, Henri. "Le cedrat kabbad: et deux autres variétés de cédrat du moyen-orient." *Al-Awamia* 8 (1963): 39–61. Online: webagris.inra.org.ma/doc/awamia/00803.pdf. Accessed Dec. 12, 2019.

Constable, Olivia Remie. *To Live Like a Moor*. Edited by Robin Vose. Philadelphia, 2018.

Corriente, Federico. *A Dictionary of Andalusi Arabic*. Leiden, 1997.

Crow, John. *Spain: The Root and the Flower*. Berkeley, 1963.

al-Damīrī, Kamāl al-Dīn Muḥammad. *Ḥayāt al-ḥayawān al-kubrā*. Edited by Ibrāhīm Ṣāliḥ. 4 vols. Damascus, 2005.

al-Darrājī, ʿAdnān. *al-Taʾthīr al-ḥaḍārī al-mutabādal bayn al-Andalus al-Islāmiyya wa Isbāniya al-Naṣrāniyya*. Cairo, 2018.

Delicado, Francisco. *Portrait of Lozana the Lusty Andalusian Woman*. English translation by Bruno Damiano. Berkeley, 1987.

Dols, Michael, trans. *Medieval Islamic Medicine: Ibn Riḍwān's Treatise "On the Prevention of Bodily Ills in Egypt."* Arabic text *Dafʿ Maḍār al-Abdān*. Edited by Adil Galal. Berkeley, 1984.

2 The name as it occurs in this edition, al-Arbūlī, has since been corrected to al-Uryūlī. I owe this information to the anonymous reviewer of this book.

Donkin, T.C. *Etymological Dictionary of Romance Languages*. Mishawaka, IN, 2016.

Dozy, Reinhart. *Takmilat al-maʿājim al-ʿArabiyya*. Translated into Arabic by Muḥammad Salīm al-Naʿīmī. 10 vols. Baghdad, 1980.

Dunlop, Fiona. *Andaluz: A Food Journey through Southern Spain*. Northampton, MA, 2019.

Ellis, A.G., and Edward Edwards. *A Descriptive List of the Arabic Manuscripts Acquired by the Trustees of the British Museum Since 1894*. London, 1912.

al-Fayrūzābādī, Majd al-Dīn Abū Ṭāhir. *al-Qāmūs al-Muḥīṭ*. Damascus, 1998.

Fikrī, Aḥmad. *Qurṭuba fī l-ʿAṣr al-Islāmī*. Alexandria, 1983.

Fregulia, Jeanette M. *A Rich and Tantalizing Brew: A History of How Coffee Connected the World*. Fayetteville, 2019.

García Sánchez, Expiración. "La gastronomía Andalusí." In *El zoco: vida económica y artes tradicionales en al-Andalus y Marruecos*, 49–57. Barcelona, 1995.

García Sánchez, Expiración. "Comida de enfermos, dieta de sanos: procesos culinarios y hábitos alimenticios en los textos médicos andalusiés." In *El banquete de las palabras: la alimentación de los textos árabes*. Edited by Manuela Marín and Christina de la Puente, 57–87. Madrid, 2005.

Gaul, Anny. "Light Enough to Travel: Couscous." In *Arablit Quarterly* 3 (2020): 108–17.

al-Ghāfiqī, Abū Jaʿfar Aḥmad. *Kitāb fī l-Adwiya al-mufrada*. MS 7508. In *The Herbal of al-Ghāfiqī: A Facsimile Edition with Critical Essays*. Edited by F. Jamil et al. Montreal, 2014.

Ghālib, Edwār. *al-Mawsūʿa fī ʿUlūm al-Ṭabīʿa*. Beirut, 1986.

al-Ghassānī, Abū al-Qāsim. *Ḥadīqat al-azhār fī māhiyyat al-ʿushb wa-l-ʿaqār*. Edited by Muḥammad al-Khaṭṭābī. Beirut, 1985.

Gitlitz, David, and Linda Davidson. *A Drizzle of Honey: The Lives and Recipes of Spain's Secret Jews*. New York, 1999.

González, Alfonso Carmona. "From the Roman to the Arab: The Rise of the City of Murcia." In *The Formation of al-Andalus*. 2 vols. Edited by Manuela Marín, 207–16. London, 1998.

Guinaudeau, Zette. *Traditional Moroccan Cooking: Recipes from Fez*, English translation by J. Harris. London, 1964.

Ḥakīma, Nūr. *Jard baʿḍ Afrān al-khubz bi-madīnat Tilimsān*. MA dissertation, University of Abū Bakr Bilqāyid, Algeria, 2015.

Hamarneh, Sami. *Catalogue of Arabic Manuscripts on Medicine and Pharmacy at the British Library*. Cairo 1975.

al-Harawī, Muḥammad b. Yūsuf. *Baḥr al-jawāhir*. Calcutta, 1871.

al-Hassan, Ahmad Y., and Donald Hill. *Islamic Technology: An Illustrated History*. UNESCO, 1992.

al-Ḥimyarī, Muḥammad b. ʿAbd al-Munʿim. *al-Rawḍ al-miʿṭār fī khabar al-aqṭār*. Edited by Iḥsān ʿAbbās. Beirut, 1974.

al-Ḥimyarī, Muḥammad b. ʿAbd al-Munʿim. *Ṣifat Jazīrat al-Andalus*. Edited by Lévi-Provençal. Beirut, 1988.

Huici Miranda, Ambrosio, ed. *Kitāb al-Ṭabīkh fī l-Maghrib wa-l-Andalus fī ʿaṣr al-Muwaḥḥidīn li-muʾallif majhūl*. In *Ṣaḥīfat Maʿhad al-Dirāsāt al-Islāmiyya fī Madrīd*. Madrid, vols. 9 and 10 (1961–2): 21–256.

al-Ḥuṣrī, Abū Isḥāq Ibrāhīm. *Jamʿ al-jawāhir fī al-mulaḥ wa l-nawādir*. Edited by ʿAlī al-Bajāwī. Beirut, 1953.

Ibn ʿAbd Rabbihi. *al-ʿIqd al-farīd*. 9 vols. Edited by Mufīd Qumayḥa. Beirut, 1983.

Ibn ʿAbd al-Raʾūf, Aḥmad b. ʿAbdallāh. *Risāla fī Ādāb al-ḥisba wa-l-muḥtasib*. In *Thalāth rasāʾil Andalusiyya fī ādāb al-ḥisba wa-l-muḥtasib*. Edited by Lévi-Provençal, 68–116. Cairo, 1955.

Ibn ʿAbdūn al-Ishbīlī, Muḥammad b. Aḥmad al-Tujībī. *Risāla fī l-Qaḍāʾ wa-l-ḥisba*. In *Thalāth rasāʾil Andalusiyya fī ādāb al-ḥisba wa-l-muḥtasib*. Edited by Lévi-Provençal, 3–66. Cairo, 1955.

Ibn Abī Uṣaybiʿa. *ʿUyūn al-anbāʾ fī ṭabqāt al-aṭibbāʾ*. Edited by Nizār Riḍā. Beirut, 1965.

Ibn al-ʿAdīm, Kamāl al-Dīn. *al-Wuṣla ilā l-ḥabīb fī waṣf al-ṭayyibāt wa-l-ṭīb*. Edited by Sulaymā Maḥjūb and Durriyya al-Khaṭīb. vol. 2. Aleppo, 1986.

Ibn al-ʿAdīm, Kamāl al-Dīn. *Scents and Flavors: A Syrian Cookbook*. English translation by Charles Perry. New York, 2017.

Ibn al-ʿAwwām, Ibn Zakariyyā Yaḥyā. *Kitāb al-Filāḥa al-Andalusiyya*. 7 vols. Edited by Anwar Suwaylim, et al. Amman, 2012.

Ibn al-ʿAwwām, Ibn Zakariyyā Yaḥyā. *Kitāb al-Filāḥa al-Andalusiyya*. 2 vols. Edited by Josef A. Banqueri. Madrid, 1802.

Ibn Baṣṣāl, Abū ʿAbdallāh Muḥammad b. Ibrāhīm. *Kitāb al-Filāḥa*. Edited with a Spanish translation, *Libro De Agricultura*, by J.M. Millás Vallicrosa and Mohamed Aziman. Tetouan, 1955.

Ibn Baṭṭūṭa, Muḥammad b. ʿAbdallāh al-Ṭanjī. *Riḥlat Ibn Baṭṭūṭa*. Edited by ʿAbd al-Hādī al-Tāzī. Rabat, 1997.

Ibn Baṭṭūṭa, Muḥammad b. ʿAbdallāh al-Ṭanjī. *Tuḥfat al-nuẓẓār fī gharāʾib al-amṣār wa ʿajāʾib al-asfār*. 2 vols. Cairo, 1904.

Ibn al-Bayṭār. *al-Jāmiʿ li-mufradāt al-adwiya wa-l-aghdhiya*. 4 vols. Beirut 1992.

Ibn Buklārish, Yūnis b. Isḥāq. *al-Mustaʿīnī fī l-adwiya al-mufrada*. MS Or. 15, Leiden University Library.

Ibn Ghālib, Muḥammad b. Ayyūb. *Farḥat al-anfus fī tārīkh al-Andalus. Maʿhad al-Makhṭūṭāt al-ʿArabiyya*, vol. 1. Cairo, 1955.

Ibn al-Ḥashshāʾ, Aḥmad b. Muḥammad. *Mufīd al-ʿulūm wa mubīd al-humūm*. Edited by G.S. Colin and Henri-Paul Renaud. Rabat, 1941.

Ibn Ḥazm, Ibn Saʿīd, and al-Shaqundī. *Faḍāʾil al-Andalus wa-ahlihā*. Edited by Ṣalāḥ al-Dīn al-Munajjid. Beirut, 1968.

Ibn Ḥawqal, Abū al-Qāsim. *Kitāb Ṣūrat al-arḍ*. Beirut, 1992.

Ibn Ḥayyān al-Qurṭubī. *al-Sifr al-thānī min Kitāb al-Muqtabis*. Edited by Maḥmūd Makkī. Riyadh, 2003.

Ibn Jazla, Yaḥyā b. ʿĪsā l-Baghdādī. *Minhāj al-bayān fīmā yastaʿmiluhu al-insān*. MS British Library, no. ADD 5934.

Ibn al-Jazzār, Abū Jaʿfar. *Kitāb fī Funūn al-ṭīb wa-l-ʿiṭr*. Edited by al-Rāḍī al-Jāzī and Fārūq al-ʿAsalī. Carthage, 2007.

Ibn al-Jazzār, Abū Jaʿfar. *Kitāb al-Iʿtimād fī al-adwiya al-mufrada*. Edited by Ibrāhīm b. Murād. London, 2019.

Ibn Khaldūn. *Muqaddimat Ibn Khaldūn*. Beirut, n.d.

Ibn al-Khaṭīb, Lisān al-Dīn. *al-Iḥāṭa fī akhbār Gharnāṭa*. Edited by Muḥammad ʿAbdullāh ʿInān. 5 vols. Cairo, 2077.

Ibn Khalṣūn, Muḥammad b. Yūsuf. *Kitāb al-Aghdhiya*. Edited and translated into French by Suzanne Gigandet. Damascus, 1996.

Ibn Luyūn, Saʿd b. Aḥmad. *Kitāb Ibdāʾ al-malāḥa wa inhāʾ al-rajāḥa fī uṣūl ṣināʿat al-filāḥa*. MS 14, Library of School of Arabic Studies, Granada. Online: http://simurg.bibliotecas.csic.es/viewer/image/CSIC001349506/1/. Accessed Nov. 17, 2020.

Ibn Manẓūr, Muḥammad b. Mukarram. *Lisān al-ʿArab*. Edited by ʿAbdallāh ʿAlī al-Kabīr et al. 6 vols. Cairo, 1998.

Ibn Manẓūr, Muḥammad b. Mukarram. *Mukhtaṣar Tārīkh Dimashq li-Ibn ʿAsākir*. Edited by Rawḥiyya al-Naḥḥās et al. 29 vols. Damascus, 1984.

Ibn Māsawayh, Abū Zakariyyā Yūḥanna. *Fī Jawāhir al-ṭīb al-mufrada*. Vollers 768–02, University Library of Leipzig. Online: https://www.refaiya.uni-leipzig.de/receive/RefaiyaBook_islamhs_00006475. Accessed March 23, 2020.

Ibn Qāḍī Baʿalbak, Badr al-Dīn al-Muẓaffar. *Mufarriḥ al-nafs*. Edited by ʿAbd al-Fattāḥ Ḥannūn and Yāsir Ṣabbāgh. Beirut, 2006.

Ibn Qayyim al-Jawziyya. *al-Ṭibb al-nabawī*. Edited by ʿAbd al-Ghanī ʿAbd al-Khāliq. Beirut, 1957.

Ibn al-Quff, Abū l-Faraj b. Yaʿqūb. *Jāmiʿ al-gharaḍ fī ḥifẓ al-ṣiḥḥa wa-dafʿ al-maraḍ*. Wellcome Library, Arabic Medicine 116. Online: www.wdl.org/ar/item/16762/. Accessed Feb. 10, 2020.

Ibn Quzmān, Muḥammad b. ʿAbd al-Malik. *Iṣābat al-aghrāḍ fī dhikr al-aʿrāḍ*. Edited by Federico Corriente. Cairo, 1995.

Ibn Rushd, Abū al-Walīd. *al-Kulliyyāt fī l-ṭibb*. Edited by Muḥammad al-Jābirī. Beirut, 1999.

Ibn Saʿīd al-Maghribi, Abū al-Ḥasan. *al-Mughrib fī ḥulā al-Maghrib*. Edited by Shawqī Ḍayf. 2 vols. Cairo, 1955.

Ibn Shuhayd al-Andalusi, Abū ʿĀmir Aḥmad. *Dīwān Ibn Shuhayd al-Andalusi*. Edited by Yaʿqūb Zakī. Cairo, 2013.

Ibn Shuhayd al-Andalusi, Abū ʿĀmir Aḥmad. *Risālat al-Tawābiʿ wa-l-zawābiʿ*. Edited by Buṭrus al-Bustānī. Beirut, 1967.

Ibn Sīnā. *al-Qānūn fi l-ṭīb*. Edited by Muḥammad al-Ḍannāwī. 3 vols. Beirut, 1999.

Ibn al-Ukhuwwa, Muḥammad b. Muḥammad al-Qurashī. *Maʿālim al-qurba fī aḥkām al-ḥisba*. Edited by Reuben Levy. London, 1938.

Ibn Wāfid, Abū al-Muṭarrif ʿAbd al-Raḥmān. *al-Adwiya al-mufrada*. Beirut, 2000.

Ibn Waḥshiyya, Abū Bakr al-Kisdānī. *al-Filāḥa al-Nabaṭiyya*. Edited by Tawfīq Fahd. 3 vols. Damascus, 1995.

Ibn al-Zayyāt, Abū Yaʿqūb. *al-Tashawwuf ilā rijāl al-taṣawwuf wa akhbār Abī al-ʿAbbās al-Sabtī*. Edited by Aḥmad al-Tawfīq. Casablanca, 1997.

Ibn Zuhr, Abū Marwān ʿAbd al-Malik. *Kitāb al-Aghdhiya*. Edited by Expiración García Sánchez. Madrid, 1992.

al-Idrīsī, Abū ʿAbdallāh al-Sharīf. *Nuzhat al-mushtāq fī ikhtirāq al-āfāq*. 2 vols. Cairo 2002.

al-Ishbīlī, Abū al-Khayr. *ʿUmdat al-ṭabīb fī maʿrifat al-nabāt*. Edited by Muḥammad al-Khaṭṭābī. 2 vols. Beirut, 1995.

al-Isrāʾīlī, Isḥāq b. Sulaymān. *Kitāb al-Aghdhiya*. 4 vols. Frankfurt, 1986.

al-Jāḥiẓ, Abū ʿUthmān. *al-Ḥayawān*. Edited by ʿAbd al-Salām Hārūn. 8 vols. Cairo, 1965.

al-Jarsīfī, ʿUmar b. ʿUthmān b. al-ʿAbbās. *Risāla fī l-Ḥisba*. In *Thalāth rasāʾil Andalusiyya fī ādāb al-ḥisba wa-l-muḥtasib*. Edited by Lévi-Provençal, 118–30. Cairo, 1955.

al-Jawbarī, ʿAbd al-Raḥīm. *al-Mukhtār fī kashf al-asrār wa hatk al-astār*. Edited by ʿIṣām Shabārū. Beirut, 1992.

Jayyusi, Salma Khadra (ed.). *The Legacy of Muslim Spain*. 2 vols. Leiden, 1992.

al-Khalīfāt, Muḥammad ʿAṭā Allāh. "Aswāq al-Andalus fī ʿaṣr al-dawla al-Umawiyya." In *Majallat al-Mishkāt* 1 (2014): 144–82.

al-Khawārizmī, Abū ʿAbdallāh. *Mafātīḥ al-ʿulūm*. Edited by Ibrāhīm al-Abyārī. Beirut, 1989.

al-Kindī, Yaʿqūb b. Isḥāq. *Al-Taraffuq fī l-ʿiṭr*. Edited by Sayf Ibn Shāhīn al-Mirrīkhī. Doha, 2010.

Koehler, Jeff. *Where the Wild Coffee Grows*. New York, 2017.

al-Lakhmī, Ibn Hishām. *al-Madkhal ilā Taqwīm al-lisān*. Edited by Ḥātam al-Ḍāmin. Beirut, 2003.

Lane, Edward. *An Arabic-English Lexicon*. 8 vols. Beirut, 1968.

Lebling, Robert. "Ziryab." In *Culinary Biographies: A Dictionary of the World's Great Historic Chefs, Cookbook Authors and Collectors, Farmers, Gourmets, Home Economists, Nutritionists, Restaurateurs, Philosophers, Physicians, Scientists, Writers, and Others Who Influenced the Way We Eat Today*. Edited by Alice Arndt, 390–2. Houston, 2006.

Leo Africanus. *Waṣf Ifrīqiyā: Ibn al-Wazzān al-Zayyātī*. Arabic translation by ʿAbd al-Raḥmān Ḥamīda. Cairo, 2005.

Levey, Martin. "Ibn Māsawaih and his Treatise on Simple Aromatic Substances." In *Journal of the History of Medicine and Allied Sciences* 16 (1961): 394–410.

Lévi-Provençal, Évariste. *Ḥaḍārat al-ʿArab fī l-Andalus*. Arabic translation by Dhūqān Qurqūṭ. Beirut, n.d.

Majmaʿ al-Lugha al-ʿArabiyya. *Al-Muʿjam al-wasīṭ*. Cairo, 2004.

Makki, Mahmud. "The Political History of al-Andalus (92/711–897/1492)." In *The Legacy of Muslim Spain*. Edited by Salma Khadra Jayyusi, i 2–87. Leiden, 1992.

al-Malik al-Muẓaffar, Yūsuf b. ʿUmar b. Rasūl al-Ghassānī. *al-Muʿtamad fi l-aʿshāb al-ṭibbiyya wa-l-adwiya al-mufrada*. Edited by Nabīl al-ʿArqāwī. Damascus, 2010.

Manniche, Lise. *An Ancient Egyptian Herbal*. London, 1989.

al-Maqqarī, Aḥmad b. Muḥammad. *Nafḥ al-ṭīb fī ghuṣn al-Andalus al-raṭīb*. 8 vols. Beirut, 1968.

al-Maqrīzī, Taqī l-Dīn Aḥmad. *al-Khiṭaṭ al-Maqrīziyya*. Edited by Muḥammad Zīnhum and Madīḥa al-Sharqāwī. 3 vols. Cairo, 1997.

Marín, Manuela. "The Cook-Book of Ibn Razīn al-Tujībī." In *Routledge Handbook of Muslim Iberia*. Edited by Maribel Fierro, 516–7. London, 2020.

Marín, Manuela. *Relieves de la mesas, acerca de la delicias de la comida y los diferentes platos*. Asturias, 2007.

Marín, Manuela. "Words for Cooking: The Culinary Lexicon in Ibn Razīn's *Fuḍālat al-khiwān*." In *The Arabic Language Across the Ages*. Edited by Juan Pedro Monferrer-Sala and Nader Al Jallad, 37–48. Wiesbaden, 2010.

Marín, Manuela. "From al-Andalus to Spain: Arab Traces in Spanish Cooking." In *Food and History* 2 (2004): 35–51.

Marín, Manuela. "Pots and Fire: The Cooking Processes in the Cookbooks of al-Andalus and the Maghreb." In *Patterns of Everyday Life*. Edited by David Waines, 289–302. Hampshire, UK, 2002.

Marks, Gil. *Encyclopedia of Jewish Food*. New Jersey, 2010.

al-Marrākushī, ʿAbd al-Wāḥid. *Tārīkh al-Andalus al-musammā al-muʿjib fī talkhīṣ akhbār al-Maghrib*. Editor not specified. Cairo, 1906.

al-Marrākushī, ʿAbd al-Wāḥid. *Wathāʾiq al-Murābiṭīn wa-l-Muwaḥḥidīn*. Edited by Ḥusayn Muʾnis. Cairo, 1997.

Martínez, María. *La Murcia andalusí* (711–1243): *Vida cotidiana*. Helsinki, 2015.

al-Marzubānī, Abū ʿUbayd Allāh. *Nūr al-qabas min muntakhab al-Muqtabas*. Edited by Rudolf Sellheim. Wiesbaden, 1964.

Mezzine, M., and L. Benkirane. *Délices de la table et les meilleurs genres de mets Fudalat al-khiwan fi tayibat at-tàam wa al alwān*. Fez, 1997.

Morro, Madeleine. "An Island's History is Coiled in a Pastry." *Boston Globe* (Jan. 1, 2016): G9.

Mūsā, ʿIzz al-Dīn Aḥmad. *al-Nashāṭ al-iqtiṣādī fī l-Maghrib al-Islāmī khilāl al-qarn al-sādis al-Hijrī*. Beirut, 1983.

al-Nābulusī, ʿAbd al-Ghanī b. Ismāʿīl. *ʿAlam al-malāḥa fī ʿilm al-filāḥa*. MS Damascus 1882. Online: ia800500.us.archive.org/3/items/kitbalamalmalahfoonbul/kitbalamalmalahfoonbul.pdf. Accessed Sept. 10, 2019.

Nadeau, Carolyn A. *Food Matters: Alonso Quijano's Diet and the Discourse of Food in Early Modern Spain*. Toronto, 2016.

Nadeau, Carolyn A. "From *Kitāb al-ṭabīj* to the *Llibre de Sent Soví*: Continuities and Shifts in the Earliest Iberian Cooking Manuals." In *Forging Communities: Food and Representation in Medieval and Early Modern Southwestern Europe*. Edited by Piera Montserrat, 21–33. Fayetteville, 2018.

Nadeau, Carolyn A. "Spanish Culinary History of Cervantes' 'Bodas de Camacho.'" 2005. *Scholarship*. Paper 8. Online: http://digitalcommons.iwu.edu/hispstu_scholarship/8. Accessed July 20, 2020.

Nasrallah, Nawal. *Dates: A Global History*. London, 2011.

al-Nuwayrī, Shihāb al-Dīn. *Nihāyat al-arab fī Funūn al-adab*. Edited by Mufīd Qumayḥa, et al. 33 vols. Beirut, 2004.

Perry, Charles. "Couscous." In *Alan Davidson: The Oxford Companion*. Edited by Tom Jaine, 220–1. Oxford, UK, 2006.

Perry, Charles. "Ushnān and Perfuming the Banquet." In *Food and Material Culture: Proceedings of the Oxford Symposium on Food and Cookery*. Edited by Mark McWilliam, 241–7. Totnes, UK, 2013.

Pliny the Elder. *The Natural History of Pliny*. Translated by John Bostock and Henry Riley. 6 vols. London, 1857.

Powel, Owen (ed. and trans.). *Galen: On the Properties of Foodstuffs*. Cambridge, UK, 2003.

al-Qalqashandī, Abū al-ʿAbbās. *Ṣubḥ al-aʿshā fī ṣināʿat al-inshā*. Edited by Muḥammad Ibrāhīm. 6 vols. Cairo, 1922.

al-Qāsimī, Jamāl al-Dīn. *Risāla fī l-Shāi wa-l-qahwa wa-l-dukhkhān*. Damascus, 1904.

Qusṭā Ibn Lūqā al-Baʿalbakī. *al-Filāḥa al-Rūmiyya*. Edited by Wāʾil ʿAbd al-Raḥīm Iʿbayd. Amman, 1999.

al-Rāzī, Abū Bakr Muḥammad b. Zakariyyā. *al-Ḥāwī fī l-ṭibb*. Edited by Muḥammad Ismāʿīl. Beirut, 2000.

al-Rāzī, Abū Bakr Muḥammad b. Zakariyyā. *Manāfiʿ al-aghdhiya wa dafʿ maḍārrihā*. Beirut, 1982.

al-Rāzī, Abū Bakr Muḥammad b. Zakariyyā. *al-Kitāb al-Manṣūrī*. MS Or. 5316, British Library. Online: https://www.qdl.qa/archive/81055/vdc_100022996955.0x000001. Accessed May 14, 2020.

Roden, Claudia. *The Food of Spain*. New York, 2011.

Rodinson, Maxime. "Studies in Arabic Manuscripts Relating to Cookery." In *Medieval Arab Cookery*, M. Rodinson, A.J. Arberry, and C. Perry, 91–164. Totnes, UK, 2001.

al-Rundī, Muḥammad b. Ibrāhīm. *Kitāb al-Aghdhiya*. In *al-Aghdhiya wa-l-adwiya ʿinda muʾallifī al-Gharb al-Islāmī: Madkhal wa Nuṣūṣ*. Edited by Muḥammad al-Khaṭṭābī, 183–208. Beirut, 1990.

al-Ṣafadī, Ṣalāḥ al-Dīn. *al-Wāfī bi-l-wafayāt*. 29 vols. Beirut, 2000.

al-Saqaṭī, Abū ʿAbdallāh. *Fī Ādāb al-ḥisba*. Edited by G.S. Colin and Lévi Provençal. Paris, 1931.

Schönig, Hanne, and Ingrid Hehmeyer (eds.). *Herbal Medicine in Yemen: Traditional Knowledge and Practice, and Their Value for Today's World*. Leiden, 2012.

Serventi, Silvano, and Françoise Sabban. *Pasta: The History of a Universal Food*. Translated by Antony Shugaar. New York, 2000.

Sevilla, María José. *Delicioso: A History of Food in Spain*. London, 2019.

al-Shantarīnī, Abū al-Ḥasan. *al-Dhakhīra fī maḥāsin ahl al-Jazīra*. Edited by Iḥsān ʿAbbās. 8 vols. Beirut, 1997.

al-Shirbīnī, Yūsuf b. Muḥammad. *Hazz al-quḥūf fī sharḥ qaṣīd Abī Shadūf*. Alexandria, 1872.

Simon, Hilda. *The Date Palm: Bread of the Desert*. New York, 1978.

Steingass, F.A. *A Comprehensive Persian-English Dictionary*. New Delhi, 2000.

al-Suyūṭī, Jalāl al-Dīn. *Ḥusn al-muḥāḍara fī akhbār Miṣr wa-l-Qāhira*. Edited by Muḥammad Ibrāhīm. 2 vols. Cairo, 1967.

al-Ṭabarī, ʿAlī b. Sahl Rabban. *Firdaws al-ḥikma fī l-ṭibb*. Edited by Muḥammad al-Ṣiddīqī. Berlin, 1928.

al-Tamīmī, Muḥammad b. Aḥmad. *Ṭīb al-ʿarūs wa-rayḥān al-nufūs fī ṣināʿat al-ʿuṭūr*. Edited by Luṭfullāh al-Qārī. Cairo, 2014.

Taniguchi, Masayukim, et al. "Preparation of Defatted Mustard by Extraction with Supercritical Carbon Dioxide." In *Agricultural and Biological Chemistry* 51 (1987): 413–7. Online: https://www.tandfonline.com/doi/abs/10.1080/00021369.1987.10868054. Accessed July 20, 2020.

al-Tanūkhī, al-Muḥsin b. ʿAlī. *Al-Faraj baʿd al-shidda*. Edited by ʿAbbūd al-Shālchī. 5 vols. Beirut, 1978.

Thompson, Campbell. *A Dictionary of Assyrian Botany*. London, 1949.

al-Ṭighnarī al-Gharnāṭī, Abū ʿAbdallāh Muḥammad. *Zahrat al-bustān wa nuzhat al-adhhān*. Edited by Expiración García Sánchez. Madrid, 2006.

al-Ṭighnarī al-Gharnāṭī, Abū ʿAbdallāh Muḥammad. *Zahrat al-bustān wa nuzhat al-adhhān*. Edited by Muḥammad al-Mashhadānī. Cairo 2005.[3]

al-Tujībī, Ibn Razīn. *Fiḍālat al-khiwān fī ṭayyibāt al-ṭaʿām wa-l-alwān*. Edited by Muḥammad b. Shaqrūn. Beirut, 1984.

al-Tujībī, Ibn Razīn. *Fiḍālat al-khiwān fī ṭayyibāt al-ṭaʿām wa-l-alwān*. Staatsbibliothek zu Berlin – Preussischer Kulturbesitz, Orientabteilung, MS Wetzstein II 1207, Berlin.

3 References in the book are from this edition unless otherwise specified.

al-Tujībī, Ibn Razīn. *Fiḍālat al-khiwān fī ṭayyibāt al-ṭaʿām wa-l-alwān. Anonymous Treatise on Cookery*. British Library: Oriental Manuscripts, Or 5927, ff. 101r–204v. In Qatar Digital Library: https://www.qdl.qa/archive/81055/vdc_100069662454.0x000002. Accessed Jan. 11, 2019.

al-Tujībī, Ibn Razīn. *Fiḍālat al-khiwān fī ṭayyibāt al-ṭaʿām wa-l-alwān*. MS 16, Collection of Gayangos, Library of the Spanish Academy of History, Madrid.

al-ʿUdhrī, Aḥmad b. ʿUmar. *Tarṣīʿ al-akhbār wa tanwīʿ al-āthār wa-l-bustān fī gharāʾib al-buldān wa-l-masālik ilā jamīʿ al-mamālik*. Edited by ʿAbd al-ʿAzīz al-Ahwānī. Cairo, n.d.

Ukers, William. *All About Coffee*. New York, 1935.

al-ʿUmarī, Ibn Faḍlullāh. *Masālik al-abṣār fī mamālik al-amṣār*. Edited by Kāmil al-Jubūrī. 27 vols. Beirut, 2010.

Viré, F. "Hare." In *Food Culture and Health in Pre-modern Islamic Societies*. Edited by David Waines, 97–100. Leiden, 2011.

Viré, F. "Orange." In *Food Culture and Health in Pre-modern Islamic Societies*. Edited by David Waines, 193–195. Leiden, 2011.

al-Wādī Āshī, Shams al-Dīn b. Jābir. *Barnāmaj al-Wādī Āshī*. Edited by Muḥammad al-Ḥabīb al-Hayla. Tunis, 1981.

Waines, David. "The Culinary Culture of al-Andalus." In *The Legacy of Muslim Spain*. Edited by Salma Khadra Jayyusi, 725–38. Leiden, 1992.

Waines, David. "Dietetics in Medieval Islamic Culture." In *Medical History* 43 (1999): 228–40.

Waines, David. *In a Caliph's Kitchen: Mediaeval Arabic Cooking for the Modern Gourmet*. London, 1989.

Waines, David. "'Luxury Foods' in Medieval Islamic Societies." In *World Archaeology* 34 (2003): 571–80.

Waines, David. "*Murrī*: The Tale of a Condiment." In *Al-Qantara* 12 (1991): 371–88.

al-Wansharīsī, Abū al-ʿAbbās. *al-Miʿyār al-Muʿrib wa-l-jāmiʿ al-mughrib*. Rabat, 1981.

al-Warrāq, Abū Muḥammad al-Muẓaffar Ibn Naṣr ibn Sayyār. *Annals of the Caliphs' Kitchens*. English translation by Nawal Nasrallah. Leiden, 2007.

al-Warrāq, Abū Muḥammad al-Muẓaffar Ibn Naṣr ibn Sayyār. *Kitāb al-Ṭabīkh*. Edited by Kaj Öhrnberg and Sahban Mroueh. Helsinki, 1987.

al-Warrāq, Abū Muḥammad al-Muẓaffar b. Naṣr b. Sayyār. *Kitāb al-Wuṣla ilā-l-ḥabīb li-yughtanā bihi ʿan jahd al-ṭabīb/Kitāb al-Ṭabāyikh* (augmented copy). MS 7322 A. 2143. Topkapi Sarayi, Istanbul.

Watson, Andrew M. *Agricultural Innovation in the Early Islamic World*. Cambridge, 1983.

Wehr, Hans. *A Dictionary of Modern Written Arabic*. Edited by J.M. Cowan. Ithaca, NY, 1971.

Wright, Clifford. *A Mediterranean Feast*. New York, 1999.

Wolfert, Paula. *Couscous and Other Good Food from Morocco*. New York, 1973.

Yaḥyā b. ʿUmar al-Andalusi. *Kitāb Aḥkām al-sūq*. Edited by Maḥmūd Makkī. In *Majallat al-Maʿhad al-ʿArabī* 4 (1956): 103–43.
Yāqūt al-Ḥamawī. *Muʿjam al-buldān*. 5 vols. Beirut, 1977.
al-Zabīdī, Muḥammad Murtaḍā. *Tāj al-ʿarūs min jawāhir al-qāmūs*. 40 vols. Kuwait, 1965–2001.
al-Zahrāwī, Abū al-Qāsim. *Kitāb al-Taṣrīf li-man ʿajiza ʿan al-taʾlīf*. In *al-Aghdhiya wa-l-adwiya ʿinda muʾallifī al-Gharb al-Islāmī: Madkhal wa Nuṣūṣ*. Edited by Muḥammad al-Khaṭṭābī, 235–302. Beirut, 1990.
al-Zajjālī, ʿUbayd Allāh b. Ahmad. *Amthāl al-ʿawām*. Edited by Muḥammad b. Sharīfa. 2 vols. Fez, 1971.
Zaouali, Lilia. *Medieval Cuisine of the Islamic World: A Concise History with 174 Recipes*. English translation by M.B. De Bevoise. Berkeley, Los Angeles, 2007.
Zozaya, Juan. "Eastern Influences in al-Andalus." In *The Formation of al-Andalus*. 2 vols. Edited by Manuela Marín, 457–68. London, 1998.

Index of People and Places

Entries marked with asterisks are not given full page citations.

ʿAbd al-Laṭīf al-Baghdādī 636n29
ʿAbd al-Malik b. Marwān 592
ʿAbd al-Raḥmān I 16n22, 27–8, 31, 44, 639n43
ʿAbd al-Raḥmān III 28, 35
Abū ʿAbdallāh b. al-Azraq al-Andalusī 18n32, 69, 127n29
Abū Ḥanīfa al-Dīnawarī 805, 807
Abū al-Qāsim Aḥmad b. Abī al-Ḥasan Nabīl (al-Tujībī's cousin) 16, 17, 20
Abū al-Qāsim al-ʿAzfī 67
Abū al-Qāsim al-Shaqūrī (al-Tujībī's grandfather) 16
Abū Yūsuf al-Manṣūr (Almohad Caliph) 473n8, 595
Algeria 17, 29, 102, 127n29, 578, 586n31
Almohads 28, 314n53
Almoravids 28
Amazigh 13, 27, 28–9, 30, 46, 48, 54, 60, 134, 569, 576, 578, 609, 610, 650, 656, 772, 780, 797
al-ʿAnṣara 52, 67
**Anwāʿ al-ṣaydala* (Andalusi cookbook) 3n2, 11, 23, 564, 566, 572, 578, 583, 595, 601, 602, 603, 608, 609, 652, 702, 753, 784
*al-Arbūlī (al-Uryūlī) 22n42, 108n16, 572, 576, 747
aswāq (markets) 41, 42, 43, 44, 56, 57–61
Atlantic Ocean 37, 38, 763
al-ʿAṭṭār al-Hārūnī 808, 811

Baghdad 31, 44, 46, 48
al-Baḥr al-Muḥīṭ/al-Muẓlim *see* Atlantic Ocean
Bijāya 14, 17, 18, 127n29, 546, 572
*Bin Sharīfa, Muḥammad 1, 15
*al-Bīrūnī 806, 812
Būrān 63, 85, 107

Carthaginians 24–5, 38, 763
Ceuta (Sabta) 17, 20, 38, 606, 762, 763
conversos 95, 100
Cordova 23, 27–8, 35, 42, 43, 100

Damascus 27, 44
Don Quixote 87, 353n1, 610

Elche (in Alicante) 29

famines 36, 44, 65
Fernando de la Granja 5
Fernando III of Castile 16
food markets see *aswāq*
Francisco Martínez Montiño, *Arte de cocina* 98n269

*Galen 619, 627, 631n22
*al-Ghāfiqī 806–7
Gibraltar 27
*Granada 28, 39–40, 94

Hafsids 17, 19
al-Ḥakam 35
Hārūn al-Rashīd 46
Ḥasan b. Muḥammad al-Wazzān *see* Leo Africanus
Hispania 25–6
Huici Miranda 3n2

Ibn ʾAbbār 17
Ibn al-ʿAdīm, *al-Wuṣla ilā l-ḥabīb* 598
*Ibn al-ʿAwwām 22, 559n2
Ibn Baṣṣāl 22, 31, 559n2
Ibn Buklārish 805
Ibn Ḥayyān al-Qurṭubī 46–52
Ibn Janāḥ 21, 539
*Ibn al-Jazzār 22, 93, 551n1
Ibn Māsawayh 805
Ibn Quzmān 65, 67, 69
Ibn Razīn *see* al-Tujībī
Ibn Rushayd 15n19, 18, 20
Ibn Saʿīd al-Maghribi 64
Ibn Shuhayd al-Andalusi 60–1, 68–9
*Ibn Sīnā 806, 809, 811, 813
Ibn al-Zaqqāq 64
*Ibn Zuhr 6n11, 21–2, 109n18, 110n25
Ibrāhīm b. al-Mahdī 46, 48–9, 315
ʿĪd al-Mahrajān (Pentecost) see *al-ʿAnṣara*

ʿĪd al-Mawlid al-Nabawī (birthday of Prophet Muḥammad) 68
ʿĪd Yanayyir (Christian New Year) 13, 52, 66, 68, 82, 142
Ifrīqiya 14, 17, 71, 130, 135n61, 207n16, 474, 546, 609, 656
Inquisition 74, 94, 95, 101, 728
Isḥāq b. Ibrāhīm al-Mawṣilī 46
Iʿtimād al-Ramīkiyya 63

Jaʿfar b. ʿUthmān al-Muṣḥafī 60
Jayyān (Jaén) 41
Jews 68, 94, 95, 101, 171n69, 584

Kushājim 803–4

Leo Africanus 99
Lisbon 38–9
Lozana see *Portrait of Lozana*

Madīnat al-Zahrāʾ 35
Madrid 35
Malaga 31, 39
al-Maʾmūn (Abbasid caliph) 63, 107
al-Maʾmūn Ibn Dhī al-Nūn (Taifa ruler of Toledo) 63
Marrakesh 28, 54n160, 155n4, 596, 599, 639, 708
Mīlād (Christmas time) 53
Moriscos 95–100
Mount Sharaf 34
Murcia 8, 14, 15–7, 20, 91, 100, 570, 622
Muslim *ʿīds* 65
al-Muʿtamid Ibn ʿAbbād (Taifa ruler of Seville) 63, 785n22
al-Mutawakkil (Abbasid caliph) 480n2, 592

Nabīl al-Rūmī (al-Tujībī's uncle) 16
Nawrūz/Nayrūz see *ʿĪd Yanayyir*
Nasrid dynasty 28, 69
Numidia 29, 576

Pergamon 619, 627
Phoenicians 25
Portrait of Lozana the Lusty Andalusian Woman 53, 70, 100

Qusṭā Ibn Lūqā 22–3

Ramadan 65, 66
al-Rāzī, Abū Bakr 54, 805
Rodinson, Maxime 1, 3n2
Romans 24–5, 26, 29n61

Ṣaqāliba (Slavic guards and servants) 35
*al-Saqaṭī 59, 60, 599
Saraqusṭā (Zaragoza) 40–1
Seville 28, 31, 34, 42, 63, 546, 761
al-Shaʿbāniyya 66
Shadhūna (Medina-Sidonia) 36–8, 653, 763
Shalūbīnya (Salobreña) 41
Shanqanīra 16
Ṣinhāj 13, 28, 35n1, 610
Solomon, King 478n2, 631
Sulaymān b. ʿAbd al-Malik (Umayyad caliph) 46
Syria 31

al-Taifa 28, 63
al-Tamīmī, Muḥammad b. Aḥmad 806
Ṭāriq b. Ziyād 27
*al-Ṭighnarī 22, 23, 30, 53
Toledo 31, 35–6, 63, 185, 708
*al-Tujībī, Ibn Razīn, life and works 15–20
Tunis 1, 14, 17, 19, 20, 130

Umayyads (al-Andalus) 41, 44, 46
(Syria) 27, 44

Valencia 8, 20, 36, 100, 153
Visigoths (al-Qūṭ) 26

al-Wādī Āshī 17
al-Wādī al-Kabīr (Guadalquivir) 34, 63, 546, 751

Yawm al-Mahrajān see *al-ʿAnṣara*
Yawm al-ṭīn (the mud say) 63

al-Zahrāwī 624, 806
Ziryāb 44–52

General Index

Entries marked with asterisks are not given full page citations.

al-ʿAjamiyya (Andalusi Romance) 8, 13, 85, 112n44, 136n67, 213, 368n25, 452n16, 571, 584, 602, 663, 683, 697, 750, 780
almadraba 38, 39, 763
anafe (portable stove) 78, 101
āniya see *inā'*
aphrodisiacs see *bāh*
awānī see *inā'*

bāh (coitus) 48, 80, 93, 133, 623, 624, 626, 642, 659, 662, 665, 667, 668, 676, 680, 688, 691, 693, 705, 710, 740, 789, 792, 795, 838
baqs (boxwood) 74, 194, 198, 573, 646, 720
bardī (papyrus) 234n40, 244n65, 716
burma (pot) 121, 246, 262n9, 711, 715

chicken, artificial incubation 41, 744
couscoussier see *qidr al-kuskusū*

dast (large brass pot) 461n5, 728
date palms (*nakhl*) 29, 643
  jarīd nakhl (stripped fronds) 179, 513, 715, 805
dhukār (caprifig) 624, 645
  ʿūd (stick) 519, 523, 645, 725, 728
  waraq (leaves) 518, 522, 645, 729
  See also *rūṭabāl*

**furn* (brick oven, bakehouse) 43, 79, 80, 87, 711–3
  farrān (operator of) 711
  kawsha 186, 711, 713

*Galen, humoral theory 93, 108, 110n24, 213n32, 246n67, 382n73, 767, 769–70
**ghaḍā* (embers) 78, 713
**ghaḍāra* (glazed bowl) 74, 713–4
**ghirbāl* (sieve) 714
  ḥalfā (esparto grass) 168, 270, 409
  ṣafīq/khafīf (fine meshed) 164, 188, 485, 501
  shaʿr (hair) 170, 249n77, 395, 397, 468, 487, 501

**ḥalfā* (esparto grass) 285n19, 393, 395, 491, 514, 520, 522, 649, 714, 720, 726
ḥantam (green-glazed vessels) 72, 109, 182n102, 711, 724
ḥaṣīr (reed mat) 166n46, 168, 715
ḥaṭab (firewood) 61, 254, 711, 715
ḥisba (market inspection) 58–60, 67, 258n115, 284n16, 599, 710, 726n16, 799

ibrīm (cauldron) 262, 715
ijjāna (large tub) 719, 723
inā' (vessel) 181, 711, 715, 729
  muḍāʿaf (double boiler) 616
  muzaffat (pithed) 498, 500, 509, 715, 733
inbīq (alembic) 516, 722
  See also *qādūs al-taqṭīr*
iskarfāj (grater) 76, 143, 280, 296, 327, 401, 442
  maṣnūʿ (steel) 417, 715

jafna (large, wide serving bowl) 74, 163, 164, 168, 190, 195, 372, 715, 728
jamr (coal fire) 73, 79, 130, 138, 162, 721, 731
jarīd nakhl *see* date palms
jild ḍa'n (sheep skin) 117, 716
jirāb (leather bag) 57

kāghad (hemp paper) 234, 243, 716
kalkha (giant fennel stalk) 463, 716
kānūn al-nār (portable stove) 49, 74, 164, 547, 716
kattān (linen cloth) 522, 536, 716, 717, 720
  mushāqat (tow linen) 432, 716
kawsha see *furn*
khābiya (large earthenware jar) 400, 495, 497, 500, 519, 523, 588, 717
  muzaffata (pitched) 490
  ṣaghīra muzayyata (small, coated with olive oil) 522
khiwān (table) see *mā'ida*

lawḥ (wooden board) 154, 163, 177, 257, 284, 295, 394, 428, 439, 464, 467, 472, 491, 501, 717
  mustaṭīl (rectangular) 193

libido see *bāh*
mafrash ḥadīd (griddle) 73, 135, 251, 276, 717
mā'ida (table) 76, 154, 163, 193, 197, 252, 486, 494, 717
malla (earthenware flat plate) 80, 119, 120, 134, 137, 142, 156, 166, 186, 366, 472, 717–8
  fakhkhār dūn muzajjaj (unglazed) 129
  ḥadīd (iron) 472
  al-kunāfa 161n27, 721
  nuḥās (copper) 186
malla (heated pit) 80n239, 254n97, 545n2, 717, 754
mighrafa (ladle) 127, 132, 518, 718
  al-bayḍ (egg ladle) 387
  kabīra (large) 146, 191, 195, 215, 247
  muthaqqaba (perforated) 467, 718
  ṣaghīra (small) 74, 491
miḥakka (scraper) 76, 136, 718
**mihrās* (mortar) 76, 85, 718
  ḥajar (stone) 152, 198, 485
  muzajjaj (glazed) 514
  nuḥās (copper) 154, 204, 250, 256, 485
  'ūd/khashab (wooden) 152, 161, 194, 198, 203, 213, 218, 229, 244, 282, 284, 289, 293, 302, 368, 401, 410, 413, 514, 658
**mi'jana* (kneading bowl) 74, 119, 144, 168, 179, 188, 275, 284, 416, 491, 496, 500, 501, 516, 520, 539, 719
mikhṭāf (iron hook) 76, 180, 181, 720
mil'aqa, baqs (boxwood spoon) 74, 194, 198, 573, 720
  ḥadīd (iron) 478
  ṣaghīra (small) 494
mindīl (piece of cloth/napkin) 117, 194, 244, 432, 470, 475, 527, 530, 720
minqāsh nuḥās (decorating copper tweezers) 76, 154, 156, 720
minshaf ghalīẓ (thick towel) 188, 720
miqdār (cheese mold) 393, 720
**miqlāt* (skillet) 73, 720
  fakhkhār (earthenware) 278, 287, 311
  al-kunāfa 161n27, 721
  muqaṣdar (tinned) 89, 163, 180, 326, 346, 385, 720
mir'āt Hindiyya/al-kunāfa (round metal pan) 73, 162n31, 721
mirwaḥa (fan) 58, 393, 721
mi'ṣara (press) 76, 506, 615, 721
**mithrad* (large, wide bowl) 74, 125, 127, 150, 156, 380, 383, 431, 461, 485, 492, 516, 721
mu'ak'ik (meatball shaper) 76, 87, 282
mukhfiyya (serving bowl) 75, 184n109, 186, 479n5, 721, 728
mulberry tree (*farṣād,* also called *tūt al-'Arab*) 39
munkhul (sieve) 109
  See also *ghirbāl*
mustawqad (stove) 77, 713

nāfikh nafsihi see *anafe*
najāsa, najis (uncleanliness, unclean) 77, 394, 522
  See also *ṭahāra*
nāranj (sour orange) tree 30, 84, 650
naṭ' (leather spread) 523
nā'ūra (noria) 26, 31

pigeon cotes 42

qadaḥ (drinking vessel) 177, 587, 721
qaḍīb ḥadīd (iron rod) 76, 274, 283, 284, 357, 721
qādūs al-taqṭīr (distilling cucurbit) 77, 516, 722
  See also *inbīq*
qālab (mold) 646
qannūṭ (reed tubes) 172, 722
qār (mineral pitch) 509, 722
**qaṣ'a* (large wide bowl) 721
qaṣab (reed stalks) 157, 179, 504, 722–3
  al-ḥalwā (confection reed) 463, 464, 465, 466, 469, 470, 723
  shubbāk min (lattice of reeds) 177
qaṣriyya (large earthenware tub) 170, 267, 495, 496, 497, 501, 532, 723
**qidr* (pot) 724
  al-kuskusū 129, 188, 274
  qudayra (small pot) 724
qim' (funnel) 76, 285, 724
qirba (leather jar) 76, 397, 724
quffa (large basket) 395, 491, 514, 724
qulla (jar) 179, 724

raḍf (heated stones) 257, 305, 314, 315, 724
raqqūja see *riqq*

riqq (leather jar) 381n64, 725
rūṭabāl (caprifig stick) 519, 725
See also *dhukār*

saffūd (spit, skewer) 130, 251, 252, 268, 318, 725
**ṣaḥfa* (wide, shallow bowl) 74, 725
ṣallāya (stone slab) 468, 475, 476, 477, 478, 479, 553, 555, 725
sāṭūr (cleaver) 76, 251, 274, 725
shakwa (butter churning vessel) 76, 399, 590, 725
shawbak/*jawbak* (rolling pin) 76, 129, 166, 176, 186, 329, 716, 725
shawk utrujj (thorns of citron tree) 549, 648
**sikkīn* (knife) 76, 122, 146, 725
al-ḥalwā (dessert knife) 67
ṣufr/*ṣifr* (brass) 466, 723, 726

ṭabaq (large platter, tray) 151, 726
zujāj (glass) 175
ṭabaq/*ṭābaq* (flat baking plate) 119n8, 718, 726
ṭabkh bayn nārayn (cooking between two fires) 734
ṭahāra, *ṭāhir* (cleanliness, clean) 77, 398, 494, 522
ṭāḥūnat al-yad (quern) 76, 726
**ṭājin* (pan) 73, 726
ḥadīd (iron) 119, 129, 159, 258, 263, 584
al-qaṭāyif 164
ṭalya (cutting wooden block/board) 13, 76, 274, 283, 284, 726
**tannūr* (domed clay oven) 79, 118, 727
ṭayfūr/*ataifor* (large deepish platter) 74, 97, 181, 727
**ṭinjīr* (cauldron) 157, 176, 254, 293, 463, 509, 728
fakhkhār (earthenware) 289, 461
nuḥās (copper) 73
nuḥās muqaṣdar (tinned copper) 171, 477, 478, 527

**wiʿāʾ* (vessel) 729
fakhkhār (earthenware) 398, 500
min ʿūd (wooden) 178
muzaffat (pitched) 498
muzajjaj (glazed) 511
zujāj (glass) 478, 492
See also *ināʾ*

ẓarf (leather container) 520, 729
zift (resinous pitch) 490, 329, 733
zīr mustaṭīl min zujāj (rectangular glass jar) 494, 730
zujāj (glass) 175, 466, 478, 479, 480, 492, 494, 514

Index of Ingredients

Entries marked with asterisks are not given full page citations.

abū khuraysh (borage) 226, 652
acacia 805, 807, 809–10, 813
ʿadas (lentils) 457, 772
afzān see *ḥarshaf*
aghlāl (edible land snails) 548–9, 740
akāriʿ (trotters) 122, 740, 747
ʿanbar (ambergris) 37, 42, 63, 239, 652–3, 673, 706, 736, 770
**anīsūn* (aniseeds) 149, 152, 156, 184, 527, 654–5
apples see *tuffāḥ*
ʿāqir qarḥā (pellitory) 257, 258, 656
aruzz (rice) 15, 20, 28, 31, 36, 71, 91, 97, 100, 101, 236, 290, 569–70
  abyaḍ (white) 194
  jashīsh (coarsely crushed) 153
ʿaṣāfīr (sparrows) 74, 80, 130, 134, 186, 253, 266, 290, 348–9, 353, 421, 427, 740–1
**ʿasal* (honey) 26, 34, 35, 39, 41, 53, 55, 60, 73, 74, 76, 86, 92, 97, 100, 591–2
  abyaḍ (white) 462, 465, 466, 467, 591
  aḥmar (red) 465, 591
  shahd (honey with its beeswax) 140, 161, 168, 171, 466, 470, 595
asparagus see *isfarāj*
ʿayn al-baqar/*ijjāṣ* (plums) 40, 208n17, 209–10, 607, 619
  See also *ihlīlaj*

**bādhinjān* (eggplants) 28, 31, 80, 97, 101, 125, 772–5
ballūṭ (acorns) 35, 65, 66, 326, 619
banīj (proso millet) 20, 119, 151, 571
**baṣal* (onions) 90, 500, 656–9
baṣal al-ʿunṣul (squills) 382, 513, 659
**basbās* (herb fennel) 659
basbās akhḍar (bulb fennel) 271, 353, 366, 370, 775
basbāsa (mace) 555, 557, 662
baṭṭ (ducks) see *laḥm iwazz*
**bayḍ* (eggs) 31, 41–2, 46, 58, 60, 61, 69, 88–90, 110, 383–9, 600, 607, 608, 735, 742–3
baysār (dried fava beans) see *fūl*
bazr, karafs (celery seeds) 370, 674
  kattān (linseeds) 110, 662
beef see *laḥm baqar*
biṭṭīkh (melon) 554, 557, 621–3
blite see *yarbūz*
bone marrow see *mukhkh*
borage see *abū khuraysh*
būdhaq (rotted bread) 519, 523, 572, 689
bunduq (hazelnuts) 51, 66, 531, 613, 623
bunk 553, 554, 555, 556, 557, 662, 803–13
bunn (coffee beans and husks) 811–3
būraq (sodium bicarbonate) 513, 534, 662–3
  See also *naṭrūn*
būshīn (Macedonian parsley) 8, 13, 213, 663, 683
  See also *maqdūnis*

cabbages see *kurunb*
cardoons see *ḥarshaf*
carrots see *jazar*
cassia see *dār Ṣīnī*
cauliflower see *qunnabīṭ*
chai/*shāh Ṣīnī* (tea) 812
chicken see *laḥm dajāj*
chickpeas see *ḥimmaṣ*
cilantro see *kuzbara*
coffee beans and husk see *bunn*
couscous see *kuskusū*
cucumbers see *khiyār* and *qiththāʾ*
cured meat see *namaksūd* and *qadīd*

**darmak* (fine white flour) 91, 117, 572, 581
  ghubār (very fine) 288, 315, 364, 372, 375, 386, 388, 472, 572, 573
  See also *samīd*
dār Ṣīnī (cassia) 172, 173, 182, 475, 558, 565, 663–5
ḍawmarān (river mint) 549, 665
  See also *ghubayrā*
ducks see *laḥm iwazz*

eggplants see *bādhinjān*
eggs see *bayḍ*

fāghira (fagara) 557, 665
faqʿ see *fuṭr*
**fatāt khubz* (breadcrumbs) 309, 374, 375, 405, 572, 599
fats and oils:
alya (sheep tail fat) 248, 252, 613
duhn bunduq (hazelnut oil) 537
duhn buṭm/ḥabba khaḍrāʾ (oil of terebinth berries) 534
duhn fustuq (pistachio oil) 537
duhn jawz (walnut oil) 161, 475, 534, 537, 613
duhn lawz (almond oil) 165, 476, 534, 537, 613, 761, 795
duhn ṣanawbar (pine nut oil) 537
duhn simsim (sesame oil) 81, 401, 534, 537, 617
**samn* (ghee) 71, 81, 92, 94, 126, 166, 399, 590
**shaḥm* (suet) 62, 81, 94, 167, 583, 608, 613, 615
**zayt* see entry
**zubd* (butter) 55, 64, 74, 76, 97, 123, 128, 141, 398–9, 402, 618
fava beans see *baysār* and *fūl*
fayjan/fayjāl (cultivated rue) 368, 451, 665
See also *sadhāb*
fish see *ḥūt*
fujl (radishes) 146, 453, 776
fūl (fava beans) 776–8
akhḍar (fresh) 127, 188, 246, 447, 448, 449, 450, 451, 452, 776
baysār/yābis (dried) 24, 51, 146, 191, 247, 452–3, 775–6
musammakh (sprouted) 451, 733, 776
fulāyū (pennyroyal) 514, 667
**fulful* (black pepper) 667
fustuq (pistachios) 41, 51, 92, 160, 172, 173, 184, 315, 468, 469, 480, 481, 593, 624
fuṭr/faqʿ (mushrooms) 331, 438, 779

geese see *laḥm iwazz*
ghazl (young vine shoots) 145, 441, 779
ghubayrā (water mint) 152, 513, 667
See also *ḍawmarān*
goats, young see *laḥm jadī*
gourds see *qarʿ*

ḥabb al-buṭm (terebinth berries) 534, 624–7
al-ḥabba al-khaḍrāʾ (terebinth berries) *see above*
hares see *laḥm arānib*
harnuwa (aloeswood fruit) 553, 555, 557, 667
ḥarshaf (cardoons) 68, 236, 436–7, 779–81
afzan/afzān (wild cardoons) 236n48, 436, 772
laṣīf (gundelia) 113n45, 236, 393, 780
qannāriyya (cultivated cardoons) 436, 780, 792
ḥimmaṣ (chickpeas) 35, 100, 129, 137, 208, 210, 223, 234, 235, 249, 256, 273, 277, 300, 302, 304, 333, 353, 388, 412, 453, 781–4
abyaḍ (white) 93, 125, 131, 133, 203, 455, 511
akhḍar (fresh in the pods) 454, 782
aswad (black) 35, 455
maṭḥūn (crushed) 55, 93, 248, 558
ḥiṣrim (sour unripe grapes) 627–8
khall (preserved juice of) see *khall*
māʾ (fresh juice) 307
ḥulba (fenugreek) 668–9
madbūgha (seeds soaked in water) 152
**ḥūt/samak* (fish) 34, 35, 38, 39, 58, 61, 186, 214, 361–82, 517, 533, 748–51
muṣayyar (preserved fish) 43, 67, 503, 601
sardīn see entry
silbāḥ (eel) 375–7, 751
ṣīr (salt cured small fish) 503, 532
tunn (tuna) *see entry*
See also glossary 749–52 for other fish varieties
ḥuwwārā see *darmak*

idhkhir (citronella) 553, 556, 557, 669–71
ihlīlaj (myrobalan plums/cherry plums) 40, 208n17, 209–10, 377, 619, 627
See also *ʿayn al-baqar*
ijjāṣ see *ʿayn al-baqar*
ʿinab (grapes) 16, 39, 40, 41, 76, 400
abyaḍ (white) 506, 533
akḥal (black) 533
ghazl al-karm (young shoots of grape vines) 145, 628
ḥiṣrim (unripe grapes) *see entry*

khall (vinegar) 506, 509
khamr (wine) see *sharāb* (alcoholic drinks)
muṣannab (sweet juice preserved with mustard seeds) 559
musṭār (recently pressed sweet juice) 528, 529, 530, 532, 533, 535n8, 560n4
rubb (grape syrup) 199, 363, 379, 382, 591, 595
thufl (grape pomace) 510, 628
waraq (leaves) 118, 398, 729
infaḥa (rennet) 393, 588, 755
innards of quadrupeds:
duwwāra (small intestine) 146, 214, 247, 256, 257, 258, 744, 760–1
fu'ād (heart) 252, 257, 262, 612
karsh (tripe) 122, 146, 203, 205, 214, 252, 258, 355, 612, 744, 755
mibʿar (large intestine) 135, 243, 290, 760
minsaj (caul fat) 122, 146, 252, 357, 612, 744, 764
qubā (omasum tripe) 289, 755
rummāna see above
sudsiyya (honeycomb tripe) 123, 211, 756
isfānākh (spinach) 28, 123, 227, 270, 271, 439, 725, 761, 784
isfarāj (asparagus) 47–8, 232, 434, 784–7

jarād (locusts) 44, 74, 545, 754
**jawz* (walnuts) 35, 39, 41, 66, 161, 362, 401, 405, 475, 533, 537, 628–30
jawzat al-ṭīb (nutmeg) 471, 553, 555, 565, 652, 671
jawz bawwa see above
jawz ḥamām see *khurʾ ḥamām*
jazar (carrots) 134, 188, 236, 353, 428, 787
jubn (cheese) 588–9
ṭarī (fresh) 128, 137, 179, 181, 182, 184, 186, 229, 260, 262, 265, 271, 296, 327, 393–5, 431
yābis (hard) 131, 143, 145, 151, 200, 246, 279, 280, 400, 401, 417, 423
juljulān/*simsim* (sesame seeds) 42, 110, 120, 176, 265, 462, 464, 465, 467, 480, 532, 671, 699

kabāba (cubeb) 555, 557, 671
kabar (capers) 90, 395, 396, 495–7, 603, 630
kāfūr (camphor) 63, 91, 154, 239, 299, 315, 316, 469, 471, 472, 473, 476, 555, 556, 557, 558, 671
kam'a (desert truffles) see *tirfās*
**kammūn* (cumin) 100, 673
karāwiya (caraway) 100, 137, 220, 245, 246, 283, 300, 319, 320, 322, 324, 327, 378, 381, 408, 409, 416, 428, 539, 676
karsh see innards
kathīrā (gum of tragacanth tree) 492, 677
**khall* (vinegar) 76, 79, 84, 85, 86, 107, 506–17
fulful (infused with black pepper) 510
ḥiṣrim (preserved juice of unripe grapes) 148, 212, 213, 243, 276, 306, 348, 379, 514–6, 678
ḥulw ḥāmiḍ (sweet and sour) 509
ʿinab (grapes) 506
līm (preserved lemon juice) 212, 242, 276, 348, 443, 515, 633, 637, 679
naʿnaʿ (infused with mint) 516
tīn (figs) 506
ʿunṣul (flavored with squills) 513
zunbūʿ (of Damascus citron) 212, 243, 276, 379, 679
khamr (grape wine) see *sharāb* (alcoholic drinks)
kharnūb (carob) 522, 532, 630–2
khass (lettuce) 127, 188, 229, 270, 271, 439, 788–9
khilāṭ see *laban*
khiyār (common cucumbers) 145, 441, 789–90
khūlanjān (galangal) 368, 369, 471, 494, 655, 679
khurʾ ḥamām (usnea variety) 556n24, 680
kundur (frankincense) 556, 680
kurunb (cabbages) 100, 123, 188, 195, 219, 220, 353, 355, 440, 599, 790–1
kuskusū (couscous) 13, 28–9, 46, 54, 69, 75, 91, 94, 97–9, 100, 188–91, 575–6, 600, 604
**kuzbara* (coriander seeds) 53–4, 65, 70, 81–2, 99, 681
**kuzbara khaḍrā'* (fresh cilantro) 48, 81, 86, 90, 99, 100, 681–2

laban (milk and yogurt) 393, 589–90
**ḥalīb* (milk) 34, 64, 74, 589
khāthir (thick yogurt) 328, 340, 398, 409, 495, 589, 590

khilāṭ (yogurt condiment) 396, 398, 589, 630
makhīḍ (buttermilk) 269, 399, 589
mays (whey) 397, 589
rāyib (yogurt) 397–8
shīrāz (very thick drained yogurt) 90, 328, 395, 397, 398, 409, 495, 590
laḥm arānib (hares and *qunilyas*) 8, 13, 24, 42, 61, 79, 86, 144–5, 210n24, 273, 275, 277–81, 353, 740, 761–2
laḥm ʿaṣāfīr (sparrows) 80, 93, 109n21, 130, 134, 186, 253, 266, 290, 348–9, 353, 421, 427, 452, 440–1, 767
laḥm baqar (beef) 84–5, 123, 124, 189, 193, 195, 203–15, 290, 353, 603, 607, 609, 734, 742, 757
baqar maʿlūf (grain-fed cows) 85, 123, 124, 742
**laḥm dajāj* (chicken) 41, 67, 69, 72, 82, 87, 101, 128, 129, 131, 133, 135, 136, 138, 142, 189, 297 332, 355, 600, 744
farrūj (young chickens) 148, 216, 306, 310, 328, 329, 398, 744, 746
khaṣiyy (capon) 127, 128, 129, 130, 142, 313, 325, 757
**laḥm ḍaʾn* (mutton) 61, 79, 126, 134, 216–59, 353, 746, 754–5, 757, 758
mislān (hip section) 126, 605, 747
laḥm firākh ḥamām (squabs) 80, 130, 139, 186, 253, 266, 317, 323, 330, 337–40, 344, 353, 355, 747
laḥm ghanam (mutton) see *laḥm ḍaʾn*
laḥm ḥajal (partridges) 42, 54, 130, 333–6, 353, 747
laḥm ʿijl (veal) 121, 221, 222, 235, 237, 239, 242, 250, 758
laḥm iwazz (geese) 41, 42, 293–6, 353, 752–3
baṭṭ/burak/iwazz al-qurṭ (ducks) 42, 293n1, 752–3
laḥm jadī (young male goat, kid) 229, 266, 440, 735, 758, 759
jadī raḍīʿ (suckling kid) 127, 216, 219, 230, 262, 271, 353, 740, 753
ṣighār al-jidāʾ (small kids) 123, 753
laḥm kharūf (lamb) 79, 126, 127, 190, 260–70, 315, 334, 746, 756
kharūf raḍīʿ (suckling lamb) 54, 262
laḥm yamām (turtledoves) 86, 253, 266, 317, 341–5, 353, 764–5
laḥm al-waḥsh (wild meats) 273–81, 353, 758–9
laḥm zarāzīr (starlings) 186, 266, 346–7, 353, 765–6
lamb see *laḥm kharūf*
**lawz* (almonds) 39, 41, 65, 66, 92, 150, 154, 155, 162, 244, 264, 298, 468, 471, 473, 476, 484, 487, 632–3
duhn (oil) 537
farīk al-lawz al-akhḍar (fresh green almonds) 235
lemons see *līm*
lettuce see *khass*
lift (turnips) 100, 188, 195, 207, 221, 353, 440, 500–2, 791–2
līm (lemon) 66, 74, 84, 633–8
khall al-līm (preserved lemon juice) see *khall*
māʾ līm (fresh lemon juice) 244, 245, 289, 299, 364, 420, 637, 638, 682
muṣayyar (pickled) 90, 242, 253, 310, 311, 317, 353, 395, 396, 492–4, 604
lisān al-thawr see *abū khuraysh*
locusts see *jarād*
lubāb (fresh wheat starch) 167n49, 169, 171, 576
lubāb al-khubz (bread crumb) 139n75, 250, 253, 313, 314, 468, 576

maḥlab 682, 812n24
māʾ maṭar (rainwater) 191, 682
maqdūnis (Macedonian parsley) 13, 81, 213, 280, 366n19, 368, 500, 663, 673, 682–3
See also *būshīn*
marzanjūsh (marjoram) 513, 553, 554, 556, 557, 683
**maṣṭakā* (mastic) 684–5
māʾ ward (rosewater) 54, 63, 85, 91, 154, 155, 156, 158, 159, 160, 165, 173, 181, 212, 239, 265, 279, 285, 300, 315, 316, 317, 329, 452, 468, 469, 471, 472, 553, 555, 565–6, 593, 596, 685
mayʿa yābisa (dry storax resin) 555, 556, 685
meat varieties see *laḥm*
**milḥ* (salt) 25, 86, 685–7
abyaḍ (white) 41, 488, 687
maghsūl (washed) 216, 297, 687
misk (musk) 42, 63, 158, 159, 160, 239, 316, 473, 555, 652, 687–8

mukhkh (bone marrow) 46, 125
murabbā al-ward al-ʿasalī (rose-petal jam) 54, 85, 211, 212, 594
murkīra (conehead thyme) 505, 696
See also *ṣaʿtar* and *shardhūn*
**murrī* (liquid fermented sauce) 84, 606–7, 688–9
al-ḥūt (fish sauce) 26, 263, 503, 504, 532, 533, 607, 689
maṭbūkh (cooked) 525–8
muʿajjal (fast) 530–2
al-musṭār (nonfermented, with sweet grape juice) 528–30
**naqīʿ* (sun-fermented) 518–25
mushrooms see *fuṭr*
musṭār (fresh juice of sweet grapes) see *ʿinab*
mutton see *laḥm ghanam*

nāfiʿ (fennel seeds) 120, 149, 150, 152, 155, 156, 659, 775
See also *basbās*
namaksūd (cured meat) 21, 539, 607–8, 761
nammām (mother of thyme) 514, 689, 696
**naʿnaʿ* (mint) 690
nāranj (sour oranges) 28, 30, 84
nashā (wheat starch) 165, 167, 169, 170, 255, 461, 462, 463, 464, 467, 471, 472, 473, 478, 480, 481, 578
naṭrūn (natron) 513, 663
nīlaj (indigo) 481, 690
noodles and pasta:
fidāwush (orzo) 192, 572
iṭriya (thin noodles) 110, 193, 573
kuskusū (couscous) *see entry*
muḥammaṣ (small balls of pasta) 193, 576, 600
taltīn (thin pasta squares) 197, 586
zabzīn (couscous balls) 151, 193, 586, 600
nukhāla (bran) 150, 152, 170, 518, 579

partridges see *laḥm ḥajal*
pasta *see* noodles and pasta
purslane see *rijla*

qadīd (cured meat) 110, 420, 426, 539, 608, 761
qamḥ (wheat berries) 152, 167, 198, 580–1
qāqulla (black cardamom) 314, 316, 368, 371, 555, 557, 691
qarʿ (gourd) 145, 230, 238, 306, 338, 405–11, 441, 792–3
**qaranful* (cloves) 82, 91, 133, 137, 154, 494, 553, 555, 556, 557, 558, 655, 691, 702
qasṭal/*shāhballūṭ* (chestnuts) 35, 39, 41, 65, 66, 326, 330, 619, 638–9
qawqan see *aghlāl*
**qirfa* (Ceylon cinnamon) 655, 665, 691–2
qiththāʾ (snake cucumbers) 145, 441, 794
qiṭniyya bayḍāʾ (white sorghum) 28, 198, 582, 602, 794
qulqās (taros) 245, 443, 457, 794–5
qumrūn (freshwater shrimps) 91, 546–7, 761
qunilya see *laḥm arānib*
qunnabīṭ (cauliflower) 223, 790, 795
qusṭ ḥulw (sweet costus) 555, 557, 692–3

rabbits see *laḥm arānib*
radishes see *fujl*
rayḥān (myrtle) 36, 252, 556, 694, 706
rijla (purslane) 230, 270, 795–6
rosewater see *māʾ ward*
rummān (pomegranates) 31, 39, 84, 245, 639–42
Safarī 31, 65

sadhāb bustānī (cultivated rue) 250, 322
See also *fayjan*
safarjal (quinces) 84, 87, 239, 324, 354, 525, 529, 532, 642
salīkha (cassia variety) 557, 694–5
**samīd* (semolina flour) 91, 117, 581, 583
khashin (coarsely crushed) 170, 583
See also *darmak*
samn (ghee) *see* fats and oils
ṣanawbar (pine nuts) 92, 156, 158, 159, 160, 172, 173, 184, 289, 325, 326, 330, 334, 356, 357, 369, 374, 407, 468, 532, 537, 613, 642–3
jumjuma (pinecone) 525, 529, 643
ʿūd (pinecone scales) 532, 643
ṣandal (sandalwood) 553, 555, 556, 557, 558, 652, 695–6, 806, 808
sardīn (sardines) 750
mumallaḥ (salt-cured) 381, 750
ṭarī (fresh) 80, 364, 365, 366, 371

**ṣaʿtar* (thyme) 91, 210, 689, 696–7
mulūkī (royal thyme) 519, 696
See also *nammām, shardhūn, murkīra,* and *shaṭriyya*
shaʿīr (barley) 16, 29n57, 85, 123n13, 511, 518, 522, 584
daqīq (flour) 525, 526, 528, 530, 531, 536, 556
jashīsh (coarsely crushed) 152, 196
marmaz (green, young barley) 196, 576
shajar al-astab (rockrose shrub) 402, 697
shamʿ (beeswax) 161, 167, 464, 697
sharāb (syrups for cooking, and diluted for nonalcoholic drinks)
ʿasal mufawwah (spiced honey syrup) 382, 564
jullāb (rosewater syrup) 160n23, 165, 472, 473, 565–6
maṣṭakā (mastic infused syrup) 165, 473, 566, 596
rubb ʿinab (grape molasses) 41, 199, 363, 379, 382, 566, 595, 627
ward (rose-petal infused syrup) 165, 315, 317, 473, 566–8, 596
sharāb/khamr (alcoholic drinks) 25, 26, 39, 69, 95, 533, 535n10, 568, 653, 689, 693
ʿasalī (honey wine) 680
aḥmar (red wine) 555, 568
ʿatīq (aged) 65
ṣirf (undiluted wine) 382
washakī (dark reddish-brown wine) 739
shardhūn (conehead thyme) 490, 504, 532, 696–7
See also *murkīra* and *ṣaʿtar*
shaṭriyya (thyme-leaved savory) 238, 697–8
See also *ṣaʿtar*
shīrāz see *laban*
shūnīz (nigella seeds) 395, 500, 503, 519, 523, 525, 526, 527, 528, 529, 530, 531, 532, 574, 698–9
silq (chard) 86, 218, 223, 355, 570, 599, 608, 761, 796–7
simsim (sesame seeds) see *juljulān*
ṣināb (mustard seeds) 487, 501, 559, 700
ṣināb (mustard sauce) 79, 250, 251, 252, 286, 287, 428, 485, 610
sorghum, white see *qiṭniyya bayḍāʾ*
sparrows see *laḥm ʿaṣāfīr*
spinach see *isfānākh*
squabs see *firākh ḥamām*
starlings see *laḥm zarāzīr*
suʿdā (cyperus) 553, 555, 556, 557, 701, 804, 812n24
sukk (aromatic pastilles) 553, 555, 557, 701
**sukkar* (sugar) 24, 46, 53, 91, 92, 127, 591–2, 596–7
abyaḍ (refined, white) 165, 469, 597
jumjuma (molded white sugar cone) 257, 597, 732
masḥūq (crushed) 160, 161, 329, 330, 408, 462, 472, 480, 481, 597
**sunbul* (spikenard) 40, 82, 91, 131, 701–2
syrups and drinks see *sharāb*

tābil (seasoning spice) 604n9, 702
tamr (dates) 29, 66, 155, 175, 643
shadānaj (dried variety) 155, 644
taro see *qulqās*
tea see *chai*
**thūm* (garlic) 13, 54, 67, 80, 8280, 82–4, 886, 125, 142, 146, 314, 343, 703–4, 767
farīk al-thūm (spring garlic) 234, 286
tīn (figs) 16, 24, 39, 97, 395, 396, 645–6, 706, 753, 794
jāff/yābis (dried) 34, 40, 42, 46, 66, 766
khall (vinegar) 506
ṭīn Armanī (Armenian clay) 556, 704
tirfās (desert truffles) 61, 127, 238, 263, 271, 431–3, 713, 797–9
truffles see *tirfās*
tuffāḥ (apples) 35, 38, 39, 84, 87, 239, 354, 377, 525, 529, 646–7, 649, 688
qushūr (peels) 554
tuna see *tunn*
tunn (tuna) 37–8, 87, 762, 4
muṣayyar fī jarra (pickled in a jar) 381
mushammaʿ/mojama (salt-cured and air dried) 25, 26, 378–81
ṭarī (fresh) 377, 378
yābis (dried) see *mushammaʿ* above
turnips see *lift*
turtledoves see *laḥm yamām*
turunjān (lemon balm) 225, 271, 306, 342, 513, 517, 704

ʿūd (aloeswood) 553, 555, 558, 652, 704–6
Hindī (Indian) 155
ʿūd al-sūs (licorice roots) 535, 706

ukrunb see *kurunb*
ʿuṣfur (safflower) 34, 500, 502, 706
utrujj (citron) 34, 648
 qishr (peels) 554, 557
 shawk (thorns) 74, 91, 549, 648, 740
 ʿurūq (roots) 535, 648
 **waraq* (leaves) 82, 84, 125, 303, 370, 553, 648

waraq (leaves) of:
 ās (myrtle) 252, 556, 706
 rand (bay laurel) 303, 370, 553, 706
 utrujj (citron) see *utrujj*
 ward aḥmar (red rose petals) 553, 556, 557, 707
wild meats see *laḥm al-waḥsh*

yarbūz (blite) 229, 270, 271, 439, 441, 799

zabīb (raisins) 40, 66, 84, 97, 307, 313, 511, 532, 648–9
 al-aghshiya (processed in baskets) 649
 aḥmar (red) 209
 ḥulw (sweet) 501
 shamsī (sundried) 648
**zaʿfarān* (saffron) 28, 36, 82, 85, 87, 90, 101, 304, 481, 707–10, 718
**zanjabīl* (ginger) 82, 86, 91, 124, 710
**zayt* (olive oil) 25, 26, 34, 44, 53, 61, 64, 69, 80, 81, 96, 615–8
 maṭbūkh (treated with heat) 423, 616
**zaytūn* (olives) 34, 39, 54, 77, 87, 130, 612
 akhḍar (green) 131, 4, 612, 650, 687
 aswad (black) 612, 650
 mutammar (oil-cured black olives) 131, 491, 612
 See also next index for table olives
zubd (butter) *see* fats and oils
zunbūʿ/kabbād (Damascus citron) 13, 28, 84, 650–1
 khall (preserved juice) see *khall*

Index of Dishes and Other Preparations

In this index, bold numbers indicate recipes. Prepared foods that are also used as cooking ingredients are included in the previous index as well. Unnamed dishes are indexed under the name of the main ingredient in the recipe, e.g., the first three entries below.

abū khuraysh (borage) **226**
ʿadas (lentils) **457–8**
aghlāl (snails) **548–9**
aḥrash (meat patties) **274–5**, **287–8**
aḥsāʾ (soups) 51, **148–51**, 853
barkūkash see entry
ḥasū al-fatāt (crumb soup) **148**, **149**
lakhṭaj **150**
zabzīn see entry
akhbāz (breads):
buyyāt (bread that goes stale fast) 60
fatāt khubz (breadcrumbs) **148**, **149**
khabīṣ (thin sheets of bread) **167–8**
khamīr (fresh yeast) **574**
khubz al-banīj (proso millet bread) **119–20**
khubz faṭīr (unleavened bread) **119**, **129**
khubz al-furn (brick-oven bread) **117**, 574
khubz ghayr maṭbūkh (unbaked bread) **140**, 575
khubz al-ḥuwwārā (fine white bread) 190, 575
khubz al-malla (thin flat bread) **119**, 575, 718
khubz muʿād al-ʿajn (twice kneaded bread) **121**
khubz mukhtamir (fermented bread) 139, 149, 313, 575
khubz samīd (semolina bread) 269, 293, 575
khubz al-tannūr (clay oven bread) **118**, 575
muwarraqāt al-isfanj **122**
ruqāq (thin sheets of bread) **126**, **316n62**, **329**, 569, 841
shabāt 13, 62, 130, 583–4
aknāf (pit-roasted meat) 80, **254**
albān (dairy foods):
ʿaqīd laban (rennet-curdled milk) **393**, 395, **396**, 397, 588
jubn (cheese) **393–5**, 400–1, 854
khilāṭ (thick yogurt with vegetables) **396**, 589
rāyib (yogurt) **397–8**, 409, 589–90
shīrāz (thick yogurt) 90, 8, **395**, 590, 818
zubd (butter) **398**
albondigas (meatballs) 101
albondiguillas (small meatballs) 100
See also *banādiq*
alcuzcuzu (couscous with chickpeas) 100
See also *kuskusū*
ampanadillas (small meat pies) 100
See also *sanbūsak*
al-ʿArabī (mutton with chickpeas) **249**
arnabī/arnabiyya 210, 380, **425**, 418, 598
arroz grasso (rice cooked in fat) 100
aruzz bi-l-laban al-ḥalīb (rice pudding with milk) **194**
aruzziyya 194n17
aruzz mufalfal (pilaf) 100, 834
ashriba see *sharāb*
ʿĀṣimī see *murūziyya*
asparagus see *isfarāj*

badawiyya (peasants' dish) 54, **314**, 598
bādhinjān (eggplant) **412–27**, 826
aqrāṣ (patties) **415**
arnabiyya **425**, 598
Būrāniyya 85, **205–6**
maḥshū (stuffed) **416–7**, **420–2**
mashwī (grilled) **424**
mirqās (sausage) **423**
mughaffar (dipped in batter) **422**
muṣayyar (pickled) **498–500**
tūma **417**
ʿujja (omelet) **422**
badīʿī (casserole dish) **260–2**, 271, 394, 598
balāja (meatloaf) 60, **257**, 599
banādiq (meatballs) 50, **135**, **139**, **203**, **218**, 270, **221**, **282–3**, **297**, 300, 302, **312**, 330, **364**, **367**, **369**, **375**, 599
baqliyyāt (vegetable dishes) 50, 91, 110, **405–43**
muzawwarāt (meatless) 599–600

barkūkas/barkūkash (soup) 151, 586, 600
See also *zabzīn*
baṣal (onion), pickled 500
basṭīla (bastilla) 102, 315, 602
r'zīma (Algerian) 102
ṭājin malṣūqa (Tunisian) 102
ūrṭa (Tunisian, meatless) 102
See also *jūdhāba*
bayḍ (eggs) 383–9
cooked in ashes 389
fried 385, 386, 387, 388
isfīriyya (thin omelet) 383
nīmbarisht (poached) 386
stuffed 385
baysār see *fūl*
bāzīn see *muʿallaka*
beef dishes see *laḥm baqarī*
beverages see *sharāb*
blite see *yarbūz*
bread see *akhbāz*
buñuelos see *isfanj*
Būrāniyya 84, 107n12, 205, 236, 373, 422, 498, 598

capers, pickled see *kabar*
cardoons see *ḥarshaf*
carrots see *jazar*
cazuela de berengenas mojíes (eggplant casserole) 100
cheese see *albān*
chicken dishes see *laḥm dajāj*
chickpeas see *ḥimmaṣ*
cookies see *ṭaʿām al-khubz*
couscous see *kuskusū*
cured meat see *namaksūd* and *qadīd*

dairy foods see *albān*
desserts, confections see *ḥalwā*

egg dishes see *bayḍ*
ensaïmada 94

faḥṣī (countryside dish) 242, 306
falyāṭil 136, 142
farīk see *marmaz*
fava beans see *fūl*
fideos 28, 100
See also noodles and pasta

fūl (fava beans) 447–53
baysār (dried), mashed with meat 247–8
baysār (dried) with couscous 191
fūl akhḍar maqlī (fresh, fried) 821
fustuqiyya (fresh, pistachio green) 246, 271, 447
rās barṭāl (sparrow's head) 452, 819
tharīda (with *baysār*) 146–7
fustuqiyya (pistachio green) 246, 447
fuṭr (mushrooms) 331, 438, 824

ghassānī/ghassāniyya (meat with honey) 189, 255, 462, 592, 600
See also *muʿassal*
ghassānī (honey pudding) see *ḥalwā*
ghāsūlāt (hand-washing compounds) 553–8
goose dishes see *laḥm iwazz*
gourd see *qarʿ*

ḥalwā (desserts, confections):
damāgh al-Wāthiq/al-Mutawakkil 480, 592
fālūdhaj (starch-based pudding) 170, 410, 463–4, 592
fānīdh (pulled sugar taffy) 478
ghassānī (honey pudding) 462, 592
ḥalwā' (confection) 463–4, 466–8, 481
ishqāqūl (hard sugar candy) 479
jawzīnaq (walnut confection) 475
juljulāniyya (nougat with sesame) 465
lawzīnaj (almond brittle) 476
muʿassal (honey pudding) 461, 593, 845
muʿqad (chewy candy) 468, 469–70
Qāhiriyya (delicate rings) 471–3
qaṣab ḥulw (reeds of candy) 477
qubbayṭ majbūdh (pulled honey taffy) 465–6
rukhāmiyya (chewy candy) 469
sanbūsak (marzipan) 473, 595
zumurrudī (emerald green pudding) 481
hare dishes see *laḥm arānib*
harīsa (wheat porridge) 198, 290, 573
ḥarshaf (cardoons) 236, 436–7
ḥasū (soup) see *aḥsā'*
ḥimmaṣ (chickpeas) 454–6

ḥiṣrimiyya (chicken with sour grape juice) 306
ḥūt (fish):
arnabī 380
aqrāṣ and banādiq (fish cakes and balls) 364, 830
basbāsiyya (with fresh bulb fennel) 370
jumlī 370
maḥshī (stuffed) 372
maqlī (fried) 367
mughaffar (coated) 372
murawwaj (quick and easy) 363
murrī (fish fermented sauce) 532–3, 689
muṣayyar (pickled large fish) 503–5, 601
muṭajjan (baked in *ṭājin*) 371, 843
rāhibī (monks' food) 369, 379
sardīn see entry
tafāyā 369–70
tunn (tuna) *see entry*
Ibrāhīmiyya (chicken stew) 49, 315, 673
ishīdhāj (white stew) 48n124, 216n2, 297n1
See also *tafāyā*
isfanākh (spinach) 227, 270, 439–40, 823
isfanj (yeasted fritters) 55–6, 58–9, 68, 69, 92, 97, 177–9, 573
isfarāj (asparagus) 48, 232–3, 434, 822, 836
isfiriyya (thin and smooth meat patties) 283, 295, 301, 303, 321, 326, 335, 355, 383, 601

Jaʿfariyya (yellow stew) 304, 601
jalīdiyya (frosty) 313
jalja (table sauce) 13, 50n136, 213–4, 602
jarād (locusts) 545
jashīsh (porridge) 152–3
jazar (carrots) 428
jināniyya 145, 441, 602
jubn see *albān*
jūdhāba (bastilla) 315–7, 602–3
See also *basṭīla*
jumlī (all-in-one dish) 203, 296, 347, 370, 603

kabar muṣayyar (pickled capers) 396, 495–7
kaʿb al-ghazāl see *ṭaʿām al-khubz*
kaʿk see *ṭaʿām al-khubz*
kamʾa (desert truffles) 238, 263, 431–3
al-kāmil 90, 253
karsh maḥshuwwa (stuffed tripe) 355
qubā (stuffed omasum tripe) 289, 755
khall (vinegar)
fulful (infused with black pepper) 510
ḥiṣrim (preserved juice of unripe grapes) 514–515, 816
ḥulw ḥāmiḍ (sweet and sour) 509
ʿinab (with grapes) 506
khamīr (vinegar base) 511
līm (preserved lemon juice) 515
naʿnaʿ (infused with mint) 516
tīn (with figs) 506
turunjān (infused with balm mint) 517
ʿunṣul (flavored with squills) 513
khass (lettuce) 439–40
khubz see *akhbāz*
khubz maḥshū (double crust pie) see *ṭaʿām al-khubz*
kurunbiyya (mutton with cabbage stew) 219
kuskusū 94, 97–9, 100, 188–91, 834

laḥm arānib (hare and *qunilya* dishes) 277–81
mughaffar (clad) 277
laḥm ʿaṣāfīr (sparrow dishes) 348–9
laḥm baqarī (beef dishes) 123–5, 203–15
arnabiyya 210
Būrāniyya (with eggplants) 295
jumlī (all-in-one dish) 203
murūziyya 207
muthallatha 207
rāhibī 211
qidr al-farsh (garnishes) 214
laḥm dajāj (chicken dishes) 128, 129, 131, 133, 135, 136, 138, 142, 148, 189, 297–332
badawiyya 314
dajājat ʿumrūs 308, 840
faḥṣī 306
ḥūtiyya 303
Ibrāhīmiyya 315
Jaʿfariyya 304
jalīdiyya 313
jūdhāba 315
kāfūriyya 299
maghmūm 317
mufattit 301
mughaffar 302
mukhallal 300

murūziyya 305
narjisiyya 312
Qurashiyya 313
tafāyā 297–8
thūmiyya 314
Turkiyya 310
Yahūdiyya 309
zīrbājiyya muḥallāt 299
laḥm firākh ḥamām (squab dishes) 139–40, 172–3, 337–40
mashwī (grilled) 340
mufarrij (comforting) 338
qarʿiyya (with gourd) 338
rāhibī (monks' food) 337
laḥm ghanamī (mutton dishes) 126–8, 134, 216–59
al-ʿArabī 249
aknāf (pit roasted) 254
balāja (meatloaf) 257
basbāsiyya (with fresh bulb fennel) 224
baysār (with dried fava beans) 247
faḥṣī 242
fustuqiyya (pistachio green) 246
ghassāniyya (with honey) 255
al-kāmil (complete) 90, 253
kurunbiyya (with cabbages) 219
lawziyya (with almonds) 244
liftiyya (with turnips) 221
maqlī fī l-qidr (pot fried) 242
muʿassal (with honey) 254
naʿnaʿiyya (with mint) 225
narjisiyya 235
qaliyya (moist fries) 258
qarʿiyya (with gourd) 238
qunnabīṭiyya (with cauliflower) 223
ra's maymūn (blessed head) 256
rijliyya (with purslane) 230
shawī al-qidr (pot roast) 243
silqiyya (with chard) 223
ṣinābī (with mustard sauce) 250
ṭabāhijiyya *see entry*
tafāyā (white and green stews) 216–8
ṭafshīla 248
turunjāniyya (with lemon balm) 225
laḥm ḥajal (partridge dishes) 333–6
ḥajala Yahūdiyya (Jewish stuffed partridge) 334n6
laḥm ʿijl (veal dishes) 221, 222, 235, 237, 239, 242, 250
laḥm iwazz (goose dishes) 293–6
laḥm jadī (young goat dishes) 230, 262, 266, 271
laḥm kharūf (lamb dishes) 126, 127, 190, 260–70
badīʿī 260
maḍīra (with milk) 268, 269
muʿallak 262
mulabbaqa 269
laḥm al-waḥsh (wild meat dishes) 273–6
laḥm yamām (turtledove dishes) 341–5
maḥshī (stuffed) 344
mashwī (salt crusted and roasted) 344
mashwī (grilled) 344
mufarrij (comforting) 341
naʿnaʿiyya (with mint) 341
laḥm zarāzīr (starling dishes) 346–7
lamb dishes see *laḥm kharūf*
laqāniq (large sausages) 287
lemons, picked see *līm muṣayyar*
lentils see *ʿadas*
lettuce see *khass*
lift (turnips) 207, 221
muṣayyar (pickled) 500–2
liftiyya (mutton with turnip stew) 221
līm muṣayyar (pickled lemons) 492–4
lisān Ṣinhājī (mock tongue) 347
lisān al-thawr see *abū khuraysh*
locusts see *jarād*

mallīn 80, 254
marmaz (green barley dish) 196
mirqās (small sausages) 58, 284–6, 423
mojama (dried tuna) see *tunn*
muʿallaka 195
muʿassal (meat dish with honey) 254–5, 605
See also *ghassānī*
muʿassal (honey pudding) see *ḥalwā*
mufarrij/*shuʿāʿ al-shams* (comforting) 212, 306, 338, 341, 606
See also *rāhibī*
mughaffar (clad/coated) 277, 302, 372, 422
mujabbana (cheese pastries) 12, 15, 55–6, 59, 68, 69, 74, 92, 179, 183
al-furn (oven baked) 184, 847
makhāriq/*muthallatha* (doughnuts) 181
oven baked, with milk 183
qayjāṭa (oven baked) 182

Sharīsh 56
Ṭulayṭuliyya (oven baked) **185**
mukhallal (vinegar-soured stew) **300**
murrī (liquid fermented sauce) 606
al-ḥūt (fish sauce) 26, **503**, **532–3**, 689
maṭbūkh (cooked) **525**, **526**, **527**, **528**, **817**
mu'ajjal (fast) **530**
al-musṭār (with sweet grape juice) **528**, **529**, **530**
naqī' (sun-fermented) **518–25**, 607
murūziyya/marwaziyya (sour plum stew) **207–10**, **305**, 607
muṣannab (sweet grape juice preserved with mustard seeds) **559**
mushamma' (dried tuna) see *tunn*
mushāsh Zubayda see *ṭa'ām al-khubz*
mushrooms see *fuṭr*
muthawwama (chicken with garlic) 67, 69, 82, **142–5**
mutton dishes see *laḥm ghanamī*

namaksūd (cured meat) 21, **539–40**, **607–8**, 761
naql (snack foods) 51, **451**, **545–6**, **546**, 595, 608, 754, 799, **819**, **821**
narjisiyya (narcissus-like) 23, **235**, **312**
nīmbarisht see *bayḍ*
noodles and pasta:
fidāwush (grain-shaped pasta) **192**, 197n27, 572
iṭriya (thin noodles) **193**, 573
kuskusū (couscous) *see entry*
muḥammaṣ (small balls of pasta) **193**, 600
taltīn (thin pasta squares) **197**, 586
zabzīn (couscous balls, in soup) **151**, 193, 586, 600

olive oil see *zayt*
olives see *zaytūn*
olla podrida 87, 353n11, 610

paella 100, 153n14, 570
partridge dishes see *laḥm ḥajal*
pasta see noodles
pastries, sweet and savory see *ṭa'ām al-khubz*

qadīd (cured meat) 420, 426, **539**, 608, 761
qar' (gourd) **405–11**, **828**
aḥrash (patties) **407**
fālūdhaj (thick pudding) **410**
qar'iyya (stew) **230**, **238**, **306**, **338**
qaṭā'if (pancakes) **164**
'Abbāsiyya (stuffed) **165**
tharīda with **135**
qawqan see *aghlāl*
qayjāṭa see *mujabbana*
qiṭniyya bayḍā' (white sorghum) **198**, 582, 794
qubā see *karsh maḥshuwwa*
qubayṭā' see *ḥalwā'*
qulqās (taro) **245**, **443**, **457**, 794–5
qumrūn (freshwater shrimps) 91, **546–7**, 761
qunilya see *laḥm arnab*
qunnabīṭiyya (mutton with cauliflower) **223**
Qurashiyya (chicken in saffron sauce) **313**

rabbit dishes see *laḥm aranib*
rāhibī (monks' food) **211**, 286, 296, **305**, **337**, **347**, **369**, **379**, **381**
See also *mufarrij*
ra's maymūn (head-shaped savory meat and egg dish) **256–7**
ra's maymūn (head-shaped sweet pastry) **171–4**

sanbūsak (marzipan) **473**, 595
sanbūsak (meat-stuffed pastries) 14, 71, 473n8, 474n11, 595
sardīn (sardines), fresh **364**, **365**, **366**, **371**
muṣayyar mumallaḥ (salt-cured sardines) **381**
sausages see *laqāniq* and *mirqās*
shalsha see *jalja*
shāqūma (*tharīda* dish) **134**
sharmūla 58
shāshiyyat ibn al-waḍī'/al-faqīr/ibn al-rafī' 13, 69, **127–8**
shawā al-qidr (pot roast) 213, **243**, **343**
shīrāz see *albān*
shrimps see *qumrūn*
ṣibāgh (dipping sauce) 50n136, 213n37, 281n28, 387n17, 605
See also *jalja*

sikbāj (vinegar-soured stew) 190n4, 300n14
See also *mukhallal*
ṣināb (mustard sauce) 251, 252, 428, **485–7**
ṣinābī (mutton dish seasoned with *ṣināb*) **250**
Ṣinhājī **353**, 610
lisān (mock tongue) **357**
soups see *aḥsā'*
snails see *aghlāl*
sparrow dishes see *laḥm 'aṣāfīr*
spinach see *isfanākh*
squab dishes see *laḥm firākh ḥamām*
starling dishes see *laḥm zarāzīr*

ṭa'ām al-khubz (sweet and savory pastries, and cookies):
ādhān maḥshuwwa (stuffed ears) **158**
aqrāṣ maḥshuwwa (stuffed discs) **159**
isfanj see entry
jawzīnaq (walnut pinwheel cookies) **161**
ka'b al-ghazāl (small cookies) **156**, **851**
ka'k (ring cookies) 154, **155–6**
khubz maḥshū (double crust pie) **186**, 575
kunāfa (starch-based crepes) **162–4**
lawzīnaq (almond pinwheel cookies) **162**
luqam al-qāḍī (judge's morsels) **157**
madā'in Yanayyir (miniature pastry towns) 66
maqrūḍ (stuffed cookie bars) **175**
mithradat al-amīr (small pie-like pastries) **160**
mujabbana see entry
muqawwara maḥshuwwa (stuffed) **158**
murakkaba (assembled crepes) **174**
mushahhada (pancakes) **135**
mushāsh Zubayda (Zubayda's ribs) **175**, **849**
qanānīṭ maḥshuwwa (stuffed mock reeds) **157**
qaṭā'if (pancakes) *see entry*
ra's maymūn (blessed head) *see entry*
ṣafanj see *isfanj*
sanbūsak (meat-stuffed pastries) 14, 71, 473n8, 474n11, 595
zalābiya (latticed fritters) 52n145, **176**, 586–7
zalābiya Shāmiyya (fried yeasted dough) 55
ṭabāhijiyya (succulently fried mutton) **245**
maghmūma (cooked in lidded pot) **246**
ṭibā'iyya (with agreeable humoral properties) **245**
tafāyā (simple stew) 48–50, 51, 72, 85–6, 611
bayḍā' (white) **216**, **297**, **369**
khaḍrā' (green) **217**, **298**, **370**, **832**
ṭafshīla (porridge with pulses) **248–9**, 611
**takhmīr* (egg-based topping) 58, 89–90, 733, 735
talbīna (thin starchy batter) 162, 586
taro see *qulqās*
tharīda (bread sop dishes) **121–46**
baysār (crushed dried fava beans) **146**
bi-l-laban al-ḥalīb (with milk) **140**, **141**, **841**
falyāṭil **136**, **142**
jinānīyya **145**
mardūda **126**
mukarrara (refined) **133**
muthawwama (with garlic) **142**
al-qaṭāyif **135**
shabāt 13, 62, **130**, 583–4
shāqūma **134**
thūmiyya (chicken with garlic) 82, 84, **314**
tuzīd fī l-bāh (invigorates coitus) **133**, **838**
tripe see *karsh*
truffles see *kam'a*
tuna see *tunn*
tunn (tuna), fresh **377–8**
muṣayyar fī jarra (jar-pickled) **381**
yābis/mushamma' (dried) **378–81**
Turkiyya (Turkish chicken dish) **310**
turnips see *lift*
turtledove dishes see *laḥm yamām*
turunjāniyya (mutton with lemon balm) **225**

'ujja (omelet) **387**, **422**
'uṣb (intestine rolls) 122, 146, 191, **267**, 612
ushnān see *ghāsūlāt*

vinegar see *khall*

wild meat dishes see *laḥm al-waḥsh*

Yahūdiyya (Jewish stuffed chicken) **309**
yarbūz (blite) 270, 271, **439–40**
yogurt see *albān*

zabzīn (couscous balls in soup) **151**, 193, 586, 600
  See also *barkūkas*
zayt (olive oil):
  making *zayt* from varieties of seeds **534**
  remedying **534–6**
zaytūn (table olives) 612
  brined green olives **490**
  maksūr (cracked) **489**
  musharraḥ (scored) **499**
  mutammar (preserved in olive oil) **491**
zīrbājiyya muḥallāt (golden chicken stew, sweetened) **299**
zubd (butter) see *albān*